AUTOCOURSE™

THE WORLD'S LEADING GRAND PRIX ANNUAL

icon
PUBLISHING LIMITED

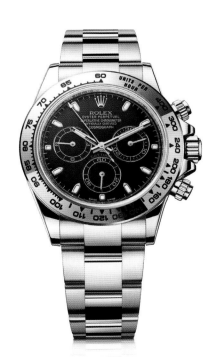

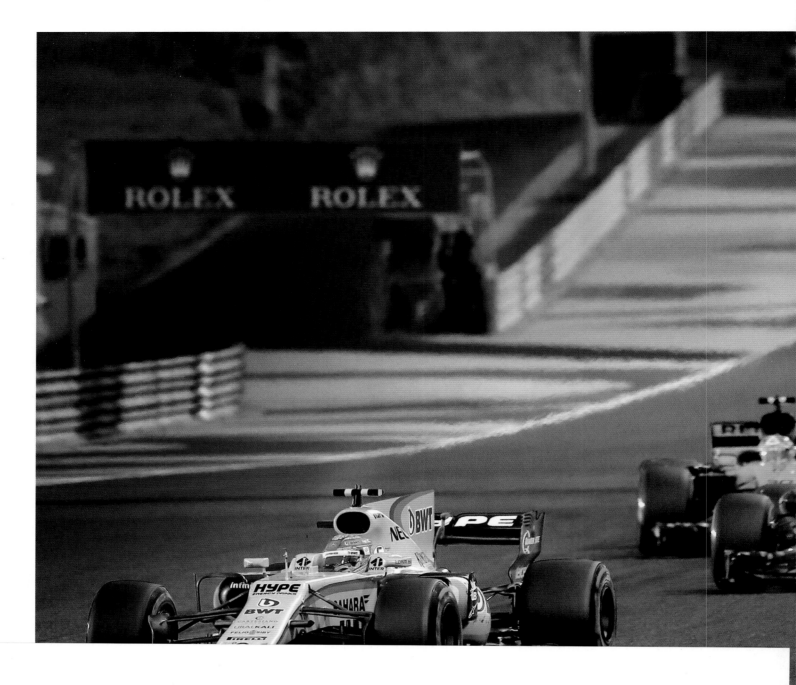

CONTENTS

AUTOCOURSE
2017–2018

is published by:
Icon Publishing Limited
16 Imperial Square
Cheltenham
Gloucestershire
GL50 1QZ
United Kingdom

Tel: +44 (0)1242 269154

Email: info@autocourse.com
Website: www.autocourse.com

Printed in Italy by
L.E.G.O. S.p.A
Viale dell'Industria, 2
I-36100 Vicenza
Email: info@legogroup.com
www.legogroup.com

ISBN: 978-1910584-26-2

DISTRIBUTORS
Gardners Books
1 Whittle Drive, Eastbourne,
East Sussex BN23 6QH
Tel: +44 (0)1323 521555
email: sales@gardners.com

Bertram Books
1 Broadland Business Park, Norwich,
Norfolk, NR7 0WF
Tel: +44 (0)871 803 6709
email: books@bertrams.com

Chaters Wholesale Ltd
25/26 Murrell Green Business Park,
Hook, Hampshire RG27 9GR
Telephone: +44 (0)1256 765443
Fax: +44 (0)1256 769900
email: books@chaters.co.uk

NORTH AMERICA
Motorbooks
Quayside Distribution Services
400 First Avenue North, Suite 300,
Minneapolis, MN 55401, USA
Tel: (612) 344 8100

publisher
STEVE SMALL
steve.small@iconpublishinglimited.com

commercial director
BRYN WILLIAMS
bryn.williams@iconpublishinglimited.com

editor
TONY DODGINS

grand prix correspondent
MAURICE HAMILTON

f1 technical editor
MARK HUGHES

text editor
IAN PENBERTHY

results and statistics
DAVID HAYHOE

lap chart compiler
PETER McLAREN

chief photographer
PETER J. FOX

chief contributing photographers
JEAN-FRANÇOIS GALERON
LUKAS GORYS
PETER NYGAARD
JAD SHERIF

f1 car and circuit illustrations
ADRIAN DEAN
f1artwork@blueyonder.co.uk

Acknowledgements

France: ACO; Fédération Française du Sport Automobile; FIA (Jean Todt, Charlie Whiting, Matteo Bonciani); **Germany:** Formula 3 Vereinigung; Mercedes-Benz (Toto Wolff, James Vowles, Bradley Lord, Felix Siggemann, Rosa Herrero Venegas); **Great Britain:** Formula One Group (Chase Carey, Ross Brawn, Sean Bratches, Norman Howell, Luca Colajanni);

STILL LEADING THE FIELD

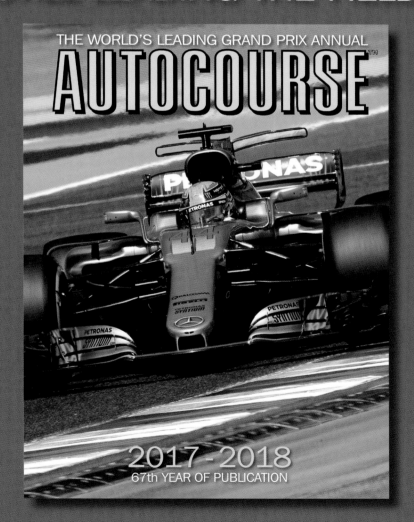

FOREWORD by LEWIS HAMILTON

FROM the opening race in Melbourne, it was clear we had a fight on our hands in 2017. It was all about us and Ferrari. I'm here to race – and I loved it; it was like, "game on". There are no friends in competition – but that doesn't mean rivals cannot respect each other. That's what Formula 1 should be all about: driver against driver, and team against team. It was a great battle, and it was fantastic to win races like Barcelona and Austin by doing the job out on track.

Twenty-seventeen has been my hardest working year in the sport and my most enjoyable year. I loved driving the car and working with the team more than ever before. Mercedes has shown such strength over the past four years, and we pulled together in a way I have never experienced until this point. I walk the corridors in Brixworth and Brackley, I see the passion and determination of my colleagues, and that inspires me to push myself to new limits. I'm very proud to be part of it.

This was a year that tested the whole team to the limits. We spent a long time chasing Sebastian and Ferrari. But it's in those moments, when the pressure is on, that you see real character. In the heat of the moment, do you stop, do you turn around or go a different direction? All the way through the tough times, Maya Angelou's poem, *Still I Rise*, was top of my mind – you get knocked down and you get back up, and you keep pushing as hard as you can. And when you eventually get there, you realise it was worth it – all the hard work, all the sacrifices by family and friends to help you reach your dream.

When you win a championship, it doesn't hit you straight away. Then people start saying things like "four-times world champion" and slowly the achievement begins to dawn on you. In the good times and bad, I know that there are a lot of people and a lot of kids watching me. So I am trying to be the brightest light that I can be, to shine that light in their direction and hopefully inspire them to chase their dreams and to never give up.

I still feel like I have a lot of races and, hopefully, championships ahead of me. We know our rivals are coming for us, and the focus now is how do we work towards the next one? My job in the winter is to focus on all those areas where I can improve for next year, to come back better than before. I fully trust in the team, and I know that, together, we can face any challenge that is put in front of us.

REACHING NEW HEIGHTS

Above: Four-times champion and potential all-time record breaker Lewis Hamilton took his fourth world drivers' title to join an elite strata of world champions.

Top right: In the pink. Sahara Force India found a new major sponsor and continued to punch above its weight to finish fourth once more in the constructors' championship.

Above right: Sebastian Vettel put Scuderia Ferrari back among the winners in 2017, but his championship challenge unravelled before the season was out.

Photos: Peter J. Fox

Right: Despite a power disadvantage, Red Bull grew stronger as the year progressed. Max Verstappen and Daniel Ricciardo both drove superbly, grabbing three victories and numerous opportunistic podiums.

Photo: Red Bull Racing/Getty Images

FOR the fourth consecutive season, Mercedes won the drivers' and constructors' titles. But they had to work for them like never before in the hybrid era. Even Lewis Hamilton was forced to scale new heights en route to a fourth world championship, which allowed him to join Michael Schumacher, Juan Manuel Fangio, Alain Prost and Sebastian Vettel in rarefied air.

The championships may have been decided with a couple of races to go, but Ferrari's SF70 was worthy opposition for the Mercedes W08, and it was only a disastrous Asian leg of the championship for the Scuderia that allowed Hamilton and Mercedes to relax a little at the final two races in Brazil and Abu Dhabi.

Increasingly, Michael Schumacher's seemingly impossible-to-match records look attainable for Hamilton. With nine race victories, he finished the 2017 season with a total of 62 GP wins, just 29 short of Schumacher's 91, and with a fractionally better wins/starts ratio. During the course of the season, he surpassed first Ayrton Senna's and then Schumacher's pole-position totals. And he is still only 32. He says he is enjoying his racing more than ever, and even if their advantage is diminishing, you cannot exactly see Mercedes falling behind the game in the remaining three years that F1 will utilise the existing power units.

The Ferrari advance was unexpected, after a promising 2015 season had become a false dawn and 2016 had gone by without a single victory. But, right from the first day of testing, Maranello was on the pace, and chairman Sergio Marchionne was right when he pointed out that a combination of driver and team errors had cost them dear. Whereas Hamilton had a flawless year without a single non-finish and had scored in every race, Vettel's rush of blood to the head in Baku, first-lap shunt in Singapore, opening-lap brushes with

Verstappen and Hamilton in Mexico, and reliability issues in Malaysia and Japan put paid to his challenge.

With more aero-centric regulations in 2017, Red Bull Racing were much fancied, but started on the back foot after correlation issues with its wind tunnel. They were much stronger in the second half of the year, and Max Verstappen scored impressive wins in Malaysia and Mexico to add to his fairy-tale debut win for the senior Red Bull team in Barcelona in 2016. Daniel Ricciardo took an opportunistic win in Azerbaijan, but then suffered more of the reliability woes that had afflicted his team-mate earlier in the year.

Force India's management shrugs whenever there is mention of a $150–200m budget cap in Formula 1. Irrelevant to us, they say, we don't spend that much… Yet again, the team did a brilliant job and confounded anyone who suggested they would struggle to match the fourth position achieved in 2016. They did so comfortably, finishing the year well clear of fifth-placed Williams, with points in every round except Monaco. They entertained, too, the rivalry between Sergio Pérez and new signing Esteban Ocon unbelievably tight.

McLaren Honda's season once more was a tale of woe. That Fernando Alonso's one-off Indy 500 appearance was the highlight of his year says it all. With luck and a working Honda, Alonso could have won at The Brickyard, though. A divorce between McLaren and its engine supplier was inevitable. The team will race with Renault power in 2018, with Toro Rosso taking up F1's supply of Hondas.

Off the track, Liberty Media completed its takeover of F1 at the beginning of the year, and Chase Carey, Sean Bratches and Ross Brawn started to prepare for a new dawn at the beginning of 2021. In the words of Christian Horner, though, there is probably a good deal of filibustering to go on before then…

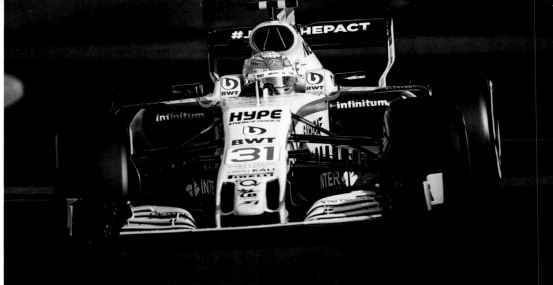

Porsche again won the World Endurance Championship and Le Mans double, with the drivers' title falling to Brendon Hartley, Timo Bernhard and Earl Bamber. As well as the French 24-hour classic, they won in Nürburgring, Mexico City and Austria. Their stiffest opposition once more came in the shape of Toyota's Sébastien Buemi, Anthony Davidson and Kazuki Nakajima, who were victorious at Silverstone, Spa, Fuji, Shanghai and Bahrain.

Charles Leclerc followed up his 2016 GP3 success with a highly impressive debut F2 (formerly GP2) championship win for Prema, and has now been confirmed at Alfa Romeo-branded Sauber for 2018. Artem Markelov also impressed and took runner-up spot in the series, having fought a season-long battle with DAMS driver Oliver Rowland. The teams' championship went right down to the wire in Abu Dhabi, with Russian Time claiming its second title in five years.

In GP3, British Mercedes junior driver George Russell took the crown, ahead of compatriot Jack Aitken. Russell tested impressively for Mercedes in Budapest, and also enjoyed FP1 outings with Force India in Interlagos and Yas Marina.

In the European F3 championship, McLaren test and reserve driver Lando Norris was the gold standard with eight wins, taking the title ahead of Joel Eriksson, Max Günther and fellow Briton Callum Ilott.

In Formula E, a delighted Lucas di Grassi won the series, with victories in Mexico and Montreal. Defending champion Sébastien Buemi was a tough rival, winning six times, before disqualifications in Berlin and Montreal, and absence in New York due to clashing Toyota commitments in the Nürburgring 6 Hours derailed his championship challenge.

On the other side of the Atlantic, Josef Newgarden won a closely-fought Indycar title, while Team Penske team-mates Simon Pagenaud, Helio Castroneves and Will Power took three of the next four places, the only interloper being Chip Ganassi's Scott Dixon, who finished the series in third place. Happily, Dixon also walked away uninjured from a big accident at Indianapolis, where he was an innocent party, as popular Japanese driver Takuma Sato got to drink the milk.

Monster Energy became backers of the NASCAR Cup, with 37-year-old five-timed winner Martin Truex Jr taking the series for Furniture Row Racing, ahead of fellow Toyota driver Kyle Busch and Ford's Kevin Harvick.

Tony Dodgins
November, 2017

Above: Porsche signed off from the WEC with a third straight win at Le Mans, courtesy of Brendon Hartley, Earl Bamber and Timo Bernhard.
Photo: Bryn Williams

Right: A golden future? Charles Leclerc was the class of the field in F2 and earned a Sauber F1 seat, alongside Marcus Ericsson, for 2018.
Photo: Formula 2 Media Services

Below right: George Russell was just as convincing in winning the GP3 title, and has already tasted F1 machinery.
Photo: GP2 Media Services

Bottom right: Lando Norris won the European F3 title and is already affiliated to McLaren.
Photo: FIA F3 Media

Top right: Indianapolis 500 winner Takuma Sato drinks the milk, having earned redemption after his last-lap disappointment of 2012.
Photo: Shwan Gritzmacher/Indycar

Top far right: Lucas di Grassi won his first Formula E title after a season-long battle with his nemesis, Sébastien Buemi.
Photo: Formula E

Top centre far right: A NASCAR title at last for 37-year-old Martin Truex.
Photo: LAT Images/Nigel Kinrade

Far right: Indycar still struggles to pull an audience, but the level of talent, all in relatively evenly matched machinery, has ensured plenty of opportunities for the drivers to shine.
Photo: Chris Owens/Indycar

FIA F1 WORLD CHAMPIONSHIP 2017
TOP TEN DRIVERS
THE EDITOR'S CHOICE

Driver Portraits by Peter J. Fox

LEWIS HAMILTON

1

THE jaw-dropping disbelief as Lewis Hamilton deposited his Mercedes into the tyre barrier at Interlagos in Q1 brought it home to you just how infrequently this man makes a mistake.

"I'm human..." he said. You do sometimes wonder. The qualifying pace is devastating and set up many a 25-point Sunday afternoon, the racecraft purely instinctive, and his ability to get the best out of a set of rubber pretty much second to none.

In a spellbinding season when Mercedes and Ferrari were so evenly matched – and indeed you could argue that the Ferrari was the quicker car over a more varied range of tracks – Hamilton often made the difference. That extra eight metres at the start of a grand prix allowed Mercedes to be on the front foot strategically, and 11 times Hamilton put his W08 on pole. From there, they didn't drop the ball.

At the high-downforce places – Monaco, Budapest, Singapore and Mexico – even Hamilton could not stop Ferrari from stealing the initiative, but you could never rule him out. As soon as you saw a wet track in Singapore, you kind of knew – and so it proved.

As his numbers became ever more impressive, he overtook Michael Schumacher's record 68 F1 poles and ended the season with a better wins/starts ratio than the seven-times champion. As the wins mounted up, he seemed more focused rather than less, which is why Brazil qualifying was such a surprise, although he made amends by finishing just 5s behind Vettel's winning Ferrari – from the pit lane...

Mentally, Lewis was in a happier place, enjoying racing against Ferrari rather than the enemy within, which is how he viewed Nico Rosberg. The relationship with new team-mate Bottas was altogether more convivial – possibly because Valtteri was less threatening. But in reality, Hamilton doesn't feel threatened by anyone, although Max Verstappen is working on it!

MAX VERSTAPPEN

2

AT Red Bull, there had been some internal debate about whether the 2017 car should have been designated RB12A – to avoid 'unlucky 13'. And certainly for the first half of the season at least, Max Verstappen must have been wishing that had been the chosen route.

Red Bull had a tough start to the year, when the new car's on-track performance did not correlate with what the team was being told by its wind tunnel and computational fluid dynamics (CFD). On top of that, the reliability was about as good as Max's luck. So much so that by the time the circus headed for Brazil, with just two rounds to go, Verstappen had done fewer laps than anyone who had competed in all 18 races to that point. Max had completed 693 of the season's 1,070 laps, which compared with Lewis Hamilton's 1,069…

It was as if he were jinxed: brake trouble in Bahrain; opening-lap accidents in Spain, Austria and Singapore, none of which he was really responsible for; electrical issues in Montreal, and power unit problems in Baku and Spa. Among it all, there was a bit of a cack-handed collision with an unimpressed Ricciardo at Turn Two in Hungary, which was his only real *faux-pas* of the year.

But finally his fortunes changed. That superb win in Malaysia was, unbelievably, his first podium appearance since round two in China. He harried Hamilton all the way to the flag in Suzuka, and then his Mexican win was one of the most dominant of the year as Hamilton and Vettel were faced with recovery drives. Indeed, as everyone headed for the season finale in Abu Dhabi, if you looked at just the previous five races, the scores among the Big Three's drivers were: Verstappen, 92; Hamilton, 80; Bottas, 68; Vettel, 67: Räikkönen, 55; Ricciardo, 38.

Having committed himself to Red Bull, his fervent hope was that the momentum would carry on into 2018.

DANIEL RICCIARDO

3

TRUTH be told, it's difficult to know in which order to rank the Red Bull pair. Going into the year, Daniel Ricciardo was hopeful that a reset with the 2017 regulations and a new RB13 would allow him to challenge for the championship. The early-season races quickly disabused him of that. The car was tricky, as evidenced by it snapping out of his control in Melbourne qualifying.

But Ricciardo was still driving at the top of his game. He and Verstappen usually qualified within a few hundredths of each other, and his instinctive racecraft was as clinical as ever. Give him half a sniff, and he always delivers, as shown by that opportunistic win in Baku from tenth on the grid. That was part of a run of five consecutive races, Spain through Austria, where he stood on the podium.

As Red Bull progressed, Ricciardo demonstrated that his overtaking capabilities are top drawer. He is tremendous on the brakes and will come from deep, often surprising an opponent without any element of 'fling it up the inside and hope'. That was particularly evident in his fine recovery drive in Brazil. Okay, some of it was DRS, but you get the feeling that if DRS were to be banned, Ricciardo would still pass people.

The latter part of the season was anti-climactic. Verstappen pipped him to the front row by three-hundredths in Singapore, where Daniel normally excels, and he had to play second fiddle to Max in both Malaysia and Japan. Then came engine problems in successive races in Austin and Mexico, making it a flat end to the season.

But write Ricciardo off at your peril. The smiley demeanour masks a steely competitiveness, and given the way Red Bull finished the season, 2018 could be the year that Daniel had been hoping for this time around. Much will depend upon Renault.

SEBASTIAN VETTEL

4

IT'S tough to rank Sebastian Vettel just fourth when he scored a hundred-plus points more than the guy in the other Ferrari and won five grands prix. And yet... Mercedes and Hamilton were formidable opposition, but you couldn't help feeling that Sebastian and Ferrari dropped the ball. Sergio Marchionne was right when he pointed to mistakes from both team and drivers.

The Asian leg – Singapore, Malaysia, Japan – was a disaster. Did Seb really have to be quite so aggressive from pole at Marina Bay with a championship at stake? The stewards held that nobody was principally to blame for an accident that took out the Ferraris and Verstappen, but few agreed.

In Malaysia, the car clearly had race-winning pace (Räikkönen qualified just 0.05s behind Hamilton), and Vettel's recovery from the back after problems in qualifying showed what might have been. Even if he hadn't beaten Hamilton in Singapore or Verstappen in Malaysia, an additional 24 points from those races could pretty much have been taken as read. Add another 15 at the very least from Suzuka without the spark plug problem, and Seb would have headed for the Abu Dhabi finale just four points shy of Hamilton, and possibly even ahead.

Maybe it's as well he didn't, because the focus might then have been Baku, where a rush of blood to the head, when he sideswiped Lewis, cost him 13 points. If that had decided the championship... His judgement was also questionable in the brushes with Verstappen and Hamilton in Mexico.

All a bit harsh? The defence barrister would cite more front-row starts than anyone – and with a qualifying engine deficit – five fine wins, consistently formidable race pace, an inclusive and supportive demeanour around a Ferrari race team under pressure, a refusal to throw his toys out of the pram when it went pear-shaped, and the key role in making 80 per cent of the 2017 season so spellbinding.

FERNANDO ALONSO

"THE terrible thing for me," Bernie Ecclestone said in an interview with *Motorsport* magazine, "is walking down the back of the grid and seeing a two-times world champion who could win the race, and knowing he has zero chance. That's what's bad."

Fernando Alonso has been wasted for three years, a victim of Honda not being at a sufficiently high level in a hybrid formula that is engine dominated. Where you rank him is entirely subjective – and tricky, because he has not been competing at the sharp end. He would not be out of place at number two – which many would say is, conservatively, his natural place in the F1 hierarchy

What's so impressive is that he never gives less than 100 per cent. No matter how many squillions are in the bank, it still matters deeply at 36, some 11 years after he won the second of his two titles. How many, within the comfort zone of the F1 bubble he knows so well, would take on the challenge of the Indy 500? And do it to a level at which, with a bit of luck, he would have won.

The F1 radio messages give him away. "So that's pole!" he'd say, whenever he figures that without his power deficit, he'd have been at the top of the time sheet. "I'm driving like an animal!" He was, too, and it didn't matter whether it was for sixth, his best finish of the season, or 16th. A competitor extraordinaire.

Then, before the season was over, he was off to test a Toyoya LMP1 car in Bahrain and had signed up for the Daytona 24 Hours with Zak Brown's United Autosports team for what will obviously be preparation for Le Mans and his stated ambition of wanting the Monaco/Le Mans/Indianapolis triple crown. He is a man who would have been in his element in another era, driving anything and everything. Can Renault put him back at the sharp end?

VALTTERI BOTTAS

6

NICO ROSBERG'S decision to retire in late 2016 gave Valtteri Bottas the best Christmas present he's ever had. It also threw him straight into the lion's den.

"When you sign for Mercedes, the target can only be the world championship," he said. But to win that, you have to beat Lewis Hamilton in the same car. And the sustained pressure of trying to do that had persuaded Rosberg to seek an easier life! Valtteri knew that Lewis, as a three-times world champion, was clearly a tough yardstick, but he readily admitted that he found Hamilton even better than expected.

Pole position for race three in Bahrain was a good start, as was a fine win in round four at Sochi, under intense pressure from Vettel. But an engine failure at the next race in Barcelona – the only reliability blemish on the works team's season – put him on the back foot in terms of a realistic championship challenge.

In truth, he was never quite at that level. Relative to Hamilton, he always seemed to do his best work on low-grip surfaces – Sochi was one, and the Red Bull Ring, where he took a second victory, another. There were times when, unlike Lewis, he couldn't get the tyre into the right operating window and consequently looked ordinary. In his defence, the team readily acknowledged that the W08 was "a bit of a diva".

Not in question was Bottas's work ethic, and his desire to use the resources and strength in depth of engineering expertise to improve his game. For all the talk of championships, if, in March, you'd offered him 81 per cent of Hamilton's points going to Abu Dhabi (Räikkönen had just 63 per cent of Vettel's at Ferrari), plus a contract extension, he'd probably have snapped your arm off. The working relationship with Hamilton is a strong one, but to keep his seat for 2019, you sense that he needs to kick on a bit.

ESTEBAN OCON certainly doesn't carry any excess weight. You'd swear he hasn't been near a calf machine or a leg press, but looks can be deceptive. From the minute the 21-year-old Frenchman first tested for Force India, the team was impressed. When many pundits were extolling the virtues of Pascal Wehrlein, Ocon was the man they wanted.

He hasn't let them down. From day one, the lanky Frenchman and Sergio Pérez have been separated by the tiniest of margins – an average in comparable qualifying of 0.003s in Pérez's favour going to Abu Dhabi – and their territorial disputes during races escalated to the point of being a problem. The most notable of their skirmishes occurred at Baku and Spa. In Belgium, Ocon accused Pérez of "trying to kill me" as the Mexican squeezed him towards the wall on the flat-out run towards Eau Rouge – for the second time…

Ocon always keeps his boot in, though, and certainly is no pushover. That characteristic shows that he knows what he's doing in close-quarter combat, particularly given the fact that his Grosjean-prompted non-finish in Brazil was the first single-seater race in which he had failed to see the chequered flag since winning the European F3 crown ahead of Max Verstappen in 2014. Punctures and bits of missing carbon fibre were enough to prompt Force India to institute team orders, though!

Heading to Abu Dhabi, Ocon had scored points 16 times in 18 races. Pérez was normally that tiny bit quicker in qualifying for the first half of the season. Ocon said that he hoped to turn it around after the summer break when they visited tracks he'd driven on (with Manor), and he was as good as his word.

How good is he? With no disrespect intended, the yardstick was Sergio Pérez, not Ayrton Senna, but for a first full F1 season, he was still mighty impressive. Together again for a second season in 2018, it will be interesting to observe the dynamic.

7 ESTEBAN OCON

8 CARLOS SAINZ

YOU could easily justify putting Carlos Sainz higher in this list, and it will be interesting to see how his first full season with the Renault works outfit goes in 2018.

For single-lap pace, it was nip and tuck between Carlos and Daniil Kvyat before Helmut Marko lost faith in the Russian post-Singapore and swept in a new Toro Rosso era with Pierre Gasly and Brendon Hartley. In the 12 races they did alongside each other in 2017 where comparisons are relevant, Sainz was 7–5 up, and the average margin between them was just 0.06s.

But that's just one part of the story. A much more astonishing statistic is that in the time they spent together as team-mates – from the point when Red Bull demoted Kvyat back to Toro Rosso for Barcelona 2016 up to Singapore in 2017 – Sainz scored 90 points for the small Faenza team, while Kvyat managed just eight. That's a chasm, and testament to Sainz's attacking, never-say-die performances on a Sunday afternoon.

The highlight was his fourth place in Singapore, after which a radio transmission from his race engineer said it all: "Bravo, Carlos, we don't let you go!" That race was a key component in sending Toro Rosso to the Abu Dhabi season finale sixth in the constructors' championship, and still ahead of the Renault works team and Haas.

When Sainz did swap teams, replacing Jolyon Palmer alongside Nico Hülkenberg at Renault in time for Austin, his new outfit was immediately impressed by its acquisition. He got straight into Q3 and finished seventh at Circuit of the Americas, then qualified close to Hülkenberg's pace in both Mexico and Brazil.

Sainz impressed Hülkenberg with both his pace and his work ethic – in Carlos Sr, he's had a good mentor! – and this pairing can do great things if Renault continues its rate of development progress into 2018.

9 NICO HÜLKENBERG

To be honest, sixth through tenth in the 2017 Top Ten are quite interchangeable, and it would be possible to build a strong case for Nico Hülkenberg being higher up the list.

For the first half of the season, the Renault was not the easiest of cars, with a tricky balance and a tendency to rapidly wear the rear tyres certainly not helping on race day. That was improved by aero updates, particularly the new floor, which was incorporated in Hülkenberg's car in time for the mid-season visit to Silverstone.

But right from the start, the team was highly impressed by Hülkenberg's single-lap pace, which did nothing for Jolyon Palmer's confidence. They did 16 races together, and forgetting Australia, where Palmer had brake issues and crashed; Baku, where his car caught fire in practice; and Silverstone, where he did not have the new floor, it was a 13–0 whitewash in favour of 'The Hulk', with an average of 0.62s between them. That was the biggest margin on the grid, wider even than Massa's advantage over rookie Stroll at Williams. The only place Palmer was anywhere near him was at Spa where, in fairness, Jolyon was quicker in Q2 before gremlins prevented his Q3 participation.

This was the same Palmer who had got the better of Kevin Magnussen in the second half of 2016 to retain his Renault seat. If anything, Hülkenberg's performance level tipped the balance in favour of replacing Palmer with Sainz before season's end.

One record that fell to Hülkenberg in 2017 was not one that he had sought: the most grand prix starts without a podium finish. Adrian Sutil had managed 128, a mark that Hülkenberg left behind in Singapore and had advanced to 135 by season's end. Given his level of ability, that's all a bit of a nonsense. Provided that Enstone and Renault make the desired winter progress, 2018 must give him a chance of leaving that behind.

PERHAPS Sergio Pérez is due a bit of an apology: he finishes 'best of the rest' outside the Big Three teams and only just squeaks into the Top Ten... But then Räikkönen and Grosjean don't make it at all, which, in Romain's case, is tough. He should probably be included for incident and entertainment value alone! Kimi? Well, he did do a whole season in Ferrari's excellent SF70 without winning a race – although he'll feel he should probably have had Monaco and Budapest.

The only reason Pérez is three slots lower than his team-mate is because of Ocon's achievements in his first full F1 season, which took a bit of doing.

Really, though, the strength and consistency of performance from Mercedes-powered Force India was such that we should probably talk about the Big Four – they headed to Abu Dhabi with almost 100 points more than fifth-placed Williams.

Pérez and Ocon were tied together by the proverbial piece of string in qualifying, and the team's best result came via Sergio's fourth place in Barcelona. He scored points everywhere except Monaco – where he usually excels – Azerbaijan and Belgium. Indeed, in Baku and Spa, those two non-scores followed spats with his team-mate. Being fair, you'd probably blame Ocon for Baku (although he was retaliating to a Pérez move he hadn't enjoyed on the exit of Turn One) and Pérez for Belgium, where he seemed to have no defence after two bites at ushering Esteban into the wall!

One of the great things about Pérez is that he is not afraid to overtake. He pulled off a couple of great moves in Australia, even if he was a little overoptimistic in Monaco. He can also be a bit lairy at times, but it's all good for 'the show'. With no top seats on offer in the higher echelons, both Pérez and Ocon go again at Force India in 2018. Take cover!

SERGIO PÉREZ

10

NO TAKING LIBERTY'S

In January 2017, the FIA World Motor Sport Council approved Liberty Media's 100 per cent F1 buy-out after the US company had paid $746m for an initial 18.7 per cent stake in 2016. Taking into account debt, the $8bn deal valued F1 at $4.4bn. TONY DODGINS looks at F1's new landscape...

Above: Ross Brawn, the man in the know and Liberty's MD Motorsport.
Photo: WRi2/Jean-François Galeron

Top right: A gladiatorial entrance by Kimi Räikkönen at Austin.
Photo: Scuderia Ferrari

Above right: Ready to rumble – boxing MC Michael Buffer.
Photo: WRi2/Jad Sherif

Right: Drivers parade with the winner's trophy before the start of the United States GP.
Photo: Scuderia Ferrari

Opening spread: Liberty Media holds a press conference in Canada.
Photo: Peter J. Fox

THE new owner of F1 is 75-year-old American billionaire John Malone, dubbed 'Darth Vader' in business circles, a moniker allegedly accorded him by Al Gore's grandmother, who lived in an area where Malone's Tele-Communications Inc (TCI) provided the cable service, and she couldn't understand why the charges had gone up!

Malone's chairman is Chase Carey, 62, Rupert Murdoch's right-hand man and 21st Century Fox vice-chairman. After a few months looking at the business, Carey told Bernie Ecclestone that he wanted his CEO position and gave the man who had effectively run the sport for the previous 40 years the title 'Chairman Emeritus'.

"I'm not sure what that means," Ecclestone said.

"It means that you probably shouldn't underestimate a man who has been a Murdoch troubleshooter for 20 years and who had the balls to effectively fire Bernie…" mused one F1 team principal.

Carey stated that Ecclestone had been a one-man team, not right in today's world, that decision making was not as effective as it should have been and needed improving. Liberty, he said, was ideally placed to exploit new technologies to grow the sport, saw Europe as the foundation of F1, but wanted to expand it to 'destination venues', particularly in the US, and promote the individual events better. He wanted 20 'Super Bowls'.

The moustachioed Carey – it hides a scar from a car accident – is now the paddock face of Liberty's Formula One Group, along with former ESPN sales and marketing man Sean Bratches (MD of commercial operations) and Ross Brawn (MD Motorsport).

With F1's existing Concorde Agreement governing the sport until the end of 2020, their hands are currently tied in terms of radical change.

So, a few months into the new reign, what has been seen?

"A relaxing of some of the red tape there previously," said Red Bull team principal Christian Horner. "Things like engagement with social media, the promoters working closer and taking different shapes with events. For the first time, investment in a promotion in London, attended by 19 of the 20 drivers, taking F1 to the people. Red Bull has done that for the last ten years with show-car programmes which have been tremendously successful."

Boxing MC Michael Buffer – he of "Let's get ready to rumble!" fame – introducing some of the top names and Danny 'The Torpeeeedo' KvyAAAAAt, amid smoke on the Austin grid, caused lots of Twitter abuse. But the Americans appeared to like it. The general feeling seemed to be fine, as long as it stayed there. It would be a bit lost on the Chinese…

Buffer, the 72-year-old announcer of choice for Top Rank and all the Trump casino fights in Las Vegas, does not come cheap. Having patented his trademark catchphrase in 1992, he is said to have earned over $400m from licensing it. Inevitably, there was a 'rumble' in the paddock about where the money was coming from. Not from our pot, we hope!

Brawn finds some of the closed thinking frustrating: "I think it's unfair if you don't recognise the investment Liberty is making. I mean, I heard a silly comment about these flash new offices we've got. But we've paid for those ourselves. It's capital equipment paid for by Liberty, and the teams don't have to pay for anything that's capital equipment.

"People twist the scenario to suit themselves. We need to be a bit more grown up about the whole commercial discussion and recognise that Liberty are in this for the long

term. They're not a venture capital company looking to flip it in five years' time for the biggest profit they can find. They're a commercial entity in it to make a profit, no one's denying that, but if you look at all their enterprises, they've been engaged with them for a long time. They're excited about where F1 can be in five years' time."

That's a good point. Contrast it with what Ecclestone told journalist Richard Williams in a recent *Motor Sport* magazine interview: "I ran the business for the last five or six years because CVC wanted to sell. All I was trying to do was set the stall up to sell it for the maximum price." In other words, maximise revenues and spend nothing.

Brawn is cautiously optimistic that F1's ownership change will create a more positive environment.

"I hope the teams think of Liberty in a different way to the previous owners," he said. "Liberty is willing to invest heavily to build the sport. I think we have to cross that cultural change. In the past, it was divide and conquer, do the side deals and so forth. We don't want that. We want to have as adult a conversation as we can. It's going to be very difficult, I know that, but Liberty's mentality is from that culture. So who knows where the discussions will lead once they start."

As far as future engines are concerned, they have already started, with a view to publishing a set of engine regulations for 2021 by the end of 2018. Discussions between the FIA, Liberty and the teams identified the following aims:

1 The power unit (PU) must be less expensive to develop and produce.
2 It must be simpler.
3 It must be road-relevant and hybrid.
4 It must sound better.
5 It must use some standard parts.
6 F1 must be a power-to-weight-related formula with the PU used by a driver at its full potential 100 per cent of the time.

With those in mind, the fundamentals of the future engine were presented to the teams by the FIA/Liberty in Paris at the end of October:

• A 1.6-litre V6 turbo hybrid.
• Engines running 3,000rpm faster to improve the sound.
• The removal of the MGU-H, the part of the hybrid system that recovers energy from the turbo and that is largely responsible for muting the sound made by the current engines.
• A more powerful MGU-K – which recovers energy from the rear axle – to make up the loss in hybrid energy from the MGU-H, and with the option for a driver to save up energy over a number of laps to add a tactical element to the racing.
• A single turbo with constraints on size and weight.
• Standard battery and control electronics.
• Research into fuel regulations.

Having already employed a consultative process, Brawn was thus somewhat taken aback by the vehemence of opposition. Ferrari's Sergio Marchionne objected to the fact that "powertrain uniqueness is not going to be one of the drivers of distinctiveness." He added, somewhat pompously, "It needs to be absolutely clear that unless we find a set of circumstances, the results of which are beneficial to the maintenance of the brand and to the strengthening of the unique position for Ferrari, Ferrari will not play."

Renault and Mercedes also voiced concerns that the new rev limit and revised fuel flow would prompt the need for a whole new engine, sparking an arms race that was unnecessary and contrary to keeping a lid on costs. It seems that the manufacturers agreed with 75 per cent of what had been placed in front of them, just not the same 75 per cent...

As to whether a new engine would be necessary, it's difficult to disagree with any of Brawn's points.

"The current engine is an incredible piece of engineering, but it's not a good racing engine," he said. "It's very expensive, it doesn't make any noise, it has componentry that in order to try to control the number of uses is creating grid penalties that make a farce of F1, there are big differentials of performance between the competitors, and we are never going to get anyone else to come in and make engines.

"We have the four manufacturers, and maybe we'll lose one or two if they continue the way they are. So we can't leave it as it is. We're four seasons into this technology and are still getting 730 grid penalties because we can't get on top of it. All credit to Mercedes, they've done a fantastic job. But no one else can catch up. That's the reality.

"I think the FIA has recognised that having the ultimate technology is perhaps too high a price, even in F1. There has to be a balance between road-relevance, technology and what is most sensible to have in F1, because the costs of this engine have got so high."

There's also the thorny topic of how you balance a sport in which the privateer teams, whose core business is motor racing alone and hence budget-limited, have to compete with big motor manufacturers, who are in the sport to move metal, but who will come and go when it suits them. An independent, competitive engine manufacturer is seen as key to that, but how do you achieve it and make it viable?

"We are aligned with the FIA, and in fairness," Brawn said, "they've done a huge amount of work on this. It gets presented as an FOM engine, but it's as much an FIA initiative as ours; Fabrice Lom and other people have put a huge amount of work into it.

"The current engine is impressive engineering, but the costs are truly amazing as well. Williams had an engine problem in Brazil – a gearbox caused an over-rev and they had to plug a new engine in – and Mercedes wanted £1m to give them another engine to do the last two races, and for Williams it wasn't viable.

"A stand-alone engine that costs £1m... we've really got to look at ourselves and ask if we're in a good spot. And I don't think we are. I think it's evolved in a way nobody could have anticipated, and we've got to learn the lessons.

"I remember the normally-aspirated engines being £200–300,000. We're now three times that. And what we're trying to do is say, let's make them last longer because they're so expensive. And that gets into a vicious cycle. To get the reliability, you have to do a huge amount of work on the dyno to sign off the engine, so you think it's great that you've only got three or four per team, but the number of engines that have gone through the system to get to that level...

"By the time we've finished 2020, this engine will have been racing for seven years, and that's not bad for a racing engine. I don't think it's unrealistic to say that now's the time for a reset, and in doing that, the model that would make it viable for an independent is essential to addressing the cost. Where do you have to get to so an independent can make a go of this, is a good canary in the coal mine for whether you are in the right place? Whether they do or don't come in, is another matter."

Surely though, the push back against the engine proposal can't really have surprised a man who has been in the business as long as Brawn. After all, isn't it standard F1 practice to complain about everything and barter from there?

"It could be," he smiled, "and I say that with a certain wryness. But can we one day get over that? All have a vision of a different sort of future. Because if we don't, it'll never change. I'm optimistic. Maybe we have to go through this process for everyone to realise that we're all in it together, and if the business gets stronger, the sport gets stronger and everybody gains. The core of Liberty's mantra is the fans. Without the fans, the business and the sport doesn't go anywhere."

You do sincerely hope Brawn is right, but F1 history over the past 37 years is none too promising (see 'How Did We Get Here?'). Or, more accurately, we get there, but only after, in the words of Christian Horner, "a whole lot of filibustering." If there was that much flak over engines, just wait until Liberty starts to talk about money and governance...

Above: Chase Carey expounds on Liberty Media's plans for Formula 1.
Photo: WRi2/Jean-François Galeron

Left: The French Grand Prix will make a comeback at Paul Ricard in 2018.

Far left: Sean Bratches with Niki Lauda on the grid in China.
Photos: WRi2/Jean-François Galeron

Above: The paddock rules have become more relaxed, witness the Heineken bar in Spain.

Above right: Ecclestone has been eased out of the picture by Liberty.

Photos: Peter J. Fox

A few years ago, Brawn, then reportedly considering a role with the FIA, said that he would be interested in trying to implement an F1 cost cap, provided that the FIA was fully committed, which at the time didn't appear to be the case. Today, as an employee of the new commercial rights holders (CRH), Brawn peddles the importance of working hand-in-glove with the governing body.

"In all these initiatives, the FIA is vital," he said. "I don't know if some of the teams expected us to align with them and discard the FIA, but that's not what we want and is never going to work. The sport needs a clear, clean regulator, whom all the fans know. They can disagree with the decisions, that's natural, but the fans know that there is an independent regulator running the sport and that they can rely on the integrity of that regulator for the way the sport is run. That's vital.

"If you are going to have a cost control system, then having the FIA implement and regulate that is the surest way of having the confidence that it is being applied fairly and consistently through all the teams. It's not a simple matter, it's a very complicated thing to achieve, but then if you look at the complexity of the technical regulations in F1, we argue about them often, but they are the core of having F1 function. And I see no reason why there shouldn't be the same process on the financial regulations, where we have a financial working group who works with the FIA and ourselves to evolve the financial regulations.

"We'll have challenges on currency rates and tax regimes in different countries, but if there is an effort from everyone involved to achieve it, I still feel that a cost control system is the best way of ensuring that we have a fair system and competition which is not tilted towards those that have got most resources.

"There's a paradox because F1 has become a victim of its own success. Manufacturers are in it as a business enterprise. They are not in F1 because they love the sport. They do enjoy it, but they see a profit on the money invested and, because F1 is so successful, it has driven up the level of investment that can be justified."

Despite $150m being previously mentioned as a possible annual operating maximum – with leading teams said to be spending as much as $400m – Brawn would not be drawn on a number because, until you have the engine finalised and a direction, it's pointless, he said.

"The teams have asked already, and I've said let's get the system worked out first and then see what a sensible number is. It's a number that can be adjusted. It will have to have a glide path between where it is now and where it will be in three or four years' time, so that teams can start to structure themselves. I'm not pre-occupied with the number because we're not absolutely sure what it will involve. And it probably won't include marketing, because if a team wants to spend a lot of money on marketing, that's great for Formula 1."

The encouraging difference between Liberty and the previous 'owner'/political climates is that, under Brawn, a team of experts is being put in place to address and improve a number of F1's main issues. Improvements cannot and will not come overnight, but they should come.

On the engine side, for example, Nick Hayes, who ran Cosworth for a number of years, is instrumental in examining future engine models. And work is ongoing on an aerodynamic project looking into improving the racing, with former Brawn/Williams man Craig Wilson part of that team.

"We've bought the geometry of the old Manor 2017 car because we wanted to have a generic model that we could use in CFD modelling to at least give us a basis," Brawn explained. "We've carried out all the initial work, and with the season finished, the teams are going to start giving us their 2017 cars to have more representative models to look at. We've been putting in place the confidentiality agreements, and they are going to start providing us with representative models to run our CFD programme. The team of people we are putting together is about 75 per cent complete. I'm quite excited about it, and there's things we'll be able to show you early next year that will demonstrate what we are trying to do.

"We don't have the limitations on CFD technology and capacity that the teams do with the regulations. The world has overtaken F1 by a long way in terms of CFD. The capacity we have and ability to do what we need to do is far in excess of any F1 team."

With Brawn's vast technical knowledge, allied to his experience in running teams, Liberty could scarcely have a better poacher-turned-gamekeeper. If the teams are smart enough to recognise that, he and Liberty should represent the best opportunity to progress F1 in the right direction, without (too much) ulterior motive, for many a decade. But, along the way, he may need the patience of Job, and there will be times when a fishing rod will appear to be a more attractive alternative…

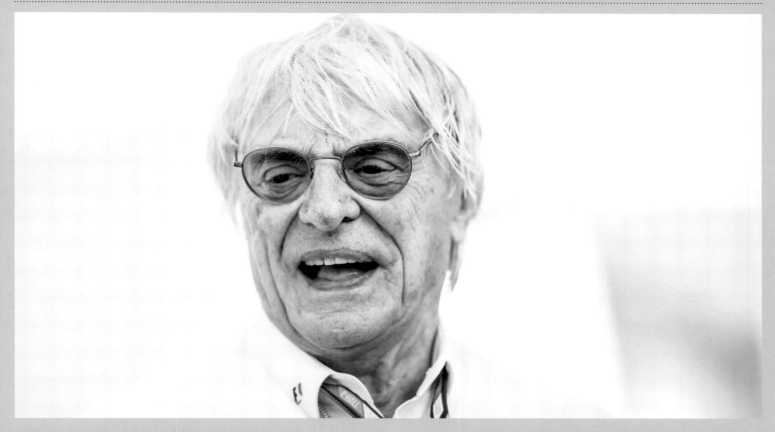

ON Monday, 23rd January, 2017, Liberty Media Corporation announced the completion of its acquisition of Formula 1. Chase Carey had been appointed CEO and Bernie Ecclestone gently shunted into the position of Chairman Emeritus.

Liberty said that Ecclestone would be "a source of advice", but that was all. The F1 world had changed. As part of the acquisition process, F1 became a company listed on the NASDAQ stock exchange in New York, and that meant new rules. Carey spoke early on about a need to create "a shared vision for the sport that will create real value for all stakeholders". F1 people didn't know what to think. It was all so very different from Ecclestone's way of doing business.

"The attitude is more collaborative and strategic," said Shaikh Mohammed bin Essa Al Khalifa, the executive chairman of McLaren. "This is something that everyone in the paddock needs to get used to. It is a completely different way of looking at things. They are going to try new things, but they have a long-term view. They seem intent to make the sport grow. They want sustainable teams and a sustainable sport, by making it exciting for the fans and sustainable for the promoters. The only way to do that is to grow the sport. We have to be patient."

Carey and his head of the commercial side of F1, Sean Bratches, have been working hard to win hearts and minds within the sport, but they are confident that they have a solid foundation for growth.

"We've a product that captivates anyone who sees it," Carey said. "We've drivers who are incredible stars. We've machines that combine power and technology in a way that cannot help but awe you. We've got fabulous brands. We've got a tremendous brand ourselves, which is identified with stars, glamour and excitement. Everything that people want and gravitate towards today. Can we improve the product? Sure. Is that a goal? Sure. You should always try to improve. You don't want to gimmick it up. You want to respect what has made the sport great. We want to take the things that have made the sport great, bring in energy and innovation, bring in more of a spirit of partnership to work with the teams, to work with the FIA, to figure out how we make the sport better."

Bratches was busy working on new races and on new kinds of media deals.

"We don't want to do straight-up contracts with media rights companies," he said. "We want to enter into deep partnerships. Most of the media companies have assets that are outside their linear broadcaster paid television platforms. We want to integrate our brand into all of that. To their benefit and to our benefit, but ultimately to serve the fan. I think each market is going to be different, and I think you're going to find a combination of both free-to-air and pay. And I think that is where it serves everyone's interest. We're trying to increase the number of sponsors who are investing in our brand, our belief and our vision. And to have a combination of the both, I think, is an appropriate mix going forward. So, we're not looking at fan engagement from any one specific platform."

In the autumn came the news that NBC would not extend its rights deal in the US market. The network explained this as being because Formula 1 was planning to stream its content directly to consumers in the future. So Bratches did a deal with ESPN and ABC instead.

"ESPN is part of the Disney empire," he said, "so they know a thing or two about the entertainment business. SportsCenter is the most powerful sports platform there is in the United States, but there is also espn.com digital, which has enormous reach. This linear and digital partnership with ESPN represents a significant step forward in achieving Formula 1's aim of broadening the sport's appeal."

ESPN won't have its own crew at races, relying instead on the feed produced by Britain's Sky Sport, but Disney is already developing ideas related to F1 for its other assets: the cinema, theme parks and so on. Bratches argued that streaming direct to the fans (otherwise known as 'over the top', or OTT) does not exclude other means of delivery.

"In France, we have just signed a new pay-TV deal with Canal+ for considerably more money than we were previously getting," he explained. "We have also done a deal with free-to-air TF1 for a number of races, including the French Grand Prix. And we will also have our OTT service in the French market as well, although we don't yet know exactly how that will work."

It was a point backed up by Carey.

"We live in world that is changing," he said. "There are multiple platforms for content delivery, with pay-TV, free-to-air, social media and over the top. There are endless possibilities for structuring deals with all the different parties involved. What we want to do is to use all of these different ways to get to as broad an audience as possible. We see OTT as being a way to deliver a lot more things to the fans, which we cannot do on linear TV. We have all this data and we are not using it. So, if you want to know about braking distances, or you want to listen to a particular driver's radio, or whatever, digital media allows you to do that. And it doesn't have to be expensive. We have to figure out the best way to get the sport across to the different age groups in different regions. And we will have to structure deals differently to meet the different requirements."

When it comes to the racing, Ross Brawn is the man in charge, and he had been busy trying to find "the right solutions to make our sport as great as possible in the future. And by great, I mean close racing, healthy teams, true meritocracy of drivers and all the things we know we have in the perfect world.

"We need as many teams to be as competitive as possible. And we need to flatten off the variation between the front and the back of the grid. So that, on a good day with a following wind and a great driver, a great team can win a race. That means, quite obviously, finding ways of limiting the potential of the regulations or limiting the resources that teams have at their availability."

The proposals put forward for engines in 2021 meet these goals, but they have prompted grumbles and gripes from some of the bigger teams. They want the status quo. Why wouldn't they? They are at the front. Liberty understands this and, although they will not say it out loud, they clearly believe that F1 is their 'train set', and if any teams don't agree with the way things are heading, then they can go and do something else...

Joe Saward

BETWEEN now and 2021, there is likely to be the usual fight for income and power among the signatories to the fragile tripartite Concorde Agreement that holds F1 together. Its history can, and does, fill books. If you are really interested and want a good grounding, read investigative journalist Terry Lovell's excellent book, *Bernie's Game*.

The Concorde Agreement used to be a bipartite agreement. In the seventies, Ecclestone began negotiating with race promoters on behalf of the Formula One Constructors Association (FOCA) – the teams – for a small, but ever growing percentage.

He regularly got into pitched battles with dictatorial, bombastic Jean-Marie Balestre, president of FISA, which governed the sport at the time on behalf of the FIA (subsequently, he became president of the FIA itself). Balestre had the manufacturers (the grandees) on his side – Ferrari, Renault and Alfa Romeo, while Ecclestone represented what Balestre saw as the grubby British *garagistes*. The *garagistes*, teams such as Tyrrell, Lotus, McLaren and Williams, with their off-the-shelf Cosworth engines, tended to be highly successful and technically innovative. When Balestre tried to ban sliding skirts, an intrinsic part of ground-effects underbody aerodynamics so successfully adopted by the British teams, it was seen as an attempt to favour the manufacturers.

A FISA/FOCA war ensued, during which Ecclestone and Max Mosley (then FOCA's lawyer) threatened a breakaway series, the World Federation of Motor Sport. Despite being almost broke, they got as far as staging a race, which brought Balestre to the negotiating table. The result was the first Concorde Agreement, which was actually hammered out with Enzo Ferrari's input, at Maranello. But such was Balestre's ego, that he insisted it be formally signed at FISA's Place de la Concorde HQ in Paris. Part of the deal gave FOCA the commercial rights for a four-year period, after which they would revert to the FIA. But that deal kept being renegotiated over time and there was no return to the original arrangement.

Amusingly, even back then, Ferrari was threatening to pull out, Enzo claiming that F1 was all the poorer for FOCA's machinations and threatening to put his money into sports car racing.

Ecclestone insisted that race organisers signed over TV rights as a condition of his deal and then set about revolutionising the broadcasting of F1, to the point where it became hugely lucrative. The next key moment came when Mosley usurped Balestre as FIA president and delegated the commercial rights to Ecclestone directly, rather than Ecclestone on behalf of the teams. All hell broke loose, but Ecclestone, usually through divide-and-conquer tactics and various 'sweetener' payments along the way, managed to keep the show together.

He had plenty of run-ins, not least with the European Commission. Attempting to cash in and float F1 in 1997, he failed to seek guidance from the European Commission to establish that his TV contracts and agreements with the FIA, broadcasters and promoters were compatible with EC competition laws.

All contracts of more than five years attracted the concern of the Comission, including his ten-year contracts with the teams and several free-to-air and pay-TV contracts, and a new 15-year agreement with the FIA.

Evidence of monopolistic practice was said to be plentiful: some of the TV contracts offered substantial discounts to broadcasters who agreed to show only F1, apparently confirming a long-held suspicion that Ecclestone had deliberately suppressed other motor sport to benefit F1.

In December, 1997, European Competition Commissioner Karel Van Miert authorised a warning letter to Ecclestone and the FIA, saying that the terms of the Concorde Agreement were a "serious restriction of competition".

Mosley dismissed it and encouraged the Commission to get its facts right. At the Court of First Instance in Luxembourg the following May, the FIA alleged that letters leaked to journalists constituted an unlawful release of confidential documents. Van Miert had given the *Wall St Journal* an interview in which he had claimed breaches of competition.

In October of the following year, after an internal investigation, Mosley received an apology, which claimed that a press release had been issued by an "inexperienced staff member". That reminded the F1 paddock somewhat of 1994, when Benetton had got away with the removal of a fuel filter, which speeded up the refuelling stop, because it "had been done by a junior member of staff". The EC was made to pay the FIA's legal costs.

With his flotation dead in the water while EC investigations went on, Ecclestone instead issued a $2bn Eurobond against future earnings. In June, 1999, the EC's Directorate-General for Competition issued a 185-page report, known as a Statement of Objections, part of which said that the FIA could not claim exclusive television rights, and that it was only one of a number of claimants, along with the organisers, promoters, track owners and teams, all of whom could reasonably claim shares. Claims to sole ownership of these rights was deemed to be an abuse of a dominant position.

Mosley hit back with a 107-page response, plus a personal letter to Mario Monti (who had been appointed to succeed Van Miert as Competition Commissioner), claiming that the Statement of Objections was hopelessly flawed. The FIA requested an

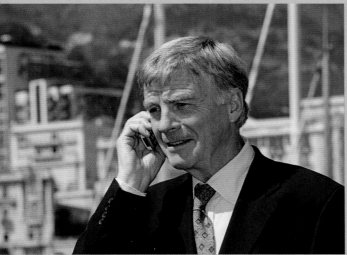

Left: Max Mosley has always been well-connected.

Far Left: Current FIA president Jean Todt, about to embark on an unopposed third term, talks to the press in Abu Dhabi.

Below: What war? Bernie Ecclestone with Jean-Marie Balestre at Magny-Cours in 2000.

Photos: WRi2/Jean-François Galeron

Mosley, it is alleged, had copied the UK property procedure of selling a leasehold so far into the distance that it was just like selling the freehold. As far as EU competition law was concerned, he believed that it would be seen as the FIA divesting itself of its F1 commercial interests to the point where it would obviously have no reason to favour F1 over any rival form of motor sport, which is one of the things the EC wanted. He also believed that as it was as good as an outright sale, it put the agreement out of the Commission's jurisdiction.

Mosley managed to persuade Monti to give his approval, despite many considering the deal to be in flagrant violation of competition law. Monti is said to have sanctioned it on the grounds that "a longer duration of exclusive arrangements can prove to be justified, particularly when an operator wishes to enter a new market with an innovative service or to introduce a new technology requiring very high risk and heavy investment."

This was held to be Ecclestone's big investment in digital TV technology, but legal opinion was highly dubious about whether this held water.

Whether it did or not, it was the foundation of Ecclestone's multi-billionaire status, confirmed when F1 was sold to CVC in 2005. A number of lawyers raised eyebrows at such an acquisition by a private equity investment company, calling it ballsy in the extreme. But if it had been a gamble, it certainly paid off for CVC, who made a 350 per cent return on investment when it sold to Liberty, and it still retains shares.

Periodically, whenever a new Concorde Agreement is due, the teams seek a better deal and more influence in the sport's governance. In the early days, they had a weak power base, but as more manufacturers entered, threats of a breakaway series carried more weight, in that they would have the financial clout to instigate one. But it never happened. Allegiances broke down and divide-and-rule won the day. In the early noughties, it was the GPMA (Grand Prix Manufacturers Association), and in the late noughties, it was FOTA (Formula One Teams Association).

In 2009, there appeared to be solidarity behind a breakaway, with Ferrari on-side, but then Red Bull and Maranello broke away, signing strong deals to commit to F1.

You can never quite believe what you are seeing. For instance, at practically the same time as FOTA chairman and then-McLaren team principal Martin Whitmarsh was photographed shaking hands with Ferrari's Luca di Montezemolo in a show of FOTA solidarity, someone else was signing Ferrari's new deal with F1… And such was Maranello's desire to be seen to have done so first that Red Bull, who actually had, was asked to change the date on its agreement…

With around $750m of an estimated $1.8bn annual revenue disappearing out of F1 to the commercial rights holder – a body that effectively didn't exist 30-odd years ago when agreements were bipartite, you might wonder why the manufacturers/teams don't just get on and run their own series, maybe calling it GP1 or some such.

For the manufacturers, the ones with the money, making cars is their core business, not running racing championships, quite apart from the legal, organisational and logistical challenges such an undertaking would mean. The idea of competing in F1 for prestige/marketing reasons, while it suits, may well be rubber-stamped by a board. Becoming involved with and committing to running a racing series is unlikely to. So the only brinkmanship that went as far as actually putting on a race was Max and Bernie's 37 years ago, and that's unlikely to change.

But, if you had just paid $8bn for something, you'd want to be sure. Which is why, if it seems to matter desperately to the manufacturers, F1's next engine might be closer to what *they* would like than perhaps the fans' ideal. Time will tell.

Tony Dodgins

oral hearing to challenge the conclusions, and said that if the hearing confirmed the objections, it would take the matter to the Court of First Instance in Luxembourg. It was a gamble: if the FIA lost, it could be fined ten per cent of its turnover.

A date in May, 2000, was set, but, in truth, neither side wanted the hearing. Ecclestone may have been concerned about having to make disclosures, and Monti, who had seen Mosley embarrass Van Miert, had bigger fish to fry than motor sport, and little stomach for pitching his budget and staff against adversaries as well-connected and well-heeled as Mosley and Ecclestone. Thus when Mosley wrote to Monti ahead of the hearing with some proposals, he received a favourable response – the hearing was cancelled and 'settlement talks' began.

The FIA was to amend sporting regulations that the EC regarded as abuses of competition law. Monti officially announced the 'peace deal' in January, 2001. Ecclestone would no longer continue as the FIA vice-president of promotional affairs and sold his interests in rallying and other motor sport except F1. His FOA would agree to limit the duration of its free-to-air broadcasting rights to five years. The FIA would no longer have commerical interest in the success of F1 and agreed to waive any broadcasting rights under the Concorde Agreement.

Then one of F1's defining moments occurred at a press conference given by Mosley at the Monaco Grand Prix in May, 2001, when it was announced that the FIA had sold the F1 commercial rights to SLEC (Kirch Group and the Ecclestone family trust) for 100 years, starting on 1st January, 2011, for $313.6m. Come again?

To put that into perspective, Kirch had just paid $600m to FIFA for 2002 football World Cup rights, while Sky had paid £1.1bn for Premiership football rights, and ITV £120m for three years of TV highlights…

Mosley then conjectured about what the FIA would do with "all the money" and talked about a new FIA Foundation to pursue safety work in particular, presenting one of its first initiatives, a safer crash helmet, of which they were "particularly proud".

If this was a diversionary tactic, it didn't really cut it, and of much greater interest was Mosley's observation: "There is something else I would like to add… nobody knows with any certainty who has what rights in the various parts of the championship: what proportion of the rights belongs to the teams who have invested in the cars and drivers; how much can be attributed to Bernie or his companies to reward him for his foresight in making Formula 1 such a valuable business; how much belongs to the FIA as the originator and proprietor of the World Championship.

"If there were to have been a dispute involving these issues, the FIA might conceivably be faced with a ruling that it is not entitled to claim as great a proportion of these rights for itself as previously it believed it owned. We have therefore followed the principle that a bird in the hand is worth two in the bush. We are therefore very satisfied with the amount of money that we have been paid for these rights."

And Ecclestone, no doubt, was absolutely ecstatic. As one disgruntled team principal commented, "So, the FIA has sold F1 to Max's old mate for 100 years for about the price of a year's NASCAR rights? As a sting, it makes Redford and Newman look like beginners…"

But how, when the EC had been getting hot under the collar about deals lasting longer than five years, had Ecclestone been able to buy the rights for a century?

FOUR TIMES A CHAMPION

n the end, Lewis Hamilton won his fourth world title by a relatively comfortable 46 points. But that doesn't begin to tell the story of his best season yet. The constants were outright speed combined with amazing consistency, as TONY DODGINS relates...

Above: Four times a champion, and it's doughnut time in Mexico City.

Photo: Mercedes AMG Petronas F1 Team

Above right and far right: Bling and tattoos have become a Lewis staple...

Right: The never-ending round of interviews for the most in-demand driver in the paddock.

Opening spread: Lewis, in familiar casual attire, finds himself in a rare moment of solitude.

Photos: Peter J. Fox

THERE'S no question Lewis is the best out there," said his three-times world champion team boss, Niki Lauda, after Hamilton had overcome Sebastian Vettel to take his ninth and final 2017 GP win in Austin, helping Mercedes seal a fourth consecutive constructors' championship.

The win was Lewis's 62nd GP victory, and it prompted Mercedes team principal Toto Wolff to say, "I've worked with him for five years, and I've never seen him operate at this level: the raw pace is spectacular; his understanding of the tyres and the ability of a car that is difficult sometimes is amazing. And it's not easy. Sustainable performance at that level, I haven't seen before."

Hamilton himself said, "I take a lot of pride and satisfaction from not making mistakes. In Mexico, I had a spin, then came Brazil, but otherwise it's been my cleanest year overall."

Records, they say, are there to be broken, and Hamilton continued to do so. He became the first four-times British world champion, with three-times champion Jackie Stewart on hand to offer his congratulations. He overhauled Ayrton Senna's 65 pole positions and then Michael Schumacher's 68. In Canada, he was touched to receive one of Ayrton's iconic race helmets from the Senna family to mark the occasion, and then to have a message from Michael's wife, Corinna, delivered to him by Ross Brawn at Spa. Suddenly, Schumacher's 91-race win record, which many had suggested would stand for all time, didn't look so far away.

But, before Hamilton could embark on his tremendous year, the air had to be cleared at Mercedes to a much greater degree than was generally appreciated, after he and Nico Rosberg had gone down to the wire in Abu Dhabi in 2016.

It was a combustible situation, literally, when Hamilton had his engine blow-up in Malaysia, had bad-mouthed Mercedes reliability and been left with backing up Rosberg into the traffic at Yas Marina as his only hope of the title. Wolff did not agree with the tactic and said so.

"We had a difficult moment," Wolff admitted. "We came back together a couple of days later and had a long evening in my kitchen, and put it all out there. All the frustrations and questions that had grown over the years were dismantled. He went off and came back with a great mindset this year, and it just got stronger all the way through. And you can see, also, the relationship with Valtteri is an important factor. The spirit is great in the team and was an essential piece of the jigsaw."

Hamilton himself admitted, "Going and seeing Toto at the end of last year was crucial in solidifying the longevity in the team. If you're at the office and your boss doesn't want you there, it's going to be a bad environment. That's just negativity drawing away from what you're great at. It was almost a purification of the relationship and a restart of the solid foundation we'd built years ago."

You could understand both points of view: Wolff would have been severely hacked off about Hamilton letting rip about reliability issues in a team that had just served him up two world championships and was paying him squillions of dollars. And Hamilton didn't appreciate criticism for doing the only thing that realistically he could have done in the Abu Dhabi finale.

But it was all buried, and Wolff, Hamilton and the entire Mercedes team had bigger concerns to focus their minds when Ferrari turned up at Barcelona pre-season testing and went quickest.

When Sebastian Vettel was able to shadow Hamilton in Melbourne, jump him at his pit stop and win the race, everyone at Mercedes could see that they had a proper fight on their hands. And that is exactly when Hamilton is at his most dangerous.

Paddy Lowe, who has deep experience of working with him at both Mercedes and McLaren, said, "If Lewis is going to have a lapse in terms of concentration, it's more likely to come when he's not under pressure. When he is, he's frighteningly good and can be almost impossible to beat."

The early-season races see-sawed: after Vettel had taken Melbourne, Hamilton won in China, and Vettel hit back in Bahrain. Round four in Sochi was one of Lewis's weaker races, and it highlighted something of a pattern: whenever there was a low-grip surface, Hamilton seemed almost to over-drive the car, whereas Valtteri Bottas would more readily accept its lower limits and get a time out of it.

That culminated in a rare second-row grid position, and while Bottas was able to convert P3 into a first-corner lead, helped by the long run and tow down to Sochi's Turn Two, Hamilton found himself running in traffic – not ideal when the closeness of the battle with Ferrari had forced Mercedes to run marginal on cooling in pursuit of small aero gains. Valtteri won and Lewis had to be content with third, behind Vettel.

Throughout those early-season races, though, Hamilton seemed at peace with the world. His relationship with new team-mate Bottas was clearly as good as could be expected with a man who was trying to beat him in the same car, and even he and Vettel seemed to constitute a mutual admiration society. But all that changed in Baku.

Vettel's rush of blood to the head in side-swiping Hamilton, after he thought the Mercedes driver had brake-tested him behind the safety car, meant that he was always going to be the villain.

Was it just symptomatic of Seb feeling the pressure? Interestingly, former Ferrari-driver-turned-TV-pundit Ivan Capelli had already said that he could see the odd mistake here and there, which indicated, he thought, that Vettel was feeling the heat of Ferrari being in a genuine championship-challenging position versus Hamilton and Mercedes.

Vettel clearly thought he had cause to be annoyed in Azerbaijan. Hamilton made a point of telling the media that his data proved he had not touched the brakes. But Nico Rosberg had previously made the observation that Lewis was always good at plausible deniability when he'd taken things to the edge – such as in past first-corner robustness at Austin

Above: Surfing the crowd after his victory at Silverstone.

Top right: The famous Hamilton helmet awaits the adornment of a fourth star.

Above right: Selfie time after his victory in Austin.
Photos: Peter J. Fox

Right: Lewis and his Mercedes, a symphony in speed under the lights in Singapore.
Photo: Mercedes AMG Petronas F1 Team

and Suzuka. Vettel felt that not picking up the throttle when Hamilton might have been expected to do so had much the same effect… But his overreaction that day meant that the sound of any violins was faint.

When opening-lap misjudgements followed from Vettel in Singapore and Mexico – although Hamilton questioned whether the Mexican contact that punctured his tyre had been deliberate after his championship rival had already damaged his front wing in a brush with Verstappen – you did wonder whether he had succeeded in getting into Vettel's head and affecting him.

"I don't know…" Lewis said. "You just keep your foot down, keep the pressure on, and when the other guy shows no sign of weakness… that's definitely difficult. Look at Federer and Nadal: at some point in the game, one will see a slight weakness in the other – even if just half a per cent. That's what they try to capitalise, which makes the difference. And that's really how it has been this year. The key for me is to be the most solid driver out there."

And he was. Hamilton was the only driver with a 100 per cent point-scoring record across all 2017 GPs. He completed every single racing lap bar one, which was a consequence of being lapped in Mexico when he had to pit after the incident with Vettel.

A revealing part of Hamilton's competitive persona is that rather than wishing to protect his advantage, to hope that any potential on-track challenge is nullified, he'd rather bring it on. He is genuinely scared of nobody. The more battling at the front, the merrier.

Speaking of his battles with Vettel, Verstappen and, in the closing laps of Mexico, Alonso, he said, "We're the four strongest drivers. I really hope we're all in the fight next year. It would be friggin' amazing! Sebastian, this year, you could say, 'Give more space.' Not in a negative way. Fernando – toughest driver there is: very hard, but fair. Friggin' heck, his racecraft is mighty. But Max's racecraft is very impressive, too. He's doing wonderful things, but he's going to grow so much over the next ten years. I don't think it will be a problem, it'll just be freaking tough. Wouldn't that be a fight? Even I'd pay to see that!" Daniel Ricciardo, you'd guess, would feel he ought to be in it, too…

Hamilton had also changed a number of aspects of his personal approach, from training alone and eating a vegan diet to the way in which he works with the team.

"My engineers and I are constantly working on improving our communication, and we've done an exceptional job this year in terms of what we do at the factory. For example, I've changed my factory days a lot compared to my time at McLaren. They were generally a bit of a waste, and when I joined Mercedes I changed the dynamic so I can extract the maximum. I'm not one who can sit in a meeting for five hours. I can't focus that long!"

Hamilton said he feels the best he's ever felt, physically and mentally, reckoning that a big factor in the former was his change to a vegan diet.

"The best decision I've ever made was moving to this team," he explained, "and the second best was changing my diet. Ultimately, you always try to live to your potential

Above: Lewis drove better than ever in 2017 to secure his fourth title.
Photo: Mercedes AMG Petronas F1 Team

Top right: Hamilton relished the battle for the championship with Ferrari's Sebastian Vettel.

Above right: Mutual respect. Lewis enjoyed a harmonious relationship with team-mate Valtteri Bottas.
Photos: Peter J. Fox

Right: A Silver Arrow and a lightning Bolt share the victory podium at Circuit of the Americas.
Photo: Mercedes AMG Petronas F1 Team

and drive to your potential, and I feel that the Austin race was one of my greatest days. I felt right in the zone. It's the greatest feeling."

If you're a cynic, you could say that any driver would feel comfortable in a team when he is not being pressed too hard by a team-mate, and Bottas, at that point, was having a tough time. Ask Lewis if the current equilibrium could have been achieved with Rosberg in the team, and the response is rapid. "No."

"No one knows what really happened in the team," he said. "I can't say it was great last year. But it's great that this year we were fighting with another team, so the focus was different. When you have two strong drivers in the team, as we had, it's like a hurricane. Strong energy, but just stuck in the room. Whereas now, we had this bundle of energy directed to the car. Overall, a much happier dynamic.

"I think Valtteri will go from strength to strength, and I'll work with him. I don't mind if he wins some races. I don't want him to win them all, but I like that he can push me, and at the beginning of the year that's what he was doing. I was just able to take the car to another level in the second half of the season.

"The W08 was a great car, but tricky to get it to work. For him to come into a new team, with a new aero-concept car, was tough." He might have added, "and take on me!"

Bottas readily admitted that he did not underestimate a three-times world champion, but found Hamilton even better than expected.

In such a tight year, Hamilton's intrinsic speed, allied, in fairness, to stronger Mercedes engine modes in qualifying, often made a key difference. Those 11 pole positions, the extra eight metres at the start, often gave his team a

strategic advantage in a super-tight fight. And, as Hamilton confirmed, he did manage to step up his level even more in the second half of the year.

"You start a weekend with the potential you and the car have, and you want to squeeze out those extra drops that no one else can get. That's where I feel my value is. Sometimes, if you go in the wrong direction, you don't even get to the car's potential. But understanding the car allowed me to get that potential and a little bit more. So even in races where we struggled, we came out with more than we hoped."

But that didn't come free, it involved work. With those landmark records becoming ever closer, how much longer did Lewis envisage putting in the necessary effort to stay in F1 and perform at the highest level?

"It's about trying to find the balance. I've currently got another year with the team, and I do want to continue, but I'm at that point where there's that question. But you can't come back to F1. Whatever happens, you're going to miss it. If it's next year, if it's five years from now, you're going to miss it when you finish. I was talking to my best friend about things that I do envy or look forward to, like living in one place, getting a routine, having game nights with my friends, my family. Each year, I stay in the sport, I delay those things. But from 40 onwards, there's so much time for it.

"But... my auntie died from cancer, and on her last day she said, 'I've worked every day with the plan of stopping one day and doing all these different things, then I ran out of time.' So I'm battling with that in my mind. I live my life day by day and try to live it to the maximum. I want to keep racing, but there are these other things I want to do. I want to have my cake and eat it." Let's hope there are no eggs in it!

ANOTHER RED DAWN?

After a disappointing 2016 season for the Prancing Horse, DIETER RENCKEN considers the resurgence that resulted in Ferrari winning again in 2017...

1:01:58 RAI RAI VET VET

10:28:02

Above: You looking at me kid? Maurizio Arrivabene stares down the lens of Foxy's camera.

Top right: When Marchionne speaks, everyone listens.
Photos: Peter J. Fox

Above right: Could have, should have? Kimi Räikkönen looked set for a victory in Monaco...
Photo: Scuderia Ferrari

Right: ...But it was Sebastian Vettel who took the honours.

Opening spread: Vettel wins in Bahrain to make it two victories from the first three races of the 2017 season.
Photos: Peter J. Fox

A S Formula 1 headed into 2017, Ferrari's stock, and, by extension, that of Sebastian Vettel, was so low that bookmakers rated the four-times champion's chances of winning the title no better than 20:1. The Scuderia had been firmly trounced in 2016 by Mercedes, as expected, but also by Red Bull Racing, using Renault power. Ferrari had not scored a single win.

Seven retirements over the season had not helped Ferrari's cause (Mercedes had posted three, two of which had come courtesy of a first-corner contretemps between its drivers in Spain). The 'would he, wouldn't he' departure of technical director James Allison mid-season created further consternation. Finally, the 2017 aero-centric regulations were deemed to be right up Red Bull's alley. On reflection, 20:1 seemed pretty fair.

Yet, come the first day of pre-season testing, and Vettel, driving the SF70, named in honour of Ferrari's *settantesimo*, stunned the paddock by topping the times at noon. Although Hamilton eventually shaded him by a tenth, the Prancing Horse had clearly leap-frogged Red Bull and was snapping at Merc's heels. Ferrari ran consistently at the sharp end thereafter.

During 2016, his second year with Ferrari as *Gestione Sportiva* managing director and team principal – after transferring from sponsor Philip Morris at the behest of

Ferrari president Sergio Marchionne – Maurizio Arrivabene restructured the team, introducing a flatter hierarchy and granting increased responsibility to younger members. Individual objectives were revised and targets redefined.

In July 2016, he promoted Mattia Binotto to the post of chief technical officer (previously the Swiss had been responsible for power units, hydraulics and electronics). The quietly-spoken Ferrari 'lifer' played a key role in leading the technical team from the front. Increased conceptual input was provided by Rory Byrne, Ferrari's legendary retired ex-designer, who had been retained as a consultant and was described in-house as "our jewel".

After F1's engine regulations had been freed up, Binotto's team substantially upgraded the power unit. If not quite up to Mercedes levels of race performance, it was not far off. Crucially, reliability was also improved. An uprated Binotto engine, Byrne's chassis magic and a team smarting from a winless 2016 proved a potent mix.

"It was soon clear that we had a very good car and a highly-motivated team," recalled Arrivabene, who freely admitted that Ferrari was pleasantly surprised by its testing form. According to race predictor software, it would be nip-and-tuck, with the SF70 holding an advantage over Mercedes on certain circuits; vice versa on others.

Fast forward to Melbourne's season-opener: Vettel started

alongside Hamilton and then shadowed the pole-man until he stopped early. Once Vettel was running in clean air, the race swung in Ferrari's favour, sending bookies around the globe into nervous spasms. The question, though, was whether Vettel's win, his team's first in 28 grands prix, was simply a flash in the pan.

All too often in the Wagnerian drama that is Ferrari, elation gives way to desolation quicker than purple Pirellis degrade on a summer Sunday, so Shanghai was awaited with bated breath. Hamilton did the business ahead of Vettel, but in the sands of Bahrain, the Red Army fought back. In Sochi, Sebastian adapted to the ultra-smooth circuit better than Lewis, but Valtteri Bottas had the measure of him – just. With the season 20 per cent done, Vettel led Hamilton by 13 points, with three wins to two.

The see-sawing continued through Spain – Hamilton won from the Ferrari – but the championship leader emphatically took the initiative in Monaco. A pattern was developing: on faster, sweeping venues, the silver car was quicker; on slower, high-downforce tracks, Vettel and Ferrari held the advantage. Taking their cars out of the equation, there was little to choose between the two multiple champions.

Then came Canada and Azerbaijan. At Île Notre-Dame, a first-lap clash cost Vettel his front wing. In Baku, his fiery temper under duress (remember his Turkish antics with

Red Bull team-mate Mark Webber, and his expletive-ridden message to Charlie Whiting in Mexico), there was another rush of blood to the head. He angrily side-swiped Hamilton after running into the back of the Merc and damaging his front wing for the second successive race as Lewis slowed the field behind the safety car.

Arguably, that cost Vettel victory and 13 points – he finished fourth after a stop/go penalty and was probably fortunate not to have been black-flagged. It certainly dented his reputation, and gave Hamilton the moral high ground. Three penalty points on his licence took his tally to nine – three points away from a race ban – and forced some circumspection in the heat of battle.

Still, Vettel drew strength from leading the title hunt and, when F1 broke for summer after Hungary at the end of July, his advantage over Hamilton was 14 points, despite a steering problem in Budapest that required the full co-operation of Kimi Räikkönen, loyally riding shotgun as designated number two. Kimi managed to fend off Hamilton, who also maintained Mercedes team equilibrium by handing the final podium place back to Bottas, having asked to be let by earlier.

Vettel and Hamilton had both claimed four wins by the summer break, and the SF70 had displayed not only front-running pace, but also inherent reliability. Punters who had presciently wagered a grand on Vettel taking his fifth title headed into summer smelling twenty big ones!

What could go wrong? Red Bull may have been on the up after a faltering start, but the team's drivers were taking

points off each other. The second half of the season kicked off with a Spa/Monza back-to-back – ultra-quick circuits, and Hamilton, perhaps not unexpectedly, won both, turning his 14-point deficit to Vettel into a three-point lead.

On the plus side, though, if Mercedes had pushed Ferrari harder than expected in Budapest, Spa was an intense race, with Sebastian harrying Lewis every inch of the way on what had been viewed as a Mercedes track. Looking at the calendar's remaining seven venues, even Mercedes was conceding that they might have their work cut out.

But then Ferrari's championship challenge went horribly awry, Mercedes clinching its fourth successive constructors' championship at Austin, and Hamilton winning his fourth drivers' championship in Mexico, with two rounds still to go. How did Ferrari slip from being serious contenders to limping losers in just four races, given their earlier sparkling form?

Fundamentally, four factors conspired against them: wrangles over 'oil-burn'; a first-lap shunt in sultry Singapore that eliminated both red cars – gifting Hamilton victory on a bogey track; manifold failure during Malaysian qualifying that forced Vettel to start from the back and eliminated front-row Räikkönen; and a dud spark plug in Japan.

Although Ferrari officially downplayed the oil burning – actually a Mercedes initiative – there is little doubt that when the FIA tightened up on teams finding clever ways to burn oil in the cylinders with a new technical directive pre-Baku, it impacted more on them than it did on Mercedes. Introducing oil into combustion chambers adds calorific value and is particularly valuable when a fuel-flow limit is in place.

However, this factor did not trigger Hamilton's post-Hungary run of five wins in six races, which was as much down to Ferrari's reliability debacles in Asia. When the pendulum swung in favour of Mercedes, it did so decisively.

There were self-inflicted set-up issues in Austin. According to a team insider, Ferrari royally screwed up on corner weights – setting up Mercedes to clinch the world title, which they duly delivered. Hamilton then sealed the drivers' title next time out in Mexico.

So, was 2017 False Dawn or Red Dawn? Certainly the latter, tinged with a touch of Red Mist. There is no doubt that Vettel's moves in Baku and Singapore cost the team dearly, with the racing incident in Canada and the opening lap in Mexico losing further points, although he only really held his hand up to the first of those: "Looking back, Baku stands out obviously, but for the rest, I think it's been okay."

Teams win or lose together, and Ferrari must shoulder the blame for the failures in Sepang and Suzuka, even if the spark plug failure, allegedly a fifty-quid NGK component, was out of its hands. However, Marchionne's swift bolstering of Ferrari's internal and supplier quality-control systems speaks volumes about his displeasure.

As is his wont, Marchionne was blunt: "I think we learned a lot, and it's a painful way of learning. The second half [of the season] revealed structural weaknesses in the manner in which we are managing the business, which are going to get rectified."

Depending upon how the resultant points swings versus Hamilton are quantified, Ferrari lost around 60 points to

Above: Vettel is wheeled to the Singapore pole, his season about to unravel.
Photo: Peter J. Fox

Top left: Hungary: Marchionne applauds his team while Piero Ferrari holds the winner's trophy.
Photo: WRi2/Studio Colombo

Above left: Seventy years of Ferrari in 2017.
Photo: Photo: Peter J. Fox

Left: Where Marchionne leads, Arrivabene and Binotto follow…
Photo: WRi2/Studio Colombo

Above: Ferraris lined up on the track after their 1-2 finish in Hungary.
Photo: Scuderia Ferrari

Above right: Arrivabene and Binotto are charged with bringing the championship back to Ferrari.
Photo: WRi2/Jean-François Galeron

Right: Vettel could only manage third at Monza, but the *tifosi* were as wild as ever.
Photo: Scuderia Ferrari

Mercedes, meaning the sport's new owners, Liberty Media, potentially had a two-car finale in Abu Dhabi on their hands before fate intervened. However, IF is F1 spelt backwards, so none of this is any consolation to a Ferrari team that can equally draw solace from its resurgence.

Arrivabene summarised the first season since 2008 when the team had mounted a sustained challenge across the full spectrum of races with a neat twist of the 'glass half full/half empty' analogy.

"To use the example of the glass: at mid-season, when we led the championship, we were thirsty, but by end of season, we were using the water to take a pill for a bit of headache…" said the gravelly-voiced former Marlboro marketing guru. "Apart from that, I think the team was pushing, pushing, really hard. They were working well. We had certain circumstances that were not in our favour."

The fact is that despite the highs and lows of 2017, the overwhelming belief at Ferrari was that the season provided a foundation upon which to build – not only for 2018, but also beyond. Vettel said as much ahead of the Abu Dhabi finale, where the suspicion was that he had finished a somewhat conservative third to consolidate that runner-up spot in the championship standings.

"Nobody expected Ferrari to be that strong," he said after win number five in Brazil. "We made the biggest step – there was a lot of talk about other people – but in the end, we were there from the start until the end.

"Of course, if you miss out, it sort of sucks, but you have to be fair as well. We hadn't been very competitive last year; we hadn't been very good developing the car, and we've made massive progress this year. You have to give credit to all the people, the whole team, for the step we made. I think we can all feel we're getting stronger, so hopefully we can carry that strength into the next couple of years, not just next year, not just the winter, but also the future. Because our objective is to bring Ferrari back properly, to get there and to dominate."

In his own summary, Marchionne expressed the same sentiments as his star driver: "If, this time last year, I'd asked anyone how well we would do in 2017, I couldn't have got a buyer for the idea that we would be that far advanced in the first half of the season. We have done well, given our starting point, but were unable to finish the task. That's a 2018 objective now. We regret not having done better, but the car is there – it is, in my view, the best car on the track today."

Ferrari came close to winning both titles for the first time in a decade, and will probably start 2018 joint favourites with Mercedes. And that is progress.

DELIVER – OR ELSE!

WHERE most teams favour stability, even when things go pear-shaped, Enzo Ferrari adopted a rolling-head approach. This culture continued within Maranello even after his death in 1988, with abrupt departures of a succession of former team principals, technical officers, drivers and even the charismatic former president, Luca di Montezemolo, attesting to Ferrari's ruthlessness in dealing with failure.

When 2017 turned against Ferrari, the word in the paddock was that team principal Maurizio Arrivabene would be handed his personal belongings in a Jiffy bag at the factory gates upon his return from Asia. Yet the Italian remains steadfastly in charge, with chairman Sergio Marchionne firmly refuting rumours that the team boss (or Mattia Binotto) would be fired. He stated that both "were at the table" when issues arose and branded such suggestions "idiotic", adding that all the duo needed was space.

A banker once said of Marchionne, 65: "If you don't deliver, you're out – he's ruthless." Has he become soft? Or is something afoot?

In typical Marchionne style, he has his eye on the long game. He retires from Fiat Chrysler Automobiles in 2019, but intends to remain Ferrari president. Freed from FCA duties, he plans to assume greater responsibility for Ferrari's political/commercial activities and will have his work cut out, given Liberty's planned changes to F1's commercial/governance structures. He intends to add sporting activities to Binotto's technical role. Arrivabene, 62 in March, 2019, remains safe until then...

REMARKABLY FRANK

Through good times and bad, sheer determination and constantly striving always to win the next race have endeared Sir Frank Williams and his independent team to legions of enthusiasts. MAURICE HAMILTON looks back at their 40-year roller-coaster ride of F1 competition...

Above: Alan Jones in the Williams FW07B heads towards victory in the 1980 British GP at Brands Hatch.

Photo: Williams F1 Team

Top right: FW on the pit wall at Zandvoort in 1980.

Top far right: The no-nonsense Alan Jones was the perfect fit for the fledgling Williams team.

Above right: Early success soon turned to tragedy. FW with Piers Courage in 1969.

Above far right: No fanfare. Frank and Alan Jones unveil the FW06 in the factory at Slough early in 1978.

Photos: Autocourse archive

Right: First win for the team. Clay Regazzoni at the start of the 1979 British Grand Prix.

Photo: LAT Images

Opening spread: The team brought together drivers past and present for a day of celebration in July, 2017.

Photo: Williams F1 Team

MORE than 40,000 fans turned up at Silverstone in early June, 2017. The reason was neither an official F1 test nor a preliminary to the British Grand Prix, but rather a celebration of the 40th anniversary of Williams. The attendance – which would have done one or two grands prix proud on a Friday – said everything about the affection held for this great team and its iconic leader, Sir Frank Williams CBE.

The pit lane and garages provided a glorious time warp as cars from across the decades represented the power behind six world champions, most of whom were present and happy to pay tribute to their former boss and his devoted team.

Although an incurable optimist, frequently for no good reason, Frank Williams would never have believed in 1977 that his fledgling race team would come to this. He had tried before with customer cars and had had painful experience of F1's demands.

Under various guises between 1969 and 1975, Frank Williams (Racing Cars) Ltd had been visited by bailiffs more often than consistent success. Even the apparent salvation of a sponsor buying the team ended uncomfortably for Frank when he was elbowed aside into the role of minion rather than manager.

All that changed with a fresh start for 1977 and two significant resolutions: after a year running a March, Frank decided he needed his own car, and he chose Patrick Head to create it.

Head may have been a relative unknown in the world of motor sport technology, but the clean sheet afforded by Williams would not only allow expression of sound engineering and sensible thinking, but also provide the

foundation for an endearing and lasting friendship. In simple terms, Patrick looked after the machinery and Frank found a way to pay for it.

Alan Jones, a similarly uncomplicated racer of the same age and ambition as his new employers, completed the package. It would be a powerful force, which found full expression in 1979, when the collection of no more than 20 individuals, operating out of a former carpet warehouse in Didcot, produced FW07, Head's interpretation of the ground-effect phenomenon pioneered by Lotus.

With significant tweaking by Frank Dernie as aerodynamicist (a new role in F1), the forerunner of a department numbering more than 100 today, FW07 not only stunned the opposition, but also left Frank open-mouthed as he stared at his stop watch during a pre-British GP test.

A half-second advantage would excite an F1 team today. On that June afternoon, Jones was *six* seconds under the F1 lap record. The benchmark may have been set a few years previously, but the massive gain would translate into the team's first win in the grand prix itself (albeit for Clay Regazzoni, Jones having been forced to retire while running in the lead).

"The 1979 British Grand Prix sticks in my mind more than any other," recalled Sir Frank. "I had been toiling in the sport for a decade at that point, with limited success, so to finally get that monkey off my back was a big relief. It broke the duck. To say it was euphoric would be a bit of an exaggeration, but it was a very happy and unforgettable day. The whole factory – such as it was in those days – was at Silverstone that weekend, and everyone was thrilled. It was a sign that we were headed in the right direction."

Above: Keke Rosberg took the Williams FW08 to the title in 1982.

Top right: Sir Frank stands proudly with his FW10 cars at the 1985 Austrian GP.
Photos: Williams F1 Team

Above right: Ayrton Senna's career with Williams would end in tragic circumstances.
Photo: Autocourse archive

Right: Nigel Mansell stormed to the championship in 1992.
Photo: LAT Images

With FW07 having arrived after the 1979 season had got going, Williams had to wait until the following year to win their first championship, after a tough contest between Jones and Brabham's Nelson Piquet.

The Brazilian went on to take the drivers' title in 1981, Williams claiming a second successive constructors' championship before finishing fourth in 1982, a topsy-turvy year encapsulated when Keke Rosberg became champion for Williams, despite winning just one race.

Along with the majority of British teams, Williams used an off-the-shelf Ford Cosworth DFV engine to power his cars. The advent of turbocharging as a more competitive option led to a switch to Honda as engine supplier for 1984, a clever move that began to produce serious results, Piquet having joined Nigel Mansell to give Williams a strong driving force for 1986. Too powerful, in fact, the rivalry and split of point scoring between these two allowing Alain Prost and McLaren-TAG to steal the drivers' championship at the final round in Australia.

Nigel Mansell had retired from the race in Adelaide when a rear tyre on his FW11 failed at high speed, marking a dramatic end to a year that had got off to an extremely distressing start. While returning to Nice airport from a pre-season test at Paul Ricard, Williams had rolled his hire car and landed on the roof. Somehow he survived a broken spinal chord, although his injuries would confine him to a wheelchair for the rest of his life.

Gloomy speculation about how long that life would be under such desperate circumstances did not take into account the same cast-iron determination that had carried Frank through previous setbacks. He was the first to pay tribute to the work of surgeons, his wife Ginny and, subsequently, his carers, but there is no doubt that his love of both the team and motor racing provided a powerful motivational force.

Indeed, it was a tribute to the structure of the team when Williams Grand Prix Engineering barely broke stride on the racetrack, every member of the workforce driven by an unspoken longing to "do it for Frank". That loyalty paid off with both championships in 1987.

The peaks and troughs endemic to F1 led to the team struggling until the dawn of a new era with Renault engines and one of the most sophisticated race cars to emerge from Williams – or any other F1 team. The FW14B not only had a semi-automatic gearbox, traction control and active suspension, but also Mansell on board to wring the neck of this beast of a machine to such good effect that he dominated the 1992 season.

Fifteen-year-old Claire Williams had accompanied her father to the British Grand Prix that year.

"That was a memorable race for me," recalled Claire. "It was at the height of 'Mansell Mania', and I remember driving in with Dad on the day of the race and the car being mobbed by fans. There was also the track invasion, with fans breaking down the fences to celebrate on the track with Nigel – it's a really iconic image in F1 and Williams history.

"My happiest memory is Nigel winning the 1992 championship, because I was in Hungary and it was one of the first races that Dad had ever taken me to by myself,

rather than just going to the British Grand Prix as a family; so that was a real treat.

"That year for Williams was so momentous. We dominated the championship, winning ten out of the 16 races, and Nigel went on to win his one and only championship in 'Red 5', one of the most iconic racing cars ever built. I can still picture Nigel at the end of the race in Hungary with all the journalists and all the fans. I can still remember the music that was playing in the garage: 'The Final Countdown'."

The arrival of Adrian Newey in 1991 had been significant. The facilities and encouragement available with this top team allowed the designer full freedom to exhibit his flair with FW14B and then FW15, used by Alain Prost to give Williams another brace of titles in 1993.

Until then, Williams had taken the sport's various trials and tribulations in their considerable stride. However, one single shocking event in 1994 would devastate both the team and the world.

Frank had felt the cold hand of tragedy in 1970. His dear friend, Piers Courage, had been killed at the wheel of a de Tomaso entered by Williams in the Dutch Grand Prix, during an era when fatalities were reluctantly viewed as part and parcel of motor sport. By 1994, however, massive strides in the acceptance of a need for safety meant that there had not been the loss of a driver during a grand prix for 12 years.

In the space of one weekend at Imola, however, two drivers were killed. One of them, Ayrton Senna, was a triple world champion and a legend. He had been driving a Williams.

"The most difficult time in our history was the death of Ayrton Senna in 1994, during the San Marino Grand Prix," said Sir Frank. "I had been close to Ayrton for many years and admired him deeply as a driver and as a man. I'm sure that if he were alive today, he would be president of Brazil. He certainly had the intellect and personality needed. The whole team was deeply affected by his death, but we knew we had to bounce back and did just that with some strong results that year, in no small part due to the leadership of Damon Hill."

Hill found himself thrust into the limelight in only his second full season. Once again, the ability of Frank and his team to negotiate stumbling blocks was proven when the driver came close to taking the championship but for

Above: Frank is flanked by wife Ginny and shareholder Toto Wolff as Williams celebrates Pastor Maldonado's Spanish GP win in 2012, the team's last victory.
Photo: Peter J. Fox

Top right: Williams believes that Keke Rosberg had the most innate skill of all his drivers.
Photo: Cahier Archive

Above right: Frank's daughter, Claire, assumed the deputy principal's role.
Photo: Peter J. Fox

Right: Damon Hill crosses the line in Suzuka to clinch the 1996 World Championship.
Photo: Cahier Archive

a controversial collision with Michael Schumacher in the final race that year. Williams won the constructors' title, taking two more in 1996 and 1997 when Hill and Jacques Villeneuve respectively became champions.

Throughout his time in F1, Williams has handled more than 50 drivers. A former (unsuccessful) racer himself, he remains in awe of the ability shown by the company's highest paid employees, and is reluctant to name a favourite.

"That's a difficult one to answer, as comparing drivers from different generations is always problematic, as the sport has changed so much," said Sir Frank. "I would say the driver born with the most innate skill was Keke Rosberg; the most intellectually superior was without doubt Senna; and Prost had an outstanding talent and level of experience when he joined us. Nigel was immensely competitive and aggressive in a good way; he wanted to win at anything he put his hand to. If I had to choose one driver, I would have to choose Ayrton. He was something really special."

In 2002, Claire joined her father's team as communications officer, before going on to become head of marketing and communications nine years later, and deputy team principal in 2013. By then, Williams had been through various iterations, growing slowly, but surely, and yet remaining proudly independent, an image that continued to strike a chord with F1 followers.

Frank received a knighthood in 1999 for services to the

sport, while Claire was made an OBE in 2017. Yet despite such high-profile recognition, the company's fundamental ethos of always striving to win the next race remains exactly as it was when Frank set out 40 years ago.

"I was always a bit of a dreamer, and I was certainly in the sport to win, but it was hard to imagine F1, or indeed Williams, growing to the size it is now," said Sir Frank. "Back then, even Ferrari had only about 250 employees, and McLaren maybe a little over 100. With Patrick's genius and the money that came into the sport with TV deals in the 1980s, Williams was well placed to capitalise. It sort of snowballed, as the more success we got, the more we had at our disposal to carry on winning."

"For a team to have been competing for 40 years is a massive achievement, and for an independent team to accomplish this makes it even more remarkable," said Claire. "Only Ferrari and McLaren have reached that figure, and someone like Ferrari has the might of a big company behind it. It's a real testament to the calibre of people working behind the scenes, who work so hard to keep us on the grid, and of course to the talent and hard work of Dad and Patrick.

"It's remarkable to think that Williams, as we know it today – over 700 employees on a 33-acre technology campus – started life being run out of a phone box with Frank fighting away the bailiffs!"

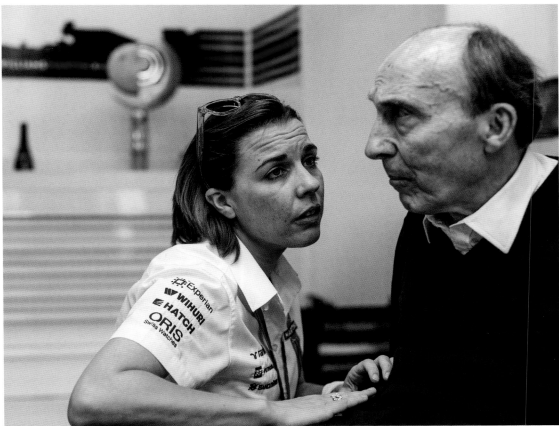

A GAME OF TWO HALVES

The 2017 season was an eventful year for Red Bull, with a poor start and eventual recovery in the second half. TONY DODGINS considers the team's performance...

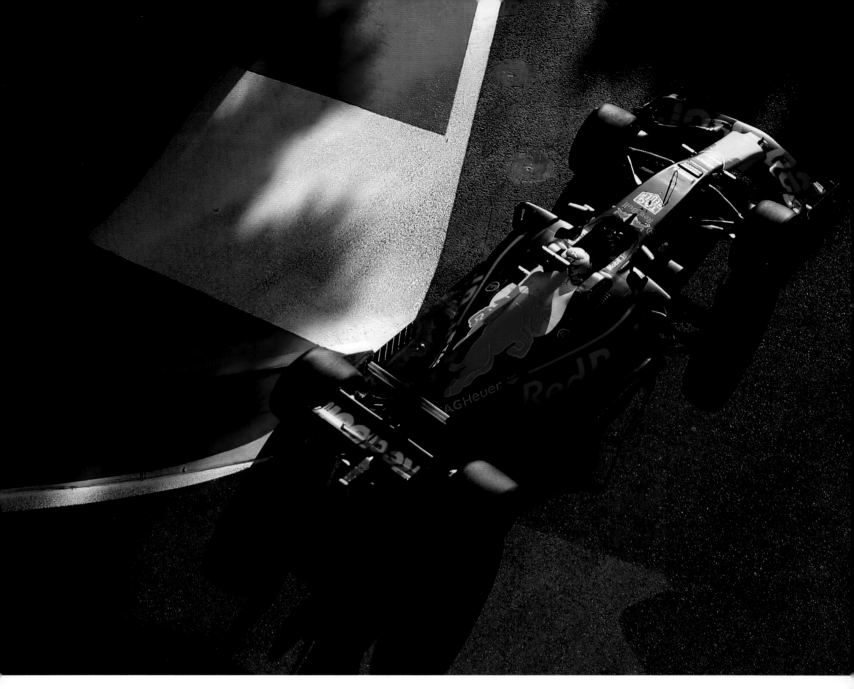

Above: Daniel Ricciardo took an opportunistic win for Red Bull in Baku.

Top right: Helmut Marko.

Above right: Daniel san, with fan.
Photos: Red Bull Racing/Getty Images

Right: Ricciardo endured a tough end to the season.
Photo: Peter J. Fox

Opening spread: Christian Horner.
Photo: Red Bull Racing/Getty Images

THE combination of more aerodynamic influence in 2017, Adrian Newey's reputation and a Daniel Ricciardo/Max Verstappen driver line-up that many rated the strongest on the grid made Red Bull pre-season favourites to take the challenge to Mercedes.

Surprisingly, though, during Barcelona testing they were some way from the pace, which was confirmed at the first race in Melbourne. Ricciardo, in particular, found the car snappy at the rear and put it into the wall during qualifying, while Verstappen was nowhere near the level of Mercedes and Ferrari.

"It was the second test when we knew we were in trouble," team principal Christian Horner explained. "We were soon on the back foot because our tools weren't correlating with what we were seeing on the track. We saw real deviation from the expectation of our simulation models, both wind tunnel and CFD.

"Predominantly, it was the wind tunnel leading us astray. I think the size of the model, the size of the tyres (bigger in 2017), in the tunnel we had gave us some spurious results, whereas previously it had been very reliable.

"It probably put us back two to two-and-a-half months. Then it was working flat-out to recoup that because the others don't stand still.

"It was around Melbourne time when we identified the issue and really Barcelona [race five] by the time we started to see good progress. I think ever since then, at each GP, we started getting more and more performance on to the car."

As well as the directional red herrings, Red Bull had reliability concerns to contend with. When they introduced the new car, there was debate about whether they should use the number 13 or name the car RB12A. They went for RB13, and probably wished they hadn't – over the course of the year, it had 13 podiums and 13 retirements!

Initially, at least, it was much unluckier for Verstappen than it was for Ricciardo. Max's driving continued to evolve to an even higher level, but he had appalling luck in four of the five races leading up to the season's mid-point at Silverstone. The car stopped in Spain; he was running second when it happened again in Montreal; and he was in a great position in Baku when the same thing happened, then was taken out in Austria. Still just 19, and hoping to fight at the very front in his second year with the senior Red Bull team, the frustration was beginning to show. There were paddock rumblings about the Verstappens checking out the lie of the land at Mercedes and Ferrari, although Horner assured everyone that Max was under lock and key.

If there's one paddock environment pretty much guaranteed to keep a driver's feet on the ground, it's Red Bull. Owner Dietrich Mateschitz's right-hand man, Helmut Marko, has been around the block a time or two, and he claimed not to be as surprised as the rest of the paddock when Verstappen actually extended his contract and committed to Red Bull until the end of 2020.

"We had a bad start, the car wasn't where it should have been, but from Hungary onwards, we had a very competitive chassis," Marko said. "But in Budapest, both drivers crashed; at Spa, one car failed and the other started from the back, so it wasn't really obvious.

"But Max saw what we are capable of doing. At one

stage – how should I say? – he was disappointed. But in a discussion, you can't show it: you're 20 years old, in an F1 car and earning good money – there's thousands who would kill for that chance! You have a technical issue and you have to overcome it – that's part of being a great driver. So, after all these discussions, we concluded we should make a contract to the end of 2020. And, if you look, what alternative did he have?"

When you hear Helmut's straight-talking, black-and-white perspective, you don't need to remind yourself of the era from which he comes. This is a man who, in 1971, had won Le Mans in the fearsome Porsche 917, which had a tubular chassis that weighed just 42kg with two 2.25-litre flat-six engines joined together and mounted to it.

Wanting an even stronger power-to-weight ratio, Porsche made some magnesium 917s, despite this being just a couple of years after Jo Schlesser had been killed at Rouen when his magnesium-chassised Honda crashed and burned awfully. "It went up like a Christmas tree," Marko recalled.

So, his Le Mans winner, was that magnesium?

"Yes," he smiled. "They told me after the race…" Then he related a story about how the long-tailed 917s used to exert so much force on the rear suspension that they were known to throw rear tyres, something that happened to him on the Daytona banking. After surviving the shunt, he set off the fire extinguisher, opened the door, rolled down the banking and set off back to the paddock to tell Porsche boss Mr Piech what he thought about it. Before he could open his mouth, though, he was informed that in 24-hour races, drivers are supposed to bring the car back, so could he please go back and check that it wouldn't still run.

"You did as you were told back then," he smiled, steadfastly unimpressed by any potential teenage histrionics. But Verstappen, no alternatives? Really?

At the time Marko was discussing this, Ferrari's championship challenge was self-destructing, and many paddock insiders were convinced that the Scuderia's post-Alonso position in 2015 had been so weak that Vettel's contract may have contained a veto over anyone he didn't fancy alongside him. If anyone was likely to know the veracity of that, it was Marko, but when asked directly, he just smiled and shrugged.

There was this funny little extra "fin" on the Engine cover /intake in 2017

Above: Max Verstappen's Mexican win was one of the year's most dominant.
Photo: Peter J. Fox

Top right: Horner and Verstappen in Malaysia with the winner's trophy.

Top far right: Verstappen climbs from the wreck after the start at Singapore.

Above right: Max takes the plaudits in Mexico.

Right: Valtteri Bottas is edged out by Ricciardo at Austin.

Photos: Red Bull Racing/Getty Images

"Max likes the Red Bull environment and wants to be in a sort of family, which is the way we and Red Bull act. He likes that. He needs it to be able to really do what he shows on the track."

Max's father, Jos, has always been close to Mercedes boss Toto Wolff, with whom he had discussions before Max joined Red Bull. At the time, Mercedes couldn't offer a race seat, and although Lewis Hamilton and Valtteri Bottas are firm for 2018, many were predicting Verstappen in a Silver Arrow in 2019.

Verstappen Sr is a pragmatist, though, and didn't see any hurry. And, being logical, perhaps it was better to earn some money before taking on Hamilton... The word was that Max's new deal included a four-fold salary increase that would see him earn around £20m in 2019. Not bad at 20!

"You forget it's only his fourth year of car racing," Horner added. "What really impressed me this year is the way that he dealt with some of the difficult moments. He kept working hard at it, kept the hours up on the simulator every week, and his application was first class. His ability is unquestionable. He has great feel, a great sensitivity to the car's limit. He's a risk taker – calculated risk, not irresponsible risk – and has a fighting spirit that's exciting to watch. The moves in Hungary [where he had taken out Ricciardo!] and Monza were his only two mistakes, and there's a fine line between hero and villain. Both drivers have done a first-class job this year."

The highlights of Verstappen's year were the two wins in Malaysia and Mexico. At Sepang, he beat Hamilton and Mercedes on merit, going aggressively inside Lewis into Turn

One early in the race and actually prompting the new four-times champion to consider whether he should have been tougher. At Autódromo Hermanos Rodriguez, he jumped Vettel into the first corner and went on to score one of the season's most dominant wins.

Over on the other side of the garage, Ricciardo again outpointed Verstappen, by 32 in 2017, and had much the better first half of the year once Red Bull started to bring some performance to the car. He went on an impressive run of five consecutive podiums, from Barcelona through Silverstone, including a fine win in Azerbaijan.

Yes, the attrition rate was high in Baku, but the foundation of his win was a fabulous overtaking move on both Williams that turned out to be decisive.

Ricciardo's ability on the brakes was more evident than ever in 2017, and passes at Interlagos, where he had started near the back, and Monza spring to mind. The latter, on Räikkönen, even impressed the man himself, so far back did he launch the move.

"Yeah," Ricciardo grinned, "I came from downtown with that one! I also enjoyed the attempts on Valtteri into Turn One in Austin – that was good racing."

But he was unimpressed at being T-boned into retirement by his team-mate at Turn Two in Hungary, having beaten Verstappen off the start, with some justification. "Sore loser," was his radio remark, and it was probably as well that he didn't see Max for the following 90 minutes...

In 2016, Ricciardo had tended to qualify better than Verstappen, who consoled himself with the thought that

Above: New boys and masters (*left to right*): Toro Rosso's Brendon Hartley and Pierre Gasly with Daniel Ricciardo and Max Verstappen.

Top right: Gasly, 2016's GP2 champion, spent the season racing in Japan, before receiving his call-up from Toro Rosso.

Photos: Red Bull Racing/Getty Images

Above right: Carlos Sainz's performances earned him promotion from Toro Rosso to Renault.

Right: Daniil Kvyat was released from the Red Bull programme.

Photos: Peter J. Fox

he would gain speed with greater experience, and that was the case. In 2017, in the second half of the season particularly, the boot was on the other foot. Strip away races where mechanical dramas made comparison redundant, and Verstappen took it 10–6 over the year, with an average 0.15s between them.

The end of Ricciardo's season rather fizzled out, his fine recovery drive in Brazil notwithstanding, as mechanical issues put paid to three of the last four races. The disappointment at the season finale in Abu Dhabi was written all over his face, after he'd had the better of Verstappen all weekend and showed every sign of being able to run with Vettel's Ferrari, until he was struck by a hydraulic problem around pit-stop time.

The engaging, jokey personality and the ever-present mile-wide grin mask a fierce competitor, but he knows that his career trajectory faces a threat from the man on the other side of the garage. It's close, but is the hugely talented Verstappen starting to do to Ricciardo what Daniel had done to Vettel at Red Bull in 2014, and Daniil Kvyat thereafter?

Kvyat, who had been demoted back to Toro Rosso in 2016 to further Verstappen's rise, was dropped again in 2017, in favour of first Pierre Gasly, then Brendon Hartley. Ultimately, he was released from the Red Bull programme altogether.

According to Marko, the chances Kvyat had were "more than enough. Something went wrong. He was bloody quick… In the first half of 2015, he was matching Ricciardo. In 2016, he lost his confidence on the brakes or in the tyres from the first test on and was much more behind Daniel."

For qualifying pace in 2017, Kvyat was pretty much a match for Carlos Sainz as well, just 7–5 down, with 0.06s between them over the first dozen races, but he didn't deliver on Sunday. Since Barcelona 2016, when Kvyat returned to Toro Rosso, Sainz outscored him 90 points to eight,

and in 2017, the Russian took more penalty points than championship points.

Marko denied that colliding with Sainz at Silverstone and crashing in Singapore, where Carlos had been a career-best fourth, had sealed Kvyat's fate. "No," he said, "Sainz saw him coming and could have moved a little. That wasn't the problem; he just didn't have his speed any more. We tried to help mentally, but he didn't recover, and we had to look forward."

Pierre Gasly, as reigning GP2 champion and a Red Bull driver, was the obvious junior team replacement, but Porsche WEC champion and Le Mans winner Brendon Hartley's recruitment, having been dropped by Red Bull in 2010, was a real feel-good story. He had called Marko and told him that if ever he was needed, he was ready. Second chances are rare, but the Austrian told Hartley he'd got the message.

"And," Helmut said, "there was the story with Sainz. Every race over at Renault, Palmer was going to stop, but we didn't really believe that it would happen. Then, all of a sudden it did. Of course, I was prepared, and then on top of that, Honda wanted Gasly for Super Formula, so…

"But that's Red Bull – we're different. Brendon was always fast, but couldn't qualify and under pressure made too many mistakes. But with his experience at Porsche and wherever else, he has overcome that. It's strange: we have a 20-year-old guy, Max, who has the maturity of a 28-year-old, and we have a 28-year-old who looks 20! And there was no one around. We were looking!"

If that doesn't exactly sound like a ringing endorsement, Marko readily acknowledged that for the short time Hartley had been able to run in clear air on his Austin debut, he was impressive, and also that both he and Gasly had been severely compromised by Renault reliability issues at the end of the year, so much so that it became publicly prickly

between Toro Rosso team principal Franz Tost and Renault's Cyril Abiteboul.

By that stage, the same issues were also impacting the senior team: in Brazil, they hurt Verstappen's pace, Red Bull having to turn down the engine. Until then, the team had come close to achieving Horner's stated aim of taking the fight to Ferrari in the second half of the season. In the first half, Milton Keynes had scored just 63 per cent of Maranello's points, but between Silverstone and Mexico, that rose to 92 per cent. It was evened out by Ferrari's nightmarish Asian leg, though.

Horner denied any drop-off in chassis performance over the last couple of races. "It was just power-sensitive circuits again," he said. "Brazil is power sensitive and, in Abu Dhabi, Mercedes were in a class of their own. Listening to their radio content, when they turned their engines up, you only have to look at the middle sector and they'd go half a second quicker or slower depending what engine mode they chose. Hats off to them, but engine performance is a key differentiator.

"By their own admission, Renault was behind the target they set themselves over the winter, but worked hard to try to recover that ground."

In 2018, of course, the four permitted power units of 2017 will be reduced to three, something about which Horner had strong views.

"There will be plenty of penalties next year, and what you'd hate to have is a championship decided on grid penalties. We are getting to the point where, with 21 races for three engines… it's nuts really. Whatever Toto [Wolff] says, his non-executive chairman [Niki Lauda] was arguing for four engines earlier in the year, because it's a false economy."

And was Horner happy with what Renault was promising for 2018?

"Ask me next February!"

Christian Horner, Daniel Ricciardo, Jonathan Wheatley, Max Verstappen and Helmut Marko celebrate Red Bull's 1-3 in Malaysia.

Photo: Red Bull Racing/Getty Images

APPRECIATIONS 2017

By MAURICE HAMILTON

JOHN SURTEES CBE

JOHN SURTEES was a world champion on two wheels and four; an unequalled achievement that only begins to scratch the surface of a career as remarkable as it was varied.

A family background in motorcycle racing and extensive success on two wheels led to a works ride with MV Agusta, for whom he won seven world championships. Such natural ability would take on a new dimension in 1960, when he switched to cars and was immediately competitive. Despite having no knowledge of either Goodwood or the intricacies of motor racing, Surtees qualified on the front row for a Formula Junior race and finished second to Jim Clark.

A couple of months later, he started the Monaco Grand Prix, and two months after that, Surtees stood on the British Grand Prix podium after finishing second in his works Lotus. He might have won in Portugal but for an incident caused by a fuel leak and his soaked shoe slipping off the brake pedal.

After such natural talent had caught the eye of Enzo Ferrari, Surtees had the temerity to turn down an offer for 1962, when he sensed the Scuderia was top-heavy with drivers and politics. It was a measure of the Englishman's standing that Ferrari made a rare second attempt for 1963. This time, Surtees acquiesced, going on to win in sports cars and score his first grand prix victory in Germany. Having helped Ferrari regain competitiveness, Surtees capitalised on his technical input with two more wins and the championship in 1964.

Intrigued by powerful Group 7 sports cars, John helped develop the Lola T70, and was fortunate to survive multiple injuries in 1965 when a front upright broke and the car landed on top of him.

He was racing again the following year, winning the Belgian Grand Prix. But life at Ferrari was never smooth, particularly for Surtees, who believed in speaking his mind in the face of the inevitable politics. Halfway through the season, he walked out following a row with Eugenio Dragoni, the irascible team manager. An immediate move to the uncompetitive Cooper team brought a surprise victory in Mexico.

Honda called upon Surtees to help sort their F1 effort in 1967, part of his cure being a marriage of the Japanese V12 with a Lola chassis. A win in the Italian Grand Prix would be his last in F1, Surtees enduring even more of a struggle with BRM in 1969.

It was almost inevitable that he would design and build his own F1 car, prompted by championship success with an F2 Surtees in the hands of Mike Hailwood. The grand prix effort lasted for nine seasons, financial difficulties and illness eventually forcing John to close the doors.

It was while running successful businesses in factory rental and building restoration that Surtees was drawn back to the sport, following the very promising progress of his son. Despite the desperate heartache when Henry, at the age of 18, was fatally struck on the head by an errant wheel during a Formula 2 race in 2009, John applied his extraordinary tenacity and quiet charm to the task of forming Headway and the Henry Surtees Foundation, charities to assist recovery from head injuries and the training of young people.

His passing, in March, 2017, at the age of 83, was mourned by the motor sport world, especially in Italy, where he will be known forever as *Il Grande John*.

Above: Surtees demonstrates his relaxed style as he rounds La Source hairpin in his Ferrari 156 at the 1963 Belgian Grand Prix.

PATRICK NEVE

PATRICK NEVE, who passed away in March, 2017, at the age of 67, is best remembered as the first driver to be signed by Williams Grand Prix Engineering in 1977. The Belgian drove a March for the new team in 11 grands prix, his best result being seventh at Monza, two races before they parted company.

Neve had worked for the Jim Russell Racing Drivers' School and occasionally raced a Formula Ford Merlyn, before embarking on a full season in 1974 and taking the STP Formula Ford championship in a Lola. Having graduated to F3 for the following season, he gave a good account of himself in a Safir powered by an elderly Ford twin-cam engine, finishing second in the Monaco GP support race. That was enough to earn a seat with the RAM F1 team, and he made an F1 debut in his home grand prix in 1976, before a lack of money ended the drive.

A breakthrough appeared to have come the following season with Williams, and Neve led an F2 race at Silverstone until suspension problems dropped him to third. When the Williams F1 drive came to a premature end, he tried to resuscitate his F1 career in 1978, but failed to qualify a March for the Belgian Grand Prix. Occasionally he raced touring cars before turning his attention to his racing team and a sports marketing company.

JOHN NICHOLSON

BEST known for founding Nicholson-McLaren Engines, New Zealander JOHN NICHOLSON was also a competitive racer. He did a lot of testing for McLaren, driving CanAm, F5000, F2 and, on occasion, F1 machinery.

The link with McLaren began soon after Nicholson arrived in the UK, his reputation growing quickly as he took responsibility for the Chevy V8 engines with which Bruce McLaren would win the 1969 CanAm title. When he took over preparing McLaren's DFV engines for the 1971 F1 season, Denny Hulme noted a useful increase in performance from the V8.

Nicholson, meanwhile, had resumed a racing career begun in New Zealand. Driving a Lyncar powered by his own BDA engines, he won the Formula Atlantic championships in 1973 and '74. He stepped up to F1 with a Lyncar-DFV in 1974, but failed to qualify for the British Grand Prix. He did make it on to the grid at Silverstone a year later, however, before crashing out in the rain.

Finding it difficult to mix racing with his growing business, Nicholson hung up his crash helmet in 1977, but not before providing championship-winning power for Emerson Fittipaldi in 1974. Nicholson-McLaren dropped out of F1 in the 1980s, but continued to gain success with Cosworth engines in many other series. Competing in powerboat racing brought multiple British titles.

Nicholson had retired to his native New Zealand a few years before his passing, at the age of 75, in September, 2017.

TIM PARNELL

ALTHOUGH from farming stock, Reg Parnell was more famous as a racing driver, and it was inevitable that his son, TIM PARNELL, would become steeped in the sport. Having tried his hand first in sports cars, he moved into single-seaters with Formula 2 and Formula Junior Coopers.

He failed to qualify a Cooper T45 for the 1959 British Grand Prix, but made his grand prix debut in his home event at Aintree two years later, retiring with clutch trouble. Tenth – and three laps behind – in the Italian Grand Prix would be his best result a few months later.

Illness curtailed Parnell's racing, but a return in 1963 resulted in a failure to qualify for the German Grand Prix. The sudden death of his father, at the age of 54, in January, 1964, resulted in Tim switching from driver to manager as he took over the running of Reg Parnell Racing for Chris Amon and Peter Revson.

Tim ran the BRM team during a successful phase at the turn of the 1970s, before managing Mallory Park and Oulton Park racetracks, and serving as vice-president of the BRDC.

Reginald Harold Haslam Parnell (his father preferred to call him Tim) passed away in April, 2017, at the age of 84.

LEO KINNUNEN

LEO KINNUNEN'S brief F1 foray in 1974 was nothing compared to his reputation and results in the World Sportscar Championship. The Finn actually had started competing in rallies and ice racing, but a switch to circuits and success with a Porsche 908/2 in the Nordic Cup for sports cars brought an offer of a test with the JW Automotive Porsche team.

Partnered with Pedro Rodriguez and Brian Redman, Kinnunen won the 1970 Daytona 24 Hours on his debut with the Porsche 917. There were further wins at Brands Hatch, Monza and Watkins Glen, but while driving to second place (with Rodriguez in a 908/3) in the Targa Florio, Kinnunen set the all-time lap record for the 44.7-mile road course.

He cleaned up the Interserie championship with 11 overall victories spread across three seasons in different versions of the powerful Porsche 917 run by AAW. The Finnish team moved to F1 with Kinnunen in 1974, when he gathered enough backing to purchase a Surtees TS16, but he did not have enough finance to run the team properly.

He qualified just once in six attempts, retiring from the Swedish Grand Prix. He returned to compete successfully for a few seasons in sports cars before retiring. Kinnunen was 73 when he passed away in July, 2017.

MASSIMO NATILI

DRIVING for the small Italian team Scuderia Centro Sud, MASSIMO NATILI took part in the 1961 British Grand Prix, being forced to retire, and failed to qualify his Cooper T51 for his home grand prix at Monza later the same year. Natili was also entered for non-championship races at Syracuse and Posillipo, but with a similar lack of success.

The privateer team had tested Natili based on the Italian's efforts with a Fiat 500 and a Giaur 750 sports. He would enjoy more success in subsequent years, even though his career was nearly ended in 1962 by a fiery accident during a Formula Junior race at Monza. A brief reappearance for Centro Sud in the 1963 F1 Rome Grand Prix ended in retirement, but he finished sixth the following year when the same race was run for F3. Natili won the 1965 F3 Rome Grand Prix and became the 1-litre national sports car champion with a Lotus 23. Following his retirement from racing, he ran a BMW dealership for many years. He passed away in September, 2017, at the age of 82.

IAN STEWART

AN accomplished driver and founding member of Ecurie Ecosse, IAN STEWART (no relation to brothers Jackie and Jimmy) came to the attention of Stirling Moss while racing a Jaguar XK120 at Charterhall in his native Scotland. Moss tipped off Jaguar, and Stewart was immediately drafted into the works team to share a C-Type at Le Mans in 1952.

The relationship continued, but it was while sharing an Ecurie Ecosse C-type with Roy Salvadori that Stewart scored an outstanding result by finishing second, behind the works Ferrari of Alberto Ascari and Giuseppe Farina, in the Nürburging 1000km round of the 1953 World Sports Car Championship.

Although his dream was to race in Formula 1, the only opportunity came when Ecurie Ecosse entered a Connaught A-type in the 1953 British Grand Prix at Silverstone. He retired with engine problems after qualifying 20th.

A bad accident while racing a C-type in Argentina brought an end to his racing career, after which he focused on the family business. He died, aged 87, in March, 2017.

MICHAEL TAYLOR

MIKE TAYLOR made a considerable name for himself at home and abroad. The Englishman embarked on a busy season in 1959. Racing a Lotus 15 sports car, he won the Grand Prix des Frontières on the very fast Chimay road circuit in Belgium and the Coupe de Paris at Monthlèry.

He took a Cooper T45 to fourth overall and first in the Formula 2 category of the non-championship Aintree 200, behind two Ferraris and a works Cooper. He was entered for the British Grand Prix at Aintree, but retired with transmission trouble.

Plans for a serious crack at F1 led to the purchase of the prototype Lotus 18 from Team Lotus. His debut with the car in the International Trophy at Silverstone would be ruined, however, by a misfire and a failure to be classified.

The next race should have been the Belgian Grand Prix at Spa-Francorchamps, where Stirling Moss had crashed heavily during practice, when a stub axle had broken on his Lotus 18. One of the first on the scene, Taylor was driving back to the pits to report the accident when the steering column failed and his Lotus flew into the trees.

He largely recovered from his serious injuries, but he never raced again. He successfully sued Lotus for career-ending damages and turned to property speculation. Michael Taylor passed away at the age of 82 in April, 2017.

ERIC BROADLEY MBE

ERIC BROADLEY, who died in May, 2017, at the age of 88, played a small, but significant part in F1 history. His Lola cars may never have won a grand prix, but he made a considerable mark in Indycar racing and on the international sports car scene.

Broadley's sports cars were so competitive that Lola was commissioned by the Bowmaker team to design and build an F1 car for the 1962 World Championship. John Surtees put the Climax-powered Lola Mk4 on pole for its first world championship race, the Dutch Grand Prix at Zandvoort. He went on to win a non-championship race at Mallory Park and came close to victory in a grand prix by finishing second in Britain and in Germany.

A contract to assist Ford in the automotive giant's efforts to beat Ferrari at Le Mans allowed Broadley to move his expanding company from Bromley to Slough and fund the construction of the Lola T70 sports car, plus the T90 Indycar. Graham Hill used the latter to win at Indianapolis in 1966, while Surtees took the first CanAm title in the same year with a T70-Chevrolet.

When Surtees struggled to make the Honda F1 car work in 1967, Broadley was asked to provide a substitute for the overweight Japanese chassis, the so-called 'Hondola' giving Surtees a late victory in the Italian Grand Prix. That would be the height of Lola's F1 success, despite subsequent efforts with Graham Hill's Embassy Lola outfit and small teams that were scarcely front line.

Indycar racing evolved into a very different story, and Lola was behind several championships and many victories for a string of drivers, including Nigel Mansell in 1993. Lola also cleaned up in other single-seater formulas, notably Formula 5000.

In 1991, Broadley was awarded the MBE for his services to motor racing.

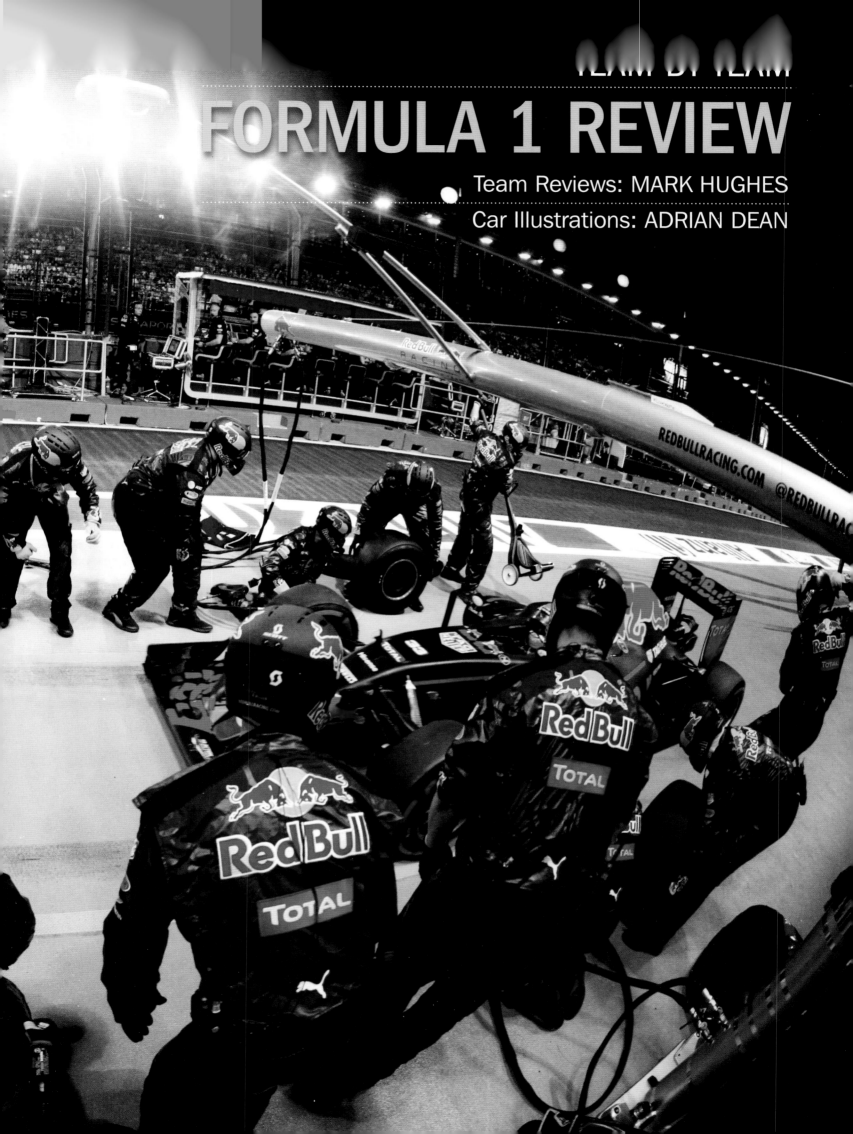

FORMULA 1 REVIEW

Team Reviews: MARK HUGHES

Car Illustrations: ADRIAN DEAN

44

LEWIS HAMILTON

77

VALTTERI BOTTAS

MERCEDES AMG PETRONAS F1 TEAM

ON paper, Mercedes' triumph in 2017 looks more resounding than perhaps it was in reality. The team comfortably clinched its fourth consecutive constructors' championship, and its lead driver, Lewis Hamilton, became world champion with two races still to go. But a significant part of that cushion came from the tribulations at Ferrari, where only a late-season reliability implosion allowed Mercedes to carry off its success with such comfort. In terms of performance, 2017 was the Mercedes team's most challenging season within the hybrid era that so far it had dominated.

When looking at the reasons why, aside from those problems suffered by its chief rival, the new chassis regulations were surely a major contributor. In addition, a further key regulation tweak on the eve of the season seemed almost calculated to rein in Merc's dominance. Nonetheless, the 'diva' W08 won 12 of the season's 20 races and set pole for 15 of them (compared to a respective 19 and 20 out of the 21 races the previous year).

During the off-season, the previous executive technical director, Paddy Lowe, had failed to reach agreement with team boss Toto Wolff on a new contract. He was replaced – albeit in a slightly different role – by James Allison, late of Ferrari and Renault, who joined just in time for the beginning of the season.

The Brackley-based team's answer to the new 2017 regulations was a significantly longer car – the longest in the field. The reasoning behind this was linked to the anticipated increase in downforce that would unfold for rival teams that had spent several seasons developing their aerodynamics around the high-rake philosophy, in contrast to Mercedes. With the wider floors of 2017, both low- and high-rake cars would generate more downforce – but the high-rake cars could expect to benefit more. Rather than start from scratch with an all-new aerodynamic philosophy, Mercedes preferred to find downforce by maximising the floor area. "Wheelbase is just a design compromise like any other," explained Allison. "Making it long puts a bit of weight on the car, which we have to manage by building the rest of it light enough. But we think it gives us more downforce, and when we go to places emphasising aero efficiency, we're usually pretty strong."

One of the downsides of that philosophy – amplified slightly by the new regulations – was the tendency for the balance to change towards understeer as the speed bled off into slower corners. In 2016, Mercedes had occasionally raced with a hydraulic heave spring with asymmetric valving that overcame this aero trait by allowing the front of the car to remain low even after the brakes had been released, only rising slowly – after the corner had been completed. This allowed a forward-biased centre of aerodynamic pressure to be maintained even at slower speeds, where a low-rake car would normally begin to lose time through understeer. This technology had been under development for several years, but the

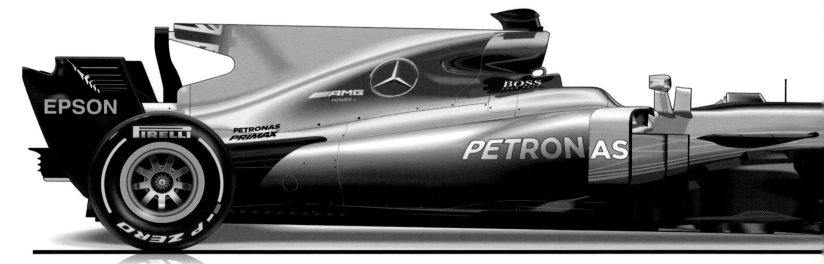

MERCEDES F1 W08 EQ POWER+

TITLE PARTNER	PETRONAS
TEAM PARTNERS	UBS • Qualcomm • Epson • Bose • HUGO BOSS • IWC Schaffhausen • Allianz • Wihuri • Monster Energy • Pure Storage TIBCO • Starwood
TEAM SUPPLIERS	PUMA • ebmpapst • TATA Communications • NetJets • DB Schenker • Rubrik • OMP • Spies Hecker • Schuberth • ASSOS • TUMI • OZ Racing • Endless • Pirelli
POWER UNIT	**Type:** Mercedes-AMG F1 M08 EQ Power+ **No. of cylinders (vee angle):** V6 (90°) **No. of valves:** 24 **Max rpm (ICE):** 15,000 **Electronics:** FIA standard ECU and FIA homologated electronic & electrical system **Instrumentation:** McLaren Applied Technology **Fuel:** PETRONAS Primax **Lubricants:** PETRONAS Syntium **Gearbox & hydraulic oil:** PETRONAS Tutela
TRANSMISSION	**Gearbox:** Eight-speed forward, one-reverse unit with carbon-fibre main case **Gear selection:** Sequential, semi-automatic, hydraulic actuation **Clutch:** Carbon plate
CHASSIS	Monocoque carbon-fibre and honeycomb composite structure **Front suspension:** Carbon-fibre wishbone and push-rod-actuated torsion springs and rockers **Rear suspension:** Carbon-fibre wishbone and pull-rod-actuated torsion springs and rockers **Brake discs and pads:** Carbone Industrie carbon/carbon with rear brake-by-wire **Brake calipers:** Brembo **Steering:** Power-assisted rack-and-pinion **Wheels:** OZ forged magnesium **Tyres:** Pirelli P Zero
DIMENSIONS	**Length:** Over 5000mm **Width:** 2000mm **Height:** 950mm **Formula weight:** 728kg, including driver and camera

Lewis Hamilton rolls out of his garage under the lights in Singapore.

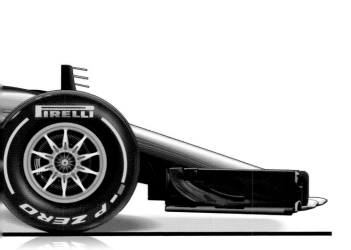

DIETER ZETSCHE AND JAMES ALLISON

MERCEDES AMG PETRONAS F1 TEAM: PERSONNEL

Non-Executive Chairman: Niki Lauda

Team Principal: Toto Wolff

**Managing Director, Mercedes AMG
High Performance Powertrains:** Andy Cowell

Technical Director: James Allison

Engineering Director: Aldo Costa

Performance Director: Mark Ellis

Technology Director: Mike Elliott

Chief Operating Officer: Rob Thomas

Digital Engineering Transformation Director:
Geoffrey Willis

Sporting Director: Ron Meadows

Trackside Engineering Director:
Andrew Shovlin

Chief Engineer Trackside: Simon Cole

Chief Strategist: James Vowles

Senior Race Engineer (Hamilton):
Peter Bonnington

Senior Race Engineer (Bottas): Tony Ross

Chief Mechanic: Matthew Deane

**Mercedes-Benz Motorsport
Communications Director:** Bradley Lord

Photos: Mercedes AMG Petronas F1 Team

TOTO WOLFF

2017 W08 was the first Mercedes to be conceived around it. Potentially, it would allow Mercedes the advantages of retaining its optimisation of a known, familiar philosophy (around which it had developed the title-winning cars of 2014 onwards) without the disadvantages. After a query from Ferrari to the FIA about the legality of such a system, on the grounds that it was an aerodynamic device, a technical directive went out to all teams that effectively banned it – on the eve of the season.

The combined result of the car's concept and the technical directive (regarding asymmetric valving within heave springs) made for a car that was tricky to set up – and that was not as flexible as the Ferrari in working well over different types of circuit, track temperature and tyre compound. When kept within its narrower operating parameters, however, it was devastatingly fast. Mercedes HPP in Brixworth again produced the standard-setting power unit, and this, together with the lower drag inherent in its aero concept, made it formidably quick on the straights.

A key part of that concept was the super-intricate array of guide vanes on the underside, between the front axle and leading edge of the floor (together with the 'W floor' feature introduced in 2016, which diverted some of the outer body flow around the sidepods to the underfloor). These assisted the acceleration of the airflow to the leading edge of the floor, helping to

energise a floor that, by definition, had a lower expansion rate than the high-rake floors of rival cars. From Barcelona onwards, one of these vanes was massively enhanced, with a more concave section – and this was just the most visible of a thorough reworking of the car's surfaces. This came in conjunction with a weight saving programme that, for the first time, brought the car beneath the weight limit (before ballast). It won the race in Barcelona, but only thanks to the fortuitous timing of a VSC and a swashbuckling attacking drive from Hamilton. The Ferrari, despite less visible upgrades, had been the faster car on race day – as it had been in Melbourne and Bahrain, and would be also in Monaco, Hungary, Spa, Singapore, Malaysia and Mexico.

Allison remained proud of the way those operating the car had found a way around its sometimes awkward traits. "We threw away two or three races at the beginning of the year because we'd not best appreciated how to adjust the car between qualifying and race. So we had cars that were comfortably on pole [Melbourne and Bahrain], but then got beaten because we didn't run the tyres well. But from Barcelona onwards, I don't think you could point to a race where we've gone backwards in the race. There were races where we just weren't quick enough, but those were defined by the car.

"Its weaknesses were that it was too nervous at

high speed, too stable at low speeds." The set-up solutions to each of those problems were, of course, in conflict – and on circuits where the important corners had a big spread of speed, the relatively narrow set-up window of the W08's concept was punished. Hence its struggles at the Hungaroring and Sepang in particular.

"On the plus side, it had a pretty good power unit, even though the gaps between power units gets smaller. The traits of the car waxed and waned a bit, but whenever the circuit demanded good aero efficiency, we tended to dominate. So our raw aero numbers are good. Plus the car ran very reliably. That's a good set of assets."

For Spa, an upgraded motor was introduced, theoretically getting around the FIA's tighter limits on oil burning for any specification of engine introduced from Monza onwards – though in reality, Mercedes did not take advantage of the greater oil usage allowed, having shifted its development emphasis away from oil burning after the pre-season ruling that sought to outlaw it.

How much pre-season rulings were responsible for the team's reduced advantage in 2017 inevitably is open to conjecture, as is the motivation behind them. But if the 2018 Mercedes is less extreme in its layout and proportions, while featuring a greater degree of rake, it would not be too much of a surprise.

Above: The Merc laid bare.
Photo: Studio Colombo/WRi2

Left: The team celebrates its fourth consecutive world championship after the US GP in Austin.

Right: Niki Lauda, always prepared to give his opinion
Photos: Mercedes AMG Petronas F1 Team

Below: Valtteri Bottas ended the season on a high in Abu Dhabi.
Photo: Peter J. Fox

5

SEBASTIAN VETTEL

7

KIMI RÄIKKÖNEN

SCUDERIA FERRARI

ALTHOUGH inevitably there was great disappointment that the Scuderia's strong title challenge had collapsed with a devastating sequence of unreliability in Malaysia and Japan (inlet manifolds and spark plug respectively), in many ways 2017 was a season of immense promise. For the first time in many years, Ferrari produced a highly original car – the SF70H – rather than simply trying to refine concepts introduced by others, as had tended to be the case in recent years. Actually, it was a more consistently competitive car than even the Mercedes, but lost out to it in qualifying and reliability. This was the first time since 2008 that Ferrari had fielded a car that could lay claim to being the season's fastest.

Innovations in the car's aerodynamics pushed the envelope of the regulations to the extreme – exactly where they should be with a top team, but a territory that Ferrari had left to others for too long. After the departure of James Allison during the previous season, this car featured much enhanced input from Ferrari's consulting genius, Rory Byrne. When Allison – and chief of aero Dirk de Beer – had left in May, 2016, all that had been established of the car was its general layout and wheelbase. Byrne had outlined its overall guiding concept, and the respective chiefs of aero and design – David Sanchez and Simone Resta – worked to that concept in keeping with the priorities, overseen by technical director Mattia Binotto. With

the 2017 regulations allowing less of a performance hit in departing from previous philosophies, it was a good time to make a clean-sheet restart, which, in essence, is what the SF70H represented. It was a well considered answer to parameters reset by the new regulations, featuring high rake as an intrinsic part of its aerodynamic philosophy.

A key demand of the new regulations was that the bodywork around the sidepod area should be angled back at 75 degrees (a regulation introduced for aesthetic reasons, to give a more swooping, dynamic look to the 2017 generation of F1 cars). Every team other than Ferrari duly laid back their sidepods to the required angle. But the regulations did not stipulate sidepod, only bodywork. That allowed Sanchez to introduce 75-degree-angled bodywork containing the required crash structures, ahead of the sidepods. The sidepods themselves, sitting just behind that point, were angled at 90 degrees, allowing a more direct capture of the airflow. This, in turn, permitted smaller radiators. The inlet ducts for those radiators, uniquely, were mounted at the tops of the sidepods, which also enhanced the mass flow to them, reducing the obstruction formed by the front suspension, as well as by the bodywork ahead of the sidepods.

This inspired detail was a crucial part in the overall layout and aerodynamic concept of the car, because it allowed the distance between the front axle and sidepod to be long enough to obtain good airflow to

FERRARI SF70H

MAJOR SPONSORS	Philip Morris • Alfa Romeo • Santander • Shell • Ray-Ban • UPS • Kaspersky Lab • Weichai • Hublot • Mahle • OMR • Singha
OFFICIAL SUPPLIERS	Pirelli • Puma • Swisse • Infor • Experis • SFK • Magneti Marelli • NGK • Brembo • Riedel • Iveco
SUPPLIERS	Bell • OZ • Honeywell • Technogym
POWER UNIT	**Type:** Ferrari 062 1.6-litre turbo **No. of cylinders** *(vee angle):* V6 (90°) **No. of valves:** 24 **Bore:** 80mm **Stroke:** 53mm **Crank height:** 90mm **Max. rpm:** 15,000 **Power output:** Approximately 600hp (ICE) + 160hp (ERS) **Fuel injection:** Direct fuel injection, limited to 500 bar **Pressure charging:** Single turbocharger, unlimited boost pressure (typical maximum 3.5 bar abs due to fuel flow limit) **Exhaust:** Single exhaust outlet, from turbine on car centreline, with two outlet pipes connected to the wastegate **Ignition:** NGK spark plugs **ERS:** Integrated hybrid energy recovery via electrical motor generator units **Energy store:** Lithium-Ion battery (up to 4MJ per lap)
TRANSMISSION	**Gearbox:** Ferrari eight-speed plus reverse, carbon-cased longitudinal, electronically-controlled sequential semi-automatic
CHASSIS	Carbon-fibre and honeycomb monocoque **Front suspension:** Upper and lower wishbones with push-rod-actuated inboard springs and dampers **Rear suspension:** Upper and lower wishbones with pull-rod-actuated inboard springs and dampers **Dampers:** ZF Sachs **Wheels:** OZ, 13in diameter **Tyres:** Pirelli P Zero **Brakes:** Brembo calipers and ventilated carbon-fibre discs
DIMENSIONS	**Height** 950mm **Track width:** 1460mm (front); 1416mm (rear) **Formula weight:** 728kg, including driver and camera

Kimi Räikkönen at speed in Bahrain.

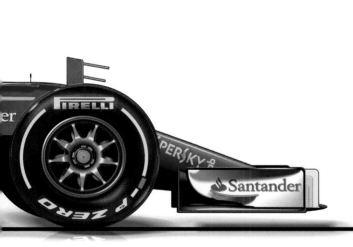

MAURIZIO ARRIVABENE

SCUDERIA FERRARI: PERSONNEL

Chairman and CEO: Sergio Marchionne

Team Principal: Maurizio Arrivabene

Technical Director: Mattia Binotto

Head of Power Unit Operations: Luigi Fraboni

Chief Designer: Simone Resta

Chief of Aerodynamics: Enrico Cardile

Head of Race Activities: Jock Clear

Race Team Manager: Diego Ioverno

Chief Race Engineer: Matteo Togninalli

Chief of Race Strategy: Inaki Rueda

Logistics: Sergio Bondi

Race Engineer (Vettel)**:** Riccardo Adami

Race Engineer (Räikkönen)**:** David Greenwood

Marketing Director: Lucia Pennesi

Head of External Relations: Alberto Antonini

External Relations Co-ordinator:
Jonathan Giacobazzi

Press Officer: Roberta Colleluori

Kimi Räikkönen Press Officer: Stefania Bocchi

MATTIA BINOTTO

Photos: Scuderia Ferrari

the sidepod area (after being disturbed by the front wheels) without having to move the front axle forward and thereby increase the length of the car. It allowed the car to combine compact dimensions (its wheelbase was 143mm shorter than that of the Mercedes) with a powerful airflow regime. The car's more compact dimensions, in turn, allowed the Ferrari to be lighter (pre-ballast) and thereby have a more favourable weight distribution. This played a crucial role in it being a more consistent and adjustable performer, with a wider set-up and track temperature window, that allowed it more easily to be quick on more than one tyre compound on any given weekend.

Aerodynamically, it had greater downforce, particularly at low speeds. The point at which more wing angle still translated to better lap times was significantly higher than on the Mercedes. But even with equivalent wing settings, it still produced more drag than the Merc (partly because of the shorter wheelbase), which, combined with an engine power shortfall of around 15bhp in qualifying, resulted in it scoring only five poles.

A lot of extra power was found over the winter (estimates put it at 50bhp) from combustion improvements, but this only matched the similar gains made by Mercedes. The engine department continued its oil-burning programme from 2016 (following Mercedes' lead), whereby oil that found its way into the combustion chambers past the piston rings and through the airbox (via valves that closed to increase crankcase pressure) provided the engine with the extra calories denied it by the regulation fuel flow limit. A technical directive on the eve of the season appeared to have outlawed this practice, after a query

from Red Bull. But post-race in Canada, oil residue was found in the exhausts of the Ferraris and the Ferrari-engined Haas cars. This initiated a further technical directive, specifically banning the use of additives in the oil to enhance combustion. Later in the season, the FIA introduced a regulation that reduced the permitted oil consumption from 1.2 litres/100km to 0.9 litres/100km. This was announced in Hungary and was set to come into effect two races later, at Monza; it would apply to any new engine *specification* introduced from that race onwards. Thus Ferrari was dismayed when Mercedes introduced a new engine specification at Spa, one race before Monza. However, it made less difference than Ferrari had feared. GPS measurements in Brazil suggested that in race trim, the Ferrari remained around 10bhp down on an equivalent-mileage Mercedes power unit, much the same as it had been all year, even though good gains were made by both.

Whether the oil-burn controversy was linked to the sudden and unexpected departure of engine chief Lorenzo Sassi mid-season was unclear. Sassi had previously been credited with the great gains made in Ferrari's power unit performances after a difficult beginning to the hybrid era in 2014.

As well as oil burn, the FIA also busied itself responding to various queries from other teams about the legality of some of the Ferrari's more progressive features. The floor – despite having to be a flat plane of uniform thickness – was shown to be flexing downwards in the area ahead of the rear wheels beyond a certain threshold of speed and load. Potentially, this may have helped stall the underbody airflow to reduce drag on the straights. Furthermore, ducts on

each side of the leading edge of the floor seemed to be there to tune the shape and distance from the ground of that leading edge under load – potentially giving a very powerful set-up tool that would allow access to more underbody downforce. There was also an 'active' blown axle, ie. below certain speeds – where the downforce gains would be greater than the drag losses – it was blown, but above that threshold, it would cease to be blown and the air would exit in the conventional way, rather than through the centre of the wheels. Ferrari was told to attend to each of these aerodynamic features at various points in the season's first half. Impressively, the aero department was able to get the car working and rebalanced going into the season's second half, despite the limitations.

As well as the usual aero developments of guide vanes, front wings and diffuser, Ferrari also worked extensively on a new front suspension, with a geometry and an enhanced heave spring that would better allow the floor's leading edge to run more consistently close to the ground (and thereby facilitate further enhanced rake). This was tried during several practices from Spa onwards, but never raced – much to the Ferrari engineers' frustration. The design necessitated a different steering arrangement, and Sebastian Vettel didn't like the feedback this gave, finding that it did not load up under cornering pressure in a way that allowed him to feel the car's behaviour accurately.

Can Ferrari use the busted promise of 2017 as the platform for ultimate title-winning success in 2018, or will history judge the season as a rare window of opportunity that was wasted? Certainly, Red Bull should get off to a better start in 2018, and McLaren will hope to join the party, too.

Left: Räikkönen – always the brides-maid in 2017.

Far left: Vettel spearheaded a true championship challenge, until a late-season meltdown.

Below: Riccardo Adami, Vettel's race engineer.

Bottom: Nothing left to chance. Vettel and his crew on a Thursday track walk at Monza.

Photos: Scuderia Ferrari

3

DANIEL RICCIARDO

33

MAX VERSTAPPEN

RED BULL RACING

RED BULL'S RB13 scored 13 podiums, but failed to finish on 13 occasions – which rather summarises the team's season. Max Verstappen and Daniel Ricciardo between them scored three victories, helping the team to third in the constructors' championship. But as had been the case ever since the hybrid formula came along in 2014, even the Red Bull's cutting-edge aerodynamics couldn't overcome the power deficit of its Renault engine.

Not that they began the season with particularly strong aero, a wind tunnel correlation problem only having become apparent as testing began. The physically wider tunnel model (replicating the greater width of the 2017-generation of cars) apparently led to distortion of the airflow data through its closer proximity to the walls. For the first few races, the drivers complained of a car in which the front and rear felt unconnected, of the impossibility of getting both ends working simultaneously.

As ever, one of the last cars to break cover, the Red Bull looked distinctively naked when it turned up for Barcelona testing, with nothing like the intricate bodywork detail of the Mercedes and Ferrari around the area between the front wheels and sidepods. The design team definitely seemed to have pitched its aero/downforce efficiencies at a different – lower-drag – point than the other two, perhaps reflecting its expectation of the respective engine power of each car. Evidently, the misleading tunnel figures had played a part in this choice, too. Its wheelbase was the equal shortest of the pack (together with the sister Toro Rosso), and it continued with the team's traditionally very aggressive rake level.

The car was tested in Barcelona with a rear heave spring damper that beyond a certain speed would sink the rear of the car and stall the underbody aerodynamics. It gave the car a significant boost in straight-line speed, but made it as much as 15kg overweight. Thus there was no plan to use it immediately, but the principle of it was set to be a development avenue before an FIA technical directive, preseason, closed it off.

The Renault motor was generally reckoned to be around 0.5s off the pace in the early-season races, but the RB13-Renault package was initially as much as 1.5s off the Mercedes/Ferrari pace. "Following either of those cars, it's clear that they have much more rear downforce than us," said Ricciardo, "and that's where the lap time is in these cars." Reliability wasn't great either, but that was more of a Renault issue than a Red Bull one.

Step forward Adrian Newey. He'd not had all that much to do with the concept of the RB13, he said. Rather he'd just fed in to the technical group – designer Rob Marshall, aero chief Dan Fallows, engineering chief (car) Paul Monaghan, engineering chief (performance) Pierre Wache – as he'd also been working on the Aston Martin Valkyrie hypercar. He'd not even taken a proper look at the new regulations, he said, until flying out to Melbourne for the

RED BULL RB13

TITLE SPONSOR	Red Bull
TEAM PARTNERS	TAG Heuer • Puma • Rauch • Mobil 1 Esso
INNOVATION PARTNERS	Citrix • IBM • Siemens • Simpivity • Hisense • Aston Martin • AT&T • HPE • Ansys
TEAM SUPPLIERS	Pirelli • Hisense • DMG Mori • PWR • Sabelt • Flir • OZ • Matrix • EARIN
POWER UNIT *Renault*	**Type:** Red Bull Racing-TAG Heuer RB13-2017 1.6-litre turbo **No. of cylinders** *(vee angle):* V6 (90°) **No. of valves:** 24 **Max. rpm** *(ICE):* 15,000 **Power output:** 900bhp **Electronics:** MESL standard electronic control unit **Fuel:** Exxon Mobil **Oil:** Exxon Mobil
TRANSMISSION	Eight-speed gearbox, longitudinally mounted with hydraulic power shift and clutch operation
CHASSIS	Composite monocoque with engine as fully stressed member **Front suspension:** Aluminium uprights, carbon-fibre double wishbones with push-rod-actuated torsion springs, dampers and anti-roll bar **Rear suspension:** Aluminium uprights, carbon-fibre double wishbones with pull-rod-actuated torsion springs, dampers and anti-roll bar **Wheel diameter:** 13in, front and rear **Wheels:** OZ Racing **Tyres:** Pirelli P Zero **Brake pads, discs and calipers:** Brembo
DIMENSIONS	Not disclosed
	Formula weight: 728kg, including driver and camera

Max Verstappen takes the Red Bull RB13 to victory in the Malaysian Grand Prix.

CHRISTIAN HORNER

BULL RACING: PERSONNEL

...rman: Dietrich Mateschitz	**Race Engineer** (Verstappen): GianPiero Lambiase
...n Principal: Christian Horner OBE	**No. 1 Race Mechanic** (Ricciardo): Chris Gent
...Bull Motorsport Consultant: Helmut Marko	**No. 1 Race Mechanic** (Verstappen): Lee Stevenson
...f Technical Officer: Adrian Newey OBE	**Head of Marketing:** Oliver Hughes
...f Engineering Officer: Rob Marshall	**Head of Red Bull Relations & Events:** Marcus Prosser
...f Engineer, Aerodynamics: Dan Fallows	**Head of Communications:** Ben Wyatt
...f Engineer, Car Engineering: Paul Monaghan	**Head of Partnerships:** Guy Richards
...f Engineer, Car Performance: Pierre Waché	**Head of Technical Partnerships:** Zoe Chilton
...e Team Manager: Jonathan Wheatley	**Press Officers:** Anna Pamin, Vicky Lloyd, James Ranson
...d of Production, supply chain and logistics: ...Field	
...e Engineer (Ricciardo): Simon Rennie	

HELMUT MARKO

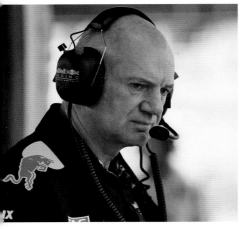

Above: Adrian Newey.

Above centre: Paul Monaghan.

Above right: Rob Marshall.

Right: Max and Daniel with their trophies in Malaysia.

Far right: Ricciardo in action.

Below: Celebration for the Verstappen crew after his win in Mexico.

Below right: Celebration for the Ricciardo crew after his win in Baku.

Photos: Red Bull Racing/Getty Images

first race… Now with the tunnel working properly, for Spain he would oversee the first part of a package of updates to unlock the car's potential. They didn't look much, but they connected the front and rear a little better, and allowed a decent underbody airflow while still getting some front-end bite. They gained around 0.4s, but there was more to come, especially in the second half of the season.

Monaghan takes up the story: "There are no magic bullets; they are incremental, and you try to improve your balance window, such that you have less oversteer and understeer in the car. Slowly, but surely, that came together."

Around Baku, their qualifying was compromised by various factors, but the underlying pace of the car was seriously good for the first time. Its mechanical traits were so good in the slow middle sector that it was able to use a Monza-type wing for the super-long 'straight' there. Ricciardo won, somewhat fortuitously (after dramas for Hamilton and Vettel). The team's campaign was at last properly under way.

There was some niggle from other teams about how the front wing endplates were flexing independently of the main plane at Silverstone, and after a word from the FIA, stiffening stays between the two were fitted for Hungary. It was at the Budapest race

that the crucial part of the upgrade package arrived, comprising reshaped sidepods, a new footplate area ahead of them, changes to the diffuser and a Mercedes-like 'W-floor', whereby serrated vanes ahead of the sidepods diverted air to the underfloor. The car had finally acquired some of the aero detailing between the front wheels and sidepods already seen on the Mercedes, Ferrari and others. Monaghan gave some background to this: "If you're going to have a lot of aerodynamic devices towards the front of the car, you can't necessarily draw a lot from the back of the car – there's only so much total pressure available down the car. We generally pursue more rake than some of our competitors, so our front wing philosophy is different, and therefore the philosophy down the rest of the car is different. So, yes, there was an evolution we had to go through to get to a point where such devices worked on our car to make it faster."

These changes really switched the car on and gave it slow corner grip that was visibly better than that of any other. That strength came into its own three races later at Singapore, where – helped by a further upgrade that included a very Ferrari-like sidepod deflector (Vettel: "I didn't know we also made them in blue!") – Verstappen qualified on the front row and Ricciardo finished second. Two weeks later, Verstap-

pen ambushed Hamilton in Sepang for his first victory of the season, and a week later chased the winning Mercedes over the line at Suzuka. Verstappen won again in Mexico from the front row.

From Austin onwards, experiments were made with a new front suspension, apparently with the intention of allowing the rake to be reduced at speed on the straight (partly replicating the pre-season version of the heave spring), and although it wasn't raced, the FIA issued a technical directive that seems to have been aimed at this system:

"Despite the directives about the legality of suspension systems regarding their influence on the aerodynamics, defined in TD/006-17, TD/010-17 and TD/014-17, we would like to add the following. We will consider a change between operating states or modes (using any mechanism, including but not limited to, switches and magnetic valves), effecting different reactions of said suspension due to different loads at the wheels at the time of driving, as a change of the suspension system, which is in breach of article 10.2.3 of the Technical Regulations."

Evidently, Red Bull's ingenuity was still fully intact. But in addition to its usual power shortfall, its season was compromised by an initially flawed design. The aim for 2018 is to hit the ground running rather better.

11

SERGIO PÉREZ

31

ESTEBAN OCON

SAHARA FORCE INDIA F1 TEAM

YET again Force India delivered an incredible bang-for-buck performance to finish fourth in the constructors' championship – all the more remarkable in 2017 because of the new regulations that, in theory, should have increased their disadvantage to teams with more resource. The Mercedes power unit and gearbox combination defined the general layout of the VJM-10 as a long-wheelbase car, but the technical team, led by Andy Green, continued with its development of the high-rake concept, in contrast to the Mercedes.

It was a basic, but effective car for the part of the grid in which the team was fighting – significantly slower than the big three and not always outright as fast as Renault – run by a very tight, efficient operation with a good tyre understanding and two strong drivers. They scored points with both Sergio Pérez and Esteban Ocon in all but three of the races.

In conceiving a car to the new regulations, Green was very aware of the potential hazards of being too aggressive: "In terms of the loads the car will see, we had to make a lot of assumptions, and you only get one go at it, especially a team like us. What we designed had to cope with the whole season, and we had to put an extra safety factor in all our calculations because we cannot afford to be redesigning or remaking; it hurts us so badly. It takes away the small resource we have for development. You'd really like to shave a bit off here and there, get the weight of the car down, give yourself a bit more ballast and

freedom on set-up. But that was a luxury I decided we couldn't afford in this first year of the regs."

That slightly conservative philosophy could also be detected in layout details, such as sidepods with a generous cooling area for the engine, which were not significantly developed through the season. The car continued with the 'nostril' nose philosophy introduced in 2016, to give the underbody enhanced flow without a particularly challenging crash test.

The conservative approach, in combination with the long wheelbase dictated by the Mercedes gearbox, meant that the car was always hovering at or just above the weight limit, meaning ballast couldn't be used to broaden the set-up window. Generally, it was aerodynamically efficient, but with a shortfall in ultimate downforce, something that was particularly apparent at the Hungaroring and Singapore, where it failed to make Q3. The aero team – led by Simon Phillips – continued to work out of the Toyota wind tunnel in Cologne

A further limiting factor of the car was a degree of instability at the rear, which was improved, but never fully cured. Although this trait was believed to be largely aero-derived, there were certain limitations of the rear suspension geometry because the Mercedes gearbox's suspension mounting points had been configured for the Merc's low-rake concept, whereas the Force India had been developed to be increasingly high-rake. In fact, by the end of the season, it was running more rake than even the Red Bull. "Although

FORCE INDIA VJM10

OFFICIAL PARTNERS	Breast Cancer Care • BWT • Cartesiano • Claro • LDNR.biz • FXTM • Hype Energy • Infinitum • Inter • Johnnie Walker • Kingfisher Magnesium Mineraliased Water • Mezasports • NEC • Quaker State • Sport Bible • Telcel • Telmex • Unifin • W66 • Vonhaucke
TECHNICAL PARTNERS	Alpinestars • Koni • Orangebus • Pirelli • Univa
OFFICIAL SUPPLIERS	3D Systems • Adaptavist • Apsley • Aqueus Guard • Bella Barista • Branded • Condeco • Farah • Gtechniq • ITEC • Schuberth Still • STL • UPS Direct • Voip unlimited • WyndyMilla • Spirit Fitness • Memento Exclusives
POWER UNIT	**Type:** Mercedes-AMG F1 M08 EQ Power+ **No. of cylinders** *(vee angle)*: V6 (90°) **No. of valves:** 24 **Max rpm** *(ICE)*: 15,000 **Electronics:** FIA standard ECU and FIA homologated electronic & electrical system **Fuels and Lubricants:** Petronas
TRANSMISSION	**Gearbox:** Mercedes AMG F1 eight-speed, semi-automatic seamless-shift
CHASSIS	Carbon-fibre composite monocoque with Zylon anti-intrusion panels **Front suspension:** Aluminium uprights with carbon-fibre composite wishbones, track rod and push-rod; inboard chassis-mounted torsion springs, dampers and anti-roll bar assembly **Rear suspension:** Aluminium uprights with carbon-fibre composite wishbones, track rod and pull-rod; hydro-mechanical springs, dampers and anti-roll bar assembly. **Wheels:** BBS, forged to Force India specification **Tyres:** Pirelli P Zero **Brake system:** AP Racing
DIMENSIONS	Not disclosed **Formula weight:** 728kg, including driver and camera

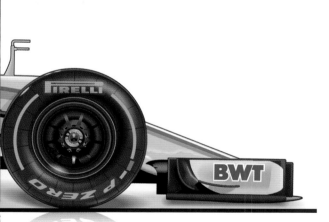

VIJAY MALLYA

OTMAR SZAFNAUER

ROBERT FERNLEY

Photos: Sahara Force India F1 Team

SAHARA FORCE INDIA F1 TEAM: PERSONNEL

Team Principal & Managing Director: Dr Vijay Mallya

Chairman & Co-owner: Subrata Roy Sahara

Shareholders: The Mol family

Deputy Team Principal: Robert Fernley

Chief Operating Officer: Otmar Szafnauer

Technical Director: Andrew Green

Sporting Director: Andy Stevenson

Production Director: Bob Halliwell

Chief Designers: Akio Haga, Ian Hall

Aerodynamics Director: Simon Phillips

Chief Engineer: Tom McCullough

Race Team Operations Manager: Mark Gray

Race Engineer (Pérez)**:** Tim Wright

Race Engineer (Ocon)**:** Bradley Joyce

No. 1 Mechanic (Pérez)**:** Michael Brown

No. 1 Mechanic (Ocon)**:** Will Vickery

Commercial Director: Stephen Curnow

Head of Communications: Will Hings

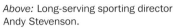

Above: Long-serving sporting director Andy Stevenson.

Above centre: Chief engineer Tom McCullough.

Above right: Technical director Andrew Green.

Right: Joint chief designer Agio Haga.

Far right: The crew prepares Sergio Pérez for action at Spa-Francor-champs for the Belgian GP.

Below right: Esteban Ocon in action during the US GP.

Below: The traditional end-of-the-year team photo taken in Mexico.

Photos: Sahara Force India F1 Team

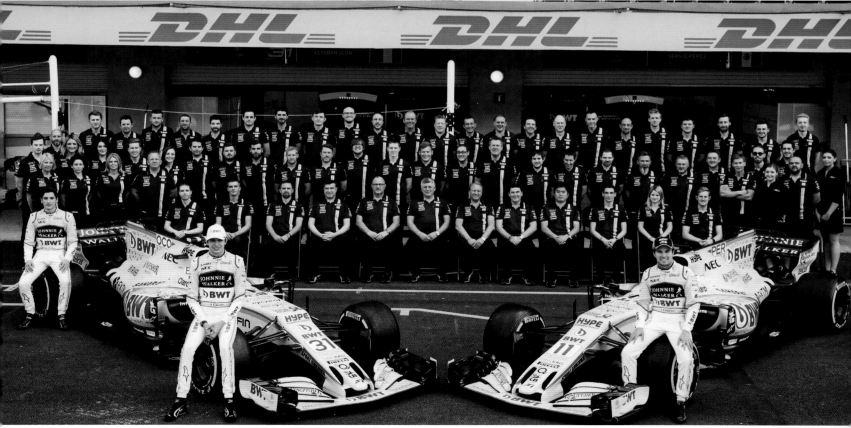

we have to take the Mercedes pick-up points, within those, they allow us to set the wishbones at the angles for high rake. They aren't designed purely for low rake. But yes, we were still compromised on that," said Green. But the aero benefit was felt to be worth the price. As in previous seasons, the blown front axle was used at higher-downforce tracks, but not where the increase in drag negated its value.

The first big upgrade came at Silverstone, with a new front wing that rebalanced the emphasis between the upper and lower elements in favour of the upper. But unlike 2016, the development continued late into the season, as with the same aero regulations in place for 2018, any upgrades bore relevance to the new car on the stocks.

So in Singapore, there was a new diffuser and T-wing, together with new, lower bargeboard elements and distinctive 'saw fish' atop the engine cover's 'shark fin'. These were tiny vortex generators, designed to speed up the airflow to the rear wing. Together with the directing effect of the T-wing, they ensured that more of the airflow reached the wing from above the main plane, rather than below, effectively increasing the flap's angle of attack, with a less than proportional increase in drag. This whole package was powerful, calculated to be worth as much as half a second. It did change the way in which the car needed to be set up, however, and this rather caught the team out in Singapore. The potential of the upgrade (together with some extra detail aero refinements), the more suitable layout of the track and the latest spec of Mercedes engine resulted in a much more competitive car two weeks later in Malaysia, where Ocon qualified a solid sixth fastest, and Pérez finished in that position in the race.

In Mexico, there was another new floor, further tweaks to the bargeboards and the introduction of new elements on the leading edge of the floor, which increased under-body airflow speed. These were quite similar to the details seen already on the Mercedes and Red Bull, and they kept the VJM-10 fighting its corner. And even if it did get left behind in the development race by Renault, its superior reliability and consistency gained the team a highly meritorious place. In summary, Force India did a near-perfect job in maximising its resource.

18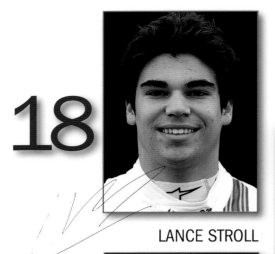

LANCE STROLL

40

PAUL DI RESTA

19

FELIPE MASSA

Lance Stroll

WILLIAMS FW40

PARTNERS	Martini • Randstad • Rexona • JCB • Avanade • BT • Hackett • Oris • Canada Life • Financial Org • Symantec • Bombardier • Michael Caines • Dtex • PPG • Pirelli • Alpinestars • Dicastal • EOS Manufacturing Solutions • Cybex • Spinal Injuries Association
POWER UNIT	**Type:** Mercedes-AMG F1 M08 EQ Power+ **No. of cylinders** *(vee angle):* V6 (90°) **No. of valves:** 24 **Bore:** 80mm **Stroke:** 53mm **Crank height:** 90mm (minimum allowed) **Max. rpm** *(ICE):* 15,000 **Fuel injection:** High-pressure direct injection (max 500 bar, one injector/cylinder) **Max. fuel flow rate:** 100kg/hr (above 10,500rpm) **Pressure charging:** Single-stage compressor and exhaust turbine on common shaft **Exhaust turbine max rpm:** 125,000 **Electronics:** FIA standard SECU and FIA homologated electronic & electrical system **ERS:** Mercedes AMG HPP **Fuel:** Petronas Primax **Lubricants:** Petronas Syntium **Gearbox & Hydraulic Oil:** Petronas Tutela
TRANSMISSION	**Gearbox:** Williams eight-speed plus reverse seamless, sequential, semi-automatic shift
CHASSIS	Monocoque, moulded carbon-fibre and honeycomb composite structure **Front suspension:** Double wishbones and push-rod-actuated springs and anti-roll bar **Rear suspension:** Double wishbones and pull-rod-actuated springs and anti-roll bar **Wheels:** APP Tech forged magnesium **Tyres:** Pirelli P Zero **Brakes:** AP six-piston front and four-piston rear calipers with carbon discs and pads **Steering:** Williams F1 power-assisted rack-and-pinion **Fuel system:** ATL Kevlar-reinforced rubber bladder
DIMENSIONS	**Length:** Not disclosed **Width:** 2000mm **Height:** 950mm **Wheelbase:** Not disclosed **Formula weight:** 728kg, including driver and camera

WILLIAMS MARTINI RACING

IN general, Williams went backwards in 2017, its development of an indifferent design proving less effective than the teams around it. Yet again, it lost out to the much smaller and identically-powered Force India team for fourth in the constructors' championship.

There was a fundamental structural change to the team between 2016 and 2017, Pat Symonds having departed as technical chief, while Paddy Lowe joined from Mercedes as chief technical officer at the start of the season. Dirk de Beer replaced Jason Sommerville as chief of aero, having formerly served in a similar role at Ferrari, but he had no part in the conception of this car, joining on 1st March. There was also a new chief of vehicle dynamics, a new project manager and a new team manager. None of these changes had an impact upon the basic conception of the FW40 (the FW39 tag was skipped to tie in with Williams' 40th anniversary celebrations), which, as before, combined the Mercedes power unit with Williams' own gearbox, the casing of which, uniquely, was fashioned not from carbon fibre, but aluminium. Similarly, its rear suspension was uniquely non-composite. Ed Wood was the chief designer, and he presided over a car in which the downforce/aero efficiency trade-off was biased more towards the latter than the former – playing its part in a car that had bigger competitive swings from track to track than any other.

Williams produced a much shorter gearbox cas-

ing than that employed by Mercedes (and provided by Mercedes to Force India), and as such, the car's wheelbase was nowhere near as long (a difference of 186mm). Consequently, it didn't have as much underbody area with which to create downforce, but it attempted to claw back as much as possible of this with continuous development around the high-rake path. In terms of the rake angle the car was able to support before it became counter-productive, Williams was somewhere in the middle of the pack. The shorter wheelbase also meant that the car had no difficulty in getting below the minimum weight limit, thereby allowing the team to use ballast as a set-up aid – this despite the biggest difference in driver weights of all the teams (15kg between the lightweight Felipe Massa and the tall Lance Stroll).

Despite the new regulations, the FW40 was visibly closely related to the 2016 car, something that Lowe considered inevitable. "The new regs were not really that new," he maintained. "A lot of stuff we had still works, even if you look at the Merc and Ferrari. The rear end plates have to be angled differently, but all the same tricks are all still working. The front wing, we've developed it further. but not in a different direction; it works same as last year. The big change in development was all the new freedom around the bargeboards. Look at a 2008 car, and they've opened that box up again, and surprise, surprise we've got the same crap back in that box." Hence the FW40,

SIR FRANK WILLIAMS

WILLIAMS MARTINI RACING: PERSONNEL

Team Principal: Sir Frank Williams

Deputy Team Principal: Claire Williams OBE

Group CEO: Mike O'Driscoll

Chief Technical Officer: Paddy Lowe

Chief Performance/Operations Engineer: Jakob Andreasen

Head of Vehicle Science: Max Nightingale

Head of Performance Engineering: Rob Smedley

Chief Designer: Ed Wood

Senior Performance Engineer: Andrew Murdoch

Head of Aerodynamics: Dirk de Beer

Senior Car Systems Engineer: Carl Gaden

Vehicle Systems Engineer: Charlie Hooper

Team Manager: Dave Redding

Car Systems Leader: Paul Leeming

Race Engineer (Massa): Dave Robson

No. 1 Mechanic (Massa): Ben Howard

Performance Engineer (Stroll): Paul Davison

Race Engineer (Stroll): James Urwin

No. 1 Mechanic (Stroll): Patric Gustafsson

Chief Mechanic: Mark Pattinson

CLAIRE WILLIAMS

Above: Paddy Lowe, Williams chief technical officer.

Above left: Paul di Resta made a late substitute appearance for Massa in Hungary.

Left: Lance Stroll had an up-and-down first season, but the youngster is learning fast...

Below: The team take a photo call in Mexico.
Photo: Williams F1 Team

Right: Felipe Massa did a thoroughly professional job in his final season.
Photo: Peter J. Fox

like all the 2017 designs, featured extensive guide vanes in that area. It also had the *de rigueur* shark-fin engine cover and T-wing ahead of the actual wing. Up front, there was an S-duct, but no blown axle. The sidepods were kept as narrow as feasible, dictated by the high-efficiency aero targets, although the undercut was more enhanced than the FW38's, and the radiator openings appeared slightly smaller. In summary, it was a very conventional design, with little visible innovation.

The rear suspension had serious geometry flaws, and a new one (entailing a new gearbox casing so that the pick-up points could be changed) was trialed at the Hungaroring tests, but it was not raced. Other changes included a switch, just prior to Montreal, to 32mm-thickness front discs, from 28mm. "We initially thought we could get through on 28mm," said Lowe, "but it quickly became clear we couldn't. There's no way we could've finished Montreal with 28mm discs." The thicker discs were used for the balance of the season.

At high-efficiency tracks, such as Sochi (where Massa qualified sixth), Montreal (where the car was quicker than the Force Indias) and Monza (where Stroll qualified fourth fastest), it was reasonably competitive. At high-downforce tracks, such as Monaco and Hungary, it was disastrously uncompetitive and it struggled to make it out of the Q1 part of the grid. So at its best, the FW40 was vying with Force India and

Renault to be 'best of the rest' after the big three. At its worst, however, it was down among the Saubers. That gives some indication of the car's mercurial nature, a natural consequence of the deliberate choice of aero targets.

In theory, Monza should have suited the car even better than it did, but the team did not run the rear wing that had been specifically designed for the track much earlier in the season. The standard low-downforce wing was found to be a better compromise and was used instead, which underlined the fact that some of the processes within the team were still not cutting-edge. "You start the programme in April for Spa/Monza, and it's very difficult to be sure," explained Lowe. "We made a whole set of wings, and by time we got to that weekend, they were clearly not what was required – all a big waste of money, time and effort."

Speed of turnaround and quality of simulation were two areas where Lowe was paying particular attention as he made the internal structural changes he considered necessary. "It's always a limitation in the F1 business generally. The quicker you can make something and learn how good or bad it is, the quicker you move forwards. So we are working hard to cut down that cycle time. There's no point where you say that's good enough. We've made some progress with it, but there's a lot further we need to go.

"The deficit is almost everywhere, not just one or

two areas. Some of our competitors are spending twice what we are able to. It's buying them more engineering, so every single item can have more time in development, be more precisely engineered, be made more efficient, lighter, stiffer whatever, more man hours going into every single part. You can use more exotic materials, more expensive ways to get it made more quickly. No disrespect to anyone in this team, who do a fantastic job with the time and materials available, but the ability to engineer detail in the car is lower than you see in the top teams, so we need to be more efficient with what we have got. You can look at something and say, 'I can solve that by writing a bigger cheque,' and I've been fortunate enough to work at teams like that for most of my career. But there's a challenge in getting a job done on a tighter set of constraints. First time around for me at Williams [in the '90s], we prided ourselves on being more ingenious than McLaren, whereas Ron Dennis prided himself on getting more sponsors and spending it on making the car quicker. That was the particular satisfaction of the '92 season at Williams, doing a dominant car on a relative shoestring. There's a bit of that element in what we're trying to do at the moment – to do a car that will over-perform relative to the budget."

It's all very much a work in progress at the moment, and the team's prospects rely heavily on the success of Lowe's vision.

27

NICO HÜLKENBERG

55

CARLOS SAINZ

30

JOLYON PALMER

Renault marked their 40th anniversary of entering F1 throughout 2017.

RENAULT R.S.17

OFFICIAL PARTNERS	APL • Bell & Ross • BP • Castrol • Eurodatacar • Genii Business Exchange • Infiniti • Mapfre • Microsoft • Pirelli • SMP Racing
TECHNICAL PARTNERS	3d Systems • Alpinestars • Digipen • Elysium • GF Machining Solutions • Matrix • PerkinElmer • Siemens
POWER UNIT	**Type:** Renault R.S.17 Hybrid **No. of cylinders** *(vee angle)*: V6 (90°) **No. of valves:** 24 **Max rpm** *(ICE)*: 15,000 **Electronics:** MES-Microsoft standard electronic control unit **Fuel:** BP **Oil:** Castrol
TRANSMISSION	**Gearbox:** Eight-speed semi-automatic titanium with reverse gear, quick-shift system **Clutch:** AP Racing
CHASSIS	Moulded carbon fibre and aluminium honeycomb composite monocoque **Front suspension:** Upper and lower carbon-fibre wishbones, push-rod-actuated torsion-bar springs, dampers and anti-roll bar **Rear suspension:** Upper and lower carbon-fibre wishbones, pull-rod actuated torsion-bar springs and transverse-mounted damper units inside gearbox casing, aluminium uprights **Wheels:** OZ magnesium **Tyres:** Pirelli P Zero **Brake pads and discs:** Carbon **Brake calipers:** Brembo **Master cylinders:** AP Racing
DIMENSIONS	**Front track:** 1600mm **Rear track:** 1550mm **Overall height:** 950mm **Overall width:** 2000mm **Formula weight:** 728kg, including driver and camera

RENAULT SPORT F1 TEAM

HERE we saw the beginning of the rebuild of the Enstone team, the R.S.17, the first car conceived by those charged with bringing Renault back as a works force. There had been a step change in performance from the very low base of 2016 as the facilities were built back up, and the car was frequently fastest of the rest after the big three teams. That did not translate in the constructors' championship, however, because of poor reliability and the fact that the second car scored only a handful of points. Renault did manage to leap-frog Toro Rosso, though, for sixth in the constructors' championship at the final round.

The car was overseen by chassis technical director Nick Chester, while Bob Bell continued in his wider role of technology director and supervisor of the upgrade of the facilities. Chief of aero when the car was conceived had been Jon Tomlinson, who would continue as assistant when Pete Machin joined (from Red Bull) to head up the aero department in July. The car was a fairly conventional take on the new 2017 regulations, albeit quite long in wheelbase (third only to Mercedes and Force India), being 8cm longer than the identically-powered Red Bull, for example. It featured tall bargeboards and some quite intricate detail on its aerodynamic surfaces. The car marked the first time in recent years that the team had followed the high-rake path popularised by Red Bull, though it had

not reached the point where it could operate at as high an angle as that team before the associated losses overwhelmed the peak downforce benefit. A large aperture was incorporated in the nose in the expectation of more complex control systems for the heave spring, but that area of development was halted pre-season by an FIA technical directive.

The architecture of the engine had been changed, though it still retained the turbo's combined compressor/turbine hung out the back. The difference was in the sizing and design of the turbo, which necessitated some changes to the shape of the engine itself. It went up in size, though was still smaller than that used by Mercedes, which had been able to justify progressively increasing the turbine/compressor size each year. The energy transfer efficiency of the power electronics and MGU-K largely determines the size of compressor that can be justified, as the increased size brings with it extra volume, weight and cooling demands. The greater the proportion of the turbo's energy that can be transferred to the crankshaft, the bigger the turbo that can be justified.

"We had to rethink what we produced for 2014," admitted Renault Sport's engine chief Rémi Taffin. "It could be that Mercedes had the right concept from the beginning and they built from that... obviously we sort of made a mistake in the first year and had to rebuild. We felt the 2016 engine was probably the

CYRIL ABITEBOUL

RENAULT SPORT F1 TEAM: PERSONNEL

President: Jérome Stoll

Managing Director: Cyril Abiteboul

Racing Consultant: Alain Prost

F1 Technology Director: Bob Bell

Chassis Technical Director: Nick Chester

Engine Technical Director: Rémi Taffin

Trackside Operations Director: Alan Permane

Chief Designer: Martin Tolliday

Head of Aerodynamics: Pete Machin

Deputy Head of Aerodynamics: Jon Tomlinson

Race Team Manager: Paul Seaby

Chief Mechanic: Robert Cherry

Team Head of Vehicle Performance: Chris Dyer

Race Engineer (Hülkenberg): Mark Slade

Race Engineer (Palmer/Sainz): Karel Loos

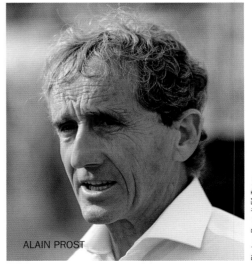

ALAIN PROST

Left: Carlos Sainz in Brazil. The Spaniard settled well into the team.

Below left: Jolyon Palmer gave his all, but alas, it was not enough to save the axe falling before the season was out.

Right: New bot in a new team. Nico Hülkenberg locks up in Melbourne.

Below: At the of a long hard season, the team overtook Toro Rosso in the final race in Abu Dhabi.

Below right: Technology director Bob Bell also oversaw the upgrading of the team's facilities.

Bottom right: Engine guru Rémi Taffin.

Photos: Renault F1 Team

ultimate potential of our original 2014 concept, and so for '17, we changed the concept."

Going hand in hand with the new turbo concept were new MGU-H and MGU-K units. Unfortunately, both proved to be unreliable during dyno testing, costing Viry around two months of development time on the engine. Ultimately, they had to revert to the 2016 specification of both components. That cost weight in both instances (around 7kg in total), but, more importantly, the MGU-H could not run at the designed shaft speeds of the new turbo without overheating. This meant that the whole compound loop was seriously compromised, and the engine never did develop the power it was theoretically capable of delivering. In addition, there were serious reliability problems – most of them associated with the overworked MGU-H – that cost many grid penalties and caused several race retirements (not just for the works team, but Viry's customers, too). In the midst of all that, it was understandable that Renault Sport was reluctant to pursue the technology of oil burn, from which Mercedes and Ferrari had found extra power. Instead, it lobbied the FIA to put an end to the practice, but was only partially successful.

That said, the power unit was estimated to be within 0.5–0.6s of the Mercedes (in race modes), although the total deficit from the front of the grid to the R.S.17 was more like 1.5s. In that respect, Viry was closer to the pace than Enstone – but Enstone was making bigger improvements year on year.

"We were still in the early stages of building up the team when this car was conceived," said Chester. "We started the tunnel programme for this car in March of 2016, at which time we were still understaffed and resourced." The Enstone head count of 460 at that time was up to 630 a year later. The long wheelbase – and the fact that Nico Hülkenberg is the heaviest driver on the grid – meant that it was a struggle to get much ballast on the car, even more so as development parts added to the weight.

"We got our start-of-year aero efficiency about right in terms of downforce and drag," said Chester, "but through the year, we've been adding more and more downforce and a bit of drag with it. That might mean we start looking at resetting those levels for next year's drag targets. You start creeping up and up, and at some point need to reset because you're putting too much drag on the car."

The initial traits of the car were that it qualified better than it raced, as it seemed to use its tyres over-aggressively. "That turned out just to be the way we were setting the car up," surmised Chester. "We had it so it was a bit nervous for qualifying and a bit too nervous for the race. That was just understanding what the drivers needed in the balance of their car. Nico was new to us this year, and it took a little while to understand what was needed." Certainly, into the season's second half, that trait had disappeared.

Significant upgrades went on the car at Barcelona (rear wing and bargeboards), but the biggest breakthrough came with a new floor/diffuser introduced on Hülkenberg's car at Silverstone and that of Jolyon Palmer at Spa. That and the accompanying changes to the bargeboards brought a very significant step in performance.

More compact sidepods appeared for Suzuka, and accompanying changes to the bargeboards a race later in Austin. Carlos Sainz, on his debut with the team, scored a strong seventh in America, with Hülkenberg following that up with a sixth at the Abu Dhabi season finale.

Onwards and upwards, but the fact remains that even if Renault produced what at its best was the fourth-fastest car, it remained almost 1s off the pace of the identically-engined Red Bull. So there's much still to do.

26

DANIIL KVYAT

10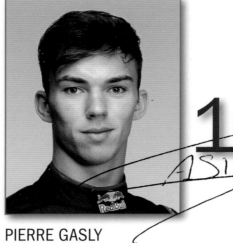

PIERRE GASLY

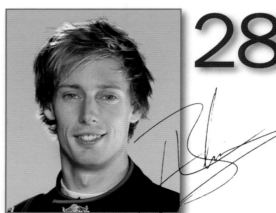

End of term for Brendon Hartley and Pierre Gasly in Abu Dhabi.

55

CARLOS SAINZ

28

BRENDON HARTLEY

TORO ROSSO STR12

PARTNERS	Red Bull • Estrella Galicia • Acronis • Edifice Casio • Gi Group
SUPPLIERS	CD-Adapco • Riedel • App Tech • Siemens• Pirelli
POWER UNIT	**Type:** Renault R.E.17 **No. of cylinders** *(vee angle)*: V6 (90°) **No. of valves:** 24 **Bore:** 80mm **Stroke:** 53mm **Crank height: 90mm** **Max rpm** *(ICE)*: 15,000 **Power output:** approximately 900bhp **Electronics:** MESL standard electronic control unit **Fuel:** Exxon Mobil **Lubricants:** Exxon Mobil
TRANSMISSION	Scuderia Toro Rosso carbon-fibre main case, eight-speed sequential, hydraulically operated
CHASSIS	Composite monocoque structure **Front suspension:** Upper and lower carbon wishbones, push-rod-actuated torsion-bar springs and anti-roll bars **Rear suspension:** Upper and lower carbon wishbones, pull-rod-actuated torsion-bar springs and anti-roll bars **Wheels:** APP Tech magnesium alloy **Tyres:** Pirelli P Zero **Brakes:** Brembo with carbon discs and pads; Scuderia Toro Rosso brake-by-wire **Fuel tank:** ATL with Scuderia Toro Rosso internals
DIMENSIONS	Not disclosed
	Formula weight: 728kg, including driver and camera

SCUDERIA TORO ROSSO

ALTHOUGH seventh place in the constructors' championship matched the team's 2016 result, 2017 generally was a less competitive season for Toro Rosso. Only once did it qualify as 'best of the rest' behind the big three – when Carlos Sainz put together a spectacular Monaco lap that was probably more driver than car – whereas even with its obsolete engine, the 2016 car had achieved that status on four occasions.

Pre-season, it was expected that, with a long-notice switch back to Renault engines (rather than year-old Ferrari units), the new STR12 would be a significant improvement. It certainly looked the part, the James Key-led technical team having produced an eye-catching design with several sophisticated little details (such as the extension on the front wheel hub that allowed the upper wishbone to be sited higher, to the benefit of the airflow to the sidepods, a detail it shared with the Mercedes). Its compact dimensions (the wheelbase was equal shortest with Red Bull) helped keep the weight down, allowing ballast to optimise the distribution of that weight. It proved to have good mechanical traits, which, together with the good weight balance, meant that it was quite good on its tyres.

It never really went as well as it looked, however, as its high drag wasn't adequately offset by downforce, and the troubled Renault engine couldn't overcome that difficulty. Nonetheless, reliability was better than in previous seasons, and only a late surge from the works Renault team prevented STR from taking sixth place overall.

"We got ourselves into a couple of sticky areas of development," said Key, "which proved surprisingly difficult to get out of. Our development rate was a bit disappointing as a result." Certainly, the team was left well behind in the development battle by McLaren and Renault, cars that had begun the season behind, but by the end were out of Toro Rosso's reach.

High-speed corner performance had been a strength of Toro Rossos of the previous two seasons, particularly in 2015, but that aspect just wasn't replicated (relative to the opposition) with this car. "There's no guarantee with such a massive difference in regs that you're going to have the same strengths and weaknesses," continued Key. "We wanted to ensure we still had that, then work on the bits we knew we needed to improve, on the basis our understanding would carry over to these regs. But we've missed that a bit, and again it's tied in with some of these sensitive areas, which have reduced the development rate compared to what we need to be achieving."

Generally, the car could be made to work adequately well on fast corners or slow, but at any circuits where there was a big spread in the speeds of critical corners – Hungary, Sepang, for example – it

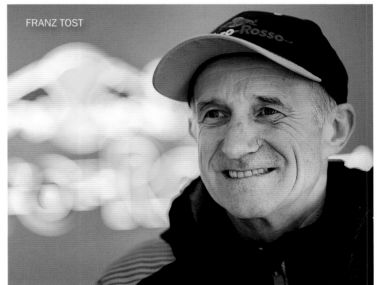

FRANZ TOST

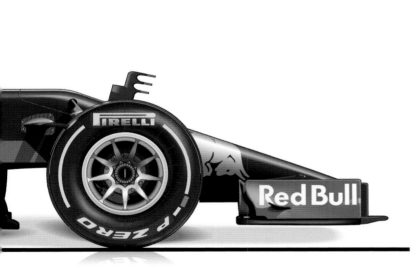

SCUDERIA TORO ROSSO: PERSONNEL

Team Owner: Dietrich Mateschitz

Team Principal: Franz Tost

Technical Director: James Key

Head of Vehicle Performance: Jody Eggington

Team Manager: Graham Watson

Chief Race Engineer: Jonathan Eddolls

Technical Co-ordinator: Sandro Parrini

Logistics Manager: Michela Fabbri

Race Engineer (Kvyat/Gasly)**:** Pierre Hamelin

Race Engineer (Sainz/Hartley)**:** Marco Matassa

Chief Mechanic: Domiziano Facchinetti

Reliability Manager: Phil Mitchell

Head of Sponsorship and Brand Management: Andrea Menth

Head of Communications: Fabiana Valenti

Press Officer: Tabatha Valls Halling

Digital Manager: Diego Mandolfo

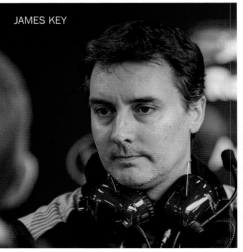

JAMES KEY

struggled. "Getting a consistency of balance has been very difficult," agreed Key. "We've been working hard on this with various mechanical tools and aero characteristics and so on."

There's a possibility that the switch to the wider cars of 2017 impacted upon the team's reliance on a 50 per cent scale tunnel (every other team now runs at 60 per cent). "It is a limitation," allowed Key. "You miss the fidelity and the stiffness of the parts, which is better at a higher scale. Possibly the 60 per cent tunnel tyre's a bit more developed as well, because there are more 60 per cent runners, so you're able to get more data and feedback. Having said that, the guys in Bicester have done a great job. The correlation of our tunnel, which isn't a million miles away in most cases, and that's tricky when you've got such different regs and wider cars and tyres. There's lots of new technology we've introduced to the tunnel over the past couple of years and will continue next year to get more out of it, to try to make up a little bit of the deficit of not having a 60 per cent."

The team's stand-out result was Sainz's fourth place in Singapore, although in reality the car had been flattered by both Sainz's performance and by the first-corner incident that took out the three fastest-qualifying cars. This was one of the Spaniard's last races for the team, before his switch to Renault. By the time he had been replaced by Brendon Hartley (concurrent with the dropping of Daniil Kvyat and his replacement by Pierre Gasly), the team was suffering badly with Renault reliability problems. In all four of Hartley's races with the team, engine penalties had forced him to start from the back. Thus it was difficult to assess the effectiveness of the aero upgrades introduced from Malaysia onwards.

But while the performance of the car was slightly disappointing, that of the operation of the team was considerably improved, helping it to a much better finishing record than previously. "It did need a lot of work," accepted Key, "but we're pretty close now to where we should be. There's a few little rough edges to smooth out, but that's taken a huge leap forward over the last year. Operationally, the team is more integrated. We've had one chassis failure this year; the others have been driver or engine related issues. We're much stronger, much more consistent, getting it right more often. Race strategy, pit stops have improved markedly as well – they're a lot quicker – so it's been a really good effort from everyone involved to pick it up. It was a weakness before and now it's a strength."

For 2018, Toro Rosso's fortunes will be aligned with Honda, with both sides very motivated to make a point to their former partners.

Above: Carlos Sainz scored the lion's share of the team's points before departing for Renault.

Top: Daniil Kvyat failed to convince and was summarily dropped by the team.

Left: Kvyat with Technical director James Key and Team Manager Graham Watson.

Above left: Gasly's Toro Rosso is wheeled on to the grid at Suzuka.

Photos: Peter J. Fox

8

ROMAIN GROSJEAN

20

KEVIN MAGNUSSEN

HAAS F1 TEAM

IT was a tough sophomore season for the smallest team on the grid, nonetheless Haas collected a consistent haul of lower-end points, but without the giant-killing highlights of its debut season. It took eighth in the constructors' championship, with a best race finish of sixth (from Romain Grosjean in Austria).

As before, the car – the VF-17 – had been conceived in Ferrari's wind tunnel, was powered by Ferrari's latest engine/gearbox, using Ferrari's suspension and running gear, was built by Dallara and operated out of a team base in Banbury. The design was overseen by Rob Taylor, with Ben Agathangelou continuing as chief of aero (supported latterly by additions to the aero department).

It followed the dimensions of the Ferrari – its wheelbase was identical, largely determined by the use of the Ferrari gearbox – but didn't have anything like as progressive an aerodynamic concept. It was a much more conventional car, but early in the season, before bigger teams developed their way clear, it was generally competitive with Williams and Renault, and occasionally made it into Q3. Aero development parts appeared regularly – there were front wing variations from as early as China, under-nose guide vane development for Spain and Japan, new sidepod flow conditioners from Montreal, further front wing development for Singapore and Austin – and Haas reckoned to

have found around 1s of lap time during the course of the season. Which, for so small a team, was commendable, but inevitably trailed some way behind, for example, Renault. Several times, production throughput was unable to keep up with the aero programme.

In summary, the car's peak performance was respectable; consistency of performance from track to track much less so. This was where the team's newness and small scale really showed. It had still been vastly under-resourced, particularly in the aero department, when the car was conceived, and as a consequence only one particular area of the car's aero map had been optimised. The general traits of the car were that it was better through fast, flowing corners than on stop/start sections.

Chief race engineer Ayao Komatsu summarised it thus: "With our aero team so small, we couldn't cover a wide range, so we have our high-downforce package – what you need for places like Budapest and Singapore, where we struggled. But also in low- to medium-downforce circuits like Baku, we are nowhere. Spa we did okay, but still not very competitive, Monza nowhere. So our range was in the middle." The competitiveness also suffered notably whenever the bodywork needed to be opened up for those tracks with a high cooling demand – and at Mexico, it was the slowest of all, largely for that reason.

The car's most competitive outings occurred in the

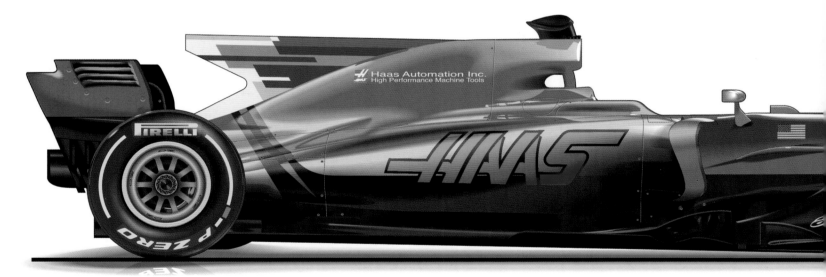

HAAS VF-17

PARTNERS	Haas Automation Inc • Alpinestars • Pirelli
POWER UNIT	**Type:** Ferrari 062 Hybrid **No. of cylinders** (vee angle): V6 (90°) **No. of valves:** 24 **Max. rpm** (ICE): 15,000 **ERS:** Integrated hybrid energy recovery via electrical motor generator units **Electronics:** FIA standard ECU and FIA homologated electronic & electrical system (as provided by MES) **Fuel and Lubricants:** Shell
TRANSMISSION	Ferrari servo-controlled hydraulic limited-slip differential with semi-automatic sequential and electronically-controlled gearbox, quick-shift (eight gears, plus reverse) **Clutch:** Carbon-carbon multi-plate
CHASSIS	Carbon-fibre and honeycomb composite structure **Suspension:** Independent, push-rod-actuated torsion-bar and damper system front and rear **Dampers:** ZF Sachs **Wheels:** Oz Racing **Wheel diameter:** 13in, front and rear **Tyres:** Pirelli P Zero **Brakes:** Carbon-fibre discs, pads and six-piston calipers **Cockpit instrumentation:** Ferrari **Fuel Cell:** ATL
DIMENSIONS	**Height:** 950mm **Overall width:** 2000mm **Wheelbase:** Not disclosed **Formula weight:** 728kg, including driver and camera

Kevin Magnussen leads Haas team-mate Romain Grosjean at Barcelona.

GENE HAAS

Photo: Haas F1 Team

HAAS F1 TEAM: PERSONNEL

Founder and Chairman: Gene Haas

Chief Operating Officer: Joe Custer

Team Principal: Guenther Steiner

Chief Designer: Rob Taylor

Team Manager: Peter Crolla

Race Team Operations Manager: Geoff Simmonds

Chief Aerodynamicist: Ben Agathangelou

Chief Race Engineer: Ayao Komatsu

Race Engineer (Grosjean): Gary Gannon

Race Engineer (Magnussen): Giuliano Salvi

Chief Mechanic: Stuart Cramp

Race Mechanic (Grosjean): Ian Staniforth

Race Mechanic (Magnussen): Toby Brown

AYAO KOMATSU

Photo: WRI2/Jean-François Galeron

GUENTHER STEINER

Photo: Haas F1 Team

first race of the year in Melbourne, where Grosjean qualified sixth, and Austria, both tracks that demand that middle level of downforce. At tracks unsuited to its narrow band of aero performance, it struggled further in generating the correct tyre temperatures. "At somewhere like Singapore," explained Komatsu, "that really made it very difficult for the drivers to understand the car, where its limit was, and be consistent. Because of this sensitivity, it doesn't take a lot between not getting out of Q1 and getting into Q3."

Using the same wind tunnel as Ferrari gave Haas confidence in what it was seeing there, allowing that to be largely eliminated when analysing any aero problems. "If Ferrari have any correlation issues, they will address it and we get the benefit. In that sense, it's very, very good," said Komatsu. "Given that the Ferrari was working very, very well, we had confidence there's nothing fundamentally wrong with the tunnel. In terms of aero personnel, we had a big recruitment drive, but that was long after this car was conceived. For next year's car, we have the right number of people for our head of aero to achieve what he wants to." There are also plans to transfer the CFD department from America to Italy, to liaise more closely with the tunnel programme.

The Banbury-based vehicle performance group was new for 2017, allowing vehicle dynamicists to work closely with the race engineering team, but there remained a difficulty in accessing the full potential of the car at every track. The vehicle performance group included just one tyre specialist. "Our tyre understanding was better than in '16," said Komatsu, "but

there's still a long way to go. I was at Brackley [then Honda, now Mercedes] 12 years ago when they introduced their tyre group, and I can only imagine what that's like now."

Grosjean, in particular, struggled – for the second consecutive year – with the feel of the brake pedal, making it difficult to avoid repeated locking up when leaning on it in qualifying.

Komatsu, who had been Grosjean's engineer during his Lotus days, understood the problem, but the solution remained a work in progress, as he explained: "Romain, if he's got the car and brakes as he wants, is very, very, very quick. But if he hasn't got the brakes or the low-speed car balance at the front end, he will struggle – a bit similar to Kimi. At Lotus, when we had Kimi and Romain, if we couldn't give them a strong front end, they really couldn't do anything. Romain's driving style is very late braking and really requires a certain feedback from the brakes, so when he hasn't got it, that's really a big disadvantage for him, but not so much for our other driver, Kevin, or even Antonio [Giovinazzi]. Fact is, we've got Romain and need to get the best out of him. Kevin can drive it like this and isn't so badly affected either way. But even when Romain's unhappy with it, and Kevin's okay, often you still see Romain pull out the lap in qualifying. You saw a good example of this in Singapore, where Romain was really struggling with the brakes. That's his potential – give him a good balance and brakes, and there's a lot you can get from Romain. It's frustrating because we know what to give him, but sometimes can't deliver it."

Part of the problem was getting the front tyres in the correct temperature window to give Grosjean the grip needed for his aggressive corner-entry speeds, another was in the feel of the pedal itself. "We've been experimenting with Carbone Industrie brakes, while with Brembo we're trying to improve their materials," explained Komatsu.

The Brembos did not give the same ultimate braking power as the Carbone Industries (CI), which furthermore allowed better modulation of the pedal – ie. the wheels could be unlocked more easily with a slight release of pedal pressure. The downside of the CI brakes was that they generated much more heat, which the disc design could only cope with at circuits where there was relatively little braking demand.

The CIs were first tried in practice at Sochi and proved to be completely beyond the cooling capacity of the design. The Brembos remained the usual Hobson's choice – and they were not of the same material as those employed by Ferrari. The reason for this was that the supplier of the material to Brembo – Honeywell – had decided to concentrate on its aerospace market and thus had ceased production of the base material that Brembo had used previously. Ferrari had stockpiled enough of the old material for Brembo to continue to supply the Scuderia with it for the full season, but Haas was forced on to the inferior material from the mid-point of the year.

Did 2017 represent the maximum potential of Haas's unique small-team/'shared parts'/sub-contracted construction concept? Or is there more giant slaying to come?

Above: Pit stop for Grosjean at Austin.

Right: One for the future? Antonio Giovinazzi.

Left: Preparations are made to run Grosjean's car.

Below: On home soil. The team lines up for a photo at the Circuit of the Americas in Austin.

Photos: Haas F1 Team

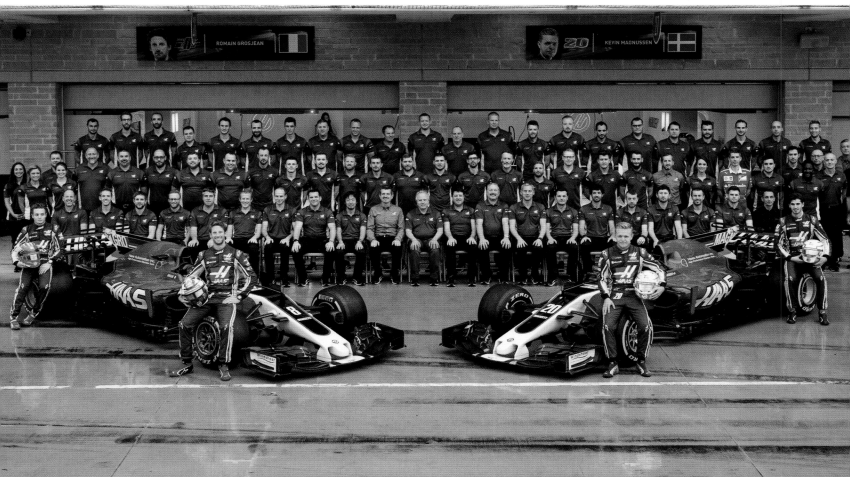

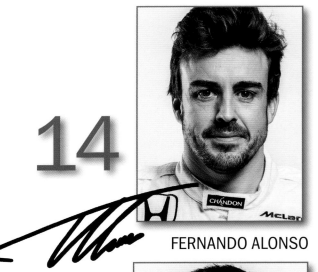

14

FERNANDO ALONSO

22

JENSON BUTTON

47

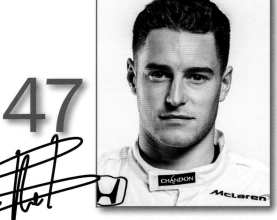

STOFFEL VANDOORNE

Fernando Alonso at Interlagos.

McLAREN HONDA MCL32

ENGINE PARTNER	Honda
TECHNOLOGY PARTNERS	Akebono • NTT Communications • Pirelli • SAP **OFFICIAL PARTNERS** Chandon • Logitech • Michael Kors
CORPORATE PARTNERS	CNN • Hilton • Johnnie Walker • Norton Rose Fulbright • Richard Mille • Santander • GREAT
OFFICIAL SUPPLIERS	AkzoNobel • Castrol • Calsonic Kansei • Enkei • Hookit • Kenwood • LAT 56 • Sparco • Stratasys • TechnoGym • Volvo Trucks • Yamazaki Mazak
POWER UNIT	**Type:** Honda RA617H Hybrid **No. of cylinders** (vee angle): V6 (90°) **No. of valves:** 24 **Max. rpm** (ICE): 15,000 **Electronics:** McLaren Applied Technologies, including chassis control, engine control, data acquisition, alternator, sensors, data analysis and telemetry **Oil:** Castrol
TRANSMISSION	**Gearbox:** McLaren eight-speed seamless-shift, carbon-composite casing **Clutch:** Electro-hydraulically operated carbon multi-plate
CHASSIS	Carbon-fibre composite monocoque **Front suspension:** Carbon-fibre wishbones, push-rod-actuated inboard torsion-bar and damper system **Rear suspension:** Carbon-fibre wishbones, pull-rod-actuated inboard torsion-bar and damper system **Wheel diameter:** 13in, front and rear **Wheels:** Enkei **Tyres:** Pirelli P Zero **Brake system:** Akebono calipers and master cylinders; Akebono brake-by-wire rear brake controls **Steering:** McLaren power-assisted rack-and-pinion **Cooling systems:** Calsonic Kansei **Instruments and electronics:** McLaren Applied Technologies **Batteries:** GS Yuasa **Radio systems:** Kenwood
DIMENSIONS	**Dimensions:** Not disclosed **Wheelbase:** Not disclosed **Formula weight:** 728kg, including driver and camera

McLAREN HONDA F1 TEAM

THAT McLaren was about to endure a third desolate Honda-powered season in succession had been suggested very strongly during winter testing, when engine reliability problems meant that the new MCL32's longest run before the first race was a mere 13 laps. As the implications of that played out over the season, it imposed a strain that the partnership could not withstand. McLaren initiated divorce proceedings, and the degree nisi, effective at the end of the year, was announced at Singapore in September.

A major – and necessary – reconfiguration of the Honda engine's architecture for 2017 set the manufacturer's programme back when that reconfiguration impacted upon reliability. The adoption of the Mercedes split turbo arrangement was justified by the need for a bigger compressor than would fit between the engine's cylinder banks. But that justification was rendered redundant by resonance issues that had not been apparent on the dyno, which effectively limited the turbo's speed. Not only was the turbo itself less effective at the speeds at which it was forced to run, but also the combustion chamber – having been designed around a different turbo speed – was inefficient. The MGU-H was said to have been the limiting factor, initiating the vibrations that enforced the lower turbo speeds, but essentially the combustion-H-turbo combination is one big efficiency loop. A weakness in one area will impact on the others, giving a more than proportionate lack of power and fuel efficiency.

Honda continued to use IHI for their turbochargers, and there was a feeling within McLaren that the supplier had not fully appreciated the nuances and complications of design in the hybrid era. Progress was made through the season, but massive grid penalties became the depressing norm for the McLaren drivers. Progress was made with reliability, Fernando Alonso scoring from unpenalised grid positions in the last three races. But performance was never at the required level. Although the peak horsepower deficit was estimated at around 80bhp to Mercedes by the season's end, that shortfall wasn't actually the biggest obstacle. Rather, it was how that deficit manifested itself – the limited electrical deployment available in the races made the cars sitting ducks on the straights. So even when they could qualify in the lower regions of the top ten, invariably they found it difficult to maintain position. Frequently, Alonso and Vandoorne would simply try to tag on to the back of a more powerful car (even if slower over a lap) and use the DRS effect from that to stay out of reach of others behind. The car had to be raced very defensively.

As the scale of the power unit limitations became apparent, the engineering side of McLaren simply readjusted its focus. "It became a matter of developing the best car we possibly could and concentrating on that, rather than getting dragged down by the results – so just stick to the engineering task, rather than the

ZAK BROWN

McLAREN HONDA F1 TEAM: PERSONNEL

Executive Director: Zak Brown

CEO, McLaren Technology Group: Jonathan Neale

Racing Director: Eric Boullier

Operations Director: Simon Roberts

Commercial and Financial Director: John Cooper

Chief Engineering Officer: Matt Morris

Chief Technical Officer (Chassis): Tim Goss

Chief Technical Officer (Aero): Peter Prodromou

Team Manager: Paul James

ERIC BOULLIER

JONATHAN NEALE

sporting task," said technical director Tim Goss.

The MCL32 (the new nomenclature reflecting the final departure of Ron Dennis) Goss presided over was a neat-looking design, one where weight saving and reduction of centre of gravity height had been allocated particular priority. The wider, fatter-wheeled cars of 2017 were particularly difficult to bring down to the weight limit. For this reason, it was relatively short in wheelbase (actually slightly shorter than the Ferrari), and it retained a standard single-casing gearbox, rather than the Mercedes/Ferrari-like cassette arrangement. An air-to-air intercooler was chosen for its weight saving over the more compact water-air type. Aerodynamically, its most visually distinctive features were the unique gills on the nose, designed to reduce the airflow losses incurred by the extensive camber of that part of the bodywork, and also to give a more consistent flow to the underbody as the car was turned. Despite the power shortfall, a very aggressive degree of rake (which brings a drag penalty) was chosen.

The lack of pre-season mileage meant that it was three or four races into the season before the team even had a full handle on the traits of the car. But generally, it proved well balanced and benign. How it compared to the top cars in terms of aero performance was difficult to assess. Certainly, by the season's end, it could usually record comparable lap times to Force India and Williams, which enjoyed Mercedes engines with a considerable power benefit over the McLaren's.

"We genuinely believe we had one of the better cars in that respect," said Goss, "but we would be wrong to assume that we've got the best car. It's difficult to tell when there's a reasonable delta in power unit performance. We're still hitting the job as hard

as we would have done if we felt we had an issue, because we won't rest until we have the best car on the grid, and even when we do have the best car, we still won't rest because you've got to keep that pace up to keep that advantage."

The aero philosophy behind the car – a benign platform, as espoused by head of aero Peter Prodromou – remained much as before, but adapted to the new regulations, as Goss explained: "The basics of what you're trying to achieve are about the same, but, for example, the flow around the wider front tyre, with an endplate sat in front of it, has got a higher pressure rise than before and just disturbs what you're trying to achieve. Similarly, with the rear corner – with the diffuser change and the wider rear tyre – you've got a similar thing going on there, and you need to get the car to somewhere where it's performing aerodynamically sensibly. Then after that, you can start working it. In the bargeboard area, where there is now a lot more real estate to work with, you have to start with something where, while you're looking for load, you're not throwing vast losses at the car. The danger is that you leap in too early on and try to crank load into it when you haven't got the basics under control… We concentrated on getting the car to work properly, then we started cranking load into it and dealing with the sensitivities and incidence tolerance – yaw, steer, etc. From the start, what we wanted to do with the base architecture of the car was to give the aerodynamicists a good canvas to work with."

That philosophy will be combined with a new engine partner – Renault – in 2018. As the team reverts to customer engine status for only the second time in three decades, it will be fascinating to compare its performance with that of the identically-powered Red Bull.

Above: Vandoorne's rookie season was a long hard one, but the Belgian driver never let his head drop.

Right: Mechanics hard at work under the lights in the garage in Singapore.

Left: Alonso drove his heart out in a car unworthy of his talents.

Below left: Could Lando Norris be McLaren's next superstar?

Bottom left: McLaren paddock HQ.

Below: The team line-up in Brazil with the Honda era drawing to a close.

Photos: McLaren Honda

9

MARCUS ERICSSON

36

ANTONIO GIOVINAZZI

12

PASCAL WEHRLEIN

Processing data in laptop city.

SAUBER C36

PRINCIPAL PARTNER	Silanna **PREMIUM PARTNERS** CNBC • Edox Swiss Watches • Modo Eyewear
OFFICIAL & TECHNICAL PARTNERS	Additive Industries • Auto Bild Motosport • Erreà Sport • Gabrielle's Angel Foundation for Cancer Research Malbuner Pocket Sandwich • Mitsubishi Electric • NetApp • OMP • Pirelli • Swiss Fibertec • Thomann Nutzfahrzeuge AG Walter Meier
PROMOTIONAL PARTNERS	Brütsch/Rüegger • carbon-connect • Hewlett Packard Enterprise • Interroll • MTO • Riedel Communications Singapore Airlines • Vebego
POWER UNIT	**Type:** Ferrari 1.6-litre turbo **No. of cylinders** (vee angle): V6 (90°) **No. of valves:** 24 **Max. rpm:** 15,000
TRANSMISSION	**Gearbox:** Ferrari eight-speed quick-shift carbon gearbox, longitudinally mounted **Clutch:** Carbon fibre
CHASSIS	Carbon-fibre monocoque **Front suspension:** Upper and lower wishbones, inboard spring and damper elements actuated by push-rods **Rear suspension:** Upper and lower wishbones, inboard spring and damper elements actuated by pull-rods **Dampers:** ZF Sachs **Wheel diameter:** 13in, front and rear **Wheels:** OZ **Tyres:** Pirelli P Zero **Brake calipers and pads:** Brembo **Discs:** Carbone Industrie **Steering wheel:** Sauber F1 Team **Instruments:** Sauber F1 Team
DIMENSIONS	**Length:** 5143mm **Width:** 2000mm **Front track:** 1615mm **Rear track:** 1530mm **Height:** 950mm
	Formula weight: 728kg, including driver and camera

SAUBER F1 TEAM

SAUBER'S 2017 season was defined by the straitened circumstances in play when the C36 had been conceived. Chief among those was the decision to run the year-old 2016 Ferrari engine (and associated transmission), which saved the team around 10 million euros compared to a supply of the 2017 power unit, but which left the Saubers ever more outpowered as the season progressed. But it wasn't only the engine; aerodynamically, the C36 was inevitably below par as an under-resourced team attempted to fully exploit the huge gains possible under the new regulations.

The purchase of the team in mid-2016 by Longbow Finance had allowed it to progress to something more than the survival mode it had been in for some time, but – much as at Renault's Enstone team – a lot of damage had been inflicted by the financial difficulties. Team principal of four years Monisha Kaltenborn split with Sauber on the eve of the Azerbaijan Grand Prix in June, and eventually she was replaced by former Enstone boss Frédéric Vasseur.

Under the new ownership, a more stable technical department was established, and Jörg Zander was recruited as technical director. He started work in January, 2017, at the factory where he had last served as chief designer 11 years earlier. He was under no illusions about the task he faced. "Some of the departments were not in good shape," he explained. "They were suffering a lack of resource, competence, accountability because of the financial pressures of the past. A lot of people had left, and some areas of the organisation were suffering quite badly – the design office, composite design, track engineering, for example. But it was a happy place – because there was now a foundation of support from the new owners, justifying the trust and belief of those who remained."

Luca Furbatto joined in June to work alongside incumbent designer Eric Gandelin. This allowed Zander to implement a system of alternating chief designer, with Furbatto concentrating on developing the C36 while Gandelin moved across to the 2018 car. "Within three months, the benefits of this became apparent," he said. "The feedback into the loop is much better because people have time for it, so it helps integrate everything better, and this was one of the problems before." Chief of aero remained Nicolas Hennel, with Xevi Pujolar as head of track engineering.

The C36 was the physical embodiment of the team's limitations at the time of its conception in 2016, as Zander explained: "The link between the vehicle performance group and aerodynamics needed to be improved, needed greater collaboration… so the parameters around which the car was conceived, the target aero maps, the weightings between the various performance factors were not appropriate. It gave us a car that was very poor in the medium speed range, even if very good in slow corners. It's all very well being slow-corner world champions, but…

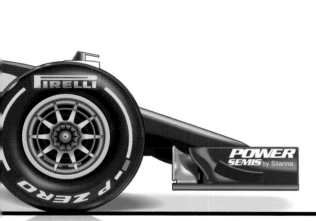

FRÉDÉRIC VASSEUR

SAUBER F1 TEAM: PERSONNEL

President of the Board of Directors: Pascal Picci

Team Principal & CEO: Frédéric Vasseur

Production Director: Axel Kruse

Technical Director: Jörg Zander

Chief Designer: Eric Gandelin, Luca Furbatto

Head of Aerodynamics:
Nicolas Hennel de Beaupreau

Head of Systems Engineering: Davide Spagnol

Team Manager: Beat Zehnder

Head of Track Engineering: Xevi Pujolar

Race Engineer (Ericsson): Julien Simon-Chautemps

Race Engineer (Wehrlein/Giovinazzi): Jörn Becker

Head of Track Operations: Timothée Guerin

Chief Mechanic: Reto Camenzind

Head of Communications: Marleen Seilheimer

Head of Marketing & Sales: Christine Uphoff

BEAT ZEHNDER

Photos: Sauber F1 Team

"This had run-on consequences. If you do not have enough downforce, you do not get the tyres in the right temperature window, reducing your grip level, in a downwards spiral. These were the fundamentals of this year's car."

Despite being one of the smallest cars on the grid, with the combined weight of car and the heavier of its drivers, Marcus Ericsson, it was actually 4–8kg over the minimum weight. The sister car of the lighter Pascal Wehrlein ran at around the weight limit, but there was no capacity to use ballast to vary the weight distribution from track to track. On average, it was the slowest car in the field, though Wehrlein twice scored points with it and three times managed to graduate to the Q2 part of qualifying.

Sauber remained the only team without access to a driver-in-loop simulator, a crucial part of extracting the maximum from the current generation of cars. Zander: "We want to do this and have a road map towards doing it. We are beginning to use a quasi-static simulator and then looking at the best way of using a driver-in-loop [DIL] approach later. But it's not just a matter of buying your system and plugging it in. It takes about two years to get it working properly. The quasi-static costs maybe 150,000 euros; the DIL around 4–4.5 million – and there's not really an upper limit."

Despite this, the track engineering group was much improved from 2016, and both drivers were impressed with how much better the car was at the first race than in winter testing, particularly its braking stability. There were two rafts of aero upgrades – Spain/Monaco and Hungary/Spa – but the weighting problem Zander referred to in the car's basic concept meant that they did not yield a lot of extra performance, certainly nowhere near enough to make up for the power unit's declining competitiveness. This was an unavoidable consequence of the budget-saving decision forced on to the team long before Zander joined it.

"I cannot criticise Ferrari; they are the perfect partner and we have a brilliant relationship with them," he said. "But in terms of the choice of the '16 engine, how can you recover a deficit of 50–70bhp? Yes, you can run the car with lower downforce and match your downforce levels to the required end-of-straight speeds, but then you're again into the downwards spiral of not putting enough energy into the tyres, their temperatures falling and losing grip, etc. So at low-efficiency tracks, we didn't stand a chance. I was surprised we were relatively good at Baku. Montreal wasn't as bad as it might've been. But when you are talking of 10bhp making 0.3s of lap time, we were 1.5s off just on bhp."

In this context, Zander's analysis of the comparison to the other engines is interesting: "At the beginning of the year, we had a big deficit to Mercedes/Ferrari '17, with Renault between one-third and one-half of that, and we were slightly ahead of Honda. By now, we are slightly behind Honda [since Silverstone], and the gap to the front and to Renault has opened up further." So what had been a state-of-the-art competitive engine in 2016 was behind even the weakest engine just 12 months later – a telling illustration of the pace of development in F1.

That's the hard truth that Sauber will be fighting against for some time to come, albeit with renewed hope for a brighter future, one that, with the involvement of Alfa Romeo, will be more closely associated with Ferrari.

Above: Wehrlein scored the team's only points.

Top right: Team principal Monisha Kaltenborn made an abrupt departure in mid-season.

Top far right: Giovinazzi was a late stand-in for Wehrlein in Melbourne.

Above right: F2 champion Charles Leclerc has been confirmed alongside Marcus Ericsson for 2018.

Above far right: Vasseur and Zehnder in discussion.

Right: Marcus Ericsson had loyal backing to cement his place on the team. He remains on board with Sauber as they embark upon a new partnership with Alfa Romeo.

Photos: Sauber F1 Team

CHASSIS LOGBOOK 2017

COMPILED BY DAVID HAYHOE

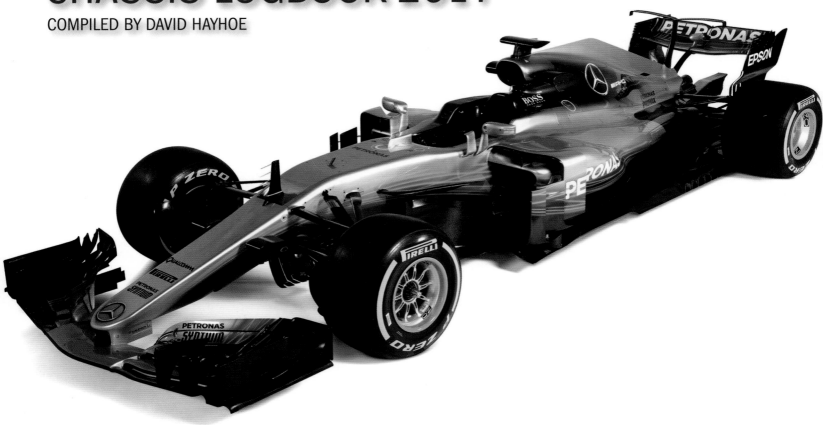

MERCEDES F1 W08 EQ Power+

ROUND 1 AUSTRALIAN GP

	MERCEDES	
44	Lewis Hamilton	F1 W08 EQ Power+/01
77	Valtteri Bottas	F1 W08 EQ Power+/03
	RED BULL-TAG HEUER	
3	Daniel Ricciardo	RB13/03
33	Max Verstappen	RB13/01
	FERRARI	
5	Sebastian Vettel	SF70H/
7	Kimi Räikkönen	SF70H/
	FORCE INDIA-MERCEDES	
11	Sergio Pérez	VJM10/02
31	Esteban Ocon	VJM10/01
	WILLIAMS-MERCEDES	
18	Lance Stroll	FW40/02
19	Felipe Massa	FW40/03
	McLAREN-HONDA	
2	Stoffel Vandoorne	MCL32/01
14	Fernando Alonso	MCL32/03
	TORO ROSSO-RENAULT	
26	Daniil Kvyat	STR12/01
55	Carlos Sainz	STR12/03
	HAAS-FERRARI	
8	Romain Grosjean	VF-17/02
20	Kevin Magnussen	VF-17/01
	RENAULT	
27	Nico Hülkenberg	R.S.17/02
30	Jolyon Palmer	R.S.17/01
	SAUBER-FERRARI	
9	Marcus Ericsson	C36/03
94	Pascal Wehrlein	C36/02
36	Antonio Giovinazzi	C36/02

ROUND 2 CHINESE GP

	MERCEDES	
44	Lewis Hamilton	F1 W08 EQ Power+/01
77	Valtteri Bottas	F1 W08 EQ Power+/03
	RED BULL-TAG HEUER	
3	Daniel Ricciardo	RB13/03
33	Max Verstappen	RB13/04
	FERRARI	
5	Sebastian Vettel	SF70H/
7	Kimi Räikkönen	SF70H/
	FORCE INDIA-MERCEDES	
11	Sergio Pérez	VJM10/02
31	Esteban Ocon	VJM10/01
	WILLIAMS-MERCEDES	
18	Lance Stroll	FW40/02
19	Felipe Massa	FW40/03
	McLAREN-HONDA	
2	Stoffel Vandoorne	MCL32/01
14	Fernando Alonso	MCL32/03
	TORO ROSSO-RENAULT	
26	Daniil Kvyat	STR12/01
55	Carlos Sainz	STR12/03
	HAAS-FERRARI	
8	Romain Grosjean	VF-17/02
20	Kevin Magnussen	VF-17/01
	RENAULT	
27	Nico Hülkenberg	R.S.17/02
30	Jolyon Palmer	R.S.17/01
	SAUBER-FERRARI	
9	Marcus Ericsson	C36/03
36	Antonio Giovinazzi	C36/02

ROUND 3 BAHRAIN GP

	MERCEDES	
44	Lewis Hamilton	F1 W08 EQ Power+/01
77	Valtteri Bottas	F1 W08 EQ Power+/03
	RED BULL-TAG HEUER	
3	Daniel Ricciardo	RB13/03
33	Max Verstappen	RB13/04
	FERRARI	
5	Sebastian Vettel	SF70H/
7	Kimi Räikkönen	SF70H/
	FORCE INDIA-MERCEDES	
11	Sergio Pérez	VJM10/02
31	Esteban Ocon	VJM10/01
	WILLIAMS-MERCEDES	
18	Lance Stroll	FW40/02
19	Felipe Massa	FW40/03
	McLAREN-HONDA	
2	Stoffel Vandoorne	MCL32/01
14	Fernando Alonso	MCL32/03
	TORO ROSSO-RENAULT	
26	Daniil Kvyat	STR12/01
55	Carlos Sainz	STR12/03
	HAAS-FERRARI	
8	Romain Grosjean	VF-17/02
20	Kevin Magnussen	VF-17/01
	RENAULT	
27	Nico Hülkenberg	R.S.17/02
30	Jolyon Palmer	R.S.17/01
	SAUBER-FERRARI	
9	Marcus Ericsson	C36/03
94	Pascal Wehrlein	C36/01

ROUND 4 RUSSIAN GP

	MERCEDES	
44	Lewis Hamilton	F1 W08 EQ Power+/01
77	Valtteri Bottas	F1 W08 EQ Power+/03
	RED BULL-TAG HEUER	
3	Daniel Ricciardo	RB13/03
33	Max Verstappen	RB13/04
	FERRARI	
5	Sebastian Vettel	SF70H/
7	Kimi Räikkönen	SF70H/
	FORCE INDIA-MERCEDES	
11	Sergio Pérez	VJM10/02
31	Esteban Ocon	VJM10/01
	WILLIAMS-MERCEDES	
18	Lance Stroll	FW40/02
19	Felipe Massa	FW40/03
	McLAREN-HONDA	
2	Stoffel Vandoorne	MCL32/01
14	Fernando Alonso	MCL32/03
	TORO ROSSO-RENAULT	
26	Daniil Kvyat	STR12/01
55	Carlos Sainz	STR12/03
	HAAS-FERRARI	
8	Romain Grosjean	VF-17/02
20	Kevin Magnussen	VF-17/01
	RENAULT	
27	Nico Hülkenberg	R.S.17/02
46	Sergey Sirotkin	R.S.17/02
30	Jolyon Palmer	R.S.17/03
	(01-Fri)	
	SAUBER-FERRARI	
9	Marcus Ericsson	C36/03
94	Pascal Wehrlein	C36/01

ROUND 5 SPANISH GP

MERCEDES
| 44 | Lewis Hamilton | F1 W08 EQ Power+/05 |
| 77 | Valtteri Bottas | F1 W08 EQ Power+/04 |

RED BULL-TAG HEUER
| 3 | Daniel Ricciardo | RB13/03 |
| 33 | Max Verstappen | RB13/04 |

FERRARI
| 5 | Sebastian Vettel | SF70H/ |
| 7 | Kimi Räikkönen | SF70H/ |

FORCE INDIA-MERCEDES
| 11 | Sergio Pérez | VJM10/02 |
| 31 | Esteban Ocon | VJM10/01 |

WILLIAMS-MERCEDES
| 18 | Lance Stroll | FW40/01 |
| 19 | Felipe Massa | FW40/03 |

McLAREN-HONDA
| 2 | Stoffel Vandoorne | MCL32/01 |
| 14 | Fernando Alonso | MCL32/03 |

TORO ROSSO-RENAULT
| 26 | Daniil Kvyat | STR12/01 |
| 55 | Carlos Sainz | STR12/03 |

HAAS-FERRARI
| 8 | Romain Grosjean | VF-17/02 |
| 20 | Kevin Magnussen | VF-17/03 |

RENAULT
27	Nico Hülkenberg	R.S.17/02
30	Jolyon Palmer	R.S.17/03
46	Sergey Sirotkin	R.S.17/03

SAUBER-FERRARI
| 9 | Marcus Ericsson | C36/03 |
| 94 | Pascal Wehrlein | C36/01 |

ROUND 6 MONACO GP

MERCEDES
| 44 | Lewis Hamilton | F1 W08 EQ Power+/05 |
| 77 | Valtteri Bottas | F1 W08 EQ Power+/04 |

RED BULL-TAG HEUER
| 3 | Daniel Ricciardo | RB13/03 |
| 33 | Max Verstappen | RB13/04 |

FERRARI
| 5 | Sebastian Vettel | SF70H/ |
| 7 | Kimi Räikkönen | SF70H/ |

FORCE INDIA-MERCEDES
| 11 | Sergio Pérez | VJM10/02 |
| 31 | Esteban Ocon | VJM10/01 |

WILLIAMS-MERCEDES
| 18 | Lance Stroll | FW40/02 |
| 19 | Felipe Massa | FW40/03 |

McLAREN-HONDA
| 2 | Stoffel Vandoorne | MCL32/04 |
| 22 | Jenson Button | MCL32/03 |

TORO ROSSO-RENAULT
| 26 | Daniil Kvyat | STR12/01 |
| 55 | Carlos Sainz | STR12/03 |

HAAS-FERRARI
| 8 | Romain Grosjean | VF-17/02 |
| 20 | Kevin Magnussen | VF-17/03 |

RENAULT
| 27 | Nico Hülkenberg | R.S.17/02 |
| 30 | Jolyon Palmer | R.S.17/03 |

SAUBER-FERRARI
| 9 | Marcus Ericsson | C36/03 |
| 94 | Pascal Wehrlein | C36/02 |

TORO ROSSO STR12

Scuderia Toro Rosso

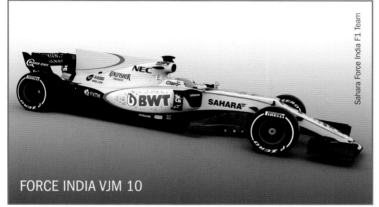

FORCE INDIA VJM 10

Sahara Force India F1 Team

RENAULT R.S.17

Renault F1 Team

ROUND 7 CANADIAN GP

MERCEDES
| 44 | Lewis Hamilton | F1 W08 EQ Power+/05 |
| 77 | Valtteri Bottas | F1 W08 EQ Power+/03 |

RED BULL-TAG HEUER
| 3 | Daniel Ricciardo | RB13/03 |
| 33 | Max Verstappen | RB13/04 |

FERRARI
| 5 | Sebastian Vettel | SF70H/ |
| 7 | Kimi Räikkönen | SF70H/ |

FORCE INDIA-MERCEDES
| 11 | Sergio Pérez | VJM10/02 |
| 31 | Esteban Ocon | VJM10/01 |

WILLIAMS-MERCEDES
| 18 | Lance Stroll | FW40/01 |
| 19 | Felipe Massa | FW40/03 |

McLAREN-HONDA
| 2 | Stoffel Vandoorne | MCL32/02 |
| 14 | Fernando Alonso | MCL32/03 |

TORO ROSSO-RENAULT
| 26 | Daniil Kvyat | STR12/01 |
| 55 | Carlos Sainz | STR12/03 |

HAAS-FERRARI
| 8 | Romain Grosjean | VF-17/02 |
| 20 | Kevin Magnussen | VF-17/03 |

RENAULT
| 27 | Nico Hülkenberg | R.S.17/04 |
| 30 | Jolyon Palmer | R.S.17/02 |

SAUBER-FERRARI
| 9 | Marcus Ericsson | C36/03 |
| 94 | Pascal Wehrlein | C36/04 |

ROUND 8 AZERBAIJAN GP

MERCEDES
| 44 | Lewis Hamilton | F1 W08 EQ Power+/05 |
| 77 | Valtteri Bottas | F1 W08 EQ Power+/03 |

RED BULL-TAG HEUER
| 3 | Daniel Ricciardo | RB13/03 |
| 33 | Max Verstappen | RB13/04 |

FERRARI
| 5 | Sebastian Vettel | SF70H/ |
| 7 | Kimi Räikkönen | SF70H/ |

FORCE INDIA-MERCEDES
| 11 | Sergio Pérez | VJM10/02 |
| 31 | Esteban Ocon | VJM10/01 |

WILLIAMS-MERCEDES
| 18 | Lance Stroll | FW40/01 |
| 19 | Felipe Massa | FW40/03 |

McLAREN-HONDA
| 2 | Stoffel Vandoorne | MCL32/02 |
| 14 | Fernando Alonso | MCL32/03 |

TORO ROSSO-RENAULT
| 26 | Daniil Kvyat | STR12/04 |
| 55 | Carlos Sainz | STR12/01 |

HAAS-FERRARI
| 8 | Romain Grosjean | VF-17/02 |
| 20 | Kevin Magnussen | VF-17/03 |

RENAULT
| 27 | Nico Hülkenberg | R.S.17/04 |
| 30 | Jolyon Palmer | R.S.17/02 |

SAUBER-FERRARI
| 9 | Marcus Ericsson | C36/03 |
| 94 | Pascal Wehrlein | C36/04 |

ROUND 9 AUSTRIAN GP

MERCEDES
44	Lewis Hamilton	F1 W08 EQ Power+/05
77	Valtteri Bottas	F1 W08 EQ Power+/03

RED BULL-TAG HEUER
3	Daniel Ricciardo	RB13/03
33	Max Verstappen	RB13/04

FERRARI
5	Sebastian Vettel	SF70H/
7	Kimi Räikkönen	SF70H/

FORCE INDIA-MERCEDES
11	Sergio Pérez	VJM10/02
34	Alfonso Celis	VJM10/02
31	Esteban Ocon	VJM10/01

WILLIAMS-MERCEDES
18	Lance Stroll	FW40/02
19	Felipe Massa	FW40/03

McLAREN-HONDA
2	Stoffel Vandoorne	MCL32/02
14	Fernando Alonso	MCL32/03

TORO ROSSO-RENAULT
26	Daniil Kvyat	STR12/04
55	Carlos Sainz	STR12/02

HAAS-FERRARI
8	Romain Grosjean	VF-17/02
20	Kevin Magnussen	VF-17/03

RENAULT
27	Nico Hülkenberg	R.S.17/04
46	Sergey Sirotkin	R.S.17/04
30	Jolyon Palmer	R.S.17/04

SAUBER-FERRARI
9	Marcus Ericsson	C36/01
94	Pascal Wehrlein	C36/04

ROUND 10 BRITISH GP

MERCEDES
44	Lewis Hamilton	F1 W08 EQ Power+/05
77	Valtteri Bottas	F1 W08 EQ Power+/03

RED BULL-TAG HEUER
3	Daniel Ricciardo	RB13/03
33	Max Verstappen	RB13/04

FERRARI
5	Sebastian Vettel	SF70H/
7	Kimi Räikkönen	SF70H/

FORCE INDIA-MERCEDES
11	Sergio Pérez	VJM10/02
31	Esteban Ocon	VJM10/01

WILLIAMS-MERCEDES
18	Lance Stroll	FW40/02
19	Felipe Massa	FW40/03

McLAREN-HONDA
2	Stoffel Vandoorne	MCL32/04
14	Fernando Alonso	MCL32/05

TORO ROSSO-RENAULT
26	Daniil Kvyat	STR12/04
55	Carlos Sainz	STR12/02

HAAS-FERRARI
8	Romain Grosjean	VF-17/02
20	Kevin Magnussen	VF-17/03
50	Antonio Giovinazzi	VF-17/03

RENAULT
27	Nico Hülkenberg	R.S.17/04
30	Jolyon Palmer	R.S.17/01

SAUBER-FERRARI
9	Marcus Ericsson	C36/01
94	Pascal Wehrlein	C36/04

ROUND 11 HUNGARIAN GP

MERCEDES
44	Lewis Hamilton	F1 W08 EQ Power+/05
77	Valtteri Bottas	F1 W08 EQ Power+/03

RED BULL-TAG HEUER
3	Daniel Ricciardo	RB13/05
33	Max Verstappen	RB13/04

FERRARI
5	Sebastian Vettel	SF70H/
7	Kimi Räikkönen	SF70H/

FORCE INDIA-MERCEDES
11	Sergio Pérez	VJM10/02
31	Esteban Ocon	VJM10/04
34	Alfonso Celis	VJM10/04

WILLIAMS-MERCEDES
18	Lance Stroll	FW40/01
19	Felipe Massa	FW40/04
40	Paul Di Resta	FW40/04

McLAREN-HONDA
2	Stoffel Vandoorne	MCL32/04
14	Fernando Alonso	MCL32/05

TORO ROSSO-RENAULT
26	Daniil Kvyat	STR12/04
55	Carlos Sainz	STR12/02

HAAS-FERRARI
8	Romain Grosjean	VF-17/02
20	Kevin Magnussen	VF-17/03
50	Antonio Giovinazzi	VF-17/03

RENAULT
27	Nico Hülkenberg	R.S.17/04
30	Jolyon Palmer	R.S.17/03

SAUBER-FERRARI
9	Marcus Ericsson	C36/03
94	Pascal Wehrlein	C36/02

ROUND 12 BELGIAN GP

MERCEDES
44	Lewis Hamilton	F1 W08 EQ Power+/05
77	Valtteri Bottas	F1 W08 EQ Power+/03

RED BULL-TAG HEUER
3	Daniel Ricciardo	RB13/05
33	Max Verstappen	RB13/04

FERRARI
5	Sebastian Vettel	SF70H/
7	Kimi Räikkönen	SF70H/

FORCE INDIA-MERCEDES
11	Sergio Pérez	VJM10/02
31	Esteban Ocon	VJM10/04

WILLIAMS-MERCEDES
18	Lance Stroll	FW40/03
19	Felipe Massa	FW40/01
	(04-Fri)	

McLAREN-HONDA
2	Stoffel Vandoorne	MCL32/04
14	Fernando Alonso	MCL32/05

TORO ROSSO-RENAULT
26	Daniil Kvyat	STR12/04
55	Carlos Sainz	STR12/02

HAAS-FERRARI
8	Romain Grosjean	VF-17/02
20	Kevin Magnussen	VF-17/03

RENAULT
27	Nico Hülkenberg	R.S.17/04
30	Jolyon Palmer	R.S.17/04

SAUBER-FERRARI
9	Marcus Ericsson	C36/02
94	Pascal Wehrlein	C36/04

RED BULL RB13

Red Bull Racing

ROUND 13 ITALIAN GP

	MERCEDES	
44	Lewis Hamilton	F1 W08 EQ Power+/05
77	Valtteri Bottas	F1 W08 EQ Power+/03
	RED BULL-TAG HEUER	
3	Daniel Ricciardo	RB13/05
33	Max Verstappen	RB13/04
	FERRARI	
5	Sebastian Vettel	SF70H/
7	Kimi Räikkönen	SF70H/
	FORCE INDIA-MERCEDES	
11	Sergio Pérez	VJM10/02
31	Esteban Ocon	VJM10/04
	WILLIAMS-MERCEDES	
18	Lance Stroll	FW40/03
19	Felipe Massa	FW40/01
	McLAREN-HONDA	
2	Stoffel Vandoorne	MCL32/04
14	Fernando Alonso	MCL32/05
	TORO ROSSO-RENAULT	
26	Daniil Kvyat	STR12/04
55	Carlos Sainz	STR12/02
	HAAS-FERRARI	
8	Romain Grosjean	VF-17/02
20	Kevin Magnussen	VF-17/03
	RENAULT	
27	Nico Hülkenberg	R.S.17/04
30	Jolyon Palmer	R.S.17/03
	SAUBER-FERRARI	
9	Marcus Ericsson	C36/02
94	Pascal Wehrlein	C36/04

ROUND 15 SINGAPORE GP

	MERCEDES	
44	Lewis Hamilton	F1 W08 EQ Power+/05
77	Valtteri Bottas	F1 W08 EQ Power+/03
	RED BULL-TAG HEUER	
3	Daniel Ricciardo	RB13/05
33	Max Verstappen	RB13/04
	FERRARI	
5	Sebastian Vettel	SF70H/
7	Kimi Räikkönen	SF70H/
	FORCE INDIA-MERCEDES	
11	Sergio Pérez	VJM10/02
31	Esteban Ocon	VJM10/04
	WILLIAMS-MERCEDES	
18	Lance Stroll	FW40/03
19	Felipe Massa	FW40/04
	McLAREN-HONDA	
2	Stoffel Vandoorne	MCL32/03
14	Fernando Alonso	MCL32/02
	TORO ROSSO-RENAULT	
10	Pierre Gasly	STR12/04
55	Carlos Sainz	STR12/01
38	Sean Gelael	STR12/01
	HAAS-FERRARI	
8	Romain Grosjean	VF-17/02
20	Kevin Magnussen	VF-17/03
50	Antonio Giovinazzi	VF-17/03
	RENAULT	
27	Nico Hülkenberg	R.S.17/04
46	Sergey Sirotkin	R.S.17/04
30	Jolyon Palmer	R.S.17/03
	SAUBER-FERRARI	
9	Marcus Ericsson	C36/02
37	Charles Leclerc	C36/02
94	Pascal Wehrlein	C36/04

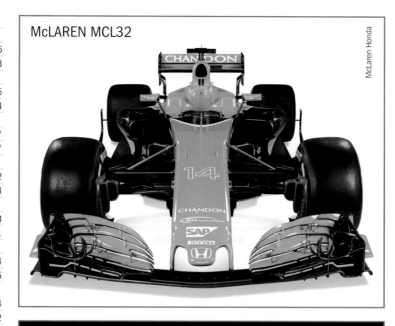

McLAREN MCL32

McLaren Honda

SAUBER C36

Sauber F1 Team

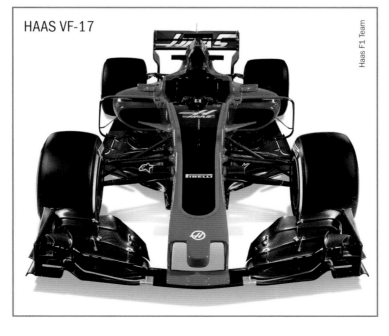

HAAS VF-17

Haas F1 Team

ROUND 14 SINGAPORE GP

	MERCEDES	
44	Lewis Hamilton	F1 W08 EQ Power+/05
77	Valtteri Bottas	F1 W08 EQ Power+/03
	RED BULL-TAG HEUER	
3	Daniel Ricciardo	RB13/05
33	Max Verstappen	RB13/06
	FERRARI	
5	Sebastian Vettel	SF70H/
7	Kimi Räikkönen	SF70H/
	FORCE INDIA-MERCEDES	
11	Sergio Pérez	VJM10/02
31	Esteban Ocon	VJM10/04
	WILLIAMS-MERCEDES	
18	Lance Stroll	FW40/01
19	Felipe Massa	FW40/04
	McLAREN-HONDA	
2	Stoffel Vandoorne	MCL32/03
14	Fernando Alonso	MCL32/02
	TORO ROSSO-RENAULT	
26	Daniil Kvyat	STR12/04
55	Carlos Sainz	STR12/01
38	Sean Gelael	STR12/01
	HAAS-FERRARI	
8	Romain Grosjean	VF-17/02
20	Kevin Magnussen	VF-17/03
50	Antonio Giovinazzi	VF-17/03
	RENAULT	
27	Nico Hülkenberg	R.S.17/04
30	Jolyon Palmer	R.S.17/03
	SAUBER-FERRARI	
9	Marcus Ericsson	C36/02
94	Pascal Wehrlein	C36/04

ROUND 16 JAPANESE GP

	MERCEDES	
44	Lewis Hamilton	F1 W08 EQ Power+/05
77	Valtteri Bottas	F1 W08 EQ Power+/03
	RED BULL-TAG HEUER	
3	Daniel Ricciardo	RB13/05
33	Max Verstappen	RB13/04
	FERRARI	
5	Sebastian Vettel	SF70H/
7	Kimi Räikkönen	SF70H/
	FORCE INDIA-MERCEDES	
11	Sergio Pérez	VJM10/02
31	Esteban Ocon	VJM10/04
	WILLIAMS-MERCEDES	
18	Lance Stroll	FW40/03
19	Felipe Massa	FW40/04
	McLAREN-HONDA	
2	Stoffel Vandoorne	MCL32/03
14	Fernando Alonso	MCL32/02
	TORO ROSSO-RENAULT	
10	Pierre Gasly	STR12/04
55	Carlos Sainz	STR12/01
	HAAS-FERRARI	
8	Romain Grosjean	VF-17/02
20	Kevin Magnussen	VF-17/03
	RENAULT	
27	Nico Hülkenberg	R.S.17/04
30	Jolyon Palmer	R.S.17/03
	SAUBER-FERRARI	
9	Marcus Ericsson	C36/02
94	Pascal Wehrlein	C36/04

FERRARI SF70H

Scuderia Ferrari

ROUND 17 UNITED STATES GP

MERCEDES
44	Lewis Hamilton	F1 W08 EQ Power+/05
77	Valtteri Bottas	F1 W08 EQ Power+/03

RED BULL-TAG HEUER
3	Daniel Ricciardo	RB13/05
33	Max Verstappen	RB13/06

FERRARI
5	Sebastian Vettel	SF70H/
7	Kimi Räikkönen	SF70H/

FORCE INDIA-MERCEDES
11	Sergio Pérez	VJM10/02
31	Esteban Ocon	VJM10/04

WILLIAMS-MERCEDES
18	Lance Stroll	FW40/03
19	Felipe Massa	FW40/04

McLAREN-HONDA
2	Stoffel Vandoorne	MCL32/04
14	Fernando Alonso	MCL32/05

TORO ROSSO-RENAULT
26	Daniil Kvyat	STR12/01
38	Sean Gelael	STR12/01
39	Brendon Hartley	STR12/04

HAAS-FERRARI
8	Romain Grosjean	VF-17/02
20	Kevin Magnussen	VF-17/03

RENAULT
27	Nico Hülkenberg	R.S.17/04
55	Carlos Sainz	R.S.17/03

SAUBER-FERRARI
9	Marcus Ericsson	C36/03
94	Pascal Wehrlein	C36/04
37	Charles Leclerc	C36/04

ROUND 18 MEXICAN GP

MERCEDES
44	Lewis Hamilton	F1 W08 EQ Power+/05
77	Valtteri Bottas	F1 W08 EQ Power+/03

RED BULL-TAG HEUER
3	Daniel Ricciardo	RB13/05
33	Max Verstappen	RB13/06

FERRARI
5	Sebastian Vettel	SF70H/
7	Kimi Räikkönen	SF70H/

FORCE INDIA-MERCEDES
11	Sergio Pérez	VJM10/02
31	Esteban Ocon	VJM10/04
34	Alfonso Celis	VJM10/04

WILLIAMS-MERCEDES
18	Lance Stroll	FW40/03
19	Felipe Massa	FW40/04

McLAREN-HONDA
2	Stoffel Vandoorne	MCL32/04
14	Fernando Alonso	MCL32/05

TORO ROSSO-RENAULT
10	Pierre Gasly	STR12/01
38	Sean Gelael	STR12/01
28	Brendon Hartley	STR12/04

HAAS-FERRARI
8	Romain Grosjean	VF-17/02
50	Antonio Giovinazzi	VF-17/02
20	Kevin Magnussen	VF-17/03

RENAULT
27	Nico Hülkenberg	R.S.17/04
55	Carlos Sainz	R.S.17/03

SAUBER-FERRARI
9	Marcus Ericsson	C36/03
37	Charles Leclerc	C36/03
94	Pascal Wehrlein	C36/04

ROUND 19 BRAZILIAN GP

MERCEDES
44	Lewis Hamilton	F1 W08 EQ Power+/05
77	Valtteri Bottas	F1 W08 EQ Power+/03

RED BULL-TAG HEUER
3	Daniel Ricciardo	RB13/05
33	Max Verstappen	RB13/06

FERRARI
5	Sebastian Vettel	SF70H/
7	Kimi Räikkönen	SF70H/

FORCE INDIA-MERCEDES
11	Sergio Pérez	VJM10/02
35	George Russell	VJM10/02
31	Esteban Ocon	VJM10/04

WILLIAMS-MERCEDES
18	Lance Stroll	FW40/03
19	Felipe Massa	FW40/04

McLAREN-HONDA
2	Stoffel Vandoorne	MCL32/04
14	Fernando Alonso	MCL32/05

TORO ROSSO-RENAULT
10	Pierre Gasly	STR12/01
28	Brendon Hartley	STR12/04

HAAS-FERRARI
8	Romain Grosjean	VF-17/02
50	Antonio Giovinazzi	VF-17/02
20	Kevin Magnussen	VF-17/03

RENAULT
27	Nico Hülkenberg	R.S.17/04
55	Carlos Sainz	R.S.17/01

SAUBER-FERRARI
9	Marcus Ericsson	C36/03
94	Pascal Wehrlein	C36/04
37	Charles Leclerc	C36/04

ROUND 20 ABU DHABI GP

MERCEDES
44	Lewis Hamilton	F1 W08 EQ Power+/05
77	Valtteri Bottas	F1 W08 EQ Power+/03

RED BULL-TAG HEUER
3	Daniel Ricciardo	RB13/05
33	Max Verstappen	RB13/06

FERRARI
5	Sebastian Vettel	SF70H/
7	Kimi Räikkönen	SF70H/

FORCE INDIA-MERCEDES
11	Sergio Pérez	VJM10/02
31	Esteban Ocon	VJM10/04
35	George Russell	VJM10/04

WILLIAMS-MERCEDES
18	Lance Stroll	FW40/03
19	Felipe Massa	FW40/04

McLAREN-HONDA
2	Stoffel Vandoorne	MCL32/04
14	Fernando Alonso	MCL32/05

TORO ROSSO-RENAULT
10	Pierre Gasly	STR12/01
28	Brendon Hartley	STR12/04

HAAS-FERRARI
8	Romain Grosjean	VF-17/02
20	Kevin Magnussen	VF-17/03
50	Antonio Giovinazzi	VF-17/03

RENAULT
27	Nico Hülkenberg	R.S.17/04
55	Carlos Sainz	R.S.17/01

SAUBER-FERRARI
9	Marcus Ericsson	C36/03
94	Pascal Wehrlein	C36/04

FIA FORMULA 1 WORLD CHAMPIONSHIP

GRANDS PRIX 2017

By TONY DODGINS and MAURICE HAMILTON

AUSTRALIAN GRAND PRIX

MELBOURNE CIRCUIT

MELBOURNE QUALIFYING

THE pre-season testing pace of Ferrari had prompted Lewis Hamilton to declare the Maranello outfit favourite to win in Melbourne, but many read that as Lewis just playing down fears of yet more domination by the Silver Arrows.

Another development that prompted some doubts was the FIA's decision to interpret suspension regulations more strictly in 2017, basically meaning that suspension needed to be just that, not a clever way to garner aerodynamic gain. The hydraulically-operated heave springs used by Mercedes and Red Bull were no more after a technical question raised by Ferrari.

Without them, both teams, the heavy bookies' pre-season favourites, were expecting a trickier task to balance their cars, but it did look very much like business as usual for Mercedes after Lewis Hamilton took an Ayrton Senna-equalling sixth Australian GP pole with a 0.27s margin over Sebastian Vettel's Ferrari. The Scuderia was obviously a lot closer, with Vettel feeling he'd attacked a little too hard on his final Q3 run and cost himself time, but not enough to have pipped Hamilton to pole.

Valtteri Bottas, who had received an early Christmas present when Nico Rosberg announced his retirement and been drafted in as his Mercedes replacement, failed to make it an all-silver front row by just a couple of hundredths, but he comfortably outpaced the second Ferrari of Kimi Räikkönen, the elder Finn having driven a couple of error-strewn laps, unhappy with his car's balance and more than half a second adrift of his team-mate.

"Third is not ideal," Bottas said, "and I'm not happy." But maybe he was being too hard on himself: Hamilton always excels around Albert Park, and Valtteri's 0.3s deficit to Lewis actually compared favourably with the delta between Hamilton and Rosberg over the two previous seasons (0.60s in 2015 and 0.36s in 2016).

In contrast to the Mercedes and Ferrari, Red Bull's RB13 looked a bit of a handful and was more than a second from the ultimate pace. Daniel Ricciardo's car snapped away from him at the fast Turn 12 and went into the barrier before he had a Q3 time on the board. A five-place grid penalty on top for the resultant gearbox damage meant that the Australian home hero would be starting 15th.

The additional downforce of the 2017-spec cars and their wider tyres did mean higher speeds and more grip in the quick corners, but when the cars did let go, they seemed to do so suddenly rather than progressively. Theories ranged from the harder tyre compounds Pirelli had employed while accommodating the loadings of F1 cars with strong aero performance at the same time as 1000bhp and significant weight, to potential wind effect on the returning long shark-fin engine covers that many found so aesthetically displeasing.

Ricciardo's shunt also compromised team-mate Max Verstappen's lap, the young Dutchman having been on schedule to knock Räikkönen off the second row had he been able to finish his lap. Thus the 19-year-old had to content himself with fifth. Sharing the third row with him was Romain Grosjean, who had driven a superlative lap in the first of the Haas cars.

Rosberg's retirement and Bottas's move had added up to a Williams reprieve for the 'retired' Felipe Massa, who qualified the FW40 seventh, just ahead of an impressive display from Toro Rosso, which put both cars through to Q3, Carlos Sainz qualifying eighth and Daniil Kvyat ninth.

At Force India, Sergio Pérez reported that the rear aerodynamics were not quite to the team's liking, but they had identified the problem and it would be addressed by the car's first significant upgrade. A more pressing difficulty in Q3 was an upshift hesitation that kept him out of Q3 and meant 11th on the grid, just a gnat's whisker ahead of erstwhile team-mate Nico Hülkenberg, now leading the Renault team. Jolyon Palmer had something of a nightmare with the second French machine, crashing heavily out of the final turn in Friday practice. His rebuilt car was plagued by both fuel system and braking troubles, the Briton propping up the entire grid sheet.

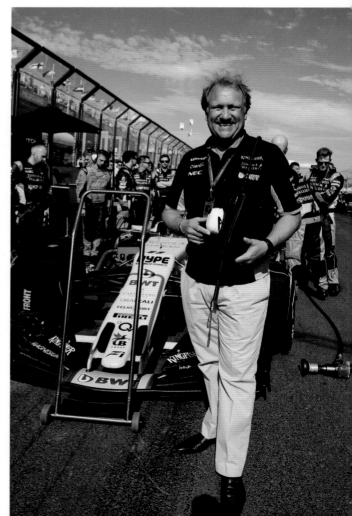

The poor form of McLaren Honda throughout winter testing was underlined at the season's opening race, although Fernando Alonso actually did better than anticipated to qualify 13th, half a second down on Hülkenberg's pace, but marginally quicker than Esteban Ocon. The young Frenchman was starting his first race as a Force India driver from 14th.

Marcus Ericsson did a solid job to get his Sauber through to Q2. In the second car, however, Pascal Wehrlein pulled out after Friday practice, not confident that his back, injured in a Race of Champions winter accident, would allow him to perform properly. Ferrari junior driver and 2016 GP2 runner-up Antonio Giovinazzi was drafted in as replacement and did a sterling job, actually looking like bouncing Ericsson out of Q2 until he ran wide on to the grass at Turn 14 on his second Q1 run. He would make his GP debut 16th.

Kevin Magnussen had a tough Haas debut, the Dane another to fall victim to Turn 12 as he tried to take it flat, like team-mate Grosjean had done to such good effect. Thus Magnussen was mired in Q1, along with Stoffel Vandoorne, whose McLaren did not have the aero upgrades fitted to Alonso's car, which were reckoned to be worth around three-tenths. The Belgian, though, trailed Alonso by the best part of a second.

Eighteen-year-old Lance Stroll, son of billionaire businessman Lawrence, was having his F1 baptism at Williams and did himself no favours when he clobbered the Turn Ten wall in final free practice on Saturday morning, to the detriment of the right-side suspension at both ends, plus the gearbox. The crew did well to get him out in qualifying, but he was half a second shy of his earlier practice best and two seconds from Massa, 19th.

THERE were groans of disbelief from the crowd as Ricciardo ground to a halt with an electrical sensor failure as he made his way to the grid. The Red Bull was towed back to the pits and a replacement fitted, but Daniel would only get to join in when the rest of the field had done two laps, ultimately retiring with a metering unit problem before half-distance.

The initial start was aborted due to a small brake fire on Kvyat's car, the race distance being reduced to 57 laps. With new clutch rules in 2017 even more manually-orientated and placing greater emphasis on driver feel, Hamilton converted his pole and led into Turn One, with the top four going through in grid order: Hamilton, Vettel, Bottas, Räikkönen.

Further back, Magnussen got out of shape over a kerb and collected Ericsson's Sauber, putting the pair into the gravel. They both extricated themselves, but ultimately retired due to the contact. Massa had passed Grosjean off the line to run sixth, behind Verstappen, and Pérez pulled off a fine move down the inside of Turn Five to displace Sainz. Stroll made a decent start, but then flat-spotted his tyres badly and needed to pit as early as the fourth lap. Ultimately he would retire with a hydraulics problem.

Part of Pirelli's 2017 brief was to provide a supply of control tyres capable of being raced harder without irreversible thermal degradation, and Hamilton set a relatively strong pace from the start. Friday afternoon's long runs on the ultrasoft tyre indicated that Mercedes was well placed versus Ferrari, but in the hotter conditions of Sunday's race – the ambient still around 37°C by the late 4pm start time – that didn't prove to be the case. When Hamilton was instructed to push to open a gap to protect against the undercut as the first (and likely only) stops approached, he found he was unable to shake Vettel's Ferrari as the pair opened up a small gap to the struggling Bottas, who had a margin to Räikkönen, the elder Finn having had an even poorer opening stint.

"After ten or twelve laps, Lewis was really pushing, trying to open a gap, and he succeeded a bit," Vettel explained. "I was struggling to keep up, but still hanging in there. I knew that if anything was to happen around the first stop, I needed to be right behind him to either put him under pressure or have a chance to jump into the pits earlier and pass him through the stop."

It was this fear of an undercut that pushed Mercedes towards an early stop, on lap 17, which brought Hamilton out behind Max Verstappen's Red Bull and cost him crucial time. Team principal Toto Wolff denied that it was a strategic error, despite some angry table-thumping as Hamilton remained trapped.

"That was just my emotions," Wolff smiled. "Maybe I need to talk to a professional about it! The Ferrari was the quicker car, seen by the way that Sebastian was able to hold on to Lewis's gearbox. We were pushing flat out and felt that the tyres wouldn't last any more, so that led us to the decision to pit to avoid the undercut. Coming out behind Max lost us the race."

Hamilton added, "I had to pit a lot earlier because I just ran out of grip. After I pitted, I got stuck, and sometimes that's just the way it goes." On the lap before Lewis stopped, the lead over Verstappen had been 18.5s with around 22s needed for a stop, so the team knew that Hamilton would pit out behind him, but were more concerned about vulnerability to an imminent Vettel undercut.

"You are trying to take on board all the information you have, in terms of tyre temperatures, grip levels, the sliding and how the driver perceives it," Wolff explained. "All that leads to a decision, and in this case the stop was probably a couple of laps too early.

"These tyres have a very narrow operating window, and you need to keep them in that window in order for them to perform well. If you are below or above the window, you

Above: Sebastian Vettel leads, while Max Verstappen blunts Lewis Hamilton's challenge.
Photo: WRi2/Jean-François Galeron

Top left: Massive disappointment for Daniel Ricciardo, who is forced to abandon his Red Bull before the start.
Photo: M-Pix/John Morris

Above left: Maurizio Arrivabene looks suitably pleased with Ferrari's start to the season.
Photo: Peter J. Fox

Left: Pretty in pink? Force India's Bob Fernley chose to colour co-ordinate his outfit with BWT, the team's new title sponsor.
Photo: Sahara Force India F1 Team

Opening spread: Sebastian Vettel and Ferrari opened the season with a win, forcing the Mercedes duo of Lewis Hamilton and Valtteri Bottas to accept a supporting role.
Photo: Peter J. Fox

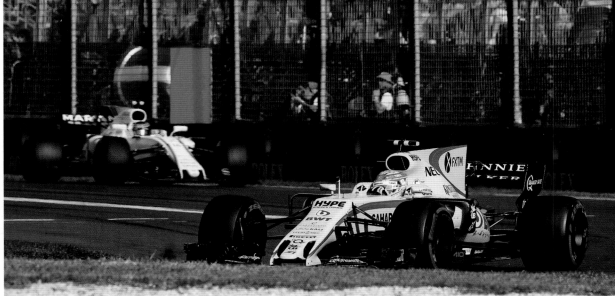

Above: Felipe Massa, back in the Williams after his brief retirement, claimed sixth place as the last un-lapped runner.
Photo: Williams Martini Racing

Left: Pastures new for Nico Hülkenberg at Renault.

Below left: Toro Rosso's Daniil Kvyat opened his season with a couple of points for ninth.

Far left: Christian Horner, Zak Brown and Toto Wolff enjoy an amiable chat before the season begins in earnest.
Photos: Peter J. Fox

Top right: Esteban Ocon opened his account for Force India, scoring the final point for tenth.
Photo: Sahara Force India F1 Team

Above right: Antonio Giovinazzi impressed as a late stand-in for the indisposed Pascal Wehrlein at Sauber.
Photo: Peter J. Fox

lose performance. That's different from last year [2016] and needs a new calibration from all of us, and an understanding of the tyres."

This was emphasised later in the race, on Pirelli's yellow-walled soft compound, the hardest tyre on offer in Melbourne. Even on that, Hamilton radioed that tyre performance was "dropping in and out." This being the first race experience of the 2017 Pirelli compounds, not knowing exactly how recoverable the tyre was in that opening stint on the purple-walled ultrasoft, persuaded Hamilton that stopping was the better option than risking a Vettel undercut or, indeed, having the Ferrari pass him on the circuit if the tyre performance did suddenly drop away.

Once freed by Hamilton's stop, there was actually no discernible increase in pace by the Ferrari. On lap 16, his last behind Hamilton, Vettel recorded a lap of 1m 22.221s, identical down to the last thousandth of a second to lap 12, when he had been giving everything to hang on as Lewis attempted to open a gap. On lap 19, Vettel found another tenth, but that was all, and the last couple of laps before his own lap-23 stop dropped off by three-tenths. By that stage, however, the Ferrari had the required 22s advantage (23.2s actually) to facilitate an overcut, with Vettel diving in as soon as the margin was there and pitting out just ahead of Verstappen/Hamilton.

Hamilton's loss of track position, therefore, was caused by the time loss behind Verstappen, rather than any significant increase in Ferrari pace in free air. At first, in fact, Hamilton had set a new fastest lap of the race (1m 27.551s) on his 'golden lap' on his fresh set of soft-compound Pirellis, which compared with Vettel's 1m 28.118s on used ultrasofts. This

lap, however, pulled him right on to the back of Verstappen's Red Bull.

It was at this point that the Mercedes pit-wall team advised Hamilton that he still had a positive delta to Vettel (meaning that Sebastian didn't have enough time to get in and out of the pits ahead), but that it was critical he pass Verstappen, who was lapping about 0.8s slower than Vettel.

Being told that you have to pass Max Verstappen is not the most welcome instruction to receive. Not a simple task in any event, the degree of difficulty was compounded in 2017 by the new aerodynamic regulations, which included a larger diffuser and created more 'dirty' air behind cars, making it more difficult to follow closely and more difficult still to overtake – already hard enough at Albert Park.

"There's no way I can get past this guy!" was the bad news radioed by Hamilton, who was trapped for six laps until Verstappen headed for his lone pit stop on lap 25, the same time that Bottas, who had taken over the race lead for three laps, also stopped. By this stage, Hamilton had fallen 6s behind Vettel's fleeing Ferrari.

"I was struggling with grip from the get-go," Hamilton admitted. "Sebastian was always able to answer in terms of lap time. Then I got a bit of traffic and the car started to overheat the tyres. I was struggling with grip to the point that I needed to come in. I was sliding around. It was my call because otherwise Sebastian probably would have come by anyway." So, widespread speculation that Hamilton had lost the race due to a poor strategy call was wide of the mark, based on information that the team had had when they made the call and backed up by Hamilton himself.

In the early stages on the ultrasoft, neither Bottas nor

Above: Valtteri Bottas took a podium on his debut for Mercedes.
Photo: Mercedes AMG Petronas F1 Team

Above right: A first win for Vettel and Ferrari since the Singapore Grand Prix in 2015.
Photo: Lukas Gorys

Right: Ferrari showed that they were back in contention, bringing hope to F1 fans everywhere that they might be able to challenge Mercedes for the championship.
Photo: Peter J. Fox

Räikkönen was able to run at the pace of their respective team-mates. Bottas, though, certainly had a race of two halves, coming on strongly once he switched to the soft-compound Pirellis.

"My main issue was the first stint," Valtteri explained. "I was always sliding around on the ultrasoft – missing front and rear grip – especially after ten laps. That wasn't easy. But once we put on the softs, I had a great feeling with the car. It's a shame it was a bit too late."

After his sole pit stop on lap 25 of the 57, Bottas rejoined 8s behind his team-mate and 14s behind the race-leading Ferrari. Twenty laps later, he was 2s behind Hamilton and 11s behind the race leader.

Having lost out to Vettel, Mercedes told Hamilton, "Okay, Lewis, we're thinking of Plan B," which was conversion to a two-stop race. But ten laps later, a further communication informed him that such a strategy was not feasible: firstly, Vettel's tyres were not dropping off; and, secondly, an additional stop would have dropped Lewis behind Räikkönen's Ferrari, requiring him to pass on track.

In fact, as Wolff explained, Pirelli's new tyres and compounds involved a steep learning curve for everyone. Hamilton's lap-44 radio communication illustrated just that. As Bottas gained on him, he complained, "The tyres are dropping in and out [of the performance window]," just as he lapped at 1m 27.033s, his quickest lap of the race, some 27 laps into his stint on the soft-compound tyre...

With nine laps remaining, Hamilton had trimmed Vettel's lead, but then dropped his pace. "I stopped significantly earlier than Sebastian and Valtteri, so I just didn't know how long the tyres were going to go," he explained. "I just took it easy, and at the end I'd got more pace, but even if I did close the gap, you can't overtake, so..."

Bottas's later stop looked to be the quicker strategy over the race distance, but the team informed him that Hamilton was backing off – coded message: "Hold station." – and the pair crossed the line 9.9s and 11.2s behind Vettel's winning Ferrari respectively.

Fourth, as in qualifying, was Räikkönen, the second Ferrari having come under pressure from Verstappen's Red Bull during the closing stages as the team put the young Dutchman on to Pirelli's supersoft as opposed to the soft for his second stint.

Massa finished a lonely sixth for Williams, comfortably clear of a tight battle between Pérez and the Toro Rosso twins, who ran different strategies. Sainz made an early stop for softs, while Kvyat ran his ultrasofts to lap 35 before bolting on supersofts. Daniil came out just behind his team-mate on much grippier tyres, and Sainz was instructed to let him by so that he could chase down Pérez's Force India. Just as Kvyat got within DRS range of the Mexican, though, he needed an extra pit visit to re-pressurise the hydraulics and dropped back behind his team-mate once again.

There was a spirited battle for the final point, with Ocon taking it to break his F1 point-scoring duck. Alonso had had it for McLaren until some great action when Esteban attempted a DRS pass of the McLaren at the same time as Hülkenberg tried the same thing on the Force India. It was Ocon who emerged from Turn One ahead. Alonso, bumped out of the points, retired the McLaren Honda a lap later. A suspension issue was blamed, the Spaniard reporting that the car was pulling to the left, but some less charitable souls suggested that the Honda was about to run short of fuel.

As the packing crates were filled on Sunday night, we were left to reflect that for the first time in F1's hybrid era – notwithstanding the anomalous race at Singapore in 2015 – the works Mercedes team did not set the pace. Events had been dictated by the nuances of tyre performance. Mercedes had been in the window with the ultrasoft on Friday afternoon, out of it on Saturday morning, back in it for qualifying and out of it again on Sunday.

"I've always said we couldn't expect it to continue for ever," Toto Wolff admitted. "In the conditions today, we underperformed. The difference was, it was much hotter on race day and clearly we weren't as good as in the long runs on Friday. But rest assured, we will come back stronger."

An ecstatic Vettel, meanwhile, praised the effort that had brought Ferrari right back on the pace, a tremendous fillip for F1 in general as everyone began to contemplate a mouthwatering battle between two top teams and drivers, something the sport had been missing for too long.

Tony Dodgins

VIEWPOINT
A SMILEY START

WAS it surprise? Was it relief? Was it simply the joy of winning again for the first time since Singapore in 2015? What did prompt the return of Sebastian Vettel's long-lost grin on the podium? Probably a mix of all three emotions.

He – we – had been there before: Ferrari consistently quick during winter testing, only for that pace to flicker and fail when the serious business of scoring championship points got under way. There was the added uncertainty created by 2016: regarded at best as being even more disappointing than the previous few seasons; considered at worst by many in Italy as a complete disaster for what amounts to the national F1 team.

Had Ferrari got it right this time? Had the rebuilding within the team worked? Had they got over the departure of James Allison? Was the SF70H any good? Fifty-seven consecutive laps of Albert Park on 26th March would ask the most important question so far.

The answer was undoubtedly positive. What a relief! Ferrari had the pace through all conditions of the grand prix to match the best Mercedes could throw at them.

Early in the race, Lewis Hamilton had asked the question as he upped his pace – and Vettel had answered it by not giving Mercedes the strategic breathing space they had become accustomed to. We had a race on our hands. And, whisper it, possibly a season-long fight for the championship as these two teams went head to head.

That was a surprise, but only insofar as Red Bull were not joining them. Seen as the most likely challenge to Mercedes's established superiority in this era of increased dependence on downforce, Red Bull had not stepped up to the plate in Melbourne. But Ferrari had. All was well with this new world, the 2017 cars looking better than had been hoped; a suitable development to welcome on board F1's new management.

Albert Park, always a good place to start any season, was even sunnier than usual, beginning with that wide smile at the top of the podium.

Maurice Hamilton

1

2017 FORMULA 1
ROLEX
AUSTRALIAN
GRAND PRIX
MELBOURNE 24–26 MARCH

OFFICIAL TIMEPIECE

RACE DISTANCE: 57 laps, 187.822 miles/302.271km

RACE WEATHER: Dry/sunny (track 30–37°C, air 23–25°C)

ALBERT PARK, MELBOURNE
Circuit: 3.295 miles / 5.303km
58 laps
100/62 kmh/mph
☼ Gear
— DRS zone

Turn 13 150/93
Turn 12 265/165
Turn 15 90/562
Turn 14 215/134
Turn 11 260/162
Turn 9 130/81
Turn 8 285/177
Turn 16 190/118
Turn 10 155/96
300/186
310/193
Turn 7 186/116
Turn 2 210/130
Turn 6 155/963
330/205
Turn 1 175/109
Turn 4 175/109
Turn 5 239/149
Turn 3 105/65

RACE – OFFICIAL CLASSIFICATION

Pos.	Driver	Nat.	No.	Entrant	Car/Engine	Laps	Time/Retirement	Speed (mph/km/h)	Gap to leader	Fastest race lap	
1	**Sebastian Vettel**	D	5	Scuderia Ferrari	Ferrari SF70H-062 V6	57	1h 24m 11.672s	133.848/215.408		1m 26.638s	53
2	**Lewis Hamilton**	GB	44	Mercedes AMG Petronas Motorsport	Mercedes F1 W08-Mercedes M08 EQ Power+ V6	57	1h 24m 21.647s	133.585/214.984	9.975s	1m 27.033s	44
3	**Valtteri Bottas**	FIN	77	Mercedes AMG Petronas Motorsport	Mercedes F1 W08-Mercedes M08 EQ Power+ V6	57	1h 24m 22.922s	133.551/214.930	11.250s	1m 26.593s	56
4	**Kimi Räikkönen**	FIN	7	Scuderia Ferrari	Ferrari SF70H-062 V6	57	1h 24m 34.065s	133.258/214.458	22.393s	1m 26.538s	56
5	**Max Verstappen**	NL	33	Red Bull Racing	Red Bull RB13-TAG Heuer RB13 V6	57	1h 24m 40.499s	133.089/214.186	28.827s	1m 26.964s	43
6	**Felipe Massa**	BR	19	Williams Martini Racing	Williams FW40-Mercedes M08 EQ Power+ V6	57	1h 25m 35.058s	131.675/211.911	1m 23.386s	1m 28.045s	49
7	**Sergio Pérez**	MEX	11	Sahara Force India Formula 1 Team	Force India VJM10-Mercedes M08 EQ Power+ V6	56			1 lap	1m 28.336s	56
8	**Carlos Sainz**	E	55	Scuderia Toro Rosso	Toro Rosso STR12-Renault R.E.17 V6	56			1 lap	1m 27.677s	53
9	**Daniil Kvyat**	RUS	26	Scuderia Toro Rosso	Toro Rosso STR12-Renault R.E.17 V6	56			1 lap	1m 26.711s	51
10	**Esteban Ocon**	F	31	Sahara Force India Formula 1 Team	Force India VJM10-Mercedes M08 EQ Power+ V6	56			1 lap	1m 28.475s	55
11	Nico Hülkenberg	D	27	Renault Sport Formula One Team	Renault R.S.17-R.E.17 V6	56			1 lap	1m 28.486s	55
12	Antonio Giovinazzi	I	36	Sauber F1 Team	Sauber C36-Ferrari 059/5 V6	55			2 laps	1m 29.052s	51
13	Stoffel Vandoorne	B	2	McLaren Honda Formula 1 Team	McLaren MCL32-Honda RA617H V6	55			2 laps	1m 29.440s	53
	Fernando Alonso	E	14	McLaren Honda Formula 1 Team	McLaren MCL32-Honda RA617H V6	50	floor			1m 30.077s	48
	Kevin Magnussen	DK	20	Haas F1 Team	Haas VF-17-Ferrari 062 V6	46	punctured tyre			1m 27.568s	46
	Lance Stroll	CDN	18	Williams Martini Racing	Williams FW40-Mercedes M08 EQ Power+ V6	40	brakes			1m 29.389s	38
	Daniel Ricciardo	AUS	3	Red Bull Racing	Red Bull RB13-TAG Heuer RB13 V6	25	power unit			1m 29.447s	21
	Marcus Ericsson	S	9	Sauber F1 Team	Sauber C36-Ferrari 059/5 V6	21	accident			1m 32.052s	18
	Jolyon Palmer	GB	30	Renault Sport Formula One Team	Renault R.S.17-R.E.17 V6	15	brakes			1m 32.195s	6
	Romain Grosjean	F	8	Haas F1 Team	Haas VF-17-Ferrari 062 V6	13	water leak			1m 30.183s	12
EW	Pascal Wehrlein	D	94	Sauber F1 Team	Sauber C36-Ferrari 059/5 V6		driver unfit, withdrew after FP2				

Race scheduled for 58 laps, but reduced by one lap due to an aborted start, Pérez having pulled into the incorrect grid slot.

Fastest race lap: Kimi Räikkönen on lap 56, 1m 26.538s, 137.078mph/220.605km/h.

Lap record: Michael Schumacher (Ferrari F2004 V10), 1m 24.125s, 141.010mph/226.933km/h (2004).

19 · PALMER · Renault   17 · MAGNUSSEN · Haas   15 · RICCIARDO · Red Bull
5-place grid penalty for replacing gearbox; started from pit lane   13 · OCON · Force India   11 · HÜLKENBERG · Renault

20 · STROLL · Williams
5-place grid penalty for replacing gearbox   18 · VANDOORNE · McLAREN   16 · GIOVINAZZI · Sauber   14 · ERICSSON · Sauber   12 · ALONSO · McLaren

Grid order	1	2	3	4	5	6	7	8	9	10	11	12	13	14	15	16	17	18	19	20	21	22	23	24	25	26	27	28	29	30	31	32	33	34	35	36	37	38	39	40	41	42	43	44	45	46
44 HAMILTON	44	44	44	44	44	44	44	44	44	44	44	44	44	44	44	44	5	5	5	5	5	5	5	77	77		5	5	5	5	5	5	5	5	5	5	5	5	5	5	5	5	5	5	5	5
5 VETTEL	5	5	5	.	5	5	5	5	5	5	5	5	5	5	5	5	77	77	77	77	77	77	77	5	5	77	44	44	44	44	44	44	44	44	44	44	44	44	44	44	44	44	44	44	44	44
77 BOTTAS	77	77	77	77	77	77	77	77	77	77	77	77	77	77	77	77	7	7	7	7	7	7	7	7	5	44	77	77	77	77	77	77	77	77	77	77	77	77	77	77	77	77	77	77	77	77
7 RÄIKKÖNEN	7	7	7	7	7	7	7	7	7	7	7	7	7	7	7	7	44	33	33	33	33	33	33	33	77	7	7	7	7	7	7	7	7	7	7	7	7	7	7	7	7	7	7	7	7	7
33 VERSTAPPEN	33	33	33	33	33	33	33	33	33	33	33	33	33	33	33	33	33	44	44	44	44	44	44	44	33	33	33	33	33	33	33	33	33	33	33	33	33	33	33	33	33	33	33	33	33	33
8 GROSJEAN	19	19	19	19	19	19	19	19	19	19	19	19	19	19	19	19	26	26	26	26	26	26	26	26	26	26	26	26	26	26	26	26	19	19	19	19	19	19	19	19	19	19	19	19	19	19
19 MASSA	8	8	8	8	8	8	8	8	8	8	8	8	8	8	8	55	55	55	26	26	19	19	19	19	19	19	19	19	19	19	11	11	11	11	11	11	11	11	11	11	11	11	11	11	11	11
55 SAINZ	55	55	55	55	55	55	55	55	55	55	55	55	55	55	11	11	11	11	26	55	11	11	11	11	11	11	11	11	11	11	55	55	55	55	55	55	55	55	55	26	26	26	26	26	26	26
26 KVYAT	11	11	11	11	11	11	11	11	11	11	11	11	11	11	26	26	26	11	11	11	55	55	55	55	55	55	55	55	55	55	26	26	26	26	26	26	26	55	55	55	55	55	55	55	55	55
11 PÉREZ	26	26	26	26	26	26	26	26	26	26	26	26	26	26	14	14	14	14	14	14	14	14	14	14	14	14	14	14	14	14	14	14	14	14	14	14	14	14	14	14	14	14	14	14	14	14
27 HÜLKENBERG	14	14	14	14	14	14	14	14	14	14	14	14	14	27	27	27	31	31	31	31	31	31	31	31	31	31	31	31	31	31	31	31	31	31	31	31	31	31	31	31	31	31	31	31	31	31
14 ALONSO	27	27	27	27	27	27	27	27	27	27	27	27	27	31	31	31	27	27	27	27	27	27	27	27	27	27	27	27	27	27	27	27	27	27	27	27	27	27	27	27	27	27	27	27	27	27
31 OCON	31	31	31	31	31	31	31	31	31	31	31	31	31	18	18	18	18	18	18	18	18	18	18	18	18	18	18	18	18	18	18	18	18	18	18	18	36	36	36	36	36	2	2	2	2	2
9 ERICSSON	18	18	18	18	30	30	30	30	30	30	18	18	18	9	9	9	9	9	9	9	9	9	36	36	36	36	36	36	36	36	36	36	36	36	36	36	18	18	36	36	36	36	2	2	2	2
3 RICCIARDO	30	30	30	30	2	2	2	2	36	36	18	18	9	36	36	36	36	36	36	36	2	2	2	2	2	2	2	2	2	2	2	2	2	2	2	2	20	20	20	20	20	20	20	20	20	20
36 GIOVINAZZI	2	2	2	2	36	36	36	36	18	18	9	9	9	30	30	2	2	2	2	20	20	20	20	20	20	20	20	20	20	20	20	20	20	20	20	20	20	20	20	20						
20 MAGNUSSEN	36	36	36	36	9	9	9	9	9	9	2	30	30	30	2	20	20	20	20	2	3	3	3	3																						
2 VANDOORNE	9	9	9	9	18	18	18	18	2	2	2	2	2	20	20	3	3	3	3	3																										
30 PALMER	20	20	20	20	20	20	20	20	20	20	20	20	20	3	3																															
18 STROLL	3	3	3	3	3	3	3	3	3	3	3	3	3																																	

TIME SHEETS

PRACTICE 1 (FRIDAY)
Weather: Dry/sunny
Temperatures: track 27–36°C, air 21–23°C

Pos.	Driver	Laps	Time
1	Lewis Hamilton	22	1m 24.220s
2	Valtteri Bottas	25	1m 24.803s
3	Daniel Ricciardo	19	1m 24.886s
4	Max Verstappen	19	1m 25.246s
5	Kimi Räikkönen	16	1m 25.372s
6	Sebastian Vettel	10	1m 25.464s
7	Felipe Massa	28	1m 26.142s
8	Romain Grosjean	20	1m 26.168s
9	Nico Hülkenberg	15	1m 26.183s
10	Sergio Pérez	29	1m 26.276s
11	Carlos Sainz	24	1m 26.450s
12	Daniil Kvyat	25	1m 26.514s
13	Lance Stroll	29	1m 26.734s
14	Fernando Alonso	18	1m 27.116s
15	Marcus Ericsson	30	1m 27.348s
16	Esteban Ocon	23	1m 27.656s
17	Kevin Magnussen	20	1m 27.667s
18	Pascal Wehrlein	22	1m 28.539s
19	Jolyon Palmer	6	1m 28.585s
20	Stoffel Vandoorne	14	1m 28.695s

PRACTICE 2 (FRIDAY)
Weather: Dry/overcast
Temperatures: track 28–32°C, air 22–23°C

Pos.	Driver	Laps	Time
1	Lewis Hamilton	34	1m 23.620s
2	Sebastian Vettel	35	1m 24.167s
3	Valtteri Bottas	34	1m 24.176s
4	Kimi Räikkönen	30	1m 24.525s
5	Daniel Ricciardo	27	1m 24.650s
6	Max Verstappen	8	1m 25.013s
7	Carlos Sainz	34	1m 25.084s
8	Romain Grosjean	29	1m 25.436s
9	Nico Hülkenberg	36	1m 25.478s
10	Daniil Kvyat	39	1m 25.493s
11	Sergio Pérez	35	1m 25.591s
12	Fernando Alonso	19	1m 26.000s
13	Esteban Ocon	37	1m 26.145s
14	Felipe Massa	6	1m 26.331s
15	Marcus Ericsson	29	1m 26.498s
16	Lance Stroll	27	1m 26.525s
17	Stoffel Vandoorne	33	1m 26.608s
18	Pascal Wehrlein	30	1m 26.919s
19	Kevin Magnussen	8	1m 27.279s
20	Jolyon Palmer	4	1m 27.549s

PRACTICE 3 (SATURDAY)
Weather: Dry/sunny
Temperatures: track 31°C, air 27°C

Pos.	Driver	Laps	Time
1	Sebastian Vettel	12	1m 23.380s
2	Valtteri Bottas	12	1m 23.859s
3	Lewis Hamilton	12	1m 23.870s
4	Kimi Räikkönen	10	1m 23.988s
5	Nico Hülkenberg	10	1m 25.063s
6	Daniel Ricciardo	15	1m 25.092s
7	Romain Grosjean	11	1m 25.581s
8	Carlos Sainz	11	1m 25.948s
9	Daniil Kvyat	11	1m 26.049s
10	Kevin Magnussen	11	1m 26.138s
11	Felipe Massa	15	1m 26.237s
12	Max Verstappen	7	1m 26.269s
13	Sergio Pérez	12	1m 26.457s
14	Fernando Alonso	7	1m 26.556s
15	Stoffel Vandoorne	9	1m 26.699s
16	Esteban Ocon	16	1m 27.103s
17	Lance Stroll	12	1m 27.327s
18	Marcus Ericsson	10	1m 27.402s
19	Jolyon Palmer	12	1m 28.320s
20	Antonio Giovinazzi	18	1m 28.583s

QUALIFYING (SATURDAY)
Weather: Dry/sunny-overcast   Temperatures: track 32–35°C, air 28–30°C

Pos.	Driver	First	Second	Third	Qualifying Tyre
1	Lewis Hamilton	1m 24.191s	1m 23.251s	1m 22.188s	Ultrasoft (new)
2	Sebastian Vettel	1m 25.210s	1m 23.401s	1m 22.456s	Ultrasoft (new)
3	Valtteri Bottas	1m 24.514s	1m 23.215s	1m 22.481s	Ultrasoft (new)
4	Kimi Räikkönen	1m 24.352s	1m 23.376s	1m 23.033s	Ultrasoft (new)
5	Max Verstappen	1m 24.482s	1m 24.092s	1m 23.485s	Ultrasoft (new)
6	Romain Grosjean	1m 25.419s	1m 24.718s	1m 24.074s	Ultrasoft (new)
7	Felipe Massa	1m 25.099s	1m 24.547s	1m 24.443s	Ultrasoft (new)
8	Carlos Sainz	1m 25.542s	1m 24.997s	1m 24.487s	Ultrasoft (new)
9	Daniil Kvyat	1m 25.970s	1m 24.864s	1m 24.512s	Ultrasoft (new)
10	Daniel Ricciardo	1m 25.383s	1m 23.989s	no time	Ultrasoft (new)
11	Sergio Pérez	1m 25.064s	1m 25.081s		
12	Nico Hülkenberg	1m 24.975s	1m 25.091s		
13	Fernando Alonso	1m 25.872s	1m 25.425s		
14	Esteban Ocon	1m 26.009s	1m 25.568s		
15	Marcus Ericsson	1m 26.236s	1m 26.465s		
16	Antonio Giovinazzi	1m 26.419s			
17	Kevin Magnussen	1m 26.847s			
18	Stoffel Vandoorne	1m 26.858s			
19	Lance Stroll	1m 27.143s			
20	Jolyon Palmer	1m 28.244s			

QUALIFYING: head to head

Hamilton	1	0	Bottas
Vettel	1	0	Räikkönen
Massa	1	0	Stroll
Ricciardo	0	1	Verstappen
Pérez	1	0	Ocon
Hülkenberg	1	0	Palmer
Kvyat	0	1	Sainz
Ericsson	1	0	Giovinazzi
Alonso	1	0	Vandoorne
Grosjean	1	0	Magnussen

FOR THE RECORD

1st GRAND PRIX: Antonio Giovinazzi, Lance Stroll
1st POINT: Esteban Ocon
10th PODIUM POSITION: Valtteri Bottas
100th RACE LED: Lewis Hamilton
3,000th LAP LED: Lewis Hamilton
15,000th LAP RACED: Fernando Alonso

POINTS

DRIVERS

1	Sebastian Vettel	25
2	Lewis Hamilton	18
3	Valtteri Bottas	15
4	Kimi Räikkönen	12
5	Max Verstappen	10
6	Felipe Massa	8
7	Sergio Pérez	6
8	Carlos Sainz	4
9	Daniil Kvyat	2
10	Esteban Ocon	1

CONSTRUCTORS

1	Ferrari	37
2	Mercedes	33
3	Red Bull	10
4	Williams	8
5	Force India	7
6	Toro Rosso	6

9 · KVYAT · Toro Rosso

7 · MASSA · Williams

5 · VERSTAPPEN · Red Bull

3 · BOTTAS · Mercedes

1 · HAMILTON · Mercedes

10 · PÉREZ · Force India

8 · SAINZ · Toro Rosso

6 · GROSJEAN · Haas

4 · RÄIKKÖNEN · Ferrari

2 · VETTEL · Ferrari

47	48	49	50	51	52	53	54	55	56	57	
5	5	5	5	5	5	5	5	5	5	5	1
44	44	44	44	44	44	44	44	44	44	44	2
77	77	77	77	77	77	77	77	77	77	77	3
7	7	7	7	7	7	7	7	7	7	7	4
33	33	33	33	33	33	33	33	33	33	33	5
19	19	19	19	19	19	19	19	19	19	19	6
11	11	11	11	11	11	11	11	11	11	11	7
26	26	55	55	55	55	55	55	55	55	55	8
55	55	26	26	26	26	26	26	26	26		9
14	14	14	14	31	31	31	31	31	31		10
31	31	31	31	27	27	27	27	27	27		
27	27	27	27	36	36	36	36	36			
36	36	36	36	2	2	2	2	2			
2	2	2	2								

20 = Pit stop   3 = One lap or more behind

RACE TYRE STRATEGIES

	Driver	Race Stint 1	Race Stint 2	Race Stint 3
1	Vettel	Ultrasoft (u): 1-23	Soft (n): 24-57	
2	Hamilton	Ultrasoft (u): 1-17	Soft (n): 18-57	
3	Bottas	Ultrasoft (u): 1-25	Soft (n): 26-57	
4	Räikkönen	Ultrasoft (u): 1-26	Soft (n): 27-57	
5	Verstappen	Ultrasoft (u): 1-25	Supersoft (n): 26-57	
6	Massa	Ultrasoft (u): 1-20	Supersoft (n): 21-57	
7	Pérez	Ultrasoft (n): 1-17	Soft (n): 18-57	
8	Sainz	Ultrasoft (u): 1-18	Soft (n): 19-57	
9	Kvyat	Ultrasoft (u): 1-34	Supersoft (n): 35-49	Ultrasoft (u): 50-57
10	Ocon	Ultrasoft (u): 1-15	Soft (n): 16-57	
11	Hülkenberg	Ultrasoft (u): 1-16	Soft (n): 17-30	Ultrasoft (u): 31-57
12	Giovinazzi	Soft (n): 1-15	Supersoft (n): 16-57	
13	Vandoorne	Ultrasoft (n): 1-9	Soft (n): 10-57	
	Alonso	Ultrasoft (n): 1-16	Supersoft (n): 17-50 (dnf)	
	Magnussen	Soft (n): 1	Supersoft (n): 2-44	Ultrasoft (u): 45-46 (dnf)
	Stroll	Supersoft (n): 1-5	Ultrasoft (u): 6-29	Ultrasoft (u): 30-40 (dnf)
	Ricciardo	Ultrasoft (u): 1-25 (dnf)		
	Ericsson	Supersoft (n): 1-21 (dnf)		
	Palmer	Soft (n): 1-15 (dnf)		
	Grosjean	Ultrasoft (u): 1-13 (dnf)		

The tyre regulations stipulate that at least two of three dry tyre specifications must be used during a dry race.

Pirelli P Zero logos are colour-coded on the tyre sidewalls: Purple = Ultrasoft; Yellow = Soft; Red = Supersoft. (n) new (u) used

Photos: Peter J. Fox

FIA FORMULA 1 WORLD CHAMPIONSHIP · ROUND 2

CHINESE GRAND PRIX

SHANGHAI CIRCUIT

SHANGHAI QUALIFYING

A FTER Melbourne had hinted at a Ferrari resurgence and a nip-and-tuck battle with Mercedes, Shanghai couldn't come fast enough. Unfortunately, the typical fog of the sprawling Chinese city permitted just a few laps on Friday morning before the session was red-flagged. The problem was the medical helicopter. There was enough visibility for it to fly at the track, but not enough at the hospital it would head for if called upon. Without any improvement, that was it for the day, and with more of the same forecast for Sunday, there was brief talk of running both qualifying and race on Saturday.

The Saturday programme eventually remained as scheduled and, at a circuit where he always excels, Lewis Hamilton took pole once again. He needed both Q3 runs to do so, however, and, if anything, the Ferrari looked the more composed chassis, even though Hamilton was able to get a quicker lap out of the Mercedes. He stopped the clock in 1m 31.678s, compared to Sebastian Vettel's 1m 31.864s. It provided nice symmetry for Mercedes with the team's 75th pole in 150 attempts.

With similar race pace evident between the top two teams, qualifying had taken on additional significance, as Lewis acknowledged: "Pole may be just an eight-metre advantage, but come the end of the season, it may amount to much more than that…"

For Valtteri Bottas, who recorded a time just 0.19s slower than Hamilton, there was the frustration of again being pipped to a front-row slot by Vettel's Ferrari. A couple of hundredths had separated them in Melbourne, but this time it was a miniscule thousandth of a second, or 6cm if you prefer.

"Lewis is definitely the quickest team-mate I've had," Valtteri admitted. "That was pretty much expected from a three-time world champion and multiple race winner. But what I'm seeing is that it's possible to match him. I know that I'm very close now and will improve. We are going to have some good fights in the future. At the moment, though, it's about getting good points and going step by step. I'm feeling better and better in the car."

Kimi Räikkönen was again slowest of the four drivers fortunate enough to have a Mercedes or Ferrari in their hands, with Red Bull once again best of the rest, this time through Daniel Ricciardo, but a whopping 1.36s adrift

of Hamilton's pace. As in Australia, the RB13 proved tricky to balance. If Ricciardo was a little frustrated, it was nothing compared to team-mate Max Verstappen, who suffered a software glitch that gave him a chronic misfire in Q1, meaning he would start from the penultimate grid slot.

Felipe Massa was a further half-second behind Ricciardo with the first of the Williams cars, teenage team-mate Lance Stroll doing well to get the second car into Q3, too, ultimately qualifying tenth, 0.72s behind Massa.

The mid-grid tussle had promised to be super-tight in 2017, and so it was proving. Nico Hülkenberg put the first Renault a fine seventh, just 0.08s behind Massa, the German with just over a tenth in hand over former Force India team-mate Sergio Pérez. The Mexican was just a hundredth quicker than Daniil Kvyat's Toro Rosso, making it four different chassis blanketed by only 0.21s.

Carlos Sainz, who regularly had got the better of Kvyat throughout 2016, was a couple of tenths adrift here, just the wrong side of the Q2 cut-off, ahead of Kevin Magnussen's Haas and Fernando Alonso's McLaren Honda. Alonso was still keen to put across the message about how hard he was driving, exclaiming on the radio, "That's all there is. I am driving like an animal!" Are you listening, Mercedes?

The Saubers of Marcus Ericsson and Antonio Giovinazzi were next, but the Ferrari test driver crashed heavily out of the last corner, which actually did his team-mate a favour, as out came the waved yellows just as Romain Grosjean, Jolyon Palmer, Esteban Ocon and Stoffel Vandoorne were on hot laps attempting to bump Ericsson. Considering the pace shown by their respective team-mates, you would certainly have placed money on Grosjean, Palmer and Ocon doing just that.

Poor Vandoorne didn't get much of a crack at Shanghai. Never having seen the track before, he was hurt as badly as anyone by the cancellation of Friday practice, and then found himself late out after an operational glitch in the McLaren pits. His Q1 time was 0.47s adrift of Alonso.

Penalties for Grosjean and Palmer for failing to slow sufficiently for the waved yellows for Giovinazzi added insult to injury, and spelled back-row starts for both.

Above: A thoughtful Carlos Sainz. The young Spaniard took a fine seventh place for Toro Rosso.

Above left: Love and kisses for Fernando from his legion of supporters.

Top left: Guenther Steiner ponders the changeable weather conditions.
Photos: Peter J. Fox

Above far left: Lewis Hamilton takes the crowd's applause after his masterful display in qualifying.
Photo: Mercedes Benz AMG Petronas F1 Team

Left: Lance Stroll did well to make Q3 in his Williams.
Photo: Williams Martini Racing

Opening spread: Lewis Hamilton takes command at the start, while Sebastian Vettel holds off Valtteri Bottas.
Photo: Mercedes Benz AMG Petronas F1 Team

FORECASTED weather for race day was unpredictable and, sure enough, a damp track confronted drivers as start time approached, meaning difficult decisions for team strategists. The headline news may have been that Hamilton converted his pole and led all the way, but winning is never straightforward in such conditions.

The first conundrum facing the teams was whether to start on Pirelli's intermediate tyre or to take a gamble on slicks. Mercedes was one of the few to explore slick-shod laps on the way to the grid, during which outing Hamilton spun at Turn 14. The conclusion was that due to the wet state of the track through Turns 14–16, slicks represented an unacceptable risk.

Carlos Sainz, starting 11th, was the only driver to take the gamble. He paid the price when lack of traction off the grid relegated him to the back before he suffered a spin.

A first-lap incident, in which Lance Stroll and Sergio Pérez made contact, gave rise to a virtual safety car and another tricky decision for team strategists: whether or not to come in at that early point for slicks and risk having insufficient grip. Among the first six, Ferrari alone opted for that strategy with Vettel, who was tracking Lewis in a first-lap race order of Hamilton, Vettel, Bottas, Ricciardo, Räikkönen and the fast-starting Kvyat.

"I think the decision was right on the margin," Hamilton confirmed. "But my intermediates were fine and there was no need to risk coming in. It's often when you want to gain something that you take that risk. I could still maintain a decent pace with the tyres that I had."

Predictably perhaps, in view of Brazil 2016, the slippery conditions were just what Verstappen needed, starting from the back, and he appeared to find grip where nobody else could. He made up a couple of positions off the grid, went down the inside of another in Turn Two and around the outside of yet another in Turn Three. By the end of lap, he'd passed an amazing nine cars to run seventh!

Mercedes concluded that with sufficient evidence of drivers struggling to stay on the track, Verstappen excluded, more incidents were likely. The trade-off to consider was an approximate 8s gain for a stop under the VSC versus the risk of going off the road on slicks or losing more time than such a gain while trying to generate tyre temperature.

Ferrari, having lost the start to Hamilton, elected to go for it with Vettel, and the tactic may well have worked for the four-times champion, but on lap four Antonio Giovinazzi – Ferrari's test driver ironically – lost his Sauber out of the final turn for the second time of the weekend and brought out the safety car proper. After making such an impressive debut in Melbourne after the 11th-hour call-up to replace the injured Wehrlein, the GP2 runner-up had rapidly gone from hero to zero.

The outcome was that Ferrari and Vettel never got to see the upside of their gamble, as the rest of the field piled into the pits under the full safety car and gained even more time, trapping the Australian GP winner behind Hamilton, both Red Bulls, team-mate Räikkönen and Bottas. The cost to Vettel could be gauged by Bottas having a problematic stop that lost him positions to both Red Bulls and Räikkönen, yet he still remained ahead of the No. 5 Ferrari.

"There was a problem with the rear jack and the car

Left: The race started on wets. Sebastian Vettel takes a wide line ahead of the Mercedes of Valtteri Bottas. Kimi Räikkönen and Daniel Ricciardo give chase.
Photo: Mercedes AMG Petronas F1 Team

Below: Wet or dry? The damp conditions inevitably brought out the best in Lewis Hamilton.
Photo: Peter J. Fox

Bottom: Max Verstappen delivered a stellar performance to take third in his Red Bull.
Photo: Red Bull Racing/Getty Images

dropped to the ground," Bottas explained. "One guy, by pure force, lifted up the rear of the car!" Then, as the safety car prepared to pull off after seven of the race's 56 laps, things went from bad to worse for the Finn, who suddenly found himself down in 12th place.

"I spun behind the safety car, a mistake I'm really not proud of…" he admitted candidly. "I got a call in Turn Seven that the safety car was coming in, so the straight out of Turn Ten was the last real chance to do some weaving and generate tyre temperature. I was trying to get the tyres warmer than the cars around so I could attack at the restart, but I went too far. I had a bit of a slide, then overcorrected and spun on to the grass – a silly mistake. These things happen, but it's really s**t when it happens to you!

"It was slow getting the car back off the grass, and I lost a lot of time and tyre temperature. Later, In free air, the car was handling pretty well except for a bit of a struggle with some understeer that was causing quite a lot of tyre wear to the front left. But the car was fast, and Lewis proved it. It was a winning car today, so I'm very disappointed with sixth.

"I think there was a chance to fight for a 1-2. I felt we were slightly quicker than Ferrari today."

Vettel apart, others to gamble on an early stop for slicks at the end of the second lap were Kvyat, Alonso, Massa, Pérez, Magnussen, Ericsson, Ocon, Grosjean, Giovinazzi and Vandoorne. Pérez had suffered a puncture in his first-lap contact with Stroll, and Ocon was waved around again while the crew dealt with Pérez, costing the young Frenchman around 16s. Sainz, already on slicks of course, had gained massively after his opening-lap spin, getting back up to seventh when so many of his rivals headed for the pits.

Hülkenberg, meanwhile, had fortune go totally against him. While Sainz was the only driver to start the race on slicks, 'The Hulk' was the only one to dive in at the end of the opening lap. That could have worked well, but no sooner had he left the pits than the VSC was notified for Stroll/Pérez, effectively ruining the Renault's race. He would attract further delay for overtaking during the safety car period. Kvyat's promising race, meanwhile, fell victim to a hydraulics problem, and Vandoorne retired with no fuel pressure.

If the cards had fallen well for Hamilton in those early laps, there was still a lot of work to be done and plenty of unknowns. Would the slick tyre make it to the end?

Those concerns were key to differing tyre selections. For example, whereas Mercedes elected to put both Hamilton and Bottas on to the soft-compound yellow-wall Pirelli slick, Red Bull went for the supersoft red-wall tyre with both Ricciardo and Verstappen. That led to Mercedes managing the situation as much as possible in the early laps until the likely direction of the race became apparent.

Communication In such conditions, where the driver has less information at his disposal than the team, is more important, hence a team radio message to Hamilton informing him that the Red Bulls, close behind, were on a softer tyre that was unlikely to be able to make it to the end. Coded message: "Don't defend too hard and risk an incident or over-use of the tyres."

Fortunately for Mercedes, Ferrari and Vettel were held up significantly by the Red Bulls, and a number of other cars also opted for the supersoft Pirellis. By instinct, that can feel the right thing to do in cold conditions, but actually a number of drivers had problems with the left front.

There were a number of radio communications between Red Bull and Verstappen alluding to the need to generate more temperature to keep the tyres alive in both sets of supersofts run by the young Dutchman. The problem was not so much wear in the punishing sector-one 'snail' section and at Turns 12/13 – the normal issues at Shanghai – but simple lack of temperature.

The soft-compound tyre chosen by Mercedes, meanwhile, had more resilience to that and was working well on the W08. So well, in fact, that Hamilton said he could comfortably have gone to the end on a single set, although that proved

Above: Mutual admiration between Vettel and Hamilton at the finish.
Photo: Peter J. Fox

Top right: Kevin Magnussen scored his first points for Haas.
Photo: Haas F1 Team

Above right: Max Verstappen and his crew celebrate an early-season podium.
Photo: Peter J. Fox

Right: Antonio Giovinazzi suffered an embarrassing crash on his second outing for Sauber.
Photo: WRi2/Studio Colombo

unnecessary. When he asked the team about such a strategy after 20 of the race's 56 laps, he was told, "We're flexible."

"From the get-go, I felt I had the pace to control the race from the front," Lewis explained, "but if it wasn't for the safety car, it would have been a flat-chat race against Sebastian with just a couple of seconds between us the whole race, probably. We were very close in lap time, but the strategist did the right job in terms of reacting to the scenarios. Sebastian was unfortunate, and I didn't really understand what was going on behind because I had the Red Bulls there and the Ferraris weren't getting past. At that time, I was quite chilled, but later, when Sebastian got behind, we had a real race on our hands, although I had a good gap."

When the race had resumed after the safety car proper, on lap eight, Verstappen snatched third from Räikkönen around the outside of Turn Eight and set off after second-placed team-mate Ricciardo, while the Finn was left to defend from his team-mate.

On lap 11, Verstappen went inside Ricciardo into Turn Six and was still within a couple of seconds of the harder-tyred leading Mercedes. Vettel, meanwhile, remained trapped behind Räikkönen until lap 20 and needed an aggressive outside pass around Turn Six to displace the No. 7 Ferrari. Negotiating his team-mate had cost the German around 6s – he would eventually lose the race to Hamilton by 6.2s – and he rapidly closed down and passed Ricciardo, the Red Bull in trouble with a lack of front tyre temperature and resulting understeer.

Next on the radar was Verstappen, whom Vettel passed with the aid of DRS on the lap before half-distance to go second, but Hamilton was now 10.6s in the distance.

The extent to which Hamilton was controlling the situation was demonstrated by his lap times. After several laps in the high 1.37s/low 1.38s, through laps 21–27 approaching half-distance, he upped the pace to 1m 37.4s on being informed that Vettel had fought his way back up into second place.

On lap 32, Lewis produced an impressive 1m 36.71s lap some 28 laps into his stint on softs, increasing his lead to almost 12.5s. Vettel pitted for a fresh set of softs two laps later and was 0.08s slower on his 'golden' first lap, finding another four-tenths next time around as he generated more temperature. Mercedes, now with ample pit window, brought in Lewis for another set of soft Pirellis two laps later. Once back out and up to speed, his lead had shrunk to 9.4s and when, on lap 40, Vettel lapped at 1m 35.423s, the Ferrari's fastest lap of the race, the margin was down to 8.26s.

"How has the gap come down from 12s to 8s?" Lewis asked on the radio.

Part of the explanation was that at the point Vettel pitted, Hamilton's lead over Räikkönen was 24.2s, just marginally more than required for a stop. Having experienced the rear jack problem with Bottas earlier in the race, however, Mercedes believed that it was wrong to target a perfect stop and risk emerging behind the second Ferrari if there was a further issue. Once the pit-stop window was available, it made sense to pit Hamilton a second time, but it was better to surrender a little of his advantage to the fresh-tyred Vettel to gain a more comfortable stop window to Räikkönen.

While it was natural for Lewis to be wary of Vettel's potential pace in the closing stages, in fact he was able to validate his team-mate's belief that the Mercedes had the legs of the Ferrari at this track in these conditions. He

VIEWPOINT
WIN SOME, LOSE MORE

FAMILIAR with the expression, "You're only as good as your last race"? If not, Antonio Giovinazzi can tell you all about it. Hero in Australia; zero in China a fortnight later.

The 24-year-old Italian was well known to F1 insiders, thanks to five wins in the 2016 GP2 series, and testing for Ferrari and then Sauber when Pascal Wehrlein was declared unfit.

Giovinazzi may not have been surprised by any of that, but he, and just about everyone in F1, was caught off guard when continuing problems for Wehrlein led to the urgent need for a substitute on Saturday morning in Melbourne.

Thrown in at the deep end, Giovinazzi had swum strongly on his first visit to Albert Park by almost qualifying for Q2 and running the full race distance to finish 12th. It was a very impressive debut by any standard.

The trend continued in China, where he briefly outpaced Marcus Ericsson in Q1. But then this tough business bit back. Hard.

A wheel over the kerb put the Sauber into the barrier in full view of the pit wall. It actually did Ericsson a favour, since the yellow flags thwarted potentially quicker laps by four others. But that's where the good news – such as it was – ended.

Both Saubers having stopped for slicks at the end of lap two, Giovinazzi watched Ericsson run wide at the exit of the final corner. In his enthusiasm to profit from his team-mate's mistake, the novice gave the Ferrari power unit too much throttle as he passed across the still-damp surface directly beneath the media centre straddling the track. For the second time in 24 hours, Sauber No. 36 attacked the same barrier, more substantially this time.

Doing further damage to his reputation was the unfortunate fact that the subsequent virtual safety car scuppered the gamble of an early tyre change for Sebastian Vettel, allowing the rest – Lewis Hamilton in particular – a free pit visit. Giovinazzi had possibly cost Ferrari the race, immediately cancelling out the goodwill generated two weeks before.

Maurice Hamilton

recorded the race's fastest lap, 1m 35.423s, some 0.05s quicker than the Ferrari, four laps after Vettel had thrown down the gauntlet. As both men throttled back in the closing stages, a delighted Lewis took the chequered flag for his first win of 2017.

Behind them, the Red Bulls were third and fourth, almost 40s in arrears, both having been caught by Räikkönen who, in turn, had Bottas bearing down on him after his earlier indiscretion, the second Mercedes taking the flag just 0.73s behind the second Ferrari. From his early race spin, Bottas had surrendered just over 20s to Hamilton in 50 laps during a race in which he had been forced to battle past Kvyat, Magnussen, Alonso and Sainz on track.

But, leaving China with a 54th GP win under his belt, there was no disguising Hamilton's pleasure at both a job well done and the prospect of a fascinating season taking on the strongest of adversaries.

"It really is great to win against Sebastian, a four-time world champion at his best who is phenomenally quick. And also with Ferrari at their best in a decade, I think. We are at our best as a team, too, and I feel like I'm at my best. The ultimate fighter always wants the best battle because when you come out on top, it's so much more satisfying. I'm loving this fight!"

The reality was that with the contest so tight, race wins looked set to go to the man and team who got it right on the day. Hamilton and Vettel were tied at the top of the drivers' championship, on 43 points apiece, and Mercedes led Ferrari by a single point, 66–65, in the constructors' battle. It was that close.

Tony Dodgins

2017 FORMULA 1
HEINEKEN
CHINESE
GRAND PRIX

SHANGHAI 7-9 APRIL

RACE DISTANCE: 56 laps, 189.559 miles/305.066km

RACE WEATHER: Wet track/drying/overcast
(track 14-15°C, air 12-13°C)

ROLEX

F1 OFFICIAL TIMEPIECE

SHANGHAI INTERNATIONAL CIRCUIT
Circuit: 3.387 miles / 5.451km
56 laps

187/116 kmh/mph
☀ Gear
DRS zone

Turn 1 230/143
Turn 2 135/84
Turn 3 95/59
Turn 4 240/149
Turn 5 295/183
Turn 6 90/56
Turn 7 270/168
Turn 8 240/149
Turn 9 130/81
Turn 12 200/124
16 195/121
Turn 15 192/120
10 210/130 11 100/62
Turn 13 240/149
Turn 14 80/50
330/205

RACE – OFFICIAL CLASSIFICATION

Pos.	Driver	Nat.	No.	Entrant	Car/Engine	Laps	Time/Retirement	Speed (mph/km/h)	Gap to leader	Fastest race lap
1	**Lewis Hamilton**	GB	44	Mercedes AMG Petronas Motorsport	Mercedes F1 W08-Mercedes M08 EQ Power+ V6	56	1h 37m 36.158s	116.529/187.535		1m 35.378s 44
2	**Sebastian Vettel**	D	5	Scuderia Ferrari	Ferrari SF70H-062 V6	56	1h 37m 42.408s	116.405/187.335	6.250s	1m 35.423s 40
3	**Max Verstappen**	NL	33	Red Bull Racing	Red Bull RB13-TAG Heuer RB13 V6	56	1h 38m 21.350s	115.637/186.099	45.192s	1m 36.722s 31
4	**Daniel Ricciardo**	AUS	3	Red Bull Racing	Red Bull RB13-TAG Heuer RB13 V6	56	1h 38m 22.193s	115.620/186.072	46.035s	1m 36.791s 36
5	**Kimi Räikkönen**	FIN	7	Scuderia Ferrari	Ferrari SF70H-062 V6	56	1h 38m 24.234s	115.580/186.008	48.076s	1m 36.003s 42
6	**Valtteri Bottas**	FIN	77	Mercedes AMG Petronas Motorsport	Mercedes F1 W08-Mercedes M08 EQ Power+ V6	56	1h 38m 24.966s	115.566/185.985	48.808s	1m 35.849s 41
7	**Carlos Sainz**	E	55	Scuderia Toro Rosso	Toro Rosso STR12-Renault R.E.17 V6	56	1h 38m 49.051s	115.096/185.229	1m 12.893s	1m 37.398s 30
8	**Kevin Magnussen**	DK	20	Haas F1 Team	Haas VF-17-Ferrari 062 V6	55			1 lap	1m 37.528s 35
9	**Sergio Pérez**	MEX	11	Sahara Force India Formula 1 Team	Force India VJM10-Mercedes M08 EQ Power+ V6	55			1 lap	1m 36.531s 55
10	**Esteban Ocon**	F	31	Sahara Force India Formula 1 Team	Force India VJM10-Mercedes M08 EQ Power+ V6	55			1 lap	1m 37.036s 55
11	Romain Grosjean	F	8	Haas F1 Team	Haas VF-17-Ferrari 062 V6	55			1 lap	1m 37.551s 50
12	Nico Hülkenberg	D	27	Renault Sport Formula One Team	Renault R.S.17-R.E.17 V6	55			1 lap	1m 38.015s 36
13	Jolyon Palmer	GB	30	Renault Sport Formula One Team	Renault R.S.17-R.E.17 V6	55			1 lap	1m 38.181s 47
14	Felipe Massa	BR	19	Williams Martini Racing	Williams FW40-Mercedes M08 EQ Power+ V6	55			1 lap	1m 36.511s 50
15	Marcus Ericsson	S	9	Sauber F1 Team	Sauber C36-Ferrari 059/5 V6	55			1 lap	1m 39.732s 50
	Fernando Alonso	E	14	McLaren Honda Formula 1 Team	McLaren MCL32-Honda RA617H V6	33	driveshaft			1m 39.496s 31
	Daniil Kvyat	RUS	26	Scuderia Toro Rosso	Toro Rosso STR12-Renault R.E.17 V6	18	hydraulics			1m 40.090s 18
	Stoffel Vandoorne	B	2	McLaren Honda Formula 1 Team	McLaren MCL32-Honda RA617H V6	17	fuel pressure			1m 41.460s 15
	Antonio Giovinazzi	I	36	Sauber F1 Team	Sauber C36-Ferrari 059/5 V6	3	accident			no time
	Lance Stroll	CDN	18	Williams Martini Racing	Williams FW40-Mercedes M08 EQ Power+ V6	0	accident			no time

Fastest race lap: Lewis Hamilton on lap 44, 1m 35.378s, 127.844mph/205.745km/h.

Lap record: Michael Schumacher (Ferrari F2004 V10), 1m 32.238s, 132.196mph/212.749km/h (2004).

19 · GROSJEAN · Haas
5-place grid penalty for failing to slow for double waved yellow flags

17 · OCON · Force India

15 · VANDOORNE · McLaren

13 · ALONSO · McLaren

11 · SAINZ · Toro Rosso

20 · PALMER · Renault
5-place grid penalty for failing to slow for double waved yellow flags

18 · GIOVINAZZI · Sauber
5-place grid penalty for replacing gearbox

16 · VERSTAPPEN · Red Bull

14 · ERICSSON · Sauber

12 · MAGNUSSEN · Haas

Grid order	1	2	3	4	5	6	7	8	9	10	11	12	13	14	15	16	17	18	19	20	21	22	23	24	25	26	27	28	29	30	31	32	33	34	35	36	37	38	39	40	41	42	43	44
44 HAMILTON	44	44	44	44	44	44	44	44	44	44	44	44	44	44	44	44	44	44	44	44	44	44	44	44	44	44	44	44	44	44	44	44	44	44	44	44	44	44	44	44	44	44	44	44
5 VETTEL	5	5	77	77	3	3	3	3	3	3	33	33	33	33	33	33	33	33	33	33	33	33	33	33	33	33	5	5	5	5	5	5	7	7	7	7	5	5	5	5	5			
77 BOTTAS	77	77	3	3	7	7	7	33	33	33	3	3	3	3	3	3	3	3	3	3	5	5	5	5	5	33	3	3	3	3	7	7	5	5	5	5	7	33	33	33	33			
7 RÄIKKÖNEN	7	33	33	33	33	33	33	7	7	7	7	7	7	7	7	7	7	5	5	3	3	3	3	3	3	7	7	7	7	33	33	33	33	33	33	3	3	3	3				
3 RICCIARDO	3	7	7	33	33	77	77	5	5	5	5	5	5	5	5	5	5	7	7	7	7	7	7	7	7	33	77	77	77	33	77	3	3	3	3	55	7	7	7				
19 MASSA	26	33	5	5	5	5	14	55	55	55	55	55	55	55	55	55	55	55	55	55	55	55	55	55	77	33	33	33	77	3	77	55	55	55	55	7	55	55	55	7				
27 HÜLKENBERG	33	26	55	55	55	14	55	14	14	14	14	14	14	14	14	14	14	14	14	14	14	14	14	14	77	77	77	77	14	14	14	14	55	55	77	77	77	77	77	77	77	5		
11 PÉREZ	14	14	31	31	14	55	26	11	11	11	11	11	11	11	11	11	11	11	77	77	77	77	14	14	14	14	55	55	55	55	14	11	11	11	11	11	11	11	11	11	11	11		
26 KVYAT	19	19	14	14	26	26	20	20	20	20	20	20	20	20	20	20	20	20	77	77	20	20	20	20	20	20	20	11	11	31	31	31	20	20	20	20	31	31	31					
18 STROLL	11	11	26	26	19	19	11	26	26	77	77	77	77	77	77	77	77	20	20	20	31	11	11	11	11	11	11	11	11	11	11	20	31	20	20	20	20	31	31	31	19	1		
55 SAINZ	27	20	19	19	11	11	20	77	77	26	26	26	26	26	26	26	26	31	31	11	31	31	31	31	31	31	31	31	31	20	8	19	19	19	19	19	19	19	19	31	3			
20 MAGNUSSEN	20	9	11	11	20	20	77	19	31	31	31	31	31	31	31	31	31	27	27	27	27	27	27	27	27	27	27	27	27	19	8	27	27	8	8	8	8	8	8					
14 ALONSO	9	31	20	20	31	31	31	31	19	19	27	27	27	27	27	27	27	19	19	19	19	19	19	30	30	8	8	8	8	8	27	27	8	27	27	27	27	27	27	27	2			
9 ERICSSON	31	55	30	30	30	30	30	2	27	27	19	19	19	19	19	19	19	30	30	30	30	30	30	8	30	30	19	19	19	30	30	30	30	30	30	30	30	30	30	30				
2 VANDOORNE	8	8	2	2	2	2	2	27	2	2	2	2	2	30	30	30	30	8	8	8	8	19	19	19	19	19	30	30	9	9	9	9	9	9	9	9	9	9	9					
33 VERSTAPPEN	2	36	9	27	27	27	27	30	30	30	30	30	30	8	9	9	9	9	9	9	9	9	9	9	9	9	9	30	30	30														
31 OCON	36	2	36	9	9	9	8	8	8	8	8	8	8	2	2	9																												
36 GIOVINAZZI	55	30	27	8	8	8	9	9	9	9	9	9	2																															
8 GROSJEAN	30	27	8																																									
30 PALMER																																												

TIME SHEETS

PRACTICE 1 (FRIDAY)
Weather: Wet/cloudy-foggy
Temperatures: track 15–16°C, air 13–14°C

Pos.	Driver	Laps	Time
1	Max Verstappen	4	1m 50.491s
2	Felipe Massa	7	1m 52.086s
3	Lance Stroll	7	1m 52.507s
4	Carlos Sainz	5	1m 52.840s
5	Romain Grosjean	6	1m 53.039s
6	Daniil Kvyat	4	1m 53.314s
7	Fernando Alonso	5	1m 53.520s
8	Daniel Ricciardo	7	1m 54.038s
9	Valtteri Bottas	4	1m 54.664s
10	Kevin Magnussen	8	1m 55.104s
11	Nico Hülkenberg	6	1m 55.608s
12	Stoffel Vandoorne	4	1m 57.445s
13	Marcus Ericsson	4	2m 15.138s
14	Antonio Giovinazzi	4	2m 15.281s
15	Jolyon Palmer	3	no time
16	Sebastian Vettel	2	no time
17	Kimi Räikkönen	1	no time
18	Esteban Ocon	2	no time
19	Sergio Pérez	3	no time
20	Lewis Hamilton	3	no time

PRACTICE 2 (FRIDAY)
Weather: Wet/foggy
Temperatures: track 15°C, air 13°C

Cancelled due to poor visibility, which prevented the medical helicopter from operating.

PRACTICE 3 (SATURDAY)
Weather: Dry/cloudy
Temperatures: track 32°C, air 20°C

Pos.	Driver	Laps	Time
1	Sebastian Vettel	20	1m 33.336s
2	Kimi Räikkönen	19	1m 33.389s
3	Valtteri Bottas	26	1m 33.707s
4	Lewis Hamilton	25	1m 33.879s
5	Felipe Massa	23	1m 34.773s
6	Max Verstappen	20	1m 34.946s
7	Daniel Ricciardo	23	1m 35.092s
8	Lance Stroll	24	1m 35.182s
9	Jolyon Palmer	21	1m 35.192s
10	Carlos Sainz	24	1m 35.223s
11	Nico Hülkenberg	22	1m 35.449s
12	Kevin Magnussen	22	1m 35.521s
13	Sergio Pérez	20	1m 35.626s
14	Romain Grosjean	22	1m 35.680s
15	Daniil Kvyat	23	1m 35.804s
16	Esteban Ocon	24	1m 35.811s
17	Fernando Alonso	17	1m 35.912s
18	Marcus Ericsson	25	1m 36.063s
19	Stoffel Vandoorne	21	1m 36.221s
20	Antonio Giovainazzi	24	1m 36.705s

QUALIFYING (SATURDAY)
Weather: Dry/sunny-overcast Temperatures: track 30–36°C, air 20–23°C

Pos.	Driver	First	Second	Third	Qualifying Tyre
1	Lewis Hamilton	1m 33.333s	1m 32.406s	1m 31.678s	Supersoft (new)
2	Sebastian Vettel	1m 33.078s	1m 32.391s	1m 31.864s	Supersoft (new)
3	Valtteri Bottas	1m 33.684s	1m 32.552s	1m 31.865s	Supersoft (new)
4	Kimi Räikkönen	1m 33.341s	1m 32.181s	1m 32.140s	Supersoft (new)
5	Daniel Ricciardo	1m 34.041s	1m 33.546s	1m 33.033s	Supersoft (new)
6	Felipe Massa	1m 34.205s	1m 33.759s	1m 33.507s	Supersoft (new)
7	Nico Hülkenberg	1m 34.453s	1m 33.636s	1m 33.580s	Supersoft (new)
8	Sergio Pérez	1m 34.657s	1m 33.920s	1m 33.706s	Supersoft (new)
9	Daniil Kvyat	1m 34.440s	1m 34.034s	1m 33.719s	Supersoft (new)
10	Lance Stroll	1m 33.986s	1m 34.090s	1m 34.220s	Supersoft (new)
11	Carlos Sainz	1m 34.567s	1m 34.150s		
12	Kevin Magnussen	1m 34.942s	1m 34.164s		
13	Fernando Alonso	1m 34.499s	1m 34.372s		
14	Marcus Ericsson	1m 34.892s	1m 35.046s		
15	Antonio Giovinazzi	1m 34.963s	no time		
16	Stoffel Vandoorne	1m 35.023s			
17	Romain Grosjean	1m 35.223s			
18	Jolyon Palmer	1m 35.279s			
19	Max Verstappen	1m 35.433s			
20	Esteban Ocon	1m 35.496s			

QUALIFYING: head to head

Hamilton	2	0	Bottas
Vettel	2	0	Räikkönen
Massa	2	0	Stroll
Ricciardo	1	1	Verstappen
Pérez	2	0	Ocon
Hülkenberg	2	0	Palmer
Kvyat	1	1	Sainz
Ericsson	2	0	Giovinazzi
Alonso	2	0	Vandoorne
Grosjean	1	1	Magnussen

FOR THE RECORD

150th GRAND PRIX: **Mercedes**

75th POLE POSITION: **Mercedes**

100th RACE WITH A PODIUM: **Red Bull**

POINTS

DRIVERS

1	Sebastian Vettel	43
2	Lewis Hamilton	43
3	Max Verstappen	25
4	Valtteri Bottas	23
5	Kimi Räikkönen	22
6	Daniel Ricciardo	12
7	Carlos Sainz	10
8	Felipe Massa	8
9	Sergio Pérez	8
10	Kevin Magnussen	4
11	Daniil Kvyat	2
12	Esteban Ocon	2

CONSTRUCTORS

1	Mercedes	66
2	Ferrari	65
3	Red Bull	37
4	Toro Rosso	12
5	Force India	10
6	Williams	8
7	Haas	4

9 · KVYAT · Toro Rosso   7 · HÜLKENBERG · Renault   5 · RICCIARDO · Red Bull   3 · BOTTAS · Mercedes   1 · HAMILTON · Mercedes

10 · STROLL · Williams   8 · PÉREZ · Force India   6 · MASSA · Williams   4 · RÄIKKÖNEN · Ferrari   2 · VETTEL · Ferrari

45	46	47	48	49	50	51	52	53	54	55	56	
44	44	44	44	44	44	44	44	44	44	44	44	1
5	5	5	5	5	5	5	5	5	5	5	5	2
33	33	33	33	33	33	33	33	33	33	33	33	3
3	3	3	3	3	3	3	3	3	3	3	3	4
7	7	7	7	7	7	7	7	7	7	7	7	5
77	77	77	77	77	77	77	77	77	77	77	77	6
55	55	55	55	55	55	55	55	55	55	55	55	7
11	11	11	20	20	20	20	20	20	20	20	20	8
20	20	20	11	11	11	11	11	11	11	11	11	9
31	31	31	31	31	31	31	31	31	31	31		10
19	19	19	8	8	8	8	8	8	8			
8	8	8	27	27	27	27	27	27	27			
27	27	27	19	30	30	30	30	30	30			
30	30	30	30	19	19	19	19	19	19			
9	9	9	9	9	9	9	9	9	9			

27 = Pit stop   *2 One lap or more behind*

 Safety car deployed on laps shown

RACE TYRE STRATEGIES

PIRELLI

	Driver	Race Stint 1	Race Stint 2	Race Stint 3	Race Stint 4
1	Hamilton	Inter (n): 1-4	Soft (n): 5-36	Soft (n): 37-56	
2	Vettel	Inter (n): 1-2	Soft (n): 3-34	Soft (u): 35-56	
3	Verstappen	Inter (n): 1-4	Supersoft (n): 5-29	Supersoft (n): 30-56	
4	Ricciardo	Inter (n): 1-4	Supersoft (n): 5-33	Supersoft (u): 34-56	
5	Räikkönen	Inter (n): 1-4	Soft (n): 5-39	Supersoft (u): 40-56	
6	Bottas	Inter (n): 1-4	Soft (n): 5-35	Soft (n): 36-56	
7	Sainz	Supersoft (n): 1-28	Soft (n): 29-56		
8	Magnussen	Inter (n): 1-2	Supersoft (n): 3-32	Supersoft (u): 33-56	
9	Pérez	Inter (n): 1-2	Supersoft (u): 3-20	Supersoft (u): 21-49	Supersoft (u): 50-56
10	Ocon	Inter (n): 1-2	Soft (n): 3-42	Supersoft (n): 43-56	
11	Grosjean	Inter (n): 1-2	Supersoft (n): 3-5	Soft (n): 6-35	Supersoft (n): 36-56
12	Hülkenberg	Inter (n): 1	Supersoft (n): 2-33	Supersoft (u): 34-56	
13	Palmer	Supersoft (n): 1-30	Soft (n): 31-56		
14	Massa	Inter (n): 1-2	Soft (n): 3-24	Supersoft (u): 25-48	Supersoft (u): 49-56
15	Ericsson	Inter (n): 1-2	Soft (n): 3-56		
	Alonso	Inter (n): 1-2	Soft (n): 3-33 (dnf)		
	Kvyat	Inter (n): 1-2	Soft (n): 3-18 (dnf)		
	Vandoorne	Inter (n): 1-2	Soft (n): 3-17 (dnf)		
	Giovinazzi	Inter (n): 1-2	Soft (n): 3 (dnf)		
	Stroll	Inter (n): 0 (dnf)			

At least two of three dry tyre specs must be used in a dry race. If Wet or Intermediate tyres are needed, this rule is suspended. Pirelli P Zero sidewall logos are colour-coded: Green = Intermediate; Yellow = Soft; Red = Supersoft. (n) new (u) used

Photos: Peter J. Fox

BAHRAIN GRAND PRIX

SAKHIR CIRCUIT

Main photo: Tyre trouble hobbled early race leader Valtteri Bottas, who eventually had to settle for third.
Photo: Peter J. Fox

Inset: Sebastian took the honours for the second time in three races. Valtteri can hardly hide his disappointment.
Photo: Mercedes AMG Petronas F1 Team

SAKHIR QUALIFYING

IN Australia, Valtteri Bottas had qualified 0.3s from Lewis Hamilton, which was closer than Nico Rosberg had been around Albert Park in five attempts. In China, Bottas had been just 0.19s away, but a spin behind the safety car and a dominant win from Lewis had fuelled the perception that the 2017 title chase could be a two-horse race between Hamilton and Sebastian Vettel. Bottas needed to fight back quickly, and Bahrain was a track on which he had never been outqualified by a team-mate. Then again, he hadn't had a team-mate like Hamilton. But, you sensed that Bottas had a real chance to claim his first career F1 pole in the heat of the desert.

The margins between the pair were narrow, Hamilton topping Q2 by just 0.02s, with Vettel another 0.04s adrift of the second Mercedes. Bottas had been quicker in sector one, with Hamilton coming on strong at the end of the lap, possibly with his supersoft Pirellis in better shape. On his second Q3 run, Bottas tempered his approach to sector one a fraction and blasted across the line three-hundredths quicker than his team-mate's first run, in 1m 28.769s. For once, Hamilton couldn't respond, losing time in the middle sector, and a delighted Bottas did indeed claim that first pole.

In the cockpit, he did a little fist pump. "You almost showed some emotion there. I'm impressed!" said engineer Tony Ross over the radio. In Q3, the Mercs had found almost three-quarters of a second, once again utilising a much more aggressive Q3 engine mode than their rivals to give the team its first all-silver front row of 2017.

Hamilton seemed genuinely pleased for his new team-mate, with team principal Toto Wolff commenting, "No driver likes to lose, but you can see the respect between them, and with Sebastian, too. It reminds you of the genuine respect you see between Roger Federer and Rafael Nadal."

Vettel could not split the Mercs this time, the cooler track temperatures of the 6pm Bahrain qualifying hour playing more to the strengths of Mercedes than Ferrari.

After such a difficult start to the season, Red Bull had made a step forward, the team's long-run pace on Friday afternoon even suggesting that they could be a factor in the race. Daniel Ricciardo did a great job to split the Ferraris, a couple of hundredths faster than Räikkönen, who was more than 0.3s down on Vettel at a circuit where he often impresses, once again finding too much understeer in the Ferrari's set-up after losing much of Friday's practice to a turbo problem.

Max Verstappen qualified the second Red Bull sixth, 0.14s behind his team-mate, but reckoned he'd left a couple of tenths on the table when his preparation lap had not gone to plan, the young Dutchman having slowed to leave sufficient gap to Massa, losing front tyre temperature in the process.

Just 0.16s behind Verstappen, Nico Hülkenberg produced another impressive qualifying performance from just the one Q3 run. "That," he said, "was one of my best qualifying laps, together with my Brazil 2010 pole." After a dreadful start to the year, team-mate Jolyon Palmer was happier to put both of the French cars into the top ten, but in Q3 selected the wrong engine mode and didn't actually beat his Q2 time, which was still a sizeable 0.73s adrift of 'The Hulk'.

Splitting the Renaults on the grid was Felipe Massa's Williams and Romain Grosjean. The latter had crashed his Haas at Turn 14 in morning practice, troubled by braking problems, and robbed his crew of a lunch break.

Daniil Kvyat missed out on Q3 by just 0.03s after locking up, while team-mate Carlos Sainz became mired in Q1 after suffering a power unit failure approaching the final turn while on a competitive lap. The young Spaniard was another to miss out on the majority of Friday practice after a broken exhaust had damaged the Toro Rosso's wiring loom.

Lance Stroll had set himself a target of qualifying within half a second of team-mate Massa, and in Bahrain he achieved that – just – by stopping the Q2 clocks 0.49s down on the Brazilian. That did not get him into Q3, and he would start 12th.

The returning Pascal Wehrlein did a great job to put the first Sauber 13th on the grid, 0.27s clear of Esteban Ocon. Force India were struggling a little with aero efficiency at the rear, and Sergio Pérez's problems were compounded when he had to back off for waved yellows for Sainz's stranded Toro Rosso, which eliminated the Mexican in Q1. The same fate had also befallen Kevin Magnussen in the second Haas.

You need grunt in Bahrain, and that was something in short supply for McLaren Honda. Fernando Alonso made it through to Q2 with six-hundredths to spare, but then suffered an MGU-H problem and failed to post a time in the second session. Team-mate Stoffel Vandoorne was 0.26s adrift of the two-times champion in Q1, after being hit by two MGU-H failures of his own, severely limiting his seat time at a track where it would have been particularly valuable to the rookie.

Above: Lewis arrives centre stage for the pre-race national anthem.
Photo: Peter J. Fox

Left: Pascal Wehrlein was back in action for Sauber and nearly made the points.

Right: Fernando Alonso and Zak Brown announce the Spaniard's intention to take part in the 2017 Indianapolis 500.
Photo: McLaren Honda

Far right: A glimpse of the stewards' room, where judgements are made and penalties handed down.
Photo: WRi2/Jean-François Galeron

THE 'under lights' format has proved hugely popular in Bahrain, the cars looking otherworldly against the desert backdrop. Some 94 minutes after the starting lights blinked out, however, Mercedes team principal Toto Wolff was left to contemplate a slightly surreal 'perfect storm' that had allowed Ferrari and Sebastian Vettel to claim a second win in three 2017 races, after the Silver Arrows had locked out the front row.

Bottas converted his pole position and led into Turn One, but Lewis struggled a little more with traction on the dirty side of the grid and could not prevent Vettel from going around his outside to snatch second.

It soon became apparent that the pace Bottas had shown on Pirelli's supersoft compound to take pole was absent, and a train of cars was able to go with him, comprising Vettel, Hamilton, Verstappen, Ricciardo, Räikkönen and Massa. Unable to break the one-second DRS delta to Vettel, Valtteri was told by Mercedes to use the overtake button to defend, but as early as lap eight, the Finn was on the radio reporting, "The tyres are not good..." The surface temperature had been hot from the start, and the pit wall team confirmed that the pressures were too high.

"Our generator broke on the grid and we couldn't bleed air from Valtteri's tyres, so we were starting with completely the wrong tyre pressures on his car and knew he'd be struggling," Wolff explained. "And, with Sebastian running second, there was nothing we could do. That opened up the opportunity for Ferrari to undercut us, and they did it quite early."

"I could feel the problem from lap two," Bottas elaborated. "I was just sliding around with the rear end, struggling to get on the power out of the corners, so the pace wasn't good, and Sebastian was really putting pressure on. Trying to extend the stint, I couldn't keep up with the pace; the tyres were just dropping."

Adopting the same aggressive strategy already seen in Melbourne and Shanghai, Vettel headed into the pits for a fresh set of supersoft Pirellis as soon as possible, just ten laps into the 57-lap race. He rejoined in tenth place, Ferrari unconcerned with traffic in the belief that those in front would soon pit or have insufficient pace to resist the freshly reshod Ferrari.

Of the leading group, Verstappen pitted on the following lap, but any potential threat from the Red Bull evaporated when he crashed following a braking problem.

The next curve ball came in the form of a lap-13 safety car, after Sainz had collected Stroll at Turn One upon re-emerging from the pits. Vettel reported a couple of missed heartbeats when momentarily it appeared that the benefits of his undercut strategy were about to be undone by the appearance of the official Mercedes for the second time in seven days! This time, he need not have worried; it was Mercedes's turn to suffer misfortune.

Above: Vettel locks up a wheel as he attacks Bottas for the lead.
Photo: Mercedes AMG Petronas F1 Team

Top left: Carlos Sainz and Lance Stroll clashed on lap 12, which eliminated both of them.
Photo: WRi2/Jerry Andre

Above left: A well-executed pit stop for Romain Grosjean on his way to eighth place.
Photo: Haas F1 Team

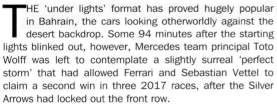

Right: Ferrari team personnel share a selfie moment in *parc fermé.*
Photo: WRi2/Jean-François Galeron

As all those who hadn't already stopped piled into the pit lane under the safety car, Bottas had a slow stop. A power loss in the garage prevented the wheel guns from operating as they should, slowing the tyre change initially, the issue compounded by the team having to wait for Ricciardo's Red Bull to go past before they could safely release their man. The upshot was that Bottas re-emerged behind Vettel's Ferrari, losing his lead. "Without the problems, it would have been close and we might have hung on," he reckoned.

Behind him, Hamilton had problems of his own. Knowing that he was going to have to wait for his team-mate's stop to be completed before his car could be serviced, he backed off to allow a gap so that he would not have to be 'stacked' in the pits, in the hope that he would not lose a position to Ricciardo. The latter would receive new tyres immediately, since team-mate Verstappen had already stopped earlier and was out of the race. But Lewis drove a little *too* slowly in the pit lane, impeding the Red Bull, and an investigation resulted in him serving a 5s penalty at his second stop.

The reality is that in such a situation, a driver is doing quite a lot – trying to manage his safety car time delta and gaps to the cars around him. In Hamilton's case, his team-mate's slow pit stop exacerbated the situation, but the three-times champion was quick to accept responsibility: "It was completely my fault with the safety car, just a misjudgement."

When the safety car pulled in and racing resumed on lap 17, Bottas, on another set of supersofts, made a valiant attempt to wrest back the lead from Vettel, trying to go around the outside of the Ferrari in Turn Four. It almost came off, but not quite. Behind, Hamilton was soon back into third position as Ricciardo, struggling to get heat into a set of the soft-compound Pirellis, dropped places to Massa and Räikkönen as well.

During his opening-stint struggle, Bottas had been told about the high tyre pressures, that he would have more grip on his second set of supersofts and to adjust the differential accordingly. Hamilton, meanwhile, had been put on to the yellow-walled soft Pirellis for the second stint. The team thinking was that running the soft tyre in the middle stint would give more options at the end of the race, as well as affording a comparison to show which tyre was better. Interestingly, for Mercedes, that turned out to be the soft, rather than the supersoft.

That soon became apparent when Bottas, who initially had thought that his second set of supersofts was better, still found himself in trouble with oversteer and struggling to hold off his team-mate on the harder tyre.

It was not long before Lewis was on the radio: "Valtteri needs to up the pace; we can't let the Ferrari get away…" The spectre of team orders reared its head for the first time.

But Hamilton was not posturing and his concerns were genuine enough. On lap 18, Vettel led Bottas by 1.56s, and the margin was growing by the lap: 2.06, 2.25, 2.68, 2.87, 3.53, 4.06, 4.88, 6.11. But it was not until lap 27 that Mercedes made the 'swap' call, Bottas initially being offered the opportunity to respond and drive to target lap times and target gaps.

"We need to be within 1s of Vettel and you have two laps to achieve it," he was told at first. But, on the supersoft tyre at least, Mercedes did not have Ferrari pace.

Around 11 laps into this second stint, Hamilton, too, was told, "We think we should be faster at this time and will review the situation." Lewis's response, that he was worried about destroying his tyres, initially gave rise to the suspicion that Mercedes might even try to get him to the end on a single set of the softs, given that Vettel, on supersofts, would obviously have to pit again. Such a move would have given Lewis the lead and track position, but it would have required 44 laps out of a soft tyre that was predicted to have a useful life expectancy of 30 or so.

"We had a short chat about it around 20 laps before the end," Wolff confirmed. "At that stage, there were 20-odd laps on the tyre already, so no chance really. The intention

Above: Sebastian Vettel remained in control at the head of the field.

Top right: Kimi on autograph duty.
Photos: Scuderia Ferrari

Above right: An electrifying late charge from Lewis Hamilton was not enough to take victory.
Photo: Mercedes AMG Petronas F1 Team

Right: Things were looking good for pole-sitter Valtteri Bottas on Saturday evening in Bahrain, but race day did not turn out as planned for the unlucky Finn.
Photo: Peter J. Fox

was to have a long middle stint and then decide whether to put the supersoft on for the last blast, or revert to the soft if it was the quicker tyre."

On the Mercedes W08 at least, everything was pointing to the soft being the better tyre. Four laps after surrendering second place to his team-mate, Bottas made his second and final pit stop on lap 30, switching to the yellow-walled Pirelli. Immediately, he began lapping significantly quicker – low 1:34s versus a couple of 1:34.9s and low 1:35s on the supersoft.

Race leader Vettel stopped three laps later for a set of softs and had 24 laps remaining, while the decision to put Lewis on to softs at his first stop had allowed him to stay out as far as lap 41. He served his 5s penalty, took on a second set of softs and blasted back into the fray, 19s behind the race-leading Ferrari and 10s behind his team-mate.

Vettel, informed that Hamilton would come back at him on fresher rubber in the closing stages, was in tyre conservation mode at this stage, but still lapping relatively quickly in the low to mid-1:34s. Hamilton's pace, though, was electrifying: 1:32.96, 32.88, 32.92, 32.79 – massively impressive high-speed consistency that propelled him up to Bottas within five laps.

"Don't hold Lewis up; he's on fresher rubber and going for the win," was the instruction to the pole man.

"As a racing driver, it's maybe the worst thing you want to hear," Bottas admitted post-race, "but that's how it was, and for sure I let him by because there was potential that Lewis could challenge Sebastian. In the end, it didn't happen, but the team tried, which I completely understand. It's tough, but that's life. I didn't have enough pace today and we need to find the reasons why."

Wolff himself conceded that he doesn't enjoy making such calls, but there was no denying that the team had been more than fair to Bottas in giving him a chance to respond. Indeed, some even argued that perhaps they had been too fair, given that Lewis was just 6.6s behind Vettel at the chequered flag, having served a 5s penalty, had clearly lost time behind Valtteri at the beginning of the second stint, and that the win might even have been there.

"It looks like on single-lap pace, we have a little edge, and

in the race it's pretty evenly matched," Wolff summarised. "That may be a bit of a bold statement after losing the race, but Lewis's pace was good throughout, and I think it's going to be close in the next couple of races.

"As regards letting Lewis past Valtteri earlier, you are always more intelligent looking back, and it's a call you don't like to make. I think both have to have a chance of winning the race and having the best possible result, and it's only when you realise that if you don't change anything you are going to lose the race, that you have to make that unpopular call. We don't like it at all, and in past years have tried to avoid it. We would probably have taken a different decision if Valtteri had run at the front with his problem on the tyres and Lewis had been second, but with Vettel between them, there was nothing we could do, which was our perfect storm."

Räikkönen closed down Bottas in the closing laps, but the younger Finn got to the chequer with 2s in hand, while Ricciardo, fifth, was 40s adrift of Hamilton, proving that Red Bull still had work to do.

Massa, aboard the lone surviving Williams, finished a further 15s adrift of Ricciardo and 8s clear of Pérez, who was satisfied with seventh place and his afternoon's work for Force India, having started 18th.

In a well-spread field, Grosjean finished 12s down on the Mexican and 5s ahead of Hülkenberg, who found the Renault heavy on its tyres, with Ocon claiming the final point and maintaining his 100 per cent scoring record with Force India thus far.

There was more radio comedy from Alonso, who fought a mighty tussle with Palmer and Kvyat for a number of laps, then came on the radio and announced that he'd never driven with such little power in his life. The thoughts of the Honda hierarchy could only be imagined...

As the paddock crates were packed, we were left to reflect on another race in which Mercedes and Ferrari had had similar pace, but the two main protagonists had not yet gone directly head to head. Vettel now led the drivers' championship by seven points, with Ferrari three ahead of Mercedes in the constructors' battle. This was beginning to shape up nicely!

Tony Dodgins

VIEWPOINT
NOT MEANT TO END THIS WAY

VALTTERI BOTTAS was on the podium for only the second time in 17 months, but you wouldn't have known it, judging by his preoccupied expression. Rather than standing on the third spot, he knew he should have been at the top. What made it worse was the course of events that had led to his team-mate finishing second.

This was the first time Mercedes had not led the constructors' championship since the beginning of 2014. Was the strain beginning to tell with a compressor problem that didn't allow Bottas's tyre pressures to be adjusted on the grid?

That may have accounted for a loss of pace in the first stint. But, along with everyone else, Bottas was wondering why he had suffered oversteer on the second and third sets. This, in turn, had led to Mercedes dealing with strategy calls forced upon them by the continuing resurgence of Ferrari as Vettel took his second win of 2017.

It was a problem Mercedes had not expected so early in the season. With the Ferrari being easier on its tyres, Mercedes had a fight on their hands. But the difference between the two teams was that Vettel would be seen as the *de facto* No. 1 after another poor race weekend for Kimi Räikkönen, whereas, according to Mercedes, there was no leader, appointed or otherwise, within their team. But how long could that last?

That must have crossed Valtteri's mind as he wondered why the lap of his life and his first pole position had led to the pit wall team asking him to move aside and let Lewis through. There was good reason for the call, and Bottas did not hesitate.

But here was proof of the need for a new kind of strategy call. In the past, such pit wall conversations had been limited to deciding which of the two Mercedes drivers was best suited to win. Now, with such a heavy threat from Ferrari, Mercedes had to think about avoiding the loss of victory by making the sort of call that, according to Bottas, "a driver never wants to hear". He needed a win. And soon.

Maurice Hamilton

3

2017 FORMULA 1
GULF AIR
BAHRAIN
GRAND PRIX

SAKHIR 14–16 APRIL

ROLEX
OFFICIAL TIMEPIECE

RACE DISTANCE: 57 laps, 191.530 miles/308.238km

RACE WEATHER: Dry/dark (track 28–35°C, air 24–26°C)

BAHRAIN INTERNATIONAL CIRCUIT, SAKHIR
Circuit: 3.363 miles / 5.412km, 57 laps
187/116 kmh/mph ✦ Gear — DRS zone

RACE – OFFICIAL CLASSIFICATION

Pos.	Driver	Nat.	No.	Entrant	Car/Engine	Laps	Time/Retirement	Speed (mph/km/h)	Gap to leader	Fastest race lap	
1	Sebastian Vettel	D	5	Scuderia Ferrari	Ferrari SF70H-062 V6	57	1h 33m 53.374s	122.397/196.979		1m 33.826s	36
2	Lewis Hamilton	GB	44	Mercedes AMG Petronas Motorsport	Mercedes F1 W08-Mercedes M08 EQ Power+ V6	57	1h 34m 00.034s	122.252/196.746	6.660s	1m 32.798s	46
3	Valtteri Bottas	FIN	77	Mercedes AMG Petronas Motorsport	Mercedes F1 W08-Mercedes M08 EQ Power+ V6	57	1h 34m 13.771s	121.955/196.268	20.397s	1m 34.087s	33
4	Kimi Räikkönen	FIN	7	Scuderia Ferrari	Ferrari SF70H-062 V6	57	1h 34m 15.849s	121.911/196.196	22.475s	1m 33.720s	55
5	Daniel Ricciardo	AUS	3	Red Bull Racing	Red Bull RB13-TAG Heuer RB13 V6	57	1h 34m 32.720s	121.548/195.612	39.346s	1m 33.495s	42
6	Felipe Massa	BR	19	Williams Martini Racing	Williams FW40-Mercedes M08 EQ Power+ V6	57	1h 34m 47.700s	121.228/195.097	54.326s	1m 34.256s	39
7	Sergio Pérez	MEX	11	Sahara Force India Formula 1 Team	Force India VJM10-Mercedes M08 EQ Power+ V6	57	1h 34m 55.980s	121.052/194.814	1m 02.606s	1m 34.609s	39
8	Romain Grosjean	F	8	Haas F1 Team	Haas VF-17-Ferrari 062 V6	57	1h 35m 08.239s	120.791/194.395	1m 14.865s	1m 34.948s	33
9	Nico Hülkenberg	D	27	Renault Sport Formula One Team	Renault R.S.17-R.E.17 V6	57	1h 35m 13.562s	120.679/194.214	1m 20.188s	1m 35.372s	40
10	Esteban Ocon	F	31	Sahara Force India Formula 1 Team	Force India VJM10-Mercedes M08 EQ Power+ V6	57	1h 35m 29.085s	120.352/193.688	1m 35.711s	1m 35.179s	39
11	Pascal Wehrlein	D	94	Sauber F1 Team	Sauber C36-Ferrari 059/5 V6	56			1 lap	1m 36.786s	43
12	Daniil Kvyat	RUS	26	Scuderia Toro Rosso	Toro Rosso STR12-Renault R.E.17 V6	56			1 lap	1m 34.985s	45
13	Jolyon Palmer	GB	30	Renault Sport Formula One Team	Renault R.S.17-R.E.17 V6	56			1 lap	1m 35.552s	43
14	Fernando Alonso	E	14	McLaren Honda Formula 1 Team	McLaren MCL32-Honda RA617H V6	54	power unit		3 laps	1m 35.595s	47
	Marcus Ericsson	S	9	Sauber F1 Team	Sauber C36-Ferrari 059/5 V6	50	gearbox			1m 35.086s	35
	Carlos Sainz	E	55	Scuderia Toro Rosso	Toro Rosso STR12-Renault R.E.17 V6	12	accident			1m 38.026s	8
	Lance Stroll	CDN	18	Williams Martini Racing	Williams FW40-Mercedes M08 EQ Power+ V6	12	accident			1m 36.303s	10
	Max Verstappen	NL	33	Red Bull Racing	Red Bull RB13-TAG Heuer RB13 V6	11	brakes/accident			1m 36.681s	4
	Kevin Magnussen	DK	20	Haas F1 Team	Haas VF-17-Ferrari 062 V6	8	electrics			1m 38.718s	6
NS	Stoffel Vandoorne	B	2	McLaren Honda Formula 1 Team	McLaren MCL32-Honda RA617H V6		water pressure on the formation lap				

Fastest race lap: Lewis Hamilton on lap 46, 1m 32.798s, 130.459mph/209.952km/h.

Lap record: Michael Schumacher (Ferrari F2004 V10), 1m 30.252s, 134.263mph/216.074km/h (2004, 3.366-mile/5.417km circuit).

Lap record (current configuration): Pedro de la Rosa (McLaren MP4-20-Mercedes V10), 1m 31.447s, 132.386mph/213.054km/h (2005).

19 · ERICSSON · Sauber

17 · VANDOORNE · McLaren
In the pit lane; did not start

15 · ALONSO · McLaren

13 · WEHRLEIN · Sauber

11 · KVYAT · Toro Rosso

20 · MAGNUSSEN · Haas

18 · PÉREZ · Force India

16 · SAINZ · Toro Rosso

14 · OCON · Force India

12 · STROLL · Williams

Grid order	1	2	3	4	5	6	7	8	9	10	11	12	13	14	15	16	17	18	19	20	21	22	23	24	25	26	27	28	29	30	31	32	33	34	35	36	37	38	39	40	41	42	43	44	45	46
77 BOTTAS	77	77	77	77	77	77	77	77	77	77	77	77	77	5	5	5	5	5	5	5	5	5	5	5	5	5	5	5	5	5	5	5	5	44	44	44	44	44	44	44	44	5	5	5	5	5
44 HAMILTON	5	5	5	5	5	5	5	5	5	44	44	44	44	77	77	77	77	77	77	77	77	77	77	77	77	77	77	44	44	44	44	44	44	7	7	5	5	5	5	77	77	77	77	77	77	77
5 VETTEL	44	44	44	44	44	44	44	44	44	33	3	3	3	3	3	3	44	44	44	44	44	44	44	44	44	44	77	77	77	77	7	7	7	5	5	7	7	77	77	77	44	44	44	44	44	44
3 RICCIARDO	33	33	33	33	33	33	33	33	33	3	33	7	19	44	44	44	19	19	19	19	19	19	19	7	7	7	7	7	7	7	3	3	3	3	3	77	3	7	7	7	7	7	7	7	7	7
7 RÄIKKÖNEN	3	3	3	3	3	3	3	3	3	5	7	19	5	19	19	19	7	7	7	7	7	7	7	19	19	19	19	19	3	3	19	19	19	77	77	77	3	7	3	3	3	3	3	3	3	3
33 VERSTAPPEN	19	19	19	19	19	19	19	7	7	7	19	27	27	7	7	7	3	3	3	3	3	3	3	3	3	3	3	19	19	11	77	77	19	19	19	19	19	19	19	19	19	19	19	19	19	19
27 HÜLKENBERG	7	7	7	7	7	7	7	19	19	19	27	5	11	27	27	27	11	11	11	11	11	11	11	11	11	11	11	11	11	77	11	11	11	11	11	31	11	11	11	11	11	11	11	11	11	11
19 MASSA	27	27	27	27	27	27	27	27	27	8	9	27	8	11	11	11	27	27	27	27	27	27	27	27	27	27	27	27	27	31	8	8	8	8	8	8	8	8	8	8	8	8	8	8	8	8
8 GROSJEAN	8	8	8	8	8	8	8	8	8	55	11	30	11	11	11	8	8	8	8	8	8	8	8	8	8	8	8	31	31	31	31	27	26	26	26	26	26	27	27	27	27					
30 PALMER	31	31	31	31	31	31	31	31	31	11	55	14	8	8	8	31	31	31	31	31	31	31	31	31	31	31	8	26	26	26	26	8	94	94	27	27	31	31	31	31						
26 KVYAT	55	55	55	55	55	55	55	55	55	5	30	26	31	31	9	9	14	14	14	14	30	30	30	30	30	26	26	14	14	14	8	94	27	31	31	94	94	94	94							
18 STROLL	30	30	30	30	11	11	11	11	11	31	14	9	9	9	14	30	30	30	26	26	14	14	30	30	8	30	30	31	31	94	94	14	14	14	14											
94 WEHRLEIN	11	11	11	11	30	30	30	30	30	30	26	31	14	14	30	94	94	8	30	14	27	14	14	14	9	9	26	26																		
31 OCON	18	18	18	18	18	18	14	14	14	9	31	26	26	26	26	9	9	94	94	94	94	94	94	94	8	94	94	94	14	9	9	30	30	26	26	26										
14 ALONSO	14	14	14	14	14	14	20	94	94	31	94	94	94	94	94	94	9	9	9	9	9	9	9	9	9	30	30	30	30	30	30															
55 SAINZ	20	20	20	20	20	20	94	26	26	9	18																																			
2 VANDOORNE	94	94	94	94	94	94	18	9	9	94	94																																			
11 PÉREZ	26	26	26	26	26	26	26	18	18	18																																				
9 ERICSSON	9	9	9	9	9	9	9																																							
20 MAGNUSSEN																																														

TIME SHEETS

PRACTICE 1 (FRIDAY)
Weather: Dry/sunny
Temperatures: track 38–48°C, air 36–38°C

Pos.	Driver	Laps	Time
1	Sebastian Vettel	21	1m 32.697s
2	Daniel Ricciardo	22	1m 33.097s
3	Max Verstappen	23	1m 33.566s
4	Sergio Pérez	22	1m 34.095s
5	Felipe Massa	24	1m 34.246s
6	Lance Stroll	25	1m 34.322s
7	Esteban Ocon	23	1m 34.332s
8	Fernando Alonso	14	1m 34.372s
9	Romain Grosjean	21	1m 34.564s
10	Lewis Hamilton	28	1m 34.636s
11	Daniil Kvyat	13	1m 34.838s
12	Nico Hülkenberg	13	1m 34.927s
13	Stoffel Vandoorne	10	1m 34.997s
14	Valtteri Bottas	27	1m 35.002s
15	Jolyon Palmer	19	1m 35.068s
16	Kevin Magnussen	21	1m 35.579s
17	Marcus Ericsson	24	1m 35.888s
18	Pascal Wehrlein	23	1m 35.959s
19	Carlos Sainz	16	1m 36.079s
20	Kimi Räikkönen	6	1m 42.333s

PRACTICE 2 (FRIDAY)
Weather: Dry/dark
Temperatures: track 31–37°C, air 30–36°C

Pos.	Driver	Laps	Time
1	Sebastian Vettel	29	1m 31.310s
2	Valtteri Bottas	35	1m 31.351s
3	Daniel Ricciardo	28	1m 31.376s
4	Kimi Räikkönen	34	1m 31.478s
5	Lewis Hamilton	35	1m 31.594s
6	Nico Hülkenberg	37	1m 31.883s
7	Felipe Massa	37	1m 32.079s
8	Max Verstappen	18	1m 32.245s
9	Romain Grosjean	34	1m 32.505s
10	Daniil Kvyat	35	1m 32.707s
11	Kevin Magnussen	33	1m 32.854s
12	Esteban Ocon	38	1m 32.875s
13	Jolyon Palmer	38	1m 32.876s
14	Fernando Alonso	31	1m 32.897s
15	Sergio Pérez	34	1m 33.319s
16	Lance Stroll	36	1m 33.361s
17	Marcus Ericsson	34	1m 33.944s
18	Carlos Sainz	5	1m 34.072s
19	Pascal Wehrlein	29	1m 34.117s
20	Stoffel Vandoorne	8	1m 34.230s

PRACTICE 3 (SATURDAY)
Weather: Dry/sunny
Temperatures: track 37–40°C, air 34–35°C

Pos.	Driver	Laps	Time
1	Max Verstappen	8	1m 32.194s
2	Lewis Hamilton	10	1m 32.304s
3	Sebastian Vettel	10	1m 32.750s
4	Valtteri Bottas	13	1m 32.754s
5	Kimi Räikkönen	9	1m 32.785s
6	Felipe Massa	12	1m 32.801s
7	Daniel Ricciardo	8	1m 32.809s
8	Nico Hülkenberg	9	1m 32.933s
9	Carlos Sainz	18	1m 33.604s
10	Daniil Kvyat	11	1m 33.744s
11	Sergio Pérez	14	1m 33.916s
12	Fernando Alonso	10	1m 33.922s
13	Pascal Wehrlein	15	1m 33.947s
14	Lance Stroll	15	1m 33.965s
15	Stoffel Vandoorne	15	1m 34.027s
16	Esteban Ocon	17	1m 34.064s
17	Kevin Magnussen	13	1m 34.198s
18	Romain Grosjean	14	1m 34.205s
19	Marcus Ericsson	15	1m 34.268s
20	Jolyon Palmer	11	1m 34.417s

QUALIFYING (SATURDAY)
Weather: Dry/dark Temperatures: track 34°C, air 29–33°C

Pos.	Driver	First	Second	Third	Qualifying Tyre
1	Valtteri Bottas	1m 31.041s	1m 29.555s	1m 28.769s	Supersoft (new)
2	Lewis Hamilton	1m 30.814s	1m 29.535s	1m 28.792s	Supersoft (new)
3	Sebastian Vettel	1m 31.037s	1m 29.596s	1m 29.247s	Supersoft (new)
4	Daniel Ricciardo	1m 31.667s	1m 30.497s	1m 29.545s	Supersoft (new)
5	Kimi Räikkönen	1m 30.988s	1m 29.843s	1m 29.567s	Supersoft (new)
6	Max Verstappen	1m 30.904s	1m 30.307s	1m 29.687s	Supersoft (new)
7	Nico Hülkenberg	1m 31.057s	1m 30.169s	1m 29.842s	Supersoft (new)
8	Felipe Massa	1m 31.373s	1m 30.677s	1m 30.074s	Supersoft (new)
9	Romain Grosjean	1m 31.691s	1m 30.857s	1m 30.763s	Supersoft (new)
10	Jolyon Palmer	1m 31.458s	1m 30.899s	1m 31.074s	Supersoft (new)
11	Daniil Kvyat	1m 31.531s	1m 30.923s		
12	Lance Stroll	1m 31.748s	1m 31.168s		
13	Pascal Wehrlein	1m 31.995s	1m 31.414s		
14	Esteban Ocon	1m 31.774s	1m 31.684s		
15	Fernando Alonso	1m 32.054s	no time		
16	Carlos Sainz	1m 32.118s			
17	Stoffel Vandoorne	1m 32.313s			
18	Sergio Pérez	1m 32.318s			
19	Marcus Ericsson	1m 32.543s			
20	Kevin Magnussen	1m 32.900s			

QUALIFYING: head to head

Hamilton	2	1	Bottas
Vettel	3	0	Räikkönen
Massa	3	0	Stroll
Ricciardo	2	1	Verstappen
Pérez	2	1	Ocon
Hülkenberg	3	0	Palmer
Kvyat	2	1	Sainz
Ericsson	2	0	Giovinazzi
Ericsson	0	1	Wehrlein
Alonso	3	0	Vandoorne
Grosjean	2	1	Magnussen

FOR THE RECORD

DID YOU KNOW?

This was the 50th grid 1-2 for Mercedes as a constructor.

POINTS

DRIVERS

1	Sebastian Vettel	68
2	Lewis Hamilton	61
3	Valtteri Bottas	38
4	Kimi Räikkönen	34
5	Max Verstappen	25
6	Daniel Ricciardo	22
7	Felipe Massa	16
8	Sergio Pérez	14
9	Carlos Sainz	10
10	Romain Grosjean	4
11	Kevin Magnussen	4
12	Esteban Ocon	3
13	Nico Hülkenberg	2
14	Daniil Kvyat	2

CONSTRUCTORS

1	Ferrari	102
2	Mercedes	99
3	Red Bull	47
4	Force India	17
5	Williams	16
6	Toro Rosso	12
7	Haas	8
8	Renault	2

9 · GROSJEAN · Haas

7 · HÜLKENBERG · Renault

5 · RÄIKKÖNEN · Ferrari

3 · VETTEL · Ferrari

1 · BOTTAS · Mercedes

10 · PALMER · Renault

8 · MASSA · Williams

6 · VERSTAPPEN · Red Bull

4 · RICCIARDO · Red Bull

2 · HAMILTON · Mercedes

47	48	49	50	51	52	53	54	55	56	57	
5	5	5	5	5	5	5	5	5	5	5	1
44	44	44	44	44	44	44	44	44	44	44	2
77	77	77	77	77	77	77	77	77	77	77	3
7	7	7	7	7	7	7	7	7	7	7	4
3	3	3	3	3	3	3	3	3	3	3	5
19	19	19	19	19	19	19	19	19	19	19	6
11	11	11	11	11	11	11	11	11	11	11	7
8	8	8	8	8	8	8	8	8	8	8	8
27	27	27	27	27	27	27	27	27	27	27	9
31	31	31	31	31	31	31	31	31	31	31	10
94	94	94	94	94	94	94	94	94	94		
14	14	14	14	14	14	14	26	26	26		
26	26	26	26	26	26	26	30	30	30		
9	9	9	9	30	30	30	14				
30	30	30	30								

5 = Pit stop   30 One lap or more behind

■ Safety car deployed on laps shown

RACE TYRE STRATEGIES · PIRELLI

	Driver	Race Stint 1	Race Stint 2	Race Stint 3
1	Vettel	Supersoft (u): 1–10	Supersoft (n): 11–33	Soft (u): 34–57
2	Hamilton	Supersoft (u): 1–13	Soft (n): 14–41	Soft (u): 42–57
3	Bottas	Supersoft (u): 1–13	Supersoft (n): 14–30	Soft (n): 31–57
4	Räikkönen	Supersoft (u): 1–12	Supersoft (u): 13–37	Soft (u): 38–57
5	Ricciardo	Supersoft (u): 1–13	Soft (n): 14–39	Supersoft (n): 40–57
6	Massa	Supersoft (u): 1–13	Soft (n): 14–37	Soft (n): 38–57
7	Pérez	Supersoft (u): 1–13	Supersoft (n): 14–36	Soft (n): 37–57
8	Grosjean	Supersoft (u): 1–12	Supersoft (u): 13–31	Soft (n): 32–57
9	Hülkenberg	Supersoft (u): 1–13	Soft (n): 14–36	Supersoft (u): 37–57
10	Ocon	Supersoft (n): 1–11	Supersoft (n): 12–37	Soft (n): 38–57
11	Wehrlein	Supersoft (n): 1–11	Soft (n): 12–57	
12	Kvyat	Supersoft (n): 1–13	Soft (n): 14–41	Soft (u): 42–57
13	Palmer	Supersoft (n): 1–13	Soft (n): 14–37	Supersoft (u): 38–57
14	Alonso	Supersoft (n): 1–13	Soft (n): 14–36	Supersoft (n): 37–54
	Ericsson	Soft (n): 1–33	Supersoft (n): 34–50 (dnf)	
	Sainz	Supersoft (n): 1–12 (dnf)		
	Stroll	Supersoft (n): 1–8	Soft (n): 9–12 (dnf)	
	Verstappen	Supersoft (u): 1–11 (dnf)		
	Magnussen	Supersoft (n): 1–8 (dnf)		
NS	Vandoorne			

The tyre regulations stipulate that at least two of three dry tyre specifications must be used during a dry race.
Pirelli P Zero logos are colour-coded on the tyre sidewalls: Red = Super-Soft; Yellow = Soft. (n) new (u) used

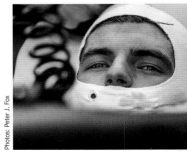

Photos: Peter J. Fox

Inset: Valtteri Bottas is congratulated by his team after his maiden grand prix victory.
Photo: Peter J. Fox

Main photo: Bottas takes his Mercedes to the chequered flag, after holding off a late charge from the Ferrari of Vettel.
Photo: Mercedes AMG Petronas

FIA FORMULA 1 WORLD CHAMPIONSHIP · ROUND 4

RUSSIAN GRAND PRIX

SOCHI CIRCUIT

SOCHI QUALIFYING

FOR the first time since the French GP at Magny-Cours in 2008, Ferrari locked out the front row of a grand prix grid and brought to an end a run of 30 races (since the anomaly of Singapore in 2015) when Mercedes had started on the front row.

The three-pointed star had arrived in Sochi having led every lap of every Russian GP since the event's inauguration in 2014. But Ferrari's race pace from FP2 on Friday looked mighty impressive, as did single-lap speed, Sebastian Vettel being 0.67s quicker than the faster Mercedes.

The Sochi Autodrom surface has always been easy on tyres, with precious little degradation. That, together with the layout, makes it a challenge to get the front tyres into their required temperature window for a qualifying lap while keeping the rears alive, and large chunks of practice sessions were spent experimenting with out-laps and multi-lap runs to find the best way of doing so.

Mercedes worked hard overnight to reduce the deficit to Ferrari, and in the final session of free practice on Saturday morning had narrowed the gap. Vettel still topped the session, but Valtteri Bottas, who was quicker than Lewis Hamilton in every session, was within three-tenths. And the suspicion that Mercedes was still able to find more than Ferrari through Q3 engine modes led you to believe that there could still be a keenly fought pole-position battle. And so it was.

After Bottas headed Q1 (which Ferrari, alone, completed on Pirelli's supersoft, rather than ultrasoft compound) and Q2, Kimi Räikkönen (1m 33.253s) set the pace on the first Q3 runs. Vettel pipped him by six-hundredths on the second run and then had to sit it out to see whether his team-mate or either of the Mercs could displace him.

The answer was no. Räikkönen lost the rear end in the final sector of the lap and failed to improve, and all eyes switched to the Mercs. Bottas, who had qualified third for Williams on each of the previous three visits to Sochi, surely fancied his chances of a front-row start here, but it was not to be and he couldn't quite match his Q2 time, ultimately ending up three-hundredths shy of Räikkönen.

Hamilton, meanwhile, was right on the pace in the first two sectors, but ran wide at Turn 15 and dropped half a second in the final sector. Never really happy with his car's balance, the three-times champion was left to contemplate a tricky Sunday afternoon, starting from the slippery side of the grid behind both Ferraris and his team-mate.

Behind Ferrari and Mercedes was a bit of a chasm, with Daniel Ricciardo's fifth-placed Red Bull more than 1.7s from the pole. The team had anticipated Sochi being somewhat challenging, given the track's power dependency (the fourth most power-sensitive venue on the calendar), and fifth was actually the team's best grid slot at the Russian track.

Team-mate Max Verstappen had appeared quicker for much of qualifying, but ran out of tyres in the final sector and was a quarter of a second adrift of his team-mate, the pair split by Felipe Massa's Williams.

Behind the Brazilian, Nico Hülkenberg maintained his strong qualifying form and put the works Renault eighth on the grid, just 0.38s shy of Ricciardo's pace. The team's Achilles heel at the previous races had been race pace, the suggestion being that the car's ability to rapidly switch on the tyres for single-lap pace hurt its tyre usage over a race stint. 'The Hulk' reckoned it was a bit more complex than that, though, and was hopeful that progress had been made at the post-Bahrain test.

The Force Indias completed the top ten qualifiers, both being in the top ten for the first time in 2017. Sergio Pérez was five-hundredths adrift of his former team-mate and seven-hundredths clear of Esteban Ocon in the second pink machine. The Mexican felt he'd left something on the table and had the potential to be a slot or two higher, while the Frenchman was satisfied with his first career Q3 appearance.

Both Toro Rosso drivers were struggling for grip throughout most of qualifying, with Carlos Sainz also laughing out loud at the FIA's statement that engine convergence had been achieved, by which they meant three of the four engine suppliers being within 0.3s of each other. The Spaniard was 11th quickest, but also had to accept a three-place grid penalty for his collision with Lance Stroll in Bahrain.

Stroll himself split the Toro Rossos, with just two-hundredths covering all three cars, with only another five-hundredths to Kevin Magnussen's Haas emphasising once again the tightness of the midfield scrap.

Fernando Alonso, as usual, drove the wheels off the McLaren Honda, but could do no better than 15th. Team-mate Stoffel Vandoorne once again joined the Saubers as Q1 victims, along with Jolyon Palmer and Romain Grosjean. Palmer's miserable beginning to 2017 continued when he lost FP3 to an engine change and then, looking more competitive, just hooked a kerb and put the car into the wall.

Grosjean, meanwhile, suffered something of a nightmare. Haas were using Carbone Industrie brakes for the first time in 2017, following the Bahrain test, but after a less-than-conclusive Friday went back to Brembo for the rest of the weekend. Grosjean just could not get the car to his liking and then, when on a decent lap in Q1, was caught out by the yellows for Palmer's accident – the third time in four races that it had happened to the team.

Above: The Liberty triumvirate of Sean Bratches, Chase Carey and Ross Brawn.
Photo: WRi2/Studio Colombo

Right: Jolyon Palmer suffered another weekend to forget.
Photo: WRi2/Jean-François Galeron

Far right: Sebastian Vettel took pole position, but despite a late rally, he could not quite overhaul Valtteri Bottas at the finish.
Photo: Scuderia Ferrari

Below: Fernando Alonso brilliantly put the McLaren Honda into Q2, but failed to make the start.
Photo: McLaren Honda

Below right: Red Bull's Max Verstappen ready for action.
Photo: Red Bull Racing/Getty Images

Bottom: Kimi Räikkönen, as inscrutable as ever behind his shades.
Photo: Peter J. Fox

FERRARI'S qualifying speed, allied to great pace and strong consistency on Pirelli's softest ultrasoft compound over the long runs during Friday practice, suggested that Mercedes was going to have its work cut out maintaining that 100 per cent Sochi record. And precious little tyre degradation added up to what was expected to be an exclusively one-stop race, limiting strategic options.

Actually, though, qualifying P3, 0.03s behind Kimi Räikkönen, but on the clean side of the grid, proved to be a cloud with a silver lining for Valtteri Bottas after the original start had to be aborted due to Alonso's McLaren Honda suffering yet more reliability woe on the formation lap. Sochi, along with Mexico, has an abnormally long run to the first corner, around 800m, which represents around ten seconds of full-throttle running when the starting lights extinguish before drivers go hard on the brakes for Turn Two (Turn One being a flat-out right-hand kink). That affords the opportunity to pick up a tow, which, if done optimally, translates into an 8–9m advantage by the Turn Two braking area.

Bottas had his mind focused on exactly that and executed it perfectly as he made a marginally better getaway than pole-man Sebastian Vettel, drafted alongside and then was able to cut across in front of the Ferrari and close the door into Turn Two to lead. Hamilton, despite starting in P4, on the dirty side of the grid, also made a strong getaway.

"I went left to get in the tow of the car in front," he explained. "Kimi got a tow from the two cars ahead, I got a tow from Valtteri, but then Seb pulled in behind him, so I couldn't brake and overtake and had to settle for fourth into Turn Two."

After difficult heavy-fuel opening stints for Bottas on the softest Pirellis in both Australia and Bahrain, it was soon evident that the Sochi script was very different as he immediately started to open out a gap to Vettel's pursuing Ferrari, increasing his lead by an average 0.3s per lap over the first 15 laps of the 52-lap race. On the evidence of Friday afternoon's long runs, that was a big surprise.

Part of the explanation proved just how intense was F1's battle between Mercedes and Ferrari. Both teams had pushed cooling to the absolute limit in search of ultimate engine performance. Opening up an extra 'cooling package' (or bodywork slot) created additional aerodynamic drag, costing an estimated 0.1s per lap, which translated to more than 5s of performance over a race distance.

Prior to qualifying, Ferrari had anticipated being able to qualify at the front and run in free air, so had gone marginal on the cooling. Mercedes, hoping to be able to overcome Maranello for single-lap pace and knowing that Sochi, along with Mexico (which also has a long run to the first corner), afforded a real opportunity to overhaul the front-row men from P3, had done likewise. On race day, though, the ambient was around five degrees higher than forecast, making cooling even more marginal.

An opening-lap safety car, following contact between Jolyon Palmer and Romain Grosjean that eliminated both, sent engine temperatures climbing as the field ran slowly behind the official Mercedes. Suspicions that the temperature situation was marginal came at the restart after four laps. Bottas's was as well-judged as his race start, but the fact that he did not come under more pressure from Vettel was likely due to Ferrari's need to control engine temperatures at a time when they wanted to be as close as possible, rather than the four-times champion being half asleep.

The two Saubers and Vandoorne, meanwhile, had started on the supersoft tyre and took the opportunity to get them out of the way and go on to the ultrasoft under the safety car, while Ricciardo was out. The Australian had lost places to team-mate Verstappen and Massa on the opening lap, and then found his rear brakes alight after the safety car laps – one to forget for Daniel, his retirement promoting the Force Indias of Pérez and Ocon. Further back, Stroll had spun to the rear trying to avoid Hülkenberg in Turn Four.

Two factors were at work in an impressive opening stint from Bottas: firstly, his Mercedes W08 feeling better "connected" front and rear on the ultrasoft tyre than at any point hitherto during the weekend and, second, Ferrari telling Vettel to allow a gap in the interests of engine cooling, possibly in the belief that they had the pace to close it down again as pit-stop time approached.

However, when Vettel upped his pace by around half a second with his fastest lap of the race to that point on lap 16 (1m 38.629s), Bottas was able to respond. He drove an amazingly consistent sequence of four laps (1:38.40, 1:38.40, 1:38.35, 1:38.37) that increased his lead to more than 5.5s. For the first time, those anticipating a Ferrari whitewash post-qualifying began to have second thoughts.

The lack of tyre degradation in Sochi meant that an early pit stop and undercut was not the normal powerful tool. That, plus the need to clear traffic and the feeling that the Mercedes W08 was better suited to the ultrasoft than the supersoft Pirelli in Russia, was the explanation behind Mercedes leaving Bottas out until half-distance on the ultra. A slick 2.5s stop allowed him to blast back into the fray just over 20s behind Vettel's now-leading Ferrari, with around 25–26s the necessary pit window.

Realising that there was little point in mirroring the Mercedes strategy, Ferrari left Vettel out for a further seven laps to have a fresher set of supersofts with which to attack in the closing stages. If Bottas was to break his F1 duck, he was going to have to earn it.

Vettel pitted with 18 laps remaining and rejoined 4.6s behind the leading Mercedes. On the red-walled Pirelli, he immediately began to cut into Bottas's margin, the gap coming down to 4.33s and then 4.04s on consecutive laps. Trying to respond, Bottas locked up and flat-spotted his left-front tyre at Turn 13 on lap 38, costing himself just over a second. Vettel was now within 3s and there were still 14 laps to go…

Over the next four laps, the race leader's pace dropped by half to three-quarters of a second and suddenly the chasing Ferrari was just 1.4s behind, dangerously close to

DRS range. With his first grand prix win so tantalisingly close, Bottas was now under the most intense pressure. It was the acid test of his composure. Suddenly, though, the Finn was lapping quicker than before his lock-up.

"After the lock-up, I lost tyre temperature, and it takes a while to get it back again at Sochi," Valtteri explained. "That was the reason for the slower laps, and at this circuit in particular, a good rhythm is so important. Thankfully, I got that back again!"

In the dying moments of the race, Bottas also faced the challenge of negotiating back-markers without tripping up. Under new regulations, they only get the cockpit warning light when the gap is less than a second, which can make things tough in Sochi's tight final sector particularly.

Vettel had the Ferrari within DRS range with two laps remaining, and Bottas hit the 'overtake' button a little earlier on the main straight to defend. In a nail-biting finish to a superb race, a delighted Valterri took the chequered flag to win his first GP, just 0.61s in front of Vettel.

"Thanks guys, amazing!" came over the team radio. "It's been a while coming, more than 80 races for me, but worth the wait!" Bottas is not renowned for outward displays of emotion, but he did seem to keep his crash helmet on a mite longer than usual. And, standing on the top step of the podium, listening to the Finnish national anthem was, he admitted, "a very special moment."

When he arrived at the post-race press conference, Bottas was greeted by a spontaneous round of applause from the world's F1 media.

"Thanks guys," he said, with a wry smile. "It's all a little bit surreal: my first win and hopefully the first of many. It was definitely one of my best ever races. I always trusted in my

Left: Valtteri Bottas takes control of the race from the Ferraris of Vettel and Räikkönen.

Below: A rare weekend to forget. Curiously, Lewis Hamilton was off the pace at Sochi; nonetheless, he stayed within reach of championship leader Vettel.

Photos: Peter J. Fox

Above: Kimi Räikkönen lacked the pace to catch team-mate Vettel, but he took third, comfortably clear of fourth-placed Hamilton.
Photo: Scuderia Ferrari

Top right: Esteban Ocon continued his impressive progress with his best race of the season so far, taking seventh, just behind team-mate Pérez.
Photo: Peter J. Fox

Above right: Max Verstappen had a lonely run to fifth.
Photo: Red Bull Racing/Getty Images

Right: A break-through victory for the popular Valtteri Bottas, who outshone team-mate Hamilton throughout the Sochi weekend.
Photo: Mercedes AMG Petronas F1 Team

ability, but it's nice to have confirmation. The pressure at the end was okay, and the main thing was the lapped cars. With these new cars, we definitely lose more downforce when we are within two or three seconds, so it was tricky to get close and pass them without losing time. I did ask for a bit more radio silence from the guys on the pit wall so I could get on with it and focus. It went quite nice and quiet, and that helped!"

Unsaid was the suspicion that Ferrari had been able to follow cars closer than Mercedes with less aerodynamic interference, making Valtteri's task in those closing laps tougher still.

Hamilton had not been a threat, his problematic weekend continuing as he took the flag a whopping 25s down on Räikkönen's third-placed Ferrari.

"I can't really explain it," Lewis admitted. "I have some ideas, but there's lots of work to be done. In the race, the car was exactly the same as in qualifying, with snaps of oversteer in sector three. And I had overheating. From lap five onwards, I had to slow down and turn down the settings and power unit. One of the cylinders was cutting because of the temperature issues, so I was going to be fourth from very early on.

"In terms of set-up, there was not a huge difference to Valtteri: a bit of difference in low- and medium-speed corners, where I struggled, and a little bit of difference on the differential. The direction he was able to go, I wasn't able to go, and I don't really understand why, because our driving styles are quite similar."

Despite his own disappointment on a day when, unusually, he had never been a factor, Hamilton was one of the first to

congratulate his team-mate on his first grand prix win. Vettel, too, was magnanimous: "Today is Valtteri's day. He drove a fantastic race, he had incredible pace, did a superb job. He deserves to win because he drove better than the rest of us. So... it's not easy to swallow."

While nothing should detract from a perfectly executed drive by Bottas, the willingness of Mercedes to push the boundaries on cooling was a contributory factor. After Friday's initial indications, this win was one that went against the head.

Underlining just how much of a two-horse race the 2017 world championship currently appeared, Verstappen brought his Red Bull home fifth, a full minute behind the winning Mercedes, the team having instructed him to wind his brake balance forward after Ricciardo's rear brake fire.

Max himself had the luxury of a 26s advantage over Pérez's Force India, with the impressive Ocon scoring points for the fourth successive race, some 8s behind his team-mate. Hülkenberg, just a second behind the second pink machine at the flag, was the last unlapped runner, with Massa and Sainz claiming the final two point-scoring positions. Stroll, meanwhile, was still searching for his first F1 point, having recovered to finish just 5s adrift of the Spaniard after his early spin.

Leaving Russia, in the drivers' championship, Vettel led with 86 points to Hamilton's 73, with F1's new first-time winner ten points behind his Mercedes team-mate. In the constructors' championship, Mercedes was now back on top, by the tightest or margins, 136 points to 135. It was roll on Barcelona.

Tony Dodgins

VIEWPOINT
LAYING DOWN A MARKER

THREE different winners in four races. But the statistic that really stood out was Valtteri Bottas claiming his first victory. It's not so much that it took the Finn 81 races to get to the top of the podium, but more the manner in which he did it.

This win was not handed to him; he really had to work for it, soaking up enormous pressure as Sebastian Vettel chased the Mercedes to the line. He also had to deal with damaged front tyres.

Having come so far without a victory, Bottas knew those final 15 laps could make or break his reputation. Do the business, and he would be the next Mika Häkkinen. Fail, and he would become the next Heikki Kovalainen: nice guy, quick – but not a consistent winner. This was pressure that went beyond the red blur growing large in his mirrors.

Given the intricate detail (*see race report*) needed to keep the Mercedes cool, Bottas had been able to run in clear air. He got to the front with a very impressive first lap, using a tow from Vettel's pole-position Ferrari to swoop into the lead on the very long run to the first braking zone. The next question was: how would he deal with back-markers?

That was the impressive part of Bottas's drive. His win depended on much more than beating Hamilton. He had to cope with Ferraris that were the favourites to win. And Vettel's final set of tyres were seven laps fresher than the damaged Pirellis on his car.

The timing of this could not have been better, since Bottas had always gone well at Sochi. Not only did he qualify 0.478s ahead of Hamilton, but also his race was world class.

Bottas came into the weekend facing questions about whether Mercedes needed to make him an unofficial number two to help Hamilton deal with the increasing threat from Ferrari. He finished it having laid down a marker that said Hamilton had a challenge from within his own team that was every bit as strong as the exciting return to form by Ferrari.

Valtteri Bottas had officially become a serious player.

Maurice Hamilton

4

2017 FORMULA 1
VTB
RUSSIAN GRAND PRIX

SOCHI 28–30 APRIL

ROLEX

OFFICIAL TIMEPIECE

RACE DISTANCE: 52 laps, 188.956 miles/303.897km

RACE WEATHER: Dry/sunny (track 39–42°C, air 25–27°C)

SOCHI OLYMPIC PARK CIRCUIT, KRASNODAR KRAI

Circuit: 3.633 / 5.848km miles
53 laps

— DRS zone

All results and data © FOM 2017

RACE – OFFICIAL CLASSIFICATION

Pos.	Driver	Nat.	No.	Entrant	Car/Engine	Laps	Time/Retirement	Speed (mph/km/h)	Gap to leader	Fastest race lap	
1	**Valtteri Bottas**	FIN	77	Mercedes AMG Petronas Motorsport	Mercedes F1 W08-Mercedes M08 EQ Power+ V6	52	1h 28m 08.743s	128.536/206.859		1m 37.367s	49
2	**Sebastian Vettel**	D	5	Scuderia Ferrari	Ferrari SF70H-062 V6	52	1h 28m 09.360s	128.521/206.835	0.617s	1m 37.312s	49
3	**Kimi Räikkönen**	FIN	7	Scuderia Ferrari	Ferrari SF70H-062 V6	52	1h 28m 19.743s	128.270/206.430	11.000s	1m 36.844s	49
4	**Lewis Hamilton**	GB	44	Mercedes AMG Petronas Motorsport	Mercedes F1 W08-Mercedes M08 EQ Power+ V6	52	1h 28m 45.063s	127.660/205.449	36.320s	1m 38.398s	18
5	**Max Verstappen**	NL	33	Red Bull Racing	Red Bull RB13-TAG Heuer RB13 V6	52	1h 29m 09.159s	127.085/204.523	1m 00.416s	1m 38.429s	47
6	**Sergio Pérez**	MEX	11	Sahara Force India Formula 1 Team	Force India VJM10-Mercedes M08 EQ Power+ V6	52	1h 29m 35.531s	126.461/203.520	1m 26.788s	1m 38.661s	51
7	**Esteban Ocon**	F	31	Sahara Force India Formula 1 Team	Force India VJM10-Mercedes M08 EQ Power+ V6	52	1h 29m 43.747s	126.268/203.209	1m 35.004s	1m 38.745s	50
8	**Nico Hülkenberg**	D	27	Renault Sport Formula One Team	Renault R.S.17-R.E.17 V6	52	1h 29m 44.931s	126.240/203.164	1m 36.188s	1m 38.418s	52
9	**Felipe Massa**	BR	19	Williams Martini Racing	Williams FW40-Mercedes M08 EQ Power+ V6	51			1 lap	1m 38.232s	45
10	**Carlos Sainz**	E	55	Scuderia Toro Rosso	Toro Rosso STR12-Renault R.E.17 V6	51			1 lap	1m 38.858s	51
11	Lance Stroll	CDN	18	Williams Martini Racing	Williams FW40-Mercedes M08 EQ Power+ V6	51			1 lap	1m 38.870s	50
12	Daniil Kvyat	RUS	26	Scuderia Toro Rosso	Toro Rosso STR12-Renault R.E.17 V6	51			1 lap	1m 38.300s	50
13	Kevin Magnussen	DK	20	Haas F1 Team	Haas VF-17-Ferrari 062 V6	51			1 lap	1m 39.566s	40
14	Stoffel Vandoorne	B	2	McLaren Honda Formula 1 Team	McLaren MCL32-Honda RA617H V6	51			1 lap	1m 39.790s	47
15	Marcus Ericsson	S	9	Sauber F1 Team	Sauber C36-Ferrari 059/5 V6	51			1 lap	1m 39.835s	48
16	Pascal Wehrlein	D	94	Sauber F1 Team	Sauber C36-Ferrari 059/5 V6	50			2 laps	1m 40.922s	37
	Daniel Ricciardo	AUS	3	Red Bull Racing	Red Bull RB13-TAG Heuer RB13 V6	5	brakes			1m 42.285s	4
	Jolyon Palmer	GB	30	Renault Sport Formula One Team	Renault R.S.17-R.E.17 V6	0	accident			no time	
	Romain Grosjean	F	8	Haas F1 Team	Haas VF-17-Ferrari 062 V6	0	accident			no time	
NS	Fernando Alonso	E	14	McLaren Honda Formula 1 Team	McLaren MCL32-Honda RA617H V6		ERS software on the parade lap			no time	

Race scheduled for 53 laps, but reduced by a lap due to Alonso stopping on the track during the parade lap.

Fastest race lap: Kimi Räikkönen on lap 49, 1m 36.844s, 135.079mph/217.388km/h (new record).

Previous lap record: Nico Rosberg (Mercedes-Benz F1 W07 V6 turbo), 1m 39.094s, 132.012mph/212.452km/h (2016).

19 · GROSJEAN · Haas   17 · WEHRLEIN · Sauber   15 · ALONSO · McLaren   13 · MAGNUSSEN · Haas   11 · STROLL · Williams

20 · VANDOORNE · McLaren
15-place grid penalty for using additional power unit elements

18 · ERICSSON · Sauber

16 · PALMER · Renault

14 · SAINZ · Toro Rosso
3-place grid penalty for causing accident in round 3

12 · KVYAT · Toro Rosso

Grid order	1	2	3	4	5	6	7	8	9	10	11	12	13	14	15	16	17	18	19	20	21	22	23	24	25	26	27	28	29	30	31	32	33	34	35	36	37	38	39	40	41	42
5 VETTEL	77	77	77	77	77	77	77	77	77	77	77	77	77	77	77	77	77	77	77	77	77	77	77	77	77	77	5	5	5	5	5	5	5	77	77	77	77	77	77	77	77	77
7 RÄIKKÖNEN	5	5	5	5	5	5	5	5	5	5	5	5	5	5	5	5	5	5	5	5	5	5	5	5	5	5	77	7	44	77	77	77	77	5	5	5	5	5	5	5	5	5
77 BOTTAS	7	7	7	7	7	7	7	7	7	7	7	7	7	7	7	7	7	7	7	7	7	7	7	7	7	7	44	44	77	7	7	7	7	7	7	7	7	7	7	7	7	7
44 HAMILTON	44	44	44	44	44	44	44	44	44	44	44	44	44	44	44	44	44	44	44	44	44	44	44	44	44	44	7	77	7	44	44	44	44	44	44	44	44	44	44	44	44	44
3 RICCIARDO	33	33	33	33	33	33	33	33	33	33	33	33	33	33	33	33	33	33	33	33	33	33	33	33	33	33	33	33	33	33	33	33	33	33	33	33	33	33	33	33	33	33
19 MASSA	19	19	19	19	19	19	19	19	19	19	19	19	19	19	19	19	19	19	19	19	11	11	11	11	11	11	11	27	27	27	27	27	27	27	27	27	27	27	27	27	19	11
33 VERSTAPPEN	3	3	3	3	11	11	11	11	11	11	11	11	11	11	11	11	11	11	11	11	19	31	31	31	31	27	27	19	19	19	19	19	19	19	19	19	19	19	19	19	11	31
27 HÜLKENBERG	11	11	11	11	31	31	31	31	31	31	31	31	31	31	31	31	31	31	31	27	27	27	27	31	19	11	11	11	11	11	11	11	11	11	11	11	11	11	11	11	31	27
11 PÉREZ	31	31	31	31	27	27	27	27	27	27	27	27	27	27	27	27	27	27	27	31	55	55	19	19	31	31	31	31	31	31	31	31	31	31	31	31	31	31	31	31	27	19
31 OCON	27	27	27	27	20	20	20	20	20	20	20	20	20	20	20	20	20	20	20	20	55	19	19	55	18	18	55	55	55	55	55	55	55	55	55	55	55	55	55	55	55	55
18 STROLL	20	20	20	20	55	55	55	55	55	55	55	55	55	55	55	55	55	55	55	55	20	18	18	18	55	55	18	18	18	18	18	18	18	18	18	18	18	18	18	18	18	18
26 KVYAT	55	55	55	55	26	26	26	26	26	26	26	26	26	26	26	26	26	26	26	18	2	2	2	26	26	26	26	26	26	26	26	26	26	26	26	26	26	26	26	26	26	26
20 MAGNUSSEN	26	26	26	26	18	18	18	18	18	18	18	18	18	18	18	18	18	18	18	26	26	26	26	20	20	20	20	20	20	20	20	20	20	20	20	20	20	20	20	20	20	20
55 SAINZ	94	18	18	18	2	2	2	2	2	2	2	2	2	2	2	2	2	2	2	20	20	20	20	2	2	2	2	2	2	2	2	2	2	2	2	2	2	2	2	2	2	2
14 ALONSO	18	2	2	2	94	94	94	94	94	94	94	94	94	94	94	94	94	94	94	2	9	9	9	9	9	9	9	9	9	9	9	9	9	9	9	9	9	9	9	9	9	9
30 PALMER	2	9	9	9	9	9	9	9	9	9	9	9	9	9	9	9	9	9	9	94	94	94	94	94	94	94	94	94	94	94	94	94	94	94	94	94	94	94	94	94	94	94
94 WEHRLEIN	9	94	94	94	3																																					
9 ERICSSON																																										
8 GROSJEAN																																										
2 VANDOORNE																																										

TIME SHEETS

PRACTICE 1 (FRIDAY)
Weather: Dry/sunny
Temperatures: track 34–37°C, air 19–22°C

Pos.	Driver	Laps	Time
1	Kimi Räikkönen	19	1m 36.074s
2	Valtteri Bottas	24	1m 36.119s
3	Lewis Hamilton	23	1m 36.681s
4	Max Verstappen	19	1m 37.174s
5	Sebastian Vettel	19	1m 37.230s
6	Daniel Ricciardo	19	1m 37.290s
7	Sergio Pérez	29	1m 37.457s
8	Felipe Massa	29	1m 37.900s
9	Lance Stroll	30	1m 37.944s
10	Esteban Ocon	28	1m 38.065s
11	Daniil Kvyat	17	1m 38.496s
12	Kevin Magnussen	23	1m 38.747s
13	Fernando Alonso	16	1m 38.813s
14	Carlos Sainz	17	1m 38.976s
15	Jolyon Palmer	16	1m 39.158s
16	Romain Grosjean	17	1m 39.533s
17	Stoffel Vandoorne	19	1m 39.541s
18	Pascal Wehrlein	21	1m 39.731s
19	Marcus Ericsson	20	1m 40.079s
20	Sergey Sirotkin	2	no time

PRACTICE 2 (FRIDAY)
Weather: Dry/sunny
Temperatures: track 34–40°C, air 21–23°C

Pos.	Driver	Laps	Time
1	Sebastian Vettel	36	1m 34.120s
2	Kimi Räikkönen	36	1m 34.383s
3	Valtteri Bottas	36	1m 34.790s
4	Lewis Hamilton	34	1m 34.829s
5	Max Verstappen	15	1m 35.540s
6	Daniel Ricciardo	26	1m 35.910s
7	Felipe Massa	39	1m 36.261s
8	Nico Hülkenberg	38	1m 36.329s
9	Kevin Magnussen	31	1m 36.506s
10	Sergio Pérez	38	1m 36.600s
11	Esteban Ocon	39	1m 36.654s
12	Fernando Alonso	27	1m 36.765s
13	Jolyon Palmer	22	1m 36.771s
14	Romain Grosjean	31	1m 37.039s
15	Carlos Sainz	36	1m 37.083s
16	Stoffel Vandoorne	25	1m 37.125s
17	Daniil Kvyat	35	1m 37.300s
18	Pascal Wehrlein	30	1m 37.441s
19	Lance Stroll	36	1m 37.747s
20	Marcus Ericsson	29	1m 37.819s

PRACTICE 3 (SATURDAY)
Weather: Dry/sunny
Temperatures: track 33°C, air 19°C

Pos.	Driver	Laps	Time
1	Sebastian Vettel	17	1m 34.001s
2	Kimi Räikkönen	16	1m 34.338s
3	Valtteri Bottas	20	1m 34.364s
4	Lewis Hamilton	19	1m 34.542s
5	Max Verstappen	21	1m 35.452s
6	Felipe Massa	17	1m 35.471s
7	Nico Hülkenberg	15	1m 35.662s
8	Daniel Ricciardo	24	1m 35.830s
9	Carlos Sainz	20	1m 36.164s
10	Kevin Magnussen	19	1m 36.556s
11	Lance Stroll	19	1m 36.649s
12	Esteban Ocon	22	1m 36.676s
13	Daniil Kvyat	18	1m 36.846s
14	Fernando Alonso	12	1m 36.869s
15	Sergio Pérez	21	1m 36.962s
16	Romain Grosjean	20	1m 37.164s
17	Stoffel Vandoorne	15	1m 37.182s
18	Marcus Ericsson	21	1m 37.503s
19	Pascal Wehrlein	17	1m 37.657s
20	Jolyon Palmer	4	no time

QUALIFYING (SATURDAY)
Weather: Dry/sunny Temperatures: track 39–41°C, air 22–25°C

Pos.	Driver	First	Second	Third	Qualifying Tyre
1	Sebastian Vettel	1m 34.493s	1m 34.038s	1m 33.194s	Ultrasoft (new)
2	Kimi Räikkönen	1m 34.953s	1m 33.663s	1m 33.289s	Ultrasoft (new)
3	Valtteri Bottas	1m 34.041s	1m 33.264s	1m 33.289s	Ultrasoft (new)
4	Lewis Hamilton	1m 34.409s	1m 33.760s	1m 33.767s	Ultrasoft (new)
5	Daniel Ricciardo	1m 35.560s	1m 35.483s	1m 34.905s	Ultrasoft (new)
6	Felipe Massa	1m 35.828s	1m 35.049s	1m 35.110s	Ultrasoft (new)
7	Max Verstappen	1m 35.301s	1m 35.221s	1m 35.161s	Ultrasoft (new)
8	Nico Hülkenberg	1m 35.507s	1m 35.328s	1m 35.285s	Ultrasoft (new)
9	Sergio Pérez	1m 36.185s	1m 35.513s	1m 35.337s	Ultrasoft (new)
10	Esteban Ocon	1m 35.372s	1m 35.729s	1m 35.430s	Ultrasoft (new)
11	Carlos Sainz	1m 35.827s	1m 35.948s		
12	Lance Stroll	1m 36.279s	1m 35.964s		
13	Daniil Kvyat	1m 35.984s	1m 35.968s		
14	Kevin Magnussen	1m 36.408s	1m 36.017s		
15	Fernando Alonso	1m 36.353s	1m 36.660s		
16	Jolyon Palmer	1m 36.462s			
17	Stoffel Vandoorne	1m 37.070s			
18	Pascal Wehrlein	1m 37.332s			
19	Marcus Ericsson	1m 37.507s			
20	Romain Grosjean	1m 37.620s			

QUALIFYING: head to head

Hamilton	2	2	Bottas
Vettel	4	0	Räikkönen
Massa	4	0	Stroll
Ricciardo	3	1	Verstappen
Pérez	3	1	Ocon
Hülkenberg	4	0	Palmer
Kvyat	2	2	Sainz
Ericsson	2	0	Giovinazzi
Ericsson	0	2	Wehrlein
Alonso	4	0	Vandoorne
Grosjean	2	2	Magnussen

FOR THE RECORD

1st WIN: Valtteri Bottas

50,000th KM RACED: Sebastian Vettel

90th PODIUM POSITION: Sebastian Vettel

400th PODIUM POSITION: Mercedes engine

500th PODIUM POSITION: Pirelli

DID YOU KNOW?

Bottas became the fifth Finn to win a grand prix.

This was the fourth time that two Finns had stood on the podium, the previous occasion being Hungary 2008 (Kovalainen and Räikkönen).

This was the first complete front row for Ferrari since France 2008 (Räikkönen and Massa).

POINTS

DRIVERS

1	Sebastian Vettel	86
2	Lewis Hamilton	73
3	Valtteri Bottas	63
4	Kimi Räikkönen	49
5	Max Verstappen	35
6	Daniel Ricciardo	22
7	Sergio Pérez	22
8	Felipe Massa	18
9	Carlos Sainz	11
10	Esteban Ocon	9
11	Nico Hülkenberg	6
12	Romain Grosjean	4
13	Kevin Magnussen	4
14	Daniil Kvyat	2

CONSTRUCTORS

1	Mercedes	136
2	Ferrari	135
3	Red Bull	57
4	Force India	31
5	Williams	18
6	Toro Rosso	13
7	Haas	8
8	Renault	6

9 · PÉREZ · Force India

7 · VERSTAPPEN · Red Bull

5 · RICCIARDO · Red Bull

3 · BOTTAS · Mercedes

1 · VETTEL · Ferrari

10 · OCON · Force India

8 · HÜLKENBERG · Renault

6 · MASSA · Williams

4 · HAMILTON · Mercedes

2 · RÄIKKÖNEN · Ferrari

43	44	45	46	47	48	49	50	51	52	
77	77	77	77	77	77	77	77	77	77	1
5	5	5	5	5	5	5	5	5	5	2
7	7	7	7	7	7	7	7	7	7	3
44	44	44	44	44	44	44	44	44	44	4
33	33	33	33	33	33	33	33	33	33	5
11	11	11	11	11	11	11	11	11	11	6
31	31	31	31	31	31	31	31	31	31	7
27	27	27	27	27	27	27	27	27	27	8
19	19	19	19	19	19	19	19	19	19	9
55	55	55	55	55	55	55	55	55	55	10
18	18	18	18	18	18	18	18	18	18	
26	26	26	26	26	26	26	26	26	26	
20	20	20	20	20	20	20	20	20	20	
2	2	2	2	2	2	2	2	2	2	
9	9	9	9	9	9	9	9	9	9	
94	94	94	94	94	94	94	94			

2 = Pit stop   *94 One lap or more behind*

■ Safety car deployed on laps shown

RACE TYRE STRATEGIES

	Driver	Race Stint 1	Race Stint 2	Race Stint 3
1	Bottas	Ultrasoft (u): 1-27	Supersoft (n): 28-52	
2	Vettel	Ultrasoft (u): 1-34	Supersoft (n): 35-52	
3	Räikkönen	Ultrasoft (u): 1-29	Supersoft (n): 30-52	
4	Hamilton	Ultrasoft (u): 1-30	Supersoft (n): 31-52	
5	Verstappen	Ultrasoft (u): 1-29	Supersoft (n): 30-52	
6	Pérez	Ultrasoft (u): 1-27	Supersoft (n): 28-52	
7	Ocon	Ultrasoft (u): 1-26	Supersoft (n): 27-52	
8	Hülkenberg	Ultrasoft (u): 1-40	Supersoft (n): 41-52	
9	Massa	Ultrasoft (u): 1-21	Supersoft (n): 22-41	Ultrasoft (u): 42-52
10	Sainz	Ultrasoft (u): 1-24	Supersoft (n): 25-52	
11	Stroll	Ultrasoft (u): 1-26	Supersoft (n): 27-52	
12	Kvyat	Ultrasoft (u): 1-21	Supersoft (n): 22-52	
13	Magnussen	Ultrasoft (u): 1-21	Supersoft (n): 22-52	
14	Vandoorne	Supersoft (n): 1	Ultrasoft (n): 2-24	Ultrasoft (n): 25-52
15	Ericsson	Supersoft (n): 1	Ultrasoft (n): 2-21	Ultrasoft (n): 22-52
16	Wehrlein	Supersoft (n): 1-2	Ultrasoft (n): 3-20	Ultrasoft (n): 21-52
	Ricciardo	Ultrasoft (u): 1-5 (dnf)		
	Palmer	0		
	Grosjean	0		
NS	Alonso			

The tyre regulations stipulate that at least two of three dry tyre specifications must be used during a dry race.
Pirelli P Zero logos are colour-coded on the tyre sidewalls: Purple = Ultrasoft; Red = Supersoft. (n) new (u) used

Photos: Peter J. Fox

SPANISH GRAND PRIX

CATALUNYA CIRCUIT

CATALUNYA QUALIFYING

AS ever for the first race of the European season, Barcelona was all about bargeboards, floors and wings. The work carried out by Mercedes had been the most visible, thanks to a concave vane between the front wheels and sidepods, with the minutiae of aero detail elsewhere more or less mirrored by Ferrari's view on the development path as the new formula got into its stride.

None of that was a surprise. But unexpected – and pleasantly so – was the way in which the furious pace of improvement had not given one leading team an advantage over the other. When it came to qualifying at the Circuit de Cataluña-Barcelona, a track the teams and drivers know intimately, it was all about the tiniest of mistakes making the difference between P1 and P4 on the grid. And when it mattered most, Lewis Hamilton's error was the least significant as he took another pole position.

The chicane turned out to be the final arbiter, in the sense that even the softest tyre (soft) was running out of performance, particularly if worked hard through the preceding corners as track temperatures nudged 45°C. It didn't amount to much, but that's all it took to give Hamilton pole by 0.051s from Sebastian Vettel, the Ferrari driver admitting he didn't get the chicane "right", not that you would have noticed given the incredibly small margin. More telling, perhaps, was the water leak from a fresh engine that had prompted a reversion to a tired Ferrari power unit for qualifying.

Valtteri Bottas would line up directly behind his Mercedes team-mate, the Finn's practice schedule having received a setback when a water leak and electrical problems led to the loss of track time in FP3 and, like Vettel, a switch to an engine that had already done active race duty. To add to Bottas's discomfort, the gusty wind caught him slightly during his best qualifying lap and accounted for the couple of tenths differential to Hamilton. Kimi Räikkönen, half a tenth further back, said with typical directness that he could have driven better after running wide more than once.

Work continued as Red Bull tried to unlock the pace so evidently lacking when compared to Ferrari and Mercedes. The result – revised bargeboards and front suspension, allowing an even steeper rake – brought Max Verstappen to just over half a second off pole, the Dutchman enjoying better balance even if out-and-out downforce was still lacking. Verstappen outqualified Daniel Ricciardo by a tidy three-tenths as the Australian struggled to carry speed through the final chicane, but he felt reasonably happy elsewhere on the 2.89-mile lap.

Despite the small improvement, Red Bull's performance was completely overshadowed by an astonishing seventh on the grid for Fernando Alonso. It mattered little that he was almost a second off the leading trio of teams; it was the fact that he was heading a pack of several cars covered by 0.2s. Even allowing for the positive vibes flowing from the home crowd, Alonso was making good use of extensive aero upgrades to the chassis and overcoming the immediate setback of a Honda engine blowing itself to bits on Friday morning – a failure that had prompted a visit by Fernando to the tennis court while fellow drivers continued to get down to business. The only unfortunate aspect of Alonso's exceptional lap was its effect on the comparison with Stoffel Vandoorne, who was unable to pinpoint exactly why he was a disappointing 19th fastest.

Alonso's position had been helped by Esteban Ocon's overenthusiastic use of the DRS button. He had pushed it too early and the flap had not opened immediately, costing the couple of tenths that would have put the Frenchman ahead of both Alonso and the other Force India. Sergio Pérez was delighted to be P8 after a troubled free practice made good by the careful management of tyres during qualifying.

Felipe Massa split the Force Indias, the Williams driver having had to work hard to bring his tyres in. The need for a two-lap warm-up had cost a set of softs in Q1, the single lap earmarked for Q3 being additionally compromised by a small mistake. Massa joined Pérez and Ocon in saying that but for that setback, he could have been ahead of Alonso. Lance Stroll had no such excuse after failing to go beyond Q1, despite getting to within 0.3s of Massa (the closest he had been thus far during the season).

Kevin Magnussen narrowly missed making Q3, the Haas driver reporting that aero upgrades were a small move in the right direction. The Dane was a couple of places ahead of his team-mate, Romain Grosjean's progress bedevilled once more with brake trouble bad enough to cause a spin and relegation to 14th, behind Carlos Sainz and Nico Hülkenberg.

Sainz, 12th, was particularly unhappy to struggle at home with a Toro Rosso that was short of breath in a straight line and not particularly good in the slow sections, 19th for Daniil Kvyat being more indicative of the team's base line after Sainz had wrung the neck of a car his team-mate described as undriveable.

The problem for Renault was more frustrating, after both drivers had showed well during Friday's practice, only to be caught out by higher temperatures on Saturday and going backwards instead of forwards. Jolyon Palmer not only failed to get out of Q1, but also finished behind the Saubers. Pascal Wehrlein was the quicker of the two and made it into Q2, even though that eventually placed him alongside Marcus Ericsson, three rows from the back of the grid.

Below: Hasagawa's expression summed up Honda's predicament.
Photo: Lukas Gorys

Below centre: Fernando Alonso's McLaren Honda ground to a halt as soon as practice began.
Photo: WRi2/Bryn Williams

Bottom: For the benefit of the fans in attendance, post-qualifying interviews were held on the grid.
Photo: Lukas Gorys

FOLLOWING four races on very different circuits, the Spanish Grand Prix was considered to be the first true indicator of form. If a car doesn't work at Barcelona, it will not be good for many of the tracks that follow. Qualifying had shown that Ferrari and Mercedes continued to be right on the money.

But how would they fare over 66 laps? With these two teams being so close, it was clear that this race would come down to strategy and aggressive driving. With track temperature getting close to the high levels experienced during qualifying and the middle-of-the-range medium tyre having proved difficult, it seemed that the soft would be the preferred option, despite the obvious durability issues. The talk was of two – possibly three – pit stops.

Before any of that, the front two rows needed to consider the 730m charge towards the first corner. Neither Hamilton nor Vettel made a perfect getaway, a touch too much wheelspin in each case allowing Bottas to consider a run down the middle. As he approached the braking zone, however, Valtteri thought better of possibly making contact with his team-mate (perhaps remembering the premature departure of both Mercedes from the same race 12 months previously) and backed off slightly.

In such close company, that was just enough to trigger the end of the race for Räikkönen and Verstappen as they attempted to run three abreast into the corner. Kimi, finding himself in the middle as Max tried to swoop around the outside of Turn One, was tagged by the left front of the Mercedes, the impact being sufficient to send the Ferrari into the Red Bull. Both cars took to the run-off area and returned to the track with various broken bits of suspension and steering arms.

There was also dust on the right-hand side of the Turn Two exit, after a great start by Massa (passing Pérez and Alonso) resulted in the Williams and McLaren touching at the exit of Turn Two as Alonso tried to make a comeback. Fernando was forced on to the grass and Felipe sent towards the pits with a puncture.

By the time the field had returned to Turn One, Vettel was leading Hamilton by more than two seconds and pulling away. Bottas was a second behind his team-mate, a gap that would open gradually as he struggled to find the balance he needed (partly due to the effects of contact with Räikkönen).

Ricciardo dropped back by a similar amount as the race settled down. There was nothing particularly wrong that more downforce couldn't cure, but at least the Red Bull was able to stay clear of the Force Indias (led by Pérez) in fifth and sixth. Hülkenberg was untroubled in seventh, but the same could not be said for Magnussen as he fended off Sainz, Grosjean receiving similar close attention from a recovering Alonso. The rest, led by Wehrlein and Stroll, began to spread out. Kvyat and Palmer joined Massa as early pit visitors, Palmer having tried an ultimately fruitless alternative strategy by starting on the medium.

Tyre and pit-stop strategy now figured large on the Mercedes and Ferrari computers as Vettel continued to lead and Hamilton did everything he could to keep the gap at around 2.5s. The impressive Ferrari pace gained Mercedes's full attention.

The pressure, however, was on the leader. With Hamilton managing to stay reasonably close, the undercut would be possible as – assuming a two-stop strategy – the first pit-stop window approached at around the 15-lap mark. Ferrari decided to jump first and brought in Vettel at the end of lap 14. With the undercut opportunity gone, how would Mercedes react?

In fact, they were quite pleased. By forcing Ferrari's hand, Vettel would rejoin behind Ricciardo who, running without pressure from behind, was not intending to stop any time soon. If Hamilton stayed out and continued at his current pace, he could gain the necessary distance to eventually rejoin ahead of the Red Bull.

Above: The field thunders towards the first turn with Vettel in the Ferrari ahead.
Photo: Lukas Gorys

Opening spread: Lewis Hamilton turned in a stellar performance to overhaul Vettel.
Photo: Mercedes AMG Petronas F1 Team

Opening spread, inset: Lewis takes a moment to savour his victory, while Sebastian ponders his defeat.
Photo: WRi2/Studio Colombo

163

But it didn't work out like that, as Vettel, running new softs, immediately caught and, with the benefit of a flat-out final corner (thanks to the 2017-spec cars and tyres) and DRS, passed Ricciardo as if he were standing still. Now what?

Hamilton's leading car was lapping at least a second slower on his aging tyres. But Mercedes had an ace card in the shape of Bottas, running second and therefore the next car for Vettel to pass as he closed down the nine-second gap by a second a lap (and sometimes more), while the Finn continued to struggle. With Valtteri consigned to finishing third more or less no matter what he did, the trick would be to bring him to the aid of Hamilton by keeping him out and delaying Vettel as much as possible. Meanwhile, Lewis could stay out for a shorter and more competitive middle and particularly final stint (on the soft).

Hamilton's first stop (for mediums) came on lap 21, and he rejoined third, seven seconds behind Vettel. Up front, Bottas was in no doubt about what he had to do as the Ferrari closed in. Two laps later, Vettel was right with the leading Mercedes, using DRS to assist a tow on the main straight. But Bottas had it covered, staying firmly on the inside line. For two laps, this went on, Hamilton getting closer to the Ferrari as Vettel lost vital seconds.

Realising that he had to do something as they started lap 25, Vettel dummied left before swooping across to the right, but Bottas covered the move. Vettel kept coming, however, to the extent that the Ferrari, DRS wide open, clipped the grass at close to 200mph and forced the inside line under braking. Ballsy stuff.

Back in the lead once more, Vettel was 4.5s ahead of Hamilton after Bottas had let his team-mate through. Job done, Valtteri was called in for what would be his only stop at the end of lap 26.

As things stood, Vettel would have to stop for mediums towards the end. Hamilton, meanwhile, would hang on in second place as Vettel stole a tenth here and there and stretched the gap to six seconds, knowing that Lewis would

be on a charge once he had his softs for the final phase. But the Ferrari had track position and Sebastian could be guaranteed not to give it up easily. This would be a tough one for Mercedes to win.

The stand-off continued through to lap 33, Vettel leading Hamilton by 7.8s. Thirteen places behind them, and a lap down, Stoffel Vandoorne was three seconds off the pace, but keeping an eye on Massa, continuing his recovery from the early pit stop. The Belgian had actually been lapping faster on fresh softs until the inevitable blue flags played havoc with progress and allowed the Williams to close in and engage DRS on the main straight. Vandoorne, aware of the threat, judged Massa to be too far back to have a go into Turn One and took the racing line – only to find the white car diving down the inside and aiming for the apex at the same moment. The collision sent the McLaren into the gravel trap, where it became stuck fast in a hazardous position.

Cue a virtual safety car – and a massive dilemma for the leading contenders. While Pérez and Ocon, peeling away from fifth and sixth places, led an exodus to the pits for mediums and a run to the finish, the decision for Ferrari and Mercedes was not clear cut. Ferrari watched Mercedes intently and assumed, as Hamilton continued past the pits, that a decision to stop had been ruled out by the thought that the softs would not last the distance. Ferrari now had no option but to leave Vettel out, since a stop would have given Hamilton track position and the chance to eek out his mediums to the finish.

Then, just as they had correctly judged the safety car period was about to end, Mercedes brought in Hamilton, Vettel having already started his 37th lap. Sure enough, by the time Ferrari responded at the end of that lap, the race had been resumed and thus Vettel lost more time than Hamilton. As the Ferrari rejoined, Vettel discovered to his great surprise that the eight-second cushion had gone, the two cars running side by side through the first corner. Sebastian was holding off Lewis, but for how long?

Above: Sahara Force India's Sergio Perez and Esteban Ocon scooped a haul of constructors' points with fourth- and fifth-place finishes.
Photo: Sahara Force India F1 Team

Top far left: A smooth run to seventh for Carlos Sainz on home soil.

Top left: Nico Hülkenberg enjoyed another strong race for Renault, netting sixth place.
Photos: WRi2/Bryn Williams

Above far left: Adrian Newey and Simon Rennie searching for more speed from the Red Bull.
Photo: Red Bull Racing/Getty Images

Above left: Daniil Kvyat joined team-mate Sainz inside the top ten, scoring his second points finish of the season so far.

Left: No quarter as Vettel fends off Hamilton's attack. The Mercedes driver would eventually prevail in their titanic tussle.
Photos: WRi2/Bryn Williams

VIEWPOINT
STOFFEL'S STRUGGLE

BEFORE the season started, there was much discussion about the likely state of play between Fernando Alonso and Stoffel Vandoorne as the promising Belgian with the stellar GP2 record embarked on his debut F1 season alongside the twice world champion.

There were those who predicted that it would be nip and tuck between them in qualifying, but in fact Alonso had shown a surprising degree of superiority over the first four fly-away races. That continued in Fernando's backyard, where he qualified an amazing seventh, aided, it must be said, by qualifying issues for a number of the expected midfield front-runners, with Vandoorne 19th. The gap between Alonso and 15th in Q2 was just a couple of tenths and yet, in Q1, there was half a second between him and his McLaren Honda team-mate, despite the Spaniard losing track time in practice when one of the Honda units grenaded itself.

"Today, we put everything together," Alonso said. "I felt confident in the car, in spite of quite windy and tricky conditions, and I need that confidence to push and gain those couple of tenths in qually."

Vandoorne, meanwhile, was at something of a loss: "I don't really know what happened today. Yesterday, I was feeling quite comfortable and confident in the car... It seems like we lost a bit of performance, and at the moment there's no real explanation why."

More Honda engine penalties meant that Stoffel started right at the back, and he quickly lost ground in the opening stint, unhappy with the balance. The performance was better after his early-race tyre stop, but then came the rather embarrassing collision with Massa, when Felipe, with DRS open, went down his inside and Vandoorne appeared not to think he was coming and simply turned in at Turn One. Result: one McLaren beached in the gravel trap, a race-influencing safety car and a three-place grid penalty for the Belgian in Monaco.

The word was that Vandoorne was finding it difficult to adapt a specific late-braking style to F1. Few doubted that he was a great talent, but his F1 baptism was clearly tougher than most – himself included – had imagined.

Tony Dodgins

With his tyres up to temperature and the bit between his teeth, Hamilton harried Vettel for several laps as the latter made good use of back-markers and the accompanying DRS. But, when that advantage disappeared and with a clear road ahead on lap 44, Hamilton took the Ferrari with comparative ease.

Ferrari clung to the hope that Hamilton's softs would not see out the remaining 22 laps, but that did not take into account the lighter fuel loads, a rubbered-in track and Hamilton's innate ability to make the tyres last. As the lead eased out to more than two seconds in ten laps, it looked like being game over.

That was certainly the case for Bottas, whose engine gave up, the Finn paying the price for using the same power unit to its maximum while winning the previous race in Russia. The first Mercedes failure since Hamilton's emotional departure from the previous year's Malaysian Grand Prix elevated Ricciardo to a distant third as some reward for the Australian's lonely race. The Force Indias, Pérez comfortably ahead of Ocon, assumed fourth and fifth, well clear of Hülkenberg, the Renault driver continuing to reap the dividends of a storming start with a car that otherwise lacked race pace.

One of the most creditable performances of the day was rounded off by Wehrlein, a brave one-stop tactic playing out perfectly, thanks to the virtual safety car and a very respectable pace from the Sauber, good enough to keep Sainz at bay – on the track at least. The Toro Rosso eventually inherited seventh place when Wehrlein received a penalty for a pit-lane infringement after running on the wrong side of the bollards.

Magnussen lost the chance to score points for ninth place when, overtaken by Kvyat, the Haas driver made a lunge into Turn Four that resulted in a puncture and an eventual 14th place. The Toro Rosso continued to score two points ahead of Grosjean, the Haas having struggled on the medium and lost out to both Wehrlein and Kvyat.

Whereas Wehrlein had the pace and the good luck (with the safety car), Ericsson had neither and trailed home 11th, ahead of Alonso, who set fourth fastest lap on his way to 12th. Palmer's struggle continued throughout the race, minor consolation coming from not being the final runner. That 'honour' belonged to Stroll who, despite having been 50s up on Massa at the end of lap two, found himself 11.5s down as his team-mate came home an unhappy 13th.

Hamilton finished 3.4s in front of Vettel, having maintained a sufficient gap to cover himself in case Ferrari brought in their driver for more softs and a late attack. In the end, stalemate prevailed, despite Sebastian's best efforts to unsettle his rival.

That makes it sound relatively easy. It wasn't. For the first time, it was possible to hear through the radio conversations just how hard Hamilton had to work. The physical effort required by the rise and fall of Barcelona, with fast sweeping corners and two periods of very heavy braking, meant he was breathing hard. Which is exactly as it should be.

The new cars for 2017 were supposed to be harder to drive – and that was definitely the case in Spain. Hamilton had to sit down just after he had climbed the stairs to the cool-down room before the podium. But that did not detract from his genuine enjoyment of a thrilling race.

Maurice Hamilton

Left: Pascal Wehrlein brought some cheer to the beleagured Sauber team with his eighth place.
Photo: Lukas Gorys

Below left: McLaren Honda's Stoffel Vandoorne struggled to match the pace of team-mate Fernando Alonso during the early-season races.
Photos: McLaren Honda

Below: Daniel Ricciardo took third for Red Bull after the early retirements of team-mate Verstappen and Ferrari's Räikkönen.
Photo: Peter J. Fox

2017 FORMULA 1
GRAN PREMIO DE ESPAÑA
PIRELLI
CATALUNYA 12–14 MAY

ROLEX

OFFICIAL TIMEPIECE

RACE DISTANCE: 66 laps, 190.826 miles/307.104km

RACE WEATHER: Dry/sunny (track 40–46°C, air 23–26°C)

CIRCUIT DE BARCELONA-CATALUNYA, BARCELONA

Circuit: 2.892 miles / 4.655km, 66 laps

Renault 265/165 · Turn 5 125/78 · Repsol 175/109 · Campsa 245/152 · Turn 2 190/118 · Turn 6 270/168 · Turn 8 220/137 · Banc Sabadell 130/81 · Europcar 140/87 · Total 165/103 · 325/202 · Turn 7 · La Caixa 95/59 · Turn 14/15 120/75 · New Holland 230/143

Gear — 187/116 kmh/mph

DRS zone

RACE – OFFICIAL CLASSIFICATION

Pos.	Driver	Nat.	No.	Entrant	Car/Engine	Laps	Time/Retirement	Speed (mph/km/h)	Gap to leader	Fastest race lap
1	**Lewis Hamilton**	GB	44	Mercedes AMG Petronas Motorsport	Mercedes F1 W08-Mercedes M08 EQ Power+ V6	66	1h 35m 56.497s	119.338/192.056		1m 23.593s 64
2	**Sebastian Vettel**	D	5	Scuderia Ferrari	Ferrari SF70H-062 V6	66	1h 35m 59.987s	119.266/191.940	3.490s	1m 23.674s 43
3	**Daniel Ricciardo**	AUS	3	Red Bull Racing	Red Bull RB13-TAG Heuer RB13 V6	66	1h 37m 12.317s	117.787/189.560	1m 15.820s	1m 23.686s 40
4	**Sergio Pérez**	MEX	11	Sahara Force India Formula 1 Team	Force India VJM10-Mercedes M08 EQ Power+ V6	65			1 lap	1m 25.755s 51
5	**Esteban Ocon**	F	31	Sahara Force India Formula 1 Team	Force India VJM10-Mercedes M08 EQ Power+ V6	65			1 lap	1m 26.276s 40
6	**Nico Hülkenberg**	D	27	Renault Sport Formula One Team	Renault R.S.17-R.E.17 V6	65			1 lap	1m 26.703s 56
7	**Carlos Sainz**	E	55	Scuderia Toro Rosso	Toro Rosso STR12-Renault R.E.17 V6	65			1 lap	1m 26.186s 61
8	**Pascal Wehrlein**	D	94	Sauber F1 Team	Sauber C36-Ferrari 059/5 V6	65	*		1 lap	1m 26.476s 58
9	**Daniil Kvyat**	RUS	26	Scuderia Toro Rosso	Toro Rosso STR12-Renault R.E.17 V6	65			1 lap	1m 25.976s 37
10	**Romain Grosjean**	F	8	Haas F1 Team	Haas VF-17-Ferrari 062 V6	65			1 lap	1m 26.871s 50
11	Marcus Ericsson	S	9	Sauber F1 Team	Sauber C36-Ferrari 059/5 V6	64			2 laps	1m 26.213s 60
12	Fernando Alonso	E	14	McLaren Honda Formula 1 Team	McLaren MCL32-Honda RA617H V6	64			2 laps	1m 23.894s 64
13	Felipe Massa	BR	19	Williams Martini Racing	Williams FW40-Mercedes M08 EQ Power+ V6	64			2 laps	1m 26.472s 64
14	Kevin Magnussen	DK	20	Haas F1 Team	Haas VF-17-Ferrari 062 V6	64			2 laps	1m 26.371s 15
15	Jolyon Palmer	GB	30	Renault Sport Formula One Team	Renault R.S.17-R.E.17 V6	64			2 laps	1m 24.843s 44
16	Lance Stroll	CDN	18	Williams Martini Racing	Williams FW40-Mercedes M08 EQ Power+ V6	64			2 laps	1m 26.838s 50
	Valtteri Bottas	FIN	77	Mercedes AMG Petronas Motorsport	Mercedes F1 W08-Mercedes M08 EQ Power+ V6	38	power unit			1m 24.696s 28
	Stoffel Vandoorne	B	2	McLaren Honda Formula 1 Team	McLaren MCL32-Honda RA617H V6	32	accident			1m 27.554s 14
	Max Verstappen	NL	33	Red Bull Racing	Red Bull RB13-TAG Heuer RB13 V6	1	accident/front suspension			no time
	Kimi Räikkönen	FIN	7	Scuderia Ferrari	Ferrari SF70H-062 V6	0	accident			no time

* includes 5-second penalty for failing to keep to the right of the pit-entry bollard – originally finished 7th.

Fastest race lap: Lewis Hamilton on lap 64, 1m 23.593s, 124.567mph/200.471km/h.

Lap record: Giancarlo Fisichella (Renault R25 V10), 1m 15.641s, 136.835mph/220.213km/h (2005, 2.875-mile/4.627km circuit).

Lap record (current configuration): Kimi Räikkönen (Ferrari F2008 V8), 1m 21.670s, 127.500mph/205.191km/h (2008).

19 · KVYAT · Toro Rosso   17 · PALMER · Renault   15 · WEHRLEIN · Sauber   13 · HÜLKENBERG · Renault   11 · MAGNUSSEN · Haas

20 · VANDOORNE · McLaren   18 · STROLL · Williams   16 · ERICSSON · Sauber   14 · GROSJEAN · Haas   12 · SAINZ · Toro Rosso

10-place grid penalty for using additional power unit elements

Grid order / lap chart

Grid order		1	2	3	4	5	6	7	8	9	10	11	12	13	14	15	16	17	18	19	20	21	22	23	24	25	26	27	28	29	30	31	32	33	34	35	36	37	38	39	40	41	42	43	44	45	46	47	48	49	50	51	52
44	HAMILTON	5	5	5	5	5	5	5	5	5	5	5	5	5	44	44	44	44	44	44	44	77	77	77	5	5	5	5	5	5	5	5	5	5	5	5	5	5	44	44	44	44	44	44	44	44	44						
5	VETTEL	44	44	44	44	44	44	44	44	44	44	44	44	44	5	77	77	77	77	77	77	77	5	5	5	77	44	44	44	44	44	44	44	44	44	44	44	44	44	44	44	44	44	44	5	5	5	5	5	5	5	5	5
77	BOTTAS	77	77	77	77	77	77	77	77	77	77	77	77	77	77	5	5	5	5	5	5	44	44	44	44	77	77	77	77	77	77	77	77	77	77	77	77	77	3	3	3	3	3	3	3	3	3	3	3	3	3	3	3
7	RÄIKKÖNEN	3	3	3	3	3	3	3	3	3	3	3	3	3	3	3	3	3	3	3	3	3	3	3	3	3	3	3	3	3	3	3	3	11	11	11	11	11	11	11	11	11	11	11	11	11	11	11	11	11	11	11	11
33	VERSTAPPEN	11	11	11	11	11	11	11	11	11	11	11	11	11	11	11	11	11	8	94	11	11	11	11	11	11	11	11	11	11	11	11	11	31	31	31	31	31	31	31	31	31	31	31	31	31	31	31	31	31	31	31	31
3	RICCIARDO	31	31	31	31	31	31	31	31	31	31	31	31	31	31	8	8	94	11	94	94	31	31	31	31	31	31	31	31	31	31	31	31	27	27	27	27	27	27	27	27	27	27	27	27	27	27	27					
14	ALONSO	27	27	27	27	27	27	27	27	27	27	27	27	27	27	8	94	94	11	31	31	31	94	94	94	94	94	94	94	94	94	55	27	27	27	94	94	94	94	94	94	94	94	94	94	94	94						
11	PÉREZ	20	20	20	20	20	20	20	20	20	20	20	8	8	94	9	31	31	27	27	27	27	27	27	27	27	27	27	8	94	94	94	94	55	55	55	55	55	55	55	55	55	55	55	55	55	55						
19	MASSA	55	55	55	55	55	55	55	55	55	55	55	55	94	94	9	27	20	20	20	20	20	20	20	20	20	20	27	8	8	94	94	94	20	20	20	20	20	20	20	20	20	20	20	20	20	20						
31	OCON	8	8	8	8	8	8	8	8	8	8	8	55	9	9	27	27	9	55	55	55	55	55	55	55	55	55	55	55	55	20	20	20	8	8	8	26	26	26	8	8	8	8	8	8	8	8						
20	MAGNUSSEN	14	14	14	14	14	14	14	14	14	14	14	94	26	20	20	20	55	8	8	8	8	8	8	8	8	8	8	20	8	8	26	26	26	26	8	8	8	8	26	26	26	8	8	8	8	8						
55	SAINZ	94	94	94	94	94	94	94	94	94	94	94	9	20	26	55	55	26	26	26	26	26	26	26	26	26	26	26	26	26	26	26	26	18	18	18	18	18	18	18	18	18	18	18	18	18	18						
27	HÜLKENBERG	18	18	18	18	18	18	18	18	18	18	18	9	26	55	55	26	26	14	14	14	14	14	14	14	14	14	9	9	9	9	18	18	18	18	18	9	9	9	9	9	9	9	9	9	9	9						
8	GROSJEAN	30	9	9	9	9	9	9	9	9	9	9	26	55	55	26	26	14	9	9	9	9	18	9	9	9	14	14	14	14	14	14	14	14	14	14	14	14	14	14	14	14	14	14	14	14	14	19					
94	WEHRLEIN	9	2	2	2	2	2	2	2	2	2	2	2	18	18	18	18	18	9	9	9	18	9	18	18	18	9	19	19	19	19	19	19	19	19	19	19	19	19	19	19	19	19	19	14	14	14	14					
9	ERICSSON	2	30	26	26	26	26	26	26	26	26	26	30	30	30	30	30	30	2	2	2	2	2	2	2	2	19	14	19	19	19	14	19	19	19	19	30	30	30	30	30	30	30	30	30	30	30						
30	PALMER	26	26	30	30	30	30	30	30	30	30	30	2	2	2	2	2	2	30	30	19	19	19	19	19	19	14	30	30	30	30	30																					
18	STROLL	19	19	19	19	19	19	19	19	19	19	19	19	19	19	19	19	19	30	30	30	30	30	30	30	30	30																										
26	KVYAT	33																																																			
2	VANDOORNE																																																					

TIME SHEETS

PRACTICE 1 (FRIDAY)
Weather: Dry/sunny
Temperatures: track 23–38°C, air 18–23°C

Pos.	Driver	Laps	Time
1	Lewis Hamilton	28	1m 21.521s
2	Valtteri Bottas	30	1m 21.550s
3	Kimi Räikkönen	24	1m 22.456s
4	Sebastian Vettel	23	1m 22.600s
5	Max Verstappen	22	1m 22.706s
6	Daniel Ricciardo	17	1m 23.084s
7	Kevin Magnussen	22	1m 23.670s
8	Romain Grosjean	23	1m 23.758s
9	Nico Hülkenberg	24	1m 23.993s
10	Carlos Sainz	21	1m 24.004s
11	Sergio Pérez	23	1m 24.188s
12	Esteban Ocon	22	1m 24.324s
13	Stoffel Vandoorne	24	1m 24.400s
14	Felipe Massa	34	1m 24.618s
15	Daniil Kvyat	18	1m 24.642s
16	Marcus Ericsson	23	1m 24.966s
17	Pascal Wehrlein	24	1m 25.182s
18	Lance Stroll	34	1m 25.919s
19	Sergey Sirotkin	10	1m 26.293s
20	Fernando Alonso	1	no time

PRACTICE 2 (FRIDAY)
Weather: Dry/sunny
Temperatures: track 39–45°C, air 24–26°C

Pos.	Driver	Laps	Time
1	Lewis Hamilton	39	1m 20.802s
2	Valtteri Bottas	38	1m 20.892s
3	Kimi Räikkönen	34	1m 21.112s
4	Sebastian Vettel	36	1m 21.220s
5	Max Verstappen	29	1m 21.438s
6	Daniel Ricciardo	35	1m 21.585s
7	Nico Hülkenberg	40	1m 21.687s
8	Jolyon Palmer	43	1m 21.992s
9	Felipe Massa	38	1m 22.015s
10	Carlos Sainz	34	1m 22.265s
11	Romain Grosjean	36	1m 22.371s
12	Esteban Ocon	37	1m 22.520s
13	Stoffel Vandoorne	36	1m 22.693s
14	Sergio Pérez	32	1m 22.722s
15	Kevin Magnussen	32	1m 23.007s
16	Marcus Ericsson	37	1m 23.082s
17	Lance Stroll	35	1m 23.221s
18	Daniil Kvyat	27	1m 23.236s
19	Pascal Wehrlein	31	1m 23.599s
20	Fernando Alonso	21	1m 24.077s

PRACTICE 3 (SATURDAY)
Weather: Dry/sunny
Temperatures: track 31°C, air 23°C

Pos.	Driver	Laps	Time
1	Kimi Räikkönen	20	1m 20.214s
2	Sebastian Vettel	7	1m 20.456s
3	Lewis Hamilton	12	1m 20.595s
4	Valtteri Bottas	7	1m 20.868s
5	Max Verstappen	14	1m 21.025s
6	Daniel Ricciardo	15	1m 21.249s
7	Nico Hülkenberg	13	1m 21.670s
8	Felipe Massa	19	1m 21.746s
9	Carlos Sainz	19	1m 21.835s
10	Fernando Alonso	16	1m 22.093s
11	Romain Grosjean	21	1m 22.128s
12	Kevin Magnussen	12	1m 22.214s
13	Sergio Pérez	19	1m 22.237s
14	Esteban Ocon	22	1m 22.297s
15	Daniil Kvyat	15	1m 22.391s
16	Marcus Ericsson	20	1m 22.513s
17	Lance Stroll	19	1m 22.574s
18	Jolyon Palmer	13	1m 22.755s
19	Stoffel Vandoorne	15	1m 22.853s
20	Pascal Wehrlein	19	1m 22.974s

QUALIFYING (SATURDAY)
Weather: Dry/sunny Temperatures: track 39–47°C, air 26–27°C

Pos.	Driver	First	Second	Third	Qualifying Tyre
1	Lewis Hamilton	1m 20.511s	1m 20.210s	1m 19.149s	Soft (new)
2	Sebastian Vettel	1m 20.939s	1m 20.295s	1m 19.200s	Soft (new)
3	Valtteri Bottas	1m 20.991s	1m 20.300s	1m 19.373s	Soft (new)
4	Kimi Räikkönen	1m 20.742s	1m 20.621s	1m 19.439s	Soft (new)
5	Max Verstappen	1m 21.430s	1m 20.722s	1m 19.706s	Soft (new)
6	Daniel Ricciardo	1m 21.704s	1m 20.855s	1m 20.175s	Soft (new)
7	Fernando Alonso	1m 22.015s	1m 21.251s	1m 21.048s	Soft (new)
8	Sergio Pérez	1m 21.998s	1m 21.239s	1m 21.070s	Soft (new)
9	Felipe Massa	1m 22.138s	1m 21.222s	1m 21.232s	Soft (new)
10	Esteban Ocon	1m 21.901s	1m 21.148s	1m 21.272s	Soft (new)
11	Kevin Magnussen	1m 21.945s	1m 21.329s		
12	Carlos Sainz	1m 21.941s	1m 21.371s		
13	Nico Hülkenberg	1m 22.091s	1m 21.397s		
14	Romain Grosjean	1m 21.822s	1m 21.517s		
15	Pascal Wehrlein	1m 22.327s	1m 21.803s		
16	Marcus Ericsson	1m 22.332s			
17	Jolyon Palmer	1m 22.401s			
18	Lance Stroll	1m 22.411s			
19	Stoffel Vandoorne	1m 22.532s			
20	Daniil Kvyat	1m 22.746s			

QUALIFYING: head to head

Hamilton	3	2	Bottas
Vettel	5	0	Räikkönen
Massa	5	0	Stroll
Ricciardo	3	2	Verstappen
Pérez	4	1	Ocon
Hülkenberg	5	0	Palmer
Kvyat	2	3	Sainz
Ericsson	2	0	Giovinazzi
Ericsson	0	3	Wehrlein
Alonso	5	0	Vandoorne
Grosjean	3	2	Magnussen

FOR THE RECORD

50th FASTEST LAP: Mercedes-Benz

DID YOU KNOW?

This was the 250th pole position for a British driver.

POINTS

DRIVERS
1	Sebastian Vettel	104
2	Lewis Hamilton	98
3	Valtteri Bottas	63
4	Kimi Räikkönen	49
5	Daniel Ricciardo	37
6	Max Verstappen	35
7	Sergio Pérez	34
8	Esteban Ocon	19
9	Felipe Massa	18
10	Carlos Sainz	17
11	Nico Hülkenberg	14
12	Romain Grosjean	5
13	Pascal Wehrlein	4
14	Kevin Magnussen	4
15	Daniil Kvyat	2

CONSTRUCTORS
1	Mercedes	161
2	Ferrari	153
3	Red Bull	72
4	Force India	53
5	Toro Rosso	21
6	Williams	18
7	Renault	14
8	Haas	9
9	Sauber	4

9 · MASSA · Williams

7 · ALONSO · McLaren

5 · VERSTAPPEN · Red Bull

3 · BOTTAS · Mercedes

1 · HAMILTON · Mercedes

10 · OCON · Force India

8 · PÉREZ · Force India

6 · RICCIARDO · Red Bull

4 · RÄIKKÖNEN · Ferrari

2 · VETTEL · Ferrari

53	54	55	56	57	58	59	60	61	62	63	64	65	66	
44	44	44	44	44	44	44	44	44	44	44	44	44	44	1
5	5	5	5	5	5	5	5	5	5	5	5	5	5	2
3	3	3	3	3	3	3	3	3	3	3	3	3	3	3
11	11	11	11	11	11	11	11	11	11	11	11	11	11	4
31	31	31	31	31	31	31	31	31	31	31	31	31		5
27	27	27	27	27	27	27	27	27	27	27	27	27		6
94	94	94	94	94	94	94	94	94	94	94	94	94		7
55	55	55	55	55	55	55	55	55	55	55	55	55		8
20	20	20	20	20	20	20	20	20	26	26	26			9
26	26	26	26	26	26	26	26	26	8	8	8			10
8	8	8	8	8	8	8	8	8	20	9				
9	9	9	9	9	9	9	9	9	9	14				
18	18	18	18	18	18	18	14	14	14	14	19			
19	19	19	19	19	19	14	18	18	18	18	20			
14	14	14	14	14	14	19	19	19	19	18	30			
30	30	30	30	30	30	30	30	30	30	30	18			

26 = Pit stop   19 One lap or more behind

 Safety car deployed on laps shown

RACE TYRE STRATEGIES

PIRELLI

	Driver	Race Stint 1	Race Stint 2	Race Stint 3	Race Stint 4
1	Hamilton	Soft (u): 1–21	Medium (n): 22–36	Soft (n): 37–66	
2	Vettel	Soft (u): 1–14	Soft (n): 15–37	Medium (n): 38–66	
3	Ricciardo	Soft (u): 1–21	Medium (n): 22–38	Soft (n): 39–66	
4	Pérez	Soft (u): 1–18	Soft (n): 19–34	Medium (n): 35–66	
5	Ocon	Soft (u): 1–16	Soft (u): 17–34	Medium (n): 35–66	
6	Hülkenberg	Soft (u): 1–15	Soft (u): 16–33	Medium (n): 34–66	
7	Sainz	Soft (u): 1–13	Soft (u): 14–34	Medium (n): 35–66	
8	Wehrlein	Soft (u): 1–33	Medium (n): 34–66		
9	Kvyat	Medium (n): 1	Soft (n): 2–33	Soft (n): 34–66	
10	Grosjean	Soft (u): 1–19	Soft (n): 20–34	Medium (n): 35–66	
11	Ericsson	Soft (u): 1–18	Soft (n): 19–32	Medium (n): 33–66	
12	Alonso	Soft (u): 1–12	Soft (u): 13–31	Medium (n): 32–51	Soft (u): 52–66
13	Massa	Soft (u): 1	Soft (n): 2–13	Soft (u): 14–33	Medium (n): 34–66
14	Magnussen	Soft (u): 1–13	Soft (n): 14–33	Medium (n): 34–63	Soft (u): 64–66
15	Palmer	Medium (n): 1–2	Soft (n): 3–21	Soft (n): 22–42	Soft (n): 43–66
16	Stroll	Soft (u): 1–12	Soft (n): 13–33	Medium (n): 34–66	
	Bottas	Soft (u): 1–26	Medium (n): 27–38 (dnf)		
	Vandoorne	Medium (n): 1–12	Soft (n): 13–32 (dnf)		
	Verstappen	Soft (u): 1 (dnf)			
	Räikkönen	0			

The tyre regulations stipulate that at least two of three dry tyre specifications must be used during a dry race.
Pirelli P Zero logos are colour-coded on the tyre sidewalls: Yellow = Soft; White = Medium. (n) new (u) used

Photos: Peter J. Fox

MONACO GRAND PRIX

MONTE CARLO CIRCUIT

CASINO DE MONTE-CAR

MONTE CARLO QUALIFYING

THINK Monaco pole-position man and you'd probably go for Hamilton, Vettel or even, car willing, Daniel Ricciardo. But not Kimi Räikkönen. Yes, the Finn had taken pole and won in 2005 with a superior McLaren, but going to the principality in 2017, he had not started first since Magny-Cours 2008.

But, with a perfectly hooked-up Ferrari SF70H, Räikkönen, who had been bested by Vettel in practice, got it together and stopped the clock in 1m 12.176s, some 0.043s quicker than his Ferrari team-mate as Maranello locked out the front row.

That put Ferrari in a strong position to dictate the race, as Valtteri Bottas had failed to split the red cars by just two-thousandths of a second. This was actually a fantastic effort from Bottas, since it had proved tricky to get the Mercedes's tyres into their correct operating window – to the extent that team-mate Lewis Hamilton was 14th, and out in Q2.

A radio instruction to Räikkönen from engineer Dave Greenwood was revealing as they sought some space on the circuit in which to turn in a hot lap, Kimi warned that while there was a gap ahead, the Mercedes in front of him was likely to be 6–7s slower on its warm-up lap, as Mercedes had opted for a two-lap run to get a decent balance of temperature between the ultrasoft fronts and rears.

Hamilton did not manage it in Q2 and pulled off an amazing save to keep the car out of the barrier when he overdid things into Massenet. Thus that run had to be aborted, and when Vandoorne clobbered the inside barrier leaving the Swimming Pool and brought out the waved yellows just as Hamilton was on his second hot lap, that was it for Lewis.

Why was Mercedes struggling? A reduction in Pirelli's minimum pressures (from 19/18 front/rear to 17/16.5) probably worked in Ferrari's favour and, when combined with the pre-season heave-spring ban, led to the Mercedes drivers suffering locked fronts and those temperature generation problems. All things considered, Bottas's lap was a top effort, using the Mercedes horsepower to set the quickest S1 time and hang on through S2 and S3.

"It's one of the best qualifyings I've had, certainly the best lap for me at Monaco," Bottas acknowledged. "It could have been a completely different Sunday with those extra five-hundredths..."

"It was an exceptional performance," Toto Wolff agreed. "Valtteri definitely outperformed the car."

In 2016, Ricciardo had taken his first F1 pole in Monaco and, with the Red Bull, had been a match for anything, but this time around, the RB13 was not quite there with Ferrari, and it was Max Verstappen who was the quicker of the two, some 0.32s from pole. Ricciardo, meanwhile, was fully half a second slower, unimpressed by finding himself in traffic on his final flying lap; he only managed to pip a fine effort from Carlos Sainz by 0.17s.

Of the Toro Rosso pair, Daniil Kvyat had been more impressive throughout practice, but an untimely call to the weighbridge messed up Q2, a situation he was on course to right when Vandoorne had his incident at the Swimming Pool.

Stoffel himself had turned in his most impressive display thus far and had done enough in Q2, during which he lapped a couple of tenths quicker than the returning Jenson Button (subbing for Fernando Alonso, who had elected to contest the Indy 500 instead – *see* Viewpoint). The Belgian was ninth quickest before the imposition of a three-place grid penalty for his Barcelona Turn One indiscretion.

Button made the top ten as well, but would start at the back due to a 15-place grid penalty for additional Honda power unit elements.

Always decent around Monaco, Sergio Pérez qualified the first Force India seventh. Team-mate Esteban Ocon was an impressive Monaco debutant, on Pérez's pace for much of practice until he clipped the barrier exiting the Swimming Pool in Saturday morning practice. The Force India crew worked feverishly to get the car out in Q1, but Ocon didn't have enough time to find his rhythm and lined up 15th.

Romain Grosjean also found it difficult to get the Haas's tyres to offer the grip he needed. He suffered a spin at Mirabeau, before producing a lap out of nowhere that got him into Q3, eighth quickest.

Nico Hülkenberg qualified 12th, but started tenth as a result of the penalties issued to the McLaren pair, 'The Hulk' another who struggled to get his tyres into the window. At least he was in better shape than Palmer, who lost much of Thursday practice when his car stopped on track.

Williams was hopeful that the FW40 might prove better suited to Monaco than its immediate predecessors, but the optimism was misplaced, as Felipe Massa could do no better than 14th on the grid after he couldn't get his first Q2 run together and then was also impeded by the yellow flags. Team-mate Lance Stroll, meanwhile, was mired in Q1, half a second down on Felipe before a hydraulic leak put paid to a second run. Behind the young Canadian, Pascal Wehrlein pipped Marcus Ericsson by a little over a tenth as the Saubers struggled for pace.

Top: Lance Stroll's first taste of the Monte Carlo barriers came in Thursday's FP2.
Photo: Lukas Gorys

Above: Close, but not touching for Valtteri Bottas in his Mercedes.

Right: Lewis Hamilton performed a burn-out on his bespoke MV Agusta.
Photos: Mercedes AMG Petronas F1 Team

Top right: Max Verstappen heads towards Portier and then the tunnel in his Red Bull.
Photo: Peter J. Fox

Right: Jean-Pierre Jabouille and Alain Prost ran some parade laps in their race-winning cars to mark Renault's 40th anniversary in F1.
Photo: WRi2/Jean-François Galeron

Below right: Prost's main duties lay in his role as the team's special advisor.
Photo: Renault F1 Team

Far right: Form an orderly queue. The cars stream around Grand Hotel (or Fairmont) hairpin on the opening lap.
Photo: Haas F1 Team

Opening spread: Winner Sebastian Vettel pitted later than his team-mate and reaped the rewards.
Photo: Peter J. Fox

Right: Daniel Ricciardo was spectacularly fast on his Pirelli ultrasoft tyres. The Red Bull driver survived a brush with the wall to claim a podium place.

Below: Pole-sitter and early race leader Kimi Räikkönen leads team-mate Sebastian Vettel up through Beau Rivage.

Photos: Peter J. Fox

THERE was much pre-race speculation about how Ferrari would play this one: would Räikkönen get a proper crack at winning after his pole position? Or, would he have to defer to Vettel?

When the lights went out, Kimi duly converted his pole and headed off up the hill to Casino Square, with Vettel tucked in behind, followed by Bottas, Verstappen, Ricciardo, Sainz, Pérez, Grosjean, Magnussen, Hülkenberg, Kvyat, Hamilton and the rest.

It was typical Monaco 'follow-the-leader' fare, with a static order until Hülkenberg stopped with a gearbox problem, while Bottas was not exactly following the leading Ferraris that closely, having dropped to almost 8s behind Räikkönen after 16 laps. Despite his stellar qualifying lap, Valtteri acknowledged that Mercedes did not have the race pace to trouble Ferrari. Again, it was about keeping the tyre in its operating window.

"It wasn't out of the window all the time," he explained, "but we struggled quite a bit with back-markers and losing front tyre temperature, then overheated one of the brake calipers, and I had to adjust the brake bias for that, so I lost quite a bit of time altogether. Finding the rhythm for this track is everything, and having to manage things makes that difficult."

Out front, Räikkönen's biggest margin over Vettel was 2.32s on lap eight, but as the potential first pit-stop window approached, the championship leader closed it back down again. With just about everyone having started on the ultrasoft and only a single stop to go on to the supersofts envisaged, and precious little degradation whatever the compound, there did not appear to be a great deal of scope for strategic thinking. Except that, importantly, the time taken to generate tyre temperature in Monaco suggested that, unusually, the overcut could prove more advantageous than the undercut. In other words, rather than pit first, the optimum strategy would probably be to run longer.

With the race planned for 78 laps, a switch from the ultrasofts to the supersofts could be anticipated at around the 30-lap stage, but with such little degradation, that was fluid. About halfway to that point, Räikkönen's pace dropped off by over half a second, and Bottas and Ricciardo were able to start reeling in the two Ferraris. In response to a radio message, Kimi speeded up again before, on lap 22, dropping his pace even more significantly. Then, with the clear potential to run mid-1m 16s laps quite comfortably, his 26th and 27th laps took 1m 17.9s and 1m 17.80s respectively.

Vettel's pace was being dictated by his team-mate, and by the end of the 27th lap, Bottas was just 3.14s off the lead. Verstappen was a further 2s adrift, with Ricciardo a similar distance further back in the second Red Bull. Significantly, the slowdown meant that Sainz's sixth-placed Toro Rosso was less than 20s from the lead – less than the required pit window for either Ferrari to stop and get back out ahead of the Spaniard.

Obviously, something was going on between the Ferrari drivers, and when asked about it later, Vettel said, "The plan was for us to pull away, which we did, but then…"

Post race, Räikkönen wasn't interested in elaborating.

Although closing on the Ferraris, Bottas was beginning to struggle with his rear tyres and had Verstappen within undercut range. With Ricciardo in the Dutchman's wheel

tracks, Red Bull could afford to cover both bases: try to undercut Bottas, whose pace was dictated by the cruising Ferraris, and leave Ricciardo out to attempt the overcut.

Red Bull pulled the trigger on lap 32, calling in Verstappen, which forced Mercedes into responding with Bottas on the next lap.

It's possible that Räikkönen had figured out that he was likely to get the call to allow Vettel through at some stage before lap 78 and thought that the best way to defend against that was to back his team-mate into the following pack, in the hope that he would be undercut by one of them.

The Ferrari pit-wall team now had to react. When Verstappen pitted, Räikkönen was still cruising around at 1m 17.6s pace, and when Bottas came in on the next lap, Ferrari needed Räikkönen out of the way – in a hurry. Alternatively, both Ferraris needed to speed up considerably to run longer so that they could both get in and out without ceding their positions.

Ferrari decided to call in Räikkönen on lap 34, despite the realisation that he would pit out in traffic, behind Wehrlein and Button.

Meanwhile, the early stop had not worked out for Verstappen, not helped by the fact that he had missed his marks slightly, costing an extra second or so in the pits, which allowed Bottas to retain his third place when he came in on the next lap. The pair also lost a bit more time behind Sainz, who did not pit his Toro Rosso for another four laps.

All this was good news for Ricciardo and Vettel. With Verstappen and Bottas out of the way, Ricciardo's Red Bull was the fastest car on the circuit, with four consecutive laps at 1m 16.0s pace, and he was just 5s behind race leader Vettel when he stopped on lap 38. He pitted out comfortably 7s ahead of Bottas and a hacked-off Verstappen.

If Ricciardo had been flying, Vettel redefined the term when he cut loose with laps of 1m 15.58s and 1m 15.23s before diving into the pits a lap after Ricciardo. He came out just in front of Räikkönen, who was about as impressed with developments as Verstappen had been at Red Bull.

For the Ferrari management, it had all worked out just fine. They were still first and second, with the 'right' man in front. In fairness, though, Vettel had only just jumped Räikkönen,

and it was close enough not to have been a sure thing, so there was some doubt as to whether this had all been orchestrated or not.

Why then the stony-faced Kimi looking daggers at Vettel and only just managing a handshake before the podium ceremony? Perhaps because Ferrari was being disingenuous by saying that as the lead driver, Räikkönen had been given priority with the first pit stop, on a day when stopping second was likely to offer an advantage. Or perhaps because his attempt to back up Vettel so that Ferrari had to pit him first had not quite come off. Among the little that Räikkönen did give away after the race was that it had not been his choice to pit when he did.

"It didn't work out very well for me," he muttered.

On fresh supersofts, Vettel quickly pulled away from a disinterested Räikkönen and was 10s to the good by lap 50, Kimi fully aware that the contest was over. Ricciardo was 6s behind the second Ferrari with a comfortable 8s margin over Bottas and team-mate Verstappen, who was running 17.5s clear of Sainz's Toro Rosso.

With Vettel headed for a 25-point maximum, how much damage limitation could Hamilton apply?

Any hopes that he might have been able to charge through the field in the manner seen in the past, albeit rarely, with late-braking moves into the harbour-front chicane, were quickly extinguished. Not only were 2017's cars wider, but also the added downforce resulting from the new regulations gave everyone better traction out of Portier, the corner before Monaco's flat-out tunnel, and better braking stability into the chicane itself. The race did not feature a single successful overtaking move. Lewis's only opportunities, therefore, came when those ahead pitted out of the way.

When he was finally in free air, Hamilton was able to turn low-1m 16s laps on ultrasofts that were 40 laps old, his pace carrying him up to seventh place when he emerged from his late, lap-45 tyre stop. With the car much more to his liking on the supersoft tyre, he rapidly closed a 10s gap to Sainz and was on the Toro Rosso's tail with 20 laps to go.

"I closed the gap up, was on the edge with the brakes, but in terms of utilising what I had, I think my race was good," Lewis explained. "I tried to get by Carlos and gave it a couple of stabs, but the chances of passing him were remote, so it was better to bank the points, turn the engine down and live to fight another day. Six points is not what we came here hoping for, but I'd like to think they could be important at the end of the year."

Team-mate Bottas, meanwhile, had a fleeting chance to recover his podium position after a late-race safety car, prompted by Button colliding with Wehrlein in a badly-judged attempt to pass into Portier. The McLaren's left front had hooked inside the Sauber's right rear, flipping it on to its side and into the barrier. Initially, there was concern for Wehrlein, only recently recovered from a neck/back injury, but he emerged unscathed.

At the restart, Ricciardo glanced the barrier hard at Sainte Devote and Bottas jinked right as they climbed the hill to Massenet.

"I thought there was a chance on the right, but I could see the guard rail coming closer and closer, and Daniel closing the gap," Valtteri said. "I could still get back across to the line and keep Verstappen behind, and that was my only small opportunity. Daniel actually properly hit the wall and can't have been far away from breaking something!"

With fourth and seventh places, Mercedes was left to reflect on a day in which Ferrari had opened a 17-point advantage in the constructors' championship and Vettel a 25-point margin over Lewis in the drivers' competition.

Further back, both Magnussen and Ocon suffered punctures, ultimately finishing tenth and twelfth. Pirelli reported that both had sustained similar damage to the left rear and pointed a finger of suspicion at a raised drain cover at the first corner.

Ricciardo was not the only driver to fall foul of Sainte Devote. Vandoorne, under attack from Pérez, found himself off-line on the marbles and ploughed into the barrier, for an ignominious end to his race. But not quite so ignominious as Ericsson's, the Sauber driver having been equally powerless to avoid an embarrassing exit on the marbles, this time while unlapping himself from the safety car…

With seven laps to go, Grosjean ran eighth as Pérez tried to separate Kvyat's Toro Rosso from ninth place with an optimistic move at Rascasse. It put the Russian out of the race and the Force India out of the points, the Mexican having to pit for a new nose. It was cack-handed at best.

Felipe Massa took advantage to scoop up the points for ninth, while team-mate Stroll had retired from his first Monaco GP some seven laps from the flag with failing brakes after a duct had become clogged with debris. Magnussen, after his unscheduled lap-42 puncture stop, completed the points scorers.

As Vettel sprayed the champagne and Räikkönen looked as if he wished he was somewhere else, the overriding question was: had Kimi been deliberately stitched up? With Ferrari operating under something of a media lockdown in 2017 – possibly because they had said too much that had gone unrealised in 2016 – the Scuderia was not disposed to reveal the whys and wherefores of its race strategy. But Kimi's demeanour probably told you as much as you needed to know…

Tony Dodgins

Above: Jenson Button was called up for duty to cover for the absent Fernando Alonso. After qualifying ninth, he was forced to start from the pit lane. His race ended unhappily when he ran into Pascal Wehrlein.
Photo: McLaren Honda

Right: Alonso's Honda is presented to the press at the Indianapolis Motor Speedway.
Photo: IMS/Chris Owens

Below right: Stoffel Vandoorne crashed in both practice and the race, but the Belgian showed a good turn of speed in the McLaren Honda.
Photo: Lukas Gorys

Above left: The safety car was called into action on lap 60.
Photo: Peter J. Fox

Left: A grim-faced Kimi Räikkönen suffers in silence while Sebastian Vettel celebrates.
Photo: Peter Nygaaard/GP Photo

ONE car in the wall and another damaged in a collision. You could understand why McLaren might have wished to divert attention away from Monaco. How about 4,500 miles across the Atlantic to the Indianapolis Motor Speedway? Another time zone, another motorsporting world – with the notable attraction of an entry bearing McLaren's distinctive papaya orange.

The pro-active communications team went to town. Not about to be coy about Fernando Alonso's absence from F1's flagship event, McLaren made much of their man's first attempt at the Indy 500.

The McLaren Honda Brand Centre, normally resplendent in several shades of grey and awash with serious issues, had been noisily transformed into 'Gasoline Alley on the Med'. The catering crew were appropriately dressed for serving burgers, fries and beer. The audience was equally appreciative of wide-screen views of an eventful race, ranging from Scott Dixon's survival of a huge accident to Alonso reminding McLaren and their guests of how life used to be as he led the race.

Of course, the only lap to lead is the last one. Fernando, his tyres in good shape, was nicely positioned as the climactic final phase rushed towards its 220mph conclusion. Then, a sudden return to desperately familiar territory as the McLaren rolled to a halt.

The audience stood and applauded the Spaniard's efforts while at the same time trying not to exchange glances with the Honda crew, who were clearly mortified. Not even a win for popular ex-F1 man Takuma Satu and his Dallara-Honda could console the Japanese contingent in the room.

The disappointing (for McLaren Honda) result aside, such a spectacle gave pause for thought. It was difficult to avoid making comparisons with the procession we had witnessed earlier in the day.

Monaco might be Monaco, as different from the Indy 500 as it's possible to be; a street-circuit classic that has its place on the international sporting calendar. But, as a lesson in the laying on of entertainment for spectators and feeding the requirements of the media, it could be argued that Indianapolis pointed towards an F1 future currently being shaped by its American owner.

On 28th May, 2017, that appeared to be no bad thing.

Maurice Hamilton

177

6

2017 FORMULA 1
GRAND PRIX DE MONACO

MONTE-CARLO 25–28 MAY

RACE DISTANCE: 78 laps, 161.880 miles/260.520km

RACE WEATHER: Dry/sunny (track 47–57°C, air 26–29°C)

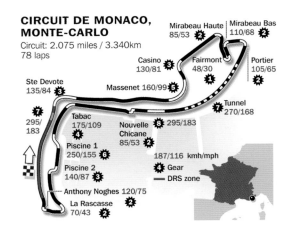

CIRCUIT DE MONACO, MONTE-CARLO
Circuit: 2.075 miles / 3.340km
78 laps

Mirabeau Haute 85/53
Mirabeau Bas 110/68
Casino 130/81
Fairmont 48/30
Portier 105/65
Ste Devote 135/84
Massenet 160/99
Tunnel 270/168
Tabac 175/109
Nouvelle Chicane 85/53
295/183
Piscine 1 250/155
295/183
187/116 kmh/mph
Piscine 2 140/87
Gear
DRS zone
Anthony Noghes 120/75
La Rascasse 70/43

ROLEX

F1 OFFICIAL TIMEPIECE

RACE – OFFICIAL CLASSIFICATION

Pos.	Driver	Nat.	No.	Entrant	Car/Engine	Laps	Time/Retirement	Speed (mph/km/h)	Gap to leader	Fastest race lap	
1	**Sebastian Vettel**	D	5	Scuderia Ferrari	Ferrari SF70H-062 V6	78	1h 44m 44.340s	92.650/149.105		1m 15.238s	38
2	**Kimi Räikkönen**	FIN	7	Scuderia Ferrari	Ferrari SF70H-062 V6	78	1h 44m 47.485s	92.603/149.030	3.145s	1m 15.527s	39
3	**Daniel Ricciardo**	AUS	3	Red Bull Racing	Red Bull RB13-TAG Heuer RB13 V6	78	1h 44m 48.085s	92.594/149.016	3.745s	1m 15.756s	51
4	**Valtteri Bottas**	FIN	77	Mercedes AMG Petronas Motorsport	Mercedes F1 W08-Mercedes M08 EQ Power+ V6	78	1h 44m 49.857s	92.568/148.974	5.517s	1m 16.439s	22
5	**Max Verstappen**	NL	33	Red Bull Racing	Red Bull RB13-TAG Heuer RB13 V6	78	1h 44m 50.539s	92.558/148.958	6.199s	1m 16.329s	56
6	**Carlos Sainz**	E	55	Scuderia Toro Rosso	Toro Rosso STR12-Renault R.E.17 V6	78	1h 44m 56.378s	92.472/148.820	12.038s	1m 16.649s	39
7	**Lewis Hamilton**	GB	44	Mercedes AMG Petronas Motorsport	Mercedes F1 W08-Mercedes M08 EQ Power+ V6	78	1h 45m 00.141s	92.417/148.731	15.801s	1m 15.825s	54
8	**Romain Grosjean**	F	8	Haas F1 Team	Haas VF-17-Ferrari 062 V6	78	1h 45m 02.490s	92.383/148.676	18.150s	1m 17.095s	45
9	**Felipe Massa**	BR	19	Williams Martini Racing	Williams FW40-Mercedes M08 EQ Power+ V6	78	1h 45m 03.785s	92.364/148.645	19.445s	1m 16.543s	50
10	**Kevin Magnussen**	DK	20	Haas F1 Team	Haas VF-17-Ferrari 062 V6	78	1h 45m 05.783s	92.335/148.598	21.443s	1m 16.313s	44
11	Jolyon Palmer	GB	30	Renault Sport Formula One Team	Renault R.S.17-R.E.17 V6	78	1h 45m 07.077s	92.315/148.567	22.737s	1m 16.614s	55
12	Esteban Ocon	F	31	Sahara Force India Formula 1 Team	Force India VJM10-Mercedes M08 EQ Power+ V6	78	1h 45m 08.065s	92.301/148.544	23.725s	1m 16.482s	52
13	Sergio Pérez	MEX	11	Sahara Force India Formula 1 Team	Force India VJM10-Mercedes M08 EQ Power+ V6	78	1h 45m 33.429s *	91.931/147.949	49.089s	1m 14.820s	76
14	Daniil Kvyat	RUS	26	Scuderia Toro Rosso	Toro Rosso STR12-Renault R.E.17 V6	71	accident damage		7 laps	1m 16.539s	43
15	Lance Stroll	CDN	18	Williams Martini Racing	Williams FW40-Mercedes M08 EQ Power+ V6	71	brakes		7 laps	1m 16.075s	71
	Stoffel Vandoorne	B	2	McLaren Honda Formula 1 Team	McLaren MCL32-Honda RA617H V6	66	accident			1m 16.665s	45
	Marcus Ericsson	S	9	Sauber F1 Team	Sauber C36-Ferrari 059/5 V6	63	accident			1m 16.829s	39
	Jenson Button	GB	22	McLaren Honda Formula 1 Team	McLaren MCL32-Honda RA617H V6	57	accident			1m 16.912s	47
	Pascal Wehrlein	D	94	Sauber F1 Team	Sauber C36-Ferrari 059/5 V6	57	accident **			1m 18.034s	25
	Nico Hülkenberg	D	27	Renault Sport Formula One Team	Renault R.S.17-R.E.17 V6	15	gearbox			1m 17.885s	13

* includes 10-second penalty for causing an accident with Kvyat.   ** includes 5-second penalty for unsafe release.

Fastest race lap: Sergio Pérez on lap 76, 1m 14.820s, 99.768mph/160.561km/h (new record for current configuration).

Lap record: Michael Schumacher (Ferrari F2004 V10), 1m 14.439s, 100.369mph/161.528km/h (2004, 2.075-mile/3.340-km circuit).

Previous lap record (current configuration): Lewis Hamilton (Mercedes-Benz F1 W07 V6 turbo), 1m 17.939s, 95.776mph/154.135km/h (2016).

20 · BUTTON · McLaren
15-place grid penalty for using additional power unit elements. Car modified in *parc fermé*; required to start from the pit lane

18 · WEHRLEIN · Sauber

16 · PALMER · Renault

14 · MASSA · Williams

12 · VANDOORNE · McLaren
3-place grid penalty for causing accident in round 5

19 · ERICSSON · Sauber
5-place grid penalty for replacing gearbox

17 · STROLL · Williams

15 · OCON · Force India

13 · HAMILTON · Mercedes

11 · MAGNUSSEN · Haas

Grid order	1	2	3	4	5	6	7	8	9	10	11	12	13	14	15	16	17	18	19	20	21	22	23	24	25	26	27	28	29	30	31	32	33	34	35	36	37	38	39	40	41	42	43	44	45	46	47	48	49	50	51	52	53	54	55	56	57	58	59	60
7 RÄIKKÖNEN	7	7	7	7	7	7	7	7	7	7	7	7	7	7	7	7	7	7	7	7	7	7	7	7	7	7	7	7	7	7	7	7	5	5	5	5	5	5	5	5	5	5	5	5	5	5	5	5	5	5	5	5	5	5	5	5	5	5	5	5
5 VETTEL	5	5	5	5	5	5	5	5	5	5	5	5	5	5	5	5	5	5	5	5	5	5	5	5	5	5	5	5	5	5	5	5	3	3	3	7	7	7	7	7	7	7	7	7	7	7	7	7	7	7	7	7	7	7	7	7	7	7	7	7
77 BOTTAS	77	77	77	77	77	77	77	77	77	77	77	77	77	77	77	77	77	77	77	77	77	77	77	77	77	77	77	77	77	77	77	77	77	7	7	3	3	3	3	3	3	3	3	3	3	3	3	3	3	3	3	3	3	3	3	3	3	3	3	3
33 VERSTAPPEN	33	33	33	33	33	33	33	33	33	33	33	33	33	33	33	33	33	33	33	33	33	33	33	33	33	33	33	33	33	33	33	33	55	55	55	77	77	77	77	77	77	77	77	77	77	77	77	77	77	77	77	77	77	77	77	77	77	77	77	77
3 RICCIARDO	3	3	3	3	3	3	3	3	3	3	3	3	3	3	3	3	3	3	3	3	3	3	3	3	3	3	3	3	3	3	3	3	55	77	77	77	77	33	33	33	33	33	33	33	33	33	33	33	33	33	33	33	33	33	33	33	33	33	33	33
55 SAINZ	55	55	55	55	55	55	55	55	55	55	55	55	55	55	55	55	55	55	55	55	55	55	55	55	55	55	55	55	55	55	55	55	33	33	33	33	33	8	8	8	44	44	44	44	44	44	55	55	55	55	55	55	55	55	55	55	55	55	55	55
11 PÉREZ	11	11	11	11	11	11	11	11	11	11	11	11	11	11	11	11	8	8	8	8	8	8	8	8	8	8	8	8	8	8	8	8	8	44	44	44	2	2	2	55	55	55	44	44	44	44	44	44	44	44	44	44	44	44	44	44	44	44	44	44
8 GROSJEAN	8	8	8	8	8	8	8	8	8	8	8	8	8	8	8	8	20	20	20	20	20	20	20	20	20	20	20	20	20	20	20	20	20	2	2	2	55	55	55	8	8	8	8	8	8	8	8	8	8	8	8	8	8	8	8	8	8	8	8	8
26 KVYAT	20	20	20	20	20	20	20	20	20	20	20	20	20	20	20	20	26	26	26	26	26	26	26	26	26	26	26	26	26	26	26	26	44	55	55	55	8	8	8	26	26	26	26	26	26	26	26	26	26	26	26	26	26	26	26	26	26	26	26	26
27 HÜLKENBERG	27	27	27	27	27	27	27	27	27	27	27	27	27	27	44	44	44	44	44	44	44	44	44	44	44	44	44	44	44	44	44	44	2	20	20	20	20	26	2	2	2	2	2	2	2	2	2	2	2	2	2	2	2	2	2	2	2	2	2	2
20 MAGNUSSEN	26	26	26	26	26	26	26	26	26	26	26	26	26	26	2	2	2	2	2	2	2	2	2	2	2	2	2	2	2	2	2	2	19	19	26	26	26	11	11	11	11	11	11	11	11	11	11	11	11	11	11	11	11	11	11	11	11	11	11	11
2 VANDOORNE	44	44	44	44	44	44	44	44	44	44	44	44	44	44	19	19	19	19	19	19	19	19	19	19	19	19	19	19	19	19	19	19	26	26	30	30	30	19	19	19	19	19	19	19	19	19	19	19	19	19	19	19	19	19	19	19	19	19	19	19
44 HAMILTON	2	2	2	2	2	2	2	2	2	2	2	2	2	2	3	31	31	31	31	31	31	31	31	31	31	31	31	31	31	31	31	31	30	30	11	11	11	11	20	20	20	20	20	20	20	20	20	20	20	20	20	20	20	20	20	20	20	20	20	20
19 MASSA	19	19	19	19	19	19	19	19	19	19	19	19	19	19	30	30	30	30	30	30	30	30	30	30	30	30	30	30	30	11	11	18	18	18	19		18	18	30	30	30	30	30	30	30	30	30	30	30	30	30	30	30	30	30	30	30	30	30	30
31 OCON	31	31	31	31	31	31	31	31	31	31	31	31	31	31	18	18	18	18	18	18	18	18	18	18	18	18	18	18	18	18	31	19	19	19	18	18	18	18	18	18	18	18	18	18	18	18	18	18	18	18	18	18	18	18	18	18	18	18	18	18
30 PALMER	30	30	30	30	30	30	30	30	30	30	30	30	30	11	11	11	11	11	11	11	11	11	11	11	11	11	11	11	11	18	18	31	31	19	31	9	9	9	9	9	9	9	9	9	9	9	9	9	9	9	9	9	9	9	9	9	9	9	9	9
18 STROLL	18	18	18	18	18	18	18	18	18	18	18	18	18	18	9	9	9	9	9	9	9	9	9	9	9	9	9	9	9	9	9	9	9	31	31	31	31	31	31	31	31	31	31	31	31	31	31	31	31	31	31	31	31	31	31	31	31	31	31	31
94 WEHRLEIN	9	9	9	9	9	9	9	9	9	9	9	9	9	9	94	94	94	94	94	94	94	94	94	94	94	94	94	94	94	94	94	94	94	94	94	94	94	94	94	94	94	94	94	94	94	94	94	94	94	94	94	94	94	94	94	94	94	94	94	94
9 ERICSSON	94	94	94	94	94	94	94	94	94	94	94	94	94	94	22	22	22	22	22	22	22	22	22	22	22	22	22	22	22	22	22	22	22	22	22	22	22	22	22	22	22	22	22	22	22	22	22	22	22	22	22	22	22	22	22	22	22	22	22	22
22 BUTTON	22	22	22	22	22	22	22	22	22	22	22	22	22	22																																															

All results and data © FOM 2017

TIME SHEETS

PRACTICE 1 (THURSDAY)
Weather: Dry/sunny
Temperatures: track 28-39°C, air 21-22°C

Pos.	Driver	Laps	Time
1	Lewis Hamilton	40	1m 13.425s
2	Sebastian Vettel	34	1m 13.621s
3	Max Verstappen	32	1m 13.771s
4	Valtteri Bottas	40	1m 13.791s
5	Daniel Ricciardo	45	1m 13.854s
6	Daniil Kvyat	42	1m 14.111s
7	Kimi Räikkönen	37	1m 14.164s
8	Sergio Pérez	32	1m 14.201s
9	Carlos Sainz	39	1m 14.333s
10	Esteban Ocon	39	1m 14.425s
11	Felipe Massa	37	1m 14.617s
12	Stoffel Vandoorne	38	1m 14.813s
13	Kevin Magnussen	34	1m 14.870s
14	Jenson Button	35	1m 14.954s
15	Romain Grosjean	33	1m 15.321s
16	Lance Stroll	44	1m 15.595s
17	Jolyon Palmer	42	1m 15.949s
18	Pascal Wehrlein	33	1m 16.258s
19	Nico Hülkenberg	3	no time
20	Marcus Ericsson	3	no time

PRACTICE 2 (THURSDAY)
Weather: Dry/sunny
Temperatures: track 39-47°C, air 22-24°C

Pos.	Driver	Laps	Time
1	Sebastian Vettel	38	1m 12.720s
2	Daniel Ricciardo	35	1m 13.207s
3	Kimi Räikkönen	46	1m 13.283s
4	Daniil Kvyat	41	1m 13.331s
5	Carlos Sainz	43	1m 13.400s
6	Max Verstappen	36	1m 13.486s
7	Sergio Pérez	45	1m 13.799s
8	Lewis Hamilton	31	1m 13.873s
9	Kevin Magnussen	46	1m 13.890s
10	Valtteri Bottas	39	1m 13.902s
11	Stoffel Vandoorne	42	1m 13.946s
12	Jenson Button	37	1m 13.981s
13	Felipe Massa	46	1m 14.003s
14	Romain Grosjean	44	1m 14.022s
15	Esteban Ocon	47	1m 14.093s
16	Lance Stroll	27	1m 14.474s
17	Nico Hülkenberg	41	1m 14.870s
18	Jolyon Palmer	8	1m 15.616s
19	Marcus Ericsson	32	1m 15.691s
20	Pascal Wehrlein	37	1m 15.695s

PRACTICE 3 (SATURDAY)
Weather: Dry/sunny
Temperatures: track 53°C, air 25°C

Pos.	Driver	Laps	Time
1	Sebastian Vettel	23	1m 12.395s
2	Kimi Räikkönen	26	1m 12.740s
3	Valtteri Bottas	29	1m 12.830s
4	Max Verstappen	27	1m 12.940s
5	Lewis Hamilton	27	1m 13.230s
6	Daniel Ricciardo	24	1m 13.392s
7	Carlos Sainz	27	1m 13.400s
8	Daniil Kvyat	23	1m 13.563s
9	Kevin Magnussen	21	1m 13.596s
10	Stoffel Vandoorne	21	1m 13.805s
11	Sergio Pérez	23	1m 13.936s
12	Jenson Button	26	1m 13.976s
13	Esteban Ocon	21	1m 14.072s
14	Felipe Massa	28	1m 14.072s
15	Nico Hülkenberg	24	1m 14.283s
16	Romain Grosjean	23	1m 14.547s
17	Lance Stroll	35	1m 14.675s
18	Jolyon Palmer	25	1m 15.164s
19	Pascal Wehrlein	29	1m 15.291s
20	Marcus Ericsson	26	1m 15.863s

QUALIFYING (SATURDAY)
Weather: Dry/sunny Temperatures: track 38-55°C, air 24-27°C

Pos.	Driver	First	Second	Third	Qualifying Tyre
1	Kimi Räikkönen	1m 13.117s	1m 12.231s	1m 12.178s	Ultrasoft (new)
2	Sebastian Vettel	1m 13.090s	1m 12.449s	1m 12.221s	Ultrasoft (new)
3	Valtteri Bottas	1m 13.325s	1m 12.901s	1m 12.223s	Ultrasoft (new)
4	Max Verstappen	1m 13.078s	1m 12.697s	1m 12.496s	Ultrasoft (new)
5	Daniel Ricciardo	1m 13.219s	1m 13.011s	1m 12.998s	Ultrasoft (new)
6	Carlos Sainz	1m 13.526s	1m 13.397s	1m 13.162s	Ultrasoft (new)
7	Sergio Pérez	1m 13.530s	1m 13.430s	1m 13.329s	Ultrasoft (new)
8	Romain Grosjean	1m 13.786s	1m 13.203s	1m 13.349s	Ultrasoft (new)
9	Jenson Button	1m 13.723s	1m 13.453s	1m 13.613s	Ultrasoft (new)
10	Stoffel Vandoorne	1m 13.476s	1m 13.249s	no time	Ultrasoft (new)
11	Daniil Kvyat	1m 13.899s	1m 13.516s		
12	Nico Hülkenberg	1m 13.787s	1m 13.628s		
13	Kevin Magnussen	1m 13.531s	1m 13.959s		
14	Lewis Hamilton	1m 13.640s	1m 14.106s		
15	Felipe Massa	1m 13.796s	1m 20.529s		
16	Esteban Ocon	1m 14.101s			
17	Jolyon Palmer	1m 14.696s			
18	Lance Stroll	1m 14.893s			
19	Pascal Wehrlein	1m 15.159s			
20	Marcus Ericsson	1m 15.276s			

QUALIFYING: head to head

Hamilton	3	3	Bottas
Vettel	5	1	Räikkönen
Massa	6	0	Stroll
Ricciardo	3	3	Verstappen
Pérez	5	1	Ocon
Hülkenberg	6	0	Palmer
Kvyat	2	4	Sainz
Ericsson	2	0	Giovinazzi
Ericsson	0	4	Wehrlein
Alonso	5	0	Vandoorne
Vandoorne	1	0	Button
Grosjean	4	2	Magnussen

FOR THE RECORD

20th PODIUM POSITION: Daniel Ricciardo

6,000th KM LED: Kimi Räikkönen

DID YOU KNOW?

This was the 75th Monaco Grand Prix, 64 of which had been within the F1 World Championship.

This was the first Ferrari win in Monaco since Michael Schumacher in 2001.

Kimi Räikkönen's interval between his previous pole (France 2008) and this one, 8 years and 340 days, beat Andretti's record.

Räikkönen's pole was the 50th for a Finnish driver.

POINTS

DRIVERS

1	Sebastian Vettel	129
2	Lewis Hamilton	104
3	Valtteri Bottas	75
4	Kimi Räikkönen	67
5	Daniel Ricciardo	52
6	Max Verstappen	45
7	Sergio Pérez	34
8	Carlos Sainz	25
9	Felipe Massa	20
10	Esteban Ocon	19
11	Nico Hülkenberg	14
12	Romain Grosjean	9
13	Kevin Magnussen	5
14	Pascal Wehrlein	4
15	Daniil Kvyat	4

CONSTRUCTORS

1	Ferrari	196
2	Mercedes	179
3	Red Bull	97
4	Force India	53
5	Toro Rosso	29
6	Williams	20
7	Renault	14
8	Haas	14
9	Sauber	4

10 · HÜLKENBERG · Renault

8 · GROSJEAN · Haas

6 · SAINZ · Toro Rosso

4 · VERSTAPPEN · Red Bull

2 · VETTEL · Ferrari

9 · KVYAT · Toro Rosso

7 · PÉREZ · Force India

5 · RICCIARDO · Red Bull

3 · BOTTAS · Mercedes

1 · RÄIKKÖNEN · Ferrari

Lap chart (partial):

62 63 64 65 66 67 68 69 70 71 72 73 74 75 76 77 78	
5 5 5 5 5 5 5 5 5 5 5 5 5 5 5 5 5	1
7 7 7 7 7 7 7 7 7 7 7 7 7 7 7 7 7	2
3 3 3 3 3 3 3 3 3 3 3 3 3 3 3 3 3	3
7 77 77 77 77 77 77 77 77 77 77 77 77 77 77 77 77	4
33 33 33 33 33 33 33 33 33 33 33 33 33 33 33 33 33	5
5 55 55 55 55 55 55 55 55 55 55 55 55 55 55 55 55	6
44 44 44 44 44 44 44 44 44 44 44 44 44 44 44 44 44	7
8 8 8 8 8 8 8 8 8 8 8 8 8 8 8 8 8	8
26 26 26 11 26 26 26 19 19 19 19 19 19 19 19 19 19	9
2 2 2 26 11 11 11 11 20 20 20 20 20 20 20 20 20	10
11 11 11 11 19 19 19 19 30 30 30 30 30 30 30	
19 19 19 20 20 20 20 31 31 31 31 31 31 31	
20 20 20 30 30 30 30 30 11 11 11 11 11 11 11	
30 30 30 30 31 31 31 31 31	
18 18 31 18 18 18 18 18	
9 31 31 18	
31	

94 = Pit stop   22 One lap or more behind

■ Safety car deployed on laps shown

RACE TYRE STRATEGIES

PIRELLI

	Driver	Race Stint 1	Race Stint 2	Race Stint 3	Race Stint 4
1	Vettel	Ultrasoft (u): 1-39	Supersoft (n): 40-78		
2	Räikkönen	Ultrasoft (u): 1-34	Supersoft (n): 35-78		
3	Ricciardo	Ultrasoft (u): 1-38	Supersoft (n): 39-78		
4	Bottas	Ultrasoft (u): 1-33	Supersoft (n): 34-78		
5	Verstappen	Ultrasoft (u): 1-32	Supersoft (n): 33-60	Ultrasoft (u): 61-78	
6	Sainz	Ultrasoft (u): 1-37	Supersoft (n): 38-78		
7	Hamilton	Ultrasoft (n): 1-46	Supersoft (n): 47-78		
8	Grosjean	Ultrasoft (u): 1-40	Supersoft (n): 41-78		
9	Massa	Ultrasoft (u): 1-38	Supersoft (n): 39-62	Ultrasoft (u): 63-78	
10	Magnussen	Ultrasoft (u): 1-37	Supersoft (n): 38-42	Ultrasoft (u): 43-78	
11	Palmer	Ultrasoft (u): 1-42	Supersoft (n): 43-78		
12	Ocon	Ultrasoft (u): 1-36	Supersoft (n): 37-39	Ultrasoft (u): 40-60	Ultrasoft (u): 61-78
13	Pérez	Ultrasoft (u): 1- 16	Supersoft (n): 17-63	Ultrasoft (u): 64-72	Ultrasoft (u): 73-78
14	Kvyat	Ultrasoft (u): 1-36	Supersoft (n): 37-71		
15	Stroll	Ultrasoft (u): 1-41	Supersoft (n): 42-67	Ultrasoft (u): 68-71	
	Vandoorne	Ultrasoft (u): 1-43	Supersoft (n): 44-66 (dnf)		
	Ericsson	Ultrasoft (u): 1-35	Supersoft (n): 36-63 (dnf)		
	Button	Ultrasoft (u): 1	Supersoft (n): 2-39	Ultrasoft (u): 40-57 (dnf)	
	Wehrlein	Supersoft (n): 1	Ultrasoft (n): 2-57 (dnf)		
	Hülkenberg	Ultrasoft (u): 1-15 (dnf)			

The tyre regulations stipulate that at least two of three dry tyre specifications must be used during a dry race.
Pirelli P Zero logos are colour-coded on the tyre sidewalls: Purple = Ultrasoft; Red = Supersoft. (n) new (u) used

Photos: Peter J. Fox

CANADIAN GRAND PRIX

MONTREAL CIRCUIT

MONTREAL QUALIFYING

AFTER the trials and tribulations of Monte Carlo, Mercedes wanted to hit back immediately in Montreal, but initial indications seemed to suggest that Ferrari's SF70H was better suited to the demands of Circuit Gilles Villeneuve than the W08. But that was on Friday. On Saturday, with the surface rubbering in and track temperature rising to the mid-forties, by the time the qualifying hour ticked around, the stage was set for another of Lewis Hamilton's barnstorming qualifying laps.

When the tyres had been reluctant to generate core temperature and had demanded careful preparation, Bottas once again looked more at home with the car's balance, but with hotter temperatures and a better front end, Hamilton left his team-mate scratching his head and contemplating a 0.72s chasm, with Vettel's Ferrari splitting the Silver Arrows.

Canada has always had emotional connotations for Hamilton. In 2007, his debut F1 season, he scored his first F1 victory at the circuit in just his sixth grand prix. Ten years on, his sixth Montreal pole allowed Lewis to equal the 65 pole positions of his childhood idol and fellow three-times world champion, Ayrton Senna.

In a lovely moment in front of the Turn Two crowd – one of the initiatives of new F1 owners Liberty to bring the drivers closer to the fans – Lewis was presented with one of Ayrton's crash helmets, donated to him in a generous gesture by the Senna family.

Why does Hamilton go so well in Montreal? Downforce levels are low and, perhaps more than any other driver, he is comfortable with any rear-end instability under heavy braking and with the rapid directional changes required by the track's four chicanes. "It's a bit like a big go-kart track!" he beamed.

It was worth bearing in mind that in 2016, a season throughout which Mercedes had been so dominant, the team had had less than 0.2s in hand over Vettel and Ferrari in Canadian qualifying. On this occasion, in such a closely fought contest, Vettel, who split the Mercs on the grid, was 0.33s behind Hamilton.

"I don't think we've discovered the Holy Grail," Mercedes team boss Toto Wolff said, "but the more data we collect, the better we can put the jigsaw together, although it's still a complicated picture. You can see that through the differences between our two cars with no major differences in set-up, and when you talk to the drivers, there's a difference in how they perceive the car. The way we put the car on the track was different to how we would have done if we hadn't had the slap in Monaco.

"And Lewis sometimes has these days where you understand why he's different. Whether it was a circuit he particularly likes or just that he got the car where he needed it, he was just stellar!"

The team's engineers and strategists echoed that. Looking at practice, they believed a 1m 11.9s qualifying lap to be the absolute limit that could be extracted from the W08, with Ferrari possibly having the slight edge. And, true to those expectations, Vettel lapped the Ferrari in 1m 11.789s. Somehow, though, aided by unexpectedly strong grip in the first sector of the lap, Hamilton produced 1m 11.459s!

Kimi Räikkönen was fourth quickest, 0.07s behind Bottas, with the Red Bull pair claiming row three. Max Verstappen was 0.15s adrift of the second Ferrari and enjoyed a similar margin over team-mate Daniel Ricciardo.

Felipe Massa was a further three-tenths down in the first of the Williams, ahead of both Force Indias, Sergio Pérez having pipped team-mate Esteban Ocon by 0.12s. The Frenchman impressed on his first visit to what can be a quirky track, which demands both confidence on the brakes and an attacking approach.

Nico Hülkenberg put Renault through into Q3 and ultimately tenth on the grid, having pushed out both Toro Rossos, Daniil Kvyat the quicker of the two and just 0.03s faster than Fernando Alonso's McLaren, which was sandwiched between them. "That's pole, then!" Alonso said over the radio when told that he was just 1.2s from Hamilton's Q2 pace and did the maths to factor in what he figured was his horsepower deficit.

Romain Grosjean was 14th with the first Haas, the generation of tyre temperature once more a problem, while Jolyon Palmer could only manage 15th with the second Renault, some 0.89s shy of team-mate Hülkenberg's Q2 pace.

Both Stoffel Vandoorne and Lance Stroll – at his first 'home' GP – fell victim to yellow flags for a crashed Pascal Wehrlein and ended their involvement in Q1, along with Kevin Magnussen and both Sauber drivers.

WITH the season's third shortest run to the tight Turns One and Two, there is always scope for a bit of early argy-bargy in Canada – Nico Rosberg had been a victim of it 12 months earlier – but in 2017, with a one-stop race looking the likely strategy for most, and hence little opportunity for strategic variation, there was even more onus to get as much as possible done on lap one.

Hamilton made a decent getaway, while Vettel's start was just okay, allowing a locked-up Bottas to go down his inside in an attempt to make it an early Mercedes 1-2. As Vettel defended, Verstappen launched a start from P5 that put you in mind of Gilles Villeneuve himself, succeeding in going around the outside of the Ferrari in Turn One, but not without his left rear wheel clipping the championship leader's right front wing. Vettel would need to pit, but didn't know it quite yet.

Further back, Sainz squeezed Grosjean on the run down to Turn Three, but the Haas kept coming, contact was made, and Sainz spun and cannoned backwards into Massa's hapless Williams, taking both out of the race and bringing out the safety car. The order was Hamilton, Verstappen, Bottas, Vettel, Ricciardo, Räikkönen, Pérez, Ocon, et al. Sainz received a three-place Baku grid penalty for his indiscretion.

When racing proper resumed on lap four, Verstappen tried an optimistic outside pass on Hamilton at the final chicane, but had to give best and then turn his attention to defending against Bottas into Turn One, the top-three order remaining unchanged.

With everyone back up to full racing speed, Vettel realised that his front wing damage was more serious than first thought as a piece flew off and the team saw load readings that suggested a failure was inevitable. They called him in at the end of lap five, fitting a new wing and a set of supersofts; Sebastian rejoined at the back half a minute adrift of Hamilton.

Increasingly, this looked like being an easy one for Lewis as he stretched a 4s advantage to Verstappen over the opening ten laps, before the Red Bull ground to a halt next time around with a loss of power out of Turn Two, prompting a four-lap virtual safety car period.

Bottas was not having the easiest opening stint either, a legacy of his Turn One lunge, but was now second, from Ricciardo's Red Bull and Pérez's Force India, with Räikkönen fifth for Ferrari.

"The lock-up and flat spot at the start compromised my opening stint," Bottas explained. "The vibration was really strong; it was difficult to see, and I think I need a dentist as well!"

Although most started the race planning a one-stopper, the VSC period came too soon for everyone to dive in and change their ultrasofts, with the race scheduled for 70 laps, but Renault thought it was worth a roll of the dice, pitting both Palmer and Hülkenberg to go on to supersofts and save the 11s that stopping under the slower-paced VSC period was worth. Ultimately, this would work out well, with 'The Hulk' bringing his car home eighth and Palmer finishing just outside the points.

With Räikkönen stuck behind Ricciardo and Pérez, Ferrari tried an aggressive undercut by bringing Kimi in after 17 laps, but when Red Bull responded with Ricciardo next time around, and Force India did likewise with Pérez on the following lap, the stalemate remained. Ocon, meanwhile, stayed out, and although he lost overall time to the stoppers, he was still setting competitive times and would be in good shape with fresher tyres later on.

Bottas pitted on lap 23 and, like Ricciardo, went on to the yellow-walled soft tyre. In an ideal world, he would have done a longer opening stint, but with his flat spot, the strategy was to take him to the point where the team felt he was secure in second, but not so far that he risked a tyre failure.

The No. 77 Mercedes pitted out behind Ocon's Force India, which ran another nine laps before making its sole pit visit. A strong Friday run on the soft tyre was behind the Mercedes decision to go that route with selection, Bottas actually preferring the feeling to both the ultrasoft and

Above: Drivers and grid personnel line up for the Canadian national anthem as race time approaches.

Far left: Max Verstappen was in brilliant form, but was forced to retire by a battery failure.

Photos: Peter J. Fox

Left: Guenther Steiner and Gene Haas contemplate a troubled race for the Haas team. They took just a single point, courtesy of Romain Grosjean.

Photo: Haas F1 Team

Below far left: An inspired Lewis Hamilton claimed his 65th pole position and was rewarded with a presentation helmet from the Senna family.

Below left: Valtteri Bottas continued his run of good results in Montreal with a second-place finish.

Photo: Mercedes AMG Petronas F1 Team

Opening spread: Lewis Hamilton covers team-mate Valtteri Bottas and takes a lead he would never surrender. Meanwhile, Sebastian Vettel and Max Verstappen are about to collide.

Photo: Peter J. Fox

Above: A big haul of points by the Sahara Force India pair of Sergio Pérez and Esteban Ocon put the team comfortably in fourth place in the constructors' standings.
Photo: Peter J. Fox

Top right: After a somewhat chastening start to his F1 career, Lance Stroll brought his Williams home ninth for his first ever points.
Photo: Lukas Gorys

Above right: Stroll indulges in some crowd surfing with his delighted fans.
Photo: Williams Martini Racing

Right: Nico Hülkenberg drove a strong race, in an underperforming Renault, to claim a valuable point for the team in its battle with Williams and Haas.
Photo: Peter J. Fox

supersoft compounds, without the hardest tyre being that far offset in terms of lap time. The move would also provide a good performance indicator when the time came for Hamilton's single stop on lap 32.

The conclusion was that in the hotter conditions of race day, the soft was not as good a tyre as the supersoft, something Ricciardo had also come to realise as he fended off Pérez, who had opted for the red-walled Pirelli.

"It took a while to get the soft going," the Australian confirmed. "Then it was good for a few laps, but you couldn't really get anything out of it. The grip was hard to find, and it was easy to make mistakes and difficult to be consistent."

Mercedes was able to take the lap time information on board, and when Hamilton pitted three laps before half-distance with a 26s lead over Ocon and Bottas, a set of the red-walled supersofts was bolted on and Hamilton resumed with a 9s advantage.

Vettel's performance level on the supersofts had further informed the Mercedes tyre choice, and the championship leader had worked his way past Wehrlein, Grosjean, Vandoorne, Kvyat, Hülkenberg, Stroll, Magnussen and Alonso, to the point where he was up to seventh, just 6s shy of team-mate Räikkönen, after 30 laps had been run.

Kimi was still trapped behind Ricciardo and Pérez, and when Ocon pitted after 32 laps, the second Force India rejoined just behind him, on fresh supersofts, and started to close him down. Montreal is not the easiest circuit on which to effect a pass, so after crunching the numbers, Ferrari brought in Räikkönen for a new set of ultrasofts, having calculated that he would be back on to Pérez with eight laps to go, but on faster rubber. They suggested the same tactic to Vettel, who was unable to pass Ocon's Force India, and after a few laps mulling it over, he too came in for a set of ultras with 21 laps remaining.

On tyres eight laps newer than Räikkönen's, Vettel halved a 7s deficit to his team-mate over the next ten laps, and then, with ten more to go, was ahead. Räikkönen had suffered a brake-by-wire failure approaching the final chicane on lap 60, and as he went through the run-off area and around the mandatory bollard to rejoin, Vettel was just going by. Engineer Dave Greenwood came on the radio with some suggested resets, none of which solved the problem, so Räikkönen had little option but to nurse the car home seventh.

Vettel, though, was on the attack, with his sights set on the Force Indias and Ricciardo. A podium from the very back was not inconceivable.

VIEWPOINT
A LOSS OF POWER AND PATIENCE

FROM the moment McLaren won the F1 raft race in Montreal, the social media comments were as predictable as a Honda power unit failure. The beleaguered team's impressive performance on the Olympic rowing lake provided an easy target. "Shows what they can do without a Honda engine" was the cynical theme.

Even while having fun, McLaren had to smile bravely and endure reminders of their current position, a dilemma that took on a more abrasive edge as McLaren F1 boss Zak Brown publicly made clear his team's reluctance to tolerate the power shortfall for much longer.

Fernando Alonso put a "maybe September" deadline on his decision to do something else if the team didn't win. But what? With his F1 choices limited, Indycar was the immediate choice in the continuing afterglow of his time at the Indy 500. In truth, there seemed to be about as much chance of him going racing at Gateway and Iowa as there was of McLaren Honda winning a grand prix between then and Alonso's 37th birthday in July, 2018.

There was some sympathy – not a lot, but some – for Yusuke Hasagawa when the Honda chief was questioned about the provocative statements.

Despite his obvious weariness – not with the questioners, but with the plight in which he found himself – Hasagawa-san was not about to be cowed, saying that Brown's threat to walk away from the relationship was "not exactly true". In terms of Japanese politeness, that amounted to a verbal lashing.

Reading between the lines, the latest development of the power unit would be made available "when we're ready". It was a cautious approach fashioned by the negative press that had accompanied public failures on the race track (Sunday in Canada being the latest as the first points finish was denied).

From day one, Honda had completely underestimated the challenge. Making all manner of threats was not going to change anything overnight. The damage had been done, and bets were being placed in the Montreal paddock that a McLaren Mercedes would be the way forward for 2018 or, if barriers went up, a McLaren Renault.

Maurice Hamilton

An internal spat at Force India helped him out. Ocon, on his fresher tyres, had caught Pérez and was convinced that he had the pace to beat both his team-mate and Ricciardo, thus giving Force India a potential podium. He suggested over the radio that Pérez should be moved aside and that if he couldn't then pass Ricciardo, he would give the place back to him.

Pérez was not impressed by that idea, however, feeling that he could have a shot at Ricciardo as they approached lapped traffic. "Just let us race, please," the Mexican responded. Sergio was then told that he had three laps to pass Ricciardo, but if he could not, he should let Ocon have a stab.

The problem was that there were only five laps remaining, and Ocon now had his mirrors full of Vettel. And, with four laps to go, Vettel was through. When Ocon tried to pass Pérez into the final chicane and ran a bit wide on the exit, Vettel seized the opportunity and bravely threw the Ferrari down the Frenchman's inside into Turn One. It was very tight, but he made it.

With just two laps to go, Vettel then demoted Pérez with a DRS move into the final chicane and finished the race right on Ricciardo's rear wing. As an exercise in damage limitation, it had been a fine afternoon's work by the Ferrari team leader.

After the problems in Monaco, though, Mercedes had hit back with its first 1-2 of 2017, Bottas taking a comfortable second, 15s clear of Ricciardo.

As the compelling see-saw season continued, with the victory count now reading Mercedes 4, Ferrari 3, Hamilton's race pace suggested that even without Vettel's troubles, the win had still been likely. He set the race's fastest lap – 1m 14.551s – on 32-lap-old supersofts with six laps remaining, not because he needed to or for the glory, but to give the team relevant feedback on the car's capability at that stage. Vettel, doing likewise, set his best lap – 1m 14.719s – on the very last lap with 21-lap-old ultrasofts.

Hamilton made a point of thanking his team for their between-race efforts. "They worked harder than ever and did an amazing job to firstly understand where we went wrong in Monaco and then figure out how we can progress."

So, what exactly did they do?

It amounted to working 24-hour shifts, running a number of simulations and driver-in-loop programmes to evaluate what they should have done in Monaco with the benefit of hindsight. Normally, not too much time is spent looking backwards, but on this occasion it was to facilitate better understanding. It provided three or four threads of information that were explored before applying the same logic to Montreal. That, in turn, led the team down a slightly different set-up avenue because, aerodynamically, the car was fundamentally exactly the same.

Behind them, Ricciardo had extracted everything that was possible for Red Bull to emerge with a podium place on a day when his young team-mate's aggressive approach had team principal Christian Horner reporting, "probably the best start in the team's history," which, sadly for Vettel, restricted him to just 12 points from a race that he had started on the front row. His lead in the championship was down to just those 12 points.

Force India went home with a driver spat to referee – it would worsen in two weeks' time – and Räikkönen was left a somewhat disgruntled seventh in a race that, two days earlier, had promised much more.

The Enstone-based squad, under whatever moniker, had never been other than operationally sharp, and Renault's use of the early VSC period to get Hülkenberg and Palmer into the pits paid off for the former, who claimed eighth, the last car to finish on the lead lap.

After a tricky start to the season, Lance Stroll hung in there to score his first F1 points in his home grand prix with ninth place, while Grosjean brought the Haas home tenth to claim the final point after his first-lap run-in with Sainz, helped by the plucky Alonso's Honda engine expiring with four laps to go.

Tony Dodgins

Above: Sir Patrick Stewart delights Daniel Ricciardo by supping from the Red Bull driver's boot.
Photo: Peter J. Fox

Top left: Winning the raft race was a little light relief for McLaren's mechanics at play.
Photo: Lukas Gorys

Above left: Back to work as they service Fernando Alonso. The Spaniard was looking good for his first point of the season, until an engine failure within five laps of the finish.
Photo: McLaren Honda

Left: Job done! Mercedes team boss Toto Wolff reaches out to congratulate Lewis Hamilton on his victory.
Photo: Peter J. Fox

7

2017 FORMULA 1
GRAND PRIX DU CANADA
MONTRÉAL 9–11 JUNE

ROLEX

OFFICIAL TIMEPIECE

RACE DISTANCE:
70 laps, 189.686 miles/305.270km

RACE WEATHER:
Dry/sunny (track 43–46°C, air 29–30°C)

CIRCUIT GILLES VILLENEUVE, MONTRÉAL

Turn 2 85/50
Turn 3/4 145/90
Pont de la Concorde 180/112
Turn 5 270/168
Turn 6 115/71
Virage Senna 160/99
Droit du Casino 339/211
301/187
Start/finish Chicane 150/93
Turn 9 145/90
Turn 8 135/84
Droite du Casino
Épingle 80/50

Circuit: 2.709 miles / 4.361km
70 laps
187/116 kmh/mph ⚙ Gear — DRS zone

RACE – OFFICIAL CLASSIFICATION

Pos.	Driver	Nat.	No.	Entrant	Car/Engine	Laps	Time/Retirement	Speed (mph/km/h)	Gap to leader	Fastest race lap
1	**Lewis Hamilton**	GB	44	Mercedes AMG Petronas Motorsport	Mercedes F1 W08-Mercedes M08 EQ Power+ V6	70	1h 33m 05.154s	122.265/196.767		1m 14.551s 64
2	**Valtteri Bottas**	FIN	77	Mercedes AMG Petronas Motorsport	Mercedes F1 W08-Mercedes M08 EQ Power+ V6	70	1h 33m 24.937s	121.833/196.072	19.783s	1m 15.894s 65
3	**Daniel Ricciardo**	AUS	3	Red Bull Racing	Red Bull RB13-TAG Heuer RB13 V6	70	1h 33m 40.451s	121.497/195.530	35.297s	1m 16.165s 67
4	**Sebastian Vettel**	D	5	Scuderia Ferrari	Ferrari SF70H-062 V6	70	1h 33m 41.061s	121.484/195.509	35.907s	1m 14.719s 70
5	**Sergio Pérez**	MEX	11	Sahara Force India Formula 1 Team	Force India VJM10-Mercedes M08 EQ Power+ V6	70	1h 33m 45.630s	121.385/195.350	40.476s	1m 16.367s 62
6	**Esteban Ocon**	F	31	Sahara Force India Formula 1 Team	Force India VJM10-Mercedes M08 EQ Power+ V6	70	1h 33m 45.870s	121.380/195.342	40.716s	1m 16.247s 68
7	**Kimi Räikkönen**	FIN	7	Scuderia Ferrari	Ferrari SF70H-062 V6	70	1h 34m 03.786s	120.995/194.722	58.632s	1m 15.388s 59
8	**Nico Hülkenberg**	D	27	Renault Sport Formula One Team	Renault R.S.17-R.E.17 V6	70	1h 34m 05.528s	120.957/194.662	1m 00.374s	1m 16.136s 64
9	**Lance Stroll**	CDN	18	Williams Martini Racing	Williams FW40-Mercedes M08 EQ Power+ V6	69			1 lap	1m 15.979s 64
10	**Romain Grosjean**	F	8	Haas F1 Team	Haas VF-17-Ferrari 062 V6	69			1 lap	1m 16.949s 58
11	Jolyon Palmer	GB	30	Renault Sport Formula One Team	Renault R.S.17-R.E.17 V6	69			1 lap	1m 16.704s 64
12	Kevin Magnussen	DK	20	Haas F1 Team	Haas VF-17-Ferrari 062 V6	69			1 lap	1m 16.341s 65
13	Marcus Ericsson	S	9	Sauber F1 Team	Sauber C36-Ferrari 059/5 V6	69			1 lap	1m 16.995s 50
14	Stoffel Vandoorne	B	2	McLaren Honda Formula 1 Team	McLaren MCL32-Honda RA617H V6	69			1 lap	1m 16.774s 69
15	Pascal Wehrlein	D	94	Sauber F1 Team	Sauber C36-Ferrari 059/5 V6	68			2 laps	1m 17.091s 66
16	Fernando Alonso	E	14	McLaren Honda Formula 1 Team	McLaren MCL32-Honda RA617H V6	66	*power unit*			1m 15.853s 63
	Daniil Kvyat	RUS	26	Scuderia Toro Rosso	Toro Rosso STR12-Renault R.E.17 V6	54	*rear wheel nut*			1m 16.713s 33
	Max Verstappen	NL	33	Red Bull Racing	Red Bull RB13-TAG Heuer RB13 V6	10	*energy store*			1m 17.187s 9
	Felipe Massa	BR	19	Williams Martini Racing	Williams FW40-Mercedes M08 EQ Power+ V6	0	*accident*			no time
	Carlos Sainz	E	55	Scuderia Toro Rosso	Toro Rosso STR12-Renault R.E.17 V6	0	*accident*			no time

Fastest race lap: Lewis Hamilton on lap 64, 1m 14.551s, 130.854mph/210.588km/h.

Lap record: Rubens Barrichello (Ferrari F2004 V10), 1m 13.622s, 132.505mph/213.246km/h (2004).

19 · ERICSSON · Sauber   17 · STROLL · Williams   15 · PALMER · Renault   13 · SAINZ · Toro Rosso   11 · KVYAT · Toro Rosso

20 · WEHRLEIN · Sauber
5-place grid penalty for replacing gearbox. Car modified in *parc fermé*; required to start from the pit lane

18 · MAGNUSSEN · Haas   16 · VANDOORNE · McLaren   14 · GROSJEAN · Haas   12 · ALONSO · McLaren

Grid order	1	2	3	4	5	6	7	8	9	10	11	12	13	14	15	16	17	18	19	20	21	22	23	24	25	26	27	28	29	30	31	32	33	34	35	36	37	38	39	40	41	42	43	44	45	46	47	48	49	50	51	52	53	54
44 HAMILTON	44	44	44	44	44	44	44	44	44	44	44	44	44	44	44	44	44	44	44	44	44	44	44	44	44	44	44	44	44	44	44	44	44	44	44	44	44	44	44	44	44	44	44	44	44	44	44	44	44	44	44	44	44	44
5 VETTEL	33	33	33	33	33	33	33	33	33	33	77	77	77	77	77	77	77	77	77	77	77	31	31	31	31	31	31	31	31	31	31	77	77	77	77	77	77	77	77	77	77	77	77	77	77	77	77	77	77	77	77	77	77	77
77 BOTTAS	77	77	77	77	77	77	77	77	77	77	3	3	3	3	3	3	3	11	31	31	31	31	77	77	77	77	77	77	77	77	77	3	3	3	3	3	3	3	3	3	3	3	3	3	3	3	3	3	3	3	3	3	3	3
7 RÄIKKÖNEN	5	5	5	5	3	3	3	3	3	3	11	11	11	11	11	11	11	31	11	3	3	3	3	3	3	3	3	3	3	3	3	11	11	11	11	11	11	11	11	11	11	11	11	11	11	11	11	11	11	11	11	11	11	11
33 VERSTAPPEN	3	3	3	11	11	11	11	11	11	11	7	7	7	7	7	7	31	3	14	14	11	11	11	11	11	11	11	11	11	11	11	31	7	7	7	7	7	7	31	31	31	31	31	31	31	31	31	31	31	31	31	31	31	31
3 RICCIARDO	7	7	7	11	7	7	7	7	7	14	14	3	11	7	7	7	7	7	7	7	7	7	7	7	31	31	31	31	31	31	5	5	5	5	5	5	5	5	5	7	7	7	7	7	5	5	5	5	5		
19 MASSA	11	11	11	7	31	31	31	31	31	26	26	26	26	14	14	7	7	7	14	14	14	14	14	5	5	5	5	5	5	5	5	7	7	7	7	7	7	5	5	5	5	5	5											
11 PÉREZ	31	31	31	31	27	27	27	27	27	14	14	14	20	20	20	20	20	5	5	5	5	5	5	14	14	14	14	14	14	14	14	14	14	14	14	27	27	27	27	27	27	27	27	27	27	27	2							
31 OCON	27	27	27	27	26	26	26	26	26	2	2	20	20	26	27	18	18	18	5	20	20	20	20	20	27	27	27	27	27	27	27	27	27	27	27	26	26	26	26	26	26	26	26	18	1								
27 HÜLKENBERG	26	26	26	26	14	14	14	14	14	20	20	2	18	18	18	5	5	18	18	18	18	18	5	27	20	20	26	26	26	26	20	20	20	20	20	18	18	18	18	18	18	18	14	1										
26 KVYAT	2	2	2	14	2	2	18	18	18	27	27	26	5	27	27	27	27	27	27	27	26	26	26	26	20	20	20	20	20	20	14	14	14	14	14	14	14	14	14	8														
14 ALONSO	14	14	14	2	20	20	20	20	20	27	27	27	2	2	2	26	26	26	26	26	26	2	2	2	2	2	2	2	2	2	2	2	2	2	18	18	8	8	8	8	8	30	30											
55 SAINZ	20	20	20	20	18	18	18	18	18	8	8	8	5	5	5	2	2	2	2	2	2	8	8	8	8	8	8	8	8	8	8	8	8	18	18	2	8	30	30	30	30	30	9											
8 GROSJEAN	30	30	30	30	30	30	30	30	94	94	5	8	8	8	8	8	8	30	30	30	30	30	30	30	18	18	18	8	30	9	9	9	9	9	9	20																		
30 PALMER	18	18	18	18	9	9	9	9	9	5	5	94	94	94	94	94	94	9	9	9	9	9	18	18	18	18	18	30	30	30	30	9	20	20	20	20	20	20	2																
2 VANDOORNE	9	9	9	8	8	94	94	94	8	30	30	30	30	30	30	30	94	94	9	9	9	9	18	94	18	18	18	18	9	9	9	9	9	9	9	9	2	2	2	2	2	2	94	9										
18 STROLL	8	8	8	8	94	94	8	8	94	18	94	18	18	18	18	94	94	94	94	94	94	94	94	94	94	94	94	94	94	94	94	94	94	94	94	94	94	94	94	26	2													
20 MAGNUSSEN	94	94	94	94	5	5	5	5	5																																													
9 ERICSSON																																																							
94 WEHRLEIN																																																							

8 = Pit stop   26 = Drive-through penalty   94 = One lap or more behind

TIME SHEETS

PRACTICE 1 (FRIDAY)
Weather: Dry/sunny-cloudy
Temperatures: track 28–30°C, air 21–22°C

Pos.	Driver	Laps	Time
1	Lewis Hamilton	36	1m 13.809s
2	Sebastian Vettel	28	1m 14.007s
3	Valtteri Bottas	21	1m 14.046s
4	Kimi Räikkönen	28	1m 14.230s
5	Sergio Pérez	34	1m 14.578s
6	Esteban Ocon	35	1m 14.785s
7	Max Verstappen	19	1m 14.861s
8	Felipe Massa	31	1m 15.106s
9	Daniel Ricciardo	23	1m 15.441s
10	Daniil Kvyat	26	1m 15.658s
11	Stoffel Vandoorne	29	1m 15.943s
12	Kevin Magnussen	25	1m 16.233s
13	Lance Stroll	36	1m 16.313s
14	Romain Grosjean	18	1m 16.345s
15	Nico Hülkenberg	27	1m 16.473s
16	Fernando Alonso	13	1m 16.521s
17	Marcus Ericsson	24	1m 16.805s
18	Jolyon Palmer	26	1m 17.004s
19	Pascal Wehrlein	28	1m 17.606s
20	Carlos Sainz	1	no time

PRACTICE 2 (FRIDAY)
Weather: Dry/sunny-cloudy
Temperatures: track 34–38°C, air 24–25°C

Pos.	Driver	Laps	Time
1	Kimi Räikkönen	41	1m 12.935s
2	Lewis Hamilton	41	1m 13.150s
3	Sebastian Vettel	41	1m 13.200s
4	Valtteri Bottas	42	1m 13.310s
5	Max Verstappen	25	1m 13.388s
6	Felipe Massa	38	1m 14.063s
7	Fernando Alonso	19	1m 14.245s
8	Esteban Ocon	46	1m 14.299s
9	Daniil Kvyat	38	1m 14.461s
10	Sergio Pérez	41	1m 14.501s
11	Romain Grosjean	33	1m 14.566s
12	Nico Hülkenberg	38	1m 14.604s
13	Carlos Sainz	43	1m 14.621s
14	Kevin Magnussen	35	1m 14.676s
15	Daniel Ricciardo	8	1m 15.072s
16	Jolyon Palmer	40	1m 15.127s
17	Lance Stroll	40	1m 15.240s
18	Marcus Ericsson	31	1m 15.611s
19	Stoffel Vandoorne	20	1m 15.624s
20	Pascal Wehrlein	31	1m 16.308s

PRACTICE 3 (SATURDAY)
Weather: Dry/sunny
Temperatures: track 30°C, air 19°C

Pos.	Driver	Laps	Time
1	Sebastian Vettel	20	1m 12.572s
2	Kimi Räikkönen	19	1m 12.864s
3	Lewis Hamilton	22	1m 12.926s
4	Max Verstappen	22	1m 12.965s
5	Valtteri Bottas	24	1m 13.210s
6	Nico Hülkenberg	20	1m 13.493s
7	Felipe Massa	22	1m 13.527s
8	Daniel Ricciardo	35	1m 13.545s
9	Esteban Ocon	26	1m 13.635s
10	Carlos Sainz	22	1m 13.667s
11	Daniil Kvyat	23	1m 13.788s
12	Fernando Alonso	18	1m 13.885s
13	Sergio Pérez	27	1m 13.956s
14	Romain Grosjean	19	1m 13.994s
15	Jolyon Palmer	22	1m 14.102s
16	Stoffel Vandoorne	22	1m 14.228s
17	Kevin Magnussen	18	1m 14.392s
18	Lance Stroll	25	1m 14.409s
19	Marcus Ericsson	25	1m 14.883s
20	Pascal Wehrlein	25	1m 14.965s

QUALIFYING (SATURDAY)
Weather: Dry/sunny-cloudy Temperatures: track 30–44°C, air 20–22°C

Pos.	Driver	First	Second	Third	Qualifying Tyre
1	Lewis Hamilton	1m 12.692s	1m 12.496s	1m 11.459s	Ultrasoft (new)
2	Sebastian Vettel	1m 13.046s	1m 12.749s	1m 11.789s	Ultrasoft (new)
3	Valtteri Bottas	1m 12.685s	1m 12.563s	1m 12.177s	Ultrasoft (new)
4	Kimi Räikkönen	1m 13.548s	1m 12.580s	1m 12.252s	Ultrasoft (new)
5	Max Verstappen	1m 13.177s	1m 12.751s	1m 12.403s	Ultrasoft (new)
6	Daniel Ricciardo	1m 13.543s	1m 12.810s	1m 12.557s	Ultrasoft (new)
7	Felipe Massa	1m 13.435s	1m 13.012s	1m 12.858s	Ultrasoft (new)
8	Sergio Pérez	1m 13.470s	1m 13.262s	1m 13.018s	Ultrasoft (new)
9	Esteban Ocon	1m 13.520s	1m 13.320s	1m 13.135s	Ultrasoft (new)
10	Nico Hülkenberg	1m 13.804s	1m 13.406s	1m 13.271s	Ultrasoft (new)
11	Daniil Kvyat	1m 13.802s	1m 13.690s		
12	Fernando Alonso	1m 13.669s	1m 13.693s		
13	Carlos Sainz	1m 14.051s	1m 13.756s		
14	Romain Grosjean	1m 13.780s	1m 13.839s		
15	Jolyon Palmer	1m 13.990s	1m 14.293s		
16	Stoffel Vandoorne	1m 14.182s			
17	Lance Stroll	1m 14.209s			
18	Kevin Magnussen	1m 14.318s			
19	Marcus Ericsson	1m 14.495s			
20	Pascal Wehrlein	1m 14.810s			

QUALIFYING: head to head

Hamilton	4	3	Bottas
Vettel	6	1	Räikkönen
Massa	7	0	Stroll
Ricciardo	3	4	Verstappen
Pérez	6	1	Ocon
Hülkenberg	7	0	Palmer
Kvyat	3	4	Sainz
Ericsson	2	0	Giovinazzi
Ericsson	1	4	Wehrlein
Alonso	6	0	Vandoorne
Vandoorne	1	0	Button
Grosjean	5	2	Magnussen

FOR THE RECORD

1st POINTS: Lance Stroll

500th POINT: Valtteri Bottas

4,000th LAP LED: Mercedes

10,000th LAP RACED: Sebastian Vettel

DID YOU KNOW?

With 65 pole positions, Lewis Hamilton joined Ayrton Senna in second place in the all-time standings. Hamilton claimed his 65th pole by 0.33 seconds, coincidentally the same margin as Senna for his 65th at San Marino, 1994

POINTS

DRIVERS

1	Sebastian Vettel	141
2	Lewis Hamilton	129
3	Valtteri Bottas	93
4	Kimi Räikkönen	73
5	Daniel Ricciardo	67
6	Max Verstappen	45
7	Sergio Pérez	44
8	Esteban Ocon	27
9	Carlos Sainz	25
10	Felipe Massa	20
11	Nico Hülkenberg	18
12	Romain Grosjean	10
13	Kevin Magnussen	5
14	Pascal Wehrlein	4
15	Daniil Kvyat	4
16	Lance Stroll	2

CONSTRUCTORS

1	Mercedes	222
2	Ferrari	214
3	Red Bull	112
4	Force India	71
5	Toro Rosso	29
6	Williams	22
7	Renault	18
8	Haas	15
9	Sauber	4

9 · OCON · Force India   7 · MASSA · Williams   5 · VERSTAPPEN · Red Bull   3 · BOTTAS · Mercedes   1 · HAMILTON · Mercedes

10 · HÜLKENBERG · Renault   8 · PÉREZ · Force India   6 · RICCIARDO · Red Bull   4 · RÄIKKÖNEN · Ferrari   2 · VETTEL · Ferrari

Lap chart

56	57	58	59	60	61	62	63	64	65	66	67	68	69	70	
44	44	44	44	44	44	44	44	44	44	44	44	44	44	44	1
77	77	77	77	77	77	77	77	77	77	77	77	77	77	77	2
3	3	3	3	3	3	3	3	3	3	3	3	3	3	3	3
11	11	11	11	11	11	11	11	11	11	11	11	5	5	11	4
31	31	31	31	31	31	31	31	31	5	5	11	11	11		5
7	7	7	5	5	5	5	5	31	31	31	31	31			6
5	5	5	7	7	7	7	7	7	7	7	7				7
27	27	27	27	27	27	27	18	27	27	27					8
18	18	18	18	18	18	18	18	18	18	18					9
14	14	14	14	14	14	14	14	14	14	8	8	8			10
8	8	8	8	8	8	8	8	8	8	30	30	30			
30	30	30	30	30	30	30	30	30	30	20	20	20			
20	20	20	20	20	20	20	20	20	20	9	9	9			
9	9	9	9	9	9	9	9	9	9	2	2	2			
2	2	2	2	2	2	2	2	2	94	94					
94	94	94	94	94	94	94	94	94	94						

■ Safety car deployed on laps shown

RACE TYRE STRATEGIES

PIRELLI

	Driver	Race Stint 1	Race Stint 2	Race Stint 3
1	Hamilton	Ultrasoft (u): 1–32	Supersoft (n): 33–70	
2	Bottas	Ultrasoft (u): 1–23	Soft (n): 24–70	
3	Ricciardo	Ultrasoft (u): 1–18	Soft (n): 19–70	
4	Vettel	Ultrasoft (u): 1–5	Supersoft (n): 6–49	Ultrasoft (u): 50–70
5	Pérez	Ultrasoft (u): 1–19	Supersoft (n): 20–70	
6	Ocon	Ultrasoft (u): 1–32	Supersoft (n): 33–70	
7	Räikkönen	Ultrasoft (u): 1–17	Supersoft (n): 18–41	Ultrasoft (u): 42–70
8	Hülkenberg	Ultrasoft (u): 1–11	Supersoft (n): 12–70	
9	Stroll	Ultrasoft (n): 1–25	Supersoft (n): 26–69	
10	Grosjean	Ultrasoft (n): 1	Supersoft (n): 2–69	
11	Palmer	Ultrasoft (n): 1–11	Supersoft (n): 12–69	
12	Magnussen	Supersoft (n): 1–46	Ultrasoft (n): 47–69	
13	Ericsson	Ultrasoft (n): 1–11	Supersoft (n): 12–69	
14	Vandoorne	Ultrasoft (n): 1–45	Supersoft (n): 46–69	
15	Wehrlein	Supersoft (n): 1	Ultrasoft (n): 2–40	Ultrasoft (n): 41–68
16	Alonso	Ultrasoft (n): 1–42	Supersoft (n): 43–66	
	Kvyat	Ultrasoft (n): 1–15	Ultrasoft (u): 16–53	Soft (n): 54 (dnf)
	Verstappen	Ultrasoft (u): 1–10 (dnf)		
	Massa	Ultrasoft (u): 0 (dnf)		
	Sainz	Ultrasoft (n): 0 (dnf)		

The tyre regulations stipulate that at least two of three dry tyre specifications must be used during a dry race.
Pirelli P Zero logos are colour-coded on the tyre sidewalls: Purple = Ultrasoft; Red = Supersoft; Yellow = Soft. (n) new (u) used

Photos: Peter J. Fox

189

AZERBAIJAN GRAND PRIX

BAKU CITY CIRCUIT

Inset, above: An elated Daniel Ricciardo lifts the winner's trophy after an extraordinary race.

Main photo: Once again, Ricciardo made the most of his opportunities to snatch victory when misfortune hit other competitors.

Photos: Red Bull Racing/Getty Images

BAKU QUALIFYING

AT round eight in Baku, qualifying was always going to be intriguing: another relatively low-grip surface with low tyre degradation and an extremely long main straight, on which tyres and brakes lost temperature, meaning that tyre preparation was going to be trickier than ever. When you considered the evidence of Sochi and Monaco, it was likely to be challenging for Mercedes, notwithstanding that ambient temperatures were higher, although they had dropped again by the near 6pm finishing time of qualifying. On the other hand, there was the Mercedes grunt and the fact that the long Baku lap played to the strengths of the three-pointed star's superior energy harvesting capabilities.

On Friday, Mercedes did indeed seem a little lost, with Valtteri Bottas again appearing more comfortable than Lewis Hamilton in these specific conditions. The situation was exacerbated by Pirelli not offering the ultrasoft compound in Azerbaijan, the official explanation being that the selections had to be made before the company had sufficient data, hence the conservatism. But great overnight work by the Mercedes engineers resulted in the W08 being better at switching on its tyres on Saturday.

After the first Q3 runs, it was indeed Bottas who topped the time sheet, but Hamilton had been on a good first run prior to getting a little overambitious in Turn 16 and losing time, so the potential was there. His task was made tougher, however, when Daniel Ricciardo clipped the Turn Six wall and brought out the red flag with just 3m 33s left on the clock. With Mercedes being the best at getting the supersoft tyre into its operating window on a second flying lap, that *modus operandi* was a luxury they were not about to enjoy...

Thus it was a great effort when, with the chips down, Hamilton produced a fantastic 1m 40.593s to claim a 66th, and Senna-beating, pole position on a single lap that he considered even better than his Montreal pole and that beat Bottas, who also improved, by 0.43s.

"The guys did fantastic work overnight," Lewis confirmed. "On that last run, I could see that Valtteri, up ahead, was on a great lap as well, and I was so happy to get the pole and proud of the lap."

Bottas didn't agree with his team-mate's assessment, however, and his face betrayed his disappointment.

"Lewis had a really good lap, and I didn't," he countered. "It was the first time we'd tried to go for it on the first lap, and I just didn't get the tyres working as well as Lewis."

The margin over Ferrari was uncharacteristically large, with third-placed Kimi Räikkönen 1.1s adrift of Hamilton's pole as Maranello faced a threat from Red Bull. There were rumours that a method of burning oil in the cylinders to boost qualifying power by around 40bhp (worth roughly 0.4s) had been neutralised by a pre-race technical directive, and that it had hit Ferrari hardest, hence the larger gap. Sebastian Vettel's cause was not aided by an engine change to an older unit, which had already completed almost 3,500km, after the final session of free practice on Saturday morning, the four-times champion qualifying 0.15s behind his team-mate.

Just three-hundredths behind him was Max Verstappen, who had looked mighty throughout, regularly quickest of all in the twisty second sector. Red Bull team principal Christian Horner had figured it might be possible to sneak a car on to the second row, but Verstappen, on a lap three-tenths quicker than previously, lost gear synchronisation in the second sector and made a small error at Turn Seven, so had to be content with fifth.

Force India, strong at Baku in 2016, when Pérez had finished on the podium, was a strong factor again, the Mexican putting his car on the third row, 0.07s quicker than teammate Esteban Ocon. The latter shared row four with an impressive Lance Stroll, who outqualified Williams team-mate Felipe Massa for the first time.

The young Canadian's confidence had been boosted by the two points he had taken at home in Montreal and the luxury of a day's test in a 2014 car at Austin, which had prioritised 'operations procedures' (read tyre warm-up) after the Canadian race. Stroll was one of only three drivers who did not initiate a yellow flag on Friday – and it wasn't because he was going slowly.

Williams technical chief Paddy Lowe was only partly happy, though, with Massa some 0.04s behind Stroll in a car that the team suspected had Force India-beating pace. In Q3, Massa tried a single-lap first run, but didn't get the tyres in, the team pitting him to allow for a two-lap final run that was scuppered by the red flag.

Behind the chastened Ricciardo, Daniil Kvyat was satisfied with 11th in the first Toro Rosso, 0.16s ahead of Carlos Sainz, who had never felt fully confident in the car from first thing on Friday and would start 15th, following the imposition of a three-place grid penalty for his Grosjean indiscretion in Canada.

Kevin Magnussen did a strong job to place the first Haas 13th, while team-mate Grosjean, in trouble with brakes yet again, failed to make it out of Q1. Nico Hülkenberg lost his second Q2 run to an electrical issue and was 14th, ahead of another strong showing by Pascal Wehrlein in the sole Sauber to progress from Q1.

McLaren's Eric Boullier labelled Baku "the most painful weekend I have experienced in the sport," as Fernando Alonso (40) and Stoffel Vandoorne (35) were hit with multiple grid penalties for engine changes; the McLaren Hondas were slow anyway. To cope with Baku's long straight, and aware that they would be starting at the back, they ran barely any rear wing, which made them slower in sector two. If there was a positive, a new 'Spec 3' engine, tried on Friday in Alonso's car, was reckoned to be worth 0.3s. Sadly, though, due to a gearbox problem, McLaren took it out after Friday practice and put it away until Austria.

Jolyon Palmer's woes continued, too, a high-pressure fuel leak setting fire to his car on Saturday morning, which left too much work to get him out for qualifying.

WITH the GP2 race as a barometer, many had expected 2016's F1 race around the streets of Baku to be an incident-packed crash festival, but in fact it passed off with barely a drama. This race made up for that...

It all began at Turn One as Hamilton converted his pole position and Vettel suffered a small lock-up as he went inside Räikkönen. Kimi was forced to back out of the throttle to allow his team-mate room, giving Bottas a sniff of an opportunity to follow Sebastian through down the inside of Turn Two. But the younger Finn used a bit too much kerb and bounced the Mercedes into the side of the Ferrari.

The contact punctured Bottas's right front, and he hobbled around to the pits, going a lap down in the process, while Räikkönen had front wing damage, but continued, losing places to Pérez and Verstappen. Further back, Ricciardo collected a piece of Räikkönen's damaged Ferrari in his front brake duct. Red Bull monitored the rising brake temperatures before pitting him after just five laps, bolting on a set of softs and sending him back out 17th for an intended 46-lap stint to the flag.

Daniel soon became the team's sole interest, after an irritated Verstappen suffered loss of oil pressure and another engine failure while running a strong fourth. A couple of laps earlier, Kvyat's Renault engine had suffered an electrical issue and he parked his Toro Rosso at Turn 12, which ultimately prompted the appearance of the safety car.

Everyone piled in for a tyre change, most opting for the yellow-walled Pirelli soft to get to the end. Ricciardo, meanwhile, came back in to jettison the softs he'd taken just eight laps earlier in favour of supersofts.

Once everyone was back in line behind the official Mercedes, the order was: Hamilton, Vettel, Pérez, Räikkönen, Massa, Ocon, Stroll, Hülkenberg, Magnussen and, back into the top ten, Ricciardo. He had managed to tow his way past Sainz and Ericsson in one go, and also demote Alonso before the safety car had made its second appearance.

The aforementioned 2016 GP2 race had produced some hairy-looking restarts as the ultra-long front straight had left cars vulnerable to being slipstreamed into Turn One, leading to late braking and robust defence. Factor in differing F1 engine performance, and many were holding their breath...

Hamilton backed up the pack and then seemed to catch Vettel on the hop. The championship leader only just managed to defend against Pérez's Mercedes-powered Force India into Turn One. However, team-mate Räikkönen could not stop either Massa's Williams or Ocon in the second Force India from demoting the second Ferrari, while Ricciardo picked up another slot when he jumped Magnussen.

Almost immediately, though, the safety car was out once more as TV monitors showed debris being sent skywards by passing cars. The field was led through the pit lane by Bernd Maylander while it was recovered. Everyone prepared themselves for opportunities provided by a second restart.

What happened next changed a thus far respectful relationship between the two championship combatants, which had bordered on being a mutual admiration society. When the safety car lights went out again to indicate that it would come in at the end of lap 19, Hamilton backed up the pack once again. Over the crest into Turn 15, he came off the throttle at a point where Vettel, having been caught napping a little first time around, was intent on staying close. Sebastian had just given the Ferrari a little squirt of throttle as Hamilton backed off. In a trice, his front wing was into the back of the Merc's diffuser, lightly damaging both.

Vettel, furious and believing he had been brake-tested, pulled alongside and deliberately clouted Hamilton's left front wheel with his own right front while offering Lewis a "What the hell are you doing?" gesture with his other hand. When race stewards examined the data later, they found that while Hamilton had lifted off, he hadn't touched the brakes, so, technically, had not 'brake-tested' the Ferrari.

Vettel's moment of deliberate impact had occurred well before the point at which Hamilton was about to launch his

Above: Mercedes pair Hamilton and Bottas lead the field at the start.
Photo: Mercedes AMG Petronas F1 Team

Top left: The mix of ancient and modern architecture makes the Baku circuit a pleasing venue for F1.
Photo: Haas F1 Team

Above left: Williams's Paddy Lowe (*left*) and Mercedes's Toto Wolff in conversation.
Photo: Peter J. Fox

Centre left: Lewis Hamilton lifts a wheel on his way to taking a stunning pole position.
Photo: Mercedes AMG Petronas F1 Team

Below left: Up the escalator. Valtteri Bottas and Kimi Räikkönen head for the interview room post-qualifying.
Photo: Lukas Gorys

Above: Race eight, and Fernando Alonso broke his duck after plugging away to earn a ninth-place finish for McLaren Honda.
Photo: McLaren Honda

Top right: Felipe Massa, Nico Hülkenberg and Kevin Magnussen run three abreast on the wide track.
Photo: Lukas Gorys

Above right: Marcus Ericsson meets the press before the race. He underlined the team's stance that both drivers were always given equal equipment.

Above far right: Pascal Wehrlein grabbed a point Sauber. The team was somewhat in disarray after the sudden departure of Monisha Kaltenborn in the week before the race.
Photos: WRi2/Jad Sherif

Right: After an early collision with Räikkönen, Valtteri Bottas staged a great comeback drive to second place. Here, the Finn locks a wheel ahead of Esteban Ocon during his charge through the field.
Photo: Peter J. Fox

restart proper, and at a snail's pace. It was something and nothing, but clearly a fit of temper and overreaction, and not an action befitting a four-times champion. Vettel had laid himself open to a penalty, and we waited to see what it would be.

"I was told at Turn Seven that the safety car was going to come in, and I'm only allowed a ten-car-length gap while its lights are still on," Hamilton explained. "Going into Turn 15, I was around that, and as the safety car went down the hill, I saw the lights go off. The leading driver sets the pace, and at that point I don't need to accelerate or speed up. I kept a consistent pace, or probably a constant deceleration down to the apex, and just didn't speed up from there.

"I did that at the first restart, and I did that again second time. But on that second time, I got a nudge. I didn't think anything about it and I still got a really good restart. It's a very hard circuit to maintain position into Turn One with such a long straight, so I made sure I was really on top of it. The first trick that you tried won't necessarily work again, and so I had to come up with different ways to make sure I was into T1 in the lead, but that's after Turn 16, not Turn 15."

Thus Hamilton successfully protected his lead for a second time, while Vettel had more to think about in defending against Pérez and Massa. Ricciardo, meanwhile, gained a place by demoting Hülkenberg.

Relations at Force India, already strained after Pérez had refused to let Ocon by in Canada, were about to deteriorate further. When the two cars banged wheels through Turn One, Ocon considered that Pérez had been too physical and launched a counter move down the inside of Turn Two. On exit, he tried to put the squeeze on the Mexican, but overdid it, and once again we had flying carbon fibre. Räikkönen, enduring a nightmare of an afternoon, ran over it, to the detriment of his floor and a punctured left rear. The Ferrari left yet more debris as it limped around to the pits, and the safety car was out again practically before it had parked.

After a handful of slow laps, Alonso informed race director Charlie Whiting on the radio that there was so much debris

on the track that a red flag would be a better option and, indeed, race control considered discretion the better part of valour. The field was led into the pits after 22 of the scheduled 51 laps.

Time to take stock. Hamilton led, from Vettel, then the two Williams – Massa ahead of Stroll; Ricciardo was up to fifth, then Hülkenberg, Magnussen, Alonso, Sainz, Grosjean, Ericsson, Vandoorne, Bottas – who had the safety cars to thank for being back on the lead lap; next came the delayed Ocon, Wehrlein and, now a lap down, the damaged Pérez and Räikkönen.

The red-flag period allowed Force India and Ferrari to effect running repairs to their cars, although they would pick up penalties for working on Pérez and Räikkönen in a restricted area once the three-minute signal had been given. And there was more comedy radio angst from poor Kimi as his car was pushed to the end of the pit lane temporarily without its steering wheel…

After a 25-minute delay, the Azerbaijan GP resumed behind the safety car for a single lap with everyone on changed supersofts before the field was released in anger once more. Across the line, Hamilton had a small margin over Vettel, and behind them just 0.18s blanketed Stroll, Hülkenberg, Massa and Ricciardo. Massa was in trouble, however, passed by his team-mate and Hülkenberg's Renault as the No. 19 Williams bucked all over the place.

"We can see the issue," the Williams team told Felipe over the radio. It was a broken rear damper, and the Brazilian toured in to retire on lap 25.

Ricciardo, meanwhile, had shot down the inside of both Stroll and Hülkenberg at Turn One to emerge third, something he couldn't possibly have imagined when forced to make a lap-five pit stop with sky-high brake temperature. Offer him an opportunity, and the Australian rarely fails to grab it. 'The Hulk's' afternoon ended prematurely, though, when he clobbered the Turn Eight wall and removed his right front wheel.

Bottas was on the move, into the top ten for the first time

Above: Lance Stroll drove with great composure to bag a podium, only narrowly losing second place to Bottas on the last lap.
Photo: Lukas Gorys

Top right: Daniel Ricciardo dispenses the champagne over Lance Stroll on the young Canadian's first ever podium visit.
Photo: Red Bull Racing/Getty Images

Above right: With the race redflagged, Lewis Hamilton waits for the restart. A loose cockpit surround would deny a probable victory for the unlucky leader.
Photo: GP Photo/Peter Nygaard

Right: In a race full of drama, Sebastian Vettel took on the role of pantomime villain after his wheel-banging escapade with Hamilton behind the safety car.
Photo: Peter J. Fox

as he demoted Vandoorne and Ericsson, and just 15s behind his race-leading team-mate.

Hamilton, though, would not be leading for much longer. His cockpit surround padding was flapping loose, and despite the fact that he and Mercedes played it down over the radio, and that he attempted to hold it in place with one hand at 220mph in eighth gear, before trying to re-attach it, there soon came a message from race control that he needed to pit to have it properly sorted.

Almost simultaneously, the race stewards announced that Vettel's earlier hot-headedness would be penalised by a 10s stop-go. So, at the end of lap 31, Hamilton's Mercedes headed in for attention, costing him a net 27s, and two laps later, the Ferrari team leader was in to serve his penalty, costing him a total of 29.3s. But a quicker in-lap from the Ferrari, allied to the fact that Hamilton had pitted out behind Pérez, meant that Vettel came out just ahead of Hamilton on the road as they ran seventh and eighth, behind Alonso.

The upshot, unbelievably, was that Ricciardo now had a 3.5s lead over Stroll, with a 13s gap to third-placed Magnussen. Ocon ran fourth, just ahead of Bottas, who had put his Mercedes into the top five, having disposed of Grosjean and Alonso.

Magnussen's third place didn't last long, as Bottas managed to pass both the Haas and Ocon's Force India at Turn One, and then the Dane had to give best to the Frenchman, and to the recovering Vettel and Hamilton.

At the start of lap 42, Vettel passed Ocon into Turn One; Hamilton did likewise a lap later in a ballsy move around the outside. Ricciardo now had a 5s lead over Stroll, with Bottas 9s back, but lapping a full second quicker. Vettel, going even quicker, was 4.5s behind Valtteri, while Hamilton, in his wheel tracks, was faster still. This would be interesting!

"You will catch Stroll on the last lap," Mercedes told Bottas eight laps out, and their prediction was spot on. With Ricciardo still 4s to the good as he stroked home to an entirely unpredictable fifth GP win, Bottas lined up Stroll

out of Turn 16 and shot by to take second place by just a tenth of a second as the chequer fell on the season's most dramatic race. Nevertheless, the young Canadian was delighted to score his first F1 podium, with less than 2s in hand over Vettel's closing Ferrari, which was just 0.2s clear of Hamilton's Mercedes.

Ocon was sixth and faced another interesting Force India debrief. Magnussen was a fighting seventh, in front of the Spanish contingent – Sainz followed by Alonso – while Wehrlein took the final point ahead of Ericsson, these 'teammates' having also made contact earlier.

Despite his rush of blood to the head, Vettel had scored two points more than Hamilton and extended his championship lead to 14 points, aided of course by the Merc's unscheduled pit stop. Hamilton, clearly, was unimpressed by that and thought that Vettel had got off lightly, and it didn't take long for the recriminations to begin.

"Today was obviously a different Sebastian that we saw," Hamilton observed. "I'd like to think that I will remain respectful and want to win this championship in the right way. We pulled away to a 24-point lead over Ferrari in the constructors' championship, so there's positives to take. Generally, the car behind wants to get as close as possible at a restart, but it was a misjudgement from him. To blame it on the car in front, you know, some people don't like to own up to their own mistakes...

"As a team, we can also look at it as another positive. We've put a lot of pressure on Ferrari, and it's not a bad thing if it shows that pressure can get to some of the best of us..."

And Vettel, you can be sure, would have gone home reflecting upon exactly that. Hamilton's points loss was a factor of his headrest issue and beyond his control. From that point on, Vettel knew he should have won the race, but he'd scored 12 points instead of 25, due to a factor totally within his control. If he ended up losing the championship by less than 13 points...

Tony Dodgins

VIEWPOINT
BUMPING, NOT BORING

A LOT of fuss about very little? Or a serious issue than needed to be addressed? The Vettel/Hamilton incident aroused as much emotion trackside and beyond as Sebastian demonstrated momentarily in the car. One argument claimed that you can't have one driver deliberately banging into a rival. Another said that this was hardly at 200mph going up Kemmel Straight; a case of handbags rather than a knife fight.

A strong thread in the first line of thinking was that this would send the wrong message to the global audience of young kart racers, for whom a quick flick of the wrist could easily become an acceptable reaction to any perceived injustice from a competitor. After all, there was no question about the role model created by a four-times world champion, even if the incident had been at a walking pace.

On the other hand, more moderate voices supported a show of emotion in a sport that was becoming increasingly sanitised by political correctness and predictable sound bites. The supporting argument ran along the lines: "People say that there are no characters in F1 any more, and then when we get one, albeit briefly, he is criticised."

Vettel's case was not helped in the immediate aftermath by a complete lack of contrition and his inaccurate assertion that Hamilton had been the guilty party because of a (wrongly) perceived brake-test. The naysayers were further incensed when the FIA followed up the ten-second stop-go penalty with what appeared to be a cosy chat with their safety ambassador and a slap on the wrist, preceded by Seb's promise that he would not be a naughty boy again.

Whatever your view of the punishment, there could be no denying that the penalty actually had a damaging effect. It not only took around 30 seconds out of his race by the time he had got in and out of the pits, but also the enforced delay had cost him an easy win. He finished fourth, his impetuous behaviour actually having cost 13 points, a huge setback in a championship as close as this.

Maurice Hamilton

8

2017 FORMULA 1
AZERBAIJAN
GRAND PRIX

ROLEX

OFFICIAL TIMEPIECE

BAKU 23–25 JUNE

RACE DISTANCE: 51 laps, 190.170 miles/306.049km

RACE WEATHER: Dry/sunny (track 38–54°C, air 27–29°C)

BAKU STREET CIRCUIT, AZERBAIJAN
Circuit: 3.730 miles / 6.003km
51 laps

RACE – OFFICIAL CLASSIFICATION

Pos.	Driver	Nat.	No.	Entrant	Car/Engine	Laps	Time/Retirement	Speed (mph/km/h)	Gap to leader	Fastest race lap	
1	**Daniel Ricciardo**	AUS	3	Red Bull Racing	Red Bull RB13-TAG Heuer RB13 V6	51	2h 03m 55.573s	92.072/148.176		1m 44.882s	46
2	**Valtteri Bottas**	FIN	77	Mercedes AMG Petronas Motorsport	Mercedes F1 W08-Mercedes M08 EQ Power+ V6	51	2h 03m 59.477s	92.024/148.098	3.904s	1m 43.925s	51
3	**Lance Stroll**	CDN	18	Williams Martini Racing	Williams FW40-Mercedes M08 EQ Power+ V6	51	2h 03m 59.582s	92.023/148.096	4.009s	1m 45.108s	44
4	**Sebastian Vettel**	D	5	Scuderia Ferrari	Ferrari SF70H-062 V6	51	2h 04m 01.549s	91.998/148.057	5.976s	1m 43.441s	47
5	**Lewis Hamilton**	GB	44	Mercedes AMG Petronas Motorsport	Mercedes F1 W08-Mercedes M08 EQ Power+ V6	51	2h 04m 01.761s	91.996/148.053	6.188s	1m 43.469s	46
6	**Esteban Ocon**	F	31	Sahara Force India Formula 1 Team	Force India VJM10-Mercedes M08 EQ Power+ V6	51	2h 04m 25.871s	91.699/147.575	30.298s	1m 45.634s	39
7	**Kevin Magnussen**	DK	20	Haas F1 Team	Haas VF-17-Ferrari 062 V6	51	2h 04m 37.326s	91.558/147.348	41.753s	1m 46.312s	45
8	**Carlos Sainz**	E	55	Scuderia Toro Rosso	Toro Rosso STR12-Renault R.E.17 V6	51	2h 04m 44.973s	91.465/147.198	49.400s	1m 45.866s	46
9	**Fernando Alonso**	E	14	McLaren Honda Formula 1 Team	McLaren MCL32-Honda RA617H V6	51	2h 04m 55.124s	91.341/146.999	59.551s	1m 45.168s	49
10	**Pascal Wehrlein**	D	94	Sauber F1 Team	Sauber C36-Ferrari 059/5 V6	51	2h 05m 24.666s	90.982/146.421	1m 29.093s	1m 47.120s	46
11	Marcus Ericsson	S	9	Sauber F1 Team	Sauber C36-Ferrari 059/5 V6	51	2h 05m 27.367s	90.949/146.369	1m 31.794s	1m 47.186s	45
12	Stoffel Vandoorne	B	2	McLaren Honda Formula 1 Team	McLaren MCL32-Honda RA617H V6	51	2h 05m 27.733s	90.945/146.362	1m 32.160s	1m 46.648s	45
13	Romain Grosjean	F	8	Haas F1 Team	Haas VF-17-Ferrari 062 V6	50			1 lap	1m 46.831s	45
14	Kimi Räikkönen	FIN	7	Scuderia Ferrari	Ferrari SF70H-062 V6	46	floor		5 laps	1m 45.542s	44
	Sergio Pérez	MEX	11	Sahara Force India Formula 1 Team	Force India VJM10-Mercedes M08 EQ Power+ V6	39	accident damage			1m 45.588s	37
	Felipe Massa	BR	19	Williams Martini Racing	Williams FW40-Mercedes M08 EQ Power+ V6	25	suspension			1m 47.340s	10
	Nico Hülkenberg	D	27	Renault Sport Formula One Team	Renault R.S.17-R.E.17 V6	24	accident/front suspension			1m 48.536s	9
	Max Verstappen	NL	33	Red Bull Racing	Red Bull RB13-TAG Heuer RB13 V6	12	engine			1m 46.398s	10
	Daniil Kvyat	RUS	26	Scuderia Toro Rosso	Toro Rosso STR12-Renault R.E.17 V6	9	electronics			1m 48.394s	9
	Jolyon Palmer	GB	30	Renault Sport Formula One Team	Renault R.S.17-R.E.17 V6	7	ignition			1m 51.673s	5

Race stopped on lap 23 due to debris on the track, then restarted for the remaining distance. Overall race times include stoppage time totalling 22m 40s.

Fastest race lap: Sebastian Vettel on lap 47, 1m 43.441s, 129.816mph/208.919km/h (new record).

Previous lap record: Nico Rosberg (Mercedes-Benz F1 W07 V6 turbo), 1m 46.485s, 126.105mph/202.946km/h (2016).

 All results and data © FOM 2017

20 · PALMER · Renault

18 · VANDOORNE · McLaren
30-place grid penalty for using additional power unit elements; 5 places for replacing gearbox

16 · GROSJEAN · Haas

14 · WEHRLEIN · Sauber

12 · MAGNUSSEN · Haas

19 · ALONSO · McLaren
40-place grid penalty for using additional power unit elements

17 · ERICSSON · Sauber

15 · SAINZ · Toro Rosso
3-place grid penalty for causing an accident in round 7

13 · HÜLKENBERG · Renault

11 · KVYAT · Toro Rosso

Grid order		1	2	3	4	5	6	7	8	9	10	11	12	13	14	15	16	17	18	19	20	21	22	23	24	25	26	27	28	29	30	31	32	33	34	35	36	37	38	39	40	41
44	HAMILTON	44	44	44	44	44	44	44	44	44	44	44	44	44	44	44	44	44	44	44	44	44	44	44	44	44	44	44	44	44	5	5	5	3	3	3	3	3	3	3
77	BOTTAS	5	5	5	5	5	5	5	5	5	5	11	5	5	5	5	5	5	5	5	5	5	5	5	44	3	3	18	18	18	18	18	18	18
7	RÄIKKÖNEN	11	11	11	11	11	11	11	11	11	11	11	11	5	11	11	11	19	18	3	3	3	3	3	3	18	18	20	20	20	31	31	77	77
5	VETTEL	33	33	33	33	33	33	33	33	33	7	7	18	7	7	19	19	19	18	18	18	27	18	18	18	18	18	20	20	31	31	31	20	77	31	31	31
33	VERSTAPPEN	7	7	7	7	7	7	7	7	7	19	19	7	19	19	31	31	31	31	3	3	3	19	27	20	20	20	20	20	14	31	77	77	77	77	20	5	5	5
11	PÉREZ	19	19	19	19	19	19	19	19	19	31	31	19	31	31	7	7	7	7	27	27	27	3	19	14	14	14	14	14	31	14	14	14	5	5	5	44	44	44
31	OCON	31	31	31	31	31	31	31	31	31	33	18	31	18	18	18	18	20	20	20	20	55	55	55	31	31	31	77	77	5	5	44	44	44	20	20	20
18	STROLL	18	18	18	18	18	18	18	18	18	18	33	27	27	27	27	27	14	14	14	14	31	31	31	55	77	77	44	44	44	14	14	14	14	14
19	MASSA	3	3	3	27	27	27	27	27	27	27	20	20	20	3	3	3	3	55	55	55	8	77	77	77	55	55	55	55	55	55	55	55	55
3	RICCIARDO	27	27	27	20	20	20	20	20	20	20	3	3	3	20	20	20	8	8	8	8	77	8	8	8	8	8	8	8	9	9	9	9	9	9
26	KVYAT	20	20	20	26	26	26	26	26	3	3	14	14	14	14	14	9	9	9	31	2	2	2	2	2	9	9	94	94	94	94	94	94
20	MAGNUSSEN	26	26	26	3	9	9	9	14	14	14	55	55	55	55	55	2	2	2	2	9	9	9	9	9	2	94	94	8	2	2	2	2
27	HÜLKENBERG	94	8	9	9	14	14	14	55	55	55	2	2	2	2	77	77	77	31	77	94	94	94	94	94	94	2	2	2	8	8	8	8
94	WEHRLEIN	8	94	94	14	55	55	55	9	9	9	9	9	9	9	31	31	77	19	11	11	11	11	11	11	11	11	11	11	11	7	7
55	SAINZ	9	9	2	14	55	30	3	3	3	94	94	94	8	8	8	9	9	11	94	94	94	94	11	7	7	7	7	7	7	7	11
8	GROSJEAN	2	14	55	94	94	94	94	94	2	2	2	94	94	94	94	77	77	31	11	11	11	11	7
9	ERICSSON	30	14	55	94	30	3	2	2	2	8	8	8	77	77	77	77	77	94	94	7	7	7	7
2	VANDOORNE	14	30	30	30	2	2	8	8	8	77	77	77
14	ALONSO	55	55	8	8	8	8	30	77	77
30	PALMER	77	77	77	77	77	77	77

77 = Pit stop   11 = Drive-through penalty

7 = One lap or more behind

TIME SHEETS

PRACTICE 1 (FRIDAY)
Weather: Dry/sunny
Temperatures: track 50–56°C, air 27–29°C

Pos.	Driver	Laps	Time
1	Max Verstappen	19	1m 44.410s
2	Daniel Ricciardo	22	1m 44.880s
3	Sebastian Vettel	20	1m 44.967s
4	Sergio Pérez	16	1m 45.398s
5	Lewis Hamilton	16	1m 45.497s
6	Valtteri Bottas	19	1m 45.737s
7	Esteban Ocon	24	1m 45.752s
8	Felipe Massa	25	1m 45.968s
9	Kimi Räikkönen	18	1m 46.000s
10	Daniil Kvyat	11	1m 46.617s
11	Lance Stroll	28	1m 46.649s
12	Kevin Magnussen	23	1m 46.721s
13	Romain Grosjean	22	1m 46.837s
14	Nico Hülkenberg	21	1m 47.217s
15	Stoffel Vandoorne	22	1m 47.446s
16	Carlos Sainz	13	1m 47.501s
17	Fernando Alonso	20	1m 47.551s
18	Jolyon Palmer	15	1m 48.525s
19	Pascal Wehrlein	19	1m 49.048s
20	Marcus Ericsson	21	1m 49.937s

PRACTICE 2 (FRIDAY)
Weather: Dry/sunny
Temperatures: track 35–45°C, air 26–29°C

Pos.	Driver	Laps	Time
1	Max Verstappen	36	1m 43.362s
2	Valtteri Bottas	32	1m 43.462s
3	Daniel Ricciardo	34	1m 43.473s
4	Kimi Räikkönen	35	1m 43.489s
5	Sebastian Vettel	35	1m 43.615s
6	Lance Stroll	27	1m 44.113s
7	Sergio Pérez	34	1m 44.306s
8	Daniil Kvyat	27	1m 44.321s
9	Esteban Ocon	37	1m 44.484s
10	Lewis Hamilton	23	1m 44.525s
11	Felipe Massa	33	1m 44.609s
12	Fernando Alonso	15	1m 45.515s
13	Carlos Sainz	34	1m 45.733s
14	Kevin Magnussen	33	1m 45.831s
15	Nico Hülkenberg	29	1m 46.003s
16	Jolyon Palmer	17	1m 46.061s
17	Stoffel Vandoorne	28	1m 46.174s
18	Pascal Wehrlein	25	1m 47.150s
19	Marcus Ericsson	25	1m 47.347s
20	Romain Grosjean	22	1m 47.722s

PRACTICE 3 (SATURDAY)
Weather: Dry/sunny
Temperatures: track 56°C, air 26°C

Pos.	Driver	Laps	Time
1	Valtteri Bottas	21	1m 42.742s
2	Kimi Räikkönen	14	1m 42.837s
3	Lewis Hamilton	23	1m 43.158s
4	Daniel Ricciardo	24	1m 43.287s
5	Esteban Ocon	21	1m 43.344s
6	Max Verstappen	16	1m 43.614s
7	Felipe Massa	18	1m 43.738s
8	Daniil Kvyat	21	1m 43.908s
9	Lance Stroll	17	1m 44.040s
10	Sergio Pérez	22	1m 44.138s
11	Nico Hülkenberg	16	1m 44.312s
12	Sebastian Vettel	7	1m 44.344s
13	Carlos Sainz	23	1m 44.401s
14	Fernando Alonso	18	1m 44.741s
15	Kevin Magnussen	20	1m 44.926s
16	Stoffel Vandoorne	17	1m 45.143s
17	Romain Grosjean	20	1m 45.491s
18	Marcus Ericsson	21	1m 45.645s
19	Pascal Wehrlein	19	1m 45.722s
20	Jolyon Palmer	4	1m 53.040s

QUALIFYING (SATURDAY)
Weather: Dry/sunny Temperatures: track 42–54°C, air 26–28°C

Pos.	Driver	First	Second	Third	Qualifying Tyre
1	Lewis Hamilton	1m 41.983s	1m 41.275s	1m 40.593s	Supersoft (new)
2	Valtteri Bottas	1m 43.026s	1m 41.502s	1m 41.027s	Supersoft (new)
3	Kimi Räikkönen	1m 42.678s	1m 42.009s	1m 41.693s	Supersoft (new)
4	Sebastian Vettel	1m 42.952s	1m 41.911s	1m 41.841s	Supersoft (new)
5	Max Verstappen	1m 42.544s	1m 41.961s	1m 41.879s	Supersoft (new)
6	Sergio Pérez	1m 43.162s	1m 42.467s	1m 42.111s	Supersoft (new)
7	Esteban Ocon	1m 43.051s	1m 42.751s	1m 42.186s	Supersoft (new)
8	Lance Stroll	1m 43.613s	1m 42.284s	1m 42.753s	Supersoft (new)
9	Felipe Massa	1m 43.165s	1m 42.735s	1m 42.798s	Supersoft (used)
10	Daniel Ricciardo	1m 42.857s	1m 42.215s	1m 43.414s	Supersoft (new)
11	Daniil Kvyat	1m 42.927s	1m 43.186s		
12	Carlos Sainz	1m 43.489s	1m 43.347s		
13	Kevin Magnussen	1m 44.029s	1m 43.796s		
14	Nico Hülkenberg	1m 43.930s	1m 44.267s		
15	Pascal Wehrlein	1m 44.317s	1m 44.603s		
16	Fernando Alonso	1m 44.334s			
17	Romain Grosjean	1m 44.468s			
18	Marcus Ericsson	1m 44.795s			
19	Stoffel Vandoorne	1m 45.030s			
20	Jolyon Palmer	no time			

QUALIFYING: head to head

Hamilton	5	3	Bottas
Vettel	6	2	Räikkönen
Massa	7	1	Stroll
Ricciardo	3	5	Verstappen
Pérez	7	1	Ocon
Hülkenberg	8	0	Palmer
Kvyat	4	4	Sainz
Ericsson	2	0	Giovinazzi
Ericsson	1	5	Wehrlein
Alonso	7	0	Vandoorne
Vandoorne	1	0	Button
Grosjean	5	3	Magnussen

FOR THE RECORD

FOR THE RECORD

1st PODIUM POSITION: **Lance Stroll**

DID YOU KNOW?

Stroll was the first Canadian on the podium since Jacques Villeneuve in Germany 2001.

POINTS

DRIVERS

1	Sebastian Vettel	153
2	Lewis Hamilton	139
3	Valtteri Bottas	111
4	Daniel Ricciardo	92
5	Kimi Räikkönen	73
6	Max Verstappen	45
7	Sergio Pérez	44
8	Esteban Ocon	35
9	Carlos Sainz	29
10	Felipe Massa	20
11	Nico Hülkenberg	18
12	Lance Stroll	17
13	Kevin Magnussen	11
14	Romain Grosjean	10
15	Pascal Wehrlein	5
16	Daniil Kvyat	4
17	Fernando Alonso	2

CONSTRUCTORS

1	Mercedes	250
2	Ferrari	226
3	Red Bull	137
4	Force India	79
5	Williams	37
6	Toro Rosso	33
7	Haas	21
8	Renault	18
9	Sauber	5
10	McLaren	2

10 · RICCIARDO · Red Bull

8 · STROLL · Williams

6 · PÉREZ · Force India

4 · VETTEL · Ferrari

2 · BOTTAS · Mercedes

9 · MASSA · Williams

7 · OCON · Force India

5 · VERSTAPPEN · Red Bull

3 · RÄIKKÖNEN · Ferrari

1 · HAMILTON · Mercedes

42	43	44	45	46	47	48	49	50	51	
3	3	3	3	3	3	3	3	3	3	1
18	18	18	18	18	18	18	18	18	77	2
77	77	77	77	77	77	77	77	77	18	3
5	5	5	5	5	5	5	5	5	5	4
31	44	44	44	44	44	44	44	44	44	5
44	31	31	31	31	31	31	31	31		6
20	20	20	20	20	20	20	20	20	20	7
14	55	55	55	55	55	55	55	55		8
55	14	14	14	14	14	14	14	14	14	9
94	94	94	94	94	94	94	94	94	94	10
9	9	9	9	9	9	9	9	9	9	
2	2	2	2	2	2	2	2	2	2	
8	8	8	8	8	8	8	8	8		
7	7	7	7	7						

Safety car deployed on laps shown

Race red-flagged

RACE TYRE STRATEGIES
PIRELLI

	Driver	Race Stint 1	Race Stint 2	Race Stint 3	Race Stint 4	Race Stint 5
1	Ricciardo	Supersoft (u): 1–5	Soft (n): 6–13	Supersoft (n): 14–22	Supersoft (u): 23–51	
2	Bottas	Supersoft (u): 1	Soft (n): 2–11	Supersoft (u): 12–22	Supersoft (u): 23–51	
3	Stroll	Supersoft (u): 1–13	Soft (n): 14–22	Supersoft (u): 23–51		
4	Vettel	Supersoft (u): 1–12	Soft (n): 13–22	Supersoft (u): 23–51		
5	Hamilton	Supersoft (u): 1–12	Soft (n): 13–22	Supersoft (u): 23–51		
6	Ocon	Supersoft (u): 1–12	Soft (n): 13–20	Supersoft (u): 21–22	Supersoft (u): 23–51	
7	Magnussen	Supersoft (n): 1–12	Soft (n): 13–22	Supersoft (u): 23–51		
8	Sainz	Supersoft (n): 1–12	Soft (n): 13–22	Supersoft (u): 23–51		
9	Alonso	Supersoft (n): 1–12	Soft (n): 13–22	Supersoft (u): 23–51		
10	Wehrlein	Supersoft (n): 1–12	Soft (n): 13	Supersoft (n): 14–22	Supersoft (u): 23–51	
11	Ericsson	Soft (n): 1–12	Supersoft (n): 13–22	Supersoft (u): 23–51		
12	Vandoorne	Soft (n): 1–5	Supersoft (n): 6–22	Supersoft (n): 23–33	Supersoft (u): 34–51	
13	Grosjean	Soft (n): 1–3	Supersoft (n): 4–14	Supersoft (n): 15–22	Supersoft (u): 23–36	Supersoft (u): 37–50
14	Räikkönen	Supersoft (u): 1–12	Soft (n): 13–20	Supersoft (u): 21–46		
	Pérez	Supersoft (u): 1–12	Soft (n): 13–20	Supersoft (u): 21–39 (dnf)		
	Massa	Supersoft (u): 1–12	Soft (n): 13–22	Supersoft (u): 23–25 (dnf)		
	Hülkenberg	Supersoft (u): 1–13	Soft (n): 14–22	Supersoft (u): 23–24 (dnf)		
	Verstappen	Supersoft (n): 1–12 (dnf)				
	Kvyat	Supersoft (n): 1–9 (dnf)				
	Palmer	Supersoft (n): 1–7 (dnf)				

The tyre regulations stipulate that at least two of three dry tyre specifications must be used during a dry race.
Pirelli P Zero logos are colour-coded on the tyre sidewalls: Red = Supersoft; Yellow = Soft. (n) new (u) used

FIA FORMULA 1 WORLD CHAMPIONSHIP · ROUND 9

AUSTRIAN GRAND PRIX

RED BULL RING

THE Mercedes team faced a tough decision when a partial inspection of Lewis Hamilton's gearbox revealed damage after the previous race in Baku – nothing to do with his controversial restart rear-ending by Sebastian Vettel incidentally. The chances of a failure and resultant non-finish in Austria, costing the team a potential minimum 15 points and Lewis as many as 25, had to be weighed against the likely loss of points arising from taking a five-place gearbox penalty. While the chances of gearbox failure were not 100 per cent, they were high enough to warrant changing the unit and putting Hamilton on the back foot.

The question then was which tyre to qualify on? For Austria, Pirelli had brought its three softest compounds – ultrasoft, supersoft and soft. With Saturday weather forecasts predicting rain at some stage during the race, anything that could extend the first stint, possibly taking Lewis deep enough into it to eliminate an extra tyre stop before the rain arrived, needed careful consideration. Hence the decision to put him on the supersoft instead of the ultrasoft in Q2 (the session that dictates a driver's race-start tyre), potentially affording him an additional ten laps or just over ten minutes on Sunday afternoon.

In fact, when Hamilton topped Friday's first practice session on the soft tyre, consideration was even given to qualifying on the hardest tyre to further extend the range of that first stint. But by Saturday afternoon, as the track rubbered in, the speed delta between the three compounds had widened enough to render that strategy just a bit too adventurous.

Hamilton cleared Q2 comfortably on the supersoft, but the downside was a lack of opportunity to assess the car's balance on the ultrasoft for Q3. He felt that his experience should have been able to overcome that, however, and he was pretty underwhelmed with a 1m 04.424s lap, which left him third, a couple of tenths shy of team-mate Valtteri Bottas, who took the second pole position of his short Mercedes career. Lewis ended up eighth once his gearbox penalty was applied. Bottas's 1m 04.251s lap bested Vettel's Ferrari by 0.04s, the Mercedes W08s arriving in Austria with a revised front wing, barge boards and diffuser, while the Ferrari still seemed a very well-sorted chassis, particularly strong through the quick Turns Nine and Ten (a relabelling of the corners meaning that the old Turn Two was now Turn Three), despite the FIA's technical team requiring Maranello to add additional floor stiffening to its SF70H.

Bottas was more than happy with the Merc's confidence-inspiring performance as well and did little to tinker with the set-up, this time on the right end of a gnat's-whisker time difference to Vettel, whose final attempt to pip him was scuppered by Grosjean's Haas grinding to a halt with an electrical issue, which brought out the yellows.

Räikkönen, in contrast, was never happy with his Ferrari's balance and admitted that they pretty much "started again from zero" in Saturday's third free practice. Around half a second's gap to Vettel over a 65s lap was not great, prompting Ferrari boss Sergio Marchionne to observe that Kimi can sometimes be "a bit of a laggard." Something of a wake-up call with contract time almost upon him...

Perhaps it was as well for Räikkönen that Red Bull did not have quite the same relative pace that they had shown in Baku, and his time was 0.12s clear of Daniel Ricciardo, who had just under a tenth in hand over team-mate Max Verstappen, Christian Horner's cars filling row three. Ricciardo lost Friday track time to problems with a revised MGU-H, which forced Renault to revert to the original version on all of its engines, while Max felt there was more in the locker but for some slight over-driving errors, which had culminated in a spin at Turn Seven.

Romain Grosjean's Haas looked a bit of a handful, but when he got it into the tyre window and on top of his usual braking issues, he was very competitive, just 0.15s shy of Ricciardo's Q2 time and fast enough in Q3 to take seventh on the grid before his electrical problem. Team-mate Kevin Magnussen was within a couple of tenths in Q1, but a broken rear wishbone precluded his involvement in Q2 and left him 15th.

The Red Bull Ring is a very power-sensitive track, and despite neither Force India driver being initially happy with the balance, Mercedes power helped them to eighth and ninth, Pérez 0.07s ahead of Ocon. Just 0.05s behind them and rounding out the top ten was Sainz's Toro Rosso, whose only new-tyre run had been interupted by the yellows. All three drivers had been quicker in Q2.

Nico Hülkenberg missed out on Q3 by five-hundredths with the first of the Renaults, while Palmer went out in Q1, adding to mounting pressure, despite a lap time that was just 0.17s shy of his team-mate.

Fernando Alonso and Stoffel Vandoorne were 12th and 13th with the two McLaren Hondas, the Spaniard reckoning that an MGU-H failure and subsequent removal of his new Spec 3 Honda prior to qualifying had cost him a slot in Q3.

Williams endured a nightmare at a track on which previously they had performed strongly. A substantial aero upgrade to the FW40 – nose, floor, barge boards, diffuser, engine cover – was rendered immaterial by an inability to access the tyre window, to the extent that it put technical chief Paddy Lowe in mind of that anomalous Singapore weekend with Mercedes in 2015. Both Felipe Massa and Lance Stroll, separated by 0.07s, were Q1 casualties, quicker only than the Saubers of Marcus Ericsson and Pascal Wehrlein. The latter needed an engine change, which meant a pit-lane start.

PRIOR evidence during the season – read Sochi – had suggested that while the Mercedes was highly competitive on the ultrasoft, it struggled more on the supersoft, hence Valtteri Bottas's need for pole position and a Sebastian Vettel-beating start to maximise his opening-stint potential.

He certainly managed that! When the red lights went out on Sunday afternoon, the No. 77 Mercedes made a lightning getaway – so good that both Vettel and Daniel Ricciardo radioed in to say that Bottas had jumped the start. Shortly afterwards came notification that the FIA was investigating.

When data from the grid sensor was examined, it revealed that Bottas's reaction time had been 0.201s, compared to 0.364s for Vettel. To prevent drivers from anticipating the start, the governing body can impose a penalty if they find that the reaction time is less than considered humanly possible. Thus anything better than 0.18s is likely to be marginal. Valtteri's start was about as good as it gets.

"I had no doubts about it," he said, "but knew it was probably the best start I'd ever had. We do a lot of start practice and reaction-time practice, and in those practices you can hit better times than that, but it was just the perfect start really."

Later he admitted that such had been his desire to lead the opening lap that in fact he had gambled a little: "With the start lights, there is always variation [in time] between all five being on and going off. But for quite a long time, the variation has not been massive, so you know more or less when it's going to be off. You are so alert at that point and you're gambling between your reaction and guessing. Sometimes you get a mega one and sometimes you're a bit

late. Today was my best reaction for the light." So, he'd been a tad lucky...

Further back, there were issues for Verstappen – a clutch problem kicking in the anti-stall – and a misfiring Sainz, which led to a concertina effect into Turn One as the pack avoided the Red Bull-backed cars. Alonso had made a decent getaway, but thought better of trying to usurp the slow-starting Verstappen into Turn One and backed off, which caught out Kvyat, the Toro Rosso rear-ending the McLaren Honda and spinning it into Verstappen. Alonso was out, while Max's rotten run of fortune continued, the young Dutchman pulling off with a broken driveshaft, right in front of an almost exclusively orange grandstand packed full of his despondent supporters.

Kvyat pitted for a new nose and later had to serve a drive-through, which put him last in the final classification, behind the Saubers, which were really struggling with their year-old Ferrari engines on such a power track. 'The Torpedo' also attracted a couple of penalty points, which put him perilously close to the 12 points that would mean a race ban.

The order at the end of the opening lap was Bottas, Vettel, Ricciardo, Grosjean, Räikkönen (delayed by a fine Ricciardo pass at Turn Three that also allowed Grosjean by), Pérez, Hamilton, Ocon, Sainz, Massa, Stroll, Palmer, Magnussen (who would ultimately retire the second Haas with hydraulic failure), Vandoorne, Hülkenberg (who also had an anti-stall issue on the grid), Ericsson and Wehrlein.

With Bottas's start under investigation, Mercedes was studying all available video and data, both at the circuit and back at the Brackley factory. They were confident it was okay, but nevertheless instructed Valtteri to build a gap at the

Left: A massive turn-out of support for Max Verstappen at the Red Bull Ring.
Photo: Peter J. Fox

Below: Disaster at the start as Daniil Kvyat's first-corner move eliminates Fernando Alonso's McLaren and the slow-starting Red Bull of Max Verstappen. To the left, Kevin Magnussen and Stoffel Vandoorne both take avoiding action.
Photo: WRi2

Opening spread: Valtteri Bottas took a brilliant pole position and sped to a dominant victory in Austria.

Above: The Force Indias of Sergio Pérez and Esteban Ocon sandwich Lewis Hamilton as the Mercedes driver makes his way through the field from eighth on the grid, having received a five-place penalty for a gearbox change.

Photo: Sahara Force India F1 Team

Above right: Daniil Kvyat's Toro Rosso is prepared on the grid. All the mechanics' meticulous work was undone at the first corner...

Right: Sebastian Vettel overcame problems mid-race on the supersoft Pirellis to storm back to second place behind Bottas.

Photos: Peter J. Fox

front, just in case. A drive-through penalty was considered most likely, which at Red Bull Ring would involve a time loss of around 14.5s. Therefore they needed that margin over what would become a Grosjean/Pérez/Ocon train, something that Bottas had achieved by lap nine. Despite upping his pace, he was lapping with amazing consistency, laps 7–10 all within 0.09s as he extended his lead over Vettel to 4.5s.

Behind, Räikkönen was able to retake fourth from Grosjean once DRS was in operation, and Hamilton was also on the move, passing Pérez for sixth on lap six and then Grosjean two laps later. Once he had cleared the Haas and set off after Räikkönen's fourth-placed Ferrari, Lewis was 14.5s behind his race-leading team-mate. The rain that his tyre strategy had been based upon had not arrived, and now it looked like a straightforward case of damage limitation and making the best of a simple one-stop race. He was also having to manage some brake temperature issues and reported a grip problem with his rear supersofts. Despite that, by lap 20 of the scheduled 71, he was within DRS range of Räikkönen, who had lost 10s to Vettel's second-placed Ferrari and was 7s adrift of Ricciardo's Red Bull.

The opportunity for Hamilton to undercut Räikkönen did not yet exist because Grosjean/Pérez/Ocon were still just 17s behind, with 20s the necessary pit-stop window.

By lap 29, Räikkönen had the necessary margin over Grosjean to stop, but Ferrari left him out. That handed the undercut opportunity to Mercedes.

"Do the opposite to Kimi," came the radio instruction to Hamilton on lap 31. As Räikkönen stayed out, Lewis dived into the pits for a set of ultrasofts. Mercedes was confident that he could get to the end on them and benefit from the better first-lap performance (Räikkönen would be going on to the supersoft after starting on the ultrasoft).

When Ferrari did not pit Räikkönen as soon as his window to Grosjean had opened, Mercedes concluded that their strategy was to leave him out and sacrifice a position to Hamilton in an attempt to have Kimi back Bottas into Vettel later on. Leaving Hamilton out, therefore, would only have lost him more time behind Räikkönen.

With the Mercedes/Ferrari/Red Bull race pace pretty evenly matched, Hamilton's stop for ultrasofts caused the leaders to react, Ricciardo pitting on lap 33 and Vettel on lap 34. It was not until lap 41, however, that Bottas headed for the pits after a long stint on his ultrasofts.

With Mercedes anticipating Ferrari's strategy with Räikkönen, Bottas was tantalisingly close to having a pit-stop window over his fellow Finn, but not quite there. Between laps 34 and 40, the gap fluctuated between 19.5s and 20.2s. Valtteri had been given a target lap time, and the Merc strategists could see that Räikkönen was going to have to lap Palmer's Renault and potentially would lose vital time. At that point, though, Bottas reported, "There's not much left in these tyres..."

Mindful that a year earlier Vettel had suffered a blow-out

in Austria when he had extended his stint, Mercedes called Bottas straight in. There was a slight delay in positioning the right front and his stop was 1.4s slower than Hamilton's. He rejoined 1.6s behind Räikkönen, with Vettel now just 3s behind him – good news for Ferrari.

The race was really hotting up, with Hamilton, on ultrasofts, also hunting down Ricciardo's Red Bull. This was not as simple a task as it might have been earlier in the season – a look at the quickest lap times over the course of the race by the top three chassis showed that they were blanketed by just 0.07s!

Intensifying the pressure on Bottas was that while he'd been able to control the race during the opening stint on ultrasofts, as in Russia, the tables turned once supersofts

had been bolted on for the second stint, the Ferrari being better suited to the red-walled Pirellis.

The first hurdle for Bottas to clear was Räikkönen's long-running Ferrari. Importantly, he was able to go by Kimi as soon as he caught him. The Ferrari driver suffered a slight lock-up into Turn Three and Valtteri went by with the aid of DRS on the run to Turn Four.

The next issue he had to deal with was a black line that appeared on his blistered left rear tyre as the laps ticked by. With the same composure he'd shown in Russia, despite Vettel being within DRS range for the last two laps, he calmly made no mistakes and blasted across the line just 0.658s ahead. In Sochi, the margin had been 0.617s...

"It was a bit of a *déjà vu* with Seb coming so close in

PIT LANE   PIT-I

Above: The McLaren Honda crew performs the only tyre change of the race for Stoffel Vandoorne on lap 14.
Photo: McLaren Honda

Top right: Vettel and Räikkönen on driver parade duties.
Photo: Peter J. Fox

Above centre right: Romain Grosjean enjoyed a fine race for Haas, finishing in sixth place.
Photo: Haas F1 Team

Above right: A thoughtful Sergio Pérez prepares for action.
Photo: Sahara Force India F1 Team

Right: Daniel Ricciardo drove a storming race to claim yet another podium. The Red Bull driver felt that this race was better than his win in Baku.
Photo: Peter J. Fox

those final laps," Valtteri smiled. "And I could feel the blister getting worse and worse. Every time I approached a right-hand corner, it was more tricky, and with the back-markers as well. It all ended well, but I was pleased the race finished when it did!"

Hamilton's damage-limitation weekend concluded with 12 points for fourth place, as he only just failed to steal the final podium position from Ricciardo on the very last lap with a bid down the outside into Turn Four. The Australian, though, braked as late as he dared and clung on.

"I've just sat and watched the replay with Daniel to see how far alongside I got and whether if I'd just been a bit more aggressive, I might have been ahead," Lewis explained post-race. "In the end, though, he just defended really well, and I don't think I could have done better. Daniel's pace was fantastic today. I was giving it hell and wasn't closing massively. But it was actually a really good race for me. I was almost 15s behind the lead when I got past Grosjean early on and just 7s behind at the end, so I was quick today."

Räikkönen crossed the line 13s behind Hamilton, his afternoon unsurprisingly compromised after Ferrari had prioritised Vettel, with Grosjean putting the Haas into the top six as the final car to finish on the lead lap. It was a fine effort to get to the flag ahead of the Force Indias – Pérez beating Ocon by 7.4s for seventh.

The final points went to the Williams pair, Massa and Stroll, the Canadian teenager scoring for the third successive

race. After their dire tyre warm-up problems in qualifying, the FW40s were a much better proposition in the race, Massa having started on the soft Pirelli and run a 47-lap opening stint. Palmer finished just out of the points for Renault, half a second behind Stroll.

As a classic season developed, Bottas's second win moved him to within 15 points of team-mate Hamilton in the drivers' championship and just 35 behind Vettel's 171 championship-leading total. He may have been helped by Lewis's head-rest problem in Baku and his gearbox penalty here, but bear in mind that he had suffered a DNF due to engine failure in Barcelona.

"Valtteri's performance this weekend was great," Hamilton said, "and when you consider the DNF, he's having a great season. He has always been in the championship fight."

Bottas is low-key, never one to make a song and dance. Muhammad Ali he is not. But faced with the inevitable 'championship' questions, he did quietly admit that once a driver is confirmed for a Mercedes seat, he can't really target anything else. His Mercedes drive was something he desperately wanted to hang on to. With no news yet about a contract extension, Austria did his cause no harm at all. In the constructors' battle, meanwhile, Mercedes extended its margin by nine points to lead Ferrari 287 to 254 as the paddock packed up and headed for the season's halfway point at Silverstone.

Tony Dodgins

VIEWPOINT
BULLISH AT HOME

AFTER a surprising early-season disappointment, Red Bull's comeback continued, appropriately enough, at the team owner's race track.

Coy when asked if the performance shortfall had been related to Adrian Newey's focus on the Aston Martin-Red Bull road car, Christian Horner preferred to suggest that the team had experienced correlation problems between wind tunnel and track, thanks to the larger proportions of the 2017 F1 cars.

Whatever the reason, Newey's presence at the pit wall, clipboard and familiar furrowed brow in evidence, was beginning to reap benefits, thanks to an upgrade package for Spain, assisted further by more recent Renault engine mode and mapping tweaks.

Any correlation issues were clearly being resolved as Daniel Ricciardo and Max Verstappen began to narrow the qualifying performance gap to Ferrari and Mercedes, both drivers ready to pounce if the leading duo hesitated – Verstappen's bad luck notwithstanding.

Baku provided the perfect canvas for such opportunism as Ricciardo – employing typical demon out-braking moves – grabbed Red Bull's first win since Malaysia 2016.

Welcome as such a 'crazy' victory may have been, Ricciardo felt that third place in Austria was actually more significant in terms of performance. Not only had he finished just six seconds behind the winning Mercedes, but also he had used guile, skill and enough raw pace to catch Hamilton's attention.

"Baku was a victory, but things happened in that race," said Ricciardo. "Today, we earned a podium on a circuit that, for sure, isn't our strength."

Ricciardo's fifth consecutive podium had elevated the Australian to fourth in the championship, 64 points behind leader Vettel. The key point for Red Bull at this stage would be to continue the qualifying improvement and position themselves for future podiums, something that Hamilton recognised after his experience in Austria.

"If they can pull that out in qualifying, then that's going to be great for the rest of the season," said Hamilton. "It means we've got a third team that is going to be battling it out with us."

Maurice Hamilton

9

2017 FORMULA 1
GROSSE PREIS VON ÖSTERREICH

ROLEX

F1 OFFICIAL TIMEPIECE

SPIELBERG 7–9 JULY

RACE DISTANCE: 71 laps, 190.420 miles/306.452km

RACE WEATHER: Dry/sunny-cloudy (track 44–51°C, air 29–30°C)

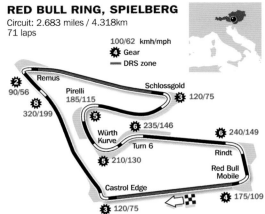

RED BULL RING, SPIELBERG
Circuit: 2.683 miles / 4.318km
71 laps

100/62 kmh/mph
Gear
DRS zone

Remus 90/56
320/199
Pirelli 185/115
Schlossgold 120/75
235/146
Würth Kurve 210/130
Turn 6
240/149
Rindt
Red Bull Mobile
Castrol Edge 120/75
175/109

RACE – OFFICIAL CLASSIFICATION

Pos.	Driver	Nat.	No.	Entrant	Car/Engine	Laps	Time/Retirement	Speed (mph/km/h)	Gap to leader	Fastest race lap
1	**Valtteri Bottas**	FIN	77	Mercedes AMG Petronas Motorsport	Mercedes F1 W08-Mercedes M08 EQ Power+ V6	71	1h 21m 48.523s	139.658/224.757		1m 07.847s 51
2	**Sebastian Vettel**	D	5	Scuderia Ferrari	Ferrari SF70H-062 V6	71	1h 21m 49.181s	139.639/224.727	0.658s	1m 07.496s 69
3	**Daniel Ricciardo**	AUS	3	Red Bull Racing	Red Bull RB13-TAG Heuer RB13 V6	71	1h 21m 54.535s	139.487/224.482	6.012s	1m 07.442s 69
4	**Lewis Hamilton**	GB	44	Mercedes AMG Petronas Motorsport	Mercedes F1 W08-Mercedes M08 EQ Power+ V6	71	1h 21m 55.953s	139.446/224.417	7.430s	1m 07.411s 69
5	**Kimi Räikkönen**	FIN	7	Scuderia Ferrari	Ferrari SF70H-062 V6	71	1h 22m 08.893s	139.080/223.828	20.370s	1m 07.486s 68
6	**Romain Grosjean**	F	8	Haas F1 Team	Haas VF-17-Ferrari 062 V6	71	1h 23m 01.683s	137.606/221.456	1m 13.160s	1m 08.590s 65
7	**Sergio Pérez**	MEX	11	Sahara Force India Formula 1 Team	Force India VJM10-Mercedes M08 EQ Power+ V6	70			1 lap	1m 08.470s 58
8	**Esteban Ocon**	F	31	Sahara Force India Formula 1 Team	Force India VJM10-Mercedes M08 EQ Power+ V6	70			1 lap	1m 08.659s 68
9	**Felipe Massa**	BR	19	Williams Martini Racing	Williams FW40-Mercedes M08 EQ Power+ V6	70			1 lap	1m 08.419s 49
10	**Lance Stroll**	CDN	18	Williams Martini Racing	Williams FW40-Mercedes M08 EQ Power+ V6	70			1 lap	1m 08.777s 67
11	Jolyon Palmer	GB	30	Renault Sport Formula One Team	Renault R.S.17-R.E.17 V6	70			1 lap	1m 08.652s 64
12	Stoffel Vandoorne	B	2	McLaren Honda Formula 1 Team	McLaren MCL32-Honda RA617H V6	70			1 lap	1m 08.422s 67
13	Nico Hülkenberg	D	27	Renault Sport Formula One Team	Renault R.S.17-R.E.17 V6	70			1 lap	1m 09.043s 64
14	Pascal Wehrlein	D	94	Sauber F1 Team	Sauber C36-Ferrari 059/5 V6	70			1 lap	1m 09.241s 60
15	Marcus Ericsson	S	9	Sauber F1 Team	Sauber C36-Ferrari 059/5 V6	69			2 laps	1m 09.284s 56
16	Daniil Kvyat	RUS	26	Scuderia Toro Rosso	Toro Rosso STR12-Renault R.E.17 V6	68			3 laps	1m 08.061s 57
	Carlos Sainz	E	55	Scuderia Toro Rosso	Toro Rosso STR12-Renault R.E.17 V6	44	engine			1m 09.150s 42
	Kevin Magnussen	DK	20	Haas F1 Team	Haas VF-17-Ferrari 062 V6	29	hydraulics			1m 10.402s 23
	Fernando Alonso	E	14	McLaren Honda Formula 1 Team	McLaren MCL32-Honda RA617H V6	1	accident/clutch			no time
	Max Verstappen	NL	33	Red Bull Racing	Red Bull RB13-TAG Heuer RB13 V6	0	accident			no time

Fastest race lap: Lewis Hamilton on lap 69, 1m 07.411s, 143.287mph/230.597km/h (new record for current configuration).

Lap record: Nigel Mansell (Williams FW11B-Honda V6 turbo), 1m 28.318s, 150.500mph/242.207km/h (1987, 3.692-mile/5.942km circuit).

Previous lap record (current configuration): Michael Schumacher (Ferrari V10), 1m 08.337s, 141.607mph/227.894km/h (2003).

The Grand Prix circuit was re-measured and from 2017 was listed as being 8 metres shorter, though in reality no layout changes have taken place.

19 · ERICSSON · Sauber   17 · MASSA · Williams   15 · MAGNUSSEN · Haas   13 · VANDOORNE · McLaren   11 · HÜLKENBERG · Renault

20 · WEHRLEIN · Sauber
Car modified in *parc fermé*; required to start from the pit lane
18 · STROLL · Williams   16 · PALMER · Renault   14 · KVYAT · Toro Rosso   12 · ALONSO · McLaren

Grid order	1	2	3	4	5	6	7	8	9	10	11	12	13	14	15	16	17	18	19	20	21	22	23	24	25	26	27	28	29	30	31	32	33	34	35	36	37	38	39	40	41	42	43	44	45	46	47	48	49	50	51	52	53	54
77 BOTTAS	77	77	77	77	77	77	77	77	77	77	77	77	77	77	77	77	77	77	77	77	77	77	77	77	77	77	77	77	77	77	77	77	77	77	77	77	77	77	77	77	77	77	7	7	77	77	77	77	77	77	77	77	77	7
5 VETTEL	5	5	5	5	5	5	5	5	5	5	5	5	5	5	5	5	5	5	5	5	5	5	5	5	5	5	5	5	5	5	5	5	5	5	5	5	5	7	7	7	7	7	77	77	5	5	5	5	5	5	5	5	5	5
7 RÄIKKÖNEN	3	3	3	3	3	3	3	3	3	3	3	3	3	3	3	3	3	3	3	3	3	3	3	3	3	3	3	3	3	3	3	3	3	7	5	5	5	5	5	5	5	5	7	3	3	3	3	3	3	3	3	3	3	3
3 RICCIARDO	8	8	7	7	7	7	7	7	7	7	7	7	7	7	7	7	7	7	7	7	7	7	7	7	7	7	7	7	7	7	7	7	7	3	3	3	3	3	3	3	3	3	3	44	44	44	44	44	44	44	44	44	44	44
33 VERSTAPPEN	7	7	8	8	8	8	8	44	44	44	44	44	44	44	44	44	44	44	44	44	44	44	44	44	44	44	44	44	44	44	44	44	44	44	44	44	44	44	44	44	44	44	44	7	7	7	7	7	7	7	7	7	7	7
8 GROSJEAN	11	11	11	11	11	44	44	8	8	8	8	8	8	8	8	8	8	8	8	8	8	8	8	8	8	8	8	8	8	8	8	8	8	8	31	31	31	31	31	19	19	19	19	19	8	8	8	8	8	8	8	8		
11 PÉREZ	44	44	44	44	44	11	11	11	11	11	11	11	11	11	11	11	11	11	11	11	11	11	11	11	11	11	11	11	11	31	31	19	19	19	19	19	31		8	8	8	8	8	11	11	11	11	11	11	11	11	11		
44 HAMILTON	31	31	31	31	31	31	31	31	31	31	31	31	31	31	31	31	31	31	31	31	31	31	31	31	31	31	31	31	31	11	19	8	8	8	8	8	11	11	11	11	11	11	31	31	31	31	31	31						
31 OCON	55	55	19	19	19	19	19	19	19	19	19	19	19	19	19	19	19	19	19	19	19	19	19	19	19	19	19	19	19	19	11	11	11	11	11	11	31	31	31	31	31	31	31	31	19	19	19	19	19	19	19	19	19	19
55 SAINZ	19	19	55	55	18	18	18	18	18	19	18	18	18	18	18	18	18	18	18	18	18	18	18	18	18	18	18	18	18	18	18	55	55	55	55	55		18	18	18	18	18	18	18	18	18	18	18	18	18	18	18	18	
27 HÜLKENBERG	18	18	18	18	55	20	20	20	20	20	20	20	20	20	20	20	20	20	20	20	20	20	20	30	30	30	30	55	18	18	18	18	18	30	30	30	30	30	30	30	30	30	30	30	30	30	30	30	30	30	30	30		
14 ALONSO	30	20	20	20	30	30	30	30	30	30	30	30	30	30	30	30	30	30	30	30	30	30	30	2	2	55	55	55	30	30	30	30	30	30	30	2	2	2	2	2	2	2	2	2	2	2	2	2	2	2	2	2		
2 VANDOORNE	20	30	30	30	30	55	2	2	2	2	2	2	2	2	2	2	2	2	2	2	2	2	2	55	55	2	94	94	94	94	2	2	2	2	55	55	55	27	27	27	27	27	27	27	27	27	27	27	27	27	2			
26 KVYAT	2	2	2	2	2	2	55	55	55	55	55	55	55	55	55	55	55	55	55	55	55	55	55	94	94	94	2	2	2	9	27	94	94	94	2	27	55	94	94	94	94	94	94	94	94	94	94	94	94	94				
20 MAGNUSSEN	27	27	27	27	27	27	27	27	27	27	27	27	94	94	94	94	94	94	94	94	94	94	94	27	27	27	27	27	55	94	94	9	27	94	94	94	94	9	9	9	9	9	9	9	9	9	9	9	9					
30 PALMER	9	9	9	9	94	94	94	94	94	94	94	94	27		9	9	9	9	9	9	9	9	9	9	20	27	27	27	27	27	9	9	9	9	9	9	9	26	26	26	26	26	26	26	26	26	26	26	26					
19 MASSA	94	94	94	94	9	9	9	9	9	9	9	9	9	27	27	27	27	27	27	27	27	27	27	26	26	26	26	26	26	26	26	26	26	26	26	26	26																	
18 STROLL	26	26	26	26	26	26	26	26	9	26	26	26	26	26	26	26	26	26	26	26	26	26	26																															
9 ERICSSON	14																																																					
94 WEHRLEIN																																																						

27 = Pit stop   26 = Drive-through penalty   *9 = One lap or more behind*

TIME SHEETS

FOR THE RECORD

80th POLE POSTION: Mercedes

500th KM LED: Valtteri Bottas

PRACTICE 1 (FRIDAY)
Weather: Dry/cloudy-sunny
Temperatures: track 34–46°C, air 23–28°C

Pos.	Driver	Laps	Time
1	Lewis Hamilton	38	1m 05.975s
2	Max Verstappen	23	1m 06.165s
3	Valtteri Bottas	35	1m 06.345s
4	Sebastian Vettel	28	1m 06.424s
5	Daniel Ricciardo	32	1m 06.620s
6	Kimi Räikkönen	24	1m 06.848s
7	Stoffel Vandoorne	31	1m 07.283s
8	Daniil Kvyat	31	1m 07.437s
9	Fernando Alonso	28	1m 07.510s
10	Esteban Ocon	39	1m 07.511s
11	Felipe Massa	29	1m 07.550s
12	Kevin Magnussen	30	1m 07.594s
13	Carlos Sainz	32	1m 07.633s
14	Jolyon Palmer	31	1m 07.649s
15	Lance Stroll	35	1m 08.041s
16	Romain Grosjean	20	1m 08.074s
17	Sergey Sirotkin	27	1m 08.586s
18	Alfonso Celis	15	1m 09.280s
19	Pascal Wehrlein	29	1m 09.323s
20	Marcus Ericsson	12	1m 10.853s

PRACTICE 2 (FRIDAY)
Weather: Dry/cloudy-sunny
Temperatures: track 38–43°C, air 29–31°C

Pos.	Driver	Laps	Time
1	Lewis Hamilton	30	1m 05.483s
2	Sebastian Vettel	50	1m 05.630s
3	Valtteri Bottas	41	1m 05.699s
4	Max Verstappen	33	1m 05.832s
5	Daniel Ricciardo	27	1m 05.873s
6	Kimi Räikkönen	54	1m 06.144s
7	Kevin Magnussen	43	1m 06.591s
8	Fernando Alonso	27	1m 06.732s
9	Nico Hülkenberg	42	1m 06.735s
10	Romain Grosjean	52	1m 06.763s
11	Esteban Ocon	50	1m 06.849s
12	Stoffel Vandoorne	37	1m 06.859s
13	Daniil Kvyat	34	1m 06.906s
14	Felipe Massa	50	1m 07.065s
15	Carlos Sainz	24	1m 07.100s
16	Lance Stroll	46	1m 07.468s
17	Sergio Pérez	41	1m 07.509s
18	Jolyon Palmer	7	1m 07.623s
19	Pascal Wehrlein	49	1m 08.782s
20	Marcus Ericsson	51	1m 08.870s

PRACTICE 3 (SATURDAY)
Weather: Dry/cloudy-sunny
Temperatures: track 33°C, air 24°C

Pos.	Driver	Laps	Time
1	Sebastian Vettel	18	1m 05.092s
2	Lewis Hamilton	21	1m 05.361s
3	Valtteri Bottas	19	1m 05.515s
4	Kimi Räikkönen	19	1m 05.611s
5	Max Verstappen	24	1m 05.784s
6	Daniel Ricciardo	29	1m 05.896s
7	Kevin Magnussen	21	1m 05.936s
8	Romain Grosjean	22	1m 06.015s
9	Daniil Kvyat	28	1m 06.279s
10	Carlos Sainz	19	1m 06.284s
11	Esteban Ocon	26	1m 06.374s
12	Nico Hülkenberg	18	1m 06.563s
13	Stoffel Vandoorne	18	1m 06.578s
14	Jolyon Palmer	22	1m 06.595s
15	Fernando Alonso	20	1m 06.599s
16	Lance Stroll	22	1m 06.776s
17	Felipe Massa	24	1m 06.865s
18	Sergio Pérez	28	1m 06.280s
19	Marcus Ericsson	21	1m 07.378s
20	Pascal Wehrlein	25	1m 07.468s

DID YOU KNOW?

This was the 30th Austrian Grand Prix.

QUALIFYING (SATURDAY)
Weather: Dry/sunny-cloudy Temperatures: track 38–44°C, air 28–30°C

Pos.	Driver	First	Second	Third	Qualifying Tyre
1	Valtteri Bottas	1m 05.760s	1m 04.316s	1m 04.251s	Ultrasoft (new)
2	Sebastian Vettel	1m 05.585s	1m 04.772s	1m 04.293s	Ultrasoft (new)
3	Lewis Hamilton	1m 05.064s	1m 04.800s	1m 04.424s	Ultrasoft (new)
4	Kimi Räikkönen	1m 05.148s	1m 05.004s	1m 04.779s	Ultrasoft (new)
5	Daniel Ricciardo	1m 05.854s	1m 05.161s	1m 04.896s	Ultrasoft (new)
6	Max Verstappen	1m 05.779s	1m 04.948s	1m 04.983s	Ultrasoft (new)
7	Romain Grosjean	1m 05.902s	1m 05.319s	1m 05.480s	Ultrasoft (used)
8	Sergio Pérez	1m 05.975s	1m 05.435s	1m 05.605s	Ultrasoft (used)
9	Esteban Ocon	1m 06.033s	1m 05.550s	1m 05.674s	Ultrasoft (used)
10	Carlos Sainz	1m 05.675s	1m 05.544s	1m 05.726s	Ultrasoft (used)
11	Nico Hülkenberg	1m 06.174s	1m 05.597s		
12	Fernando Alonso	1m 06.158s	1m 05.602s		
13	Stoffel Vandoorne	1m 06.316s	1m 05.741s		
14	Daniil Kvyat	1m 05.990s	1m 05.884s		
15	Kevin Magnussen	1m 06.143s	no time		
16	Jolyon Palmer	1m 06.345s			
17	Felipe Massa	1m 06.534s			
18	Lance Stroll	1m 06.608s			
19	Marcus Ericsson	1m 06.857s			
20	Pascal Wehrlein	1m 07.011s			

QUALIFYING: head to head

Hamilton	5	4	Bottas
Vettel	7	2	Räikkönen
Massa	8	1	Stroll
Ricciardo	4	5	Verstappen
Pérez	8	1	Ocon
Hülkenberg	9	0	Palmer
Kvyat	4	5	Sainz
Ericsson	2	0	Giovinazzi
Ericsson	2	5	Wehrlein
Alonso	8	0	Vandoorne
Vandoorne	1	0	Button
Grosjean	6	3	Magnussen

POINTS

DRIVERS

1	Sebastian Vettel	171
2	Lewis Hamilton	151
3	Valtteri Bottas	136
4	Daniel Ricciardo	107
5	Kimi Räikkönen	83
6	Sergio Pérez	50
7	Max Verstappen	45
8	Esteban Ocon	39
9	Carlos Sainz	29
10	Felipe Massa	22
11	Lance Stroll	18
12	Nico Hülkenberg	18
13	Romain Grosjean	18
14	Kevin Magnussen	11
15	Pascal Wehrlein	5
16	Daniil Kvyat	4
17	Fernando Alonso	2

CONSTRUCTORS

1	Mercedes	287
2	Ferrari	254
3	Red Bull	152
4	Force India	89
5	Williams	40
6	Toro Rosso	33
7	Haas	29
8	Renault	18
9	Sauber	5
10	McLaren	2

 9 · OCON · Force India
 7 · PÉREZ · Force India
5 · VERSTAPPEN · Red Bull
3 · RÄIKKÖNEN · Ferrari
 1 · BOTTAS · Mercedes

10 · SAINZ · Toro Rosso
 8 · HAMILTON · Mercedes
5-place grid penalty for replacing gearbox
 6 · GROSJEAN · Haas
 4 · RICCIARDO · Red Bull
2 · VETTEL · Ferrari

56	57	58	59	60	61	62	63	64	65	66	67	68	69	70	71
77	77	77	77	77	77	77	77	77	77	77	77	77	77	77	77
5	5	5	5	5	5	5	5	5	5	5	5	5	5	5	2
3	3	3	3	3	3	3	3	3	3	3	3	3	3	3	3
44	44	44	44	44	44	44	44	44	44	44	44	44	44	44	44
7	7	7	7	7	7	7	7	7	7	7	7	7	7	7	7
8	8	8	8	8	8	8	8	8	8	8	8	8	8	8	6
11	11	11	11	11	11	11	11	11	11	11	11	11	11	11	11
31	31	31	31	31	31	31	31	31	31	31	31	31	31	31	8
19	19	19	19	19	19	19	19	19	19	19	19	19	19	19	9
18	18	18	18	18	18	18	18	18	18	18	18	18	18	18	10
30	30	30	30	30	30	30	30	30	30	30	30	30	30		
2	2	2	2	2	2	2	2	2	2	2	2	2	2	2	
27	27	27	27	27	27	27	27	27	27	27	27	27	27		
94	94	94	94	94	94	94	94	94	94	94	94	94	94		
9	9	9	9	9	9	9	9	9	9	9	9	9	9		
26	26	26	26	26	26	26	26	26	26	26	26				

RACE TYRE STRATEGIES — PIRELLI

	Driver	Race Stint 1	Race Stint 2	Race Stint 3
1	Bottas	Ultrasoft (u): 1–41	Supersoft (n): 42–71	
2	Vettel	Ultrasoft (u): 1–34	Supersoft (n): 35–71	
3	Ricciardo	Ultrasoft (u): 1–33	Supersoft (n): 34–71	
4	Hamilton	Supersoft (u): 1–31	Ultrasoft (n): 32–71	
5	Räikkönen	Ultrasoft (u): 1–44	Supersoft (n): 45–71	
6	Grosjean	Ultrasoft (u): 1–36	Supersoft (n): 37–71	
7	Pérez	Ultrasoft (u): 1–35	Supersoft (n): 36–70	
8	Ocon	Ultrasoft (u): 1–42	Supersoft (n): 43–70	
9	Massa	Soft (n): 1–47	Ultrasoft (n): 48–70	
10	Stroll	Supersoft (n): 1–35	Ultrasoft (n): 36–70	
11	Palmer	Soft (n): 1–34	Ultrasoft (n): 35–70	
12	Vandoorne	Ultrasoft (n): 1–31	Supersoft (n): 32–70	
13	Hülkenberg	Supersoft (n): 1–14	Soft (n): 15–70	
14	Wehrlein	Supersoft (n): 1–35	Ultrasoft (n): 36–70	
15	Ericsson	Ultrasoft (n): 1–34	Supersoft (n): 35–69	
16	Kvyat	Ultrasoft (n): 1	Soft (n): 2–55	Ultrasoft (u): 56–68
	Sainz	Ultrasoft (u): 1–40	Supersoft (n): 41–44 (dnf)	
	Magnussen	Supersoft (n): 1–29 (dnf)		
	Alonso	Ultrasoft (n): 1 (dnf)		
	Verstappen	Ultrasoft (u): 0 (dnf)		

The tyre regulations stipulate that at least two of three dry tyre specifications must be used during a dry race.
Pirelli P Zero logos are colour-coded on the tyre sidewalls: Purple = Ultrasoft; Red = Supersoft; Yellow = Soft. (n) new (u) used

Photos: Peter J. Fox

Lewis Hamilton enjoys the moment.
Photo: Peter J. Fox

BRITISH GRAND PRIX

SILVERSTONE CIRCUIT

SILVERSTONE QUALIFYING

THIS would be the perfect start to Lewis Hamilton's weekend. After the disappointment of Austria, he needed a result at home. And it was as if the Mercedes W08 had been designed specifically for such a spectacularly quick race track. The 2017 cars, with extra downforce and performance, were always likely to be in their element around the fast Northamptonshire sweeps. But Hamilton was not alone in being impressed by a step up in the thrill factor that came with taking on the likes of Copse, Maggotts and Becketts.

"The downforce is incredible," Hamilton said. "One of the reasons why this track is so great is that we generally have a headwind into Copse. It's like being in a wind tunnel with just the optimum downforce package. Copse… obviously we were building up to it because it was a little bit damp at the beginning of qualifying [when everyone started on intermediates].

"You can take it flat in eighth, but it's not necessarily the quickest way – you scrub quite a lot of speed off and then the rpm potentially drops a little bit too much, so I don't personally do it flat, and that didn't seem to cost me any time. Then, when you come through Maggotts and Becketts, that section is just on fire; you just can't imagine how incredible it is when you come through Turns 10, 11… Ten is obviously always flat, 11 has been flat for years, 12, from 2007 to now, just bit by bit, you're letting off later and later, and now you're kind of still on the gas through 12, or into 12 at least.

"And then 13 [Becketts] is a fantastic corner because it's very bumpy through there. You've got maximum downforce, a lot of compression on the tyres, and it's all about the exit. And then obviously coming down to Stowe, where you're turning already as you start to brake. You only dab the brake and you're straight back on the gas. It's unbelievable!"

It was clear that if Hamilton could string every corner together when it mattered in Q3, no one would get near him. That's exactly what happened, and Lewis claimed his 67th pole by over half a second from a Ferrari, albeit that of Kimi Räikkönen and not his team-mate. Sebastian Vettel was third fastest – and not happy to be there after Ferrari had released the championship leader into traffic for his final run in Q3, thus having a negative effect on tyre preparation. On such fine details are grid positions established during such an intense fight at the front.

Even if Q3 had gone according to plan, Vettel was the first to admit that Hamilton had been out of reach, the Mercedes having a marginal, but critical, advantage through the fast sweeps. At least Seb was ahead of Valtteri Bottas, the Finn having been compromised by a five-place grid penalty for an unscheduled gearbox change, in the same way that Hamilton had been in Austria. Bottas had run the soft (rather than the supersoft) Pirellis during Q2, thus earning strategic leeway, as he would start the race and potentially run longer with the harder Pirelli. The downside for Q3, as Lewis had found the previous weekend, was unfamiliarity with the supersoft – another fine detail that translated into fourth fastest and thus a ninth-place start.

Both Ferrari and Mercedes had brought significant engine upgrades, which, combined with the power emphasis of Silverstone, exacerbated the shortfall at Renault. That was underlined by Max Verstappen driving the wheels off his Red Bull, but finding himself fifth fastest, 1.5 seconds from pole. As frustrating as that may have been, at least he was running, unlike Daniel Ricciardo, who had been sidelined in Q1 by a broken turbo and relegated to the back.

At Renault, a new floor bolstered Nico Hülkenberg's growing confidence in the package, and he qualified an impressive sixth. Jolyon Palmer's struggle was not helped by being stuck with the old one. He failed to make Q3 by just under a tenth of a second after a commendable effort.

The increasingly intense in-house Force India battle continued, Sergio Pérez reversing the free practice trend as he edged Esteban Ocon when it mattered most in Q3, the pink cars lining up ahead of Stoffel Vandoorne in the McLaren Honda. The Belgian's best qualifying of 2017 was a surprise and a credit, given the power-sensitive nature of the track. Honda's usual problems were loaded on to Fernando Alonso, as various replacements amounted to 30 places of penalties and the back row.

Romain Grosjean was tenth quickest, but Haas reckoned he would have been eighth had his final corner not been upset by the turbulent air of a Mercedes as Hamilton set off on his quick lap. Silverstone held its breath as the stewards launched an investigation, before deciding that Hamilton had 'affected', but not 'impeded' Grosjean, thus escaping a three-place penalty.

Either way, Grosjean's performance emphasised a struggle for his team-mate, Kevin Magnussen continuing to be mystified over a lap worth no more than 17th fastest and barely quicker than the Saubers of Pascal Wehrlein and Marcus Ericsson.

Lance Stroll had his first experience of F1 in the damp, but it was a disappointing day for Williams, as Felipe Massa failed to get to grips with the changing conditions, the Brazilian beaten by Toro Rosso, a team that did not expect to go well. A suspension problem for Carlos Sainz in Q2 meant giving best to Daniil Kyvat, the pair almost four seconds from Hamilton's searing pace at the front.

WITH a dry track and wide-open spaces beckoning, the first lap was always going to be a busy one as early advantages were either sought or stolen. But first, a delay and another formation lap.

If Palmer hadn't had bad luck, he'd have had none at all, the Englishman ruefully waving to the sympathetic crowd as he walked away from his Renault, parked on Hangar Straight with a hydraulic leak. The race was shortened by a lap, but in the meantime, brakes were overheating as drivers desperately tried to maintain core temperatures in the hubs and tyres.

As the cars formed up on the grid again, Vettel appeared to be in serious trouble, smoke increasing in strength from the rear of his Ferrari. He was slow off the mark, Verstappen immediately sensing his opportunity and getting alongside into the first corner, only to find progress checked by Räikkönen as Vettel quickly restored the status quo. If Seb thought that was the end of it, then he had made no allowance for the irrepressible Max as Räikkönen, this time dead ahead of his team-mate, gave the Red Bull a chance to run all the way around the outside of the loop and slice ahead as the pack entered Wellington Straight. Vettel's afternoon had suddenly become a lot worse as he immediately realised that it would be difficult to get the place back, while up ahead, Hamilton and Räikkönen were set to pull away.

There was action aplenty elsewhere. The Force India fight kicked off immediately as Ocon not only got ahead of Pérez, but also Hülkenberg. But not for long. With a brave and impressive move, 'The Hulk' slipstreamed Ocon on Hangar Straight and took fifth back on the outside of Stowe. Pérez, meanwhile, was suffering further frustration after Bottas (who had started on softs) ran around his outside at Village.

Some side-by-side moves, however, were destined to end in tears. And one of them was always likely to come from within Toro Rosso as its drivers struggled for status with a difficult car. Sainz had actually dared to run around the outside of Copse, as brave a move as you would see going into and through the blind right-hander at more than 180mph. The tight exit meant the Spaniard's momentum would be checked as he took to the kerb, Kvyat drawing alongside as the pair headed, pedal to the metal, for Maggotts and Becketts. Trying to leave room, Kvyat ran wide, but didn't lift off. His subsequent oversteery return brought contact with his team-mate, Sainz spinning on to the grass and back across the track.

In the middle of this mayhem, Magnussen's Haas took a glancing blow, but the Dane was able to continue. Which was more than could be said for Sainz as he climbed from a badly damaged car. Kvyat managed to make it back to the pits and would rejoin, later receiving a drive-through (for an unsafe return at the scene of the original crime), just to make Toro Rosso's miserable day complete.

The appearance of the safety car sent the strategists into overdrive as the situation was assessed before the restart at the end of the fourth lap. Not much changed at the front as Hamilton took command once more and seemed able to ease ahead of Räikkönen, Vettel having failed to make the most of a slim opportunity to jump Verstappen.

Bottas was on the move, however, taking Ocon on lap five and, two laps later, doing the same to Hülkenberg, thanks to a neat slipstream down into Stowe. Further back, the informed crowd watched the progress of Ricciardo – 19th to 13th by lap four – only to share the Aussie's disappointment as an overambitious move on Grosjean at Luffield ended in a visit to the gravel and a return to the back of the field. Undaunted, he set about doing it all again.

Above: The start of the race at Silverstone, as Hamilton, Räikkönen and Verstappen lead the field away.
Photo: WRi2/Bryn Williams

Top left: The F1 experience. Zsolt Baumgartner gave the lucky few a taste of speed in an F1 car.

Above centre left: Renault marked the 40th anniversary of their Silverstone debut by running the RS01. Former grand prix winner René Arnoux, complete with bespoke carbon-fibre teapot, was the centre of attention.

Above left: Lewis Hamilton acknowledges the fans after taking a brilliant pole position.
Photos: WRi2/Jean-François Galeron

Left: With qualifying looming, Christian Horner surveys the ever-changeable weather conditions.
Photo: WRi2/Bryn Williams

Below left: With Vettel installed, Maurizio Arrivabene and his crew discuss the aero screen used briefly in first practice.
Photo: Lukas Gorys

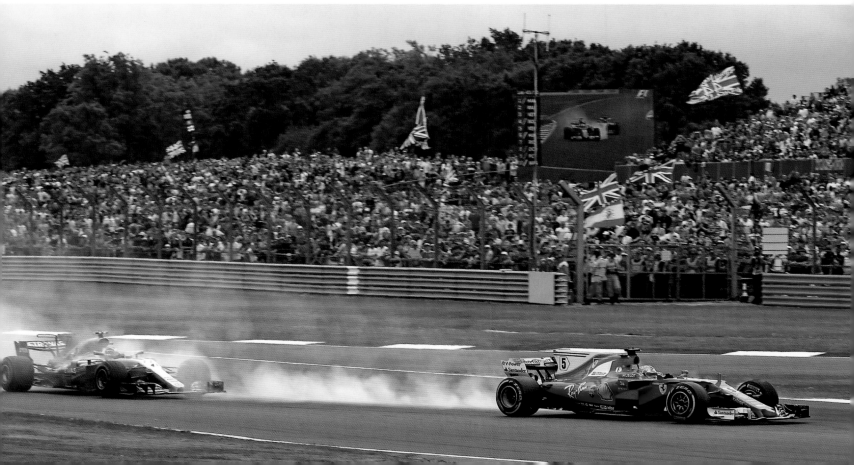

Alonso had also been closely monitored as a likely charger, his early progress to 13th being halted once he got stuck behind Stroll and the Mercedes power of the white Williams. In fact, the Spaniard was destined to go nowhere at all, for the Honda suffered a loss of fuel pressure after 32 laps, by which time, the leading four had made their first stops.

The received wisdom on tyres suggested that the supersofts would manage at least 25 laps, which would be the minimum if, as suspected, a one-stop turned out to be the best strategy. But for Hamilton, with Räikkönen less than four seconds away, there was always the threat of the undercut. The Englishman then found the best part of a second a lap and was ten seconds clear when Ferrari blinked first on lap 24 and brought in Kimi. Mercedes responded on the following lap, Hamilton rejoining still in the lead, but with Bottas now 3.2 seconds behind and ahead of both Ferraris. Räikkönen was leading his team-mate, who had been the first to stop, on lap 18.

Vettel had lost ground thanks to energetic and entertaining attempts to get by Verstappen into Stowe. He had got alongside on lap 13, only for the Dutchman to hold his ground on the outside. On one occasion, the Ferrari driver went off the road before successfully getting back on terms as they shot into Vale, the Red Bull having the inside for Club. The crowd loved it; not so Vettel, who used the radio to broadcast his view that Verstappen was moving around excessively in the braking zone.

The call to bring in Vettel on lap 18 – with Verstappen stopping a lap later – paid off, but only because a sticking wheel nut on the Red Bull's left rear had cost half a second. The problem now for Vettel would be making the softs last on a track that was not being kind to the Ferrari's left front. Proof that fast corners such as Copse, Becketts and Stowe were not causing as much grief for Mercedes came when Bottas had no trouble in staying out for 32 laps on the soft-compound Pirelli, even while heavy with fuel. Hamilton had pulled away once he had rejoined in front of his team-mate, allowing Valtteri to focus on making up time on the Ferraris and Verstappen. He was revelling in the handling of his car and forcing the Ferrari drivers to push their tyres harder than they would have liked – a crucial development that would play out late in the race.

Ricciardo, meanwhile, was working wonders with his supersofts while pushing to the limit and moving up to sixth before his first stop 32 laps into such a dramatic, but typically well-managed drive. He rejoined not far behind the warring Force Indias, Ocon holding up Pérez (according to Sergio). Taking his new rubber (nine laps fresher) to the maximum, Ricciardo used Stowe to overhaul them both on successive laps, before setting off after Hülkenberg's sixth place. The ten-second gap would slowly decrease, 'The Hulk' not helped by a leaking exhaust that was affecting the efficiency of the Renault power unit.

Bottas, on quicker tyres after his later stop, was also edging closer to his prey, the Mercedes getting on to the back of Vettel's Ferrari by lap 42. Using DRS, Bottas pulled alongside and tried to run around the outside at Stowe, but Vettel forced the Mercedes on to the exit kerb. Perhaps energised by such stout defence, the Finn immediately attacked into Club. Although it didn't pay off, this turned out to be a significant move, as Vettel locked up and did more damage to his fronts, particularly the left one. Making

Above: Valtteri Bottas backed up his team-mate with a fine second place.
Photo: Peter J. Fox

Top left: Suffering an exhaust leak on his Renault, Nico Hülkenberg was just pipped by Ricciardo and had to settle for sixth place after a gutsy drive.
Photo: Wri2/Bryn Williams

Above far left: Vettel limps to the pits with a puncture.
Photo: Wri2/Jad Sherif

Above left: Kimi Räikkönen, who also suffered a tyre failure, appears de-flated, despite rescuing a podium.
Photo: Scuderia Ferrari

Left: Vettel locks up, flat-spotting his left front, in a desperate attempt to fend off the attention of Bottas.
Photo: WRi2/Studio Colombo

Above: A typically feisty drive from Max Verstappen brought the Red Bull driver fourth place.
Photo: Red Bull Racing/Getty Images

Above right: Red, white and blue were the overwhelming colours of the day.
Photo: Peter J. Fox

Top right: The Force Indias of Ocon and Pérez brought the Silverstone-based team points in their home race. No doubt members and guests watching from the BRDC clubhouse were pondering the long-term future of the circuit's premier event.
Photo: Mercedes AMG Petronas F1 Team

Right: Old pals act. Jenson Button assumed MC duties to interview Lewis on the podium.
Photo: Lukas Gorys

it worse for the German on the following lap, Bottas timed his move into Stowe to perfection and took third. Räikkönen was ten seconds ahead – and also nursing his tyres. There were eight laps remaining.

As he had done from the start, Hamilton was controlling the race, running at his own pace and helped by Räikkönen dropping back, the gap now exceeding ten seconds. With no pressure from behind, Kimi was hanging on, hoping his front Pirellis would do the same.

But as he headed towards Copse with three laps to go, the tread on the left front came adrift. The tyre remained inflated, however, allowing Räikkönen to limp to the pits, where subsequent inspection revealed damage to two separate areas at the edge of the belt, close to the internal shoulder area. According to Pirelli, this was consistent with "contact against an external body", leading to partial separation of the belt from the carcass; part of the tread had also become detached.

Vettel, however, would not be so fortunate – if that's the right word. A lap later, his left front let go completely, forcing him to crawl back to the pits. In this case, a slow puncture of the completely worn tyre was deemed to be the cause. He would lose places and points as he rejoined seventh, Räikkönen having dropped just one place to third, thanks, in part, to Verstappen being brought in for a precautionary tyre change.

In the end, it was a Mercedes 1-2; a perfect result that reflected top performances by Hamilton and Bottas with

cars that were the class of the field – and, judging by their smiling faces in the cool-down room, a pleasure to drive. Räikkönen, by contrast, sat slumped in a corner, red-faced and disappointed – yet again. Red Bull came away with a clutch of points for fourth and fifth, Ricciardo having got by Hülkenberg into Stowe just as all the excitement was kicking off elsewhere during the final laps. Nonetheless, it was a fine result for Renault, helped by Vettel's woes.

Ocon managed to stay ahead of Pérez for 51 laps, with Massa nicking the final point after Vandoorne had been delayed during his pit stop. Magnussen, not having struggled quite so much in the race, finished 12th and was the first of the Haas drivers, but only because Grosjean had lost ground with a two-stop strategy after making contact with Ericsson.

The Swede came home 13th, four places ahead of Wehrlein, who had suffered due to a strategy call that had relied on the use of the medium tyre for one lap during the early safety car period and then an unsuccessful attempt to run to the finish on softs. Splitting the Saubers, Kvyat had put his first-lap problems behind him and battled on to finish 15th, 10s ahead of Stroll, who had to cope with unexplained bodywork damage during the conclusion of a mediocre weekend.

For Hamilton, the tenth round of the championship had been anything but, and he soaked up a rapturous reception, celebrating his Jim Clark/Alain Prost record-equalling fifth British GP win and his fourth in succession.

Maurice Hamilton

VIEWPOINT
POSTURING OR HOBSON'S CHOICE?

THE British GP took place against a backdrop of uncertainty over the race's future beyond 2019. In the week of the race came the news that Silverstone's owners, the British Racing Drivers Club (BRDC), had activated a break clause in its contract to run the race until 2026.

BRDC chairman John Grant said, "It is not financially viable for us to deliver the British GP under the terms of our current contract. We sustained losses of £2.8m in 2015 and £4.8m in 2016, and expect to lose a similar amount this year. We have reached the tipping point where we can no longer let our passion for the sport rule our heads."

At the centre of the problem was one of Bernie Ecclestone's escalator deals, involving a 5 per cent compounding annual fee increase, which had taken Silverstone's costs from £11.5m when the deal had been signed in 2010 to £16.2m in 2017; and it was due to rise to £25m by the end of the 17-year deal.

Although this arrangement was favourable in comparison to fees charged to other circuits on the F1 calendar, unlike those circuits, Silverstone did not receive any central or local government support.

The terms of Silverstone's deal required them to exercise the break clause by the week of the 2017 GP if they were going to do so, but Formula One Group (Liberty) indicated they'd been happy to extend the discussion deadline, having previously said they were unwilling to renegotiate. Mixed messages...

We'd been here before, of course. But was it coincidence that on the Wednesday before the British GP, 19 of F1's 20 drivers had attended a specially-organised 'London Live' demonstration in the capital?

The one driver who hadn't attended the event was Lewis Hamilton, and the media flak he took for that masked the potential political significance of London Live.

The logistical, safety and financial hurdles of organising a London GP by 2020 were widely believed to be insurmountable and not a realistic alternative for a British GP, which had been on the calendar since the world championship began in 1950. Liberty, too, peddled the importance of maintaining a balance between new events and F1's 'classic' races.

To a man, the drivers said it would be a shame to lose Silverstone, Daniel Ricciardo reckoning that Copse through Stowe provided the biggest buzz of the season. But just how 'classic' is the Northamptonshire former wartime bomber base? In the two decades when the British GP alternated between Silverstone and Brands Hatch, many preferred the trip to Kent...

You found yourself agreeing with Christian Horner when he expressed slight dismay at the BRDC exercising its break clause at precisely the time that Liberty was emphasising its desire to take F1 to 'destination' cities. Maybe it really was Hobson's choice. If one of the season's best-attended races is unviable, something's wrong.

Tony Dodgins

10

2017 FORMULA 1
ROLEX
BRITISH
GRAND PRIX

SILVERSTONE 14–16 JULY

ROLEX

OFFICIAL TIMEPIECE

RACE DISTANCE: 51 laps, 186.602 miles/300.307km

RACE WEATHER: Dry/cloudy (track 28–33°C, air 22–24°C)

SILVERSTONE GRAND PRIX CIRCUIT
Circuit: 3.660 miles / 5.891km, 52 laps

Club 1 130/81
Club 2 240/149
Luffield 125/78
Woodcote 285/177
Vale 115/71
Abbey 300/186
Brooklands 190/118
Stowe 255/158
Farm 305/190
Wellington Straight
305/190 Village
The Loop
Copse 285/177
Hangar Straight 325/202
Chapel 252/157
Aintree
Maggotts 305/190
Becketts 220/137
295/183
249/155

⚙ Gear
187/116 kmh/mph
— DRS zone

RACE – OFFICIAL CLASSIFICATION

Pos.	Driver	Nat.	No.	Entrant	Car/Engine	Laps	Time/Retirement	Speed (mph/km/h)	Gap to leader	Fastest race lap
1	**Lewis Hamilton**	GB	44	Mercedes AMG Petronas Motorsport	Mercedes F1 W08-Mercedes M08 EQ Power+ V6	51	1h 21m 27.430s	137.448/221.201		1m 30.621s 48
2	**Valtteri Bottas**	FIN	77	Mercedes AMG Petronas Motorsport	Mercedes F1 W08-Mercedes M08 EQ Power+ V6	51	1h 21m 41.493s	137.053/220.566	14.063s	1m 30.905s 46
3	**Kimi Räikkönen**	FIN	7	Scuderia Ferrari	Ferrari SF70H-062 V6	51	1h 22m 04.000s	136.427/219.558	36.570s	1m 31.517s 44
4	**Max Verstappen**	NL	33	Red Bull Racing	Red Bull RB13-TAG Heuer RB13 V6	51	1h 22m 19.555s	135.997/218.866	52.125s	1m 30.678s 51
5	**Daniel Ricciardo**	AUS	3	Red Bull Racing	Red Bull RB13-TAG Heuer RB13 V6	51	1h 22m 33.385s	135.617/218.255	1m 05.955s	1m 31.874s 47
6	**Nico Hülkenberg**	D	27	Renault Sport Formula One Team	Renault R.S.17-R.E.17 V6	51	1h 22m 35.539s	135.558/218.160	1m 08.109s	1m 32.577s 43
7	**Sebastian Vettel**	D	5	Scuderia Ferrari	Ferrari SF70H-062 V6	51	1h 23m 01.419s	134.854/217.027	1m 33.989s	1m 31.872s 38
8	**Esteban Ocon**	F	31	Sahara Force India Formula 1 Team	Force India VJM10-Mercedes M08 EQ Power+ V6	50			1 lap	1m 33.521s 39
9	**Sergio Pérez**	MEX	11	Sahara Force India Formula 1 Team	Force India VJM10-Mercedes M08 EQ Power+ V6	50			1 lap	1m 33.504s 42
10	**Felipe Massa**	BR	19	Williams Martini Racing	Williams FW40-Mercedes M08 EQ Power+ V6	50			1 lap	1m 33.562s 39
11	Stoffel Vandoorne	B	2	McLaren Honda Formula 1 Team	McLaren MCL32-Honda RA617H V6	50			1 lap	1m 33.464s 43
12	Kevin Magnussen	DK	20	Haas F1 Team	Haas VF-17-Ferrari 062 V6	50			1 lap	1m 32.683s 41
13	Romain Grosjean	F	8	Haas F1 Team	Haas VF-17-Ferrari 062 V6	50			1 lap	1m 32.290s 45
14	Marcus Ericsson	S	9	Sauber F1 Team	Sauber C36-Ferrari 059/5 V6	50			1 lap	1m 33.119s 30
15	Daniil Kvyat	RUS	26	Scuderia Toro Rosso	Toro Rosso STR12-Renault R.E.17 V6	50			1 lap	1m 33.594s 29
16	Lance Stroll	CDN	18	Williams Martini Racing	Williams FW40-Mercedes M08 EQ Power+ V6	50			1 lap	1m 33.400s 44
17	Pascal Wehrlein	D	94	Sauber F1 Team	Sauber C36-Ferrari 059/5 V6	50			1 lap	1m 33.342s 34
	Fernando Alonso	E	14	McLaren Honda Formula 1 Team	McLaren MCL32-Honda RA617H V6	32	fuel pump			1m 34.263s 22
	Carlos Sainz	E	55	Scuderia Toro Rosso	Toro Rosso STR12-Renault R.E.17 V6	0	accident			no time
NS	Jolyon Palmer	GB	30	Renault Sport Formula One Team	Renault R.S.17-R.E.17 V6		hydraulics			no time

Race scheduled for 52 laps, but reduced by one lap due to an aborted start, with Palmer retiring on the formation lap.

Fastest race lap: Lewis Hamilton on lap 48, 1m 30.621s, 145.417mph/234.025km/h (new record for current configuration).

Lap record: Nigel Mansell (Williams FW11B-Honda V6 turbo), 1m 09.832s, 153.059mph/246.324km/h (1987, 2.969-mile/4.778km circuit).

Previous lap record (current configuration): Fernando Alonso (Ferrari F10 V8), 1m 30.874s, 145.012mph/233.373km/h (2010)

19 · RICCIARDO · Red Bull
5-place grid penalty for replacing gearbox; 10 places for using additional power unit elements

17 · WEHRLEIN · Sauber

15 · STROLL · Williams

13 · SAINZ · Toro Rosso

11 · Palmer · Renault

20 · ALONSO · McLaren
30-place grid penalty for using additional power unit elements

18 · ERICSSON · Sauber

16 · MAGNUSSEN · Haas

14 · MASSA · Williams

12 · KVYAT · Toro Rosso

Grid order	1	2	3	4	5	6	7	8	9	10	11	12	13	14	15	16	17	18	19	20	21	22	23	24	25	26	27	28	29	30	31	32	33	34	35	36	37	38	39	40	41
44 HAMILTON	44	44	44	44	44	44	44	44	44	44	44	44	44	44	44	44	44	44	44	44	44	44	44	44	44	44	44	44	44	44	44	44	44	44	44	44	44	44	44	44	44
7 RÄIKKÖNEN	7	7	7	7	7	7	7	7	7	7	7	7	7	7	7	7	7	7	7	7	7	7	7	7	77	77	77	77	77	77	77	77	7	7	7	7	7	7	7	7	7
5 VETTEL	33	33	33	33	33	33	33	33	33	33	33	33	33	33	33	33	33	33	33	77	77	77	77	77	7	7	7	7	7	7	7	7	5	5	5	5	5	5	5	5	5
33 VERSTAPPEN	5	5	5	5	5	5	5	5	5	5	5	5	5	5	5	5	5	5	5	33	77	27	5	5	5	5	5	5	5	5	5	5	77	77	77	77	77	77	77	77	77
27 HÜLKENBERG	27	27	27	27	27	27	27	27	77	77	77	77	77	77	77	77	77	77	27	5	27	5	33	33	33	33	33	33	33	33	33	33	33	33	33	33	33	33	33	33	33
11 PÉREZ	31	31	31	31	77	77	27	27	27	27	27	27	27	27	27	27	27	27	5	33	33	27	27	27	3	3	3	3	3	3	3	3	27	27	27	27	27	27	27	27	27
31 OCON	77	77	77	77	31	31	31	31	31	31	31	31	31	31	31	31	31	31	31	11	11	11	3	2	2	27	27	27	27	27	20	20	3	3	3	3	3	3	3	3	3
2 VANDOORNE	11	11	11	11	11	11	11	11	11	11	11	11	11	11	11	11	11	11	2	3	3	2	19	27	20	20	20	20	20	20	31	3	20	20	20	31	31	31	31		
77 BOTTAS	2	2	2	2	2	2	2	2	2	2	2	2	2	2	2	2	2	2	3	2	19	27	20	31	31	31	31	31	31	11	31	31	31	31	11	11	11	11		
8 GROSJEAN	19	19	19	19	19	19	19	19	19	19	19	19	19	19	19	19	19	3	3	19	20	20	31	11	11	11	11	11	11	3	11	11	11	11	19	19	19	19		
30 PALMER	8	8	8	8	8	8	8	8	8	8	8	8	8	8	3	3	3	19	19	19	8	8	8	31	31	11	9	19	19	19	19	19	19	19	2	2	2			
26 KVYAT	18	18	18	18	18	18	18	18	18	18	18	18	3	8	8	8	8	8	8	8	18	18	20	11	11	9	19	9	2	2	2	2	2	2	8	8	8			
55 SAINZ	20	20	20	3	14	14	14	14	14	14	3	3	18	18	18	18	18	18	20	20	31	9	9	94	2	2	8	8	8	8	8	8	8	8	18	20	20	20			
19 MASSA	3	94	3	20	20	20	3	3	14	14	14	14	14	14	14	14	9	31	9	94	94	19	8	14	14	18	18	18	18	18	18	18	18	18	18	18	18			
18 STROLL	9	3	94	14	94	94	20	20	20	20	20	20	20	20	20	20	31	9	94	8	8	94	14	18	18	14	9	9	9	9	9	9	9	9							
20 MAGNUSSEN	14	9	9	9	9	3	94	94	94	9	9	9	9	9	9	9	94	94	14	14	14	14	94	94	94	14	26	26	26	26	26	26	26	26							
94 WEHRLEIN	94	14	14	94	26	9	9	9	9	94	94	94	94	94	94	94	14	26	26	18	18	18	18	9	9	26	94	94	94	94	94	94									
9 ERICSSON	26	26	26	3	26	26	26	26	26	26	26	26	26	26	26	26	14	14	18	26	26	26	26	26	26	94															
3 RICCIARDO																																									
14 ALONSO																																									

94 = Pit stop   26 = Drive-through penalty   9 = One lap or more behind

All results and data © FOM 2017

TIME SHEETS

PRACTICE 1 (FRIDAY)
Weather: Dry/cloudy
Temperatures: track 21–32°C, air 15–17°C

Pos.	Driver	Laps	Time
1	Valtteri Bottas	29	1m 29.106s
2	Lewis Hamilton	29	1m 29.184s
3	Max Verstappen	26	1m 29.604s
4	Daniel Ricciardo	19	1m 29.942s
5	Kimi Räikkönen	19	1m 30.137s
6	Sebastian Vettel	19	1m 30.517s
7	Daniil Kvyat	21	1m 30.895s
8	Fernando Alonso	20	1m 30.993s
9	Felipe Massa	26	1m 30.999s
10	Stoffel Vandoorne	27	1m 31.041s
11	Carlos Sainz	24	1m 31.200s
12	Esteban Ocon	32	1m 31.210s
13	Sergio Pérez	34	1m 31.297s
14	Romain Grosjean	24	1m 31.610s
15	Lance Stroll	24	1m 31.684s
16	Antonio Giovinazzi	24	1m 32.031s
17	Nico Hülkenberg	19	1m 32.171s
18	Jolyon Palmer	16	1m 32.450s
19	Pascal Wehrlein	23	1m 33.029s
20	Marcus Ericsson	26	1m 33.399s

PRACTICE 2 (FRIDAY)
Weather: Dry/cloudy
Temperatures: track 30–34°C, air 22–23°C

Pos.	Driver	Laps	Time
1	Valtteri Bottas	31	1m 28.496s
2	Lewis Hamilton	35	1m 28.543s
3	Kimi Räikkönen	36	1m 28.828s
4	Sebastian Vettel	36	1m 28.956s
5	Max Verstappen	32	1m 29.098s
6	Daniel Ricciardo	35	1m 29.586s
7	Nico Hülkenberg	37	1m 29.936s
8	Felipe Massa	36	1m 30.006s
9	Fernando Alonso	28	1m 30.238s
10	Esteban Ocon	42	1m 30.383s
11	Carlos Sainz	26	1m 30.555s
12	Daniil Kvyat	34	1m 30.562s
13	Sergio Pérez	43	1m 30.624s
14	Romain Grosjean	33	1m 30.661s
15	Lance Stroll	37	1m 30.695s
16	Stoffel Vandoorne	31	1m 30.782s
17	Kevin Magnussen	33	1m 30.835s
18	Jolyon Palmer	25	1m 30.879s
19	Marcus Ericsson	27	1m 31.616s
20	Pascal Wehrlein	30	1m 31.929s

PRACTICE 3 (SATURDAY)
Weather: Dry-wet/cloudy
Temperatures: air 25°

Pos.	Driver	Laps	Time
1	Lewis Hamilton	18	1m 28.063s
2	Sebastian Vettel	14	1m 28.095s
3	Valtteri Bottas	20	1m 28.137s
4	Kimi Räikkönen	15	1m 28.732s
5	Nico Hülkenberg	14	1m 29.480s
6	Daniel Ricciardo	15	1m 29.612s
7	Romain Grosjean	14	1m 29.819s
8	Max Verstappen	13	1m 29.904s
9	Felipe Massa	19	1m 29.959s
10	Stoffel Vandoorne	19	1m 30.088s
11	Fernando Alonso	17	1m 30.138s
12	Esteban Ocon	19	1m 30.172s
13	Kevin Magnussen	15	1m 30.270s
14	Jolyon Palmer	16	1m 30.302s
15	Sergio Pérez	16	1m 30.416s
16	Daniil Kvyat	20	1m 30.504s
17	Carlos Sainz	19	1m 30.515s
18	Pascal Wehrlein	24	1m 30.621s
19	Marcus Ericsson	24	1m 30.630s
20	Lance Stroll	18	1m 31.358s

QUALIFYING (SATURDAY)
Weather: Light showers/cloudy Temperatures: track 20–22°C, air 16–18°C

Pos.	Driver	First	Second	Third	Qualifying Tyre
1	Lewis Hamilton	1m 39.069s	1m 27.893s	1m 26.600s	Supersoft (new)
2	Kimi Räikkönen	1m 40.455s	1m 28.992s	1m 27.147s	Supersoft (new)
3	Sebastian Vettel	1m 39.962s	1m 28.978s	1m 27.356s	Supersoft (new)
4	Valtteri Bottas	1m 39.698s	1m 28.732s	1m 27.376s	Supersoft (new)
5	Max Verstappen	1m 38.912s	1m 29.431s	1m 28.130s	Supersoft (new)
6	Nico Hülkenberg	1m 39.201s	1m 29.340s	1m 28.856s	Supersoft (new)
7	Sergio Pérez	1m 42.009s	1m 29.824s	1m 28.902s	Supersoft (new)
8	Esteban Ocon	1m 39.738s	1m 29.701s	1m 29.074s	Supersoft (new)
9	Stoffel Vandoorne	1m 40.011s	1m 30.105s	1m 29.418s	Supersoft (new)
10	Romain Grosjean	1m 42.042s	1m 29.966s	1m 29.549s	Supersoft (new)
11	Jolyon Palmer	1m 41.404s	1m 30.193s		
12	Daniil Kvyat	1m 41.726s	1m 30.355s		
13	Fernando Alonso	1m 37.598s	1m 30.600s		
14	Carlos Sainz	1m 41.114s	1m 31.368s		
15	Felipe Massa	1m 41.874s	1m 31.482s		
16	Lance Stroll	1m 42.573s			
17	Kevin Magnussen	1m 42.577s			
18	Pascal Wehrlein	1m 42.593s			
19	Marcus Ericsson	1m 42.633s			
20	Daniel Ricciardo	1m 42.966s			

QUALIFYING: head to head

Hamilton	6	4	Bottas
Vettel	7	3	Räikkönen
Massa	9	1	Stroll
Ricciardo	4	6	Verstappen
Pérez	9	1	Ocon
Hülkenberg	10	0	Palmer
Kvyat	5	5	Sainz
Ericsson	2	0	Giovinazzi
Ericsson	2	6	Wehrlein
Alonso	8	1	Vandoorne
Vandoorne	1	0	Button
Grosjean	7	3	Magnussen

FOR THE RECORD

50th GRAND PRIX: Kevin Magnussen, Carlos Sainz, **Max Verstappen**

70th WIN: Mercedes

DID YOU KNOW?

Lewis Hamilton equalled Jim Clark's record of five British GP wins. He also drew level with Fangio's record of four consecutive wins at the same home circuit.

POINTS

DRIVERS

1	Sebastian Vettel	177
2	Lewis Hamilton	176
3	Valtteri Bottas	154
4	Daniel Ricciardo	117
5	Kimi Räikkönen	98
6	Max Verstappen	57
7	Sergio Pérez	52
8	Esteban Ocon	43
9	Carlos Sainz	29
10	Nico Hülkenberg	26
11	Felipe Massa	23
12	Lance Stroll	18
13	Romain Grosjean	18
14	Kevin Magnussen	11
15	Pascal Wehrlein	5
16	Daniil Kvyat	4
17	Fernando Alonso	2

CONSTRUCTORS

1	Mercedes	330
2	Ferrari	275
3	Red Bull	174
4	Force India	95
5	Williams	41
6	Toro Rosso	33
7	Haas	29
8	Renault	26
9	Sauber	5
10	McLaren	2

9 · BOTTAS · Mercedes
5-place grid penalty for replacing gearbox

7 · OCON · Force India

5 · HÜLKENBERG · Renault

3 · VETTEL · Ferrari

1 · HAMILTON · Mercedes

10 · GROSJEAN · Haas

8 · VANDOORNE · McLaren

6 · PÉREZ · Force India

4 · VERSTAPPEN · Red Bull

2 · RÄIKKÖNEN · Ferrari

42	43	44	45	46	47	48	49	50	51	
44	44	44	44	44	44	44	44	44	44	1
7	7	7	7	7	7	7	77	77	77	2
5	77	77	77	77	77	77	7	7	7	3
77	5	5	5	5	5	5	5	33	33	4
33	33	33	33	33	33	33	33	3	3	5
27	27	27	27	27	27	27	27	5	27	6
3	3	3	3	3	3	3	3	27	5	7
31	31	31	31	31	31	31	31	31		8
11	11	11	11	11	11	11	11	11		9
19	19	19	19	19	19	19	19	19		10
2	2	2	2	2	2	2	2			
8	8	20	20	20	20	20	20	20		
20	20	9	8	8	8	8	8	8		
18	9	8	9	9	9	9	9	9		
9	18	18	18	26	26	26	26	26		
26	26	26	26	18	18	18	18	18		
94	94	94	94	94	94	94	94	94		

■ Safety car deployed on laps shown

RACE TYRE STRATEGIES
PIRELLI

	Driver	Race Stint 1	Race Stint 2	Race Stint 3	Race Stint 4
1	Hamilton	Supersoft (u): 1–25	Soft (n): 26–51		
2	Bottas	Soft (u): 1–32	Supersoft (n): 33–51		
3	Räikkönen	Supersoft (u): 1–24	Soft (n): 25–49	Supersoft (u): 50–51	
4	Verstappen	Supersoft (u): 1–19	Soft (n): 20–49	Supersoft (n): 50–51	
5	Ricciardo	Supersoft (n): 1–32	Soft (n): 33–51		
6	Hülkenberg	Supersoft (u): 1–24	Soft (n): 25–51		
7	Vettel	Supersoft (u): 1–18	Soft (n): 19–50	Supersoft (u): 51	
8	Ocon	Supersoft (u): 1–20	Soft (n): 21–50		
9	Pérez	Supersoft (u): 1–23	Soft (n): 24–50		
10	Massa	Soft (n): 1–25	Supersoft (n): 26–50		
11	Vandoorne	Supersoft (u): 1–26	Soft (n): 27–50		
12	Magnussen	Soft (n): 1–37	Supersoft (n): 38–50		
13	Grosjean	Supersoft (u): 1– 23	Soft (n): 24–43	Supersoft (n): 44–50	
14	Ericsson	Soft (n): 1–28	Supersoft (n): 29–50		
15	Kvyat	Supersoft (n): 1	Soft (n): 2–27	Supersoft (n): 28–50	
16	Stroll	Soft (n): 1–22	Supersoft (n): 23–42	Supersoft (n): 43–50	
	Wehrlein	Soft (n): 1–2	Medium (n): 3	Soft (n): 4–31	Supersoft (n): 32–50 (dnf)
	Alonso	Supersoft (n): 1–20	Soft (n): 21–32 (dnf)		
	Sainz	Supersoft (n): 0 (dnf)			
	Palmer	Supersoft (n): 0 (dnf)			

The tyre regulations stipulate that at least two of three dry tyre specifications must be used during a dry race.
Pirelli P Zero logos are colour-coded on the tyre sidewalls: Red = Supersoft; Yellow = Soft; White = Medium. (n) new (u) used

Photos: Peter J. Fox

HUNGARIAN GRAND PRIX

HUNGARORING CIRCUIT

Inset, above: Vettel leads Räikkönen
home to a Ferrari 1-2 finish.
Photo: Lukas Gorys

Inset, above: Vettel stretched his championship lead over Hamilton to 24 points by taking victory at the Hungaroring.

Main photo: Countdown to the race. The grid girls take up position as they await the arrival of the cars.

Photos: Peter J. Fox

HUNGARORING QUALIFYING

OFF the pace two weeks before at Silverstone, Ferrari responded by making a spectacular comeback, taking their first pole position in Hungary since Michael Schumacher in 2005. In 2017, the honour went to Sebastian Vettel with a scorching lap, faster than anyone had ever gone around the Hungaroring.

"It's fantastic, and a tribute to the entire team," said Vettel. "We've been working hard and we made a big step forward this weekend. It's all about making these steps, never giving up. We're very happy as a team, particularly when you remember where we were 12 months ago, and compare that struggle with where we are now. I was confident going into Q3. I went flat out, but I think I asked a bit too much of the tyres at one point. Even so, the car was phenomenal."

A modified floor played its part, but overall the Ferrari was better suited than the Mercedes to the relentless succession of corners at the Hungaroring. With the left rear being the limiting tyre here, the Ferrari's benign balance was actually enhanced during qualifying when the track temperature rose to the mid-50s, a couple of degrees higher than it had been on the Friday.

Kimi Räikkönen backed up his team-mate by jumping ahead of the Mercedes and Red Bull drivers. But despite getting on to the front row, the Finn was disappointed, having genuinely believed he could have been on pole.

"The start and the end of the lap was good, but I braked on the kerb at the chicane [Turns Six and Seven] and lost a little time," said Räikkönen. "That was a little disappointing because we managed to improve the car. It hadn't been so good on Friday."

Lewis Hamilton could do no better than fourth, a few tenths of a second behind his Mercedes team-mate, Valtteri Bottas, who managed to get more from the W08, which veered towards understeer in the slow stuff and snap oversteer through the faster corners. Whereas Bottas tended to nurse his car around the lap, Hamilton's more aggressive style did not pay off, forcing the abandonment of his first Q3 run, which was followed by a more conservative start to his final attempt and a 0.17s deficit to Bottas at the end of it.

"We've struggled a bit with the car, but it improved during qualifying," said Hamilton. "My laps were generally good, except in the final part of qualifying. We knew Ferrari would be quick, so I think we did quite well."

Hamilton was actually fortunate to be ahead of Max Verstappen and Daniel Ricciardo, the Red Bulls having been fastest on Friday and enjoying the fruits of much development work, predominantly reshaped sidepods, a new footplate area ahead of them and a revised diffuser. Despite the benefit of additional grip at the front, Verstappen added more front wing for his final Q3 run – and regretted it when the resulting move towards oversteer cost the tenth of a second that separated the Dutchman from Hamilton. Ricciardo, fastest in FP1 and FP2, felt he could have been ahead but for the effect of lost track time during FP3 due to a hydraulics problem.

Nico Hülkenberg's top form continued with seventh fastest, albeit with the Renault being just over half a second off the Red Bulls and the knowledge that the German would pay the price of an unscheduled gearbox change. That penalty placed him 12th on the grid, directly behind Jolyon Palmer, who had recovered from two offs on Friday, improved the balance and just missed out on a place in Q3. It was minor consolation for the Englishman during a weekend of mounting pressure as stories of a Kubica comeback gathered strength. Eventually, he was more than half a second from his team-mate.

A slightly better comparison was to be had at McLaren, where Stoffel Vandoorne was three-tenths from his team-mate, after Fernando Alonso had produced a trademark stonking lap to qualify eighth on a track that was better suited than most to the customary Honda shortfall.

On the other hand, there was an even larger discrepancy between the Toro Rosso drivers, Carlos Sainz having turned in an excellent lap to reach Q3, while Daniil Kvyat found himself in all sorts of trouble. Apart from spinning through Turn Eight during Q1, the Russian's method of rejoining was deemed to have impeded Lance Stroll, costing the Williams driver time. Kvyat received a three-place penalty, which dropped him to 16th.

The Force Indias, focused on race set-up rather than qualifying, slotted in behind Palmer, Esteban Ocon leading the way by a couple of tenths after Sergio Pérez admitted that a poor first lap had upset preparation for his final Q2 run. The Haas drivers, meanwhile, were struggling with a lack of mechanical grip, Romain Grosjean heading Kevin Magnussen after the Dane had lost track time waiting for repairs to be completed on his car, following a shunt by Antonio Giovinazzi during FP1.

Most disappointing by far, Williams had to make do with 17th for the impeded Stroll and a brave effort by Paul di Resta. The team's reserve driver, having had absolutely no experience of the 2017 car (not even time in the simulator), stepped in at the last minute and qualified 19th after Felipe Massa had been affected by dizzy spells on Saturday morning. Di Resta did not put a foot wrong and split the updated Saubers, Pascal Wehrlein (recovering from a huge shunt on Friday) ahead of Marcus Ericsson (delayed by Kvyat).

Up front, Vettel was in no doubt that there was still a long way to go. "My main task comes in the race," he said. "We have a big boost from race fans here and at home in Italy. It's going to be a very tough race on this track: one corner after another with no time to relax. Starting from pole is obviously an advantage, but there is a lot of work to do, particularly with these guys behind me!"

FORMULA 1 PIRELLI MAGYAR NAGYDÍJ 2017

Clockwise, from top left:
There was much excitement over the return of Robert Kubica to the cockpit of a 2017 Renault during the post-race tests.
Photo: Lukas Gorys

A tough season for Marcus Ericsson, with the Swede still searching for a championship point.
Photo: WRi2/Jean-François Galeron

Paul di Resta was pressed into duty at Williams to substitute for the indisposed Felipe Massa.
Photo: WRi2/Studio Colombo

Laurent Mekies, Charlie Whiting and Matteo Bonciani expound on the FIA's decision to introduce the cockpit halo into F1 for 2018.

Right: Frédéric Vasseur, the former Renault boss, was installed as the new supremo at Sauber.
Photos: WRi2/Jean-François Galeron

THE drivers on row two knew they would have their work cut out. All things being equal, the Ferrari should have had the legs of the Mercedes in all conditions throughout 71 laps. But in motor racing, all things are rarely equal – as Vettel discovered the moment his car was lowered from the jacks on the starting grid.

As he set off on the parade lap, Seb noted that the steering was pulling slightly to the left. The rear of his Ferrari had been in pieces earlier in the day to allow the replacement of a hydraulic control unit and moog valve. Had that work caused this potential problem?

Putting it to the back of his mind, Vettel turned his attention to the start and the run to the first corner. Both of the Ferraris made strong getaways, Räikkönen sweeping in behind his team-mate and, crucially, having to back off marginally as they scrambled through the first corner. That, in turn, caught out Verstappen, who had got ahead of Hamilton and then run around the outside of Bottas through the right-hander. The subsequent visit to the exit kerb by the Red Bull allowed Bottas to regain his place, however. Meanwhile, Ricciardo had got ahead of Hamilton on the inside and accelerated into fourth, just as Verstappen recovered on the left of his team-mate.

Anxious – desperate, even – not to lose more ground (particularly to Ricciardo) after having potentially gained so much, Verstappen dived down the inside on the approach to Turn Two, misjudged his braking and hit the side of Ricciardo, damaging his radiator and puncturing a tyre. In a typical piece of racing irony, Verstappen was able to continue while a furious Ricciardo could not. With oil, water and debris sprayed around Turn Two, the safety car was called.

Red Bull was not the only team to suffer the frustration of watching their drivers fight among themselves rather than against the competition. As had become almost a matter of routine in recent races, the Force India drivers were at it, banging wheels as Pérez forced his way past Ocon coming out of Turn One. Their cars did not emerge unscathed: Ocon came off worse, with a broken floor that would compromise his race performance; Pérez got away with minor damage to a nose wing and having the buffer of Vandoorne between them in ninth place.

The subsequent five-lap intervention by the official Mercedes eased the option towards the faster one-stop strategy, which was good news for the kind-to-its-tyres Ferrari, but not so good for Mercedes. On the other hand, the Red Bull contretemps and an impending ten-second penalty for Verstappen would remove the threat of an undercut to the Mercedes one-stop plan. But everything remained open as they took the restart.

Vettel showed no outward sign of the steering problem as he pulled away from Räikkönen who, in turn, was opening a similar 0.5s gap every lap to Bottas. Neither Valtteri nor Lewis (in fifth, behind Verstappen) were able to even think about attacking as they worked to protect their rear tyres and keep everything cool in the scorching temperatures. As the laps ticked by and everyone held station, Mercedes began to accept that a one-stop would be physically possible. But what about Ferrari?

As the laps completed reached double figures, Vettel began to notice that the steering problem was growing worse. He had eased out a 3s lead, but on lap 15, that began to shrink as he was forced to drive on the straights

Above: Sebastian Vettel locks a wheel as the Ferraris take control of the race from the start.
Photo: WRi2/Jean-François Galeron

223

while applying lock, Indy oval racing style, leaving Mercedes to wonder if the reduction in pace had been caused by Seb needing to take care of his tyres. In any case, Mercedes had a problem of its own.

A cracked fibre-optics cable was causing havoc with the team's communication system: while the drivers were able to receive occasional bursts from the pit wall, the engineers were unable to hear the drivers' comments about tyres, and there was an increasing need to know exactly what was going on, particularly with the leading Ferrari.

Ferrari's wish not to reveal Vettel's problem over the airwaves meant that Räikkönen was also in the dark as he tried to figure out why Vettel was coming to him at a time when Bottas was staying on their pace, maintaining a gap of around eight seconds. Surely, this was not in the game plan of a team that really ought to be commanding the race?

Bottas was the first of the leading bunch to stop for fresh softs at the end of lap 30, his rear supersofts on their last legs. In the absence of information from Hamilton, it was assumed that he was in a similar situation. In fact, he felt that there was life left in his rubber and was reluctant to heed the call to come in a lap later.

With the Mercedes pair immediately lapping a second faster, Ferrari responded by bringing in Vettel on lap 32; Räikkönen a lap later. Kimi's state of confusion was compounded by his in-lap being 1.6s faster than the struggling Vettel. This – plus a marginally faster stop – meant that he rejoined just as Seb was powering along the pit straight. At Force India, say, this would have been a recipe for wheel banging through Turn One, but Kimi knew his place and offered no challenge for what had become second behind the yet-to-stop Verstappen. Even so, he was soon on the radio enquiring (politely, by his standards) about the team's wisdom in not leaving him out on tyres that were good enough to allow an overcut and save him from potential attack by the advancing Mercedes.

Just as Räikkönen was unaware of his team-mate's predicament, the radio silence meant that Mercedes were not completely informed of Hamilton's opinion that he could have used fresher tyres and an overcut on Bottas to get closer to the Ferraris.

"Without the radio problem," said Toto Wolff, "we could have had the discussion probably a couple of laps earlier.

Later, when we could hear him, he told us he could have gone much quicker, and he even said that the first set of tyres were in good shape, and we could probably have tried to leave him out and that could have had a potentially massive outcome on the race because we were so close to the Ferraris at the end.

"Our whole comms and data systems broke down, and we didn't have any communications on the 'fantasy island' [the central computer console in the garage] or on the pit wall. No radio comms, no data, no TV feed, and we somehow managed to get it back occasionally."

Verstappen stayed out for another ten laps, then stopped at his pit for ten seconds before the crew sprang to life and banged on a new set of softs. He rejoined fifth, 17s ahead of Hülkenberg, who was about to make a pit stop during an eventful race. A forceful brush with Grosjean in Turn One on the first lap had briefly tipped the Haas on to two wheels, a move that did not earn the approval of either the Frenchman or Magnussen, who witnessed the collision. Magnussen would later take revenge on behalf of Haas by forcing Hülkenberg wide as the Renault tried to take 11th place; a rough tactic that would earn him a five-second penalty and spark a colourful exchange between the two in the post-race TV interview compound.

More civilised, if abrupt, words were continuing to flow from Ferrari No. 7 as Räikkönen expressed his discomfort at having Bottas at close quarters when, by rights, the Ferrari – both Ferraris, in fact – should have been out of harm's reach. But each time Bottas got close and considered triggering DRS on the main straight, the front of the Mercedes would wash out through the pair of long, slow final corners. There was nothing he could do about it.

Hamilton, feeling he had stronger pace, used the revived radio link to request permission to have a go, on the understanding that he would give third back to Bottas if the mission failed. The team agreed, but, mindful of Verstappen's fast approach on fresher tyres, they gave Lewis five laps to get the job done, and Valtteri moved aside without hesitation at the start of lap 46.

Within a handful of laps, Hamilton had closed down the 3.7s gap to what should have been striking distance. But, just like his team-mate, he hit the same aero wall as he tried to break into the 1s DRS activation gap.

Above: A smart pit stop by Toro Rosso helped Carlos Sainz take an excellent seventh place.

Left: Deep in thought. Maurizio Arrivabene oversaw a dominant performance from his drivers.

Right: Max Verstappen overcame a needless collision with team-mate Daniel Ricciardo to claim fifth place for Red Bull.

Photos: Peter J. Fox

Above: Kimi Räikkönen played the team game and protected leader Sebastian Vettel, who was struggling with damaged steering gear on his winning Ferrari.
Photo: Scuderia Ferrari

Top right: Even in cartoon form, Fernando Alonso appears to shun Vettel's victory celebration.
Photo: Wri2/Jad Sherif

Above right: Valtteri Bottas ended up on the podium.
Photo: Mercedes AMG Petronas F1 Team

Right: Lewis Hamilton moved ahead of Bottas to try to attack the Ferraris, but having failed, he handed back third place to his team-mate.
Photo: Lukas Gorys

This was a major relief for Räikkönen, who remained right with Vettel, and by now, he had realised there was something amiss with the leading Ferrari. Seb was responding to instruction from his team to stay off the kerbs for fear of exacerbating the steering problem – a crippling handicap on a circuit where attacking the kerbs is the fastest way forward. Bizarrely, this race was being dictated by a broken Ferrari and a Mercedes that could not overtake.

Bottas, meanwhile, had dropped back, the better to save his tyres for the inevitable final attack from Verstappen. With Hamilton unable to do anything about Räikkönen, Bottas was told to close up and benefit from the agreed switch of positions. But it wasn't that simple.

"It was difficult," said Bottas. "They [back-markers] were getting out the way of the first three because they were running together in a train, but I'd have to find my own way through. Then you get off line, you pick up dirt on the tyres, they lose their grip and temperature, and it takes a lap or two to get them back."

While keeping an eye on the Ferraris ahead and hoping for a mistake, Hamilton was also looking in his mirrors, waiting for his team-mate to catch up. Neither was happening – and Verstappen was closing by at least half a second a lap.

The Red Bull was a long way clear of Alonso, who was pressing on, having finally dealt with Sainz at the end of a lively battle between the Spaniards. The Toro Rosso driver had got the attention of the stewards – not to mention Alonso – with some pretty aggressive stuff as he muscled ahead of the McLaren on the first lap and strongly defended his position. The stewards decided that the move had been just on the right side of marginal, by which time Alonso, having backed off slightly to allow things to cool in every sense, launched an attack, the two running nose to tail before and after their pit stops on lap 35.

Alonso finally did the job two laps later, starting with a DRS-assisted move alongside into Turn One and finishing it decisively around the outside of Turn Two. As the fuel load lightened, the McLaren driver began to relish the handling, pulling away and making his penultimate lap the fastest of anyone; satisfying for Fernando and a handy reminder for the watching world.

With Sainz holding seventh, the final points were heading the way of Pérez, Ocon and Vandoorne, who had lost P9 thanks to overshooting his pit. Hülkenberg would have been in the mix but for his contretemps with Magnussen, and then ending a busy race with gearbox and brake trouble a couple of laps from home. Palmer, having been instructed earlier to let Hülkenberg through, lost two more places when undercut by Magnussen and Kvyat, the Haas and Toro Rosso finishing 11th and 12th.

The disappointing weekend for Stroll had continued when overheating tyres caused the Canadian to drop away badly in the second half, di Resta's tidy drive in the other Williams having ended with ten laps to go due to a loss of oil pressure. The Saubers brought up the rear. Wehrlein was ahead, despite a slow puncture that had prompted an early stop, while Ericsson's race had been compromised from the start by flat-spotted front tyres at Turn One. A subsequent pit stop and an attempt to make the fresh set last the distance ended with another stop several laps from the finish.

The Swede's pit visit went unnoticed, as all eyes were on the leading quartet being chased down by Verstappen. The Red Bull's menacing presence appeared to rule out the planned Mercedes shuffle, but Hamilton managed to let Bottas through at the final corner and cross the line with half a second to spare.

Hamilton's honorable move had cost him three points on a day when Vettel had considered himself lucky to have scored the maximum. As F1 headed for its summer break, Lewis probably did not want to think about the consequences if he was three points short of a title at the end of the season (*see* Viewpoint). On the other hand, Bottas, still a championship contender, might be very grateful.

Maurice Hamilton

VIEWPOINT
MERCEDES TOPS FAIR PLAY LEAGUE

AT Ferrari, Sebastian Vettel was the team leader and Kimi Räikkönen played the supporting role. Mercedes, ostensibly, was an equal-opportunities employer. But was it really? In Bahrain, we had seen Valtteri Bottas instructed to let the better-performing Lewis Hamilton past (twice). While Valtteri had found that difficult, he had acquiesced and later was thanked by Lewis, who said he would do the same if the boot was on the other foot. There were those who thought that the situation would never arise and, if it did, doubted that Hamilton would actually pull over.

In Budapest, though, Lewis was put to the test and passed. Bottas had outqualified him, but could not get into a position to make a move stick on the race-leading Ferraris. Hamilton, behind him, thought he could. Bottas was told to move over so that Lewis could attack, on the understanding that if he couldn't displace the Ferraris, Valtteri would get his third place back.

Problem one: on the single lap when Bottas had let Hamilton through, he dropped 3s while cleaning up his dirty tyres. Problem two: the back-marker traffic was less obliging to Valtteri than to the leading three-car train, and he fell to more than 7s behind Hamilton. Problem three: Max Verstappen had closed to just over a second behind the second Mercedes. So, what to do?

Toto Wolff admitted that it had been the hardest decision he'd had to take in five years: "Sometimes, doing it the right way and standing by your values is f***ing tough. And it was today, believe me. I feel cr*p." But do it Mercedes did, asking Hamilton to give the podium position back to Bottas on the last lap. Admirably, he complied. It would have been easy not to have done so and fought his corner later.

The switch cost Lewis three points in his drivers' title bid, as race winner Vettel stretched his championship lead to 14. It kept Bottas properly in the fight and also sent him a strong message that the team could be trusted.

Did Mercedes do the right thing? Some won't have liked part of Wolff's explanation: "We have seen the backlash of decisions that were ruthless and cold-blooded [Ferrari's nonsense in Austria 2002], and the effect it had on the brand."

To hell with brands, they would have said, F1 is about drivers. Hamilton said all the right things about wanting to win the championship in the right way, but he couldn't disguise the fact that he was a bit hacked off and hoped it didn't all come back to bite him on the bum when the points were totalled up in Abu Dhabi…

You had to doff your cap to Mercedes for upholding their sporting values. "They have won us six championships and will win us more in the years to come," Wolff said. "If the consequences are as much as losing this championship, we'll take it. Long-term, that approach is better." Fair play all around.

Tony Dodgins

11

2017 FORMULA 1
PIRELLI
MAGYAR NAGYDÍJ
BUDAPEST 28–30 JULY

ROLEX

F1 OFFICIAL TIMEPIECE

RACE DISTANCE: 70 laps, 190.531 miles/306.630km

RACE WEATHER: Dry/sunny (track 51–56°C, air 30–32°C)

HUNGARORING MOGYORÓD, BUDAPEST
Circuit: 2.722 miles / 4.381km
70 laps

Turn 1 110/68
Turn 14 140/87
Turn 2 145/90
Turn 3 240/149
Turn 4 250/155
Turn 13 105/65
Turn 12 130/81
Turn 8 185/115
Turn 7 130/81
Turn 5 160/99
Turn 10 260/162
Turn 6 115/71
187/116 kmh/mph
Turn 11 230/143
Turn 9 150/93
Gear
DRS zone

RACE – OFFICIAL CLASSIFICATION

Pos.	Driver	Nat.	No.	Entrant	Car/Engine	Laps	Time/Retirement	Speed (mph/km/h)	Gap to leader	Fastest race lap
1	**Sebastian Vettel**	D	5	Scuderia Ferrari	Ferrari SF70H-062 V6	70	1h 39m 46.713s	114.572/184.386		1m 20.807s 69
2	**Kimi Räikkönen**	FIN	7	Scuderia Ferrari	Ferrari SF70H-062 V6	70	1h 39m 47.621s	114.555/184.358	0.908s	1m 20.461s 70
3	**Valtteri Bottas**	FIN	77	Mercedes AMG Petronas Motorsport	Mercedes F1 W08-Mercedes M08 EQ Power+ V6	70	1h 39m 59.175s	114.334/184.003	12.462s	1m 21.214s 68
4	**Lewis Hamilton**	GB	44	Mercedes AMG Petronas Motorsport	Mercedes F1 W08-Mercedes M08 EQ Power+ V6	70	1h 39m 59.598s	114.326/183.990	12.885s	1m 20.818s 66
5	**Max Verstappen**	NL	33	Red Bull Racing	Red Bull RB13-TAG Heuer RB13 V6	70	1h 39m 59.989s	114.319/183.978	13.276S	1m 20.490s 44
6	**Fernando Alonso**	E	14	McLaren Honda Formula 1 Team	McLaren MCL32-Honda RA617H V6	70	1h 40m 57.936s	113.225/182.218	1m 11.223s	1m 20.182s 69
7	**Carlos Sainz**	E	55	Scuderia Toro Rosso	Toro Rosso STR12-Renault R.E.17 V6	69			1 lap	1m 21.871s 67
8	**Sergio Pérez**	MEX	11	Sahara Force India Formula 1 Team	Force India VJM10-Mercedes M08 EQ Power+ V6	69			1 lap	1m 22.105s 68
9	**Esteban Ocon**	F	31	Sahara Force India Formula 1 Team	Force India VJM10-Mercedes M08 EQ Power+ V6	69			1 lap	1m 22.431s 60
10	**Stoffel Vandoorne**	B	2	McLaren Honda Formula 1 Team	McLaren MCL32-Honda RA617H V6	69			1 lap	1m 21.960s 44
11	Daniil Kvyat	RUS	26	Scuderia Toro Rosso	Toro Rosso STR12-Renault R.E.17 V6	69			1 lap	1m 21.631s 42
12	Jolyon Palmer	GB	30	Renault Sport Formula One Team	Renault R.S.17-R.E.17 V6	69			1 lap	1m 21.589s 68
13	Kevin Magnussen	DK	20	Haas F1 Team	Haas VF-17-Ferrari 062 V6	69	*		1 lap	1m 22.100s 67
14	Lance Stroll	CDN	18	Williams Martini Racing	Williams FW40-Mercedes M08 EQ Power+ V6	69			1 lap	1m 22.830s 53
15	Pascal Wehrlein	D	94	Sauber F1 Team	Sauber C36-Ferrari 059/5 V6	68			2 laps	1m 23.573s 50
16	Marcus Ericsson	S	9	Sauber F1 Team	Sauber C36-Ferrari 059/5 V6	68			2 laps	1m 21.752s 66
17	Nico Hülkenberg	D	27	Renault Sport Formula One Team	Renault R.S.17-R.E.17 V6	67	accident		3 laps	1m 21.611s 61
	Paul di Resta	GB	40	Williams Martini Racing	Williams FW40-Mercedes M08 EQ Power+ V6	60	oil leak			1m 23.242s 49
	Romain Grosjean	F	8	Haas F1 Team	Haas VF-17-Ferrari 062 V6	20	rear wheel loose			1m 24.702s 19
	Daniel Ricciardo	AUS	3	Red Bull Racing	Red Bull RB13-TAG Heuer RB13 V6	0	accident			no time
EW	Felipe Massa	BR	40	Williams Martini Racing	Williams FW40-Mercedes M08 EQ Power+ V6		driver unwell, withdrew after FP3			

* includes 5-second penalty for forcing Hülkenberg off the track – originally finished 11th.

Fastest race lap: Fernando Alonso on lap 69, 1m 20.182s, 122.222mph/196.697km/h.

Lap record: Michael Schumacher (Ferrari F2004 V10), 1m 19.071s, 123.939mph/199.461km/h (2004).

19 · DI RESTA · Williams

17 · STROLL · Williams

15 · MAGNUSSEN · Haas

13 · PÉREZ · Force India

11 · OCON · Force India

20 · ERICSSON · Sauber

18 · WEHRLEIN · Sauber

16 · KVYAT · Toro Rosso
3-place grid penalty for impeding another driver

14 · GROSJEAN · Haas

12 · HÜLKENBERG · Renault
5-place grid penalty for replacing gearbox

Grid order	1	2	3	4	5	6	7	8	9	10	11	12	13	14	15	16	17	18	19	20	21	22	23	24	25	26	27	28	29	30	31	32	33	34	35	36	37	38	39	40	41	42	43	44	45	46	47	48	49	50	51	52	53
5 VETTEL	5	5	5	5	5	5	5	5	5	5	5	5	5	5	5	5	5	5	5	5	5	5	5	5	5	5	5	5	5	5	5	7	33	33	33	33	33	33	33	33	33	5	5	5	5	5	5	5	5	5	5	5	5
7 RÄIKKÖNEN	7	7	7	7	7	7	7	7	7	7	7	7	7	7	7	7	7	7	7	7	7	7	7	7	7	7	7	7	7	7	7	5	33	5	5	5	5	5	5	5	5	7	7	7	7	7	7	7	7	7	7	7	7
77 BOTTAS	77	77	77	77	77	77	77	77	77	77	77	77	77	77	77	77	77	77	77	77	77	77	77	77	77	77	77	77	77	77	77	33	33	33	5	7	7	7	7	7	7	7	7	77	44	44	44	44	44	44	44	44	4
44 HAMILTON	33	33	33	33	33	33	33	33	33	33	33	33	33	33	33	33	33	33	33	33	33	33	33	33	33	33	33	33	33	33	33	77	44	77	77	77	77	77	77	77	77	44	44	44	77	77	77	77	77	77	77	77	7
33 VERSTAPPEN	44	44	44	44	44	44	44	44	44	44	44	44	44	44	44	44	44	44	44	44	44	44	44	44	44	44	44	44	44	44	44	44	77	44	44	44	44	44	44	44	44	33	33	33	33	33	33	33	33	33	33	33	3
3 RICCIARDO	55	55	55	55	55	55	55	55	55	55	55	55	55	55	55	55	55	55	55	55	55	55	55	55	55	55	55	55	55	55	55	2	2	2	2	2	27	27	27	27	14	14	14	14	14	14	14	14	1
14 ALONSO	14	14	14	14	14	14	14	14	14	14	14	14	14	14	14	14	14	14	14	14	14	14	14	14	14	14	14	14	14	14	14	27	27	27	27	27	2	14	14	14	55	55	55	55	55	55	55	55	5
2 VANDOORNE	11	11	11	11	11	11	11	11	11	11	11	11	11	11	11	11	11	11	11	11	11	11	11	11	11	11	11	11	11	11	11	2	30	30	30	30	30	30	30	55	55	11	11	11	11	11	11	11	1
55 SAINZ	2	2	2	2	2	2	2	2	2	2	2	2	2	2	2	2	2	2	2	2	2	2	2	2	2	2	2	2	2	2	2	27	55	14	14	14	14	14	55	2	2	31	31	31	31	31	31	31	3
30 PALMER	31	31	31	31	31	31	31	31	31	31	31	31	31	31	31	31	31	31	31	31	31	31	31	31	31	31	31	31	31	31	31	14	55	55	55	55	55	11	11	30	2	2	2	2	2	2	2	2	2
31 OCON	30	30	30	30	30	30	30	30	30	30	30	30	30	30	30	30	30	27	27	27	27	27	27	27	27	27	27	27	27	30	11	11	11	11	11	11	11	31	31	31	30	20	20	20	20	20	20	20	2
27 HÜLKENBERG	27	27	27	27	27	27	27	27	27	27	27	27	27	27	27	27	30	30	30	30	30	30	30	30	30	30	30	30	30	11	26	26	26	26	31	31	31	2	2	2	20	27	27	27	27	27	27	27	2
11 PÉREZ	20	20	20	20	20	20	20	20	20	20	20	20	20	20	20	20	20	20	20	20	20	26	26	26	26	26	26	26	26	26	31	31	31	31	26	20	20	20	20	20	27	26	26	26	26	26	26	26	2
8 GROSJEAN	26	26	26	26	26	26	26	26	26	26	26	26	26	26	26	26	26	26	26	26	26	20	20	20	20	20	20	20	20	20	20	20	20	20	20	26	26	26	26	26	30	30	30	30	30	30	30	30	1
20 MAGNUSSEN	18	18	18	18	18	18	18	18	18	18	18	18	18	18	18	18	18	18	18	18	18	18	18	18	18	18	18	18	18	18	18	18	18	18	18	18	18	18	18	18	18	18	18	18	18	18	18	18	18
26 KVYAT	8	8	8	8	8	8	8	8	8	8	8	8	8	8	8	8	8	8	8	8	8	8	40	40	40	40	40	40	40	18	40	40	40	9	9	9	9	9	9	9	9	9	9	9	9	9	9	9	9
18 STROLL		9	94	94	40	40	40	40	40	40	40	40	40	40	40	40	40	40	40	94	94	94	94	94	94	94	94		9	9	9	9	40	94	94	94	94	94	94	94	94	94	94	94	94	94	94	94	9
94 WEHRLEIN		94	40	40	9	9	9	94	94	94	94	94	94	94	94	94	94	94	9	9	9	9	9	9	9	9	9	9	94	94	94	94	9	40	40	40	40	40	40	40	40	40	40	40	40	40	40	40	4
40 DI RESTA		40	9	9	94	94	94	9	9	9	9	9	9	9	9	9	9	9																															
9 ERICSSON																																																	

9 = Pit stop   94 = One lap or more behind

All results and data © FOM 2017

TIME SHEETS

PRACTICE 1 (FRIDAY)
Weather: Dry/sunny-cloudy
Temperatures: track 26–31°C, air 22–24°C

Pos.	Driver	Laps	Time
1	Daniel Ricciardo	31	1m 18.486s
2	Kimi Räikkönen	20	1m 18.720s
3	Lewis Hamilton	31	1m 18.858s
4	Max Verstappen	27	1m 19.162s
5	Valtteri Bottas	30	1m 19.248s
6	Sebastian Vettel	21	1m 19.563s
7	Fernando Alonso	21	1m 19.987s
8	Stoffel Vandoorne	24	1m 20.005s
9	Nico Hülkenberg	25	1m 20.150s
10	Jolyon Palmer	27	1m 20.461s
11	Felipe Massa	28	1m 20.540s
12	Sergio Pérez	23	1m 20.574s
13	Daniil Kvyat	27	1m 20.780s
14	Carlos Sainz	25	1m 20.917s
15	Lance Stroll	29	1m 20.974s
16	Romain Grosjean	20	1m 21.313s
17	Alfonso Celis	24	1m 21.602s
18	Marcus Ericsson	31	1m 21.785s
19	Antonio Giovinazzi	8	1m 22.251s
20	Pascal Wehrlein	29	1m 22.490s

PRACTICE 2 (FRIDAY)
Weather: Dry/sunny-cloudy
Temperatures: track 30–36°C, air 25–27°C

Pos.	Driver	Laps	Time
1	Daniel Ricciardo	32	1m 18.455s
2	Sebastian Vettel	28	1m 18.638s
3	Valtteri Bottas	33	1m 18.656s
4	Kimi Räikkönen	28	1m 18.755s
5	Lewis Hamilton	31	1m 18.779s
6	Max Verstappen	25	1m 18.951s
7	Nico Hülkenberg	33	1m 19.714s
8	Fernando Alonso	31	1m 19.815s
9	Carlos Sainz	35	1m 19.834s
10	Stoffel Vandoorne	18	1m 19.909s
11	Esteban Ocon	34	1m 20.126s
12	Sergio Pérez	33	1m 20.266s
13	Daniil Kvyat	37	1m 20.577s
14	Lance Stroll	31	1m 20.791s
15	Felipe Massa	22	1m 20.869s
16	Jolyon Palmer	12	1m 21.175s
17	Kevin Magnussen	11	1m 21.345s
18	Romain Grosjean	25	1m 21.504s
19	Marcus Ericsson	31	1m 21.559s
20	Pascal Wehrlein	16	1m 21.722s

PRACTICE 3 (SATURDAY)
Weather: Dry/Sunny
Temperatures: track 44°C, air 24°C

Pos.	Driver	Laps	Time
1	Sebastian Vettel	17	1m 17.017s
2	Kimi Räikkönen	16	1m 17.492s
3	Valtteri Bottas	15	1m 17.914s
4	Max Verstappen	25	1m 18.194s
5	Lewis Hamilton	14	1m 18.434s
6	Stoffel Vandoorne	18	1m 18.638s
7	Nico Hülkenberg	20	1m 18.699s
8	Daniel Ricciardo	7	1m 18.714s
9	Fernando Alonso	14	1m 18.884s
10	Jolyon Palmer	19	1m 18.956s
11	Carlos Sainz	22	1m 19.300s
12	Esteban Ocon	22	1m 19.352s
13	Daniil Kvyat	23	1m 19.455s
14	Sergio Pérez	22	1m 19.609s
15	Romain Grosjean	21	1m 19.622s
16	Kevin Magnussen	19	1m 19.895s
17	Felipe Massa	12	1m 20.255s
18	Lance Stroll	24	1m 20.379s
19	Pascal Wehrlein	24	1m 20.446s
20	Marcus Ericsson	19	1m 20.748s

QUALIFYING (SATURDAY)
Weather: Dry/sunny Temperatures: track 55–58°C, air 26–28°C

Pos.	Driver	First	Second	Third	Qualifying Tyre
1	Sebastian Vettel	1m 17.244s	1m 16.802s	1m 16.276s	Supersoft (new)
2	Kimi Räikkönen	1m 17.364s	1m 17.207s	1m 16.444s	Supersoft (new)
3	Valtteri Bottas	1m 18.058s	1m 17.362s	1m 16.530s	Supersoft (new)
4	Lewis Hamilton	1m 17.492s	1m 16.693s	1m 16.707s	Supersoft (new)
5	Max Verstappen	1m 17.266s	1m 17.028s	1m 16.797s	Supersoft (new)
6	Daniel Ricciardo	1m 17.702s	1m 17.698s	1m 16.818s	Supersoft (new)
7	Nico Hülkenberg	1m 18.137s	1m 17.655s	1m 17.468s	Supersoft (new)
8	Fernando Alonso	1m 18.395s	1m 17.919s	1m 17.549s	Supersoft (new)
9	Stoffel Vandoorne	1m 18.479s	1m 18.000s	1m 17.894s	Supersoft (new)
10	Carlos Sainz	1m 18.948s	1m 18.311s	1m 18.912s	Supersoft (new)
11	Jolyon Palmer	1m 18.699s	1m 18.415s		
12	Esteban Ocon	1m 18.843s	1m 18.495s		
13	Daniil Kvyat	1m 18.702s	1m 18.538s		
14	Sergio Pérez	1m 19.095s	1m 18.639s		
15	Romain Grosjean	1m 19.085s	1m 18.771s		
16	Kevin Magnussen	1m 19.095s			
17	Lance Stroll	1m 19.102s			
18	Pascal Wehrlein	1m 19.839s			
19	Paul di Resta	1m 19.868s			
20	Marcus Ericsson	1m 19.972s			

QUALIFYING: head to head

Hamilton	6	5	Bottas
Vettel	8	3	Räikkönen
Massa	9	1	Stroll
Stroll	1	0	Di Resta
Ricciardo	4	7	Verstappen
Pérez	9	2	Ocon
Hülkenberg	11	0	Palmer
Kvyat	5	6	Sainz
Ericsson	2	0	Giovinazzi
Ericsson	2	7	Wehrlein
Alonso	9	1	Vandoorne
Vandoorne	1	0	Button
Grosjean	8	3	Magnussen

FOR THE RECORD

15,000th KM LED: Sebastian Vettel

5,000th LAP RACED: Valtteri Bottas

DID YOU KNOW?

This was only the fifth time in F1 history that the top five on the grid finished in exactly the same positions.

POINTS

DRIVERS

1	Sebastian Vettel	202
2	Lewis Hamilton	188
3	Valtteri Bottas	169
4	Daniel Ricciardo	117
5	Kimi Räikkönen	116
6	Max Verstappen	67
7	Sergio Pérez	56
8	Esteban Ocon	45
9	Carlos Sainz	35
10	Nico Hülkenberg	26
11	Felipe Massa	23
12	Lance Stroll	18
13	Romain Grosjean	18
14	Kevin Magnussen	11
15	Fernando Alonso	10
16	Pascal Wehrlein	5
17	Daniil Kvyat	4
18	Stoffel Vandoorne	1

CONSTRUCTORS

1	Mercedes	357
2	Ferrari	318
3	Red Bull	184
4	Force India	101
5	Williams	41
6	Toro Rosso	39
7	Haas	29
8	Renault	26
9	McLaren	11
10	Sauber	5

 9 · SAINZ · Toro Rosso

 7 · ALONSO · McLaren

 5 · VERSTAPPEN · Red Bull

 3 · BOTTAS · Mercedes

1 · VETTEL · Ferrari

 10 · PALMER · Renault

8 · VANDOORNE · McLaren

6 · RICCIARDO · Red Bull

4 · HAMILTON · Mercedes

2 · RÄIKKÖNEN · Ferrari

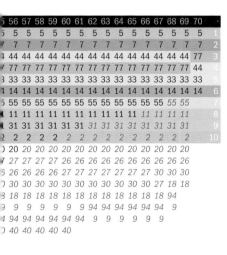

	56	57	58	59	60	61	62	63	64	65	66	67	68	69	70	
5	5	5	5	5	5	5	5	5	5	5	5	5	5	5	5	1
7	7	7	7	7	7	7	7	7	7	7	7	7	7	7	7	2
44	44	44	44	44	44	44	44	44	44	44	44	44	44	44	77	3
77	77	77	77	77	77	77	77	77	77	77	77	77	77	77	44	4
33	33	33	33	33	33	33	33	33	33	33	33	33	33	33	33	5
14	14	14	14	14	14	14	14	14	14	14	14	14	14	14	14	6
55	55	55	55	55	55	55	55	55	55	55	55	55	55	55	55	7
11	11	11	11	11	11	11	11	11	11	11	11	11	11	11	11	8
31	31	31	31	31	31	31	31	31	31	31	31	31	31	31	31	9
2	2	2	2	2	2	2	2	2	2	2	2	2	2	2	2	10
20	20	20	20	20	20	20	20	20	20	20	20	20	20	20		
27	27	27	27	26	26	26	26	26	26	26	26	26	26			
26	26	26	26	27	27	27	27	27	27	30	30	30				
30	30	30	30	30	30	30	30	27	27	18	18					
18	18	18	18	18	18	18	18	18	18	94						
9	9	9	9	9	9	94	94	94	94	94	9					
94	94	94	94	94	94	9	9	9	9	9						
40	40	40	40	40	40											

 ▓ Safety car deployed on laps shown

RACE TYRE STRATEGIES

PIRELLI

	Driver	Race Stint 1	Race Stint 2	Race Stint 3
1	Vettel	Supersoft (u): 1–32	Soft (n): 33–70	
2	Räikkönen	Supersoft (u): 1–33	Soft (n): 34–70	
3	Bottas	Supersoft (u): 1–30	Soft (n): 31–70	
4	Hamilton	Supersoft (u): 1–31	Soft (n): 32–70	
5	Verstappen	Supersoft (u): 1–42	Soft (n): 43–70	
6	Alonso	Supersoft (u): 1–35	Soft (n): 36–70	
7	Sainz	Supersoft (u): 1–35	Soft (n): 36–69	
8	Pérez	Supersoft (n): 1–34	Soft (n): 35–69	
9	Ocon	Supersoft (n): 1–35	Soft (n): 36–69	
10	Vandoorne	Supersoft (u): 1–42	Soft (n): 43–69	
11	Kvyat	Soft (n): 1–40	Supersoft (n): 41–69	
12	Palmer	Supersoft (n): 1–46	Soft (n): 47–69	
13	Magnussen	Supersoft (n): 1–31	Soft (n): 32–69	
14	Stroll	Supersoft (n): 1–29	Soft (n): 30–69	
15	Wehrlein	Supersoft (n): 1–3	Soft (n): 4–28	Soft (n): 29–68
16	Ericsson	Supersoft (n): 1	Soft (n): 2–63	Supersoft (u): 64–68
17	Hülkenberg	Supersoft (u): 1–45	Soft (n): 46–67	
	Di Resta	Soft (n): 1–34	Supersoft (n): 35–60 (dnf)	
	Grosjean	Supersoft (n): 1–20	Soft (n): 0 (dnf)	
	Ricciardo	Supersoft (u): 0 (dnf)		

The tyre regulations stipulate that at least two of three dry tyre specifications must be used during a dry race.
Pirelli P Zero logos are colour-coded on the tyre sidewalls: Red = Supersoft; Yellow = Soft. (n) new (u) used

Photos: Peter J. Fox

BELGIAN GRAND PRIX

SPA-FRANCORCHAMPS CIRCUIT

Game on. Vettel chases Hamilton
through Eau Rouge.
Photo: Peter J. Fox

SPA-FRANCORCHAMPS QUALIFYING

IF Mercedes had pushed Ferrari harder than expected in Budapest before the summer break, the boot was on the other foot in Belgium. With the high-speed demands of sectors one and three at Spa playing to the strengths of Mercedes, this was supposed to be a banker race for the Silver Arrows. But such was the Ferrari pace through the twisty sector two that the red cars were a bit too close for the Mercedes management's comfort, despite their new engines, introduced in Belgium, having an upgraded ERS-K.

But that did not stop a fabulous 1m 42.553s qualifying lap – during which he took the demanding Pouhon downhill left-hander flat – from giving Lewis Hamilton his 68th F1 pole position, equalling the all-time record of Michael Schumacher. Hamilton, therefore, had started slightly better than one in three of his grands prix from pole...

An emotional moment for the English driver occurred when Ross Brawn greeted him with a message of congratulations from Corinna Schumacher, on behalf of Michael's family.

"I remember coming here in 1996, my first grand prix, and watching Michael come by out of Turn One," Hamilton said. "The engine just shook my rib cage, it was incredible. And that was when my love for the sport took another step. To think that I'm now equal to him on poles... It's surreal and very much a humbling experience."

After showing impressive race pace in the second session of free practice on Friday afternoon, championship leader Sebastian Vettel was delighted to split the Mercedes and put his Ferrari on the front row, just 0.24s behind Lewis.

For Valtteri Bottas, Spa had been a happy hunting ground in his Williams days, with both a top-three qualifying position and a podium on his CV. But this time, Bottas was finding the track a challenge and had to work hard to qualify third, just over half a second adrift of his team-mate. "The balance felt really good," Valtteri said. "I've just really been lacking overall grip and losing a lot of time in the high-speed corners in sector two. It would have been nice to at least be second."

If Bottas had been struggling throughout relative to his team-mate, the same could not be said of Kimi Räikkönen at Ferrari. The Finn is always quick at Spa, with four wins to his name, and he had looked quicker than Vettel right up to Q3. But, with the chips down, he ran wide at Liège and spoiled the most crucial lap of the weekend. Having done so, and knowing he couldn't improve, he selflessly positioned himself to give Vettel a tow from Blanchimont to the Bus Stop chicane, reckoned to be worth a couple of tenths. Sebastian would probably have outqualified Bottas any way, but that made sure.

The Renault-powered Red Bulls were struggling for grunt here relative to Mercedes and Ferrari, with no amount of drag/downforce experimentation getting them close enough to challenge. Max Verstappen won their inter-team battle, pipping Daniel Ricciardo to fifth place as the RB13s filled row three, the best part of a second behind Hamilton's pace.

A similar margin separated Christian Horner's cars from Nico Hülkenberg with the first of the Renaults. For the first time in the season, Jolyon Palmer seemed to have the better of the 'The Hulk', being quicker in Q2, which only added to his frustration when a gearbox leak prevented him from contesting Q3 and sentenced him to a five-place grid demotion.

Force India had trimmed its cars right out, opting for speed on the straight rather than pace through sector two, with Sergio Pérez and Esteban Ocon qualifying eighth and ninth, separated by their customary fag paper's width.

McLaren Honda looked more threatening than perhaps they had the right to expect at a power track, but Stoffel Vandoorne knew that he would be incurring an obscene amount of engine penalties – all 65 of them! – and so was used purely to try to tow team-mate Fernando Alonso into Q3, doing a fine job along the Kemmel Straight. The McLaren chassis looked highly accomplished through sector two, which is where Alonso came to grief, for the oddest of reasons. When he took Pouhon flat for the first time, it baffled the algorithm controlling the power unit's electric power deployment, which concluded that the car was somewhere else on the track and gave no additional energy assistance.

"No power!" a frustrated Alonso bellowed over the team radio. The glitch cost him the best part of half a second and kept him out of Q3. To say that he was not best pleased didn't make a start on it...

The Haas twins qualified 12th and 13th, Romain Grosjean ahead of Kevin Magnussen; then came Carlos Sainz's Toro Rosso and Vandoorne, who did not complete his Alonso aid lap.

Out in Q1 went both Williams. Felipe Massa, back in the cockpit after his illness in Hungary, crashed quite heavily at Turn Eight early on Friday morning when he took too much inside kerb. He played catch-up thereafter, also incurring a five-place grid penalty for failing to respect waved yellows. Lance Stroll suffered rear wing endplate damage that the team suspected had been caused by an extreme rear tyre standing wave.

Daniil Kvyat also took a five-place grid hit for a changed gearbox; and, at Sauber, Marcus Ericsson pipped Pascal Wehrlein.

Above: Renault's Nick Chester and Cyril Abiteboul.
Photo: Renault F1 Team

Right: Ross Brawn embraces Lewis Hamilton after his record-equalling 68th pole position.
Photo: Lukas Gorys

Below: Mick Schumacher was the centre of attention when he demonstrated his father's Benetton-Ford.
Photo: WRi2/Jean-François Galeron

Bottom: Bike racer and TV personality Guy Martin was invited to participate as a pit-stop crew member for TV.
Photo: Williams Martini Racing

LA SOURCE hairpin on the opening lap of the Belgian GP is best described as 'busy'. This time, though, the first three rows went around in grid order and the action occurred further behind as Hülkenberg battled the faster-starting Force Indias of Pérez and Ocon, and Alonso, from tenth, went around the outside of all three to claim an early seventh!

On the run down to Eau Rouge, Pérez had forgotten to select his starting mode and found himself down on power as he tried to pull alongside Hülkenberg. Ocon saw the opportunity to force through further to the right, causing a heart-in-the-mouth moment at Force India as the pink cars rubbed wheels and the Frenchman only just squeaked through between his team-mate and the pit wall. This would be revisited later...

Hamilton saw that first run through the mighty Eau Rouge and down Kemmel Straight into Les Combes as the first hurdle to be overcome in his bid to win. Concerned at Ferrari's potential race pace, he needed to keep Vettel behind. Over the top of Raidillon, the Ferrari was tucked under Lewis's rear wing, flicking out of the slipstream, but without quite enough to challenge Hamilton at the top of the hill.

Evidently, though, this was going to be no easy afternoon for Mercedes: after the first couple of laps, Vettel radioed in that he was able to follow Lewis quite comfortably.

Pirelli's pre-race predictions said that a one-stop race, going from the ultrasoft on to the soft tyre was likely to be the optimum strategy. Thus it was vital for Hamilton to protect against any possible Ferrari undercut. And such was the pace of the leading pair that by one-quarter distance (11 laps into the race's 44), Bottas, running third, was almost 8s behind his team-mate, who had a 17.9s advantage over Ricciardo's fifth-placed Red Bull.

Having successfully kept Vettel out of DRS range throughout the opening stint, Lewis headed for the pits at the end of the following lap, once he had the necessary 18s pit-stop window to Ricciardo and the pit-wall crew felt that he was in range of the finish on a single set of softs.

If defending the undercut was the prime consideration for Hamilton and Mercedes, there were a couple of potential curve balls. First, the early stop would commit Lewis to 32 laps on the soft-compound Pirelli. Second, Ferrari could use Räikkönen – with a newly-extended contract and 6s further up the road from Ricciardo – to slow Lewis down. They were confident, though, that they had enough straight-line speed to deal with that threat if it arose, and so it proved.

After a first-rate Hamilton stop – the fastest of the afternoon at 22.03s overall pit-lane duration versus the 22.44s next best for Vettel at Ferrari two laps later – the status quo at the front remained, with Lewis flashing across the line still 2s clear of Vettel at the end of lap 15, both cars now on the yellow-walled Pirelli soft.

Bottas, meanwhile, was pitted the lap after Hamilton and increased his margin over Räikkönen, who came in two laps later, to 10s. Any potential threat from the second Ferrari was temporarily extinguished when Kimi was given a stop-go penalty for failing to respect yellow flags for a stationary Verstappen, and was forced to pit again two laps later, rejoining half a minute behind Ricciardo.

A stationary Verstappen? Yes, there was yet more bad luck for the young Dutchman when a sensor picked up a drop in cylinder pressure and shut the engine down on lap eight, Max coasting to a halt on Kemmel Straight. It did not take long for Christian Horner to fire another shot at Renault: "We pay a hell of a lot of money for the engine, and they need to sort it out..."

Alonso, meanwhile, was hardly being PR gold for Honda as the world and his wife went by the Spaniard on the long

Above: Romain Grosjean safely negotiates La Source in the Haas-Ferrari, on his way to an eventual seventh-place finish.

Photo: Haas F1 Team

233

Kemmel Straight. The two-times champion, who had been repassed by Hülkenberg on the opening lap, rapidly lost out in a straight line to both Force Indias and Grosjean as well. "Just embarrassing…" he shouted.

Both Mercedes and both Ferraris had gone on to the Pirelli soft, while Red Bull went for the supersoft with Ricciardo, more or less confirmation of a two-stop strategy. Force India did the same with Ocon and Pérez. The Mexican, however, re-emerged behind Grosjean's earlier-stopping Haas and, in a battle at Les Combes, went off and rejoined. The stewards decreed that Pérez should have given the place back to Grosjean and awarded him a 5s time penalty.

At the front, Hamilton was being forced to demonstrate his best race management. With his W08 tending to overheat even the hardest Pirelli soft compound, he was having to trade off looking after his rubber against keeping Vettel out of DRS range – no easy task. The decision on whether to try to get to the end on those tyres or stop again was taken out of his hands when the Force Indias hit each other – again!

Pérez had recaught Ocon and, with Hülkenberg just ahead, informed the team that he had more pace. But rather than tell Ocon to move aside, Force India brought Pérez in first, mindful of his 5s penalty. Ocon came in on the next lap and was unimpressed to find himself pitting out behind his team-mate.

With the pair of them closing on Massa's Williams, Ocon attempted to reassert himself on the run down to Eau Rouge on lap 29, after a better exit from La Source. But Pérez, for the second time, put a somewhat unsophisticated squeeze on the young Frenchman, and this time they made contact. Pérez suffered a punctured right rear and Ocon damaged his left front wing

"What's he doing?" a furious Ocon shouted over the radio. Pérez, meanwhile, claimed that the move was too optimistic and that Ocon should have attacked on the

Kemmel Straight in more conventional fashion. The upshot, though, was that both were headed for the pits, jettisoning debris and prompting a safety car, which was a pleasing sight for Räikkönen, who was brought back into play, but not for Hamilton.

"Why is the safety car out?" a frustrated Lewis wanted to know. "There is literally no debris…" The official Mercedes appeared right at the point where those in two minds about a one- or two-stop race were going to have to commit and effectively removed any decision that had to be made.

Red Bull had already committed to a two-stop by putting Ricciardo on to the supersoft Pirelli at his first stop, but the likelihood was that Mercedes would have one-stopped Hamilton and two-stopped Bottas.

The No. 77 Mercedes was experiencing more tyre degradation than the No. 44 car, which, at the time of the safety car, only had a 1.9s lead over Vettel's Ferrari. Hamilton, however, did have slight blistering to the right rear tyre that the team was concerned might need changing.

Although leading the race, Mercedes was slightly on the defensive.

Their problem was that if Vettel had elected to two-stop, the fact that he was within 2s of Hamilton meant that there was not a big enough margin to cover him by pitting Lewis on the following lap without potentially losing track position. Also, Vettel's softs were a couple of laps fresher and Lewis was going to have to defend that at the end of the race while trying to keep the Ferrari out of DRS range.

The safety car solved that issue, but, as Lewis was well aware, created another one. Whereas Ferrari had a new set of ultrasofts to bolt on, Mercedes did not. Going back to qualifying, the team had used two sets of ultrasofts in Q2, while Ferrari had used just one. You could argue that those two Q2 runs had given Lewis the feel to take his vital pole position, which had given him all-important track position on Sunday, but now he was going to have to defend against a Ferrari on quicker tyres at the restart.

"It would have been a less comfortable race without the safety car because we would have needed to decide whether to pit Lewis because of the blistered rear tyre," Toto Wolff opined. "It wasn't critical, but there were 14 laps left, and it would have put us and Lewis in a very difficult situation. Annoying as the safety car looked, with hindsight it was actually optimum for us and Lewis at that stage."

At the time, though, such thoughts were not uppermost in Hamilton's mind as the temperatures of his soft yellow-walled Pirellis dropped behind the official Mercedes and he contemplated having to defend against Vettel on ultrasofts initially more than a second a lap quicker. The restart was going to be all important.

When the official Mercedes pulled in, Lewis got a decent jump on Vettel as he accelerated hard through Blanchimont, the fast left-hander before the final chicane, but then he selected the wrong engine mode, and the Ferrari was upon him once more as they headed out of La Source and down to Eau Rouge. That turned out to be a disguised blessing, too.

"Initially, it felt like a mistake, but was actually a really good thing," Hamilton explained, "because if I'd gone into Turn One with that gap, Sebastian, on the softer tyre, would have had the momentum to really propel out of the corner and get a really good tow. So it worked out perfect."

There was no small degree of tactical skill and judgement involved, too.

"Going down the straight [between La Source and Eau Rouge]," Hamilton continued, "I let off the power a little bit just to keep him on my tail. If he was further away, he would have had the chance to gain momentum through Eau Rouge and pass in the slipstream. That's what he wanted, so I didn't give him that. As we were going up Eau Rouge, I gave it full power and he had no space to really propel, so he could only just pull alongside and I could defend. I was really pleased with that."

Above: Nico Hülkenberg hustles his Renault between Esteban Ocon's Force India (31) and Fernando Alonso's McLaren (14) on the Kemmel Straight.

Photo: Sahara Force India F1 Team

Left: Max Verstappen exits on a bike after his engine failure.

Photo: WRi2/Fritz Van Eldik

Below left: Sergio Pérez limps into the pits after his clash with team-mate Esteban Ocon.

Photos: Lukas Gorys

Far left: The overwhelming colour at Spa was orange, but ultimately fans of Max Verstappen would leave disappointed after the Dutchman's early retirement.

Photo: Peter J. Fox

Above: Lewis Hamilton holds off the challenge of Sebastian Vettel on the first lap. Thereafter, he took control of proceedings.
Photo: WRi2/Jean-François Galeron

Right: Feeling blue? Daniil Kvyat was subjected to increasing pressure at Toro Rosso.

Centre right: Spa-Francorchamps provides a choice of superb vantage points for spectators.

Top far right: Lewis Hamilton embraces his crew in *parc fermé* as the cameras record the moment.
Photos: Peter J. Fox

Above far right: Daniel Ricciardo celebrates another podium, this one at a circuit that should have disadvantaged Red Bull.
Photo: Red Bull Racing/Getty Images

Right: Kimi Räikkönen, having been confirmed at Ferrari for 2018, continued to play the support role at Spa.
Photo: WRi2/Jad Sherif

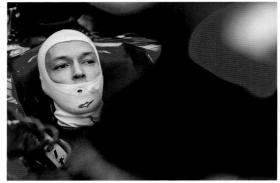

There was slightly more to it than that, as well. Television pictures from the rear showed the Ferrari driver's de-rate light (to warn following drivers when a car has run out of ERS-K boost) coming on as they approached Les Combes, while Hamilton's did not. As the extra ERS boost becomes less effective at the end of the straight, it is normal to deploy it at a more advantageous location on the lap, but Mercedes had worked at setting up their system to allow that extra bit of boost specifically to defend in just such a situation.

"After that, it was a cool battle," Hamilton enthused. "Nine or ten laps of qualifying. The Ferrari was very quick, and I had to do some really fast laps to stay ahead. I was just thinking: I want to win this race. I've come here, I've told you what I'm coming here for and I'm not leaving here without it!"

The outcome of the restart was somewhat different for Bottas. Like his team-mate, he was on the soft-compound Pirelli and facing attacks from Ricciardo and Räikkönen, both on ultrasofts. With the Mercedes struggling for traction out of La Source all afternoon, both the Red Bull and Ferrari got better exits on the softer rubber and went either side of him at the top of the hill into Les Combes, relegating him to fifth.

"I was just lacking a bit of pace the whole weekend, but it was difficult to see exactly where I was losing out," Bottas elaborated. "I could see when I was behind Kimi that out of the last corner and out of Turn One, I was definitely losing out on traction. And behind the safety car, I just couldn't get the soft tyre into the window. I was struggling with the temperature, and it felt pretty much like driving on ice.

"At the restart, I had a poor Turn One – poor overall grip, poor traction, a bad exit on to the back straight, and then the guys came both sides of me. I tried to brake late for Turn Five, but still couldn't stop the car and went straight. I'm really disappointed to lose the podium, and obviously if two guys overtake you in one corner, it's not a good feeling…"

Behind the Mercs, Ferraris and Ricciardo, Hülkenberg scored a top-six finish for Renault, ahead of a tight battle between Grosjean, Massa and Ocon, with Sainz's Toro Rosso claiming the final point.

It had been an absorbing battle, and winning it took a delighted Hamilton to within three points of Vettel in the championship. The foundation was that fine pole, but nobody at Mercedes was ignoring the strength of Ferrari's pace at a track seen by many as a Silver Arrows banker.

Tony Dodgins

VIEWPOINT
REMAINING IN THE RED...

YOU could gauge the mounting tension in the championship battle when Ferrari eschewed their once traditional, maximum-effect Monza press release to promote early inner calm by announcing Sebastian Vettel's long-term future.

The statement was short and to the point: Vettel would be staying for another three seasons. If the new contract was not exactly a surprise, its duration was. Vettel was said to have been angling for a single season, the better to keep his options open when other seats (specifically Lewis Hamilton's at Mercedes) might come up for grabs at the end of 2018.

Looking at it another way, Vettel's decision immediately put the lid on any suggestion that Hamilton might want the kudos of a Ferrari drive on his CV, particularly if he clinched a fourth – and possibly fifth – title with Mercedes.

For all their chumminess on the early-season podiums, there was no way that Seb would want Lewis in the other Ferrari. He'd had enough of in-house difficulties with Mark Webber during his time at Red Bull.

On which subject, the retention of Kimi Räikkönen for one more year was an unspoken confirmation that Ferrari was Vettel's team with Kimi riding shotgun and capable of stepping up to the plate should Seb run into problems.

In more immediate terms, Räikkönen's continued presence in the team would be reassuring from Vettel's point of view for the rest of 2017. He and Ferrari were now in a position to focus totally on dealing with the opposition and making the most of the problem within Mercedes that Ferrari had neatly avoided.

If Räikkönen was some distance from the top of the championship, the same could not be said of Valtteri Bottas at Mercedes, who continued to entertain thoughts, publicly at least, of going for the title.

Hamilton may have known in his heart of hearts that he was the faster of the two, but that would not lessen the worry of the other silver car taking a run down the inside, given half a chance. That was a problem no more – if it ever had been in the first place – in the red camp.

Maurice Hamilton

12

2017 FORMULA 1
SHELL
BELGIAN
GRAND PRIX

ROLEX

F1 OFFICIAL TIMEPIECE

SPA-FRANCORCHAMPS 25–27 AUGUST

RACE DISTANCE: 44 laps, 191.415 miles/308.052km

RACE WEATHER: Dry/sunny-cloudy (track 30–37°C, air 22–25°C)

CIRCUIT DE SPA-FRANCORCHAMPS
Circuit: 4.352 miles / 7.004km
44 laps

Campus 170/106
Paul Frère 245/152
Rivage 140/87
Fagnes 175/109
310/193
187/116 kmh/mph
Gear
— DRS zone
Blanchimont 325/202
Pouhon 290/180
Chicane 110/68
La Source 95/59
Malmedy 190/118
Les Combes 170/106
Kemmel 335/208
Radillon 310/193
Eau Rouge 320/199

RACE – OFFICIAL CLASSIFICATION

Pos.	Driver	Nat.	No.	Entrant	Car/Engine	Laps	Time/Retirement	Speed (mph/km/h)	Gap to leader	Fastest race lap	
1	**Lewis Hamilton**	GB	44	Mercedes AMG Petronas Motorsport	Mercedes F1 W08-Mercedes M08 EQ Power+ V6	44	1h 24m 42.820s	135.573/218.183		1m 46.603s	35
2	**Sebastian Vettel**	D	5	Scuderia Ferrari	Ferrari SF70H-062 V6	44	1h 24m 45.178s	135.510/218.082	2.358s	1m 46.577s	41
3	**Daniel Ricciardo**	AUS	3	Red Bull Racing	Red Bull RB13-TAG Heuer RB13 V6	44	1h 24m 53.611s	135.286/217.721	10.791s	1m 47.549s	44
4	**Kimi Räikkönen**	FIN	7	Scuderia Ferrari	Ferrari SF70H-062 V6	44	1h 24m 57.291s	135.188/217.564	14.471s	1m 47.730s	36
5	**Valtteri Bottas**	FIN	77	Mercedes AMG Petronas Motorsport	Mercedes F1 W08-Mercedes M08 EQ Power+ V6	44	1h 24m 59.276s	135.135/217.479	16.456s	1m 47.721s	37
6	**Nico Hülkenberg**	D	27	Renault Sport Formula One Team	Renault R.S.17-R.E.17 V6	44	1h 25m 10.907s	134.828/216.984	28.087s	1m 48.922s	39
7	**Romain Grosjean**	F	8	Haas F1 Team	Haas VF-17-Ferrari 062 V6	44	1h 25m 14.373s	134.736/216.837	31.553s	1m 49.087s	37
8	**Felipe Massa**	BR	19	Williams Martini Racing	Williams FW40-Mercedes M08 EQ Power+ V6	44	1h 25m 19.469s	134.602/216.621	36.649s	1m 49.637s	37
9	**Esteban Ocon**	F	31	Sahara Force India Formula 1 Team	Force India VJM10-Mercedes M08 EQ Power+ V6	44	1h 25m 20.974s	134.562/216.557	38.154s	1m 49.721s	37
10	**Carlos Sainz**	E	55	Scuderia Toro Rosso	Toro Rosso STR12-Renault R.E.17 V6	44	1h 25m 22.267s	134.529/216.503	39.447s	1m 49.709s	39
11	Lance Stroll	CDN	18	Williams Martini Racing	Williams FW40-Mercedes M08 EQ Power+ V6	44	1h 25m 31.819s	134.278/216.100	48.999s	1m 50.543s	41
12	Daniil Kvyat	RUS	26	Scuderia Toro Rosso	Toro Rosso STR12-Renault R.E.17 V6	44	1h 25m 32.760s	134.253/216.060	49.940s	1m 49.708s	39
13	Jolyon Palmer	GB	30	Renault Sport Formula One Team	Renault R.S.17-R.E.17 V6	44	1h 25m 36.059s	134.167/215.921	53.239s	1m 49.283s	44
14	Stoffel Vandoorne	B	2	McLaren Honda Formula 1 Team	McLaren MCL32-Honda RA617H V6	44	1h 25m 39.898s	134.067/215.760	57.078s	1m 49.907s	44
15	Kevin Magnussen	DK	20	Haas F1 Team	Haas VF-17-Ferrari 062 V6	44	1h 25m 50.082s	133.802/215.333	1m 07.262s	1m 49.126s	36
16	Marcus Ericsson	S	9	Sauber F1 Team	Sauber C36-Ferrari 059/5 V6	44	1h 25m 52.531s	133.738/215.231	1m 09.711s	1m 50.775s	25
17	Sergio Pérez	MEX	11	Sahara Force India Formula 1 Team	Force India VJM10-Mercedes M08 EQ Power+ V6	42	accident damage		2 laps	1m 48.300s	27
	Fernando Alonso	E	14	McLaren Honda Formula 1 Team	McLaren MCL32-Honda RA617H V6	25	engine			1m 51.720s	12
	Max Verstappen	NL	33	Red Bull Racing	Red Bull RB13-TAG Heuer RB13 V6	7	engine			1m 51.022s	5
	Pascal Wehrlein	D	94	Sauber F1 Team	Sauber C36-Ferrari 059/5 V6	2	rear suspension			no time	

Fastest race lap: Sebastian Vettel on lap 41, 1m 46.577s, 147.006mph/236.583km/h (new record for current configuration).

Lap record: Kimi Räikkönen (McLaren MP4-19B-Mercedes Benz V8), 1m 45.108s, 148.465mph/238.931km/h (2004, 4.335-mile/6.976km circuit).

Previous lap record (current configuration): Lewis Hamilton (Mercedes-Benz F1 W07 V6 turbo), 1m 17.939s, 95.776 mph/ 154.135 km/h (2016).

20 · VANDOORNE · McLaren
60-place grid penalty for using additional power unit elements; 5-place penalty for replacing gearbox

18 · WEHRLEIN · Sauber
5-place grid penalty for replacing gearbox

16 · MASSA · Williams
5-place grid penalty for failing to slow for yellow flags

14 · PALMER · Renault
5-place grid penalty for replacing gearbox

12 · MAGNUSSEN · Haas

19 · KVYAT · Toro Rosso
20-place grid penalty for using additional power unit elements

17 · ERICSSON · Sauber
5-place grid penalty for replacing gearbox

15 · STROLL · Williams

13 · SAINZ · Toro Rosso

11 · GROSJEAN · Haas

Grid order	1	2	3	4	5	6	7	8	9	10	11	12	13	14	15	16	17	18	19	20	21	22	23	24	25	26	27	28	29	30	31	32	33	34	35
44 HAMILTON	44	44	44	44	44	44	44	44	44	44	44	5	5	5	44	44	44	44	44	44	44	44	44	44	44	44	44	44	44	44	44	44	44	44	44
5 VETTEL	5	5	5	5	5	5	5	5	5	5	5	44	77	7	5	5	5	5	5	5	5	5	5	5	5	5	5	5	5	5	5	5	5	5	5
77 BOTTAS	77	77	77	77	77	77	77	77	77	77	77	77	44	77	77	77	77	77	77	77	77	77	77	77	77	77	77	77	77	77	77	77	77	3	3
7 RÄIKKÖNEN	7	7	7	7	7	7	7	7	7	7	7	7	44	3	77	7	3	3	3	3	3	3	3	3	3	3	3	3	3	3	3	3	3	7	7
33 VERSTAPPEN	33	33	33	33	33	33	33	3	3	3	3	3	3	77	3	3	7	27	27	27	27	27	27	7	7	7	7	7	7	7	7	7	7	77	77
3 RICCIARDO	3	3	3	3	3	27	27	27	27	11	27	27	27	27	31	7	7	7	7	7	7	27	27	27	27	27	27	27	27	27	27	27	27	27	27
27 HÜLKENBERG	27	14	27	27	27	27	27	31	31	11	11	55	55	55	55	31	31	7	31	31	31	31	31	31	31	31	8	8	20	8	8	8	8	8	
11 PÉREZ	14	27	14	31	31	31	31	11	31	55	27	31	31	31	55	11	11	11	11	11	11	11	8	20	8	19	19	19	19	19					
31 OCON	31	31	31	14	11	11	11	8	8	8	19	26	26	11	11	11	55	55	8	8	20	19	19	19	20	20	20	31	31		31	31			
14 ALONSO	20	20	11	11	14	8	8	14	14	19	26	31	8	8	8	8	55	20	20	20	20	20	19	19	11	31	31	31	31	55	55				
8 GROSJEAN	11	11	20	8	8	14	14	20	19	55	2	2	11	26	26	26	26	20	20	19	19	19	19	19	11	11	31	55	26	55	55	55	18	18	
20 MAGNUSSEN	8	8	8	20	20	20	20	19	55	14	31	8	2	2	2	20	20	19	19	14	14	14	14	14	55	55	55	26	55	18	18	18	11	11	
55 SAINZ	30	30	30	30	19	19	19	55	20	8	20	20	20	20	2	19	26	14	30	30	30	30	55	18	18	18	18	30	30	26	26	11	26	30	
30 PALMER	19	19	19	19	30	30	55	18	55	2	20	14	14	14	19	2	18	30	18	18	18	18	18	11	11	26	26	11	26	26					
18 STROLL	18	55	55	55	55	55	30	26	2	20	14	19	19	19	14	14	14	30	18	55	55	55	55	18	26	30	30	30	2	2	30	30	30	2	2
19 MASSA	55	18	18	18	18	18	2	18	30	30	30	30	30	30	18	26	26	26	26	26	2	2	2	2	11	11	2	2	2	9	9				
9 ERICSSON	26	26	26	26	26	26	26	30	30	18	18	18	18	18	18	2	2	2	2	2	2	2	9	9	9	9	9	9	9	9	9	20	20		
94 WEHRLEIN	2	2	2	2	2	2	9	9	9	9	9	9	9	9	9	9	9	9	9	9															
26 KVYAT	9	9	9	9	9	9	9																												
2 VANDOORNE	94	94																																	

30 = Pit stop   9 = One lap or more behind

TIME SHEETS

PRACTICE 1 (FRIDAY)
Weather: Dry/sunny-cloudy
Temperatures: track 22–29°C, air 18–21°C

Pos.	Driver	Laps	Time
1	Kimi Räikkönen	13	1m 45.502s
2	Lewis Hamilton	19	1m 45.555s
3	Sebastian Vettel	13	1m 45.647s
4	Max Verstappen	18	1m 46.302s
5	Daniel Ricciardo	22	1m 46.352s
6	Valtteri Bottas	20	1m 46.424s
7	Carlos Sainz	22	1m 47.446s
8	Esteban Ocon	27	1m 47.670s
9	Daniil Kvyat	20	1m 47.851s
10	Stoffel Vandoorne	18	1m 47.865s
11	Jolyon Palmer	14	1m 47.930s
12	Nico Hülkenberg	15	1m 48.037s
13	Fernando Alonso	18	1m 48.252s
14	Sergio Pérez	19	1m 48.452s
15	Lance Stroll	24	1m 48.541s
16	Kevin Magnussen	20	1m 48.615s
17	Romain Grosjean	20	1m 48.626s
18	Marcus Ericsson	21	1m 50.160s
19	Pascal Wehrlein	13	1m 51.263s
20	Felipe Massa	3	no time

PRACTICE 2 (FRIDAY)
Weather: Dry-wet/sunny-cloudy
Temperatures: track 20–31°C, air 22–23°C

Pos.	Driver	Laps	Time
1	Lewis Hamilton	17	1m 44.753s
2	Kimi Räikkönen	21	1m 45.015s
3	Valtteri Bottas	17	1m 45.180s
4	Max Verstappen	16	1m 45.225s
5	Sebastian Vettel	20	1m 45.235s
6	Daniel Ricciardo	15	1m 46.072s
7	Nico Hülkenberg	24	1m 46.441s
8	Esteban Ocon	19	1m 46.473s
9	Carlos Sainz	19	1m 46.561s
10	Jolyon Palmer	23	1m 46.670s
11	Fernando Alonso	20	1m 46.743s
12	Sergio Pérez	18	1m 46.984s
13	Romain Grosjean	15	1m 47.285s
14	Stoffel Vandoorne	17	1m 47.303s
15	Daniil Kvyat	12	1m 47.450s
16	Kevin Magnussen	15	1m 47.556s
17	Lance Stroll	13	1m 47.861s
18	Marcus Ericsson	12	1m 49.214s
19	Pascal Wehrlein	18	1m 49.725s
–	Felipe Massa	–	–

PRACTICE 3 (SATURDAY)
Weather: Damp-dry/cloudy-sunny
Temperatures: track 22–26°C, air 21–22°C

Pos.	Driver	Laps	Time
1	Kimi Räikkönen	17	1m 43.916s
2	Sebastian Vettel	15	1m 44.113s
3	Lewis Hamilton	11	1m 44.114s
4	Max Verstappen	13	1m 45.034s
5	Valtteri Bottas	18	1m 45.230s
6	Daniel Ricciardo	18	1m 45.286s
7	Jolyon Palmer	11	1m 45.491s
8	Sergio Pérez	14	1m 45.857s
9	Carlos Sainz	18	1m 45.942s
10	Fernando Alonso	12	1m 46.060s
11	Nico Hülkenberg	11	1m 46.064s
12	Esteban Ocon	14	1m 46.179s
13	Romain Grosjean	14	1m 46.196s
14	Stoffel Vandoorne	14	1m 46.300s
15	Lance Stroll	18	1m 46.620s
16	Felipe Massa	22	1m 46.667s
17	Kevin Magnussen	13	1m 46.690s
18	Daniil Kvyat	7	1m 47.903s
19	Pascal Wehrlein	17	1m 48.296s
20	Marcus Ericsson	6	1m 48.300s

QUALIFYING (SATURDAY)
Weather: Dry/sunny-cloudy Temperatures: track 33–37°C, air 24–25°C

Pos.	Driver	First	Second	Third	Qualifying Tyre
1	Lewis Hamilton	1m 44.184s	1m 42.927s	1m 42.553s	Ultrasoft (new)
2	Sebastian Vettel	1m 44.275s	1m 43.987s	1m 42.795s	Ultrasoft (new)
3	Valtteri Bottas	1m 44.773s	1m 43.249s	1m 43.094s	Ultrasoft (new)
4	Kimi Räikkönen	1m 44.729s	1m 43.700s	1m 43.270s	Ultrasoft (new)
5	Max Verstappen	1m 44.535s	1m 43.940s	1m 43.380s	Ultrasoft (new)
6	Daniel Ricciardo	1m 45.114s	1m 44.224s	1m 43.863s	Ultrasoft (new)
7	Nico Hülkenberg	1m 45.280s	1m 44.988s	1m 44.982s	Ultrasoft (new)
8	Sergio Pérez	1m 45.591s	1m 44.894s	1m 45.244s	Ultrasoft (new)
9	Esteban Ocon	1m 45.277s	1m 45.006s	1m 45.369s	Ultrasoft (new)
10	Jolyon Palmer	1m 45.447s	1m 44.843s	no time	Ultrasoft (new)
11	Fernando Alonso	1m 45.668s	1m 45.090s		
12	Romain Grosjean	1m 45.728s	1m 45.133s		
13	Kevin Magnussen	1m 45.535s	1m 45.400s		
14	Carlos Sainz	1m 45.374s	1m 45.439s		
15	Stoffel Vandoorne	1m 45.441s	no time		
16	Felipe Massa	1m 45.823s			
17	Daniil Kvyat	1m 46.028s			
18	Lance Stroll	1m 46.915s			
19	Marcus Ericsson	1m 47.214s			
20	Pascal Wehrlein	1m 47.679s			

QUALIFYING: head to head

Hamilton	7	5	Bottas
Vettel	9	3	Räikkönen
Massa	10	1	Stroll
Stroll	1	0	Di Resta
Ricciardo	4	8	Verstappen
Pérez	10	2	Ocon
Hülkenberg	12	0	Palmer
Kvyat	5	7	Sainz
Ericsson	2	0	Giovinazzi
Ericsson	3	7	Wehrlein
Alonso	10	1	Vandoorne
Vandoorne	1	0	Button
Grosjean	9	3	Magnussen

FOR THE RECORD

200th GRAND PRIX: Lewis Hamilton

90th RACE LED: Mercedes

30th FASTEST LAP: Sebastian Vettel

DID YOU KNOW?

Lewis Hamilton equalled Michael Schumacher's record of 68 pole positions.

This was the 50th grand prix at Spa-Francorchamps.

POINTS

DRIVERS

1	Sebastian Vettel	220
2	Lewis Hamilton	213
3	Valtteri Bottas	179
4	Daniel Ricciardo	132
5	Kimi Räikkönen	128
6	Max Verstappen	67
7	Sergio Pérez	56
8	Esteban Ocon	47
9	Carlos Sainz	36
10	Nico Hülkenberg	34
11	Felipe Massa	27
12	Romain Grosjean	24
13	Lance Stroll	18
14	Kevin Magnussen	11
15	Fernando Alonso	10
16	Pascal Wehrlein	5
17	Daniil Kvyat	4
18	Stoffel Vandoorne	1

CONSTRUCTORS

1	Mercedes	392
2	Ferrari	348
3	Red Bull	199
4	Force India	103
5	Williams	45
6	Toro Rosso	40
7	Haas	35
8	Renault	34
9	McLaren	11
10	Sauber	5

10 · ALONSO · McLaren   8 · PÉREZ · Force India   6 · RICCIARDO · Red Bull   4 · RÄIKKÖNEN · Ferrari   2 · VETTEL · Ferrari

9 · OCON · Force India   7 · HÜLKENBERG · Renault   5 · VERSTAPPEN · Red Bull   3 · BOTTAS · Mercedes   1 · HAMILTON · Mercedes

	36	37	38	39	40	41	42	43	44	
	44	44	44	44	44	44	44	44	44	1
	5	5	5	5	5	5	5	5	5	2
	3	3	3	3	3	3	3	3	3	3
	7	7	7	7	7	7	7	7	7	4
	77	77	77	77	77	77	77	77	77	5
	27	27	27	27	27	27	27	27	27	6
	8	8	8	8	8	8	8	8	8	7
	19	19	19	19	19	19	19	19	19	8
	31	31	31	31	31	31	31	31	31	9
	55	55	55	55	55	55	55	55	55	10
	18	18	18	18	18	18	18	18	18	
	11	11	11	26	26	26	26	26	26	
	26	26	26	11	11	30	30	30	30	
	30	30	30	30	30	11	2	2	2	
	2	2	2	2	2	2	9	9	20	
	9	9	9	9	9	9	20	20	9	
	20	20	20	20	20	20	11			

Safety car deployed on laps shown

RACE TYRE STRATEGIES

	Driver	Race Stint 1	Race Stint 2	Race Stint 3	Race Stint 4
1	Hamilton	Ultrasoft (u): 1–12	Soft (n): 13–30	Soft (n): 31–44	
2	Vettel	Ultrasoft (u): 1–14	Soft (n): 15–30	Ultrasoft (n): 31–44	
3	Ricciardo	Ultrasoft (u): 1–14	Supersoft (n): 15–30	Ultrasoft (n): 31–44	
4	Räikkönen	Ultrasoft (u): 1–15	Soft (n): 16–29	Ultrasoft (n): 30–44	
5	Bottas	Ultrasoft (u): 1–13	Soft (n): 14–30	Soft (n): 31–44	
6	Hülkenberg	Ultrasoft (u): 1–11	Soft (n): 12–29	Ultrasoft (u): 30–44	
7	Grosjean	Ultrasoft (u): 1–10	Soft (n): 11–29	Supersoft (n): 30–44	
8	Massa	Supersoft (n): 1–11	Soft (n): 12–29	Ultrasoft (n): 30–44	
9	Ocon	Ultrasoft (u): 1–10	Supersoft (n): 11–27	Supersoft (n): 28–29	Ultrasoft (u): 30–44
10	Sainz	Ultrasoft (u): 1–19	Soft (n): 20–29	Supersoft (n): 30–44	
11	Stroll	Supersoft (n): 1–9	Soft (u): 10–29	Ultrasoft (n): 30–44	
12	Kvyat	Supersoft (n): 1–18	Ultrasoft (n): 19–30	Ultrasoft (n): 31–44	
13	Palmer	Ultrasoft (u): 1–8	Soft (n): 9–30	Ultrasoft (n): 31–44	
14	Vandoorne	Ultrasoft (u): 1–18	Ultrasoft (n): 19–30	Ultrasoft (n): 31–44	
15	Magnussen	Ultrasoft (u): 1–9	Soft (n): 10–30	Supersoft (n): 31–34	Ultrasoft (u): 35–44
16	Ericsson	Supersoft (n): 1–8	Soft (n): 9–23	Soft (n): 24–29	Ultrasoft (n): 30–44
17	Pérez	Ultrasoft (u): 1–12	Supersoft (n): 13–25	Supersoft (n): 26–29	Ultrasoft (u): 30–42
	Alonso	Ultrasoft (u): 1–10	Soft (n): 11–25 (dnf)		
	Verstappen	Ultrasoft (u): 1–7 (dnf)			
	Wehrlein	Soft (n): 1–2 (dnf)			

The tyre regulations stipulate that at least two of three dry tyre specifications must be used during a dry race.
Pirelli P Zero logos are colour-coded on the tyre sidewalls: Purple = Ultrasoft; Yellow = Soft; Red = Supersoft. (n) new (u) used

Photos: Peter J. Fox

ITALIAN GRAND PRIX

MONZA CIRCUIT

LEWIS HAMILTON claimed a record 69th pole position, but, thanks to untypically wet weather for Monza in September, qualifying took much longer than it should have done. The running was interrupted after several minutes when heavy rain brought the risk of aquaplaning – confirmed when Romain Grosjean spun his Haas into the barriers.

There may have been questions about the heavy application of the Frenchman's right foot, but there was no doubt that the incident highlighted a problem created by a new patch of tarmac on the pit straight, which failed to drain the water away.

After much indecision – some of the drivers and most of the crowd felt the rain had abated enough to allow the resumption of action – qualifying resumed over an hour later on a track that remained treacherous in places, specifically under the trees and on the new surface.

It was testament to the star quality of the field that there were no further serious incidents during what turned out to be an intense battle for grid positions.

The Q3 shoot-out was run in continuing rain, which made tyre choice difficult. It proved impossible to get temperature into the favoured Pirelli intermediate, drivers switching to wets as the session went on.

With the emphasis no longer on maximum engine power on such a fast track, Red Bull made good use of their car's handling, and towards the end, Max Verstappen and Daniel Ricciardo topped the times. But with less than a minute remaining, Hamilton produced an absolutely stunning lap to claim pole and beat Michael Schumacher's record.

"Getting in and out of the car, waiting for qualifying to continue, meant it was difficult to stay in the zone and continually focused," he said. "Being in the wet in these cars is such a challenge. It's an epic circuit, and the difficulty is trying to find where the grip is on such an old surface. I really, really enjoyed it."

"It was hard to switch on the inter," said Verstappen. "I couldn't get temperature into the tyre and the car was sliding around everywhere. I felt the inter should have been better, but the extreme [wet] turned out to be faster. When Q3 started, it was raining quite a bit. We were on the inter and decided straight away to go back to extreme. That was the right choice. I did my time – I knew it was pole position then, but I kept asking my engineer what Lewis was doing; I knew he would be the guy to beat."

"In Q1 and Q2, we were nowhere," said Ricciardo. "There was no grip and we were struggling. But when we got into Q3 and put on extremes, we had a lot more grip. It felt like a different car. I was fastest, but then Max came through and then Lewis. It was close between us. It was a good recovery. At least the wait was worthwhile for all the fans who stayed out in the rain to watch."

The hard work by the Red Bull drivers would count for nothing, however, as engine penalties (deliberately taken to allow maximum power unit performance for the next race in Singapore) moved them towards the back of the grid. That allowed surprising starting positions for Lance Stroll and Esteban Ocon, the novice Williams and Force India drivers having made the most of impressive qualifying performances in the wet: they moved into second and third on the grid.

Hamilton might have really enjoyed his pole lap, but part of that pleasure came from knowing that Ferrari were in trouble – Kimi Räikkönen and Sebastian Vettel were seventh and eighth. While Ferrari would have come to Monza in the knowledge that it was one of their worst tracks of the season, aquaplaning on the wet surface exacerbated their discomfort in front of a home crowd that would not necessarily have understood how these things worked – or didn't work in the case of the SF70H. The increased diameter of the wet-weather tyre raised the chassis just enough to tip the handling from difficult to undriveable.

They were not alone. Valtteri Bottas struggled with tyre temperature, the grip falling away as the rain increased, putting the Mercedes driver five places behind a team-mate who, at this moment, was on an entirely different level.

The irony was that the quietly intense Bottas probably thought about the technicalities too much, whereas Stroll simply got in and drove an F1 car in the wet for the first time without any preconceived notions. "I felt free," was how the Canadian described going with the flow and finding that his delicate, but comparatively unsophisticated style generated just enough heat to make the inters work and give F1 its youngest ever front-row starter. Felipe Massa was 1.2s slower in the other Williams.

A much smaller margin – 0.002s – had a significant effect on the Force India drivers. That was the difference between them in Q2, Ocon making Q3 (and greater things), while Sergio Pérez (also about to take a gearbox penalty) had to simmer in 11th place.

A penalty (ERS replacement) would be the undoing of a fine performance by Stoffel Vandoorne, the McLaren driver having got into Q3 before the problem struck after a couple of laps. Fernando Alonso, meanwhile, was forced to accept back-of-the-grid penalties from the outset because of planned power unit replacements. The good news was that the latest Honda engine (3.7 spec) was considered an improvement – when everything worked.

Qualifying performances generally became something of an irrelevance as penalties rained down. It was as if names had been thrown into a hat and drivers given grid positions at random. With Nico Hülkenberg setting 12th fastest time, pressure on Jolyon Palmer went up another notch when a decision to stop for inters did him no favours at a time when a continuation on wets could have put him into Q2.

Kevin Magnussen made the same strategic error with tyres, while Danill Kvyat and Carlos Sainz must have wished their problems were that simple as they fought an impossible fight with Toro Rossos that were fully trimmed out to extract the maximum (which wasn't much) for race day, leaving them passengers in the wet. Grosjean's progress was arrested by the wall, of course, while the Saubers, led by Marcus Ericsson, travelled further up the penalty-stricken grid from qualifying positions at the back.

Above: Seventieth anniversary celebrations merely ramped up the pressure on Vettel and Ferrari at Monza.
Photo: Scuderia Ferrari

Top: Verstappen heads the queue in an interrupted Q3 qualifying session.
Photo: WRi2/Jad Sherif

Above left: Daniel was well prepared for the expected weather conditions.
Photo: Red Bull Racing/Getty Images

Top left: In the wet conditions, Lewis Hamilton was on scintillating form during qualifying.
Photo: Peter J. Fox

Left: Hamilton celebrates his record-breaking 69th pole position.
Photo: Mercedes AMG Petronas F1 Team

Opening spread: Valtteri Bottas and Kimi Räikkönen jostle for position on the opening lap, while Sebastian Vettel waits to pounce.
Photo: Wri2/Bryn Williams

243

WHEN 93,000 fans – the largest Monza attendance for more than a decade – turned up on a typically warm September morning, most arrived in hope rather than expectation. The local media might have been talking up the possibility of a Ferrari success in broad terms, but informed *Tifosi* knew that the devil lay in the downforce detail.

Quite simply, the red cars were no match for the silver ones, either through the few corners or along the predominant straights. There was little to choose between the skinny wing profiles of both cars, thus underlining the overall efficiency of the Mercedes on a track like this. And Ferrari knew it.

They had come to their home race expecting to be beaten, off-the-record comments to trusted members of the Italian press earlier in the week having suggested that fifth and sixth would be a realistic result. But that had been before Red Bull elected to take their penalties. Maybe, just maybe, a podium was possible.

Lewis Hamilton's more immediate concern was the potentially over-excitable behaviour of the comparative novices surrounding him when they reached the first braking zone, some 638 metres from the start line. Would the chance of leading a grand prix prove too much?

Their teams were wise to this, both Lance Stroll and Esteban Ocon having been briefed that their fights were with Force India and Williams respectively, not Mercedes. Even so, the effect of barrelling into such a cauldron of emotion at Turn One might have prompted hearts to rule young heads.

Hamilton banished any such notion when he made a clean getaway and immediately moved right to block Stroll's potential advance. Not only did this send a clear message to the Williams driver, but it also checked his pace just enough to allow Ocon to run around the outside as they swung right and into the chicane.

That left Stroll at the potential mercy of Kimi Räikkönen as he bumped wheels with Valtteri Bottas and edged into fourth place on the run towards the Roggia chicane. But then came momentary relief for Stroll when Kimi made a poor exit from Ascari, allowing Bottas to take a run at the Ferrari into and through Parabolica. Bottas's momentum was helped greatly when Räikkönen moved right on the main straight to start his defence for the chicane braking zone and left the Mercedes free to grab a tow from the cars ahead. By the time he had reached the chicane, Bottas was a clear fourth with Stroll now in his sights.

The most spectacular – and anticipated – progress had been made by Max Verstappen, the Red Bull jumping six places to P8. Daniel Ricciardo's first lap was comparatively more measured, the prelude to a great drive beginning with just a couple of passes during the first two laps. This was part of the master plan, as Red Bull had chosen the soft tyre for the early skirmishes before running longer and then switching to the supersoft for the final attacks; a strategy diametrically opposed to the majority of the field. This was going to be interesting.

By the fifth lap, Hamilton was 3.6 seconds ahead of his team-mate, Bottas having used DRS to easily take third from Stroll on lap three, before repeating the main-straight move on Ocon a lap later. There was less than a second between the Force India and the Williams, but Sebastian Vettel was soon among them, having got the better of a troubled Räikkönen on lap three. The Finn was struggling with no grip at the rear and becoming frustrated by an inability to attack the corners.

Having easily moved ahead of Stroll and Ocon by lap eight, Vettel was six seconds behind Bottas and nine adrift of Hamilton. The Ferrari being consistently half a second slower than the leaders told its own story, one that was picked up by the Mercedes engineers. With Hamilton cruising and maintaining the gap to Bottas, both drivers were told to

turn down their engines, a considerable luxury, prompted by thoughts of Singapore to come.

Verstappen's flying progress had come to a halt against the side of Felipe Massa's Williams at the first chicane, the Red Bull puncturing the right rear and being forced to crawl slowly back to the pits at the end of lap four. Max was destined to continue lapping quickly – but at the back of the field.

With Vettel's pace at its maximum, Ferrari considered their options and decided to try Räikkönen on the supersoft, thinking that it might cure his handling problem as well as giving useful tyre information for Vettel. Kimi duly stopped from sixth at the end of lap 15, a move that prompted Force India and Williams to bring in Ocon and Stroll on successive laps. A problem with the left rear on the Williams allowed Räikkönen to move up one place

All of this promoted Ricciardo to fifth, the Australian really in the groove, which he demonstrated with a typically precise and dramatic pass on Sergio Pérez into the Roggia chicane. When Räikkönen pulled a DRS move on Ocon on lap 26, he found himself 14 seconds behind the other Force India. Although able to reduce that gap by around half a second a lap, his times on the supersoft had not been good enough to prompt Ferrari to bring in third-placed Vettel sooner than had been planned.

That stop finally came on lap 31. With Vettel around 20 seconds behind the leaders, Mercedes were able to bring in Hamilton and then Bottas on successive laps without serious threat. Bottas was able to stay within 3–4s of his team-mate, the Finn saying that the W08 felt as good as it had ever been. Hamilton obviously felt the same, as he responded each time Bottas set what looked like being fastest race lap.

Vettel having stopped, Ricciardo was third on the road, his laps fast and a model of consistency, right down to a hundredth of a second. But that was not quite enough to pull out a pit-stop gap on Räikkönen, and he rejoined fifth, 2.5

Above: After a stellar performance in wet qualifying, Lance Stroll held off the challenge of team-mate Massa in the race. The Williams pair took seventh and eighth places at the finish.
Photo: WRi2/Bryn Williams

Top right: Sebastian Vettel rescued a podium for Ferrari with third, keeping himself within three points of the championship lead.
Photo: Scudria Ferrari

Above right: Esteban Ocon delivered another accomplished drive to score a sixth for Force India, ahead of Williams drivers Stroll and Massa.
Photo: Sahara Force India F1 Team

Right: Despite the *tifosi's* display of red ticker-tape, the Mercedes pair of Hamilton and Bottas took a 1-2 win at Monza.
Photo: Peter J. Fox

seconds behind the Ferrari after pitting on lap 37. Now, of course, the flying Red Bull had the added advantage of fresh supersofts, worth perhaps half a second a lap.

When told Räikkönen was vulnerable, Ricciardo gleefully replied, "Great. I like 'em vulnerable!" Sure enough, the Red Bull closed in. When they passed the pits to start lap 41, Räikkönen routinely checked his mirrors and noted that Ricciardo was too far back to launch an attack into the chicane. Wrong!

The Australian caught Kimi completely by surprise when the Red Bull arrived alongside with not a hint of tyre smoke, despite having come from so far back and having left his braking impossibly late. If Marchionne and Co at Maranello had not noted the 'Honey Badger's' brilliance before, they were aware of it at home as he then set about reducing the 11s gap to Vettel in P3. There were 12 laps remaining. It may have been a tall order, but it was giving this race a much-needed edge.

A feisty drive by Massa, fending off constant attacks by Pérez, brought the Brazilian on to the tail of his team-mate as Stroll sat behind Ocon without being able to find enough impetus to get alongside. Feeling he could do more to relieve the Force India of sixth place, Massa gave the Williams management a few anxious moments as he threatened Stroll more than once.

Along the way, Massa had overhauled Stoffel Vandoorne, whose impressive midfield run (having passed Carlos Sainz) had come to an end thanks to another faulty MGU-K. McLaren's continuing misery was increased when Fernando Alonso retired with a gearshift problem, but not before he had become involved in a mildly controversial incident on lap 13, when Jolyon Palmer had got ahead by cutting the Roggia chicane and not given the place back. Alonso allowed his

state of agitation to show when he claimed it was "karma" upon receiving the news that Palmer had eventually retired with transmission trouble.

A three-way battle continued for most of the race between Kevin Magnussen, Daniil Kvyat and Nico Hülkenberg. Magnussen had overtaken the Toro Rosso on lap one, and then Kvyat was jumped by the Renault in the pits, only to get the place back from the struggling Hülkenberg on lap 36.

All three were soon joined by the flying Verstappen, the Red Bull having worked its way through and taken tenth from Magnussen with eight laps remaining. Sainz was happy to see the race over and take 14th place, clear of the recovering Grosjean (who had a damaged front wing from an early clash with a Red Bull) and Pascal Wehrlein, the sole Sauber survivor after Marcus Ericsson had retired with an intercooler problem.

A succession of fastest laps by Ricciardo reduced the gap to Vettel to 7.7s. Sebastian responded with personal bests, locking up and taking to the first chicane escape road on one occasion. On another, a hefty handful of opposite lock triggered a power steering malfunction, but by the time that had corrected itself, the threat from Ricciardo was subsiding as his supersofts began to wilt under the searing pace. Vettel would be more than happy with a podium finish on a day when Ferrari had expected much less.

It was a sign of the close championship contest that Hamilton's victory marked the first back-to-back wins of 2017. A small section of the crowd packed beneath the prominent podium booed the appearance of Hamilton. He didn't care about that. As he said quite pointedly – and truthfully – Mercedes had done the better job, and here he was, clear leader of the championship for the first time.

Maurice Hamilton

VIEWPOINT
ABOUT TURN...

MONZA was a perfect illustration of the intriguing see-saw nature of the Mercedes/Ferrari contest that enlivened F1 in 2017.

Just seven days earlier, Ferrari had pushed Mercedes harder than anyone expected at Spa, where Lewis Hamilton had to run qualifying laps for the last quarter of the race to keep Sebastian Vettel at bay.

So what had changed in a week that allowed Hamilton to beat Vettel by more than half a minute in Ferrari's backyard at Monza and Mercedes to turn its engines down at quarter-distance?

"I think the job the guys did analysing the deficits we had at Spa was awesome," Toto Wolff explained. "We had some very strong sectors in Spa and sacrificed raw speed for race speed, and therefore lacked low-downforce performance, braking stability, apex stability and traction. We tried to understand and optimise that for Monza, and straight from the get-go we had a car that was a really good drive."

Valtteri Bottas elaborated: "Spa is such a different track. There's a lot of high- and medium-speed corners, so in general you need a much stiffer car, and then the traction can be really poor. Here at Monza, though, there's not really high-speed corners, and so you can set the car up a bit more for the chicanes and for traction."

But if Mercedes had got it right, Ferrari clearly had not, a point that Wolff acknowledged: "It looks like this weekend, Ferrari made a step back somehow. They didn't perform the way everyone expected. Red Bull started from the back of the grid and almost finished P3, so something's out of synch. That's not how it should be."

Ferrari's low-downforce configuration was clearly nothing like as efficient as Mercedes's. Okay, Monza is a bit of a one-off, but with Hamilton taking the championship lead for the first time in the year, one left Italy feeling that Maranello needed to hit back. Quickly.

Tony Dodgins

2017 FORMULA 1
GRAN PREMIO
HEINEKEN
D'ITALIA

MONZA 1–3 SEPTEMBER

RACE DISTANCE: 53 laps, 190.587 miles/306.720km

RACE WEATHER: Dry/sunny (track 37–39°C, air 24–26°C)

ROLEX

OFFICIAL TIMEPIECE

AUTODROMO NAZIONALE DI MONZA

Circuit: 3.600 miles / 5.793km, 53 laps

Lesmo 2 185/115
Lesmo 1 200/124
Curva del Serraglio 305/190
Seconda Variante 130/81
Curva Vialone 220/137
Variante Ascari 240/149 340/211
Prima Variante 70/43
Curva Biassono 305/190
Rettifilo Tribune 350/217
Curva Parabolica 270/168

187/116 kmh/mph — Gear — DRS zone

RACE – OFFICIAL CLASSIFICATION

Pos.	Driver	Nat.	No.	Entrant	Car/Engine	Laps	Time/Retirement	Speed (mph/km/h)	Gap to leader	Fastest race lap
1	**Lewis Hamilton**	GB	44	Mercedes AMG Petronas Motorsport	Mercedes F1 W08-Mercedes M08 EQ Power+ V6	53	1h 15m 32.312s	151.382/243.626		1m 23.488s 50
2	**Valtteri Bottas**	FIN	77	Mercedes AMG Petronas Motorsport	Mercedes F1 W08-Mercedes M08 EQ Power+ V6	53	1h 15m 36.783s	151.233/243.386	4.471s	1m 23.722s 53
3	**Sebastian Vettel**	D	5	Scuderia Ferrari	Ferrari SF70H-062 V6	53	1h 16m 08.629s	150.179/241.690	36.317s	1m 23.897s 51
4	**Daniel Ricciardo**	AUS	3	Red Bull Racing	Red Bull RB13-TAG Heuer RB13 V6	53	1h 16m 12.647s	150.047/241.477	40.335s	1m 23.361s 49
5	**Kimi Räikkönen**	FIN	7	Scuderia Ferrari	Ferrari SF70H-062 V6	53	1h 16m 32.394s	149.402/240.439	1m 00.082s	1m 25.054s 43
6	**Esteban Ocon**	F	31	Sahara Force India Formula 1 Team	Force India VJM10-Mercedes M08 EQ Power+ V6	53	1h 16m 43.840s	149.030/239.841	1m 11.528s	1m 25.652s 53
7	**Lance Stroll**	CDN	18	Williams Martini Racing	Williams FW40-Mercedes M08 EQ Power+ V6	53	1h 16m 46.468s	148.945/239.704	1m 14.156s	1m 25.625s 51
8	**Felipe Massa**	BR	19	Williams Martini Racing	Williams FW40-Mercedes M08 EQ Power+ V6	53	1h 16m 47.146s	148.923/239.669	1m 14.834s	1m 25.477s 30
9	**Sergio Pérez**	MEX	11	Sahara Force India Formula 1 Team	Force India VJM10-Mercedes M08 EQ Power+ V6	53	1h 16m 47.588s	148.909/239.646	1m 15.276s	1m 24.968s 48
10	**Max Verstappen**	NL	33	Red Bull Racing	Red Bull RB13-TAG Heuer RB13 V6	52			1 lap	1m 24.351s 48
11	Kevin Magnussen	DK	20	Haas F1 Team	Haas VF-17-Ferrari 062 V6	52			1 lap	1m 26.037s 48
12	Daniil Kvyat	RUS	26	Scuderia Toro Rosso	Toro Rosso STR12-Renault R.E.17 V6	52			1 lap	1m 25.894s 43
13	Nico Hülkenberg	D	27	Renault Sport Formula One Team	Renault R.S.17-R.E.17 V6	52			1 lap	1m 26.131s 46
14	Carlos Sainz	E	55	Scuderia Toro Rosso	Toro Rosso STR12-Renault R.E.17 V6	52			1 lap	1m 26.210s 46
15	Romain Grosjean	F	8	Haas F1 Team	Haas VF-17-Ferrari 062 V6	52			1 lap	1m 25.020s 48
16	Pascal Wehrlein	D	94	Sauber F1 Team	Sauber C36-Ferrari 059/5 V6	51			2 laps	1m 26.547s 47
17	Fernando Alonso	E	14	McLaren Honda Formula 1 Team	McLaren MCL32-Honda RA617H V6	50	gearbox		3 laps	1m 25.871s 44
18	Marcus Ericsson	S	9	Sauber F1 Team	Sauber C36-Ferrari 059/5 V6	49	accident damage		4 laps	1m 27.663s 20
	Stoffel Vandoorne	B	2	McLaren Honda Formula 1 Team	McLaren MCL32-Honda RA617H V6	33	power unit			1m 26.912s 30
	Jolyon Palmer	GB	30	Renault Sport Formula One Team	Renault R.S.17-R.E.17 V6	29	transmission			1m 25.752s 27

Fastest race lap: Daniel Ricciardo on lap 49, 1m 23.361s, 155.451mph/250.174km/h.

Lap record: Rubens Barrichello (Ferrari F2004 V10), 1m 21.046s, 159.892mph/257.320km/h (2004).

19 · ALONSO · McLaren 35-place grid penalty for using additional power unit elements

17 · PALMER · Renault 15-place grid penalty for using additional power unit elements

15 · SAINZ · Toro Rosso 10-place grid penalty for using additional power unit elements

13 · VERSTAPPEN · Red Bull 20-place grid penalty for using additional power unit elements

11 · ERICSSON · Sauber

 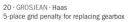 

20 · GROSJEAN · Haas 5-place grid penalty for replacing gearbox

18 · VANDOORNE · McLaren 25-place grid penalty for using additional power unit elements

16 · RICCIARDO · Red Bull 20-place grid penalty for using additional power unit elements; 5-place penalty for replacing gearbox

14 · HÜLKENBERG · Renault 10-place grid penalty for using additional power unit elements

12 · WEHRLEIN · Sauber

Grid order	1	2	3	4	5	6	7	8	9	10	11	12	13	14	15	16	17	18	19	20	21	22	23	24	25	26	27	28	29	30	31	32	33	34	35	36	37	38	39	40	41	42
44 HAMILTON	44	44	44	44	44	44	44	44	44	44	44	44	44	44	44	44	44	44	44	44	44	44	44	44	44	44	44	44	44	44	44	77	77	44	44	44	44	44	44	44	44	44
18 STROLL	31	31	31	77	77	77	77	77	77	77	77	77	77	77	77	77	77	77	77	77	77	77	77	77	77	77	77	77	77	77	77	44	44	77	77	77	77	77	77	77	77	77
31 OCON	18	18	77	31	31	31	31	5	5	5	5	5	5	5	5	5	5	5	5	5	5	5	5	5	5	5	5	5	5	5	5	3	3	3	3	3	3	5	5	5	5	5
77 BOTTAS	77	77	18	18	5	5	5	31	31	31	31	31	31	31	31	31	18	19	19	19	19	3	3	3	3	3	3	3	3	3	3	5	5	5	5	5	7	7	7	3	3
7 RÄIKKÖNEN	7	7	5	5	18	18	18	18	18	18	18	18	18	18	18	31	18	3	3	11	11	11	11	11	11	11	11	11	11	11	7	7	7	7	7	3	3	3	7	7	
5 VETTEL	5	5	7	7	7	7	7	7	7	7	7	7	7	7	7	19	3	11	11	11	19	31	31	31	31	7	7	7	7	7	7	31	31	31	31	31	31	31	31	31	31	
19 MASSA	19	19	19	19	19	19	19	19	19	19	19	19	19	19	11	11	11	26	2	2	31	7	7	7	7	31	31	31	31	31	31	18	18	18	18	18	18	18	18	18	18	
26 KVYAT	33	33	11	11	11	11	11	11	11	11	11	11	11	11	7	3	26	2	31	31	7	18	18	18	18	18	18	18	18	18	18	19	19	19	19	19	19	19	19	19	19	
20 MAGNUSSEN	11	11	20	20	20	20	3	3	3	3	3	3	3	3	26	2	31	7	7	2	2	2	2	2	2	20	20	20	20	20	20	11	11	11	11	11	11	11	11	11	11	
11 PÉREZ	20	20	26	26	2	2	20	20	20	20	26	26	26	26	2	31	7	26	18	18	19	19	2	2	2	2	2	20	20	20	20	20	20	20	20	20	20	20	20	20	20	
9 ERICSSON	26	26	27	27	3	26	26	26	26	26	2	2	2	2	7	7	18	30	30	30	30	30	14	14	14	14	20	20	27	27	27	26	26	26	26	26	26	26	26	26	26	
94 WEHRLEIN	27	27	3	3	27	27	27	2	2	20	55	30	30	30	30	30	30	14	14	14	14	20	20	20	27	27	26	26	26	27	27	27	27	27	27	27	27					
33 VERSTAPPEN	55	55	55	55	55	2	2	55	55	55	14	55	14	14	14	14	14	20	20	20	27	27	27	14	26	26	2	55	55	55	55	55	55	55	55	33						
27 HÜLKENBERG	9	3	2	2	55	55	55	14	14	14	30	14	14	30	20	20	20	27	27	27	26	26	26	26	55	55	55	33	33	33	33	33	33	33	33	55						
55 SAINZ	3	2	14	14	14	14	14	27	30	9	9	9	9	20	20	27	27	26	26	26	55	55	55	55	14	14	33	14	14	14	14	14	14	14	14	14						
3 RICCIARDO	2	9	9	9	9	9	30	30	9	94	20	20	20	27	94	55	55	55	55	55	33	33	30	8	8	33	8	14	8	94	94	94	94									
30 PALMER	14	14	94	94	30	30	9	9	9	94	94	20	27	27	94	55	55	33	33	33	33	33	30	30	8	30	33	8	8	8	94	8	94	8	94	94	94	94	94	94		
2 VANDOORNE	8	8	30	30	94	94	94	94	27	27	27	27	55	55	55	9	33	94	8	8	8	8	33	33	9	94	94	9	9	9	9	9	9									
14 ALONSO	30	94	8	8	8	8	8	8	8	8	33	33	33	33	9	8	8	8	9	9	9	9	9	9	94	9	9	9														
8 GROSJEAN	94	30	33	33	33	33	33	33	33	33	33	33	33	8	8	8	9	9	9	94	94	94	94	94	94	94	94															

All results and data © FOM 2017

TIME SHEETS

FOR THE RECORD

PRACTICE 1 (FRIDAY)

Weather: Dry/partly cloudy
Temperatures: track 24–28°C, air 22–23°C

Pos.	Driver	Laps	Time
1	Lewis Hamilton	28	1m 21.537s
2	Valtteri Bottas	31	1m 21.972s
3	Sebastian Vettel	24	1m 22.652s
4	Kimi Räikkönen	28	1m 22.689s
5	Daniel Ricciardo	28	1m 22.742s
6	Max Verstappen	23	1m 22.749s
7	Sergio Pérez	36	1m 23.317s
8	Esteban Ocon	34	1m 23.400s
9	Stoffel Vandoorne	24	1m 23.465s
10	Felipe Massa	37	1m 23.561s
11	Carlos Sainz	22	1m 23.680s
12	Kevin Magnussen	22	1m 23.973s
13	Lance Stroll	30	1m 23.991s
14	Daniil Kvyat	27	1m 24.012s
15	Fernando Alonso	17	1m 24.015s
16	Romain Grosjean	22	1m 24.079s
17	Nico Hülkenberg	17	1m 24.542s
18	Jolyon Palmer	21	1m 25.166s
19	Pascal Wehrlein	26	1m 25.223s
20	Marcus Ericsson	17	1m 25.687s

PRACTICE 2 (FRIDAY)

Weather: Dry/partly sunny
Temperatures: track 33–41°C, air 25–28°C

Pos.	Driver	Laps	Time
1	Valtteri Bottas	25	1m 21.406s
2	Lewis Hamilton	24	1m 21.462s
3	Sebastian Vettel	33	1m 21.546s
4	Kimi Räikkönen	34	1m 21.804s
5	Max Verstappen	34	1m 22.409s
6	Daniel Ricciardo	22	1m 22.752s
7	Stoffel Vandoorne	31	1m 22.947s
8	Fernando Alonso	31	1m 22.968s
9	Esteban Ocon	43	1m 22.977s
10	Felipe Massa	42	1m 22.985s
11	Carlos Sainz	21	1m 23.150s
12	Nico Hülkenberg	14	1m 23.272s
13	Jolyon Palmer	34	1m 23.317s
14	Sergio Pérez	43	1m 23.352s
15	Lance Stroll	36	1m 23.403s
16	Romain Grosjean	31	1m 23.567s
17	Kevin Magnussen	20	1m 23.650s
18	Daniil Kvyat	28	1m 24.253s
19	Marcus Ericsson	39	1m 24.894s
20	Pascal Wehrlein	25	1m 25.295s

PRACTICE 3 (SATURDAY)

Weather: Rain/cloudy
Temperatures: 17°C, air 13°C

Pos.	Driver	Laps	Time
1	Felipe Massa	4	1m 40.660s
2	Lance Stroll	4	1m 40.888s
3	Nico Hülkenberg	4	1m 41.491s
4	Carlos Sainz	5	1m 41.515s
5	Jolyon Palmer	4	1m 44.369s
6	Marcus Ericsson	3	1m 44.701s
7	Daniil Kvyat	4	1m 45.033s
8	Daniel Ricciardo	1	no time
9	Max Verstappen	1	no time
10	Sebastian Vettel	3	no time
11	Kimi Räikkönen	4	no time
12	Fernando Alonso	2	no time
13	Stoffel Vandoorne	4	no time
14	Romain Grosjean	1	no time
15	Kevin Magnussen	1	no time
16	Esteban Ocon	2	no time
17	Pascal Wehrlein	2	no time
18	Valtteri Bottas	1	no time
19	Sergio Pérez	1	no time
20	Lewis Hamilton	1	no time

QUALIFYING (SATURDAY)

Weather: Heavy rain at first/cloudy Temperatures: track 15–18°C, air 14–15°C

Pos.	Driver	First	Second	Third	Qualifying Tyre
1	Lewis Hamilton	1m 36.009s	1m 34.660s	1m 35.554s	Wet (new)
2	Max Verstappen	1m 37.344s	1m 36.113s	1m 36.702s	Wet (new)
3	Daniel Ricciardo	1m 38.304s	1m 37.313s	1m 36.841s	Wet (new)
4	Lance Stroll	1m 37.653s	1m 37.002s	1m 37.032s	Wet (new)
5	Esteban Ocon	1m 38.775s	1m 37.580s	1m 37.719s	Wet (new)
6	Valtteri Bottas	1m 35.716s	1m 35.396s	1m 37.833s	Wet (new)
7	Kimi Räikkönen	1m 38.235s	1m 37.031s	1m 37.987s	Wet (new)
8	Sebastian Vettel	1m 37.198s	1m 36.223s	1m 38.064s	Wet (new)
9	Felipe Massa	1m 38.338s	1m 37.456s	1m 38.251s	Wet (used)
10	Stoffel Vandoorne	1m 38.767s	1m 37.471s	1m 39.157s	Wet (new)
11	Sergio Pérez	1m 38.511s	1m 37.582s		
12	Nico Hülkenberg	1m 39.242s	1m 38.059s		
13	Fernando Alonso	1m 39.134s	1m 38.202s		
14	Daniil Kvyat	1m 39.183s	1m 38.245s		
15	Carlos Sainz	1m 39.788s	1m 38.526s		
16	Kevin Magnussen	1m 40.489s			
17	Jolyon Palmer	1m 40.646s			
18	Marcus Ericsson	1m 41.732s			
19	Pascal Wehrlein	1m 41.875s			
20	Romain Grosjean	1m 43.355s			

QUALIFYING: head to head

Hamilton	8	5	Bottas
Vettel	9	4	Räikkönen
Massa	10	2	Stroll
Stroll	1	0	Di Resta
Ricciardo	4	9	Verstappen
Pérez	10	3	Ocon
Hülkenberg	13	0	Palmer
Kvyat	6	7	Sainz
Ericsson	2	0	Giovinazzi
Ericsson	4	7	Wehrlein
Alonso	10	2	Vandoorne
Vandoorne	1	0	Button
Grosjean	9	4	Magnussen

FOR THE RECORD

1st FRONT ROW POSITION: Lance Stroll

150th FRONT ROW POSITION: Mercedes

DID YOU KNOW?

Lewis Hamilton, with 69 pole positions, broke Michael Schumacher's all-time record.
Lance Stroll became the youngest driver to achieve an F1 front row, at 18 years and 309 days, beating Max Verstappen by 24 days.

POINTS

DRIVERS

1	Lewis Hamilton	238
2	Sebastian Vettel	235
3	Valtteri Bottas	197
4	Daniel Ricciardo	144
5	Kimi Räikkönen	138
6	Max Verstappen	68
7	Sergio Pérez	58
8	Esteban Ocon	55
9	Carlos Sainz	36
10	Nico Hülkenberg	34
11	Felipe Massa	31
12	Lance Stroll	24
13	Romain Grosjean	24
14	Kevin Magnussen	11
15	Fernando Alonso	10
16	Pascal Wehrlein	5
17	Daniil Kvyat	4
18	Stoffel Vandoorne	1

CONSTRUCTORS

1	Mercedes	435
2	Ferrari	373
3	Red Bull	212
4	Force India	113
5	Williams	55
6	Toro Rosso	40
7	Haas	35
8	Renault	34
9	McLaren	11
10	Sauber	5

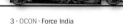

9 · MAGNUSSEN · Haas   7 · MASSA · Williams   5 · RÄIKKÖNEN · Ferrari   3 · OCON · Force India   1 · HAMILTON · Mercedes

10 · PÉREZ · Force India   8 · KVYAT · Toro Rosso   6 · VETTEL · Ferrari   4 · BOTTAS · Mercedes   2 · STROLL · Williams
5-place grid penalty for replacing gearbox

43	44	45	46	47	48	49	50	51	52	53	
44	44	44	44	44	44	44	44	44	44	44	1
77	77	77	77	77	77	77	77	77	77	77	2
5	5	5	5	5	5	5	5	5	5	5	3
3	3	3	3	3	3	3	3	3	3	3	4
7	7	7	7	7	7	7	7	7	7	7	5
31	31	31	31	31	31	31	31	31	31	31	6
18	18	18	18	18	18	18	18	18	18	18	7
19	19	19	19	19	19	19	19	19	19	19	8
11	11	11	11	11	11	11	11	11	11	11	9
20	20	20	33	33	33	33	33	33	33		10
26	26	33	20	20	20	20	20	20	20		
33	33	26	26	26	26	26	26	26	26		
27	27	27	27	27	27	27	27	27	27		
55	55	55	55	55	55	55	55	55	55		
14	14	14	14	14	14	14	14	14	8		
8	8	8	8	8	8	8	94				
94	94	94	94	94	94	94	94				
9	9	9	9	9	9	9					

8 = Pit stop   9 = One lap or more behind

RACE TYRE STRATEGIES

PIRELLI

	Driver	Race Stint 1	Race Stint 2	Race Stint 3
1	Hamilton	Supersoft (n): 1-32	Soft (n): 33-53	
2	Bottas	Supersoft (n): 1-33	Soft (n): 34-53	
3	Vettel	Supersoft (n): 1-31	Soft (n): 32-53	
4	Ricciardo	Soft (n): 1-37	Supersoft (n): 38-53	
5	Räikkönen	Supersoft (n): 1-15	Soft (n): 16-53	
6	Ocon	Supersoft (n): 1-16	Soft (n): 17-53	
7	Stroll	Supersoft (n): 1-17	Soft (n): 18-53	
8	Massa	Supersoft (n): 1-21	Soft (n): 22-53	
9	Pérez	Supersoft (n): 1-32	Soft (n): 33-53	
10	Verstappen	Soft (n): 1-3	Supersoft (n): 4-27	Supersoft (n): 28-52
11	Magnussen	Supersoft (n): 1-11	Soft (n): 12-52	
12	Kvyat	Supersoft (n): 1-19	Soft (n): 20-52	
13	Hülkenberg	Supersoft (n): 1-9	Soft (n): 10-52	
14	Sainz	Supersoft (n): 1-13	Soft (n): 14-52	
15	Grosjean	Supersoft (n): 1-3	Soft (n): 4-34	Supersoft (n): 35-52
16	Wehrlein	Supersoft (n): 1-20	Soft (n): 21-51	
17	Alonso	Soft (n): 1-30	Supersoft (n): 31-50	
18	Ericsson	Supersoft (n): 1-18	Soft (n): 19-49	
	Vandoorne	Supersoft (n): 1-33 (dnf)		
	Palmer	Soft (n): 1-25	Supersoft (n): 26-29 (dnf)	

The tyre regulations stipulate that at least two of three dry tyre specifications must be used during a dry race.
Pirelli P Zero logos are colour-coded on the tyre sidewalls: Red = Supersoft; Yellow = Soft. (n) new (u) used

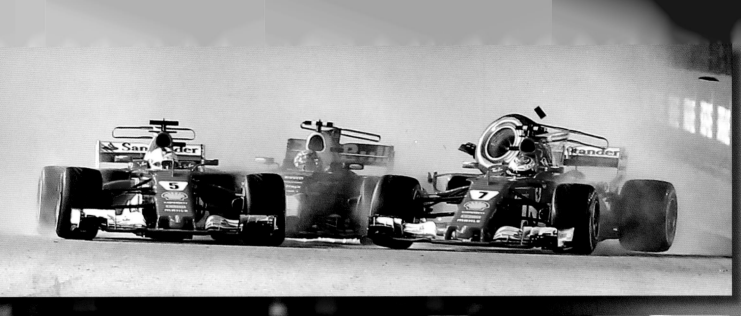

GAPORE

2017 FORMULA 1
SINGAPORE AIRLINES
SINGAPORE GRAND PRIX

FIA FORMULA 1 WORLD CHAMPIONSHIP · ROUND 14

SINGAPORE GRAND PRIX

MARINA BAY CIRCUIT

nsets, above: **Both Mercedes drivers look somewhat nonplussed on
the podium.**
Photos: WRi2/Jean-François Galeron & Jad Sherif

Main photo: **Lewis Hamilton avoided
the first-corner carnage and soon
began to stamp his authority on
proceedings**
Photo: Peter J. Fox

MARINA BAY QUALIFYING

FROM Monza, the least physical track with the shortest race time to Singapore's Marina Bay, a tough 23-corner lap and the longest race, always pushing the two-hour duration maximum.

From the Monza Royal Park, where Ferrari's low-downforce package had underperformed, to the extent that Lewis Hamilton had more than half a minute in hand over the first red car when the chequer fell, to Singapore, where the Ferrari was expected to be the pace setter, as it had been at high-downforce Monte Carlo and Budapest.

Sebastian Vettel, though, refused to buy into the hype. He preferred to wait and feel the car under him when practice started. And he didn't entirely like it. Then he hit the wall and damaged the suspension, the car compromised during Friday afternoon's long runs, when the two Red Bulls looked mighty impressive. Mercedes, Hamilton admitted, also had work to do, with Valtteri Bottas looking even more at sea with a total lack of rear-end grip. For him at least, it was starting to look like 2015 all over again.

The Red Bulls looked a genuine pole threat, too, notwithstanding that Renault didn't have the ability to turn up the engines for Q3 to the same extent that Mercedes and Ferrari could. But after Max Verstappen and Daniel Ricciardo topped Q1 and Q2 (where they had a couple of tenths in hand over Vettel and Kimi Räikkönen), Vettel dug out a totally on-the-limit 1m 39.491s to take a great fourth Singapore pole, the lap including a hefty clout of the Turn 19 wall.

Vettel's face betrayed what it meant to him, the adrenaline still flowing as he climbed out of the Ferrari.

"Turn 19 was no brush, it was a hit!" he admitted. "I felt a bit of vibration, but kept going, and when they confirmed pole I really screamed! I'm very, very happy. Yesterday we were caught a bit off guard, the car not behaving as we wanted. The effort has been huge. Charles [Leclerc] has been in the simulator and answered a lot of questions that we couldn't. And I've had a lot of support from the guys. I don't know when they went to bed, probably around lunch time!" (The F1 paddock stays on European time in Singapore.)

At Red Bull, meanwhile, as they announced "P2, Max, good job," rather than being happy with a second fastest, 1m 39.814s qualifying performance, which equalled his best at Spa in 2016, Verstappen's radio response needed to be bleeped out. He had wanted pole, nothing less.

Verstappen and Ricciardo were evenly matched throughout practice and qualifying – Max ahead, but fractionally. The margin was five-hundredths in Q1, five-hundredths in Q2 and then three-hundredths in Q3. It was *that* tight.

"I'll accept a little bit of defeat today," Ricciardo grimaced, "but I still think we can win. I thought pole would be on, too, but we couldn't quite run with Sebastian. It's a long lap; you gain a bit, you lose a bit, but in the end three-tenths was quite significant."

Kimi Räikkönen did not attack Marina Bay with quite the same gusto as his team-mate. Just when Ferrari could have done with a repeat of their front-row lock-outs in Monaco and Budapest to protect Vettel from the Red Bull race threat, Räikkönen was almost six-tenths adrift, down in fourth place. Significantly, though, that was sufficient to put him 0.06s clear of Lewis Hamilton's Mercedes. As in 2015, both Silver Arrows ended up on the third row.

"We just lack a load of grip," Hamilton said. "We were already holding on for dear life in Q1 and Q2, and I wasn't driving badly – I got everything out of every lap."

Bearing that out was Bottas's time, which was almost 0.7s slower.

"It's our yearly wake-up call," grimaced Toto Wolff.

Bottas had precious little rear grip on Friday, prompting wholesale overnight changes. In Saturday's third practice session, though, the car felt even worse.

"Valtteri, do we go back to yesterday or develop from here?" Bottas was asked over the radio as he prepared to enter the pits with half an hour of Saturday morning practice remaining.

"That's a good question," he replied. They did revert to Friday's settings, then made more changes, and thus Bottas went into qualifying pretty much blind.

The rest of the top ten was filled by drivers and teams all very much in the news. Nico Hülkenberg went into the weekend convinced that Renault could be best of the rest in Singapore as the team targeted fifth place in the constructors' championship by year-end. He delivered on that with seventh best qualifying time.

With the paddock alive with the end of the McLaren Honda partnership and the team's subsequent move to Renault power for 2018, it was ironic that Fernando Alonso and Stoffel Vandoorne put both of Woking's cars into the top ten for the first time all season. It was not wholly unexpected, mind you, given the circuit layout and the competence of the McLaren chassis.

One of the outcomes of the negotiations that had culminated in McLaren moving to Renault, and Toro Rosso concluding a deal with Honda for three years, was that Carlos Sainz would move to the Renault works team to partner Hülkenberg in 2018, on a single year's piece of Red Bull elastic. After qualifying a fine sixth in Singapore in 2016, the Spaniard put James Key's car into the top ten once more.

Jolyon Palmer, again having to fend off questions about his continued occupation of the second Renault, was 11th, but more than 0.8s from Hülkenberg in Q2.

Force India had never managed to qualify a car in the top ten in Singapore, and that state of affairs continued: Sergio Pérez and Esteban Ocon, 21 on race day, lined up 12th and 14th respectively.

Haas also had a difficult time, Romain Grosjean hauling one of the cars into Q2, while Kevin Magnussen joined the two Williams and two Sauber drivers as Q1 victims. Felipe Massa, the pole man in 2008, clipped the wall, and Lance Stroll struggled for pace on his Marina Bay debut.

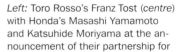

Above: Vettel accepts the plaudits after taking pole position.
Photo: Peter J. Fox

Left: Toro Rosso's Franz Tost (*centre*) with Honda's Masashi Yamamoto and Katsuhide Moriyama at the announcement of their partnership for the 2018 season.
Photo: Lukas Gorys

Centre left: Aston Martin CEO Andy Palmer with Red Bull team principal Christian Horner.
Photo: Red Bull Racing/Getty Images

Below centre left: McLaren's Zak Brown, delighted to be joining forces with Renault's Cyril Abiteboul.

Left: Still searching for horsepower. Honda's Yusuke Hasagawa,
Photos: Jean-François Galeron/WRi2

Far Left: Vettel edged out the Red Bull pair of Ricciardo and Verstappen.
Photo: Scuderia Ferrari

253

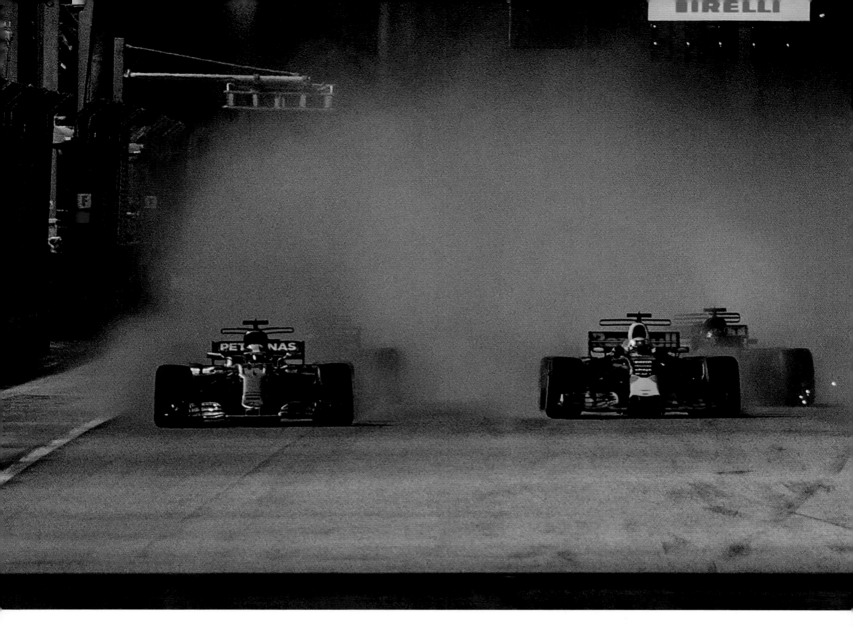

Above: Having edged his Ferrari to the left, Sebastian Vettel is collected by team-mate Kimi Räikkönen, following the Finn's collision with Max Verstappen's Red Bull.

Right: The luckless Fernando Alonso and his McLaren Honda were punted into retirement by the entangled Verstappen and Räikkönen.

Photos: Peter J. Fox

Below right: The Mercedes safety car holds the leaders following the first-corner mayhem. There would be two further interventions, after both Daniil Kvyat and Marcus Ericsson hit the barriers.

Photo: WRi2/Jad Sherif

IT began to look as though this could be Lewis Hamilton's day, against the odds, when rain fell before the 8pm start time and a glistening surface greeted drivers as they pulled out of the pits.

Wet tyres were required, but which ones? When the covers came off on the grid, there was an exact 50/50 split between drivers who had opted for the intermediate Pirelli and those who had selected the blue-walled extreme wet. Significantly, the top six had all gone for the intermediate. Initial lap times would be right on the crossover point, but team information was that the rain was passing – and the probability of an early safety car in Singapore is always high.

With track position more crucial than just about anywhere bar Monaco, all eyes were on the front-row men as the lights blinked out. Verstappen got a slightly better getaway than Vettel, and immediately Sebastian went defensive, edging left. To the left of the Dutchman, though, Räikkönen got an absolute flier and was already alongside the Red Bull.

At that point, Vettel started to move much more aggressively towards the left and Verstappen, pincered, was left with nowhere to go. The initial contact was between Verstappen and Räikkönen. Kimi's car immediately flicked to the right, into his team-mate's Ferrari, which suffered heavy impact to the left-hand pod, damaging an oil radiator.

Both Räikkönen and Verstappen speared off to the right, where they collected Alonso, who had made a stupendous start and was attempting to run right around the outside into Turn One. The McLaren was briefly flicked up on to two wheels and came down hard, but Fernando continued on his way, with damage, behind Vettel and Hamilton.

Vettel's Ferrari was leaking oil on to the rear tyres, and before Turn Three he spun and rolled backwards into retirement. It was the first time in Ferrari history that both cars had been eliminated on the opening lap of a race.

Hamilton couldn't believe his luck. When he had seen the

wet track, he figured on being able to take the fight to Vettel, but with less than half a lap gone, he didn't need to.

Alonso, who also had looked forward to seeing what he could do in the conditions – "a podium was sure," he reckoned – was deeply frustrated to have to retire his damaged car after a handful of laps. So much so, that he punched a hole in his driver's room back at McLaren's paddock enclave!

There were varying opinions about what had happened at the start, but there can be little doubt that Vettel's acute swerve to the left triggered the sequence of events, although stewards labelled it a racing incident.

"My start was a little bit better than Seb's," Verstappen said. "I think he saw that and so tried to move left to squeeze me a bit, but didn't know Kimi was on my other side. It wasn't the smartest move, and you can't make excuses for it when you are fighting for a world championship. Kimi had a great start and was alongside me very quickly. I didn't try to defend, as I knew it would be a long race, but he started to squeeze me also, at which point there wasn't a lot I could do. The rear wheels are wider than the fronts, so I was locked in the sandwich."

Study the footage and it appears that after beginning to edge across gently, Vettel makes his more aggressive swoop at the point where he probably picked up the rapid-starting Räikkönen in his peripheral vision. But whether he realised that it was Kimi is another question. Under lights, with a lot of spray, he may suddenly have just been aware of the presence of another car. Defending so hard against a team-mate, who would have had to defer to him anyway, did not appear to make much sense. Easy to say with hindsight; a lot more difficult in the moment. Perhaps he thought it was Ricciardo from row two. Whatever, the safety car maintained its 100 per cent involvement in the Singapore GP.

Hamilton had managed to get around Ricciardo, who saw

what was developing ahead of him and backed off, while Hülkenberg and Pérez were early beneficiaries, finding themselves third and fourth in line behind the safety car, with Bottas fifth.

Suddenly, a race Hamilton had gone into intent on damage limitation afforded him a golden opportunity, with his main championship rival non-scoring. When the safety car pulled off after four laps, he immediately opened out a 3.5s margin over Ricciardo and had extended that to 5s by the time Daniil Kvyat crashed his Toro Rosso at Turn Five, bringing out Bernd Maylander for a second time, on lap 11.

Whereas in 2016, Red Bull had tended to be superior on the intermediate Pirelli, that pattern was not re-emerging with the altered specification of the 2017 tyres. Putting on intermediates changes the car's ride-height characteristics, and the tyre seal region reacts differently because the sidewalls flex in a different way. As seen in wet qualifying at Monza, where Hamilton was electrifying, perhaps the Mercedes W08 was better suited to those circumstances than Red Bull's RB13 because, in spite of Hamilton's undisputed brilliance, both Red Bull drivers had demonstrated that they, too, were better than handy in the wet.

There was another factor. Ricciardo was losing gearbox oil pressure and was instructed to short-shift and lift-and-coast where possible as Red Bull tried to get him to the end of the race, which they felt was a long shot.

The second safety car allowed those on extremes to switch to intermediates without too big a penalty. With the track drying slowly, it was too soon to make the move on to slicks, but Ricciardo had a big enough margin over those behind to dive in for a fresh set of intermediates. He was helped by Hülkenberg, Pérez and Palmer adopting the same approach, the Red Bull only briefly surrendering track position to Palmer, but it was right back behind Hamilton, on fresh tyres, when the safety car pulled off at the end of

Above: A well-drilled pit stop for Daniel Ricciardo on his way to taking second place.
Photo: Red Bull Racing/Getty Images

Top right: Jolyon Palmer finally scored points for Renault with a trouble-free race to sixth, ahead of Stoffel Vandoorne's McLaren Honda.
Photo: WRi2/Jad Sherif

Above right: Carlos Sainz drove brilliantly to take a career-best fourth for Toro Rosso.
Photo: Peter J. Fox

Right: The tension shows on Vettel's face before the start.
Photo: Scuderia Ferrari

lap 14. Bottas who, like Hamilton, did not pit now ran third, ahead of Sainz, Hülkenberg and Pérez.

Hamilton expressed concern over the radio that stopping for fresh tyres would have been better. His team, however, immediately explained the reasoning why not. First, if Lewis had pitted, Red Bull would have left Ricciardo out. Around Marina Bay, track position is king, and it would be better to be leading the race on worn intermediates than running second on fresh ones. Second, on a drying surface, sometimes it's better to be on thinner-gauge worn intermediates than thicker-gauge new ones, which can be more prone to overheating. The team was happy with Hamilton's lap times and the condition of his tyres, so they left him out.

It proved to be the right call. Racing in anger once again, Lewis was able to extend his lead. At the end of lap 16, it was 2.32s, and on successive laps it grew to 2.79s; 3.05s; 3.41s; 3.96s and 4.96s. In spite of Ricciardo's new rubber. Impressive. And vindication of the team's strategy.

The next decision that had to be called correctly was the point at which to go from intermediates to slicks. The leading teams with most to lose don't gamble, taking cues from the sector times of the first car to stop, which in this case was Kevin Magnussen's Haas, the Dane pitting for ultrasofts after 24 laps. The Mercedes team's metrics showed that this was slightly too early, that the track was still 0.8s off.

The other consideration was that when the first cars go on to dry tyres, there is increased risk. What if there is another safety car at that point? If so, not everyone would be on slicks, and those who had changed would face the tricky situation of restarting on slicks that had lost temperature. For those reasons, the front-runners tend to be reactive rather than proactive.

Ricciardo headed for the pits four laps later, at the end of lap 28, the same lap on which Mercedes brought in Bottas.

Hamilton was in at the end of lap 29. Once the lead pair was back up to speed, Lewis had an 8.6s lead over Daniel. But now, on ultrasofts on a drying track, would Hamilton be vulnerable to the impressive dry pace Red Bull had displayed in Friday's second practice?

No. Hamilton was actually able to extend his advantage, with Bottas unable to run at anything like the same pace in third, the second Mercedes actually under pressure from Hülkenberg's well-driven Renault. One of F1's anomalies was that 'The Hulk' was on course to break Adrian Sutil's record for most GP starts without a podium. Suddenly one was up for grabs. He should have known better. The Renault developed a hydraulic leak that required him to pit and then retire for good ten laps later...

That secured Sainz's Toro Rosso – the only car on supersofts rather than ultrasofts – in fourth place, the Spaniard resolutely and impressively defending against Pérez's Force India. Palmer ran sixth, with Vandoorne close behind, the Belgian taking advantage and passing Stroll when the Williams glanced a wall.

Bernd Maylander's evening was not yet done. On lap 36, Marcus Ericsson spun his Sauber over the Anderson Bridge and blocked the track. The C36 had to be craned away, so out came the official Mercedes again, once more wiping out Hamilton's margin – almost 6s – over Ricciardo. Lewis wasn't impressed. "Why couldn't it be a VSC?" he asked.

The field closed up again until being let off the leash at the end of the 41st lap, for what would be an additional 17 laps, the race ending three laps before the scheduled 61 because of the maximum two-hour time limitation.

Once again, Hamilton was able to drop Ricciardo quickly at the restart, 2.2s clear at the end of lap 42 and 4.28s ahead next time around. But, Lewis's 44th lap was almost 2.5s slower and his lead suddenly back down to 1.7s. Was

VIEWPOINT
WHAT A DIFFERENCE A DAY MAKES...

O N Saturday, Sebastian Vettel had trembled as adrenalin coursed though his veins following one of those pole-position laps that make you realise just why **F1** drivers operate in a different zone.

Twenty-four hours later, shoulders hunched, head down, he was devastated. After a misjudgement that had lasted a millisecond, he had gone a long way towards possibly throwing away a year's work.

This was no kissing a wall and getting away with it (as he had done when necessarily hanging it out during qualifying). It was an error that went beyond the excruciating and rare statistic of eliminating both Ferraris. Instead of positioning himself to take back the championship momentum, Vettel had literally cleared the way for Lewis Hamilton to lead it by 28 points.

If only Seb had read the script written by his old friend, Christian Horner. When assessing the chances of his drivers starting second and third, Horner had said, "The race is not won on a Saturday. We've got nothing to lose, but Seb has a championship to think about and can't take too many risks."

It might have been a fair point had the Red Bull boss been talking about anyone other than his former driver. With memories of 2010 and Vettel's infamous reaction to a challenge by Mark Webber in Turkey, coupled with the four-times champion's impetuous behaviour in Baku, Horner ought to have guessed that calm reason could quickly become a red mist if Max Verstappen so much as showed his nose alongside.

These two had history, going back to Verstappen's tactics in Mexico 2016, when Vettel's salty language had been even more controversial than the moves he had been complaining about. Even allowing for Sebastian's understandable failure to realise that Kimi Räikkönen might have made such a demon start in Singapore, it was one thing to ease across on the fellow front-row man (knowing you've made an average getaway) and quite another to attempt a shut-out when there's every chance – being Verstappen – that he would be coming down the inside, no matter what.

Maurice Hamilton

Mercedes slowing Hamilton down to back Ricciardo into Bottas and going for a 1-2?

The reality was more complex. At the end of the 2016 race, won by Nico Rosberg, Ricciardo had almost closed down the lead Mercedes on fresher tyres after a late stop, facilitated by having a sufficiently large pit window behind him. The concern now was that if Hamilton set a storming pace at the front and pulled Ricciardo along with him, that same window might open up behind the Red Bull if Bottas and Sainz were unable to run at similar pace. A further safety car could then leave Hamilton exposed. The intention was that Lewis should ease off slightly, but, confused, he slowed significantly, to a pace he wasn't comfortable at, prompting Peter Bonnington to get back on the radio and tell him just to do his own thing.

Lewis duly reeled off the remaining laps without further drama for a win that nobody could have predicted on Saturday evening. Ricciardo and Bottas joined him on the podium, while Sainz pulled off his best F1 finish. Engineer Marco Mattaza was delighted: "Bravo Carlos, we're not letting you go!" he said, referring to the Spaniard's imminent departure to Renault.

Pérez scored more points for the impressively consistent Force India, and Palmer finally had a 2017 score on the board for his top-six finish. Vandoorne, Stroll, Grosjean and Ocon completed the points scorers.

Reflecting on a highly unlikely Mercedes win, Toto Wolff said, "I've said it before: on a difficult day, you'd like Lewis in the car! This was another example. In the morning, we were talking about damage limitation, and then we go away with a 1-3! It's a great result, but you can kind of feel for Ferrari. I've been in the situation of losing both cars on lap one and can relate to how awful that feels."

Tony Dodgins

14

2017 FORMULA 1
SINGAPORE AIRLINES
SINGAPORE
GRAND PRIX

SINGAPORE 15–17 SEPTEMBER

ROLEX

F1 OFFICIAL TIMEPIECE

RACE DISTANCE: 58 laps, 182.455 miles/293.633km

RACE WEATHER: Rain at start/dark (track 30–32°C, air 28–29°C)

MARINA BAY STREET CIRCUIT, SINGAPORE
Circuit: 3.147 miles / 5.065km
61 laps

187/116 kmh/mph · Gear — DRS zone

RACE – OFFICIAL CLASSIFICATION

Pos.	Driver	Nat.	No.	Entrant	Car/Engine	Laps	Time/Retirement	Speed (mph/km/h)	Gap to leader	Fastest race lap
1	**Lewis Hamilton**	GB	44	Mercedes AMG Petronas Motorsport	Mercedes F1 W08-Mercedes M08 EQ Power+ V6	58	2h 03m 23.544s	88.719/142.780		1m 45.008s 55
2	**Daniel Ricciardo**	AUS	3	Red Bull Racing	Red Bull RB13-TAG Heuer RB13 V6	58	2h 03m 28.051s	88.665/142.693	4.507s	1m 45.301s 57
3	**Valtteri Bottas**	FIN	77	Mercedes AMG Petronas Motorsport	Mercedes F1 W08-Mercedes M08 EQ Power+ V6	58	2h 03m 32.344s	88.614/142.610	8.800s	1m 45.405s 54
4	**Carlos Sainz**	E	55	Scuderia Toro Rosso	Toro Rosso STR12-Renault R.E.17 V6	58	2h 03m 46.366s	88.447/142.341	22.822s	1m 46.537s 52
5	**Sergio Pérez**	MEX	11	Sahara Force India Formula 1 Team	Force India VJM10-Mercedes M08 EQ Power+ V6	58	2h 03m 48.903s	88.416/142.292	25.359s	1m 46.731s 52
6	**Jolyon Palmer**	GB	30	Renault Sport Formula One Team	Renault R.S.17-R.E.17 V6	58	2h 03m 50.803s	88.394/142.256	27.259s	1m 46.722s 52
7	**Stoffel Vandoorne**	B	2	McLaren Honda Formula 1 Team	McLaren MCL32-Honda RA617H V6	58	2h 03m 53.932s	88.356/142.196	30.388s	1m 46.722s 57
8	**Lance Stroll**	CDN	18	Williams Martini Racing	Williams FW40-Mercedes M08 EQ Power+ V6	58	2h 04m 05.240s	88.222/141.980	41.696s	1m 47.512s 55
9	**Romain Grosjean**	F	8	Haas F1 Team	Haas VF-17-Ferrari 062 V6	58	2h 04m 06.826s	88.204/141.950	43.282s	1m 47.637s 54
10	**Esteban Ocon**	F	31	Sahara Force India Formula 1 Team	Force India VJM10-Mercedes M08 EQ Power+ V6	58	2h 04m 08.339s	88.186/141.921	44.795s	1m 47.677s 52
11	Felipe Massa	BR	19	Williams Martini Racing	Williams FW40-Mercedes M08 EQ Power+ V6	58	2h 04m 10.080s	88.165/141.888	46.536s	1m 47.055s 58
12	Pascal Wehrlein	D	94	Sauber F1 Team	Sauber C36-Ferrari 059/5 V6	56	2h 04m 50.858s	84.660/136.247	2 laps	1m 49.061s 56
	Kevin Magnussen	DK	20	Haas F1 Team	Haas VF-17-Ferrari 062 V6	50	power unit			1m 47.585s 44
	Nico Hülkenberg	D	27	Renault Sport Formula One Team	Renault R.S.17-R.E.17 V6	48	oil leak			1m 48.011s 37
	Marcus Ericsson	S	9	Sauber F1 Team	Sauber C36-Ferrari 059/5 V6	35	accident			1m 52.496s 35
	Daniil Kvyat	RUS	26	Scuderia Toro Rosso	Toro Rosso STR12-Renault R.E.17 V6	10	accident			2m 10.512s 10
	Fernando Alonso	E	14	McLaren Honda Formula 1 Team	McLaren MCL32-Honda RA617H V6	8	accident damage			2m 13.579s 6
	Sebastian Vettel	D	5	Scuderia Ferrari	Ferrari SF70H-062 V6	0	accident			
	Max Verstappen	NL	33	Red Bull Racing	Red Bull RB13-TAG Heuer RB13 V6	0	accident			
	Kimi Räikkönen	FIN	7	Scuderia Ferrari	Ferrari SF70H-062 V6	0	accident			

Race scheduled for 61 laps, but stopped after the 2-hour time limit.

Fastest race lap: Lewis Hamilton on lap 55, 1m 45.008s, 107.897mph/173.643km/h (new record).

Previous lap record: Kimi Räikkönen (Ferrari F2008 V8), 1m 45.599s, 107.336mph/172.740km/h (2008, 3.148-mile/5.067km circuit).

20 · ERICSSON · Sauber
5-place grid penalty for replacing gearbox

18 · STROLL · Williams

16 · MAGNUSSEN · Haas

14 · OCON · Force India

12 · PÉREZ · Force India

19 · WEHRLEIN · Sauber

17 · MASSA · Williams

15 · GROSJEAN · Haas

13 · KVYAT · Toro Rosso

11 · PALMER · Renault

Grid order	1	2	3	4	5	6	7	8	9	10	11	12	13	14	15	16	17	18	19	20	21	22	23	24	25	26	27	28	29	30	31	32	33	34	35	36	37	38	39	40	41	42	43	44	45	46
5 VETTEL	44	44	44	44	44	44	44	44	44	44	44	44	44	44	44	44	44	44	44	44	44	44	44	44	44	44	44	44	44	44	44	44	44	44	44	44	44	44	44	44	44	44	44	44	44	44
33 VERSTAPPEN	3	3	3	3	3	3	3	3	3	3	3	27	3	3	3	3	3	3	3	3	3	3	3	3	3	3	3	3	3	3	3	3	3	3	3	3	3	3	3	3	3	3	3	3	3	3
3 RICCIARDO	27	27	27	27	27	27	27	27	27	27	27	3	77	77	77	77	77	77	77	77	77	77	77	77	77	77	77	30	77	77	77	77	77	77	77	77	77	77	77	77	77	77	77	77	77	77
7 RÄIKKÖNEN	11	11	11	11	11	11	11	11	11	11	11	80	55	55	55	55	55	55	55	55	55	55	55	55	55	55	27	27	27	27	27	27	27	27	27	27	55	55	55	55	55	55	55	55	55	55
44 HAMILTON	77	77	77	77	30	30	30	30	30	30	11	30	27	27	27	27	27	27	27	27	27	27	27	27	27	11	27	77	55	55	55	55	55	55	55	11	11	11	11	11	11	11	11	11	11	11
77 BOTTAS	30	30	30	30	77	77	77	77	77	77	77	55	11	11	11	11	11	11	11	11	11	11	11	11	11	30	11	55	11	11	11	11	11	11	11	30	30	30	30	30	30	30	30	30	30	30
27 HÜLKENBERG	2	2	2	2	2	2	2	2	2	2	2		30	30	30	30	30	30	30	30	30	30	30	30	30	55	55	11	30	30	30	30	30	30	30	2	2	2	2	2	2	2	2	2	2	2
14 ALONSO	31	31	31	31	31	31	31	31	55	55	55	11	18	18	18	18	18	18	2	2	2	2	2	2	2	2	2	2	2	2	2	2	2	2	2	18	18	18	18	18	18	18	18	18		
2 VANDOORNE	55	55	55	55	55	55	55	55	31	31	31	18	2	2	2	2	2	18	18	18	18	18	18	18	18	18	18	18	18	18	18	18	18	8	8	8	8	8	8	8	8	8	8	8		
55 SAINZ	20	20	20	20	20	20	20	20	20	20	18	19	19	19	19	8	8	8	8	8	8	8	8	31	20	20	20	20	8	8	8	8	8	27	27	27	27	27	27	27						
30 PALMER	26	26	26	26	26	26	26	26	26	20	8	8	8	8	19	20	20	20	20	20	20	31	31	31	18	8	8	8	8	20	31	31	31	31	31	31	31	31	31	31						
11 PÉREZ	14	14	14	14	14	14	18	18	18	18	19	31	31	31	31	20	31	31	31	31	31	20	9	9	9	31	31	31	31	31	20	20	20	20	20	20	19	19	19	19						
26 KVYAT	18	18	18	18	18	18	19	19	19	19	94	9	9	94	20	31	9	9	9	9	9	20	20	20	19	19	19	19	19	19	19	19	19	19	20	20	20	20								
31 OCON	19	19	19	19	19	14		8	8	8	9	94	20	20	94	94	94	94	94	19	19	9	19	19	19	9	9	9	9	9	9	9	94	94	94	94	94	94	94	94						
8 GROSJEAN	8	8	8	8	8	8	8	9	9	9			2	19	19	19	9	94	94	94	94	94	94	94	9	9	9	94	94	94	94	94														
20 MAGNUSSEN	9	9	9	9	9	9	9	94	94	94																																				
19 MASSA	94	94	94	94	94	94	94	14																																						
18 STROLL																																														
94 WEHRLEIN																																														
9 ERICSSON																																														

44 = Pit stop   94 = One lap or more behind

All results and data © FOM 2017

TIME SHEETS

PRACTICE 1 (FRIDAY)
Weather: Dry/sunny
Temperatures: track 33–35°C, air 29–31°C

Pos.	Driver	Laps	Time
1	Daniel Ricciardo	21	1m 42.489s
2	Sebastian Vettel	21	1m 42.598s
3	Max Verstappen	23	1m 42.610s
4	Lewis Hamilton	27	1m 42.904s
5	Sergio Pérez	25	1m 43.423s
6	Valtteri Bottas	27	1m 43.434s
7	Kimi Räikkönen	25	1m 43.734s
8	Fernando Alonso	19	1m 43.759s
9	Nico Hülkenberg	24	1m 44.101s
10	Daniel Kvyat	25	1m 44.220s
11	Stoffel Vandoorne	25	1m 44.340s
12	Jolyon Palmer	25	1m 44.961s
13	Esteban Ocon	25	1m 45.053s
14	Felipe Massa	27	1m 45.084s
15	Romain Grosjean	20	1m 46.456s
16	Antonio Giovinazzi	27	1m 46.782s
17	Lance Stroll	11	1m 47.190s
18	Sean Gelael	26	1m 47.570s
19	Marcus Ericsson	23	1m 47.699s
20	Pascal Wehrlein	24	1m 47.886s

PRACTICE 2 (FRIDAY)
Weather: Dry/dark
Temperatures: track 33°C, air 29–30°C

Pos.	Driver	Laps	Time
1	Daniel Ricciardo	33	1m 40.852s
2	Max Verstappen	28	1m 41.408s
3	Lewis Hamilton	36	1m 41.555s
4	Valtteri Bottas	35	1m 42.104s
5	Nico Hülkenberg	33	1m 42.448s
6	Stoffel Vandoorne	34	1m 42.501s
7	Fernando Alonso	32	1m 42.788s
8	Sergio Pérez	35	1m 42.826s
9	Kimi Räikkönen	30	1m 42.835s
10	Esteban Ocon	34	1m 43.054s
11	Sebastian Vettel	33	1m 43.104s
12	Carlos Sainz	38	1m 43.236s
13	Daniil Kvyat	32	1m 43.608s
14	Jolyon Palmer	32	1m 43.795s
15	Felipe Massa	32	1m 43.836s
16	Lance Stroll	32	1m 44.301s
17	Kevin Magnussen	32	1m 44.417s
18	Romain Grosjean	29	1m 44.928s
19	Pascal Wehrlein	34	1m 45.673s
20	Marcus Ericsson	35	1m 45.721s

PRACTICE 3 (SATURDAY)
Weather: Dry/dusk
Temperatures: track 39°C, air 30–32°C

Pos.	Driver	Laps	Time
1	Max Verstappen	12	1m 41.829s
2	Sebastian Vettel	13	1m 41.901s
3	Lewis Hamilton	16	1m 41.971s
4	Fernando Alonso	11	1m 42.383s
5	Stoffel Vandoorne	13	1m 42.439s
6	Daniel Ricciardo	11	1m 42.517s
7	Nico Hülkenberg	10	1m 42.549s
8	Valtteri Bottas	16	1m 42.592s
9	Kimi Räikkönen	16	1m 42.708s
10	Sergio Pérez	14	1m 43.010s
11	Esteban Ocon	15	1m 43.109s
12	Carlos Sainz	17	1m 43.356s
13	Jolyon Palmer	11	1m 43.368s
14	Daniil Kvyat	17	1m 43.574s
15	Felipe Massa	17	1m 43.724s
16	Kevin Magnussen	16	1m 44.041s
17	Lance Stroll	18	1m 44.223s
18	Romain Grosjean	16	1m 44.295s
19	Pascal Wehrlein	15	1m 45.760s
20	Marcus Ericsson	7	1m 46.339s

QUALIFYING (SATURDAY)
Weather: Dry/dark Temperatures: track 33–34°C, air 28–29°C

Pos.	Driver	First	Second	Third	Qualifying Tyre
1	Sebastian Vettel	1m 43.336s	1m 40.529s	1m 39.491s	Ultrasoft (new)
2	Max Verstappen	1m 42.010s	1m 40.332s	1m 39.814s	Ultrasoft (new)
3	Daniel Ricciardo	1m 42.063s	1m 40.385s	1m 39.840s	Ultrasoft (new)
4	Kimi Räikkönen	1m 43.328s	1m 40.525s	1m 40.069s	Ultrasoft (new)
5	Lewis Hamilton	1m 42.455s	1m 40.577s	1m 40.126s	Ultrasoft (new)
6	Valtteri Bottas	1m 43.137s	1m 41.409s	1m 40.810s	Ultrasoft (new)
7	Nico Hülkenberg	1m 42.586s	1m 41.277s	1m 41.013s	Ultrasoft (new)
8	Fernando Alonso	1m 42.086s	1m 41.442s	1m 41.179s	Ultrasoft (new)
9	Stoffel Vandoorne	1m 42.222s	1m 41.227s	1m 41.398s	Ultrasoft (new)
10	Carlos Sainz	1m 42.176s	1m 41.826s	1m 42.056s	Ultrasoft (new)
11	Jolyon Palmer	1m 42.472s	1m 42.107s		
12	Sergio Pérez	1m 43.594s	1m 42.246s		
13	Daniil Kvyat	1m 42.544s	1m 42.338s		
14	Esteban Ocon	1m 43.626s	1m 42.760s		
15	Romain Grosjean	1m 43.627s	1m 43.883s		
16	Kevin Magnussen	1m 43.756s			
17	Felipe Massa	1m 44.014s			
18	Lance Stroll	1m 44.728s			
19	Pascal Wehrlein	1m 45.059s			
20	Marcus Ericsson	1m 45.570s			

QUALIFYING: head to head

Hamilton	9	5	Bottas
Vettel	10	4	Räikkönen
Massa	11	2	Stroll
Stroll	1	0	Di Resta
Ricciardo	4	10	Verstappen
Pérez	11	3	Ocon
Hülkenberg	14	0	Palmer
Kvyat	6	8	Sainz
Ericsson	2	0	Giovinazzi
Ericsson	4	8	Wehrlein
Alonso	11	2	Vandoorne
Vandoorne	1	0	Button
Grosjean	10	4	Magnussen

POINTS

DRIVERS
1	Lewis Hamilton	263
2	Sebastian Vettel	235
3	Valtteri Bottas	212
4	Daniel Ricciardo	162
5	Kimi Räikkönen	138
6	Max Verstappen	68
7	Sergio Pérez	68
8	Esteban Ocon	56
9	Carlos Sainz	48
10	Nico Hülkenberg	34
11	Felipe Massa	31
12	Lance Stroll	28
13	Romain Grosjean	26
14	Kevin Magnussen	11
15	Fernando Alonso	10
16	Jolyon Palmer	8
17	Stoffel Vandoorne	7
18	Pascal Wehrlein	5
19	Daniil Kvyat	4

CONSTRUCTORS
1	Mercedes	475
2	Ferrari	373
3	Red Bull	230
4	Force India	124
5	Williams	59
6	Toro Rosso	52
7	Renault	42
8	Haas	37
9	McLaren	17
10	Sauber	5

10 · SAINZ · Toro Rosso

8 · ALONSO · McLaren

6 · BOTTAS · Mercedes

4 · RÄIKKÖNEN · Ferrari

2 · VERSTAPPEN · Red Bull

9 · VANDOORNE · McLaren

7 · HÜLKENBERG · Renault

5 · HAMILTON · Mercedes

3 · RICCIARDO · Red Bull

1 · VETTEL · Ferrari

47	48	49	50	51	52	53	54	55	56	57	58	
44	44	44	44	44	44	44	44	44	44	44	44	1
3	3	3	3	3	3	3	3	3	3	3	3	2
77	77	77	77	77	77	77	77	77	77	77	77	3
55	55	55	55	55	55	55	55	55	55	55	55	4
11	11	11	11	11	11	11	11	11	11	11	11	5
30	30	30	30	30	30	30	30	30	30	30	30	6
2	2	2	2	2	2	2	2	2	2	2	2	7
18	18	18	18	18	18	18	18	18	18	18	18	8
8	8	8	8	8	8	8	8	8	8	8	8	9
27	31	31	31	31	31	31	31	31	31	31	31	10
31	19	19	19	19	19	19	19	19	19	19	19	
19	20	20	20	94	94	94	94	94	94			
20	27	94	94									
94	94											

■ Safety car deployed on laps shown

RACE TYRE STRATEGIES

	Driver	Race Stint 1	Race Stint 2	Race Stint 3	Race Stint 4	Race Stint 5
1	Hamilton	Inter (n): 1–29	Ultrasoft (u): 30–58			
2	Ricciardo	Inter (n): 1–11	Inter (n): 12–28	Ultrasoft (u): 29–58		
3	Bottas	Inter (n): 1–28	Ultrasoft (u): 29–58			
4	Sainz	Inter (n): 1–27	Supersoft (n): 28–58			
5	Pérez	Wet (n): 1–11	Inter (n): 12–28	Ultrasoft (n): 29–58		
6	Palmer	Wet (n): 1–12	Inter (n): 13–29	Ultrasoft (u): 30–58		
7	Vandoorne	Wet (n): 1–12	Inter (n): 13–27	Ultrasoft (u): 28–58		
8	Stroll	Inter (n): 1–26	Ultrasoft (u): 27–58			
9	Grosjean	Inter (n): 1–27	Ultrasoft (u): 28–58			
10	Ocon	Wet (n): 1–11	Inter (n): 12–27	Ultrasoft (n): 28–38	Ultrasoft (n): 39–58	
11	Massa	Wet (n): 1–17	Inter (n): 18–24	Ultrasoft (n): 25–37	Ultrasoft (n): 38–58	
12	Wehrlein	Wet (n): 1–2	Wet (n): 3–21	Inter (n): 22–28	Ultrasoft (n): 29–37	Ultrasoft (n): 38–56
	Magnussen	Wet (n): 1–11	Inter (n): 12–24	Ultrasoft (n): 25–38	Ultrasoft (n): 39–50 (dnf)	
	Hülkenberg	Wet (n): 1–12	Inter (n): 13–28	Ultrasoft (n): 29–38	Ultrasoft (n): 39–48 (dnf)	
	Ericsson	Wet (n): 1–2	Wet (n): 3–13	Inter (n): 14–27	Soft (n): 28–31	Ultrasoft (n): 32–35 (dnf)
	Kvyat	Inter (n): 1–10 (dnf)				
	Alonso	Wet (n): 1–8 (dnf)				
	Vettel	Inter (n): 0 (dnf)				
	Verstappen	Inter (n): 0 (dnf)				
	Räikkönen	Inter (n): 0 (dnf)				

At least two of three dry tyre specs must be used in a dry race. If Wet or Intermediate tyres are needed, this rule is suspended.

Pirelli P Zero sidewall logos are colour-coded: Green = Intermediate; Blue = Wet; Purple = Ultrasoft; Red = Supersoft; Yellow = Soft. (n) new (u) used

FIA FORMULA 1 WORLD CHAMPIONSHIP · ROUND 15

MALAYSIAN GRAND PRIX

SEPANG CIRCUIT

SEPANG QUALIFYING

THE chances of Lewis Hamilton setting a 70th career pole on F1's final visit to Sepang looked remote indeed after the opening day's running in Malaysia. Mercedes had a new aero package to try, but, new or old, they didn't seem to have any answer to either Ferrari's single-lap or long-run pace.

At the conclusion of FP2, Hamilton and Valtteri Bottas were sixth and seventh, a huge 1.4s adrift of Sebastian Vettel's ultimate pace. And it wasn't just Ferrari. They were also slower than both Red Bulls.

With most of FP1 having been lost to rain, there was much work to be done. But on Saturday morning, the tide began to turn. The Mercs were closer, Bottas just over four-tenths behind Räikkönen's Ferrari. And, after the unexpected gift of Singapore, the gods seemed to be smiling on them again. In FP3, Vettel was in trouble, cruising back to the pits with no power. In the two hours preceding qualifying, the crew changed engines, to his fourth and last power unit before penalties would be applied.

But when Vettel took to the track again, there was another problem, and he cruised back to the pits. "It feels like there's no turbo," he said. Cue frantic activity around the back of the car. A new set of supersoft Pirellis was bolted on, but he did not re-emerge. On the back of his Singapore disaster, he was out in Q1 without a time and would start 20th and last.

At Mercedes, Hamilton had gone back to the standard aero package, while teammate Bottas had remained with the new version. The set-up changes helped, as did the cooler track temperature of the later qualifying hour, allowing the team to get its tyres into the correct operating window and generate grip, which had not been the case on Friday.

If ever Ferrari needed Räikkönen to step up to the plate it was now, but ultimately he came up five-hundredths short, Hamilton's first Q3 run stopping the clocks in 1m 30.076s; Kimi could only manage 1m 30.121s.

Hamilton's lap was a fantastic effort, almost a second quicker than his Q2 time, the kind of thing that, more than once during the season, had made the difference. You don't take 70 poles by accident...

Hamilton was also coping with an MGU-K de-rate issue, involving loss of additional power from the energy recovery system. As Toto Wolff explained, solving that was a team effort, which involved engine and data engineers both at the circuit and at Brixworth and Brackley. Their rapid response prompted a radio message to Lewis, telling him to "hold the RS button for ten seconds", which overrode the problem and helped secure his all-important pole.

Having topped Q2 and found an extra 0.05s, Bottas, in the other W08, was nowhere near, separated from Hamilton by almost seven-tenths – and two Red Bulls.

"Mid-corner, I'm losing a lot of front end, and it's tricky to get the car turned," Valtteri explained. "That overheats the front left tyre, and I'm also four-wheel sliding in high-speed corners. If I go quicker, I just slide more and struggle with tyre temperatures."

Even without the benefit of strong Q3 engine modes, Max Verstappen and Daniel Ricciardo were a couple of tenths quicker than Bottas, and Christian Horner's men annexed the second row. The gap between them was the usual five-hundredths, the Dutchman, on his 20th birthday, just shading the Australian.

Esteban Ocon produced the best qualifying performance of his short F1 career when he put the first Force India an impressive sixth on the grid, albeit more than seven-tenths from Bottas and a tenth quicker than an equally impressive Stoffel Vandoorne in the McLaren Honda. The mid-grid battle was as fiercely contested as ever, with Nico Hülkenberg just a couple of hundredths behind the Belgian and five-hundredths clear of Sergio Pérez in the second Force India. The Mexican was a similar margin ahead of Fernando Alonso, who was not used to qualifying three slots shy of his team-mate!

Pérez was fortunate to be on the grid at all, as he was suffering from a debilitating virus that had weakened him considerably and forced him to contemplate withdrawal. Not the sort of affliction you want in the heat and humidity of Sepang.

The latest-specification Merc engines, debuted by the works team at Spa, were available to Force India and Williams for the first time in Malaysia, but weren't quite enough to put Massa through to Q3. He missed out to Alonso by a couple of hundredths, being separated from Williams team-mate Lance Stroll by Jolyon Palmer.

The Toro Rossos also went out in Q2, Carlos Sainz a tenth behind Stroll and 0.15s quicker than an impressive F1 debut performance from French reigning GP2 champion Pierre Gasly, drafted into the Faenza squad in place of Daniil Kvyat.

Malaysian practice and qualifying were not kind to the Haas team. Romain Grosjean suffered a big shunt on Friday afternoon, when a faulty drain cover weld at Turn 12 allowed the cover to be flicked up. Grosjean ran over it, shredding his right rear Pirelli in the process, which pitched the Haas into the barrier at high speed. Thankfully he was okay, but the damage was estimated to be the thick end of half a million quid. Team principal Guenther Steiner did not see why the team should foot the bill, but with F1 not due to return to Malaysia any time soon, was not wholly confident that an invoice to the circuit would bear fruit...

Both Grosjean and Kevin Magnussen joined Sauber men Pascal Wehrlein and Marcus Ericsson as Q1 victims, along with the hapless Vettel.

DESPITE Hamilton's pole position, fellow front-row starter Räikkönen was a heavy pre-race favourite, so it was yet another hammer blow to Ferrari when he reported no power and an empty battery on the way to the grid.

The crew descended on the car, the engine cover came off, but the signs were not good. Before the formation lap, Räikkönen's car was pushed off the grid and back into the Ferrari garage, where work continued, but to no avail. The problem was traced to a similar issue to that which had hobbled Vettel in qualifying – a component between the compressor and engine. The wheels had totally fallen off Maranello's title challenge, and head honcho Sergio Marchionne was left demanding an overhaul of quality control procedures.

Such had been Ferrari's race pace on Friday that this truly was the one that got away. The question now was: could Hamilton run away from the Red Bulls? He'd enjoyed half a second over them in qualifying, but almost all of that could be accounted for by qualifying engine modes, and nobody at Mercedes was kidding themselves that this was going to be an easy one.

The track was still slightly damp from a pre-race shower, but when the lights went out, Hamilton got the power down from the slightly drier right-hand side of the grid and converted his pole. Bottas took full advantage of Räikkönen's absence to flick left and go around the outside of both Red Bulls at Turn One. He pulled it off with Ricciardo, but spirited defence and savvy car placement by Verstappen meant that the No. 33 car ran second and immediately started hassling the lead Mercedes.

Hamilton was having de-rate issues again. When, on lap three, Red Bull heard Mercedes tell him over the radio that his battery was not fully charged, they told Verstappen to attack immediately. Using DRS, he flicked out of the Merc's slipstream heading into Turn One for the fourth time and dived down the inside to take the lead. Hamilton, against his racer's instincts, but mindful of the bigger picture, elected not to close the door. He also had a de-rate at that point,

too. Verstappen, with pace to spare, had been able to save some energy.

"I had de-rate problems again," Hamilton confirmed. "There's switch settings and something different we have, and they're going to reassess and work on it for the future so we don't have those kinds of issues. We've not had it for a while. We had some new configurations, and I'd make a change and it threw a spanner into the mix. I was having some de-rates which enabled Max to get closer, but even if I didn't, it would have just delayed the inevitable, because they were quicker in so many areas."

Unable to run at the pace of the leading duo, Bottas was 6s behind after five laps and under intense pressure from Ricciardo. He managed to keep the Australian at bay until lap nine, when Daniel made it a Red Bull 1-3 by running around the outside of Turn One and claiming the inside at Turn Two. The battle continued all the way to Turn Four, where Daniel decisively claimed the inside.

By this point, Vettel – having started from the back on Pirelli's soft tyre, rather than the supersofts of the top ten qualifiers – had worked his way into the top ten. He was 25s behind the race leader and just 12s from Bottas, although about to lose some time behind a stubborn Alonso.

Behind Ricciardo, Vandoorne had made a fine start to run fifth, while there was a close call between the Force Indias – again! – at Turn Two as Pérez went for the inside and Ocon, accommodating him, clattered into Massa. He needed to pit for a new nose, while Felipe suffered a damaged floor and had lost out to both Force Indias and team-mate Stroll by the time he had sorted himself out.

Pérez was not driving like a man weakened by illness and usurped Vandoorne's fifth place when Stoffel ran wide at Turn Two. The Mexican's former Force India team-mate, Hülkenberg, was not having a stellar afternoon. Having dropped to 12th from his eighth grid slot and frustrated, he elected to stop as early as lap nine in a bid to undercut a tightly-packed group ahead, which included Magnussen, Alonso and the Williams pair.

Williams responded by pitting Massa, who was more

Above: Max Verstappen grabs his opportunity to attack Lewis Hamilton on the main straight.
Photo: Red Bull Racing/Getty Images

Top left: Can I have my wheel back? Sebastian Vettel thanks Pascal Wehrlein for his impromptu post-race lift back to the pits.
Photo: WRi2/Jerry Andre

Above left: Toro Rosso's Pierre Gasly prepares for his F1 baptism.
Photo: Peter J. Fox

Left: Terminal problems for Kimi Räikkönen as his Ferrari receives attention on the grid.
Photo: Lukas Gorys

Below left: A free practice outing for newly-crowned Formula 2 champion Charles Leclerc, seen here with his manager, Nicolas Todt.
Photo: Sauber F1 Team

Opening spread: Man of the moment. A victorious Max Verstappen is hoisted above the scrum as the photographers scramble desperately for a picture.
Photo: Red Bull Racing/Getty Images

vulnerable to being undercut with his damaged car. They brought in Stroll on the following lap, with the result that the team effectively undercut Felipe ahead of his team-mate, much to Stroll's disgust.

To play fair, and given that Stroll's car was healthy, Massa was asked to let Lance back past, but there was also Vandoorne to consider. The lead McLaren had only been 4s ahead of Massa when Felipe had pitted, and now, after completing a further two laps, it was not guaranteed to get back out ahead of the Williams pair. It didn't, but Vandoorne was just able to scythe back through at Turn Two amid the confusion as Massa and Stroll played 'after you'. Not ideal…

Hülkenberg, having triggered a set of early reactive stops, was great for Vettel, who found cars that might have been difficult to get by pitting out of his way. It didn't work out so well for Hülkenberg, however, as higher than anticipated tyre degradation on the soft meant he would be the only man other than Grosjean to require a fairly disastrous second

stop, which sentenced him to an eventual 16th place, ahead of only the Saubers. Contrast that with Ocon, who went the distance and claimed the final point on a set of softs bolted on when he had stopped on lap two for damage.

Vettel was sixth by lap 13 and less than 7s behind Pérez's Force India, in turn only a couple of seconds shy of Bottas's Mercedes. Six laps later, the Ferrari was with the Force India and, by lap 17, was actually in Hamilton's pit-stop window, meaning that the second-placed Mercedes, now 8.5s behind Verstappen, could not pit without falling behind the longer-running prime-shod Ferrari.

On lap 21 of the 56, Vettel passed Pérez to go fifth and, for three consecutive laps, was the fastest car on the track, lapping a couple of tenths faster than race leader Verstappen, despite being on the harder tyre. That brought him within DRS range of Bottas on lap 24.

With the second Mercedes lapping in the mid-1m 37s, however, a full second slower than Vettel had been going,

the following three laps trapped behind Bottas pushed Vettel just back out of Hamilton's pit-stop window. That allowed Mercedes to pit the No. 44 car on lap 26.

"Lewis's front tyres were just starting to take a drop, and the worst thing we could have done was get him behind Vettel and have the two collide," confirmed a team strategist.

Mercedes might then have been expected to pit Bottas on the next lap, while still in front of Vettel, but only the Ferrari came in on lap 27. Bottas stopped next time around.

"We knew there was a very strong risk that Vettel could undercut us on that lap, but what we wanted to do was force Vettel to either go really long or stop. We didn't think we'd have defended Vettel with Valtteri, even if we stopped first. Vettel, on brand new supersofts, would probably have just driven past. This way at least forced Vettel to stop on that lap, which created the best situation for Lewis at the end of the race, because Sebastian's supersofts were going to be that bit older."

It was a reflection of Ferrari's superiority that Mercedes was having to become tactical to defend against a car that had started from the back of the grid. Malaysia, without doubt, was the toughest race of the season for the defending champions.

Despite starting last, Vettel looked like he could still threaten the podium. Having undercut his way past Bottas, he set lap record after lap record as he closed the gap to third-placed Ricciardo. He was 26s behind Hamilton's

second place with 26 laps to go and started to reduce that margin by more than the required second per lap. The further the Ferrari went into its supersoft stint, though, the greater its relative tyre degradation would become.

Vettel reached DRS range of Ricciardo's third-placed Red Bull with 11 laps to go; Hamilton was a further 8s in front. His supersofts still appeared to have strong pace (lap 45 was a 1m 34.386s compared to his 1m 34.080s record lap on lap 41), but four laps behind the Red Bull in the mid-1m 35s meant that was as far as the Ferrari would climb. Ricciardo defended resolutely into Turn One, and now Vettel was running short of fuel. He backed off significantly in the closing stages, to the tune of 5–6s on the final lap.

Ferrari had light-fuelled Vettel to help him get through the field in the early stages, in anticipation of assistance from rain, a safety car, or both to help balance the books, but neither was forthcoming.

While Hamilton and Mercedes did not have Ferrari or Red Bull race pace at Sepang, they were in control in that final stint. Hamilton was given target times to drive to, evidenced by a trio of laps in the mid-1m 34s from laps 47 to 49, Mercedes calculating that even if Vettel had passed Ricciardo immediately and hadn't backed off, he would not have come closer to Lewis than 2s – impressive nonetheless!

Although he could do nothing about Verstappen, Hamilton did have sufficient pace to control his margin to Ricciardo who, admittedly, had the edge taken off his initial supersofts

Above: Best of the rest. Sergio Pérez fought off a virus to bring home his Force India sixth.
Photo: Sahara Force India F1 Team

Above left: Stoffel Vandoorne out-paced team-mate Alonso throughout the weekend, delivering his best F1 drive to date to take seventh for McLaren Honda.
Photo: Peter J. Fox

Left: Once Max Verstappen had made his decisive pass on Lewis Hamilton, the Dutchman pulled away to finish 12 seconds clear.
Photo: Lukas Gorys

Above: Verstappen's convincing win is cheered by the Red Bull mechanics.
Photo: Peter J. Fox

Above right: It was like this. Lewis Hamilton and Max Verstappen discuss their respective races.
Photo: Red Bull Racing/Getty Images

Right: Farewell Sepang. A crowd of over 56,000 turned out to see Formula 1 cars running in anger in Malaysia's last F1 grand prix.
Photo: Peter J. Fox

by his struggle to get past Bottas. Red Bull then left Daniel out a bit longer to ensure that he had decent tyres with which to resist Vettel later on.

Vettel's fourth place came after a fine drive, but there was more drama to come for Ferrari when he collided with Stroll at Turn Five on the slowdown lap as both picked up some rubber off-line. The impact to his left rear was heavy, and there was an initial fear that it would mean a fresh gearbox and a grid penalty for Japan, which somehow turned out not to be the case.

Conspiracy theorists suggested that perhaps Vettel knew that he did not have the litre of fuel left to provide the requisite sample. When he took his steering wheel with him (which may have provided a fuel read-out) and hitched a ride back on Wehrlein's Sauber, that fanned the flames. He explained that with the wheels turned and the car immobile, he couldn't reattach the steering wheel and thought better of leaving it in the seat with the crowd potentially spilling on to the track to pinch it.

Against the conspiracies, it's worth pointing out that with almost 19s in hand over Bottas at the flag, Vettel could actually have backed off even more if need be.

Behind Bottas, the brave Pérez was a drained sixth, ahead

of an impressive Vandoorne, who had managed to stave off both Williams by the best part of ten seconds. It's not often that someone beats Fernando Alonso over a race distance in the same car, and the Spaniard made no excuses. "Stoffel just did a better job in practice, qualifying and the race," he acknowledged.

Verstappen was delighted. "A great way to start your next decade," Christian Horner told him over the radio. His debut win for the team at Barcelona in 2016 may have been strategy assisted, but he'd won this one completely on merit, and beaten Hamilton and Mercedes in a straight fight.

"I knew that Lewis was fighting for the championship and wouldn't take too many risks, so I just went for it," Max smiled. "As soon as I passed him, I knew from there onwards I could control the race."

Hamilton couldn't help but beat himself up a little about not fighting harder, but he knew that it had been in the interest of the bigger picture. From two consecutive races where he had been up against it and Ferrari had had conclusively the fastest car, somehow he had emerged with a 34-point championship lead. All of a sudden, Vettel's Singapore start was looking very expensive. And, you could bet, he knew it.

Tony Dodgins

VIEWPOINT
CONSIDERING THE LONG GAME

COMPARE and contrast. One weekend in Singapore, a contender seems to forget that the championship is the ultimate aim as he eliminates both himself and his team-mate. At the next race in Malaysia, the same man's rival demonstrates how world titles are constructed over a season and not through the work of a moment at the start of one race.

Racing drivers hate losing – none more so than Lewis Hamilton, who usually looks like he wishes he was somewhere else other than on the second or third step of the podium. For these guys, it's as if the top step should be theirs by right because … well, "Nobody is faster than me," and that's an end to the discussion.

That's why Hamilton was not exactly a bundle of joy when the trophies were handed out in Sepang. In his heart of hearts, he knew that he and Mercedes should have had the measure of Max Verstappen and Red Bull. But other matters – the championship and, as the accompanying report points out, a de-rate issue – dictated otherwise.

Hamilton had to show massive self-control as he raced towards Sepang's first corner, knowing that a young upstart – 12 years his junior – was going to have a go in exactly the same way that he would have done when he went for everything in sight back in the day.

Lewis also knew that Max Verstappen would be working on the assumption that he would probably show the degree of prudence necessary when fighting for the championship. In other words, the Red Bull driver would use that to add even more impetus – if that were possible – to his attack.

When the moment came at the start of lap four, Hamilton adopted a sensible approach and kept resistance to a level far below what it might have been had there been just this race to play for.

Unlike Sebastian Vettel in the highly charged seconds after the start in Singapore, Hamilton had plenty of time to think this through. But that's the only reasonable caveat when comparing crucial and very different approaches to the long game.

Maurice Hamilton

15

2017 FORMULA 1
PETRONAS
MALAYSIAN
GRAND PRIX

ROLEX

OFFICIAL TIMEPIECE

KUALA LUMPUR 29 SEPTEMBER–1 OCTOBER

RACE DISTANCE: 56 laps, 192.879 miles/310.408km

RACE WEATHER: Dry/cloudy (track 37–42°C, air 30–32°C)

SEPANG INTERNATIONAL CIRCUIT, KUALA LUMPUR
Circuit: 3.444 miles / 5.543km, 56 laps
187/116 kmh/mph
Gear
DRS zone

Turn 6 255/158
Turn 4 110/68
Turn 7 175/109
Turn 3 265/165
Hairpin 88/55
Turn 5 235/146
Turn 8 180/112
Turn 2 65/40
335/208
340/211
Turn 9 74/46
Turn 1 90/56
Turn 10 195/121
Turn 14 110/68
Turn 10 125/78
Turn 12 200/124
Turn 13

RACE – OFFICIAL CLASSIFICATION

Pos.	Driver	Nat.	No.	Entrant	Car/Engine	Laps	Time/Retirement	Speed (mph/km/h)	Gap to leader	Fastest race lap	
1	**Max Verstappen**	NL	33	Red Bull Racing	Red Bull RB13-TAG Heuer RB13 V6	56	1h 30m 01.290s	128.555/206.889		1m 34.467s	50
2	**Lewis Hamilton**	GB	44	Mercedes AMG Petronas Motorsport	Mercedes F1 W08-Mercedes M08 EQ Power+ V6	56	1h 30m 14.060s	128.252/206.401	12.770s	1m 34.452s	48
3	**Daniel Ricciardo**	AUS	3	Red Bull Racing	Red Bull RB13-TAG Heuer RB13 V6	56	1h 30m 23.809s	128.021/206.030	22.519s	1m 34.770s	55
4	**Sebastian Vettel**	D	5	Scuderia Ferrari	Ferrari SF70H-062 V6	56	1h 30m 38.652s	127.671/205.467	37.362s	1m 34.080s	41
5	**Valtteri Bottas**	FIN	77	Mercedes AMG Petronas Motorsport	Mercedes F1 W08-Mercedes M08 EQ Power+ V6	56	1h 30m 57.311s	127.235/204.765	56.021s	1m 35.284s	44
6	**Sergio Pérez**	MEX	11	Sahara Force India Formula 1 Team	Force India VJM10-Mercedes M08 EQ Power+ V6	56	1h 31m 19.920s	126.710/203.920	1m 18.630s	1m 35.591s	32
7	**Stoffel Vandoorne**	B	2	McLaren Honda Formula 1 Team	McLaren MCL32-Honda RA617H V6	55			1 lap	1m 35.931s	49
8	**Lance Stroll**	CDN	18	Williams Martini Racing	Williams FW40-Mercedes M08 EQ Power+ V6	55			1 lap	1m 36.627s	46
9	**Felipe Massa**	BR	19	Williams Martini Racing	Williams FW40-Mercedes M08 EQ Power+ V6	55			1 lap	1m 36.944s	44
10	**Esteban Ocon**	F	31	Sahara Force India Formula 1 Team	Force India VJM10-Mercedes M08 EQ Power+ V6	55			1 lap	1m 37.075s	36
11	Fernando Alonso	E	14	McLaren Honda Formula 1 Team	McLaren MCL32-Honda RA617H V6	55			1 lap	1m 36.501s	55
12	Kevin Magnussen	DK	20	Haas F1 Team	Haas VF-17-Ferrari 062 V6	55			1 lap	1m 37.192s	46
13	Romain Grosjean	F	8	Haas F1 Team	Haas VF-17-Ferrari 062 V6	55			1 lap	1m 35.796s	49
14	Pierre Gasly	F	10	Scuderia Toro Rosso	Toro Rosso STR12-Renault R.E.17 V6	55			1 lap	1m 37.170s	45
15	Jolyon Palmer	GB	30	Renault Sport Formula One Team	Renault R.S.17-R.E.17 V6	55			1 lap	1m 37.186s	45
16	Nico Hülkenberg	D	27	Renault Sport Formula One Team	Renault R.S.17-R.E.17 V6	55			1 lap	1m 34.266s	52
17	Pascal Wehrlein	D	94	Sauber F1 Team	Sauber C36-Ferrari 059/5 V6	55			1 lap	1m 36.395s	53
18	Marcus Ericsson	S	9	Sauber F1 Team	Sauber C36-Ferrari 059/5 V6	54			2 laps	1m 36.630s	54
	Carlos Sainz	E	55	Scuderia Toro Rosso	Toro Rosso STR12-Renault R.E.17 V6	29	electrics			1m 38.123s	27
NS	Kimi Räikkönen	FIN	7	Scuderia Ferrari	Ferrari SF70H-062 V6		power unit				

Fastest race lap: Sebastian Vettel on lap 41, 1m 34.080s, 131.796mph/212.104km/h (new record).

Previous lap record: Juan Pablo Montoya (Williams FW26-BMW V10), 1m 34.223s, 131.596mph/211.782km/h (2004).

20 · VETTEL · Ferrari
20-place grid penalty for using additional power unit elements

18 · WEHRLEIN · Sauber
16 · GROSJEAN · Haas

14 · SAINZ · Toro Rosso
12 · PALMER · Renault

19 · ERICSSON · Sauber
17 · MAGNUSSEN · Haas
15 · GASLY · Toro Rosso
13 · STROLL · Williams
11 · MASSA · Williams

Grid order	1	2	3	4	5	6	7	8	9	10	11	12	13	14	15	16	17	18	19	20	21	22	23	24	25	26	27	28	29	30	31	32	33	34	35	36	37	38	39	40	41	42	43	44
44 HAMILTON	44	44	44	33	33	33	33	33	33	33	33	33	33	33	33	33	33	33	33	33	33	33	33	33	33	33	33	33	3	3	33	33	33	33	33	33	33	33	33	33	33	33	33	
7 RÄIKKÖNEN	33	33	33	44	44	44	44	44	44	44	44	44	44	44	44	44	44	44	44	44	44	44	44	44	44	44	44	3	33	33	44	44	44	44	44	44	44	44	44	44	44	44	44	44
33 VERSTAPPEN	77	77	77	77	77	77	77	77	3	3	3	3	3	3	3	3	3	3	3	3	3	3	3	3	3	3	3	44	44	44	3	3	3	3	3	3	3	3	3	3	3	3	3	3
3 RICCIARDO	3	3	3	3	3	3	3	77	77	77	77	77	77	77	77	77	77	77	77	77	77	77	77	77	77	77	77	11	11	5	5	5	5	5	5	5	5	5	5	5	5	5	5	5
77 BOTTAS	2	2	2	2	2	2	2	11	11	11	11	11	11	11	11	11	11	11	11	11	5	5	5	5	5	5	5	5	11	5	77	77	77	77	77	77	77	77	77	77	77	77	77	77
31 OCON	11	11	11	11	11	11	11	2	2	2	2	2	5	5	5	5	5	5	5	5	11	11	11	11	11	11	5	77	77	11	11	11	11	11	11	11	11	11	11	11	11	11	11	11
2 VANDOORNE	31	18	18	18	18	18	18	18	18	18	18	5	2	14	14	14	14	14	14	14	14	14	14	14	15	55	55	55	2	2	2	2	2	2	2	2	2	2	2	2	2	2	2	2
27 HÜLKENBERG	18	19	19	19	19	19	19	19	19	19	5	18	14	55	55	55	55	55	55	55	55	55	55	55	55	14	2	2	18	18	18	18	18	18	18	18	18	18	18	18	18	18	18	18
11 PÉREZ	19	20	20	20	20	20	20	20	5	5	19	14	55	31	31	31	31	31	31	31	31	31	31	31	2	2	18	18	55	19	19	19	19	19	19	19	19	19	19	19	19	19	19	19
14 ALONSO	20	14	14	14	14	14	14	5	14	14	14	30	30	2	2	2	2	2	2	2	2	2	2	2	18	18	19	19	19	31	31	31	31	31	31	31	31	31	31	31	31	31	31	31
19 MASSA	14	31	5	5	5	5	5	14	14	30	30	55	31	94	18	18	18	18	18	18	18	18	18	18	19	19	31	31	31	27	27	27	27	27	27	27	27	27	27	27	27	27	27	27
30 PALMER	27	5	27	27	27	27	27	27	30	20	55	10	94	18	94	19	19	19	19	19	19	19	19	19	31	31	20	27	27	30	30	30	30	30	14	14	14	14	14	14	14	14	14	14
18 STROLL	5	27	30	30	30	30	30	55	55	10	31	19	19	19	94	94	94	20	20	20	20	20	20	20	20	30	30	20	14	14	14	14	14	30	20	20	20	20	20	20	20	20	20	20
55 SAINZ	30	30	55	55	55	55	55	10	10	8	94	18	20	20	20	2	27	27	27	27	27	27	27	30	30	20	14	20	20	20	20	10	20	10	10	10	10	10	10	10	10	10	10	
10 GASLY	55	10	10	10	10	10	10	27	8	31	19	9	27	27	27	30	30	30	30	30	30	14	14	14	10	10	10	14	10	10	10	20	10	20	30	30	30	30	30	30	30	30	30	
8 GROSJEAN	10	10	8	8	8	8	8	8	94	94	9	20	9	30	30	20	20	14	94	94	94	10	10	10	10	94	94	94	94	94	94	94	94	94	94	8	8	8	8	8	8	8	8	
20 MAGNUSSEN	94	94	94	94	94	94	94	94	31	9	9	27	30	9	9	10	10	10	10	10	10	94	94	94	94	8	8	8	8	8	8	8	94	94	94	94	94	94	94	94	94	94	94	
94 WEHRLEIN	9	8	9	9	9	9	9	31	31	9	20	27	10	10	10	9	9	9	9	9	8	8	8	8	8	9	9	9	9	9	9	9	9	9	9	9	9	9	9	9	9	9	9	
9 ERICSSON	8	9	31	31	31	31	31	9	9	27	27	8	8	8	8	8	8	8	8	9	9	9	9	9	9	9	9	9	9															
5 VETTEL																																												

TIME SHEETS

PRACTICE 1 (FRIDAY)
Weather: Rain/cloudy
Temperatures: track 27–31°C, air 24–27°C

Pos.	Driver	Laps	Time
1	Max Verstappen	11	1m 48.962s
2	Daniel Ricciardo	12	1m 49.719s
3	Fernando Alonso	6	1m 50.597s
4	Kimi Räikkönen	12	1m 50.734s
5	Sebastian Vettel	12	1m 51.009s
6	Lewis Hamilton	8	1m 51.518s
7	Valtteri Bottas	10	1m 52.007s
8	Lance Stroll	9	1m 52.295s
9	Pierre Gasly	14	1m 52.380s
10	Sergey Sirotkin	10	1m 53.521s
11	Jolyon Palmer	10	1m 53.625s
12	Stoffel Vandoorne	10	1m 53.771s
13	Esteban Ocon	6	1m 53.896s
14	Sean Gelael	13	1m 54.610s
15	Sergio Pérez	4	1m 54.669s
16	Charles Leclerc	10	1m 55.280s
17	Pascal Wehrlein	10	1m 55.652s
18	Romain Grosjean	8	1m 56.211s
19	Antonio Giovinazzi	6	1m 56.339s
20	Felipe Massa	3	no time

PRACTICE 2 (FRIDAY)
Weather: Dry/sunny-cloudy
Temperatures: track 39–44°C, air 29–31°C

Pos.	Driver	Laps	Time
1	Sebastian Vettel	23	1m 31.261s
2	Kimi Räikkönen	19	1m 31.865s
3	Daniel Ricciardo	19	1m 32.099s
4	Max Verstappen	11	1m 32.109s
5	Fernando Alonso	14	1m 32.564s
6	Lewis Hamilton	15	1m 32.677s
7	Valtteri Bottas	21	1m 32.720s
8	Sergio Pérez	20	1m 32.862s
9	Nico Hülkenberg	24	1m 33.060s
10	Esteban Ocon	24	1m 33.096s
11	Jolyon Palmer	26	1m 33.381s
12	Felipe Massa	20	1m 33.394s
13	Stoffel Vandoorne	15	1m 33.673s
14	Lance Stroll	16	1m 33.818s
15	Pierre Gasly	22	1m 34.043s
16	Carlos Sainz	19	1m 34.104s
17	Romain Grosjean	18	1m 34.118s
18	Kevin Magnussen	17	1m 34.343s
19	Pascal Wehrlein	29	1m 35.246s
20	Marcus Ericsson	27	1m 35.697s

PRACTICE 3 (SATURDAY)
Weather: Dry/sunny
Temperatures: track 43–46°C, air 31–32°C

Pos.	Driver	Laps	Time
1	Kimi Räikkönen	19	1m 31.880s
2	Sebastian Vettel	14	1m 32.042s
3	Daniel Ricciardo	16	1m 32.091s
4	Valtteri Bottas	24	1m 32.329s
5	Lewis Hamilton	20	1m 32.539s
6	Max Verstappen	17	1m 32.579s
7	Sergio Pérez	20	1m 33.209s
8	Felipe Massa	20	1m 33.240s
9	Esteban Ocon	21	1m 33.290s
10	Stoffel Vandoorne	16	1m 33.321s
11	Fernando Alonso	17	1m 33.530s
12	Lance Stroll	21	1m 33.538s
13	Kevin Magnussen	10	1m 33.787s
14	Nico Hülkenberg	14	1m 33.871s
15	Carlos Sainz	22	1m 33.924s
16	Pierre Gasly	24	1m 34.206s
17	Jolyon Palmer	12	1m 34.475s
18	Romain Grosjean	19	1m 34.914s
19	Marcus Ericsson	19	1m 34.936s
20	Pascal Wehrlein	19	1m 35.045s

QUALIFYING (SATURDAY)
Weather: Dry/partly cloudy Temperatures: track 43–53°C, air 30–34°C

Pos.	Driver	First	Second	Third	Qualifying Tyre
1	Lewis Hamilton	1m 31.605s	1m 30.977s	1m 30.076s	Supersoft (new)
2	Kimi Räikkönen	1m 32.259s	1m 30.926s	1m 30.121s	Supersoft (new)
3	Max Verstappen	1m 31.920s	1m 30.931s	1m 30.541s	Supersoft (new)
4	Daniel Ricciardo	1m 32.416s	1m 31.061s	1m 30.595s	Supersoft (new)
5	Valtteri Bottas	1m 32.254s	1m 30.803s	1m 30.758s	Supersoft (new)
6	Esteban Ocon	1m 32.527s	1m 31.651s	1m 31.478s	Supersoft (new)
7	Stoffel Vandoorne	1m 32.838s	1m 31.848s	1m 31.582s	Supersoft (new)
8	Nico Hülkenberg	1m 32.586s	1m 31.778s	1m 31.607s	Supersoft (new)
9	Sergio Pérez	1m 32.768s	1m 31.484s	1m 31.658s	Supersoft (new)
10	Fernando Alonso	1m 33.049s	1m 32.010s	1m 31.704s	Supersoft (new)
11	Felipe Massa	1m 32.267s	1m 32.034s		
12	Jolyon Palmer	1m 32.576s	1m 32.100s		
13	Lance Stroll	1m 33.000s	1m 32.307s		
14	Carlos Sainz	1m 32.650s	1m 32.402s		
15	Pierre Gasly	1m 32.547s	1m 32.558s		
16	Romain Grosjean	1m 33.308s			
17	Kevin Magnussen	1m 33.434s			
18	Pascal Wehrlein	1m 33.483s			
19	Marcus Ericsson	1m 33.970s			
20	Sebastian Vettel	no time			

QUALIFYING: head to head

Hamilton	10	5	Bottas
Vettel	10	5	Räikkönen
Massa	12	2	Stroll
Stroll	1	0	Di Resta
Ricciardo	4	11	Verstappen
Pérez	11	4	Ocon
Hülkenberg	15	0	Palmer
Kvyat	6	8	Sainz
Gasly	0	1	Sainz
Ericsson	2	0	Giovinazzi
Ericsson	4	9	Wehrlein
Alonso	11	3	Vandoorne
Vandoorne	1	0	Button
Grosjean	10	5	Magnussen

FOR THE RECORD

1st GRAND PRIX: Pierre Gasly

70th POLE POSITION: Lewis Hamilton

POINTS

DRIVERS

1	Lewis Hamilton	281
2	Sebastian Vettel	247
3	Valtteri Bottas	222
4	Daniel Ricciardo	177
5	Kimi Räikkönen	138
6	Max Verstappen	93
7	Sergio Pérez	76
8	Esteban Ocon	57
9	Carlos Sainz	48
10	Nico Hülkenberg	34
11	Felipe Massa	33
12	Lance Stroll	32
13	Romain Grosjean	26
14	Stoffel Vandoorne	13
15	Kevin Magnussen	11
16	Fernando Alonso	10
17	Jolyon Palmer	8
18	Pascal Wehrlein	5
19	Daniil Kvyat	4

CONSTRUCTORS

1	Mercedes	503
2	Ferrari	385
3	Red Bull	270
4	Force India	133
5	Williams	65
6	Toro Rosso	52
7	Renault	42
8	Haas	37
9	McLaren	23
10	Sauber	5

10 · ALONSO · McLaren

8 · HÜLKENBERG · Renault

6 · OCON · Force India

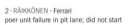
4 · RICCIARDO · Red Bull

2 · RÄIKKÖNEN · Ferrari
poer unit failure in pit lane; did not start

9 · PÉREZ · Force India

7 · VANDOORNE · McLaren

5 · BOTTAS · Mercedes

3 · VERSTAPPEN · Red Bull

1 · HAMILTON · Mercedes

45	46	47	48	49	50	51	52	53	54	55	56	
33	33	33	33	33	33	33	33	33	33	33	33	1
44	44	44	44	44	44	44	44	44	44	44	44	2
3	3	3	3	3	3	3	3	3	3	3	3	3
5	5	5	5	5	5	5	5	5	5	5	5	4
77	77	77	77	77	77	77	77	77	77	77	77	5
11	11	11	11	11	11	11	11	11	11	11	11	6
2	2	2	2	2	2	2	2	2	2	2	2	7
18	18	18	18	18	18	18	18	18	18	18	18	8
19	19	19	19	19	19	19	19	19	19	19	19	9
31	31	31	31	31	31	31	31	31	31	31	31	10
27	27	27	27	14	14	14	14	14	14			
14	14	14	14	14	20	20	20	20	20	20		
20	20	20	20	20	10	10	10	10	8	8		
10	10	10	10	10	27	8	8	8	10	10		
30	30	30	30	8	8	30	30	30	30	30		
8	8	8	8	30	30	27	27	27	27	27		
94	94	94	94	94	94	94	94	94	94	94		
9	9	9	9	9	9	9	9	9	9	9		

31 = Pit stop   9 = One lap or more behind

RACE TYRE STRATEGIES

PIRELLI

	Driver	Race Stint 1	Race Stint 2	Race Stint 3
1	Verstappen	Supersoft (u): 1-27	Soft (n): 28-56	
2	Hamilton	Supersoft (u): 1-26	Soft (n): 27-56	
3	Ricciardo	Supersoft (u): 1-29	Soft (n): 30-56	
4	Vettel	Soft (n): 1-27	Supersoft (n): 28-56	
5	Bottas	Supersoft (u): 1-28	Soft (n): 29-56	
6	Pérez	Supersoft (u): 1-30	Soft (n): 31-56	
7	Vandoorne	Supersoft (u): 1-13	Soft (n): 14-55	
8	Stroll	Supersoft (n): 1-12	Soft (n): 13-55	
9	Massa	Supersoft (n): 1-11	Soft (n): 12-55	
10	Ocon	Supersoft (u): 1-2	Soft (n): 3-55	
11	Alonso	Supersoft (u): 1-26	Soft (n): 27-55	
12	Magnussen	Supersoft (n): 1-10	Soft (n): 11-55	
13	Grosjean	Supersoft (n): 1-11	Soft (n): 12-33	Supersoft (n): 34-55
14	Gasly	Supersoft (n): 1-12	Soft (n): 13-55	
15	Palmer	Supersoft (n): 1-13	Soft (n): 14-55	
16	Hülkenberg	Supersoft (u): 1-9	Soft (n): 10-50	Supersoft (u): 51-55
17	Wehrlein	Soft (n): 1-37	Supersoft (n): 38-55	
18	Ericsson	Soft (n): 1-38	Supersoft (n): 39-54	
	Sainz	Supersoft (n): 1-29 (dnf)		
NS	Räikkönen			

The tyre regulations stipulate that at least two of three dry tyre specifications must be used during a dry race.
Pirelli P Zero logos are colour-coded on the tyre sidewalls: Red = Super-Soft; Yellow = Soft. (n) new (u) used

Photos: Peter J. Fox.

269

2017/10/08

FIA FORMULA 1 WORLD CHAMPIONSHIP · ROUND 16

JAPANESE GRAND PRIX

SUZUKA CIRCUIT

SUZUKA QUALIFYING

ASK about a drivers' track and the answer is always Spa or Suzuka. Which is why it was one of F1's great anomalies that among Lewis Hamilton's record 70 pole positions heading to Japan, he could count every current F1 circuit among them, except Suzuka…

By 3pm Saturday, Hamilton had put that to rights. The cooler ambient temperature and the 3.6-mile 'cross-over' layout was much more Mercedes territory than Malaysia, and Hamilton was relieved to be right in the ballpark from Friday's rain-effected opening practice session. He topped all three qualifying sessions to take that 71st pole with a 0.34s margin over Mercedes team-mate Valtteri Bottas.

"It's always fantastic driving here, even if it hasn't quite come together for me in qualifying in the past," Hamilton told the media, "but in these 2017 cars, it's unbelievable, a real roller-coaster ride, just awesome. I wish you guys could experience what we are feeling."

Bottas, who admitted to having had a bit of a confidence crisis post-Malaysia, flirted with disaster at Degner in practice, and then ran wide and glanced the barrier exiting Spoon Curve 20 minutes into FP3, but he still ended the session with quickest time. A qualifying time 0.14s quicker than Sebastian Vettel meant that he had done the job required of him, but his efforts were negated by a five-place grid penalty for an unscheduled gearbox change.

Vettel's Ferrari had not needed a new gearbox after his slowdown-lap shunt with Lance Stroll at Sepang. And, knowing that both Bottas and team-mate Räikkönen did have five-place grid penalties for fresh boxes, the German was pretty sure of a front-row start, so long as he had the legs of the Red Bulls. In fact, the margin to the RB13s was comfortable at around half a second.

Räikkönen's gearbox issue had been self-inflicted when he shunted at Degner 2 in the final session of free practice on Saturday morning, and then he never seemed to quite catch up. He abandoned his first Q3 run when he ran wide at the first Degner and could do no better than sixth, a couple of tenths behind the Red Bulls and fully seven-tenths from Vettel.

Perhaps 70 per cent of Red Bull's half-second deficit to Vettel was due to Renault's lack of qualifying engine modes. It was Daniel Ricciardo's turn to pip Max Verstappen by three-hundredths, but the race pace was going to be interesting. With Friday afternoon washed out, there wasn't a lot to go on, but the respective rear gunners for Hamilton and Vettel would both start the race behind the RB13s, which thus would have the opportunity to show their true pace.

The Force Indias were next, helped around by their Mercedes grunt. Esteban Ocon was around six-tenths slower than Räikkönen and fractionally quicker than team-mate Sergio Pérez throughout practice and the business end of qualifying. Normally only hundredths would separate these two, but the Frenchman was luxuriating in fully a tenth-and-a-half at Suzuka.

Felipe Massa was ninth for Williams, a couple of tenths quicker than Fernando Alonso's McLaren Honda. To Japanese embarrassment at the venue built as a Honda test track in 1962, Alonso was hit by a 35-place penalty because of the need to fit a whole new Spec 3.7 power unit.

Given that situation, it was perhaps surprising that Alonso bumped team-mate Stoffel Vandoorne out of Q3 by three-hundredths. That is until you remembered that Vandoorne had outqualified Alonso in Malaysia. At least the Belgian had the consolation of free tyre choice.

The Renaults struggled for grunt at Suzuka, and Nico Hülkenberg had to be content with 12th on the grid, 0.15s quicker than team-mate Jolyon Palmer, the pair sandwiching Kevin Magnussen's Haas. This would be Palmer's last race for the team, Renault having announced that Carlos Sainz would be in the car from Austin onwards. To boost his chances in the US, Renault had replaced Palmer's engine, sentencing him to a lowly starting position, ahead of just Alonso. Thanks, guys…

Sainz and Toro Rosso also lacked horsepower in Japan, and they, too, took an engine penalty by changing units in the Spaniard's car. They announced that Pierre Gasly and Daniil Kvyat would drive in the US, which was not best received by Honda, who wanted Gasly to try to win them the Japanese Super Formula title on the same day.

The Frenchman was out in Q1 this time, unable to get his second lap in after Romain Grosjean had a heavy shunt – his third in four races – at The Esses, red-flagging the session. Stroll also missed out and, along with Grosjean and the two Sauber drivers, completed the Q1 victims.

WITH everyone anticipating a great battle between the championship protagonists, and with the Red Bulls also potentially in the mix, it was a real dampener when Ferrari suffered yet more mechanical woes before the Japanese GP was even under way. A suspected spark-plug issue meant that as soon as Vettel took to the track, he could feel that he was down on power. Once more, the Ferrari crew descended on the car and went to work on the grid, but the formation lap confirmed that the problem was still present.

Vettel's initial getaway was not half bad for a car firing on only five healthy cylinders, and he managed to protect second place behind Hamilton as the field blasted through Turns One and Two.

Behind, Verstappen had attacked aggressively down the inside of his team-mate into Turn One, and Ricciardo had been forced to give him space, compromising his exit, which allowed Ocon to bump the Australian down another place as they ran up into The Esses. Then came Pérez, Massa, Hülkenberg and Räikkönen, who hit Vandoorne, the Belgian losing places as he sorted himself out on the grass. Further around the lap, Räikkönen also dropped down the order when he tried to run around the outside of Hülkenberg at Spoon, found zero grip and briefly ran off, losing out to both Haas cars, Stroll and Gasly.

Verstappen could see that all was not well with Vettel and immediately shot down the inside of the Ferrari into the Hairpin on the opening lap, to take second and focus on Hamilton's lead for the second race in succession.

Meanwhile, Sainz's Toro Rosso career ended in ignominious fashion when he tried to make up ground around the outside of Turn Two, but thumped into the tyre barrier. "Sorry guys…" he said, sounding truly despondent.

Vettel's cause was hopeless, and he was soon swamped by Ocon and Ricciardo, who went either side of him, with Bottas following them through. There was a two-lap VSC period while Sainz's Toro Rosso was craned away, and upon resumption, Pérez, Massa and Hülkenberg all came streaming past the Ferrari driver, who returned to the pits to retire, his championship challenge surely over.

Thus we had the same duo fighting at the front as in Malaysia. On that track, on that day, the Red Bull had the superior race pace, but this was a different layout on a cooler day.

There was another two-lap VSC interruption when Ericsson crashed his Sauber at the second Degner. On resumption, Hamilton led Verstappen by 3s, with Ricciardo a further 6s behind his team-mate as he finally managed to repass Ocon. Bottas was within a second of the Frenchman and about to go by, followed by Pérez with a 3s advantage over Massa and the recovering Räikkönen, who had enjoyed more success with his second attempt to pass Hülkenberg. Behind the Renault came the Haas twins, from Gasly and Palmer, a gap to Alonso, then an 18s gap to Stroll and Vandoorne. The last two had both pitted – the Canadian after five laps when he had punctured a tyre running off at Spoon; the Belgian to gain time under the Ericsson VSC after his opening-lap contretemps with Räikkönen.

As in Malaysia, a one-stop race was the quicker route, and the pit stops would be crucial. For Hamilton, it was all about achieving and maintaining a sufficiently large lead over Verstappen to protect against a possible undercut at that all-important stop, on red-walled supersoft tyres that had sometimes proven difficult on the Merc.

Felipe Massa was the first of the top ten qualifiers to pit for a set of Pirelli prime tyres after 17 laps, giving him a 36-lap second stint to the end of the race, which was a more marginal one-stopper than recent tracks.

Simulations suggested that the one-stopper would be around 2.5s quicker over the 53 laps, and possibly 3.5s if a driver pushed harder. The reason the call was more marginal in Japan was because the tyres are taken to much higher degradation levels. Whereas normally tyre degradation levels might be taken to 2s or so, at Suzuka it's up around 3s, which feels awful to the drivers, but is still faster than doing an extra pit stop and having to make their way through traffic on a circuit where overtaking is so difficult.

Above: Already in trouble, Sebastian Vettel is about to be engulfed by the pursuing pack, headed by Ocon, Ricciardo and Bottas.
Photo: WRi2/Jad Sherif

Far left: Kimi Räikkönen crashed out in practice and ended up taking a grid penalty for a replacement gearbox.
Photo: WRi2/Jean-François Galeron

Left: Jolyon Palmer was racing for Renault for the final time, after learning that he would be replaced by Carlos Sainz in Austin.
Photo: Renault F1 Team

Below far left: A 35-place grid penalty consigned Fernando Alonso's McLaren Honda to the back of the grid.
Photo: McLaren Honda

Below left: Vettel congratulates Lewis Hamilton on another dominant qualifying effort for Mercedes.
Photo: WRi2/Studio Colombo

Opening spread: Hamilton takes command at the start, ahead of Vettel's Ferrari, which was already running on five cylinders.
Photo: Peter J. Fox

At the time Massa pitted, Hamilton did not have the necessary 22s pit window to the Force Indias, running fifth and sixth, 2s apart. Räikkönen's Ferrari had also recovered to be right on their tail, on a set of Pirelli softs on which he would run a longer opening stint.

Mercedes strategists were confident that so long as Hamilton had a 3s cushion to Verstappen, they could afford to react to a Red Bull stop on the next lap. When the Dutchman headed in for soft-compound Pirellis on lap 21, Hamilton's margin over Räikkönen was also now big enough (26.7s), and Lewis was able to stop on lap 22 and still pit out in front of Verstappen and the Ferrari.

Ricciardo now led, 4.3s ahead of Bottas, with both cars yet to pit, while Lewis's margin over Verstappen was down below 2s, thanks to the Red Bull stopping a lap sooner. The No. 44 Mercedes, on its fresh rubber, was now also just 3.7s behind team-mate Bottas.

Ricciardo made his lone supersoft-to-soft pit stop on lap 25, but Mercedes kept Bottas out until lap 30 on his softs. Two laps into those additional five, Hamilton was right with Bottas, who pulled over to let him by as they entered the chicane on lap 28. The switch cost Bottas a couple of seconds, but allowed Hamilton to extend his lead over Verstappen by a similar margin before the second Mercedes pitted out of the way to go on to supersofts for the final 23 laps. Bottas rejoined 10s behind Ricciardo, but on the quicker tyre and not without hope of a podium.

On lap 31, Hamilton radioed in that he was "struggling a bit with the rears", and Verstappen started to cut into his lead by a tenth or a tenth-and-a-half over the next few laps, the gap coming down to 2.2s with 12 laps ramaining.

Hamilton responded and picked up the pace, setting three consecutive laps in the high 1m 33s to stretch the margin to over 3s again. If Mercedes was surprised by any facet of the race, it was that whereas at previous events the supersoft Pirelli had proven to be something of a weakness relative to car performance on the soft, in Japan it seemed to be the other way around.

While Hamilton seemed to have the opening supersoft stint under control, his cause had been partially aided by Verstappen slightly blistering his left front tyre. Once on to the soft compound, however, the Red Bull looked a genuine threat, and a third VSC with five laps to go was a challenge Hamilton could have done without. Stroll had suffered a left front tyre failure as he went through The Esses, stranding the Williams in the gravel.

Drivers must maintain a specific time delta, and it was interesting that Lewis's lead before the VSC period (2.59s) was out to 5.19s after the first lap of VSC running, but back to 2.54s after the first lap back under pukka racing conditions. Why?

Perhaps one of the less widely appreciated aspects of running under the VSC is that more than anything else, the gaps boil down to how much weaving a driver does on the straight to maintain tyre temperature. The delta is a distance-based algorithm, so there are two choices: either warm the rubber or minimise the distance. One maximises the lead, the other provides warmer tyres and hence time upon the restart. Take your pick.

Certainly, Verstappen's Red Bull had its tyres working again more quickly than Hamilton's Mercedes, Max setting his fastest lap of the race with two laps to go, just as the pair

Above: Esteban Ocon enhanced his already burgeoning reputation with a fine drive to sixth for Force India.

Top left: Night shift. Mercedes mechanics busy at work under the lights.

Above left: The enthusiasm of the fans was infectious.

Left: Under a sunny race-day sky, Max Verstappen took the fight to Lewis Hamilton once again.

Photos: Peter J. Fox

275

Above: Lewis Hamilton controlled proceedings, despite pressure from Verstappen, before the Red Bull driver encountered blistering of his tyres.

Above right: Lewis Hamilton tries on Takuma Sato's Indianapolis 500 winner's ring for size.

Photos: Lukas Gorys

Top right: Third-placed Daniel Ricciardo takes a Japanese bow on entering the podium.

Photo: WRi2/Studio Colombo

Centre right: A happy Haas team celebrates both drivers delivering points scoring finishes.

Below right: Magnussen and teammate Grosjean took eighth and ninth places respectively for Haas.

Photos: Haas F1 Team

Centre far right: Pierre Gasly admitted to over-driving as he struggled to adapt to the Toro Rosso. Eventually, he finished 13th.

Photo: Peter J. Fox

Below far right: After being consigned to the back of the grid, Carlos Sainz ended his final race with a whimper, crashing out on the opening lap.

Photo: Lukas Gorys

of them hit traffic in the form of a battling Massa and Alonso. Another phenomenon already noted in 2017 was that the Mercedes W08 seemed to be affected significantly more by turbulence from cars in front, than its main rivals.

So this was real pressure for Hamilton. Verstappen was almost within DRS range, but the traffic actually worked in the leader's favour, and he used it cannily, holding the Red Bull at bay to score a fine 61st GP victory and his eighth of the season. He had one hand on that fourth title.

"Today, I was kind of thinking, he [Max] won the last race; I'm not letting him have this one!" Lewis smiled afterwards, while paying tribute to Verstappen's speed and consistency, as well as the race pace shown by Red Bull. "I'm enjoying being in an era with such great young talent coming through. Max will be here far beyond when I stop, but until then, I'll try not to give him too many poles or wins…"

A strong final stint on his supersofts put Bottas back to within less than a second of Ricciardo and a podium finish. "The pace was good and I had the quickest lap of the race," he pointed out. "The balance was quite a lot better in the second stint, I could attack, and I got quite close to Daniel in the end, but the whole race was obviously compromised by the gearbox penalty."

Räikkönen was a lonely fifth, 22s further back in what was potentially the quickest car in the race. A 28-lap stint on his initial set of soft tyres had allowed him to leapfrog the Force Indias, pitting out 2s ahead of them, but too far (20s) behind Ricciardo to be any kind of threat in a race that, like that of Bottas, was shaped by his gearbox dramas, although Kimi's had been self-inflicted.

You could almost always bank on the Force Indias for some excitement.

"Can I attack Esteban?" Pérez asked over the radio as the pair circulated together, reminding everyone that the team had lain down the law after a series of on-track disputes had culminated in rather more serious contact at Spa. The answer was in the negative, so he backed off to look after his rubber. They took the chequer sixth and seventh for another healthy helping of points.

At Haas, similar questions were being asked. Grosjean, on supersofts that were four laps newer, was pressing Magnussen as the pair hassled Massa. The Dane solved the issue himself by taking no prisoners and forcing through on the inside of the Williams at Turns One and Two with 11 laps to go.

"Good boy!" was Magnussen's radio approval. Massa was much less impressed. Kevin's aggressive approach had actually made contact and forced Felipe wide on to the marbles, so that he could do nothing to stop Grosjean from coming through as well.

The additional points were sufficient to leapfrog the American team above Renault into seventh place in that tight mid-grid constructors' battle.

Massa was left to fend off Alonso for the final point – the fight that Hamilton and Verstappen had closed in on over the final laps. Doing his utmost to use the situation to get on terms, Alonso received a couple of penalty points for not moving over quickly enough, and ultimately he had to settle for 11th.

Hülkenberg's usual lack of good fortune continued. Having started on the Pirelli soft, he ran as far as lap 38 before having to come in without a sufficiently large pit window and pitted out right behind the fighting Massa/Magnussen/Grosjean/Gasly group. He negotiated Gasly promptly enough and was looking forward to some fun on his supersofts when his DRS stuck open. Cue retirement and a 'Hulk' who was fit to be tied.

And so, with four races remaining, Mercedes looked well set to seal a fourth consecutive manufacturers' crown in Austin, while Hamilton left the Far East leg of the world championship with a 59-point lead, thanks to Ferrari's dreadful run in Singapore, Malaysia and Japan.

"It's kind of unbelievable," Lewis reflected. "Sebastian has been incredibly unfortunate, but it's about reliability, and our whole team performance has shown over the year that we have a very solid platform. Mercedes are the leaders in that area." You couldn't really take issue with him on that…

Tony Dodgins

VIEWPOINT
A LITTLE LOCAL DIFFICULTY

I F they go so far as to check the precise alignment of tea cups across the rows before the Japanese Parliament sits (perfectly true!), you begin to get the picture of how the Honda motor sport hierarchy must have been feeling about F1's latest and typically selfish political play.

The root of the difficulty lay in Renault's desire to have Carlos Sainz on board for the US Grand Prix, rather than wait until 2018. News of this gathered momentum when Renault revealed that Japan would be Jolyon Palmer's last race in yellow and black.

Toro Rosso then formally announced Sainz's imminent departure, as if this had been their plan all along, even though the Red Bull junior squad had clearly been caught on the hop. Answering questions about Sainz's substitute was proving more difficult.

The initial response was a recall of Daniil Kvyat to partner Pierre Gasly. Cue some throat clearing by the Honda contingent and a reminder that, with the deepest respect, Austin clashed with the final round of the Japanese Super Formula Championship, in which young Gasly was just half a point off the lead.

The predictably arrogant response of the F1 *cognoscenti* was to point out that Gasly was only racing in Japan as a means of marking time while waiting for the call to F1. And now that he'd received that call (two weeks before in Malaysia), no way was he going to give up racing in the USA.

More polite clearing of throats and another gentle reminder that Gasly-san was – *is* – racing in Japan for Team Mugen (with Honda engines), and his championship rival drives for a team that is four points ahead in their version of the constructors' championship. And the rival team – ahem – runs Toyota engines.

Oh, and one final thing, Toro Rosso-san: your F1 engine for next season will be what?

Indeed! A Honda! And you've suddenly realised you overlooked the date clash and Gasly-san will be racing in Japan after all? Of course he will! Enter Brendon Hartley...

Tea anyone?

Maurice Hamilton

16

2017 FORMULA 1
JAPANESE GRAND PRIX

SUZUKA 6–8 OCTOBER

RACE DISTANCE: 53 laps, 191.054 miles/307.471km

RACE WEATHER: Dry/sunny (track 39–45°C, air 26–27°C)

ROLEX

F1 **OFFICIAL TIMEPIECE**

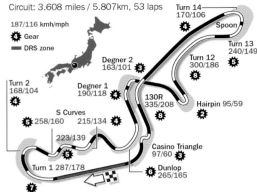

SUZUKA INTERNATIONAL RACING COURSE, SUZUKA-CITY
Circuit: 3.608 miles / 5.807km, 53 laps

187/116 kmh/mph
⚙ Gear
▬ DRS zone

Turn 14 170/106
Spoon
Turn 13 240/149
Turn 12 300/186
Degner 2 163/101
Degner 1 190/118
130R 335/208
Hairpin 95/59
Turn 2 168/104
S Curves 258/160 215/134
223/139
Casino Triangle 97/60
Turn 1 287/178
Dunlop 265/165

All results and data © FOM 2017

RACE – OFFICIAL CLASSIFICATION

Pos.	Driver	Nat.	No.	Entrant	Car/Engine	Laps	Time/Retirement	Speed (mph/km/h)	Gap to leader	Fastest race lap
1	**Lewis Hamilton**	GB	44	Mercedes AMG Petronas Motorsport	Mercedes F1 W08-Mercedes M08 EQ Power+ V6	53	1h 27m 31.194s	130.978/210.789		1m 33.780s 43
2	**Max Verstappen**	NL	33	Red Bull Racing	Red Bull RB13-TAG Heuer RB13 V6	53	1h 27m 32.405s	130.948/210.740	1.211s	1m 33.730s 51
3	**Daniel Ricciardo**	AUS	3	Red Bull Racing	Red Bull RB13-TAG Heuer RB13 V6	53	1h 27m 40.873s	130.737/210.401	9.679s	1m 33.694s 52
4	**Valtteri Bottas**	FIN	77	Mercedes AMG Petronas Motorsport	Mercedes F1 W08-Mercedes M08 EQ Power+ V6	53	1h 27m 41.774s	130.715/210.365	10.580s	1m 33.144s 50
5	**Kimi Räikkönen**	FIN	7	Scuderia Ferrari	Ferrari SF70H-062 V6	53	1h 28m 03.816s	130.169/209.487	32.622s	1m 33.175s 50
6	**Esteban Ocon**	F	31	Sahara Force India Formula 1 Team	Force India VJM10-Mercedes M08 EQ Power+ V6	53	1h 28m 38.982s	129.309/208.102	1m 07.788s	1m 34.843s 50
7	**Sergio Pérez**	MEX	11	Sahara Force India Formula 1 Team	Force India VJM10-Mercedes M08 EQ Power+ V6	53	1h 28m 42.618s	129.220/207.960	1m 11.424s	1m 34.744s 23
8	**Kevin Magnussen**	DK	20	Haas F1 Team	Haas VF-17-Ferrari 062 V6	53	1h 29m 00.147s	128.797/207.278	1m 28.953s	1m 35.338s 50
9	**Romain Grosjean**	F	8	Haas F1 Team	Haas VF-17-Ferrari 062 V6	53	1h 29m 01.077s	128.774/207.242	1m 29.883s	1m 35.347s 50
10	**Felipe Massa**	BR	19	Williams Martini Racing	Williams FW40-Mercedes M08 EQ Power+ V6	52			1 lap	1m 35.943s 50
11	Fernando Alonso	E	14	McLaren Honda Formula 1 Team	McLaren MCL32-Honda RA617H V6	52			1 lap	1m 35.111s 45
12	Jolyon Palmer	GB	30	Renault Sport Formula One Team	Renault R.S.17-R.E.17 V6	52			1 lap	1m 34.095s 50
13	Pierre Gasly	F	10	Scuderia Toro Rosso	Toro Rosso STR12-Renault R.E.17 V6	52			1 lap	1m 34.533s 45
14	Stoffel Vandoorne	B	2	McLaren Honda Formula 1 Team	McLaren MCL32-Honda RA617H V6	52			1 lap	1m 33.724s 49
15	Pascal Wehrlein	D	94	Sauber F1 Team	Sauber C36-Ferrari 059/5 V6	51			2 laps	1m 36.430s 27
	Lance Stroll	CDN	18	Williams Martini Racing	Williams FW40-Mercedes M08 EQ Power+ V6	45	*front suspension*			1m 34.548s 37
	Nico Hülkenberg	D	27	Renault Sport Formula One Team	Renault R.S.17-R.E.17 V6	40	*DRS*			1m 35.883s 28
	Marcus Ericsson	S	9	Sauber F1 Team	Sauber C36-Ferrari 059/5 V6	7	*accident*			1m 38.596s 7
	Sebastian Vettel	D	5	Scuderia Ferrari	Ferrari SF70H-062 V6	4	*spark plug*			2m 06.457s 2
	Carlos Sainz	E	55	Scuderia Toro Rosso	Toro Rosso STR12-Renault R.E.17 V6	0	*spin*			no time

Fastest race lap: Valtteri Bottas on lap 50, 1m 33.144s, 139.460mph/224.439km/h.

Lap record: Kimi Räikkönen (McLaren MP4-20-Mercedes Benz V10), 1m 31.540s, 141.904mph/228.372km/h (2005).

19 · SAINZ · Toro Rosso
20-place grid penalty for using additional power unit elements

17 · WEHRLEIN · Sauber

15 · STROLL · Williams

13 · GROSJEAN · Haas

11 · HÜLKENBERG · Renault

20 · ALONSO · McLaren
35-place grid penalty for using additional power unit elements

18 · PALMER · Renault
20-place grid penalty for using additional power unit elements

16 · ERICSSON · Sauber

14 · GASLY · Toro Rosso

12 · MAGNUSSEN · Haas

Grid order	1	2	3	4	5	6	7	8	9	10	11	12	13	14	15	16	17	18	19	20	21	22	23	24	25	26	27	28	29	30	31	32	33	34	35	36	37	38	39	40	41	42
44 HAMILTON	44	44	44	44	44	44	44	44	44	44	44	44	44	44	44	44	44	44	44	44	44	44	3	3	3	77	77	44	44	44	44	44	44	44	44	44	44	44	44	44	44	44
5 VETTEL	33	33	33	33	33	33	33	33	33	33	33	33	33	33	33	33	33	33	33	33	33	33	3	77	77	77	44	44	77	77	33	33	33	33	33	33	33	33	33	33	33	33
3 RICCIARDO	5	31	31	31	31	31	31	31	31	31	3	3	3	3	3	3	3	3	3	3	3	3	77	44	44	44	33	33	33	33	77	3	3	3	3	3	3	3	3	3	3	3
33 VERSTAPPEN	31	3	3	3	3	3	3	3	3	3	31	77	77	77	77	77	77	77	77	77	77	33	33	33	33	7	7	3	3	77	77	77	77	77	77	77	77	77	77	77	77	77
31 OCON	3	77	77	77	77	77	77	77	77	77	77	77	31	31	31	31	31	31	31	31	7	7	7	7	7	3	7	27	27	27	7	7	7	7	7	7	7	7	7	7	7	7
77 BOTTAS	77	5	5	11	11	11	11	11	11	11	11	11	11	11	11	11	11	11	11	31	11	27	27	27	27	27	27	7	7	7	27	27	27	27	31	31	31	31	31
11 PÉREZ	11	11	11	19	19	19	19	19	19	19	19	19	7	7	7	7	7	7	11	27	8	8	31	31	31	31	31	31	31	31	31	31	31	31	11	11	11	11	11
19 MASSA	19	19	19	27	27	27	27	7	7	7	7	7	19	19	19	27	27	27	27	8	10	30	30	11	11	11	11	11	11	11	11	11	11	11	27	19	19	19	20
2 VANDOORNE	27	27	27	20	7	7	7	27	27	27	27	27	27	27	27	19	20	8	8	10	30	31	11	30	30	30	19	30	30	30	30	30	30	30	30	30	30	20	20	8
7 RÄIKKÖNEN	20	20	20	7	20	20	20	20	20	20	20	20	20	20	20	20	8	20	10	30	31	11	14	19	19	19	19	19	19	19	19	19	19	8	19	8	8
27 HÜLKENBERG	18	18	18	7	8	8	8	8	8	8	8	8	8	8	8	8	10	10	30	31	14	14	19	14	20	20	20	20	20	20	20	20	20	8	27	14	14
20 MAGNUSSEN	10	8	8	10	10	10	10	10	10	10	10	10	10	10	10	10	30	30	14	14	11	19	20	20	8	8	8	8	8	8	8	8	27	14	30	30
8 GROSJEAN	8	10	10	30	30	30	30	30	30	30	30	30	30	30	30	14	14	19	19	19	20	8	8	10	10	10	10	10	10	10	10	10	10	10	10	30	10	10
10 GASLY	30	7	7	9	9	9	14	14	14	14	14	14	14	14	14	19	19	20	20	20	10	10	18	18	18	18	18	18	18	14	14	14	14	10	18	18
18 STROLL	7	30	30	5	14	14	2	18	18	18	18	18	18	18	18	8	2	18	18	14	14	18	18	18	18	18	18
9 ERICSSON	9	9	9	14	2	2	18	2	2	2	2	2	2	2	2	2	14	2	2	2	2	2	2	2	2	2	94	94
94 WEHRLEIN	14	14	14	2	18	18	94	94	94	94	94	94	94	94	94	94	94	94	94	94	94	94	94	94	94	94	94	94	94	94	94	94	94	94	94	94
30 PALMER	2	2	2	18	94	94	94
55 SAINZ	94	94	94	94
14 ALONSO																																										

TIME SHEETS

PRACTICE 1 (FRIDAY)
Weather: Light rain/cloudy
Temperatures: track 23–24°C, air 19–20°C

Pos.	Driver	Laps	Time
1	Sebastian Vettel	23	1m 29.166s
2	Lewis Hamilton	29	1m 29.377s
3	Daniel Ricciardo	27	1m 29.541s
4	Kimi Räikkönen	22	1m 29.638s
5	Valtteri Bottas	30	1m 30.151s
6	Max Verstappen	26	1m 30.762s
7	Esteban Ocon	22	1m 30.899s
8	Nico Hülkenberg	24	1m 30.974s
9	Romain Grosjean	22	1m 31.032s
10	Stoffel Vandoorne	24	1m 31.202s
11	Kevin Magnussen	15	1m 31.216s
12	Fernando Alonso	19	1m 31.235s
13	Sergio Pérez	23	1m 31.530s
14	Lance Stroll	22	1m 31.602s
15	Jolyon Palmer	22	1m 31.757s
16	Felipe Massa	20	1m 31.912s
17	Carlos Sainz	14	1m 32.252s
18	Pierre Gasly	18	1m 32.501s
19	Pascal Wehrlein	29	1m 32.897s
20	Marcus Ericsson	28	1m 33.397s

PRACTICE 2 (FRIDAY)
Weather: Heavy rain/cloudy
Temperatures: track 17–18°C, air 15–16°C

Pos.	Driver	Laps	Time
1	Lewis Hamilton	4	1m 48.719s
2	Esteban Ocon	3	1m 49.518s
3	Sergio Pérez	3	1m 51.345s
4	Felipe Massa	3	1m 52.146s
5	Lance Stroll	4	1m 52.343s
6	Kimi Räikkönen	1	no time
7	Nico Hülkenberg	1	no time
8	Jolyon Palmer	1	no time
9	Marcus Ericsson	3	no time
10	Sebastian Vettel	1	no time
11	Fernando Alonso	2	no time
12	Pascal Wehrlein	2	no time
13	Carlos Sainz	1	no time
14	Stoffel Vandoorne	1	no time
–	Valtteri Bottas	–	–
–	Pierre Gasly	–	–
–	Romain Grosjean	–	–
–	Kevin Magnussen	–	–
–	Daniel Ricciardo	–	–
–	Max Verstappen	–	–

PRACTICE 3 (SATURDAY)
Weather: Cry/cloudy
Temperatures: 28°C, air 22°C

Pos.	Driver	Laps	Time
1	Valtteri Bottas	9	1m 29.055s
2	Lewis Hamilton	19	1m 29.069s
3	Sebastian Vettel	23	1m 29.379s
4	Max Verstappen	15	1m 29.910s
5	Daniel Ricciardo	13	1m 30.018s
6	Esteban Ocon	12	1m 30.109s
7	Nico Hülkenberg	19	1m 30.315s
8	Fernando Alonso	13	1m 30.424s
9	Sergio Pérez	12	1m 30.563s
10	Jolyon Palmer	22	1m 30.764s
11	Felipe Massa	21	1m 30.764s
12	Stoffel Vandoorne	18	1m 30.770s
13	Carlos Sainz	23	1m 30.799s
14	Kevin Magnussen	12	1m 30.982s
15	Lance Stroll	20	1m 31.011s
16	Pierre Gasly	25	1m 31.353s
17	Romain Grosjean	13	1m 31.459s
18	Marcus Ericsson	22	1m 32.579s
19	Pascal Wehrlein	21	1m 32.698s
20	Kimi Räikkönen	12	1m 33.962s

QUALIFYING (SATURDAY)
Weather: Dry/sunny-cloudy Temperatures: track 25–28°C, air 22–23°C

Pos.	Driver	First	Second	Third	Qualifying Tyre
1	Lewis Hamilton	1m 29.047s	1m 27.819s	1m 27.319s	Supersoft (used)
2	Valtteri Bottas	1m 29.332s	1m 28.543s	1m 27.651s	Soft (used)
3	Sebastian Vettel	1m 29.352s	1m 28.225s	1m 27.791s	Supersoft (used)
4	Daniel Ricciardo	1m 29.475s	1m 28.935s	1m 28.306s	Supersoft (used)
5	Max Verstappen	1m 29.181s	1m 28.747s	1m 28.332s	Supersoft (used)
6	Kimi Räikkönen	1m 29.163s	1m 29.079s	1m 28.498s	Soft (used)
7	Esteban Ocon	1m 30.115s	1m 29.199s	1m 29.111s	Supersoft (used)
8	Sergio Pérez	1m 29.696s	1m 29.343s	1m 29.260s	Supersoft (used)
9	Felipe Massa	1m 30.352s	1m 29.687s	1m 29.480s	Supersoft (used)
10	Fernando Alonso	1m 30.525s	1m 29.749s	1m 30.687s	Supersoft(used)
11	Stoffel Vandoorne	1m 30.654s	1m 29.778s		
12	Nico Hülkenberg	1m 30.252s	1m 29.879s		
13	Kevin Magnussen	1m 30.774s	1m 29.972s		
14	Jolyon Palmer	1m 30.516s	1m 30.022s		
15	Carlos Sainz	1m 30.565s	1m 30.413s		
16	Romain Grosjean	1m 30.849s			
17	Pierre Gasly	1m 31.317s			
18	Lance Stroll	1m 31.409s			
19	Marcus Ericsson	1m 31.597s			
20	Pascal Wehrlein	1m 31.885s			

QUALIFYING: head to head

Hamilton	11	5	Bottas
Vettel	11	5	Räikkönen
Massa	13	2	Stroll
Stroll	1	0	Di Resta
Ricciardo	5	11	Verstappen
Pérez	11	5	Ocon
Hülkenberg	16	0	Palmer
Kvyat	6	8	Sainz
Sainz	2	0	Gasly
Ericsson	2	0	Giovinazzi
Ericsson	5	9	Wehrlein
Alonso	12	3	Vandoorne
Vandoorne	1	0	Button
Grosjean	11	5	Magnussen

FOR THE RECORD

POINTS

DRIVERS

1	Lewis Hamilton	306
2	Sebastian Vettel	247
3	Valtteri Bottas	234
4	Daniel Ricciardo	192
5	Kimi Räikkönen	148
6	Max Verstappen	111
7	Sergio Pérez	82
8	Esteban Ocon	65
9	Carlos Sainz	48
10	Nico Hülkenberg	34
11	Felipe Massa	34
12	Lance Stroll	32
13	Romain Grosjean	28
14	Kevin Magnussen	15
15	Stoffel Vandoorne	13
16	Fernando Alonso	10
17	Jolyon Palmer	8
18	Pascal Wehrlein	5
19	Daniil Kvyat	4

CONSTRUCTORS

1	Mercedes	540
2	Ferrari	395
3	Red Bull	303
4	Force India	147
5	Williams	66
6	Toro Rosso	52
7	Haas	43
8	Renault	42
9	McLaren	23
10	Sauber	5

9 · VANDOORNE · McLaren

7 · PÉREZ · Force India

5 · OCON · Force India

3 · RICCIARDO · Red Bull

1 · HAMILTON · Mercedes

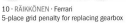

10 · RÄIKKÖNEN · Ferrari
5-place grid penalty for replacing gearbox

8 · MASSA · Williams

6 · BOTTAS · Mercedes
5-place grid penalty for replacing gearbox

4 · VERSTAPPEN · Red Bull

2 · VETTEL · Ferrari

43	44	45	46	47	48	49	50	51	52	53	
44	44	44	44	44	44	44	44	44	44	44	1
33	33	33	33	33	33	33	33	33	33	33	2
3	3	3	3	3	3	3	3	3	3	3	3
77	77	77	77	77	77	77	77	77	77	77	4
7	7	7	7	7	7	7	7	7	7	7	5
31	31	31	31	31	31	31	31	31	31	31	6
11	11	11	11	11	11	11	11	11	11	11	7
20	20	20	20	20	20	20	20	20	20	20	8
8	8	8	8	8	8	8	8	8	8	8	9
19	19	19	19	19	19	19	19	19	19	19	10
14	14	14	14	14	14	14	14	14	14		
30	30	30	30	30	30	30	30	30	30		
10	10	10	10	10	10	10	10	10	10		
18	18	18	2	2	2	2	2	2	2		
2	2	2	94	94	94	94	94	94			
94	94	94									

94 = Pit stop   2 = One lap or more behind

RACE TYRE STRATEGIES

PIRELLI

	Driver	Race Stint 1	Race Stint 2	Race Stint 3	Race Stint 4
1	Hamilton	Supersoft (u): 1–22	Soft (n): 23–53		
2	Verstappen	Supersoft (u): 1–21	Soft (n): 22–53		
3	Ricciardo	Supersoft (u): 1–25	Soft (n): 26–53		
4	Bottas	Soft (u): 1–30	Supersoft (n): 31–53		
5	Räikkönen	Soft (u): 1–28	Supersoft (n): 29–53		
6	Ocon	Supersoft (u): 1–20	Soft (n): 21–53		
7	Pérez	Supersoft (u): 1–21	Soft (n): 22–53		
8	Magnussen	Supersoft (n): 1–19	Soft (n): 20–53		
9	Grosjean	Supersoft (n): 1–23	Soft (n): 24–53		
10	Massa	Supersoft (u): 1–17	Soft (n): 18–52		
11	Alonso	Supersoft (u): 1–25	Soft (n): 26–52		
12	Palmer	Soft (n): 1–39	Supersoft (n): 40–52		
13	Gasley	Supersoft (u): 1–22	Soft (n): 23–39	Supersoft (n): 40–52	
14	Vandoorne	Supersoft (n): 1–9	Soft (n): 10–34	Supersoft (u): 35–52	
15	Wehrlein	Soft (n): 1–2	Supersoft (u): 3	Soft (n): 4–25	Soft (u): 26–51
	Stroll	Supersoft (n): 1–4	Soft (n): 5–35	Supersoft (n): 36–45 (dnf)	
	Hülkenberg	Soft (n): 1–38	Supersoft (n): 39–40 (dnf)		
	Ericsson	Soft (n): 1–7 (dnf)			
	Vettel	Supersoft (n): 1–4 (dnf)			
	Sainz	Soft (n): 0 (dnf)			

The tyre regulations stipulate that at least two of three dry tyre specifications must be used during a dry race.
Pirelli P Zero logos are colour-coded on the tyre sidewalls: Red = Super-Soft; Yellow = Soft.   (n) new   (u) used

Photos: Peter J. Fox

UNITED STATES GRAND PRIX

CIRCUIT OF THE AMERICAS

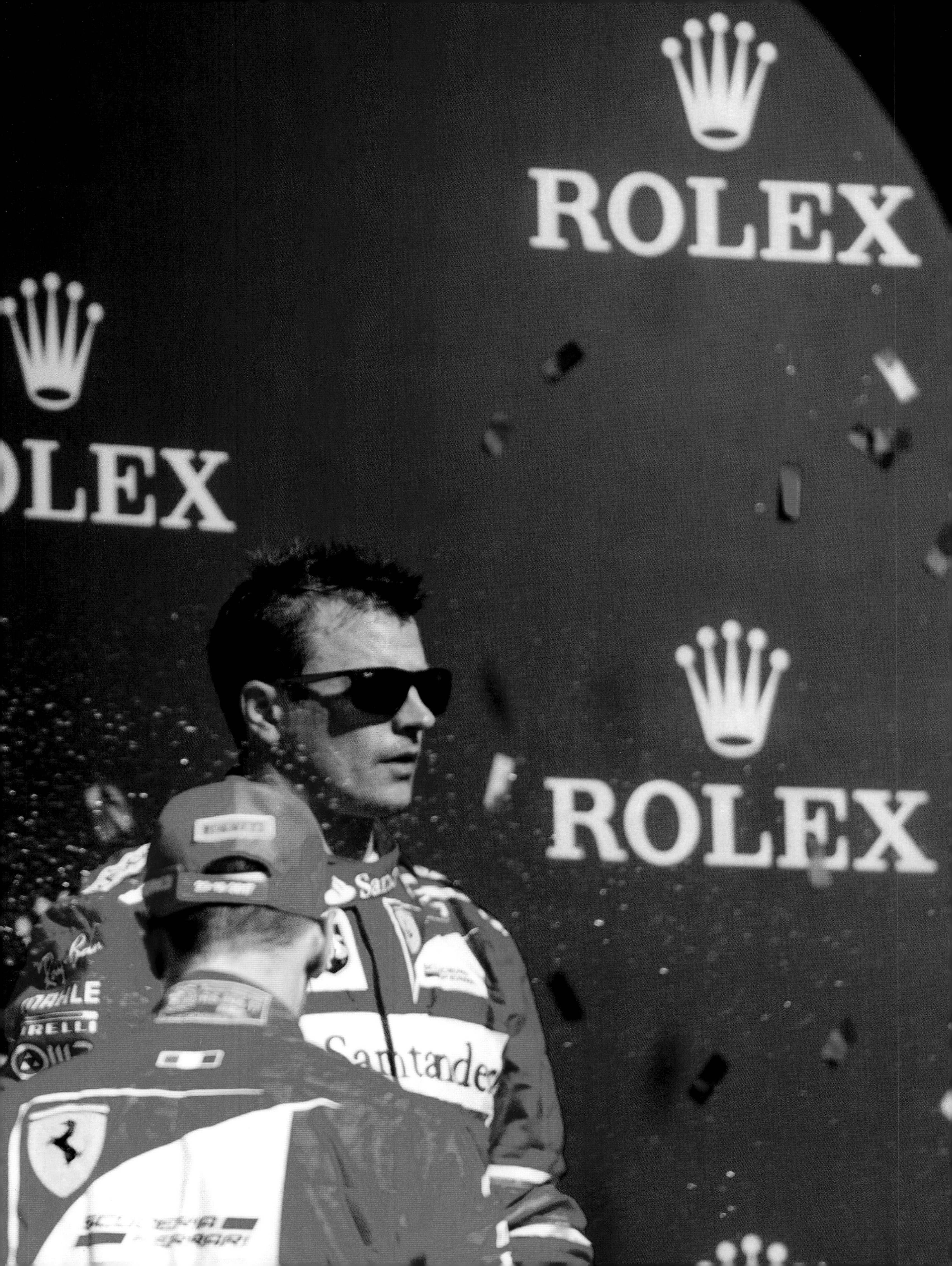
ROLEX
ROLEX
MAHLE

CIRCUIT OF THE AMERICAS QUALIFYING

LEWIS HAMILTON arrived in Austin a strong favourite and with a fourth world title within sight, after Ferrari's Asian nightmare. He might have won four of the previous five grands prix and four of the previous five Austin encounters, but he was taking nothing for granted, figuring that Ferrari and Red Bull would be serious threats.

In the final analysis, though, Lewis was the man to beat once again, topping every session of free practice and qualifying, and scorching to a 72nd pole position, and a new-record 117 front-row F1 starts – with a 1m 33.108s lap. Rising temperature and changing wind direction gave him bigger problems than any of his rivals, but he was revelling in the Circuit of the Americas layout, especially the high-speed sector one.

After a tricky start, Ferrari got it together well enough for Sebastian Vettel to get within a quarter of a second and put his SF70 on the front row, a couple of tenths quicker than Valtteri Bottas. On Friday afternoon, Vettel had spun early in FP2 and reported that the car felt very strange – jelly-like – at the front end. The team changed a cracked chassis overnight.

"I didn't find the rhythm early in qualifying, but on the final run I was closer than perhaps we expected," Vettel admitted, "although I struggled a bit into T8/9, which was probably the wind direction."

Less then a tenth of a second covered the next four cars, with Bottas just a hundredth quicker than Daniel Ricciardo's Red Bull. The Australian recorded the same time as Kimi Räikkönen down to the last thousandth of a second – 1m 33.577s – but claimed the second-row spot by dint of setting the time first, by 18 seconds!

Team-mate Max Verstappen was just 0.08s adrift. His RB13 was fitted with a development-spec Renault engine, but the resultant 15-place grid penalty meant that he would be forced to come through from the back on Sunday, which dictated an alternative qualifying strategy. The young Dutchman (who announced a Red Bull contract extension to the end of 2020 on Saturday morning) elected to qualify on Pirelli's supersoft tyre, rather than the ultrasoft.

Esteban Ocon was under the weather with stomach problems and a headache, but he did a fine job to qualify seventh for Force India, although the best part of a second from Verstappen. That put him ahead of a great Renault debut by Carlos Sainz, who set eighth best time. The young Spaniard and Nico Hülkenberg had been evenly matched throughout practice, but one of the new Renault-spec engines – reckoned to be potentially worth a couple of tenths through a stronger qualifying mode – had also sentenced 'The Hulk' to a tricky Sunday from the back through its attendant penalties. He proved the potential in Q1 with a top-ten time from just a single run, then elected to save engine mileage, knowing that whatever he did was going to mean a lowly grid position – another negative of F1's unpopular penalty system.

Just 0.15s behind Sainz was Fernando Alonso's McLaren Honda, a strong effort with a new front wing, the latest element in McLaren's ongoing aero development. There was only one, and Stoffel Vandoorne got to try it in FP1 when Alonso suffered a hydraulic issue. It was an obvious gain because, when Alonso reclaimed it on Saturday, Vandoorne found his chassis ill-balanced when running the old wing, and he lined up 13th, six-tenths adrift of Fernando in Q2.

Alonso was a tenth-and-a-half quicker than a distinctly unimpressed Sergio Pérez. The Mexican had been blocked by Kevin Magnussen's Haas in Q1, the Dane believing that Pérez was on a warm-up lap, which meant the use of another set of rubber in Q1, which limited Pérez to just one run on the ultras in Q3 and a time half a second shy of his seventh-placed team-mate.

Felipe Massa missed out on Q3 by just four-hundredths, while team-mate Lance Stroll – with ex-Ferrari man and mentor Luca Baldisserri acting as engineer while regular race engineeer James Urwin attended the birth of his child – went out in Q1 thanks to a significant de-rate on the back straight, not helped by an additional three-place grid penalty for impeding Romain Grosjean out of the final turn.

Daniil Kvyat, who had been dropped in favour of Pierre Gasly at Suzuka, was back in the Toro Rosso while Gasly attempted to clinch the Japanese Super Formula title (he was thwarted by a typhoon). Sainz had left for Renault, and Porsche's Le Mans/WEC champion, Brendon Hartley, who had been dropped from the Red Bull programme in 2010, was given a rare second chance and was drafted in for an F1 debut. Kvyat did a decent job to qualify 12th, but had no guarantees for the future beyond the weekend.

It was a big ask of Hartley, who had not driven a single-seater since 2012. Despite being 0.8s away from Kvyat, he aquitted himself well: his long-run pace was decent – despite his crash helmet trying to lift itself from his head! – and predictably his qualifying pace was affected by unfamiliarity with the nuances of F1 tyre preparation. He was quicker than the Saubers and within four-hundredths of the delayed Stroll after a session in which he did just one Q1 run, knowing that grid penalties for a replacement Renault would put him at the back any way.

Romain Grosjean qualified a couple of tenths behind Vandoorne in Q2, while gripless Haas team-mate Kevin Magnussen was half a second slower in Q1 and last of all, behind both Saubers, Ericsson more than three-tenths faster than an unhappy Wehrlein.

THE first Austin GP since new F1 owners Liberty Media had taken charge was enlivened by the appearance of celebrities from the sporting, entertainment and political arenas – from Usain Bolt to Bill Clinton – as well as a new pre-race introductory format that rather polarised opinion.

The pre-race build-up had well-known boxing MC Michael Buffer – he of "Let's get ready to rumble!" fame – introducing the drivers to an appreciative near-capacity crowd, setting the scene for the widely anticipated Hamilton versus Vettel showdown. Only in America? Let's hope so, muttered more than a few...

It sort of worked, but you couldn't help feeling that F1 was missing its Muhammad Ali figure. Where were Hamilton's staring eyes? And why wasn't he finger-jabbing Vettel, Ali/Frazier style?

"Sebastian who? At Monza, I beat him by half a minute. How in the hell he EVER gonna win it...?" Etcetera.

Despite Hamilton's 8m pole-position advantage, when the starting lights dimmed, it was Vettel's Ferrari that made the slightly better getaway, Sebastian able to go inside Lewis into the wide, uphill Turn One and emerge in front. Behind, Bottas defended from a determined Ricciardo, then Ocon, Räikkönen, Alonso, Sainz, Massa, Pérez, Kvyat, Grosjean, the rapidly advancing Verstappen – up three places on the opening lap from 16th – Ericsson, Stroll, Hülkenberg, Vandoorne, Wehrlein and Hartley.

This was interesting: Ferrari's problems in Asia had prevented them from demonstrating the SF70's true potential, and here was Vettel with a clear track in front of him. But while there were 2017 races where the Ferrari had superior race pace, Austin wasn't one of them, despite conditions that conventional wisdom suggested may have played into their hands. These included a morning rain storm, which potentially made the track more abrasive, and a hotter track temperature that was likely to increase tyre degradation.

Actually, a Mercedes engineer explained that a rain-washed track pushing a marginal one/two-stop race towards the two-stop is a bit of a myth.

"It's an interesting thing with storms," he said. "They can make the track dirtier, and in slowing down the pace at the beginning of the race, it puts less energy into the tyres, the less sliding you have and therefore the less wear you have. So, actually, in a race where the optimum strategy is very close between a one- and two-stopper, as it was here, it can help you do a one-stop rather than force you into a two. In the old days, the reason storms were a problem was that you got abrasion damage and tyre graining, but these tyres don't suffer from that."

Mercedes fears that Vettel could have opened a lead were calmed when Hamilton radioed in: "The pace is good." He was still just 1s behind as they blasted over the line at the end of the fifth lap. Once the tyre temperatures stabilised, he started to have a look at passing the Ferrari. He made a strong exit from Turn 11 on lap six and, with the aid of DRS, went down the inside of Vettel into Turn 12 to relieve him of the lead, Sebastian not offering a great deal of defence.

Once through, Hamilton began to ease away, his 0.88s advantage at the end of lap six out to 1.20s next time around, then 1.86s, 1.91s, 2.31s, 3.35s, 3.39s, 3.94s, 4.08s and 4.45s by the end of lap 15.

Mercedes strategists, having scheduled a one-stop race,

Above: Esteban Ocon continued to impress with sixth place and another haul of points.

Photo: Sahara Force India F1 Team

Top left: The 'gladiators' are called into the arena. Marcus Ericsson is the first to receive the call amid the razzmatazz introductions.

Photo: Sauber F1 Team

Above left: All for nothing. Another great performance from Fernando Alonso put him into Q3, but yet more points were lost when he retired with another engine failure.

Photo: Terry Griffin

Centre left: The championship's two protagonists are introduced to the near-capacity crowd.

Left: New boy Brendon Hartley gives his view on his first taste of F1.

Opening spread: A jubilant Lewis Hamilton sprays the Carbon, having strengthened his grip on the championship.

Photos: Peter J. Fox

Above: Kimi Räikkönen once again went largely under the radar, but he inherited third place after the race when a late charging Max Verstappen was adjudged to have exceeded the track limits.
Photo: Scuderia Ferrari

Top right: Felipe Massa's Williams was locked in battle with Sergio Pérez's Force India, with the Mexican eventually taking the honour for eighth.
Photo: Lukas Gorys

Above right: Making his point? Daniil Kvyat was dropped by Toro Rosso after his strongest race of the season ended with a tenth-place finish.
Photo: Jean-François Galeron/WRi2

Right: Toto Wolff and Niki Lauda congratulate each other after Mercedes clinched another constructors' title. Reserve driver and GP3 star George Russell enjoys the moment, too.
Photo: Mercedes AMG Petronas F1 Team

had planned to get Lewis as far as lap 18 or 19 on his starting ultrasoft Pirellis, to give him the range to complete the 56-lap race on a single set of softs. Vettel, however, dived into the pits for a set of softs after just 16 laps, potentially making a one-stop race for Ferrari a bit marginal. While losing ground to Hamilton, he had also reported blistering his left front Pirelli.

Red Bull and Ricciardo, meanwhile, still bottled up behind Bottas and almost 10s behind the leading Mercedes after it had all got a bit physical out of Turn One, had gone for an even more aggressive lap-12 stop on to the supersofts – signifying a two-stop race – in an attempt to undercut Valtteri. Sadly, though, the Australian's threat was extinguished when he crawled to a halt on lap 15 with a power unit problem. He joined Hülkenberg (no oil pressure after three laps) and Wehrlein, whose Sauber had been damaged in a spat with Magnussen at Turn 12, as early casualties.

The spirited dice with Ricciardo had left Bottas with car damage, after a hugely late lunge down the inside of Turn One from the Red Bull on lap four had forced No. 77 off on the exit, the pair rubbing wheels as a stubborn Bottas refused to cede.

"He dived inside, I tried to defend and he basically didn't leave me any space, so I had to go off the track," Valtteri said. "It was all okay, just close racing, but at some point I picked up damage to the floor. Maybe it was in the contact with Daniel."

Surprisingly, perhaps, Mercedes elected to pit Bottas first, after 18 laps, to protect his position against Räikkönen, whose Ferrari was running just 2.5s behind and within undercut range. That made it tight for Hamilton to retain his

lead when he pitted on the next lap, three laps later than Vettel, and rejoined still in front. Just.

"How did he get so close?" a surprised Hamilton asked.

Mercedes admitted that they could have pitted a lap earlier, but also had been surprised by Vettel's speed profile early in his second stint. After a fast out-lap on new softs, his first flying lap – the so-called 'golden' lap – was fast (1m 39.702s). The next lap is usually slower, and had it been, the situation would have been that much more comfortable for Hamilton. But in fact, Vettel's second flying lap was actually nearly half a second quicker (1m 39.379s) than the golden lap and included running off track on the exit of Turn 19, where there is time to be had. Track limits had been a controversial issue all weekend and would become even more so as a result of the race's last lap…

Race stewards looked into Vettel's Turn 19 with the aid of their numerous mini-sector data points and were satisfied that the Ferrari's time gain had not been made there, surprising as that seemed. Hamilton himself was sceptical about the matter when he raised it with Charlie Whiting in the drivers' briefing in Mexico.

Mercedes had anticipated Hamilton rejoining with 1.0– 1.5s in hand – still a bit tight, you might think – but in fact, his margin was just 0.6s. The reason for extending his stint, apart from protecting Bottas, was to make sure that his second set of tyres was in as good a state as possible at the end of the race, with Ferrari, they thought, likely to convert to a two-stopper.

At this point, Max Verstappen was leading briefly, some 3s ahead of Hamilton, having gone further on his longer-range supersofts than the top ten qualifiers on their ultrasofts. He

had disposed of Grosjean and Kvyat on lap two, Pérez on lap three, Massa on lap four, Sainz on lap six, Alonso on lap seven and Ocon on lap ten, before Bottas, Räikkönen and Hamilton pitted out of his way. Who said this overtaking lark was difficult? At COTA at any rate, it wasn't, although Autódromo Hermanos Rodriguez a week later would prove a different story…

Hamilton closed down Verstappen quickly on his new softs and retook the race lead on lap 23, having extended his margin over Vettel to 3s again. From that point, he was always in control.

As soon as Hamilton was back past him, Verstappen pitted for a set of fresh softs and rejoined fifth, just 10s behind Räikkönen's Ferrari, which had been brought in on lap 20, Ferrari seemingly throwing away the undercut opportunity on Bottas. Initially, the Red Bull cut Räikkönen's advantage to 6s, but then Kimi raised his pace and started to match Verstappen's times, prompting Red Bull to begin thinking about a two-stop, given that behind Max, Ocon's sixth-placed Force india was well out of the pit-stop window.

Pérez was right behind his team-mate, but was denied permission to attack, as Ocon was in tyre management mode after a lap-14 stop, and the team figured that Sergio should be doing likewise, having stopped two laps earlier than Esteban in a successful attempt to undercut Sainz, a tactic that would require 44 laps out of his softs. They had both been closing on Massa, whose Williams had yet to stop, having started on supersofts, but Felipe soon pitted out of their way. When he did so, Ocon rapidly proved that he had no problem in extending his advantage over Pérez who, in fact, had his hands full with Sainz, who nailed him with a

VIEWPOINT
OVER THE EDGE

Right: Hamilton slips his Mercedes inside the Ferrari of Sebastian Vettel on lap six, before heading for his record sixth victory in the United States Grand Prix.

Photo: Studio Colombo/WRi2

Below: As the field starts to settle, Max Verstappen begins his climb through from a lowly sixteenth place on the grid.

Photo: Peter J. Fox

MAX VERSTAPPEN'S pass on Kimi Räikkönen might have taken F1 into a grey area in the regulations (and, literally, on to the edge of the track), but opinion in the wider world was black and white.

You either thought the move was audacious and exactly what motor racing is all about. Or you held the view that the Red Bull driver had broken the rules by gaining an unfair advantage and deserved to be punished.

The overall effect – as the debate raged across comment columns during the following week – was to make F1 look muddled and incapable. There seemed to be no precise definition of the track limits, which lay at the very heart of the problem.

There were endless examples of drivers putting all four wheels across the white line and getting away with it. An answer – of sorts – could be found in the wording of the stewards' decisions.

In FIA Document 45, Valtteri Bottas was called to account for leaving the track at Turn One, but received no punishment because "the driver did not gain a lasting advantage". In Document 48, however, the four stewards unanimously declared that Verstappen had gained "a lasting advantage".

It was suggested elsewhere that Räikkönen had either forced Verstappen into this position or that Max had gone off to prevent the Ferrari from closing the door – as Kimi had every right to do. The stewards clearly felt that such arguments were irrelevant. Verstappen had gained an advantage by going off the road and gathering a momentum he would not otherwise have enjoyed. End of discussion.

The incident was further elevated into controversy by the fact that it had happened on the last lap. This was seen by many as a thrilling opportunist move and exactly the sort of thing F1 needs in an era when overtaking is made unnecessarily difficult by the absurd influence of aerodynamics.

Debate covered many issues (some given an unnecessary hard edge by Verstappen's language in connection with one of the stewards), ranging from the absence of kerbs to dumbing down a racing driver's natural instincts.

But there was one positive. Had Sebastian Vettel, rather than Räikkönen, been elevated to the podium, the championship conspiracy theories would have taken this debate to another level entirely.

Maurice Hamilton

fine move down the inside on the run to Turn 19 on lap 33. Alonso, too, had been in this fight until the McLaren Honda had suddenly lost power and forced yet another retirement.

What of debutant Hartley? Last at the end of the opening lap, he'd taken advantage of the Wehrlein/Magnussen debacle and then shot by Vandoorne with the aid of DRS down into Turn 12. Stoffel got him back through Turns 15, 16 and 17, and then Hartley became stuck behind Ericsson's Sauber. Wanting to assess his true pace, Toro Rosso brought him in super-early, after just eight laps, and for the next five laps, on supersofts, he showed highly impressive speed, before Stroll, another early stopper, passed him with DRS on lap 15. Although quicker than the Williams overall, Hartley couldn't get close enough to the Mercedes-powered car and spent most of the rest of his debut bottled up behind the Canadian and Vandoorne.

The headline figures – 0.8s from Kvyat in qualifying and 27s behind him at the flag – might not have looked spectacular, but the detail suggested something a bit different. The Kiwi's attitude and feedback impressed, too.

At the front, Hamilton had built a 7s gap over Vettel again with 20 laps to go. Bottas was just 2.3s behind the Ferrari, while Räikkönen was within DRS range of him, with Verstappen just 2s behind the second Ferrari. At this point, Red Bull went for the two-stopper with Max, bringing him in for a set of new supersofts. Vettel, struggling a little on his softs, did likewise a lap later. By that time, it was too late for Bottas and Räikkönen to follow suit, as they would have been undercut by Verstappen, so both were committed to getting through on a one-stopper.

Once everyone was back up to speed, Hamilton led team-mate Bottas by almost 9s, with Räikkönen tucked up behind, then a 14s gap to the re-shod Vettel, who had a couple of seconds in hand over Verstappen. Vettel was 23s behind Hamilton with 16 laps to go and lapping about 1s quicker than the race leader.

"How are the tyres, Lewis?" the pit-wall team asked.

"Good," said Hamilton, confident that he could have won on either strategy, but certainly not looking to pit again.

Aware of the potential late-race threat from Vettel and Verstappen, Räikkönen upped his pace and took second with a DRS-assisted pass of Bottas on lap 42. In just another seven laps, Vettel had also closed to within DRS range of Bottas. Valtteri defended for a couple of laps, but on lap 51, the German went around his outside into Turn One, squeezing between the Mercedes and a lapped Vandoorne at the same time, and going on to record fastest lap of the race on that same lap.

Team-mate Räikkönen, who was running low on fuel, let Vettel through on the next lap and turned his attention to the closing Verstappen. Sebastian, clocking what was going on, backed off by a full second on lap 54 to try to ensure

that Kimi picked up DRS from him to help defend against the Red Bull.

It looked as though the tactic had worked, but on the last lap, Verstappen went down the inside at Turn 16 and, as Räikkönen turned in, put all four wheels off to the right, kept his boot in and emerged in front. The fans loved it and Verstappen, rightly, took the 'Driver of the Day' accolade. The race stewards were somewhat less impressed, though, and judged that Max had gained "a lasting advantage" because of the abuse of track limits, adding 5s to his race time.

For the second time in a year (Mexico 2016 the other occasion), while Verstappen was enjoying some post-race banter in the pre-podium room, he was told that he would not be required on the podium after all.

In the heat of the moment, he referred to "an idiot steward" who had been present at both races and had it in for him. It wasn't the wisest use of language perhaps, as emotions ran high and accusations of inconsistency regarding track limits were levelled at the FIA.

"Shame on you, FIA," Jos Verstappen posted on Twitter. Which led to an amusing line from Christian Horner when it was suggested to the Red Bull team principal that it was inappropriate for a driver's father to be putting out his opinion on social media.

"Well," said Horner, "if the American president can do it, I don't see why Jos Verstappen can't."

For the record, though, despite Niki Lauda thinking it was the worst decision he'd ever seen, rules are rules. The Red Bull was off the track, and it wasn't just one steward – the voting was 4–0.

Thus Verstappen dropped to fourth in the final classification. Bottas was fifth, having stopped for a new pair of boots for the last handful of laps after Verstappen had passed him. Ocon held off Sainz for sixth, ahead of the lapped Pérez, Massa and Kvyat.

Mercedes had its fourth straight constructors' championship, and a delighted Toto Wolff said, "Achieving the title in Austin, three races early, feels really unbelievable. It is proper reward for so many hardworking people. You always try to identify silver bullets that make the difference, but the fact is that we have really great dynamics in this team. We enjoy doing what we do and putting it all together."

He also had high praise for the race winner: "I've worked with Lewis for five years, and I've never seen him operate at this level: the raw pace is spectacular, and understanding the tyres and the ability of a car that can be difficult sometimes is not easy. The sustained performance on that level, I haven't seen before."

A fourth drivers' title for Hamilton now looked a mere formality. He needed just a fifth place in Mexico City a week later, whatever Vettel's result. As good as done.

Tony Dodgins

2017 FORMULA 1
UNITED STATES GRAND PRIX

AUSTIN 20–22 OCTOBER

ROLEX

F1 **OFFICIAL TIMEPIECE**

RACE DISTANCE: 56 laps, 191.634 miles/308.405km

RACE WEATHER: Dry/sunny (track 34–37°C, air 25–27°C)

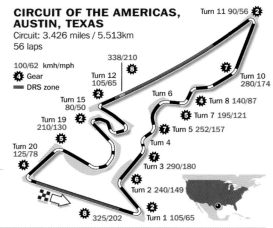

CIRCUIT OF THE AMERICAS, AUSTIN, TEXAS
Circuit: 3.426 miles / 5.513km
56 laps

100/62 kmh/mph
⚙ Gear
▬ DRS zone

Turn 11 90/56
Turn 12 105/65
Turn 15 80/50
Turn 19 210/130
Turn 20 125/78
Turn 10 280/174
Turn 8 140/87
Turn 7 195/121
Turn 6
Turn 5 252/157
Turn 4
Turn 3 290/180
Turn 2 240/149
Turn 1 105/65
338/210
325/202

RACE – OFFICIAL CLASSIFICATION

Pos.	Driver	Nat.	No.	Entrant	Car/Engine	Laps	Time/Retirement	Speed (mph/km/h)	Gap to leader	Fastest race lap
1	**Lewis Hamilton**	GB	44	Mercedes AMG Petronas Motorsport	Mercedes F1 W08-Mercedes M08 EQ Power+ V6	56	1h 33m 50.991s	122.515/197.169		1m 38.776s 48
2	**Sebastian Vettel**	D	5	Scuderia Ferrari	Ferrari SF70H-062 V6	56	1h 34m 01.134s	122.295/196.814	10.143s	1m 37.766s 51
3	**Kimi Räikkönen**	FIN	7	Scuderia Ferrari	Ferrari SF70H-062 V6	56	1h 34m 06.770s	122.173/196.618	15.779s	1m 38.809s 42
4	**Max Verstappen**	NL	33	Red Bull Racing	Red Bull RB13-TAG Heuer RB13 V6	56	1h 34m 07.759s *	122.151/196.583	16.768s	1m 38.060s 39
5	**Valtteri Bottas**	FIN	77	Mercedes AMG Petronas Motorsport	Mercedes F1 W08-Mercedes M08 EQ Power+ V6	56	1h 34m 25.958s	121.759/195.952	34.967s	1m 37.767s 54
6	**Esteban Ocon**	F	31	Sahara Force India Formula 1 Team	Force India VJM10-Mercedes M08 EQ Power+ V6	56	1h 35m 21.971s	120.567/194.034	1m 30.980s	1m 40.499s 53
7	**Carlos Sainz**	E	55	Renault Sport Formula One Team	Renault R.S.17-R.E.17 V6	56	1h 35m 23.935s	120.526/193.967	1m 32.944s	1m 40.462s 43
8	**Sergio Pérez**	MEX	11	Sahara Force India Formula 1 Team	Force India VJM10-Mercedes M08 EQ Power+ V6	55			1 lap	1m 40.851s 14
9	**Felipe Massa**	BR	19	Williams Martini Racing	Williams FW40-Mercedes M08 EQ Power+ V6	55			1 lap	1m 40.131s 36
10	**Daniil Kvyat**	RUS	26	Scuderia Toro Rosso	Toro Rosso STR12-Renault R.E.17 V6	55			1 lap	1m 40.971s 19
11	Lance Stroll	CDN	18	Williams Martini Racing	Williams FW40-Mercedes M08 EQ Power+ V6	55			1 lap	1m 39.666s 38
12	Stoffel Vandoorne	B	2	McLaren Honda Formula 1 Team	McLaren MCL32-Honda RA617H V6	55			1 lap	1m 40.349s 27
13	Brendon Hartley	NZ	39	Scuderia Toro Rosso	Toro Rosso STR12-Renault R.E.17 V6	55			1 lap	1m 39.979s 47
14	Romain Grosjean	F	8	Haas F1 Team	Haas VF-17-Ferrari 062 V6	55			1 lap	1m 41.259s 36
15	Marcus Ericsson	S	9	Sauber F1 Team	Sauber C36-Ferrari 059/5 V6	55	**		1 lap	1m 41.041s 42
16	Kevin Magnussen	DK	20	Haas F1 Team	Haas VF-17-Ferrari 062 V6	55			1 lap	1m 37.893s 51
	Fernando Alonso	E	14	McLaren Honda Formula 1 Team	McLaren MCL32-Honda RA617H V6	24	engine			1m 41.537s 21
	Daniel Ricciardo	AUS	3	Red Bull Racing	Red Bull RB13-TAG Heuer RB13 V6	14	engine			1m 40.102s 14
	Pascal Wehrlein	D	94	Sauber F1 Team	Sauber C36-Ferrari 059/5 V6	5	accident			1m 47.073s 2
	Nico Hülkenberg	D	27	Renault Sport Formula One Team	Renault R.S.17-R.E.17 V6	3	oil pressure			1m 44.270s 2

* includes 5-second penalty for leaving the track and gaining an advantage (originally finished 3rd). ** includes 5-second penalty for causing an accident.

Fastest race lap: Sebastian Vettel on lap 51, 1m 37.766s, 126.140mph/203.003km/h (new record).

Previous lap record: Sebastian Vettel, 1m 39.347s, 124.133mph/199.772km (2012).

20 · VANDOORNE · McLaren
30-place grid penalty for using additional power unit elements

18 · HÜLKENBERG · Renault
20-place grid penalty for using additional power unit elements

16 · VERSTAPPEN · Red Bull
15-place grid penalty for using additional power unit elements

14 · WEHRLEIN · Sauber

12 · GROSJEAN · Haas

19 · HARTLEY · Toro Rosso
25-place grid penalty for using additional power unit elements

17 · MAGNUSSEN · Haas
3-place grid penalty for impeding another driver

15 · STROLL · Williams
3-place grid penalty for impeding another driver

13 · ERICSSON · Sauber

11 · KVYAT · Toro Rosso

Grid order	1	2	3	4	5	6	7	8	9	10	11	12	13	14	15	16	17	18	19	20	21	22	23	24	25	26	27	28	29	30	31	32	33	34	35	36	37	38	39	40	41	42	43	44
44 HAMILTON	5	5	5	5	5	44	44	44	44	44	44	44	44	44	44	44	44	44	44	7	33	33	44	44	44	44	44	44	44	44	44	44	44	44	44	44	44	44	44	44	44	44	44	44
5 VETTEL	44	44	44	44	44	5	5	5	5	5	5	5	5	5	5	5	5	77	77	7	33	44	44	33	33	5	5	5	5	5	5	5	5	5	5	5	5	5	5	77	77	77	7	7
77 BOTTAS	77	77	77	77	77	77	77	77	77	77	77	77	77	77	77	77	77	7	33	44	5	5	5	77	77	77	77	77	77	77	77	77	77	77	77	77	77	77	7	7	7	77	77	77
3 RICCIARDO	3	3	3	3	3	3	3	3	3	3	3	3	3	7	7	7	33	33	5	5	77	77	77	77	7	7	7	7	7	7	7	7	7	7	7	7	7	7	5	5	5	5	5	5
7 RÄIKKÖNEN	31	7	7	7	7	7	7	7	7	7	7	7	7	33	33	33	5	5	77	77	7	7	7	7	33	33	33	33	33	33	33	33	33	33	33	33	33	33	33	33	33	33	33	33
31 OCON	7	31	31	31	31	31	31	31	31	33	33	33	31	31	55	55	55	55	55	19	19	19	19	19	19	19	19	19	19	31	31	31	31	31	31	31	31	31	31	31	31	31	31	31
55 SAINZ	14	14	14	14	14	14	33	33	33	31	31	31	14	14	19	19	19	19	19	31	31	31	31	31	31	31	31	31	31	11	11	11	55	55	55	55	55	55	55	55	55	55	55	55
14 ALONSO	55	55	55	55	55	55	14	14	14	14	14	14	55	55	3	26	26	26	31	31	14	14	14	14	11	11	11	11	11	55	55	11	11	11	11	11	11	11	11	11	11	11	11	11
11 PÉREZ	19	19	19	33	33	55	55	55	55	55	55	55	3	55	8	2	2	2	2	11	11	11	11	55	55	55	55	26	26	26	26	26	26	26	26	26	26	26	26	26	26	26	26	26
19 MASSA	11	11	33	19	19	19	19	19	19	19	19	19	19	19	2	2	31	14	14	2	2	2	55	26	26	26	26	26	26	8	8	8	8	8	8	8	19	19	19	19	19	19		
26 KVYAT	26	33	11	11	11	11	11	11	11	11	11	11	11	26	26	31	31	14	11	11	55	55	55	2	2	2	8	8	8	20	20	19	19	19	19	19	8	8	8	8	8	8	19	19
8 GROSJEAN	8	26	26	26	26	26	26	26	26	26	26	26	8	8	14	14	11	9	9	26	26	26	26	8	8	20	20	20	20	19	19	20	20	20	2	2	2	2	2	2	2	2		
9 ERICSSON	33	8	8	8	8	8	8	8	8	8	8	8	2	9	11	9	26	26	9	8	8	20	20	18	18	18	2	2	2	2	2	20	20	20	20	20	20	20	20	20	20	20		
94 WEHRLEIN	9	9	9	18	18	18	2	2	2	9	9	11	9	20	20	8	8	8	20	14	18	39	39	2	2	39	39	39	9	9	9	9	9	9	9	9	9	9	9	9	9	9		
18 STROLL	18	18	18	2	2	2	18	18	18	9	11	11	20	8	20	20	18	18	8	9	2	39	39	39	39	39	39	39	18	18	9	18	18	18	18	18	18	18	18					
33 VERSTAPPEN	27	27	2	9	9	9	9	9	9	20	20	20	18	18	18	18	18	18	39	39	39	9	9	9	9	9	9	9	39	39	39	39	39	39	39	39	39	39	39					
20 MAGNUSSEN	2	2	27	39	39	39	39	39	20	20	39	39	39	39	9	39	39	39	39	9	9	9																						
27 HÜLKENBERG	20	39	39	20	20	20	20	20	39	39	18	18	18	18																														
39 HARTLEY	94	94	94	94	94																																							
2 VANDOORNE	39	20	20																																									

TIME SHEETS

PRACTICE 1 (FRIDAY)
Weather: Wet track at first/overcast
Temperatures: track 22–24°C, air 20–21°C

Pos.	Driver	Laps	Time
1	Lewis Hamilton	18	1m 36.335s
2	Sebastian Vettel	20	1m 36.928s
3	Valtteri Bottas	10	1m 36.979s
4	Max Verstappen	21	1m 37.339s
5	Stoffel Vandoorne	26	1m 37.352s
6	Felipe Massa	23	1m 37.570s
7	Kimi Räikkönen	20	1m 37.598s
8	Esteban Ocon	25	1m 37.808s
9	Sergio Pérez	20	1m 37.861s
10	Carlos Sainz	24	1m 38.093s
11	Kevin Magnussen	16	1m 38.408s
12	Lance Stroll	25	1m 38.534s
13	Nico Hülkenberg	19	1m 38.904s
14	Brendon Hartley	28	1m 39.267s
15	Romain Grosjean	17	1m 39.336s
16	Daniel Ricciardo	14	1m 39.366s
17	Sean Gelael	25	1m 40.406s
18	Marcus Ericsson	19	1m 40.448s
19	Charles Leclerc	25	1m 40.828s
20	Fernando Alonso	4	no time

PRACTICE 2 (FRIDAY)
Weather: Dry/overcast
Temperatures: track 30–35°C, air 22–23°C

Pos.	Driver	Laps	Time
1	Lewis Hamilton	26	1m 34.668s
2	Max Verstappen	30	1m 35.065s
3	Sebastian Vettel	11	1m 35.192s
4	Valtteri Bottas	39	1m 35.279s
5	Daniel Ricciardo	24	1m 35.463s
6	Kimi Räikkönen	29	1m 35.514s
7	Fernando Alonso	28	1m 36.304s
8	Felipe Massa	30	1m 36.460s
9	Sergio Pérez	28	1m 36.481s
10	Esteban Ocon	34	1m 36.490s
11	Carlos Sainz	30	1m 36.529s
12	Nico Hülkenberg	18	1m 36.534s
13	Daniil Kvyat	40	1m 36.761s
14	Kevin Magnussen	17	1m 37.285s
15	Stoffel Vandoorne	31	1m 37.463s
16	Lance Stroll	27	1m 37.788s
17	Brendon Hartley	41	1m 37.987s
18	Pascal Wehrlein	35	1m 38.165s
19	Marcus Ericsson	22	1m 38.262s
20	Romain Grosjean	26	1m 38.387s

PRACTICE 3 (SATURDAY)
Weather: Dry/overcast
Temperatures: track - not available, air 26°C

Pos.	Driver	Laps	Time
1	Lewis Hamilton	15	1m 34.478s
2	Sebastian Vettel	19	1m 34.570s
3	Valtteri Bottas	17	1m 34.692s
4	Kimi Räikkönen	17	1m 34.755s
5	Max Verstappen	14	1m 35.103s
6	Felipe Massa	11	1m 35.346s
7	Nico Hülkenberg	21	1m 35.608s
8	Carlos Sainz	16	1m 35.650s
9	Daniel Ricciardo	17	1m 35.723s
10	Sergio Pérez	16	1m 35.802s
11	Esteban Ocon	17	1m 35.965s
12	Lance Stroll	12	1m 36.118s
13	Fernando Alonso	15	1m 36.239s
14	Stoffel Vandoorne	14	1m 36.599s
15	Brendon Hartley	26	1m 36.818s
16	Kevin Magnussen	16	1m 37.271s
17	Marcus Ericsson	17	1m 37.319s
18	Pascal Wehrlein	15	1m 37.807s
19	Romain Grosjean	9	1m 37.891s
20	Daniil Kvyat	6	1m 38.500s

QUALIFYING (SATURDAY)
Weather: Dry/partly sunny Temperatures: track 39–41°C, air 31–32°C

Pos.	Driver	First	Second	Third	Qualifying Tyre
1	Lewis Hamilton	1m 34.822s	1m 33.437s	1m 33.108s	Ultrasoft (new)
2	Sebastian Vettel	1m 35.420s	1m 34.103s	1m 33.347s	Ultrasoft (new)
3	Valtteri Bottas	1m 35.309s	1m 33.769s	1m 33.568s	Ultrasoft (new)
4	Daniel Ricciardo	1m 35.991s	1m 34.495s	1m 33.577s	Ultrasoft (new)
5	Kimi Räikkönen	1m 35.649s	1m 33.840s	1m 33.577s	Ultrasoft (new)
6	Max Verstappen	1m 34.899s	1m 34.716s	1m 33.658s	Ultrasoft (new)
7	Esteban Ocon	1m 35.849s	1m 35.113s	1m 34.647s	Ultrasoft (new)
8	Carlos Sainz	1m 35.517s	1m 34.899s	1m 34.852s	Ultrasoft (new)
9	Fernando Alonso	1m 35.712s	1m 35.046s	1m 35.007s	Ultrasoft (new)
10	Sergio Pérez	1m 36.358s	1m 34.789s	1m 35.148s	Ultrasoft (used)
11	Felipe Massa	1m 35.603s	1m 35.155s		
12	Daniil Kvyat	1m 36.073s	1m 35.529s		
13	Stoffel Vandoorne	1m 36.286s	1m 35.641s		
14	Romain Grosjean	1m 36.835s	1m 35.870s		
15	Nico Hülkenberg	1m 35.740s	no time		
16	Marcus Ericsson	1m 36.842s			
17	Lance Stroll	1m 36.868s			
18	Brendon Hartley	1m 36.889s			
19	Pascal Wehrlein	1m 37.179s			
20	Kevin Magnussen	1m 37.394s			

QUALIFYING: head to head

Hamilton	12	5	Bottas
Vettel	12	5	Räikkönen
Massa	14	2	Stroll
Stroll	1	0	Di Resta
Ricciardo	6	11	Verstappen
Pérez	11	6	Ocon
Hülkenberg	16	0	Palmer
Hülkenberg	0	1	Sainz
Kvyat	6	8	Sainz
Sainz	2	0	Gasly
Kvyat	1	0	Hartley
Ericsson	2	0	Giovinazzi
Ericsson	6	9	Wehrlein
Alonso	13	3	Vandoorne
Vandoorne	1	0	Button
Grosjean	12	5	Magnussen

FOR THE RECORD

4th CONSTRUCTORS' CHAMPIONSHIP: Mercedes
1st GRAND PRIX: Brendon Hartley
50,000th KM LED: Mercedes engine
14,000th LAP RACED: Kimi Räikkönen
150th PODIUM POSITION: Mercedes

DID YOU KNOW?

Brendon Hartley became the 9th New Zealander to start a GP, the first since Mike Thackwell in Canada, 1984.

Ocon's 26 races without a retirement from his debut, beats that set by Max Chilton.

POINTS

DRIVERS

1	Lewis Hamilton	331
2	Sebastian Vettel	265
3	Valtteri Bottas	244
4	Daniel Ricciardo	192
5	Kimi Räikkönen	163
6	Max Verstappen	123
7	Sergio Pérez	86
8	Esteban Ocon	73
9	Carlos Sainz	54
10	Felipe Massa	36
11	Nico Hülkenberg	34
12	Lance Stroll	32
13	Romain Grosjean	28
14	Kevin Magnussen	15
15	Stoffel Vandoorne	13
16	Fernando Alonso	10
17	Jolyon Palmer	8
18	Pascal Wehrlein	5
19	Daniil Kvyat	5

CONSTRUCTORS

1	Mercedes	575
2	Ferrari	428
3	Red Bull	315
4	Force India	159
5	Williams	68
6	Toro Rosso	53
7	Renault	48
8	Haas	43
9	McLaren	23
10	Sauber	5

0 · MASSA · Williams   8 · ALONSO · McLaren   6 · OCON · Force India   4 · RICCIARDO · Red Bull   2 · VETTEL · Ferrari

9 · PÉREZ · Force India   7 · SAINZ · Renault   5 · RÄIKKÖNEN · Ferrari   3 · BOTTAS · Mercedes   1 · HAMILTON · Mercedes

45	46	47	48	49	50	51	52	53	54	55	56	
44	44	44	44	44	44	44	44	44	44	44	44	1
7	7	7	7	7	7	7	5	5	5	5	5	2
77	77	77	77	77	77	5	7	7	7	7	33	3
5	5	5	5	5	5	77	33	33	33	33	7	4
33	33	33	33	33	33	33	77	77	77	77	77	5
31	31	31	31	31	31	31	31	31	31	31		6
55	55	55	55	55	55	55	55	55	55	55		7
11	11	11	11	11	11	11	11	11	11	11		8
26	26	26	26	26	26	26	19	19	19	19		9
19	19	19	19	19	19	19	26	26	26	26		10
8	8	8	8	8	8	8	8	8	2	18		
2	2	2	2	2	2	2	2	2	18	2		
20	9	18	18	18	18	18	18	18	39	39		
9	18	9	9	39	39	9	9	39	8	8		
18	39	39	39	9	9	9	9	9	9	9		
39	20	20	20	20	20	20	20	20	20	20		

20 = Pit stop   39 = One lap or more behind

RACE TYRE STRATEGIES

  PIRELLI

	Driver	Race Stint 1	Race Stint 2	Race Stint 3
1	Hamilton	Ultrasoft (u): 1–19	Soft (n): 20–56	
2	Vettel	Ultrasoft (u): 1–16	Soft (n): 17–38	Supersoft (u): 39–56
3	Räikkönen	Ultrasoft (u): 1–20	Soft (n): 21–56	
4	Verstappen	Supersoft (u): 1–24	Soft (n): 25–37	Supersoft (u): 38–56
5	Bottas	Ultrasoft (u): 1–18	Soft (n): 19–52	Ultrasoft (u): 53–56
6	Ocon	Ultrasoft (u): 1–14	Soft (n): 15–56	
7	Sainz	Ultrasoft (u): 1–19	Soft (n): 20–56	
8	Pérez	Ultrasoft (u): 1–12	Soft (n): 13–55	
9	Massa	Supersoft (n): 1–29	Ultrasoft (n): 30–55	
10	Kvyat	Ultrasoft (n): 1–17	Soft (n): 18–55	
11	Stroll	Supersoft (n): 1–10	Soft (n): 11–36	Ultrasoft (n): 37–55
12	Vandoorne	Supersoft (n): 1–25	Ultrasoft (n): 26–55	
13	Hartley	Ultrasoft (u): 1–8	Supersoft (n): 9–35	Supersoft (u): 36–55
14	Grosjean	Ultrasoft (u): 1–16	Soft (n): 17–55	
15	Ericsson	Supersoft (n): 1–21	Soft (n): 22–55	
16	Magnussen	Supersoft (n): 1	Soft (n): 2–49	Ultrasoft (n): 50–55
	Alonso	Ultrasoft (u): 1–14	Soft (n): 15–24 (dnf)	
	Ricciardo	Ultrasoft (u): 1–12	Supersoft (u): 13–14 (dnf)	
	Wehrlein	Soft (n): 1–3	Soft (u): 4–5 (dnf)	
	Hülkenberg	Ultrasoft (u): 1–3 (dnf)		

The tyre regulations stipulate that at least two of three dry tyre specifications must be used during a dry race.
Pirelli P Zero logos are colour-coded on the tyre sidewalls: Purple = Ultrasoft; Yellow = Soft; Red = Supersoft. (n) new (u) used

Photos: Peter J. Fox

MEXICAN GRAND PRIX

MEXICO CITY CIRCUIT

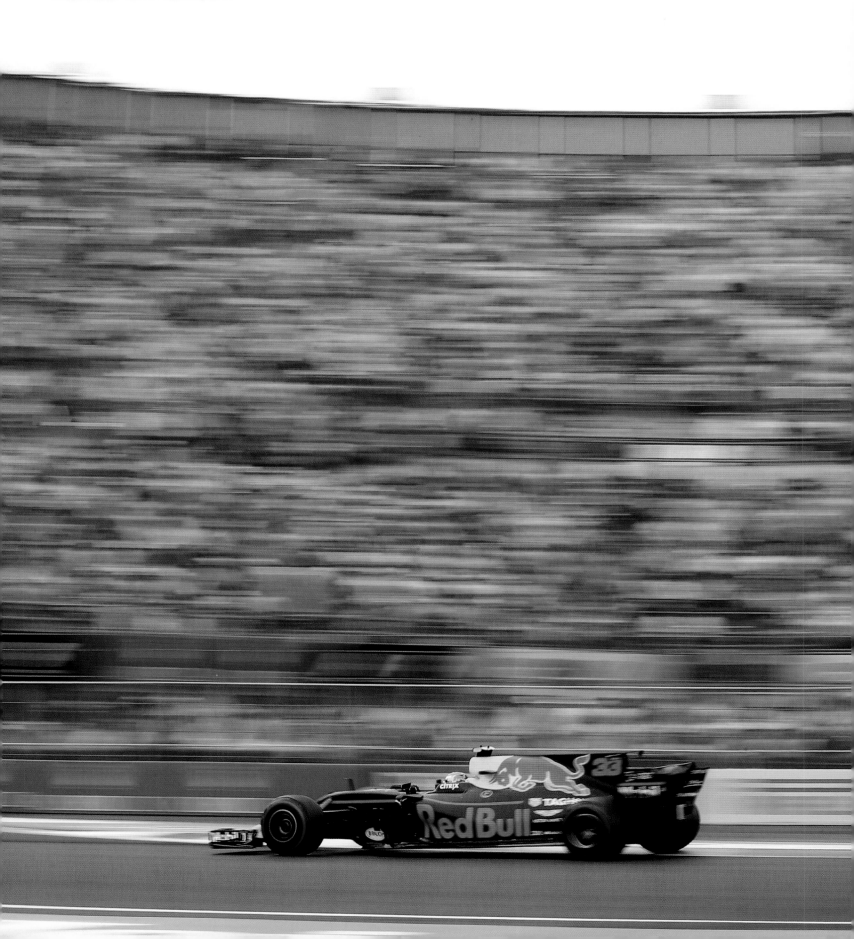

MEXICO CITY QUALIFYING

FROM Austin to the altitude of Mexico City, where, despite high-downforce aero packages, the thin air means that an F1 car actually generates less downforce than even at Monza.

Lewis Hamilton arrived knowing that a fifth place would be good enough to admit him to that exclusive four-times world champions' club, the select membership of which comprised just Michael Schumacher, Juan-Manuel Fangio, Alain Prost and Sebastian Vettel. Hamilton wasn't thinking like that, though; he wanted to win it in style. But it soon became apparent that if he was to win at Autódromo Hermanos Rodriguez, he wasn't going to have things all his own way.

Mercedes team-mate Valtteri Bottas topped the first session of free practice, Daniel Ricciardo the second and Max Verstappen the third. Moreover, Red Bull, Mercedes and Ferrari all seemed to have similar single-lap and race pace.

Illustrating that point, in Saturday morning's final session of practice, Verstappen's Red Bull was quickest in the first sector of the 2.6-mile lap, Hamilton's Mercedes in the second and Vettel's Ferrari in the third.

The low-grip surface meant that sometimes the first lap on a set of tyres wasn't the quickest, and the secret was to get the tyres 'in' for the first sector of the lap. After the first Q3 run, Verstappen was happy, with a handy margin over Vettel and Hamilton, his 1m 16.574s significantly quicker than both of them. But, a great final run by Vettel was enough to stop Max from taking his first F1 pole position, by less than a tenth. It was Vettel's 50th F1 pole and his fourth of the season. Thus, in high-downforce trim, Ferrari had taken pole in Monaco, Budapest, Singapore and now Mexico.

"Yes, guys! *Grazie!*" exclaimed Vettel on the radio, before explaining, "Max was very quick in Q2 [0.35s quicker than the Ferrari] and I don't know where he pulled that one from! The asphalt is slippery and it's very easy to make a mistake. Around here, it's very difficult to understand where the limit is, where you can push and where you can't. And he goes four-tenths quicker than anyone else. How did he do that?

"But I knew that if I got the first sector together, I had a better chance. I had a moment in sixth gear and nearly lost the car, but held it together. Crossing the line, I knew it would be close. When I heard "P1", it was like an explosion in the car. And certainly a better one than yesterday when the fire extinguisher set itself off!"

Verstappen blamed the tyres for failing to improve on his final run. A small energy deployment issue had also cost him a few hundredths. We had the same front row as Singapore, with Verstappen's lap good enough to relegate Mercedes to the second row, Hamilton beating team-mate Bottas by just 0.02s. Whenever presented with a low-grip surface, Valtteri always seems much more on par with Lewis.

You had to wonder what Kimi Räikkönen was doing, some three-quarters of a second shy of Vettel as he put the second Ferrari fifth, joined on the third row by Esteban Ocon's Force India. This being Mexico, the home of Sergio Pérez, with whom Ocon had had many an on-track altercation, the young Frenchman had actually received death threats on social media! With the pair split by an average of 0.07s in qualifying over the season, Sergio ahead more often than not, it won't have gone down well with the home supporters that Ocon chose this race to outqualify Pérez by 0.37s and four places!

A somewhat bemused seventh was Daniel Ricciardo, almost nine-tenths adrift of his front-row-starting Red Bull team-mate. "We've been strong all weekend, but in qualifying, we just didn't have any grip. We tried experimenting in Q3 and doing an extra warm-up lap to try and give the tyres something extra, but it seemed that the grip I had when I left the box was the grip I had until the end of each run. Sometimes you get one set of tyres that you can't turn on or warm up properly, and you might lose some time, but every run it seemed to be the same story."

Weighing their options, Red Bull decided to take new engine components, meaning that Ricciardo would start 16th.

Renault, with its new Nico Hülkenberg/Carlos Sainz driver line-up, had skipped ahead of Haas for seventh place in the constructors' championship by dint of Sainz's fine seventh in Austin, and now was just five points behind Toro Rosso and 20 shy of Williams in fifth place. Overhauling Sir Frank's men would be a tall order, but that was the target.

Hülkenberg turned in a fine lap to qualify eighth, a decent 0.33s ahead of Sainz, as the Renaults looked set to fight a keen 'best of the rest' battle behind Ferrari, Mercedes and Red Bull.

Williams was a couple of tenths behind Pérez, Massa ahead of Stroll, while none of the remaining Q2 men (Brendon Hartley, and McLaren drivers Stoffel Vandoorne and Fernando Alonso) recorded a time. All faced a hatful of engine penalties and so went into tyre conservation mode for the race. Kiwi Hartley, confirmed in the Toro Rosso squad alongside Pierre Gasly for the rest of the season, actually did a strong job to split the Williams pair in Q2 before his power unit failed.

Marcus Ericsson outpaced Sauber team-mate Pascal Wehrlein, the Hinwil cars ahead of both Haas machines. The Haas was not at its best in high-downforce trim, and the team's suspicions that they would struggle proved on the money. Gasly, meanwhile, brought up the rear, awful reliability scuppering most of free practice and robbing him of the chance to take any part in qualifying.

THE run down to Turns One and Two in Mexico is long, and with overtaking sure to be difficult for the rest of the afternoon, there was even more onus on getting as much done on the opening lap as possible. It was going to be busy…

"Initially," said Verstappen, "I almost touched the limiter and so my start wasn't great, but then, actually because of that, I was in a good position because I had a good slipstream from Sebastian."

The Ferrari moved to protect the inside into Turn One and briefly they were almost three abreast as Hamilton made up ground from P3, to the left of Verstappen.

Turning in, Vettel had the inside, but Verstappen took a plunge around the outside. "I just saw that we had a little bit of a touch, but didn't really feel anything," he said. "I got through Turn Two in front, and from then on, I could do my own race, which was crucial."

A piece of Vettel's left front wing flew into the air, and Hamilton, seeing the opportunity to gain as well, accelerated through the right-hander at Turn Three in second place. Vettel, though, ran slightly wide on exit, his damaged wing snagging Hamilton's right rear tyre and puncturing it. Both championship protagonists headed for the pits with damage, Hamilton, with his deflating right rear, at considerably slower pace. Bottas, meanwhile, took advantage to snatch second place, ahead of Ocon, Hülkenberg, Sainz, Pérez, Massa, Räikkönen, Stroll, Ricciardo (up from 16th on the grid), Magnussen, Vandoorne, Ericsson, Grosjean, Alonso, Wehrlein, Hartley and Gasly.

"Did he [Vettel] do it on purpose?" Lewis asked over the team radio.

"Don't know, Lewis," came the reply. It seemed unlikely, given that to stand any chance of keeping his slim title hopes alive, Vettel needed to win the race or finish second. On the other hand, knowing that he was compromised straight away, it didn't harm that Hamilton was, too. The race stewards, meanwhile, decreed that no investigation into the incident was necessary.

Thus both title contenders faced recovery drives. Across the line at the end of the second lap, Vettel's Ferrari, with its replacement nose, was 19th, 35s behind leader Verstappen and 10s behind his first target, Gasly. Lewis was dead last, a further 24s in arrears. At their pit stops, both the Ferrari and Mercedes had been fitted with the hardest-compound Pirelli tyre on offer, the yellow-walled soft, giving both the capability to run to the end of the 71-lap race.

Hamilton, however, suffered another bad break when Carlos Sainz, who had been running fifth, spun his Renault on the second lap, suspected he might have had a puncture and pitted for fresh tyres, also going on to the softs. He rejoined 11s behind Vettel and 13s ahead of Hamilton.

With Verstappen comfortable in the lead, 2s ahead after the opening couple of laps and dropping Bottas by 0.3–0.4s per lap, Ricciardo was also going well in the second Red Bull, gaining two places on lap three at the expense of Williams. He passed Lance Stroll and Felipe Massa, who was headed for the pits with a slow puncture to his left front. That put Ricciardo seventh, just a second-and-a-half behind Räikkönen's Ferrari, which had made a poor start and was stuck behind Pérez's Force India.

It was not Ricciardo's weekend, though. After his struggle in qualifying and the decision to take a new power unit and its attendant penalties, Daniel was out after five laps with more Renault power unit issues. The ERS-H was fingered this time.

Hamilton had closed down the gap to Sainz by lap 16,

Above: Fernando Alonso drove with his usual verve and determination to claim a point for McLaren Honda.
Photo: McLaren Honda

Centre from top: Cigars, sombreros and senoritas provided a rich palette of colour.
Photos: Peter J. Fox

Above left: A golden glow surrounds F2 champion and Sauber's driver prospect, Charles Leclerc.
Photo: Sauber F1 Team

Centre left: Lance Stroll made good use of his qualifying position to bring his Williams home sixth.
Photo: Lukas Gorys

Left: Sergio Pérez salutes the fans at his home race.
Photo: Sahara Force India F1 Team

Opening spread, main: Max Verstappen took charge on the opening lap and sped to an untroubled victory.
Photo: Peter J. Fox

Opening spread, inset: Max was triumphant, leaving Valtteri Bottas to trail home nearly 20 seconds adrift.
Photo: Jad Sherif/WRi2

Above: The race win was effectively decided on the opening lap, after Sebastian Vettel's Ferrari ran into Lewis Hamilton's Mercedes, giving the Red Bull of Max Verstappen a free run.
Photo: Mercedes AMG Petronas F1 Team

Right: Following a pit stop for a new front wing, Sebastian Vettel climbed back through the field to fourth place, but by then his slim championship chances had long gone.
Photo: Scuderia Ferrari

but now the Renault was on the tail of Wehrlein's Sauber and unable to get past. Compounding Lewis's struggle was Sainz picking up the DRS from Wehrlein each lap, making the Renault almost impossible to pass.

"Jeez, I just can't get past these guys," a frustrated Hamilton said over the radio. Initially, Vettel and Hamilton had been able to lap within half a second of leader Verstappen's ultrasoft-shod Red Bull on their softs, but now car No. 44's pace was 2.5s slower than the leading Red Bull. That forced Hamilton to react to blue flags and let the race leader lap him after 21 laps! Vettel, meanwhile, was making progress, the Ferrari up to 13th after 20 laps.

The characteristics of the Mexico lap, and the relative ineffectiveness of slipstreaming and DRS in the thin air, meant that one of the biggest speed deltas of the season was needed to mount an effective overtaking bid – something in the order of 1.3–1.4s. Looking at their respective Q3 times, Hamilton only had a 0.86s margin over Sainz, so it was hardly surprising that he was unable to pass the Spaniard. It would have been tough enough any way, even without the Renault picking up DRS from the Sauber.

It was as frustrating for the Mercedes strategists as it was for Hamilton. When Mercedes had put him on the soft-compound Pirelli at his opening-lap stop, they obviously hadn't known that Sainz would spin on the following lap, stop and pit out in front of them. Had they known, they would have fitted ultrasofts and accepted the need to make a second stop.

Renault's afternoon, so promising when Hülkenberg and Sainz had run fourth and fifth on the opening lap, soon fell apart completely with yet more unreliability. By lap 18, 'The Hulk' had fallen around 4s behind Ocon, but had a similar margin over Pérez and Räikkönen when Force India went for the undercut with their home hero. Renault responded on the next lap with Hülkenberg, who pitted out still ahead of the Force India, now behind Magnussen, Stroll and Räikkönen. Four laps later, though, Pérez was past, Hülkenberg reporting, "No power", before grinding to a halt on lap 25.

Six laps later, Hartley's Renault-powered Toro Rosso also stopped with a power unit issue, after another solid drive by the Kiwi. He had run at a very similar pace to Alonso, albeit that the Spaniard had started on supersofts, rather than ultrasofts, with a view to running a longer stint. Increasingly, Hartley and Gasly were looking like Toro Rosso's line-up heading into 2018.

Ocon had a 7s lead over Räikkönen when he pitted from third on lap 20, but when Pérez had pitted out of his way two laps earlier, Kimi's Ferrari was the fastest car on the circuit. His pace was sufficient for Ferrari to attempt overcutting Ocon, a strategy that paid dividends, as Kimi ran to lap 32 on his original ultrasofts before pitting for softs and rejoining 5.5s ahead of the Force India. During those dozen laps, he'd actually reduced his deficit to race leader Verstappen by a second. It suggested that but for Vettel's first-lap brush with the Dutchman, Ferrari certainly had race-winning pace.

At the front, though, Verstappen was in total control, leading Bottas by 6.3s at the 20-lap stage.

"I don't think our car was quite good enough here," Valtteri said. "We couldn't keep up with Max and fight for the win today, which was unfortunate. Handling-wise, it wasn't too bad, just sliding around a bit and missing grip in the corners. I think that's where Red Bull is still at an advantage at places like this."

Hamilton finally made it past Sainz on lap 28 at the end of the main straight; two laps later, he was past Wehrlein. Vettel, by this stage, was up to eighth, 10s behind Magnussen's seventh-placed Haas.

Spending so much time in traffic was not good for even the hardest-compound tyre, not to mention brake and engine cooling, and Hamilton duly reported his scepticism about his softs actually making it to the end. In the event, they didn't need to, a brief virtual safety car period while Hartley's Toro Rosso was recovered affording the opportunity for a relatively cheap pit stop. More than half the field took advantage, including Vettel and Hamilton. The Ferrari switched to ultrasofts, while Mercedes bolted a fresh set of

the red-walled supersofts on to Hamilton's car, believing that there was precious little to choose from between the two softest compounds.

At half-distance, Verstappen led Bottas by 7.5s, with Räikkönen's Ferrari 24s further behind, ahead of Ocon, Stroll, Pérez, Magnussen, Vettel, Alonso, Vandoorne, Ericsson, Gasly, Wehrlein, Grosjean and Hamilton.

"It sucked being back there!" Lewis admitted, his team striving to put his mind at rest regarding the championship; Vettel was still over a minute behind Bottas's second place.

"Vettel is P8 and he needs P2," Hamilton was told. "Our best projection for him is P4, so just keep doing what you're doing and get up into the points."

"Understood," Lewis came back. It wasn't the way he wanted to win it, but it was the hand he'd been dealt. Aiming for those lower points positions, he passed Grosjean on lap 36, Wehrlein on lap 38, Gasly on lap 43, Ericsson on lap 46 and Vandoorne on lap 53, putting himself into the points for the first time, tenth. Massa's Williams fell four laps later, and then Hamilton set his sights on the eighth place that would mean Vettel needed to win the race to keep his slim hopes alive. The next car up the road, though, was Alonso's…

Fernando himself was trying to pass Magnussen's spiritedly-driven eighth-placed Haas as the American team battled for every point in its fight with Renault in the constructors' championship. As with Sainz and Wehrlein earlier in the race, Hamilton was faced with Alonso picking up DRS from Magnussen.

By now, Vettel had passed Ocon for fourth, and Räikkönen could be counted on to move over for him if need be, but the Ferrari was still more than 50s behind Bottas's second place. No doubt this was one occasion when the Mercedes pit-wall crew sympathised with Christian Horner's tapping

Above: After his first-lap puncture, Lewis Hamilton could only finish ninth, but the 2017 champion indulged himself with some celebratory doughnuts.
Photo: Studio Colombo/WRi2

Top right: The four-times champion flies the flag.
Photo: Peter J. Fox

Above centre right: Kimi Räikkönen took a lonely third place for Ferrari.
Photo: Scuderia Ferrari

Above right: For the record. Lewis and Sebastian give their post-race views in the TV pen.
Photo: Lukas Gorys

Right: Carlos Sainz in the Renault proved to be a difficult man for Hamilton to pass.
Photo: Renault F1 Team

foot in the hope that leader Verstappen did not suffer the same fate as the other Renault-engined cars. Sainz, too, retired after 59 laps. If Vettel got up to second, Hamilton needed to be eighth to clinch the championship.

Caution, though, did not stop the racer in Lewis indulging in an entertaining scrap with Alonso. The tactical approach was to attack hard, costing Alonso time in defence and breaking his DRS assistance from Magnussen, with the idea then of picking off the McLaren Honda when it was on its own. It took a while for the strategy to work, but Lewis finally nailed Fernando around the outside of Turn Four and into Turn Five in what some of the Mercedes team thought was one of the passes of the year.

"Was that okay, or did he have all four wheels off the track?" Alonso asked his team on the radio.

"It was okay, Fernando, just hard racing," they confirmed.

"Fernando… that is one tough Mofo!" Lewis laughed afterwards. "Wait 'til the guy gets a good engine. McLaren has a special place in my heart, and I hope next year they have a better engine and car." A sentiment Alonso no doubt shared…

Vettel reduced what had been a 43.5s deficit to Räikkönen on lap 31 to just 16s over the remaining 40 laps, repeatedly setting new lap records as he did so. Verstappen replied to take back fastest lap of the race on lap 65, prompting Vettel to hit back with a lap a couple of tenths quicker with three to go.

Not for the first time came stern instructions from the pit wall for Verstappen to slow down. "Let's just say we have a

bonus system for fastest lap," Christian Horner said, "but I told Max's race engineer that under no circumstances was he to inform him what lap time Sebastian had just done."

After 71 laps, Verstappen crossed the line with almost 20s in hand over Bottas to win his second grand prix of the final four. Räikkönen was a further 34s behind, and fourth was not enough for Vettel. Ocon's excellent fifth equalled his best F1 finish in Barcelona, and a good effort from Stroll, sixth, split the Force India pair as Pérez had to accept seventh on home turf. Magnussen managed to hang on to a hard-earned four points for eighth, half a second ahead of Hamilton, and close Haas to within a point of the luckless Renault team in the constructors' championship.

Finally it was done, Hamilton's ninth place securing his membership of that four-times world champions' club. The mouthwatering three-way fight between the sport's current leading teams had not quite materialised, and there was much discussion about what might have transpired if it had.

"I think in a clean race, Lewis could have won, because our pace with a damaged car was very good," said Toto Wolff.

Red Bull had a very different opinion: Verstappen, they said, had been cruising. And Ferrari's pace was such that Maranello appeared to have had about a tenth or a tenth-and-a-half in hand over the Silver Arrows in Mexico. But it was all conjecture. The hour belonged to Verstappen and Hamilton as F1 appeared to be in ruder health than for quite some time.

Tony Dodgins

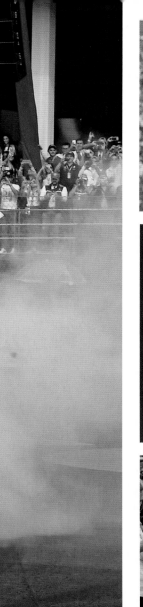

VIEWPOINT
STUCK IN THIN AIR

LEWIS HAMILTON: P19: stuck behind Carlos Sainz for a dozen laps and more: going nowhere. Having become accustomed to car No. 44 cutting through the field, this was difficult to fathom.

It was tempting to wonder if Hamilton's head had dropped for the first time in 2017, after being relegated to unfamiliar territory at the back. After all, Sebastian Vettel had also been forced to make an early stop, and there were two more races for Lewis to gather the handful of points needed for the title. Why take unnecessary risks when trying to deal with Sainz, particularly as the Renault driver was busy trying to get by Pascal Wehrlein?

Sainz was also unable to make headway – and there was the clue. The familiar negative effect of F1 aerodynamics on the following car was exacerbated hugely by the substance of this track and its geographical circumstances.

The low-grip surface was made even more difficult to deal with by Mexico City's altitude. The thin air pushed brake and engine cooling to critical when following another car for any length of time. After a couple of failed overtaking attempts, it was necessary to either drop back or run in echelon. DRS was of little help, since its effect was reduced thanks to less drag in the first place.

Throw in the quick contour of a final corner that allowed the leading car to ease ahead just sufficiently to remain out of reach, even on a straight as long as this one, and you had the recipe for follow-my-leader. Plus, in the singular case of Hamilton's all-or-nothing move on Fernando Alonso's slower (in theory) McLaren Honda, a spectacular and brave candidate for 'overtake of the year'.

Doubtless Liberty Media will have taken note, particularly when comparing Autódromo Hermanos Rodriguez with Circuit of the Americas. The contrast between T17 at the former and the wide, multi-line entries into T1 and T11 at COTA will hopefully have prompted the thought that the layout of a track requires just as much attention as its outer limits.

Maurice Hamilton

18

2017 FORMULA 1
GRAN PREMIO DE MÉXICO

MEXICO CITY 27–29 OCTOBER

RACE DISTANCE: 71 laps, 189.738 miles/305.354km

RACE WEATHER: Dry/sunny (track 38–43°C, air 22–24°C)

ROLEX

F1 OFFICIAL TIMEPIECE
Formula 1

AUTODROMO HERMANOS RODRIGUEZ, MEXICO CITY
Circuit: 2.674 miles / 4.304km 70 laps

Recta Principale

🔧 Gear
— DRS zone

RACE – OFFICIAL CLASSIFICATION

Pos.	Driver	Nat.	No.	Entrant	Car/Engine	Laps	Time/Retirement	Speed (mph/km/h)	Gap to leader	Fastest race lap
1	**Max Verstappen**	NL	33	Red Bull Racing	Red Bull RB13-TAG Heuer RB13 V6	71	1h 36m 26.552s	118.042/189.970		1m 18.892s 65
2	**Valtteri Bottas**	FIN	77	Mercedes AMG Petronas Motorsport	Mercedes F1 W08-Mercedes M08 EQ Power+ V6	71	1h 36m 46.230s	117.642/189.326	19.678s	1m 19.374s 70
3	**Kimi Räikkönen**	FIN	7	Scuderia Ferrari	Ferrari SF70H-062 V6	71	1h 37m 20.559s	116.950/188.213	54.007s	1m 20.054s 59
4	**Sebastian Vettel**	D	5	Scuderia Ferrari	Ferrari SF70H-062 V6	71	1h 37m 36.630s	116.630/187.697	1m 10.078s	1m 18.785s 68
5	**Esteban Ocon**	F	31	Sahara Force India Formula 1 Team	Force India VJM10-Mercedes M08 EQ Power+ V6	70			1 lap	1m 20.946s 67
6	**Lance Stroll**	CDN	18	Williams Martini Racing	Williams FW40-Mercedes M08 EQ Power+ V6	70			1 lap	1m 21.062s 53
7	**Sergio Pérez**	MEX	11	Sahara Force India Formula 1 Team	Force India VJM10-Mercedes M08 EQ Power+ V6	70			1 lap	1m 19.929s 54
8	**Kevin Magnussen**	DK	20	Haas F1 Team	Haas VF-17-Ferrari 062 V6	70			1 lap	1m 21.214s 68
9	**Lewis Hamilton**	GB	44	Mercedes AMG Petronas Motorsport	Mercedes F1 W08-Mercedes M08 EQ Power+ V6	70			1 lap	1m 19.945s 69
10	**Fernando Alonso**	E	14	McLaren Honda Formula 1 Team	McLaren MCL32-Honda RA617H V6	70			1 lap	1m 21.014s 50
11	Felipe Massa	BR	19	Williams Martini Racing	Williams FW40-Mercedes M08 EQ Power+ V6	70			1 lap	1m 21.136s 55
12	Stoffel Vandoorne	B	2	McLaren Honda Formula 1 Team	McLaren MCL32-Honda RA617H V6	70			1 lap	1m 20.972s 66
13	Pierre Gasly	F	10	Scuderia Toro Rosso	Toro Rosso STR12-Renault R.E.17 V6	70			1 lap	1m 20.859s 70
14	Pascal Wehrlein	D	94	Sauber F1 Team	Sauber C36-Ferrari 059/5 V6	69			2 laps	1m 21.638s 56
15	Romain Grosjean	F	8	Haas F1 Team	Haas VF-17-Ferrari 062 V6	69			2 laps	1m 20.345s 64
	Carlos Sainz	E	55	Renault Sport Formula One Team	Renault R.S.17-R.E.17 V6	59	steering			1m 21.360s 34
	Marcus Ericsson	S	9	Sauber F1 Team	Sauber C36-Ferrari 059/5 V6	55	rear suspension			1m 21.686s 54
	Brendon Hartley	NZ	28	Scuderia Toro Rosso	Toro Rosso STR12-Renault R.E.17 V6	30	power unit			1m 22.572s 28
	Nico Hülkenberg	D	27	Renault Sport Formula One Team	Renault R.S.17-R.E.17 V6	24	power unit			1m 21.691s 18
	Daniel Ricciardo	AUS	3	Red Bull Racing	Red Bull RB13-TAG Heuer RB13 V6	5	turbo			1m 22.789s 4

Fastest race lap: Sebastian Vettel on lap 68, 1m 18.785s, 122.203mph/196.666km/h (new record for current configuration).

Lap record: Nigel Mansell (Williams FW14 - Renault V10), 1m 16.788s, 128.790mph/207.267km (1991, 2.747-mile/4.421km circuit).

Previous lap record (current configuration): Nico Rosberg (Mercedes F1 W06 V6 turbo), 1m 20.521s, 119.568mph/192.426km/h (2015).

19 · VANDOORNE · McLaren
35-place grid penalty for using additional power unit elements

17 · HARTLEY · Toro Rosso
20-place grid penalty for using additional power unit elements

15 · GROSJEAN · Haas

13 · WEHRLEIN · Sauber

11 · STROLL · Williams

20 · GASLY · Toro Rosso
20-place grid penalty for using additional power unit elements

18 · ALONSO · McLAREN
20-place grid penalty for using additional power unit elements

16 · RICCIARDO · Red Bull
20-place grid penalty for using additional power unit elements

14 · MAGNUSSEN · Haas

12 · ERICSSON · Sauber

5 = Pit stop   44 = One lap or more behind

All results and data © FOM 2017

TIME SHEETS

PRACTICE 1 (FRIDAY)

Weather: Dry/sunny
Temperatures: track 28-37°C, air 16-20°C

Pos.	Driver	Laps	Time
1	Valtteri Bottas	42	1m 17.824s
2	Lewis Hamilton	35	1m 18.290s
3	Max Verstappen	16	1m 18.395s
4	Daniel Ricciardo	28	1m 18.421s
5	Sebastian Vettel	28	1m 18.586s
6	Kimi Räikkönen	27	1m 19.008s
7	Sergio Pérez	21	1m 19.240s
8	Fernando Alonso	20	1m 19.346s
9	Felipe Massa	32	1m 19.443s
10	Nico Hülkenberg	19	1m 19.552s
11	Carlos Sainz	24	1m 19.554s
12	Lance Stroll	34	1m 19.772s
13	Kevin Magnussen	16	1m 20.644s
14	Pascal Wehrlein	30	1m 20.971s
15	Antonio Giovinazzi	26	1m 21.269s
16	Charles Leclerc	28	1m 21.446s
17	Sean Gelael	29	1m 21.639s
18	Brendon Hartley	10	1m 21.747s
19	Alfonso Celis	17	1m 22.342s
20	Stoffel Vandoorne	3	no time

PRACTICE 2 (FRIDAY)

Weather: Dry/sunny
Temperatures: track 45-48°C, air 22-25°C

Pos.	Driver	Laps	Time
1	Daniel Ricciardo	26	1m 17.801s
2	Lewis Hamilton	40	1m 17.932s
3	Max Verstappen	17	1m 17.964s
4	Sebastian Vettel	35	1m 18.051s
5	Kimi Räikkönen	40	1m 18.142s
6	Valtteri Bottas	43	1m 18.299s
7	Fernando Alonso	26	1m 18.508s
8	Sergio Pérez	41	1m 18.728s
9	Nico Hülkenberg	19	1m 18.775s
10	Esteban Ocon	42	1m 18.822s
11	Carlos Sainz	30	1m 19.060s
12	Felipe Massa	37	1m 19.206s
13	Brendon Hartley	40	1m 19.423s
14	Lance Stroll	42	1m 19.524s
15	Stoffel Vandoorne	32	1m 19.844s
16	Pascal Wehrlein	38	1m 20.306s
17	Kevin Magnussen	35	1m 20.318s
18	Marcus Ericsson	38	1m 20.362s
19	Pierre Gasly	10	1m 21.745s
20	Romain Grosjean	3	1m 25.526s

PRACTICE 3 (SATURDAY)

Weather: Dry/sunny
Temperatures: air 20°C

Pos.	Driver	Laps	Time
1	Max Verstappen	20	1m 17.113s
2	Lewis Hamilton	23	1m 17.188s
3	Sebastian Vettel	21	1m 17.230s
4	Valtteri Bottas	18	1m 17.283s
5	Daniel Ricciardo	10	1m 17.361s
6	Kimi Räikkönen	27	1m 17.517s
7	Sergio Pérez	20	1m 18.040s
8	Esteban Ocon	18	1m 18.165s
9	Carlos Sainz	21	1m 18.208s
10	Nico Hülkenberg	21	1m 18.380s
11	Brendon Hartley	23	1m 18.602s
12	Felipe Massa	23	1m 18.690s
13	Lance Stroll	20	1m 19.066s
14	Kevin Magnussen	19	1m 19.205s
15	Marcus Ericsson	27	1m 19.331s
16	Fernando Alonso	22	1m 19.565s
17	Romain Grosjean	22	1m 19.586s
18	Pascal Wehrlein	16	1m 19.826s
19	Stoffel Vandoorne	25	1m 20.030s
20	Pierre Gasly	2	no time

QUALIFYING (SATURDAY)

Weather: Dry/sunny Temperatures: track 43-50°C, air 19-22°C

Pos.	Driver	First	Second	Third	Qualifying Tyre
1	Sebastian Vettel	1m 17.665s	1m 16.870s	1m 16.488s	Ultrasoft (new)
2	Max Verstappen	1m 17.630s	1m 16.524s	1m 16.574s	Ultrasoft (new)
3	Lewis Hamilton	1m 17.518s	1m 17.035s	1m 16.934s	Ultrasoft (new)
4	Valtteri Bottas	1m 17.578s	1m 17.161s	1m 16.958s	Ultrasoft (new)
5	Kimi Räikkönen	1m 18.148s	1m 17.534s	1m 17.238s	Ultrasoft (new)
6	Esteban Ocon	1m 18.336s	1m 17.827s	1m 17.437s	Ultrasoft (new)
7	Daniel Ricciardo	1m 18.208s	1m 17.631s	1m 17.447s	Ultrasoft (new)
8	Nico Hülkenberg	1m 18.322s	1m 17.792s	1m 17.466s	Ultrasoft (new)
9	Carlos Sainz	1m 18.405s	1m 17.753s	1m 17.794s	Ultrasoft (new)
10	Sergio Pérez	1m 18.020s	1m 17.868s	1m 17.807s	Ultrasoft (new)
11	Felipe Massa	1m 18.570s	1m 18.099s		
12	Lance Stroll	1m 18.902s	1m 19.159s		
13	Brendon Hartley	1m 18.683s	no time		
14	Fernando Alonso	1m 17.710s	no time		
15	Stoffel Vandoorne	1m 18.578s	no time		
16	Marcus Ericsson	1m 19.176s			
17	Pascal Wehrlein	1m 19.333s			
18	Kevin Magnussen	1m 19.443s			
19	Romain Grosjean	1m 19.473s			
–	Pierre Gasly	–			

QUALIFYING: head to head

Hamilton	13	5	Bottas
Vettel	13	5	Räikkönen
Massa	15	2	Stroll
Stroll	1	0	Di Resta
Ricciardo	6	12	Verstappen
Pérez	11	7	Ocon
Hülkenberg	16	0	Palmer
Hülkenberg	1	1	Sainz
Kvyat	6	8	Sainz
Sainz	2	0	Gasly
Kvyat	1	0	Hartley
Gasly	0	1	Hartley
Ericsson	2	0	Giovinazzi
Ericsson	7	9	Wehrlein
Alonso	14	3	Vandoorne
Vandoorne	1	0	Button
Grosjean	12	6	Magnussen

FOR THE RECORD

4th WORLD DRIVERS' CHAMPIONSHIP:
Lewis Hamilton

90th PODIUM POSITION: Kimi Räikkönen

50th POLE POSITION: Sebastian Vettel

20th PODIUM POSITION: Valtteri Bottas

DID YOU KNOW?

This was the fourth time that the drivers' championship was decided in Mexico; previously 1964 (Surtees), 1967 (Hulme) and 1968 (Graham Hill).

POINTS

DRIVERS

1	Lewis Hamilton	333
2	Sebastian Vettel	277
3	Valtteri Bottas	262
4	Daniel Ricciardo	192
5	Kimi Räikkönen	178
6	Max Verstappen	148
7	Sergio Pérez	92
8	Esteban Ocon	83
9	Carlos Sainz	54
10	Lance Stroll	40
11	Felipe Massa	36
12	Nico Hülkenberg	34
13	Romain Grosjean	28
14	Kevin Magnussen	19
15	Stoffel Vandoorne	13
16	Fernando Alonso	11
17	Jolyon Palmer	8
18	Pascal Wehrlein	5
19	Daniil Kvyat	5

CONSTRUCTORS

1	Mercedes	595
2	Ferrari	455
3	Red Bull	340
4	Force India	175
5	Williams	76
6	Toro Rosso	53
7	Renault	48
8	Haas	47
9	McLaren	24
10	Sauber	5

9 · PÉREZ · Force India

7 · HÜLKENBERG · Renault

5 · RÄIKKÖNEN · Ferrari

3 · HAMILTON · Mercedes

1 · VETTEL · Ferrari

10 · MASSA · Williams

8 · SAINZ · Renault

6 · OCON · Force India

4 · BOTTAS · Mercedes

2 · VERSTAPPEN · Red Bull

56	57	58	59	60	61	62	63	64	65	66	67	68	69	70	71	
33	33	33	33	33	33	33	33	33	33	33	33	33	33	33	33	1
77	77	77	77	77	77	77	77	77	77	77	77	77	77	77	77	2
7	7	7	7	7	7	7	7	7	7	7	7	7	7	7	7	3
31	5	5	5	5	5	5	5	5	5	5	5	5	5	5	5	4
5	31	31	31	31	31	31	31	31	31	31	31	31	31	31	31	5
18	18	18	18	18	18	18	18	18	18	18	18	18	18	18	18	6
11	11	11	11	11	11	11	11	11	11	11	11	11	11	11	11	7
20	20	20	20	20	20	20	20	20	20	20	20	20	20	20	20	8
14	14	14	14	14	14	14	14	14	14	14	14	14	14	14	14	9
44	44	44	44	44	44	44	44	44	44	14	14	14	14	14	14	10
19	19	19	19	19	19	19	19	19	19	19	19	19	19			
2	2	2	2	2	2	2	2	2	2	2	2	2	2			
10	10	10	10	10	10	10	10	10	10	10	10	10	10			
94	94	94	94	94	94	94	94	94	94	94	94	94	94			
8	8	8	8	8	8	8	8	8	8	8	8					
55	55	55	55													

■ Safety car deployed on laps shown

RACE TYRE STRATEGIES

PIRELLI

	Driver	Race Stint 1	Race Stint 2	Race Stint 3
1	Verstappen	Ultrasoft (u): 1-32	Supersoft (n): 33-71	
2	Bottas	Ultrasoft (u): 1-32	Supersoft (n): 33-71	
3	Räikkönen	Ultrasoft (u): 1-32	Soft (n): 33-71	
4	Vettel	Ultrasoft (u): 1	Soft (n): 2-32	Ultrasoft (n): 33-71
5	Ocon	Ultrasoft (u): 1-20	Soft (n): 21-70	
6	Stroll	Ultrasoft (n): 1-32	Supersoft (n): 33-70	
7	Pérez	Ultrasoft (u): 1-18	Soft (n): 19-50	Ultrasoft (u): 51-70
8	Magnussen	Ultrasoft (u): 1-31	Soft (n): 32-70	
9	Hamilton	Ultrasoft (u): 1	Soft (n): 2-31	Supersoft (n): 32-70
10	Alonso	Supersoft (n): 1-32	Ultrasoft (n): 33-70	
11	Massa	Ultrasoft (n): 1-3	Soft (n): 4-70	
12	Vandoorne	Ultrasoft (u): 1-31	Supersoft (n): 32-70	
13	Gasly	Ultrasoft (n): 1-31	Supersoft (n): 32-70	
14	Wehrlein	Ultrasoft (n): 1-4	Soft (n): 5-69	
15	Grosjean	Supersoft (n): 1-31	Soft (n): 32-62	Ultrasoft (n): 63-69
	Sainz	Ultrasoft (u): 1-2	Soft (n): 3-31	Ultrasoft (u): 32-59 (dnf)
	Ericsson	Ultrasoft (u): 1-28	Supersoft (n): 29-55 (dnf)	
	Hartley	Ultrasoft (u): 1-30 (dnf)		
	Hülkenberg	Ultrasoft (u): 1-19	Soft (n): 20-24 (dnf)	
	Ricciardo	Ultrasoft (u): 1-5 (dnf)		

The tyre regulations stipulate that at least two of three dry tyre specifications must be used during a dry race.
Pirelli P Zero logos are colour-coded on the tyre sidewalls: Purple = Ultrasoft; Red = Supersoft; Yellow = Soft. (n) new (u) used

Photos: Peter J. Fox

BRAZILIAN GRAND PRIX

INTERLAGOS CIRCUIT

INTERLAGOS QUALIFYING

VALTTERI BOTTAS claimed pole position for the third time in 2017. Lewis Hamilton was the first driver to congratulate his Mercedes team-mate – not because he had been beaten by fractions of a second, but because, unusually, the world champion had played no part in Q3.

Hamilton's car had been in the garage with the left side hanging off. He had made a rare mistake (one of very few in 2017). Even more surprising was the timing. Hamilton had slid off the road on his first out-lap, the considerably cooler track temperature, lower tyre pressures and a car grounding more than usual catching him out as he powered into the uphill Turn Six. He was sideways and into the tyre wall in an instant.

Would pole have been a given for Hamilton? Even with his record number recorded in 2017, it was by no means certain on a track that suited Ferrari and Mercedes quite markedly in different places. The Mercedes had an advantage on the power sections in S1 and S3, but the Ferrari could make up for that through the twists of S2. There was nothing in it.

Well, there was: 0.038s to be precise, the difference between Bottas and Sebastian Vettel in P2. Or, put another way, 0.038s accounted for Seb's misjudgement when, with typical honesty, he said that he had "chickened out a bit" when braking for the first corner and spent the rest of an excellent lap knowing he could never make that up in his fight not only for pole, but also second in the world championship.

"It feels really good," said Bottas. "It's a shame Lewis was not able to fight for pole, so I'm happy to have been able to deliver. I knew I had to improve on my last run after Sebastian had been just a bit quicker on the previous lap. I could see and feel that I was improving corner after corner."

Any hopes that Kimi Räikkönen might improve were thwarted from the start as he struggled to get the front tyres up to temperature, had similar braking problems to Vettel and failed to tap into what should have been a strong performance. Nonetheless, the Ferrari's pace – or a comparative lack of it from the Red Bull – meant a comfortable third place.

The Renault power unit was always going to be short of grunt on the uphill section. Nonetheless, Max Verstappen wrung the Red Bull's neck and then, remembering his remarkable performance in 2016, checked the weather forecast for salvation on race day.

"Fourth is the best we could have hoped for," said the Dutchman. "To be honest, we never expected to beat Mercedes and Ferrari because this track doesn't really suit our car. We were losing something like half a second on the straight. We need a bit of luck to win this race and, yes, a wet race would be very good."

Daniel Ricciardo was worse off, knowing that a ten-place penalty was looming. With the mid-grid start in mind, Red Bull ran the soft (rather than the super-soft) in Q2 to allow a long first stint before switching to the faster (allegedly) tyre for the final phase of the race. But when Ricciardo got to Q3 and switched to the supersoft, the performance was not there, and he complained of a vibration and an inability to generate temperature in the left front. Fifth fastest, 0.4s off his team-mate, would translate into P14 once the penalty shuffles elsewhere had been taken into account.

Sergio Pérez was very pleased with sixth fastest time after sitting out FP1 (George Russell had been making his official F1 debut) and then having to work hard at fine-tuning the set-up as the learning process with the Mexico upgrade continued. His sunny disposition was probably helped by Esteban Ocon not making Q3 and qualifying 11th after failing to cope with the cooler conditions on the second day.

Similar difficulties for Stoffel Vandoorne on Saturday added to a personal struggle, as he felt unwell, the Belgian half a second off the flying pace of team-mate Fernando Alonso, who produced lap after lap on the very edge. On such a power-dependent circuit, particularly with the long uphill climb, P7 indicated that the McLaren-Honda was continuing to close the gap to Renault, aided by another aero upgrade.

Nico Hülkenberg regained the bragging rights – only just – at Renault, as both drivers made it through to Q3, Carlos Sainz qualifying ninth after his first Q3 run had been compromised by a mix-up with Felipe Massa over track space.

The Brazilian, already stoked up for his final home grand prix, made no bones about where the fault lay, blaming Sainz for "disturbing me on purpose." Massa reckoned he would have been seventh (based on his Q2 lap) rather than the tenth place gained on his one clean lap in Q3. Either way, that was better than Lance Stroll, who was having one of those weekends when he never got to grips with the track, not helped by a gearbox failure that limited his FP3 track time. This damaged the engine and committed Stroll to an old unit that could not be used in qualifying mode, which helped account for 18th and Q1 elimination.

There was a discrepancy of three-tenths of a second between the Haas drivers, Romain Grosjean having done an impressive job with the recalcitrant car to qualify 12th, two places ahead of Kevin Magnussen. Brendon Hartley made it to Q2, but, with engine penalties looming, Toro Rosso chose not to waste tyres and limited the Kiwi to standing laps in which he could gain useful start practice at the end of the pit lane. Pierre Gasly, a whisker away in the other car, was also strapped with grid penalties, relegating him to the back

row of the grid. The Toro Rosso pair were split by the Saubers, Marcus Ericsson having gone a tenth quicker than Pascal Wehrlein.

Joining them at the back of the field would be the newly crowned four-times world champion.

"Lewis is very upset with himself," said Niki Lauda. "We have no problem with this; mistakes can happen, and Lewis has had such a great season, driving perfectly. For us, this is a fantastic result for Valtteri – and at a good time for him. With Valtteri at the front and Lewis coming through from the back, it's going to be a very interesting race."

WITH not much to lose, Mercedes went for broke and changed everything on Hamilton's car. The penalty-free status associated with a pit-lane start would mean a new power unit that 'only' needed to do two races and therefore could be thrashed. In addition, tyre choice was free, allowing a first phase on the soft with, in contrast to the front-runners, the supersoft available for the final phase. That said, one factor to be considered would be temperatures in traffic and thermal degradation as the track reached a baking 60°C.

Meanwhile, at the front, the immediate concern was tyre grip. With nothing to choose between Ferrari and Mercedes, Bottas and Vettel knew the short uphill surge to the first corner would be absolutely crucial.

As soon as the red lights went out and he released the clutch, Valtteri realised that he might be in trouble, as traction was not all that it should have been. Sebastian immediately sensed his opportunity, but, in the excitement, gave a touch too much throttle, and he, too, thought the opportunity had been lost.

Looking quickly across at the Mercedes, Vettel then realised that he was in with a shout and aimed for the narrowing gap between the pit wall on his left and the silver car on his right. Bottas, for his part, knew the Ferrari would be coming, but couldn't determine its exact position. He had confirmation when a right front wheel and a flash of red drew alongside as they crested the rise and reached the braking area, Seb leaving the crucial moment a fraction later. Job done by Vettel with a bold move. Just the 71 laps to go.

As he sat at the end of the pit lane, Hamilton could hear the commotion high above and to his right. His getaway would not be easy thanks to the contorted pit-lane exit, sweeping left, then downhill and right before arcing left in its narrow confines and finally release on to the straight leading to Descida do Lago (Turn Four). This would cost five valuable seconds. More than ever, he needed an early safety car. The

Mercedes had barely joined the back straight before race control had ordered an answer to Hamilton's prayer.

Going into the first corner, Räikkönen had kept Verstappen in check, but Alonso and Massa were about to pounce on Pérez. Further back, cars two and three abreast would lead to trouble as they funnelled into Turn Two. Magnussen made heavy contact with Vandoorne on his left. He, in turn, hit Ricciardo – already up on the exit kerb – and spun the Red Bull across the track, luckily without further contact. But the Haas and McLaren were badly damaged and about to retire.

Meanwhile, the pack was tackling the start of the inside loop at the point where Hamilton had visited the tyre barrier during qualifying. Trying to run around the outside of Grosjean, but leaving him little room, Ocon tightened the line and caused the Haas to oversteer – into the side of the Force India, giving Ocon two punctures for his trouble. It had to come some time; this would be the Frenchman's first failure to finish a grand prix. Having spun harmlessly, Grosjean got going again, but was set to run at the back for the rest of the afternoon and due – with justification – to be peeved over a subsequent ten-second penalty for allegedly causing the accident.

The series of incidents had hindered some drivers and assisted others – none more than Hamilton, who found himself 14th in the safety car queue without having actually overtaken anyone. He was directly behind Gasly, Ericsson, Hartley and Stroll, all of whom would be relatively easy meat once the race was restarted on lap six.

In the meantime, the field was being directed through the pit lane to allow the clearance of debris at Turn Two, Wehrlein, Grosjean and Ricciardo dropping back after stopping in their respective pit boxes. The safety car would help Ferrari and Mercedes particularly when it came to fuel consumption, since both teams had been running as light as they dared, every fraction of a kilogram counting in a fight as close as this.

Above: Using the Ferrari's superior traction, Sebastian Vettel dives to the inside of pole-sitter Valtteri Bottas and gains an advantage he would never lose.
Photo: Scuderia Ferrari

Left: A rare mistake in Q1 led to Lewis Hamilton hitting the barrier.
Photo: Peter J. Fox

Below left: Friends reunited. Sir Jackie Stewart and Emerson Fittipaldi.
Photo: Studio Colombo/WRi2

Opening spread: A glorious hot and sunny day at Interlagos ended with Sebastian Vettel scoring his fifth win of the season.
Photo: Peter J. Fox

Above: Fernando Alonso prepares for another long afternoon, which this time brought some reward, with eighth place in the McLaren Honda.
Photo: McLaren Honda

Top right: The Red Bull pair of Max Verstappen and Daniel Ricciardo drove superbly, but had to be content with fifth and sixth respectively.
Photo: Lukas Gorys

Above right: After a run of misfortune, Nico Hülkenberg was glad to reach the finish at last, albeit in tenth.
Photo: Renault F1 Team

Right: The Interlagos circuit may be in need of substantial refurbishment, but the track still proves a massive challenge to the drivers.
Photo: Lukas Gorys

On the other hand, the safety car did not help when the crew turned off the flashing orange lights quite late, meaning that Vettel had to back up the field to ensure he had enough of a gap to gun the Ferrari without overtaking the official Merc before it reached the designated safety line. If it was tricky for Vettel, it was even worse for Bottas as he tried to second-guess the leader's intentions – and was caught out when Seb booted it at the bottom of the hill, finding a couple of car lengths by the time they crossed the start/finish line.

Massa, on the other hand, was poised to use his Mercedes power to the maximum while overhauling Alonso's McLaren Honda. Everyone else held station – with the exception of Lewis Hamilton.

On the move immediately, the Mercedes was into tenth two laps later, before picking off Sainz and Hülkenberg, and moving into seventh at the expense of Pérez on lap 14. Alonso was three seconds ahead, having used Massa to bring in DRS and pull away from the Force India, rather than waste time and energy re-passing the Williams; typical racecraft from the veteran. At the same time, Ricciardo was exercising his role as a serial overtaker, a few demon moves helping the Red Bull climb from last and into the points by lap 14.

Vettel was two seconds ahead and working very hard in the middle sector to maintain the slender DRS-free advantage, knowing that the following Mercedes had an 8km/h boost that Bottas was very keen to use given half a chance. Assuming a favoured one-stop strategy (two stops would mean another 22 seconds lost, plus the possibility of becoming snared in the narrow pit lane with its time-consuming exit), the Mercedes and Ferrari strategists were already considering their choices.

If Vettel could maintain the two-second advantage, he would be reasonably free from the undercut. But when Bottas began to shave tenths off the gap and go with the Ferrari as Vettel upped his pace, all options were on the table. Which way was this race going to go?

Choosing the right moment to stop was also governed by finding free space on the out-lap. Mercedes knew an overcut was not going to work, so they needed to pull the trigger first. The flies in this particular ointment were Massa and Alonso. As soon as the Williams and McLaren were far enough back not to present a time-consuming obstacle on Valtteri's out-lap, Mercedes brought him in at the end of lap 27, Ferrari predictably reacting at the end of the next lap. They had been separated by 1.6s at the end of lap 26. This was going to be very close.

And it was! They rejoined a tenth of a second apart, with Vettel still in front. Bottas had produced faster in- and out-laps (there was nothing left in Vettel's rear tyres), while the Ferrari stop had been marginally faster – but a tiny mistake coming out of Junçao possibly cost Bottas the tenth that made the difference between P2 and P1; between winning and losing.

The start of the pit stops prompted Red Bull to bring in Verstappen (3.5s behind Räikkönen) on the same lap as Vettel, with Kimi (previously 4.5s behind Bottas) stopping a lap later. Whereas the switch to softs would suit Räikkönen much more than the supersoft phase, the reverse was true for Bottas, as he began to fall away from Seb and held a 4–5 second gap to Kimi, who would begin to reduce it in the later stages.

What of Hamilton in all of this? Showing very impressive pace on the soft, he was in the lead following the round of pit stops at the front. His lap times were such that he was able to maintain a 3.5s gap to Vettel. Lewis was obviously due to stop at some point, but the thought occurred that in the meantime he might be asked to back Vettel towards the other Mercedes (for the sake of P2 in the championship). When that didn't happen, Mercedes seemed content to let this race play out a more natural course. They felt that Lewis would be in a strong position in any case, once he had made his stop.

After he had eked out consistent performance from the softs for 43 laps, the switch came with 28 to go. He rejoined fifth, 18s behind the leader, 11s behind Verstappen in P4 – and with an engine that could be worked hard compared to the conservative endurance strategy necessary elsewhere, particularly at Red Bull following the disasters at altitude two weeks before in Mexico. (All the Renaults had their turbo speeds reduced by 5,000rpm to avoid overheating and further problems with the ERS-H.)

It took Hamilton just 14 laps to catch and overtake Verstappen, Max defending strongly into the first corner, only to feel helpless as the Mercedes breezed past on the way to Descida do Lago. Ferrari and Räikkönen – three seconds up the road – knew he was coming…

If Lewis could pull a similar clean overtake on Kimi, it would pose another conundrum: would Mercedes ask Valtteri to let his team-mate through so that he could use his better-equipped car to challenge Vettel for the 25 points – thus helping Bottas's championship in the process? Although we didn't know it, the decision had already been made: Bottas was free to run his own race. Nonetheless, it was tempting to wonder how the Finn felt about car No. 44 having got so close after starting from the pit lane. Demoralised is probably not far off the mark.

In the event, Bottas would be saved from the disheartening vision of Hamilton in his mirrors thanks to Räikkönen showing good pace. It took Lewis ten laps to reduce the gap, and just as he did so, the final ounce of competitiveness was taken from his well-used supersofts by a brake-locking moment into Turn One. At that point, Räikkönen knew that if he used all his experience on a tight track such as this, plus a more potent engine mode, he could keep the Mercedes driver off the podium.

Hamilton had set a jaw-dropping lap of 1m 11.845s late in his charge, but that would be beaten after Verstappen, bored with struggling in a lonely P5 with knackered rear

Above: Valtteri Bottas took pole, but too much wheelspin at the start and a problematic pit stop left him power-less to challenge Vettel.
Photo: WRi2/Jean-François Galeron

Top right: Before... Felipe Massa is wheeled on to the Interlagos grid for his final F1 race in Brazil.
Photo: Peter J. Fox

Above right: And after... Massa bade an emotional farewell to his fans from the podium.
Photo: Jad Sherif/WRi2s

Right: All in a day's work for Lewis Hamilton, who took his Mercedes from the pit lane to fourth, only a sec-ond behind Kimi Räikkönen's Ferrari.
Photo: Studio Colombo/Wri2

Below right: Valtteri looks none too pleased to be holding up the second-place trophy.
Photo: Mercedes AMG Petronas F1 Team

Far right: Not exactly Monte Carlo. Continuing safety and security issues at Interlagos could endanger the long-term future of the race.
Photo: Peter J. Fox

rubber, had made a stop for supersofts. Without losing a place, he rejoined to enjoy himself over the final nine laps by blitzing the lap record.

Ricciardo had more or less mirrored Hamilton's strategy, the Red Bull having to re-pass the Massa/Alonso battle on the way to P6 after stopping for supersofts on lap 43. In an occasionally terse discussion with his team about the equipment at his disposal, Alonso had made it clear that he was more interested in the gap to Massa – to be able to retain DRS – than he was about defending against the closing Pérez. The preference was to use DRS to stay away from the Force India, rather than draft past Massa, only to be overtaken again. All three crossed the finishing line covered by 0.6s, Massa delighted to be 'best of the rest' at the end of a final and exhilarating home grand prix.

With his Renault's performance curtailed, Hülkenberg had no chance of doing anything about chasing down Pérez, the German at least privately satisfied with claiming the final point and finishing one place ahead of his new team-mate after Sainz's much vaunted switch to Renault.

Pierre Gasly clung on to his first-lap place gains to finish 12th for Toro Rosso (Hartley, who had been behind his team-mate, having been forced to retire when the Renault engine consumed too much oil). The Frenchman was fortunate that the race had not run another lap longer, his engine cutting out as he crossed the line – but with enough momentum to stay ahead of Ericsson, who had passed his Sauber team-mate three laps from the end after Wehrlein had run for a remarkable 69 laps on a set of softs. Stroll was the final finisher in P16, one place behind Grosjean and two laps down, to complete a weekend that had been a struggle from start to finish, with tyre delamination and lock-ups.

No such difficulties for Vettel, who had turned in a peerless performance while keeping Bottas in check and giving Ferrari its first win since Hungary three months before. It was an indication of what might have been had Ferrari and Vettel not collectively dropped the ball during that crucial Asian leg of the season.

Maurice Hamilton

VIEWPOINT
ONCE TOO OFTEN?

ON Friday evening, having left Interlagos at around 10pm, a Mercedes team minibus was held up at gunpoint when it stopped at nearby traffic lights. Valuables were stolen and one crew member had a gun put to his head. Separate incidents involved the Williams and Sauber teams and FIA personnel.

Lewis Hamilton articulated the feelings of many: "I was horrified to hear what happened. You can't imagine what they were feeling or going through, but the most frustrating thing is that I've been in F1 for ten years, and every single year that has happened to somebody in the paddock.

"It continues to happen, and that's obviously an issue that I'm sure the government here are fighting. There are protocols that are put in place to help, for example when we go to Mexico, that weren't there for these guys. Generally, the people at the top need to take action. It's not just about me having security and the bosses having security, I think everyone needs to be looked after. I hope there's some way we can move forward so that doesn't happen ever again."

Then, a couple of days later, a statement from Pirelli: "Following a robbery attempt, neutralised by Pirelli security, on a Pirelli van at the Interlagos circuit last Sunday – after a weekend where similar episodes occurred with other teams – it has been decided to cancel the tyre test planned on Tuesday 14 and Wednesday 15 on the Brazilian circuit with Team McLaren. The decision, shared with McLaren, FIA and Formula 1, was made in the interest of the safety of the personnel, both McLaren's and our own, who would have participated in the test." A serious message?

With Brazil set to have no F1 driver for the first time since Interlagos first ran in 1972, Liberty wanting to take F1 to 'destination venues' and talk of Interlagos being sold (although retaining its use as a race track), what are the chances of the track having its place on the F1 calendar post-2020, when its current deal expires? Perhaps all those Argentine flags that the cameras picked up during FP1 were not coincidence…

Tony Dodgins

19

2017 FORMULA 1
GRAN PRÊMIO
HEINEKEN
DO BRASIL

SÃO PAULO 10–12 NOVEMBER

RACE DISTANCE: 71 laps, 190.083 miles/305.909km

RACE WEATHER: Dry/sunny (track 54–60°C, air 28–30°C)

ROLEX · OFFICIAL TIMEPIECE

AUTODROMO JOSÉ CARLOS PACE, INTERLAGOS
Circuit: 2.677 miles / 4.309km, 71 laps

187/116 kmh/mph ☼ Gear
▬ DRS zone

Descida do Lago 182/113
Reta Oposta 340/211
Turn 5 272/169
Junção 127/79
Murgulho 215/134
Pinheirinho 123/76
Curva do Sol 275/171
Ferradura 230/143
Laranja 82/51
Subido dos Boxes 295/183
Senna-S 178/111
345/214
Bico de Pato 90/56
Arquibancadas 335/208
Descida do Sol 135/84

RACE – OFFICIAL CLASSIFICATION

Pos.	Driver	Nat.	No.	Entrant	Car/Engine	Laps	Time/Retirement	Speed (mph/km/h)	Gap to leader	Fastest race lap
1	**Sebastian Vettel**	D	5	Scuderia Ferrari	Ferrari SF70H-062 V6	71	1h 31m 26.262s	124.729/200.732		1m 12.539s 63
2	**Valtteri Bottas**	FIN	77	Mercedes AMG Petronas Motorsport	Mercedes F1 W08-Mercedes M08 EQ Power+ V6	71	1h 31m 29.024s	124.666/200.631	2.762s	1m 12.466s 58
3	**Kimi Räikkönen**	FIN	7	Scuderia Ferrari	Ferrari SF70H-062 V6	71	1h 31m 30.862s	124.625/200.564	4.600s	1m 12.492s 61
4	**Lewis Hamilton**	GB	44	Mercedes AMG Petronas Motorsport	Mercedes F1 W08-Mercedes M08 EQ Power+ V6	71	1h 31m 31.730s	124.605/200.532	5.468s	1m 11.845s 63
5	**Max Verstappen**	NL	33	Red Bull Racing	Red Bull RB13-TAG Heuer RB13 V6	71	1h 31m 59.202s	123.985/199.534	32.940s	1m 11.044s 64
6	**Daniel Ricciardo**	AUS	3	Red Bull Racing	Red Bull RB13-TAG Heuer RB13 V6	71	1h 32m 14.953s	123.632/198.966	48.691s	1m 12.029s 71
7	**Felipe Massa**	BR	19	Williams Martini Racing	Williams FW40-Mercedes M08 EQ Power+ V6	71	1h 32m 35.144s	123.182/198.243	1m 08.882s	1m 13.452s 60
8	**Fernando Alonso**	E	14	McLaren Honda Formula 1 Team	McLaren MCL32-Honda RA617H V6	71	1h 32m 35.625s	123.172/198.226	1m 09.363s	1m 13.451s 57
9	**Sergio Pérez**	MEX	11	Sahara Force India Formula 1 Team	Force India VJM10-Mercedes M08 EQ Power+ V6	71	1h 32m 35.762s	123.169/198.221	1m 09.500s	1m 13.052s 61
10	Nico Hülkenberg	D	27	Renault Sport Formula One Team	Renault R.S.17-R.E.17 V6	70			1 lap	1m 13.758s 57
11	Carlos Sainz	E	55	Renault Sport Formula One Team	Renault R.S.17-R.E.17 V6	70			1 lap	1m 13.625s 67
12	Pierre Gasly	F	10	Scuderia Toro Rosso	Toro Rosso STR12-Renault R.E.17 V6	70			1 lap	1m 13.323s 61
13	Marcus Ericsson	S	9	Sauber F1 Team	Sauber C36-Ferrari 059/5 V6	70			1 lap	1m 13.666s 70
14	Pascal Wehrlein	D	94	Sauber F1 Team	Sauber C36-Ferrari 059/5 V6	70			1 lap	1m 14.812s 60
15	Romain Grosjean	F	8	Haas F1 Team	Haas VF-17-Ferrari 062 V6	69			2 laps	1m 13.532s 66
16	Lance Stroll	CDN	18	Williams Martini Racing	Williams FW40-Mercedes M08 EQ Power+ V6	69			2 laps	1m 11.862s 69
	Brendon Hartley	NZ	28	Scuderia Toro Rosso	Toro Rosso STR12-Renault R.E.17 V6	40	engine			1m 14.658s 29
	Esteban Ocon	F	31	Sahara Force India Formula 1 Team	Force India VJM10-Mercedes M08 EQ Power+ V6	0	accident			no time
	Stoffel Vandoorne	B	2	McLaren Honda Formula 1 Team	McLaren MCL32-Honda RA617H V6	0	accident			no time
	Kevin Magnussen	DK	20	Haas F1 Team	Haas VF-17-Ferrari 062 V6	0	accident			no time

Fastest race lap: Max Verstappen on lap 64, 1m 11.044s, 135.676mph/218.349km/h.

Previous lap record: Juan Pablo Montoya (Williams FW26-BMW V10), 1m 11.473s, 134.862mph/217.038km/h (2004)

All results and data © FOM 2017

20 · HAMILTON · Mercedes
Car modified in *parc fermé*; required to start from the pit lane

18 · HARTLEY · Toro Rosso
10-place grid penalty for using additional power unit elements

16 · STROLL · Williams
5-place grid penalty for replacing gearbox

14 · RICCIARDO · Red Bull
10-place grid penalty for using additional power unit elements

12 · VANDOORNE · McLaren

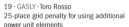

19 · GASLY · Toro Rosso
25-place grid penalty for using additional power unit elements

17 · ERICSSON · Sauber
5-place grid penalty for replacing gearbox

15 · WEHRLEIN · Sauber

13 · MAGNUSSEN · Haas

11 · GROSJEAN · Haas

Grid order	1 2 3 4 5 6 7 8 9 10 11 12 13 14 15 16 17 18 19 20 21 22 23 24 25 26 27 28 29 30 31 32 33 34 35 36 37 38 39 40 41 42 43 44 45 46 47 48 49 50 51 52 53 54 5
77 BOTTAS	5 5 5 5 5 5 5 5 5 5 5 5 5 5 5 5 5 5 5 5 5 5 5 5 5 5 5 5 7 44 44 44 44 44 44 44 44 44 44 44 44 5 5 5 5 5 5 5 5 5 5 5
5 VETTEL	77 77 77 77 77 77 77 77 77 77 77 77 77 77 77 77 77 77 77 77 77 77 77 77 77 77 77 7 7 44 5 5 5 5 5 5 5 5 5 5 5 5 44 77 77 77 77 77 77 77 77 77 77 77 7
7 RÄIKKÖNEN	7 7 7 7 7 7 7 7 7 7 7 7 7 7 7 7 7 7 7 7 7 7 7 7 7 7 77 44 7 7 77 77 77 77 77 77 77 77 77 77 7 7 7 7 7 7 7 7 7 7
33 VERSTAPPEN	33 33 33 33 33 33 33 33 33 33 33 33 33 33 33 33 33 33 33 33 33 33 33 33 33 33 33 77 7 7 7 7 7 7 7 7 7 7 33 33 33 33 33 33 33 33 33 33 33 33
11 PÉREZ	14 14 14 14 19 19 19 19 19 19 19 19 19 19 19 19 19 19 19 19 44 44 44 44 44 44 44 77 3 3 3 33 33 33 33 33 33 33 33 33 44 44 44 44 44 44 44 44 44
14 ALONSO	19 19 19 19 14 14 14 14 14 14 14 14 14 14 14 19 19 19 19 19 11 11 33 33 33 3 3 3 3 3 3 3 3 3 19 19 19 3 3 3 3 3 3 3
27 HÜLKENBERG	11 11 11 11 11 11 11 11 11 11 11 11 11 44 44 44 44 44 14 14 14 14 14 14 14 11 33 11 11 11 11 11 11 19 19 19 19 19 19 14 3 19 19 19 19 19 19 19
55 SAINZ	27 27 27 27 27 27 27 27 27 27 44 44 11 11 11 11 11 11 11 11 11 11 14 27 27 19 19 19 19 14 14 14 3 14 14 14 14 14 14 14 14 14
19 MASSA	55 55 55 55 55 44 27 27 27 27 27 27 27 27 3 3 3 3 3 3 19 55 55 14 14 14 14 11 11 11 11 11 11 11 11 11 11 11 11 11 11
31 OCON	10 10 10 10 10 10 10 44 55 55 55 55 55 3 3 3 3 27 27 27 27 27 27 55 19 55 10 10 27 27 27 27 27 27 27 27 27 27 27 27 27 2
8 GROSJEAN	9 9 9 9 9 9 44 10 10 10 10 10 3 55 55 55 55 55 55 55 55 55 55 19 14 14 10 94 27 27 27 27 10 10 55 55 55 55 55 55 55 55 55 5
2 VANDOORNE	28 28 28 28 28 18 9 9 9 9 3 3 10 10 10 10 10 10 10 10 10 10 10 94 27 94 94 94 55 55 55 10 94 94 94 94 94 94 94 94 94 9
20 MAGNUSSEN	18 18 18 18 18 44 18 18 18 18 9 18 18 18 18 18 18 18 18 94 94 27 9 55 55 55 94 94 94 94 94 94 94 10 18 18 10 10 10 10 10 10 1
3 RICCIARDO	94 94 94 94 94 94 3 3 28 28 28 28 28 28 28 28 28 28 28 28 94 94 9 9 9 55 9 9 9 8 10 18 18 18 18 18 18 18 1
94 WEHRLEIN	8 94 94 94 94 94 3 28 28 28 28 28 8 9 9 9 9 94 94 94 94 28 9 9 9 55 9 9 9 8 8 10 18 10 10 10 10 10 10 1
18 STROLL	44 8 8 8 8 94 94 94 94 94 94 94 94 94 9 9 9 9 8 18 18 18 18 18 18 18 18 18 18 9 9 8 8 8 8 8 8 8
9 ERICSSON	3 3 3 3 3 8 8 8 8 8 8 8 8 8 8 8 8 28 28 28 28 28 28 28 28 28 28 28 28 28
28 HARTLEY	
10 GASLY	
44 HAMILTON	

5 = Pit stop   *28* = One lap or more behind

TIME SHEETS

PRACTICE 1 (FRIDAY)
Weather: Dry/sunny
Temperatures: track 39–50°C, air 25–27°C

Pos.	Driver	Laps	Time
1	Lewis Hamilton	36	1m 09.202s
2	Valtteri Bottas	43	1m 09.329s
3	Kimi Räikkönen	32	1m 09.744s
4	Max Verstappen	31	1m 09.750s
5	Daniel Ricciardo	38	1m 09.828s
6	Sebastian Vettel	32	1m 09.984s
7	Felipe Massa	28	1m 10.102s
8	Stoffel Vandoorne	26	1m 10.402s
9	Esteban Ocon	36	1m 10.454s
10	Fernando Alonso	24	1m 10.476s
11	Lance Stroll	42	1m 10.632s
12	George Russell	29	1m 11.047s
13	Romain Grosjean	29	1m 11.188s
14	Kevin Magnussen	30	1m 11.463s
15	Carlos Sainz	32	1m 11.467s
16	Nico Hülkenberg	35	1m 11.608s
17	Charles Leclerc	32	1m 11.802s
18	Marcus Ericsson	28	1m 11.898s
19	Pierre Gasly	5	1m 14.034s
20	Brendon Hartley	2	no time

PRACTICE 2 (FRIDAY)
Weather: Dry/partly cloudy
Temperatures: track 43–55°C, air 29–31°C

Pos.	Driver	Laps	Time
1	Lewis Hamilton	42	1m 09.515s
2	Valtteri Bottas	45	1m 09.563s
3	Daniel Ricciardo	37	1m 09.743s
4	Sebastian Vettel	48	1m 09.875s
5	Max Verstappen	38	1m 09.886s
6	Kimi Räikkönen	45	1m 10.117s
7	Esteban Ocon	49	1m 10.306s
8	Felipe Massa	42	1m 10.373s
9	Nico Hülkenberg	39	1m 10.396s
10	Fernando Alonso	31	1m 10.655s
11	Carlos Sainz	42	1m 10.685s
12	Sergio Pérez	43	1m 10.695s
13	Stoffel Vandoorne	38	1m 10.902s
14	Lance Stroll	44	1m 11.064s
15	Romain Grosjean	39	1m 11.300s
16	Pierre Gasly	44	1m 11.422s
17	Brendon Hartley	54	1m 11.821s
18	Pascal Wehrlein	43	1m 11.857s
19	Marcus Ericsson	17	1m 11.989s
20	Antonio Giovinazzi	37	1m 12.417s

PRACTICE 3 (SATURDAY)
Weather: Damp-drying/overcast
Temperatures: track 26–28°C, air 19–20°C

Pos.	Driver	Laps	Time
1	Valtteri Bottas	24	1m 09.281s
2	Lewis Hamilton	26	1m 09.284s
3	Kimi Räikkönen	20	1m 09.326s
4	Sebastian Vettel	21	1m 09.339s
5	Daniel Ricciardo	14	1m 10.244s
6	Fernando Alonso	15	1m 10.288s
7	Sergio Pérez	21	1m 10.322s
8	Esteban Ocon	23	1m 10.357s
9	Max Verstappen	9	1m 10.495s
10	Carlos Sainz	23	1m 10.599s
11	Stoffel Vandoorne	21	1m 10.637s
12	Felipe Massa	14	1m 10.671s
13	Kevin Magnussen	19	1m 10.721s
14	Nico Hülkenberg	18	1m 10.743s
15	Romain Grosjean	20	1m 10.762s
16	Pierre Gasly	32	1m 10.981s
17	Brendon Hartley	30	1m 11.085s
18	Pascal Wehrlein	25	1m 11.126s
19	Marcus Ericsson	27	1m 11.480s
20	Lance Stroll	1	no time

QUALIFYING (SATURDAY)
Weather: Dry-light rain/cloudy Temperatures: track 26–29°C, air 17–19°C

Pos.	Driver	First	Second	Third	Qualifying Tyre
1	Valtteri Bottas	1m 09.452s	1m 08.638s	1m 08.322s	Supersoft (new)
2	Sebastian Vettel	1m 09.643s	1m 08.494s	1m 08.360s	Supersoft (new)
3	Kimi Räikkönen	1m 09.405s	1m 09.116s	1m 08.538s	Supersoft (new)
4	Max Verstappen	1m 09.820s	1m 09.050s	1m 08.925s	Supersoft (new)
5	Daniel Ricciardo	1m 09.828s	1m 09.533s	1m 09.330s	Supersoft (new)
6	Sergio Pérez	1m 10.145s	1m 09.760s	1m 09.598s	Supersoft (new)
7	Fernando Alonso	1m 10.172s	1m 09.593s	1m 09.617s	Supersoft (new)
8	Nico Hülkenberg	1m 10.078s	1m 09.726s	1m 09.703s	Supersoft (new)
9	Carlos Sainz	1m 10.227s	1m 09.768s	1m 09.805s	Supersoft (new)
10	Felipe Massa	1m 09.789s	1m 09.612s	1m 09.841s	Supersoft (new)
11	Esteban Ocon	1m 10.168s	1m 09.830s		
12	Romain Grosjean	1m 10.148s	1m 09.879s		
13	Stoffel Vandoorne	1m 10.286s	1m 10.116s		
14	Kevin Magnussen	1m 10.521s	1m 10.154s		
15	Brendon Hartley	1m 10.625s	no time		
16	Pascal Wehrlein	1m 10.678s			
17	Pierre Gasly	1m 10.686s			
18	Lance Stroll	1m 10.776s			
19	Marcus Ericsson	1m 10.875s			
20	Lewis Hamilton	no time			

QUALIFYING: head to head

Hamilton	13	6	Bottas
Vettel	14	5	Räikkönen
Massa	16	2	Stroll
Stroll	1	0	Di Resta
Ricciardo	6	13	Verstappen
Pérez	12	7	Ocon
Hülkenberg	16	0	Palmer
Hülkenberg	2	1	Sainz
Kvyat	6	8	Sainz
Sainz	2	0	Gasly
Kvyat	1	0	Hartley
Gasly	0	2	Hartley
Ericsson	2	0	Giovinazzi
Ericsson	7	10	Wehrlein
Alonso	15	3	Vandoorne
Vandoorne	1	0	Button
Grosjean	13	6	Magnussen

POINTS

DRIVERS

1	Lewis Hamilton	345
2	Sebastian Vettel	302
3	Valtteri Bottas	280
4	Daniel Ricciardo	200
5	Kimi Räikkönen	193
6	Max Verstappen	158
7	Sergio Pérez	94
8	Esteban Ocon	83
9	Carlos Sainz	54
10	Felipe Massa	42
11	Lance Stroll	40
12	Nico Hülkenberg	35
13	Romain Grosjean	28
14	Kevin Magnussen	19
15	Fernando Alonso	15
16	Stoffel Vandoorne	13
17	Jolyon Palmer	8
18	Pascal Wehrlein	5
19	Daniil Kvyat	5

CONSTRUCTORS

1	Mercedes	625
2	Ferrari	495
3	Red Bull	358
4	Force India	177
5	Williams	82
6	Toro Rosso	53
7	Renault	49
8	Haas	47
9	McLaren	28
10	Sauber	5

10 · OCON · Force India   8 · SAINZ · Renault   6 · ALONSO · McLaren   4 · VERSTAPPEN · Red Bull   2 · VETTEL · Ferrari

9 · MASSA · Williams   7 · HÜLKENBERG · Renault   5 · PÉREZ · Force India   3 · RÄIKKÖNEN · Ferrari   1 · BOTTAS · Mercedes

RACE TYRE STRATEGIES

	Driver	Race Stint 1	Race Stint 2	Race Stint 3
1	Vettel	Supersoft (u): 1–28	Soft (n): 29–71	
2	Bottas	Supersoft (u): 1–27	Soft (n): 28–71	
3	Räikkönen	Supersoft (u): 1–29	Soft (n): 30–71	
4	Hamilton	Soft (n): 1–43	Supersoft (n): 44–71	
5	Verstappen	Supersoft (u): 1–28	Soft (n): 29–62	Supersoft (u): 63–71
6	Ricciardo	Soft (u): 1	Soft (u): 2–43	Supersoft (n): 44–71
7	Massa	Supersoft (u): 1–27	Soft (n): 28–71	
8	Alonso	Supersoft (u): 1–28	Soft (n): 29–71	
9	Pérez	Supersoft (u): 1–35	Soft (n): 36–71	
10	Hülkenberg	Supersoft (u): 1–30	Soft (n): 31–70	
11	Sainz	Supersoft (u): 1–31	Soft (n): 32–70	
12	Gasly	Soft (n): 1–44	Supersoft (n): 45–70	
13	Ericsson	Soft (n): 1–44	Supersoft (n): 45–70	
14	Wehrlein	Supersoft (n): 1	Soft (n): 2–70	
15	Grosjean	Supersoft (n): 1	Soft (n): 2–48	Supersoft (u): 49–69
16	Stroll	Supersoft (n): 1–28	Soft (n): 29–67	Supersoft (n): 68–69
	Hartley	Supersoft (n): 1–27	Soft (n): 28–40 (dnf)	
	Ocon	Supersoft (n): 0 (dnf)		
	Magnussen	Supersoft (n): 0 (dnf)		
	Vandoorne	Supersoft (n): 0 (dnf)		

The tyre regulations stipulate that at least two of three dry tyre specifications must be used during a dry race.
Pirelli P Zero logos are colour-coded on the tyre sidewalls: Red = Super-Soft; Yellow = Soft. (n) new (u) used

56	57	58	59	60	61	62	63	64	65	66	67	68	69	70	71	
5	5	5	5	5	5	5	5	5	5	5	5	5	5	5	5	1
77	77	77	77	77	77	77	77	77	77	77	77	77	77	77	77	2
7	7	7	7	7	7	7	7	7	7	7	7	7	7	7	7	3
33	33	33	44	44	44	44	44	44	44	44	44	44	44	44	44	4
44	44	44	33	33	33	33	33	33	33	33	33	33	33	33	33	5
3	3	3	3	3	3	3	3	3	3	3	3	3	3	3	3	6
19	19	19	19	19	19	19	19	19	19	19	19	19	19	19	19	7
14	14	14	14	14	14	14	14	14	14	14	14	14	14	14	14	8
11	11	11	11	11	11	11	11	11	11	11	11	11	11	11	11	9
27	27	27	27	27	27	27	27	27	27	27	27	27	27	27		10
55	55	55	55	55	55	55	55	55	55	55	55	55	55	55		
94	94	10	10	10	10	10	10	10	10	10	10	10	10	10		
10	10	94	94	94	94	94	94	94	94	94	94	9	9	9		
18	18	18	18	18	18	18	18	18	9	94	94	94				
9	9	9	9	9	9	9	9	9	9	9	8					
8	8	8	8	8	8	8	8	8	18	18	18					

■ Safety car deployed on laps shown

ABU DHABI GRAND PRIX

YAS MARINA CIRCUIT

YAS MARINA QUALIFYING

IN qualifying, the order was mixed up rather more than expected. Mercedes may have locked out the front row of the grid for the 50th time, but it was Valtteri Bottas who claimed pole position, not the reigning world champion.

"It's only the fourth pole of my whole career, and I had to beat some pretty good qualifiers, so it's a great feeling to start from P1," said Bottas. "It was a really good qualifying, clean and smooth. With the changes we made, the car was behaving much better than it did in free practice. Run after run, I could always find some time here and there; I really worked on the details."

Having been fastest in FP2 and FP3, it was expected that Hamilton would make the most of a car that clearly had an edge on the opposition, making up for losses in sector three with the power sectors in one and two, and mostly generating more temperature in the tyres than Ferrari or Red Bull could manage. From the get-go, it seemed that Hamilton was on course as he blasted down the long straight and into sector two, his time glowing magenta for the fastest thus far.

"I think I was up about a tenth-and-a-half out of Turn One," said Hamilton. "But then I lost time somewhere else through the rest of the lap. But congratulations to Valtteri; he did a fantastic job. It's good to see him performing at this level, particularly at the end of the season, which puts him into a great position for next year – and the race."

Although having raised false hope with fastest time in FP1, Sebastian Vettel knew the losses in the first two sectors were too much to overcome in the final half-minute. Nonetheless, P3 put him in an attacking position on the grid.

"We tried everything," said Vettel. "I think the balance of the car was good all weekend; we trimmed it in the right way, and qualifying really came together, so I'm happy with that. The gap [to Mercedes] is big, but also it's a long lap, so naturally the gaps are a bit more spread. But for the race, I'm fairly optimistic."

One of the stand-out performances of qualifying came from Daniel Ricciardo. The Red Bull driver, happier with his car than team-mate Max Verstappen, split the Ferraris of Vettel and Kimi Räikkönen.

"I'm so happy to have jumped Ferrari, and the second row is good," said Ricciardo. "We thought we could get close to Ferrari, but as qualifying went on, it looked like they were too quick. I knew we could get a lot more out of the car; we just had to figure it out. We understood the tyre temperature a little better, and then it was a much quicker lap at the end.

"It hasn't been the perfect year of Saturdays for me, so it's nice to finish 2017 with a good one. I think we can have a chance for the podium. I don't think the start will be straightforward. It's the last race of the year, and everyone wants to win – so there could be some action! Hopefully I'm there to be a part of it!"

Räikkönen had struggled more than Vettel under circumstances such as these. A consistent performance from his tyres was the biggest problem, allied to snap oversteer, particularly at the exit of Turn 11, compromising the latent speed through the following tight corners.

Verstappen had not been happy with his car at any stage, searching for more grip and unable to find the best set-up. Time spent running an experimental 2018 front suspension on Friday probably detracted from a true understanding of how to deal with the sensitive issue of tyre temperature. Changes made for FP3 didn't work, allowing no time to continue the search for improvement and committing Max to a continued fight with the car for qualifying that resulted in sixth fastest time.

The top six were a second clear of the remaining 14, 'Best of the Rest' went to Nico Hülkenberg, after what he considered to be one of his best qualifying laps of the season in Q2 to reach the shootout and provide a boost for Renault's fight with Toro Rosso for sixth in the championship.

Hülkenberg had put himself ahead of Force India, whose drivers were having such an intense battle that they probably didn't notice the Renault creeping up and stealing a tenth of a second. In a game of swings and roundabouts, Sergio Pérez aced Esteban Ocon by 0.023s over the 3.5-mile lap, the Frenchman not happy about traffic and the feeling that he had not maximised the performance of his car during the tricky phase when the track temperature dropped.

Arguably the most emotional performance of qualifying came from Felipe Massa as he squeezed into Q3. "It's tough out there competing in the midfield to get those places in Q3," said Paddy Lowe, chief technical officer at Williams. "Felipe did a tremendous job to achieve that. It was very difficult conditions, with changing temperatures and the way that affects the tyres, to try and make the tyres last through all three sectors. Putting that perfect lap together is really difficult, but we saw on Felipe's final lap he did a great job. On Lance's side, it has been a tough day for him, trying to put the right lap together. He was able to get through into Q2 [Stroll qualified P15], but wasn't able to improve from there."

Massa was responsible for knocking Fernando Alonso out of Q3, exacerbating the disappointment for McLaren Honda after being unable to translate promising form in free practice and early qualifying to match the changing conditions as dusk closed in and temperatures fell.

Splitting Alonso and Stoffel Vandoorne, Carlos Sainz was disappointed with P12 (particularly in the light of Hülkenberg's performance), after failing to put enough temperature in his tyres during his out-lap following promising times in Q1. Kevin Magnussen was Haas's sole representative in Q2, after Romain Grosjean, having lost a practice session due to an electrical failure, had trouble dealing with the front end and qualified in 16th place.

The Toro Rosso drivers, never on the pace due to a constant struggle with balance, were split by the Saubers as Pascal Wehrlein found a couple of hundredths of a second to ease Marcus Ericsson into 19th place, ahead of the troubled Brendon Hartley, 0.7s down on Pierre Gasly and in a different world to the Mercedes at the front.

Above: Valtteri Bottas edged out team-mate Hamilton for pole, thus putting himself in a position to control the race from the front.

Left: A practice pit stop under the lights for Toro Rosso's Pierre Gasly.

Far left: Max Verstappen struggled with the Red Bull throughout the weekend, but persisted to claim fifth place in the race.

Opening spread: Valtteri Bottas produced a flawless performance. The race of his career so far?

Photos: Peter J. Fox

313

BOTTAS did not need reminding that he had started from pole in Brazil two weeks previously, but failed to win. "I've got a second opportunity and a clear target," he said quietly – but with obvious determination. Mercedes thought that their long-run pace might be marginal compared to Ferrari, but maybe two-tenths up on Red Bull. For this reason, it was important for Bottas to make a good start – and just as important if he wanted to keep Hamilton behind, otherwise, on a track like this, he could lose a second race in succession.

Special attention had been paid to tyre characteristics and clutch pedal mapping, and it paid off when Bottas made as clean a getaway as he could have hoped for, keeping his team-mate behind on the 304m run to the first corner.

Behind the silver cars, Vettel locked up, but held third place ahead of Räikkönen, who was receiving heavy attention from Ricciardo; Verstappen was still sixth, having failed to gain his usual first-corner advantage. Pérez got the jump on Hülkenberg, only for the Renault to exceed the track limit to retake P7. Further back, Magnussen was squeezed out on the exit of Turn One, but kept his foot in it. The deviation from line, however, eventually caused a huge spin on to the infield after he had crested the rise at Turn Two. Contact between Massa and Vandoorne resulted in enough bodywork damage to cause the McLaren to lose rear downforce, run off the road later in the lap and drop to 15th, behind a battling Stroll and Grosjean.

The fight for seventh continued unabated as Pérez slipstreamed ahead of Hülkenberg on the long main straight, the Renault coming back at the Force India on the run down to Turn 11. Hülkenberg didn't quite make it, locked up and took to the run-off – which was inevitable any way, as Pérez had claimed the full width of the exit. All fair in love and war so far.

But then it became controversial when Hülkenberg missed out the following chicane, rejoined in front of Pérez and showed no intention of giving the place back. This prompted an angry radio call from car No. 11 and an equally predictable five-second penalty for Hülkenberg's intransigence; not what Renault needed in this fight to overhaul Toro Rosso for P6 in the championship.

As things would turn out, this battle, although brief, would be one of the few to savour. Up front, Bottas was 1.2 seconds ahead of Hamilton, with Vettel a similar distance behind. And so it would continue, Hamilton constantly between one and two seconds behind, with Bottas keeping him out of the DRS zone. It was already clear that the high demand on fuel at this track was leading to early fuel saving and the absence of anything remotely close to place changing among the top six.

But what about strategy? Low degradation meant that a one-stop tactic was the only way to go, with little to be gained on the undercut and possibly more on the overcut, depending on the long-term performance of the ultrasoft (the popular starting choice for all except the Saubers and Hartley, who had gone for the supersoft).

If they were fortunate enough to have their drivers running 1-2, Mercedes had agreed to bring in the leader first, with the second taking the chance on making the overcut work. On that basis, Bottas knew that the longer he could extend the first stint, the more difficult it would be for Hamilton to find time as he stayed out.

Lewis, for his part, could work out Valtteri's game plan as the leader ran consistently and at sufficient pace to just stay out of reach, and was hanging back to save his tyres as best he could for the overcut that would come his way. With Vettel dropping back by a couple of tenths every lap as Ferrari sought to protect his equipment – and, with it, the second place in the drivers' championship they could not afford to lose – here was the recipe for a stalemate the race could have done without.

Searching for conflict, the TV producer found the lively battle for P13 between Stroll and Grosjean, the Williams driver working hard with tyres that simply would not come up to a decent temperature. They swapped places – clumsily at times – before the Haas got ahead for good on lap 11. Stroll pitted immediately in the hope of some sort of respite with a fresh set of supersofts, even though they were unlikely to last the remaining 44 laps. Vandoorne gave up his particular struggle a lap later, when he brought in the sliding McLaren for more tyres.

A more strategic stop followed two laps later, when Red Bull pitted Verstappen in the hope of undercutting Räikkönen in P5. It didn't work, the Ferrari, despite a slow stop, remaining ahead. That turn of events was noted by Mercedes and others, as Verstappen's new supersofts were clearly not performing brilliantly, thus making the overcut on the long-running ultras a serious option.

Above: Sebastian Vettel had a lonely race into third for Ferrari.
Photo: Scuderia Ferrari

Left: Renault personnel are jubilant on the pit wall as Hülkenberg finishes sixth to claim the same spot in the constructors' championship.
Photo: Renault F1 Team

Right: The season ended on a low note for Daniel Ricciardo.
Photo: Peter J. Fox

The other Red Bull was fourth, pulling roughly the same lap times as Vettel and running three seconds behind the Ferrari. On lap 19, a vibration from the front prompted Ricciardo, believing he had a puncture, to make a late dive into the pits. The scramble for tyres added a couple of seconds to the stop, but there would be a more significant delay when he glanced the barriers on his out-lap and then, a few corners later, slowed completely with a hydraulics failure. This would have a bearing on the race, never mind ending his mixed season on a low note.

With yellow flags at Turn Five covering the Red Bull as it pulled on to the infield, there was the thought that a safety car of some sort might be needed to aid recovery of the stricken car. Rather than risk having the leader lap at safety car speeds when others further back, and yet to pass the pit-lane entry, made a free stop for tyres, Mercedes brought in their man on lap 21. The downside was a continuation of the yellows, meaning that Bottas couldn't go for it on his out-lap. And Hamilton, 19 seconds ahead, was now the leader.

Much depended on what Hamilton – and race control – did next. Mercedes considered bringing him in on the lap following Valtteri, but Lewis, with an eye on the overcut, particularly if the safety car appeared at the right moment, asked to stay out. The team agreed.

The Red Bull was eventually removed without drama, during which time Hamilton had made up 1.6s on his team-mate. With the chance of closing further being negated by

Above: Felipe Massa managed to score a point in his very last grand prix appearance.
Photo: Jad Sherif/WRi2

Top right: Massa is congratulated by Hamilton on the grid at the end of the race.

Above right: "You've earned a bonus!" Cyril Abiteboul congratulates Hülkenberg on his controlled performance.
Photo: Jean-François Galeron/WRi2

Right: Follow-my-leader. The Force Indias of Pérez and Ocon run together in the midfield convoy.
Photo: Sahara Force India F1 Team

back-markers, Mercedes brought in Lewis at the end of lap 24. He found further time on his in-lap and therefore was surprised to rejoin 1.8s behind Bottas.

Facing the same problem as before when trying to find the 1.4s lap delta needed for overtaking momentum, Lewis was keen to use the extra engine mode afforded by his power unit (fresh for Brazil), compared to the more tired unit in the back of Valtteri's car. In earlier conversation, the team had been against this, restricting both drivers to exactly the same mode level. But this being the last race, with championships settled and nothing to lose, it was decided to let Hamilton try to make a race of it.

On one occasion, at the end of the straight, car No. 44 was almost attached to the gearbox of No. 77, after a serious piece of late braking. But Bottas played his personal ace by remaining totally calm and then gradually pulling away, making the most of the negative effect created by dirty air on Hamilton's car as they worked through the turns skirting the Viceroy Hotel.

Bottas teased the gap to more than a second and stayed there, the Mercedes men matching each other with a lock-up each as an indication of how hard they were trying. Nonetheless, despite Lewis's heroics, it begged the question of his attitude, now that the championship had been settled. Had it been Vettel in front and the title to play for, might his attack mode have been even stronger?

Hamilton would later admit that that might have been the situation, but in the meantime, he chased Bottas home, the two silver cars triggering a cascade of fireworks and the blaring of boat horns as they crossed the finishing line for the final time.

Vettel was 15 seconds in arrears, despite finding the Ferrari at its most competitive as the fuel load lightened. But it was too late and, in any case, it didn't matter now that second in the championship had been secured to give Ferrari a crumb of consolation and reduce the chance of criticism

from home. Räikkönen was fifth, a frustrated Verstappen on his tail.

When it came to tension on the pit wall, there was none more acute than at Renault, where the move to sixth in the championship depended entirely on Hülkenberg bringing his car home in the same position. Sainz had lost the chance of overcutting his way past Massa and Alonso (into what would become P9) when the left front wheel came off as he left the pits to start his 32nd lap.

Hülkenberg duly earned Renault their financial bonus by finishing ahead of Pérez, even after taking the five-second penalty during his stop on lap 17. Force India were furious, attacking the stewards for their inconsistency over such lenient punishment after Hülkenberg had failed to give the place back.

Ocon had tried unsuccessfully to overcut his team-mate and had to finish the season behind Pérez, but ahead of Alonso and Massa, the McLaren having got in front when Felipe lost performance due to an empty battery that required recharging after his pit stop. Nonetheless, claiming a championship point was a nice way for the popular Brazilian to sign off his F1 career.

Grosjean was on his own in P11, clear of a tight battle between the compromised Vandoorne and the delayed Magnussen, a scrap that was joined later by Wehrlein and Hartley, running ahead of Toro Rosso team-mate Gasly, who had spun on lap 16. Ericsson finished 17th, ahead of Stroll, whose miserable weekend generated a third stop after he flat-spotted another set of tyres. It was not the way the novice wanted to end a mixed season.

For Bottas, with fastest lap to add to pole and victory, the result was the perfect way to go into the off-season. For F1 as a whole, however, the Abu Dhabi GP and its lack of action had been a poor advert and an inadequate reflection of an otherwise engaging and, at times, highly dramatic season.

Maurice Hamilton

VIEWPOINT
PASSING SHOT

IF Lewis Hamilton and Max Verstappen can't overtake, then you've got a problem. Hamilton, with his fresher engine and reversed tyre strategy, had provided relief from the follow-the-leader stuff of a fortnight earlier at Interlagos, but at Yas Marina, even he had to trail team-mate Valtteri Bottas without much hope. It was the same story for Verstappen staring at the rear wing of Kimi Räikkönen's Ferrari.

And, probably, Nico Hülkenberg understood the futility of trying to get his Renault past a Mercedes-powered Force India and so just missed out a chicane and took a 5s hit, which he managed to overcome quite comfortably.

"He was so far off, he might as well have gone shopping in Dubai and come back again," said Force India's irritated Bob Fernley.

And all this despite two relatively long straights and a double DRS zone.

The Mercedes engineers had pointed out to Hamilton that he needed a 1.4s (per lap) speed advantage over the guy in front to have any realistic hope of getting by. And with the top six on the grid covered by 1.1s, guess what? You weren't likely to see much racing...

Post-race, Hamilton said he was surprised that TV commentators don't spell that out to viewers more often. And you can see his point. Please tell them, it's not me not trying...

But commentators are fans of the sport, too, and it's not going to grow F1's audience much if they say, "Well folks, nothing much doing here for the next 90 minutes, you might as well nip down to the shops and come back again. You might even bump into 'The Hulk' while you're there!"

Not great either, that as the last two races on the calendar, Interlagos and Abu Dhabi are more likely than not to be championship-deciding venues.

The problem at Abu Dhabi is that drivers can't follow closely enough through sector three and the following flat-out sector one, to be near enough to take advantage of DRS.

Ross Brawn was excited about the potential of his 75 per cent complete aero team looking into how to improve overtaking, with the aid of CFD and current car information from teams after the signing of confidentiality agreements. Let's hope they get a shift on!

Tony Dodgins

2017 FORMULA 1
ETIHAD AIRWAYS
ABU DHABI
GRAND PRIX

YAS MARINA 24–26 NOVEMBER

ROLEX

OFFICIAL TIMEPIECE

RACE DISTANCE: 55 laps, 189.739 miles/305.355km

RACE WEATHER: Dry/sunny-dark (track 28–31°C, air 24–25°C)

YAS MARINA CIRCUIT, ABU DHABI
Circuit: 3.451 miles / 5.554km
55 laps

Turn 7 65/40
348/216
Turn 8 85/53
4
300/186
Turns 5 & 6 100/62
Turn 9 105/65
Turn 21 192/119
Turn 3 283/176
Turn 10 215/134
20
Turn 2 262/163
19 131/185
17
Turn 1 182/113
Turn 18
Turn 16
Turn 15 297/185
Turn 11 115/71
Turn 14 115/71
Turn 12&13 132/82
116/187 mph/kmh
Gear
DRS zone

RACE – OFFICIAL CLASSIFICATION

Pos.	Driver	Nat.	No.	Entrant	Car/Engine	Laps	Time/Retirement	Speed (mph/km/h)	Gap to leader	Fastest race lap
1	**Valtteri Bottas**	FIN	77	Mercedes AMG Petronas Motorsport	Mercedes F1 W08-Mercedes M08 EQ Power+ V6	55	1h 34m 14.062s	120.808/194.422		1m 40.650s 52
2	**Lewis Hamilton**	GB	44	Mercedes AMG Petronas Motorsport	Mercedes F1 W08-Mercedes M08 EQ Power+ V6	55	1h 34m 17.961s	120.725/194.288	3.899s	1m 41.473s 51
3	**Sebastian Vettel**	D	5	Scuderia Ferrari	Ferrari SF70H-062 V6	55	1h 34m 33.392s	120.397/193.760	19.330s	1m 40.770s 55
4	**Kimi Räikkönen**	FIN	7	Scuderia Ferrari	Ferrari SF70H-062 V6	55	1h 34m 59.448s	119.846/192.874	45.386s	1m 42.338s 53
5	**Max Verstappen**	NL	33	Red Bull Racing	Red Bull RB13-TAG Heuer RB13 V6	55	1h 35m 00.331s	119.828/192.844	46.269s	1m 42.028s 43
6	**Nico Hülkenberg**	D	27	Renault Sport Formula One Team	Renault R.S.17-R.E.17 V6	55	1h 35m 39.775s	119.004/191.519	1m 25.713s	1m 42.376s 53
7	**Sergio Pérez**	MEX	11	Sahara Force India Formula 1 Team	Force India VJM10-Mercedes M08 EQ Power+ V6	55	1h 35m 46.124s	118.873/191.307	1m 32.062s	1m 42.689s 52
8	**Esteban Ocon**	F	31	Sahara Force India Formula 1 Team	Force India VJM10-Mercedes M08 EQ Power+ V6	55	1h 35m 52.973s	118.731/191.079	1m 38.911s	1m 42.609s 47
9	**Fernando Alonso**	E	14	McLaren Honda Formula 1 Team	McLaren MCL32-Honda RA617H V6	54			1 lap	1m 41.669s 54
10	**Felipe Massa**	BR	19	Williams Martini Racing	Williams FW40-Mercedes M08 EQ Power+ V6	54			1 lap	1m 43.026s 45
11	Romain Grosjean	F	8	Haas F1 Team	Haas VF-17-Ferrari 062 V6	54			1 lap	1m 42.437s 51
12	Stoffel Vandoorne	B	2	McLaren Honda Formula 1 Team	McLaren MCL32-Honda RA617H V6	54			1 lap	1m 43.986s 50
13	Kevin Magnussen	DK	20	Haas F1 Team	Haas VF-17-Ferrari 062 V6	54			1 lap	1m 43.928s 50
14	Pascal Wehrlein	D	94	Sauber F1 Team	Sauber C36-Ferrari 059/5 V6	54			1 lap	1m 43.867s 50
15	Brendon Hartley	NZ	28	Scuderia Toro Rosso	Toro Rosso STR12-Renault R.E.17 V6	54			1 lap	1m 43.897s 52
16	Pierre Gasly	F	10	Scuderia Toro Rosso	Toro Rosso STR12-Renault R.E.17 V6	54			1 lap	1m 43.844s 33
17	Marcus Ericsson	S	9	Sauber F1 Team	Sauber C36-Ferrari 059/5 V6	54			1 lap	1m 43.567s 36
18	Lance Stroll	CDN	18	Williams Martini Racing	Williams FW40-Mercedes M08 EQ Power+ V6	54			1 lap	1m 42.324s 52
	Carlos Sainz	E	55	Renault Sport Formula One Team	Renault R.S.17-R.E.17 V6	31	wheel loose			1m 43.378s 26
	Daniel Ricciardo	AUS	3	Red Bull Racing	Red Bull RB13-TAG Heuer RB13 V6	20	hydraulics			1m 42.757s 13

Fastest race lap: Valtteri Bottas on lap 52, 1m 40.650s, 123.437mph/198.652km/h.

Lap record: Sebastian Vettel (Red Bull RB5-Renault V8), 1m 40.279s, 123.894mph/199.387km/h (2009).

20 · HARTLEY · Toro Rosso
10-place grid penalty for using additional power unit elements

18 · WEHRLEIN · Sauber

16 · GROSJEAN · Haas

14 · MAGNUSSEN · Haas

12 · SAINZ · Renault

19 · ERICSSON · Sauber

17 · GASLY · Toro Rosso

15 · STROLL · Williams

13 · VANDOORNE · McLaren

11 · ALONSO · McLaren

Grid order	1	2	3	4	5	6	7	8	9	10	11	12	13	14	15	16	17	18	19	20	21	22	23	24	25	26	27	28	29	30	31	32	33	34	35	36	37	38	39	40	41	42	43	44
77 BOTTAS	77	77	77	77	77	77	77	77	77	77	77	77	77	77	77	77	77	77	77	77	77	77	44	44	44	77	77	77	77	77	77	77	77	77	77	77	77	77	77	77	77	77	77	7
44 HAMILTON	44	44	44	44	44	44	44	44	44	44	44	44	44	44	44	44	44	44	44	44	44	44	77	77	77	44	44	44	44	44	44	44	44	44	44	44	44	44	44	44	44	44	44	44
5 VETTEL	5	5	5	5	5	5	5	5	5	5	5	5	5	5	5	5	5	5	5	5	5	5	5	5	5	5	5	5	5	5	5	5	5	5	5	5	5	5	5	5	5	5	5	5
3 RICCIARDO	3	3	3	3	3	3	3	3	3	3	3	3	3	3	3	3	3	3	3	3	7	7	7	7	7	7	7	7	7	7	7	7	7	7	7	7	7	7	7	7	7	7	7	7
7 RÄIKKÖNEN	7	7	7	7	7	7	7	7	7	7	7	7	7	7	7	7	27	27	7	7	33	33	33	33	33	33	33	33	33	33	33	33	33	33	33	33	33	33	33	33	33	33	33	33
33 VERSTAPPEN	33	33	33	33	33	33	33	33	33	33	33	33	33	33	27	7	7	33	33	33	31	31	31	31	31	31	31	31	31	31	31	27	27	27	27	27	27	27	27	27	27	27	27	27
27 HÜLKENBERG	27	27	27	27	27	27	27	27	27	27	27	27	27	11	11	33	31	31	31	55	55	55	55	55	55	55	55	55	55	11	11	11	11	11	11	11	11	11	11	11	11
11 PÉREZ	11	11	11	11	11	11	11	11	11	11	11	11	11	31	33	31	19	19	19	55	19	27	27	27	27	27	27	27	27	31	31	31	31	31	31	31	31	31	31	31	31
31 OCON	31	31	31	31	31	31	31	31	31	31	31	31	31	19	31	14	14	14	11	11	11	11	11	11	11	11	8	14	14	14	14	14	14	14	14	14	14	14	14
19 MASSA	19	19	19	19	19	19	19	19	19	19	19	19	14	55	55	55	27	11	8	8	8	8	8	8	8	8	14	19	19	19	19	19	19	19	19	19	19	19	19
14 ALONSO	14	14	14	14	14	14	14	14	14	14	14	14	55	8	27	27	8	8	14	14	14	14	14	14	14	14	19	8	8	8	8	8	8	8	8	8	8	8	8
55 SAINZ	55	55	55	55	55	55	55	55	55	55	55	55	8	27	8	8	11	19	19	19	19	19	19	19	19	2	2	2	2	2	2	2	2	2	2	2
2 VANDOORNE	18	18	18	18	18	18	18	18	18	8	8	8	11	11	11	11	94	94	94	94	94	94	94	10	10	2	20	20	20	20	20	20	20	20	20	20
20 MAGNUSSEN	8	8	8	8	8	8	8	8	18	10	10	10	94	94	94	94	20	28	28	10	10	10	9	20	94	94	94	94	94	94	94	94	94
18 STROLL	2	2	2	2	2	2	2	2	2	2	94	94	94	20	20	20	28	10	10	9	9	18	2	20	2	10	10	10	10	10	10	10	10
8 GROSJEAN	10	10	10	10	10	10	10	10	10	94	20	20	28	28	28	10	9	9	18	18	18	2	20	18	18	18	18	18	18
10 GASLY	94	94	94	94	94	94	94	94	94	20	28	28	10	10	10	9	18	18	2	2	20	94	10	18	9	9	9
94 WEHRLEIN	28	28	28	28	28	28	28	28	28	18	18	18	9	9	9	18	2	2	20	20	94	18	18
9 ERICSSON	9	9	9	9	9	9	20	20	20	9	9	9	18	18	18	2	2	20	20	20	28	28	28	18	9
28 HARTLEY	20	20	20	20	20	9	9	9	9	28	2	2	2	2	2	20

TIME SHEETS

PRACTICE 1 (FRIDAY)
Weather: Dry/sunny
Temperatures: track 43–45°C, air 26–27°C

Pos.	Driver	Laps	Time
1	Sebastian Vettel	23	1m 39.006s
2	Lewis Hamilton	25	1m 39.126s
3	Max Verstappen	15	1m 39.154s
4	Kimi Räikkönen	22	1m 39.518s
5	Valtteri Bottas	30	1m 39.741s
6	Sergio Pérez	24	1m 40.293s
7	Fernando Alonso	20	1m 40.522s
7	Stoffel Vandoorne	15	1m 40.569s
8	Felipe Massa	27	1m 40.723s
9	Daniel Ricciardo	29	1m 40.773s
10	George Russell	26	1m 41.131s
11	Romain Grosjean	24	1m 41.306s
12	Lance Stroll	27	1m 41.581s
13	Pierre Gasly	29	1m 41.646s
14	Carlos Sainz	23	1m 41.748s
15	Pascal Wehrlein	26	1m 41.752s
16	Nico Hülkenberg	26	1m 41.864s
17	Antonio Giovinazzi	21	1m 42.065s
19	Marcus Ericsson	28	1m 42.344s
20	Brendon Hartley	35	1m 42.585s

PRACTICE 2 (FRIDAY)
Weather: Dry/twilight
Temperatures: track 30–32°C, air 25–26°C

Pos.	Driver	Laps	Time
1	Lewis Hamilton	39	1m 37.877s
2	Sebastian Vettel	37	1m 38.026s
3	Daniel Ricciardo	34	1m 38.180s
4	Kimi Räikkönen	35	1m 38.352s
5	Valtteri Bottas	33	1m 38.537s
6	Max Verstappen	34	1m 38.894s
7	Sergio Pérez	33	1m 39.323s
8	Esteban Ocon	36	1m 39.333s
9	Nico Hülkenberg	41	1m 39.529s
10	Fernando Alonso	28	1m 39.559s
11	Felipe Massa	36	1m 39.635s
12	Stoffel Vandoorne	31	1m 39.671s
13	Carlos Sainz	38	1m 40.201s
14	Lance Stroll	30	1m 40.329s
15	Pierre Gasly	39	1m 40.694s
16	Kevin Magnussen	31	1m 41.128s
17	Pascal Wehrlein	43	1m 41.270s
18	Marcus Ericsson	40	1m 41.302s
19	Brendon Hartley	39	1m 41.496s
20	Romain Grosjean	12	1m 41.560s

PRACTICE 3 (SATURDAY)
Weather: Dry/sunny
Temperatures: track 43°C, air 25°C

Pos.	Driver	Laps	Time
1	Lewis Hamilton	19	1m 37.627s
2	Valtteri Bottas	21	1m 37.900s
3	Kimi Räikkönen	22	1m 38.157s
4	Sebastian Vettel	22	1m 38.174s
5	Daniel Ricciardo	16	1m 38.340s
6	Max Verstappen	14	1m 38.587s
7	Fernando Alonso	15	1m 39.155s
8	Stoffel Vandoorne	18	1m 39.277s
9	Carlos Sainz	15	1m 39.340s
10	Sergio Pérez	19	1m 39.367s
11	Felipe Massa	16	1m 39.383s
12	Nico Hülkenberg	18	1m 39.396s
13	Esteban Ocon	18	1m 39.500s
14	Kevin Magnussen	19	1m 39.831s
15	Romain Grosjean	19	1m 40.079s
16	Pascal Wehrlein	20	1m 40.307s
17	Lance Stroll	16	1m 40.572s
18	Pierre Gasly	21	1m 40.737s
19	Marcus Ericsson	21	1m 40.789s
20	Brendon Hartley	23	1m 40.883s

QUALIFYING (SATURDAY)
Weather: Dry/twilight Temperatures: track 29–32°C, air 24–25°C

Pos.	Driver	First	Second	Third	Qualifying Tyre
1	Valtteri Bottas	1m 37.356s	1m 36.822s	1m 36.231s	Ultrasoft (new)
2	Lewis Hamilton	1m 37.391s	1m 36.742s	1m 36.403s	Ultrasoft (new)
3	Sebastian Vettel	1m 37.817s	1m 37.023s	1m 36.777s	Ultrasoft (new)
4	Daniel Ricciardo	1m 38.016s	1m 37.583s	1m 36.959s	Ultrasoft (new)
5	Kimi Räikkönen	1m 37.453s	1m 37.302s	1m 36.985s	Ultrasoft (new)
6	Max Verstappen	1m 38.021s	1m 37.777s	1m 37.328s	Ultrasoft (new)
7	Nico Hülkenberg	1m 38.781s	1m 38.138s	1m 38.282s	Ultrasoft (new)
8	Sergio Pérez	1m 38.601s	1m 38.359s	1m 38.374s	Ultrasoft (new)
9	Esteban Ocon	1m 38.896s	1m 38.392s	1m 38.397s	Ultrasoft (new)
10	Felipe Massa	1m 38.629s	1m 38.565s	1m 38.550s	Ultrasoft (new)
11	Fernando Alonso	1m 38.820s	1m 38.636s		
12	Carlos Sainz	1m 38.810s	1m 38.725s		
13	Stoffel Vandoorne	1m 38.777s	1m 38.808s		
14	Kevin Magnussen	1m 39.395s	1m 39.298s		
15	Lance Stroll	1m 39.503s	1m 39.646s		
16	Romain Grosjean	1m 39.516s			
17	Pierre Gasly	1m 39.724s			
18	Pascal Wehrlein	1m 39.930s			
19	Marcus Ericsson	1m 39.994s			
20	Brendon Hartley	1m 40.471s			

QUALIFYING: head to head

Hamilton	13	7	Bottas
Vettel	15	5	Räikkönen
Massa	17	2	Stroll
Stroll	1	0	Di Resta
Ricciardo	7	13	Verstappen
Pérez	13	7	Ocon
Hülkenberg	16	0	Palmer
Hülkenberg	3	1	Sainz
Kvyat	6	8	Sainz
Sainz	2	0	Gasly
Kvyat	1	0	Hartley
Gasly	1	2	Hartley
Ericsson	2	0	Giovinazzi
Ericsson	7	11	Wehrlein
Alonso	16	3	Vandoorne
Vandoorne	1	0	Button
Grosjean	13	7	Magnussen

FOR THE RECORD

400th RACE STARTED: Honda engine

100th RACE WITH A PODIUM: Mercedes

100th RACE WITH A FRONT ROW: Mercedes

DID YOU KNOW?

Lewis Hamilton became the third F1 driver to score points in every grand prix of a season, the other two being Fangio in 1954 and '55, and Michael Schumacher in 2002.

POINTS

DRIVERS

1	Lewis Hamilton	363
2	Sebastian Vettel	317
3	Valtteri Bottas	305
4	Kimi Räikkönen	205
5	Daniel Ricciardo	200
6	Max Verstappen	168
7	Sergio Pérez	100
8	Esteban Ocon	87
9	Carlos Sainz	54
10	Nico Hülkenberg	43
11	Felipe Massa	43
12	Lance Stroll	40
13	Romain Grosjean	28
14	Kevin Magnussen	19
15	Fernando Alonso	17
16	Stoffel Vandoorne	13
17	Jolyon Palmer	8
18	Pascal Wehrlein	5
19	Daniil Kvyat	5

CONSTRUCTORS

1	Mercedes	668
2	Ferrari	522
3	Red Bull	368
4	Force India	187
5	Williams	83
6	Renault	57
7	Toro Rosso	53
8	Haas	47
9	McLaren	30
10	Sauber	5

10 · MASSA · Williams

8 · PÉREZ · Force India

6 · VERSTAPPEN · Red Bull

4 · RICCIARDO · Red Bull

2 · HAMILTON · Mercedes

9 · OCON · Force India

7 · HÜLKENBERG · Renault

5 · RÄIKKÖNEN · Ferrari

3 · VETTEL · Ferrari

1 · BOTTAS · Mercedes

	45	46	47	48	49	50	51	52	53	54	55	
	77	77	77	77	77	77	77	77	77	77	77	1
14	44	44	44	44	44	44	44	44	44	44	44	2
5	5	5	5	5	5	5	5	5	5	5	5	3
	7	7	7	7	7	7	7	7	7	7	7	4
33	33	33	33	33	33	33	33	33	33	33	33	
27	27	27	27	27	27	27	27	27	27	27	27	6
11	11	11	11	11	11	11	11	11	11	11	11	7
31	31	31	31	31	31	31	31	31	31	31	31	8
14	14	14	14	14	14	14	14	14	14	14	14	9
19	19	19	19	19	19	19	19	19	19	19	19	10
8	8	8	8	8	8	8	8	8	8	8		
2	2	2	2	2	2	2	2	2	2	2		
20	20	20	20	20	20	20	20	20	20	20		
94	94	94	94	94	94	94	94	94	94	94		
28	28	28	28	28	28	28	28	28	28	28		
10	10	10	10	10	10	10	10	10	10	10		
9	9	9	9	9	9	9	9	9	9	9		
18	18	18	18	18	18	18	18	18	18	18		

18 = Pit stop   2 = One lap or more behind

RACE TYRE STRATEGIES

PIRELLI

	Driver	Race Stint 1	Race Stint 2	Race Stint 3	Race Stint 4
1	Bottas	Ultrasoft (u): 1–21	Supersoft (n): 22–55		
2	Hamilton	Ultrasoft (u): 1–24	Supersoft (n): 25–55		
3	Vettel	Ultrasoft (u): 1–20	Supersoft (n): 21–55		
4	Räikkönen	Ultrasoft (u): 1–15	Supersoft (n): 16–55		
5	Verstappen	Ultrasoft (u): 1–14	Supersoft (n): 15–55		
6	Hülkenberg	Ultrasoft (u): 1–17	Supersoft (n): 18–55		
7	Pérez	Ultrasoft (u): 1–16	Supersoft (n): 17–55		
8	Ocon	Ultrasoft (u): 1–31	Supersoft (n): 32–55		
9	Alonso	Ultrasoft (u): 1–21	Supersoft (n): 22–54		
10	Massa	Ultrasoft (u): 1–22	Supersoft (n): 23–54		
11	Grosjean	Ultrasoft (n): 1–32	Supersoft (n): 33–54		
12	Vandoorne	Ultrasoft (u): 1–12	Supersoft (n): 13–54		
13	Magnussen	Ultrasoft (u): 1– 22	Supersoft (n): 23–54		
14	Wehrlein	Supersoft (n): 1–28	Ultrasoft (n): 29–54		
15	Hartley	Supersoft (n): 1–26	Ultrasoft (n): 27–54		
16	Gasly	Ultrasoft (n): 1–30	Supersoft (n): 31–54		
17	Ericsson	Supersoft (n): 1–30	Ultrasoft (n): 31–54		
18	Stroll	Ultrasoft (u): 1–11	Supersoft (n): 12–29	Ultrasoft (u): 30–35	Ultrasoft (u): 36–54
	Sainz	Ultrasoft (n): 1–31 (dnf)			
	Ricciardo	Ultrasoft (u): 1–19	Supersoft (n): 20 (dnf)		

The tyre regulations stipulate that at least two of three dry tyre specifications must be used during a dry race.
Pirelli P Zero logos are colour-coded on the tyre sidewalls: Purple = Ultrasoft; Red = Supersoft. (n) new (u) used

Photos: Peter J. Fox

DRIVERS' POINTS TABLE 2017

Place	Driver	Nationality	Date of birth	Car	Australia	China	Bahrain	Russia	Spain	Monaco	Canada	Azerbaijan	Austria	Britain	Hungary	Belgium	Italy	Singapore	Malaysia	Japan	United States	Mexico	Brazil	Abu Dhabi	Points
1	Lewis HAMILTON	GB	7/1/85	Mercedes	2p	1pf	2f	4	1pf	7	1pf	5p	4f	1pf	4	1p	1p	1f	2p	1p	1p	9	4	2	**363**
2	Sebastian VETTEL	D	3/7/87	Ferrari	1	2	1	2p	2	1	4	4f	2	7	1p	2f	3	Rp	4f	R	2f	4pf	1	3	**317**
3	Valtteri BOTTAS	FIN	28/8/89	Mercedes	3	6	3p	1	R	4	2	2	1p	2	3	5	2	3	5	4f	5	2	2p	1pf	**305**
4	Kimi RÄIKKÖNEN	FIN	17/10/79	Ferrari	4f	5	4	3f	R	2p	7	14*	5	3	2	4	5	R	NS	5	3	3	3	4	**205**
5	Daniel RICCIARDO	AUS	1/7/89	Red Bull-TAG Heuer	R	4	5	R	3	3	3	1	3	5	R	3	4f	2	3	3	R	R	6	R	**200**
6	Max VERSTAPPEN	NL	30/9/97	Red Bull-TAG Heuer	5	3	R	5	R	5	R	R	R	4	5	R	10	R	1	2	4	1	5f	5	**168**
7	Sergio PÉREZ	MEX	26/1/90	Force India-Mercedes	7	9	7	6	4	13f	5	R	7	9	8	17*	9	5	6	7	8	7	9	7	**100**
8	Esteban OCON	F	17/9/96	Force India-Mercedes	10	10	10	7	5	12	6	6	8	8	9	9	6	10	10	6	6	5	6	8	**87**
9	Carlos SAINZ	E	1/9/94	Toro Rosso-Renault	8	7	R	10	7	6	R	8	R	R	7	10	14	4	R	R	–	–	–	–	
				Renault	–	–	–	–	–	–	–	–	–	–	–	–	–	–	–	–	7	R	11	R	**54**
10	Nico HÜLKENBERG	D	19/8/87	Renault	11	12	9	8	6	R	8	R	13	6	17*	6	13	R	16	R	R	R	10	6	**43**
11	Felipe MASSA	BR	25/4/81	Williams-Mercedes	6	14	6	9	13	9	R	R	9	10	EW	8	8	11	9	10	9	11	7	10	**43**
12	Lance STROLL	CDN	29/10/98	Williams-Mercedes	R	R	R	11	16	15*	9	3	10	16	14	11	7	8	8	R	11	6	16	18	**40**
13	Romain GROSJEAN	F	17/4/86	Haas-Ferrari	R	11	8	R	10	8	10	13	6	13	R	7	15	9	13	9	14	15	15	11	**28**
14	Kevin MAGNUSSEN	DK	5/10/92	Haas-Ferrari	R	8	R	13	14	10	12	7	R	12	13	15	11	R	12	8	16	8	R	13	**19**
15	Fernando ALONSO	E	29/7/81	McLaren-Honda	R	R	14*	NS	12	–	16*	9	R	R	6f	R	17*	R	11	11	R	10	8	9	**17**
16	Stoffel VANDOORNE	B	26/3/92	McLaren-Honda	13	R	NS	14	R	R	14	12	12	11	10	14	R	7	7	14	12	12	R	12	**13**
17	Jolyon PALMER	GB	20/1/91	Renault	R	13	13	R	15	11	R	11	NS	12	13	R	6	15	12	–	–	–	–	–	**8**
18	Pascal WEHRLEIN	D	18/10/94	Sauber-Ferrari	EW	–	11	16	8	R	15	10	14	17	15	R	16	12	17	15	R	14	14	14	**5**
19	Daniil KVYAT	RUS	26/4/94	Toro Rosso-Renault	9	R	12	12	9	14*	R	R	16	15	11	12	12	R	–	–	10	–	–	–	**5**
	Marcus ERICSSON	S	2/9/90	Sauber-Ferrari	R	15	R	15	11	R	15	11	15	14	16	16	18*	R	18	R	15	R	13	17	**–**
	Pierre GASLY	F	7/2/96	Toro Rosso-Renault	–	–	–	–	–	–	–	–	–	–	–	–	–	–	14	13	–	13	12	16	**–**
	Antonio GIOVINAZZI	I	14/12/93	Sauber-Ferrari	12	R	–	–	–	–	–	–	–	–	–	–	–	–	–	–	–	–	–	–	
				Haas-Ferrari	–	–	–	–	–	–	–	–	–	AP	AP	–	–	AP	AP	–	–	AP	AP	AP	**–**
	Brendon HARTLEY	NZ	10/11/89	Toro Rosso-Renault	–	–	–	–	–	–	–	–	–	–	–	–	–	–	–	–	13	R	R	15	**–**
	Jenson BUTTON	GB	19/1/80	McLaren-Honda	–	–	–	–	–	R	–	–	–	–	–	–	–	–	–	–	–	–	–	–	**–**
	Paul DI RESTA	GB	16/4/86	Williams-Mercedes	–	–	–	–	–	–	–	–	–	–	R	–	–	–	–	–	–	–	–	–	**–**

FRIDAY TESTERS

Place	Driver	Nationality	Date of birth	Car	Australia	China	Bahrain	Russia	Spain	Monaco	Canada	Azerbaijan	Austria	Britain	Hungary	Belgium	Italy	Singapore	Malaysia	Japan	United States	Mexico	Brazil	Abu Dhabi	Points
	Charles LECLERC	MC	16/10/97	Sauber-Ferrari	–	–	–	–	–	–	–	–	–	–	–	–	–	–	AP	–	AP	AP	AP	–	**–**
	Alfonso CELIS	MEX	18/9/96	Force India-Mercedes	–	–	–	–	–	–	–	–	AP	AP	–	–	–	–	–	–	–	–	–	–	**–**
	George RUSSELL	GB	15/2/98	Force India-Mercedes	–	–	–	–	–	–	–	–	–	–	–	–	–	–	–	–	–	–	AP	AP	**–**
	Sergey SIROTKIN	RUS	27/8/95	Renault	–	–	AP	AP	–	–	–	–	AP	–	–	–	–	–	–	–	AP	–	–	–	**–**
	Sean GELAEL	RI	1/11/96	Toro Rosso-Renault	–	–	–	–	–	–	–	–	–	–	–	–	–	–	AP	AP	–	AP	AP	–	**–**

KEY: AP – Also practised   EW – Entry withdrawn   NC – Non-classified   NS – Non-starter   R – Retired   * – Placed, but retired   f – fastest lap   p – pole position

POINTS AND PERCENTAGES

GRID POSITIONS: 2017

Pos	Driver	Starts	Best	Worst	Average
1	Sebastian Vettel	20	1	20	3.15
2	Valtteri Bottas	20	1	9	3.35
3	Lewis Hamilton	20	1	20	3.60
4	Kimi Räikkönen	19	1	10	3.95
5	Max Verstappen	20	2	16	6.10
6	Daniel Ricciardo	20	3	19	7.75
7	Sergio Pérez	20	5	18	8.85
8	Esteban Ocon	20	3	17	9.50
9	Nico Hülkenberg	20	5	18	9.65
10	Felipe Massa	19	6	17	10.26
11	Carlos Sainz	20	6	19	11.65
12	Daniil Kvyat	15	8	19	12.27
13	Fernando Alonso	18	6	20	12.61
14	Romain Grosjean	20	6	20	13.20
15	Lance Stroll	20	2	20	14.15
16	Kevin Magnussen	20	9	20	14.20
17	Stoffel Vandoorne	19	7	20	14.47
18	Jolyon Palmer	15	10	20	15.40
19	Pascal Wehrlein	18	12	20	16.44
20	Marcus Ericsson	20	11	20	16.85
21	Pierre Gasly	5	14	20	17.00
22	Antonio Giovinazzi	2	16	18	17.00
23	Brendon Hartley	4	17	20	18.50
24	Paul di Resta	1	19	19	19.00
25	Jenson Button	1	20	20	20.00

RETIREMENTS: 2017

Number of cars to have retired

Grand Prix	Starters	At 1/4-distance	At 1/2-distance	At 3/4-distance	At full distance	Percentage of finishers
Australia	20	1	4	5	7	65.0
China	20	2	4	5	5	75.0
Bahrain	19	4	4	4	6	68.4
Russia	19	3	3	3	3	84.2
Spain	20	2	3	4	4	80.0
Monaco	20	1	1	3	7	65.0
Canada	20	3	3	3	5	75.0
Azerbaijan	20	3	5	5	7	65.0
Austria	20	2	3	4	4	80.0
Britain	19	1	1	2	2	89.5
Hungary	20	2	3	3	4	80.0
Belgium	20	2	2	3	4	80.0
Italy	20	0	0	2	4	80.0
Singapore	20	5	5	6	8	60.0
Malaysia	19	0	0	2	1	94.7
Japan	20	3	3	3	5	75.0
United States	20	3	4	4	4	80.0
Mexico	20	1	3	3	5	75.0
Brazil	20	3	3	4	4	80.0
Abu Dhabi	20	0	1	2	2	90.0

LAP LEADERS: 2017

Grand Prix	Hamilton	Vettel	Bottas	Verstappen	Räikkönen	Ricciardo	Total
Australia	16	38	2	–	1	–	57
China	56	–	–	–	–	–	56
Bahrain	8	36	13	–	–	–	57
Russia	–	8	44	–	–	–	52
Spain	31	32	3	–	–	–	66
Monaco	–	45	–	–	33	–	78
Canada	70	–	–	–	–	–	70
Azerbaijan	30	3	–	–	–	18	51
Austria	–	–	69	–	2	–	71
Britain	51	–	–	–	–	–	51
Hungary	–	59	–	9	2	–	70
Belgium	41	3	–	–	–	–	44
Italy	51	–	2	–	–	–	53
Singapore	58	–	–	–	–	–	58
Malaysia	3	–	–	51	–	2	56
Japan	48	–	2	–	–	3	53
United States	48	5	–	2	1	–	56
Mexico	–	–	–	71	–	–	71
Brazil	13	57	–	–	1	–	71
Abu Dhabi	3	–	52	–	–	–	55
Total	**527**	**286**	**187**	**133**	**40**	**23**	**1196**
(Per cent)	44.1	23.9	15.6	11.1	3.3	1.9	100.0

CAREER PERFORMANCES: 2017

Driver	Nationality	Races	Championships	Wins	2nd places	3rd places	4th places	5th places	6th places	7th places	8th places	9th places	10th places	Pole positions	Fastest laps	Points
Fernando Alonso	E	**291**	2	32	37	28	26	22	16	15	8	6	10	22	23	**1849**
Valtteri Bottas	FIN	**97**	–	3	8	11	7	14	5	7	5	3	4	5	9	**716**
Jenson Button	GB	**306**	1	15	15	20	24	27	19	12	20	14	14	8	8	**1235**
Paul di Resta	GB	**59**	–	–	–	–	2	–	3	6	6	4	5	–	–	**121**
Marcus Ericsson	S	**76**	–	–	–	–	–	–	–	–	1	1	3	–	–	**9**
Pierre Gasly	BR	**5**	–	–	–	–	–	–	–	–	–	–	–	–	–	**–**
Antonio Giovinazzi	I	**2**	–	–	–	–	–	–	–	–	–	–	–	–	–	**–**
Romain Grosjean	F	**122**	–	–	2	8	2	1	6	9	9	5	6	–	1	**344**
Lewis Hamilton	GB	**208**	4	62	32	23	17	17	6	7	4	5	2	72	38	**2610**
Brendon Hartley	NZ	**4**	–	–	–	–	–	–	–	–	–	–	–	–	–	**–**
Nico Hülkenberg	D	**135**	–	–	–	3	7	15	14	15	7	13	1	1	2	**405**
Daniil Kvyat	RUS	**72**	–	–	1	3	1	2	2	–	9	8	–	1	1	**133**
Kevin Magnussen	DK	**60**	–	–	1	–	–	4	4	4	5	5	–	–	–	**81**
Felipe Massa	BR	**269**	–	11	13	17	21	24	21	27	18	16	26	17	16	15	**1167**
Esteban Ocon	F	**29**	–	–	–	–	–	2	5	1	3	2	5	–	–	**87**
Jolyon Palmer	GB	**35**	–	–	–	–	1	–	–	1	–	–	1	–	–	**9**
Sergio Pérez	MEX	**134**	–	–	2	5	2	7	9	15	13	15	12	–	4	**467**
Kimi Räikkönen	FIN	**271**	1	20	34	37	25	23	17	13	11	9	10	17	45	**1565**
Daniel Ricciardo	AUS	**129**	–	5	6	16	11	8	6	6	4	5	9	1	9	**816**
Carlos Sainz	E	**60**	–	–	–	1	–	4	5	7	6	4	–	–	–	**118**
Lance Stroll	CDN	**20**	–	–	–	1	–	1	1	2	1	–	–	–	–	**40**
Stoffel Vandoorne	B	**20**	–	–	–	–	–	–	2	–	2	–	2	–	–	**14**
Max Verstappen	NL	**60**	–	3	5	3	7	2	2	5	3	3	–	2	**421**
Sebastian Vettel	D	**198**	4	47	26	26	26	15	8	4	6	2	–	50	33	**2425**
Pascal Wehrlein	D	**39**	–	–	–	–	–	1	1	–	2	–	–	–	–	**6**

Note: As is now common practice, drivers retiring on the formation lap are not counted as having started. Where races have been subjected to a restart, those retiring during an initial race are included as having started (Alonso and Räikkönen in Belgium, 2001 are affected).

ALL-TIME RECORDS: 2017

STARTS

Rubens Barrichello	323
Michael Schumacher	307
Jenson Button	306
Fernando Alonso	291
Kimi Räikkönen	271
Felipe Massa	269
Riccardo Patrese	256
Jarno Trulli	252
David Coulthard	246
Giancarlo Fisichella	229
Mark Webber	215
Gerhard Berger	210

FASTEST LAPS

Michael Schumacher	77
Kimi Räikkönen	45
Alain Prost	41
Lewis Hamilton	38
Sebastian Vettel	33
Nigel Mansell	30
Jim Clark	28
Mika Häkkinen	25
Niki Lauda	24
Fernando Alonso	23
Juan Manuel Fangio	23
Nelson Piquet	23

WINS

Michael Schumacher	91
Lewis Hamilton	62
Alain Prost	51
Sebastian Vettel	47
Ayrton Senna	41
Fernando Alonso	32
Nigel Mansell	31
Jackie Stewart	27
Jim Clark	25
Niki Lauda	25
Juan Manuel Fangio	24
Nelson Piquet	23
Nico Rosberg	23

POLE POSITIONS

Lewis Hamilton	72
Michael Schumacher	68
Ayrton Senna	65
Sebastian Vettel	50
Jim Clark	33
Alain Prost	33
Nigel Mansell	32
Nico Rosberg	30
Juan Manuel Fangio	29
Mika Häkkinen	26
Niki Lauda	24
Nelson Piquet	24

PODIUMS

Michael Schumacher	155
Lewis Hamilton	117
Alain Prost	106
Sebastian Vettel	99
Fernando Alonso	97
Kimi Räikkönen	91
Ayrton Senna	80
Rubens Barrichello	68
David Coulthard	62
Nelson Piquet	60
Nigel Mansell	59
Nico Rosberg	57

YOUNGEST STARTERS

Max Verstappen	17y 166d
Jaime Alguersuari	19y 125d
Mike Thackwell	19y 182d
Ricardo Rodríguez	19y 208d
Fernando Alonso	19y 218d
Esteban Tuero	19y 320d
Chris Amon	19y 324d
Daniil Kvyat	19y 324d
Esteban Ocon	19y 346d
Sebastian Vettel	19y 349d
Eddie Cheever	20y 53d
Jenson Button	20y 53d

YOUNGEST WINNERS

Max Verstappen	18y 228d
Sebastian Vettel	21y 73d
Fernando Alonso	22y 26d
Bruce McLaren	22y 104d
Lewis Hamilton	22y 154d
Kimi Räikkönen	23y 157d
Robert Kubica	23y 184d
Jacky Ickx	23y 188d
Michael Schumacher	23y 240d
Emerson Fittipaldi	23y 296d
Mike Hawthorn	24y 86d
Jody Scheckter	24y 131d

YOUNGEST CHAMPIONS

Sebastian Vettel	23y 134d
Lewis Hamilton	23y 300d
Fernando Alonso	24y 58d
Emerson Fittipaldi	25y 273d
Michael Schumacher	25y 314d
Niki Lauda	26y 197d
Jacques Villeneuve	26y 200d
Jim Clark	27y 188d
Kimi Räikkönen	28y 4d
Jochen Rindt	28y 169d
Ayrton Senna	28y 223d
James Hunt	29y 56d

YOUNGEST ON POLE

Sebastian Vettel	21y 73d
Fernando Alonso	21y 237d
Rubens Barrichello	22y 97d
Lewis Hamilton	22y 154d
Andrea de Cesaris	22y 308d
Nico Hülkenberg	23y 80d
Robert Kubica	23y 121d
Jacky Ickx	23y 216d
Kimi Räikkönen	23y 255d
David Coulthard	24y 13d
Jenson Button	24y 97d
Eugenio Castellotti	24y 238d

WORLD CHAMPIONSHIPS

Michael Schumacher	7	Ayrton Senna	3	Mario Andretti	1	Nigel Mansell	1
Juan Manuel Fangio	5	Jackie Stewart	3	Jenson Button	1	Kimi Räikkönen	1
Lewis Hamilton	4	Fernando Alonso	2	Giuseppe Farina	1	Keke Rosberg	1
Alain Prost	4	Alberto Ascari	2	Mike Hawthorn	1	Nico Rosberg	1
Sebastian Vettel	4	Jim Clark	2	Phil Hill	1	Jody Scheckter	1
Jack Brabham	3	Emerson Fittipaldi	2	Denny Hulme	1	John Surtees	1
Niki Lauda	3	Mika Häkkinen	2	James Hunt	1	Jacques Villeneuve	1
Nelson Piquet	3	Graham Hill	2	Alan Jones	1		

F2 REVIEW by CRAIG LLEWELLYN
KING CHARLES

Above: Charles Leclerc's decision to join Prema for his tilt at the Formula 2 crown proved to be inspired, and the Monegasque driver constantly showed his class in winning seven races against top-quality opposition.

Right: On the way to Formula 1? Under the wing of the Ferrari Driver Academy, Leclerc seems destined for a full-time seat at Sauber in 2018.

Photos: F2 Media Services

AFTER 12 seasons running under the GP2 Series banner, Formula 1's primary feeder championship reverted to the more logical F2 designation for 2017, aligning itself with the FIA's Global Pathway initiative, designed to create a clear linear progression from domestic F4 series right through to the top tier of single-seater racing.

The rebranding, however, extended only to marketing purposes, as the series retained the GP2 regulations used for the previous dozen campaigns and employed the same Dallara chassis, which had made its debut in 2011, along with the existing four-litre Mecachrome V8 engine – which had been used since the inaugural 2005 season – prior to an entirely new package being introduced for 2018.

When the season kicked off in Bahrain in mid-April, it marked the first FIA-sanctioned F2 event since former F1 driver Jonathan Palmer's centrally run series had been shut down in 2012. Prior to that, F2 had been the recognised second step for some 37 seasons, before being replaced by F3000 in 1985. Regardless of the name change, however, the purpose of the series remained the same, namely opening the door to the top flight for the latest batch of young hopefuls, and the 2017 field comprised the usual mix of GP2 veterans and rookies eager to jump the queue, some with at least a foot already in the F1 door.

Norman Nato, fifth overall for Racing Engineering in 2016, was the highest-placed returnee but, like all but one of those coming back with a top-ten championship finish under their belts, he would be in different colours in 2017. While his reversion to Arden at least brought some familiarity, former team-mate Jordan King and fellow potential title threats Luca Ghiotto and Oliver Rowland were venturing into the unknown at MP Motorsport, Russian Time and DAMS respectively.

Of the 2016 top ten, therefore, only Artem Markelov stayed put, hoping to use his close ties to the Russian Time team to good effect. Interestingly, given their relative success in 2016, Nato and Markelov were the ones without F1 links, an anomaly given even greater emphasis when the lower-ranked Nicholas Latifi, Nobuharu Matsushita and Sean Gelael all boasted ties to the top flight. Of the new faces, three of the top four had already impressed enough on their way up the ladder to have attracted the attention of the F1 talent scouts – GP3 champion Charles Leclerc and Prema team-mate Antonio Fuoco with Ferrari, and Nyck de Vries with McLaren – while the other, Alexander Albon, had briefly enjoyed not one, but two opportunities.

The only change on the team front was the withdrawal of Carlin, which had decided to focus on its nascent Indy Lights programme after six seasons in GP2, reducing the field to ten squads. The calendar, meanwhile, waved goodbye to Hockenheim – a casualty of Germany falling off the F1 schedule – and Sepang, with Bahrain returning after a one-year hiatus to open the season and Jerez being granted stand-alone status on what was, remarkably, its series debut.

If Leclerc was under less pressure to succeed than either Pierre Gasly or Stoffel Vandoorne before him – both of whom had the expectations of F1 paymasters to fulfil – he was also undoubtedly helped by signing with the team *du jour*, joining former GP3 rival and fellow Ferrari protégé Fuoco at Prema Racing. The Monegasque had raced at the previous level with all-conquering ART, but his decision to join the reigning GP2 champion left the French team to go with veteran Matsushita, alongside another 'home-grown' GP3 graduate in Albon. Leclerc's decision looked a wise move from the off.

The youngster proved a quick study, too, shadowing veterans Rowland and Markelov in Bahrain practice before unleashing a qualifying lap fully seven-tenths quicker than the next man, fellow rookie de Vries, could manage. There was still some learning to do, though, with tyre strategy and

management in the sweltering Sakhir heat proving Leclerc's undoing in the first race. Having initially squandered the lead to Nato during the pit stops, the Prema driver faded to a distant third as Markelov charged through from seventh on the grid, after running longer on his first set of tyres. He spent that evening studying his data, however, and returned on Sunday to turn the outside of row three into the top step of the podium by swapping from medium- to soft-compound tyres mid-race and then making up a 14-place, 24-second deficit to emerge with a comfortable points lead heading back to Europe.

Lest anyone thought Leclerc's Bahrain form had been a fluke – and there can only have been a handful, given the punishment he had meted out in GP3 – he set them straight in Barcelona. Admitting that the biggest improvements were coming from him and not the already well-fettled Prema Dallara, the Monegasque continued to get to grips with the importance of preserving his Pirellis, but not before he had blitzed both practice and qualifying to secure a second straight pole. The margins were smaller this time, but that did not bother Leclerc who, aided by a handily timed safety car, eased to a three-second win over Ghiotto and Rowland.

Climbing from eighth to fourth on Sunday subsequently stretched Leclerc's points lead to 26 as the series turned towards his home rounds, but rare misfortune would prevent a conqueror's return – and briefly allow his rivals a chance to close in. The weekend had begun in typical Leclerc fashion, with the rookie defying a lack of Monaco circuit experience to top practice again, before heading the faster qualifying group to claim another four points.

He appeared on course for another feature-race maximum as well, before the safety car upset his dominance. A broken suspension upright ultimately might have wrought similar frustration as Leclerc posted his first DNF of the campaign and, when a second followed on Saturday, after he collided with Nato while trying to come from the back, those pole points were all he added to his tally.

Leclerc's loss in the Principality was Rowland's gain, the Briton finally gaining a breakthrough at this level. He had started directly behind his rival on the grid, having been drawn in the same qualifying group, but benefited from the timing of the safety car to emerge ahead of the Prema driver after his stop. Once in front, he was able to control the gap to those behind, eventually crossing the line 0.8s clear of Markelov. Although he narrowly missed another point in race two, Rowland left Monaco just three points off the championship lead, while Markelov also closed the gap with a third and fifth on the weekend.

If either man had aspirations of snatching top spot overall at round four in Azerbaijan, however, they would be sorely disappointed: Leclerc produced a near-perfect performance, ruined only by a race-two penalty for failing to slow under yellow flags. Another pole position – his fourth in as many rounds – allowed him to lead from the front in a feature race beset with caution periods and eventually ended by red flags, after Gelael hit the wall. A clean sweep – complete with a brace of fastest laps – appeared on the cards when Leclerc assumed the lead of Sunday's sprint race with three laps remaining on the streets of Baku. Unfortunately for the Monegasque, he was then assessed a nine-second time penalty, which promoted Nato after the chequer.

Leclerc's 45-point haul was all the more remarkable given that he had been competing just three days after the death of his father, Hervé, at the age of just 54. Coming less than 12 months after the passing of childhood friend Jules Bianchi, it was an emotional blow, but he responded with a maturity well beyond his 19 years. With neither Rowland – who had suffered gearbox failure on Sunday – nor Markelov, who had scored twice, but missed the podium on both occasions, able to make inroads, Leclerc's championship lead was extended to 42 points heading to Austria.

The gap grew further at the Red Bull Ring, but at least Leclerc was made to work for his gains. Sadly for DAMS, however, it wasn't Rowland bearing down on the Monegasque in race one. Instead, as the championship leader converted another pole into victory, it was Latifi who gradu-

Above: Oliver Rowland was a feisty and tenacious opponent to Leclerc and often was a match for the champion. However, the DAMS driver also suffered misfortunes, such as two disqualifications, which cost him a win and a third place – and second in the championship.

Top right: Nobuharu Matsushita celebrates his sprint-race win in Budapest, one of two victories by the Japanese driver.

Above right: With two second-place finishes, Alexander Albon enjoyed a very creditable rookie season.

Above far right: Although largely overshadowed by his team-mate, Markelov, Luca Ghiotto nabbed a sprint-race win for Russian Time on home ground in Monza.

Right: Antonio Fuoco also had to play second fiddle to Leclerc at Prema. But the Italian managed a single win and three further podiums for the team.

Photos: F2 Media Services

ally filled his mirrors, their respective strategies converging to produce a nail-biting finish. Another couple of laps, and the Canadian might have had his first win – having thrown one away in Barcelona after being distracted by a missing mirror. Despite being the fastest man on track, instead he had to settle for a fourth podium in six outings.

Rowland's bid to join his team-mate among the silverware had been thwarted by the second Prema entry, in which Fuoco was enjoying easily his best weekend of the season. Having lapped close enough to Leclerc to join the points leader on the front row, the Italian looked set for second on the road, only to be overhauled by Latifi's superior tyre choice with two laps remaining.

The two Prema cars were even closer on Sunday, but not in a way that the Italian team would have wanted. Leclerc was caught out by Fuoco having to lift to avoid a moment between Rowland and Albon, and broke a wishbone against his team-mate's right rear, posting his third – and final – non-classification of the season. Markelov and Rowland limited their losses by sandwiching Albon – racing with a broken collarbone after missing Baku due to a mountain-bike accident – on the podium, the Russian taking his first win since the opening round.

Normal order was resumed at Silverstone, where Leclerc equalled Vandoorne's record for consecutive pole positions at six, before going on to claim victory in the feature race. Success was not without its drama, however, as the Prema car began spewing oil smoke immediately prior to its pit stop, but the emissions came to nought and win number five came a comfortable ten seconds ahead of Nato.

Again, Rowland and Markelov limited the damage to their ambitions by taking third and fourth respectively, but any hope the Briton had of turning the tables in front of his home crowd disappeared in race two, when a brace of penalties – for over-aggressive defence against his Russian rival and then a dicey safety car restart – dropped him from fourth to 17th in the sprint. Markelov capitalised with the final podium spot, behind Ghiotto and Latifi – who finally claimed that

elusive first win – which was enough for him to swap places with Rowland in the standings, albeit now 67 points adrift of Leclerc as the season passed its halfway mark.

Whereas the 2016 campaign had cycled through overall leaders on a round-by-round basis prior to Silverstone, the top six was already firming up by the same point in 2017. Markelov's return to second overall was the first time he'd been that high since the opening round, and he and Rowland distanced themselves from fourth, which had been Ghiotto's until Latifi's podium run edged him ahead in Austria.

Matsushita held a watching brief over the top five, until he was deposed by Nato's solid Silverstone performance. The Frenchman's win in Baku, however, would remain his sole success of the season, putting him on a par with both Matsushita (Barcelona sprint) and de Vries (Monaco sprint) as the only drivers to keep the Leclerc-Rowland-Markelov triumvirate off the top step heading into the summer.

With rumours of a possible Sauber F1 seat for 2018 beginning to circulate, Leclerc showed little sign of slowing his pursuit of the title, and he would have broken Vandoorne's qualifying record at the Hungaroring had it not been for Prema's decision to fit a brass shim to its differential, instead of the mandated steel type. The team insisted that there was no performance advantage, but Rowland inherited top spot while the championship leader would have to come from the back of the grid.

Leclerc did his part, gaining eight places in a single lap before going on to take fourth in the feature, but for the most part, the race was about his nearest rivals. Markelov got the better of the start, but Rowland was back ahead after the pit stops, only for the Russian to benefit from a late safety car, closing back in on the Briton. The battle ended in tears, however, when a decisive block from Rowland squeezed Markelov on to the grass and into the Turn One barriers, which not only sealed his fate, but also a DAMS 1-2.

Rowland's best weekend at this level was completed with a strong run to second behind Matsushita in the sprint. With Markelov only able to rise to ninth – albeit with fastest lap

– their championship positions switched again, only this time with a 35-point cushion in Rowland's favour. Leclerc, meanwhile, salvaged another fourth place in spite of clutch and gearbox issues, which ensured he went into the summer break with a 50-point advantage over his nearest rival.

The price of Prema's shim sham was amplified when the season resumed at Spa, for Leclerc again produced the fastest time in qualifying and would have forced another alteration to the record books had it been an eighth straight pole. As it was, the Hungaroring exclusion had paled in significance by the end of Saturday in Belgium, for a commanding win was scrubbed from the ledger when the No. 1 machine was found to have a worn underside plank. With Rowland, third on the road, also ejected for the same reason, luck was still on Leclerc's side, although second-placed Markelov – who had survived another frenetic scrap with the Briton that resulted in offsetting last-corner penalties – took advantage to rack up a third win of the year and eat into the points deficit.

Markelov's fortune would have been greater had he been able to make hay while the championship leaders had to come from the back on Sunday, but instead his car let him down for the first time all year, allowing Leclerc and Rowland, fifth and eighth respectively behind first-time winner Sérgio Sette Câmara, to salvage something from the weekend.

If the top three thought that they had had it bad in Belgium, however, it was nothing compared to Monza, which they left with a combined total of two points from three days of toil. Once again, it was Markelov who came off 'best', but he remained seven marks shy of Rowland when there had been a chance to not only overhaul the DAMS driver, but also take a chunk out of Leclerc's 68-point advantage. The Russian's mediocre haul came from ninth in a wet feature race, where he had clashed with both Albon and Roberto Merhi

Above: Artem Markelov was the third stand-out driver, along with Leclerc and Rowland. The Russian scored five wins to finish the season in a clear second place.

Top right: The highlight of Gustav Malja's season was a podium in the sprint race at Monaco.

Top far right: Brazilian Sérgio Sette Câmara was largely unspectacular, until he bounced to a win at Spa and a second place at Monza for MP Motorsport.

Above centre right: Canadian Nicholas Latifi was an admirably consistent points scorer for DAMS throughout the season, taking one win and adding a further seven podiums.

Above centre far right: Norman Nato's stand-out performance came with his sprint-race win in Baku.

Above right: Rapax gained their only victory of the season when Nyck de Vries took the win in the Monaco sprint race. The ambitious Dutch driver switched teams to Racing Engineering mid-season and will be looking for more glory in 2018, when he takes up a seat at Prema Racing.

Right: Oliver Rowland gave his all in a campaign that just fell short. What does the future hold now for the talented Yorkshireman?

Photos: F2 Media Services

early on, but it was still better than either Rowland – who had lost a wheel after a late pit stop – and Leclerc, whose race had ended in the barriers at Curva Grande following a last-lap coming-together with de Vries while contesting the lead.

Coming from the back on Sunday, Leclerc made it to ninth and Rowland to 11th, while Markelov went backwards from row five to end up an unusually lowly 15th. That left the door open for some lesser lights to take to the podium, with Ghiotto eventually claiming the sprint-race spoils. It could have been so much better for the local favourite, however, for he had also benefited from the Leclerc-de Vries clash to 'win' on Saturday, only to be assessed a five-second penalty for cutting the Rettifilio chicane. Thus Fuoco inherited his first win at this level, holding off Matsushita who, on Friday, had claimed a maiden pole just days after suffering "the biggest crash of [his] life" at Eau Rouge.

Latifi took third in the feature to continue his recovery from a rare DNS in Belgium, while Sette Câmara and Fuoco completed Sunday's top three. The Brazilian carried his Spa form – where he had claimed that first win thanks to a blinding start from row two – to Italy to extend his late scoring run to four races. Prior to that, Matsushita had racked up a second sprint win of the year, in Hungary, to cement sixth place overall heading to the stand-alone event at Jerez de la Frontera. All attention, however, would be on Leclerc who, ironically, away from the eyes of the Suzuka-bound F1 paddock, could finally put his sizeable points advantage to good use and wrap up the title.

He looked set to do so in comfortable fashion, having approached his weekend strategy with a quick settlement in mind. Pole and feature victory were the target to rule out any late challenge from the pair behind him, and things worked out almost to plan, until a late safety car and inaccurate lap count from his own pit – which led to the tyre-troubled Prema car sliding around the 'extra' two laps – caused Leclerc some undue concern. Eventually he crossed the line just a couple of tenths ahead of Rowland, but it was enough.

"I think we've had a really good year," Leclerc said of the partnership with Prema. "We worked very hard from winter testing and we focused on ourselves. In Bahrain, I wasn't sure whether we had been lucky, but arriving in Barcelona, it became clear that, if we were doing the job correctly, we had

the pace to win the championship. Obviously, I've had some lows during the season, most of all on the personal side, and I would like to dedicate this title to my father. Winning the championship is an amazing way for me to honour him."

The final rounds of the season, in Abu Dhabi, were an excuse for Leclerc, as if he needed one, to parade his abilities before the F1 circus. He did so with another podium brace, including a seventh win of the year, which, in fitting fashion, he waited until the final lap to claim, out-punching Albon to the line. Prior to that, he had claimed second spot, a little more fortuitously, in the feature race, after winner Rowland and third-placed Fuoco were excluded by the stewards.

Rowland's DSQ – again because of plank irregularities – promoted Markelov to the top spot and, with Ghiotto inheriting the final step of the podium, all but sealed both second in the championship for the driver and the teams' title for Russian Time. Ghiotto's haul also edged him closer to the Briton overall, but overtaking him in the sprint remained a tall order, and when Rowland climbed from the back of the grid to seventh, hope faded completely. Markelov finished between the pair, sixth on the road, to end the season fully 72 points adrift of Leclerc.

Latifi and Matsushita also scored in both races – the former with third place in the sprint – to cement their positions in the standings. Behind the top six, de Vries, Fuoco and Nato remained closely matched almost to the end, with the Dutchman only edging away in Abu Dhabi. A factor for points almost everywhere, the McLaren protégé took a lone win in Monaco and split his remaining four podium finishes between two teams, having started the year with Rapax, before swapping seats with Louis Delétraz and finishing at Racing Engineering. Fuoco and Nato took a win apiece, the Italian adding four third places and the Frenchman a brace of runner-up spots, but they were inconsistent elsewhere, preventing them from challenging higher overall.

Sette Câmara was the only other driver to win a race, but his two-round purple patch, covering Spa and Monza, was far from enough to boost him into the top ten. Instead, he finished 12th overall, behind rookie Albon. The Thai was a persistent threat for points through the first half of the year, but evidently felt the effects of his broken shoulder thereafter, although a win had looked possible prior to Leclerc's

charge in the final race. King was similarly unable to rack up a win, having left Racing Engineering over the winter; he also tailed off during the second half.

Behind Sette Câmara, Gustav Malja led the Racing Engineering cause prior to the arrival of de Vries, but he recorded just one podium – in Monaco – in a relatively lean year for Alfonso de Orléans-Borbón's team. The departed Delétraz topped out with fourth place with Rapax at Monza and finished 17th overall. The pair sandwiched a trio of relative veterans, with Sergio Canamasas (14th) and Johnny Cecotto Jr (16th) making prolonged cameo appearances, the Venezuelan finishing second in Monaco. Gelael, at least, completed the year, but 15th overall – with only four scoring finishes – hardly confirmed him as worthy of his Toro Rosso test runs or a Prema seat alongside de Vries in 2018.

In all, 29 drivers took in at least one round, while 17 completed the season, but it was still surprising not to see Prema at the head of the team standings for the second time in as many years in their brief history at this level. Instead, with both DAMS and Russian Time within six points heading to Yas Marina, there was some intrigue to the finale, and the combination of Markelov and Ghiotto won out, propelling the latter from third to first over the weekend. Rowland's DSQ hurt DAMS, keeping it behind Prema who, in turn, trailed the champions by 15 points in the final reckoning. ART finished a long way adrift in fourth overall, but comfortably ahead of the rest, headed by Rapax.

When F2 returns for the second season of its latest incarnation, it will do so with a different look, following the unveiling of the F2/2018, the car that will take the category through its next three-year cycle. The Dallara-built machine will comply with the latest F1 safety standards, including – regrettably for many – the halo cockpit protection. It will feature a 3.4-litre turbocharged Mecachrome engine, delivering 620hp, and benefit from other developments, including a drag reduction system (DRS) and virtual safety car (VSC) technology. Tyres, once again, will be supplied by Pirelli.

Unlike his immediate predecessors, Leclerc looked set to translate his title straight into an F1 seat and, with both Vandoorne and Gasly joining him following Japanese detours, the principal feeder series appears back on track with regard to its main purpose. Long live F2.

PRINCE GEORGE

Above: George Russell takes his ART Grand Prix car to victory at the Red Bull Ring, one of four wins in an ultra-consistent season for the lanky 19-year-old from Norfolk.

Top right: The cream of the GP3 crop on the Monza podium. Winner Russell is flanked by ART team-mates Jack Aitken (*left*) and Anthoine Hubert.

Above right: Aitken was second in the standings, but, on 141, a long way short of Russell's winning 220.

Right: Pleased as punch. Nirei Fukuzumi savours the moment after his win in Catalunya.

Below right: A famous name makes his mark. Giuliano Alesi took his first victory at Silverstone, then followed it up with another at the Hungaroring.

Bottom right: Finland's latest hotshot? Niko Kari came good for Arden International with an end-of-season win in Abu Dhabi.

Photos: GP3 Media

GEORGE RUSSELL'S increasingly inexorable path towards Formula 1, possibly as a successor to four-times world champion Lewis Hamilton at Mercedes, took a definitive step forward as he cruised to the 2017 GP3 Series title and a bigger role with the Silver Arrows.

The 2014 McLaren *Autosport* BRDC Award winner had arrived in the series on the back of a successful second season in the FIA F3 European Championship, and had attracted the attention of Mercedes, which revealed him as an addition to its line-up at the beginning of 2017.

Having eased Hitech into European F3, Russell's GP3 bid was undoubtedly helped by a seat at series juggernaut ART Grand Prix, although he would still have to overcome the in-house threat brought about by joining the team to beat. Although it would field a largely overhauled line-up, ART's prowess not only attracted Russell, but also fellow Brit Jack Aitken – from series rival Arden – and Russell's erstwhile F3 opponent, Anthoine Hubert, to line up alongside second-year protégé Nirei Fukuzumi.

Aitken (Renault) and Fukuzumi (Honda) were both backed by manufacturers with ties to F1, and were the highest-placed returnees from the previous season, having finished fifth and seventh respectively. The rest of the field was largely an unknown quantity at GP3 level, with those already possessing experience yet to back it up with results.

Experience, and the ART factor, told from the start, with Aitken putting the No. 1 car on pole for the opening round in Barcelona, and Fukuzumi picking up the feature-race win after his team-mate cruelly suffered an engine sensor failure that had ended the battle between them. With DRS having been introduced to the category for the first time in a bid to liven up the racing, an entertaining scrap for honours had been on the cards, but Aitken's DNF – and resulting back-of-the-grid start for Sunday's sprint – was an early blow.

Newcomer Leonardo Pulcini, from Euroformula F3, and Alessio Lorandi filled out the race-one podium after Russell and Hubert left themselves with work to do, the former after excessive wheelspin off the line, and ART was without a driver on the podium in the sprint – won by Jenzer's Arjun Maini – although the French team still left Catalunya with the series lead.

Fukuzumi's points advantage lasted fully eight weeks as the sort of hiatus that has blighted recent GP3 seasons kept the drivers from competition until mid-July at the Red Bull Ring. They did have the benefit of a group test in Hungary during that break, however, and that proved to be key to Russell's title march, the Briton admitting to being able to work on flaws that had become apparent in Barcelona.

The preparation clearly paid off, for he claimed pole and victory in the feature in Austria, and repeated the feat twice in the next three races, either side of an unexpected poor weekend, ironically, at the Hungaroring. Russell had to fend off Aitken for much of race one at the Red Bull Ring, as ART capitalised on an unfortunate series of events for Arden to bring its cars home 1-2-3-4, Fukuzumi and Hubert swapping places post-race after the Frenchman was assessed a ten-second penalty for contact with Arden's Pulcini.

A repeat performance on home soil at Silverstone belied the fact that Russell had to overcome initial opposition from Hubert, who had made a better start than the pole-man, but, having arrived in the UK just a point behind Fukuzumi in the standings, the Briton left with a near 40-point advantage, his team-mate having suffered a nightmare weekend and failed to add to his tally. Hubert also overhauled Fukuzumi, while Aitken closed to within a couple of points as ART emphasised its championship dominance.

Russell had scored in all six races to that point, but was prevented from stretching his advantage going into the summer break by a sensor problem of his own ahead of race one in Budapest. Unable to take up his front-row spot, he could only watch as Aitken, from pole, claimed a vital victory. Neither would score on Sunday, though, as they came together in an incident largely caused by Aitken already having picked up a puncture. When the tyre let go, Russell – into the points from last on the grid – had nowhere to go; he limped home 11th after stopping for a new nose.

During the three-week 'holiday' between Hungary and Belgium, ART filled the top four spots in the drivers' championship, with just 20 points splitting Russell from fourth-placed Fukuzumi, but with others close enough to believe that they still had a say in how things might play out over the remaining four rounds. While ART had dominated qualifying and the feature race through rounds 1–4 – claiming pole and victory at each – the Sunday event, with its reversed-top-eight grid, at least provided opportunities for the rest of the field to dispute the silverware.

Maini's sprint-race win in Spain was followed by a maiden victory for Raoul Hyman and Campos Racing in Austria, and a similar first for Giuliano Alesi at Silverstone. A repeat for the son of former Ferrari favourite Jean in Hungary, at the head of a Trident 1-2-3-4, was enough to position the Frenchman as the principal threat to the ART quartet heading to Spa, with just six points separating him from Fukuzumi.

battle that ultimately was settled by the latter's forceful early move at Turn Two.

The ART pair were at it again in race two, with Russell in touching distance of the crown, but not afraid to put a move on his rival. Aitken was unimpressed, but could do little thereafter to prevent his countryman from going on to claim the points he needed, fourth place bolstered by the bonus for fastest lap, as he took his first title since edging Maini and Hyman to win BRDC F4 in 2014.

"At the start of the year, Mercedes set a clear goal for me, and that was to go out and win this title no matter how I did it," Russell said. "I could win every race or finish second in every race as Esteban [Ocon] almost did in 2015. After the Barcelona disappointment, we had a test in Budapest, and I set myself the goal to put it on pole every single race from then until the end of the season – and it was almost there.

"Mercedes played a big part [in my success]. Being part of their team and spending time in their debriefs really helped me, but it also helped to have three extremely fast and intelligent team-mates. I think it's quite easy for us to say ART had the best car, and they are fairly used to winning this category, but the reason behind it was that we worked so well as a team."

While Russell was away and clear at the top of the table, Aitken headed to the finale – again after a lengthy break between rounds – only six points ahead of Fukuzumi, with Hubert also in with a shout of mixing up the final ART order at the top of the table. As it turned out, however, the French team failed to dominate as it had done throughout the season, allowing some lesser lights to take on leading roles.

Although Russell had claimed his fourth pole of the year, making light of switching between his regular mount and Force India's F1 machine on Friday, to ensure a qualifying clean sweep for ART, he was jumped at the start by practice pace-setter Niko Kari. The latter proceeded to defy his fringe top-ten championship position by resisting pressure from behind – and a couple of virtual safety car periods – to claim his first win in GP3, and a first of the year for Arden. Russell was also demoted by the second Arden car of Pulcini, but he reclaimed the position at the final restart to add another podium to his collection.

There was another first-time winner in the sprint, Boccolacci obtaining some measure of reward for a solid season. Having started second on the partially-reversed grid, the Frenchman made short work of pole-man and Trident team-mate Tveter to blast into a lead he would not lose. The American also lost a place to DAMS' Dan Ticktum, the Red Bull-backed Brit having joined the series at Monza. Between rounds, Ticktum won Macau's F3 Grand Prix, and it showed in an aggressive drive from fifth on the grid – although a five-second track-limits penalty ultimately cost him runner-up honours.

While Russell claimed fourth to ensure that, Hungary aside, he took points from every race, his team-mates were comparatively nowhere. Aitken only managed 14th and eighth, Fukuzumi 15th and 14th, and Hubert 11th and fifth. While that wasn't sufficient to dislodge any of them from their championship positions, it provided a surprising anomaly to an otherwise dominant season.

Behind the ART steamroller, Alesi's prowess in the sprint races kept him clear of fellow winners Lorandi – who claimed the Jerez sprint – and Boccolacci in the standings. Indeed, with the exception of Alesi, and early-round sprinters Maini and Hyman, no one outside of ART won races until Jerez, and even then the team's victories were shared between three drivers not four, as Hubert missed out.

Tveter, Kari and Kevin Jörg (Trident) hoovered up the remaining podium finishes, finishing eighth, tenth and twelfth in the standings respectively, surrounding Maini – who had inherited third in the feature at Yas Marina – and Ticktum. Hyman was pushed back to 13th overall at the finale.

ART's points haul was more than double that of any of its rivals, with Trident leading the five teams in pursuit of the champions. In all, 22 drivers took part in the season, despite there potentially being as many as 24 cars available from round to round. Bottom of the table DAMS will make way for MP Motorsport in 2018, while talks continue about combining GP3 and F3 on a streamlined international single-seater ladder from 2019. That would probably benefit everyone.

Any hopes Alesi, or almost anyone else, had of battling for the title pretty much evaporated in Belgium, however, as Russell produced the best result combination of the year. No doubt bolstered by his success there the previous season, the Briton claimed the four-point pole bonus in a wet qualifying session and went on to win the feature with fastest lap. It wasn't all plain sailing, as he had to overcome fast-starting Fukuzumi, which he did using DRS after a VSC, but he was never headed after that.

Aitken dicing with the Japanese driver kept things interesting for the fans at least, but Russell did more damage to his rivals' ambitions on Sunday, waltzing through from eighth to second to claim as much as he could behind now serial sprint winner Alesi. With Aitken only 18th after being hobbled by contact with Dorian Boccolacci – an error the Briton admitted to – Russell's lead was suddenly 36 points, with Fukuzumi and Alesi close enough to keep second overall honest.

Unsurprisingly, ART sewed up the teams' title well before the end of the season, and only needed one race at Monza to do so. Which was just as well, as there was only one race, thanks to a September deluge that threatened to derail the entire programme, from F1 on down. Qualifying on Saturday morning was washed away, with Fukuzumi ultimately pocketing the pole points by virtue of topping Friday evening's practice, and the feature race was eventually postponed until Sunday morning, when it started without the pole-sitter, who took his turn to suffer an ART sensor problem…

Without Fukuzumi alongside, Russell, from P2, seized the early lead, but the race was interrupted by a series of incidents that prevented him from drawing away. Hubert was the first to capitalise, briefly taking the lead after a mid-race restart, before Aitken tried his hand in similar fashion, passing both ART team-mates as Russell struggled with radio issues. The two Britons continued to battle until Russell sneaked back in front just before a race-ending shunt brought the safety car back out, extending his lead to 43 points and leaving Aitken, especially, hoping that the axed sprint race could be rescheduled at the stand-alone Jerez round.

Despite the lack of an F1-style TV schedule in southern Spain, Aitken would not get his wish, but he set about trying to do all he could to wrest the title fight at least to the season finale in Abu Dhabi. Although Fukuzumi had qualified fastest for his first true GP3 pole, Aitken lined up alongside, demoting Russell to row two. Fukuzumi was not cowed by the title fight brewing in his wake either, pulling clear to claim his first win since the series was last in Iberia, and leaving Aitken and Russell to duke it out around the narrow Jerez circuit, a

CURTAIN CALL

Above: Sporting the same famous helmet design as worn by his grandfather, Pietro Fittipaldi continued the family's illustrious racing tradition by becoming the final champion of the Formula V8 3.5 series.

Top right: Series stalwart Roy Nissany recorded a single win in the RP Motorsport Dallara.

Top far right: Aiming for the top. A pensive Fittipaldi no doubt ponders a bright future in the sport.
Photos: Formula V8 3.5

Above centre right: Alfonso Celis only managed a single win for Fortec, but his consistency earned him third place in the championship.
Photo: Bryn Williams

Above right: Fittipaldi's team-mate, Rene Binder, prepares for action in the rain at the Nürburgring. The Austrian driver scored four wins for the Lotus team.

Right: Matevos Isaakyan, driving for SMP Racing by AVF, was Fittipaldi's closest challenger in a season of twists and turns.
Photos: Formula V8 3.5

It wouldn't be hyperbole to describe the demise of the Formula 3.5 category as nothing less than a huge blow for the motor sport community. The latest – and final – iteration of the increasingly beleaguered junior series, characterised by depleted grid numbers, was sounding the death knell long before the inevitable was confirmed on the eve of what would become its final event. However, such an anti-climactic conclusion shouldn't diminish the legacy of a championship that has featured so prominently in moulding many of today's F1 stars.

As recently as 2015, the Formula 3.5 Championship had been thriving under Renault stewardship and finance. But the French company's withdrawal of support ahead of the 2016 season signalled an immediate and damaging effect on team commitment, despite the noble efforts of the RPM group, which had assumed responsibility to retain interest.

That's not to say that the championship's last hurrah in 2017 failed to drum up some eye-catching headlines. The series was rebranded as the World Series Formula V8 3.5, to reflect a deal reached to headline the support bill for the FIA World Endurance Championship, and as a result the cars raced outside Europe for the first time.

However, the attractive billing – which comprised six of the nine scheduled rounds – did little to enthuse the teams. An already sparse grid was reduced further when Arden withdrew and reigning champions AVF joined forces with SMP Racing to form a single entry. As a result, only 12 cars regularly made the start-line over the course of the year.

Nevertheless, the series did benefit from a degree of continuity among the drivers, with six of the top ten from 2016 returning for the opportunity to succeed Tom Dilmann as the final winner of the 3.5 era. They included Egor Orudzhev (SMP Racing by AVF), Roy Nissany (RP Motorsport), Rene Binder (Lotus), Yu Kanamaru (RP Motorsport) and Matevos Isaakyan (SMP Racing by AVF).

Come November, though, it was another sophomore racer who had his name etched into the title trophy. Pietro Fittipaldi, grandson of two-times F1 world champion Emerson Fittipaldi, was immortalised as the series' last ever champion.

Fittipaldi's title bid had been set in motion during the opening rounds, the Brazilian – having switched from Fortec to the Charouz-Racing Lotus-branded team – demonstrating his title credentials out of the box with a double win at Silverstone. That set him well on the path to success seven months later.

From that beginning, Fittipaldi didn't stray far from the head of the standings at any stage in the year, the occasional indifferent result never dropping him more than 16 points shy of the overall lead. Indeed, for the most part, he was the driver to beat in 2017. His Silverstone success was complemented by timely mid-season wins in Jerez and Motorland Aragon, while another comprehensive double win in Mexico, towards the end of the year, went a long way to pushing him towards the crown.

Even so, Fittipaldi was made to work hard for his eventual prize, and there were eight different race winners over the course of the season, the scant grid numbers making any non-scoring slip-ups more costly. In the light of this, it is no coincidence that the Brazilian underpinned his title bid by demonstrating greater race-finishing consistency than his direct rivals, taking the chequered flag on all but two occasions in 2017.

While six drivers went into the season finale in Bahrain with a mathematical chance of being crowned champion, ultimately Fittipaldi's greater consistency won out, giving him an eventual 44-point advantage over the competition.

The challenge to Fittipaldi's campaign came from several directions, during a season when five of the overall top six each enjoyed a moment atop the standings, most notable among them, during the latter stages, being SMP Racing by AVF's Isaakyan.

The Russian youngster put in a spirited mid-season run of eight podiums in ten races, which included wins at Spa and the Nürburgring, to briefly usurp Fittipaldi at the head of the standings going into the final rounds in Mexico, Austin and Bahrain. However, indifferent results when it mattered in those flyaways led to Isaakyan's title bid fading, even before an ill-timed technical issue during the finale in Bahrain al-

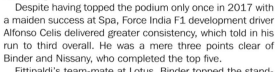

lowed his rival to wrap up the title at a canter with one race remaining.

Despite having topped the podium only once in 2017 with a maiden success at Spa, Force India F1 development driver Alfonso Celis delivered greater consistency, which told in his run to third overall. He was a mere three points clear of Binder and Nissany, who completed the top five.

Fittipaldi's team-mate at Lotus, Binder topped the standings for a time during the early stages of the season, courtesy of a double win at Monza. A moderate run of form mid-season, however, ensured that even another two victories, in the United States and Bahrain, couldn't haul him back into contention when it mattered.

Similarly, Nissany's five podiums from the opening seven races, including a win in Jerez, earmarked the RP Motorsport driver as a potential threat initially, only for him to fade as the season progressed.

A multiple race winner at Formula 3.5 V8 level over the previous two seasons, SMP Racing by AVF's Orudzhev added to his career tally with wins at Motorland Aragon and Austin. Six failures to score over the course of the year, however, spoke volumes for his eventual run to sixth in the championship standings.

Elsewhere, Teo Martin Motorsport's Yu Kanamaru and Konstantin Tereshchenko enjoyed moments on the podium en route to seventh and eighth overall. Fortec's Diego Menchaca followed in ninth place for Fortec.

Despite entering only six races for Teo Martin Motorsport, Alex Palou notched up a win at the Nürburgring and enough points to secure tenth in the overall standings. Formula Renault 2.0 Eurocup graduate Henrique Chaves was also a race winner during an impressive one-off outing for AVF in the season-ending Bahrain finale.

Alas, the curtain call for Formula 3.5 proved a low-key affair when considered against the talents who had used the series as a springboard into the upper echelons of motor sport during its heyday.

Indeed, a glance at the 2017 Formula 1 grid revealed that seven of its 20 drivers had competed in Formula 3.5 on their way to the top, including title winners Carlos Sainz and Kevin Magnussen, not to mention Daniel Ricciardo and for a time Sebastian Vettel. You can even trace Fernando Alonso's participation back to the series' more domestic early days, under the largely Spanish-based Formula Nissan Series banner.

It had been Renault's decision to take the series Europe-wide under a 'World Series' format in 2005, which established it as a worthy alternative route to F1 in addition to F3, GP2 and latterly GP3. It gave us champions in Robert Kubica, Giedo van der Garde and Oliver Rowland, as well as the aforementioned Sainz and Magnussen.

In light of the FIA's eagerness to establish a more structured and regulated motor sport ladder, through F2, F3 and F4, it is difficult to imagine how a privateer series could exist successfully on the fringes of the mighty governing body, so it seems unlikely that a revival of the series could occur any time soon.

Nevertheless, the series' eye-catching roll-call of champions and alumni will become its legacy, and its status as a veritable 'star maker' is one it richly deserves.

GREAT EXPECTATIONS

Above: Lando Norris, driving a Dallara-Volkswagen, took nine wins and seven second places to lift the European F3 crown at his first attempt.

Top right: Norris was snapped up by McLaren as a reserve driver, but staying with Carlin, he will step up to Formula 2 in 2018.

Above right: Prema Powerteam's Callum Ilott won six times and will become the first English driver to join the Ferrari Driver Academy in 2018.

Right: Sweden's Joel Eriksson led Motopark's challenge and scored seven wins on his way to second in the final standings, pipping Maximilian Günther by just five points.

Photos: FIA F3 Media

DO you recall the first time you heard the name Lewis Hamilton? For many, his rise to superstardom in the eyes of the public may have begun with his spectacular rookie season in Formula 1, but for those in the know, it was his prior dominant campaigns in GP2 and European Formula 3 (*née* Euroseries) that first earmarked him as the future of British motor sport.

Since then, however, despite notable successes in the junior ranks by the likes of Jolyon Palmer, Alex Lynn and Oliver Rowland, winning the GP2, GP3 and Formula Renault 3.5 championships respectively, no British driver has come close to forging a similar path as Hamilton to the pinnacle of the sport.

Nevertheless, as Hamilton wrapped up a fourth F1 world title a decade on from his headline-grabbing F1 debut, the buzz of anticipation was beginning to generate around a young driver many were tipping as Britain's next world beater – introducing Lando Norris

The statistics make for compelling reading. At just 18 years old and in only three seasons of car racing, Norris notched up five titles, including the Formula Renault 2.0 Eurocup in 2016 – joining a champion's roll-call that includes Stoffel Vandoorne and Valtteri Bottas – and in 2017, the European Formula 3 Championship, a series that has propelled more than half of the current F1 grid towards the upper echelons of the sport, most recently champions Esteban Ocon and Lance Stroll.

Hype will inevitably dub Norris 'the next Lewis Hamilton' – or perhaps more fittingly 'the next Max Verstappen' – but it's worth pointing out that even Hamilton took two seasons to clinch his European F3 title, whereas his present-day counterpart largely dominated it at the first attempt.

Indeed, few drivers have made their European F3 debut shouldering the burden of such lofty expectations on the back of relatively little experience, Norris going toe to toe

with drivers who had invested more time competing in this championship alone than his motor sport career had thus far spanned.

And yet, by the season's end, it was the novice who would prevail over more experienced contenders Joel Eriksson and Maximilian Günther.

In fact, while the 2017 European F3 Championship appeared to have all the hallmarks of becoming a classic title showdown midway into the season, Norris ultimately would surge clear when it mattered to emerge as the comfortable winner in a clinical display of late-season dominance that – fittingly – mirrored Hamilton's route to the 2017 F1 title.

With an intriguing blend of eye-catching new talent and more proficient returnees, what the 2017 European Formula 3 Championship lacked somewhat in quantity – five teams entering around four drivers each – it undoubtedly made up for in terms of quality and breadth.

Norris headed up a deep talent pool of first-timers, having put pen to paper with fellow Brits Carlin, the F3 stalwarts eager to bounce back from a lean campaign a year earlier, which had yielded its lowest ever ranking at European level.

By stark contrast, perennial front-runners Italian outfit Prema Powerteam started 2017 pitching for an unprecedented seventh consecutive drivers' title, headed by 2016's runner-up Günther and another Briton, Callum Ilott. In addition, Mick Schumacher, the son of seven-times F1 world champion and motor sport legend Michael Schumacher, made his much vaunted European racing debut with the team.

Elsewhere, Eriksson, who had been fifth in 2016, entered his second season of European F3 racing, once more with Motopark. Meanwhile, Hitech's challenge was headed by another British talent, Jake Hughes.

With Silverstone heralding the start of the ten-round, 30-race campaign, Norris confirmed that his pre-season hype had been justified by winning straight out of the box on home

soil, an early title credential he'd establish further during round two at Monza, where he took a second win. Better still, he succeeded in Italy by demonstrating an impressively varied skill set during wheel-to-wheel combat after a poor start had demoted him initially to a low of fifth place.

In fact, tardy getaways would prove a frustrating stumbling block for Norris on several occasions during the first half of the season. His mighty performances over a single lap – enough to secure eight pole positions during the course of the season – were often undone by an unusual failure to reach Turn One without losing a lot of positions. Indeed, he didn't always make it easy for himself early on in his F3 inauguration, the compromising starts – most notably in the remaining Silverstone races, Monza and Hungaroring – sacrificing valuable points and preventing him from topping the podium again until round five at the Norisring.

After a frustrating suspension failure-induced crash out of the lead in Pau and a clumsy last-lap collision while disputing victory with Hughes at the Norisring, by the mid-point of the year, Norris was seen as the relative title outsider, having slipped 38 points in arrears after 15 races. The error-prone start to his title campaign meant that it was left largely to Eriksson and Günther to make the early running. They shared the championship lead and the lion's share of the wins during an otherwise closely contested five events.

Considered the driver to watch pre-season, after an impressive podium-peppered latter half of his rookie European F3 season in 2016, Eriksson quickly established his title credentials by assuming the series lead from Norris with a victory at Silverstone, before notching up wins in round two at Monza and another on the streets of Pau. That was enough to keep his rivals at bay at the summit of the standings until the end of round three, when an ill-timed DNF allowed Günther to take over at the top.

The pre-season title favourite by virtue of Prema Powerteam's sheer stranglehold on the series in recent years (six drivers' titles in six consecutive campaigns), Günther had also been runner-up to 2016 champion Stroll, which simply added credence to his status as the driver to beat. Slipping under the radar initially with a series of solid points finishes and podiums at Silverstone and Monza, he took a pair of wins at Pau to haul himself back into contention. By the end of round three, the German, Norris and Eriksson were split by a mere two points.

A third win in a row, as the series headed east to Budapest's Hungaroring, allowed Günther to strengthen his position at the top of the standings, a position he'd retain to the end of round five at the Norisring, the mid-point of the season. Indeed, though it remained close race by race as momentum swung between the trio, Günther's greater consistency, combined with his four race wins, would allow him to pull out a solid 34-point lead over Eriksson after 15 races, with Norris staring at a 38-point margin to the top.

Going into the second half of the year with headway to make up, Norris – apparently having overcome his start-line woes – quickly reasserted his authority in the title hunt. He took two convincing wins from three races at Spa-Francorchamps, before a third in four races during round seven at Zandvoort put him back on the cusp of the championship lead. A third in race two and a seventh win of the season in race three – coupled to lowly results for his two rivals – meant that he left the Netherlands having turned his fortunes around entirely to reassume the championship lead.

With momentum now on his side, Norris stretched the margin during round eight at the Nürburgring. His two wins from the three races – including a mesmerising plus-20s win in the wet – were complemented by a relative slump in consistency from Eriksson and Günther, allowing him to multiply his advantage.

Indeed, such was the extent of his sparkling form over those three events, that Norris had turned a 38-point deficit at the start of round six into a 73-point advantage nine

Above: Maximilian Günther won two of the three races held at Pau.

Top right: On the way up? F3 rookie aspirants Joey Mawson, Jehan Daruvala and Mick Schumacher share the podium at Spielberg.

Above centre right: Hitech's Jake Hughes could only manage a single win, but he still finished fifth in the championship.

Above right: Guanyu Zhou finished the season strongly with a couple of podiums at Hockenheim after a largely disappointing campaign.

Below right: The highlight of the season for popular Austrian Ferdinand Habsburg came with a victory at Spa.

Photos: FIA F3 Media

races later, leaving him with one hand on the trophy and two rounds remaining.

Title glory surely would have come during the penultimate event at the Red Bull Ring had Norris not been cruelly spun into retirement on the final lap. But during the Hockenheimring season finale, he achieved his crowning moment, courtesy of a 20th podium in 30 races.

The first champion since Esteban Ocon in 2014 to succeed in his rookie season, Norris's formidable march through the junior ranks showed little sign of stopping. He was expected to move into Formula 2 for 2018, where he will seek to emulate the runaway success of Charles Leclerc, arguably the only other burgeoning youngster capable of mirroring his hype as tomorrow's potential world champion in waiting

Norris's success also allowed Carlin to prevent the Prema Powerteam from lifting the drivers' trophy for the first time since the European F3 Championship had been refreshed in its current guise in 2012. However, the Italian team would do enough to resist its rivals for a seventh straight teams' title.

With Norris having quickly turned a championship fight into a runaway success during the second half of the year, Günther and Eriksson were left to dispute a distant runner-up spot, the Swede ultimately emerging ahead by five points.

Though he often matched Norris for pace, Eriksson's title bid lost its way with just six points from a five-race stretch during the critical seventh and eighth rounds. He spared his blushes, however, with a run of three consecutive wins in Austria and Germany to resist Günther for 'vice champion' status. The latter, meanwhile, had to rely on consistency rather than headlines when it mattered, taking just one further win during the season finale.

Despite the focus on the top three, European F3 2017 was a showcase of emerging talent, with seven drivers in all spraying the winner's champagne over the course of the year. Moreover, an impressive 15 drivers would enjoy a moment on the podium.

Another of the pre-season favourites – alongside country-

man Norris and team-mate Günther – Ilott made a promising start to his campaign with Prema, taking two wins from the opening two rounds. A subsequent run of bad form, however, caused him to lose ground that he was never quite able to make up, preventing the championship battle from becoming a four-way fight. Nonetheless, six wins represented a good return and a solid springboard for the future, after troubled 2015 and 2016 campaigns.

Making it three British drivers inside the top five, Hughes led Hitech's cause with a distant, but worthy, fifth. A win at the Nürburgring was bolstered by six trips to the podium.

Such was Carlin's confidence in Norris that it gave its other full-time seats to two more series newcomers: Jehan Daruvala, a product of India's burgeoning junior driver programme; and Ferdinand Habsburg, a descendent of Austria's former royal Habsburg dynasty. Justifying Carlin's faith in their abilities, both claimed impressive wins at the Norisring (Daruvala) and Spa (Habsburg) en route to sixth and seventh overall as the highest placed rookies after their title-winning team-mate.

By contrast, Guanyu Zhou and Ralf Aron struggled to live up to pre-season expectations following their own eye-catching rookie campaigns of 2016. They scored four and two podiums respectively, ending the year down in eighth and ninth.

Force India F1 development driver Nikita Mazepin scored a trio of maiden podiums with his solid run to tenth overall, ahead of another driver who made strides in his sophomore campaign, Harrison Newey. He, in turn, led the way in an otherwise disappointing winless season for the erstwhile successful Van Amersfoot Racing team.

Garnering much pre-season attention by virtue of his world-renowned lineage, Schumacher Junior's progress was keenly observed, and a podium place in round two at Monza certainly did its bit to leave fans and commentators misty-eyed. The 18-year-old's season generated scant headlines thereafter, but a campaign built on the solid foundation of consistency – having reached the chequered flag in 29 of

ternational line-up of drivers from as far afield as the USA, South Africa, Venezuela and Brazil.

Nevertheless, it was local drivers who reigned supreme by the season's end, with Enaam Ahmed cruising to comfortable title glory for Carlin. Four victories straight out of the box allowed the second-year racer to power to a comfortable early lead that he'd retain to the end of the 24-race season, with nine more trips to the top of the podium establishing a winning margin of 164 points over team-mate James Pull.

Fourteen podiums – albeit no wins – allowed Pull to clinch the runner-up spot over fellow Brits Ben Hingeley of Fortec and Toby Sowery of Lanan Racing. American Cameron Das completed the top five.

A three-times race winner in 2016, despite having started only eight races, Mitsunori Takaboshi committed to a full campaign of All-Japan Formula 3 action in 2017 and subsequently powered to championship glory. It was a season of two halves for the B-MAX Racing driver. While he had appeared well on course for a dominant title by the mid-point of the year, after winning six of the opening eight races, a powerful second-half run of nine wins from the concluding 11 races quickly brought Toyota Racing protégé Sho Tsuboi back into contention.

Mercifully for Takaboshi, despite topping the podium only once more during the second half of the year, his results behind TOM's factory racer Tsuboi remained consistent enough to withstand his rival by a mere eight points during a tense final-round showdown in Sugo. Elsewhere, Spanish former GP3 racer Alex Palou usurped the Japanese driver stronghold at the forefront of the field with three wins en route to third overall, ahead of locals Rotomo Miyata and Hiroki Otsu.

The Union Jack reigned supreme over a bevy of young talents in the 2017 Euroformula Open Championship, where Harrison Scott romped to dominant title success. A rival of Norris at Formula Renault Eurocup 2.0 level in 2016, Scott, in the RP Motorsport Dallara, was barely challenged en route to an extraordinary 12 wins from the 14 races he started. The 21-year-old established a huge winning margin of 118 points, despite skipping the final round altogether. Rookie Russian racer Nikita Troitskiy finished a distant runner-up, while Canada's Devlin DeFrancesco was third overall and classified winner of the Spanish F3 sub-category. India's Ameya Vaidyanathan and Jannes Fittje of Germany completed the top five.

Down under, young rookie Calan Williams prevailed to clinch the 2017 Australian Formula 3 Premier Series at the wheel of his Gilmour Racing Dallara. The 17-year-old forged clear in what initially had been a tight title fight, after main rival John Magro – series leader after three rounds – skipped two of the final three events following the birth of his daughter. Nevertheless, Magro would return to retain the runner-up spot from Nathan Kumar, with Roman Krumins succeeding in the National Class.

In South America, with two rounds still remaining as AUTOCOURSE closed for press, Guilherme Samaia was firmly on track to become 2017 Formula 3 Brasil champion. Runner-up behind Matheus Iorio in 2016, Cesario Racing's Samaia needed only a handful of points from the final four races to ensure that he went one better in 2017, ahead of Giuliano Raucci.

Nevertheless, the 2017 F3 season belonged to Lando Norris, and not just in F3 terms. Hamilton may have been crowned world champion once again with Mercedes, but perhaps it was no coincidence that Norris had been courted by McLaren for its junior development programme. The team that ultimately moulded Hamilton into the four-times title-winning legend he is today, McLaren no doubt will draw upon those experiences to ensure that Norris hits the ground running as and when he is given his F1 chance.

Indeed, while Hamilton is far from yesterday's news just yet, few would disagree that Norris seems well on course to follow in his footsteps as Britain's next racing superstar...

Just remember you read it here first!

the 30 races – was likely to set the tone for a bigger push in 2018.

With F3 descending on Asia for the traditional end-of-year showdown at the Macau Grand Prix, the stage appeared set for Norris to conclude his season in fitting style. The finale would stray beyond the anticipated script, however, by producing a wholly unexpected – and little known – winner.

Indeed, Norris may have been the favourite, but it was an F3 debutant who would sweep to a shock victory. Red Bull junior Dan Ticktum confounded expectations and avoided the carnage to become the first British Macau Grand Prix winner since Alex Lynn in 2013.

Capitalising fully on his F3 shot with Motopark, following a successful maiden season in the Formula Renault Eurocup 2.0, Ticktum's success was the headline-grabbing outcome of a thrilling race full of flash points around the gruelling Guia street circuit.

The drama began when initial front-runners Eriksson and Ilott collided and retired while disputing the lead. That promoted Sergio Sette Camara – back from Formula 2 for a one-off outing – and Carlin's Habsburg into an unlikely victory battle, but both crashed sensationally in separate incidents at the final corner, just as the latter had attempted an audacious, but ultimately overambitious, pass around the outside. Their cruel misfortune allowed Ticktum to pick up the pieces over the remaining 100m and take the chequered flag. Norris salvaged second, having started down the order, thanks to qualifying-race issues, while Ralf Aron – driving for Van Amersfoot this time – completed the podium.

The latest iteration of the BRDC British Formula 3 Championship may share little more than a name with the once illustrious series that had propelled the likes of Ayrton Senna, Nelson Piquet and Daniel Ricciardo towards F1, but the remastered series nevertheless benefited from sizeable grids and competitive racing in 2017. Using 2-litre, 230bhp Tatuus-Cosworth single-seaters similar to those raced in the increasingly popular Formula 4 class, it also attracted an in-

FORMULA E REVIEW by SCOTT MITCHELL

MAKING A BREAKTHROUGH

Above: Three wins in a row. Sébastien Buemi continued where he had left off when the series resumed in the 2017 opener in Buenos Aires.

Top right: Jumping for joy. Lucas di Grassi celebrates his unlikely title victory in Montreal after his rival Buemi hit trouble.

Above right: The dominant force. Buemi was a six-times winner (out of the ten races in which he participated), but events conspired against the Swiss driver in his bid to retain the title.

Right: Paris provided the kind of backdrop that Formula E craved. Nick Heidfeld heads towards the third of his five podiums in the Mahindra.

Photos: Formula E

WHETHER Formula E goes on to enjoy a prosperous, long future or not, 2017 should be looked back on as the year it 'made it'. On track, the electric single-seater series crowned its third different champion in three years, while Jaguar completed its first season in major international motor racing for 13 years.

Off-track, the progress was even greater. Audi confirmed that it would take the Abt-run FE team into its works programme from the 2017/18 season. BMW announced that it would enter a fully-fledged factory effort run by Andretti. Mercedes indicated it would be taking up its option to join the series from 2018/19, quitting the DTM (after the 2018 season) to do so. Porsche stated it was axing its LMP1 programme from the end of 2017 and joining FE at the same time as Mercedes. And then Nissan said that it would be taking over the Renault entry from 2018/19, to become the first Japanese manufacturer in FE.

With three final-round title deciders in three seasons and a host of committed major manufacturers, FE has ingredients most championship organisers can only dream of. It is the most sought after motor racing category in the world from a manufacturer's perspective, and it remains an extremely attractive entertainment for fans longing for good old-fashioned engineering, wheel-to-wheel racing and contests decided by people in the pit lane and drivers in the cockpits, not brains at the factories, fancy swoops on bodywork or overly-complicated turbo-hybrids beneath engine covers.

The strength of FE, which had become apparent by the end of 2017, had not looked assured at the start of the year. It was facing the prospect of a pitiful title battle, after reigning champion Sébastien Buemi had cantered to victories in Hong Kong and Marrakech at the end of 2016. Even a three-month wait until the next race wasn't enough for his

and Renault e.dams' rivals to regroup; in Buenos Aires, he was outqualified by Abt Audi's Lucas di Grassi (who scored his first FE pole in the process) and Techeetah's Jean-Eric Vergne, powered by a customer Renault powertrain. No matter for Buemi – he outgunned them in the race and eased to a comfortable win. Three for three, the first such run in FE's short history.

Hope sprang eternal in FE, though, such had been the topsy-turvy nature of the opening two seasons. Buemi was a late arrival at the next race, skipping the drivers' briefing and the shakedown after dashing on an overnight flight from Monza to Mexico City. He had been at the official launch of Toyota's LMP1 programme at the World Endurance Championship's pre-season test in Italy, and the last-minute travel – with Toyota team-mates Stéphane Sarrazin (Venturi) and José Maria López (DS Virgin Racing) – was the compromise. Disruptions from the WEC would impact Buemi in a far bigger way later in the season.

Buemi and di Grassi were both hamstrung in qualifying in Mexico by being drawn in the opening group, for which the Autódromo Hermanos Rodríguez was at its dustiest. Buemi lined up seventh, di Grassi 15th. And then something quite remarkable happened.

A strategy gamble propelled di Grassi from last, after pitting with a broken rear wing on the third lap, to his first win of the season. His first pit stop was rescued by a safety car, while his early move to swap cars under a second caution period – seven laps before anyone else – vaulted him to the front, but would have been more successful had the safety car stayed on track longer than just one more lap. A second safety car, which obliterated the 30-second lead he held over cars that had significantly more energy left, was his most concerning moment.

After swapping cars so much earlier than the rest of the field, di Grassi had around a third less energy than the front-runners when the remainder of the stops had been completed by lap 25 of 45. His saving grace was Jérôme d'Ambrosio, who adopted the same strategy as the Brazilian and was a superb 'rear gunner' as somehow he kept the chasing pack at bay.

Buemi arguably would have cleared d'Ambrosio and been able to hunt down di Grassi had he been leading the pursuit, but he wasn't. In fact, he wasn't even in the points. He was sixth in the first half of the race and in the lead group, but he lost time in the pit stops. Eager to make amends, he attempted to pass Felix Rosenqvist around the outside into Turn One – just as Lôpez spun at the same corner – and ultimately finished 13th. Buemi salvaged a point for fastest lap, but his lead was slashed from 29 points to five.

He retaliated by claiming his first pole position of the season in Monaco, then led from start to finish, fending off a late attack from di Grassi to clinch his fourth win from five races. In Paris a week later, he won from pole again, this time keeping Vergne at bay until the Techeetah driver crumpled his car against a wall after suffering what looked like a suspension breakage. That shunt helped make Buemi's win simpler; another made it far more significant – di Grassi didn't finish.

It was a disaster of a weekend for the Brazilian. First, after qualifying poorly, he collided with António Félix da Costa for 13th position. Di Grassi had passed the Andretti driver on the outside, then squeezed him on the run to the next corner and moved across for the apex in the braking zone, where he was hit by the Portuguese, who had kept his nose just on the inside.

That speared both into the barriers, although di Grassi was able to rejoin and make it back to the pits as a full-course yellow was thrown because of da Costa's immobilised car. He picked up a drive-through penalty for a pit stop that was well under the minimum time, then crashed out two laps from the end while pushing for fastest lap.

Di Grassi said that it was simply an example of how "frus-

Above: Lucas di Grassi sits on pole for the first race in Berlin. Two podiums over the weekend consolidated the Brazilian's championship bid, especially after his rival Buemi was disqualified from Saturday's race.

Top right: Jaguar's season was hugely disappointing, but rookie driver Mitch Evans shone, despite the limitations of the car.

Above centre right: Despite scoring a couple of podiums, José Maria López had a mixed season in the second Virgin car.

Above right: Nick Heidfeld's experience was crucial to the Mahindra team's development.

Above far right: Daniel Abt was a consistent points scorer, but the German struggled to make the podium.

Right: Felix Rosenqvist emerged as the new star of the series with a victory in Berlin and three second places, ensuring the Swede finished third overall, behind di Grassi and Buemi.

Photos: Formula E

trating" FE can be, after topping practice, and it left him 43 points behind Buemi. He explained that he and the team needed to "reset" for the double-header in Berlin – and indeed, there the championship would edge back in his favour.

By the end of the weekend at the former Tempelhof Airport, Buemi had another win in his pocket, but he also had picked up an exclusion from the opening race. He had qualified poorly, but charged from 14th to fifth. However, post-race checks revealed that all four tyres on both of his cars had been below the minimum pressure stipulated by Michelin. Di Grassi inherited second place – now it was Buemi who had to regroup.

He did so with an inherited victory on the Sunday, after Mahindra's rookie sensation, Felix Rosenqvist, had picked up a penalty. Rosenqvist had claimed Mahindra's maiden victory, and his own first win in FE, at only the seventh attempt on the Saturday. Then he qualified on pole on Sunday as the Indian team starred. He finished first on the road, 2.9s clear of Buemi, but was slapped with a ten-second time penalty for an unsafe release during the car swaps. He had pulled away in his second car as his team-mate, Nick Heidfeld, had entered the garage.

Although briefly delayed, Rosenqvist's strong in-lap had boosted his buffer to Buemi by just enough to retain the lead, then the penalty for unsafe release was confirmed with 13 laps remaining. Buemi, who was within a second of the leader, was happy not to attack so that Rosenqvist could maintain a big enough gap to keep second ahead of di Grassi.

The fortunate win undid some of the damage of Saturday's exclusion, but the net result of the weekend was a small gain for di Grassi, for whom a pole, a second and a third helped nibble 11 points out of Buemi's lead. A 32-point advantage with four races to go would have looked very healthy in any other season, but the ties to the WEC – which had been loosely draped around Buemi and Renault e.dams all season – were about to tighten.

The WEC had caused surprise by scheduling its 2017 Nürburgring round against an FE double-header in New York, despite a pre-existing gentlemen's agreement between them to avoid that very situation. Despite extensive negotiations between Renault and Toyota, Buemi (and DS Virgin Racing driver Lôpez) had to miss FE's first visit to New York. Thus he was a sitting duck – di Grassi had two races in which to bag as many points as possible in his absence.

As it transpired, the damage could have been far greater. Di Grassi was never close to contention for either win, as Sam Bird snapped up a superb double for DS Virgin.

It was Bird's team-mate for the weekend, debutant Alex Lynn, who initially stole the headlines by claiming a stunning pole position. But Bird got the jump on Vergne into Turn One to run behind Lynn, and eventually he was allowed past on lap nine of 43. Then he swiftly started to attack Daniel Abt – who had beaten Lynn into Turn One at the start – and took the lead from the Abt Audi driver with an aggressive dive down the inside at Turn One. Bird survived a two-lap shoot-out, caused by a late safety car, to beat Vergne to the win by 1.3 seconds, while di Grassi rose to fourth to cut the absent Buemi's points lead to 20.

The going was similarly hard for di Grassi in the second leg. The Brazilian started ninth and worked his way up to fifth, but he had no answer to the pace of the race's leading quartet. He finished off the podium again, but another top-five finish meant that he would travel to the final two races in Montreal just ten points adrift.

With di Grassi neutered, Bird, the Mahindra team and Buemi's rookie stand-in, Pierre Gasly, were free to play out the race as the star performers. Bird started from pole, but lost the lead to Rosenqvist on the run to Turn One. He stayed glued to the Swede's rear bumper and made a lunge at the tight Turn Six hairpin on lap ten, wresting back the lead with a superb and aggressive pass.

Bird eventually won by a commanding 11.3s to vault to fourth in the drivers' championship, having started the week-

end eighth in the points. Heidfeld tried to follow Bird past Rosenqvist when the Briton nicked the lead, and although he failed, he shadowed his team-mate throughout. Red Bull Formula 1 protégé Gasly caught the pair at the end, and the three closed right up through the final corner, with Gasly throwing his Renault e.dams around the outside of Heidfeld.

Rosenqvist retained second, and Heidfeld third. Gasly ran wide, though, hitting the wall on the exit and then on the other side of the track as well as he crossed the line with a crumpled front end. Fourth was still a superb result for the 2016 GP2 champion, who beat his much more experienced team-mate, Nico Prost, in both races on his debut – and, of course, took points off di Grassi.

It wasn't talked about at the time, but Gasly's crash could have been costly for Buemi. Had he damaged the gearbox in that unnecessary final-corner shunt, he would have forced Buemi to take a grid penalty – Renault had already used up its one free change earlier in the season, and the motor/gearbox/inverter allowances are assigned to the cars, not the drivers. It would have been very unfortunate if Buemi had started the Montreal weekend knowing he had a grid penalty.

Once in Canada, however, Buemi wrecked more than just the gearbox with a huge FP2 shunt. He clipped the wall on the entry to one of the chicanes, which sent him almost head-on into the barrier that marked the inside of the next part of the corner. The impact was so violent that the car rebounded to the outside of the track, where it came to rest against the wall. It was a massive accident that had severe consequences and set the tone for a hectic few hours.

Despite having started 12th, thanks to the ten-place penalty, Buemi ended up being denied a shock podium on the final lap. He had always been at risk of midfield aggravation at the start, and he fell to 17th on an awful opening lap, picking up mild steering damage in the process.

He regrouped and was into a points-paying tenth place by the end of the opening stint, then had a bizarre altercation with di Grassi's team-mate, Daniel Abt, entering the pits, nudging the German's rear end and gesticulating because he felt that Abt was deliberately holding him up.

Buemi was released side by side with Abt after swapping cars, but got ahead of the German before receiving a punt in the rear after appearing to slow suddenly at the pit-lane exit. Later it emerged that Abt had switched off his pit-lane speed limiter, while Buemi's had remained active because they were rejoining the track under a virtual safety car.

Buemi complained furiously over the radio, then set about recovering further ground (in a partially-liveried second car, because his practice crash had forced Renault e.dams into a barely-completed rebuild around a new tub).

He made steady progress to sixth, which became fourth after an actual safety car period, when team-mate Prost had moved aside without fuss and Rosenqvist had hit the wall exiting the final corner, damaging his left rear.

Despite catching Stéphane Sarrazin and launching a final-lap assault, which included wheel banging and side-by-side squabbling through three corners, Buemi was forced to settle for fourth. Afterwards, he lost his cool. He was filmed in the post-race coverage seeking out Robin Frijns and then addressing Abt in the pit lane, having been hit by both drivers. The former had damaged his steering into Turn One on the opening lap, while the latter had collided with him at the end of the pit lane.

Though furious, Buemi had at least minimised the damage to his title bid after starting 12th – the problem was that di Grassi had won from pole with his most emphatic drive of the season.

Then the situation became even worse for Buemi. In a terrible case of *déjà vu*, he was thrown out – this time because his car was underweight. During the hasty rebuild, there had not been enough time to weigh the car, and despite the team reportedly having added 4kg of additional ballast as an insurance policy, the car was still below the 880kg limit. The penalty was immediate disqualification from the race, meaning

Above: In July, New York joined the roster of major cities to host a Formula E race. DS Virgin Racing's Sam Bird triumphed in both races.

Top right: António Félix da Costa locks a wheel on his Amlin Andretti. The Portuguese driver endured a tough season and will be hoping for better results with BMW support in 2018.

Above right: It all came right for Jean-Eric Vergne in the season finale weekend in Montreal, where he finally broke his long winless streak to take victory in race two.

Right: The Montreal track drew praise from the competitors. Stéphane Sarrazin heads towards third place in race one.

Photos: Formula E

that Buemi was 18 points behind di Grassi heading into the season finale. Disaster.

It didn't get much better on Sunday morning. Buemi was drawn in the first qualifying group and paid the price of driving in worse conditions, after starting from 13th on the grid.

As on Saturday, that put him in the firing line at the start, and he picked up mild bodywork damage when the pack closed up at Turn One, after Sarrazin had spun following contact from Abt.

Buemi was flagged into the pits for repairs, and although the offending part fell off, his Renault e.dams team still forced him to stop. The impromptu trip to the pit lane ruined his race and made a difficult task almost impossible.

Though he charged back up the order, Buemi finished out of the points in 11th, his misfortune allowing di Grassi to coast to the end of the race and seal the title with seventh place. The Brazilian – who had finished third in the first season and second, behind Buemi, in 2015/16 – was in tears on his in-lap, after snatching a title that had looked unlikely for a long time.

The waxing and waning of title fortunes distracted attention from Vergne's first win in FE, a feat he had been waiting to achieve since claiming pole on his debut in round three of the inaugural campaign. He had to catch and pass pole man and star rookie Rosenqvist in the second half of the race, after the Mahindra driver had stopped a lap earlier than his pursuer to swap cars. That gave the Swede a five-second lead once the Frenchman had stopped, but it also meant he had to go a lap longer in his second car, while Vergne gradually ate into the advantage before executing a relatively simple move and easing clear to score his and Techeetah's first victory in FE.

Vergne's win, made by possible by Techeetah's gradual improvement over its first season, was a quietly encouraging way for FE's track action to end. Buemi and di Grassi had monopolised the title battle again, but faced more competition on individual race weekends than they had done during the previous campaign. And by the time pre-season testing rolled around in October, at Valencia in Spain, the incredibly close one-lap pace between Renault, Audi, Mahindra, Techeetah, DS Virgin and NIO (formerly NextEV) suggested that the race-by-race contest was going to be more intense than ever. Audi's long-run pace looked immense, but testing is one thing and racing quite another...

With the 2017/18 season due to kick off in Hong Kong as the calendar year drew to a close, the narrow margins between teams in testing would have been extremely heartening for the series. Testing of the new 2018/19 car – the first FE machine that will complete an entire race distance, with mid-race car swaps becoming a thing of the past after the coming season – had started; Nissan's announcement was made before the opening round, and rumours circulated about Mercedes and Porsche already examining proxy entries in 2018.

FE enjoyed plenty of positive rhetoric in the off-season, but it needed something that would maintain the momentum when the racing started again. The indications are that the series will enjoy a more compressed grid than ever, and double the money has been pumped into the TV budget. They could be crucial developments – better, closer racing than ever, and a better TV product to put in front of new and existing supporters. Growing its fan base during a supposed 'holding season' – before the manufacturers join in swathes and the new car makes its debut – would be the best possible way for FE to build on the momentum it had developed over the course of a breakthrough 2017.

STRIKE THREE AND OUT!

Inset, above: The Jackie Chan DC Racing ORECA 07 came close to pulling off a shock win for an LMP2 car at Le Mans, but eventually finished second overall.

Inset, left: Aston Martin took LM GTE Pro honours at the Sarthe circuit. The Vantage was handled by Darren Turner, Jonny Adam and Daniel Serra.

Main photo: Despite losing an hour with axle trouble, Porsche was able to get its No. 2 car back on track and complete a hat trick of Le Mans victories.

Photos: WEC

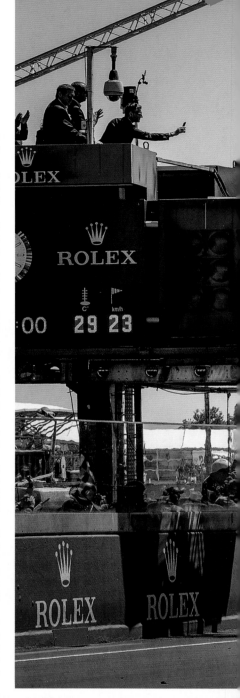

IN years to come, a brief glance at the history books no doubt will give the impression that Porsche dominated what turned out to be its final campaign in the FIA World Endurance Championship with the 919 Hybrid. The German manufacturer completed a hat trick of hat tricks with a third clean sweep in three years of all the big prizes on offer – victory in the Le Mans 24 Hours, and the drivers' and manufacturers' championships. Yet it was Toyota, its only rival in the LMP1 division after Audi's withdrawal at the end of 2016, that had the faster car for much of the season.

The latest version of the Toyota TS050 Hybrid was on top at the beginning and end of the season, each time pushing home its advantage to notch up a string of race victories, but at Le Mans, it dramatically failed to do so. A win for the Porsche of Brendon Hartley, Timo Bernhard and Earl Bamber in the double-points round of the WEC in June proved to be the foundation stone for the trio's championship success.

It wasn't just that they collected 50 points for their victory in the French enduro to take a handy lead in the championship, but that, as significantly, they left Le Mans with a 55-point advantage over team-mates André Lotterer, Nick Tandy and Neel Jani, which shifted the focus of Porsche's campaign in their favour. Twice in the following three races, the Lotterer/Tandy/Jani Porsche had to yield position to give the victory to the eventual champions at a time when the 919 was in the ascendant.

A run of victories for Hartley, Bernhard and Bamber at the Nürburgring, Mexico City and then the Circuit of the Americas all but assured them of the title. It didn't matter that the Toyota trio of Sébastien Buemi, Anthony Davidson and Kazuki Nakajima added another three victories to the two they'd won at the start of the year. Both drivers' and manufacturers' championships were all but out of reach by the time the TS050 started winning again.

New aerodynamic regulations were devised to reduce the downforce of the factory hybrid P1s – or at least keep the rate of development under control – at the same time as the limit on the number of bodywork configurations was reduced from three to two. That essentially allowed Porsche and Toyota a high-downforce package for the regular six-hour races, held exclusively on Formula 1 tracks, and a low-downforce version for the unique demands of the Circuit de la Sarthe at Le Mans.

Porsche opted to leave its high-downforce design in the wind tunnel and take its Le Mans car to the opening two rounds of the series at Silverstone and Spa. This was a variation of a strategy that had worked in the past: in each of the three seasons since its P1 debut, Porsche had waited until the first post-Le Mans round before debuting its full-house sprint car.

However, the decision meant that the factory team went to the opening two WEC rounds before Le Mans effectively with one hand tied behind its back. Damage limitation was the name of the game, but in a year when only two manufacturers were battling out at the front, it was a risk Porsche felt it could take. The worst its cars would do, given a reliable run, would be to finish third and fourth.

Porsche almost pulled off an upset at Silverstone, in a race interrupted by rain and safety cars of the real and virtual variety. It wasn't so close to victory three weeks later, however, in round two at Spa, on a track where a low-downforce-configuration car should have been more competitive.

Toyota retained its advantage at Le Mans, where it gave a race debut to the low-downforce version of the TS050. Just as in 2016, it had the fastest car on the 8.47-mile circuit; witness Kamui Kobayashi's record-breaking lap in qualifying. What it didn't have, as in previous years, was the luck to notch up a first victory in the 24 Hours 30 years on from its first full factory assault on the big race.

The Japanese manufacturer contrived to find new ways to lose that coveted victory in endurance racing's 'big one'. After the last-gasp heartbreak of 12 months before, it lost out in 2017 through a bizarre sequence of events that couldn't have been dreamt up by even the wildest of imaginations.

Kobayashi and team-mates Mike Conway and Stéphane Sarrazin, who had stepped into the No. 7 car after a late reshuffle of the Toyota driver line-up, were looking good for victory in the tenth hour. They had a clear lead of around a minute – and crucially the pace to maintain it – when Kobayashi encountered a red light at the end of the pit lane during a safety car period.

An orange-clad figure, whom the Japanese driver presumed to be a marshal, appeared to wave him through the signal. The team told him to stop immediately, and when he did try to get going, he did so using the conventional internal-combustion engine rather than its twin electric motors, the normal procedure by which the TS050 would leave the pits.

Above: Last man standing. The No. 2 Porsche takes the chequered flag to win the Le Mans 24 Hours. It was the only LMP1 hybrid ahead of the LMP2 challengers at the finish.

Photo: WEC

Left: The Priaulx/Tinknell/Derani Ford GT won the LM GTE Pro class in the season-opener at Silverstone.

Centre left: Clearwater Racing's Ferrari 488 GTE took the LM GTE Am honours at the season-opener.

Photos: Bryn Williams

Left: Rusinov, Thiriet and Lynn handled the LMP2 G-Drive Racing ORECA-Gibson.

Photo: WEC

Far left: Toyotas take charge at the start of the 6 Hours of Silverstone. The No. 8 car of Buemi/Davidson/Nakajima would triumph, after the sister car suffered accident damage.

Photo: Bryn Williams

Above: Big beasts running three abreast at the start of the 6 Hours of Spa-Francorchamps.

Top right: Three Toyota TS050 Hybrids and their drivers are presented to the press and public in the streets of Le Mans during the big race build-up.

Above right: All lit up. The Vaillante Rebellion ORECA of Bruno Senna, Nicolas Prost and Julien Canal flashes past the pits.
Photos: WEC

Right: Joy for the winning Porsche trio of Earl Bamber, Brendon Hartley and Timo Bernhard.
Photo: LAT Images

The problem was that the car's transmission was not designed to support such a getaway. In his attempt to get moving, he irrevocably damaged the clutch. After one lap behind the safety car, the clutch gave up the ghost, and after a valiant attempt to get the car around the long Le Mans lap on hybrid power, Kobayashi was forced to park up within sight of the pit lane, its battery completely flat.

Toyota laid no blame at Kobayashi's door for trying to restart on petrol power in what had been a confusing moment for the driver. It turned out that the man in orange who'd waved him through was not a marshal, but a driver. Frenchman Vincent Capillaire, who was driving for the Algarve Pro LMP2 team housed in the final garage before pit-out, subsequently admitted that he'd waved to Kobayashi in encouragement to the race leader.

Toyota's hopes of victory had not entirely disappeared, despite the Buemi/Davidson/Nakajima car losing a couple of minutes short of two hours in the pits for repairs. The Japanese manufacturer had entered three cars at Le Mans for the first time since its return to top-flight sports car racing on the rebirth of the WEC in 2012, and it was the third that now carried its hopes.

The extra TS050 was driven by Toyota returnee Nicolas Lapierre and Le Mans debutants Yuji Kunimoto and José Maria Lôpez, who had lost his place alongside Kobayashi and Conway after shunting at Silverstone and missing Spa as a result of the concussion he had sustained. They had fallen off the lead lap early in the race when a malfunctioning illuminated panel had required attention. But they were still very much in the hunt and, as events turned out, were well placed to take Toyota's first Le Mans victory.

But it wasn't to be. Less than half an hour after the No. 7 car had ground to a halt, Lapierre had the misfortune to be hit in the rear by an LMP2 car when he suffered an unexpected fuel cut at the end of the start/finish straight. The Frenchman was tapped into a spin through the gravel, but more significantly, the initial impact damaged a rear wheel.

As he drove back to the pits, rubber flailing from the disintegrating tyre took out the gearbox hydraulics, forcing Lapierre into all-electric mode just like Kobayashi. He, too, failed to make it around the long lap.

The Porsche that went on to win had hit similar problems to the No. 8 Toyota early in the race. The Bernhard/Hartley/Bamber 919 needed a change of its energy-retrieval motor generator unit. Unlike the Toyota, it didn't also need its battery replacing. That meant its stay in the pits was just over an hour, compared with the Toyota's two hours – time that would turn out to be crucial in the championship fight.

Bernhard and his team-mates looked out of contention, but as the other LMP1s slowly dropped by the wayside, suddenly it was in with a chance of making it to the podium. When the sister Porsche retired from a big lead with engine failure shortly after the 20-hour mark on Sunday morning, it wasn't just Porsche's chances that rested on the No. 2 919 Hybrid. If it didn't win the race, a car from the secondary LMP2 prototype division would do so.

The delays for all the remaining factory LMP1 cars – not to mention the early retirement of the only P1 privateer car in the field, the ByKolles ENSO CLM-AER P1/01 – meant that the P2 class Jackie Chan DC Racing ORECA-Gibson 07, shared by Oliver Jarvis, Ho-Pin Tung and Thomas Laurent, took over the lead on the No. 1 Porsche's retirement.

Above: The Jani/Lotterer/Tandy Porsche 919 leads the field into Turn One at the Circuit of the Americas. The No. 1 car trio would obey team orders and give way to the better placed Porsche to strengthen the team's championship points tally.

Top right: André Lotterer, Nick Tandy and Neel Jani were destined to play a support role in Porsche's successful championship challenge.
Photos: WEC

Above centre right: The No. 63 Corvette C7.R, in the hands of Jordan Taylor, put up a strong challenge to Aston Martin at Le Mans.
Photo: Bryn Williams

Above right: Delight for the Jackie Chan DC Racing squad, who took a sensational second place at Le Mans.

Right: Toyota's winning trio of Naka-jima, Davidson and Buemi celebrate their victory at Fuji.
Photos: WEC

Catching the best of the LMP2s wasn't as straightforward as it might have been in previous years. A new breed of P2 machinery had been introduced for 2017. More powerful to the tune of 100bhp, and with more downforce, the cars were up to eight seconds faster around the Le Mans lap than their predecessors. The Porsche only caught the leader with little more than 60 minutes to go – nearly eighteen-and-a-half hours after getting going again following its hybrid problems.

Buemi and Co could only recover to eighth place at the fin-ish, as the sixth WEC-registered finisher home. That meant they collected just 16 points compared to the 50 of their ri-vals. The balance in the championship had swung and would swing again – and in the same direction – when the WEC resumed at the Nürburgring in mid-July.

The belated, but very much planned, arrival of the 919 Hybrid's high-downforce aero kit gave the Porsche driv-ers an advantage. Toyota, which had always claimed it was "resource-limited" in comparison to its rivals, once again de-veloped its sprint package out of its Le Mans car and found itself on the back foot for the six-hour races.

Porsche was on top on home ground in Germany in July, and it maintained that advantage through the Mexico City and Austin races. The fact that the 919s had a margin on the TS050s allowed the German manufacturer to maximise its chances in the championship through blatant team orders, for which it made no apologies.

Lotterer was given an extra dump of fuel when the cars came in for their final splash-and-dash stops at the 'Ring, which reversed the positions of the two Porsches at the front of the field. Hartley, Bernhard and Bamber made it two vic-tories in two starts.

They won again in the high altitude of Mexico City, though there was no need for any late-race reshuffling of the order, after the Lotterer/Tandy/Jani car was delayed by a stop/go penalty for speeding in the pit lane.

Come Austin later in September, Tandy had to move over for Bamber again – and actually did so twice – to make sure that Porsche's best-placed car in the championship took maximum points.

The WEC headed for the three-race Asian leg of the cham-pionship with Bernhard and Co in what appeared to be an unassailable 51-point lead over Buemi, Davidson and Na-kajima in the standings. Toyota admitted that the end-of-season silverware, particularly the drivers' crown, was out of reach, but it didn't give up the fight. Or rather it set itself a new target.

At this point in the season, Toyota would normally have been developing its car for the following year, but with the need to do that having been removed, in the wake of Por-sche's mid-season announcement that it would not be re-turning in 2018, resources were diverted into development of the existing car. The aerodynamic rules, which limited the manufacturers to a set number of bodywork configurations, didn't allow Toyota massive scope, but it was able to improve the aero efficiency of the car at the same time as removing a bit of weight from the design.

The renewed push wasn't so much aimed at an attempt to win either of the championships, as to win races. The consolation prize on offer was ending the season with more race victories from the nine WEC rounds, and Toyota wanted that badly.

Toyota triumphed in a shortened race on home ground

at Fuji, the track on the second half of the schedule requiring the least amount of downforce. However, the rain that caused two red-flag stoppages, and eventually resulted in the clock stopping with only a handful of minutes left, masked any advantage that Toyota might have gained.

When the WEC arrived in Shanghai, there were more new parts on the Toyota, and it was immediately apparent that the TS050 now had an advantage over the 919. Buemi, Davidson and Nakajima won again, although victory might have gone to the sister car of Kobayashi, Conway and Lôpez but for two incidents involving the last-named driver.

Second place was more than enough to give Hartley, Bernhard and Bamber the title. The issues for the No. 7 TS050 also handed Porsche the manufacturers' crown: Toyota had needed to finish 1-2 to keep the championship mathematically open going to the Bahrain finale.

Buemi, Davidson and Nakajima would win again in Bahrain to give Toyota a fifth victory, in a season in which Porsche only won four times. After that, it was difficult to argue against Toyota Motorsport technical director Pascal Vasselon's verdict that "Porsche didn't win the championships, we lost them."

The Jackie Chan DC Racing squad could have made the same case for the loss of the LMP2 titles. Jarvis, Tung and Laurent led the LMP2 rankings through the season, only to fall behind Bruno Senna and Julien Canal, who shared their Rebellion ORECA-Gibson with Nicolas Prost in eight of the nine races, after the penultimate round in Shanghai. Then they were back on course for the title until midway through the Bahrain finale when a fuel problem struck.

An inability to pick up the last 15 litres of fuel in the tank forced the lead Chan/DC car to make an extra pit stop during the closing stages, which handed a narrow victory to their championship rivals from Rebellion. And with that, Senna and Canal took a title that Prost couldn't share, because he was away on Formula E duty with the e.dams team on the weekend of the Nürburgring event.

It was a galling way for Chan/DC to lose the title, although arguably more significant in the championship battle was the problem that left it last in class in Mexico. That was

Lights out and lights on. The No. 1
Porsche 919 Hybrid of Neel Jani,
Nick Tandy and André Lotterer grabs
the lead at the start of the 6 Hours
of Bahrain, the season's finale, but
Toyota would take the victory.
Photo: WEC

Above: Bruno Senna and Julien Canal led the Anglo-Swiss Rebellion team to the LMP2 title in a gripping final race in Bahrain.
Photo: WEC

Top right: Memo Rojas, Ryo Hirakawa and Léo Roussel took their G-Drive Racing ORECA 07-Gibson to the European Le Mans series title.

Above right: The Lamborghini Huracan GT3 driven by Christian Engelhart and Mirko Bortolotti was a consistent front-runner in GT classes around the globe.
Photos: LAT Images

Centre right: Ferrari 488 GTE drivers Colado and Guidi emerged as GT champions ahead of AF Corse team-mates Bird and Rigon.
Photo: Scuderia Ferrari

Centre far right: A title at last for GTE Am winners Mathias Lauda, Paul Dalla Lana and Pedro Lamy.
Photo: WEC

Right: In a chaotic accident-strewn event, Edoardo Mortara took his Mercedes-AMG GT3 to victory in the FIA GT World Cup races in Macau.
Photo: Daimler AG

Far right: Jules Gounon, Christopher Haase and Markus Winkelhock, in the works-backed Team Sainteloc Audi R8 LMS, scored a prestigious victory for the marque in the Spa 24-hour race.
Photo: Audi Communications Motorsport

even more exasperating for the team – an errant washer had jammed the clutch pedal.

Jarvis, Tung and Laurent had hit the ground running, scoring a victory at Silverstone. After the high of their overall podium at Le Mans, they took another class win at the Nürburgring. Rebellion, previously the dominant team in the privateer P1 ranks, grew stronger over the season as it got to grips with LMP2 and the ORECA-Gibson. Undoubtedly it had the edge over the final races, though not in Bahrain, and a run of three victories in four races allowed Senna and Canal to overhaul the long-time leaders with one round remaining.

Ferrari claimed both GT drivers' and manufacturers' titles – now full FIA world championships, rather than the previous cups – after winning the GTE Pro class in five of the six races. James Calado and Alessandro Pier Guidi took the title with three wins in their factory AF Corse Ferrari 488 GTE, while team-mates Sam Bird and Davide Rigon won twice.

The Ferrari was the most consistent of the GTE Pro cars over the course of a closely fought season. A new automated system used to calculate the Balance of Performance – the means by which the performance of a disparate range of cars is equated – appeared to work. The UK-based Ganassi team won twice, Andy Priaulx and Harry Tincknell triumphing in their Ford GT at Silverstone, with Luis Felipe 'Pipo' Derani, and then as a duo in Shanghai. Aston Martin also claimed two victories, while Porsche remained in contention for the drivers' title with Richard Lietz and Frédéric Makowiecki, despite failing to win a race with its new rear-engined 911 RSR.

Aston Martin Racing never really looked like retaining the drivers' title it had won in 2016, but it did take the most important victory of the season at Le Mans with the Vantage GTE shared by Darren Turner, Jonny Adam and Daniel Serra. Adam came out on top in a thrilling battle with Jordan Taylor in the best of the factory Chevrolet Corvette C7.Rs over the final couple of hours.

Aston Martin drivers Pedro Lamy and Paul Dalla Lana finally took the GTE Am title in their fourth season of trying, and their third together with Mathias Lauda. They won four of the races, not to mention taking seven pole positions, to put the heartbreak of previous seasons behind them.

The European Le Mans Series was won by the G-Drive Racing ORECA-Gibson run by the US DragonSpeed squad.

It claimed the drivers' title with Memo Rojas and Léo Roussel, despite winning only once to the two victories apiece for each of its nearest rivals. Rojas and Roussel, who were joined by Toyota protégé Ryo Hirakawa in four of the six races, enjoyed a consistent season, however. They were second no fewer than four times.

The Anglo-American United Autosports squad won twice with a Ligier-Gibson JSP217 shared by Filipe Albuquerque, Will Owen and Hugo de Sadeleer, but only made it on to the podium on one other occasion. The third-placed Graff Racing crew of Richard Bradley, Gustavo Yacaman and James Allen had a slow start to the season, before coming on strong to win the final two races.

GTE honours in the ELMS went to the British JMW Motorsport Ferrari squad after a strong season that yielded a series victory to go with its class crown at Le Mans. Jody Fannin and Robert Smith won the title driving two different cars – a 458 and then a 488 – and with three different team-mates over the course of the season. United Autosports retained its LMP3 title, this time with Americans Sean Rayhall and John Falb driving the championship car.

The Blancpain GT Series continued to flourish, as did the GT3 category in general. The Endurance Cup segment of the BGTS attracted more than 30 pro-class cars among its full-season entry, which turned out to be too many for series boss and GT3 founder Stéphane Ratel. Before the season was out, he had announced a 26-car cap on the number of pro entries allowed for 2018.

Lamborghini was the big winner across the Endurance and Sprint Cups. The trio of factory drivers in the lead car run by the Austrian Grasser squad, Mirko Bortolotti, Christian Engelhart and Andrea Caldarelli, came from behind in the season finale at Barcelona to win the Endurance Cup title, while Bortolotti and Engelhart also claimed the overall BGTS title.

Lamborghini's title success in the five-race Endurance Cup was founded on back-to-back victories in the opening two races at Monza and Silverstone, as well as a big scoring weekend at the double-points Spa 24 Hours. Bortolotti and his team-mates were second and first at the six- and 12-hour marks, when the first tranches of points were awarded, but they missed out on a shot at victory after a braking problem put the Huracan GT3 into the barriers in the 17th hour.

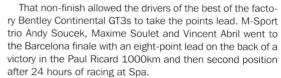

That non-finish allowed the drivers of the best of the factory Bentley Continental GT3s to take the points lead. M-Sport trio Andy Soucek, Maxime Soulet and Vincent Abril went to the Barcelona finale with an eight-point lead on the back of a victory in the Paul Ricard 1000km and then second position after 24 hours of racing at Spa.

The Lambo trio had been heading for the title even before the Bentley retired from the Spanish event shortly after half-distance. Victory in the teams' championship appeared to be of little consolation to either Bentley or M-Sport.

The big one at Spa was won by the full-factory Audi R8 LMS entered by the French Sainteloc team for Markus Winkelhock, Christopher Haase and Jules Gounon. They ended up just 11 seconds ahead of the Bentley, while the French Auto Sport Promotion team took third with the Mercedes-AMG GT3 driven by Raffaele Marciello, Edoardo Mortara and Michael Meadows.

The pairing of Bortolotti and Engelhart took both of the one-hour Sprint Cup races at Brands Hatch and notched up further podiums at the Hungaroring to end up fourth in the championship. Their points total was enough, however, to give them the overall BGTS crown.

The Belgian WRT Audi squad retained its Sprint Cup title. Factory driver Robin Frijns and Stuart Leonard overhauled team-mates Markus Winkelhock and Dries Vanthoor in a thrilling finale at the Nürburgring, into which no fewer than 13 drivers had gone with a mathematical chance of the title. Franck Perera and Maximilian Buhk had appeared on course for the crown until a puncture put the latter out of the lead late in the race.

CLOSE-QUARTER COMBAT

Above: Ready, steady, go! Nestor Girolami (Volvo S60 – 61), Esteban Guerrieri (Chevrolet RML Cruze – 86) and Mehdi Bennani (Citroën C-Elysee – 25) fight for the lead at Vila Real.

Top right: Bennani in the Sébastien Loeb Racing Citroën C-Elysee. The Moroccan driver was locked in a tight battle for third place in the series with Nicky Catsburg and Tom Chilton.

Above right: Volvo S60 driver Thed Björk was a serious contender all year and clinched the title at the season's finale in Qatar.

Centre right: Tiago Monteiro was a favourite for the title, until a massive testing accident during the mid-season break sidelined the Portuguese for the remainder of the season.

Centre far right: Tom Chilton crashes the curves in his Citroën C-Elysee.

Right: Veteran Tom Coronel was as competitive as ever in his Chevrolet RML Cruze TC1.

Far right: Championship winner: Polestar Cyan Racing's Thed Björk.

Photos: Courtesy WTCC

AS usual, there was action aplenty in the touring car world during 2017, and while familiar faces had been on top in 2016, there were new ones firmly in the mix for top honours.

As AUTOCOURSE closed for press, the battle for the World Touring Car Championship was finally settled, with Volvo's Polestar Cyan Racing's Thed Björk ultimately beating Norbert Michelisz to the title, while in the British Touring Car Championship, the German DTM series and the TCR International Series, new drivers secured the titles for the first time.

In the Supercars Championship in Australia, however, a familiar face saw off huge pressure to secure a record-breaking seventh championship title.

WORLD TOURING CAR CHAMPIONSHIP

Having been the dominant force for three seasons, Citroën's decision to leave the World Touring Car Championship to focus on the WRC posed many questions about who would emerge as the team to beat.

While championship winners José María López, Yvan Muller and Gabriele Tarquini all departed – the last-named after LADA joined Citroën in pulling the plug on its works programme – a field high in talent, if low in numbers, was assembled for 2017, with 16 full-season entries being announced ahead of the opening meeting.

Among them was an expanded three-car team from Volvo, alongside three cars from Honda, with privateer entries keeping the likes of Citroën, LADA and Chevrolet present on the grid.

One of those privateers would take opening honours when the season kicked off in Morocco, as the Campos Racing Chevrolet of Esteban Guerrieri emerged on top in a dramatic first race in which only ten cars made it to the finish. Race two would go the way of pole-man Tiago Monteiro, who took an early lead in the championship standings for Honda as a result.

The wide-open nature of the title battle was reflected by the fact that in the second round, at Monza, two more drivers

tasted victory – marking the first time since 2008 that there were four different winners from the opening four races.

After Thed Björk gave Volvo a first pole position in qualifying, the reverse-grid opening race went the way of Tom Chilton's Citroën, the Briton having made the most of contact between Mehdi Bennani and Norbert Michelisz early on to take victory. Then Björk converted his pole into a win in race two, with Monteiro managing to maintain his advantage in the points with two podiums, at a circuit that hadn't been expected to favour his Honda Civic.

Monteiro became the first double winner of the year in the opening race in Hungary, extending his lead in the standings in the process as rivals Björk and Michelisz ran into problems after a collision on the opening lap.

Bennani secured his first victory of the year in the main race, with Monteiro leaving Hungary with a lead of 38 points in the standings over Volvo's Nicky Catsburg, who had maintained a solid run of early-season points to emerge as the Portuguese driver's closest rival.

The field headed for the fearsome Nürburgring Nordschleife for round four, but trouble was brewing ahead of qualifying, as a number of drivers struggled with tyre failures through testing and practice; an issue that had also been problematic 12 months earlier.

A potential tyre issue caused Catsburg to miss out on pole to Michelisz, who sprung a surprise to put Honda on the front of the grid. In the opening race of the weekend, both Monteiro and Nestor Girolami ran into problems with tyres, while Björk took victory for Volvo.

The Swedish manufacturer doubled up in race two as Catsburg stormed to victory. That moved him into the championship lead after Monteiro failed to score, having been forced to start from the pits when the team was unable to repair race-one damage during the tight 15-minute gap between races.

With just eight points covering the top three drivers, the series headed for Portugal for the fifth meeting of the campaign. There, a new 'joker lap', similar to that used regularly in rallycross competition, was introduced, with each driver

required to take the joker lap once in each race. Approximately two seconds slower than a regular lap of the Villa Real street circuit, it would add an extra layer of intrigue to proceedings.

Slight changes were made to the layout of the joker lap over the weekend, but it proved a success come race day, when Bennani and Michelisz shared the victories, and Monteiro jumped back into the points lead on the back of two podium finishes.

Not everything went to plan, however, the FIA being forced to open an investigation into how Tom Coronel had been able to collide with a support vehicle during practice, after a crash barrier hadn't been put in the correct position.

Portugal marked the end of the European season, with the field then heading for Argentina to kick-start the second half of the campaign. Monteiro, Björk and Catsburg were split by just ten points.

Catsburg would pick up the bonus points for pole in controversial fashion at the Termas de Rio Hondo circuit, after running off track on his quickest lap. Race day was disastrous for the Dutchman, however, as he failed to score after suffering punctures in both races.

In the opening race, Chilton had crossed the line first, only for victory to be handed to the privateer LADA of Yann Ehrlacher after the Citroën driver was hit with a time penalty for a move on the Frenchman on the opening lap. Then Michelisz headed Monteiro for a Honda 1-2 in race two, having taken full advantage of Catsburg's puncture while leading. Monteiro retained his points lead over Björk in the standings, while Michelisz jumped up to third going into a three-month midseason break.

Before the season could resume in China, however, the battle for the title would take an unexpected twist after

Above: After team-mate Monteiro's testing mishap, Norbert Michelisz took the title challenge to Björk in the Team Castrol Honda Civic.

Top right: Jean-Karl Vernay holds aloft his third-place trophy at Oschersleben. Although he only scored a single victory, consistency proved the key to the Frenchman's success.

Top far right: Vernay took his tyre-scuffed Volkswagen Golf GTI to maximum points in Zhejiang, China.

Above right: Pepe Oriola won two races in his Lukoil Craft-Bamboo Racing SEAT León.

Above far right: Fast approaching 50, Gianni Morbidelli showed no signs of slowing down as he took a double win at Oschersleben.

Centre right: Outgoing champion Stefano Comini was always a factor in his Audi RS3 LMS, taking three wins.

Right: Hungarian teenager Attila Tassi stormed into the series with his M1RA Honda Civic Type R, finishing second to the experienced Vernay in the battle for the title.

Photos: Courtesy WTCC

Monteiro suffered a high-speed accident during a testing session in Barcelona. It would be 16 days before he was discharged from hospital to return home, and there was little surprise when Monteiro was ruled out of the Chinese weekend. Ultimately, the incident would end his championship bid and he would sit out the remainder of the season.

Björk moved into the points lead in China, where the weather played havoc with the proceedings, despite failing to score in race one after retiring with suspension damage.

Guerrieri and Girolami shared the victories, while third place in the second race, which was abandoned after just three laps due to the conditions, meant that Björk moved half a point clear in the standings heading to Japan.

Ahead of Motegi, Honda dropped away from the lead of the manufacturers' championship, after its cars were excluded from the previous meeting in China for running non-compliant fuel injectors.

Back on track, the opening race was dominated by Chilton's Citroën, while the main championship contenders found themselves battling hard in the midfield pack. In race two, shortened again by poor weather, Michelisz gave Honda a home win and moved up to second, behind Björk, as the series returned to Macau for the first time since 2014.

In race one on the infamous Guia circuit, Bennani took his third win of the year, while Björk and Michelisz finished fourth and fifth, the latter despite being the cause of a red flag that ended the race early. Then Rob Huff romped to a record-breaking ninth Macau win in race two. Second place for Michelisz allowed him to cut Björk's lead to just 6.5 points. With 60 available in the season finale in Qatar, a further four drivers remained in contention.

Ultimately, Chilton and Guerrieri shared the wins in Qatar, but a fifth in race one and a fourth in race two were enough for Björk to lift the championship crown.

Meanwhile, Volvo held a slender lead in the manufacturers' championship, while in the Independents' standings, Chilton and Bennani were split by half a point, with Chilton's first-race Qatar win ultimately propelling him to the title.

As the year headed towards its close, talks aimed at securing the future of the series were ongoing, with a need to cut costs to maintain a full grid of cars. A move to adopt TCR regulations seemed likely, although that was still to be officially confirmed as AUTOCOURSE closed for press.

TCR INTERNATIONAL SERIES

The second season of the TCR International Series had drawn to a close in somewhat farcical fashion after AUTOCOURSE 2016–2017 had closed for press, with Stefano Comini emerging from chaos on the streets of Macau to successfully defend his title.

Neither race of the season finale, which had been shaping up to be an interesting four-way title fight, made it to half-distance due to incidents and delays, with Comini managing to edge out James Nash to take the title on a weekend that proved to be frustrating for everyone concerned.

The third season of TCR competition kicked off at a new venue in Georgia, and it was home driver Davit Kajaia who claimed the early lead in the standings, having taken a dominant pole position and race-one win in his Alfa Romeo. He was ahead of teenager Attila Tassi and race-two winner Pepe Oriola as they headed for Bahrain for round two.

The F1 support races would go the way of Honda driver Roberto Colciago and Kajaia's GE-Force team-mate, Dušan Borkovic, with the points lead passing to Jean-Karl Vernay as the series returned to Europe for round three at Spa.

Comini took his first victory of the year – and a first for Audi – in the first race, while Vernay was victorious in race two to maintain his position at the head of the standings.

Vernay remained out front after round four at Monza, where the wins had gone to Colciago and Comini on a weekend when leading outfit Westcoast Racing threatened to quit the series in protest at what it felt had been poor driving standards through the opening races of the campaign. It was an issue that had been debated at length after a multitude of controversial clashes in the opening meetings, but it was put

to one side in Austria after a series of high-speed incidents overshadowed the Salzburgring weekend.

First, Tassi destroyed his Honda in a crash during testing, while both Rob Huff and WRT team-mate Vernay went off at the same corner in the opening race with punctures.

There were also very public arguments over balance of performance and the legality of certain cars on the grid, and there was the small matter of wins for Borkovic and Colciago.

Vernay's failure to score in either race allowed Comini to take the points lead, but a double success for Tassi in Hungary vaulted him into top spot in the title race.

Subsequently, Tassi was caught up in one of a number of messy incidents at Oschersleben, losing the lead to Vernay. Both races were won by Gianni Morbidelli. In the second, only eight of the 23 cars made it to the finish following a multi-car shunt at the start.

The visiting Norbert Michelisz and WTCC refugee Aurélien Panis shared the wins in Thailand, before the series headed for China and the long awaited debut of Hyundai's first TCR machine. It appeared in a non-scoring capacity in the hands of Gabriele Tarquini and Alain Menu.

While Tarquini romped through from the midfield to win race one, Vernay scored maximum points. Huff took victory in the second race, before the series headed to Dubai for the season finale.

With Vernay 21 points clear of Tassi in the standings, the title was won in the opening race when the Frenchman took third behind Oriola and visiting BTCC ace Gordon Shedden. Outgoing champion Comini took the final victory of the season in race two.

Heading into 2018, the continued growth of TCR as a formula was demonstrated by the announcement of a new series in the UK, due to run across seven events spread throughout England and Scotland, and an expanded European Trophy.

Updated versions of the Honda Civic and Peugeot 308, and a new Renault Megane, were among the cars set to join the Hyundai on track.

BRITISH TOURING CAR CHAMPIONSHIP

As has become the norm, the fight for honours in the British Touring Car Championship would go right to the wire, with the title only being decided in the 30th and final race of the campaign at Brands Hatch. That brought to a close a frenetic fight for the championship crown that had begun at the same circuit earlier in the year, in somewhat surprising fashion, after Jeff Smith secured the first pole position of the season in a rain-affected qualifying session.

The first victory of 2017 went the way of Tom Ingram at the wheel of his Toyota – as it had done 12 months earlier. Defending champion Gordon Shedden and Andrew Jordan won races two and three, the latter on his debut for West Surrey Racing.

Conspicuous by their absence towards the front of the field were the Team BMR Subarus, which were off the pace throughout the weekend. Team leader Jason Plato, in particular, endured a meeting to forget, an accident at the start of race two having left him with a damaged car that was unable to start race three.

After Aiden Moffat took his first career victory in the opening race at Donington Park, Ingram became the first driver to win twice with a strong showing in the second. Then Shedden thought that he had taken a second win himself in the final race, only to be excluded for failing the ride-height test. That meant victory was handed to Colin Turkington, the first for Team BMW on its return as a manufacturer outfit.

Ingram's strong form through the opening two rounds meant that he led the championship standings as the field headed to Thruxton for round three. There, Matt Neal moved level with Andy Rouse, on 60 career wins, with victory in race one. That came a day after the Honda driver had ended a five-year run without a pole position in qualifying.

Rob Collard secured victory on home soil in race two, which was shortened by a heavy crash at Church for Dan Lloyd's MG. Turkington took his second win of the year in race three.

Subaru's struggles had continued, despite some impressive drives from Ash Sutton. They turned a corner at Oulton Park, however, after BTCC officials revealed that they would analyse the turbo boost of the Mountune-engined cars.

Sutton duly took the team's first victory of the season with a dominant drive in race two, having earlier finished behind Jordan and Neal on the race-one podium. Then race three, and the championship lead, went to Shedden, after a nightmare weekend in which Ingram picked up just a single point.

The season reached the halfway point at Croft, but the weekend was overshadowed by a huge accident in qualifying that left three drivers requiring hospital treatment. In total, a dozen drivers had been caught up in the incident, which occurred after Luke Davenport's Ford Focus dropped oil in challenging wet conditions at the quickest part of the circuit.

Davenport was the most seriously injured of the drivers, and he would miss the remainder of the season, as would round-one pole-sitter Smith. MG's Aron Taylor-Smith suffered a fractured leg, but was able to return to action in the second half of the year.

On track, Sutton was in fine form again in race one, beating Turkington to victory. The positions were reversed in race two, when Turkington saw off his Subaru rival to take top honours. Given what had happened the previous day, there was high emotion all round when Davenport's Motorbase team-mate, Mat Jackson, took victory in race three.

Shedden held the points lead into the summer break and retained his advantage at the top of the standings when the season resumed at Snetterton, taking victory in the final race of the weekend. Earlier, Sutton had done the double in races one and two, putting himself firmly into contention in the title race, despite his zero score in the season-opener.

While Sutton had impressed, team-mate Plato had struggled to extract any kind of performance from his car after the incident at Brands Hatch. He finally took to the top step of the podium, however, during round seven at Knockhill. But by then, he had assumed a supporting role for Sutton, who moved to within four points of new leader Turkington with

Above: Out in front. Two wins at Snetterton in July heralded the beginning of Ashley Sutton's charge to the title for Subaru Racing.

Left: Winners all on the Brands Hatch podium: (*left to right*) BTCC champion Ashley Sutton, surprise race winner Aiden Moffat and overall top Independent Tom Ingram.

Above right: Two outright wins for Aiden Moffat, who impressed in his independent Mercedes A-class.

Below right: Rob Collard was a consistent front-runner, until a nasty accident at Silverstone curtailed his season.

Far right: Reigning champion Gordon Shedden on two wheels in his Team Dynamics Honda Civic.

Photos: BTCC/Jakob Ebrey

Above: Tom Ingram was the star of the weekend at Silverstone's September meeting, taking a first, a second and a fourth over the three races in his Toyota Avensis.

Top right: West Surrey Racing's Andrew Jordan celebrates his win in race three at Rockingham.

Top far right: Fender benders. Stephen Jelley's Ford Focus and Josh Cook's MG6 need booking into the repair shop after their collision at Snetterton.

Above right: The perennial Matt Neal scored his 60th career BTCC victory at Thruxton.

Right: Colin Turkington and Ashley Sutton battled it out for the title in a thrilling Brands Hatch finale.

Photos: BTCC/Jakob Ebrey

another victory in race two. Ingram returned to the top of the podium in race three to remain in contention for the crown, having lost ground following a number of below-par rounds.

Sutton's seemingly relentless charge towards the top of the standings eventually resulted in him moving into the top spot after the opening race at Rockingham. There, he had followed team-mate James Cole home in a Subaru 1-2. Then he made it six wins in five meetings with victory in race two; race three went to Jordan's BMW.

That meant Sutton led Turkington by just 12 points in what was increasingly becoming a two-horse race, both Shedden and Collard having lost serious ground in the standings heading to Silverstone.

Collard's title bid ended in dramatic fashion when he was caught up in a huge accident in race one, which finished his season. The race went the way of Ingram, keeping his title bid alive.

Jack Goff's Honda won race two, but the real drama was just down the road, after Sutton was penalised for a last-lap move on Turkington for third place. A third strike of the year, it meant that he was demoted to the back of the grid for race three, but he still extended his lead by coming through to 11th in a race won by Neal. Turkington, by contrast, didn't score, having been forced to pit after an incident on the second lap.

Thus four drivers headed back to Brands Hatch still in mathematical contention for the title, although both Shedden and Ingram needed something akin to a miracle to stand any chance of ending the year on top.

Out front, Sutton held a ten-point lead over Turkington, and after qualifying, the Subaru man was in the box seat, having taken third place on the grid. Turkington was down in 17th after encountering mechanical issues.

Sutton extended his lead with third place in the opening race and had one hand firmly on the title when Turkington only made it to 15th – meaning that the championship would

be won in race two unless Turkington finished ahead. As it was, the BMW man produced arguably the drive of the season, storming through the pack to victory, with Sutton going the other way and slipping back to 12th by the finish

Turkington's charge meant that he trailed Sutton by just six points going into race three, but any hope of a grandstand finish to the year ended on the second lap, when he was forced out with damaged suspension. As Rob Austin took the race win, Sutton ended the season as champion with third place, eventually finishing 21 points clear at the top of the standings.

"I feel worn out from the emotions of it all," Sutton said afterwards. "The team has been fantastic all season. I knew it would be tough to fight back from the start we had at Brands Hatch, and it was only really from Oulton Park that we got our arses in gear.

"The team never gave up, and we were on the podium and around the top six for the rest of the year. Absolutely nothing can top this. It's just an unreal feeling."

Despite ending the year in second, Turkington helped BMW to take both the manufacturers' and teams' championships on its return, while Ingram and his Speedworks Motorsport team picked up Independent honours. Top rookie was the impressive Senna Proctor, who won half of the 30 races to wrap up the Jack Sears Trophy with five races to spare in his Vauxhall Astra.

A big season lay ahead for the BTCC in 2018, when the series will celebrate its 60th anniversary. While the calendar will retain a similar look to recent seasons, the final race of the weekend at Snetterton will run to an extended length and will award double points as part of the championship's celebrations.

Another manufacturer will also make a return to the grid, albeit not in a works capacity, HMS Racing having announced that it would build an Alfa Romeo Giulietta for the new season.

GERMAN TOURING CAR CHAMPIONSHIP

A reduced grid of 18 drivers fought for the DTM title, and there would be a different name on the trophy come the end of the season for the third year in a row.

The season kicked off at Hockenheim, where Lucas Auer took the first victory of the year for Mercedes, after an impressive drive from pole position. The Austrian held the early advantage in the title race after a solid fourth place in race two. That race went to Jamie Green, who mastered tricky weather conditions and a five-second stop/go penalty to give Audi its first win of the year.

It was a similar story at Lausitz, where Auer took an un-challenged race-one win, while Green recovered from being excluded from qualifying for race one by winning race two.

Hungary proved to be a tough weekend for the two early-season pace-setters, however. Auer failed to score in either race, and Green was excluded from race one for a technical infringement. That meant a new leader emerged in the points race, René Rast's maiden victory in race two having vaulted him to the head of the standings. Former Formula 1 racer Paul di Resta had earlier taken the top honours in race one.

After a tough start to the year for BMW, there was reason to cheer at the Norisring, where Bruno Spengler and Maxime Martin shared the victories. Spengler's success ended a win drought going back to 2013.

Meanwhile, Mattias Ekström moved into the points lead, having prioritised the DTM over his parallel programme in World Rallycross. However, Rast would come to within a point

of his Audi stablemate in Moscow, where he took victory in race one. Maro Engel picked up victory for Mercedes in race two, but then the manufacturer dropped a bombshell by revealing that it would quit the series after 2018 to move to Formula E.

While work began behind the scenes to deal with the announcement, the on-track action headed for Zandvoort, where Timo Glock took BMW's third win of the season in race one. Defending champion Marco Wittmann won race two, only to be excluded for not having enough fuel in his car at the finish, which handed victory to Mike Rockenfeller.

Auer and Rob Wickens shared victory at the Nürburgring, before Ekström finally took his first win of the season in the opening race at the Red Bull Ring. Victory for Rast in race two, after late gearbox issues for the previously dominant Green, meant that he would go into the season finale at Hockenheim as Ekström's closest challenger in the points – with Green, Wittmann, Rockenfeller and Auer all still in with a chance.

Green put himself right back into contention with victory in the opening race of the finale, placing him nine points behind Ekström, who failed to score. Both drivers took grid penalties into the final race of the year, however, and that handed the title initiative back to Rast, despite the fact that he went into the race third in the points.

Having qualified on the front row of the grid, Rast took second behind outgoing champion Wittmann, to lift the crown by just three points over Ekström. Green was three

Left: Lucas Auer after his victory at the Nürburgring. The Austrian youngster scored three wins and was the highest ranked Mercedes driver.
Photo: Mercedes AMG

Below left: The best result of BMW's season came at Zandvoort, where Marco Wittmann, Timo Glock and Maxime Martin took a 1-2-3 in the first race.
Photo: BMW Press Club

Below: Robert Wickens spent six happy years with Mercedes, but after the Stuttgart marque's decision to withdraw from DTM competition, the popular Canadian will move to IndyCar with Schmidt Peterson in 2018.
Photo: Mercedes AMG

Bottom: René Rast was the surprise package of the season in his Audi Sport Team Rosberg Audi RS5 DTM.
Photo: Audi Communications Motorsport

points further back after one of the most tightly contested title battles in recent memory.

"My goal was to become the best rookie," Rast said. "I wanted to learn, regularly score points and always finish a race well. Before the season, who'd have thought that I'd instantly be battling for the title? That's why, in the finale, I actually couldn't lose any more. I approached the weekend without pressure, and now am overjoyed that it all worked out."

Given that the top three were all Audi drivers, it was little surprise that Audi also wrapped up the manufacturers' and teams' titles once again. That left Mercedes and BMW without any silverware going into 2018 and what would be the final season when the three German giants would go head to head for honours.

SUPERCARS CHAMPIONSHIP

Five drivers were still in contention for the Supercars Championship title in Australia when the series headed to Newcastle for the season finale, but it would be a familiar face that emerged on top after one of the most dramatic weekends of the season.

Jamie Whincup was in the box seat with a slender lead in the standings over DJR Team Penske pair Scott McLaughlin and Fabian Coulthard, with Chaz Mostert and Shane van Gisbergen also still in contention.

McLaughlin moved into the lead after winning race one of the finale, while Whincup ran into trouble, leaving the youngster only needing a top-11 result in race two to take his first crown. However, three penalties left him down in 18th place, and Whincup picked up a victory that handed him the title for a record-breaking seventh time.

McLaughlin had been arguably the quickest driver in the field, with no fewer than eight wins and an astonishing 16 pole positions. These included a record-breaking display at Bathurst, where he became the first driver to break the 2m 04s mark.

The 60th running of the Great Race produced a surprise result, however. The unfancied Erebus Motorsport pair of David Reynolds and Luke Youlden emerged victorious after the big names fell by the wayside.

For 2018, the first cars built to the Gen2 Supercar regulations are set to appear on the grid. In addition, a new turbo V6 engine is scheduled to run in selected events as a wildcard – the first time a non-V8 car will have competed in the series in more than 20 years.

Among other changes for the new season are an event at the all-new Bend Motorsport Park, while the traditional Australian GP support races will now form part of the championship for the first time.

Above: René Rast went from an unheralded rookie to become the 2017 DTM champion.

Left: Mattias Ekström fell just three points short of a third DTM title.
Photos: Audi Communications Motorsport

Far left: Marco Wittmann ended the season on a high for BMW, with a win in the final race at Hockenheim. The former champion was best of the rest, finishing fifth in the standings, behind the Audi juggernaut.
Photo: BMW Press Club

Below left: Although he notched just one win, at Zandvoort, Mike Rockenfeller finished the season strongly to take fourth place.

Below far left: Three wins for Audi's Jamie Green, including race one at the October meeting.
Photos: Audi Communications Motorsport

Below: In Supercars, Scott McLaughlin showed astonishing speed in the DJR Team Penske Ford, but lost out to Jamie Whincup in the dramatic Newcastle finale.
Photo: LAT Images/Daniel Kalisz

Below right: A record-breaking seventh title for Jamie Whincup in the Triple Eight Race Engineering Holden.
Photo: Red Bull

THRILL OF THE CHASE

At 37 years of age, Martin Truex finally claimed his first NASCAR title at the Homestead showdown.
Photo: LAT Images/Matthew T. Thacker

Above: Kyle Busch, in the Joe Gibbs Racing Skittles Toyota Camry, leads the field as the Monster Energy NASCAR Cup Series gets under way with the Brickyard 400 at the Indianapolis Motor Speedway.
Photo: LAT Images/Russell LaBounty

Above right: Celebrating 'The Big One'. Busch after his win in the 2017 Daytona 500.
Photo: LAT Images/Rusty Jarrett

Top far right: NASCAR continued to make occasional forays on to traditional road courses, such as Watkins Glen. Chase Elliott leads Jamie McMurray in their Chevrolets.
Photo: LAT Images/John Harrelson

Above far right: A pit stop for Jimmie Johnson in the Hendrick Motorsports Lowe's Chevrolet. The thinly populated stands demonstrate how the racing has lost much of its lustre.
Photo: LAT Images/Rusty Jarrett

Right: The field goes green at the Daytona 500, with Kevin Harvick at the front of the pack.
Photo: LAT Images/Michael L. Levitt

NASCAR remains by far the most visible and strongest form of racing in the United States. Consider that seven-times champion Jimmie Johnson earned US$21.8 million in 2016 in salary, endorsements, and his share of prize money and licensing. Dale Earnhardt Jr was a close second with US$21.1 million in income, despite missing half the 2016 season. Over the year, NASCAR's top 12 drivers' combined earnings were an estimated US$168 million, a decline from 2013's high of US$192 million.

Meanwhile, *Forbes* magazine estimated that Rick Hendrick's four-car team was worth US$350 million, followed by Joe Gibbs Racing at US$250 million and Stewart-Haas at US$225 million. NASCAR also enjoys many name brand sponsors who have long-term contracts with some of the top teams and drivers.

These days, the season-opening Daytona 500 is known as 'America's Race' and pulls TV ratings three or four times larger than the Indy 500, while NASCAR as a whole defines motor racing to the average American. Most of NASCAR's 36 first-division Cup races are run at Daytona-like superspeedways in almost every region of the United States. NASCAR's current television contracts with NBC and Fox are worth $8 billion over ten years, and in 2015 the Cup races paid a grand total of more than $220 million in prize money to drivers and teams.

But NASCAR reached its peak in the early 21st century, and over the past ten years it has suffered a steady decline in both crowds at a lot of the races and TV ratings. At many traditional tracks, ticket sales have fallen substantially, and some have taken down grandstands rather than have so many empty seats. The most spectacular failure was the Brickyard 400 at Indianapolis, which had made its debut in 1994 in front of a full house. The race continued to draw well for a handful of years before falling into a steep decline, with barely a tenth of the IMS's 250,000 seats occupied more recently. In 2018, the Brickyard 400 will be moved from mid-summer to the autumn in the hope of preventing the race from dying.

Some tracks have begun to improve and modernise existing facilities to attract today's increasingly discerning fans. Meanwhile, NASCAR's TV ratings have fallen, almost precipitously. As a result, sponsorship income has dropped substantially in recent years, and everyone in NASCAR is wondering what the future will bring and what the solutions may be to the sport's problems.

Faced with an increasing challenge of how to reverse a long downward slide in TV ratings and crowds at many races, NASCAR has made an incessant series of changes and tweaks in an attempt to create more excitement. This started with the introduction of 'The Chase for the Cup' back in 2004; then in 2007 came the 'Car of Tomorrow' spec car; 2017's brainwave was to split each race into three parts, with bonus points awarded for each segment. It's called 'stage racing', with the yellow flag being waved at the end of the first and second stages of each race.

NASCAR believed that the unpredictable, almost random nature of 'The Chase' would create more interest among fans, TV viewers and the media in general. Thanks to the fiendishly complex 'Chase' rules, it's impossible to predict who will win the championship until the last of the 36 races. In recent years, changes have been made to the format that theoretically compel the drivers and teams to be more aggressive at all times. The latest move to break each race into segments was another step in trying to make NASCAR more aggressive and appealing.

Yet the TV ratings continue to fall. They have been in steady decline for a dozen years, shrinking 45 per cent since 2005, from nearly nine million viewers per race to 4.6 million in 2016. Most races in 2016 and 2017 were down substantially from 2015, and the last dozen races of 2017, including all the 'Chase' races, plunged to record low ratings.

NASCAR enjoys American racing's biggest and best TV package by far, with plenty of income from handsome rights fees and acres of TV time and space. IndyCar and IMSA are seriously hobbled on this front, with little more than race coverage and no leverage to negotiate better rights fees.

Above: Kyle Larson and Chase Elliott on the inside line at the Dover International Speedway.
Photo: LAT Images/Nigel Kinrade

Top right: Chip Ganassi Racing's Kyle Larson, one of the leading drivers of the younger generation.
Photo: LAT Images/Barry C. Cantrell

Above centre right: Hendrick Motorsports are looking to the future with a big talent in Chase Elliott.
Photo: LAT Images/Nigel Kinrade

Above centre far right: Erik Jones took over at Joe Gibbs Racing.
Photo: LAT Images/Logan Whitton

Above right: Ryan Blaney raced for Wood Brothers in 2017.
Photo: LAT Images/Rusy Jarrett

Right: Homestead marked the end of a gruelling 36-race series.
Photo: LAT Images/John Harrelson

NASCAR, on the other hand, is in the opening years of a pair of ten-year contracts with NBC and Fox that are due to run until 2024 and that are worth more than US$8 billion. So NASCAR enjoys plenty of room to find a way to rebound before the time comes to renew its TV contracts. If the current decline continues, however, the rights fees are sure to be much smaller.

NASCAR continues to enjoy star power from its top drivers, but it's going through a big transition, with Jeff Gordon, Tony Stewart and Carl Edwards having retired at the end of 2016, and its most popular driver, Dale Earnhardt Jr, hanging up his helmet at the end of the 2017 season. The likes of Jimmie Johnson, 2015 champion Kyle Busch, Martin Truex, Joey Logano and Brad Keselowski don't seem to inspire the same passion from the fans, and it will be interesting to see whether newcomers like Kyle Larson, Chase Elliott, Ryan Blaney and Erik Jones can become major personalities or superstars. Will any of them rise to the occasion and begin to match the appeal Richard Petty, Dale Earnhardt Sr and Jeff Gordon had for older generations and thereby help NASCAR right its foundering ship?

One element in racing's struggles in the marketplace is the sport's failure to make itself a common cultural component of life in America. Most major sports – football, baseball, basketball, hockey and increasingly soccer – are played by kids in school and college, and every family in every corner of the country is exposed to these sports, which are deeply rooted as essential parts of community life in America.

Not so motor racing. No fewer than 200 sanctioning bodies vye to sell their products, ranging from NASCAR, IndyCar, IMSA and NHRA, through off-road racing, midgets and sprint cars, and modifieds, to a wide variety of road racing. There's an endless array of different types of race car, with their brand names or logos, competing with each other for identity and media space. The giant jumble of sanctioning bodies is a tremendous celebration of diversity, but it's a very bad thing for the sport as whole.

Another problem for racing is that the drivers have become marketing tools, sublimating their personalities to the need to promote and service their sponsors. This is a plague on all forms of racing, as young drivers learn market-speak from an early age in the eternal quest for sponsorship. The days of Dale Earnhardt habitually using his fender, laughing it off and speaking his mind are long gone.

If either Bill France Sr or Jr returned to earth today, they surely would be disgusted with the giant bureaucracy that runs NASCAR. And when they heard that NASCAR had been working with fan focus groups and a drivers' council to determine policy and rules, I can just hear Bill Jr saying, "Who the hell are all these people? Fire their asses!" More than ever, the sport cries out for powerful, inspired leadership in the style of Bills Sr and Jr.

Martin Truex wins NASCAR title

The man to beat in NASCAR during 2017 was Martin Truex, a 37-year-old from New Jersey who had been racing at NASCAR's top level since 2005. Truex won more races (eight) and led more laps than anyone else, driving a Toyota for Furniture Row Racing, but none of that ensured that he would win the championship.

The key to winning NASCAR's modern championship is making the final cut-off of four finalists for the season-closing race at Homestead-Miami Speedway. The top 16 drivers in points qualify for NASCAR's play-offs over the final ten races of the season. The field is trimmed to 12 after three play-off races, and further cut to eight after another trio of races before the final four are determined for the year's last race. This system guarantees that the championship remains open down to the closing laps of the last race, with the highest finisher among the final four taking the title. In 2017, the Homestead finalists were Truex, Kyle Busch, Kevin Harvick and Brad Keselowski.

Truex took his first championship in style, winning the season-closer after a fierce battle with Busch and Harvick. Furniture Row Racing is owned by Barney Visser, and the team is based in Denver, 2,000 miles west of the Charlotte, North Carolina area where most NASCAR teams are based. Truex was picked up four years ago by Visser's fledgling team after a fuel-cheating scandal resulted in him losing his seat with Michael Waltrip's now-defunct team. With Visser's team, Truex responded immediately, running up front in many races and establishing himself as a regular winner.

Visser's team runs as a satellite operation to Joe Gibbs's four-car factory Toyota team, with cars built at Gibbs's shop in North Carolina and engines from TRD (Toyota Racing Development) in Southern California. It was the second year in a row that Toyota had won NASCAR's manufacturers' championship.

Busch finished second in the championship, aboard one of Joe Gibbs's four Toyotas. Champion in 2015, Busch was the man to beat in many races, and he chased Truex across the line in the season-closer. He won five races in 2017. Harvick, NASCAR's 2014 champion, was very competitive in many races, less so in others, and he finished a fighting third in the season's finale, driving one of Stewart-Haas Racing's four Fords. Keselowski, the 2012 champion, was very strong in some races with one of Penske Racing's Fords, but he went through a frustrating second half of the season, struggling occasionally to break out of the midfield.

Among those who failed to make the final cut was seven-times champion Jimmie Johnson, who endured a tough year. He won three races in the first half of the season, but rarely contended in the second half, often qualifying and running outside the top ten. Johnson, 42, signed a new three-year contract with Hendrick Motorsports through to 2020, and it will be interesting to see if, at the end of his career, he is able to muster a run for what would be a record-setting eighth championship.

Other potential 2017 championship contenders included Denny Hamlin, Chase Elliott, Kyle Larson and Matt Kenseth. Each of them had appeared likely at one stage or another to make the final cut, but mechanical failures and crashes conspired to eliminate them. Youngsters Elliott and Larson have established themselves as possible future champions.

Former champion Kenseth (in 2003) reluctantly retired at the end of the year, at 45. His contract for 2018 wasn't renewed by Joe Gibbs Racing and he was unable to find a top replacement ride. His place in the team was taken by 21-year-old Erik Jones. Also retiring at the end of the season was Dale Earnhardt Jr, 43, who had raced Cup cars for 18 years. Although he never won a championship, Earnhardt was a front-runner throughout most of his career, and for the last 15 years he was perennially NASCAR's most popular driver. Earnhardt will join NASCAR's television broadcasting team, but his presence on the track will be sorely missed.

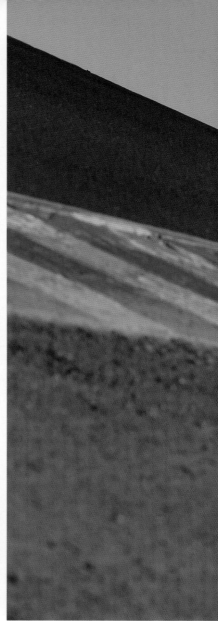

Penske's 15th Indy car title

Josef Newgarden took the lead of the Verizon IndyCar championship by scoring his third win of the season at Mid-Ohio at the end of July. In his first year with Team Penske, the 26-year-old went on to win his first IndyCar title after finishing second to team-mate Will Power in the Pocono 500, beating team-mate and defending champion Simon Pagenaud at Gateway, and recovering from a mistake while exiting the pits at Watkins Glen to take the pole for the season finale at Sonoma and lead most of the race before finishing a close second behind Pagenaud.

UK Formula Ford Festival winner in 2008 and Indy Lights champion in 2011, Newgarden moved to Indy car racing with Sarah Fisher in 2012. He scored his first big-league victory in 2015 and earned his seat at Team Penske with an impressive win at Iowa in 2016, a few weeks after breaking his collarbone in a big accident at Texas. He is an aggressive, but smart driver, and it was no surprise to see him earn his first, and Penske's 15th, Indy car championship in his first season with the team.

"There are a couple of races that stand out," Newgarden said. "The first was Barber Motorsport Park, where we got our first win of the year. That was a very exciting weekend, a solid weekend and a lot of fun. We had a test day there, so we knew what to do. We were quick in practice and we took some risks in qualifying that didn't pan out, but we were quick in the race and were able to win.

"Another solid weekend was Detroit. We got two top-fives from the two races in Detroit, and that was a good result and recovery after the difficulties we had at Indianapolis. Then we had a great weekend in Toronto and won the race, and followed that up with good races at Mid-Ohio and Pocono."

Newgarden battled with Will Power at Mid-Ohio and Pocono. He made a superb pass on his team-mate at Mid-Ohio to score his third win of the year, and fought hard to finish a close second behind a resourceful Power in the Pocono 500. At Gateway, he muscled his way inside Pagenaud to record his fourth win of the year. After messing up at Watkins Glen, he came back to take the pole, lead most laps and finish a strong second in the season closer at Sonoma.

"It's great to be able to race with your team-mates, especially as it came down to the closing races," Newgarden said. "Will is one of the best, and it was great to race with him at Mid-Ohio and Pocono, and with Simon at Gateway and Sonoma. We were pretty racey at Gateway, and that was a hard battle with Simon. Same thing at Sonoma, where he and his guys really used their heads.

"All my team-mates are very talented and very quick. You can't hide anything nowadays, with all the data, and we work together. That's the way the team operates. We work together as a team. We push each other in a positive way, and in this environment you're so quick to learn. Everyone learns from everyone else, and it creates a dialogue where you can apply the lessons.

"We all want to beat each other, and that makes for a strong dialogue between us. There's lots of conversation about improving the race set-up. Everyone has different philosophies and ideas they bring to the table each weekend to improve our performance."

All this cross-pollination helped the team dominate the last half of the season and finish 1-2-4-5 in the championship. Defending champion Pagenaud took second, ahead of Ganassi's number one, Scott Dixon, 2014 champion Will Power and veteran Helio Castroneves, who had been with Penske for 18 years, but had never won a championship. Penske's cars usually looked great on the track, working

Above left: Golden boy. A move to Team Penske was the opportunity for Josef Newgarden to demonstrate his talent. He showed great speed and crucially learned from his mistakes, taking the IndyCar crown in a very accomplished manner.
Photo: IndyCar/Joe Skibinski

Above: Newgarden clinched his title at Sonoma, where he kept his head and settled for a second place, behind team-mate Simon Pagenaud.
IndyCar/Chris Owens

Right: Roger Penske and his juggernaut team celebrated a 15th Indy car title, his drivers having taken four of the top five places.
Photo: IndyCar/Joe Skibinski

Above: Pagenaud took his Penske to victory at Phoenix and was ultra-consistent throughout the season, but even a dramatic four-stop strategy on his way to victory at Sonoma could not help him retain his crown.

Right: In his time honoured tradition, Helio Castroneves climbs the fence after his win in Iowa. The popular Brazilian led the standings mid-season, but would not make the top three thereafter, and his title challenge eventually fell short.
Photos: IndyCar/Chris Owens

Top right: James Hinchcliffe grabbed a win for Schmidt Petersen at Long Beach, but after that his season's bright start faded.
Photo: IndyCar/Hadar Goren

Above right: Graham Rahal took a double victory at Detroit. His never-say-die attitude earned him sixth place in the final standings.
Photo: IndyCar/Brett Kelley

Right: Scott Dixon fought against the odds with the Ganassi Honda, only managing a single win. The veteran champion was the only man to break the Penske stranglehold.
Photo: IndyCar/Chris Owens

smoothly and progressively. Newgarden found Penske's Dallaras a little less forgiving than what he had been used to, but very effective.

"It really is amazing how much capability we have at this team," he said. "They are able to produce different feels in the car's platform. Sometimes it doesn't feel so good, but the cars always produce a lot of lateral grip. If you can get past the feel, you discover there's a lot of performance underneath it.

"I've always preferred a car that felt good and would react very quickly at the rear so I knew where I was. The Penske team has a little different philosophy, and I had to take the car by the ears to get comfortable with it. But I've discovered that the performance is always there, even if the comfort is not the best."

Newgarden commented on the fierce competition from Scott Dixon and Chip Ganassi's team. At 37, Dixon is a four-times IndyCar champion (all with Ganassi) and the series' leading active driver with 41 wins. "Scott has a great team behind him, and he's proven that he can adapt to any situation," Newgarden said. "He's got lots of experience and doesn't make mistakes. This year, we had a great battle with Ganassi's team, and with Honda versus Chevrolet. There was a lot of back and forth between Honda and Chevrolet. Our cars were a little bit better on some tracks, and theirs were a little better on other tracks. But Scott is a guy who is good everywhere. You can never discount him."

Newgarden pointed out that Michael Andretti's four-car team, including Alex Rossi and Takuma Sato, winners of the previous two years' Indy 500s, and former Indy winner and champion Ryan Hunter-Reay, are also tough customers. Rossi, Sato and Hunter-Reay finished seventh, eighth and ninth in the 2017 championship. "Of course, the Andretti guys were often very quick," Newgarden said. "They have a

strong team and have been the guys to beat at Indianapolis in recent years. They've been the toughest competitors in the 500 over the last couple of years."

Newgarden also has great respect for Graham Rahal, who won in Detroit and finished sixth in the championship with his father's Honda-powered Rahal-Letterman team. Sato was set to join Rahal at Rahal-Letterman in 2018. "Graham is very quick and a great racer," Newgarden said. "He should be even stronger next year in a two-car team with Sato. We will have to work very hard to have those guys covered."

Like all the IndyCar drivers, Newgarden was looking forward to racing the much more attractive 2018 Dallara, with its substantially revised aerodynamic package. "Juan Pablo Montoya and Oriol Servia have tested the car," he said. "It sounds like the new package will make the cars more difficult to drive and better for racing, which is what everyone hoped for. You have to work hard to keep the new car underneath you and work hard to stay on top of the car. There's more downforce from the bottom on the new car and less from the wings. That should bring the field even closer together, and enable us to run closer and race better. So I think it should be more exciting for everyone. I'm really looking forward to it."

Like most of his fellow drivers, Newgarden would love to see IndyCar allow them more power. "All we need is 150 more horsepower and then we'd be all set," he grinned. "We would have a car that would be even harder to drive, and it would show the difference between the drivers. It would be great to have more power."

As a Team USA scholarship winner, Newgarden won the UK's Formula Ford Kent Festival in 2008, and raced Formula Fords and GP3 cars in the UK and Europe in 2009 and 2010. He won nine Brit FF1600 races in 2009, finishing second in the championship, and has an ambition to race in Formula 1.

If Chase Carey and Liberty Media want to build F1 into a major sport in America, it's essential to have a talented American driving for one of the top teams, like Mario Andretti back in the seventies. Mario broke into F1 with Lotus, scored his first GP win with Ferrari and took the world championship with Lotus in 1978, pushing F1 to new heights in the United States. Newgarden has shown that he has the talent, and it surely would be a great thing for the sport if Carey could manoeuvre a seat for him in one of F1's top teams – Mercedes, Ferrari or Red Bull. Anything less wouldn't do the job for Newgarden or F1 in America. "I'd love to have that opportunity," he grinned. "That would be great. Formula 1 has always been a dream for me."

Meanwhile, Newgarden was looking forward to 2018 and many more productive seasons to follow with Team Penske. "I'm really excited about it," he said. "There's definitely room for improvement. I was surprised how well we were able to do this year, with the errors I made at Watkins Glen and elsewhere. I'm looking forward to doubling down and doing a better job next year. We started testing the new car in October, and if we can continue to grow and develop like this year, we should be very competitive. So I'm very excited."

It's great to see Newgarden arrive at the top of the sport with one of the best teams in the business. He should be able to build an impressive record in the coming years.

Above: All action at Watkins Glen as the field thunders towards Turn One. It was a breakout race for Andretti's Alexander Rossi (98), who dominated proceedings to take his first road-course win.

Photo: IndyCar/Brett Kelley

Top left: After winning the Indy Lights title in 2016, Brit Ed Jones took the second seat at Dale Coyne Racing and went on to gain Rookie of the Year honours. The highlight of his year was third place at the Indianapolis 500. In a surprise move, he will join Chip Ganassi in 2018, in place of the experienced Tony Kanaan.

Above left: Sébastien Bourdais was a surprise winner of the opening race at St Petersburg, but a massive crash at Indianapolis curtailed his season.

Photos: IndyCar/Chris Owens

Left: Will Power was often the fastest man in the series, with three wins, but doses of bad luck thwarted his title challenge.

Photo: IndyCar/Shawn Gritzmacher

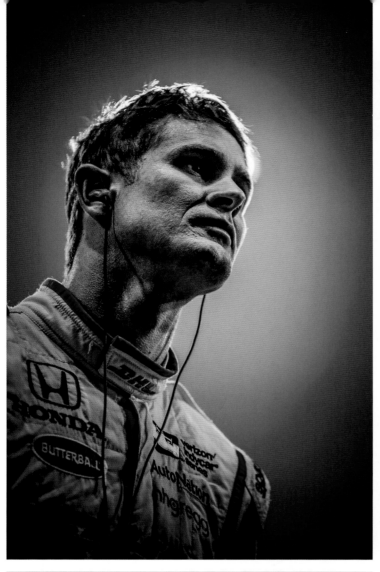

Left: Helio Castroneves called an end to his full-time Indy car career, but the three-times 500 winner will be back at the Speedway in May, 2018, looking for that elusive fourth win.

Right: Will Power drove with all his considerable verve and commitment.

Far left: Andretti's long-term mainstay, Ryan Hunter-Reay, could do no better than three third places in a season of toil without much reward.

Below far left: Max Chilton, in his sophomore season with Ganassi, just missed out on the top ten in the final points standings.

Below left: Graham Rahal extracted the most from his Honda-powered Rahal Letterman Lanigan Dallara.
Photos: IndyCar/Shawn Gritzmacher

Below: Immaculate and ultra-professional Simon Pagenaud.
Photo: IndyCar/Chris Owens

Bottom: The irrepressible Tony Kanaan will join forces with A.J. Foyt for 2018.

Below right: Marco Andretti was consistent, but still sought the win that had eluded him since 2011.
Photos: IndyCar/Shawn Gritzmacher

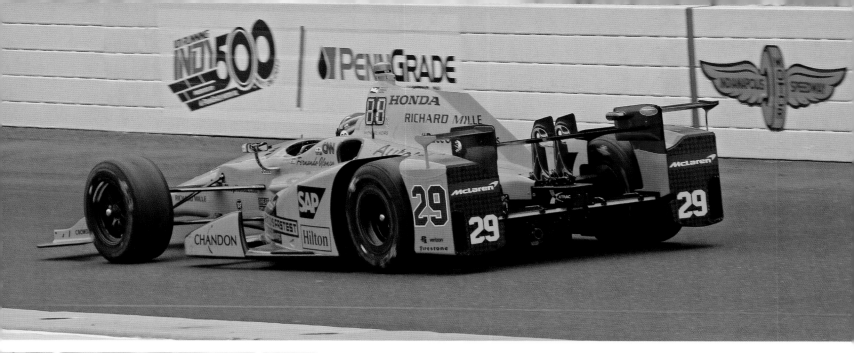

Above: Fernando Alonso flashes past the famous winged-wheel logo during his impressive Indy 500 debut.
Photo: IndyCar/Michel Harding

Left: Alonso adapted to the 'Month of May' with considerable aplomb.
Photo: Indycar/Chris Owens

Far left: The grid buzzes with activity before the start of the 101st running of the Indianapolis 500.
Photo: Indycar/Jason Porter

Below left: I can't believe it! Castroneves with Roger Penske after his failed bid to win a fourth 500.
Photo: IndyCar/Michel Harding

Below far left: Duel in the sun. Takuma Sato takes the chequer just ahead of Castroneves for a perfectly judged win.
Photo: Indycar/Walt Kuhn

Below: Gil de Ferran, winner of the 2003 Indianapolis 500 (*left*), passes on his wealth of experience to Alonso during qualifying. McLaren's Zak Brown, who had made the whole deal possible, listens in.
Photo: Indycar/Chris Owens

Alonso and the Indy 500

The 101st running of the Indy 500 was won by Takumo Sato, who became the first Japanese driver to win the big race in Indiana. Sato had been racing Indy cars for eight years and had come close to winning the 500 in 2012, only to crash on the last lap as he attempted to take the lead from Dario Franchitti. In 2017, he qualified fourth and ran with the leaders all the way. In the end, it came down to a duel between Sato and three-times Indy winner Castroneves, with the former doing the job perfectly this time, taking the lead with five laps to go and holding off Castroneves by 0.211 of a second on the run to the chequered flag.

The big news at Indianapolis in 2017 was Fernando Alonso's first appearance in the 500 or any oval-track race. The Spaniard drove a Honda-powered Andretti Autosport entry organised by Zak Brown and McLaren, thus forsaking the Monaco GP. The two-times world champion did an excellent job, quickly getting up to speed and qualifying fifth in the middle of the second row. He went on to drive an even more impressive race, making some superb passes around the outside, which defines the greatest of oval racers. He took the lead for the first time on lap 48 (of 200), and was able to head a total of 27 laps before his engine blew with only 21 to go. Without doubt, it was one of the most impressive Indy 500 debuts in recent years.

After the race, Alonso discussed his rookie experience.

"Obviously, I'm disappointed not to finish the race, because every race you compete, you want to be at the chequered flag," he said. "Today was not possible, but the last two weeks here was a great experience. I came here basically to prove myself, to challenge myself. I know that I can be as quick as anyone in an F1 car. I didn't know if I can be as quick as anyone in an IndyCar.

"It was nice to have this competitive feeling, even leading the Indy 500. I was passing, watching the [scoring] tower and saw the No. 29 on top of it. I was thinking at that moment if Zak [Brown, McLaren boss] or someone from the team was taking a picture, because I want that picture at home. Thanks to IndyCar for an amazing experience. Thanks to Indianapolis. Thanks to the fans. I felt at home. I'm not American, but I felt really proud to race here.

"Even with some unlucky moments on the yellow flags, we were in the group, in the mix. So it felt okay. Obviously, when you are eighth or seventh, you know the last 20 laps were intense, but I was taking care a bit of the front tyres in the first couple laps of the last stint, because I knew the race would be decided in the last six or seven laps. I think I had a little bit in the pocket before the engine blew up.

"Obviously, if I come back here, at least I know how it is with everything. It will not be the first time I do restarts, pit stops, all these kind of things. So it will be an easier, let's say, adaptation. Let's see what happens in the following years. I need to keep pursuing this challenge, because winning the Indy 500 is not completed. It holds a new challenge for me."

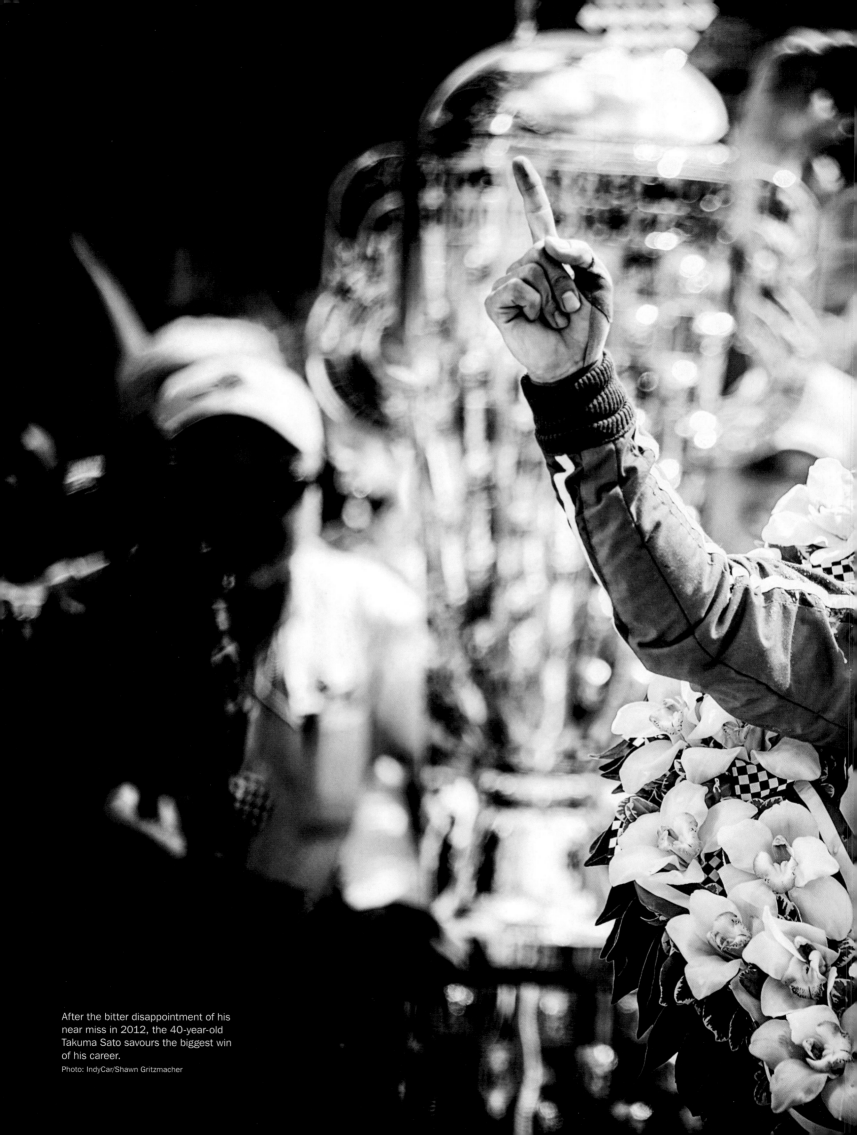

After the bitter disappointment of his near miss in 2012, the 40-year-old Takuma Sato savours the biggest win of his career.
Photo: IndyCar/Shawn Gritzmacher

Mazda Road to Indy champions

Kyle Kaiser, a 21-year-old Californian, clinched the 2017 Indy Lights championship along with a Mazda Scholarship valued at US$1 million to ensure his entry in at least three IndyCar Series races in 2018, including the Indianapolis 500. Victor Franzoni, a 21-year-old Brazilian, won the Pro Mazda championship and a scholarship worth $790,300 to graduate to Indy Lights. The USF2000 Championship Powered by Mazda was won by 20-year-old Floridian Oliver Askew, who picked up a US$325,000 bonus to move on to Pro Mazda in 2018. A total of more than US$2.6 million in Mazda Scholarships and other awards was paid in 2017 to the top competitors in Mazda's Road to Indy ladder system.

Taylor brothers dominate IMSA series

IMSA's WeatherTech SportsCar series was won by brothers Jordan and Ricky Taylor driving a Cadillac DPi for their father, Wayne Taylor. They kicked off the year by winning the season-opening Daytona 24 Hours, repeating the feat at Sebring in March. Three more mid-season wins followed, enabling them to wrap up their first IMSA championship.

"This is something that our family has been around my whole life, and I built it up in my mind what it's going to be like," said Ricky Taylor. "This is obviously a dream come true. I never would've imagined that I'd get to share this experience with my family and such a great group of guys and great group of partners."

Cadillac also took IMSA's Prototype and Patrón Endurance Cup manufacturers' championships with additional wins from each of the two Action Express Cadillacs, driven by Dane Cameron and Eric Curran, and Christian Fittipaldi and João Barbosa. Fittipaldi and Barbosa also won the Patrón Endurance Cup team and driver championships, with Filipe Albuquerque joining them for the long-distance races.

The final year of IMSA's second-level Prototype Challenge class was dominated by Performance Tech Motorsports. The team won seven of eight races with James French and Patricio O'Ward, who were joined in the longer races by Kyle Masson. IMSA's hotly contested GT Le Mans (GTLM) class was taken by Chevrolet and Corvette Racing, which won both the drivers' and manufacturers' titles. Antonio Garcia and Jan Magnussen won three races and recorded a top-five finish in every race aboard one of two factory Corvette C7.Rs.

The majority of IMSA's field comprised GT Daytona cars, a total of eight manufacturers competing full time, seven of them winning at least one race each. Defending champions Alessandro Balzan and Christina Nielsen repeated their 2016 title run aboard a Scuderia Corsa Ferrari 488 GT3.

Above: João Barbosa, Christian Fittipaldi and Filipe Albuquerque won the teams' and drivers' titles in the Patrón Endurance Cup.
Photo: LAT Images/Richard Dole

Left: Ricky and Jordan Taylor wrapped up their first IMSA championship for the family team.
Photo: LAT Images/Michael L. Levitt

Above centre: Victor Franzoni, a 21-year-old Brazilian, won the Pro Mazda Championship to graduate to Indy Lights.
Photo: Indycar/Chris Owens

Top: Kyle Kaiser took the Indy Lights crown and won the chance to break into Indycar in 2018.
Photo: Indycar/Brent Kelley

Appreciations by Gordon Kirby

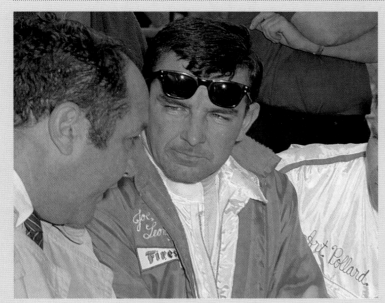

IMS

Joe Leonard

JOE LEONARD, 84, passed away in April, 2017. He had achieved the rare distinction of winning three AMA Grand National motorcycle championships in 1954, '56 and '57, and two USAC Indy car titles in 1971 and '72. He is the only man to have done so. Leonard won 27 AMA races, including the 1957 and '58 Daytona 200s, before retiring from motorcycle racing in 1961. He made his USAC Indy car debut in 1964 and scored his first win at Milwaukee in 1965, driving for Dan Gurney's All American Racers.

Leonard drove one of three STP Lotus turbines at Indianapolis in 1968, replacing the injured Jackie Stewart. He qualified on the pole, setting a new track record of 171.599mph, and led 31 laps in the 500 before his fuel driveshaft broke with only nine laps to go. After joining Vel's Parnelli Jones Racing in 1970, he won the USAC championship the following two years. He also won the California 500 in 1971 and finished second to Mark Donohue in the Pocono 500. In 1972, he took victory in the Pocono 500 and also won 200-mile races at Michigan and Milwaukee.

Although Leonard continued with VPJ for two more years, the team was struggling. He crashed after a tyre failure in the 1974 California 500, and his feet and legs were badly broken. He attempted a comeback in 1975, but failed USAC's physical fitness test, which ended his career.

Jim McElreath

JIM McELREATH died in May, 2017, at the age of 89. Born and raised just outside Dallas, Texas, he started racing stock cars when he was 17, continuing for 15 years while earning his living as a bricklayer. He broke into USAC racing in 1961 with Lindsey Hopkins's team and raced Indy cars for 23 years, starting 178 races, including 15 Indy 500s. Over the years, he won five USAC races and finished second to Mario Andretti in the 1966 USAC championship. He was third in USAC points in 1963, '65 and '70. McElreath scored his biggest win in the inaugural California 500 in 1970, driving a Coyote for A.J. Foyt.

McElreath's son, James, was killed in a sprint car accident in October, 1977. A talented driver, James had tried unsuccessfully to qualify for the Indy 500 earlier that year. Jim's daughter, Shirley, was married to racing driver and CART team owner Tony Bettenhausen Jr, but both lost their lives when their private plane crashed in Kentucky in February, 2000.

Rolla Vollstedt

When he died in October, 2017, ROLLA VOLLSTEDT was 99 years old. He had built and entered Indy cars for almost 30 years, from the 1960s through to the 1990s, and had achieved early success at Indianapolis in 1964 with a rear-engined Offenhauser-powered car driven by Len Sutton.

At Riverside in 1967, Jim Clark drove a Vollstedt-Ford, the only time he raced a non-Lotus single-seater. Clark qualified second to Dan Gurney and led the race before missing a shift and blowing his engine.

In 1976 and '77, Vollstedt entered one of his cars at Indianapolis for Janet Guthrie, who became the first woman to qualify for the 500 in the latter year. Guthrie started the 500 from the ninth row, but she retired early in the race with timing-gear failure.

Vollstedt's final appearance as a team owner at Indianapolis was in 1982, when Tom Bigelow qualified a Vollstedt Eagle-Chevy on the 11th row. He dropped out with a blown engine at half-distance.

David Steele

A top American midget and sprint car driver, DAVID STEELE died in a racing accident in March, 2017. He was 42. Between 1996 and 2007, he had scored 60 wins in USAC midgets, sprint cars and Silver Crown cars, winning the Silver Crown championship in 2004 and '05.

Steele had been taking part in a Southern Sprint Car Shootout Series race at Desoto Speedway in Florida, when his front wheel hit the rear wheel of a fellow competitor, which launched him into the wall. He died instantly.

Horst Kroll

HORST KROLL started his career as a factory Porsche mechanic in Stuttgart, but emigrated to Canada in 1958 and found success as a Porsche mechanic and racing driver. He won the Canadian Formula Vee championship in 1965 and later drove a Kelly-Porsche sports/racer to win the overall Canadian Championship in 1968.

In 1969, Kroll began competing in Canada's Formula A series and continued for a few years before expanding into the USA's F5000 series in 1973 and '74. He carried on racing for many years and won the last Can-Am championship in 1986, aboard his own Frissbee-Chevrolet, at 50 years of age.

He also helped launch a teenage Paul Tracy's career by giving him a ride in his Can-Am car. Kroll died in October, 2017, at the age of 81.

Chuck Weyant

Prior to CHUCK WEYANT'S death in January, 2017, at the age of 93, he had been the oldest living Indy 500 veteran. He had started racing in dirt cars before the Second World War, scoring his first win in 1947 and going on to win at least 64 feature races on the dirt. Weyant raced AAA and USAC Indy cars between 1952 and 1959, and started four Indy 500s in 1955, '57, '58 and '59.

Robert Yates

ROBERT YATES was a top NASCAR engine builder and former owner of Yates Racing from 1988 to 2007. As a youth, he had raced his own dragster in the late 1950s. He graduated from Wilson Technical College in North Carolina with a degree in mechanical engineering, and his engines won NASCAR's championship in 1983 with Bobby Alison and DiGard Motorsports.

Yates purchased his team from Harry Ranier in 1988, with talented up-and-comer Davey Allison driving. The team finished second in its first race, the 1988 Daytona 500, Allison having chased his father Bobby across the finish line. Allison contended NASCAR's championship in 1991 and '92, finishing third in points with five wins in both years. But the young driver was killed in a helicopter accident in 1993.

Yates replaced Allison with Ernie Irvan, who continued to win races for the team until he was seriously injured in a crash at Michigan. Yates hired Dale Jarrett to replace Irvan, who came back later in the year to drive a second car beside Jarrett. In 1996, Jarrett won the Busch Clash at Daytona, the Daytona 500, the Charlotte 600 and the Brickyard 400, finishing third in the championship. Three years later, he won his and Yates's first and only championship, having taken four race victories.

Yates's last win came with Jarrett at Talladega in October, 2005. He retired as a NASCAR team owner at the end of 2007, handing the team over to his son, Doug. In 2010, he came out of retirement to form a new company, Robert Yates Racing Engines. He was diagnosed with liver cancer in 2016 and succumbed to the disease a year later, in October, 2017. He was 74.

MAJOR RESULTS

OTHER CHAMPIONSHIP RACING SERIES WORLDWIDE

Compiled by DAVID HAYHOE and JOÃO PAULO CUNHA - www.forix.com

FIA Formula E Championship

2015–16

HONG KONG EPRIX, Hong Kong Central HarbourFront Circuit, China, 9 October. Round 1. 45 laps of the 1.156-mile/1.860km circuit, 52.009 miles/83.700km.
1 Sébastien Buemi, CH (Renault Z.E.16), 53m 13.298s, 58.632mph/94.360km/h; **2** Lucas di Grassi, BR (Abt Schaeffler FE02), +2.477s; **3** Nick Heidfeld, D (Mahindra M3ELECTRO), +5.522s; **4** Nicolas Prost, F (Renault Z.E.16), +7.360s; **5** António Félix da Costa, P (Andretti ATEC-02), +17.987s; **6** Robin Frijns, NL (Andretti ATEC-02), +21.161s; **7** Jérôme d'Ambrosio, B (Penske 701-EV), +28.443s; **8** Oliver Turvey, GB (NextEV NIO), +30.355s; **9** Maro Engel, D (Venturi VM200-FE-02), +30.898s; **10** Stéphane Sarrazin, F (Venturi VM200-FE-02), +31.734s; **11** Nelson Piquet Jr, BR (NextEV NIO), +35.256s; **12** Adam Carroll, GB (Jaguar I-type 1), +43.839s; **13** Sam Bird, GB (Virgin DSV-02), +48.058s; **14** Loïc Duval, F (Penske 701-EV), -2 laps; **15** Felix Rosenqvist, S (Mahindra M3ELECTRO), -2; Daniel Abt, D (Abt Schaeffler FE02), -11 (DNF-out of energy); Jean-Éric Vergne, F (Renault Z.E.16), -14 (DNF-out of energy); Mitch Evans, NZ (Jaguar I-type 1), -21 (DNF-mechanical); José María López, RA (Virgin DSV-02), -30 (DNF-accident); Ma Qing Hua, CHN (Renault Z.E.16), -44 (DNF-accident).
Fastest race lap: Rosenqvist, 1m 02.947s, 66.098mph/106.375km/h.
Pole position: Piquet Jr, 1m 03.099s, 65.939mph/106.118km/h.
Championship points
Drivers: 1 Buemi, 25; **2** di Grassi, 18; **3** Heidfeld, 15; **4** Prost, 12; **5** da Costa, 10; **6** Frijns, 8.
Teams: 1 Renault e.Dams, 37; **2** ABT Schaeffler Audi Sport, 18; **3** Andretti Formula E, 18.

MARRAKESH EPRIX, Circuit International Automobile Moulay El Hassan, Agdal, Marrakesh, Morocco, 12 November. Round 2. 33 laps of the 1.846-mile/2.971km circuit, 60.921 miles/98.043km.
1 Sébastien Buemi, CH (Renault Z.E.16), 47m 40.840s, 76.661mph/123.374km/h; **2** Sam Bird, GB (Virgin DSV-02), +2.457s; **3** Felix Rosenqvist, S (Mahindra M3ELECTRO), +7.195s; **4** Nicolas Prost, F (Renault Z.E.16), +11.586s; **5** Lucas di Grassi, BR (ABT Schaeffler FE02), +13.771s; **6** Daniel Abt, D (ABT Schaeffler FE02), +18.233s; **7** Oliver Turvey, GB (NextEV NIO), +21.710s; **8** Jean-Éric Vergne, F (Renault Z.E.16), +28.011s; **9** Nick Heidfeld, D (Mahindra M3ELECTRO), +33.699s; **10** José María López, RA (Virgin DSV-02), +33.863s; **11** Robin Frijns, NL (Andretti ATEC-02), +37.092s; **12** Stéphane Sarrazin, F (Venturi VM200-FE-02), +40.683s; **13** Jérôme d'Ambrosio, B (Penske 701-EV), +42.034s; **14** Adam Carroll, GB (Jaguar I-type 1), +49.026s; **15** Ma Qing Hua, CHN (Renault Z.E.16), +50.433s; **16** Nelson Piquet Jr, BR (NextEV NIO), +1m 15.452s; **17** Mitch Evans, NZ (Jaguar I-type 1), -1 lap; **18** Loïc Duval, F (Penske 701-EV), -3; Maro Engel, D (Venturi VM200-FE-02), -7 (DNF); António Félix da Costa, P (Andretti ATEC-02), -12 (DNF).
Fastest race lap: Duval, 1m 22.600s, 80.459mph/129.486km/h.
Pole position: Rosenqvist, 1m 21.509s, 81.536mph/131.219km/h.

BUENOS AIRES EPRIX, Circuit de Puerto Madero, Buenos Aires, Argentina, 18 February. Round 3. 37 laps of the 1.541-mile/2.480km circuit, 57.017 miles/91.760km.
1 Sébastien Buemi, CH (Renault Z.E.16), 45m 45.623s, 74.759mph/120.313km/h; **2** Jean-Éric Vergne, F (Renault Z.E.16), +2.996s; **3** Lucas di Grassi, BR (ABT Schaeffler FE02), +6.921s; **4** Nicolas Prost, F (Renault Z.E.16), +8.065s; **5** Nelson Piquet Jr, BR (NextEV NIO), +9.770s; **6** Loïc Duval, F (Penske 701-EV), +35.103s; **7** Daniel Abt, D (ABT Schaeffler FE02), +35.801s; **8** Jérôme d'Ambrosio, B (Penske 701-EV), +36.335s; **9** Oliver Turvey, GB (NextEV NIO), +37.111s; **10** José María López, RA (Virgin DSV-02), +38.206s; **11** António Félix da Costa, P (Andretti ATEC-02), +43.740s; **12** Stéphane Sarrazin, F (Venturi VM200-FE-02), +44.243s; **13** Mitch Evans, NZ (Jaguar I-Type 1), +44.918s *; **14** Robin Frijns, NL (Andretti ATEC-02), +49.683s; **15** Nick Heidfeld, D (Mahindra M3ELECTRO), +51.456s; **16** Ma Qing Hua, CHN (Renault Z.E.16), -1 lap; **17** Adam Carroll, GB (Jaguar I-Type 1), -1; **18** Felix Rosenqvist, S (Mahindra M3ELECTRO), -3; Maro Engel, D (Venturi VM200-FE-02), -11 (NC); Sam Bird, GB (Virgin DSV-02), -17 (DNF-accident).
** includes 5s penalty for speeding under Full Course Yellow.*
Fastest race lap: Rosenqvist, 1m 09.467s, 79.859mph/128.521km/h.
Pole position: di Grassi, 1m 09.404s, 79.932mph/128.638km/h.
Championship points
Drivers: 1 Buemi, 75; **2** di Grassi, 46; **3** Prost, 36; **4** Vergne, 22; **5** Rosenqvist, 20; **6** Bird, 18.
Teams: 1 Renault e.Dams, 111; **2** ABT Schaeffler Audi Sport, 60; **3** Mahindra Racing, 37.

MEXICO CITY EPRIX, Autódromo Hermanos Rodríguez, Mexico City, D.F., Mexico, 1 April. Round 4. 45 laps of the 1.301-mile/2.093km circuit, 58.524 miles/94.185km.
1 Lucas di Grassi, BR (ABT Schaeffler FE02), 56m 27.535s, 62.194mph/100.092km/h; **2** Jean-Éric Vergne, F (Renault Z.E.16), +1.966s; **3** Sam Bird, GB (Virgin DSV-02), +7.480s *; **4** Mitch Evans, NZ (Jaguar I-Type 1), +9.770s; **5** Nicolas Prost, F (Renault Z.E.16), +9.956s; **6** José María López, RA (Virgin DSV-02), +10.631s; **7** Daniel Abt, D (ABT Schaeffler FE02), +11.694s; **8** Adam Carroll, GB (Jaguar I-Type 1), +13.722s; **9** Nelson Piquet Jr, BR (NextEV NIO), +14.156s; **10** Esteban Gutiérrez, MEX (Renault Z.E.16), +15.717s; **11** Robin Frijns, NL (Andretti ATEC-02), +21.459s; **12** Nick Heidfeld, D (Mahindra M3ELECTRO), +27.232s; **13** Sébastien Buemi, CH (Renault Z.E.16), +1m 01.365s; **14** Jérôme d'Ambrosio, B (Penske 701-EV), +1m 09.646s **; **15** Stéphane Sarrazin, F (Venturi VM200-FE-02), -1 lap; **16** Felix Rosenqvist, S (Mahindra M3ELECTRO), -2 (DNF-accident); Maro Engel, D (Venturi VM200-FE-02), -7 (DNF-lost power); António Félix da Costa, P (Andretti ATEC-02), -13 (DNF-gearbox); Loïc Duval, F (Penske 701-EV), -20 (DNF-electrical); Oliver Turvey, GB (NextEV NIO), -33 (DNF-electrical).
** includes 2s penalty for unsafe release.*
*** includes 37s penalty for short-cutting.*
Fastest race lap: Buemi, 1m 03.102s, 74.195mph/119.406km/h.
Pole position: Turvey, 1m 02.867s, 74.473mph/119.853km/h.
Championship points
Drivers: 1 Buemi, 76; **2** di Grassi, 71; **3** Prost, 46; **4** Vergne, 40; **5** Bird, 33; **6** Rosenqvist, 20.
Teams: 1 Renault e.Dams, 122; **2** ABT Schaeffler Audi Sport, 91; **3** DS Virgin Racing, 43.

MONACO EPRIX, Monte-Carlo Street Circuit, Monaco, 13 May. Round 5. 51 laps of the 1.097-mile/1.765km circuit, 55.933 miles/90.015km.
1 Sébastien Buemi, CH (Renault Z.E.16), 51m 05.488s, 65.685mph/105.710km/h; **2** Lucas di Grassi, BR (ABT Schaeffler FE02), +0.320s; **3** Nick Heidfeld, D (Mahindra M3ELECTRO), +13.678s; **4** Nelson Piquet Jr, BR (NextEV NIO), +19.074s; **5** Maro Engel, D (Venturi VM200-FE-02), +19.518s; **6** Felix Rosenqvist, S (Mahindra M3ELECTRO), +19.599s; **7** Daniel Abt, D (ABT Schaeffler FE02), +20.430s; **8** Esteban Gutiérrez, MEX (Renault Z.E.16), +32.295s; **9** Nicolas Prost, F (Renault Z.E.16), +35.667s; **10** Mitch Evans, NZ (Jaguar I-Type 1), +38.410s; **11** António Félix da Costa, P (Andretti ATEC-02), +1m 08.330s *; **12** Robin Frijns, NL (Andretti ATEC-02), +1m 14.053s; **13** Oliver Turvey, GB (NextEV NIO), -1 lap; **14** Adam Carroll, GB (Jaguar I-Type 1), -1; **15** Stéphane Sarrazin, F (Venturi VM200-FE-02), -2; José María López, RA (Virgin DSV-02), -8 (NC); Jérôme d'Ambrosio, B (Penske 701-EV), -8 (NC); Loïc Duval, F (Penske 701-EV), -11 (NC); Sam Bird, GB (Virgin DSV-02), -15 (NC); Jean-Éric Vergne, F (Renault Z.E.16), -31 (DNF-accident).
** includes 33s penalty.*
Fastest race lap: Bird, 53.822s, 73.356mph/118.055km/h.
Pole position: Buemi, 53.313s, 74.056mph/119.182km/h.
Championship points
Drivers: 1 Buemi, 104; **2** di Grassi, 89; **3** Prost, 48; **4** Vergne, 40; **5** Bird, 34; **6** Heidfeld, 32.
Teams: 1 Renault e.Dams, 152; **2** ABT Schaeffler Audi Sport, 115; **3** Mahindra Racing, 60.

PARIS EPRIX, Circuit des Invalides, Paris, France, 20 May. Round 6. 49 laps of the 1.193-mile/1.920km circuit, 58.459 miles/94.080km.
1 Sébastien Buemi, CH (Renault Z.E.16), 59m 41.125s, 58.766mph/94.575km/h; **2** José María López, RA (Virgin DSV-02), +0.707s; **3** Nick Heidfeld, D (Mahindra M3ELECTRO), +2.043s; **4** Felix Rosenqvist, S (Mahindra M3ELECTRO), +2.621s; **5** Nicolas Prost, F (Renault Z.E.16), +3.521s; **6** Robin Frijns, NL (Andretti ATEC-02), +7.999s *; **7** Nelson Piquet Jr, BR (NextEV NIO), +32.420s; **8** Tom Dillmann, F (Venturi VM200-FE-02), +32.929s; **9** Mitch Evans, NZ (Jaguar I-Type 1), +33.369s; **10** Stéphane Sarrazin, F (Venturi VM200-FE-02), +34.051s; **11** Esteban Gutiérrez, MEX (Renault Z.E.16), +36.197s **; **12** Oliver Turvey, GB (NextEV NIO), +40.082s ***; **13** Daniel Abt, D (ABT Schaeffler FE02), -1 lap (DNF-battery); **14** Mike Conway, GB (Penske 701-EV), -1; **15** Adam Carroll, GB (Jaguar I-Type 1), -1; **16** Sam Bird, GB (Virgin DSV-02), -2; Lucas di Grassi, BR (ABT Schaeffler FE02), -11 (DNF-accident); Jérôme d'Ambrosio, B (Penske 701-EV), -14 (DNF-withdrew); Jean-Éric Vergne, F (Renault Z.E.16), -16 (DNF-accident); António Félix da Costa, P (Andretti ATEC-02), -31 (DNF-accident).
** includes 5s penalty for speeding under yellow flag.*
*** includes 5s penalty for speeding under yellow flag.*
**** includes 5s penalty for speeding under yellow flag.*
Fastest race lap: Bird, 1m 02.422s, 68.804mph/110.730km/h.
Pole position: Buemi, 1m 02.319s, 68.918mph/110.913km/h.
Championship points
Drivers: 1 Buemi, 132; **2** di Grassi, 89; **3** Prost, 58; **4** Heidfeld, 47; **5** Vergne, 40; **6** Rosenqvist, 40.
Teams: 1 Renault e.Dams, 190; **2** ABT Schaeffler Audi Sport, 115; **3** Mahindra Racing, 87.

BERLIN EPRIX, Tempelhof Airport Street Circuit, Berlin, Germany, 10/11 June. Round 7. 44 and 46 laps of the 1.415-mile/2.277km circuit.
Race 1 (62.254 miles/100.188km).
1 Felix Rosenqvist, S (Mahindra M3ELECTRO), 53m 19.661s, 70.043mph/112.723km/h; **2** Lucas di Grassi, BR (ABT Schaeffler FE02), +2.232s; **3** Nick Heidfeld, D (Mahindra M3ELECTRO), +4.058s; **4** José María López, RA (Virgin DSV-02), +13.638s; **5** Nicolas Prost, F (Renault Z.E.16), +19.068s; **6** Daniel Abt, D (ABT Schaeffler FE02), +19.799s; **7** Sam Bird, GB (Virgin DSV-02), +20.065s; **8** Jean-Éric Vergne, F (Renault Z.E.16), +20.689s *; **9** Maro Engel, D (Venturi VM200-FE-02), +39.030s; **10** Oliver Turvey, GB (NextEV NIO), +40.985s; **11** Stéphane Sarrazin, F (Renault Z.E.16), +42.682s; **12** Nelson Piquet Jr, BR (NextEV NIO), +42.980s; **13** Jérôme d'Ambrosio, B (Penske 701-EV), +45.712s; **14** Adam Carroll, GB (Jaguar I-Type 1), +49.658s; **15** Loïc Duval, F (Penske 701-EV), +59.010s; **16** António Félix da Costa, P (Andretti ATEC-02), +1m 00.269s; **17** Robin Frijns, NL (Andretti ATEC-02), +1m 02.463s; **18** Tom Dillmann, F (Venturi VM200-FE-02), +1m 07.695s; Mitch Evans, NZ (Jaguar I-Type 1), -28 laps (NC).
** includes 5s penalty for unsafe release.*
Disqualified: Sébastien Buemi, CH (Renault Z.E.16), +17.888s (incorrect tyre pressures-originally finished 5th).
Fastest race lap: Evans, 1m 10.224s, 72.532mph/116.729km/h.
Pole position: di Grassi, 1m 08.312s, 74.562mph/119.996km/h.

Race 2 (65.084 miles/104.742km).
1 Sébastien Buemi, CH (Renault Z.E.16), 56m 02.155s, 69.687mph/112.151km/h; **2** Felix Rosenqvist, S (Mahindra M3ELECTRO), +7.195s *; **3** Lucas di Grassi, BR (ABT Schaeffler FE02), +10.862s; **4** Daniel Abt, D (ABT Schaeffler FE02), +13.631s; **5** José María López, RA (Virgin DSV-02), +20.324s; **6** Jean-Éric Vergne, F (Renault Z.E.16), +20.751s; **7** Sam Bird, GB (Virgin DSV-02), +21.959s; **8** Nicolas Prost, F (Renault Z.E.16), +22.155s; **9** Oliver Turvey, GB (NextEV NIO), +34.949s; **10** Nick Heidfeld, D (Mahindra M3ELECTRO), +35.814s; **11** António Félix da Costa, P (Andretti ATEC-02), +44.057s; **12** Nelson Piquet Jr, BR (NextEV NIO), +44.439s; **13** Jérôme d'Ambrosio, B (Penske 701-EV), +47.336s; **14** Stéphane Sarrazin, F (Renault Z.E.16), +51.653s; **15** Tom Dillmann, F (Venturi VM200-FE-02), +56.977s; **16** Adam Carroll, GB (Jaguar I-Type 1), +1m 05.426s; **17** Mitch Evans, NZ (Jaguar I-Type 1), +1m 07.018s; **18** Robin Frijns, NL (Andretti ATEC-02), +1m 12.083s; Loïc Duval, F (Penske 701-EV), -13 laps (DNF-technical); Maro Engel, D (Venturi VM200-FE-02), -32 (NC).
** includes 10s penalty for unsafe release.*
Fastest race lap: Engel, 1m 09.509s, 73.278mph/117.930km/h.
Pole position: Rosenqvist, 1m 08.208s, 74.676mph/120.179km/h.
Championship points
Drivers: 1 Buemi, 157; **2** di Grassi, 125; **3** Rosenqvist, 86; **4** Prost, 72; **5** Heidfeld, 63; **6** Vergne, 52.
Teams: 1 Renault e.Dams, 229; **2** ABT Schaeffler Audi Sport, 171; **3** Mahindra Racing, 149.

QUALCOMM NEW YORK CITY EPRIX, Brooklyn Street Circuit, New York, USA, 15/16 July. Round 8. 43 and 49 laps of the 1.214-mile/1.953km circuit.
Race 1 (52.182 miles/83.979km).
1 Sam Bird, GB (Virgin DSV-02), 52m 29.275s, 59.650mph/95.998km/h; **2** Jean-Éric Vergne, F (Renault Z.E.16), +1.354s; **3** Stéphane Sarrazin, F (Renault Z.E.16), +4.392s; **4** Lucas di Grassi, BR (ABT Schaeffler FE02), +6.155s; **5** Loïc Duval, F (Penske 701-EV), +8.428s; **6** Oliver Turvey, GB (NextEV NIO), +8.952s; **7** Pierre Gasly, F (Renault Z.E.16), +9.321s; **8** Nicolas Prost, F (Renault Z.E.16), +10.036s; **9** Robin Frijns, NL (Andretti ATEC-02), +11.019s; **10** Adam Carroll, GB (Jaguar I-Type 1), +12.073s; **11** Nelson Piquet Jr, BR (NextEV NIO), +12.977s; **12** António Félix da Costa, P (Andretti ATEC-02), +13.341s; **13** Tom Dillmann, F (Venturi VM200-FE-02), +16.337s; **14** Daniel Abt, D (ABT Schaeffler FE02), -1 lap; **15** Felix Rosenqvist, S (Mahindra M3ELECTRO), -1; Nick Heidfeld, D (Mahindra M3ELECTRO), -8 (DNF-wheel); Maro Engel, D (Venturi VM200-FE-02), -13 (NC); Alex Lynn, GB (Virgin DSV-02), -20 (DNF-driveshaft); Jérôme d'Ambrosio, B (Penske 701-EV), -21 (DNF); Mitch Evans, NZ (Jaguar I-Type 1), -25 (NC).
Fastest race lap: Engel, 1m 03.883s, 68.386mph/110.057km/h.
Pole position: Lynn, 1m 03.296s, 69.020mph/111.078km/h.

Race 2 (59.463 miles/95.697km).
1 Sam Bird, GB (Virgin DSV-02), 58m 09.388s, 61.348mph/98.730km/h; **2** Felix Rosenqvist, S (Mahindra M3ELECTRO), +11.381s; **3** Nick Heidfeld, D (Mahindra M3ELECTRO), +12.319s; **4** Pierre Gasly, F (Renault Z.E.16), +12.355s; **5** Lucas di Grassi, BR (ABT Schaeffler FE02), +23.451s; **6** Nicolas Prost, F (Renault Z.E.16), +30.470s; **7** Tom Dillmann, F (Venturi VM200-FE-02), +41.862s; **8** Jean-Éric Vergne, F (Renault Z.E.16), +52.292s; **9** Robin Frijns, NL (Andretti ATEC-02), +1m 00.475s; **10** Jérôme d'Ambrosio, B (Penske 701-EV), +1m 12.659s; **11** Adam Carroll, GB (Jaguar I-Type 1), +1m 41.134s; **12** Stéphane Sarrazin, F (Renault Z.E.16), -1 lap; **13** Loïc Duval, F (Penske 701-EV), -1; **14** Oliver Turvey, GB (NextEV NIO), -1; **15** António Félix da Costa, P (Andretti ATEC-02), -1; **16** Nelson Piquet Jr, BR (NextEV NIO), -3; Maro Engel, D (Venturi VM200-FE-02), -27 (DNF-steering); Alex Lynn, GB (Virgin DSV-02), -30 (DNF-electronics); Daniel Abt, D (ABT Schaeffler FE02), -31 (NC); Mitch Evans, NZ (Jaguar I-Type 1), -44 (DNF-battery).
Fastest race lap: Abt, 1m 03.898s, 68.370mph/110.031km/h.
Pole position: Bird, 1m 02.285s, 70.141mph/112.881km/h.
Championship points
Drivers: 1 Buemi, 157; **2** di Grassi, 147; **3** Rosenqvist, 104; **4** Bird, 100; **5** Prost, 84; **6** Heidfeld, 78.
Teams: 1 Renault e.Dams, 259; **2** ABT Schaeffler Audi Sport, 194; **3** Mahindra Racing, 182.

HYDRO-QUÉBEC MONTRÉAL EPRIX, Montréal Street Circuit, Québec, Canada, 29/30 July. Round 9. 35 and 37 laps of the 1.706-mile/2.745km circuit.
Race 1 (59.698 miles/96.075km).
1 Lucas di Grassi, BR (ABT Schaeffler FE02), 56m 55.592s, 62.921mph/101.262km/h; **2** Jean-Éric Vergne, F (Renault Z.E.16), +0.350s; **3** Stéphane Sarrazin, F (Renault Z.E.16), +7.869s; **4** Daniel Abt, D (ABT Schaeffler FE02), +8.592s; **5** Sam Bird, GB (Virgin DSV-02), +8.913s; **6** Nicolas Prost, F (Renault Z.E.16), +10.058s; **7** Mitch Evans, NZ (Jaguar I-Type 1), +10.457s; **8** Robin Frijns, NL (Andretti ATEC-02), +15.836s; **9** Felix Rosenqvist, S (Mahindra M3ELECTRO), +16.764s; **10** Tom Dillmann, F (Venturi VM200-FE-02), +19.320s; **11** Jérôme d'Ambrosio, B (Penske 701-EV), +20.229s; **12** Maro Engel, D (Venturi VM200-FE-02), +22.314s; **13** Nelson Piquet Jr, BR (NextEV NIO), +23.145s; **14** António Félix da Costa, P (Andretti ATEC-02), +34.786s; **15** Oliver Turvey, GB (NextEV NIO), +46.996s; **16** Adam Carroll, GB (Jaguar I-Type 1), +49.612s; Loïc Duval, F (Penske 701-EV), -9 laps (NC); José María López, RA (Virgin DSV-02), -12 (DNF-acci-

dent); Nick Heidfeld, D (Mahindra M3ELECTRO), -22 (DNF-accident).
Disqualified: Sébastien Buemi, CH (Renault Z.E.16), +8.256s (originally finished 4th).
Fastest race lap: Duval, 1m 24.536s, 72.636mph/116.896km/h.
Pole position: di Grassi, 1m 22.869s, 74.097mph/119.248km/h.

Race 2 (63.110 miles/101.565km).
1 Jean-Éric Vergne, F (Renault Z.E.16), 54m 12.606s, 69.849mph/112.412km/h; **2** Felix Rosenqvist, S (Mahindra M3ELECTRO), +0.896s; **3** José María López, RA (Virgin DSV-02), +4.468s; **4** Sam Bird, GB (Virgin DSV-02), +7.114s; **5** Nick Heidfeld, D (Mahindra M3ELECTRO), +21.933s; **6** Daniel Abt, D (ABT Schaeffler FE02), +24.444s; **7** Lucas di Grassi, BR (ABT Schaeffler FE02), +24.855s; **8** Stéphane Sarrazin, F (Renault Z.E.16), +26.038s; **9** Jérôme d'Ambrosio, B (Penske 701-EV), +28.282s; **10** Tom Dillmann, F (Venturi VM200-FE-02), +28.591s; **11** Sébastien Buemi, CH (Renault Z.E.16), +35.170s; **12** Mitch Evans, NZ (Jaguar I-Type 1), +36.548s; **13** Robin Frijns, NL (Andretti ATEC-02), +36.826s; **14** Adam Carroll, GB (Jaguar I-Type 1), +36.972s; **15** António Félix da Costa, P (Andretti ATEC-02), +39.720s; **16** Nelson Piquet Jr, BR (NextEV NIO), +46.751s; **17** Oliver Turvey, GB (NextEV NIO), +49.116s; **18** Maro Engel, D (Venturi VM200-FE-02), +1m 33.530s; **19** Loïc Duval, F (Penske 701-EV), -3 laps (DNF-not running); Nicolas Prost, F (Renault Z.E.16), -5 (NC).
Fastest race lap: Prost, 1m 23.444s, 73.586mph/118.426km/h.
Pole position: Rosenqvist, 1m 22.344s, 74.569mph/120.008km/h.

Final championship points
Drivers
1 Lucas di Grassi, BR, 181; **2** Sébastien Buemi, CH, 157; **3** Felix Rosenqvist, S, 127; **4** Sam Bird, GB, 122; **5** Jean-Éric Vergne, F, 117; **6** Nicolas Prost, F, 93; **7** Nick Heidfeld, D, 88; **8** Daniel Abt, D, 67; **9** José María López, RA, 65; **10** Stéphane Sarrazin, F, 36; **11** Nelson Piquet Jr, BR, 33; **12** Oliver Turvey, GB, 26; **13** Robin Frijns, NL, 24; **14** Mitch Evans, NZ, 22; **15** Loïc Duval, F, 20; **16** Pierre Gasly, F, 18; **17** Maro Engel, D, 16; **18** Jérôme d'Ambrosio, B, 13; **19** Tom Dillmann, F, 12; **20** António Félix da Costa, P, 10; **21** Esteban Gutiérrez, MEX, 5; **22** Adam Carroll, GB, 5; **23** Alex Lynn, GB, 3.

Teams
1 Renault e.Dams, 268; **2** ABT Schaeffler Audi Sport, 248; **3** Mahindra Racing, 215; **4** DS Virgin Racing, 190; **5** Techeetah, 156; **6** NextEV NIO, 59; **7** Andretti Formula E, 34; **8** Faraday Future Dragon Racing, 33; **9** Venturi Formula E, 30; **10** Panasonic Jaguar Racing, 27.

FIA Formula 2 Championship

All cars are Dallara GP2-11-Renault GP2.

FIA FORMULA 2 CHAMPIONSHIP, Bahrain International Circuit, Sakhir, Bahrain, 15/16 April. Round 1. 32 and 23 laps of the 3.363-mile/5.412km circuit.
Race 1 (107.459 miles/172.938km).
1 Artem Markelov, RUS, 58m 18.977s, 110.716mph/178.181km/h; **2** Norman Nato, F, +7.891s; **3** Charles Leclerc, MC, +13.780s; **4** Jordan King, GB, +17.478s; **5** Oliver Rowland, GB, +18.144s; **6** Alexander Albon, T, +19.744s; **7** Luca Ghiotto, I, +27.056s; **8** Nobuharu Matsushita, J, +29.971s; **9** Antonio Fuoco, I, +30.950s; **10** Nyck de Vries, NL, +35.726s; **11** Nicholas Latifi, CDN, +47.578s; **12** Ralph Boschung, CH, +52.529s; **13** Sérgio Sette Câmara, BR, +55.146s *; **14** Sergio Canamasas, E, +56.311s; **15** Johnny Cecotto Jr, YV, +1m 06.723s; **16** Stefano Coletti, MC, +1m 12.903s; **17** Sean Gelael, RI, +1m 18.579s **; **18** Gustav Malja, S, +1m 24.483s; **19** Nabil Jeffri, MAL, +1m 38.982s; **20** Louis Delétraz, CH, +1m 39.106s.
** includes 5s penalty for forcing another driver off the track.*
*** includes 5s penalty for speeding in the pit lane.*
Fastest race lap: Coletti, 1m 45.843s, 114.379mph/184.076km/h.
Pole position: Leclerc, 1m 38.907s, 122.400mph/196.985km/h.

Race 2 (77.193 miles/124.230km).
1 Charles Leclerc, MC, 43m 01.023s, 107.879mph/173.615km/h; **2** Luca Ghiotto, I, +1.569s; **3** Oliver Rowland, GB, +2.898s; **4** Nicholas Latifi, CDN, +7.575s; **5** Jordan King, GB, +9.962s; **6** Nyck de Vries, NL, +10.865s; **7** Alexander Albon, T, +11.382s; **8** Artem Markelov, RUS, +18.953s; **9** Johnny Cecotto Jr, YV, +19.150s; **10** Antonio Fuoco, I, +19.983s; **11** Sergio Canamasas, E, +28.829s; **12** Louis Delétraz, CH, +31.187s; **13** Gustav Malja, S, +33.622s; **14** Nobuharu Matsushita, J, +34.392s; **15** Stefano Coletti, MC, +35.901s; **16** Nabil Jeffri, MAL, +41.595s; **17** Sean Gelael, RI, +52.029s; **18** Sérgio Sette Câmara, BR, +1m 08.570s; Ralph Boschung, CH, -14 laps (DNF-suspension); Norman Nato, F, -23 (DNF-accident).
Fastest race lap: Sette Câmara, 1m 43.950s, 116.462mph/187.428km/h.
Pole position: Matsushita.
Championship points
Drivers: 1 Leclerc, 36; **2** Markelov, 28; **3** Rowland, 20; **4** Ghiotto, 18; **5** Nato, 18; **6** King, 18.
Teams: 1 RUSSIAN TIME, 46; **2** Prema Racing, 38; **3** DAMS, 28.

FIA FORMULA 2 CHAMPIONSHIP, Circuit de Catalunya, Montmeló, Barcelona, Spain, 13/14 May. Round 2. 37 and 26 laps of the 2.892-mile/4.655km circuit.
Race 1 (106.944 miles/172.109km).
1 Charles Leclerc, MC, 1h 02m 33.684s, 102.639mph/165.182km/h; **2** Luca Ghiotto, I, +3.730s; **3** Oliver Rowland, GB, +11.146s; **4** Nobuharu Matsushita, J, +14.103s; **5** Alexander Albon, T, +17.319s; **6** Nicholas Latifi, CDN, +23.879s; **7** Gustav Malja, S, +24.779s; **8** Artem Markelov, RUS, +25.403s; **9** Jordan King, GB, +30.967s; **10** Nyck de Vries, NL, +43.832s; **11** Louis Delétraz, CH, +50.283s; **12** Ralph Boschung, CH, +58.201s *; **13** Antonio Fuoco, I, +1m 05.970s **; **14** Sérgio Sette Câmara, BR, +1m 05.973s ***; **15** Sean Gelael, RI, +1m 08.333s; **16** Norman Nato, F, +1m 09.241s; **17** Johnny Cecotto Jr, YV, +1m 27.784s ****; **18** Nabil Jeffri, MAL, +1m 29.521s; **19** Roberto Merhi, E, -4 laps (DNF-broken floor); Sergio Canamasas, E, -29 (DNF-electrics).
** includes 15s penalty for leaving the track + exceeding the VSC speed limit exiting the pit lane.*
*** includes 10s penalty for causing an accident.*
**** includes 20s penalty which includes causing an accident.*
***** includes 20s penalty.*
Fastest race lap: Markelov, 1m 34.294s, 110.430mph/177.720km/h.
Pole position: Leclerc, 1m 29.285s, 116.625mph/187.691km/h.

Race 2 (75.126 miles/120.904km).
1 Nobuharu Matsushita, J, 42m 20.450s, 106.569mph/171.506km/h; **2** Oliver Rowland, GB, +3.309s; **3** Nicholas Latifi, CDN, +4.621s; **4** Charles Leclerc, MC, +9.177s; **5** Jordan King, GB, +15.333s; **6** Gustav Malja, S, +17.987s; **7** Luca Ghiotto, I, +18.092s; **8** Alexander Albon, T, +21.135s; **9** Artem Markelov, RUS, +21.552s; **10** Johnny Cecotto Jr, YV, +30.744s; **11** Sergio Canamasas, E, +31.549s; **12** Roberto Merhi, E, +34.434s; **13** Norman Nato, F, +35.271s; **14** Louis Delétraz, CH, +38.090s; **15** Sérgio Sette Câmara, BR, +39.446s; **16** Sean Gelael, RI, +46.950s *; **17** Ralph Boschung, CH, +50.226s; **18** Nabil Jeffri, MAL, +59.912s; Nyck de Vries, NL, -26 laps (DNF-accident); Antonio Fuoco, I, -26 (DNF-accident).
** includes 10s penalty for overtaking under safety car conditions.*
Fastest race lap: Boschung, 1m 34.670s, 109.991mph/177.014km/h.
Pole position: Markelov.
Championship points
Drivers: 1 Leclerc, 73; **2** Rowland, 47; **3** Ghiotto, 38; **4** Markelov, 34; **5** Matsushita, 31; **6** Latifi, 28.
Teams: 1 Prema Racing, 75; **2** DAMS, 75; **3** RUSSIAN TIME, 72.

FIA FORMULA 2 CHAMPIONSHIP, Monte-Carlo Street Circuit, Monaco, 26/27 May. Round 3. 41 and 30 laps of the 2.074-mile/3.337km circuit.
Race 1 (85.014 miles/136.817km).
1 Oliver Rowland, GB, 1h 00m 46.545s, 83.929mph/135.070km/h; **2** Artem Markelov, RUS, +0.864s; **3** Nobuharu Matsushita, J, +13.769s; **4** Alexander Albon, T, +19.738s; **5** Luca Ghiotto, I, +24.657s; **6** Gustav Malja, S, +28.082s; **7** Nyck de Vries, NL, +28.453s; **8** Johnny Cecotto Jr, YV, +29.125s; **9** Jordan King, GB, +45.552s; **10** Sergio Canamasas, E, +46.581s; **11** Antonio Fuoco, I, +47.818s; **12** Ralph Boschung, CH, +50.772s; **13** Sean Gelael, RI, +53.694s; **14** Nabil Jeffri, MAL, -1 lap; **15** Louis Delétraz, CH, -2; Sérgio Sette Câmara, BR, -8 (DNF-driveshaft); Charles Leclerc, MC, -15 (DNF-suspension); Norman Nato, F, -18 (DNF-suspension); Robert Visoiu, RO, -21 (DNF-accident); Nicholas Latifi, CDN, -35 (DNF-battery).
Fastest race lap: Leclerc, 1m 21.403s, 91.700mph/147.576km/h.
Pole position: Leclerc, 1m 19.309s, 94.121mph/151.473km/h.

Race 2 (62.205 miles/100.110km).
1 Nyck de Vries, NL, 41m 51.284s, 89.173mph/143.510km/h; **2** Johnny Cecotto Jr, YV, +9.834s; **3** Gustav Malja, S, +10.415s; **4** Luca Ghiotto, I, +10.881s; **5** Artem Markelov, RUS, +11.258s; **6** Alexander Albon, T, +11.901s; **7** Nobuharu Matsushita, J, +13.627s; **8** Jordan King, GB, +13.970s; **9** Oliver Rowland, GB, +28.993s; **10** Antonio Fuoco, I, +29.051s; **11** Nabil Jeffri, MAL, +34.041s; **12** Sean Gelael, RI, +42.732s; **13** Nicholas Latifi, CDN, +43.430s; **14** Sérgio Sette Câmara, BR, +46.423s; **15** Robert Visoiu, RO, +47.007s; **16** Louis Delétraz, CH, +53.179s *; **17** Sergio Canamasas, E, +55.677s; Charles Leclerc, MC, -10 laps (DNF-accident damage); Ralph Boschung, CH, -16 (DNF-gearbox); Norman Nato, F, -28 (DNF-accident damage).
** includes 3s penalty for causing an accident.*
Fastest race lap: Markelov, 1m 21.674s, 91.395mph/147.087km/h.
Pole position: Cecotto Jr.
Championship points
Drivers: 1 Leclerc, 77; **2** Rowland, 74; **3** Markelov, 60; **4** Ghiotto, 56; **5** Matsushita, 48; **6** Albon, 37.
Teams: 1 RUSSIAN TIME, 116; **2** DAMS, 102; **3** ART Grand Prix, 85.

FIA FORMULA 2 CHAMPIONSHIP, Baku City Circuit, Azerbaijan, 24/25 June. Round 4. 24 and 21 laps of the 3.730-mile/6.003km circuit.
Race 1 (89.458 miles/143.968km).
1 Charles Leclerc, MC, 52m 33.196s, 102.206mph/164.485km/h; **2** Nyck de Vries, NL, +3.469s; **3** Nicholas Latifi, CDN, +6.390s; **4** Artem Markelov, RUS, +11.694s; **5** Norman Nato, F, +17.074s; **6** Jordan King, GB, +18.570s; **7** Oliver Rowland, GB, +19.090s *; **8** Ralph Boschung, CH, +21.348s; **9** Sergio Canamasas, E, +22.870s; **10** Sergey Sirotkin, RUS, +24.042s; **11** Gustav Malja, S, +24.828s; **12** Nobuharu Matsushita, J, +25.696s; **13** Sérgio Sette Câmara, BR, +29.675s *; **14** Sean Gelael, RI, +33.101s *; **15** Robert Visoiu, RO, +33.320s *; **16** Luca Ghiotto, I, +49.207s; Louis Delétraz, CH, -13 laps (DNF-accident); Nabil Jeffri, MAL, -15 (DNF-accident); Antonio Fuoco, I, -18 (DNF-accident); Johnny Cecotto Jr, YV, -24 (DNF-accident).
** includes 10s penalty for failing to slow for yellow flags.*
Fastest race lap: Leclerc, 1m 54.025s, 117.766mph/189.526km/h.
Pole position: Leclerc, 1m 52.129s, 119.757mph/192.731km/h.

Race 2 (78.267 miles/125.959km).
1 Norman Nato, F, 40m 37.601s, 115.684mph/186.176km/h; **2** Charles Leclerc, MC, +8.717s *; **3** Nicholas Latifi, CDN, +11.574s; **4** Sergey Sirotkin, RUS, +12.792s; **5** Artem Markelov, RUS, +12.890s; **6** Nobuharu Matsushita, J, +14.472s; **7** Luca Ghiotto, I, +16.888s; **8** Ralph Boschung, CH, +21.387s; **9** Sérgio Sette Câmara, BR, +27.343s; **10** Sean Gelael, RI, +27.827s; **11** Robert Visoiu, RO, +31.612s; **12** Antonio Fuoco, I, +32.664s; **13** Gustav Malja, S, +34.645s; **14** Johnny Cecotto Jr, YV, +35.789s; **15** Sergio Canamasas, E, +49.243s *; **16** Louis Delétraz, CH, +57.152s; **17** Nabil Jeffri, MAL, +1m 38.931s; Nyck de Vries, NL, -13 laps (DNF-accident); Oliver Rowland, GB, -14 (DNF-gearbox).
** includes 10s penalty for failing to slow for yellow flags.*
Disqualified: Jordan King, GB, +12.505s (tyres below minimum pressure-originally finished 4th).
Fastest race lap: Leclerc, 1m 53.635s, 118.170mph/190.177km/h.
Pole position: Boschung.
Championship points
Drivers: 1 Leclerc, 122; **2** Rowland, 80; **3** Markelov, 78; **4** Ghiotto, 58; **5** Latifi, 53; **6** Matsushita, 52.
Teams: 1 RUSSIAN TIME, 136; **2** DAMS, 133; **3** Prema Racing, 124.

FIA FORMULA 2 CHAMPIONSHIP, Red Bull Ring, Spielberg, Austria, 8/9 July. Round 5. 40 and 28 laps of the 2.683-mile/4.318km circuit.
Race 1 (107.245 miles/172.594km).
1 Charles Leclerc, MC, 52m 21.629s, 122.981mph/197.918km/h; **2** Nicholas Latifi, CDN, +1.345s; **3** Antonio Fuoco, I, +5.160s; **4** Oliver Rowland, GB, +5.682s; **5** Alexander Albon, T, +9.846s; **6** Nobuharu Matsushita, J, +12.179s; **7** Ralph Boschung, CH, +19.400s; **8** Artem Markelov, RUS, +20.385s; **9** Jordan King, GB, +30.481s; **10** Sean Gelael, RI, +33.662s; **11** Robert Visoiu, RO, +35.636s; **12** Gustav Malja, S, +36.011s; **13** Nyck de Vries, NL, +44.145s; **14** Luca Ghiotto, I, +46.896s; **15** Sergio Canamasas, E, +48.883s; **16** Sérgio Sette Câmara, BR, +50.940s; **17** Louis Delétraz, CH, +53.423s; **18** Nabil Jeffri, MAL, +56.881s; **19** Raffaele Marciello, I, -1 lap; Norman Nato, F, -35 (DNF-driveshaft).
Fastest race lap: Matsushita, 1m 15.854s, 127.337mph/204.930km/h.
Pole position: Leclerc, 1m 13.396s, 131.602mph/211.793km/h.

Race 2 (75.048 miles/120.778km).
1 Artem Markelov, RUS, 40m 32.190s, 111.196mph/178.953km/h; **2** Alexander Albon, T, +1.458s; **3** Oliver Rowland, GB, +2.055s; **4** Luca Ghiotto, I, +5.840s; **5** Antonio Fuoco, I, +6.629s; **6** Jordan King, GB, +10.515s; **7** Norman Nato, F, +13.656s; **8** Nicholas Latifi, CDN, +15.922s *; **9** Sergio Canamasas, E, +15.979s; **10** Sérgio Sette Câmara, BR, +16.282s; **11** Sean Gelael, RI, +18.849s; **12** Nabil Jeffri, MAL, +20.948s; **13** Louis Delétraz, CH, +21.301s; **14** Nobuharu Matsushita, J, +22.443s; **15** Gustav Malja, S, +1m 07.922s; **16** Nyck de Vries, NL, -2 laps (DNF-accident damage); **17** Robert Visoiu, RO, -3 (DNF-accident damage); Ralph Boschung, CH, -13 (DNF-accident damage); Charles Leclerc, MC, -24 (DNF-accident); Raffaele Marciello, I, -28 (DNF-accident).
** includes 5s penalty for speeding in the pit lane.*
Fastest race lap: Markelov, 1m 16.119s, 126.894mph/204.217km/h.
Pole position: Markelov.
Championship points
Drivers: 1 Leclerc, 151; **2** Rowland, 102; **3** Markelov, 99; **4** Latifi, 72; **5** Ghiotto, 66; **6** Matsushita, 62.
Teams: 1 Prema Racing, 174; **2** DAMS, 174; **3** RUSSIAN TIME, 165.

FIA FORMULA 2 CHAMPIONSHIP, Silverstone Arena Grand Prix Circuit, Towcester, Northamptonshire, Great Britain, 15/16 July. Round 6. 28 and 21 laps of the 3.660-mile/5.891km circuit.
Race 1 (102.411 miles/164.814km).
1 Charles Leclerc, MC, 49m 23.075s, 124.524mph/200.402km/h; **2** Norman Nato, F, +8.866s; **3** Oliver Rowland, GB, +9.605s; **4** Artem Markelov, RUS, +17.743s; **5** Sergio Canamasas, E, +18.715s; **6** Luca Ghiotto, I, +24.284s; **7** Jordan King, GB, +26.498s; **8** Nicholas Latifi, CDN, +27.805s; **9** Sean Gelael, RI, +28.904s; **10** Nobuharu Matsushita, J, +34.560s; **11** Ralph Boschung, CH, +44.764s; **12** Louis Delétraz, CH, +46.536s; **13** Sérgio Sette Câmara, BR, +47.050s; **14** Gustav Malja, S, +50.673s; **15** Nabil Jeffri, MAL, +56.457s; **16** Antonio Fuoco, I, +1m 01.355s; **17** Robert Visoiu, RO, +1m 09.543s; **18** Alexander Albon, T, +1m 12.549s; **19** Callum Ilott, GB, -1 lap.
Did not start: Nyck de Vries, NL -driveshaft.
Fastest race lap: Matsushita, 1m 42.512s, 128.548mph/206.879km/h.
Pole position: Leclerc, 1m 38.427s, 133.883mph/215.465km/h.

Race 2 (76.787 miles/123.577km).
1 Nicholas Latifi, CDN, 37m 17.053s, 123.703mph/199.081km/h; **2** Luca Ghiotto, I, +1.717s; **3** Artem Markelov, RUS, +5.300s; **4** Sergio Canamasas, E, +7.698s; **5** Charles Leclerc, MC, +7.943s; **6** Norman Nato, F, +8.279s; **7** Nyck de Vries, NL, +8.801s; **8** Nobuharu Matsushita, J, +9.484s; **9** Gustav Malja, S, +10.618s; **10** Oliver Rowland, GB, +12.263s *; **11** Alexander Albon, T, +13.262s; **12** Robert Visoiu, RO, +13.535s; **13** Antonio Fuoco, I, +13.825s; **14** Louis Delétraz, CH, +14.386s; **15** Callum Ilott, GB, +14.665s; **16** Sérgio Sette Câmara, BR, +14.925s; **17** Sean Gelael, RI, +15.871s; **18** Nabil Jeffri, MAL, +45.918s; Ralph Boschung, CH, -4 laps (DNF-accident); Jordan King, GB, -20 (DNF-accident damage).
** includes 5s penalty for forcing another driver off the track.*
Fastest race lap: Leclerc, 1m 43.219s, 127.668mph/205.462km/h.
Pole position: Latifi.
Championship points
Drivers: 1 Leclerc, 188; **2** Markelov, 121; **3** Rowland, 117; **4** Latifi, 91; **5** Ghiotto, 86; **6** Nato, 67.
Teams: 1 Prema Racing, 211; **2** DAMS, 208; **3** RUSSIAN TIME, 207.

FIA FORMULA 2 CHAMPIONSHIP, Hungaroring, Mogyoród, Budapest, Hungary, 29/30 July. Round 7. 36 and 28 laps of the 2.722-mile/4.381km circuit.
Race 1 (97.975 miles/157.676km).
1 Oliver Rowland, GB, 58m 37.062s, 100.310mph/161.434km/h; **2** Nicholas Latifi, CDN, +0.235s; **3** Nyck de Vries, NL, +0.673s; **4** Charles Leclerc, MC, +1.405s; **5** Nobuharu Matsushita, J, +1.633s; **6** Luca Ghiotto, I, +2.534s; **7** Norman Nato, F, +3.079s; **8** Alexander Albon, T, +3.350s; **9** Santino Ferrucci, USA, +4.238s; **10** Louis Delétraz, CH, +6.627s; **11** Ralph Boschung, CH, +7.550s; **12** Nabil Jeffri, MAL, +8.179s; **13** Gustav Malja, S, +9.462s; **14** Sean Gelael, RI, +13.911s *; **15** Jordan King, GB, +16.126s **; **16** Sérgio Sette Câmara, BR, +19.069s *; **17** Artem Markelov, RUS, -3 laps (DNF-accident); Robert Visoiu, RO, -12 (DNF-accident); Sergio Canamasas, E, -12 (DNF-accident); Antonio Fuoco, I, -25 (DNF-oil pressure).
** includes 10s penalty for activating DRS before completing 2 laps.*
*** includes 10s penalty for leaving the track and rejoining unsafely.*
Fastest race lap: Latifi, 1m 30.153s, 108.704mph/174.942km/h.
Pole position: Rowland, 1m 26.731s, 112.993mph/181.845km/h.

Race 2 (76.198 miles/122.628km).
1 Nobuharu Matsushita, J, 44m 52.900s, 101.897mph/163.988km/h; **2** Oliver Rowland, GB, +4.307s; **3** Nyck de Vries, NL, +7.143s; **4** Charles Leclerc, MC, +11.635s; **5** Norman Nato, F, +12.458s; **6** Nicholas Latifi, CDN, +13.485s; **7** Alexander Albon, T, +16.754s; **8** Luca Ghiotto, I, +24.843s; **9** Artem Markelov, RUS, +25.577s; **10** Sean Gelael, RI, +33.887s; **11** Jordan King, GB, +35.770s; **12** Louis Delétraz, CH, +35.823s; **13** Sérgio Sette Câmara, BR, +41.847s; **14** Santino Ferrucci, USA, +42.122s; **15** Nabil Jeffri, MAL, +1m 26.947s *; **16** Ralph Boschung, CH, -1 lap; **17** Antonio Fuoco, I, -1; Gustav Malja, S, -5 (NC); Sergio Canamasas, E, -7 (DNF-accident); Robert Visoiu, RO, -8 (DNF-accident).
** includes 10s penalty for causing an accident.*
Fastest race lap: Fuoco, 1m 29.121s, 109.963mph/176.968km/h.
Pole position: Albon.
Championship points
Drivers: 1 Leclerc, 208; **2** Rowland, 158; **3** Markelov, 123; **4** Latifi, 115; **5** Ghiotto, 95; **6** Matsushita, 91.

Teams: **1** DAMS, 273; **2** Prema Racing, 231; **3** RUSSIAN TIME, 218.

FIA FORMULA 2 CHAMPIONSHIP, Circuit de Spa-Francorchamps, Stavelot, Belgium, 26/27 August. Round 8. 25 and 18 laps of the 4.352-mile/7.004km circuit.
Race 1 (108.725 miles/174.976km).
1 Artem Markelov, RUS, 52m 55.172s, 123.358mph/198.526km/h *; **2** Luca Ghiotto, I, +1.057s; **3** Antonio Fuoco, I, +1.446s; **4** Gustav Malja, S, +14.912s; **5** Nyck de Vries, NL, +16.149s; **6** Sérgio Sette Câmara, BR, +24.356s; **7** Roberto Merhi, E, +28.479s; **8** Norman Nato, F, +30.611s; **9** Santino Ferrucci, USA, +37.735s; **10** Robert Visoiu, RO, +39.133s; **11** Nabil Jeffri, MAL, +42.608s; **12** Alexander Albon, T, +54.552s *; **13** Ralph Boschung, CH, +55.217s; **14** Louis Delétraz, CH, +56.070s; **15** Sean Gelael, RI, +1m 09.082s; **16** Nobuharu Matsushita, J, -1 lap; Jordan King, GB, -24 (DNF-puncture/differential).
** includes 5s penalty for leaving the track and gaining an advantage.*
Disqualified: Charles Leclerc, MC, 52m 23.537s (originally finished 1st); Oliver Rowland, GB, +26.707s (originally finished 2nd).
Did not start: Nicholas Latifi, CDN (engine).
Fastest race lap: Markelov, 2m 00.204s, 130.340mph/209.763km/h.
Pole position: Leclerc, 2m 20.842s, 111.241mph/179.026km/h.

Race 2 (78.260 miles/125.948km).
1 Sérgio Sette Câmara, BR, 39m 40.215s, 118.481mph/190.678km/h; **2** Nyck de Vries, NL, +0.623s; **3** Luca Ghiotto, I, +2.403s; **4** Norman Nato, F, +3.109s; **5** Charles Leclerc, MC, +3.820s; **6** Roberto Merhi, E, +4.894s; **7** Antonio Fuoco, I, +5.448s; **8** Oliver Rowland, GB, +5.828s; **9** Nicholas Latifi, CDN, +6.690s; **10** Santino Ferrucci, USA, +9.202s; **11** Gustav Malja, S, +9.629s; **12** Louis Delétraz, CH, +10.556s; **13** Ralph Boschung, CH, +10.865s; **14** Jordan King, GB, +11.095s; **15** Nabil Jeffri, MAL, +12.070s; **16** Robert Visoiu, RO, +13.709s; **17** Sean Gelael, RI, +14.121s; **18** Alexander Albon, T, +17.543s; Nobuharu Matsushita, J, -4 laps (DNF-accident); Artem Markelov, RUS, -6 (DNF-exhaust).
Fastest race lap: King, 1m 59.965s, 130.600mph/210.181km/h.
Pole position: Nato.
Championship points
Drivers: **1** Leclerc, 218; **2** Rowland, 159; **3** Markelov, 150; **4** Ghiotto, 123; **5** Latifi, 115; **6** de Vries, 96.
Teams: **1** DAMS, 274; **2** RUSSIAN TIME, 273; **3** Prema Racing, 258.

FIA FORMULA 2 CHAMPIONSHIP, Autodromo Nazionale di Monza, Milan, Italy, 2/3 September. Round 9. 23 and 21 laps of the 3.600-mile/5.793km circuit.
Race 1 (82.599 miles/132.930km).
1 Antonio Fuoco, I, 44m 10.800s, 112.434mph/180.945km/h; **2** Nobuharu Matsushita, J, +0.351s; **3** Nicholas Latifi, CDN, +1.477s; **4** Luca Ghiotto, I, +3.085s *; **5** Sean Gelael, RI, +3.844s; **6** Sérgio Sette Câmara, BR, +5.268s; **7** Louis Delétraz, CH, +6.031s; **8** Gustav Malja, S, +6.930s; **9** Artem Markelov, RUS, +7.878s; **10** Jordan King, GB, +8.219s; **11** Roberto Merhi, E, +9.712s **; **12** Nabil Jeffri, MAL, +11.679s; **13** Norman Nato, F, +11.979s; **14** Alexander Albon, T, +12.046s ***; **15** Ralph Boschung, CH, +12.406s **; **16** Robert Visoiu, RO, +13.531s **; **17** Charles Leclerc, MC, +33.989s; **18** Nyck de Vries, NL, +1m 12.409s ****; Oliver Rowland, GB, -5 laps (DNF-wheel lost); Santino Ferrucci, USA, -18 (DNF-engine).
** includes 5s penalty for leaving the track and gaining an advantage.*
*** includes 5s penalty.*
**** includes 10s penalty for causing an accident.*
***** includes 20s penalty for causing an accident.*
Fastest race lap: Latifi, 1m 47.648s, 120.379mph/193.731km/h.
Pole position: Matsushita, 1m 30.982s, 142.430mph/229.218km/h.

Race 2 (75.400 miles/121.344km).
1 Luca Ghiotto, I, 33m 15.078s, 136.397mph/219.510km/h; **2** Sérgio Sette Câmara, BR, +2.296s; **3** Antonio Fuoco, I, +4.505s; **4** Louis Delétraz, CH, +6.246s; **5** Roberto Merhi, E, +11.803s; **6** Sean Gelael, RI, +17.305s; **7** Nobuharu Matsushita, J, +20.010s; **8** Alexander Albon, T, +20.588s; **9** Charles Leclerc, MC, +23.263s; **10** Norman Nato, F, +23.704s; **11** Oliver Rowland, GB, +27.419s; **12** Nyck de Vries, NL, +29.307s; **13** Ralph Boschung, CH, +29.659s; **14** Santino Ferrucci, USA, +29.906s; **15** Artem Markelov, RUS, +32.045s; **16** Nicholas Latifi, CDN, +32.965s; **17** Nabil Jeffri, MAL, +33.237s; **18** Gustav Malja, S, +57.447s; **19** Robert Visoiu, RO, +1m 00.129s; **20** Jordan King, GB, +1m 06.302s.
Fastest race lap: King, 1m 32.921s, 139.457mph/224.435km/h.
Pole position: Malja.
Championship points
Drivers: **1** Leclerc, 218; **2** Rowland, 159; **3** Markelov, 152; **4** Ghiotto, 150; **5** Latifi, 132; **6** Matsushita, 115.
Teams: **1** RUSSIAN TIME, 302; **2** Prema Racing, 295; **3** DAMS, 291.

FIA FORMULA 2 CHAMPIONSHIP, Circuito Permanente de Jerez, Jerez de la Frontera, Spain, 7/8 October. Round 10. 39 and 28 laps of the 2.751-mile/4.428km circuit.
Race 1 (107.306 miles/172.692km).
1 Charles Leclerc, MC, 1h 01m 31.999s, 104.631mph/168.388km/h; **2** Oliver Rowland, GB, +0.230s; **3** Antonio Fuoco, I, +0.917s; **4** Nicholas Latifi, CDN, +1.236s; **5** Artem Markelov, RUS, +2.685s; **6** Jordan King, GB, +6.744s; **7** Luca Ghiotto, I, +8.017s; **8** Alex Palou, E, +8.262s; **9** Nabil Jeffri, MAL, +14.483s; **10** Sérgio Sette Câmara, BR, +16.226s; **11** Norman Nato, F, +16.256s; **12** Alexander Albon, T, +17.122s; **13** Nyck de Vries, NL, +17.657s; **14** Gustav Malja, S, +24.855s; **15** Rene Binder, A, +26.942s; **16** Sean Gelael, RI, -1 lap; **17** Louis Delétraz, CH, -1; **18** Nobuharu Matsushita, J, -1; Santino Ferrucci, USA, -8 (DNF-accident); Ralph Boschung, CH, -12 (DNF-engine overheating).
Fastest race lap: Rowland, 1m 29.906s, 110.172mph/177.305km/h.
Pole position: Leclerc, 1m 24.682s, 116.968mph/188.243km/h.

Race 2 (77.040 miles/123.984km).
1 Artem Markelov, RUS, 43m 01.086s, 107.452mph/172.928km/h; **2** Nicholas Latifi, CDN, +11.840s; **3** Oliver Rowland, GB, +13.286s; **4** Luca Ghiotto, I, +14.691s; **5** Antonio Fuoco, I, +16.497s; **6** Nyck de Vries, NL, +20.201s; **7** Charles Leclerc, MC, +20.510s; **8** Alex Palou, E, +25.027s; **9** Alexander Albon, T, +25.613s; **10** Norman Nato, F, +30.411s; **11** Nobuharu Matsushita, J, +34.059s; **12** Louis Delétraz, CH, +38.074s; **13** Santino Ferrucci, USA, +44.257s; **14** Sérgio Sette Câmara, BR, +52.036s; **15** Nabil Jeffri, MAL, +52.395s; **16** Sean Gelael, RI, +52.516s; **17** Rene Binder, A, +52.658s; **18** Gustav Malja, S, +1m 04.836s; **19** Ralph Boschung, CH, -1 lap; Jordan King, GB, -25 (DNF-engine).
Fastest race lap: Binder, 1m 29.032s, 111.253mph/179.045km/h.
Pole position: Palou.
Championship points
Drivers: **1** Leclerc, 249; **2** Rowland, 189; **3** Markelov, 177; **4** Ghiotto, 164; **5** Latifi, 156; **6** Matsushita, 115.
Teams: **1** Prema Racing, 347; **2** DAMS, 345; **3** RUSSIAN TIME, 341.

FIA FORMULA 2 CHAMPIONSHIP, Yas Marina Circuit, Abu Dhabi, United Arab Emirates, 25/26 November. Round 11. 31 and 22 laps of the 3.451-mile/5.554km circuit.
Race 1 (106.913 miles/172.059km).
1 Artem Markelov, RUS, 59m 34.767s, 107.738mph/173.388km/h; **2** Charles Leclerc, MC, +16.265s; **3** Luca Ghiotto, I, +25.438s; **4** Nyck de Vries, NL, +27.181s; **5** Nicholas Latifi, CDN, +29.697s; **6** Nobuharu Matsushita, J, +31.974s; **7** Alexander Albon, T, +34.618s; **8** Jordan King, GB, +40.639s; **9** Sérgio Sette Câmara, BR, +43.305s; **10** Louis Delétraz, CH, +52.356s; **11** Gustav Malja, S, +1m 01.198s; **12** Alex Palou, E, +1m 04.596s *; **13** Norman Nato, F, +1m 12.209s; **14** Santino Ferrucci, USA, +1m 21.496s; **15** Sean Gelael, RI, +1m 23.795s; **16** Roberto Merhi, E, -1 lap; Lando Norris, GB, -26 (DNF); Nabil Jeffri, MAL, -31 (DNF).
** includes 5s penalty for speeding in the pit lane.*
Disqualified: Oliver Rowland, GB, 59m 28.088s (skid block thickness-originally finished 1st); Antonio Fuoco, I, +16.250s (front tyre pressure-originally finished 3rd).
Fastest race lap: Albon, 1m 50.314s, 112.623mph/181.249km/h.
Pole position: Markelov, 1m 47.181s, 115.915mph/186.547km/h.

Race 2 (75.853 miles/122.073km).
1 Charles Leclerc, MC, 41m 36.188s, 109.496mph/176.217km/h; **2** Alexander Albon, T, +1.293s; **3** Nicholas Latifi, CDN, +3.207s; **4** Nobuharu Matsushita, J, +4.105s; **5** Luca Ghiotto, I, +4.952s; **6** Artem Markelov, RUS, +14.758s; **7** Oliver Rowland, GB, +15.446s; **8** Sérgio Sette Câmara, BR, +24.795s; **9** Nyck de Vries, NL, +29.261s; **10** Roberto Merhi, E, +29.689s; **11** Antonio Fuoco, I, +29.912s; **12** Alex Palou, E, +30.999s; **13** Lando Norris, GB, +31.564s *; **14** Sean Gelael, RI, +38.714s; **15** Santino Ferrucci, USA, +39.605s; **16** Nabil Jeffri, MAL, +43.310s; **17** Gustav Malja, S, +49.659s *; **18** Norman Nato, F, -3 laps; Louis Delétraz, CH, -4 (DNF); Jordan King, GB, -11 (DNF).
** includes 5s penalty for leaving the track and gaining an advantage.*
Fastest race lap: King, 1m 51.315s, 111.610mph/179.619km/h.
Pole position: King.

Final championship points
Drivers
1 Charles Leclerc, MC, 282; **2** Artem Markelov, RUS, 210; **3** Oliver Rowland, GB, 191; **4** Luca Ghiotto, I, 185; **5** Nicholas Latifi, CDN, 178; **6** Nobuharu Matsushita, J, 131; **7** Nyck de Vries, NL, 114; **8** Antonio Fuoco, I, 98; **9** Norman Nato, F, 91; **10** Alexander Albon, T, 86; **11** Jordan King, GB, 62; **12** Sérgio Sette Câmara, BR, 47; **13** Gustav Malja, S, 44; **14** Sergio Canamasas, E, 21; **15** Sean Gelael, RI, 17; **16** Johnny Cecotto Jr, YV, 16; **17** Louis Delétraz, CH, 16; **18** Roberto Merhi, E, 16; **19** Ralph Boschung, CH, 11; **20** Sergey Sirotkin, RUS, 9; **21** Alex Palou, E, 5; **22** Santino Ferrucci, USA, 4; **23** Nabil Jeffri, MAL, 2; **24** Robert Visoiu, RO, 1.

Teams
1 RUSSIAN TIME, 395; **2** Prema Racing, 380; **3** DAMS, 369; **4** ART Grand Prix, 226; **5** Rapax, 137; **6** MP Motorsport, 109; **7** Pertamina Arden, 108; **8** Racing Engineering, 87; **9** Campos Racing, 17; **10** Trident, 9.

Japanese Championship Super Formula

All cars are Dallara SF14.

JAPANESE CHAMPIONSHIP SUPER FORMULA, Suzuka International Racing Course, Suzuka-shi, Mie Prefecture, Japan, 23 April. Round 1. 35 laps of the 3.608-mile/5.807km circuit, 126.291 miles/203.245km.
1 Kazuki Nakajima, J (-Toyota), 1h 03m 18.440s, 119.693mph/192.627km/h; **2** Naoki Yamamoto, J (-Honda), +5.086s; **3** Yuji Kunimoto, J (-Toyota), +8.823s; **4** Hiroaki Ishiura, J (-Toyota), +9.408s; **5** André Lotterer, D (-Toyota), +10.800s; **6** Koudai Tsukakoshi, J (-Honda), +11.266s; **7** Daisuke Nakajima, J (-Honda), +16.907s; **8** Takuya Izawa, J (-Honda), +18.307s; **9** Kamui Kobayashi, J (-Toyota), +18.950s; **10** Pierre Gasly, F (-Honda), +21.561s.
Fastest race lap: Tsukakoshi, 1m 40.404s, 129.376mph/208.211km/h.
Pole position: Nakajima, 1m 35.907s, 135.443mph/217.974km/h.

JAPANESE CHAMPIONSHIP SUPER FORMULA, Okayama International Circuit (TI Circuit Aida), Aida Gun, Okayama Prefecture, Japan, 27/28 May. Round 2. 30 and 51 laps of the 2.301-mile/3.703km circuit.
Race 2 (69.028 miles/111.090km).
1 André Lotterer, D (-Toyota), 37m 58.782s, 109.050mph/175.499km/h; **2** Yuhi Sekiguchi, J (-Toyota), +1.948s; **3** Nick Cassidy, NZ (-Toyota), +7.786s; **4** Kamui Kobayashi, J (-Toyota), +11.558s; **5** Naoki Yamamoto, J (-Honda), +14.919s; **6** Jann Mardenborough, GB (-Toyota), +15.492s; **7** Kenta Yamashita, J (-Toyota), +17.496s; **8** Hiroaki Ishiura, J (-Toyota), +18.752s; **9** Kazuki Nakajima, J (-Toyota), +25.369s; **10** Yuji Kunimoto, J (-Toyota), +28.965s.
Fastest race lap: Felix Rosenqvist, S (-Toyota), 1m 15.072s, 110.339mph/177.574km/h.
Pole position: Sekiguchi, 1m 13.387s, 112.873mph/181.651km/h.

Race 3 (117.348 miles/188.853km).
1 Yuhi Sekiguchi, J (-Toyota), 1h 09m 02.975s, 101.968mph/164.102km/h; **2** Hiroaki Ishiura, J (-Toyota), +0.408s; **3** André Lotterer, D (-Toyota), +2.586s; **4** Felix Rosenqvist, S (-Toyota), +3.252s; **5** Kamui Kobayashi, J (-Toyota), +5.922s; **6** Kenta Yamashita, J (-Toyota), +8.034s; **7** Pierre Gasly, F (-Honda), +10.233s; **8** Naoki Yamamoto, J (-Honda), +14.287s; **9** Yuji Kunimoto, J (-Toyota), +17.087s; **10** Tomoki Nojiri, J (-Honda), +17.732s.
Fastest race lap: Kobayashi, 1m 15.631s, 109.524mph/176.261km/h.
Pole position: Ishiura, 1m 13.918s, 112.062mph/180.346km/h.

JAPANESE CHAMPIONSHIP SUPER FORMULA, Fuji International Speedway, Sunto-gun, Shizuoka Prefecture, Japan, 9 July. Round 3. 55 laps of the 2.835-mile/4.563km circuit, 155.754 miles/250.661km.
1 Hiroaki Ishiura, J (-Toyota), 1h 20m 09.046s, 116.735mph/187.867km/h; **2** Felix Rosenqvist, S (-Toyota), +7.269s; **3** André Lotterer, D (-Toyota), +22.842s; **4** Yuhi Sekiguchi, J (-Toyota), +41.786s; **5** Pierre Gasly, F (-Honda), +41.821s; **6** Takuya Izawa, J (-Honda), +43.384s; **7** Kazuki Nakajima, J (-Toyota), +44.067s; **8** Jann Mardenborough, GB (-Toyota), +44.361s; **9** Koudai Tsukakoshi, J (-Honda), +44.910s; **10** Tomoki Nojiri, J (-Honda), +46.192s.
Fastest race lap: Rosenqvist, 1m 25.581s, 119.269mph/191.944km/h.
Pole position: Yuji Kunimoto, J (-Toyota), 1m 23.044s, 122.912mph/197.808km/h.

JAPANESE CHAMPIONSHIP SUPER FORMULA, Twin Ring Motegi, Motegi-machi, Haga-gun, Tochigi Prefecture, Japan, 20 August. Round 4. 52 laps of the 2.983-mile/4.801km circuit, 155.139 miles/249.672km.
1 Pierre Gasly, F (-Honda), 1h 24m 26.817s, 110.227mph/177.393km/h; **2** Kamui Kobayashi, J (-Toyota), +18.583s; **3** Felix Rosenqvist, S (-Toyota), +19.507s; **4** Hiroaki Ishiura, J (-Toyota), +20.195s; **5** Nick Cassidy, NZ (-Toyota), +26.089s; **6** Kenta Yamashita, J (-Toyota), +39.339s; **7** André Lotterer, D (-Toyota), +40.898s; **8** Tomoki Nojiri, J (-Honda), +47.104s; **9** Koudai Tsukakoshi, J (-Honda), +49.690s; **10** Kazuya Oshima, J (-Toyota), +57.342s.
Fastest race lap: Tsukakoshi, 1m 34.259s, 113.945mph/183.377km/h.
Pole position: Yamashita, 1m 32.030s, 116.705mph/187.819km/h.

JAPANESE CHAMPIONSHIP SUPER FORMULA, Autopolis International Racing Course, Kamit-sue-mura, Hita-gun, Oita Prefecture, Japan, 10 September. Round 5. 54 laps of the 2.904-mile/4.674km circuit, 156.832 miles/252.396km.
1 Pierre Gasly, F (-Honda), 1h 24m 28.619s, 111.390mph/179.265km/h; **2** Felix Rosenqvist, S (-Toyota), +1.558s; **3** Kazuya Oshima, J (-Toyota), +7.638s; **4** Hiroaki Ishiura, J (-Toyota), +8.555s; **5** Yuji Kunimoto, J (-Toyota), +9.009s; **6** Kazuki Nakajima, J (-Toyota), +9.457s; **7** Kamui Kobayashi, J (-Toyota), +14.463s; **8** Jann Mardenborough, GB (-Toyota), +14.980s; **9** Koudai Tsukakoshi, J (-Honda), +31.150s; **10** Yuhi Sekiguchi, J (-Toyota), +44.699s.
Fastest race lap: Mardenborough, 1m 30.197s, 115.918mph/186.552km/h.
Pole position: Tomoki Nojiri, J (-Honda), 1m 26.196s, 121.298mph/195.211km/h.

JAPANESE CHAMPIONSHIP SUPER FORMULA, Sportsland-SUGO International Course, Shibata-gun, Miyagi Prefecture, Japan, 24 September. Round 6. 68 laps of the 2.302-mile/3.704km circuit, 156.517 miles/251.889km.
1 Yuhi Sekiguchi, J (-Toyota), 1h 19m 00.439s, 118.863mph/191.291km/h; **2** Pierre Gasly, F (-Honda), +0.243s; **3** Kazuki Nakajima, J (-Toyota), +1.174s; **4** Yuji Kunimoto, J (-Toyota), +6.754s; **5** Felix Rosenqvist, S (-Toyota), +11.472s; **6** Hiroaki Ishiura, J (-Toyota), +12.646s; **7** Kamui Kobayashi, J (-Toyota), +19.452s; **8** Takuya Izawa, J (-Honda), +20.741s; **9** Jann Mardenborough, GB (-Toyota), +21.459s; **10** André Lotterer, D (-Toyota), +28.971s.
Fastest race lap: Ishiura, 1m 07.697s, 122.401mph/196.985km/h.
Pole position: Nick Cassidy, NZ (-Toyota), 1m 04.910s, 127.657mph/205.443km/h.

JAPANESE CHAMPIONSHIP SUPER FORMULA, Suzuka International Racing Course, Suzuka-shi, Mie Prefecture, Japan, 22 October. Round 7. 19 and 36 laps of the 3.608-mile/5.807km circuit.
Race 8 (68.558 miles/110.333km).
Race 9 (129.899 miles/209.052km).
Both races cancelled due to a typhoon.

Final championship points
Drivers
1 Hiroaki Ishiura, J, 33.5; **2** Pierre Gasly, F, 33; **3** Felix Rosenqvist, S, 28.5; **4** Yuhi Sekiguchi, J, 25; **5** Kazuki Nakajima, J, 22; **6** André Lotterer, D, 21; **7** Kamui Kobayashi, J, 16.5; **8** Yuji Kunimoto, J, 16; **9** Naoki Yamamoto, J, 10.5; **10** Nick Cassidy, NZ, 8; **11** Kenta Yamashita, J, 6.5; **12** Kazuya Oshima, J, 6; **13** Takuya Izawa, J, 5; **14** Jann Mardenborough, GB, 4.5; **15** Koudai Tsukakoshi, J, 3; **16** Daisuke Nakajima, J, 2; **17** Tomoki Nojiri, J, 2.

Teams
1 Project μ/cerumo-Inging, 47.5; **2** Team Mugen, 43.5; **3** Vantelin Team TOM'S, 41; **4** Sunoco Team Lemans, 34.5; **5** ITOCHU ENEX Team Impul, 27.5; **6** KCMG, 16.5; **7** Kondo Racing, 12.5; **8** DoCoMo Team Dandelion Racing, 6; **9** Real Racing, 3; **10** TCS Nakajima Racing, 2.

GP3 Series

All cars are Dallara GP3/16 – Mecachrome GP3.

GP3 SERIES, Circuit de Catalunya, Montmeló, Barcelona, Spain, 13/14 May. Round 1. 22 and 17 laps of the 2.892-mile/4.655km circuit.
Race 1 (63.556 miles/102.284km).
1 Nirei Fukuzumi, J, 36m 41.269s, 104.068mph/167.481km/h; **2** Leonardo Pulcini, I, +7.433s; **3** Alessio Lorandi, I, +7.889s; **4** George Russell, GB, +11.807s; **5** Anthoine Hubert, F, +12.159s; **6** Dorian Boccolacci, F, +14.364s; **7** Arjun Maini, IND, +14.906s; **8** Raoul Hyman, ZA, +30.986s; **9** Santino Ferrucci, USA, +31.314s; **10** Marcos Siebert, RA, +31.357s; **11** Julien Falchero, F, +31.912s; **12** Ryan Tveter, USA, +32.228s; **13** Kevin Jörg, CH, +32.916s; **14** Tatiana Calderón, CO, +33.288s; **15** Niko Kari, FIN, +35.996s; **16** Bruno Baptista, BR, +37.783s; **17** Giuliano Alesi, F, +38.240s; **18** Steijn Schothorst, NL, +39.412s; Jack Aitken, GB, -6 laps (DNF-engine sensor).
Fastest race lap: Hubert, 1m 39.386s, 104.772mph/168.615km/h.
Pole position: Aitken, 1m 34.187s, 110.556mph/177.922km/h.

Race 2 (49.094 miles/79.009km).
1 Arjun Maini, IND, 28m 05.908s, 104.998mph/168.978km/h; **2** Dorian Boccolacci, F, +6.060s; **3** Alessio Lorandi, I, +7.171s; **4** Anthoine Hubert, F, +8.268s; **5** George Russell, GB, +9.335s; **6** Nirei Fukuzumi, J, +11.309s; **7** Raoul Hyman, ZA, +14.085s; **8** Santino Ferrucci, USA, +16.638s; **9** Kevin Jörg, CH, +17.813s; **10** Julien Falchero, F, +20.265s; **11** Giuliano Alesi,

F, +23.251s; **12** Jack Aitken, GB, +23.511s; **13** Bruno Baptista, BR, +26.863s; **14** Niko Kari, FIN, +27.888s *; **15** Steijn Schothorst, NL, +29.709s; **16** Marcos Siebert, RA, +31.093s; **17** Leonardo Pulcini, I, +1m 06.654s; **18** Ryan Tveter, USA, -1 lap; Tatiana Calderón, CO, -6 (DNF-accident damage).
** includes 5s penalty for forcing another driver off the track.*
Fastest race lap: Pulcini, 1m 37.654s, 106.630mph/171.605km/h.
Pole position: Hyman.
Championship points
Drivers: **1** Fukuzumi, 29; **2** Lorandi, 25; **3** Maini, 21; **4** Boccolacci, 20; **5** Hubert, 20; **5** Russell, 20.
Teams: **1** ART Grand Prix, 73; **2** Jenzer Motorsport, 46; **3** Trident, 20.

GP3 SERIES, Red Bull Ring, Spielberg, Austria, 8/9 July. Round 2. 24 and 18 laps of the 2.683-mile/4.318km circuit.
Race 1 (64.316 miles/103.506km).
1 George Russell, GB, 34m 13.306s, 112.898mph/181.692km/h; **2** Jack Aitken, GB, +2.390s; **3** Nirei Fukuzumi, J, +5.646s; **4** Anthoine Hubert, F, +14.051s *; **5** Ryan Tveter, USA, +23.181s; **6** Giuliano Alesi, F, +23.885s; **7** Alessio Lorandi, I, +24.363s; **8** Raoul Hyman, ZA, +24.930s; **9** Dorian Boccolacci, F, +25.920s; **10** Arjun Maini, IND, +26.229s; **11** Kevin Jörg, CH, +28.975s; **12** Marcos Siebert, RA, +29.198s; **13** Tatiana Calderón, CO, +30.489s **; **14** Bruno Baptista, BR, +31.654s **; **15** Julien Falchero, F, -1 lap *; Niko Kari, FIN, -10 (DNF-accident damage); Santino Ferrucci, USA, -21 (DNF-suspension); Steijn Schothorst, NL, -22 (DNF-accident damage); Leonardo Pulcini, I, -24 (DNF-accident).
** includes 10s penalty for causing an accident.*
*** includes 5s penalty for overtaking under yellow flag conditions.*
Fastest race lap: Hubert, 1m 21.298s, 118.810mph/191.207km/h.
Pole position: Russell, 1m 19.114s, 122.090mph/196.486km/h.

Race 2 (48.217 miles/77.598km).
1 Raoul Hyman, ZA, 24m 34.848s, 117.883mph/189.715km/h; **2** Giuliano Alesi, F, +0.938s; **3** Nirei Fukuzumi, J, +5.799s; **4** Ryan Tveter, USA, +7.107s; **5** Jack Aitken, GB, +7.949s; **6** George Russell, GB, +8.997s; **7** Anthoine Hubert, F, +9.172s; **8** Alessio Lorandi, I, +14.677s; **9** Kevin Jörg, CH, +15.310s; **10** Marcos Siebert, RA, +15.890s; **11** Julien Falchero, F, +16.487s; **12** Tatiana Calderón, CO, +16.926s; **13** Santino Ferrucci, USA, +17.106s; **14** Leonardo Pulcini, I, +17.867s; **15** Steijn Schothorst, NL, +18.673s; **16** Arjun Maini, IND, +20.459s; **17** Dorian Boccolacci, F, -1 lap; **18** Niko Kari, FIN, -1; Bruno Baptista, BR, -9 (DNF-driver discomfort).
Fastest race lap: Maini, 1m 21.252s, 118.878mph/191.315km/h.
Pole position: Hyman.
Championship points
Drivers: **1** Fukuzumi, 54; **2** Russell, 53; **3** Hubert, 38; **4** Lorandi, 32; **5** Aitken, 28; **6** Hyman, 25.
Teams: **1** ART Grand Prix, 159; **2** Trident, 60; **3** Jenzer Motorsport, 54.

GP3 SERIES, Silverstone Arena Grand Prix Circuit, Towcester, Northamptonshire, Great Britain, 15/16 July. Round 3. 20 and 15 laps of the 3.660-mile/5.891km circuit.
Race 1 (73.127 miles/117.686km).
1 George Russell, GB, 40m 20.435s, 108.886mph/175.235km/h; **2** Anthoine Hubert, F, +1.128s; **3** Alessio Lorandi, I, +1.555s; **4** Jack Aitken, GB, +8.316s; **5** Niko Kari, FIN, +10.134s; **6** Arjun Maini, IND, +10.731s; **7** Giuliano Alesi, F, +10.990s; **8** Dorian Boccolacci, F, +14.183s *; **9** Kevin Jörg, CH, +15.205s; **10** Julien Falchero, F, +17.329s; **11** Leonardo Pulcini, I, +19.371s; **12** Marcos Siebert, RA, +26.859s; **13** Steijn Schothorst, NL, +28.536s; **14** Tatiana Calderón, CO, +30.283s; **15** Bruno Baptista, BR, +45.967s **; **16** Raoul Hyman, ZA, +58.289s; Ryan Tveter, USA, -7 laps (DNF-electrics/fuel system); Santino Ferrucci, USA, -13 (DNF-floor); Nirei Fukuzumi, J, -20 (DNF-lost power).
** includes 5s penalty for causing an accident.*
*** includes 20s penalty for VSC infringement.*
Fastest race lap: Alesi, 1m 49.838s, 119.974mph/193.080km/h.
Pole position: Russell, 1m 46.608s, 123.609mph/198.930km/h.

Race 2 (54.824 miles/88.231km).
1 Giuliano Alesi, F, 30m 04.801s, 109.521mph/176.257km/h; **2** Jack Aitken, GB, +0.724s; **3** Niko Kari, FIN, +1.431s; **4** George Russell, GB, +1.857s; **5** Arjun Maini, IND, +5.900s; **6** Alessio Lorandi, I, +7.257s; **7** Kevin Jörg, CH, +8.099s; **8** Anthoine Hubert, F, +8.447s; **9** Santino Ferrucci, USA, +10.744s; **10** Marcos Siebert, RA, +11.712s; **11** Raoul Hyman, ZA, +12.387s; **12** Leonardo Pulcini, I, +17.079s; **13** Ryan Tveter, USA, +17.645s; **14** Bruno Baptista, BR, +22.595s; **15** Tatiana Calderón, CO, +23.280s; **16** Nirei Fukuzumi, J, +28.539s *; Julien Falchero, F, -12 laps (DNF-accident damage); Steijn Schothorst, NL, -12 (DNF-accident).
** includes 10s penalty for overtaking under safety car conditions.*
Did not start: Dorian Boccolacci, F (gearbox/hydraulics).

Fastest race lap: Russell, 1m 48.862s, 121.050mph/194.811km/h.
Pole position: Boccolacci.
Championship points
Drivers: **1** Russell, 92; **2** Hubert, 57; **3** Fukuzumi, 54; **4** Aitken, 52; **5** Lorandi, 51; **6** Alesi, 43.
Teams: **1** ART Grand Prix, 241; **2** Trident, 91; **3** Jenzer Motorsport, 87.

GP3 SERIES, Hungaroring, Mogyoród, Budapest, Hungary, 29/30 July. Round 4. 22 and 17 laps of the 2.722-mile/4.381km circuit.
Race 1 (59.864 miles/96.342km).
1 Jack Aitken, GB, 37m 23.211s, 96.112mph/154.677km/h; **2** Nirei Fukuzumi, J, +4.489s; **3** Anthoine Hubert, F, +8.946s; **4** Alessio Lorandi, I, +16.563s; **5** Dorian Boccolacci, F, +20.303s; **6** Giuliano Alesi, F, +20.890s; **7** Kevin Jörg, CH, +21.618s; **8** Ryan Tveter, USA, +22.772s; **9** Niko Kari, FIN, +25.082s; **10** Bruno Baptista, BR, +25.460s; **11** Marcos Siebert, RA, +28.209s; **12** Matthieu Vaxivière, F, +28.700s; **13** Julien Falchero, F, +29.196s; **14** Raoul Hyman, ZA, +29.795s; **15** Leonardo Pulcini, I, +30.303s; Steijn Schothorst, NL, -19 laps (DNF-input shaft); Tatiana Calderón, CO, -22 (DNF-accident damage); Arjun Maini, IND, -22 (DNF-clutch).
Did not start: George Russell, GB.
Fastest race lap: Aitken, 1m 34.440s, 103.769mph/167.001km/h.
Pole position: Aitken, 1m 31.754s, 106.807mph/171.890km/h.

Race 2 (46.253 miles/74.437km).
1 Giuliano Alesi, F, 29m 05.379s, 95.451mph/153.614km/h; **2** Ryan Tveter, USA, +0.620s; **3** Kevin Jörg, CH, +2.418s; **4** Dorian Boccolacci, F, +4.190s; **5** Anthoine Hubert, F, +6.955s; **6** Niko Kari, FIN, +8.903s; **7** Raoul Hyman, ZA, +9.858s; **8** Arjun Maini, IND, +12.740s; **9** Marcos Siebert, RA, +31.642s *; **10** Leonardo Pulcini, I, +42.876s; **11** George Russell, GB, +1m 12.795s; **12** Matthieu Vaxivière, F, +1m 24.137s *; **13** Tatiana Calderón, CO, -1 lap; Julien Falchero, F, -4 (DNF-puncture); Jack Aitken, GB, -4 (DNFpuncture); Bruno Baptista, BR, -9 (DNF-electrics); Alessio Lorandi, I, -10 (DNF-puncture); Steijn Schothorst, NL, -11 (DNF-engine overheating); Nirei Fukuzumi, J, -16 (DNF-accident damage).
** includes 20s penalty.*
Fastest race lap: Russell, 1m 33.715s, 104.572mph/168.293km/h.
Pole position: Tveter.
Championship points
Drivers: **1** Russell, 92; **2** Aitken, 83; **3** Hubert, 78; **4** Fukuzumi, 72; **5** Alesi, 66; **6** Lorandi, 63.
Teams: **1** ART Grand Prix, 311; **2** Trident, 152; **3** Jenzer Motorsport, 100.

GP3 SERIES, Circuit de Spa-Francorchamps, Stavelot, Belgium, 26/27 August. Round 5. 17 and 13 laps of the 4.352-mile/7.004km circuit.
Race 1 (73.908 miles/118.944km).
1 George Russell, GB, 37m 47.103s, 117.482mph/189.069km/h; **2** Jack Aitken, GB, +7.460s; **3** Nirei Fukuzumi, J, +7.807s; **4** Arjun Maini, IND, +9.259s; **5** Dorian Boccolacci, F, +14.409s; **6** Ryan Tveter, USA, +15.106s; **7** Giuliano Alesi, F, +15.502s; **8** Julien Falchero, F, +23.361s; **9** Niko Kari, FIN, +26.210s; **10** Kevin Jörg, CH, +26.514s; **11** Leonardo Pulcini, I, +27.620s; **12** Alessio Lorandi, I, +29.201s; **13** Steijn Schothorst, NL, +35.149s; **14** Raoul Hyman, ZA, +38.400s; **15** Juan Manuel Correa, USA, +38.625s; **16** Tatiana Calderón, CO, +43.005s *; Marcos Siebert, RA, -3 laps (DNF-gearbox); Matthieu Vaxivière, F, -10 (DNF-accident damage); Anthoine Hubert, F, -13 (DNF-radiator); Bruno Baptista, BR, -15 (DNF-accident).
*** includes 10s penalty for causing an accident.*
Fastest race lap: Russell, 2m 08.433s, 121.989mph/196.323km/h.
Pole position: Russell, 2m 27.042s, 106.551mph/171.477km/h.

Race 2 (56.500 miles/90.928km).
1 Giuliano Alesi, F, 27m 50.961s, 121.890mph/196.164km/h; **2** George Russell, GB, +3.323s; **3** Ryan Tveter, USA, +7.089s; **4** Nirei Fukuzumi, J, +10.902s; **5** Julien Falchero, F, +12.670s; **6** Arjun Maini, IND, +14.395s; **7** Anthoine Hubert, F, +14.667s; **8** Kevin Jörg, CH, +18.291s; **9** Niko Kari, FIN, +18.544s *; **10** Raoul Hyman, ZA, +19.419s; **11** Leonardo Pulcini, I, +21.689s; **12** Steijn Schothorst, NL, +22.074s; **13** Tatiana Calderón, CO, +22.490s; **14** Alessio Lorandi, I, +23.413s; **15** Matthieu Vaxivière, F, +27.895s; **16** Bruno Baptista, BR, +30.361s; **17** Dorian Boccolacci, F, +1m 37.635s; **18** Jack Aitken, GB, -2 laps **; Marcos Siebert, RA, -3 (DNF-oil temperature); Juan Manuel Correa, USA, -4 (DNF-engine).
** includes 5s penalty for forcing another driver off the track.*
*** includes 10s penalty for causing an accident.*
Fastest race lap: Russell, 2m 06.961s, 123.404mph/198.599km/h.
Pole position: Falchero.
Championship points
Drivers: **1** Russell, 137; **2** Aitken, 101; **3** Fukuzumi, 95; **4** Alesi, 87; **5** Hubert, 80; **6** Lorandi, 63.
Teams: **1** ART Grand Prix, 399; **2** Trident, 202; **3** Jenzer Motorsport, 116.

GP3 SERIES, Autodromo Nazionale di Monza, Milan, Italy, 3 September. Round 6. 21 and 17 laps of the 3.600-mile/5.793km circuit.
Race 1 (75.400 miles/121.344km).
1 George Russell, GB, 44m 15.898s, 102.459mph/164.893km/h; **2** Jack Aitken, GB, +1.526s; **3** Anthoine Hubert, F, +2.361s; **4** Marcos Siebert, RA, +2.959s; **5** Ryan Tveter, USA, +5.026s; **6** Giuliano Alesi, F, +5.351s; **7** Tatiana Calderón, CO, +6.448s; **8** Julien Falchero, F, +7.044s; **9** Kevin Jörg, CH, +7.207s; **10** Bruno Baptista, BR, +8.879s; **11** Raoul Hyman, ZA, +9.567s; **12** Steijn Schothorst, NL, +9.645s *; **13** Dan Ticktum, GB, +16.268s; **14** Dorian Boccolacci, F, +40.836s; **15** Niko Kari, FIN, -2 laps (DNF-accident); **16** Arjun Maini, IND, -3 (DNF-accident damage); Juan Manuel Correa, USA, -9 (DNF-accident); Leonardo Pulcini, I, -21 (DNF-accident); Alessio Lorandi, I, -21 (DNF-accident).
** includes 5s penalty.*
Did not start: Nirei Fukuzumi, J.
Fastest race lap: Hubert, 1m 40.232s, 129.285mph/208.065km/h.
Pole position: Fukuzumi, 1m 38.594s, 131.433mph/211.521km/h.

Race 2 (61.001 miles/98.172km).
Cancelled due to heavy rain.
Championship points
Drivers: **1** Russell, 162; **2** Aitken, 119; **3** Fukuzumi, 99; **4** Hubert, 97; **5** Alesi, 95; **6** Lorandi, 63.
Teams: **1** ART Grand Prix, 463; **2** Trident, 222; **3** Jenzer Motorsport, 116.

GP3 SERIES, Circuito Permanente de Jerez, Jerez de la Frontera, Spain, 7/8 October. Round 7. 23 and 17 laps of the 2.751-mile/4.428km circuit.
Race 1 (63.283 miles/101.844km).
1 Nirei Fukuzumi, J, 35m 57.969s, 105.570mph/169.899km/h; **2** George Russell, GB, +1.559s; **3** Jack Aitken, GB, +3.128s; **4** Dan Ticktum, GB, +5.459s; **5** Anthoine Hubert, F, +8.146s; **6** Niko Kari, FIN, +10.299s; **7** Dorian Boccolacci, F, +12.514s; **8** Alessio Lorandi, I, +19.393s; **9** Giuliano Alesi, F, +18.055s *; **10** Julien Falchero, F, +19.984s; **11** Steijn Schothorst, NL, +21.574s; **12** Ryan Tveter, USA, +21.869s; **13** Tatiana Calderón, CO, +22.371s; **14** Leonardo Pulcini, I, +23.131s; **15** Juan Manuel Correa, USA, +23.710s; **16** Bruno Baptista, BR, +30.610s; **17** Arjun Maini, IND, +31.203s; **18** Marcos Siebert, RA, +1m 09.306s; **19** Raoul Hyman, ZA, +1m 20.941s; **20** Kevin Jörg, CH, -1 lap.
** includes 1-place penalty.*
Fastest race lap: Hyman, 1m 33.073s, 106.423mph/171.272km/h.
Pole position: Fukuzumi, 1m 30.678s, 109.234mph/175.795km/h.

Race 2 (46.774 miles/75.276km).
1 Alessio Lorandi, I, 28m 05.939s, 99.877mph/160.737km/h; **2** Dorian Boccolacci, F, +0.743s; **3** Anthoine Hubert, F, +1.696s; **4** George Russell, GB, +2.722s; **5** Nirei Fukuzumi, J, +3.065s; **6** Jack Aitken, GB, +3.617s; **7** Giuliano Alesi, F, +4.077s; **8** Tatiana Calderón, CO, +4.376s; **9** Julien Falchero, F, +5.198s; **10** Steijn Schothorst, NL, +5.563s; **11** Leonardo Pulcini, I, +5.948s; **12** Arjun Maini, IND, +6.576s; **13** Bruno Baptista, BR, +6.960s; **14** Ryan Tveter, USA, +7.228s; **15** Raoul Hyman, ZA, +7.723s; **16** Juan Manuel Correa, USA, +8.096s; **17** Marcos Siebert, RA, +8.637s; **18** Kevin Jörg, CH, +8.746s; **19** Niko Kari, FIN, +11.510s *; Dan Ticktum, GB, -4 laps (DNF).
** includes 10s penalty for causing an accident.*
Fastest race lap: Russell, 1m 32.279s, 107.339mph/172.745km/h.
Pole position: Lorandi.
Championship points
Drivers: **1** Russell, 190; **2** Aitken, 140; **3** Fukuzumi, 134; **4** Hubert, 117; **5** Alesi, 99; **6** Lorandi, 82.
Teams: **1** ART Grand Prix, 553; **2** Trident, 244; **3** Jenzer Motorsport, 135.

GP3 SERIES, Yas Marina Circuit, Abu Dhabi, United Arab Emirates, 25/26 November. Round 8. 18 and 14 laps of the 3.451-mile/5.554km circuit.
Race 1 (62.048 miles/99.857km).
1 Niko Kari, FIN, 37m 28.944s, 99.437mph/160.028km/h; **2** George Russell, GB, +2.748s; **3** Arjun Maini, IND, +7.532s; **4** Dan Ticktum, GB, +13.745s *; **5** Alessio Lorandi, I, +25.884s; **6** Steijn Schothorst, NL, +29.890s; **7** Dorian Boccolacci, F, +34.339s; **8** Ryan Tveter, USA, +35.815s; **9** Kevin Jörg, CH, +36.374s; **10** Bruno Baptista, BR, +37.837s; **11** Anthoine Hubert, F, +40.003s *; **12** Juan Manuel Correa, USA, +41.362s; **13** Raoul Hyman, ZA, +50.566s; **14** Jack Aitken, GB, +57.811s; **15** Nirei Fukuzumi, J, +1m 15.635s; **16** Tatiana Calderón, CO, +1m 20.614s; **17** Leonardo Pulcini, I, -2 laps; Giuliano Alesi, F, -9 (DNF); Marcos Siebert, RA, -15 (DNF).
** includes 5s for exceeding 80km/h behind the VSC.*
Did not start: Julien Falchero, F.
Fastest race lap: Fukuzumi, 1m 57.544s, 105.696mph/170.101km/h.
Pole position: Russell, 1m 54.751s, 108.268mph/174.241km/h.

Race 2 (48.244 miles/77.641km).
1 Dorian Boccolacci, F, 27m 38.145s, 104.895mph/168.813km/h; **2** Ryan Tveter, USA, +5.581s; **3** Dan Ticktum, GB, +8.510s *; **4** George Russell, GB, +9.981s; **5** Anthoine Hubert, F, +13.169s; **6** Arjun Maini, IND, +18.681s; **7** Kevin Jörg, CH, +19.557s; **8** Jack Aitken, GB, +20.745s; **9** Giuliano Alesi, F, +22.389s; **10** Bruno Baptista, BR, +23.501s *; **11** Raoul Hyman, ZA, +23.946s; **12** Juan Manuel Correa, USA, +26.766s; **13** Niko Kari, FIN, +27.323s **; **14** Nirei Fukuzumi, J, +27.607s; **15** Tatiana Calderón, CO, +28.814s; **16** Julien Falchero, F, +31.359s; **17** Alessio Lorandi, I, +1m 17.433s; **18** Steijn Schothorst, NL, -1 lap; Marcos Siebert, RA, -13 (DNF); Leonardo Pulcini, I, -14 (DNF).
** includes 5s penalty for leaving the track and gaining an advantage.*
*** includes 10s penalty for causing an accident.*
Fastest race lap: Fukuzumi, 1m 57.662s, 105.590mph/169.930km/h.
Pole position: Tveter.

Final championship points
Drivers
1 George Russell, GB, 220; **2** Jack Aitken, GB, 141; **3** Nirei Fukuzumi, J, 134; **4** Anthoine Hubert, F, 123; **5** Giuliano Alesi, F, 99; **6** Dorian Boccolacci, F, 93; **7** Alessio Lorandi, I, 92; **8** Ryan Tveter, USA, 78; **9** Arjun Maini, IND, 72; **10** Niko Kari, FIN, 63; **11** Dan Ticktum, GB, 36; **12** Kevin Jörg, CH, 28; **13** Raoul Hyman, ZA, 27; **14** Leonardo Pulcini, I, 20; **15** Julien Falchero, F, 16; **16** Marcos Siebert, RA, 13; **17** Steijn Schothorst, NL, 8; **18** Tatiana Calderón, CO, 7; **19** Santino Ferrucci, USA, 3; **20** Bruno Baptista, BR, 3.

Teams
1 ART Grand Prix, 590; **2** Trident, 285; **3** Jenzer Motorsport, 164; **4** Arden International, 91; **5** Campos Racing, 56; **6** DAMS, 49.

FIA Formula 3 European Championship

FIA FORMULA 3 EUROPEAN CHAMPIONSHIP, Silverstone Arena Grand Prix Circuit, Towcester, Northamptonshire, Great Britain, 14/16 April. Round 1. 16, 19 and 19 laps of the 3.667-mile/5.901km circuit.
Race 1 (58.667 miles/94.416km).
1 Lando Norris, GB (Dallara F317-Volkswagen), 36m 34.049s, 96.261mph/154.917km/h; **2** Jake Dennis, GB (Dallara F316-Volkswagen), +1.683s; **3** Maximilian Günther, D (Dallara F316-Mercedes Benz), +2.432s; **4** Joel Eriksson, S (Dallara F315-Volkswagen), +3.207s; **5** Joey Mawson, AUS (Dallara F316-Mercedes Benz), +4.991s; **6** Harrison Newey, GB (Dallara F316-Mercedes Benz), +9.376s; **7** Guan Yu Zhou, CHN (Dallara F315-Mercedes Benz), +13.253s; **8** Mick Schumacher, D (Dallara F317-Mercedes Benz), +14.154s; **9** Pedro Piquet, BR (Dallara F316-Mercedes Benz), +14.644s; **10** Jehan Daruvala, IND (Dallara F315-Volkswagen), +15.574s.
Fastest race lap: Norris, 1m 51.183s, 118.724mph/191.068km/h.
Pole position: Norris, 1m 50.094s, 119.899mph/192.958km/h.

Race 2 (69.668 miles/112.119km).
1 Joel Eriksson, S (Dallara F315-Volkswagen), 35m 26.312s, 117.952mph/189.825km/h; **2** Callum Ilott, GB (Dallara F317-Mercedes Benz), +2.336s; **3** Jake Hughes, GB (Dallara F315-Mercedes Benz), +15.397s; **4** Maximilian Günther, D (Dallara F316-Mercedes Benz), +18.679s; **5** Jake Dennis, GB (Dallara F316-Volkswagen), +19.202s; **6** Mick Schumacher, D (Dallara F317-Mercedes Benz), +23.124s; **7** Guan Yu Zhou, CHN (Dallara F315-Mercedes Benz), +23.779s; **8** Jehan Daruvala, IND (Dallara F315-Volkswagen), +24.829s; **9** Lando Norris, GB (Dallara F317-Volkswagen), +25.412s; **10** Harrison Newey, GB (Dallara F316-Mercedes Benz), +25.942s.
Fastest race lap: Eriksson, 1m 51.193s, 118.713mph/191.051km/h.
Pole position: Ilott, 1m 50.482s, 119.477mph/192.281km/h.

Race 3 (69.668 miles/112.119km).
1 Callum Ilott, GB (Dallara F317-Mercedes Benz), 35m 32.355s, 117.617mph/189.287km/h; **2** Joel Eriksson, S (Dallara F315-Volkswagen), +6.815s; **3** Lando Norris, GB (Dallara F317-Volkswagen), +7.626s; **4** Maximilian Günther, D (Dallara F316-Mercedes Benz), +10.974s; **5** Jake Dennis, GB (Dallara F316-Volkswagen), +11.755s; **6** Jehan Daruvala, IND (Dallara F315-Volkswagen), +14.734s; **7** Nikita Mazepin, RUS (Dallara F316-Mercedes Benz), +19.509s; **8** Joey Mawson, AUS (Dallara F316-Mercedes Benz), +20.019s; **9** Harrison Newey, GB (Dallara F316-Mercedes Benz), +24.171s; **10** Ralf Aron, EST (Dallara F316-Mercedes Benz), +26.587s.
Fastest race lap: Ilott, 1m 51.253s, 118.649mph/190.948km/h.
Pole position: Ilott, 1m 50.503s, 119.455mph/192.244km/h.

FIA FORMULA 3 EUROPEAN CHAMPIONSHIP, Autodromo Nazionale di Monza, Milan, Italy, 29/30 April. Round 2. 3 x 20 laps of the 3.600-mile/5.793km circuit.
Race 1 (71.992 miles/115.860km).
1 Lando Norris, GB (Dallara F317-Volkswagen), 35m 00.127s, 123.407mph/198.605km/h; **2** Jehan Daruvala, IND (Dallara F315-Volkswagen), +0.649s; **3** Ferdinand Habsburg, A (Dallara F315-Volkswagen), +5.360s; **4** Joel Eriksson, S (Dallara F315-Volkswagen), +5.803s; **5** Guan Yu Zhou, CHN (Dallara F315-Mercedes Benz), +17.245s; **6** Mick Schumacher, D (Dallara F317-Mercedes Benz), +17.937s; **7** Maximilian Günther, D (Dallara F316-Mercedes Benz), +19.334s; **8** Ralf Aron, EST (Dallara F316-Mercedes Benz), +22.580s; **9** Callum Ilott, GB (Dallara F317-Mercedes Benz), +22.947s; **10** Jake Hughes, GB (Dallara F315-Mercedes Benz), +22.975s.
Fastest race lap: Norris, 1m 44.288s, 124.257mph/199.973km/h.
Pole position: Daruvala, 1m 44.105s, 124.475mph/200.324km/h.

Race 2 (71.992 miles/115.860km).
1 Joel Eriksson, S (Dallara F315-Volkswagen), 34m 53.980s, 123.769mph/199.188km/h; **2** Lando Norris, GB (Dallara F317-Volkswagen), +0.735s; **3** Mick Schumacher, D (Dallara F317-Mercedes Benz), +9.037s; **4** Maximilian Günther, D (Dallara F316-Mercedes Benz), +13.533s; **5** Ferdinand Habsburg, A (Dallara F315-Volkswagen), +14.829s; **6** Guan Yu Zhou, CHN (Dallara F315-Mercedes Benz), +15.347s; **7** Callum Ilott, GB (Dallara F317-Mercedes Benz), +15.930s; **8** Jehan Daruvala, IND (Dallara F315-Volkswagen), +18.991s; **9** Ralf Aron, EST (Dallara F316-Mercedes Benz), +22.615s; **10** Nikita Mazepin, RUS (Dallara F316-Mercedes Benz), +23.826s.
Fastest race lap: Ilott, 1m 43.989s, 124.614mph/200.548km/h.
Pole position: Eriksson, 1m 43.720s, 124.938mph/201.068km/h.

Race 3 (71.992 miles/115.860km).
1 Callum Ilott, GB (Dallara F317-Mercedes Benz), 35m 05.538s, 123.090mph/198.094km/h; **2** Lando Norris, GB (Dallara F317-Volkswagen), +0.736s; **3** Maximilian Günther, D (Dallara F316-Mercedes Benz), +2.705s; **4** Joel Eriksson, S (Dallara F315-Volkswagen), +9.074s; **5** Ferdinand Habsburg, A (Dallara F315-Volkswagen), +9.762s; **6** Mick Schumacher, D (Dallara F317-Mercedes Benz), +12.135s; **7** Pedro Piquet, BR (Dallara F316-Mercedes Benz), +13.627s; **8** Ralf Aron, EST (Dallara F316-Mercedes Benz), +14.980s; **9** Jehan Daruvala, IND (Dallara F315-Volkswagen), +15.371s; **10** Guan Yu Zhou, CHN (Dallara F315-Mercedes Benz), +17.436s.
Fastest race lap: Eriksson, 1m 44.452s, 124.062mph/199.659km/h.
Pole position: Eriksson, 1m 43.790s, 124.853mph/200.932km/h.

FIA FORMULA 3 EUROPEAN CHAMPIONSHIP, Circuit de Pau Ville, Pau, France, 20/21 May. Round 3. 23, 29 and 28 laps of the 1.715-mile/2.760km circuit.
Race 1 (39.445 miles/63.480km).
1 Joel Eriksson, S (Dallara F315-Volkswagen), 34m 59.570s, 67.633mph/108.845km/h; **2** Lando Norris, GB (Dallara F317-Volkswagen), +0.243s; **3** Maximilian Günther, D (Dallara F316-Mercedes Benz), +2.636s; **4** Nikita Mazepin, RUS (Dallara F316-Mercedes Benz), +3.560s; **5** Ralf Aron, EST (Dallara F316-Mercedes Benz), +3.970s; **6** Harrison Newey, GB (Dallara F316-Mercedes Benz), +4.564s; **7** Pedro Piquet, BR (Dallara F312-Mercedes Benz), +5.383s; **8** Ferdinand Habsburg, A (Dallara F315-Volkswagen), +6.637s; **9** Mick Schumacher, D (Dallara F317-Mercedes Benz), +5.825s *; **10** Jehan Daruvala, IND (Dallara F315-Volkswagen), +7.201s.
** includes 1-place penalty for overtaking under yellow flags.*
Fastest race lap: Norris, 1m 10.394s, 87.705mph/141.148km/h.
Pole position: Callum Ilott, GB (Dallara F317-Mercedes Benz), 1m 09.514s, 88.815mph/142.935km/h.

Race 2 (49.735 miles/80.040km).
1 Maximilian Günther, D (Dallara F316-Mercedes Benz), 34m 14.016s, 87.167mph/140.283km/h; **2** Lando Norris, GB (Dallara F317-Volkswagen), +1.953s; **3** Callum Ilott, GB (Dallara F317-Mercedes Benz), +5.287s; **4** Harrison Newey, GB (Dallara F316-Mercedes Benz), +11.883s; **5** Ralf Aron, EST (Dallara F316-Mercedes Benz), +12.596s; **6** Jake Hughes, GB (Dallara F315-Mercedes Benz), +13.411s; **7** Nikita Mazepin, RUS (Dallara F316-Mercedes Benz), +15.873s; **8** Ferdinand Habsburg, A (Dallara F315-Volkswagen), +17.371s; **9** Jehan Daruvala, IND (Dallara F315-Volkswagen), +18.009s; **10** Jake Dennis, GB (Dallara F316-Volkswagen), +20.084s.
Fastest race lap: Günther, 1m 09.788s, 88.467mph/142.374km/h.
Pole position: Norris, 1m 09.085s, 89.367mph/143.822km/h.

Race 3 (48.020 miles/77.280km).
1 Maximilian Günther, D (Dallara F316-Mercedes Benz), 34m 23.254s, 83.785mph/134.839km/h; **2** Callum Ilott, GB (Dallara F317-Mercedes Benz), +1.952s; **3** Ralf Aron, EST (Dallara F316-Mercedes Benz), +3.237s; **4** Harrison Newey, GB (Dallara F316-Mercedes Benz), +6.786s; **5** Joel Eriksson, S (Dallara F315-Volkswagen), +8.386s; **6** Ferdinand Habsburg, A (Dallara F315-Volkswagen), +9.395s; **7** Tadasuke Makino, J (Dallara F317-Mercedes Benz), +11.453s; **8** Pedro Piquet, BR (Dallara F312-Mercedes Benz), +11.979s; **9** Jake Dennis, GB (Dallara F316-Volkswagen), +12.272s; **10** Guan Yu Zhou, CHN (Dallara F315-Mercedes Benz), +17.826s.
Fastest race lap: Lando Norris, GB (Dallara F317-Volkswagen), 1m 10.124s, 88.043mph/141.691km/h.
Pole position: Norris, 1m 09.308s, 89.079mph/143.360km/h.

FIA FORMULA 3 EUROPEAN CHAMPIONSHIP, Hungaroring, Mogyoród, Budapest, Hungary, 17/18 June. Round 4. 21, 22 and 22 laps of the 2.722-mile/4.381km circuit.
Race 1 (57.167 miles/92.001km).
1 Maximilian Günther, D (Dallara F316-Mercedes Benz), 35m 37.466s, 96.282mph/154.951km/h; **2** Jake Hughes, GB (Dallara F315-Mercedes Benz), +5.873s; **3** Jehan Daruvala, IND (Dallara F315-Volkswagen), +6.509s; **4** Joey Mawson, AUS (Dallara F316-Mercedes Benz), +7.142s; **5** Callum Ilott, GB (Dallara F314-Mercedes Benz), +9.473s; **6** Harrison Newey, GB (Dallara F316-Mercedes Benz), +12.034s; **7** Guan Yu Zhou, CHN (Dallara F315-Mercedes Benz), +13.726s; **8** Lando Norris, GB (Dallara F317-Volkswagen), +14.313s; **9** Mick Schumacher, D (Dallara F317-Mercedes Benz), +21.944s; **10** Joel Eriksson, S (Dallara F315-Volkswagen), +22.406s.
Fastest race lap: Ferdinand Habsburg, A (Dallara F315-Volkswagen), 1m 35.829s, 102.265mph/164.580km/h.
Pole position: Günther, 1m 49.369s, 89.605mph/144.205km/h.

Race 2 (59.889 miles/96.382km).
1 Callum Ilott, GB (Dallara F314-Mercedes Benz), 35m 15.865s, 101.897mph/163.987km/h; **2** Joel Eriksson, S (Dallara F315-Volkswagen), +8.600s; **3** Guan Yu Zhou, CHN (Dallara F315-Mercedes Benz), +9.757s; **4** Jake Hughes, GB (Dallara F315-Mercedes Benz), +11.262s; **5** David Beckmann, D (Dallara F316-Volkswagen), +16.380s; **6** Maximilian Günther, D (Dallara F316-Mercedes Benz), +19.291s; **7** Joey Mawson, AUS (Dallara F316-Mercedes Benz), +21.634s; **8** Jehan Daruvala, IND (Dallara F315-Volkswagen), +22.471s; **9** Mick Schumacher, D (Dallara F317-Mercedes Benz), +23.537s; **10** Ferdinand Habsburg, A (Dallara F315-Volkswagen), +29.781s.
Fastest race lap: Ilott, 1m 35.619s, 102.490mph/164.942km/h.
Pole position: Ilott, 1m 34.890s, 103.277mph/166.209km/h.

Race 3 (59.889 miles/96.382km).
1 Joel Eriksson, S (Dallara F315-Volkswagen), 35m 37.495s, 100.865mph/162.327km/h; **2** Callum Ilott, GB (Dallara F314-Mercedes Benz), +1.882s; **3** Lando Norris, GB (Dallara F317-Volkswagen), +6.408s; **4** Guan Yu Zhou, CHN (Dallara F315-Mercedes Benz), +10.519s *; **5** David Beckmann, D (Dallara F316-Volkswagen), +12.146s; **6** Maximilian Günther, D (Dallara F316-Mercedes Benz), +12.790s; **7** Jake Hughes, GB (Dallara F315-Mercedes Benz), +13.167s; **8** Joey Mawson, AUS (Dallara F316-Mercedes Benz), +13.953s; **9** Jehan Daruvala, IND (Dallara F315-Volkswagen), +15.023s; **10** Nikita Mazepin, RUS (Dallara F316-Mercedes Benz), +17.410s.
** includes 5s penalty.*
Fastest race lap: Eriksson, 1m 36.250s, 101.818mph/163.860km/h.
Pole position: Eriksson, 1m 35.267s, 102.868mph/165.551km/h.

FIA FORMULA 3 EUROPEAN CHAMPIONSHIP, Norisring, Nürnberg (Nuremberg), Germany, 1/2 July. Round 5. 38, 42 and 39 laps of the 1.429-mile/2.300km circuit.
Race 1 (54.308 miles/87.400km).
1 Maximilian Günther, D (Dallara F316-Mercedes Benz), 33m 54.166s, 96.112mph/154.677km/h; **2** Pedro Piquet, BR (Dallara F317-Mercedes Benz), +1.507s; **3** Guan Yu Zhou, CHN (Dallara F315-Mercedes Benz), +2.134s; **4** Joel Eriksson, S (Dallara F315-Volkswagen), +4.421s; **5** Harrison Newey, GB (Dallara F316-Mercedes Benz), +15.640s; **6** Jehan Daruvala, IND (Dallara F315-Volkswagen), +15.717s; **7** Mick Schumacher, D (Dallara F317-Mercedes Benz), +16.480s; **8** Tadasuke Makino, J (Dallara F317-Mercedes Benz), +17.907s; **9** Ralf Aron, EST (Dallara F316-Mercedes Benz), +18.508s; **10** Nikita Mazepin, RUS (Dallara F316-Mercedes Benz), +19.426s.
Fastest race lap: Aron, 48.368s, 106.371mph/171.187km/h.
Pole position: Jake Hughes, GB (Dallara F315-Mercedes Benz), 48.231s, 106.673mph/171.673km/h.

Race 2 (60.024 miles/96.600km).
1 Lando Norris, GB (Dallara F317-Volkswagen), 34m 15.834s, 105.109mph/169.157km/h; **2** Jake Hughes, GB (Dallara F315-Mercedes Benz), +1.134s; **3** Maximilian Günther, D (Dallara F316-Mercedes Benz), +2.176s; **4** Jehan Daruvala, IND (Dallara F315-Volkswagen), +3.378s; **5** Ralf Aron, EST (Dallara F316-Mercedes Benz), +4.167s; **6** Pedro Piquet, BR (Dallara F317-Mercedes Benz), +4.554s; **7** Harrison Newey, GB (Dallara F316-Mercedes Benz), +5.074s; **8** Guan Yu Zhou, CHN (Dallara F315-Mercedes Benz), +5.624s; **9** Callum Ilott, GB (Dallara F314-Mercedes Benz), +6.504s; **10** Joel Eriksson, S (Dallara F315-Volkswagen), +7.848s.
Fastest race lap: Ilott, 47.977s, 107.237mph/172.582km/h.
Pole position: Aron, 47.859s, 107.502mph/173.008km/h.

Race 3 (55.737 miles/89.700km).
1 Jehan Daruvala, IND (Dallara F315-Volkswagen), 34m 29.733s, 96.946mph/156.020km/h; **2** Maximilian Günther, D (Dallara F316-Mercedes Benz), +0.458s; **3** Lando Norris, GB (Dallara F317-Volkswagen), +3.088s; **4** Ralf Aron, EST (Dallara F316-Mercedes Benz), +4.021s; **5** Jake Hughes, GB (Dallara F315-Mercedes Benz), +4.548s; **6** David Beckmann, D (Dallara F316-Volkswagen), +5.009s; **7** Joel Eriksson, S (Dallara F315-Volkswagen), +5.753s; **8** Ferdinand Habsburg, A (Dallara F315-Volkswagen), +6.843s; **9** Callum Ilott, GB (Dallara F314-Mercedes Benz), +8.165s; **10** Nikita Mazepin, RUS (Dallara F316-Mercedes Benz), +9.223s.
Fastest race lap: Ilott, 47.949s, 107.300mph/172.683km/h.
Pole position: Günther, 47.965s, 107.264mph/172.625km/h.

FIA FORMULA 3 EUROPEAN CHAMPIONSHIP, Circuit de Spa-Francorchamps, Stavelot, Belgium, 28/29 July. Round 6. 15, 16 and 15 laps of the 4.352-mile/7.004km circuit.
Race 1 (65.281 miles/105.060km).
1 Lando Norris, GB (Dallara F317-Volkswagen), 36m 47.067s, 106.481mph/171.365km/h; **2** Nikita Mazepin, RUS (Dallara F316-Mercedes Benz), +2.807s; **3** Maximilian Günther, D (Dallara F316-Mercedes Benz), +6.665s; **4** Jehan Daruvala, IND (Dallara F315-Volkswagen), +9.593s; **5** Joey Mawson, AUS (Dallara F316-Mercedes Benz), +10.014s; **6** Mick Schumacher, D (Dallara F317-Mercedes Benz), +10.759s; **7** Harrison Newey, GB (Dallara F316-Mercedes Benz), +16.620s; **8** Ferdinand Habsburg, A (Dallara F315-Volkswagen), +18.748s; **9** Joel Eriksson, S (Dallara F315-Volkswagen), +19.387s; **10** Pedro Piquet, BR (Dallara F317-Mercedes Benz), +20.427s.
Fastest race lap: Mazepin, 2m 12.309s, 118.415mph/190.572km/h.
Pole position: Norris, 2m 12.144s, 118.563mph/190.810km/h.

Race 2 (69.633 miles/112.064km).
1 Ferdinand Habsburg, A (Dallara F315-Volkswagen), 35m 38.003s, 117.249mph/188.694km/h; **2** Joel Eriksson, S (Dallara F315-Volkswagen), +2.117s; **3** Maximilian Günther, D (Dallara F316-Mercedes Benz), +3.557s; **4** Jake Hughes, GB (Dallara F315-Mercedes Benz), +4.321s; **5** Jehan Daruvala, IND (Dallara F315-Volkswagen), +7.920s; **6** Callum Ilott, GB (Dallara F314-Mercedes Benz), +8.925s; **7** Nikita Mazepin, RUS (Dallara F316-Mercedes Benz), +9.787s *; **8** Ralf Aron, EST (Dallara F316-Mercedes Benz), +10.048s; **9** Mick Schumacher, D (Dallara F317-Mercedes Benz), +12.721s; **10** Joey Mawson, AUS (Dallara F316-Mercedes Benz), +13.328s.
** includes 2s penalty for forcing another driver off the track.*
Fastest race lap: Habsburg, 2m 12.634s, 118.125mph/190.105km/h.
Pole position: Lando Norris, GB (Dallara F317-Volkswagen), 2m 11.120s, 119.489mph/192.300km/h.

Race 3 (65.281 miles/105.060km).
1 Lando Norris, GB (Dallara F317-Volkswagen), 35m 36.677s, 109.989mph/177.011km/h; **2** Joel Eriksson, S (Dallara F315-Volkswagen), +2.393s; **3** Guan Yu Zhou, CHN (Dallara F315-Mercedes Benz), +4.142s; **4** Callum Ilott, GB (Dallara F314-Mercedes Benz), +4.701s; **5** Jehan Daruvala, IND (Dallara F315-Volkswagen), +7.890s; **6** Ferdinand Habsburg, A (Dallara F315-Volkswagen), +10.177s; **7** Ralf Aron, EST (Dallara F316-Mercedes Benz), +10.973s; **8** Mick Schumacher, D (Dallara F317-Mercedes Benz), +11.957s; **9** Harrison Newey, GB (Dallara F316-Mercedes Benz), +12.643s; **10** Joey Mawson, AUS (Dallara F316-Mercedes Benz), +17.728s.
Fastest race lap: Eriksson, 2m 11.992s, 118.700mph/191.029km/h.
Pole position: Ilott, 2m 11.388s, 119.246mph/191.907km/h.

FIA FORMULA 3 EUROPEAN CHAMPIONSHIP, Circuit Park Zandvoort, Netherlands, 19/20 August. Round 7. 21, 22 and 24 laps of the 2.676-mile/4.307km circuit.
Race 1 (56.201 miles/90.447km).
1 Lando Norris, GB (Dallara F317-Volkswagen), 34m 40.756s, 97.235mph/156.486km/h; **2** Joel Eriksson, S (Dallara F315-Volkswagen), +8.974s; **3** Maximilian Günther, D (Dallara F316-Mercedes Benz), +11.653s; **4** Ferdinand Habsburg, A (Dallara F315-Volkswagen), +12.493s; **5** Callum Ilott, GB (Dallara F314-Mercedes Benz), +13.002s; **6** Mick Schumacher, D (Dallara F317-Mercedes Benz), +20.000s; **7** Pedro Piquet, BR (Dallara F317-Mercedes Benz), +21.066s; **8** Jake Hughes, GB (Dallara F315-Mercedes Benz), +21.761s; **9** Jehan Daruvala, IND (Dallara F315-Volkswagen), +22.989s; **10** Harrison Newey, GB (Dallara F316-Mercedes Benz), +24.258s.
Fastest race lap: Norris, 1m 28.204s, 109.229mph/175.787km/h.
Pole position: Norris, 1m 28.362s, 109.034mph/175.473km/h.

Race 2 (58.877 miles/94.754km).
1 Callum Ilott, GB (Dallara F314-Mercedes Benz), 34m 52.414s, 101.298mph/163.024km/h; **2** Jake Hughes, GB (Dallara F315-Mercedes Benz), +7.371s; **3** Lando Norris, GB (Dallara F317-Volkswagen), +8.742s; **4** Harrison Newey, GB (Dallara F316-Mercedes Benz), +14.993s; **5** David Beckmann, D (Dallara F316-Volkswagen), +15.650s; **6** Ferdinand Habsburg, A (Dallara F315-Volkswagen), +20.059s; **7** Maximilian Günther, D (Dallara F316-Mercedes Benz), +20.756s; **8** Guan Yu Zhou, CHN (Dallara F315-Mercedes Benz), +21.837s; **9** Mick Schumacher, D (Dallara F317-Mercedes Benz), +22.405s; **10** Ralf Aron, EST (Dallara F316-Mercedes Benz), +23.367s.
Fastest race lap: Ilott, 1m 28.234s, 109.192mph/175.728km/h.
Pole position: Ilott, 1m 28.161s, 109.282mph/175.873km/h.

Race 3 (64.230 miles/103.368km).
1 Lando Norris, GB (Dallara F317-Volkswagen), 35m 44.299s, 107.833mph/173.541km/h; **2** Ferdinand Habsburg, A (Dallara F315-Volkswagen), +6.646s; **3** Maximilian Günther, D (Dallara F316-Mercedes Benz), +11.530s; **4** Guan Yu Zhou, CHN (Dallara F315-Mercedes Benz), +15.058s; **5** Jake Hughes, GB (Dallara F315-Mercedes Benz), +31.078s; **6** Pedro Piquet, BR (Dallara F317-Mercedes Benz), +31.541s; **7** Harrison Newey, GB (Dallara F316-Mercedes Benz), +31.936s; **8** Ralf Aron, EST (Dallara F316-Mercedes Benz), +32.461s; **9** Joey Mawson, AUS (Dallara F316-Mercedes Benz), +32.817s; **10** Nikita Mazepin, RUS (Dallara F316-Mercedes Benz), +32.976s.
Fastest race lap: Callum Ilott, GB (Dallara F314-Mercedes Benz), 1m 28.688s, 108.633mph/174.828km/h.
Pole position: Norris, 1m 28.271s, 109.146mph/175.654km/h.

FIA FORMULA 3 EUROPEAN CHAMPIONSHIP, Nürburgring, Nürburg/Eifel, Germany, 9/10 September. Round 8. 20, 26 and 25 laps of the 2.255-mile/3.629km circuit.
Race 1 (45.099 miles/72.580km).
1 Lando Norris, GB (Dallara F317-Volkswagen), 35m 11.010s, 76.909mph/123.773km/h; **2** Jake Hughes, GB (Dallara F315-Mercedes Benz), +17.562s; **3** Joey Mawson, AUS (Dallara F316-Mercedes Benz), +35.435s; **4** Callum Ilott, GB (Dallara F314-Mercedes Benz), +36.251s; **5** Ferdinand Habsburg, A (Dallara F315-Volkswagen), +37.242s; **6** Jehan Daruvala, IND (Dallara F315-Volkswagen), +38.271s; **7** Tadasuke Makino, J (Dallara F317-Mercedes Benz), +40.990s *; **8** Mick Schumacher, D (Dallara F317-Mercedes Benz), +44.750s; **9** Guan Yu Zhou, CHN (Dallara F315-Mercedes Benz), +45.424s; **10** Joel Eriksson, S (Dallara F315-Volkswagen), +50.510s.
** includes 5s penalty.*
Fastest race lap: Max Defourny, B (Dallara F317-Mercedes Benz), 1m 36.824s, 83.841mph/134.929km/h.
Pole position: Norris, 1m 35.601s, 84.913mph/136.655km/h.

Race 2 (58.629 miles/94.354km).
1 Jake Hughes, GB (Dallara F315-Mercedes Benz), 35m 37.113s, 98.761mph/158.940km/h; **2** Lando Norris, GB (Dallara F317-Volkswagen), +0.539s; **3** Callum Ilott, GB (Dallara F314-Mercedes Benz), +12.767s; **4** Tadasuke Makino, J (Dallara F317-Mercedes Benz), +13.814s; **5** Ralf Aron, EST (Dallara F316-Mercedes Benz), +15.205s; **6** Ferdinand Habsburg, A (Dallara F315-Volkswagen), +16.196s; **7** Joey Mawson, AUS (Dallara F316-Mercedes Benz), +26.790s; **8** Harrison Newey, GB (Dallara F316-Mercedes Benz), +33.639s; **9** Joel Eriksson, S (Dallara F315-Volkswagen), +36.104s; **10** Jehan Daruvala, IND (Dallara F315-Volkswagen), +37.452s.
Fastest race lap: Hughes, 1m 21.377s, 99.755mph/160.541km/h.
Pole position: Hughes, 1m 37.002s, 83.687mph/134.681km/h.

Race 3 (56.374 miles/90.725km).
1 Lando Norris, GB (Dallara F317-Volkswagen), 35m 44.949s, 94.615mph/152.269km/h; **2** Jake Hughes, GB (Dallara F315-Mercedes Benz), +0.794s; **3** Ralf Aron, EST (Dallara F316-Mercedes Benz), +2.197s; **4** Callum Ilott, GB (Dallara F314-Mercedes Benz), +5.225s; **5** Jehan Daruvala, IND (Dallara F315-Volkswagen), +8.658s; **6** Harrison Newey, GB (Dallara F316-Mercedes Benz), +19.698s; **7** Maximilian Günther, D (Dallara F316-Mercedes Benz), +20.361s; **8** Joel Eriksson, S (Dallara F315-Volkswagen), +20.851s; **9** Max Defourny, B (Dallara F317-Mercedes Benz), +24.961s; **10** Sacha Fenestraz, F (Dallara F312-Volkswagen), +28.384s.

Fastest race lap: Norris, 1m 21.866s, 99.160mph/159.582km/h.
Pole position: Ilott, 1m 37.386s, 83.357mph/134.150km/h.

FIA FORMULA 3 EUROPEAN CHAMPIONSHIP, Red Bull Ring, Spielberg, Austria, 23/24 September. Round 9. 25, 25 and 24 laps of the 2.683-mile/4.318km circuit.
Race 1 (67.077 miles/107.950km).
1 Callum Ilott, GB (Dallara F317-Mercedes Benz), 34m 59.668s, 115.007mph/185.086km/h; **2** Joel Eriksson, S (Dallara F315-Volkswagen), +1.828s; **3** Maximilian Günther, D (Dallara F316-Mercedes Benz), +5.141s; **4** Lando Norris, GB (Dallara F317-Volkswagen), +8.940s; **5** Tadasuke Makino, J (Dallara F317-Mercedes Benz), +10.119s; **6** Ferdinand Habsburg, A (Dallara F315-Volkswagen), +14.599s; **7** Mick Schumacher, D (Dallara F317-Mercedes Benz), +15.598s; **8** David Beckmann, D (Dallara F316-Volkswagen), +19.574s; **9** Guan Yu Zhou, CHN (Dallara F315-Mercedes Benz), +21.330s; **10** Pedro Piquet, BR (Dallara F317-Mercedes Benz), +22.568s.
Fastest race lap: Ilott, 1m 23.355s, 115.878mph/186.489km/h.
Pole position: Ilott, 1m 23.301s, 115.954mph/186.610km/h.

Race 2 (67.077 miles/107.950km).
1 Joel Eriksson, S (Dallara F315-Volkswagen), 35m 02.436s, 114.855mph/184.842km/h; **2** Lando Norris, GB (Dallara F317-Volkswagen), +0.896s; **3** Nikita Mazepin, RUS (Dallara F316-Mercedes Benz), +7.303s; **4** Callum Ilott, GB (Dallara F317-Mercedes Benz), +7.842s; **5** Jehan Daruvala, IND (Dallara F315-Volkswagen), +11.634s; **6** Ralf Aron, EST (Dallara F316-Mercedes Benz), +13.412s; **7** Maximilian Günther, D (Dallara F316-Mercedes Benz), +24.461s; **8** Joey Mawson, AUS (Dallara F316-Mercedes Benz), +25.141s; **9** Ferdinand Habsburg, A (Dallara F315-Volkswagen), +25.504s; **10** Mick Schumacher, D (Dallara F317-Mercedes Benz), +26.661s.
Fastest race lap: Norris, 1m 23.688s, 115.417mph/185.747km/h.
Pole position: Eriksson, 1m 23.431s, 115.773mph/186.319km/h.

Race 3 (64.394 miles/103.632km).
1 Joel Eriksson, S (Dallara F315-Volkswagen), 35m 04.815s, 110.137mph/177.248km/h; **2** Nikita Mazepin, RUS (Dallara F316-Mercedes Benz), +5.737s; **3** Tadasuke Makino, J (Dallara F317-Mercedes Benz), +8.978s; **4** Ferdinand Habsburg, A (Dallara F315-Volkswagen), +9.206s *; **5** Maximilian Günther, D (Dallara F316-Mercedes Benz), +9.652s; **6** Jehan Daruvala, IND (Dallara F315-Volkswagen), +10.644s; **7** Joey Mawson, AUS (Dallara F316-Mercedes Benz), +11.286s *; **8** Mick Schumacher, D (Dallara F317-Mercedes Benz), +11.482s; **9** David Beckmann, D (Dallara F316-Volkswagen), +19.592s; **10** Marino Sato, J (Dallara F314-Volkswagen), +20.273s.
** includes 5s penalty for leaving the track and gaining an advantage.*
Fastest race lap: Jake Hughes, GB (Dallara F315-Mercedes Benz), 1m 23.697s, 115.405mph/185.727km/h.
Pole position: Eriksson, 1m 23.545s, 115.615mph/186.064km/h.

FIA FORMULA 3 EUROPEAN CHAMPIONSHIP, Hockenheimring Grand Prix Circuit, Heidelberg, Germany, 14/15 October. Round 10. 23, 21 and 22 laps of the 2.842-mile/4.574km circuit.
Race 1 (65.369 miles/105.202km).
1 Joel Eriksson, S (Dallara F315-Volkswagen), 35m 45.712s, 109.674mph/176.504km/h; **2** Lando Norris, GB (Dallara F317-Volkswagen), +0.725s; **3** Ferdinand Habsburg, A (Dallara F316-Volkswagen), +3.988s; **4** Callum Ilott, GB (Dallara F314-Mercedes Benz), +9.036s; **5** Jehan Daruvala, IND (Dallara F315-Volkswagen), +12.520s; **6** Nikita Mazepin, RUS (Dallara F316-Mercedes Benz), +15.639s; **7** Pedro Piquet, BR (Dallara F316-Mercedes Benz), +17.218s; **8** Ralf Aron, EST (Dallara F316-Mercedes Benz), +17.815s; **9** Tadasuke Makino, J (Dallara F317-Mercedes Benz), +19.436s; **10** Maximilian Günther, D (Dallara F316-Mercedes Benz), +25.250s.
Fastest race lap: Norris, 1m 32.635s, 110.452mph/177.755km/h.
Pole position: Ilott, 1m 31.646s, 111.644mph/179.673km/h.

Race 2 (59.685 miles/96.054km).
1 Callum Ilott, GB (Dallara F314-Mercedes Benz), 32m 41.110s, 109.563mph/176.325km/h; **2** Maximilian Günther, D (Dallara F316-Mercedes Benz), +11.339s; **3** Guan Yu Zhou, CHN (Dallara F315-Mercedes Benz), +14.174s; **4** Joel Eriksson, S (Dallara F315-Volkswagen), +14.707s; **5** Jake Hughes, GB (Dallara F315-Mercedes Benz), +23.183s; **6** Nikita Mazepin, RUS (Dallara F316-Mercedes Benz), +23.977s; **7** Pedro Piquet, BR (Dallara F316-Mercedes Benz), +25.279s*; **8** Jehan Daruvala, IND (Dallara F315-Volkswagen), +26.941s; **9** Tadasuke Makino, J (Dallara F317-Mercedes Benz), +27.527s *; **10** Ralf Aron, EST (Dallara F316-Mercedes Benz), +27.716s.
** includes 5s penalty.*
Fastest race lap: Ilott, 1m 32.694s, 110.381mph/177.642km/h.
Pole position: Ilott, 1m 31.685s, 111.596mph/179.597km/h.

Race 3 (62.527 miles/100.628km).
1 Maximilian Günther, D (Dallara F316-Mercedes Benz), 35m 31.488s, 105.606mph/169.956km/h; **2** Joel Eriksson, S (Dallara F315-Volkswagen), +3.585s; **3** Guan Yu Zhou, CHN (Dallara F315-Mercedes Benz), +14.264s; **4** Lando Norris, GB (Dallara F317-Volkswagen), +14.780s; **5** Callum Ilott, GB (Dallara F314-Mercedes Benz), +16.085s; **6** Pedro Piquet, BR (Dallara F316-Mercedes Benz), +23.872s; **7** Nikita Mazepin, RUS (Dallara F316-Mercedes Benz), +24.718s; **8** Jake Hughes, GB (Dallara F315-Mercedes Benz), +24.918s *; **9** Joey Mawson, AUS (Dallara F316-Mercedes Benz), +25.559s; **10** David Beckmann, D (Dallara F316-Volkswagen), +27.603s.
** includes 5s penalty.*
Fastest race lap: Günther, 1m 32.271s, 110.887mph/178.456km/h.
Pole position: Günther, 1m 31.961s, 111.261mph/179.058km/h.

Final championship points
Drivers
1 Lando Norris, GB, 441; **2** Joel Eriksson, S, 388; **3** Maximilian Günther, D, 383; **4** Callum Ilott, GB, 344; **5** Jake Hughes, GB, 207; **6** Jehan Daruvala, IND, 191; **7** Ferdinand Habsburg, A, 186; **8** Guan Yu Zhou, CHN, 149; **9** Ralf Aron, EST, 123; **10** Nikita Mazepin, RUS, 108; **11** Harrison Newey, GB, 106; **12** Mick Schumacher, D, 94; **13** Joey Mawson, AUS, 83; **14** Pedro Piquet, BR, 80; **15** Tadasuke Makino, J, 57; **16** David Beckmann, D, 45; **17** Jake Dennis, GB, 41; **18** Max Defourny, B, 2; **19** Marino Sato, J, 1; **20** Sacha Fenestraz, F, 1.

Teams
1 Prema Powerteam, 829; **2** Carlin, 702; **3** Motopark, 614; **4** HitechGP, 463; **5** Van Amersfoort Racing, 357.

BRDC British Formula 3 Championship

All cars are Tatuus F4-016-Cosworth.

BRDC BRITISH FORMULA 3 CHAMPIONSHIP, Oulton Park Circuit, Tarporley, Cheshire, Great Britain, 17 April. 11, 4 and 14 laps of the 2.692-mile/4.332km circuit.
Round 1 (29.612 miles/47.656km).
1 Enaam Ahmed, GB, 18m 47.816s, 94.521mph/152.118km/h; **2** James Pull, GB, +2.897s; **3** Toby Sowery, GB, +12.639s; **4** Ben Hingeley, GB, +14.063s; **5** Cameron Das, USA, +14.695s; **6** Harry Hayek, AUS, +19.051s; **7** Callan O'Keeffe, ZA, +19.979s; **8** Omar Ismail, GB, +27.257s; **9** Petru Florescu, RO, +29.251s; **10** Tristan Charpentier, F, +31.573s.
Fastest race lap: Ahmed, 1m 41.505s, 95.475mph/153.652km/h.
Pole position: Das, 1m 30.457s, 107.135mph/172.418km/h.

Round 2 (10.768 miles/17.329km).
1 Enaam Ahmed, GB, 6m 32.071s, 98.871mph/159.118km/h; **2** Ben Hingeley, GB, +7.749s; **3** Callan O'Keeffe, ZA, +8.119s; **4** James Pull, GB, +8.234s; **5** Nicolai Kjaergaard, DK, +11.067s; **6** Cameron Das, USA, +11.794s; **7** Manuel Maldonado, YV, +22.804s; **8** Chase Owen, USA, +22.901s; **9** Tristan Charpentier, F, +24.252s; **10** Nick Worm, D, +25.557s.
Fastest race lap: Ahmed, 1m 34.972s, 102.042mph/164.221km/h.
Pole position: Ismail.

Round 3 (37.688 miles/60.653km).
1 Enaam Ahmed, GB, 21m 20.292s, 105.973mph/170.547km/h; **2** Cameron Das, USA, +1.833s; **3** James Pull, GB, +8.704s; **4** Callan O'Keeffe, ZA, +12.993s; **5** Omar Ismail, GB, +16.011s; **6** Ben Hingeley, GB, +16.482s; **7** Toby Sowery, GB, +17.233s; **8** Nicolai Kjaergaard, DK, +19.689s; **9** Aaron Di Comberti, GB, +26.777s; **10** Harry Hayek, AUS, +27.821s.
Fastest race lap: Ahmed, 1m 30.687s, 106.864mph/171.981km/h.
Pole position: Ahmed, 1m 34.972s, 102.042mph/164.221km/h.

BRDC BRITISH FORMULA 3 CHAMPIONSHIP, Rockingham Motor Speedway, Corby, Northamptonshire, Great Britain, 29/30 April. 3 x 14 laps of the 1.940-mile/3.122km circuit.
Round 4 (27.160 miles/43.710km).
1 Enaam Ahmed, GB, 17m 38.139s, 92.403mph/148.709km/h; **2** Cameron Das, USA, +1.011s; **3** Callan O'Keeffe, ZA, +2.028s; **4** Ben Hingeley, GB, +3.618s; **5** James Pull, GB, +7.339s; **6** Omar Ismail, GB, +8.517s; **7** Nicolai Kjaergaard, DK, +11.366s; **8** Jamie Chadwick, GB, +17.207s; **9** Guilherme Samaia, BR, +17.524s; **10** Toby Sowery, GB, +17.840s.
Fastest race lap: Das, 1m 14.622s, 93.591mph/150.621km/h.
Pole position: Das, 1m 13.470s, 95.059mph/152.982km/h.

Round 5 (27.160 miles/43.710km).
1 Cameron Das, USA, 17m 42.861s, 91.993mph/148.048km/h; **2** Omar Ismail, GB, +6.436s; **3** Jamie Chadwick, GB, +7.627s; **4** Ben Hingeley, GB, +8.139s; **5** Callan O'Keeffe, ZA, +15.759s; **6** Toby Sowery, GB, +16.207s; **7** Harry Hayek, AUS, +16.505s; **8** Enaam Ahmed, GB, +17.906s; **9** Aaron Di Comberti, GB, +18.546s; **10** Manuel Maldonado, YV, +19.365s.
Fastest race lap: Das, 1m 14.659s, 93.545mph/150.546km/h.
Pole position: Chadwick.

Round 6 (27.160 miles/43.710km).
1 Ben Hingeley, GB, 20m 01.945s, 81.348mph/130.917km/h; **2** James Pull, GB, +0.987s; **3** Cameron Das, USA, +1.788s; **4** Toby Sowery, GB, +2.990s; **5** Callan O'Keeffe, ZA, +3.449s; **6** Jeremy Wahome, EAK, +8.568s; **7** Chase Owen, USA, +8.799s; **8** Enaam Ahmed, GB, +9.211s; **9** Guilherme Samaia, BR, +9.728s; **10** Jamie Chadwick, GB, +11.114s.
Fastest race lap: Hingeley, 1m 15.744s, 92.205mph/148.390km/h.
Pole position: Das, 1m 14.622s, 93.591mph/150.621km/h.

BRDC BRITISH FORMULA 3 CHAMPIONSHIP, Snetterton Circuit, Thetford, Norfolk, Great Britain, 27/28 May. 3 x 10 laps of the 2.969-mile/4.778km circuit.
Round 7 (29.689 miles/47.780km).
1 Enaam Ahmed, GB, 20m 35.558s, 86.503mph/139.214km/h; **2** James Pull, GB, +2.960s; **3** Toby Sowery, GB, +3.872s; **4** Callan O'Keeffe, ZA, +4.381s; **5** Ben Hingeley, GB, +10.275s; **6** Cameron Das, USA, +10.655s; **7** Jamie Chadwick, GB, +12.629s; **8** Jordan Cane, GB, +12.929s; **9** Chase Owen, USA, +18.705s; **10** Aaron Di Comberti, GB, +20.219s.
Fastest race lap: Ahmed, 1m 44.903s, 101.884mph/163.967km/h.
Pole position: Pull, 2m 00.192s, 88.924mph/143.110km/h.

Round 8 (29.689 miles/47.780km).
1 Jordan Cane, GB, 17m 37.303s, 101.087mph/162.684km/h; **2** Cameron Das, USA, +1.489s; **3** Callan O'Keeffe, ZA, +2.295s; **4** Ben Hingeley, GB, +5.587s; **5** Toby Sowery, GB, +6.625s; **6** Enaam Ahmed, GB, +7.819s; **7** Jamie Chadwick, GB, +13.587s; **8** Nicolai Kjaergaard, DK, +13.992s; **9** Chase Owen, USA, +20.184s; **10** Guilherme Samaia, BR, +20.524s.
Fastest race lap: Ahmed, 1m 43.383s, 103.382mph/166.378km/h.
Pole position: Cane.

Round 9 (29.689 miles/47.780km).
1 Enaam Ahmed, GB, 17m 38.986s, 100.927mph/162.426km/h; **2** Toby Sowery, GB, +2.103s; **3** James Pull, GB, +3.092s; **4** Jordan Cane, GB, +6.374s; **5** Callan O'Keeffe, ZA, +6.999s; **6** Cameron Das, USA, +8.224s; **7** Ben Hingeley, GB, +12.003s; **8** Nicolai Kjaergaard, DK, +20.333s; **9** Omar Ismail, GB, +21.027s; **10** Aaron Di Comberti, GB, +21.447s.
Fastest race lap: Ahmed, 1m 44.582s, 102.197mph/164.471km/h.
Pole position: Ahmed, 1m 43.383s, 103.382mph/166.378km/h.

BRDC BRITISH FORMULA 3 CHAMPIONSHIP, Silverstone Arena Grand Prix Circuit, Towcester, Northamptonshire, Great Britain, 10/11 June. 3 x 10 laps of the 3.660-mile/5.891km circuit.
Round 10 (36.604 miles/58.908km).
1 Toby Sowery, GB, 19m 44.362s, 111.261mph/179.058km/h; **2** Enaam Ahmed, GB, +5.265s; **3** James Pull, GB, +5.779s; **4** Callan O'Keeffe, ZA, +7.949s; **5** Ben Hingeley, GB, +12.089s; **6** Cameron Das, USA, +14.813s; **7** Nicolai Kjaergaard, DK, +19.068s; **8** Manuel Maldonado, YV, +20.701s; **9** Jamie Chadwick, GB, +31.713s; **10** Omar Ismail, GB, +32.276s.
Fastest race lap: Sowery, 1m 57.924s, 111.745mph/179.836km/h.
Pole position: Sowery, 1m 57.146s, 112.487mph/181.030km/h.

Round 11 (36.604 miles/58.908km).
1 Ben Hingeley, GB, 19m 46.440s, 111.067mph/178.745km/h; **2** Toby Sowery, GB, +2.075s; **3** James Pull, GB, +2.278s; **4** Callan O'Keeffe, ZA, +4.680s; **5** Enaam Ahmed, GB, +7.425s; **6** Manuel Maldonado, YV, +10.212s; **7** Cameron Das, USA, +10.774s; **8** Jeremy Wahome, EAK, +14.865s; **9** Chase Owen, USA, +18.786s; **10** Jamie Chadwick, GB, +24.679s.
Fastest race lap: Sowery, 1m 57.152s, 112.481mph/181.021km/h.
Pole position: Maldonado.

Round 12 (36.604 miles/58.908km).
1 Toby Sowery, GB, 19m 48.263s, 110.896mph/178.470km/h; **2** James Pull, GB, +3.935s; **3** Enaam Ahmed, GB, +4.475s; **4** Chase Owen, USA, +9.245s; **5** Cameron Das, USA, +9.859s; **6** Jordan Cane, GB, +10.579s; **7** Nicolai Kjaergaard, DK, +12.850s; **8** Guilherme Samaia, BR, +22.632s *; **9** Jeremy Wahome, EAK, +23.230s; **10** Ben Hingeley, GB, +24.643s.
** includes 10s penalty for false start.*
Fastest race lap: Ahmed, 1m 58.229s, 111.456mph/179.372km/h.
Pole position: Sowery, 1m 57.152s, 112.481mph/181.021km/h.

BRDC BRITISH FORMULA 3 CHAMPIONSHIP, Circuit de Spa-Francorchamps, Stavelot, Belgium, 7/8 July. 3 x 9 laps of the 4.352-mile/7.004km circuit.
Round 13 (39.169 miles/63.036km).
1 Ben Hingeley, GB, 20m 52.077s, 112.618mph/181.242km/h; **2** Enaam Ahmed, GB, +1.123s; **3** Guilherme Samaia, BR, +3.159s; **4** Toby Sowery, GB, +4.426s; **5** Jordan Cane, GB, +8.647s; **6** Jamie Chadwick, GB, +9.255s; **7** Cameron Das, USA, +9.988s; **8** James Pull, GB, +10.500s; **9** Callan O'Keeffe, ZA, +11.100s; **10** Chase Owen, USA, +11.218s.
Fastest race lap: Sowery, 2m 18.350s, 113.245mph/182.250km/h.
Pole position: Ahmed, 2m 18.081s, 113.466mph/182.605km/h.

Round 14 (39.169 miles/63.036km).
1 Enaam Ahmed, GB, 20m 49.892s, 112.815mph/181.559km/h; **2** James Pull, GB, +1.449s; **3** Toby Sowery, GB, +2.358s; **4** Cameron Das, USA, +4.664s; **5** Callan O'Keeffe, ZA, +6.877s; **6** Jordan Cane, GB, +10.169s; **7** Chase Owen, USA, +14.118s; **8** Tristan Charpentier, F, +15.779s; **9** Linus Lundqvist, S, +16.360s; **10** Jamie Chadwick, GB, +18.487s.
Fastest race lap: Ahmed, 2m 17.568s, 113.889mph/183.286km/h.
Pole position: Pull.

Round 15 (39.169 miles/63.036km).
1 Enaam Ahmed, GB, 21m 03.109s, 111.635mph/179.659km/h; **2** Toby Sowery, GB, +0.797s; **3** Ben Hingeley, GB, +4.441s; **4** James Pull, GB, +6.272s; **5** Cameron Das, USA, +7.026s; **6** Chase Owen, USA, +7.905s; **7** Linus Lundqvist, S, +9.466s; **8** Tristan Charpentier, F, +10.001s; **9** Callan O'Keeffe, ZA, +12.547s; **10** Nicolai Kjaergaard, DK, +13.241s.
Fastest race lap: Ahmed, 2m 19.404s, 112.389mph/180.872km/h.
Pole position: Ahmed, 2m 17.568s, 113.889mph/183.286km/h.

BRDC BRITISH FORMULA 3 CHAMPIONSHIP, Brands Hatch Grand Prix Circuit, West Kingsdown, Dartford, Kent, Great Britain, 5/6 August. 8, 14 and 14 laps of the 2.433-mile/3.916km circuit.
Round 16 (19.466 miles/31.327km).
1 Enaam Ahmed, GB, 11m 18.122s, 103.338mph/166.307km/h; **2** James Pull, GB, +0.747s; **3** Toby Sowery, GB, +2.716s; **4** Callan O'Keeffe, ZA, +4.689s; **5** Jordan Cane, GB, +9.729s; **6** Jeremy Wahome, EAK, +12.234s; **7** Nicolai Kjaergaard, DK, +12.696s; **8** Krishnaraaj Mahadik, IND, +13.692s; **9** Chase Owen, USA, +14.921s; **10** Manuel Maldonado, YV, +17.744s.
Fastest race lap: Sowery, 1m 21.562s, 107.397mph/172.838km/h.
Pole position: Ahmed, 1m 20.746s, 108.482mph/174.585km/h.

Round 17 (34.065 miles/54.822km).
1 Krishnaraaj Mahadik, IND, 21m 11.890s, 96.418mph/155.169km/h; **2** James Pull, GB, +2.307s; **3** Enaam Ahmed, GB, +4.432s; **4** Omar Ismail, GB, +5.148s; **5** Jamie Chadwick, GB, +6.035s; **6** Chase Owen, USA, +6.693s; **7** Callan O'Keeffe, ZA, +6.907s; **8** Manuel Maldonado, YV, +7.467s; **9** Nick Worm, D, +11.251s; **10** Cameron Das, USA, +11.487s.
Fastest race lap: Ahmed, 1m 21.047s, 108.079mph/173.937km/h.
Pole position: Mahadik.

Round 18 (34.065 miles/54.822km).
1 Enaam Ahmed, GB, 19m 07.210s, 106.896mph/172.034km/h; **2** Cameron Das, USA, +6.169s; **3** James Pull, GB, +7.193s; **4** Callan O'Keeffe, ZA, +8.131s; **5** Ben Hingeley, GB, +14.401s; **6** Nicolai Kjaergaard, DK, +14.655s; **7** Toby Sowery, GB, +16.564s; **8** Krishnaraaj Mahadik, IND, +22.470s; **9** Chase Owen, USA, +22.796s; **10** Jeremy Wahome, EAK, +25.707s.
Fastest race lap: Sowery, 1m 21.182s, 107.899mph/173.647km/h.
Pole position: Ahmed, 1m 21.047s, 108.079mph/173.937km/h.

BRDC BRITISH FORMULA 3 CHAMPIONSHIP, Snetterton Circuit, Thetford, Norfolk, Great Britain, 26/27 August. 3 x 10 laps of the 2.969-mile/4.778km circuit.
Round 19 (29.689 miles/47.780km).
1 Enaam Ahmed, GB, 17m 37.141s, 101.103mph/162.709km/h; **2** Toby Sowery, GB, +0.942s; **3** James Pull, GB, +5.616s; **4** Ben Hingeley, GB, +9.030s; **5** Krishnaraaj Mahadik, IND, +9.326s; **6** Cameron Das, USA, +10.334s; **7** Jordan Cane, GB, +11.926s; **8** Guilherme Samaia, BR, +16.930s; **9** Jamie Chadwick, GB, +18.226s; **10** Callan O'Keeffe, ZA, +18.720s.
Fastest race lap: Ahmed, 1m 44.118s, 102.653mph/165.204km/h.
Pole position: Ahmed, 1m 43.202s, 103.564mph/166.670km/h.

Round 20 (29.689 miles/47.780km).
1 Jordan Cane, GB, 17m 30.958s, 101.698mph/163.667km/h; **2** Guilherme Samaia, BR,

+6.431s; **3** Ben Hingeley, GB, +6.902s; **4** Toby Sowery, GB, +7.413s; **5** Enaam Ahmed, GB, +8.692s; **6** Krishnaraaj Mahadik, IND, +11.570s; **7** Jamie Chadwick, GB, +12.595s; **8** Omar Ismail, GB, +15.881s; **9** Chase Owen, USA, +17.915s; **10** Nicolai Kjaergaard, DK, +21.298s.
Fastest race lap: Cameron Das, USA, 1m 43.099s, 103.667mph/166.837km/h.
Pole position: Samaia.

Round 21 (29.689 miles/47.780km).
1 Enaam Ahmed, GB, 17m 46.295s, 100.235mph/161.313km/h; **2** Toby Sowery, GB, +0.455s; **3** Jordan Cane, GB, +4.810s; **4** Callan O'Keeffe, ZA, +5.427s; **5** Krishnaraaj Mahadik, IND, +11.182s; **6** Chase Owen, USA, +11.529s; **7** James Pull, GB, +12.934s; **8** Cameron Das, USA, +14.759s; **9** Ben Hingeley, GB, +16.401s *; **10** Guilherme Samaia, BR, +17.706s.
** includes 2s penalty for dangerous driving.*
Fastest race lap: Sowery, 1m 44.847s, 101.939mph/164.055km/h.
Pole position: Das, 1m 43.099s, 103.667mph/166.837km/h.

BRDC BRITISH FORMULA 3 CHAMPIONSHIP, Donington Park National Circuit, Castle Donington, Great Britain, 23/24 September. 3 x 12 laps of the 2.487-mile/4.003km circuit.
Round 22 (29.848 miles/48.035km).
1 Ben Hingeley, GB, 17m 19.584s, 103.359mph/166.341km/h; **2** Enaam Ahmed, GB, +0.415s; **3** Cameron Das, USA, +2.297s; **4** James Pull, GB, +3.400s; **5** Jordan Cane, GB, +4.586s; **6** Chase Owen, USA, +5.855s; **7** Callan O'Keeffe, ZA, +7.289s; **8** Nicolai Kjaergaard, DK, +11.542s; **9** Jamie Chadwick, GB, +14.266s; **10** Manuel Maldonado, YV, +16.244s.
Fastest race lap: Owen, 1m 25.466s, 104.770mph/168.611km/h.
Pole position: Hingeley, 1m 25.108s, 105.210mph/169.320km/h.

Round 23 (29.848 miles/48.035km).
1 Jordan Cane, GB, 17m 19.865s, 103.332mph/166.296km/h; **2** Chase Owen, USA, +1.088s; **3** James Pull, GB, +2.793s; **4** Cameron Das, USA, +3.125s; **5** Ben Hingeley, GB, +6.752s; **6** Enaam Ahmed, GB, +7.300s; **7** Manuel Maldonado, YV, +9.006s; **8** Guilherme Samaia, BR, +11.388s; **9** Alex Quinn, GB, +12.625s; **10** Pavan Ravishankar, SGP, +17.438s.
Fastest race lap: Das, 1m 25.165s, 105.140mph/169.207km/h.
Pole position: Kjaergaard.

Round 24 (29.848 miles/48.035km).
1 Enaam Ahmed, GB, 17m 17.227s, 103.594mph/166.719km/h; **2** Jordan Cane, GB, +0.773s; **3** Alex Quinn, GB, +4.979s; **4** Ben Hingeley, GB, +6.204s; **5** James Pull, GB, +6.923s; **6** Chase Owen, USA, +7.494s; **7** Jamie Chadwick, GB, +8.943s; **8** Nicolai Kjaergaard, DK, +12.356s; **9** Manuel Maldonado, YV, +14.450s; **10** Pavan Ravishankar, SGP, +17.640s.
Fastest race lap: Ahmed, 1m 25.570s, 104.642mph/168.406km/h.
Pole position: Cameron Das, USA, 1m 25.165s, 105.140mph/169.207km/h.

Final championship points
Drivers
1 Enaam Ahmed, GB, 654; **2** James Pull, GB, 490; **3** Ben Hingeley, GB, 444; **4** Toby Sowery, GB, 432; **5** Cameron Das, USA, 425; **6** Callan O'Keeffe, ZA, 373; **7** Chase Owen, USA, 302; **8** Jordan Cane, GB, 288; **9** Jamie Chadwick, GB, 264; **10** Nicolai Kjaergaard, DK, 247; **11** Omar Ismail, GB, 216; **12** Manuel Maldonado, YV, 205; **13** Guilherme Samaia, BR, 195; **14** Jeremy Wahome, EAK, 165; **15** Nick Worm, D, 159; **16** Aaron Di Comberti, GB, 112; **17** Krishnaraaj Mahadik, IND, 104; **18** Tristan Charpentier, F, 53; **19** Harry Hayek, AUS, 51; **20** Alex Quinn, GB, 46; **21** Linus Lundqvist, S, 32; **22** Petru Florescu, RO, 22; **23** Pavan Ravishankar, SGP, 31.

All-Japan Formula 3 Championship

ALL-JAPAN FORMULA 3 CHAMPIONSHIP, Okayama International Circuit (TI Circuit Aida), Aida Gun, Okayama Prefecture, Japan, 1/2 April. 25, 18 and 18 laps of the 2.301-mile/3.703km circuit.
Round 1 (57.523 miles/92.575km).
1 Mitsunori Takaboshi, J (Dallara F312-Volkswagen), 34m 34.084s, 99.844mph/160.683km/h; **2** Sho Tsuboi, J (Dallara F317-Toyota), +4.609s; **3** Ritomo Miyata, J (Dallara F314-Toyota), +5.323s; **4** Alex Palou, E (Dallara F314-Threebond), +6.117s; **5** Hiroki Ohtsu, J (Dallara F316-Toda), +15.628s; **6** Sena Sakaguchi, J (Dallara F316-Toda), +25.215s; **7** Yoshiaki Katayama, J (Dallara F315-Mercedes Benz), +25.570s; **8** Hong Li Ye, CHN (Dallara F315-Volkswagen), +26.545s; **9** Ai Miura, J (Dallara F312-Volkswagen), +37.171s; **10** Tairoku Yamaguchi, J (Dallara F316-Volkswagen), +38.215s.
Fastest race lap: Takaboshi, 1m 22.010s, 101.004mph/162.551km/h.
Pole position: Palou, 1m 22.965s, 99.842mph/160.680km/h.

Round 2 (41.417 miles/66.654km).
1 Alex Palou, E (Dallara F314-Threebond), 24m 44.011s, 100.471mph/161.693km/h; **2** Mitsunori Takaboshi, J (Dallara F312-Volkswagen), +2.994s; **3** Ritomo Miyata, J (Dallara F314-Toyota), +20.140s; **4** Hong Li Ye, CHN (Dallara F315-Volkswagen), +21.515s; **5** Sena Sakaguchi, J (Dallara F316-Toda), +26.933s; **6** Tairoku Yamaguchi, J (Dallara F316-Volkswagen), +32.674s; **7** Hiroki Ohtsu, J (Dallara F316-Toda), +55.177s *; **8** Shigetomo Shimono, J (Dallara F306-Toyota), +1m 23.705s; **9** Sho Tsuboi, J (Dallara F317-Toyota), -1 lap; **10** Ryoya Hasegawa, J (Dallara F308-Toyota), -1.
** includes 40s penalty.*
Fastest race lap: Palou, 1m 21.380s, 101.786mph/163.809km/h.
Pole position: Palou, 1m 22.974s, 99.831mph/160.662km/h.

Round 3 (41.417 miles/66.654km).
1 Mitsunori Takaboshi, J (Dallara F312-Volkswagen), 24m 43.017s, 100.539mph/161.802km/h; **2** Alex Palou, E (Dallara F314-Threebond), +1.682s; **3** Ritomo Miyata, J (Dallara F314-Toyota), +3.399s; **4** Hiroki Ohtsu, J (Dallara F316-Toda), +9.239s; **5** Sho Tsuboi, J (Dallara F317-Toyota), +10.244s; **6** Hong Li Ye, CHN (Dallara F315-Volkswagen), +17.291s; **7** Sena Sakaguchi, J (Dallara F316-Toda), +22.078s; **8** Yoshiaki Katayama, J (Dallara F315-Mercedes Benz), +22.602s; **9** Ai Miura, J (Dallara F312-Volkswagen), +25.647s; **10** Tairoku Yamaguchi, J (Dallara F316-Volkswagen), +45.801s.
Fastest race lap: Takaboshi, 1m 21.524s, 101.607mph/163.520km/h.
Pole position: Palou.

ALL-JAPAN FORMULA 3 CHAMPIONSHIP, Suzuka International Racing Course, Suzuka-shi, Mie Prefecture, Japan, 22/23 April. 12 and 17 laps of the 3.608-mile/5.807km circuit.
Round 4 (43.300 miles/69.684km).
1 Mitsunori Takaboshi, J (Dallara F312-Volkswagen), 22m 33.048s, 115.206mph/185.405km/h; **2** Alex Palou, E (Dallara F314-Threebond), +3.768s; **3** Sho Tsuboi, J (Dallara F317-Toyota), +6.094s; **4** Sena Sakaguchi, J (Dallara F316-Toda), +11.173s; **5** Ai Miura, J (Dallara F312-Volkswagen), +20.596s; **6** Hong Li Ye, CHN (Dallara F315-Volkswagen), +22.173s; **7** Bruno Carneiro, USA (Dallara F315-Mercedes Benz), +31.995s; **8** Yoshiaki Katayama, J (Dallara F315-Mercedes Benz), +51.423s; **9** Shigetomo Shimono, J (Dallara F306-Toyota), +1m 06.451s; **10** Dragon, J (Dallara F306-Toyota), +1m 09.721s.
Fastest race lap: Takaboshi, 1m 52.166s, 115.810mph/186.377km/h.
Pole position: Takaboshi, 1m 50.999s, 117.027mph/188.337km/h.

Round 5 (61.341 miles/98.719km).
1 Mitsunori Takaboshi, J (Dallara F312-Volkswagen), 32m 00.297s, 114.997mph/185.069km/h; **2** Alex Palou, E (Dallara F314-Threebond), +5.159s; **3** Hiroki Ohtsu, J (Dallara F316-Toda), +8.596s; **4** Sena Sakaguchi, J (Dallara F316-Toda), +20.164s; **5** Yoshiaki Katayama, J (Dallara F315-Mercedes Benz), +21.399s; **6** Ai Miura, J (Dallara F312-Volkswagen), +29.248s; **7** Bruno Carneiro, USA (Dallara F315-Mercedes Benz), +31.831s; **8** Hong Li Ye, CHN (Dallara F315-Volkswagen), +33.465s; **9** Sho Tsuboi, J (Dallara F317-Toyota), +39.438s *; **10** Tairoku Yamaguchi, J (Dallara F316-Volkswagen), +46.300s.
** includes 30s penalty.*
Fastest race lap: Takaboshi, 1m 52.213s, 115.761mph/186.299km/h.
Pole position: Takaboshi, 1m 51.159s, 116.859mph/188.066km/h.

ALL-JAPAN FORMULA 3 CHAMPIONSHIP, Fuji International Speedway, Sunto-gun, Shizuoka Prefecture, Japan, 13/14 May. 15 and 21 laps of the 2.835-mile/4.563km circuit.
Round 6 (42.341 miles/68.141km).
1 Alex Palou, E (Dallara F314-Threebond), 27m 50.470s, 91.651mph/147.498km/h; **2** Hiroki Ohtsu, J (Dallara F316-Toda), +15.192s; **3** Hong Li Ye, CHN (Dallara F315-Volkswagen), +25.734s; **4** Sena Sakaguchi, J (Dallara F316-Toda), +27.195s; **5** Ritomo Miyata, J (Dallara F314-Toyota), +30.947s; **6** Bruno Carneiro, USA (Dallara F315-Mercedes Benz), +33.620s; **7** Sho Tsuboi, J (Dallara F317-Toyota), +44.789s; **8** Yoshiaki Katayama, J (Dallara F315-Mercedes Benz), +46.224s; **9** Ai Miura, J (Dallara F312-Volkswagen), +58.652s; **10** Dragon, J (Dallara F306-Toyota), +1m 23.914s.
Fastest race lap: Tsuboi, 1m 50.138s, 92.676mph/149.147km/h.
Pole position: Palou, 1m 51.649s, 91.422mph/147.129km/h.

Round 7 (59.353 miles/95.519km).
1 Mitsunori Takaboshi, J (Dallara F312-Volkswagen), 33m 27.952s, 106.747mph/171.793km/h; **2** Sho Tsuboi, J (Dallara F317-Toyota), +2.012s; **3** Ritomo Miyata, J (Dallara F314-Toyota), +7.033s; **4** Alex Palou, E (Dallara F314-Threebond), +11.079s; **5** Hiroki Ohtsu, J (Dallara F316-Toda), +19.551s; **6** Ai Miura, J (Dallara F312-Volkswagen), +36.778s; **7** Bruno Carneiro, USA (Dallara F315-Mercedes Benz), +37.231s; **8** Tairoku Yamaguchi, J (Dallara F316-Volkswagen), +37.735s; **9** Yoshiaki Katayama, J (Dallara F315-Mercedes Benz), +38.234s; **10** Hong Li Ye, CHN (Dallara F315-Volkswagen), +39.295s.
Fastest race lap: Tsuboi, 1m 34.831s, 107.635mph/173.222km/h.
Pole position: Palou, 1m 51.867s, 91.244mph/146.842km/h.

ALL-JAPAN FORMULA 3 CHAMPIONSHIP, Okayama International Circuit (TI Circuit Aida), Aida Gun, Okayama Prefecture, Japan, 27/28 May. 18 and 25 laps of the 2.301-mile/3.703km circuit.
Round 8 (41.417 miles/66.654km).
1 Mitsunori Takaboshi, J (Dallara F312-Volkswagen), 25m 05.039s, 99.068mph/159.434km/h; **2** Ritomo Miyata, J (Dallara F314-Toyota), +1.155s; **3** Sho Tsuboi, J (Dallara F317-Toyota), +3.634s; **4** Ai Miura, J (Dallara F312-Volkswagen), +17.700s; **5** Hong Li Ye, CHN (Dallara F315-Volkswagen), +18.355s; **6** Sena Sakaguchi, J (Dallara F316-Toda), +25.027s; **7** Tairoku Yamaguchi, J (Dallara F316-Volkswagen), +28.684s; **8** Alex Palou, E (Dallara F314-Threebond), +29.189s; **9** Dragon, J (Dallara F306-Toyota), +1m 18.359s; **10** Masayuki Ueda, J (Dallara F308-Toyota), +1m 19.462s.
Fastest race lap: Takaboshi, 1m 22.617s, 100.262mph/161.357km/h.
Pole position: Takaboshi, 1m 22.315s, 100.630mph/161.949km/h.

Round 9 (57.523 miles/92.575km).
1 Alex Palou, E (Dallara F314-Threebond), 34m 53.714s, 98.908mph/159.176km/h; **2** Ritomo Miyata, J (Dallara F314-Toyota), +0.936s; **3** Sho Tsuboi, J (Dallara F317-Toyota), +2.966s; **4** Mitsunori Takaboshi, J (Dallara F312-Volkswagen), +13.382s; **5** Hiroki Ohtsu, J (Dallara F316-Toda), +14.621s; **6** Ai Miura, J (Dallara F312-Volkswagen), +21.137s; **7** Yoshiaki Katayama, J (Dallara F315-Mercedes Benz), +22.079s; **8** Hong Li Ye, CHN (Dallara F315-Volkswagen), +30.225s; **9** Sena Sakaguchi, J (Dallara F316-Toda), +32.586s; **10** Bruno Carneiro, USA (Dallara F315-Mercedes Benz), +38.498s.
Fastest race lap: Miyata, 1m 23.085s, 99.698mph/160.448km/h.
Pole position: Palou, 1m 21.892s, 101.150mph/162.785km/h.

ALL-JAPAN FORMULA 3 CHAMPIONSHIP, Suzuka International Racing Course, Suzuka-shi, Mie Prefecture, Japan, 24/25 June. 12 and 17 laps of the 3.608-mile/5.807km circuit.
Round 10 (43.300 miles/69.684km).
1 Sho Tsuboi, J (Dallara F317-Toyota), 22m 50.657s, 113.726mph/183.023km/h; **2** Ritomo Miyata, J (Dallara F314-Toyota), +0.901s; **3** Mitsunori Takaboshi, J (Dallara F312-Volkswagen), +3.057s; **4** Alex Palou, E (Dallara F314-Threebond), +6.500s; **5** Hiroki Ohtsu, J (Dallara F316-Toda), +14.412s; **6** Hong Li Ye, CHN (Dallara F315-Volkswagen), +16.127s; **7** Sena Sakaguchi, J (Dallara F316-Toda), +16.796s; **8** Yoshiaki Katayama, J (Dallara F315-Mercedes Benz), +19.096s; **9** Bruno Carneiro, USA (Dallara F315-Mercedes Benz), +22.845s; **10** Ai Miura, J (Dallara F312-Volkswagen), +25.693s.
Fastest race lap: Takaboshi, 1m 53.858s, 114.089mph/183.608km/h.
Pole position: Tsuboi, 1m 52.746s, 115.214mph/185.419km/h.

Round 11 (61.341 miles/98.719km).
1 Sho Tsuboi, J (Dallara F317-Toyota), 32m 16.893s, 114.012mph/183.484km/h; **2** Alex Palou, E (Dallara F314-Threebond), +0.960s; **3** Mitsunori Takaboshi, J (Dallara F312-Volkswagen), +2.413s; **4** Ritomo Miyata, J (Dallara F314-Toyota), +3.192s; **5** Hiroki Ohtsu, J (Dallara F316-Toda), +20.700s; **6** Yoshiaki Katayama, J (Dallara F315-Mercedes Benz), +31.256s; **7** Ai Miura, J (Dallara F312-Volkswagen), +35.747s; **8** Bruno Carneiro, USA (Dallara F315-Mercedes Benz), +40.514s; **9** Hong Li Ye, CHN (Dallara F315-Volkswagen), +41.600s; **10** Tairoku Yamaguchi, J (Dallara F316-Volkswagen), +54.224s.
Fastest race lap: Palou, 1m 53.270s, 114.681mph/184.561km/h.
Pole position: Tsuboi, 1m 53.116s, 114.837mph/184.812km/h.

ALL-JAPAN FORMULA 3 CHAMPIONSHIP, Fuji International Speedway, Sunto-gun, Shizuoka Prefecture, Japan, 8/9 July. 15 and 21 laps of the 2.835-mile/4.563km circuit.
Round 12 (42.341 miles/68.141km).
1 Mitsunori Takaboshi, J (Dallara F312-Volkswagen), 24m 06.559s, 105.838mph/170.329km/h; **2** Hiroki Ohtsu, J (Dallara F316-Toda), +2.715s; **3** Alex Palou, E (Dallara F314-Threebond), +5.369s; **4** Sena Sakaguchi, J (Dallara F316-Toda), +9.536s; **5** Ai Miura, J (Dallara F312-Volkswagen), +11.677s; **6** Ritomo Miyata, J (Dallara F314-Toyota), +12.384s; **7** Hong Li Ye, CHN (Dallara F315-Volkswagen), +17.274s; **8** Bruno Carneiro, USA (Dallara F315-Mercedes Benz), +29.842s; **9** Dragon, J (Dallara F306-Toyota), +1m 03.134s; **10** Masayuki Ueda, J (Dallara F308-Toyota), +1m 11.395s.
Fastest race lap: Takaboshi, 1m 35.791s, 106.556mph/171.486km/h.
Pole position: Sho Tsuboi, J (Dallara F317-Toyota), 1m 34.167s, 108.394mph/174.443km/h.

Round 13 (59.353 miles/95.519km).
1 Sho Tsuboi, J (Dallara F317-Toyota), 33m 35.057s, 106.371mph/171.187km/h; **2** Mitsunori Takaboshi, J (Dallara F312-Volkswagen), +1.229s; **3** Hiroki Ohtsu, J (Dallara F316-Toda), +14.536s; **4** Alex Palou, E (Dallara F314-Threebond), +16.683s; **5** Ritomo Miyata, J (Dallara F314-Toyota), +23.260s; **6** Sena Sakaguchi, J (Dallara F316-Toda), +23.979s; **7** Hong Li Ye, CHN (Dallara F315-Volkswagen), +24.756s; **8** Ai Miura, J (Dallara F312-Volkswagen), +26.367s; **9** Tairoku Yamaguchi, J (Dallara F316-Volkswagen), +43.333s; **10** Dragon, J (Dallara F306-Toyota), +1m 16.009s.
Fastest race lap: Takaboshi, 1m 35.452s, 106.935mph/172.095km/h.
Pole position: Tsuboi, 1m 34.191s, 108.366mph/174.399km/h.

ALL-JAPAN FORMULA 3 CHAMPIONSHIP, Twin Ring Motegi, Motegi-machi, Haga-gun, Tochigi Prefecture, Japan, 29/30 July. 14, 14 and 20 laps of the 2.983-mile/4.801km circuit.
Round 14 (41.768 miles/67.219km).
1 Sho Tsuboi, J (Dallara F317-Toyota), 24m 37.391s, 101.778mph/163.795km/h; **2** Mitsunori Takaboshi, J (Dallara F312-Volkswagen), +0.894s; **3** Hiroki Ohtsu, J (Dallara F316-Toda), +8.358s; **4** Ritomo Miyata, J (Dallara F314-Toyota), +9.361s; **5** Yoshiaki Katayama, J (Dallara F315-Mercedes Benz), +18.939s; **6** Tairoku Yamaguchi, J (Dallara F316-Volkswagen), +25.420s; **7** Sena Sakaguchi, J (Dallara F316-Toda), +46.491s; **8** Dragon, J (Dallara F306-Toyota), +1m 09.127s; **9** Yuya Taira, J (Dallara F306-Toyota), +1m 09.396s; **10** Alex Yang, CHN (Dallara F306-Toyota), +1m 25.155s.
Fastest race lap: Takaboshi, 1m 44.880s, 102.406mph/164.807km/h.
Pole position: Tsuboi, 1m 44.200s, 103.075mph/165.883km/h.

Round 15 (41.768 miles/67.219km).
1 Sho Tsuboi, J (Dallara F317-Toyota), 24m 42.466s, 101.429mph/163.234km/h; **2** Mitsunori Takaboshi, J (Dallara F312-Volkswagen), +0.986s; **3** Alex Palou, E (Dallara F314-Threebond), +4.339s; **4** Hiroki Ohtsu, J (Dallara F316-Toda), +11.773s; **5** Yoshiaki Katayama, J (Dallara F315-Mercedes Benz), +18.031s; **6** Sena Sakaguchi, J (Dallara F316-Toda), +19.771s; **7** Ai Miura, J (Dallara F312-Volkswagen), +20.569s; **8** Ritomo Miyata, J (Dallara F314-Toyota), +21.950s; **9** Hong Li Ye, CHN (Dallara F315-Volkswagen), +28.913s; **10** Tairoku Yamaguchi, J (Dallara F316-Volkswagen), +30.220s.
Fastest race lap: Tsuboi, 1m 45.197s, 102.098mph/164.310km/h.
Pole position: Tsuboi, 1m 44.377s, 102.900mph/165.601km/h.

Round 16 (59.669 miles/96.028km).
1 Sho Tsuboi, J (Dallara F317-Toyota), 35m 23.235s, 101.170mph/162.817km/h; **2** Mitsunori Takaboshi, J (Dallara F312-Volkswagen), +0.841s; **3** Hiroki Ohtsu, J (Dallara F316-Toda), +11.159s; **4** Ritomo Miyata, J (Dallara F314-Toyota), +11.863s; **5** Yoshiaki Katayama, J (Dallara F315-Mercedes Benz), +23.517s; **6** Sena Sakaguchi, J (Dallara F316-Toda), +24.175s; **7** Alex Palou, E (Dallara F314-Threebond), +24.710s; **8** Tairoku Yamaguchi, J (Dallara F316-Volkswagen), +31.357s; **9** Hong Li Ye, CHN (Dallara F315-Volkswagen), +31.950s; **10** Ai Miura, J (Dallara F312-Volkswagen), +32.650s.
Fastest race lap: Takaboshi, 1m 45.551s, 101.755mph/163.759km/h.
Pole position: Tsuboi.

ALL-JAPAN FORMULA 3 CHAMPIONSHIP, Autopolis International Racing Course, Kamitsue-mura, Hita-gun, Oita Prefecture, Japan, 9/10 September. 15 and 21 laps of the 2.904-mile/4.674km circuit.
Round 17 (43.564 miles/70.110km).
1 Sho Tsuboi, J (Dallara F317-Toyota), 24m 47.314s, 105.446mph/169.699km/h; **2** Alex Palou, E (Dallara F314-Threebond), +12.805s; **3** Mitsunori Takaboshi, J (Dallara F312-Volkswagen), +13.470s; **4** Ritomo Miyata, J (Dallara F314-Toyota), +13.904s; **5** Sena Sakaguchi, J (Dallara F316-Toda), +16.911s; **6** Yoshiaki Katayama, J (Dallara F315-Mercedes Benz), +36.300s; **7** Ai Miura, J (Dallara F312-Volkswagen), +37.797s; **8** Tairoku Yamaguchi, J (Dallara F316-Volkswagen), +44.665s; **9** Bruno Carneiro, USA (Dallara F315-Mercedes Benz), +44.786s; **10** Hiroki Ohtsu, J (Dallara F316-Toda), +44.999s.
Fastest race lap: Tsuboi, 1m 38.646s, 105.990mph/170.574km/h.
Pole position: Tsuboi, 1m 37.412s, 107.332mph/172.734km/h.

Round 18 (60.990 miles/98.154km).
1 Sho Tsuboi, J (Dallara F317-Toyota), 34m 57.505s, 104.679mph/168.464km/h; **2** Ritomo Miyata, J (Dallara F314-Toyota), +3.083s; **3** Mitsunori Takaboshi, J (Dallara F312-Volkswagen), +10.564s; **4** Alex Palou, E (Dallara F314-Threebond), +12.783s; **5** Hiroki Ohtsu, J (Dallara F316-Toda), +15.781s; **6** Sena Sakaguchi, J (Dallara F316-Toda), +20.213s; **7** Bruno Carneiro, USA (Dallara F315-Mercedes Benz), +30.771s; **8** Ai Miura, J (Dallara F312-Volkswagen), +42.840s; **9** Yoshiaki Katayama, J (Dallara F315-Mercedes

Benz), +54.301s; **10** Tairoku Yamaguchi, J (Dallara F316-Volkswagen), +1m 12.819s.
Fastest race lap: Takaboshi, 1m 39.364s, 105.224mph/169.341km/h.
Pole position: Tsuboi, 1m 37.925s, 106.770mph/171.829km/h.

ALL-JAPAN FORMULA 3 CHAMPIONSHIP, Sportsland-SUGO International Course, Shibata-gun, Miyagi Prefecture, Japan, 23/24 September. 18 and 25 laps of the 2.302-mile/3.704km circuit.
Round 19 (41.431 miles/66.677km).
1 Sho Tsuboi, J (Dallara F317-Toyota), 26m 34.327s, 93.551mph/150.556km/h; **2** Ritomo Miyata, J (Dallara F314-Toyota), +1.231s; **3** Sena Sakaguchi, J (Dallara F316-Toda), +2.856s; **4** Mitsunori Takaboshi, J (Dallara F312-Volkswagen), +3.775s; **5** Alex Palou, E (Dallara F314-Threebond), +5.232s; **6** Yoshiaki Katayama, J (Dallara F315-Mercedes Benz), +6.468s; **7** Bruno Carneiro, USA (Dallara F315-Mercedes Benz), +8.834s; **8** Ai Miura, J (Dallara F312-Volkswagen), +12.053s; **9** Dragon, J (Dallara F315-Volkswagen), +15.618s; **10** Tairoku Yamaguchi, J (Dallara F316-Volkswagen), +16.126s.
Fastest race lap: Miyata, 1m 13.180s, 113.230mph/182.226km/h.
Pole position: Hiroki Ohtsu, J (Dallara F316-Toda), 1m 12.588s, 114.154mph/183.712km/h.

Round 20 (57.543 miles/92.606km).
1 Hiroki Ohtsu, J (Dallara F316-Toda), 34m 15.112s, 100.800mph/162.221km/h; **2** Sho Tsuboi, J (Dallara F317-Toyota), +0.226s; **3** Ritomo Miyata, J (Dallara F314-Toyota), +1.687s; **4** Mitsunori Takaboshi, J (Dallara F312-Volkswagen), +1.746s; **5** Alex Palou, E (Dallara F314-Threebond), +3.442s; **6** Ai Miura, J (Dallara F312-Volkswagen), +8.708s; **7** Bruno Carneiro, USA (Dallara F315-Mercedes Benz), +8.737s; **8** Yoshiaki Katayama, J (Dallara F315-Mercedes Benz), +11.318s; **9** Sena Sakaguchi, J (Dallara F316-Toda), +34.756s *; **10** Shi Jie Hong, CHN (Dallara F315-Volkswagen), +38.931s.
** includes 30s penalty.*
Fastest race lap: Palou, 1m 14.621s, 111.044mph/178.707km/h.
Pole position: Ohtsu, 1m 12.980s, 113.540mph/182.726km/h.

Final championship points
Drivers
1 Mitsunori Takaboshi, J, 148; **2** Sho Tsuboi, J, 140; **3** Alex Palou, E, 102; **4** Ritomo Miyata, J, 79; **5** Hiroki Ohtsu, J, 64; **6** Sena Sakaguchi, J, 27; **7** Hong Li Ye, CHN, 13; **8** Ai Miura, J, 11; **9** Yoshiaki Katayama, J, 11; **10** Tairoku Yamaguchi, J, 2; **11** Bruno Carneiro, USA, 1.

Drivers (National Class)
1 Dragon, J, 136; **2** Masayuki Ueda, J, 92; **3** Ryoya Hasegawa, J, 77; **4** Alex Yang, CHN, 75; **5** Shigetomo Shimono, J, 52; **6** Katsuaki Kubota, J, 49; **7** Yuya Taira, J, 29; **8** Yuya Motojima, J, 24; **9** Motoyoshi Yoshida, J, 18; **10** Shinji Sawada, J, 14; **11** Ryu Ohtsuka, J, 10; **12** Takashi Fujii, J, 8; **13** Syuji, J, 4; **14** Makoto Hotta, J, 3.

Teams
1 TOM'S, 143; **2** B-MAX Racing Team with NDDP, 134; **3** ThreeBond Racing with Drago Corse, 94; **4** Toda Racing, 62.

Major Non-Championship Formula 3

64TH FORMULA 3 MACAU GRAND PRIX, Circuito da Guia, Macau, 18/19 November. 10 and 15 laps of the 3.803-mile/6.120km circuit.
Race 1 (57.042 miles/91.800km).
1 Dan Ticktum, GB (Dallara F317-Volkswagen), 39m 56.648s, 85.682mph/137.892km/h; **2** Lando Norris, GB (Dallara F317-Volkswagen), +0.568s; **3** Ralf Aron, EST (Dallara F317-Mercedes Benz), +1.763s; **4** Ferdinand Habsburg, A (Dallara F316-Volkswagen), +1.953s; **5** Maximilian Günther, D (Dallara F316-Mercedes Benz), +4.463s; **6** Pedro Piquet, BR (Dallara F316-Mercedes Benz), +5.141s; **7** Sacha Fenestraz, F (Dallara F312-Volkswagen), +5.386s; **8** Guan Yu Zhou, CHN (Dallara F315-Mercedes Benz), +6.483s; **9** Tadasuke Makino, J (Dallara F316-Volkswagen), +7.626s; **10** Jehan Daruvala, IND (Dallara F315-Volkswagen), +10.455s.
Fastest race lap: Mick Schumacher, D (Dallara F317-Mercedes Benz), 2m 12.651s, 103.203mph/166.089km/h.
Pole position: Callum Ilott, GB (Dallara F314-Mercedes Benz).

Race 2 (38.028 miles/61.200km).
1 Callum Ilott, GB (Dallara F314-Mercedes Benz), 22m 18.077s, 102.311mph/164.654km/h; **2** Joel Eriksson, S (Dallara F315-Volkswagen), +7.957s; **3** Sérgio Sette Câmara, BR (Dallara F315-Volkswagen), +8.643s; **4** Maximilian Günther, D (Dallara F316-Mercedes Benz), +9.798s; **5** Ferdinand Habsburg, A (Dallara F316-Volkswagen), +10.391s; **6** Pedro Piquet, BR (Dallara F316-Mercedes Benz), +10.821s; **7** Lando Norris, GB (Dallara F317-Volkswagen), +11.966s; **8** Dan Ticktum, GB (Dallara F317-Volkswagen), +12.657s; **9** Yuhi Sekiguchi, J (Dallara F312-Volkswagen), +13.418s; **10** Guan Yu Zhou, CHN (Dallara F315-Mercedes Benz), +14.715s.
Fastest race lap: Ticktum, 2m 12.281s, 103.492mph/166.554km/h.
Pole position: Eriksson, 2m 10.720s, 104.728mph/168.543km/h.

Formula V8 3.5

All cars are Dallara FR35-12-Zytek.

FORMULA V8 3.5, Silverstone Arena Grand Prix Circuit, Towcester, Northamptonshire, Great Britain, 15/16 April. Round 1. 24 and 22 laps of the 3.667-mile/5.901km circuit.
Race 1 (88.001 miles/141.624km).
1 Pietro Fittipaldi, BR, 42m 05.753s, 125.429mph/201.859km/h; **2** Egor Orudzhev, RUS, +0.749s; **3** Alfonso Celis, MEX, +1.584s; **4** Matevos Isaakyan, RUS, +6.295s; **5** Rene Binder, A, +13.977s; **6** Damiano Fioravanti, I, +16.208s; **7** Nelson Mason, CDN, +16.506s; **8** Konstantin Tereschenko, RUS, +42.969s; **9** Diego Menchaca, MEX, +44.276s; **10** Yu Kanamaru, J, +59.534s.
Fastest race lap: Celis, 1m 43.545s, 127.482mph/205.162km/h.
Pole position: Fittipaldi, 1m 41.660s, 129.846mph/208.967km/h.

Race 2 (80.668 miles/129.822km).
1 Pietro Fittipaldi, BR, 41m 50.035s, 115.697mph/186.196km/h; **2** Egor Orudzhev, RUS, +2.623s; **3** Roy Nissany, IL, +5.404s; **4** Rene Binder, A, +6.298s; **5** Konstantin Tereschenko, RUS, +6.930s; **6** Alfonso Celis, MEX, +7.913s; **7** Diego Menchaca, MEX, +13.423s; **8** Damiano Fioravanti, I, +14.077s; **9** Giuseppe Cipriani, I, +29.837s; Matevos Isaakyan, RUS, -12 laps (DNF).
Fastest race lap: Nelson Mason, CDN, 1m 43.386s, 127.678mph/205.478km/h.
Pole position: Fittipaldi, 1m 47.787s, 122.465mph/197.088km/h.

FORMULA V8 3.5, Circuit de Spa-Francorchamps, Stavelot, Belgium, 5/6 May. Round 2. 2 x 21 laps of the 4.352-mile/7.004km circuit.
Race 1 (91.392 miles/147.082km).
1 Alfonso Celis, MEX, 43m 10.639s, 127.000mph/204.387km/h; **2** Roy Nissany, IL, +2.929s; **3** Egor Orudzhev, RUS, +24.857s; **4** Diego Menchaca, MEX, +34.230s; **5** Yu Kanamaru, J, +40.360s; **6** Rene Binder, A, +41.993s; **7** Damiano Fioravanti, I, +42.331s; **8** Pietro Fittipaldi, BR, +49.342s; **9** Nelson Mason, CDN, +59.602s; **10** Konstantin Tereschenko, RUS, +1m 20.541s.
Fastest race lap: Nissany, 2m 02.369s, 128.033mph/206.049km/h.
Pole position: Celis, 1m 59.387s, 131.231mph/211.195km/h.

Race 2 (91.392 miles/147.082km).
1 Matevos Isaakyan, RUS, 43m 49.000s, 125.147mph/201.405km/h; **2** Rene Binder, A, +3.009s; **3** Alfonso Celis, MEX, +5.715s; **4** Roy Nissany, IL, +8.550s; **5** Diego Menchaca, MEX, +13.064s; **6** Pietro Fittipaldi, BR, +21.767s; **7** Egor Orudzhev, RUS, +27.639s; **8** Yu Kanamaru, J, +31.944s; **9** Nelson Mason, CDN, +33.611s; **10** Damiano Fioravanti, I, +34.184s.
Fastest race lap: Isaakyan, 2m 02.842s, 127.540mph/205.255km/h.
Pole position: Fittipaldi, 1m 58.731s, 131.956mph/212.362km/h.

FORMULA V8 3.5, Autodromo Nazionale di Monza, Milan, Italy, 13/14 May. Round 3. 26 and 24 laps of the 3.600-mile/5.793km circuit.
Race 1 (93.590 miles/150.618km).
1 Rene Binder, A, 42m 18.590s, 132.720mph/213.592km/h; **2** Roy Nissany, IL, +3.120s *; **3** Matevos Isaakyan, RUS, +13.611s; **4** Alfonso Celis, MEX, +24.053s; **5** Egor Orudzhev, RUS, +34.635s; **6** Nelson Mason, CDN, +35.294s; **7** Diego Menchaca, MEX, +35.381s; **8** Konstantin Tereschenko, RUS, +52.242s; **9** Pietro Fittipaldi, BR, -1 lap; **10** Giuseppe Cipriani, I, -1 **.
** includes 5s penalty. ** includes 1-place penalty.*
Fastest race lap: Fittipaldi, 1m 36.712s, 133.991mph/215.638km/h.
Pole position: Fittipaldi, 1m 34.808s, 136.682mph/219.968km/h.

Race 2 (86.390 miles/139.032km).
1 Rene Binder, A, 40m 34.981s, 127.724mph/205.551km/h; **2** Roy Nissany, IL, +7.065s; **3** Yu Kanamaru, J, +11.315s; **4** Pietro Fittipaldi, BR, +11.694s; **5** Matevos Isaakyan, RUS, +28.945s; **6** Nelson Mason, CDN, +32.119s; **7** Konstantin Tereschenko, RUS, +33.342s *; **8** Giuseppe Cipriani, I, +1m 59.065s **; Alfonso Celis, MEX, -17 laps (DNF); Egor Orudzhev, RUS, -19 (DNF).
** includes 5s penalty.*
*** includes 60s penalty.*
Fastest race lap: Nissany, 1m 35.626s, 135.513mph/218.087km/h.
Pole position: Fittipaldi, 1m 33.813s, 138.131mph/222.301km/h.

FORMULA V8 3.5, Circuito Permanente de Jerez, Jerez de la Frontera, Spain, 27/28 May. Round 4. 26 and 27 laps of the 2.751-mile/4.428km circuit.
Race 1 (71.537 miles/115.128km).
1 Roy Nissany, IL, 42m 24.972s, 101.193mph/162.854km/h; **2** Pietro Fittipaldi, BR, +0.556s; **3** Matevos Isaakyan, RUS, +1.415s; **4** Rene Binder, A, +5.664s; **5** Nelson Mason, CDN, +25.198s; **6** Alfonso Celis, MEX, +25.318s; **7** Yu Kanamaru, J, +25.948s; **8** Konstantin Tereschenko, RUS, +31.429s; **9** Diego Menchaca, MEX, +31.655s; **10** Giuseppe Cipriani, I, +59.252s.
Fastest race lap: Egor Orudzhev, RUS, 1m 31.219s, 108.586mph/174.753km/h.
Pole position: Orudzhev, 1m 26.811s, 114.100mph/183.626km/h.

Race 2 (74.289 miles/119.556km).
1 Pietro Fittipaldi, BR, 41m 45.053s, 106.759mph/171.813km/h; **2** Egor Orudzhev, RUS, +4.373s; **3** Matevos Isaakyan, RUS, +7.577s; **4** Alfonso Celis, MEX, +8.164s; **5** Rene Binder, A, +10.657s; **6** Damiano Fioravanti, I, +11.171s; **7** Konstantin Tereschenko, RUS, +28.597s; **8** Nelson Mason, CDN, +29.865s; **9** Diego Menchaca, MEX, +30.226s; **10** Yu Kanamaru, J, +30.489s.
Fastest race lap: Fittipaldi, 1m 30.014s, 110.040mph/177.092km/h.
Pole position: Fittipaldi, 1m 26.515s, 114.490mph/184.254km/h.

FORMULA V8 3.5, MotorLand Aragón, Alcañiz, Aragon, Spain, 24/25 June. Round 5. 23 and 24 laps of the 3.321-mile/5.344km circuit.
Race 1 (76.374 miles/122.912km).
1 Egor Orudzhev, RUS, 41m 48.398s, 109.610mph/176.400km/h; **2** Matevos Isaakyan, RUS, +13.134s; **3** Alfonso Celis, MEX, +19.577s; **4** Roy Nissany, IL, +20.084s; **5** Rene Binder, A, +20.217s; **6** Konstantin Tereschenko, RUS, +29.415s; **7** Yu Kanamaru, J, +37.911s; **8** Damiano Fioravanti, I, +38.606s; **9** Diego Menchaca, MEX, +38.946s; **10** Giuseppe Cipriani, I, +50.849s.
Fastest race lap: Orudzhev, 1m 44.473s, 114.423mph/184.147km/h.
Pole position: Pietro Fittipaldi, BR, 1m 41.222s, 118.098mph/190.061km/h.

Race 2 (79.695 miles/128.256km).
1 Pietro Fittipaldi, BR, 42m 26.477s, 112.665mph/181.317km/h; **2** Alfonso Celis, MEX, +2.381s; **3** Egor Orudzhev, RUS, +11.554s; **4** Yu Kanamaru, J, +16.570s; **5** Matevos Isaakyan, RUS, +20.087s; **6** Roy Nissany, IL, +29.252s; **7** Diego Menchaca, MEX, +30.863s; **8** Damiano Fioravanti, I, +35.204s; **9** Nelson Mason, CDN, +44.461s; **10** Giuseppe Cipriani, I, +1m 16.934s.
Fastest race lap: Orudzhev, 1m 44.139s, 114.790mph/184.737km/h.
Pole position: Fittipaldi, 1m 40.765s, 118.634mph/190.923km/h.

FORMULA V8 3.5, Nürburgring, Nürburg/Eifel, Germany, 15/16 July. Round 6. 25 and 20 laps of the 3.199-mile/5.148km circuit.
Race 1 (79.970 miles/128.700km).
1 Matevos Isaakyan, RUS, 43m 26.086s, 110.469mph/177.783km/h; **2** Alfonso Celis, MEX, +6.357s; **3** Egor Orudzhev, RUS, +19.145s; **4** Roy Nissany, IL, +19.792s; **5** Yu Kanamaru, J, +35.361s; **6** Rene Binder, A, +35.828s; **7** Pietro Fittipaldi, BR, +36.134s; **8** Diego Menchaca, MEX, +42.254s; **9** Konstantin Tereschenko, RUS, +43.421s; **10** Damiano Fioravanti, I, +55.198s.
Fastest race lap: Isaakyan, 1m 43.791s, 110.951mph/178.558km/h.
Pole position: Alex Palou, E, 1m 42.174s, 112.707mph/181.384km/h.

Race 2 (63.976 miles/102.960km).
1 Alex Palou, E, 42m 06.724s, 91.151mph/146.694km/h; **2** Matevos Isaakyan, RUS, +9.541s; **3** Egor Orudzhev, RUS, +14.319s; **4** Konstantin Tereschenko, RUS, +18.692s *; **5** Roy Nissany, IL, +20.873s; **6** Pietro Fittipaldi, BR, +29.918s; **7** Yu Kanamaru, J, +41.830s; **8** Alfonso Celis, MEX, +44.482s *; **9** Rene Binder, A, +1m 02.432s; **10** Diego Menchaca, MEX, -1 lap.
** includes 10s penalty for crossing the white line at pit exit.*
Fastest race lap: Palou, 1m 48.716s, 105.925mph/170.469km/h.
Pole position: Palou, 1m 40.840s, 114.198mph/183.784km/h.

FORMULA V8 3.5, Autódromo Hermanos Rodriguez, Mexico City, D.F., Mexico, 2/3 September. Round 7. 27 and 25 laps of the 2.674-mile/4.304km circuit.
Race 1 (72.208 miles/116.208km).
1 Pietro Fittipaldi, BR, 43m 03.238s, 100.629mph/161.947km/h; **2** Matevos Isaakyan, RUS, +3.227s; **3** Alex Palou, E, +5.912s; **4** Konstantin Tereschenko, RUS, +8.253s; **5** Alfonso Celis, MEX, +10.437s; **6** Rene Binder, A, +15.517s; **7** Yu Kanamaru, J, +24.577s; **8** Diego Menchaca, MEX, +40.922s *; **9** Roy Nissany, IL, +41.594s *; **10** Giuseppe Cipriani, I, +1m 07.042s.
** includes 10s penalty.*
Fastest race lap: Isaakyan, 1m 32.524s, 104.057mph/167.463km/h.
Pole position: Fittipaldi, 1m 31.382s, 105.357mph/169.556km/h.

Race 2 (66.860 miles/107.600km).
1 Pietro Fittipaldi, BR, 42m 15.595s, 94.926mph/152.768km/h; **2** Alfonso Celis, MEX, +1.062s; **3** Konstantin Tereschenko, RUS, +2.023s; **4** Matevos Isaakyan, RUS, +11.178s; **5** Diego Menchaca, MEX, +39.362s; **6** Giuseppe Cipriani, I, +51.059s; **7** Yu Kanamaru, J, +57.867s; **8** Roy Nissany, IL, -2 laps; Rene Binder, A, -12 (DNF); Alex Palou, E, -24 (DNF).
Fastest race lap: Isaakyan, 1m 32.144s, 104.486mph/168.154km/h.
Pole position: Fittipaldi, 1m 30.635s, 106.225mph/170.953km/h.

FORMULA V8 3.5, Circuit of the Americas, Austin, Texas, USA, 15/16 September. Round 8. 22 and 23 laps of the 3.426-mile/5.513km circuit.
Race 1 (75.364 miles/121.286km).
1 Rene Binder, A, 43m 14.765s, 104.560mph/168.273km/h; **2** Egor Orudzhev, RUS, +1.249s; **3** Pietro Fittipaldi, BR, +10.899s; **4** Matevos Isaakyan, RUS, +21.513s; **5** Alex Palou, E, +13.671s *; **6** Roy Nissany, IL, +22.842s; **7** Yu Kanamaru, J, +24.926s; **8** Alfonso Celis, MEX, +27.159s; **9** Diego Menchaca, MEX, +30.672s; Konstantin Tereschenko, RUS, -5 laps (DNF).
** includes drop of 1 place.*
Fastest race lap: Binder, 1m 52.800s, 109.328mph/175.946km/h.
Pole position: Binder, 1m 49.764s, 112.352mph/180.813km/h.

Race 2 (78.789 miles/126.799km).
1 Egor Orudzhev, RUS, 43m 42.573s, 108.153mph/174.056km/h; **2** Alex Palou, E, +5.418s; **3** Diego Menchaca, MEX, +22.194s; **4** Roy Nissany, IL, +42.044s; **5** Alfonso Celis, MEX, +45.063s; **6** Matevos Isaakyan, RUS, +52.896s; **7** Yu Kanamaru, J, +1m 48.790s; **8** Konstantin Tereschenko, RUS, +2m 01.104s; **9** Giuseppe Cipriani, I, -1 lap; **10** Rene Binder, A, -1.
Fastest race lap: Binder, 1m 51.437s, 110.665mph/178.098km/h.
Pole position: Palou, 1m 49.411s, 112.714mph/181.396km/h.

FORMULA V8 3.5, Bahrain International Circuit, Sakhir, Bahrain, 17/18 November. Round 9. 2 x 23 laps of the 3.363-mile/5.412km circuit.
Race 1 (77.346 miles/124.476km).
1 Henrique Chaves Jr, P, 42m 07.489s, 110.166mph/177.295km/h; **2** Pietro Fittipaldi, BR, +1.654s; **3** Roy Nissany, IL, +3.752s; **4** Yu Kanamaru, J, +7.447s; **5** Tatiana Calderón, CO, +9.334s; **6** Alfonso Celis, MEX, +11.791s; **7** Konstantin Tereschenko, RUS, +17.075s; **8** Diego Menchaca, MEX, +23.509s; **9** Rene Binder, A, -1 lap; Matevos Isaakyan, RUS, -5 (DNF).
Fastest race lap: Chaves Jr, 1m 48.627s, 111.448mph/179.358km/h.
Pole position: Isaakyan, 1m 44.727s, 115.598mph/186.037km/h.

Race 2 (77.346 miles/124.476km).
1 Rene Binder, A, 42m 29.001s, 109.236mph/175.799km/h; **2** Pietro Fittipaldi, BR, +2.542s; **3** Tatiana Calderón, CO, +13.573s; **4** Roy Nissany, IL, +21.904s; **5** Henrique Chaves Jr, P, +22.890s; **6** Yu Kanamaru, J, +23.796s; **7** Diego Menchaca, MEX, +31.879s; **8** Alfonso Celis, MEX, +1m 17.722s *; **9** Matevos Isaakyan, RUS, +1m 25.427s; Konstantin Tereschenko, RUS, -23 laps (DNF).
** includes 20s penalty due to pit stop out of window.*
Fastest race lap: Kanamaru, 1m 48.216s, 111.871mph/180.039km/h.
Pole position: Binder, 1m 44.730s, 115.595mph/186.032km/h.

Final championship points
Drivers
1 Pietro Fittipaldi, BR, 259; **2** Matevos Isaakyan, RUS, 215; **3** Alfonso Celis, MEX, 204; **4** Rene Binder, A, 201; **5** Roy Nissany, IL, 201; **6** Egor Orudzhev, RUS, 198; **7** Yu Kanamaru, J, 115; **8** Konstantin Tereschenko, RUS, 94; **9** Diego Menchaca, MEX, 94; **10** Alex Palou, E, 68; **11** Nelson Mason, CDN, 42; **12** Damiano Fioravanti, I, 36; **13** Henrique Chaves Jr, P, 35; **14** Tatiana Calderón, CO, 25; **15** Giuseppe Cipriani, I, 21.

Teams
1 Lotus, 460; **2** SMP Racing by AVF, 419; **3** Rp Motorsport, 342; **4** Fortec Motorsports, 298; **5** Teo Martin Motorsport, 198; **6** AVF, 35; **7** Il Barone Rampante, 33.

FIA World Endurance Championship

6 HOURS OF SILVERSTONE, Silverstone Arena Grand Prix Circuit, Towcester, Northamptonshire, Great Britain, 16 April. Round 1. 197 laps of the 3.667-mile/5.901km circuit, 722.342 miles/1162.497km.
1 Sébastien Buemi/Anthony Davidson/Kazuki Nakajima, CH/GB/J (Toyota TS050 HYBRID), 6h 00m 33.211s, 120.205mph/193.452km/h; **2** Timo Bernhard/Earl Bamber/Brendon Hartley, D/NZ/NZ (Porsche 919 Hybrid '17), +6.173s; **3** Neel Jani/André Lotterer/Nick Tandy, CH/D/GB (Porsche 919 Hybrid '17), +46.956s; **4** Ho-Pin Tung/Oliver Jarvis/Thomas Laurent, CHN/GB/F (ORECA 07-Gibson), -13 laps; **5** Julien Canal/Nicolas Prost/

Bruno Senna, F/F/BR (ORECA 07-Gibson), -13; **6** François Perrodo/Matthieu Vaxivière/Emmanuel Collard, F/F/F (ORECA 07-Gibson), -13; **7** Nicolas Lapierre/Gustavo Menezes/Matt Rao, F/USA/GB (Alpine A470-Gibson), -14; **8** Roman Rusinov/Pierre Thiriet/Alex Lynn, RUS/F/GB (ORECA 07-Gibson), -14; **9** Tor Graves/Jonathan Hirschi/Jean-Éric Vergne, GB/CH/F (ORECA 07-Gibson), -14; **10** Roberto González/Simon Trummer/Vitaly Petrov, MEX/CH/RUS (ORECA 07-Gibson), -15.
Fastest race lap: Mike Conway, GB (Toyota TS050 HYBRID), 1m 39.656s, 132.457mph/213.169km/h.
Pole position: Mike Conway/Kamui Kobayashi/José María López, GB/J/RA (Toyota TS050 HYBRID), 1m 37.304s, 135.658mph/218.321km/h.

6 HOURS OF SPA-FRANCORCHAMPS, Circuit de Spa-Francorchamps, Stavelot, Belgium, 6 May. Round 2. 173 laps of the 4.352-mile/7.004km circuit, 752.900 miles/1211.675km.
1 Sébastien Buemi/Anthony Davidson/Kazuki Nakajima, CH/GB/J (Toyota TS050 HYBRID), 6h 00m 11.490s, 125.416mph/201.838km/h; **2** Mike Conway/Kamui Kobayashi, GB/J (Toyota TS050 HYBRID), +1.992s; **3** Timo Bernhard/Earl Bamber/Brendon Hartley, D/NZ/NZ (Porsche 919 Hybrid '17), +35.283s; **4** Neel Jani/André Lotterer/Nick Tandy, CH/D/GB (Porsche 919 Hybrid '17), +1m 25.438s; **5** Stéphane Sarrazin/Yuji Kunimoto/Nicolas Lapierre, F/J/F (Toyota TS050 HYBRID), -2 laps; **6** Oliver Webb/Dominik Kraihamer/James Rossiter, GB/A/GB (ENSO CLM P1/01-NISMO), -12; **7** Roman Rusinov/Pierre Thiriet/Alex Lynn, RUS/F/GB (ORECA 07-Gibson), -13; **8** Julien Canal/Nicolas Prost/Bruno Senna, F/F/BR (ORECA 07-Gibson), -13; **9** Ho-Pin Tung/Oliver Jarvis/Thomas Laurent, CHN/GB/F (ORECA 07-Gibson), -13; **10** Mathias Beche/David Heinemeier Hansson/Nelson Piquet Jr, CH/DK/BR (ORECA 07-Gibson), -14.
Fastest race lap: Hartley, 1m 57.638s, 133.182mph/214.335km/h.
Pole position: Jani/Lotterer/Tandy, 1m 54.097s, 137.315mph/220.987km/h.

24 HEURES DU MANS, Circuit International Du Mans, Les Raineries, Le Mans, France, 17 June. Round 3. 367 laps of the 8.469-mile/13.629km circuit, 3108.001 miles/5001.843km.
1 Timo Bernhard/Earl Bamber/Brendon Hartley, D/NZ/NZ (Porsche 919 Hybrid), 24h 01m 14.075s, 129.389mph/208.232km/h; **2** Ho-Pin Tung/Thomas Laurent/Oliver Jarvis, CHN/F/GB (ORECA 07-Gibson), -1 lap; **3** David Cheng/Tristan Gommendy/Alex Brundle, USA/F/GB (ORECA 07-Gibson), -4; **4** Nelson Panciatici/Pierre Ragues/André Negrão, F/F/BR (Alpine A470-Gibson), -5; **5** Will Owen/Hugo de Sadeleer/Filipe Albuquerque, USA/CH/P (Ligier JS P217-Gibson), -5; **6** James Allen/Franck Matelli/Richard Bradley, AUS/F/GB (ORECA 07-Gibson), -6; **7** Tor Graves/Jonathan Hirschi/Jean-Éric Vergne, GB/CH/F (ORECA 07-Gibson), -7 *; **8** Sébastien Buemi/Anthony Davidson/Kazuki Nakajima, CH/GB/J (Toyota TS050 HYBRID), -9; **9** Roberto Lacorte/Giorgio Sernagiotto/Andrea Belicchi, I/I/I (Dallara P217-Gibson), -14; **10** Romain Dumas/Gustavo Menezes/Matt Rao, F/USA/GB (Alpine A470-Gibson), -16; **11** Nigel Moore/Phil Hanson/Karun Chandhok, GB/GB/IND (Ligier JS P217-Gibson), -16; **12** Patrice Lafargue/Paul Lafargue/David Zollinger, F/F/F (Ligier JS P217-Gibson), -23; **13** Jan Lammers/Frits van Eerd/Rubens Barrichello, NL/NL/BR (Dallara P217-Gibson), -23; **14** Henrik Hedman/Ben Hanley/Felix Rosenqvist, S/GB/S (ORECA 07-Gibson), -24; **15** Jacques Nicolet/Pierre Nicolet/Erik Maris, F/F/F (Ligier JS P217-Gibson), -26; **16** Nicolas Prost/Julien Canal/Bruno Senna, F/F/BR (ORECA 07-Gibson), -27; **17** Darren Turner/Jonny Adam/Daniel Serra, GB/GB/BR (Aston Martin Vantage), -27; **18** Andy Priaulx/Harry Tincknell/Pipo Derani, GB/GB/BR (Ford GT), -27; **19** Jan Magnussen/Antonio García/Jordan Taylor, DK/E/USA (Chevrolet Corvette C7.R), -27; **20** Richard Lietz/Frédéric Makowiecki/Patrick Pilet, A/F/F (Porsche 911 RSR), -28; **21** Davide Rigon/Sam Bird/Miguel Molina, I/GB/E (Ferrari 488 GTE), -28; **22** Joey Hand/Dirk Müller/Tony Kanaan, USA/D/BR (Ford GT), -28; **23** Ryan Briscoe/Richard Westbrook/Scott Dixon, AUS/GB/NZ (Ford GT), -30; **24** Oliver Gavin/Tommy Milner/Marcel Fässler, GB/USA/CH (Chevrolet Corvette C7.R), -32; **25** Nicki Thiim/Marco Sørensen/Richie Stanaway, DK/DK/NZ (Aston Martin Vantage), -33; **26** Rob Smith/Will Stevens/Dries Vanthoor, GB/GB/B (Ferrari 488 GTE), -34; **27** Stefan Mücke/Olivier Pla/Billy Johnson, D/F/USA (Ford GT), -35; **28** Duncan Cameron/Aaron Scott/Marco Cioci, GB/GB/I (Ferrari 488 GTE), -36; **29** Cooper MacNeil/Bill Sweedler/Townsend Bell, USA/USA/USA (Ferrari 488 GTE), -36; **30** Andrew Howard/Ross Gunn/Oliver Bryant, GB/GB/GB (Aston Martin Vantage), -36; **31** Mok Weng Sun/Keita Sawa/Matt Griffin, MAL/J/IRL (Ferrari 488 GTE), -37; **32** Mark Patterson/Matt McMurry/Vincent Capillaire, USA/USA/F (Ligier JS P217-Gibson), -37; **33** Mikhail Aleshin/Sergey Sirotkin/Victor Shaytar, RUS/RUS/RUS (Dallara P217-Gibson), -37; **34** Christian Ried/Matteo Cairoli/Marvin Dienst, D/I/D (Porsche 911 RSR), -38; **35** Salih Yoluc/Euan Hankey/Rob Bell, TR/GB/GB (Aston Martin Vantage), -38; **36** Paul Dalla Lana/Pedro Lamy/Mathias Lauda, CDN/P/A (Aston Martin Vantage), -38; **37** Patrick Long/Abdulaziz Al Faisal/Mike Hedlund, USA/SA/USA (Porsche 911 RSR), -38; **38** Mike Wainwright/Ben Barker/Nick Foster, GB/GB/AUS (Porsche 911 RSR), -39; **39** Memo Rojas/Ryo Hirakawa/Jose Gutierrez, MEX/J/MEX (ORECA 07-Gibson), -40; **40** Richard Wee/Hiroki Katoh/Álvaro Parente, SGP/J/P (Ferrari 488 GTE), -40; **41** Thomas Flohr/Francesco Castellacci/Olivier Beretta, CH/I/MC (Ferrari 488 GTE), -41; **42** Tracy Krohn/Nic Jönsson/Andrea Bertolini, USA/S/I (Ferrari 488 GTE), -47; **43** Enzo Guibbert/Eric Trouillet/James Winslow, F/F/GB (ORECA 07-Gibson), -49; **44** Christina Nielsen/Alessandro Balzan/Bret Curtis, DK/I/USA (Ferrari 488 GTE), -53; **45** Miro Konopka/Konstantins Calko/Rik Breukers, SK/LV/NL (Ligier JS P217-Gibson), -53 **; **46** James Calado/Alessandro Pier Guidi/Michele Rugolo, GB/I/I (Ferrari 488 GTE), -55; **47** Ben Keating/Jeroen Bleekemolen/Ricky Taylor, USA/NL/USA (Riley Mk. 30-Gibson), -55; **48** Fernando Rees/Romain Brandela/Christian Philippon, BR/F/F (Chevrolet Corvette Z06), -58; Neel Jani/André Lotterer/Nick Tandy, CH/D/GB (Porsche 919 Hybrid), -49 (DNF-engine); Fabien Barthez/Timothé Buret/Nathanaël Berthon, F/F/F (Ligier JS P217-Gibson), -71 (DNF-gearbox); François Perrodo/Matthieu Vaxivière/Emmanuel Collard, F/F/F (ORECA 07-Gibson), -154 (DNF-accident); Michael Christensen/Kévin Estre/Dirk Werner, DK/F/D (Porsche 911 RSR), -188 (DNF-accident damage); Nicolas Lapierre/Yuji Kunimoto/José María López, F/J/RA (Toyota TS050 HYBRID), -207 (DNF-puncture damage); Mike Conway/Kamui Kobayashi/Stéphane Sarrazin, GB/J/F (Toyota TS050 HYBRID), -213 (DNF-clutch); Roberto González/Simon Trummer/Vitaly Petrov, MEX/CH/RUS (ORECA 07-Gibson), -215 (DNF-accident); Toni Vilander/Giancarlo Fisichella/Pierre Kaffer, FIN/I/D (Ferrari 488 GTE), -295 (DNF-accident); Roman Rusinov/Pierre Thiriet/Alex Lynn, RUS/F/GB (ORECA 07-Gibson), -347 (DNF-accident damage); Klaus Bachler/Stéphane Lemeret/Khaled Al Qubaisi, A/B/UAE (Porsche 911 RSR), -349 (DNF-accident damage); Oliver Webb/Dominik Kraihamer/Marco Bonanomi, GB/A/I (ENSO CLM P1/01-Nissan), -360 (DNF-engine).
** includes 35s penalty.*
*** includes 2m 02.136s penalty.*
Disqualified: Nelson Piquet Jr/David Heinemeier Hansson/Mathias Beche, BR/DK/CH (ORECA 07-Gibson), -3.
Fastest race lap: Buemi, 3m 18.604s, 153.508mph/247.046km/h.
Pole position: Conway/Kobayashi/Sarrazin, 3m 14.791s, 156.512mph/251.882km/h.

6 HOURS OF NÜRBURGRING, Nürburgring, Nürburg/Eifel, Germany, 16 July. Round 4. 204 laps of the 3.199-mile/5.148km circuit, 652.559 miles/1050.192km.
1 Timo Bernhard/Earl Bamber/Brendon Hartley, D/NZ/NZ (Porsche 919 Hybrid '17), 6h 00m 09.607s, 108.711mph/174.954km/h; **2** Neel Jani/André Lotterer/Nick Tandy, CH/D/GB (Porsche 919 Hybrid '17), +1.606s; **3** Mike Conway/Kamui Kobayashi/José María López, GB/J/RA (Toyota TS050 HYBRID), +1m 04.768s; **4** Sébastien Buemi/Anthony Davidson/Kazuki Nakajima, CH/GB/J (Toyota TS050 HYBRID), -5 laps; **5** Ho-Pin Tung/Oliver Jarvis/Thomas Laurent, CHN/GB/F (ORECA 07-Gibson), -13; **6** Julien Canal/Bruno Senna/Filipe Albuquerque, F/BR/P (ORECA 07-Gibson), -14; **7** Nicolas Lapierre/Gustavo Menezes/Matt Rao, F/USA/GB (Alpine A470-Gibson), -14; **8** Mathias Beche/David Heinemeier Hansson/Pipo Derani, CH/DK/BR (ORECA 07-Gibson), -14; **9** David Cheng/Alex Brundle/Tristan Gommendy, USA/GB/F (ORECA 07-Gibson), -15; **10** Roman Rusinov/Pierre Thiriet/Ben Hanley, RUS/F/GB (ORECA 07-Gibson), -16.
Fastest race lap: Kobayashi, 1m 40.633s, 114.433mph/184.162km/h.
Pole position: Conway/Kobayashi/López, 1m 38.118s, 117.366mph/188.882km/h.

6 HOURS OF MEXICO, Autódromo Hermanos Rodríguez, Mexico City, D.F., Mexico, 3 September. Round 5. 240 laps of the 2.674-mile/4.304km circuit, 641.852 miles/1032.960km.
1 Timo Bernhard/Earl Bamber/Brendon Hartley, D/NZ/NZ (Porsche 919 Hybrid '17), 6h 00m 05.757s, 106.946mph/172.114km/h; **2** Neel Jani/André Lotterer/Nick Tandy, CH/D/GB (Porsche 919 Hybrid '17), +7.141s; **3** Sébastien Buemi/Anthony Davidson/Kazuki Nakajima, CH/GB/J (Toyota TS050 HYBRID), -1 lap; **4** Mike Conway/Kamui Kobayashi/José María López, GB/J/RA (Toyota TS050 HYBRID), -1; **5** Julien Canal/Nicolas Prost/Bruno Senna, F/F/BR (ORECA 07-Gibson), -21; **6** Nicolas Lapierre/Gustavo Menezes/André Negrão, F/USA/BR (Alpine A470-Gibson), -21; **7** Matt Rao/Ben Hanley/Jean-Éric Vergne, GB/GB/F (ORECA 07-Gibson), -21; **8** Roman Rusinov/Pierre Thiriet/Alex Lynn, RUS/F/GB (ORECA 07-Gibson), -21; **9** Mathias Beche/David Heinemeier Hansson/Nelson Piquet Jr, CH/DK/BR (ORECA 07-Gibson), -22; **10** David Cheng/Alex Brundle/Tristan Gommendy, USA/GB/F (ORECA 07-Gibson), -22.
Fastest race lap: Hartley, 1m 25.730s, 112.303mph/180.734km/h.
Pole position: Bernhard/Bamber/Hartley, 1m 24.562s, 113.854mph/183.231km/h.

6 HOURS OF CIRCUIT OF THE AMERICAS, Circuit of the Americas, Austin, Texas, USA, 16 September. Round 6. 192 laps of the 3.426-mile/5.513km circuit, 657.719 miles/1058.496km.
1 Timo Bernhard/Earl Bamber/Brendon Hartley, D/NZ/NZ (Porsche 919 Hybrid '17), 6h 00m 52.444s, 109.354mph/175.988km/h; **2** Neel Jani/André Lotterer/Nick Tandy, CH/D/GB (Porsche 919 Hybrid '17), +0.276s; **3** Sébastien Buemi/Stéphane Sarrazin/Kazuki Nakajima, CH/F/J (Toyota TS050 HYBRID), +21.956s; **4** Mike Conway/Kamui Kobayashi/José María López, GB/J/RA (Toyota TS050 HYBRID), +45.026s; **5** Nicolas Lapierre/Gustavo Menezes/André Negrão, F/USA/BR (Alpine A470-Gibson), -15 laps; **6** Mathias Beche/David Heinemeier Hansson/Nelson Piquet Jr, CH/DK/BR (ORECA 07-Gibson), -16; **7** Julien Canal/Nicolas Prost/Bruno Senna, F/F/BR (ORECA 07-Gibson), -16 *; **8** Ho-Pin Tung/Oliver Jarvis/Thomas Laurent, CHN/GB/F (ORECA 07-Gibson), -16; **9** David Cheng/Alex Brundle/Tristan Gommendy, USA/GB/F (ORECA 07-Gibson), -17; **10** Matt Rao/Ben Hanley/Jean-Éric Vergne, GB/GB/F (ORECA 07-Gibson), -17.
** includes 10s penalty.*
Fastest race lap: Jani, 1m 47.149s, 115.094mph/185.226km/h.
Pole position: Jani/Lotterer/Tandy, 1m 44.741s, 117.740mph/189.484km/h.

6 HOURS OF FUJI, Fuji International Speedway, Sunto-gun, Shizuoka Prefecture, Japan, 15 October. Round 7. 113 laps of the 2.835-mile/4.563km circuit, 320.391 miles/515.619km.
1 Sébastien Buemi/Anthony Davidson/Kazuki Nakajima, CH/GB/J (Toyota TS050 HYBRID), 4h 24m 50.950s, 72.582mph/116.810km/h; **2** Mike Conway/Kamui Kobayashi/José María López, GB/J/RA (Toyota TS050 HYBRID), +1.498s; **3** Neel Jani/André Lotterer/Nick Tandy, CH/D/GB (Porsche 919 Hybrid '17), +2.272s; **4** Timo Bernhard/Earl Bamber/Brendon Hartley, D/NZ/NZ (Porsche 919 Hybrid '17), -1 lap; **5** Julien Canal/Nicolas Prost/Bruno Senna, F/F/BR (ORECA 07-Gibson), -3; **6** Nicolas Lapierre/Gustavo Menezes/André Negrão, F/USA/BR (Alpine A470-Gibson), -3; **7** Ho-Pin Tung/Oliver Jarvis/Thomas Laurent, CHN/GB/F (ORECA 07-Gibson), -3; **8** François Perrodo/Matthieu Vaxivière/Emmanuel Collard, F/F/F (ORECA 07-Gibson), -3; **9** Matt Rao/Ben Hanley/Jean-Éric Vergne, GB/GB/F (ORECA 07-Gibson), -3; **10** Roman Rusinov/Pierre Thiriet/James Rossiter, RUS/F/GB (ORECA 07-Gibson), -3.
Fastest race lap: Bamber, 1m 37.702s, 104.472mph/168.131km/h.
Pole position: Bernhard/Bamber/Hartley, 1m 35.160s, 107.262mph/172.622km/h.

6 HOURS OF SHANGHAI, Shanghai International Circuit, Shanghai, China, 5 November. Round 8. 195 laps of the 3.387-mile/5.451km circuit, 660.483 miles/1062.945km.
1 Sébastien Buemi/Anthony Davidson/Kazuki Nakajima, CH/GB/J (Toyota TS050 HYBRID), 6h 00m 40.777s, 109.873mph/176.823km/h; **2** Timo Bernhard/Earl Bamber/Brendon Hartley, D/NZ/NZ (Porsche 919 Hybrid '17), -1 lap; **3** Neel Jani/André Lotterer/Nick Tandy, CH/D/GB (Porsche 919 Hybrid '17), -1; **4** Mike Conway/Kamui Kobayashi/José María López, GB/J/RA (Toyota TS050 HYBRID), -7 *; **5** Julien Canal/Nicolas Prost/Bruno Senna, F/F/BR (ORECA 07-Gibson), -12; **6** Nicolas Lapierre/Gustavo Menezes/André Negrão, F/USA/BR (Alpine A470-Gibson), -12; **7** Mathias Beche/David Heinemeier Hansson/Nelson Piquet Jr, CH/DK/BR (ORECA 07-Gibson), -13; **8** Ho-Pin Tung/Oliver Jarvis/Thomas Laurent, CHN/GB/F (ORECA 07-Gibson), -13; **9** Roberto González/Simon Trummer/Vitaly Petrov, MEX/CH/RUS (ORECA 07-Gibson), -13; **10** François Perrodo/Matthieu Vaxivière/Emmanuel Collard, F/F/F (ORECA 07-Gibson), -13.
** includes 10s penalty.*
Fastest race lap: Buemi, 1m 45.892s, 115.150mph/185.317km/h.
Pole position: Conway/Kobayashi/López, 1m 42.832s, 118.577mph/190.831km/h.

6 HOURS OF BAHRAIN, Bahrain International Circuit, Sakhir, Bahrain, 18 November. Round 9. 199 laps of the 3.363-mile/5.412km circuit, 669.209 miles/1076.988km.
1 Sébastien Buemi/Anthony Davidson/Kazuki Nakajima, CH/GB/J (Toyota TS050 HYBRID), 6h 01m 26.294s, 111.091mph/178.783km/h; **2** Timo Bernhard/Earl Bamber/Brendon Hartley, D/NZ/NZ (Porsche 919 Hybrid '17), -1 lap; **3** Neel Jani/André Lotterer/Nick Tandy, CH/D/GB (Porsche 919 Hybrid '17), -1; **4** Mike Conway/Kamui Kobayashi/José María López, GB/J/RA (Toyota TS050 HYBRID), -3; **5** Julien Canal/Nicolas Prost/Bruno Senna, F/F/BR (ORECA 07-Gibson), -13; **6** Ho-Pin Tung/Oliver Jarvis/Thomas Laurent, CHN/GB/F (ORECA 07-Gibson), -13; **7** Mathias Beche/David Heinemeier Hansson/Nelson Piquet Jr, CH/DK/BR (ORECA 07-Gibson), -14; **8** Nicolas Lapierre/Gustavo Menezes/André Negrão, F/USA/BR (Alpine A470-Gibson), -14; **9** Roberto González/Simon Trummer/Vitaly Petrov, MEX/CH/RUS (ORECA 07-Gibson), -14; **10** Matt Rao/Ben Hanley/Jean-Éric Vergne, GB/GB/F (ORECA 07-Gibson), -14.
Fastest race lap: Lotterer, 1m 42.862s, 117.694mph/189.411km/h.
Pole position: Jani/Lotterer/Tandy, 1m 39.383s, 121.814mph/196.041km/h.

Final championship points
Drivers
1 Timo Bernhard, D, 208; 1 Earl Bamber, NZ, 208; 1 Brendon Hartley, NZ, 208; **2** Kazuki Nakajima, J, 183; **2** Sébastien Buemi, CH, 183; **3** Anthony Davidson, GB, 168; **4** Nick Tandy, GB, 129; **4** André Lotterer, D, 129; **4** Neel Jani, CH, 129; **5** Kamui Kobayashi, J, 103.5; **5** Mike Conway, GB, 103.5; **6** José María López, RA, 84.5; **7** Oliver Jarvis, GB, 82.5; **7** Thomas Laurent, F, 82.5; **7** Ho-Pin Tung, CHN, 82.5; **8** Julien Canal, F, 76; **8** Bruno Senna, BR, 76; **9** Nicolas Prost, F, 68; **10** André Negrão, BR, 62.5.

Drivers (LMP2)
1 Julien Canal, F, 186; 1 Bruno Senna, BR, 186; **2** Ho-Pin Tung, CHN, 175; **2** Oliver Jarvis, GB, 175; **2** Thomas Laurent, F, 175; **3** Nicolas Prost, F, 168.

Drivers (GT)
1 Alessandro Pier Guidi, I, 153; 1 James Calado, GB, 153; **2** Frédéric Makowiecki, F, 145; **2** Richard Lietz, A, 145; **3** Andy Priaulx, GB, 142.5; **3** Harry Tincknell, GB, 142.5.

Drivers (LMGTE Am)
1 Mathias Lauda, A, 192; 1 Paul Dalla Lana, CDN, 192; 1 Pedro Lamy, P, 192; **2** Christian Ried, D, 168; **2** Marvin Dienst, D, 168; **2** Matteo Cairoli, I, 168; **3** Mok Weng Sun, MAL, 165; **3** Keita Sawa, J, 165; **3** Matt Griffin, IRL, 165.

Manufacturers
1 Porsche, 337; **2** Toyota, 286.5.

Manufacturers (GT)
1 Ferrari, 305; **2** Ford, 237.5; **3** Porsche, 223.5; **4** Aston Martin, 207.

Teams (LMP2)
1 Vaillante Rebellion (31), 186; **2** Jackie Chan DC Racing (38), 175; **3** Signature Alpine Matmut (36), 151.

Teams (LMGTE Pro)
1 AF Corse (51), 164; **2** Ford Chip Ganassi Team UK (67), 146; **3** Porsche GT Team (91), 145.

Teams (LMGTE Am)
1 Aston Martin Racing (98), 198; **2** Clearwater Racing (61), 179; **3** Dempsey - Proton Racing (77), 174.

European Le Mans Series

4 HOURS OF SILVERSTONE, Silverstone Arena Grand Prix Circuit, Towcester, Northamptonshire, Great Britain, 15 April. Round 1. 126 laps of the 3.667-mile/5.901km circuit, 462.006 miles/743.526km.
1 Will Owen/Hugo de Sadeleer/Filipe Albuquerque, USA/CH/P (Ligier JS P217-Gibson), 4h 01m 24.751s, 114.825mph/184.793km/h; **2** Memo Rojas/Ryo Hirakawa/Leo Roussel, MEX/J/F (ORECA 07-Gibson), +6.339s; **3** Dennis Andersen/Anders Fjordbach, DK/DK (Dallara P217-Gibson), +28.158s; **4** James Allen/Franck Matelli/Richard Bradley, AUS/F/GB (ORECA 07-Gibson), +53.426s; **5** Nigel Moore/Philip Hanson, GB/GB (Ligier JS P217-Gibson), +1m 00.297s; **6** Roberto Lacorte/Giorgio Sernagiotto/Andrea Belicchi, I/I/I (Dallara P217-Gibson), +1m 44.440s; **7** Eric Trouillet/Paul Petit/Enzo Guibbert, F/F/F (ORECA 07-Gibson), -1 lap; **8** Patrice Lafargue/Paul Lafargue/David Zollinger, F/F/F (Ligier JS P217-Gibson), -3; **9** Fabien Barthez/Timothé Buret/Nathanaël Berthon, F/F/F (Ligier JS P217-Gibson), -3; **10** Henrik Hedman/Nicolas Lapierre/Benjamin Hanley, S/F/GB (ORECA 07-Gibson), -6.
Fastest race lap: Hanley, 1m 47.474s, 122.821mph/197.662km/h.
Pole position: Hedman/Lapierre/Hanley, 1m 44.040s, 126.875mph/204.186km/h.

4 HOURS OF MONZA, Autodromo Nazionale di Monza, Milan, Italy, 14 May. Round 2. 132 laps of the 3.600-mile/5.793km circuit, 475.148 miles/764.676km.
1 Memo Rojas/Ryo Hirakawa/Leo Roussel, MEX/J/F (ORECA 07-Gibson), 4h 01m 43.628s, 117.938mph/189.803km/h; **2** Henrik Hedman/Nicolas Lapierre/Benjamin Hanley, S/F/GB (ORECA 07-Gibson), +2.245s; **3** Dennis Andersen/Anders Fjordbach, DK/DK (Dallara P217-Gibson), +7.215s; **4** Eric Trouillet/Paul Petit/Enzo Guibbert, F/F/F (ORECA 07-Gibson), +33.980s; **5** Roberto Lacorte/Giorgio Sernagiotto/Andrea Belicchi, I/I/I (Dallara P217-Gibson), +54.798s; **6** Will Owen/Hugo de Sadeleer/Filipe Albuquerque, USA/CH/P (Ligier JS P217-Gibson), +1m 06.385s; **7** Fabien Barthez/Timothé Buret, F/F (Ligier JS P217-Gibson), +1m 38.640s; **8** James Allen/Franck Matelli/Richard Bradley, AUS/F/GB (ORECA 07-Gibson), -1 lap; **9** Patrice Lafargue/Paul Lafargue/Olivier Pla, F/F/F (Ligier JS P217-Gibson), -3; **10** Jan Lammers/Frits van Eerd, NL/NL (Dallara P217-Gibson), -5.
Fastest race lap: Bradley, 1m 38.673s, 131.328mph/211.352km/h.
Pole position: Trouillet/Petit/Guibbert, 1m 36.526s, 134.249mph/216.053km/h.

4 HOURS OF RED BULL RING, Red Bull Ring, Spielberg, Austria, 23 July. Round 3. 169 laps of the 2.683-mile/4.318km circuit, 453.441 miles/729.742km.
1 Will Owen/Hugo de Sadeleer/Filipe Albuquerque, USA/CH/P (Ligier JS P217-Gibson), 4h 00m

57.876s, 112.906mph/181.705km/h; **2** Memo Rojas/Nicolas Minassian/Leo Roussel, MEX/F/F (ORECA 07-Gibson), +4.554s; **3** Eric Trouillet/Paul Petit/Enzo Guibbert, F/F/F (ORECA 07-Gibson), -1 lap; **4** James Allen/Richard Bradley/Gustavo Yacamán, AUS/GB/CO (ORECA 07-Gibson), -1; **5** Fabien Barthez/Timothé Buret/Nathanaël Berthon, F/F/F (Ligier JS P217-Gibson), -2; **6** Matevos Isaakyan/Egor Orudzhev, RUS/RUS (Dallara P217-Gibson), -2 *; **7** Jan Lammers/Frits van Eerd, NL/NL (Dallara P217-Gibson), -4; **8** Dennis Andersen/Anders Fjordbach, DK/DK (Dallara P217-Gibson), -10; **9** Giorgio Mondini/Davide Uboldi, CH/I (Ligier JS P3-Nissan), -12; **10** John Falb/Sean Rayhall, USA/USA (Ligier JS P3-Nissan), -12 **.
** includes 1m penalty.*
*** includes 25s drive-through substitute penalty.*
Fastest race lap: Roussel, 1m 20.177s, 120.472mph/193.881km/h.
Pole position: Rojas/Minassian/Roussel, 1m 18.435s, 123.147mph/198.187km/h.

4 HOURS OF PAUL RICARD, Circuit ASA Paul Ricard, Le Beausset, France, 27 August. Round 4. 115 laps of the 3.630-mile/5.842km circuit, 417.456 miles/671.830km.
1 Matevos Isaakyan/Egor Orudzhev, RUS/RUS (Dallara P217-Gibson), 4h 00m 16.217s, 104.246mph/167.768km/h; **2** Memo Rojas/Nicolas Minassian/Leo Roussel, MEX/F/F (ORECA 07-Gibson), +1m 27.817s; **3** Eric Trouillet/Paul Petit/Enzo Guibbert, F/F/F (ORECA 07-Gibson), -1 lap; **4** Fabien Barthez/Timothé Buret/Nathanaël Berthon, F/F/F (Ligier JS P217-Gibson), -1; **5** Will Owen/Hugo de Sadeleer/Filipe Albuquerque, USA/CH/P (Ligier JS P217-Gibson), -1 *; **6** James Allen/Richard Bradley/Gustavo Yacamán, AUS/GB/CO (ORECA 07-Gibson), -1; **7** Henrik Hedman/Nicolas Lapierre/Ben Hanley, S/F/GB (ORECA 07-Gibson), -1; **8** Andrea Roda/Matt McMurry/Andréa Pizzitola, I/USA/F (Ligier JS P217-Gibson), -2; **9** Dennis Andersen/Anders Fjordbach, DK/DK (Dallara P217-Gibson), -3; **10** Roberto Lacorte/Giorgio Sernagiotto/Andrea Belicchi, I/I/I (Dallara P217-Gibson), -4.
** includes 30s penalty.*
Fastest race lap: Roussel, 1m 55.252s, 113.387mph/182.480km/h.
Pole position: Hedman/Lapierre/Hanley, 1m 52.761s, 115.892mph/186.511km/h.

4 HOURS OF SPA-FRANCORCHAMPS, Circuit de Spa-Francorchamps, Stavelot, Belgium, 24 September. Round 5. 97 laps of the 4.352-mile/7.004km circuit, 422.146 miles/679.378km.
1 James Allen/Richard Bradley/Gustavo Yacamán, AUS/GB/CO (ORECA 07-Gibson), 4h 01m 40.666s, 104.803mph/168.665km/h; **2** Memo Rojas/Ryo Hirakawa/Leo Roussel, MEX/J/F (ORECA 07-Gibson), +0.581s; **3** Matevos Isaakyan/Egor Orudzhev, RUS/RUS (Dallara P217-Gibson), +16.069s; **4** Will Owen/Hugo de Sadeleer/Filipe Albuquerque, USA/CH/P (Ligier JS P217-Gibson), +17.018s; **5** Henrik Hedman/Nicolas Lapierre/Ben Hanley, S/F/GB (ORECA 07-Gibson), +39.161s; **6** Jonathan Hirschi/Paul Petit/Enzo Guibbert, CH/F/F (ORECA 07-Gibson), +1m 02.572s; **7** Roberto Lacorte/Giorgio Sernagiotto/Andrea Belicchi, I/I/I (Dallara P217-Gibson), +1m 56.228s; **8** Dennis Andersen/Anders Fjordbach, DK/DK (Dallara P217-Gibson), -1 lap; **9** Fabien Barthez/Timothé Buret/Nathanaël Berthon, F/F/F (Ligier JS P217-Gibson), -1; **10** Patrice Lafargue/Paul Lafargue/Paul-Loup Chatin, F/F/F (Ligier JS P217-Gibson), -1 *.
** includes 30s penalty.*
Fastest race lap: Roussel, 2m 05.236s, 125.102mph/201.332km/h.
Pole position: Hedman/Lapierre/Hanley, 2m 02.457s, 127.941mph/205.901km/h.

4 HOURS OF ALGARVE, Autódromo Internacional do Algarve, Portimão, Portugal, 22 October. Round 6. 139 laps of the 2.891-mile/4.652km circuit, 401.796 miles/646.628km.
1 James Allen/Richard Bradley/Gustavo Yacamán, AUS/GB/CO (ORECA 07-Gibson), 4h 01m 17.867s, 99.908mph/160.787km/h; **2** Will Owen/Hugo de Sadeleer/Filipe Albuquerque, USA/CH/P (Ligier JS P217-Gibson), +38.169s; **3** Matevos Isaakyan/Egor Orudzhev, RUS/RUS (Dallara P217-Gibson), +59.254s; **4** Memo Rojas/Ryo Hirakawa/Leo Roussel, MEX/J/F (ORECA 07-Gibson), +1m 01.198s; **5** Roberto Lacorte/Giorgio Sernagiotto/Andrea Belicchi, I/I/I (Dallara P217-Gibson), -1 lap; **6** Fabien Barthez/Timothé Buret/Nathanaël Berthon, F/F/F (Ligier JS P217-Gibson), -1; **7** Dennis Andersen/Anders Fjordbach, DK/DK (Dallara P217-Gibson), -2; **8** Jan Lammers/Frits van Eerd, NL/NL (Dallara P217-Gibson), -2; **9** Henrik Hedman/Nicolas Lapierre/Ben Hanley, S/F/GB (ORECA 07-Gibson), -2; **10** Patrice Lafargue/Paul Lafargue/Paul-Loup Chatin, F/F/F (Ligier JS P217-Gibson), -2 *
** includes 42s penalty.*
Fastest race lap: Hanley, 1m 35.048s, 109.483mph/176.197km/h.
Pole position: Barthez/Buret/Berthon, 1m 33.575s, 111.207mph/178.970km/h.

Final championship points
Drivers (LMP2)
1 Memo Rojas, MEX, 110; 1 Leo Roussel, F, 110; **2** Filipe Albuquerque, P, 98; **2** Will Owen, USA, 98; **2** Hugo de Sadeleer, CH, 98; **3** Richard Bradley, GB, 86; **3** James Allen, AUS, 86; **4** Ryo Hirakawa, J, 73; **5** Gustavo Yacamán, CO, 70; **6** Matevos Isaakyan, RUS, 63; **6** Egor Orudzhev, RUS, 63; **7** Enzo Guibbert, F, 57; **7** Paul Petit, F, 57; **8** Eric Trouillet, F, 49; **9** Anders Fjordbach, DK, 46; **9** Dennis Andersen, DK, 46; **10** Fabien Barthez, F, 41; **10** Timothé Buret, F, 41.

Drivers (LMP3)
1 John Falb, USA, 103; 1 Sean Rayhall, USA, 103; **2** Alexandre Cougnaud, F, 81; **2** Antoine Jung, F, 81; **2** Romano Ricci, F, 81; **3** Christian England, GB, 63; **3** Mark Patterson, USA, 63; **3** Wayne Boyd, GB, 63; **4** François Heriau, F, 61; **4** Jean-Baptiste Lahaye, F, 61; **4** Matthieu Lahaye, F, 61; **5** Martin Hippe, D, 56; **5** Jakub Smiechowski, PL, 56; **6** Alexander Talkanitsa, BY, 54; **6** Alexander Talkanitsa Jr, BY, 54; **6** Mikkel Jensen, DK, 54; **7** Giorgio Mondini, CH, 49; **8** Nicolas Schatz, F, 37.5; **8** Antonin Borga, F, 37.5; **8** David Droux, CH, 37.5; **9** Davide Uboldi, I, 35; **10** Ricky Capo, AUS, 30.5.

Drivers (LMGTE)
1 Jody Fannin, GB, 104; 1 Rob Smith, GB, 104; **2** Salih Yoluc, TR, 102; **2** Nicki Thiim, DK, 102; **2** Euan Hankey, GB, 102; **3** Christian Ried, D, 80; **3** Matteo Cairoli, I, 80; **3** Joël Camathias, CH, 80; **4** Matt Griffin, IRL, 77; **4** Aaron Scott, GB, 77; **4** Duncan Cameron, GB, 77; **5** Darren Turner, GB, 75; **5** Andrew Howard, GB, 75; **6** Giorgio Roda, I, 70; **6** Andrea Bertolini, I, 70; **7** Ross Gunn, GB, 63; **8** Jonathan Cocker, GB, 58; **9** Gianluca Roda, I, 45; **10** Will Stevens, GB, 36.

Teams (LMP2)
1 G-Drive Racing (car 110), 22; **2** United Autosports (98), 32; **3** Graff (86), 40; **4** SMP Racing (63), 27; **5** Graff (57), 39; **6** High Class Racing (46), 49.

Teams (LMP3)
1 United Autosports (car 2), 103; **2** M.Racing - YMR (18), 81; **3** United Autosports (3), 63; **4** Ultimate (17), 61; **5** Inter Europol Competition (13), 56; **6** AT Racing (9), 54.

Teams (LMGTE)
1 JMW Motorsport (car 66), 104; **2** TF Sport (90), 102; **3** Proton Competition (77), 80; **4** Spirit of Race (55), 77; **5** Beechdean AMR (99), 75; **6** Spirit of Race (51), 70.

IMSA WeatherTech Sportscar Championship

IMSA WEATHERTECH SPORTSCAR CHAMPIONSHIP, Daytona International Speedway, Daytona Beach, Florida, USA, 28 January. 659 laps of the 3.560-mile/5.729km circuit, 2346.040 miles/3775.585km.
1 Ricky Taylor/Jordan Taylor/Max Angelelli/Jeff Gordon, USA/USA/I/USA (Cadillac DPi-V.R), 24h 00m 57.343s, 97.687mph/157.212km/h; **2** João Barbosa/Christian Fittipaldi/Filipe Albuquerque, P/BR/P (Cadillac DPi-V.R), +0.671s; **3** Marc Goossens/Renger van der Zande/René Rast, B/NL/D (Riley Mk. 30-Gibson), -1 lap; **4** Scott Sharp/Ryan Dalziel/Luis Derani, USA/GB/BR (Nissan Onroak DPi), -3; **5** Dirk Müller/Joey Hand/Sébastien Bourdais, D/USA/F (Ford GT '17), -7; **6** Patrick Pilet/Dirk Werner/Frédéric Makowiecki, F/D/F (Porsche 911 RSR), -7; **7** Giancarlo Fisichella/James Calado/Toni Vilander, I/GB/FIN (Ferrari 488 GTE), -7; **8** Antonio García/Jan Magnussen/Mike Rockenfeller, E/DK/D (Chevrolet Corvette C7.R), -7; **9** Harry Tincknell/Andy Priaulx/Tony Kanaan, GB/GB/BR (Ford GT '17), -7; **10** Kévin Estre/Laurens Vanthoor/Richard Lietz, F/B/A (Porsche 911 RSR), -7.
Fastest race lap: Albuquerque, 1m 36.269s, 133.127mph/214.247km/h.
Pole position: Barbosa/Fittipaldi/Albuquerque, 1m 36.903s, 132.256mph/212.845km/h.

IMSA WEATHERTECH SPORTSCAR CHAMPIONSHIP, Sebring International Raceway, Florida, USA, 18 March. 348 laps of the 3.740-mile/6.019km circuit, 1301.520 miles/2094.593km.
1 Ricky Taylor/Jordan Taylor/Alex Lynn, USA/USA/GB (Cadillac DPi-V.R), 12h 01m 09.681s, 108.285mph/174.268km/h; **2** João Barbosa/Christian Fittipaldi/Filipe Albuquerque, P/BR/P (Cadillac DPi-V.R), +13.614s; **3** Dane Cameron/Eric Curran/Mike Conway, USA/USA/GB (Cadillac DPi-V.R), -2 laps; **4** Chris Miller/Stephen Simpson/Mikhail Goikhberg, USA/ZA/CDN (ORECA 07-Gibson), -4; **5** James French/Patricio O'Ward/Kyle Masson, USA/MEX/USA (ORECA FLM09-Chevrolet), -10; **6** Garett Grist/Max Hanratty/Sean Rayhall, CDN/USA/USA (ORECA FLM09-Chevrolet), -12; **7** Antonio García/Jan Magnussen/Mike Rockenfeller, E/DK/D (Chevrolet Corvette C7.R), -14; **8** Dirk Müller/Joey Hand/Sébastien Bourdais, D/USA/F (Ford GT '17), -14; **9** Toni Vilander/James Calado/Giancarlo Fisichella, FIN/GB/I (Ferrari 488 GTE), -14; **10** Ryan Briscoe/Richard Westbrook/Scott Dixon, AUS/GB/NZ (Ford GT '17), -14.
Fastest race lap: Conway, 1m 49.629s, 122.814mph/197.650km/h.
Pole position: Sébastien Buemi/Nick Heidfeld/Neel Jani, CH/D/CH (ORECA 07-Gibson), 1m 48.178s, 124.462mph/200.301km/h.

BUBBA BURGER SPORTS CAR GRAND PRIX AT LONG BEACH, Long Beach Street Circuit, California, USA, 8 April. 63 laps of the 1.968-mile/3.167km circuit, 123.984 miles/199.533km.
1 Ricky Taylor/Jordan Taylor, USA/USA (Cadillac DPi-V.R), 1h 40m 37.481s, 73.929mph/118.977km/h; **2** Scott Sharp/Ryan Dalziel, USA/GB (Nissan Onroak DPi), +6.349s; **3** Tristan Nunez/Jonathan Bomarito, USA/USA (Mazda RT24-P), +15.735s; **4** Stephen Simpson/Mikhail Goikhberg, ZA/CDN (ORECA 07-Gibson), +18.176s; **5** Tom Kimber-Smith/Will Owen, GB/USA (Ligier JS P217-Gibson), +1m 05.741s; **6** Oliver Gavin/Tommy Milner, GB/USA (Chevrolet Corvette C7.R), +1m 09.399s; **7** Ryan Briscoe/Richard Westbrook, AUS/GB (Ford GT '17), +1m 11.229s; **8** Kévin Estre/Laurens Vanthoor, F/B (Porsche 911 RSR), +1m 11.873s; **9** Bill Auberlen/Alexander Sims, USA/GB (BMW M6 GTLM), +1m 14.238s; **10** Antonio García/Jan Magnussen, E/DK (Chevrolet Corvette C7.R), +1m 25.009s.
Fastest race lap: Dalziel, 1m 14.367s, 95.268mph/153.319km/h.
Pole position: Taylor/Taylor, 1m 13.549s, 96.328mph/155.024km/h.

ADVANCE AUTO PARTS SPORTSCAR SHOWDOWN, Circuit of the Americas, Austin, Texas, USA, 6 May. 73 laps of the 3.400-mile/5.472km circuit, 248.200 miles/399.439km.
1 Ricky Taylor/Jordan Taylor, USA/USA (Cadillac DPi-V.R), 2h 41m 14.508s, 92.358mph/148.636km/h; **2** Dane Cameron/Eric Curran, USA/USA (Cadillac DPi-V.R), +18.855s; **3** João Barbosa/Christian Fittipaldi, P/BR (Cadillac DPi-V.R), +19.818s; **4** Mikhail Goikhberg/Stephen Simpson, CDN/ZA (ORECA 07-Gibson), +27.393s; **5** Ed Brown/Johannes van Overbeek, USA/USA (Nissan Onroak DPi), -1 lap; **6** James French/Patricio O'Ward, USA/MEX (ORECA FLM09-Chevrolet), -1; **7** Jan Magnussen/Antonio García, DK/E (Chevrolet Corvette C7.R), -2; **8** Bill Auberlen/Alexander Sims, USA/GB (BMW M6 GTLM), -2; **9** Stefan Wilson/Nick Boulle, GB/USA (ORECA FLM09-Chevrolet), -2; **10** John Michael Edwards/Martin Tomczyk, USA/D (BMW M6 GTLM), -2.
Fastest race lap: Taylor, 1m 57.198s, 104.439mph/168.078km/h.
Pole position: Taylor/Taylor, 1m 54.809s, 106.612mph/171.575km/h.

CHEVROLET SPORTS CAR CLASSIC, The Raceway at Belle Isle, Detroit, Michigan, USA, 3 June. 65 laps of the 2.350-mile/3.782km circuit, 152.750 miles/245.827km.
1 Ricky Taylor/Jordan Taylor, USA/USA (Cadillac DPi-V.R), 1h 40m 49.514s, 90.900mph/146.289km/h; **2** Dane Cameron/Eric Curran, USA/USA (Cadillac DPi-V.R), +4.948s; **3** Tom Long/Joel Miller, USA/USA (Mazda RT24-P), +34.502s; **4** João Barbosa/Christian Fittipaldi, P/BR (Cadillac DPi-V.R), +40.007s; **5** Tristan Nunez/Jonathan Bomarito, USA/USA (Mazda RT24-P), +41.888s; **6** Mikhail Goikhberg/Stephen Simpson, CDN/ZA (ORECA 07-Gibson), +1m 07.765s; **7** Ed Brown/Johannes van Overbeek, USA/USA (Nissan Onroak DPi), +1m 19.995s; **8** James French/Patricio O'Ward, USA/MEX (ORECA FLM09-Chevrolet), -1 lap; **9** Tomy Drissi/Bruno Junqueira, USA/BR (ORECA FLM09-Chevrolet), -2; **10** Don Yount/Ryan Lewis, USA/GB (ORECA FLM09-Chevrolet), -3.
Fastest race lap: Taylor, 1m 23.107s, 101.796mph/163.826km/h.
Pole position: Barbosa/Fittipaldi, 1m 25.931s, 98.451mph/158.442km/h.

SAHLEN'S SIX HOURS OF THE GLEN, Watkins Glen International, New York, USA, 2 July. 200 laps of the 3.400-mile/5.472km circuit, 680.000 miles/1094.354km.
1 João Barbosa/Christian Fittipaldi/Filipe Albuquerque, P/BR/P (Cadillac DPi-V.R), 6h 01m 18.592s, 112.922mph/181.731km/h; **2** Chris Miller/Mikhail Goikhberg/Stephen Simpson, USA/CDN/ZA (ORECA 07-Gibson), +1.183s; **3** Tristan Nunez/Jonathan Bomarito/Spencer Pigot, USA/USA/USA (Mazda RT24-P), +8.546s; **4** Jose Gutierrez/Olivier Pla, MEX/F (Ligier JS P217-Gibson), +17.583s; **5** Marc Goossens/Renger van der Zande, B/NL (Riley Mk. 30-Gibson), -2 laps; **6** Ricky Taylor/Jordan Taylor, USA/USA (Cadillac DPi-V.R), -3; **7** James French/Patricio O'Ward/Kyle Masson, USA/MEX/USA (ORECA FLM09-Chevrolet), -5; **8** Bill Auberlen/Alexander Sims, USA/GB (BMW M6 GTLM), -8; **9** Ryan Briscoe/Richard Westbrook, AUS/GB (Ford GT '17), -8; **10** Jan Magnussen/Antonio García, DK/E (Chevrolet Corvette C7.R), -8.
Fastest race lap: Pla, 1m 33.314s, 131.170mph/211.098km/h.
Pole position: Scott Sharp/Ryan Dalziel/Pipo Derani, USA/GB/BR (Nissan Onroak DPi), 1m 34.405s, 129.654mph/208.658km/h.

MOBIL 1 SPORTSCAR GRAND PRIX, Mosport International Raceway, Bowmanville, Ontario, Canada, 9 July. 122 laps of the 2.459-mile/3.957km circuit, 299.998 miles/482.800km.
1 Dane Cameron/Eric Curran, USA/USA (Cadillac DPi-V.R), 2h 42m 36.619s, 110.693mph/178.144km/h; **2** Mikhail Goikhberg/Stephen Simpson, CDN/ZA (ORECA 07-Gibson), +8.295s; **3** Scott Sharp/Ryan Dalziel, USA/GB (Nissan Onroak DPi), +12.420s; **4** Tristan Nunez/Jonathan Bomarito, USA/USA (Mazda RT24-P), +13.234s; **5** Tom Long/Joel Miller, USA/USA (Mazda RT24-P), +14.716s; **6** João Barbosa/Christian Fittipaldi, P/BR (Cadillac DPi-V.R), +21.083s; **7** Ricky Taylor/Jordan Taylor, USA/USA (Cadillac DPi-V.R), -2 laps; **8** James French/Patricio O'Ward, USA/MEX (ORECA FLM09-Chevrolet), -5; **9** Bill Auberlen/Alexander Sims, USA/GB (BMW M6 GTLM), -5; **10** John Michael Edwards/Martin Tomczyk, USA/D (BMW M6 GTLM), -5.
Fastest race lap: Simpson, 1m 08.915s, 128.454mph/206.727km/h.
Pole position: Taylor/Taylor, 1m 08.459s, 129.310mph/208.103km/h.

NORTHEAST GRAND PRIX, Lime Rock Park, Lakeville, Connecticut, USA, 22 July. 181 laps of the 1.474-mile/2.372km circuit, 266.794 miles/429.363km.
1 Patrick Pilet/Dirk Werner, F/D (Porsche 911 RSR), 2h 40m 18.956s, 99.851mph/160.694km/h; **2** Laurens Vanthoor/Gianmaria Bruni, B/I (Porsche 911 RSR), +14.500s; **3** John Michael Edwards/Martin Tomczyk, USA/D (BMW M6 GTLM), +39.946s; **4** Jan Magnussen/Antonio García, DK/E (Chevrolet Corvette C7.R), +40.203s; **5** Ryan Briscoe/Richard Westbrook, AUS/GB (Ford GT '17), +52.302s; **6** Bill Auberlen/Alexander Sims, USA/GB (BMW M6 GTLM), -1 lap; **7** Dirk Müller/Joey Hand, D/USA (Ford GT '17), -4; **8** Patrick Lindsey/Jörg Bergmeister, USA/D (Porsche 991 GT3 R), -6; **9** Bryan Sellers/Madison Snow, USA/USA (Lamborghini Huracán GT3), -6; **10** Patrick Long/Daniel Morad, USA/CDN (Porsche 991 GT3 R), -6.
Fastest race lap: García, 50.780s, 104.498mph/168.173km/h.
Pole position: Vanthoor/Bruni, 50.404s, 105.277mph/169.427km/h.

CONTINENTAL TIRE ROAD RACE SHOWCASE AT ROAD AMERICA, Road America, Elkhart Lake, Wisconsin, USA, 6 August. 71 laps of the 4.048-mile/6.515km circuit, 287.408 miles/462.538km.
1 Johannes van Overbeek/Pipo Derani, USA/BR (Nissan Onroak DPi), 2h 40m 35.461s, 107.381mph/172.814km/h; **2** Ricky Taylor/Jordan Taylor, USA/USA (Cadillac DPi-V.R), +2.356s; **3** Scott Sharp/Ryan Dalziel, USA/GB (Nissan Onroak DPi), +2.718s; **4** Dane Cameron/Eric Curran, USA/USA (Cadillac DPi-V.R), +5.385s; **5** Marc Goossens/Renger van der Zande, B/NL (Riley Mk. 30-Gibson), +6.999s; **6** João Barbosa/Christian Fittipaldi, P/BR (Cadillac DPi-V.R), +9.714s; **7** Jose Gutierrez/Olivier Pla, MEX/F (Ligier JS P217-Gibson), +11.219s; **8** Mikhail Goikhberg/Stephen Simpson, CDN/ZA (ORECA 07-Gibson), +1m 37.992s; **9** James French/Patricio O'Ward, USA/MEX (ORECA FLM09-Chevrolet), -1 lap; **10** Mark Kvamme/Gustavo Yacamán, USA/CO (ORECA FLM09-Chevrolet), -1.
Fastest race lap: Simpson, 1m 54.095s, 127.725mph/205.554km/h.
Pole position: Taylor/Taylor, 1m 53.058s, 128.897mph/207.439km/h.

IMSA WEATHERTECH SPORTSCAR CHAMPIONSHIP, Virginia International Raceway, Alton, Virginia, USA, 27 August. 93 laps of the 3.270-mile/5.263km circuit, 304.110 miles/489.418km.
1 Jan Magnussen/Antonio García, DK/E (Chevrolet Corvette C7.R), 2h 41m 17.089s, 113.133mph/182.070km/h; **2** Ryan Briscoe/Richard Westbrook, AUS/GB (Ford GT '17), +12.031s; **3** Giancarlo Fisichella/Toni Vilander, I/FIN (Ferrari 488 GTE), +12.649s; **4** Bill Auberlen/Alexander Sims, USA/GB (BMW M6 GTLM), +28.026s; **5** Dirk Müller/Joey Hand, D/USA (Ford GT '17), +1m 08.064s; **6** Oliver Gavin/Tommy Milner, GB/USA (Chevrolet Corvette C7.R), +1m 39.084s; **7** Laurens Vanthoor/Gianmaria Bruni, B/I (Porsche 911 RSR), -1 lap; **8** Patrick Pilet/Dirk Werner, F/D (Porsche 911 RSR), -1; **9** Jeroen Mul/Corey Lewis, NL/USA (Lamborghini Huracán GT3), -2; **10** Jens Klingmann/Jesse Krohn, D/FIN (BMW M6 GT3), -2.
Fastest race lap: Fisichella, 1m 41.253s, 116.263mph/187.108km/h.
Pole position: Müller/Hand, 1m 40.211s, 117.472mph/189.053km/h.

AMERICA'S TIRE 250, Mazda Raceway Laguna Seca, Monterey, California, USA, 24 September. 114 laps of the 2.238-mile/3.602km circuit, 255.132 miles/410.595km.
1 Marc Goossens/Renger van der Zande, B/NL (Riley Mk. 30-Gibson), 2h 41m 04.538s, 95.036mph/152.945km/h; **2** Dane Cameron/Eric Curran, USA/USA (Cadillac DPi-V.R), +2.248s; **3** Ricky Taylor/Jordan Taylor, USA/USA (Cadillac DPi-V.R), +8.391s; **4** Mikhail Goikhberg/Stephen Simpson, CDN/ZA (ORECA 07-Gibson), +9.321s; **5** João Barbosa/Christian Fittipaldi, P/BR (Cadillac DPi-V.R), +10.411s; **6** Scott Sharp/Ryan Dalziel, USA/GB (Nissan Onroak DPi), +21.241s; **7** Jose Gutierrez/Olivier Pla, MEX/F (Ligier JS P217-Gibson), +52.076s; **8** Johannes van Overbeek/Pipo Derani, USA/BR (Nissan Onroak DPi), -1 lap; **9** John Michael Edwards/Martin Tomczyk, USA/D (BMW M6 GTLM), -4; **10** Giancarlo Fisichella/Toni Vilander, I/FIN (Ferrari 488 GTE), -4.
Fastest race lap: Pla, 1m 17.921s, 103.397mph/166.401km/h.
Pole position: Taylor/Taylor, 1m 16.853s, 104.834mph/168.714km/h.

MOTUL PETIT LE MANS, Road Atlanta Motorsports Center, Braselton, Georgia, USA, 7 October. 402 laps of the 2.540-mile/4.088km circuit, 1021.080 miles/1643.269km.
1 Scott Sharp/Ryan Dalziel/Brendon Hartley, USA/GB/NZ (Nissan Onroak DPi), 10h 00m 22.867s, 102.043mph/164.223km/h; **2** Dane Cameron/Eric Curran/Mike Conway, USA/USA/GB (Cadillac DPi-V.R), +7.633s; **3** Juan Pablo Montoya/Hélio Castroneves/Simon Pagenaud, CO/BR/F (ORECA 07-Gibson), +8.058s; **4** Johannes van Overbeek/Pipo Derani/Bruno Senna, USA/BR/BR (Nissan Onroak DPi), +19.285s; **5** João Barbosa/Christian Fittipaldi/Filipe Albuquerque, P/BR/P (Cadillac DPi-V.R), -1 lap; **6** Chris Miller/Stephen Simpson/Mikhail Goikhberg, USA/ZA/CDN (ORECA 07-Gibson), -3; **7** Bill Auberlen/Alexander Sims/Kuno Wittmer, USA/GB/CDN (BMW M6 GTLM), -10; **8** Jan Magnussen/Mike Rockenfeller/Antonio García, DK/D/E (Chevrolet Corvette C7.R), -10; **9** Giancarlo Fisichella/Toni Vilander/Alessandro Pier Guidi, I/FIN/I (Ferrari 488 GTE), -10; **10** Oliver Gavin/Tommy Milner/Marcel Fässler, GB/USA/CH (Chevrolet Corvette C7.R), -10.
Fastest race lap: Derani, 1m 12.563s, 126.015mph/202.801km/h.
Pole position: Montoya/Castroneves/Pagenaud, 1m 11.314s, 128.222mph/206.353km/h.

Final championship points
Drivers (Prototype)
1 Jordan Taylor, USA, 310; 1 Ricky Taylor, USA, 310; **2** Dane Cameron, USA, 291; **2** Eric Curran, USA, 291; **3** Christian Fittipaldi, BR, 284; **3** João Barbosa, P, 284; **4** Mikhail Goikhberg, CDN, 277; **4** Stephen Simpson, ZA, 277; **5** Ryan Dalziel, GB, 273; **5** Scott Sharp, USA, 273; **6** Johannes van Overbeek, USA, 249; **7** Marc Goossens, B, 233; **7** Renger van der Zande, NL, 233; **8** Jonathan Bomarito, USA, 205; **9** Pipo Derani, BR, 181; **10** Tristan Nunez, USA, 181.

Drivers (Prototype Challenge)
1 James French, USA, 283; 1 Patricio O'Ward, MEX, 283; **2** Don Yount, USA, 244; **3** Buddy Rice, USA, 182; **4** Kyle Masson, USA, 139; **5** Gustavo Yacamán, CO, 121; **6** Garett Grist, CDN, 97; **7** Daniel Burkett, CDN, 92; **8** Mark Kvamme, USA, 90; **9** Nick Boulle, USA, 68; **10** Tomy Drissi, USA, 67.

Drivers (GT Le Mans)
1 Antonio García, E, 334; 1 Jan Magnussen, DK, 334; **2** Alexander Sims, GB, 317; **2** Bill Auberlen, USA, 317; **3** Dirk Müller, D, 306; **3** Joey Hand, USA, 306; **4** Richard Westbrook, GB, 306; **4** Ryan Briscoe, AUS, 306; **5** Dirk Werner, D, 295; **5** Patrick Pilet, F, 295; **6** Laurens Vanthoor, B, 287.

Drivers (GT Daytona)
1 Alessandro Balzan, I, 340; 1 Christina Nielsen, DK, 340; **2** Jeroen Bleekemolen, NL, 320; **3** Patrick Lindsey, USA, 298; **4** Jens Klingmann, D, 294; **5** Ben Keating, USA, 290; **6** Andy Lally, USA, 286; **6** Katherine Legge, GB, 286.

Manufacturers (Prototype)
1 Cadillac, 344; **2** Nissan, 320; **3** Mazda, 216.

Manufacturers (GT Le Mans)
1 Chevrolet, 348; **2** BMW, 342; **3** Ford, 338.

Manufacturers (GT Daytona)
1 Ferrari, 352; **2** Mercedes-AMG, 348; **3** Porsche, **3** Porsche, 345.

Teams (Prototype)
1 Konica Minolta Cadillac DPI-V.R (10), 310; **2** Whelen Engineering Racing (31), 291; **3** Mustand Sampling Racing (5), 284.

Teams (Prototype Challenge)
1 Performance Tech Motorsports (38), 283; **2** Bari Motorsports (26), 252; **3** Bari Motorsports (20), 244.

Teams (GT Le Mans)
1 Corvette Racing (3), 334; **2** BMW Team RLL (25), 317; **3** Ford Chip Ganassi Racing (66), 306.

Teams (GT Daytona)
1 Scuderia Corsa (63), 340; **2** Riley Motorsports-Team AMG (33), 320; **3** Park Place Motorsports (73), 298.

Autobacs Super GT Series (Japan)

AUTOBACS SUPER GT SERIES, Okayama International Circuit (TI Circuit Aida), Aida Gun, Okayama Prefecture, Japan, 9 April. Round 1. 81 laps of the 2.301-mile/3.703km circuit, 186.376 miles/299.943km.
1 Ryo Hirakawa/Nick Cassidy, J/NZ (Lexus LC 500), 2h 12m 39.626s, 84.294mph/135.658km/h; **2** Kazuya Oshima/Andrea Caldarelli, J/I (Lexus LC 500), +1.503s; **3** Heikki Kovalainen/Kohei Hirate, FIN/J (Lexus LC 500), +2.761s; **4** Yuji Tachikawa/Hiroaki Ishiura, J/J (Lexus LC 500), +2.939s; **5** Kazuki Nakajima/James Rossiter, J/GB (Lexus LC 500), +7.607s; **6** Yuhi Sekiguchi/Yuji Kunimoto, J/J (Lexus LC 500), +9.219s; **7** Tsugio Matsuda/Ronnie Quintarelli, J/I (Nissan GT-R), +20.096s; **8** Hironobu Yasuda/Jann Mardenborough, J/GB (Nissan GT-R), +32.360s; **9** Hideki Mutoh/Daisuke Nakajima, J/J (Honda NSX-GT), +40.195s; **10** Daiki Sasaki/João Paulo de Oliveira, J/BR (Nissan GT-R), +51.691s.
Fastest race lap: Oshima, 1m 19.784s, 103.822mph/167.086km/h.
Pole position: Tomoki Nojiri/Takashi Kobayashi, J/J (Honda NSX-GT), 1m 18.620s, 105.359mph/169.559km/h.

AUTOBACS SUPER GT SERIES, Fuji International Speedway, Sunto-gun, Shizuoka Prefecture, Japan, 4 May. Round 2. 110 laps of the 2.835-mile/4.563km circuit, 311.885 miles/501.930km.
1 Yuji Tachikawa/Hiroaki Ishiura, J/J (Lexus LC 500), 2h 52m 28.925s, 108.492mph/174.602km/h; **2** Kazuya Oshima/Andrea Caldarelli, J/I (Lexus LC 500), +4.797s; **3** Ryo Hirakawa/Nick Cassidy, J/NZ (Lexus LC 500), +25.196s; **4** Tsugio Matsuda/Ronnie Quintarelli, J/I (Nissan GT-R), +31.792s; **5** Daisuke Ito/James Rossiter, J/GB (Lexus LC 500), +33.567s; **6** Naoki Yamamoto/Takuya Izawa, J/J (Honda NSX-GT), +35.071s; **7** Heikki Kovalainen/Kohei Hirate, FIN/J (Lexus LC 500), +51.376s; **8** Koudai Tsukakoshi/Takashi Kogure, J/J (Honda NSX-GT), +55.931s; **9** Tomoki Nojiri/Takashi Kobayashi, J/J (Honda NSX-GT), +1m 11.115s; **10** Yuhi Sekiguchi/Kenta Yamashita, J/J (Lexus LC 500), -1 lap.
Fastest race lap: Rossiter, 1m 30.480s, 112.811mph/181.551km/h.
Pole position: Tachikawa/Ishiura, 1m 27.825s, 116.221mph/187.040km/h.

AUTOBACS SUPER GT SERIES, Autopolis International Racing Course, Kamit-sue-mura, Hita-gun, Oita Prefecture, Japan, 21 May. Round 3. 65 laps of the 2.904-mile/4.674km circuit, 188.779 miles/303.810km.
1 Kazuki Nakajima/James Rossiter, J/GB (Lexus LC 500), 1h 59m 56.800s, 94.431mph/151.972km/h; **2** Koudai Tsukakoshi/Takashi Kogure, J/J (Honda NSX-GT), +26.592s; **3** Naoki Yamamoto/Takuya Izawa, J/J (Honda NSX-GT), +26.756s; **4** Satoshi Motoyama/Katsumasa Chiyo, J/J (Nissan GT-R), +27.138s; **5** Tsugio Matsuda/Ronnie Quintarelli, J/I (Nissan GT-R), +27.779s; **6** Ryo Hirakawa/Nick Cassidy, J/NZ (Lexus LC 500), +28.399s; **7** Hironobu Yasuda/Jann Mardenborough, J/GB (Nissan GT-R), +40.435s; **8** Yuhi Sekiguchi/Yuji Kunimoto, J/J (Lexus LC 500), +42.295s; **9** Daiki Sasaki/João Paulo de Oliveira, J/BR (Nissan GT-R), +1m 07.194s; **10** Yuji Tachikawa/Hiroaki Ishiura, J/J (Lexus LC 500), +1m 18.578s.
Fastest race lap: Yamamoto, 1m 35.661s, 109.296mph/175.896km/h.
Pole position: Yamamoto/Izawa, 1m 33.740s, 111.536mph/179.500km/h.

AUTOBACS SUPER GT SERIES, Sportsland-SUGO International Course, Shibata-gun, Miyagi Prefecture, Japan, 23 July. Round 4. 81 laps of the 2.302-mile/3.704km circuit, 186.439 miles/300.045km.
1 Heikki Kovalainen/Kohei Hirate, FIN/J (Lexus LC 500), 2h 09m 13.878s, 86.560mph/139.305km/h; **2** Satoshi Motoyama/Katsumasa Chiyo, J/J (Nissan GT-R), +1.022s; **3** Kazuya Oshima/Andrea Caldarelli, J/I (Lexus LC 500), -1 lap; **4** Tsugio Matsuda/Ronnie Quintarelli, J/I (Nissan GT-R), -1; **5** Tomoki Nojiri/Takashi Kobayashi, J/J (Honda NSX-GT), -1; **6** Hideki Mutoh/Daisuke Nakajima, J/J (Honda NSX-GT), -1; **7** Kazuki Nakajima/James Rossiter, J/GB (Lexus LC 500), -1; **8** Bertrand Baguette/Kosuke Matsuura, B/J (Honda NSX-GT), -1; **9** Naoki Yamamoto/Takuya Izawa, J/J (Honda NSX-GT), -2; **10** Ryo Hirakawa/Nick Cassidy, J/NZ (Lexus LC 500), -2.
Fastest race lap: Kobayashi, 1m 14.219s, 111.645mph/179.675km/h.
Pole position: Nojiri/Kobayashi, 1m 10.915s, 116.846mph/188.046km/h.

AUTOBACS SUPER GT SERIES, Fuji International Speedway, Sunto-gun, Shizuoka Prefecture, Japan, 6 August. Round 5. 66 laps of the 2.835-mile/4.563km circuit, 187.131 miles/301.158km.
1 Tomoki Nojiri/Takashi Kobayashi, J/J (Honda NSX-GT), 1h 44m 39.955s, 107.273mph/172.639km/h; **2** Tsugio Matsuda/Ronnie Quintarelli, J/I (Nissan GT-R), +1.530s; **3** Yuji Tachikawa/Hiroaki Ishiura, J/J (Lexus LC 500), +2.203s; **4** Kazuki Nakajima/James Rossiter, J/GB (Lexus LC 500), +13.300s; **5** Hironobu Yasuda/Jann Mardenborough, J/GB (Nissan GT-R), +14.938s; **6** Ryo Hirakawa/Nick Cassidy, J/NZ (Lexus LC 500), +15.244s; **7** Yuhi Sekiguchi/Yuji Kunimoto, J/J (Lexus LC 500), +19.525s; **8** Naoki Yamamoto/Takuya Izawa, J/J (Honda NSX-GT), +19.603s; **9** Kazuya Oshima/Andrea Caldarelli, J/I (Lexus LC 500), +19.666s; **10** Heikki Kovalainen/Kohei Hirate, FIN/J (Lexus LC 500), +22.480s.
Fastest race lap: Nojiri, 1m 31.851s, 111.127mph/178.841km/h.
Pole position: Nojiri/Kobayashi, 1m 29.104s, 114.553mph/184.355km/h.

AUTOBACS SUPER GT SERIES, Suzuka International Racing Course, Suzuka-shi, Mie Prefecture, Japan, 27 August. Round 6. 171 laps of the 3.608-mile/5.807km circuit, 617.020 miles/992.997km.
1 Bertrand Baguette/Kosuke Matsuura, B/J (Honda NSX-GT), 5h 51m 16.244s, 105.392mph/169.612km/h; **2** Tsugio Matsuda/Ronnie Quintarelli, J/I (Nissan GT-R), +10m 12.150s; **3** Naoki Yamamoto/Takuya Izawa/Nattapong Horthongkum, J/J/T (Honda NSX-GT), +10m 15.737s; **4** Yuhi Sekiguchi/Yuji Kunimoto/Kamui Kobayashi, J/J/J (Lexus LC 500), +10m 32.852s; **5** Daiki Sasaki/João Paulo de Oliveira, J/BR (Nissan GT-R), +10m 34.089s; **6** Ryo Hirakawa/Nick Cassidy, J/NZ (Lexus LC 500), +10m 36.330s; **7** Kazuya Oshima/Andrea Caldarelli, J/I (Lexus LC 500), +10m 37.012s; **8** Tomoki Nojiri/Takashi Kobayashi, J/J (Honda NSX-GT), +11m 58.410s; **9** Kazuki Nakajima/James Rossiter, J/GB (Lexus LC 500), -1 lap; **10** Yuji Tachikawa/Hiroaki Ishiura, J/J (Lexus LC 500), -2.
Fastest race lap: Oliveira, 1m 51.524s, 116.476mph/187.450km/h.
Pole position: Sasaki/Oliveira, 1m 47.074s, 121.316mph/195.240km/h.

AUTOBACS SUPER GT SERIES, Buriram International Circuit, Buriram, Thailand, 8 October. Round 7. 66 laps of the 2.830-mile/4.554km circuit, 186.762 miles/300.564km.
1 Ryo Hirakawa/Nick Cassidy, J/NZ (Lexus LC 500), 1h 42m 48.674s, 108.993mph/175.407km/h; **2** Kazuya Oshima/Andrea Caldarelli, J/I (Lexus LC 500), +12.121s; **3** Koudai Tsukakoshi/Takashi Kogure, J/J (Honda NSX-GT), +30.120s; **4** Yuji Tachikawa/Hiroaki Ishiura, J/J (Lexus LC 500), +41.028s; **5** Kazuki Nakajima/James Rossiter, J/GB (Lexus LC 500), +1m 08.598s; **6** Heikki Kovalainen/Kohei Hirate, FIN/J (Lexus LC 500), +1m 13.029s; **7** Naoki Yamamoto/Takuya Izawa, J/J (Honda NSX-GT), +1m 14.712s; **8** Bertrand Baguette/Kosuke Matsuura, B/J (Honda NSX-GT), +1m 27.292s; **9** Tsugio Matsuda/Ronnie Quintarelli, J/I (Nissan GT-R), -1 lap; **10** Satoshi Motoyama/Katsumasa Chiyo, J/J (Nissan GT-R), -1.
Fastest race lap: Jann Mardenborough, GB (Nissan GT-R), 1m 25.499s, 119.147mph/191.749km/h.
Pole position: Hirakawa/Cassidy, 1m 25.011s, 119.831mph/192.850km/h.

AUTOBACS SUPER GT SERIES, Twin Ring Motegi, Motegi-machi, Haga-gun, Tochigi Prefecture, Japan, 12 November. Round 8. 53 laps of the 2.983-mile/4.801km circuit, 158.122 miles/254.473km.
1 Tsugio Matsuda/Ronnie Quintarelli, J/I (Nissan GT-R), 1h 31m 44.581s, 103.412mph/166.425km/h; **2** Ryo Hirakawa/Nick Cassidy, J/NZ (Lexus LC 500), +6.263s; **3** Yuji Tachikawa/Hiroaki Ishiura, J/J (Lexus LC 500), +13.353s; **4** Koudai Tsukakoshi/Takashi Kogure, J/J (Honda NSX-GT), +19.962s; **5** Naoki Yamamoto/Takuya Izawa, J/J (Honda NSX-GT), +20.537s; **6** Satoshi Motoyama/Katsumasa Chiyo, J/J (Nissan GT-R), +20.857s; **7** Hironobu Yasuda/Jann Mardenborough, J/GB (Nissan GT-R), +38.909s; **8** Heikki Kovalainen/Kohei Hirate, FIN/J (Lexus LC 500), +46.745s; **9** Tomoki Nojiri/Takashi Kobayashi, J/J (Honda NSX-GT), +1m 01.721s; **10** Bertrand Baguette/Kosuke Matsuura, B/J (Honda NSX-GT), +1m 28.669s.
Fastest race lap: Quintarelli, 1m 40.077s, 107.321mph/172.716km/h.
Pole position: Matsuda/Quintarelli, 1m 36.316s, 111.511mph/179.460km/h.

Final championship points
Drivers (GT500)
1 Ryo Hirakawa, J, 84; 1 Nick Cassidy, NZ, 84; **2** Ronnie Quintarelli, I, 82; **2** Tsugio Matsuda, J, 82; **3** Kazuya Oshima, J, 63; **3** Andrea Caldarelli, I, 63; **4** Hiroaki Ishiura, J, 62; **4** Yuji Tachikawa, J, 62; **5** James Rossiter, GB, 53; **6** Kazuki Nakajima, J, 47; **7** Naoki Yamamoto, J, 45; **7** Takuya Izawa, J, 45; **8** Heikki Kovalainen, FIN, 44; **8** Kohei Hirate, J, 44; **9** Tomoki Nojiri, J, 37; **9** Takashi Kobayashi, J, 37; **10** Koudai Tsukakoshi, J, 37; **10** Takashi Kogure, J, 37.

Drivers (GT300)
1 Nobuteru Taniguchi, J, 77; 1 Tatsuya Kataoka, J, 77; **2** Naoya Gamou, J, 72; **2** Haruki Kurosawa, J, 72; **3** Sho Tsuboi, J, 61; **3** Yuichi Nakayama, J, 61.

Other Sportscar races

65TH ANNUAL MOBIL 1 TWELVE HOURS OF SEBRING FUELED BY FRESH FROM FLORIDA, Sebring International Raceway, Florida, USA, 18 March. 348 laps of the 3.740-mile/6.019km circuit, 1301.520 miles/2094.593km.
1 Ricky Taylor/Jordan Taylor/Alex Lynn, USA/USA/GB (Cadillac DPi-V.R), 12h 01m 09.681s, 108.285mph/174.268km/h; **2** João Barbosa/Christian Fittipaldi/Filipe Albuquerque, P/BR/P (Cadillac DPi-V.R), +13.614s; **3** Dane Cameron/Eric Curran/Mike Conway, USA/USA/GB (Cadillac DPi-V.R), -2 laps; **4** Chris Miller/Stephen Simpson/Mikhail Goikhberg, USA/ZA/CDN (ORECA 07-Gibson), -4; **5** James French/Patricio O'Ward/Kyle Masson, USA/MEX/USA (ORECA FLM09-Chevrolet), -10; **6** Garett Grist/Max Hanratty/Sean Rayhall, CDN/USA/USA (ORECA FLM09-Chevrolet), -12; **7** Antonio García/Jan Magnussen/Mike Rockenfeller, E/DK/D (Chevrolet Corvette C7.R), -14; **8** Dirk Müller/Joey Hand/Sébastien Bourdais, D/USA/F (Ford GT '17), -14; **9** Toni Vilander/James Calado/Giancarlo Fisichella, FIN/GB/I (Ferrari 488 GTE), -14; **10** Ryan Briscoe/Richard Westbrook/Scott Dixon, AUS/GB/NZ (Ford GT '17), -14.
Fastest race lap: Conway, 1m 49.629s, 122.814mph/197.650km/h.
Pole position: Sébastien Buemi/Nick Heidfeld/Neel Jani, CH/D/CH (ORECA 07-Gibson), 1m 48.178s, 124.462mph/200.301km/h.

ADAC ZURICH NURBURGRING 24-HOUR RACE, Nürburgring, Nürburg/Eifel, Germany, 27 May. 158 laps of the 15.769-mile/25.378km circuit, 2491.527 miles/4009.724km.
1 Connor De Phillippi/Christopher Mies/Markus Winkelhock/Kelvin van der Linde, USA/D/D/ZA (Audi R8 LMS), 24h 02m 28.858s, 103.635mph/166.784km/h; **2** Markus Palttala/Nicky Catsburg/Alexander Sims/Richard Westbrook, FIN/NL/GB/GB (BMW M6 GT3), +29.418s; **3** Nico Müller/Marcel Fässler/Robin Frijns/René Rast, CH/CH/NL/D (Audi R8 LMS), +50.622s; **4** Marco Wittmann/Tom Blomqvist/Martin Tomczyk/Augusto Farfus, D/GB/D/BR (BMW M6 GT3), +6m 54.159s; **5** Maro Engel/Adam Christodoulou/Yelmer Buurman/Manuel Metzger, D/GB/NL/D (Mercedes AMG GT3), +7m 10.835s; **6** Norbert Siedler/Michael Christensen/Klaus Bachler/Lucas Luhr, A/DK/A/D (Porsche 991 GT3 R), -1 lap; **7** Georg Weiss/Oliver Kainz/Daniel Keilwitz/Jochen Krumbach, D/D/D/D (Ferrari 488 GT3), -1; **8** Peter Dumbreck/Alexandre Imperatori/Stef Dusseldorp/Marco Seefried, GB/CH/NL/D (BMW M6 GT3), -1; **9** Uwe Alzen/Lance David Arnold/Maximilian Götz/Renger van der Zande, D/D/D/NL (Mercedes AMG GT3), -1; **10** Philipp Eng/Maxime Martin/Marc Basseng, A/B/D (BMW M6 GT3), -1.
Fastest race lap: Weiss/Kainz/Keilwitz/Krumbach, 8m 19.375s, 113.680mph/182.950km/h.
Pole position: Jeff Westphal/Franck Mailleux/Andreas Simonsen/Felipe Fernández Laser, USA/F/S/D (SCG 003c), 8m 15.427s, 114.586mph/184.408km/h.

SPA 24 HOURS, Circuit de Spa-Francorchamps, Stavelot, Belgium, 29 July. 546 laps of the 4.352-mile/7.004km circuit, 2376.238 miles/3824.184km.
1 Markus Winkelhock/Christopher Haase/Jules Gounon, D/D/F (Audi R8 LMS), 24h 00m 51.980s, 98.950mph/159.245km/h; **2** Andy Soucek/Maxime Soulet/Vincent Abril, E/B/F (Bentley Continental GT3), +11.862s; **3** Michael Meadows/Raffaele Marciello/Edoardo Mortara, GB/I/I (Mercedes AMG GT3), +52.855s; **4** Laurens Vanthoor/Kévin Estre/Michael Christensen, B/F/DK (Porsche 991 GT3 R), +1m 07.247s; **5** Connor De Phillippi/Christopher Mies/Frédéric Vervisch, USA/D/B (Audi R8 LMS), +1m 30.566s; **6** Antonio García/Nico Müller/René Rast, E/CH/D (Audi R8 LMS), +1m 49.955s; **7** Edward Sandström/Fabian Schiller/Dominik Baumann, S/D/A (Mercedes AMG GT3), -1 lap; **8** Adam Christodoulou/Yelmer Buurman/Luca Stolz, GB/NL/D (Mercedes AMG GT3), -1; **9** Pierre Kaffer/Kelvin van der Linde/Frank Stippler, D/ZA/D (Audi R8 LMS), -3; **10** Bruno Spengler/Nicky Catsburg/Tom Blomqvist, CDN/NL/GB (BMW M6 GT3), -4.
Fastest race lap: Winkelhock, 2m 19.756s, 112.106mph/180.417km/h.
Pole position: Giancarlo Fisichella/Marco Cioci/James Calado, I/I/GB (Ferrari 488 GT3), 2m 17.390s, 114.037mph/183.524km/h.

FIA GT WORLD CUP, Circuito da Guia, Macau, 19/18 November. 18 and 11 laps of the 3.803-mile/6.120km circuit.
Race 1 (68.450 miles/110.160km).
1 Edoardo Mortara, I (Mercedes AMG GT3), 51m 52.822s, 79.163mph/127.400km/h; **2** Robin Frijns, NL (Audi R8 LMS), +0.618s; **3** Maro Engel, D (Mercedes AMG GT3), +1.357s; **4** Augusto Farfus, BR (BMW M6 GT3), +12.312s; **5** Chaz Mostert, AUS (BMW M6 GT3), +13.041s; **6** Marco Wittmann, D (BMW M6 GT3), +18.031s; **7** Romain Dumas, F (Porsche 911 GT3 R), +22.616s; **8** Daniel Juncadella, E (Mercedes AMG GT3), +23.019s; **9** Hiroki Yoshimoto, J (Porsche 911 GT3 R), +54.804s; Nico Müller, CH (Audi R8 LMS), -7 laps (DNF).
Fastest race lap: Engel, 2m 20.196s, 97.649mph/157.151km/h.
Pole position: Mortara.

Race 2 (41.831 miles/67.320km).
1 Edoardo Mortara, I (Mercedes AMG GT3), 1h 16m 04.117s, 32.994mph/53.099km/h; **2** Augusto Farfus, BR (BMW M6 GT3), +1.566s; **3** Raffaele Marciello, I (Mercedes AMG GT3), +2.794s; **4** Robin Frijns, NL (Audi R8 LMS), +4.974s; **5** Chaz Mostert, AUS (BMW M6 GT3), +7.129s; **6** Darryl O'Young, HK (Porsche 911 GT3 R), +34.873s; **7** Hiroki Yoshimoto, J (Porsche 911 GT3 R), +1m 01.611s; **8** Maro Engel, D (Mercedes AMG GT3), -1 lap; Daniel Juncadella, E (Mercedes AMG GT3), -11 (DNF); Nico Müller, CH (Audi R8 LMS), -11 (DNF).
Fastest race lap: Frijns, 2m 19.153s, 98.381mph/158.329km/h.
Pole position: Mortara, 2m 17.565s, 99.516mph/160.157km/h.

Virgin Australia Supercars Championship

Cars are: Holden Commodore VF; Ford Falcon FG; Mercedes E63 AMG, Nissan Altima L33; Volvo S60.

2016

The following races were run after AUTOCOURSE 2016–2017 went to press.

COATES HIRE SYDNEY 500, Sydney Olympic Park Street Race, New South Wales, Australia, 3/4 December. Round 14. 74 and 73 laps of the 2.125-mile/3.420km circuit.
Race 1 (157.257 miles/253.080km).
1 Jamie Whincup, AUS (Holden), 1h 55m 51.3313s, 81.441mph/131.066km/h; **2** Garth Tander, AUS (Holden), +6.8393s; **3** Shane van Gisbergen, NZ (Holden), +9.8342s; **4** Scott McLaughlin, NZ (Volvo), +10.3900s; **5** James Courtney, AUS (Holden), +10.8347s; **6** Rick Kelly, AUS (Nissan), +17.3639s; **7** Will Davison, AUS (Holden), +17.9567s; **8** Craig Lowndes, AUS (Holden), +23.3167s; **9** Tim Slade, AUS (Holden), +25.0335s; **10** David Reynolds, AUS (Holden), +26.5982s.
Fastest race lap: van Gisbergen, 1m 27.9481s, 86.986mph/139.991km/h.
Pole position: van Gisbergen, 1m 26.6272s, 88.313mph/142.126km/h.

Race 2 (155.132 miles/249.660km).
1 Shane van Gisbergen, NZ (Holden), 1h 59m 59.1235s, 77.575mph/124.845km/h; **2** Garth Tander, AUS (Holden), +1.0246s; **3** David Reynolds, AUS (Holden), +2.3858s; **4** Jamie Whincup, AUS (Holden), +2.7922s; **5** Scott McLaughlin, NZ (Volvo), +4.2638s; **6** James Courtney, AUS (Holden), +4.7314s; **7** Tim Slade, AUS (Holden), +6.3462s; **8** Will Davison, AUS (Holden), +9.4362s; **9** Craig Lowndes, AUS (Holden), +9.7837s; **10** James Moffat, AUS (Volvo), +10.0201s.
Fastest race lap: Courtney, 1m 28.1700s, 86.767mph/139.639km/h.
Pole position: Tander, 1m 27.1524s, 87.780mph/141.269km/h.

Final championship points
Drivers
1 Shane van Gisbergen, NZ, 3368; **2** Jamie Whincup, AUS, 3168; **3** Scott McLaughlin, NZ, 2806; **4** Craig Lowndes, AUS, 2770; **5** Will Davison, AUS, 2589; **6** Mark Winterbottom, AUS, 2489; **7** Chaz Mostert, AUS, 2361; **8** Tim Slade, AUS, 2263; **9** Garth Tander, AUS, 2252; **10** Michael Caruso, AUS, 2239; **11** James Courtney, AUS, 2162; **12** Fabian Coulthard, NZ, 2078; **13** Rick Kelly, AUS, 1835; **14** Todd Kelly, AUS, 1808; **15** Scott Pye, AUS, 1807; **16** David Reynolds, AUS, 1564; **17** Jason Bright, AUS, 1459; **18** Nick Percat, AUS, 1430; **19** Cameron Waters, AUS, 1423; **20** James Moffat, AUS, 1419.

Teams
1 Red Bull Racing Australia, 6546; **2** Holden Racing Team, 4434; **3** Wilson Security Racing GRM, 4250; **4** Prodrive Racing Australia, 3962; **5** DJR Team Penske, 3855.

2017

CLIPSAL 500, Adelaide Steet Circuit, South Australia, Australia, 4/5 March. Round 1. 2 x 78 laps of the 2.001-mile/3.220km circuit.
Race 1 (156.064 miles/251.160km).
1 Shane van Gisbergen, NZ (Holden), 1h 49m 25.8502s, 85.568mph/137.708km/h; **2** Fabian Coulthard, NZ (Ford), +14.7120s; **3** James Courtney, AUS (Holden), +15.5603s; **4** Cameron Waters, AUS (Ford), +22.8775s; **5** Rick Kelly, AUS (Nissan), +23.4185s; **6** Jamie Whincup, AUS (Holden), +24.2242s; **7** Nick Percat, AUS (Holden), +28.9073s; **8** Craig Lowndes, AUS (Holden), +32.7547s; **9** Chaz Mostert, AUS (Ford), +33.8808s; **10** James Moffat, AUS (Holden), +35.2057s.
Fastest race lap: van Gisbergen, 1m 20.9659s, 88.962mph/143.171km/h.
Pole position: van Gisbergen, 1m 19.5723s, 90.520mph/145.678km/h.

Race 2 (156.064 miles/251.160km).
1 Shane van Gisbergen, NZ (Holden), 1h 47m 18.8595s, 87.255mph/140.424km/h; **2** Scott McLaughlin, NZ (Ford), +10.1229s; **3** Chaz Mostert, AUS (Ford), +19.5439s; **4** James Courtney, AUS (Holden), +21.1883s; **5** Fabian Coulthard, NZ (Ford), +29.5178s; **6** Jamie Whincup, AUS (Holden), +31.4192s; **7** Tim Slade, AUS (Holden), +33.8694s; **8** Cameron Waters, AUS (Ford), +40.6792s; **9** Todd Kelly, AUS (Nissan), +42.1935s; **10** Craig Lowndes, AUS (Holden), +43.7709s.
Fastest race lap: McLaughlin, 1m 20.4210s, 89.565mph/144.141km/h.
Pole position: van Gisbergen, 1m 19.7545s, 90.313mph/145.346km/h.

TYREPOWER TASMANIA SUPERSPRINT, Symmons Plains Raceway, Launceston, Tasmania, Australia, 8/9 April. Round 2. 4 and 76 laps of the 1.491-mile/2.400km circuit.
Race 1 (5.965 miles/9.600km).
1 Shane van Gisbergen, NZ (Holden), 54m 29.0032s, 6.569mph/10.572km/h; **2** Jamie Whincup, AUS (Holden), +0.3952s; **3** Craig Lowndes, AUS (Holden), +0.7230s; **4** David Reynolds, AUS (Holden), +1.2641s; **5** Chaz Mostert, AUS (Ford), +1.7370s; **6** Jason Bright, AUS (Ford), +2.1496s; **7** Mark Winterbottom, AUS (Ford), +2.7013s; **8** Todd Kelly, AUS (Nissan), +3.9659s; **9** Cameron Waters, AUS (Ford), +4.5085s; **10** Fabian Coulthard, NZ (Ford), +5.1666s.
Fastest race lap: Mostert, 1m 04.1043s, 83.748mph/134.780km/h.
Pole position: Scott McLaughlin, NZ (Ford), 57.4178s, 93.501mph/150.475km/h.

Race 2 (113.338 miles/182.400km).
1 Fabian Coulthard, NZ (Ford), 1h 23m 36.5118s, 81.334mph/130.895km/h; **2** Scott McLaughlin, NZ (Ford), +0.6906s; **3** Jamie Whincup, AUS (Holden), +1.1425s; **4** Craig Lowndes, AUS (Holden), +1.5404s; **5** David Reynolds, AUS (Holden), +2.1798s; **6** Cameron Waters, AUS (Ford), +2.8739s; **7** Chaz Mostert, AUS (Ford), +3.2337s; **8** Tim Slade, AUS (Holden), +4.5562s; **9** Shane van Gisbergen, NZ (Holden), +4.8085s; **10** Garth Tander, AUS (Holden), +5.3105s.
Fastest race lap: Lowndes, 51.4370s, 104.373mph/167.972km/h.
Pole position: Whincup, 58.3971s, 91.933mph/147.952km/h.

WD-40 PHILLIP ISLAND SUPERSPRINT, Phillip Island Grand Prix Circuit, Cowes, Victoria, Australia, 22/23 April. Round 3. 51 and 57 laps of the 2.762-mile/4.445km circuit.
Race 1 (140.862 miles/226.695km).
1 Fabian Coulthard, NZ (Ford), 1h 36m 25.3805s, 87.652mph/141.062km/h; **2** Jamie Whincup, AUS (Holden), +0.9352s; **3** Garth Tander, AUS (Holden), +1.0261s; **4** Shane van Gisbergen, NZ (Holden), +3.8136s; **5** Michael Caruso, AUS (Nissan), +4.0906s; **6** Todd Kelly, AUS (Nissan), +4.3781s; **7** Jason Bright, AUS (Ford), +4.7022s; **8** Mark Winterbottom, AUS (Ford), +6.3804s; **9** Will Davison, AUS (Holden), +8.5156s; **10** Scott McLaughlin, NZ (Ford), +9.3563s.
Fastest race lap: McLaughlin, 1m 31.5867s, 108.565mph/174.719km/h.
Pole position: McLaughlin, 1m 29.3632s, 111.267mph/179.066km/h.

Race 2 (157.434 miles/253.365km).
1 Chaz Mostert, AUS (Ford), 1h 38m 54.3876s, 95.504mph/153.699km/h; **2** Mark Winterbottom, AUS (Ford), +2.9040s; **3** David Reynolds, AUS (Holden), +3.5476s; **4** James Moffat, AUS (Holden), +9.9341s; **5** Lee Holdsworth, AUS (Holden), +10.6153s; **6** Cameron Waters, AUS (Ford), +16.3874s; **7** Garth Tander, AUS (Holden), +17.7569s; **8** Dale Wood, AUS (Holden), +21.2174s; **9** Rick Kelly, AUS (Nissan), +22.3449s; **10** Michael Caruso, AUS (Nissan), +22.5345s.
Fastest race lap: Scott McLaughlin, NZ (Ford), 1m 31.2142s, 109.009mph/175.433km/h.
Pole position: McLaughlin, 1m 29.0621s, 111.643mph/179.672km/h.

PERTH SUPERSPRINT, Barbagallo Raceway Wanneroo, Perth, Western Australia, Australia, 6/7 May. Round 4. 50 and 83 laps of the 1.504-mile/2.420km circuit.
Race 1 (75.186 miles/121.000km).
1 Scott McLaughlin, NZ (Ford), 48m 58.8956s, 92.098mph/148.218km/h; **2** Fabian Coulthard, NZ (Ford), +1.2995s; **3** Jamie Whincup, AUS (Holden), +7.4826s; **4** Shane van Gisbergen, NZ (Holden), +12.7819s; **5** Mark Winterbottom, AUS (Ford), +13.3064s; **6** Chaz Mostert, AUS (Ford), +17.9595s; **7** Craig Lowndes, AUS (Holden), +19.3706s; **8** Will Davison, AUS (Holden), +21.9874s; **9** David Reynolds, AUS (Holden), +24.1046s; **10** Garth Tander, AUS (Holden), +24.5760s.
Fastest race lap: Nick Percat, AUS (Holden), 56.7466s, 95.395mph/153.524km/h.
Pole position: Coulthard, 54.6667s, 99.025mph/159.365km/h.

Race 2 (124.809 miles/200.860km).
1 Scott McLaughlin, NZ (Ford), 1h 22m 17.6422s, 90.997mph/146.445km/h; **2** Chaz Mostert, AUS (Ford), +4.6115s; **3** Jamie Whincup, AUS (Holden), +5.8812s; **4** Mark Winterbottom, AUS (Ford), +13.1549s; **5** Will Davison, AUS (Holden), +14.7002s; **6** Shane van Gisbergen, NZ (Holden), +15.0737s; **7** Fabian Coulthard, NZ (Ford), +16.4181s; **8** Craig Lowndes, AUS (Holden), +31.2127s; **9** Garth Tander, AUS (Holden), +36.8102s; **10** Nick Percat, AUS (Holden), +40.7107s.
Fastest race lap: Coulthard, 56.4314s, 95.928mph/154.382km/h.
Pole position: McLaughlin, 54.5730s, 99.195mph/159.639km/h.

WINTON SUPERSPRINT, Winton Motor Raceway, Benalla, Victoria, Australia, 20/21 May. Round 5. 40 and 67 laps of the 1.864-mile/3.000km circuit.
Race 1 (74.565 miles/120.000km).
1 Scott McLaughlin, NZ (Ford), 54m 58.0579s, 81.391mph/130.986km/h; **2** Jamie Whincup, AUS (Holden), +1.6242s; **3** Fabian Coulthard, NZ (Ford), +2.4242s; **4** David Reynolds, AUS (Holden), +10.3785s; **5** Will Davison, AUS (Holden), +17.2544s; **6** Craig Lowndes, AUS (Holden), +18.9771s; **7** Garth Tander, AUS (Holden), +20.4237s; **8** Shane van Gisbergen, NZ (Holden), +20.7514s; **9** Mark Winterbottom, AUS (Ford), +23.1229s; **10** Nick Percat, AUS (Holden), +42.3733s.
Fastest race lap: Reynolds, 1m 20.3297s, 83.540mph/134.445km/h.
Pole position: McLaughlin, 1m 19.3807s, 84.539mph/136.053km/h.

Race 2 (124.896 miles/201.000km).
1 Shane van Gisbergen, NZ (Holden), 1h 35m 19.8233s, 78.608mph/126.507km/h; **2** Jamie Whincup, AUS (Holden), +1.2617s; **3** Fabian Coulthard, NZ (Ford), +1.7088s; **4** Cameron Waters, AUS (Ford), +2.8814s; **5** Scott McLaughlin, NZ (Ford), +6.2445s; **6** Garth Tander, AUS (Holden), +7.9100s; **7** David Reynolds, AUS (Holden), +10.6537s; **8** Chaz Mostert, AUS (Ford), +11.3218s; **9** Will Davison, AUS (Holden), +11.7159s; **10** Lee Holdsworth, AUS (Holden), +12.7948s.
Fastest race lap: van Gisbergen, 1m 20.0020s, 83.883mph/134.996km/h.
Pole position: McLaughlin, 1m 19.0721s, 84.869mph/136.584km/h.

CROWNBET DARWIN TRIPLE CROWN, Hidden Valley Raceway, Darwin, Northern Territory, Australia, 17/18 June. Round 6. 42 and 70 laps of the 1.783-mile/2.870km circuit.
Race 1 (74.900 miles/120.540km).
1 Fabian Coulthard, NZ (Ford), 52m 28.2817s, 85.646mph/137.835km/h; **2** Scott McLaughlin, NZ (Ford), +0.3776s; **3** Nick Percat, AUS (Holden), +1.3454s; **4** Jamie Whincup, AUS (Holden), +1.7691s; **5** Chaz Mostert, AUS (Ford), +2.3189s; **6** Cameron Waters, AUS (Ford), +4.1925s; **7** Craig Lowndes, AUS (Holden), +8.7772s; **8** David Reynolds, AUS (Holden), +9.3492s; **9** James Moffat, AUS (Holden), +9.9180s; **10** Lee Holdsworth, AUS (Holden), +10.6443s.
Fastest race lap: Moffat, 1m 06.9824s, 95.846mph/154.249km/h.
Pole position: Rick Kelly, AUS (Nissan), 1m 05.7114s, 97.700mph/157.232km/h.

Race 2 (124.833 miles/200.900km).
1 Scott McLaughlin, NZ (Ford), 1h 21m 04.2733s, 92.388mph/148.684km/h; **2** Jamie Whincup, AUS (Holden), +2.2818s; **3** Shane van Gisbergen, NZ (Holden), +23.8443s; **4** Fabian Coulthard, NZ (Ford), +24.9884s; **5** Tim Slade, AUS (Holden), +25.2383s; **6** Craig Lowndes, AUS (Holden), +25.8131s; **7** David Reynolds, AUS (Holden), +27.2470s; **8** Scott Pye, AUS (Holden), +28.3198s; **9** Cameron Waters, AUS (Ford), +31.7694s; **10** Rick Kelly, AUS (Nissan), +33.9243s.
Fastest race lap: McLaughlin, 1m 06.6747s, 96.288mph/154.961km/h.
Pole position: McLaughlin, 1m 05.7233s, 97.682mph/157.204km/h.

TOWNSVILLE 400, Townsville Street Circuit, Queensland, Australia, 8/9 July. Round 7. 2 x 70 laps of the 1.777-mile/2.860km circuit.
Race 1 (124.399 miles/200.200km).
1 Scott McLaughlin, NZ (Ford), 1h 28m 19.7419s, 84.501mph/135.991km/h; **2** Jamie Whincup, AUS (Holden), +4.0955s; **3** Mark Winterbottom, AUS (Ford), +15.4057s; **4** Chaz Mostert, AUS (Ford), +20.2589s; **5** Cameron Waters, AUS (Ford), +28.5221s; **6** Craig Lowndes, AUS (Holden), +34.1691s; **7** Shane van Gisbergen, NZ (Holden), +37.0222s; **8** Garth Tander, AUS (Holden), +37.1170s; **9** David Reynolds, AUS (Holden), +37.5962s; **10** Fabian Coulthard, NZ (Ford), +39.9157s.
Fastest race lap: McLaughlin, 1m 13.1279s, 87.485mph/140.794km/h.
Pole position: McLaughlin, 1m 12.0731s, 88.765mph/142.854km/h.

Race 2 (124.399 miles/200.200km).
1 Jamie Whincup, AUS (Holden), 1h 28m 12.5243s, 84.616mph/136.176km/h; **2** Scott McLaughlin, NZ (Ford), +1.6494s; **3** Shane van Gisbergen, NZ (Holden), +7.3193s; **4** Mark Winterbottom, AUS (Ford), +31.4243s; **5** Chaz Mostert, AUS (Ford), +34.6192s; **6** Garth Tander, AUS (Holden), +35.0159s; **7** James Moffat, AUS (Holden), +40.0452s; **8** Will Davison, AUS (Holden), +46.6986s; **9** James Courtney, AUS (Holden), +49.1262s; **10** Craig Lowndes, AUS (Holden), +1m 00.6046s.
Fastest race lap: Nick Percat, AUS (Holden), 1m 12.9311s, 87.721mph/141.174km/h.
Pole position: McLaughlin, 1m 11.9908s, 88.867mph/143.018km/h.

COATES HIRE IPSWICH SUPERSPRINT, Queensland Raceway, Ipswich, Queensland, Australia, 29/30 July. Round 8. 39 and 65 laps of the 1.939-mile/3.120km circuit.
Race 1 (75.608 miles/121.680km).
1 Scott McLaughlin, NZ (Ford), 46m 36.5253s, 97.331mph/156.640km/h; **2** Chaz Mostert, AUS (Ford), +3.2470s; **3** Shane van Gisbergen, NZ (Holden), +4.7006s; **4** Tim Slade, AUS (Holden), +5.1589s; **5** Craig Lowndes, AUS (Holden), +9.0852s; **6** Fabian Coulthard, NZ (Ford), +9.5797s; **7** Nick Percat, AUS (Holden), +14.4562s; **8** Rick Kelly, AUS (Nissan), +17.2439s; **9** Mark Winterbottom, AUS (Ford), +17.4372s; **10** David Reynolds, AUS (Holden), +20.6650s.
Fastest race lap: James Courtney, AUS (Holden), 1m 09.7225s, 100.100mph/161.095km/h.
Pole position: McLaughlin, 1m 08.8167s, 101.417mph/163.216km/h.

Race 2 (126.014 miles/202.800km).
1 Chaz Mostert, AUS (Ford), 1h 21m 42.7652s, 92.529mph/148.911km/h; **2** Scott McLaughlin, NZ (Ford), +0.7329s; **3** Shane van Gisbergen, NZ (Holden), +1.2266s; **4** Jamie Whincup, AUS (Holden), +2.7317s; **5** Fabian Coulthard, NZ (Ford), +3.2528s; **6** Craig Lowndes, AUS (Holden), +4.5190s; **7** Tim Slade, AUS (Holden), +4.9121s; **8** Cameron Waters, AUS (Ford), +5.5413s; **9** David Reynolds, AUS (Holden), +7.1110s; **10** Mark Winterbottom, AUS (Ford), +10.1359s.
Fastest race lap: McLaughlin, 1m 09.8167s, 99.965mph/160.878km/h.
Pole position: McLaughlin, 1m 08.4208s, 102.004mph/164.160km/h.

RED ROOSTER SYDNEY SUPERSPRINT, Sydney Motorsport Park, Eastern Creek, New South Wales, Australia, 19/20 August. Round 9. 31 and 52 laps of the 2.442-mile/3.930km circuit.
Race 1 (75.702 miles/121.830km).
1 Fabian Coulthard, NZ (Ford), 49m 29.1701s, 91.785mph/147.714km/h; **2** Chaz Mostert, AUS (Ford), +3.9836s; **3** Jamie Whincup, AUS (Holden), +7.4476s; **4** Mark Winterbottom, AUS (Ford), +8.7821s; **5** Scott Pye, AUS (Holden), +9.3242s; **6** Michael Caruso, AUS (Nissan), +10.1871s; **7** Craig Lowndes, AUS (Holden), +10.3811s; **8** David Reynolds, AUS (Holden), +17.0385s; **9** Garth Tander, AUS (Holden), +17.4563s; **10** Tim Blanchard, AUS (Holden), +19.0782s.
Fastest race lap: Nick Percat, AUS (Holden), 1m 30.5482s, 97.088mph/156.248km/h.
Pole position: Scott McLaughlin, NZ (Ford), 1m 28.3209s, 99.536mph/160.188km/h.

Race 2 (126.983 miles/204.360km).
1 Jamie Whincup, AUS (Holden), 1h 24m 01.8616s, 90.668mph/145.917km/h; **2** Fabian Coulthard, NZ (Ford), +9.8630s; **3** Shane van Gisbergen, NZ (Holden), +13.9601s; **4** Scott McLaughlin, NZ (Ford), +14.1025s; **5** Chaz Mostert, AUS (Ford), +15.9242s; **6** Nick Percat, AUS (Holden), +20.8056s; **7** Michael Caruso, AUS (Nissan), +20.8459s; **8** Jason Bright, AUS (Ford), +25.6430s; **9** David Reynolds, AUS (Holden), +32.7804s; **10** Todd Kelly, AUS (Nissan), +36.7436s.
Fastest race lap: Mostert, 1m 30.1577s, 97.508mph/156.925km/h.
Pole position: McLaughlin, 1m 28.2259s, 99.643mph/160.361km/h.

WILSON SECURITY SANDOWN 500, Sandown International Motor Raceway, Melbourne, Victoria, Australia, 17 September. Round 10. 125 laps of the 1.926-mile/3.100km circuit, 240.781 miles/387.500km.
1 Cameron Waters/Richie Stanaway, AUS/NZ (Ford), 3h 31m 35.7850s, 68.275mph/109.878km/h; **2** Scott McLaughlin/Alexandre Prémat, NZ/F (Ford), +0.6746s; **3** Chaz Mostert/Steve Owen, AUS/AUS (Ford), +22.5748s; **4** Garth Tander/James Golding, AUS/AUS (Holden), +27.1675s; **5** Fabian Coulthard/Tony D'Alberto, NZ/AUS (Ford), +27.7198s; **6** Jamie Whincup/Paul Dumbrell, AUS/AUS (Holden), +36.3955s; **7** James Moffat/Richard Muscat, AUS/AUS (Holden), +37.3387s; **8** Lee Holdsworth/Karl Reindler, AUS/AUS (Holden), +38.7756s; **9** Mark Winterbottom/Dean Canto, AUS/AUS (Ford), +43.9399s; **10** James Courtney/Jack Perkins, AUS/AUS (Holden), +47.2303s.
Fastest race lap: Mostert/Owen, 1m 09.2289s, 100.167mph/161.204km/h.
Pole position: Waters/Stanaway.

SUPERCHEAP AUTO BATHURST 1000, Mount Panorama, Bathurst, New South Wales, Australia, 8 October. Round 11. 161 laps of the 3.861-mile/6.213km circuit, 621.553 miles/1000.293km.
1 David Reynolds/Luke Youlden, AUS/AUS (Holden), 7h 11m 45.5456s, 86.375mph/139.007km/h; **2** Scott Pye/Warren Luff, AUS/AUS (Holden), +3.8995s; **3** Fabian Coulthard/Tony D'Alberto, NZ/AUS (Ford), +4.5913s; **4** Dale Wood/Chris Pither, AUS/NZ (Holden), +6.3450s; **5** Shane van Gisbergen/Matt Campbell, NZ/AUS (Holden), +10.6260s; **6** Michael Caruso/Dean Fiore, AUS/AUS (Nissan), +13.6874s; **7** Todd Kelly/Jack Le Brocq, AUS/AUS (Nissan), +24.3004s; **8** Jason Bright/Garry Jacobson, AUS/AUS (Ford), +28.1647s; **9** Tim Slade/Andre Heimgartner, AUS/NZ (Holden), +29.6276s; **10** Chaz Mostert/Steve Owen, AUS/AUS (Ford), +59.3060s.
Fastest race lap: Reynolds/Youlden, 2m 07.5013s, 109.003mph/175.424km/h.
Pole position: Scott McLaughlin/Alexandre Prémat, NZ/F (Ford), 2m 03.8312s, 112.234mph/180.623km/h.

VODAFONE GOLD COAST 600, Surfer's Paradise Steet Circuit, Queensland, Australia, 21/22 October. Round 12. 94 and 102 laps of the 1.854-mile/2.984km circuit.
Race 1 (174.292 miles/280.496km).
1 Chaz Mostert/Steve Owen, AUS/AUS (Ford), 2h 18m 28.8455s, 75.516mph/121.531km/h; **2** Cameron Waters/Richie Stanaway, AUS/NZ (Ford), +2.4916s; **3** Tim Slade/Andre Heimgartner, AUS/NZ (Holden), +5.5391s; **4** Shane van Gisbergen/Matt Campbell, NZ/AUS (Holden), +7.0041s; **5** Michael Caruso/Dean Fiore, AUS/AUS (Nissan), +21.2713s; **6** Jamie Whincup/Paul Dumbrell, AUS/AUS (Holden), +26.8865s; **7** Craig Lowndes/Steven Richards, AUS/NZ (Holden), +28.2674s; **8** Mark Winterbottom/Dean Canto, AUS/AUS (Ford), +43.3660s; **9** Jason Bright/Garry Jacobson, AUS/AUS (Ford), +47.5501s; **10** Rick Kelly/David Wall, AUS/AUS (Nissan), +48.7763s.
Fastest race lap: Mostert/Owen, 1m 21.3994s, 82.003mph/131.971km/h.
Pole position: Mostert/Owen, 1m 21.5486s, 81.853mph/131.730km/h.

Race 2 (189.126 miles/304.368km).
1 Scott McLaughlin/Alexandre Prémat, NZ/F (Ford), 2h 05m 17.3924s, 90.570mph/145.758km/h; **2** Jamie Whincup/Paul Dumbrell, AUS/AUS (Holden), +1.4752s; **3** Shane van Gisbergen/Matt Campbell, NZ/AUS (Holden), +2.5170s; **4** Craig Lowndes/Steven Richards, AUS/NZ (Holden), +21.0491s; **5** Mark Winterbottom/Dean Canto, AUS/AUS (Ford), +25.8166s; **6** James Courtney/Jack Perkins, AUS/AUS (Holden), +28.4383s; **7** Chaz Mostert/Steve Owen, AUS/AUS (Ford), +31.4405s; **8** Lee Holdsworth/Karl Reindler, AUS/AUS (Holden), +31.5831s; **9** Fabian Coulthard/Tony D'Alberto, NZ/AUS (Ford), +31.9997s; **10** Nick Percat/Macauley Jones, AUS/AUS (Holden), +44.5534s.
Fastest race lap: van Gisbergen/Campbell, 1m 11.4604s, 93.408mph/150.326km/h.
Pole position: van Gisbergen/Campbell, 1m 10.8384s, 94.228mph/151.646km/h.

ITM AUCKLAND SUPERSPRINT, Pukekohe Park Raceway, Auckland, New Zealand, 4/5 November. Round 13. 66 and 70 laps of the 1.808-mile/2.910km circuit.
Race 1 (119.341 miles/192.060km).
1 Shane van Gisbergen, NZ (Holden), 1h 23m 58.8115s, 85.263mph/137.218km/h; **2** Mark Winterbottom, AUS (Ford), +0.8172s; **3** Scott McLaughlin, NZ (Ford), +1.4249s; **4** Jamie Whincup, AUS (Holden), +1.8797s; **5** Jason Bright, AUS (Ford), +2.5530s; **6** Tim Slade, AUS (Holden), +3.1602s; **7** Garth Tander, AUS (Holden), +3.9512s; **8** Craig Lowndes, AUS (Holden), +4.3147s; **9** Cameron Waters, AUS (Ford), +4.7579s; **10** Lee Holdsworth, AUS (Holden), +5.2802s.
Fastest race lap: McLaughlin, 1m 03.5775s, 102.386mph/164.775km/h.
Pole position: van Gisbergen.

Race 2 (126.573 miles/203.700km).
1 Jamie Whincup, AUS (Holden), 1h 17m 11.7118s, 98.379mph/158.325km/h; **2** Scott McLaughlin, NZ (Ford), +5.9059s; **3** Cameron Waters, AUS (Ford), +8.6596s; **4** Craig Lowndes, AUS (Holden), +18.7898s; **5** Fabian Coulthard, NZ (Ford), +25.6058s; **6** Garth Tander, AUS (Holden), +29.4981s; **7** Chaz Mostert, AUS (Ford), +31.9024s; **8** Jason Bright, AUS (Ford), +32.3789s; **9** James Moffat, AUS (Holden), +38.3326s; **10** Scott Pye, AUS (Holden), +39.3094s.
Fastest race lap: Whincup, 1m 03.6772s, 102.226mph/164.517km/h.
Pole position: Whincup, 1m 02.5148s, 104.127mph/167.576km/h.

COATES HIRE NEWCASTLE 500, Newcastle Street Circuit, New South Wales, Australia, 25/26 November. Round 14. 91 and 95 laps of the 1.634-mile/2.629km circuit.
Race 1 (148.656 miles/239.239km).
1 Scott McLaughlin, NZ (Ford), 2h 00m 01.7051s, 74.310mph/119.591km/h; **2** Fabian Coulthard, NZ (Ford), +2.4430s; **3** Tim Slade, AUS (Holden), +3.5060s; **4** Lee Holdsworth, AUS (Holden), +4.1874s; **5** David Reynolds, AUS (Holden), +10.9000s; **6** Chaz Mostert, AUS (Ford), +11.8228s; **7** Scott Pye, AUS (Holden), +12.9853s; **8** Nick Percat, AUS (Holden), +13.8657s; **9** Will Davison, AUS (Holden), +14.3288s; **10** Rick Kelly, AUS (Nissan), +15.6008s.
Fastest race lap: Jamie Whincup, AUS (Holden), 1m 10.9158s, 82.928mph/133.459km/h.
Pole position: McLaughlin, 1m 09.9065s, 84.125mph/135.386km/h.

Race 2 (155.191 miles/249.755km).
1 Jamie Whincup, AUS (Holden), 2h 00m 09.8054s, 77.489mph/124.707km/h; **2** Shane van Gisbergen, NZ (Holden), +4.4812s; **3** David Reynolds, AUS (Holden), +5.7168s; **4** Rick Kelly, AUS (Nissan), +6.6820s; **5** Michael Caruso, AUS (Nissan), +7.5502s; **6** Nick Percat, AUS (Holden), +8.8470s; **7** Mark Winterbottom, AUS (Ford), +9.7854s; **8** Lee Holdsworth, AUS (Holden), +10.2893s; **9** Will Davison, AUS (Holden), +10.6255s; **10** Todd Kelly, AUS (Nissan), +12.2158s.
Fastest race lap: Reynolds, 1m 10.6403s, 83.251mph/133.980km/h.
Pole position: Scott McLaughlin, NZ (Ford), 1m 10.5212s, 83.392mph/134.206km/h.

Final championship points
Drivers
1 Jamie Whincup, AUS, 3042; **2** Scott McLaughlin, NZ, 3021; **3** Fabian Coulthard, NZ, 2812; **4** Shane van Gisbergen, NZ, 2769; **5** Chaz Mostert, AUS, 2748; **6** Mark Winterbottom, AUS, 2208; **7** David Reynolds, AUS, 2196; **8** Cameron Waters, AUS, 2173; **9** Garth Tander, AUS, 2169; **10** Craig Lowndes, AUS, 2160; **11** Tim Slade, AUS, 1812; **12** Scott Pye, AUS, 1804; **13** Michael Caruso, AUS, 1776; **14** Rick Kelly, AUS, 1773; **15** Will Davison, AUS, 1659; **16** Lee Holdsworth, AUS, 1647; **17** James Moffat, AUS, 1542; **18** Todd Kelly, AUS, 1536; **19** Nick Percat, AUS, 1527; **20** Jason Bright, AUS, 1524.

Teams
1 Shell V-Power Racing Team, 5868; **2** Red Bull Holden Racing Australia, 5811; **3** Prodrive Racing Australia, 4416; **4** Wilson Security Racing GRM, 3711; **5** Erebus Motorsport, 3477.

Other Australian V8 races

COATES HIRE SUPERCARS CHALLENGE, Albert Park Circuit, Melbourne, Victoria, Australia, 24/26 March. 13, 11, 13 and 13 laps of the 3.295-mile/5.303km circuit.
Race 1 (42.837 miles/68.939km).
1 Scott McLaughlin, NZ (Ford), 27m 13.5519s, 94.402mph/151.926km/h; **2** Fabian Coulthard, NZ (Ford), +0.3590s; **3** Chaz Mostert, AUS (Ford), +1.4422s; **4** Jamie Whincup, AUS (Holden), +2.2748s; **5** Michael Caruso, AUS (Nissan), +2.4978s; **6** Shane van Gisbergen, NZ (Holden), +4.9277s; **7** James Moffat, AUS (Holden), +5.1316s; **8** Mark Winterbottom, AUS (Ford), +6.1815s; **9** David Reynolds, AUS (Holden), +7.0755s; **10** James Courtney, AUS (Holden), +7.5189s.
Fastest race lap: McLaughlin, 1m 57.0198s, 101.371mph/163.141km/h.
Pole position: Coulthard, 1m 54.3972s, 103.695mph/166.881km/h.

Race 2 (36.246 miles/58.333km).
1 Fabian Coulthard, NZ (Ford), 27m 09.0306s, 80.101mph/128.910km/h; **2** Scott McLaughlin, NZ (Ford), +1.7229s; **3** Michael Caruso, AUS (Nissan), +2.8075s; **4** Garth Tander, AUS (Holden), +3.6783s; **5** Will Davison, AUS (Holden), +4.3614s; **6** Mark Winterbottom, AUS (Ford), +5.2714s; **7** Jamie Whincup, AUS (Holden), +8.0226s; **8** Cameron Waters, AUS (Ford), +8.0238s; **9** Craig Lowndes, AUS (Holden), +8.2131s; **10** Tim Slade, AUS (Holden), +8.5579s.
Fastest race lap: Chaz Mostert, AUS (Ford), 1m 56.6025s, 101.734mph/163.725km/h.
Pole position: Coulthard, 1m 54.8949s, 103.246mph/166.158km/h.

Race 3 (42.837 miles/68.939km).
1 Fabian Coulthard, NZ (Ford), 25m 37.8132s, 100.280mph/161.385km/h; **2** Jamie Whincup, AUS (Holden), +0.8063s; **3** Scott McLaughlin, NZ (Ford), +5.9126s; **4** Chaz Mostert, AUS (Ford), +7.8959s; **5** James Courtney, AUS (Holden), +8.9418s; **6** David Reynolds, AUS (Holden), +12.5319s; **7** Michael Caruso, AUS (Nissan), +12.9994s; **8** Will Davison, AUS (Holden), +15.5026s; **9** James Moffat, AUS (Holden), +15.6994s; **10** Todd Kelly, AUS (Nissan), +19.1832s.
Fastest race lap: Coulthard, 1m 56.6730s, 101.672mph/163.626km/h.
Pole position: Coulthard, 1m 54.5983s, 103.513mph/166.588km/h.

Race 4 (42.837 miles/68.939km).
1 Chaz Mostert, AUS (Ford), 25m 38.1620s, 100.257mph/161.348km/h; **2** Shane van Gisbergen, NZ (Holden), +9.7197s; **3** Tim Slade, AUS (Holden), +13.7350s; **4** Todd Kelly, AUS (Nissan), +15.7434s; **5** Michael Caruso, AUS (Nissan), +16.8286s; **6** James Courtney, AUS (Holden), +16.4657s; **7** Scott Pye, AUS (Holden), +17.5675s; **8** Will Davison, AUS (Holden), +19.3047s; **9** Jason Bright, AUS (Ford), +21.1277s; **10** David Reynolds, AUS (Holden), +22.2490s.
Fastest race lap: Fabian Coulthard, NZ (Ford), 1m 56.5701s, 101.762mph/163.770km/h.
Pole position: Jamie Whincup, AUS (Holden), 1m 54.6607s, 103.457mph/166.498km/h.

Final championship points
Drivers
1 Fabian Coulthard, NZ, 241; **2** Scott McLaughlin, NZ, 235; **3** Chaz Mostert, AUS, 223; **4** Michael Caruso, AUS, 222; **5** Jamie Whincup, AUS, 201; **6** Will Davison, AUS, 181; **7** James Courtney, AUS, 175; **8** Todd Kelly, AUS, 169; **9** Mark Winterbottom, AUS, 162; **10** David Reynolds, AUS, 160.

FIA World Touring Car Championship

FIA WORLD TOURING CAR CHAMPIONSHIP, Circuit Moulay El Hassan, Agdal, Marrakesh, Morocco, 9 April. 20 and 23 laps of the 1.846-mile/2.971km circuit.
Round 1 (36.922 miles/59.420km).
1 Esteban Guerrieri, RA (Chevrolet RML Cruze TC1), 31m 30.426s, 70.311mph/113.155km/h; **2** Thed Björk, S (Volvo S60 Polestar), +0.654s; **3** Mehdi Bennani, MA (Citroën C-Elysée WTCC), +1.289s; **4** Nicky Catsburg, NL (Volvo S60 Polestar), +1.921s; **5** Norbert Michelisz, H (Honda Civic WTCC), +2.201s; **6** Tiago Monteiro, P (Honda Civic WTCC), +2.803s; **7** Tom Chilton, GB (Citroën C-Elysée WTCC), +14.032s; **8** Tom Coronel, NL (Chevrolet RML Cruze TC1), +20.390s; **9** Néstor Girolami, RA (Volvo S60 Polestar), +20.858s; **10** Aurélien Panis, F (Honda Civic WTCC), +21.950s.
Fastest race lap: Dániel Nagy, H (Honda Civic WTCC), 1m 24.513s, 78.638mph/126.555km/h.
Pole position: Coronel.

Round 2 (42.460 miles/68.333km).
1 Tiago Monteiro, P (Honda Civic WTCC), 34m 00.997s, 74.893mph/120.528km/h; **2** Norbert Michelisz, H (Honda Civic WTCC), +0.751s; **3** Néstor Girolami, RA (Volvo S60 Polestar), +2.120s; **4** Nicky Catsburg, NL (Volvo S60 Polestar), +3.702s; **5** Tom Chilton, GB (Citroën C-Elysée WTCC), +4.519s; **6** Mehdi Bennani, MA (Citroën C-Elysée WTCC), +4.847s *; **7** Thed Björk, S (Volvo S60 Polestar), +5.073s; **8** Tom Coronel, NL (Chevrolet RML Cruze TC1), +6.363s; **9** Rob Huff, GB (Citroën C-Elysée WTCC), +7.658s; **10** Ryo Michigami, J (Honda Civic WTCC), +12.197s.
** includes 2s penalty for causing an accident.*
Fastest race lap: Esteban Guerrieri, RA (Chevrolet RML Cruze TC1), 1m 23.624s, 79.474mph/127.901km/h.
Pole position: Monteiro, 1m 21.792s, 81.254mph/130.765km/h.

FIA WORLD TOURING CAR CHAMPIONSHIP, Autodromo Nazionale di Monza, Milan, Italy, 30 April. 9 and 12 laps of the 3.600-mile/5.793km circuit.
Round 3 (32.396 miles/52.137km).
1 Tom Chilton, GB (Citroën C-Elysée WTCC), 17m 17.330s, 112.430mph/180.938km/h; **2** Rob Huff, GB (Citroën C-Elysée WTCC), +0.329s; **3** Tiago Monteiro, P (Honda Civic WTCC), +2.630s; **4** Esteban Guerrieri, RA (Chevrolet RML Cruze TC1), +6.899s; **5** Thed Björk, S (Volvo S60 Polestar), +7.793s *; **6** Tom Coronel, NL (Chevrolet RML Cruze TC1), +11.100s; **7** John Filippi, F (Citroën C-Elysée WTCC), +12.928s; **8** Nicky Catsburg, NL (Volvo S60 Polestar), +18.067s; **9** Kevin Gleason, USA (Lada Vesta WTCC), +18.449s; **10** Dániel Nagy, H (Honda Civic WTCC), +19.200s.
** includes 1s penalty.*
Fastest race lap: Björk, 1m 53.976s, 113.695mph/182.975km/h.
Pole position: Coronel.

Round 4 (43.195 miles/69.516km).
1 Thed Björk, S (Volvo S60 Polestar), 23m 51.974s, 108.593mph/174.764km/h; **2** Tiago Monteiro, P (Honda Civic WTCC), +2.174s; **3** Rob Huff, GB (Citroën C-Elysée WTCC), +2.779s; **4** Nicky Catsburg, NL (Volvo S60 Polestar), +3.269s; **5** Néstor Girolami, RA (Volvo S60 Polestar), +6.180s; **6** Norbert Michelisz, H (Honda Civic WTCC), +6.181s; **7** Mehdi Bennani, MA (Citroën C-Elysée WTCC), +9.582s; **8** Esteban Guerrieri, RA (Chevrolet RML Cruze TC1), +11.522s; **9** Yann Ehrlacher, F (Lada Vesta WTCC), +11.877s; **10** John Filippi, F (Citroën C-Elysée WTCC), +12.077s.
Fastest race lap: Björk, 1m 53.381s, 114.292mph/183.935km/h.
Pole position: Björk, 1m 52.505s, 115.182mph/185.367km/h.

FIA WORLD TOURING CAR CHAMPIONSHIP, Hungaroring, Mogyoród, Budapest, Hungary, 14 May. 12 and 17 laps of the 2.722-mile/4.381km circuit.
Round 5 (32.667 miles/52.572km).
1 Tiago Monteiro, P (Honda Civic WTCC), 22m 28.644s, 87.198mph/140.332km/h; **2** Tom Chilton, GB (Citroën C-Elysée WTCC), +0.768s; **3** Rob Huff, GB (Citroën C-Elysée WTCC), +2.296s; **4** Néstor Girolami, RA (Volvo S60 Polestar), +4.537s; **5** Nicky Catsburg, NL (Volvo S60 Polestar), +5.221s; **6** Esteban Guerrieri, RA (Chevrolet RML Cruze TC1), +10.308s; **7** Mehdi Bennani, MA (Citroën C-Elysée WTCC), +10.893s; **8** Yann Ehrlacher, F (Lada Vesta WTCC), +13.183s; **9** Tom Coronel, NL (Chevrolet RML Cruze TC1), +21.703s; **10** Aurélien Panis, F (Honda Civic WTCC), +37.886s.
Fastest race lap: Guerrieri, 1m 50.854s, 88.404mph/142.273km/h.
Pole position: Filippi.

Round 6 (46.278 miles/74.477km).
1 Mehdi Bennani, MA (Citroën C-Elysée WTCC), 33m 21.822s, 83.224mph/133.936km/h; **2** Nicky Catsburg, NL (Volvo S60 Polestar), +0.654s; **3** Tom Chilton, GB (Citroën C-Elysée WTCC), +3.553s; **4** Norbert Michelisz, H (Honda Civic WTCC), +7.309s; **5** Tiago Monteiro, P (Honda Civic WTCC), +9.532s; **6** Esteban Guerrieri, RA (Chevrolet RML Cruze TC1), +10.875s; **7** Thed Björk, S (Volvo S60 Polestar), +11.865s; **8** Yann Ehrlacher, F (Lada Vesta WTCC), +14.547s; **9** Tom Coronel, NL (Chevrolet RML Cruze TC1), +20.783s; **10** Rob Huff, GB (Citroën C-Elysée WTCC), +21.212s.
Fastest race lap: Huff, 1m 50.478s, 88.705mph/142.757km/h.
Pole position: Huff, 1m 48.264s, 90.519mph/145.677km/h.

FIA WORLD TOURING CAR CHAMPIONSHIP, Nürburgring, Nürburg/Eifel, Germany, 27 May. 2 x 3 laps of the 15.769-mile/25.378km circuit.
Round 7 (47.307 miles/76.134km).
1 Thed Björk, S (Volvo S60 Polestar), 26m 24.961s, 107.451mph/172.926km/h; **2** Mehdi Bennani, MA (Citroën C-Elysée WTCC), +2.538s; **3** Rob Huff, GB (Citroën C-Elysée WTCC), +3.096s; **4** Tom Chilton, GB (Citroën C-Elysée WTCC), +3.732s; **5** Esteban Guerrieri, RA (Chevrolet RML Cruze TC1), +8.487s; **6** Nicky Catsburg, NL (Volvo S60 Polestar), +8.910s; **7** Norbert Michelisz, H (Honda Civic WTCC), +16.496s; **8** Tom Coronel, NL (Chevrolet RML Cruze TC1), +16.796s; **9** Yann Ehrlacher, F (Lada Vesta WTCC), +19.481s; **10** John Filippi, F (Citroën C-Elysée WTCC), +22.889s.
Fastest race lap: Chilton, 8m 47.063s, 107.708mph/173.339km/h.
Pole position: Girolami.

Round 8 (47.307 miles/76.134km).
1 Nicky Catsburg, NL (Volvo S60 Polestar), 26m 20.680s, 107.742mph/173.395km/h; **2** Norbert Michelisz, H (Honda Civic WTCC), +3.065s; **3** Rob Huff, GB (Citroën C-Elysée WTCC), +3.401s; **4** Thed Björk, S (Volvo S60 Polestar), +4.167s; **5** Tom Chilton, GB (Citroën C-Elysée WTCC), +5.763s; **6** Mehdi Bennani, MA (Citroën C-Elysée WTCC), +11.239s; **7** Tom Coronel, NL (Chevrolet RML Cruze TC1), +14.614s; **8** Esteban Guerrieri, RA (Chevrolet RML Cruze TC1), +14.939s; **9** Yann Ehrlacher, F (Lada Vesta WTCC), +20.540s; **10** John Filippi, F (Citroën C-Elysée WTCC), +21.928s.
Fastest race lap: Catsburg, 8m 45.647s, 107.998mph/173.806km/h.
Pole position: Michelisz, 8m 38.072s, 109.577mph/176.347km/h.

FIA WORLD TOURING CAR CHAMPIONSHIP, Circuito Internacional de Vila Real, Portugal, 25 June. 11 and 13 laps of the 2.976-mile/4.790km circuit.
Round 9 (32.740 miles/52.690km).
1 Mehdi Bennani, MA (Citroën C-Elysée WTCC), 22m 00.741s, 89.240mph/143.619km/h; **2** Tiago Monteiro, P (Honda Civic WTCC), +0.799s; **3** Thed Björk, S (Volvo S60 Polestar), +1.632s; **4** Tom Chilton, GB (Citroën C-Elysée WTCC), +2.447s; **5** Nicky Catsburg, NL (Volvo S60 Polestar), +4.459s; **6** Rob Huff, GB (Citroën C-Elysée WTCC), +4.855s; **7** Norbert Michelisz, H (Honda Civic WTCC), +6.040s; **8** Néstor Girolami, RA (Volvo S60 Polestar), +12.317s; **9** Yann Ehrlacher, F (Lada Vesta WTCC), +13.151s; **10** John Filippi, F (Citroën C-Elysée WTCC), +16.210s.
Fastest race lap: Michelisz, 1m 58.654s, 90.303mph/145.330km/h.
Pole position: Michigami.

Round 10 (38.693 miles/62.270km).
1 Norbert Michelisz, H (Honda Civic WTCC), 25m 47.552s, 90.009mph/144.855km/h; **2** Thed Björk, S (Volvo S60 Polestar), +0.480s; **3** Tiago Monteiro, P (Honda Civic WTCC), +2.200s; **4** Nicky Catsburg, NL (Volvo S60 Polestar), +4.457s; **5** Rob Huff, GB (Citroën C-Elysée WTCC), +4.587s; **6** Tom Chilton, GB (Citroën C-Elysée WTCC), +8.834s; **7** Mehdi Bennani, MA (Citroën C-Elysée WTCC), +20.846s; **8** Esteban Guerrieri, RA (Chevrolet RML Cruze TC1), +23.834s; **9** Néstor Girolami, RA (Volvo S60 Polestar), +24.864s; **10** John Filippi, F (Citroën C-Elysée WTCC), +25.384s.
Fastest race lap: Huff, 1m 57.929s, 90.859mph/146.223km/h.
Pole position: Michelisz, 1m 55.846s, 92.492mph/148.852km/h.

FIA WORLD TOURING CAR CHAMPIONSHIP, Autódromo Termas de Río Hondo, Santiago del Estero, Argentina, 16 July. 11 and 13 laps of the 2.986-mile/4.806km circuit.
Round 11 (32.849 miles/52.866km).
1 Yann Ehrlacher, F (Lada Vesta WTCC), 19m 23.991s, 101.596mph/163.504km/h; **2** Mehdi Bennani, MA (Citroën C-Elysée WTCC), +0.726s; **3** Esteban Guerrieri, RA (Chevrolet RML Cruze TC1), +1.326s; **4** Tom Chilton, GB (Citroën C-Elysée WTCC), +1.573s *; **5** Tiago Monteiro, P (Honda Civic WTCC), +1.677s; **6** Thed Björk, S (Volvo S60 Polestar), +2.322s; **7** Rob Huff, GB (Citroën C-Elysée WTCC), +3.668s; **8** John Filippi, F (Citroën C-Elysée WTCC), +10.369s; **9** Tom Coronel, NL (Chevrolet RML Cruze TC1), +10.960s; **10** Ryo Michigami, J (Honda Civic WTCC), +11.379s.
** includes 5s penalty for causing an accident.*
Fastest race lap: Björk, 1m 44.727s, 102.654mph/165.206km/h.
Pole position: Ehrlacher.

Round 12 (38.822 miles/62.478km).
1 Norbert Michelisz, H (Honda Civic WTCC), 22m 39.375s, 102.811mph/165.458km/h; **2** Tiago Monteiro, P (Honda Civic WTCC), +0.505s; **3** Thed Björk, S (Volvo S60 Polestar), +1.381s; **4** Esteban Guerrieri, RA (Chevrolet RML Cruze TC1), +6.379s; **5** Mehdi Bennani, MA (Citroën C-Elysée WTCC), +14.281s; **6** Néstor Girolami, RA (Volvo S60 Polestar), +14.675s; **7** Tom Chilton, GB (Citroën C-Elysée WTCC), +20.386s; **8** Yann Ehrlacher, F (Lada Vesta WTCC), +20.750s; **9** Rob Huff, GB

(Citroën C-Elysée WTCC), +20.999s; **10** Tom Coronel, NL (Chevrolet RML Cruze TC1), +21.983s.
Fastest race lap: Nicky Catsburg, NL (Volvo S60 Polestar), 1m 43.480s, 103.891mph/167.197km/h.
Pole position: Catsburg, 1m 43.088s, 104.286mph/167.833km/h.

FIA WORLD TOURING CAR CHAMPIONSHIP, Ningbo International Speedpark, Zhejiang, China, 15 October. 15 and 2 laps of the 2.492-mile/4.010km circuit.
Round 13 (37.375 miles/60.150km).
1 Esteban Guerrieri, RA (Chevrolet RML Cruze TC1), 33m 29.509s, 66.957mph/107.757km/h; **2** Yann Ehrlacher, F (Lada Vesta WTCC), +2.893s; **3** Nicky Catsburg, NL (Volvo S60 Polestar), +11.671s; **4** John Filippi, F (Citroën C-Elysée WTCC), +23.760s; **5** Kevin Gleason, USA (Lada Vesta WTCC), +24.522s; **6** Filipe Souza, MAC (Lada Vesta WTCC), +27.243s; **7** Tom Coronel, NL (Chevrolet RML Cruze TC1), -2 laps; Thed Björk, S (Volvo S60 Polestar), -5 (DNF); Mehdi Bennani, MA (Citroën C-Elysée WTCC), -8 (DNF); Tom Chilton, GB (Citroën C-Elysée WTCC), -9 (DNF).
Disqualified: Norbert Michelisz, H (Honda Civic WTCC), +17.409s (originally 4th); Gabriele Tarquini, I (Honda Civic WTCC), +17.840s (originally 5th); Dániel Nagy, H (Honda Civic WTCC), +24.946s (originally 8th); Ryo Michigami, J (Honda Civic WTCC), +26.334s (originally 9th).
Fastest race lap: Guerrieri, 2m 03.753s, 72.484mph/116.651km/h.
Pole position: Ehrlacher.

Round 14 (4.983 miles/8.020km).
1 Néstor Girolami, RA (Volvo S60 Polestar), 4m 59.154s, 59.969mph/96.512km/h; **2** Thed Björk, S (Volvo S60 Polestar), +2.537s; **3** Tom Chilton, GB (Citroën C-Elysée WTCC), +4.562s; **4** Esteban Guerrieri, RA (Chevrolet RML Cruze TC1), +6.691s; **5** Nicky Catsburg, NL (Volvo S60 Polestar), +8.113s; **6** John Filippi, F (Citroën C-Elysée WTCC), +9.722s; **7** Kevin Gleason, USA (Lada Vesta WTCC), +12.118s; **8** Yann Ehrlacher, F (Lada Vesta WTCC), +13.656s; **9** Tom Coronel, NL (Chevrolet RML Cruze TC1), +16.721s; **10** Filipe Souza, MAC (Lada Vesta WTCC), +18.403s.
Disqualified: Norbert Michelisz, H (Honda Civic WTCC), +0.851s (originally 2nd); Gabriele Tarquini, I (Honda Civic WTCC), +3.347s (originally 4th); Ryo Michigami, J (Honda Civic WTCC), +11.250s (originally 9th).
Fastest race lap: Souza, 2m 25.745s, 61.546mph/99.049km/h.
Pole position: Girolami, 1m 58.049s, 75.986mph/122.288km/h.

FIA WORLD TOURING CAR CHAMPIONSHIP, Twin Ring Motegi, Motegi-machi, Haga-gun, Tochigi Prefecture, Japan, 29 October. 11 and 9 laps of the 2.983-mile/4.801km circuit.
Round 15 (32.815 miles/52.811km).
1 Tom Chilton, GB (Citroën C-Elysée WTCC), 23m 53.262s, 82.423mph/132.648km/h; **2** Yann Ehrlacher, F (Lada Vesta WTCC), +13.158s; **3** Esteban Guerrieri, RA (Honda Civic WTCC), +15.288s; **4** Thed Björk, S (Volvo S60 Polestar), +15.846s; **5** Mehdi Bennani, MA (Citroën C-Elysée WTCC), +19.053s; **6** Kevin Gleason, USA (Lada Vesta WTCC), +20.659s; **7** Norbert Michelisz, H (Honda Civic WTCC), +27.349s; **8** Rob Huff, GB (Citroën C-Elysée WTCC), +36.278s; **9** Nicky Catsburg, NL (Volvo S60 Polestar), +36.629s; **10** Ryo Michigami, J (Honda Civic WTCC), +37.104s.
Fastest race lap: Chilton, 2m 09.388s, 83.002mph/133.579km/h.
Pole position: Gleason.

Round 16 (26.849 miles/43.209km).
1 Norbert Michelisz, H (Honda Civic WTCC), 22m 17.924s, 72.243mph/116.264km/h; **2** Nicky Catsburg, NL (Volvo S60 Polestar), +0.392s; **3** Néstor Girolami, RA (Volvo S60 Polestar), +1.798s; **4** Esteban Guerrieri, RA (Honda Civic WTCC), +3.306s; **5** Thed Björk, S (Volvo S60 Polestar), +5.554s; **6** Mehdi Bennani, MA (Citroën C-Elysée WTCC), +6.196s; **7** Yann Ehrlacher, F (Lada Vesta WTCC), +7.063s; **8** Kevin Gleason, USA (Lada Vesta WTCC), +7.537s; **9** John Filippi, F (Citroën C-Elysée WTCC), +7.911s; **10** Tom Chilton, GB (Citroën C-Elysée WTCC), +8.764s.
Fastest race lap: Catsburg, 2m 10.990s, 81.987mph/131.945km/h.
Pole position: Michelisz, 2m 08.890s, 83.323mph/134.095km/h.

FIA WORLD TOURING CAR CHAMPIONSHIP, Circuito da Guia, Macau, 18/19 November. 5 and 13 laps of the 3.803-mile/6.120km circuit.
Round 17 (19.014 miles/30.600km).
1 Mehdi Bennani, MA (Citroën C-Elysée WTCC), 12m 26.832s, 91.654mph/147.503km/h; **2** Tom Coronel, NL (Chevrolet RML Cruze TC1), +1.952s; **3** Ryo Michigami, J (Honda Civic WTCC), +3.265s; **4** Thed Björk, S (Volvo S60 Polestar), +3.627s; **5** Norbert Michelisz, H (Honda Civic WTCC), +4.577s; **6** Esteban Guerrieri, RA (Honda Civic WTCC), +5.379s; **7** Rob Huff, GB (Citroën C-Elysée WTCC), +6.635s; **8** Tom Chilton, GB (Citroën C-Elysée WTCC), +8.068s; **9** Nicky Catsburg, NL (Volvo S60 Polestar), +10.688s; **10** Kevin Gleason, USA (Lada Vesta WTCC), +12.040s.
Fastest race lap: Huff, 2m 26.469s, 93.467mph/150.420km/h.
Pole position: Bennani.

Round 18 (49.436 miles/79.560km).
1 Rob Huff, GB (Citroën C-Elysée WTCC), 38m 15.740s, 77.522mph/124.759km/h; **2** Norbert Michelisz, H (Honda Civic WTCC), +8.142s; **3** Tom Chilton, GB (Citroën C-Elysée WTCC), +8.684s; **4** Esteban Guerrieri, RA (Honda Civic WTCC), +9.228s; **5** Thed Björk, S (Volvo S60 Polestar), +21.237s; **6** Tom Coronel, NL (Chevrolet RML Cruze TC1), +25.818s; **7** Mehdi Bennani, MA (Citroën C-Elysée WTCC), +28.693s; **8** Kevin Gleason, USA (Lada Vesta WTCC), +31.583s; **9** Néstor Girolami, RA (Volvo S60 Polestar), +34.326s; **10** Zsolt Dávid Szabó, H (Honda Civic WTCC), +41.598s.
Fastest race lap: Ma Qing Hua, CHN (Citroën C-Elysée WTCC), 2m 47.045s, 81.954mph/131.892km/h.
Pole position: Huff, 2m 23.995s, 95.073mph/153.005km/h.

FIA WORLD TOURING CAR CHAMPIONSHIP, Losail International Circuit, Doha, Qatar, 1 December. 10 and 12 laps of the 3.343-mile/5.380km circuit.
Round 19 (33.430 miles/53.800km).
1 Tom Chilton, GB (Citroën C-Elysée WTCC), 20m 44.557s, 96.698mph/155.621km/h; **2** Mehdi Bennani, MA (Citroën C-Elysée WTCC), +2.175s; **3** Kevin Gleason, USA (Lada Vesta WTCC), +6.178s; **4** John Filippi, F (Citroën C-Elysée WTCC), +7.054s; **5** Thed Björk, S (Volvo S60 Polestar), +7.571s; **6** Yvan Muller, F (Volvo S60 Polestar), +7.945s; **7** Rob Huff, GB (Citroën C-Elysée WTCC), +8.577s; **8** Nicky Catsburg, NL (Volvo S60 Polestar), +9.248s; **9** Norbert Michelisz, H (Honda Civic WTCC), +9.537s; **10** Esteban Guerrieri, RA (Honda Civic WTCC), +10.304s.
Fastest race lap: Bennani, 2m 02.496s, 98.245mph/158.111km/h.
Pole position: Gleason.

Round 20 (40.116 miles/64.560km).
1 Esteban Guerrieri, RA (Honda Civic WTCC), 24m 43.996s, 97.316mph/156.614km/h; **2** Rob Huff, GB (Citroën C-Elysée WTCC), +3.708s; **3** Nicky Catsburg, NL (Volvo S60 Polestar), +7.319s; **4** Thed Björk, S (Volvo S60 Polestar), +7.466s; **5** Tom Chilton, GB (Citroën C-Elysée WTCC), +8.785s; **6** Kris Richard, CH (Chevrolet RML Cruze TC1), +10.589s; **7** Yvan Muller, F (Volvo S60 Polestar), +11.459s; **8** Norbert Michelisz, H (Honda Civic WTCC), +12.023s; **9** John Filippi, F (Citroën C-Elysée WTCC), +15.942s; **10** Ryo Michigami, J (Honda Civic WTCC), +22.140s.
Fastest race lap: Guerrieri, 2m 01.774s, 98.828mph/159.048km/h.
Pole position: Guerrieri, 2m 00.893s, 99.548mph/160.207km/h.

Final championship points
Drivers
1 Thed Björk, S, 283.5; **2** Norbert Michelisz, H, 255; **3** Tom Chilton, GB, 248.5; **4** Esteban Guerrieri, RA, 241; **5** Nicky Catsburg, NL, 238.5; **6** Mehdi Bennani, MA, 234; **7** Rob Huff, GB, 215; **8** Tiago Monteiro, P, 200; **9** Néstor Girolami, RA, 112; **10** Yann Ehrlacher, F, 90; **11** Tom Coronel, NL, 69; **12** John Filippi, F, 48; **13** Kevin Gleason, USA, 47.5; **14** Ryo Michigami, J, 20; **15** Yvan Muller, F, 16; **16** Kris Richard, CH, 10; **17** Filipe Souza, MAC, 8.5; **18** Aurélien Panis, F, 2; **19** Dániel Nagy, H, 1; **20** Zsolt Dávid Szabó, H, 1.

Manufacturers
1 Volvo, 804.5; **2** Honda, 792.

TCR International Series

TCR INTERNATIONAL SERIES, Rustavi International Motorpark, Rustavi, Georgia, 2 April. 15 and 17 laps of the 2.560-mile/4.120km circuit.
Round 1 (38.401 miles/61.800km).
1 Davit Kajaia, GE (Alfa Romeo Giulietta TCR), 25m 56.717s, 88.803mph/142.916km/h; **2** Ferenc Ficza, H (SEAT León TCR), +0.374s; **3** Stefano Comini, CH (Audi RS3 LMS TCR), +1.176s; **4** Roberto Colciago, I (Honda Civic Type-R TCR), +1.478s; **5** Attila Tassi, H (Honda Civic Type-R TCR), +1.783s; **6** Jean-Karl Vernay, F (Volkswagen Golf Gti TCR), +6.667s; **7** Pepe Oriola, E (SEAT León TCR), +7.480s; **8** Giacomo Altoè, I (Volkswagen Golf Gti TCR), +7.841s; **9** Dušan Borkovic, SRB (Alfa Romeo Giulietta TCR), +10.842s; **10** Gianni Morbidelli, I (Volkswagen Golf Gti TCR), +11.388s.
Fastest race lap: Kajaia, 1m 49.626s, 84.069mph/135.296km/h.
Pole position: Kajaia, 1m 40.693s, 91.527mph/147.299km/h.

Round 2 (43.521 miles/70.040km).
1 Pepe Oriola, E (SEAT León TCR), 29m 40.114s, 88.014mph/141.644km/h; **2** Attila Tassi, H (Honda Civic Type-R TCR), +4.823s; **3** Jean-Karl Vernay, F (Volkswagen Golf Gti TCR), +5.466s; **4** Dušan Borkovic, SRB (Alfa Romeo Giulietta TCR), +16.878s; **5** James Nash, GB (SEAT León TCR), +19.012s; **6** Davit Kajaia, GE (Alfa Romeo Giulietta TCR), +19.835s; **7** Gianni Morbidelli, I (Volkswagen Golf Gti TCR), +20.271s; **8** Pierre-Yves Corthals, B (Opel Astra TCR), +33.498s; **9** Hugo Valente, F (SEAT León TCR), +34.056s *; **10** Giacomo Altoè, I (Volkswagen Golf Gti TCR), +34.127s.
** 30s penalty for overtaking under yellow flags.*
Fastest race lap: Oriola, 1m 42.657s, 89.776mph/144.481km/h.
Pole position: Altoè.

TCR INTERNATIONAL SERIES, Bahrain International Circuit, Sakhir, Bahrain, 15/16 April. 2 x 9 laps of the 3.363-mile/5.412km circuit.
Round 3 (30.113 miles/48.462km).
1 Roberto Colciago, I (Honda Civic Type-R TCR), 20m 15.241s, 89.653mph/144.284km/h; **2** Hugo Valente, F (SEAT León TCR), +5.502s; **3** Jean-Karl Vernay, F (Volkswagen Golf Gti TCR), +7.637s; **4** Dušan Borkovic, SRB (Alfa Romeo Giulietta TCR), +8.763s; **5** Pierre-Yves Corthals, B (Opel Astra TCR), +9.661s; **6** Pepe Oriola, E (SEAT León TCR), +9.912s; **7** James Nash, GB (SEAT León TCR), +11.284s; **8** Stefano Comini, CH (Audi RS3 LMS TCR), +11.581s; **9** Gianni Morbidelli, I (Volkswagen Golf Gti TCR), +12.200s; **10** Giacomo Altoè, I (Volkswagen Golf Gti TCR), +19.061s.
Fastest race lap: Davit Kajaia, GE (Alfa Romeo Giulietta TCR), 2m 13.635s, 90.592mph/145.794km/h.
Pole position: Corthals, 2m 12.451s, 91.402mph/147.097km/h.

Round 4 (30.113 miles/48.462km).
1 Dušan Borkovic, SRB (Alfa Romeo Giulietta TCR), 20m 20.221s, 89.288mph/143.695km/h; **2** James Nash, GB (SEAT León TCR), +4.154s; **3** Hugo Valente, F (SEAT León TCR), +4.861s; **4** Jean-Karl Vernay, F (Volkswagen Golf Gti TCR), +5.391s; **5** Roberto Colciago, I (Honda Civic Type-R TCR), +5.690s; **6** Ferenc Ficza, H (SEAT León TCR), +9.161s; **7** Pepe Oriola, E (SEAT León TCR), +14.967s; **8** Attila Tassi, H (Honda Civic Type-R TCR), +15.154s; **9** Stefano Comini, CH (Audi RS3 LMS TCR), +15.261s; **10** Gianni Morbidelli, I (Volkswagen Golf Gti TCR), +16.525s.
Fastest race lap: Borkovic, 2m 13.476s, 90.700mph/145.967km/h.
Pole position: Ficza.

TCR INTERNATIONAL SERIES, Circuit de Spa-Francorchamps, Stavelot, Belgium, 5/6 May. 2 x 9 laps of the 4.352-mile/7.004km circuit.
Round 5 (39.168 miles/63.035km).
1 Stefano Comini, CH (Audi RS3 LMS TCR), 23m 07.903s, 101.596mph/163.503km/h; **2** Benjamin Lessennes, B (Honda Civic Type-R TCR), +3.547s; **3** Attila Tassi, H (Honda Civic Type-R TCR), +8.343s; **4** Jean-Karl Vernay, F (Volkswagen Golf Gti TCR), +8.764s; **5** Frédéric Vervisch, B (Audi RS3 LMS TCR), +9.063s; **6** Rob Huff, GB (Volkswagen Golf Gti TCR), +9.325s; **7** Edouard Mondron, B (Volkswagen Golf Gti TCR), +9.619s; **8** Tom Coronel, NL (Honda Civic Type-R TCR), +10.550s; **9** Pepe Oriola, E (SEAT León TCR), +11.790s; **10** Pierre-Yves Corthals, B (Opel Astra TCR), +12.075s.
Fastest race lap: Comini, 2m 32.101s, 103.005mph/165.771km/h.
Pole position: Comini, 2m 30.794s, 103.898mph/167.208km/h.

Round 6 (39.168 miles/63.035km).
1 Jean-Karl Vernay, F (Volkswagen Golf Gti TCR), 23m 13.917s, 101.157mph/162.797km/h; **2** Rob Huff, GB (Volkswagen Golf Gti TCR), +0.720s; **3** Stefano Comini, CH (Audi RS3 LMS TCR), +2.325s; **4** Edouard Mondron, B (Volkswagen Golf Gti TCR), +3.888s; **5** Benjamin Lessennes, B (Honda Civic Type-R TCR), +4.907s; **6** Frédéric Vervisch, B (Audi RS3 LMS TCR), +5.909s; **7** Davit Kajaia, GE (Alfa Romeo Giulietta TCR), +11.790s; **8** James Nash, GB (SEAT León TCR), +12.398s; **9** Attila Tassi, H (Honda Civic Type-R TCR), +13.116s; **10** Giacomo Altoè, I (Volkswagen Golf Gti TCR), +13.817s.
Fastest race lap: Comini, 2m 32.593s, 102.673mph/165.237km/h.
Pole position: Potty.

TCR INTERNATIONAL SERIES, Autodromo Nazionale di Monza, Milan, Italy, 13/14 May. 2 x 11 laps of the 3.600-mile/5.793km circuit.
Round 7 (39.596 miles/63.723km).
1 Roberto Colciago, I (Honda Civic Type-R TCR), 22m 14.954s, 106.778mph/171.843km/h; **2** Attila Tassi, H (Honda Civic Type-R TCR), +1.613s; **3** Pepe Oriola, E (SEAT León TCR), +2.258s; **4** Jean-Karl Vernay, F (Volkswagen Golf Gti TCR), +2.408s; **5** Frédéric Vervisch, B (Audi RS3 LMS TCR), +5.881s; **6** Hugo Valente, F (SEAT León TCR), +8.591s; **7** Mat'o Homola, SK (Opel Astra TCR), +10.686s; **8** Stefano Comini, CH (Audi RS3 LMS TCR), +13.338s; **9** Dušan Borkovic, SRB (Alfa Romeo Giulietta TCR), +14.005s; **10** Ferenc Ficza, H (SEAT León TCR), +15.209s *.
** includes 10s penalty for gaining unfair advantage.*
Fastest race lap: Vervisch, 2m 00.106s, 107.892mph/173.636km/h.
Pole position: Vervisch, 1m 58.997s, 108.898mph/175.254km/h.

Round 8 (39.596 miles/63.723km).
1 Stefano Comini, CH (Audi RS3 LMS TCR), 22m 14.501s, 106.814mph/171.901km/h; **2** Roberto Colciago, I (Honda Civic Type-R TCR), +0.170s; **3** Frédéric Vervisch, B (Audi RS3 LMS TCR), +1.273s; **4** James Nash, GB (SEAT León TCR), +1.797s; **5** Jean-Karl Vernay, F (Volkswagen Golf Gti TCR), +2.052s; **6** Mat'o Homola, SK (Opel Astra TCR), +2.240s; **7** Davit Kajaia, GE (Alfa Romeo Giulietta TCR), +2.369s; **8** Pepe Oriola, E (SEAT León TCR), +2.789s; **9** Attila Tassi, H (Honda Civic Type-R TCR), +3.361s; **10** Ferenc Ficza, H (SEAT León TCR), +3.754s.
Fastest race lap: Tassi, 1m 59.958s, 108.025mph/173.850km/h.
Pole position: Valente.

TCR INTERNATIONAL SERIES, Salzburgring, Salzburg, Austria, 11 June. 14 and 17 laps of the 2.635-mile/4.240km circuit.
Round 9 (36.885 miles/59.360km).
1 Dušan Borkovic, SRB (Alfa Romeo Giulietta TCR), 24m 50.968s, 89.059mph/143.327km/h; **2** Mat'o Homola, SK (Opel Astra TCR), +0.873s; **3** Stefano Comini, CH (Audi RS3 LMS TCR), +1.465s; **4** Thomas Jäger, A (Opel Astra TCR), +1.964s; **5** Pepe Oriola, E (SEAT León TCR), +2.638s; **6** James Nash, GB (SEAT León TCR), +3.098s; **7** Davit Kajaia, GE (Alfa Romeo Giulietta TCR), +4.006s; **8** Jens Møller, DK (Honda Civic Type-R TCR), +4.631s; **9** Attila Tassi, H (Honda Civic Type-R TCR), +4.855s; **10** Frédéric Vervisch, B (Audi RS3 LMS TCR), +5.373s.
Fastest race lap: Comini, 1m 26.791s, 109.281mph/175.870km/h.
Pole position: Homola, 1m 25.481s, 110.955mph/178.565km/h.

Round 10 (44.788 miles/72.080km).
1 Roberto Colciago, I (Honda Civic Type-R TCR), 27m 50.474s, 96.522mph/155.337km/h; **2** Attila Tassi, H (Honda Civic Type-R TCR), +1.267s; **3** Stefano Comini, CH (Audi RS3 LMS TCR), +1.503s; **4** Thomas Jäger, A (Opel Astra TCR), +1.945s; **5** Gianni Morbidelli, I (Volkswagen Golf Gti TCR), +2.453s; **6** James Nash, GB (SEAT León TCR), +2.815s; **7** Daniel Lloyd, GB (SEAT León TCR), +6.777s; **8** Giacomo Altoè, I (Volkswagen Golf Gti TCR), +7.436s; **9** Jens Møller, DK (Honda Civic Type-R TCR), +8.337s; **10** Mat'o Homola, SK (Opel Astra TCR), +9.431s.
Fastest race lap: Jäger, 1m 26.583s, 109.543mph/176.293km/h.
Pole position: Colciago.

TCR INTERNATIONAL SERIES, Hungaroring, Mogyoród, Budapest, Hungary, 18 June. 2 x 14 laps of the 2.722-mile/4.381km circuit.
Round 11 (38.111 miles/61.334km).
1 Attila Tassi, H (Honda Civic Type-R TCR), 26m 56.484s, 84.875mph/136.594km/h; **2** Norbert Michelisz, H (Honda Civic Type-R TCR), +0.865s; **3** Jean-Karl Vernay, F (Volkswagen Golf Gti TCR), +1.744s; **4** Roberto Colciago, I (Honda Civic Type-R TCR), +12.769s; **5** Pepe Oriola, E (SEAT León TCR), +14.029s; **6** Daniel Lloyd, GB (SEAT León TCR), +14.959s; **7** James Nash, GB (SEAT León TCR), +22.569s; **8** Giacomo Altoè, I (Volkswagen Golf Gti TCR), +25.074s; **9** Gianni Morbidelli, I (Volkswagen Golf Gti TCR), +27.448s; **10** Mat'o Homola, SK (Opel Astra TCR), +27.869s.
Fastest race lap: Michelisz, 1m 54.252s, 85.775mph/138.042km/h.
Pole position: Michelisz, 1m 52.740s, 86.925mph/139.893km/h.

Round 12 (38.111 miles/61.334km).
1 Attila Tassi, H (Honda Civic Type-R TCR), 29m 20.272s, 77.942mph/125.436km/h; **2** Pepe Oriola, E (SEAT León TCR), +1.861s; **3** Jens Møller, DK (Honda Civic Type-R TCR), +3.283s; **4** Giacomo Altoè, I (Volkswagen Golf Gti TCR), +3.765s; **5** Roberto Colciago, I (Honda Civic Type-R TCR), +4.397s; **6** Norbert Michelisz, H (Honda Civic Type-R TCR), +4.980s; **7** Jean-Karl Vernay, F (Volkswagen Golf Gti TCR), +5.372s; **8** Stian Paulsen, N (SEAT León TCR), +6.254s; **9** James Nash, GB (SEAT León TCR), +12.055s; **10** Stefano Comini, CH (Audi RS3 LMS TCR), +17.135s.
Fastest race lap: Oriola, 1m 54.330s, 85.716mph/137.948km/h.
Pole position: Møller.

TCR INTERNATIONAL SERIES, Motorsport Arena Oschersleben, Germany, 9 July. 19 and 15 laps of the 2.279-mile/3.667km circuit.
Round 13 (43.293 miles/69.673km).
1 Gianni Morbidelli, I (Volkswagen Golf Gti TCR), 31m 28.263s, 82.538mph/132.832km/h; **2** Daniel Lloyd, GB (SEAT León TCR), +2.314s; **3** Rob Huff, GB (Volkswagen Golf Gti TCR), +5.890s; **4** James Nash, GB (SEAT León TCR), +6.454s; **5** Giacomo Altoè, I (Volkswagen Golf Gti TCR), +9.938s; **6** Stefano Comini, CH (Audi RS3 LMS TCR), +16.300s; **7** Mat'o Homola, SK (Opel Astra TCR), +16.794s; **8** Jaap van Lagen, NL (Volkswagen Golf Gti TCR), +16.992s; **9** Danny Kroes, NL (SEAT León TCR), +23.892s; **10** Frédéric Vervisch, B (Audi RS3 LMS TCR), +27.858s.
Fastest race lap: Morbidelli, 1m 32.610s, 88.574mph/142.546km/h.
Pole position: Morbidelli, 1m 31.426s, 89.721mph/144.392km/h.

Round 14 (34.179 miles/55.005km).
1 Gianni Morbidelli, I (Volkswagen Golf Gti TCR), 23m 29.470s, 87.297mph/140.491km/h; **2** Mat'o Homola, SK (Opel Astra TCR), +0.434s;

3 Jean-Karl Vernay, F (Volkswagen Golf Gti TCR), +0.716s; **4** Daniel Lloyd, GB (SEAT León TCR), +0.908s; **5** Stefano Comini, CH (Audi RS3 LMS TCR), +16.127s; **6** Frédéric Vervisch, B (Audi RS3 LMS TCR), +27.291s; **7** Duncan Ende, USA (SEAT León TCR), +31.037s; **8** Jens Møller, DK (Honda Civic Type-R TCR), +1m 06.803s; **9** Davit Kajaia, GE (Alfa Romeo Giulietta TCR), -2 laps; **10** Ferenc Ficza, H (KIA Cee'd TCR), -2.
Fastest race lap: Morbidelli, 1m 32.496s, 88.683mph/142.721km/h.
Pole position: Homola.

TCR INTERNATIONAL SERIES, Buriram International Circuit, Buriram, Thailand, 3 September. 2 x 14 laps of the 2.830-mile/4.554km circuit.
Round 15 (39.616 miles/63.756km).
1 Norbert Michelisz, H (Honda Civic Type-R TCR), 24m 44.820s, 96.050mph/154.578km/h; **2** Dušan Borkovic, SRB (Alfa Romeo Giulietta TCR), +3.769s; **3** Attila Tassi, H (Honda Civic Type-R TCR), +5.923s; **4** Jean-Karl Vernay, F (Volkswagen Golf Gti TCR), +6.211s; **5** Rob Huff, GB (Volkswagen Golf Gti TCR), +6.428s; **6** Giacomo Altoè, I (Honda Civic Type-R TCR), +7.358s; **7** Stefano Comini, CH (Audi RS3 LMS TCR), +10.610s; **8** Davit Kajaia, GE (Alfa Romeo Giulietta TCR), +11.142s; **9** Daniel Lloyd, GB (SEAT León TCR), +14.196s; **10** Gianni Morbidelli, I (Volkswagen Golf Gti TCR), +15.050s.
Fastest race lap: Mat'o Homola, SK (Opel Astra TCR), 1m 44.834s, 97.172mph/156.384km/h.
Pole position: Homola, 1m 43.093s, 98.813mph/159.025km/h.

Round 16 (39.616 miles/63.756km).
1 Aurélien Panis, F (Honda Civic Type-R TCR), 24m 34.503s, 96.722mph/155.660km/h; **2** Giacomo Altoè, I (Honda Civic Type-R TCR), +1.274s; **3** Stefano Comini, CH (Audi RS3 LMS TCR), +6.120s; **4** Attila Tassi, H (Honda Civic Type-R TCR), +7.994s; **5** Jean-Karl Vernay, F (Volkswagen Golf Gti TCR), +9.414s; **6** Dušan Borkovic, SRB (Alfa Romeo Giulietta TCR), +12.632s; **7** James Nash, GB (SEAT León TCR), +13.369s; **8** Rob Huff, GB (Volkswagen Golf Gti TCR), +13.861s; **9** Mat'o Homola, SK (Opel Astra TCR), +18.084s; **10** Kantadhee Kusiri, T (Volkswagen Golf Gti TCR), +18.830s.
Fastest race lap: Panis, 1m 44.446s, 97.533mph/156.965km/h.
Pole position: Panis.

TCR INTERNATIONAL SERIES, Zhejiang International Circuit, Shaoxing Shi, Zhejiang, China, 8 October. 2 x 19 laps of the 1.983-mile/3.191km circuit.
Round 17 (37.673 miles/60.629km).
1 Gabriele Tarquini, I (Hyundai i30 N TCR), 30m 15.966s, 74.683mph/120.191km/h; **2** Jean-Karl Vernay, F (Volkswagen Golf Gti TCR), +1.626s; **3** Rob Huff, GB (Volkswagen Golf Gti TCR), +1.970s; **4** Gianni Morbidelli, I (Volkswagen Golf Gti TCR), +3.016s; **5** Pepe Oriola, E (SEAT León TCR), +7.035s; **6** Frédéric Vervisch, B (Audi RS3 LMS TCR), +11.787s; **7** Roberto Colciago, I (Honda Civic Type-R TCR), +15.380s; **8** Davit Kajaia, GE (Alfa Romeo Giulietta TCR), +16.972s; **9** James Nash, GB (SEAT León TCR), +19.028s; **10** Aurélien Panis, F (Honda Civic Type-R TCR), +19.679s.
Fastest race lap: Tarquini, 1m 33.924s, 75.998mph/122.307km/h.
Pole position: Huff, 1m 33.173s, 76.610mph/123.293km/h.

Round 18 (37.673 miles/60.629km).
1 Rob Huff, GB (Volkswagen Golf Gti TCR), 30m 23.840s, 74.361mph/119.672km/h; **2** Gianni Morbidelli, I (Volkswagen Golf Gti TCR), +2.403s; **3** James Nash, GB (SEAT León TCR), +3.511s; **4** Alain Menu, CH (Hyundai i30 N TCR), +23.435s; **5** Pepe Oriola, E (SEAT León TCR), +24.206s; **6** Gabriele Tarquini, I (Hyundai i30 N TCR), +24.668s; **7** Zhang Zhen Dong, CHN (Audi RS3 LMS TCR), +25.442s; **8** Roberto Colciago, I (Honda Civic Type-R TCR), +26.902s; **9** Attila Tassi, H (Honda Civic Type-R TCR), +36.852s; **10** Rafaël Galiana, F (Volkswagen Golf Gti TCR), +50.687s.
Fastest race lap: Morbidelli, 1m 34.111s, 75.847mph/122.064km/h.
Pole position: Vervisch.

TCR INTERNATIONAL SERIES, Dubai Autodrome, Motor City, Dubai, UAE, 18 November. 19 and 17 laps of the 2.212-mile/3.560km circuit.
Round 19 (42.030 miles/67.640km).
1 Pepe Oriola, E (SEAT León TCR), 30m 57.563s, 81.454mph/131.087km/h; **2** Gordon Shedden, GB (Volkswagen Golf Gti TCR), +4.445s; **3** Jean-Karl Vernay, F (Volkswagen Golf Gti TCR), +6.410s; **4** James Nash, GB (SEAT León TCR), +7.451s; **5** Attila Tassi, H (Honda Civic Type-R TCR), +7.632s; **6** Josh Files, GB (Honda Civic Type-R TCR), +8.024s; **7** Stefano Comini, CH (Audi RS3 LMS TCR), +11.326s; **8** Dušan Borkovic, SRB (Alfa Romeo Giulietta TCR), +14.194s; **9** Davit Kajaia, GE (Alfa Romeo Giulietta TCR), +15.287s; **10** Duncan Ende, USA (SEAT León TCR), +17.323s.
Fastest race lap: Oriola, 1m 28.733s, 89.746mph/144.433km/h.
Pole position: Shedden, 1m 27.849s, 90.649mph/145.886km/h.

Round 20 (37.605 miles/60.520km).
1 Stefano Comini, CH (Audi RS3 LMS TCR), 25m 37.323s, 88.061mph/141.721km/h; **2** Gianni Morbidelli, I (Volkswagen Golf Gti TCR), +1.190s; **3** Josh Files, GB (Honda Civic Type-R TCR), +5.008s; **4** Frédéric Vervisch, B (Audi RS3 LMS TCR), +6.815s; **5** Alain Menu, CH (Hyundai i30 N TCR), +9.232s; **6** Benjamin Leuchter, D (Volkswagen Golf Gti TCR), +9.483s; **7** Gordon Shedden, GB (Volkswagen Golf Gti TCR), +11.453s; **8** Dušan Borkovic, SRB (Alfa Romeo Giulietta TCR), +15.440s; **9** Gabriele Tarquini, I (Hyundai i30 N TCR), +17.117s; **10** Davit Kajaia, GE (Alfa Romeo Giulietta TCR), +21.421s.
Fastest race lap: Tarquini, 1m 28.912s, 89.566mph/144.142km/h.
Pole position: Tassi.

Final championship points
Drivers
1 Jean-Karl Vernay, F, 226; **2** Attila Tassi, H, 197; **3** Stefano Comini, CH, 196; **4** Pepe Oriola, E, 164; **5** Roberto Colciago, I, 161; **6** Gianni Morbidelli, I, 132; **7** James Nash, GB, 129; **8** Dušan Borkovic, SRB, 118; **9** Rob Huff, GB, 106; **10** Frédéric Vervisch, B, 84; **11** Davit Kajaia, GE, 77; **12** Mat'o Homola, SK, 76; **13** Giacomo Altoè, I, 63; **14** Norbert Michelisz, H, 59; **15** Daniel Lloyd, GB, 50; **16** Hugo Valente, F, 46; **17** Ferenc Ficza, H, 32; **18** Benjamin Lessennes, B, 31; **19** Gordon Shedden, GB, 31; **20** Aurélien Panis, F, 27.

Teams
1 M1RA, 439; **2** Lukoil Craft-Bamboo Racing, 377; **3** Leopard Racing Team WRT, 375; **4** Comtoyou Racing, 289; **5** West Coast Racing, 201; **6** GE-Force, 199; **7** DG Sport Compétition, 99; **8** Boutsen Ginion Racing, 64; **9** Zele Racing, 32; **10** Reno Racing, 25.

German Touring Car Championship (DTM)

GERMAN TOURING CAR CHAMPIONSHIP (DTM), Hockenheimring Grand Prix Circuit, Heidelberg, Germany, 6/7 May. Round 1. 36 and 32 laps of the 2.842-mile/4.574km circuit.
Race 1 (102.317 miles/164.664km).
1 Lucas Auer, A (Mercedes C 63 DTM), 57m 23.598s, 106.965mph/172.143km/h; **2** Timo Glock, D (BMW M4 DTM), +1.942s; **3** Mike Rockenfeller, D (Audi RS 5 DTM), +3.351s; **4** Edoardo Mortara, I (Mercedes C 63 DTM), +3.984s; **5** Mattias Ekström, S (Audi RS 5 DTM), +4.275s; **6** René Rast, D (Audi RS 5 DTM), +5.855s; **7** Gary Paffett, GB (Mercedes C 63 DTM), +6.956s; **8** Paul Di Resta, GB (Mercedes C 63 DTM), +13.648s; **9** Nico Müller, CH (Audi RS 5 DTM), +17.510s; **10** Marco Wittmann, D (BMW M4 DTM), +19.190s.
Fastest race lap: Ekström, 1m 33.201s, 109.782mph/176.676km/h.
Pole position: Auer, 1m 30.849s, 112.624mph/181.250km/h.

Race 2 (90.949 miles/146.368km).
1 Jamie Green, GB (Audi RS 5 DTM), 56m 53.264s, 95.925mph/154.376km/h; **2** Gary Paffett, GB (Mercedes C 63 DTM), +4.936s; **3** Marco Wittmann, D (BMW M4 DTM), +8.191s; **4** Lucas Auer, A (Mercedes C 63 DTM), +16.985s; **5** Nico Müller, CH (Audi RS 5 DTM), +26.959s; **6** Paul Di Resta, GB (Mercedes C 63 DTM), +27.426s; **7** Mike Rockenfeller, D (Audi RS 5 DTM), +31.315s; **8** Timo Glock, D (BMW M4 DTM), +1m 06.250s; **9** Bruno Spengler, CDN (BMW M4 DTM), +1m 08.538s; **10** Maro Engel, D (Mercedes C 63 DTM), +1m 12.117s.
Fastest race lap: Green, 1m 33.614s, 109.297mph/175.897km/h.
Pole position: Glock, 1m 31.406s, 111.937mph/180.146km/h.

GERMAN TOURING CAR CHAMPIONSHIP (DTM), EuroSpeedway Lausitz, Klettwitz, Dresden, Germany, 20/21 May. Round 2. 2 x 43 laps of the 2.161-mile/3.478km circuit.
Race 1 (92.929 miles/149.554km).
1 Lucas Auer, A (Mercedes C 63 DTM), 56m 37.503s, 98.467mph/158.468km/h; **2** Robert Wickens, CDN (Mercedes C 63 DTM), +3.613s; **3** René Rast, D (Audi RS 5 DTM), +12.581s; **4** Maxime Martin, B (BMW M4 DTM), +17.660s; **5** Mike Rockenfeller, D (Audi RS 5 DTM), +17.810s; **6** Gary Paffett, GB (Mercedes C 63 DTM), +20.253s; **7** Edoardo Mortara, I (Mercedes C 63 DTM), +21.366s; **8** Mattias Ekström, S (Audi RS 5 DTM), +22.319s; **9** Maro Engel, D (Mercedes C 63 DTM), +26.361s; **10** Jamie Green, GB (Audi RS 5 DTM), +29.960s.
Fastest race lap: Rast, 1m 17.343s, 100.592mph/161.887km/h.
Pole position: Auer, 1m 16.193s, 102.110mph/164.330km/h.

Race 2 (92.929 miles/149.554km).
1 Jamie Green, GB (Audi RS 5 DTM), 56m 20.480s, 98.963mph/159.266km/h; **2** Mattias Ekström, S (Audi RS 5 DTM), +6.295s; **3** Robert Wickens, CDN (Mercedes C 63 DTM), +7.034s; **4** Gary Paffett, GB (Mercedes C 63 DTM), +7.387s; **5** Mike Rockenfeller, D (Audi RS 5 DTM), +9.750s; **6** Nico Müller, CH (Audi RS 5 DTM), +13.039s; **7** René Rast, D (Audi RS 5 DTM), +16.370s; **8** Maxime Martin, B (BMW M4 DTM), +18.115s; **9** Marco Wittmann, D (BMW M4 DTM), +19.540s; **10** Lucas Auer, A (Mercedes C 63 DTM), +26.283s.
Fastest race lap: Rast, 1m 17.098s, 100.911mph/162.401km/h.
Pole position: Wickens, 1m 16.299s, 101.968mph/164.102km/h.

GERMAN TOURING CAR CHAMPIONSHIP (DTM), Hungaroring, Mogyoród, Budapest, Hungary, 17/18 June. Round 3. 34 and 35 laps of the 2.722-mile/4.381km circuit.
Race 1 (92.556 miles/148.954km).
1 Paul Di Resta, GB (Mercedes C 63 DTM), 57m 52.984s, 95.941mph/154.402km/h; **2** Timo Glock, D (BMW M4 DTM), +1.393s; **3** Bruno Spengler, CDN (BMW M4 DTM), +4.598s; **4** Mike Rockenfeller, D (Audi RS 5 DTM), +4.948s; **5** Mattias Ekström, S (Audi RS 5 DTM), +8.937s; **6** René Rast, D (Audi RS 5 DTM), +9.561s; **7** Gary Paffett, GB (Mercedes C 63 DTM), +31.014s; **8** Marco Wittmann, D (BMW M4 DTM), +31.577s; **9** Edoardo Mortara, I (Mercedes C 63 DTM), +32.651s; **10** Nico Müller, CH (Audi RS 5 DTM), +33.106s.
Fastest race lap: Rockenfeller, 1m 37.101s, 100.926mph/162.425km/h.
Pole position: Rast, 1m 34.742s, 103.439mph/166.469km/h.

Race 2 (95.278 miles/153.335km).
1 René Rast, D (Audi RS 5 DTM), 58m 01.592s, 98.518mph/158.550km/h; **2** Mattias Ekström, S (Audi RS 5 DTM), +1.041s; **3** Maxime Martin, B (BMW M4 DTM), +1.506s; **4** Nico Müller, CH (Audi RS 5 DTM), +1.861s; **5** Jamie Green, GB (Audi RS 5 DTM), +5.772s; **6** Paul Di Resta, GB (Mercedes C 63 DTM), +7.884s; **7** Timo Glock, D (BMW M4 DTM), +8.694s; **8** Robert Wickens, CDN (Mercedes C 63 DTM), +11.999s; **9** Gary Paffett, GB (Mercedes C 63 DTM), +12.653s; **10** Mike Rockenfeller, D (Audi RS 5 DTM), +13.159s.
Fastest race lap: Ekström, 1m 36.725s, 101.318mph/163.056km/h.
Pole position: Rast, 1m 34.740s, 103.441mph/166.472km/h.

GERMAN TOURING CAR CHAMPIONSHIP (DTM), Norisring, Nürnberg (Nuremberg), Germany, 1/2 July. Round 4. 61 and 66 laps of the 1.429-mile/2.300km circuit.
Race 1 (87.178 miles/140.300km).
1 Bruno Spengler, CDN (BMW M4 DTM), 53m 15.532s, 98.213mph/158.058km/h; **2** Maxime Martin, B (BMW M4 DTM), +4.385s; **3** Mattias Ekström, S (Audi RS 5 DTM), +4.776s; **4** Marco Wittmann, D (BMW M4 DTM), +10.812s; **5** Timo Glock, D (BMW M4 DTM), +12.151s; **6** Tom Blomqvist, GB (BMW M4 DTM), +12.828s; **7** Jamie Green, GB (Audi RS 5 DTM), +18.573s; **8** Edoardo Mortara, I (Mercedes C 63 DTM), +20.328s; **9** Nico Müller, CH (Audi RS 5 DTM), +21.355s; **10** Gary Paffett, GB (Mercedes C 63 DTM), +34.707s.
Fastest race lap: Blomqvist, 48.345s, 106.422mph/171.269km/h.
Pole position: Martin, 47.472s, 108.379mph/174.419km/h.

Race 2 (94.324 miles/151.800km).
1 Maxime Martin, B (BMW M4 DTM), 1h 29m 22.150s, 63.327mph/101.914km/h; **2** Lucas Auer, A (Mercedes C 63 DTM), +2.903s; **3** Edoardo Mortara, I (Mercedes C 63 DTM), +4.460s; **4** Mattias Ekström, S (Audi RS 5 DTM), +4.462s; **5** Marco Wittmann, D (BMW M4 DTM), +4.487s; **6** Paul Di Resta, GB (Mercedes C 63 DTM), +5.708s; **7** Augusto Farfus, BR (BMW M4 DTM), +11.613s; **8** Jamie Green, GB (Audi RS 5 DTM), +12.064s; **9** Tom Blomqvist, GB (BMW M4 DTM), +12.694s; **10** Timo Glock, D (BMW M4 DTM), +13.347s.
Fastest race lap: Bruno Spengler, CDN (BMW M4 DTM), 47.846s, 107.532mph/173.055km/h.
Pole position: Blomqvist, 47.252s, 108.883mph/175.231km/h.

GERMAN TOURING CAR CHAMPIONSHIP (DTM), Moscow Raceway, Volokolamsk Oblast, Russia, 22/23 July. Round 5. 38 and 36 laps of the 2.443-mile/3.931km circuit.
Race 1 (92.819 miles/149.378km).
1 René Rast, D (Audi RS 5 DTM), 57m 50.085s, 96.294mph/154.970km/h; **2** Mike Rockenfeller, D (Audi RS 5 DTM), +0.770s; **3** Marco Wittmann, D (BMW M4 DTM), +3.899s; **4** Robert Wickens, CDN (Mercedes C 63 DTM), +6.098s; **5** Timo Glock, D (BMW M4 DTM), +9.498s; **6** Lucas Auer, A (Mercedes C 63 DTM), +14.663s; **7** Gary Paffett, GB (Mercedes C 63 DTM), +17.696s; **8** Mattias Ekström, S (Audi RS 5 DTM), +17.795s; **9** Jamie Green, GB (Audi RS 5 DTM), +24.310s; **10** Maro Engel, D (Mercedes C 63 DTM), +25.329s.
Fastest race lap: Wickens, 1m 29.573s, 98.170mph/157.990km/h.
Pole position: Rast, 1m 27.155s, 100.894mph/162.373km/h.

Race 2 (87.934 miles/141.516km).
1 Maro Engel, D (Mercedes C 63 DTM), 56m 41.087s, 93.077mph/149.793km/h; **2** Mattias Ekström, S (Audi RS 5 DTM), +0.376s; **3** Bruno Spengler, CDN (BMW M4 DTM), +3.981s; **4** René Rast, D (Audi RS 5 DTM), +4.702s; **5** Jamie Green, GB (Audi RS 5 DTM), +5.410s; **6** Marco Wittmann, D (BMW M4 DTM), +7.192s; **7** Tom Blomqvist, GB (BMW M4 DTM), +8.391s; **8** Lucas Auer, A (Mercedes C 63 DTM), +8.564s; **9** Robert Wickens, CDN (Mercedes C 63 DTM), +8.982s; **10** Edoardo Mortara, I (Mercedes C 63 DTM), +9.942s.
Fastest race lap: Green, 1m 28.436s, 99.432mph/160.021km/h.
Pole position: Spengler, 1m 26.579s, 101.565mph/163.453km/h.

GERMAN TOURING CAR CHAMPIONSHIP (DTM), Circuit Park Zandvoort, Netherlands, 19/20 August. Round 6. 2 x 37 laps of the 2.676-mile/4.307km circuit.
Race 1 (99.021 miles/159.359km).
1 Timo Glock, D (BMW M4 DTM), 57m 18.491s, 103.672mph/166.844km/h; **2** Marco Wittmann, D (BMW M4 DTM), +0.178s; **3** Maxime Martin, B (BMW M4 DTM), +0.840s; **4** Mike Rockenfeller, D (Audi RS 5 DTM), +2.530s; **5** Jamie Green, GB (Audi RS 5 DTM), +3.164s; **6** Augusto Farfus, BR (BMW M4 DTM), +4.173s; **7** Paul Di Resta, GB (Mercedes C 63 DTM), +4.771s; **8** Gary Paffett, GB (Mercedes C 63 DTM), +5.382s; **9** René Rast, D (Audi RS 5 DTM), +5.911s; **10** Nico Müller, CH (Audi RS 5 DTM), +6.278s.
Fastest race lap: Rast, 1m 30.160s, 106.860mph/171.974km/h.
Pole position: Glock, 1m 27.823s, 109.703mph/176.551km/h.

Race 2 (99.021 miles/159.359km).
1 Mike Rockenfeller, D (Audi RS 5 DTM), 56m 33.404s, 105.050mph/169.061km/h; **2** Loïc Duval, F (Audi RS 5 DTM), +16.581s; **3** Mattias Ekström, S (Audi RS 5 DTM), +58.073s; **4** Nico Müller, CH (Audi RS 5 DTM), +58.620s; **5** Gary Paffett, GB (Mercedes C 63 DTM), +58.848s; **6** Maxime Martin, B (BMW M4 DTM), +59.390s; **7** Timo Glock, D (BMW M4 DTM), +59.928s; **8** Augusto Farfus, BR (BMW M4 DTM), +1m 00.069s; **9** Jamie Green, GB (Audi RS 5 DTM), +1m 02.405s; **10** Bruno Spengler, CDN (BMW M4 DTM), +1m 12.009s *.
** includes 10s penalty.*
Fastest race lap: Duval, 1m 29.168s, 108.049mph/173.887km/h.
Pole position: Farfus, 1m 27.475s, 110.140mph/177.253km/h.

GERMAN TOURING CAR CHAMPIONSHIP (DTM), Nürburgring, Nürburg/Eifel, Germany, 9/10 September. Round 7. 33 and 40 laps of the 2.255-mile/3.629km circuit.
Race 1 (74.414 miles/119.757km).
1 Lucas Auer, A (Mercedes C 63 DTM), 54m 12.443s, 82.365mph/132.554km/h; **2** Paul Di Resta, GB (Mercedes C 63 DTM), +0.794s; **3** Robert Wickens, CDN (Mercedes C 63 DTM), +1.568s; **4** Maro Engel, D (Mercedes C 63 DTM), +5.344s; **5** René Rast, D (Audi RS 5 DTM), +9.758s; **6** Jamie Green, GB (Audi RS 5 DTM), +24.531s; **7** Edoardo Mortara, I (Mercedes C 63 DTM), +31.593s; **8** Augusto Farfus, BR (BMW M4 DTM), +49.335s; **9** Marco Wittmann, D (BMW M4 DTM), +56.886s; **10** Gary Paffett, GB (Mercedes C 63 DTM), +59.072s.
Fastest race lap: Nico Müller, CH (Audi RS 5 DTM), 1m 31.420s, 88.797mph/142.905km/h.
Pole position: Auer, 1m 25.968s, 94.429mph/151.968km/h.

Race 2 (90.198 miles/145.160km).
1 Robert Wickens, CDN (Mercedes C 63 DTM), 56m 49.795s, 95.230mph/153.257km/h; **2** Paul Di Resta, GB (Mercedes C 63 DTM), +0.362s; **3** Marco Wittmann, D (BMW M4 DTM), +7.589s; **4** Bruno Spengler, CDN (BMW M4 DTM), +7.955s; **5** Maro Engel, D (Mercedes C 63 DTM), +15.995s; **6** Mattias Ekström, S (Audi RS 5 DTM), +20.549s; **7** Jamie Green, GB (Audi RS 5 DTM), +22.887s; **8** Timo Glock, D (BMW M4 DTM), +40.196s; **9** Augusto Farfus, BR (BMW M4 DTM), +40.307s; **10** Tom Blomqvist, GB (BMW M4 DTM), +41.818s.
Fastest race lap: René Rast, D (Audi RS 5 DTM), 1m 22.308s, 98.628mph/158.726km/h.
Pole position: Wittmann, 1m 20.936s, 100.300mph/161.416km/h.

GERMAN TOURING CAR CHAMPIONSHIP (DTM), Red Bull Ring, Spielberg, Austria, 23/24 September. Round 8. 40 and 39 laps of the 2.683-mile/4.318km circuit.
Race 1 (107.323 miles/172.720km).
1 Mattias Ekström, S (Audi RS 5 DTM), 57m 00.812s, 112.945mph/181.767km/h; **2** Jamie Green, GB (Audi RS 5 DTM), +0.398s; **3** Nico Müller, CH (Audi RS 5 DTM), +0.602s; **4** Robert Wickens, CDN (Mercedes C 63 DTM), +21.625s; **5** Marco Wittmann, D (BMW M4 DTM), +22.118s; **6** Maxime Martin, B (BMW M4 DTM), +22.748s; **7** Mike Rockenfeller, D (Audi RS 5 DTM), +23.067s; **8** Lucas Auer, A (Mercedes C 63 DTM), +23.452s; **9** Edoardo Mortara, I (Mercedes C 63 DTM), +23.761s; **10** Timo Glock, D (BMW M4 DTM), +25.559s.
Fastest race lap: Green, 1m 23.742s, 115.343mph/185.627km/h.
Pole position: Green, 1m 21.973s, 117.833mph/189.633km/h.

Race 2 (104.640 miles/168.402km).
1 René Rast, D (Audi RS 5 DTM), 57m 21.893s, 109.447mph/176.138km/h; **2** Mike Rockenfeller, D (Audi RS 5 DTM), +1.025s; **3** Nico Müller, CH (Audi RS 5 DTM), +1.824s; **4** Gary Paffett, GB (Mercedes C 63 DTM), +3.741s; **5** Mattias Ekström, S (Audi RS 5 DTM), +6.136s; **6** Marco Wittmann, D (BMW M4 DTM), +7.968s; **7** Timo Glock, D (BMW M4 DTM), +8.181s; **8** Loïc Duval, F (Audi RS 5 DTM), +8.457s; **9** Paul Di Resta, GB (Mercedes C 63 DTM), +9.328s; **10** Robert Wickens, CDN (Mercedes C 63 DTM), +11.305s.
Fastest race lap: Jamie Green, GB (Audi RS 5 DTM), 1m 23.474s, 115.714mph/186.223km/h.
Pole position: Green, 1m 21.955s, 117.858mph/189.675km/h.

GERMAN TOURING CAR CHAMPIONSHIP (DTM), Hockenheimring Grand Prix Circuit, Heidelberg, Germany, 14/15 October. Round 9. 2 x 36 laps of the 2.842-mile/4.574km circuit.
Race 1 (102.317 miles/164.664km).
1 Jamie Green, GB (Audi RS 5 DTM), 56m 52.478s, 107.940mph/173.713km/h; **2** Mike Rockenfeller, D (Audi RS 5 DTM), +3.939s; **3** Timo Glock, D (BMW M4 DTM), +5.666s; **4** Maxime Martin, B (BMW M4 DTM), +10.448s; **5** Edoardo Mortara, I (Mercedes C 63 DTM), +12.962s; **6** René Rast, D (Audi RS 5 DTM), +14.752s; **7** Robert Wickens, CDN (Mercedes C 63 DTM), +16.196s; **8** Lucas Auer, A (Mercedes C 63 DTM), +23.633s; **9** Gary Paffett, GB (Mercedes C 63 DTM), +24.615s; **10** Bruno Spengler, CDN (BMW M4 DTM), +25.027s.
Fastest race lap: Rockenfeller, 1m 32.819s, 110.233mph/177.403km/h.
Pole position: Glock, 1m 30.648s, 112.873mph/181.652km/h.

Race 2 (102.317 miles/164.664km).
1 Marco Wittmann, D (BMW M4 DTM), 56m 47.699s, 108.091mph/173.956km/h; **2** René Rast, D (Audi RS 5 DTM), +3.143s; **3** Mike Rockenfeller, D (Audi RS 5 DTM), +6.280s; **4** Gary Paffett, GB (Mercedes C 63 DTM), +15.844s; **5** Jamie Green, GB (Audi RS 5 DTM), +17.835s; **6** Maxime Martin, B (BMW M4 DTM), +19.372s; **7** Augusto Farfus, BR (BMW M4 DTM), +20.386s; **8** Mattias Ekström, S (Audi RS 5 DTM), +21.229s; **9** Edoardo Mortara, I (Mercedes C 63 DTM), +22.902s; **10** Lucas Auer, A (Mercedes C 63 DTM), +29.260s.
Fastest race lap: Green, 1m 32.456s, 110.666mph/178.100km/h.
Pole position: Tom Blomqvist, GB (BMW M4 DTM), 1m 30.491s, 113.069mph/181.967km/h.

Final championship points
Drivers
1 René Rast, D, 179; **2** Mattias Ekström, S, 176; **3** Jamie Green, GB, 173; **4** Mike Rockenfeller, D, 167; **5** Marco Wittmann, D, 160; **6** Lucas Auer, A, 136; **7** Timo Glock, D, 133; **8** Maxime Martin, B, 132; **9** Robert Wickens, CDN, 119; **10** Gary Paffett, GB, 102; **11** Paul Di Resta, GB, 99; **12** Nico Müller, CH, 81; **13** Bruno Spengler, CDN, 75; **14** Edoardo Mortara, I, 61; **15** Maro Engel, D, 51; **16** Augusto Farfus, BR, 35; **17** Tom Blomqvist, GB, 25; **18** Loïc Duval, F, 22.

Manufacturers
1 Audi, 798; **2** Mercedes, 568; **3** BMW, 560.

Teams
1 Audi Sport Team Rosberg, 352; **2** Audi Sport Team Abt Sportsline, 257; **3** Mercedes-AMG Motorsport Mercedes me, 221; **4** BMW Team RBM, 207; **5** Mercedes-AMG Motorsport BWT, 197; **6** BMW Team RMG, 195; **7** Audi Sport Team Phoenix, 189; **8** BMW Team RMR, 158; **9** Mercedes-AMG Motorsport SILBERPFEIL Energy, 150.

British Touring Car Championship

BRITISH TOURING CAR CHAMPIONSHIP, Brands Hatch Indy Circuit, West Kingsdown, Dartford, Kent, Great Britain, 2 April. 27, 23 and 24 laps of the 1.208-mile/1.944km circuit.
Round 1 (32.613 miles/52.486km).
1 Tom Ingram, GB (Toyota Avensis), 24m 23.405s, 80.229mph/129.116km/h; **2** Gordon Shedden, GB (Honda Civic Type-R), +3.181s; **3** Adam Morgan, GB (Mercedes A-Class), +3.348s; **4** Jack Goff, GB (Honda Civic Type-R), +12.387s; **5** Rob Austin, GB (Toyota Avensis), +16.410s; **6** Andrew Jordan, GB (BMW 125i M Sport), +16.610s; **7** Rob Collard, GB (BMW 125i M Sport), +16.760s; **8** Mat Jackson, GB (Ford Focus ST), +18.109s; **9** Michael Epps, GB (Volkswagen Passat CC), +18.326s; **10** Tom Chilton, GB (Vauxhall Astra), +18.632s.
Fastest race lap: Shedden, 48.742s, 89.213mph/143.575km/h.
Pole position: Jeff Smith, GB (Honda Civic Type-R), 48.367s, 89.905mph/144.688km/h.

Round 2 (27.782 miles/44.710km).
1 Gordon Shedden, GB (Honda Civic Type-R), 20m 46.471s, 80.237mph/129.130km/h; **2** Rob Collard, GB (BMW 125i M Sport), +0.870s; **3** Tom Ingram, GB (Toyota Avensis), +2.657s; **4** Adam Morgan, GB (Mercedes A-Class), +4.565s; **5** Mat Jackson, GB (Ford Focus ST), +5.125s; **6** Andrew Jordan, GB (BMW 125i M Sport), +5.140s; **7** Josh Cook, GB (Ford Focus ST), +8.013s; **8** Tom Chilton, GB (Vauxhall Astra), +8.197s; **9** Colin Turkington, GB (BMW 125i M Sport), +9.441s; **10** Michael Epps, GB (Volkswagen Passat CC), +9.492s.
Fastest race lap: Turkington, 48.657s, 89.369mph/143.825km/h.
Pole position: Ingram.

Round 3 (28.990 miles/46.654km).
1 Andrew Jordan, GB (BMW 125i M Sport), 19m 53.418s, 87.448mph/140.734km/h; **2** Colin Turkington, GB (BMW 125i M Sport), +0.315s; **3** Tom Chilton, GB (Vauxhall Astra), +4.692s; **4** Matt Neal, GB (Honda Civic Type-R), +7.558s; **5** Adam Morgan, GB (Mercedes A-Class), +10.205s; **6** Rob Collard, GB (BMW 125i M Sport), +10.812s; **7** Gordon Shedden, GB (Honda Civic Type-R), +11.719s; **8** Jack Goff, GB (Honda Civic Type-R), +12.141s; **9** Michael Epps, GB (Volkswagen Passat CC), +12.970s; **10** Jake Hill, GB (Volkswagen Passat CC), +14.367s.
Fastest race lap: Turkington, 48.713s, 89.266mph/143.660km/h.
Pole position: Chilton.

BRITISH TOURING CAR CHAMPIONSHIP, Donington Park National Circuit, Castle Donington, Great Britain, 16 April. 16, 16 and 17 laps of the 1.979-mile/3.185km circuit.
Round 4 (31.626 miles/50.897km).
1 Aiden Moffat, GB (Mercedes A-Class), 18m 59.693s, 100.017mph/160.962km/h; **2** Matt Neal, GB (Honda Civic Type-R), +1.504s; **3** Rob Austin, GB (Toyota Avensis), +2.164s; **4** Colin Turkington, GB (BMW 125i M Sport), +2.433s; **5** Tom Ingram, GB (Toyota Avensis), +14.539s; **6** Rob Collard, GB (BMW 125i M Sport), +14.984s; **7** Gordon Shedden, GB (Honda Civic Type-R), +15.358s; **8** Adam Morgan, GB (Mercedes A-Class), +15.668s *; **9** Jeff Smith, GB (Honda Civic Type-R), +17.996s; **10** Josh Cook, GB (Ford Focus ST), +18.095s.
** includes 0.5s penalty.*
Fastest race lap: Turkington, 1m 10.193s, 101.497mph/163.344km/h.
Pole position: Austin, 1m 09.514s, 102.488mph/164.939km/h.

Round 5 (31.626 miles/50.897km).
1 Tom Ingram, GB (Toyota Avensis), 19m 09.281s, 99.182mph/159.619km/h; **2** Rob Collard, GB (BMW 125i M Sport), +3.865s; **3** Ash Sutton, GB (Subaru Levorg GT), +4.085s; **4** Josh Cook, GB (Ford Focus ST), +10.112s; **5** Colin Turkington, GB (BMW 125i M Sport), +14.134s; **6** Gordon Shedden, GB (Honda Civic Type-R), +15.340s; **7** Matt Neal, GB (Honda Civic Type-R), +20.817s; **8** Dave Newsham, GB (Chevrolet Cruze), +21.912s; **9** Jack Goff, GB (Honda Civic Type-R), +24.793s; **10** Tom Chilton, GB (Vauxhall Astra), +27.670s.
Fastest race lap: Andrew Jordan, GB (BMW 125i M Sport), 1m 10.409s, 101.185mph/162.842km/h.
Pole position: Moffat.

Round 6 (33.605 miles/54.082km).
1 Colin Turkington, GB (BMW 125i M Sport), 23m 56.681s, 84.300mph/135.669km/h; **2** Adam Morgan, GB (Mercedes A-Class), +9.476s; **3** Ash Sutton, GB (Subaru Levorg GT), +9.637s; **4** Dave Newsham, GB (Chevrolet Cruze), +10.492s; **5** Tom Ingram, GB (Toyota Avensis), +10.769s; **6** Jack Goff, GB (Honda Civic Type-R), +10.976s; **7** Josh Cook, GB (Ford Focus ST), +14.909s; **8** Aiden Moffat, GB (Mercedes A-Class), +15.500s; **9** Árón Taylor-Smith, IRL (MG **6** GT), +15.835s; **10** Senna Proctor, GB (Vauxhall Astra), +18.672s.
Disqualified: Gordon Shedden, GB (Honda Civic Type-R), 23m 52.096 (failed ride height check-originally finished 1st).
Fastest race lap: Daniel Lloyd, GB (MG **6** GT), 1m 20.511s, 88.489mph/142.410km/h.
Pole position: Newsham.

BRITISH TOURING CAR CHAMPIONSHIP, Thruxton Circuit, Andover, Hampshire, Great Britain, 7 May. 16, 6 and 16 laps of the 2.356-mile/3.792km circuit.
Round 7 (37.696 miles/60.666km).
1 Matt Neal, GB (Honda Civic Type-R), 20m 59.855s, 107.715mph/173.350km/h; **2** Gordon Shedden, GB (Honda Civic Type-R), +0.290s; **3** Jack Goff, GB (Honda Civic Type-R), +1.372s; **4** Tom Ingram, GB (Toyota Avensis), +1.772s; **5** Adam Morgan, GB (Mercedes A-Class), +2.230s; **6** Ash Sutton, GB (Subaru Levorg GT), +2.474s; **7** Colin Turkington, GB (BMW 125i M Sport), +5.060s; **8** Mat Jackson, GB (Ford Focus ST), +5.940s; **9** Rob Austin, GB (Toyota Avensis), +6.366s; **10** Rob Collard, GB (BMW 125i M Sport), +7.302s.
Fastest race lap: Sutton, 1m 17.619s, 109.272mph/175.856km/h.
Pole position: Neal, 1m 16.040s, 111.541mph/179.508km/h.

Round 8 (14.136 miles/22.750km).
1 Rob Collard, GB (BMW 125i M Sport), 7m 56.984s, 106.690mph/171.701km/h; **2** Gordon Shedden, GB (Honda Civic Type-R), +0.212s; **3** Tom Ingram, GB (Toyota Avensis), +0.507s; **4** Jack Goff, GB (Honda Civic Type-R), +1.575s; **5** Rob Austin, GB (Toyota Avensis), +2.791s; **6** Colin Turkington, GB (BMW 125i M Sport), +2.971s; **7** Adam Morgan, GB (Mercedes A-Class), +3.327s; **8** Ash Sutton, GB (Subaru Levorg GT), +4.143s; **9** Aiden Moffat, GB (Mercedes A-Class), +5.152s; **10** Jeff Smith, GB (Honda Civic Type-R), +5.623s.
Fastest race lap: Matt Neal, GB (Honda Civic Type-R), 1m 17.444s, 109.519mph/176.253km/h.
Pole position: Neal.

Round 9 (37.696 miles/60.666km).
1 Colin Turkington, GB (BMW 125i M Sport), 20m 56.728s, 107.983mph/173.782km/h; **2** Tom Ingram, GB (Toyota Avensis), +2.576s; **3** Jack Goff, GB (Honda Civic Type-R), +4.081s; **4** Gordon Shedden, GB (Honda Civic Type-R), +5.836s; **5** Rob Austin, GB (Toyota Avensis), +10.002s; **6** Ash Sutton, GB (Subaru Levorg GT), +10.756s; **7** Rob Collard, GB (BMW 125i M Sport), +11.732s; **8** Aiden Moffat, GB (Mercedes A-Class), +12.414s; **9** Adam Morgan, GB (Mercedes A-Class), +12.989s; **10** Matt Neal, GB (Honda Civic Type-R), +13.225s.
Fastest race lap: Tom Chilton, GB (Vauxhall Astra), 1m 17.380s, 109.609mph/176.399km/h.
Pole position: Turkington.

BRITISH TOURING CAR CHAMPIONSHIP, Oulton Park Circuit, Tarporley, Cheshire, Great Britain, 21 May. 15, 14 and 18 laps of the 2.226-mile/3.582km circuit.
Round 10 (33.390 miles/53.736km).
1 Andrew Jordan, GB (BMW 125i M Sport), 21m 57.078s, 91.265mph/146.877km/h; **2** Matt Neal, GB (Honda Civic Type-R), +0.284s; **3** Ash Sutton, GB (Subaru Levorg GT), +11.987s; **4** Aiden Moffat, GB (Mercedes A-Class), +17.642s; **5** Rob Collard, GB (BMW 125i M Sport), +18.750s; **6** Mat Jackson, GB (Ford Focus ST), +19.325s; **7** Gordon Shedden, GB (Honda Civic Type-R), +20.259s; **8** Josh Cook, GB (Ford Focus ST), +20.561s; **9** Rob Austin, GB (Toyota Avensis), +21.469s; **10** Jake Hill, GB (Volkswagen Passat CC), +22.046s.
Fastest race lap: Neal, 1m 26.811s, 92.310mph/148.559km/h.
Pole position: Neal, 1m 26.151s, 93.018mph/149.698km/h.

Round 11 (31.164 miles/50.154km).
1 Ash Sutton, GB (Subaru Levorg GT), 20m 31.536s, 91.097mph/146.607km/h; **2** Rob Collard, GB (BMW 125i M Sport), +1.066s; **3** Matt Neal, GB (Honda Civic Type-R), +9.795s; **4** Gordon Shedden, GB (Honda Civic Type-R), +10.096s; **5** Andrew Jordan, GB (BMW 125i M Sport), +10.443s; **6** Josh Cook, GB (Ford Focus ST), +10.863s; **7** Mat Jackson, GB (Ford Focus ST), +12.560s; **8** Rob Austin, GB (Toyota Avensis), +13.196s; **9** Jake Hill, GB (Volkswagen Passat CC), +13.966s; **10** Michael Epps, GB (Volkswagen Passat CC), +14.596s.
Fastest race lap: Sutton, 1m 26.902s, 92.214mph/148.404km/h.
Pole position: Jordan.

Round 12 (40.068 miles/64.483km).
1 Gordon Shedden, GB (Honda Civic Type-R), 29m 41.142s, 80.984mph/130.331km/h; **2** Matt Neal, GB (Honda Civic Type-R), +0.279s; **3** Andrew Jordan, GB (BMW 125i M Sport), +1.722s; **4** Ash Sutton, GB (Subaru Levorg GT), +4.272s; **5** Colin Turkington, GB (BMW 125i M Sport), +4.375s; **6** Rob Collard, GB (BMW 125i M Sport), +4.590s; **7** Rob Austin, GB (Toyota Avensis), +5.509s; **8** Michael Epps, GB (Volkswagen Passat CC), +7.045s; **9** Jake Hill, GB (Volkswagen Passat CC), +8.418s; **10** Luke Davenport, GB (Ford Focus ST), +8.736s.
Fastest race lap: Tom Ingram, GB (Toyota Avensis), 1m 26.911s, 92.204mph/148.389km/h.
Pole position: Cook.

BRITISH TOURING CAR CHAMPIONSHIP, Croft Racing Circuit, Croft-on-Tees, North Yorkshire, Great Britain, 11 June. 15, 15 and 16 laps of the 2.125-mile/3.420km circuit.
Round 13 (31.875 miles/51.298km).
1 Ash Sutton, GB (Subaru Levorg GT), 21m 52.260s, 87.444mph/140.728km/h; **2** Colin Turkington, GB (BMW 125i M Sport), +0.671s; **3** Mat Jackson, GB (Ford Focus ST), +8.653s; **4** Rob Collard, GB (BMW 125i M Sport), +11.307s; **5** Gordon Shedden, GB (Honda Civic Type-R), +11.858s; **6** Andrew Jordan, GB (BMW 125i M Sport), +12.984s; **7** Josh Cook, GB (MG **6** GT), +18.764s; **8** Tom Ingram, GB (Toyota Avensis), +19.585s; **9** Tom Chilton, GB (Vauxhall Astra), +19.995s; **10** Jason Plato, GB (Subaru Levorg GT), +35.408s.
Fastest race lap: Turkington, 1m 26.003s, 88.950mph/143.151km/h.
Pole position: Sutton, 1m 33.182s, 82.097mph/132.122km/h.

Round 14 (31.875 miles/51.298km).
1 Colin Turkington, GB (BMW 125i M Sport), 21m 48.750s, 87.679mph/141.105km/h; **2** Ash Sutton, GB (Subaru Levorg GT), +2.445s; **3** Rob Collard, GB (BMW 125i M Sport), +2.890s; **4** Gordon Shedden, GB (Honda Civic Type-R), +14.954s; **5** Andrew Jordan, GB (BMW 125i M Sport), +17.864s; **6** Jason Plato, GB (Subaru Levorg GT), +18.029s; **7** Mat Jackson, GB (Ford Focus ST), +21.310s; **8** Rob Austin, GB (Toyota Avensis), +22.523s; **9** Ollie Jackson, GB (Audi S3 Saloon), +23.920s; **10** Martin Depper, GB (Ford Focus ST), +24.265s.
Fastest race lap: Turkington, 1m 25.571s, 89.399mph/143.874km/h.
Pole position: Sutton.

Round 15 (34.000 miles/54.718km).
1 Mat Jackson, GB (Ford Focus ST), 24m 06.484s, 84.618mph/136.181km/h; **2** Ash Sutton, GB (Subaru Levorg GT), +0.877s; **3** Jason Plato, GB (Subaru Levorg GT), +16.032s; **4** Rob Austin, GB (Toyota Avensis), +16.073s; **5** Matt Neal, GB (Honda Civic Type-R), +16.517s; **6** Colin Turkington, GB (BMW 125i M Sport), +16.779s; **7** Andrew Jordan, GB (BMW 125i M Sport), +17.575s; **8** Rob Collard, GB (BMW 125i M Sport), +19.360s; **9** Gordon Shedden, GB (Honda Civic Type-R), +21.336s; **10** Ollie Jackson, GB (Audi S3 Saloon), +21.800s.
Fastest race lap: Jackson, 1m 25.933s, 89.022mph/143.268km/h.
Pole position: Jackson.

BRITISH TOURING CAR CHAMPIONSHIP, Snetterton Circuit, Thetford, Norfolk, Great Britain, 30 July. 12, 14 and 12 laps of the 2.969-mile/4.778km circuit.
Round 16 (35.627 miles/57.336km).
1 Ash Sutton, GB (Subaru Levorg GT), 23m 38.526s, 90.415mph/145.509km/h; **2** Jack Goff, GB (Honda Civic Type-R), +2.332s; **3** Matt Neal, GB (Honda Civic Type-R), +6.707s; **4** Andrew Jordan, GB (BMW 125i M Sport), +6.916s; **5** Jason Plato, GB (Subaru Levorg GT), +7.743s; **6** Jake Hill, GB (Volkswagen Passat CC), +12.145s; **7** Colin Turkington, GB (BMW 125i M Sport), +12.378s; **8** Tom Ingram, GB (Toyota Avensis), +19.459s; **9** Rob Collard, GB (BMW 125i M Sport), +22.446s; **10** Tom Chilton, GB (Vauxhall Astra), +22.792s.
Fastest race lap: Turkington, 1m 56.269s, 91.925mph/147.939km/h.
Pole position: Goff, 1m 55.786s, 92.308mph/148.556km/h.

Round 17 (41.565 miles/66.892km).
1 Ash Sutton, GB (Subaru Levorg GT), 29m 51.887s, 83.505mph/134.389km/h; **2** Colin Turkington, GB (BMW 125i M Sport), +2.955s; **3** Rob Collard, GB (BMW 125i M Sport), +3.657s; **4** Mat Jackson, GB (Ford Focus ST), +5.494s; **5** Jack Goff, GB (Honda Civic Type-R), +8.166s; **6** Andrew Jordan, GB (BMW 125i M Sport), +8.419s; **7** Gordon Shedden, GB (Honda Civic Type-R), +8.901s; **8** James Cole, GB (Subaru Levorg GT), +9.388s; **9** Matt Neal, GB (Honda Civic Type-R), +10.792s; **10** Tom Ingram, GB (Toyota Avensis), +11.765s.
Fastest race lap: Josh Price, GB (Subaru Levorg GT), 1m 57.494s, 90.966mph/146.396km/h.
Pole position: Sutton.

Round 18 (35.627 miles/57.336km).
1 Gordon Shedden, GB (Honda Civic Type-R), 23m 53.888s, 89.446mph/143.950km/h; **2** Rob Collard, GB (BMW 125i M Sport), +0.712s; **3** Colin Turkington, GB (BMW 125i M Sport), +1.007s; **4** Mat Jackson, GB (Ford Focus ST), +7.260s; **5** James Cole, GB (Subaru Levorg GT), +7.743s; **6** Tom Ingram, GB (Toyota Avensis), +7.953s; **7** Jake Hill, GB (Volkswagen Passat CC), +10.260s; **8** Jack Goff, GB (Honda Civic Type-R), +10.559s; **9** Senna Proctor, GB (Vauxhall Astra), +11.424s; **10** Tom Chilton, GB (Vauxhall Astra), +11.763s.
Fastest race lap: Collard, 1m 57.830s, 90.707mph/145.979km/h.
Pole position: Cole.

BRITISH TOURING CAR CHAMPIONSHIP, Knockhill Racing Circuit, Dunfermline, Fife, Scotland, Great Britain, 13 August. 24, 22 and 27 laps of the 1.271-mile/2.046km circuit.
Round 19 (30.511 miles/49.103km).
1 Jason Plato, GB (Subaru Levorg GT), 21m 06.158s, 86.750mph/139.612km/h; **2** Ash Sutton, GB (Subaru Levorg GT), +0.216s; **3** Colin Turkington, GB (BMW 125i M Sport), +0.902s; **4** Rob Collard, GB (BMW 125i M Sport), +1.580s; **5** James Cole, GB (Subaru Levorg GT), +11.188s; **6** Tom Ingram, GB (Toyota Avensis), +16.492s; **7** Senna Proctor, GB (Vauxhall Astra), +21.946s; **8** Adam Morgan, GB (Mercedes A-Class), +28.348s; **9** Matt Neal, GB (Honda Civic Type-R), +29.167s; **10** Dave Newsham, GB (Chevrolet Cruze), +29.991s.
Fastest race lap: Turkington, 52.112s, 87.823mph/141.338km/h.
Pole position: Plato, 52.579s, 87.043mph/140.083km/h.

Round 20 (27.969 miles/45.011km).
1 Ash Sutton, GB (Subaru Levorg GT), 19m 25.761s, 86.370mph/138.999km/h; **2** Jason Plato, GB (Subaru Levorg GT), +0.238s; **3** Colin Turkington, GB (BMW 125i M Sport), +3.198s; **4** Rob Collard, GB (BMW 125i M Sport), +5.063s; **5** James Cole, GB (Subaru Levorg GT), +6.831s; **6** Gordon Shedden, GB (Honda Civic Type-R), +9.401s; **7** Dave Newsham, GB (Chevrolet Cruze), +25.803s; **8** Tom Ingram, GB (Toyota Avensis), +25.954s; **9** Rory Butcher, GB (Ford Focus ST), +26.361s; **10** Ant Whorton-Eales, GB (Audi S3 Saloon), +28.889s.
Fastest race lap: Plato, 52.457s, 87.246mph/140.409km/h.
Pole position: Plato.

Round 21 (34.325 miles/55.241km).
1 Tom Ingram, GB (Toyota Avensis), 26m 33.852s, 77.529mph/124.771km/h; **2** Gordon Shedden, GB (Honda Civic Type-R), +1.167s; **3** Colin Turkington, GB (BMW 125i M Sport), +1.556s; **4** Ash Sutton, GB (Subaru Levorg GT), +4.172s; **5** James Cole, GB (Subaru Levorg GT), +4.463s; **6** Jason Plato, GB (Subaru Levorg GT), +5.179s; **7** Mat Jackson, GB (Ford Focus ST), +5.538s; **8** Matt Neal, GB (Honda Civic Type-R), +5.784s; **9** Rory Butcher, GB (Ford Focus ST), +6.333s; **10** Dave Newsham, GB (Chevrolet Cruze), +7.193s.
Fastest race lap: Ingram, 52.045s, 87.936mph/141.520km/h.
Pole position: Whorton-Eales.

BRITISH TOURING CAR CHAMPIONSHIP, Rockingham Motor Speedway, Corby, Northamptonshire, Great Britain, 27 August. 16, 18 and 17 laps of the 1.940-mile/3.122km circuit.
Round 22 (31.040 miles/49.954km).
1 James Cole, GB (Subaru Levorg GT), 22m 49.936s, 81.568mph/131.272km/h; **2** Ash Sutton, GB (Subaru Levorg GT), +2.571s; **3** Jack Goff, GB (Honda Civic Type-R), +3.167s; **4** Josh Cook, GB (MG **6** GT), +3.308s; **5** Matt Neal, GB (Honda Civic Type-R), +4.946s; **6** Colin Turkington, GB (BMW 125i M Sport), +5.245s; **7** Mat Jackson, GB (Ford Focus ST), +7.937s; **8** Adam Morgan, GB (Mercedes A-Class), +8.458s; **9** Josh Price, GB (Subaru Levorg GT), +8.698s; **10** Jason Plato, GB (Subaru Levorg GT), +10.157s.
Fastest race lap: Neal, 1m 24.130s, 83.014mph/133.598km/h.
Pole position: Cole, 1m 23.187s, 83.955mph/135.113km/h.

Round 23 (34.920 miles/56.198km).
1 Ash Sutton, GB (Subaru Levorg GT), 26m 57.861s, 77.702mph/125.050km/h; **2** Mat Jackson, GB (Ford Focus ST), +2.438s; **3** Colin Turkington, GB (BMW 125i M Sport), +2.730s; **4** Jason Plato, GB (Subaru Levorg GT), +7.110s; **5** Jack Goff, GB (Honda Civic Type-R), +9.513s; **6** Adam Morgan, GB (Mercedes A-Class), +10.101s; **7** Andrew Jordan, GB (BMW 125i M Sport), +10.569s; **8** Rob Collard, GB (BMW 125i M Sport), +10.756s; **9** Tom Ingram, GB (Toyota Avensis), +14.802s; **10** Chris Smiley, GB (Chevrolet Cruze), +15.349s.
Fastest race lap: Sutton, 1m 24.011s, 83.131mph/133.787km/h.
Pole position: Cole.

Round 24 (32.980 miles/53.076km).
1 Andrew Jordan, GB (BMW 125i M Sport), 24m 59.347s, 79.186mph/127.438km/h; **2** Adam Morgan, GB (Mercedes A-Class), +1.724s; **3** Jason Plato, GB (Subaru Levorg GT), +2.025s; **4** Jack Goff, GB (Honda Civic Type-R), +5.214s; **5** Ash Sutton, GB (Subaru Levorg GT), +5.561s; **6** Colin Turkington, GB (BMW 125i M Sport), +5.908s; **7** Senna Proctor, GB (Vauxhall Astra), +6.506s; **8** Tom Ingram, GB (Toyota Avensis), +6.786s; **9** Chris Smiley, GB (Chevrolet Cruze), +7.331s; **10** Dave Newsham, GB (Chevrolet Cruze), +7.775s.
Fastest race lap: Sutton, 1m 24.788s, 82.370mph/132.561km/h.
Pole position: Jordan.

BRITISH TOURING CAR CHAMPIONSHIP, Silverstone National Circuit, Towcester, Northamptonshire, Great Britain, 17 September. 18, 22 and 25 laps of the 1.640-mile/2.640km circuit.
Round 25 (29.527 miles/47.519km).
1 Tom Ingram, GB (Toyota Avensis), 20m 36.912s, 85.938mph/138.304km/h; **2** Jack Goff, GB (Honda Civic Type-R), +0.728s; **3** Adam Morgan, GB (Mercedes A-Class), +1.754s; **4** Colin Turkington, GB (BMW 125i M Sport), +2.973s; **5** Ash Sutton, GB (Subaru Levorg GT), +3.775s; **6** Ant Whorton-Eales, GB (Audi S3 Saloon), +5.107s; **7** Dave Newsham, GB (Chevrolet Cruze), +6.525s; **8** Aiden Moffat, GB (Mercedes A-Class), +7.339s; **9** Rob Austin, GB (Toyota Avensis), +8.704s; **10** Michael Epps, GB (Volkswagen Passat CC), +9.588s.
Fastest race lap: Morgan, 59.506s, 99.241mph/159.713km/h.
Pole position: Goff, 58.653s, 100.684mph/162.035km/h.

Round 26 (36.089 miles/58.079km).
1 Jack Goff, GB (Honda Civic Type-R), 21m 57.764s, 98.591mph/158.666km/h; **2** Tom Ingram, GB (Toyota Avensis), +4.910s; **3** Colin Turkington, GB (BMW 125i M Sport), +5.703s; **4** Ash Sutton, GB (Subaru Levorg GT), +6.528s *; **5** Rob Austin, GB (Toyota Avensis), +7.749s; **6** Adam Morgan, GB (Mercedes A-Class), +8.438s; **7** Gordon Shedden, GB (Honda Civic Type-R), +8.680s; **8** Rob Huff, GB (Vauxhall Astra), +9.038s; **9** Dave Newsham, GB (Chevrolet Cruze), +9.280s; **10** Michael Epps, GB (Volkswagen Passat CC), +9.547s.
** includes 1s penalty.*
Fastest race lap: Shedden, 59.290s, 99.602mph/160.294km/h.
Pole position: Ingram.

Round 27 (41.010 miles/65.999km).
1 Matt Neal, GB (Honda Civic Type-R), 28m 15.455s, 87.077mph/140.137km/h; **2** Rob Huff, GB (Vauxhall Astra), +0.728s; **3** Dave Newsham, GB (Chevrolet Cruze), +0.997s; **4** Tom Ingram, GB (Toyota Avensis), +1.434s; **5** Rob Austin, GB (Toyota Avensis), +1.865s; **6** Adam Morgan, GB (Mercedes A-Class), +3.006s; **7** Chris Smiley, GB (Chevrolet Cruze), +3.626s; **8** Andrew Jordan, GB (BMW 125i M Sport), +3.761s; **9** Jack Goff, GB (Honda Civic Type-R), +5.568s; **10** Mat Jackson, GB (Ford Focus ST), +6.457s.
Fastest race lap: Senna Proctor, GB (Vauxhall Astra), 59.476s, 99.291mph/159.793km/h.
Pole position: Newsham.

BRITISH TOURING CAR CHAMPIONSHIP, Brands Hatch Grand Prix Circuit, West Kingsdown, Dartford, Kent, Great Britain, 1 October. 15, 15 and 17 laps of the 2.433-mile/3.916km circuit.
Round 28 (36.498 miles/58.738km).
1 Aiden Moffat, GB (Mercedes A-Class), 24m 10.915s, 90.558mph/145.739km/h; **2** Tom Ingram, GB (Toyota Avensis), +0.345s; **3** Ash Sutton, GB (Subaru Levorg GT), +1.499s; **4** Mat Jackson, GB (Ford Focus ST), +14.474s; **5** Tom Chilton, GB (Vauxhall Astra), +15.802s; **6** Senna Proctor, GB (Vauxhall Astra), +16.195s; **7** Gordon Shedden, GB (Honda Civic Type-R), +19.140s; **8** Dave Newsham, GB (Chevrolet Cruze), +29.547s; **9** Rob Austin, GB (Toyota Avensis), +31.577s; **10** Matt Neal, GB (Honda Civic Type-R), +41.344s.
Fastest race lap: Shedden, 1m 33.715s, 93.469mph/150.425km/h.
Pole position: Jack Goff, GB (Honda Civic Type-R), 1m 30.802s, 96.468mph/155.250km/h.

Round 29 (36.498 miles/58.738km).
1 Colin Turkington, GB (BMW 125i M Sport), 23m 27.896s, 93.325mph/150.193km/h; **2** Gordon Shedden, GB (Honda Civic Type-R), +1.605s; **3** Matt Neal, GB (Honda Civic Type-R), +2.246s; **4** Mat Jackson, GB (Ford Focus ST), +3.756s; **5** Aiden Moffat, GB (Mercedes A-Class), +5.923s; **6** Tom Ingram, GB (Toyota Avensis), +6.486s; **7** Tom Chilton, GB (Vauxhall Astra), +6.832s; **8** Jack Goff, GB (Honda Civic Type-R), +7.252s; **9** Rob Austin, GB (Toyota Avensis), +7.584s; **10** Michael Epps, GB (Volkswagen Passat CC), +8.001s.
Fastest race lap: Turkington, 1m 31.741s, 95.480mph/153.661km/h.
Pole position: Moffat.

Round 30 (41.364 miles/66.570km).
1 Rob Austin, GB (Toyota Avensis), 31m 25.679s, 78.969mph/127.089km/h; **2** Jack Goff, GB (Honda Civic Type-R), +3.185s; **3** Ash Sutton, GB (Subaru Levorg GT), +4.741s; **4** Tom Ingram, GB (Toyota Avensis), +10.965s; **5** Michael Epps, GB (Volkswagen Passat CC), +13.978s; **6** Gordon Shedden, GB (Honda Civic Type-R), +15.024s; **7** Mat Jackson, GB (Ford Focus ST), +15.330s; **8** Matt Neal, GB (Honda Civic Type-R), +16.008s; **9** Adam Morgan, GB (Mercedes A-Class), +22.924s; **10** Jake Hill, GB (Volkswagen Passat CC), +24.538s.
Fastest race lap: Martin Depper, GB (Ford Focus ST), 1m 42.610s, 85.367mph/137.385km/h.
Pole position: Epps.

Final championship points
Drivers
1 Ash Sutton, GB, 372; **2** Colin Turkington, GB, 351; **3** Tom Ingram, GB, 311; **4** Gordon Shedden, GB, 309; **5** Rob Collard, GB, 256; **6** Jack Goff, GB, 245; **7** Matt Neal, GB, 243; **8** Mat Jackson, GB, 210; **9** Andrew Jordan, GB, 203; **10** Adam Morgan, GB, 187; **11** Rob Austin, GB, 174; **12** Jason Plato, GB, 146; **13** Aiden Moffat, GB, 121; **14** Dave Newsham, GB, 108; **15** Tom Chilton, GB, 100; **16** James Cole, GB, 79; **17** Michael Epps, GB, 77; **18** Josh Cook, GB, 75; **19** Senna Proctor, GB, 63; **20** Jake Hill, GB, 63; **21** Chris Smiley, GB, 45; **22** Ollie Jackson, GB, 42; **23** Ant Whorton-Eales, GB, 34; **24** Matt Simpson, GB, 30; **25** Rob Huff, GB, 26; **26** Jeff Smith, GB, 25; **27** Árón Taylor-Smith, IRL, 25; **28** Martin Depper, GB, 22; **29** Rory Butcher, GB, 20; **30** Brett Smith, GB, 13; **31** Josh Price, GB, 9; **32** Luke Davenport, GB, 6; **33** Daniel Lloyd, GB, 6; **34** Stephen Jelley, GB, 2.

Drivers (Independents)
1 Tom Ingram, GB, 418; **2** Jack Goff, GB, 379; **3** Mat Jackson, GB, 344; **4** Adam Morgan, GB, 293; **5** Rob Austin, GB, 286; **6** Dave Newsham, GB, 268; **7** Aiden Moffat, GB, 243; **8** Michael Epps, GB, 199; **9** Ollie Jackson, GB, 199; **10** Jake Hill, GB, 194.

Drivers (Jack Sears Trophy)
1 Senna Proctor, GB, 503; **2** Ant Whorton-Eales, GB, 410; **3** Josh Price, GB, 295; **4** Will Burns, GB, 269; **5** Brett Smith, GB, 197; **6** Rory Butcher, GB, 168; **7** Luke Davenport, GB, 157; **8** Dennis Strandberg, S, 43.

Manufacturers
1 BMW, 782; **2** Subaru, 751; **3** Honda, 726; **4** Vauxhall, 580; **5** MG, 369.

Teams
1 Team BMW, 594; **2** Halfords Yuasa Racing, 545; **3** Adrian Flux Subaru Racing, 513; **4** Speedworks Motorsport, 307; **5** Eurotech Racing, 286; **6** Team Shredded Wheat Racing with Duo, 235; **7** Power Maxed Racing, 201; **8** BMW Pirtek Racing, 200; **9** Ciceley Motorsport, 191; **10** Handy Motorsport, 173.

Verizon Indycar Series

All cars are Dallara DW12.

FIRESTONE GRAND PRIX OF ST. PETERSBURG, St. Petersburg Street Circuit, Florida, USA, 12 March. Round 1. 110 laps of the 1.800-mile/2.897km circuit, 198.000 miles/318.650km.
1 Sébastien Bourdais, F (-Honda), 2h 04m 32.4153s, 95.391mph/153.517km/h; **2** Simon Pagenaud, F (-Chevrolet), +10.3508s; **3** Scott Dixon, NZ (-Honda), +27.4985s; **4** Ryan Hunter-Reay, USA (-Honda), +36.1147s; **5** Takuma Sato, J (-Honda), +36.1675s; **6** Hélio Castroneves, BR (-Chevrolet), +42.0285s; **7** Marco Andretti, USA (-Honda), +49.5217s; **8** Josef Newgarden, USA (-Chevrolet), +50.0443s; **9** James Hinchcliffe, CDN (-Honda), +58.8628s; **10** Ed Jones, GB (-Honda), +1m 01.8611s; **11** Alexander Rossi, USA (-Honda), -1 lap; **12** Tony Kanaan, BR (-Honda), -1; **13** J.R. Hildebrand, USA (-Chevrolet), -1; **14** Mikhail Aleshin, RUS (-Honda), -1; **15** Conor Daly, USA (-Chevrolet), -1; **16** Max Chilton, GB (-Honda), -1; **17** Graham Rahal, USA (-Honda), -2; **18** Charlie Kimball, USA (-Honda), -5; **19** Will Power, AUS (-Chevrolet), -11 (DNF-fuel feed); **20** Spencer Pigot, USA (-Chevrolet), -39 (DNF-brakes); **21** Carlos Muñoz, CO (-Chevrolet), -78 (DNF-suspension).
Most laps led: Bourdais, 69.
Fastest race lap: Dixon, 1m 02.0786s, 104.384mph/167.989km/h.
Pole position: Power, 1m 01.0640s, 106.118mph/170.781km/h.
Championship points
Drivers: **1** Bourdais, 53; **2** Pagenaud, 41; **3** Dixon, 35; **4** Hunter-Reay, 32; **5** Sato, 31; **6** Castroneves, 28.

TOYOTA GRAND PRIX OF LONG BEACH, Long Beach Street Circuit, California, USA, 9 April. Round 2. 85 laps of the 1.968-mile/3.167km circuit, 167.280 miles/269.211km.
1 James Hinchcliffe, CDN (-Honda), 1h 50m 28.9818s, 90.845mph/146.200km/h; **2** Sébastien Bourdais, F (-Honda), +1.4940s; **3** Josef Newgarden, USA (-Chevrolet), +2.3160s; **4** Scott Dixon, NZ (-Honda), +2.7832s; **5** Simon Pagenaud, F (-Chevrolet), +3.3934s; **6** Ed Jones, GB (-Honda), +5.7951s; **7** Carlos Muñoz, CO (-Chevrolet), +6.9393s; **8** Spencer Pigot, USA (-Chevrolet), +9.0570s; **9** Hélio Castroneves, BR (-Chevrolet), +9.3403s; **10** Graham Rahal, USA (-Honda), +17.8632s; **11** J.R. Hildebrand, USA (-Chevrolet), -1 lap (DNF-accident); **12** Mikhail Aleshin, RUS (-Honda), -1; **13** Will Power, AUS (-Chevrolet), -1; **14** Max Chilton, GB (-Honda), -1; **15** Tony Kanaan, BR (-Honda), -1; **16** Conor Daly, USA (-Chevrolet), -1; **17** Ryan Hunter-Reay, USA (-Honda), -6 (DNF-electrical); **18** Takuma Sato, J (-Honda), -7 (DNF-mechanical); **19** Alexander Rossi, USA (-Honda), -23 (DNF-mechanical); **20** Marco Andretti, USA (-Honda), -71 (DNF-electrical); **21** Charlie Kimball, USA (-Honda), -84 (DNF-accident).
Most laps led: Dixon, 32.
Fastest race lap: Castroneves, 1m 07.7696s, 104.542mph/168.245km/h.
Pole position: Castroneves, 1m 06.2254s, 106.980mph/172.168km/h.
Championship points
Drivers: **1** Bourdais, 93; **2** Hinchcliffe, 74; **3** Pagenaud, 71; **4** Dixon, 70; **5** Newgarden, 59; **6** Castroneves, 51.

HONDA GRAND PRIX OF ALABAMA, Barber Motorsports Park, Birmingham, Alabama, USA, 23 April. Round 3. 90 laps of the 2.300-mile/3.701km circuit, 207.000 miles/333.134km.
1 Josef Newgarden, USA (-Chevrolet), 1h 54m 08.7076s, 108.809mph/175.111km/h; **2** Scott Dixon, NZ (-Honda), +1.0495s; **3** Simon Pagenaud, F (-Chevrolet), +2.5706s; **4** Hélio Castroneves, BR (-Chevrolet), +11.1592s; **5** Alexander Rossi, USA (-Honda), +12.0469s; **6** James Hinchcliffe, CDN (-Honda), +12.5905s; **7** Tony Kanaan, BR (-Honda), +15.4105s; **8** Sébastien Bourdais, F (-Honda), +16.0651s; **9** Takuma Sato, J (-Honda), +20.1764s; **10** Mikhail Aleshin, RUS (-Honda), +20.7064s; **11** Ryan Hunter-Reay, USA (-Honda), +22.2061s; **12** Max Chilton, GB (-Honda), +22.9713s; **13** Graham Rahal, USA (-Honda), +24.3457s; **14** Will Power, AUS (-Chevrolet), +26.3177s; **15** Charlie Kimball, USA (-Honda), +35.4868s; **16** Ed Jones, GB (-Honda), +39.5644s; **17** Carlos Muñoz, CO (-Chevrolet), +50.3679s; **18** Conor Daly, USA (-Chevrolet), +51.2029s; **19** Zach Veach, USA (-Chevrolet), +56.2545s; **20** Spencer Pigot, USA (-Chevrolet), -1 lap; **21** Marco Andretti, USA (-Honda), -3.
Most laps led: Power, 60.
Fastest race lap: Power, 1m 08.2763s, 121.272mph/195.168km/h.
Pole position: Power, 1m 06.9614s, 123.653mph/199.001km/h.
Championship points
Drivers: **1** Bourdais, 117; **2** Dixon, 111; **3** Newgarden, 110; **4** Pagenaud, 106; **5** Hinchcliffe, 102; **6** Castroneves, 84.

DESERT DIAMOND WEST VALLEY PHOENIX GRAND PRIX, Phoenix International Raceway, Arizona, USA, 29 April. Round 4. 250 laps of the 1.022-mile/1.645km circuit, 255.500 miles/411.187km.
1 Simon Pagenaud, F (-Chevrolet), 1h 46m 24.9473s, 144.058mph/231.838km/h; **2** Will Power, AUS (-Chevrolet), +9.1028s; **3** J.R. Hildebrand, USA (-Chevrolet), +9.3417s; **4** Hélio Castroneves, BR (-Chevrolet), +16.5864s; **5** Scott Dixon, NZ (-Honda), -1 lap; **6** Tony Kanaan, BR (-Honda), -1; **7** Ed Carpenter, USA (-Chevrolet), -2; **8** Charlie Kimball, USA (-Honda), -2; **9** Josef Newgarden, USA (-Chevrolet), -2; **10** Carlos Muñoz, CO (-Chevrolet), -3; **11** Ed Jones, GB (-Honda), -3; **12** James Hinchcliffe, CDN (-Honda), -4; **13** Ryan Hunter-Reay, USA (-Honda), -30 (DNF-accident damage); **14** Conor Daly, USA (-Chevrolet), -70; **15** Alexander Rossi, USA (-Honda), -109 (DNF-accident); **16** Takuma Sato, J (-Honda), -115 (DNF-accident); **17** Mikhail Aleshin, RUS (-Honda), -250 (DNF-accident); **18** Marco Andretti, USA (-Honda), -250 (DNF-accident); **19** Sébastien Bourdais, F (-Honda), -250 (DNF-accident); **20** Max Chilton, GB (-Honda), -250 (DNF-accident); **21** Graham Rahal, USA (-Honda), -250 (DNF-accident).
Most laps led: Pagenaud, 116.
Fastest race lap: Power, 19.7446s, 186.340mph/299.884km/h.
Pole position: Castroneves, 37.7538s, 194.905mph/313.669km/h (over **2** laps).
Championship points
Drivers: **1** Pagenaud, 159; **2** Dixon, 141; **3** Newgarden, 133; **4** Bourdais, 128; **5** Hinchcliffe, 120; **6** Castroneves, 118.

INDYCAR GRAND PRIX, Indianapolis Motor Speedway, Speedway, Indiana, USA, 13 May. Round 5. 85 laps of the 2.439-mile/3.925km circuit, 207.315 miles/333.641km.
1 Will Power, AUS (-Chevrolet), 1h 42m 57.6108s, 120.813mph/194.429km/h; **2** Scott Dixon, NZ (-Honda), +5.2830s; **3** Ryan Hunter-Reay, USA (-Honda), +12.0296s; **4** Simon Pagenaud, F (-Chevrolet), +17.0668s; **5** Hélio Castroneves, BR (-Chevrolet), +20.6072s; **6** Graham Rahal, USA (-Honda), +25.1039s; **7** Max Chilton, GB (-Honda), +25.7054s; **8** Alexander Rossi, USA (-Honda), +29.3214s; **9** Spencer Pigot, USA (-Chevrolet), +36.5878s; **10** Juan Pablo Montoya, CO (-Chevrolet), +41.8238s; **11** Josef Newgarden, USA (-Chevrolet), +48.3846s; **12** Takuma Sato, J (-Honda), +56.2212s; **13** James Hinchcliffe, CDN (-Honda), +1m 02.6805s; **14** J.R. Hildebrand, USA (-Chevrolet), -1 lap; **15** Carlos Muñoz, CO (-Chevrolet), -1; **16** Marco Andretti, USA (-Honda), -1; **17** Conor Daly, USA (-Chevrolet), -1; **18** Mikhail Aleshin, RUS (-Honda), -1; **19** Ed Jones, GB (-Honda), -1; **20** Tony Kanaan, BR (-Honda), -2; **21** Charlie Kimball, USA (-Honda), -53 (DNF-mechanical); **22** Sébastien Bourdais, F (-Honda), -82 (DNF-engine).
Most laps led: Power, 61.
Fastest race lap: Newgarden, 1m 09.3888s, 126.539mph/203.645km/h.
Pole position: Power, 1m 07.7044s, 129.687mph/208.711km/h.
Championship points
Drivers: **1** Pagenaud, 191; **2** Dixon, 181; **3** Newgarden, 152; **4** Castroneves, 149; **5** Power, 145; **6** Hinchcliffe, 137.

101ST RUNNING OF THE INDIANAPOLIS 500 PRESENTED BY PENNGRADE MOTOR OIL, Indianapolis Motor Speedway, Speedway, Indiana, USA, 28 May. Round 6. 200 laps of the 2.500-mile/4.023km circuit, 500.000 miles/804.672km.
1 Takuma Sato, J (-Honda), 3h 13m 03.3584s, 155.395mph/250.085km/h; **2** Hélio Castroneves, BR (-Chevrolet), +0.2011s; **3** Ed Jones, GB (-Honda), +0.5278s; **4** Max Chilton, GB (-Honda), +1.1365s; **5** Tony Kanaan, BR (-Honda), +1.6472s; **6** Juan Pablo Montoya, CO (-Chevrolet), +1.7154s; **7** Alexander Rossi, USA (-Honda), +2.4222s; **8** Marco Andretti, USA (-Honda), +2.5410s; **9** Gabby Chaves, CO (-Chevrolet), +3.8311s; **10** Carlos Muñoz, CO (-Chevrolet), +4.5319s; **11** Ed Carpenter, USA (-Chevrolet), +4.6228s; **12** Graham Rahal, USA (-Honda), +5.0310s; **13** Mikhail Aleshin, RUS (-Honda), +5.6993s; **14** Simon Pagenaud, F (-Chevrolet), +6.0513s; **15** Sebastian Saavedra, CO (-Chevrolet), +12.6668s; **16** J.R. Hildebrand, USA (-Chevrolet), +33.2191s; **17** Pippa Mann, GB (-Honda), -1 lap; **18** Spencer Pigot, USA (-Chevrolet), -6; **19** Josef Newgarden, USA (-Chevrolet), -14; **20** James Davison, AUS (-Honda), -17 (DNF-accident); **21** Oriol Servià, E (-Honda), -17 (DNF-accident); **22** James Hinchcliffe, CDN (-Honda), -17 (DNF-accident); **23** Will Power, AUS (-Chevrolet), -17 (DNF-accident); **24** Fernando Alonso, E (-Honda), -21 (DNF-engine); **25** Charlie Kimball, USA (-Honda), -34 (DNF-engine); **26** Zach Veach, USA (-Chevrolet), -45 (DNF-battery); **27** Ryan Hunter-Reay, USA (-Honda), -64 (DNF-engine); **28** Sage Karam, USA (-Chevrolet), -75 (DNF-alternator); **29** Buddy Lazier, USA (-Chevrolet), -82 (DNF-accident); **30** Conor Daly, USA (-Chevrolet), -135 (DNF-accident); **31** Jack Harvey, GB (-Honda), -135 (DNF-accident); **32** Scott Dixon, NZ (-Honda), -148 (DNF-accident); **33** Jay Howard, GB (-Honda), -155 (DNF-accident).
Did not start: Sébastien Bourdais, F (-Honda) – accident in qualifying.

Most laps led: Chilton, 50.
Fastest race lap: Sato, 39.7896s, 226.190mph/364.017km/h.
Pole position: Dixon, 2m 35.0630s, 232.164mph/373.631km/h (over 4 laps).
Championship points
Drivers: 1 Castroneves, 245; **2** Pagenaud, 234; **3** Sato, 234; **4** Dixon, 234; **5** Rossi, 190; **6** Kanaan, 188.

CHEVROLET DETROIT GRAND PRIX PRESENTED BY LEAR RACE 1, The Raceway at Belle Isle, Detroit, Michigan, USA, 3/4 June. Round 7. 2 x 70 laps of the 2.350-mile/3.782km circuit. Race 1 (164.500 miles/264.737km).
1 Graham Rahal, USA (-Honda), 1h 35m 48.7028s, 103.015mph/165.786km/h; **2** Scott Dixon, NZ (-Honda), +6.1474s; **3** James Hinchcliffe, CDN (-Honda), +9.1688s; **4** Josef Newgarden, USA (-Chevrolet), +10.0930s; **5** Alexander Rossi, USA (-Honda), +25.5556s; **6** Mikhail Aleshin, RUS (-Honda), +31.3644s; **7** Hélio Castroneves, BR (-Chevrolet), +33.1052s; **8** Takuma Sato, J (-Honda), +47.4696s; **9** Ed Jones, GB (-Honda), +53.6531s; **10** Spencer Pigot, USA (-Chevrolet), +54.0726s; **11** Max Chilton, GB (-Honda), +55.2547s; **12** Marco Andretti, USA (-Honda), +58.3402s; **13** Ryan Hunter-Reay, USA (-Honda), +59.1348s; **14** Carlos Muñoz, CO (-Chevrolet), +1m 00.7310s; **15** Tony Kanaan, BR (-Honda), +1m 01.9596s; **16** Simon Pagenaud, F (-Chevrolet), +1m 02.1492s; **17** J.R. Hildebrand, USA (-Chevrolet), +1m 06.0717s; **18** Will Power, AUS (-Chevrolet), -1 lap; **19** Esteban Gutiérrez, MEX (-Honda), -1; **20** Oriol Servià, E (-Honda), -1; **21** Charlie Kimball, USA (-Honda), -1; **22** Conor Daly, USA (-Chevrolet), -45 (DNF-mechanical).
Most laps led: Rahal, 55.
Fastest race lap: Newgarden, 1m 14.2062s, 114.007mph/183.476km/h.
Pole position: Rahal, 1m 13.9681s, 114.374mph/184.067km/h.

Race 2 (164.500 miles/264.737km).
1 Graham Rahal, USA (-Honda), 1h 33m 36.3769s, 105.442mph/169.692km/h; **2** Josef Newgarden, USA (-Chevrolet), +1.1772s; **3** Will Power, AUS (-Chevrolet), +2.6228s; **4** Takuma Sato, J (-Honda), +3.8535s; **5** Simon Pagenaud, F (-Chevrolet), +4.0810s; **6** Scott Dixon, NZ (-Honda), +4.6005s; **7** Alexander Rossi, USA (-Honda), +6.1978s; **8** Charlie Kimball, USA (-Honda), +6.6823s; **9** Hélio Castroneves, BR (-Chevrolet), +6.8439s; **10** Tony Kanaan, BR (-Honda), +7.7201s; **11** Carlos Muñoz, CO (-Chevrolet), +8.1160s; **12** Conor Daly, USA (-Chevrolet), +8.7847s; **13** Marco Andretti, USA (-Honda), +9.6103s; **14** Esteban Gutiérrez, MEX (-Honda), +13.1325s; **15** Max Chilton, GB (-Honda), -1 lap; **16** Mikhail Aleshin, RUS (-Honda), -1; **17** Ryan Hunter-Reay, USA (-Honda), -1; **18** J.R. Hildebrand, USA (-Chevrolet), -1; **19** Oriol Servià, E (-Honda), -1; **20** James Hinchcliffe, CDN (-Honda), -5 (DNF-mechanical); **21** Spencer Pigot, USA (-Chevrolet), -5 (DNF-mechanical); **22** Ed Jones, GB (-Honda), -10 (DNF-mechanical).
Most laps led: Rahal, 41.
Fastest race lap: Newgarden, 1m 14.6385s, 113.346mph/182.413km/h.
Pole position: Sato, 1m 13.6732s, 114.831mph/184.803km/h.
Championship points
Drivers: 1 Dixon, 303; **2** Castroneves, 295; **3** Sato, 292; **4** Pagenaud, 278; **5** Newgarden, 259; **6** Rahal, 251.

RAINGUARD WATER SEALERS 600, Texas Motor Speedway, Fort Worth, Texas, USA, 10 June. Round 8. 248 laps of the 1.440-mile/2.317km circuit, 357.120 miles/574.729km.
1 Will Power, AUS (-Chevrolet), 2h 32m 31.0118s, 140.491mph/226.098km/h; **2** Tony Kanaan, BR (-Honda), +0.1978s; **3** Simon Pagenaud, F (-Chevrolet), +0.3740s; **4** Graham Rahal, USA (-Honda), +0.8112s; **5** Gabby Chaves, CO (-Chevrolet), +1.8984s; **6** Marco Andretti, USA (-Honda), +4.1632s; **7** Conor Daly, USA (-Chevrolet), -1 lap; **8** Max Chilton, GB (-Honda), -3; **9** Scott Dixon, NZ (-Honda), -5 (DNF-accident); **10** Takuma Sato, J (-Honda), -5 (DNF-accident); **11** Ed Carpenter, USA (-Chevrolet), -24 (DNF-accident) *; **12** J.R. Hildebrand, USA (-Chevrolet), -33 *; **13** Josef Newgarden, USA (-Chevrolet), -47 (DNF-accident); **14** James Hinchcliffe, CDN (-Honda), -97 (DNF-accident); **15** Mikhail Aleshin, RUS (-Honda), -97 (DNF-accident); **16** Tristan Vautier, F (-Honda), -97 (DNF-accident); **17** Ed Jones, GB (-Honda), -97 (DNF-accident); **18** Carlos Muñoz, CO (-Chevrolet), -97 (DNF-accident); **19** Ryan Hunter-Reay, USA (-Honda), -97 (DNF-accident); **20** Hélio Castroneves, BR (-Chevrolet), -158 (DNF-accident); **21** Charlie Kimball, USA (-Honda), -207 (DNF-oil leak); **22** Alexander Rossi, USA (-Honda), -212 (DNF-accident).
** includes 2-lap penalty for unapproved work under red flag.*
Most laps led: Power, 180.
Fastest race lap: Kanaan, 23.0816s, 224.594mph/361.450km/h.
Pole position: Kimball, 46.5861s, 222.556mph/358.169km/h (over 2 laps).
Championship points
Drivers: 1 Dixon, 326; **2** Pagenaud, 313; **3** Sato, 312; **4** Castroneves, 305; **5** Power, 286; **6** Rahal, 283.

INDYCAR SERIES, Road America, Elkhart Lake, Wisconsin, USA, 25 June. Round 9. 55 laps of the 4.014-mile/6.460km circuit, 220.770 miles/355.295km.
1 Scott Dixon, NZ (-Honda), 1h 47m 18.9870s, 123.431mph/198.643km/h; **2** Josef Newgarden, USA (-Chevrolet), +0.5779s; **3** Hélio Castroneves, BR (-Chevrolet), +4.1918s; **4** Simon Pagenaud, F (-Chevrolet), +4.9721s; **5** Will Power, AUS (-Chevrolet), +5.7227s; **6** Charlie Kimball, USA (-Honda), +14.7178s; **7** Ed Jones, GB (-Honda), +21.6338s; **8** Graham Rahal, USA (-Honda), +22.2273s; **9** Max Chilton, GB (-Honda), +23.3076s; **10** Mikhail Aleshin, RUS (-Honda), +24.3586s; **11** Carlos Muñoz, CO (-Chevrolet), +26.1402s; **12** Spencer Pigot, USA (-Chevrolet), +33.4983s; **13** Alexander Rossi, USA (-Honda), +38.1370s; **14** Ryan Hunter-Reay, USA (-Honda), +39.8433s; **15** Conor Daly, USA (-Chevrolet), +43.1988s; **16** J.R. Hildebrand, USA (-Chevrolet), +1m 16.5039s; **17** Esteban Gutiérrez, MEX (-Honda), +1m 28.4634s; **18** Marco Andretti, USA (-Honda), -1 lap; **19** Takuma Sato, J (-Honda), -1; **20** James Hinchcliffe, CDN (-Honda), -2; **21** Tony Kanaan, BR (-Honda), -11 (DNF-accident).
Most laps led: Dixon, 24.
Fastest race lap: Newgarden, 1m 43.4651s, 139.664mph/224.768km/h.
Pole position: Castroneves, 1m 41.3007s, 142.649mph/229.571km/h.
Championship points
Drivers: 1 Dixon, 379; **2** Pagenaud, 345; **3** Castroneves, 342; **4** Sato, 323; **5** Newgarden, 318; **6** Power, 316.

IOWA CORN 300, Iowa Speedway, Newton, Iowa, USA, 9 July. Round 10. 300 laps of the 0.894-mile/1.439km circuit, 268.200 miles/431.626km.
1 Hélio Castroneves, BR (-Chevrolet), 1h 55m 11.2807s, 139.702mph/224.829km/h; **2** J.R. Hildebrand, USA (-Chevrolet), +3.9647s; **3** Ryan Hunter-Reay, USA (-Honda), +4.5845s; **4** Will Power, AUS (-Chevrolet), +5.7403s; **5** Graham Rahal, USA (-Honda), +10.1811s; **6** Josef Newgarden, USA (-Chevrolet), +11.0500s; **7** Simon Pagenaud, F (-Chevrolet), +12.2562s; **8** Scott Dixon, NZ (-Honda), +14.3653s; **9** Tony Kanaan, BR (-Honda), +15.1184s; **10** James Hinchcliffe, CDN (-Honda), +15.8243s; **11** Alexander Rossi, USA (-Honda), -1 lap; **12** Ed Carpenter, USA (-Chevrolet), -1; **13** Esteban Gutiérrez, MEX (-Honda), -1; **14** Max Chilton, GB (-Honda), -1; **15** Charlie Kimball, USA (-Honda), -2; **16** Takuma Sato, J (-Honda), -2; **17** Marco Andretti, USA (-Honda), -2; **18** Ed Jones, GB (-Honda), -3; **19** Conor Daly, USA (-Chevrolet), -132 (DNF-accident damage); **20** Carlos Muñoz, CO (-Chevrolet), -170 (DNF-accident damage); **21** Mikhail Aleshin, RUS (-Honda), -244 (DNF-accident).
Most laps led: Castroneves, 217.
Fastest race lap: Castroneves, 18.1486s, 177.336mph/285.395km/h.
Pole position: Power, 34.7541s, 185.210mph/298.066km/h (over 2 laps).
Championship points
Drivers: 1 Dixon, 403; **2** Castroneves, 395; **3** Pagenaud, 372; **4** Power, 350; **5** Newgarden, 347; **6** Rahal, 337.

HONDA INDY TORONTO, Toronto Street Circuit, Ontario, Canada, 16 July. Round 11. 85 laps of the 1.786-mile/2.874km circuit, 151.810 miles/244.315km.
1 Josef Newgarden, USA (-Chevrolet), 1h 35m 05.3522s, 95.790mph/154.159km/h; **2** Alexander Rossi, USA (-Honda), +1.8704s; **3** James Hinchcliffe, CDN (-Honda), +4.7020s; **4** Marco Andretti, USA (-Honda), +18.7408s; **5** Simon Pagenaud, F (-Chevrolet), +19.4274s; **6** Ryan Hunter-Reay, USA (-Honda), +27.3905s; **7** Max Chilton, GB (-Honda), +28.3386s; **8** Hélio Castroneves, BR (-Chevrolet), +28.9415s; **9** Graham Rahal, USA (-Honda), +29.7693s; **10** Scott Dixon, NZ (-Honda), +30.3369s; **11** Sebastian Saavedra, CO (-Honda), +32.7668s; **12** Charlie Kimball, USA (-Honda), +36.4821s; **13** J.R. Hildebrand, USA (-Chevrolet), +52.8910s; **14** Esteban Gutiérrez, MEX (-Honda), +53.9858s; **15** Carlos Muñoz, CO (-Chevrolet), +57.2777s; **16** Takuma Sato, J (-Honda), +1m 01.8457s; **17** Conor Daly, USA (-Chevrolet), +1m 02.3752s; **18** Spencer Pigot, USA (-Chevrolet), -1 lap; **19** Tony Kanaan, BR (-Honda), -2; **20** Ed Jones, GB (-Honda), -10 (DNF-oil line); **21** Will Power, AUS (-Chevrolet), -85 (DNF-accident).
Most laps led: Newgarden, 58.
Fastest race lap: Pagenaud, 1m 00.2357s, 106.741mph/171.782km/h.
Pole position: Pagenaud, 58.9124s, 109.138mph/175.641km/h.
Championship points
Drivers: 1 Dixon, 423; **2** Castroneves, 420; **3** Pagenaud, 404; **4** Newgarden, 400; **5** Power, 359; **6** Rahal, 359.

HONDA INDY 200 AT MID-OHIO, Mid-Ohio Sports Car Course, Lexington, Ohio, USA, 30 July. Round 12. 90 laps of the 2.258-mile/3.634km circuit, 203.220 miles/327.051km.
1 Josef Newgarden, USA (-Chevrolet), 1h 46m 19.5989s, 114.677mph/184.554km/h; **2** Will Power, AUS (-Chevrolet), +5.1556s; **3** Graham Rahal, USA (-Honda), +6.3129s; **4** Simon Pagenaud, F (-Chevrolet), +6.8807s; **5** Takuma Sato, J (-Honda), +7.3092s; **6** Alexander Rossi, USA (-Honda), +9.0266s; **7** Hélio Castroneves, BR (-Chevrolet), +11.6809s; **8** Ryan Hunter-Reay, USA (-Honda), +12.3623s; **9** Scott Dixon, NZ (-Honda), +18.1857s; **10** Conor Daly, USA (-Chevrolet), +20.5661s; **11** James Hinchcliffe, CDN (-Honda), +27.3241s; **12** Marco Andretti, USA (-Honda), +29.9928s; **13** Charlie Kimball, USA (-Honda), +31.1248s; **14** Mikhail Aleshin, RUS (-Honda), +32.5958s; **15** Max Chilton, GB (-Honda), +33.1095s; **16** Tony Kanaan, BR (-Honda), +36.1997s; **17** J.R. Hildebrand, USA (-Chevrolet), +1m 00.8248s; **18** Carlos Muñoz, CO (-Chevrolet), -1 lap; **19** Spencer Pigot, USA (-Chevrolet), -1; **20** Esteban Gutiérrez, MEX (-Honda), -1; **21** Ed Jones, GB (-Honda), -2.
Most laps led: Newgarden, 73.
Fastest race lap: Rossi, 1m 05.9696s, 123.220mph/198.304km/h.
Pole position: Power, 1m 04.1720s, 126.672mph/203.859km/h.
Championship points
Drivers: 1 Newgarden, 453; **2** Castroneves, 446; **3** Dixon, 445; **4** Pagenaud, 436; **5** Power, 401; **6** Rahal, 395.

ABC SUPPLY 500, Pocono Raceway, Long Pond, Pennsylvania, USA, 20 August. Round 13. 200 laps of the 2.500-mile/4.023km circuit, 500.000 miles/804.672km.
1 Will Power, AUS (-Chevrolet), 2h 43m 16.6005s, 183.737mph/295.696km/h; **2** Josef Newgarden, USA (-Chevrolet), +0.5268s; **3** Alexander Rossi, USA (-Honda), +0.7112s; **4** Simon Pagenaud, F (-Chevrolet), +0.8770s; **5** Tony Kanaan, BR (-Honda), +2.9056s; **6** Scott Dixon, NZ (-Honda), +3.3544s; **7** Hélio Castroneves, BR (-Chevrolet), +3.7273s; **8** Ryan Hunter-Reay, USA (-Honda), +4.0833s; **9** Graham Rahal, USA (-Honda), +4.6884s; **10** Carlos Muñoz, CO (-Chevrolet), +6.9330s; **11** Marco Andretti, USA (-Honda), +9.4607s; **12** Ed Carpenter, USA (-Chevrolet), +10.4503s; **13** Takuma Sato, J (-Honda), +11.2388s; **14** Conor Daly, USA (-Chevrolet), +19.8050s; **15** Gabby Chaves, CO (-Chevrolet), +20.6790s; **16** Charlie Kimball, USA (-Honda), +24.4523s; **17** Ed Jones, GB (-Honda), +25.0689s; **18** Max Chilton, GB (-Honda), -71 laps (DNF-turbo wastegate); **19** J.R. Hildebrand, USA (-Chevrolet), -76 (DNF-accident); **20** James Hinchcliffe, CDN (-Honda), -76 (DNF-accident); **21** Sebastian Saavedra, CO (-Honda), -86 (DNF-accident); **22** Esteban Gutiérrez, MEX (-Honda), -177 (DNF-accident).
Most laps led: Dixon, 51.
Fastest race lap: Kanaan, 41.2230s, 218.325mph/351.360km/h.
Pole position: Sato, 1m 21.9526s, 219.639mph/353.475km/h (over 2 laps).
Championship points
Drivers: 1 Newgarden, 494; **2** Dixon, 476; **3** Castroneves, 472; **4** Pagenaud, 468; **5** Power, 452; **6** Rahal, 418.

BOMMARITO AUTOMOTIVE GROUP 500 PRESENTED BY VALVOLINE, Gateway Motorsports Park, Madison, Illinois, USA, 26 August. Round 14. 248 laps of the 1.250-mile/2.012km circuit, 310.000 miles/498.897km.
1 Josef Newgarden, USA (-Chevrolet), 2h 13m 22.0358s, 139.465mph/224.446km/h; **2** Scott Dixon, NZ (-Honda), +0.6850s; **3** Simon Pagenaud, F (-Chevrolet), +0.9743s; **4** Hélio Castroneves, BR (-Chevrolet), +1.5668s; **5** Conor Daly, USA (-Chevrolet), +1.7446s; **6** Alexander Rossi, USA (-Honda), +2.9101s; **7** Charlie Kimball, USA (-Honda), +4.2365s; **8** James Hinchcliffe, CDN (-Honda), +4.8498s; **9** Carlos Muñoz, CO (-Chevrolet), +7.8832s; **10** Sébastien Bourdais, F (-Honda), +8.1831s; **11** Sebastian Saavedra, CO (-Honda), +8.6604s; **12** Graham Rahal, USA (-Honda), +8.8457s; **13** Ed Jones, GB (-Honda), +12.3444s; **14** Marco Andretti, USA (-Honda), +19.8702s; **15** Ryan Hunter-Reay, USA (-Honda), -43 laps (DNF-accident); **16** Tony Kanaan, BR (-Honda), -80 (DNF-mechanical); **17** Max Chilton, GB (-Honda), -84 (DNF-accident); **18** J.R. Hildebrand, USA (-Chevrolet), -148 (DNF-accident); **19** Takuma Sato, J (-Honda), -242 (DNF-accident damage); **20** Will Power, AUS (-Chevrolet), -243 (DNF-accident); **21** Ed Carpenter, USA (-Chevrolet), -243 (DNF-accident).
Most laps led: Newgarden, 170.
Fastest race lap: Newgarden, 24.6317s, 182.691mph/294.013km/h.
Pole position: Power, 47.4579s, 189.642mph/305.199km/h (over 2 laps).
Championship points
Drivers: 1 Newgarden, 547; **2** Dixon, 516; **3** Castroneves, 505; **4** Pagenaud, 504; **5** Power, 464; **6** Rahal, 436.

INDYCAR GRAND PRIX AT THE GLEN, Watkins Glen International, New York, USA, 3 September. Round 15. 60 laps of the 3.370-mile/5.423km circuit, 202.200 miles/325.409km.
1 Alexander Rossi, USA (-Honda), 1h 42m 03.9024s, 118.865mph/191.295km/h; **2** Scott Dixon, NZ (-Honda), +0.9514s; **3** Ryan Hunter-Reay, USA (-Honda), +7.1592s; **4** Hélio Castroneves, BR (-Chevrolet), +8.8938s; **5** Graham Rahal, USA (-Honda), +11.8863s; **6** Will Power, AUS (-Chevrolet), +15.3787s; **7** Charlie Kimball, USA (-Honda), +16.1639s; **8** Max Chilton, GB (-Honda), +28.0410s; **9** Simon Pagenaud, F (-Chevrolet), +28.2941s; **10** Carlos Muñoz, CO (-Chevrolet), +29.4972s; **11** Conor Daly, USA (-Chevrolet), +30.2436s; **12** Spencer Pigot, USA (-Chevrolet), +32.3478s; **13** Ed Jones, GB (-Honda), +33.1533s; **14** Jack Harvey, GB (-Honda), +35.6826s; **15** J.R. Hildebrand, USA (-Chevrolet), +41.5905s; **16** Marco Andretti, USA (-Honda), +52.7948s; **17** Sébastien Bourdais, F (-Honda), +54.0444s; **18** Josef Newgarden, USA (-Chevrolet), -2 laps; **19** Takuma Sato, J (-Honda), -4; **20** Tony Kanaan, BR (-Honda), -14 (DNF-accident); **21** James Hinchcliffe, CDN (-Honda), -55 (DNF-engine).
Most laps led: Rossi, 32.
Fastest race lap: Bourdais, 1m 23.9166s, 144.572mph/232.666km/h.
Pole position: Rossi, 1m 22.4639s, 147.119mph/236.765km/h.
Championship points
Drivers: 1 Newgarden, 560; **2** Dixon, 557; **3** Castroneves, 538; **4** Pagenaud, 526; **5** Power, 492; **6** Rossi, 476.

GOPRO GRAND PRIX OF SONOMA, Infineon Raceway, Sears Point, Sonoma, California, USA, 17 September. Round 16. 85 laps of the 2.385-mile/3.838km circuit, 202.725 miles/326.254km.
1 Simon Pagenaud, F (-Chevrolet), 1h 55m 52.6840s, 104.968mph/168.930km/h; **2** Josef Newgarden, USA (-Chevrolet), +1.0986s; **3** Will Power, AUS (-Chevrolet), +1.6139s; **4** Scott Dixon, NZ (-Honda), +12.0870s; **5** Hélio Castroneves, BR (-Chevrolet), +22.5022s; **6** Graham Rahal, USA (-Honda), +23.5289s; **7** Marco Andretti, USA (-Honda), +23.9788s; **8** Ryan Hunter-Reay, USA (-Honda), +24.5140s; **9** Sébastien Bourdais, F (-Honda), +49.9911s; **10** Conor Daly, USA (-Chevrolet), +55.6650s; **11** Charlie Kimball, USA (-Honda), +1m 21.0203s; **12** Max Chilton, GB (-Honda), +1m 24.5038s; **13** Spencer Pigot, USA (-Chevrolet), -1 lap; **14** J.R. Hildebrand, USA (-Chevrolet), -1; **15** Carlos Muñoz, CO (-Chevrolet), -1; **16** Tony Kanaan, BR (-Honda), -1; **17** Zachary Claman, CDN (-Honda), -1; **18** Jack Harvey, GB (-Honda), -1; **19** Ed Jones, GB (-Honda), -16 (DNF-suspension); **20** Takuma Sato, J (-Honda), -23 (DNF-engine); **21** Alexander Rossi, USA (-Honda), -25; **22** James Hinchcliffe, CDN (-Honda), -33 (DNF-electrics).
Most laps led: Pagenaud, 41Newgarden, 41.
Fastest race lap: Pagenaud, 1m 18.3576s, 109.575mph/176.343km/h.
Pole position: Newgarden, 1m 15.5205s, 113.691mph/182.968km/h.

Final championship points
Drivers
1 Josef Newgarden, USA, 642; **2** Simon Pagenaud, F, 629; **3** Scott Dixon, NZ, 621; **4** Hélio Castroneves, BR, 598; **5** Will Power, AUS, 562; **6** Graham Rahal, USA, 522; **7** Alexander Rossi, USA, 494; **8** Takuma Sato, J, 441; **9** Ryan Hunter-Reay, USA, 421; **10** Tony Kanaan, BR, 403; **11** Max Chilton, GB, 396; **12** Marco Andretti, USA, 388; **13** James Hinchcliffe, CDN, 376; **14** Ed Jones, GB, 354; **15** J.R. Hildebrand, USA, 347; **16** Carlos Muñoz, CO, 328; **17** Charlie Kimball, USA, 327; **18** Conor Daly, USA, 305; **19** Mikhail Aleshin, RUS, 237; **20** Spencer Pigot, USA, 218; **21** Sébastien Bourdais, F, 214; **22** Ed Carpenter, USA, 169; **23** Gabby Chaves, CO, 98; **24** Juan Pablo Montoya, CO, 93; **25** Esteban Gutiérrez, MEX, 91; **26** Sebastian Saavedra, CO, 80; **27** Oriol Servià, E, 61; **28** Jack Harvey, GB, 57; **29** Fernando Alonso, E, 47; **30** Pippa Mann, GB, 32; **31** Zachary Claman, CDN, 26; **32** Jay Howard, GB, 24; **33** Zach Veach, USA, 23; **34** Sage Karam, USA, 23; **35** James Davison, AUS, 21; **36** Tristan Vautier, F, 15; **37** Buddy Lazier, USA, 14.

Rookies
1 Ed Jones, 354; **2** Esteban Gutiérrez, 91; **3** Jack Harvey, 57.

Engine manufacturers
1 Chevrolet, 1399; **2** Honda, 1294.

NASCAR Monster Energy Cup

THE 59TH ANNUAL DAYTONA 500, Daytona International Speedway, Daytona Beach, Florida, USA, 26 February. Round 1. 200 laps of the 2.500-mile/4.023km circuit, 500.000 miles/804.672km.
1 Kurt Busch, USA (Ford Fusion), 3h 29m 31s, 143.187mph/230.437km/h; **2** Ryan Blaney, USA (Ford Fusion), +0.228s; **3** A.J. Allmendinger, USA (Chevrolet SS), +0.419s; **4** Aric Almirola, USA (Ford Fusion), +1.195s; **5** Paul Menard, USA (Chevrolet SS), +1.564s; **6** Joey Logano, USA (Ford Fusion), +2.196s; **7** Kasey Kahne, USA (Chevrolet SS), +2.288s; **8** Michael Waltrip, USA (Toyota Camry), +8.826s; **9** Matt DiBenedetto, USA (Ford Fusion), +9.451s; **10** Trevor Bayne, USA (Ford Fusion), +9.581s.
Pole position: Chase Elliott, USA (Chevrolet SS), 46.663s, 192.872mph/310.398km/h.

Championship points
Drivers: 1 Busch (Kurt), 56; **2** Blaney, 44; **3** Logano, 43; **4** Harvick, 42; **5** Allmendinger, 39; **6** Almirola, 37.

58TH ANNUAL FOLDS OF HONOR QUIKTRIP 500, Atlanta Motor Speedway, Hampton, Georgia, USA, 5 March. Round 2. 325 laps of the 1.540-mile/2.478km circuit, 500.500 miles/805.477km.
1 Brad Keselowski, USA (Ford Fusion), 3h 33m 08s, 140.898mph/226.753km/h; **2** Kyle Larson, USA (Chevrolet SS), +0.564s; **3** Matt Kenseth, USA (Toyota Camry), +1.465s; **4** Kasey Kahne, USA (Chevrolet SS), +1.938s; **5** Chase Elliott, USA (Chevrolet SS), +2.222s; **6** Joey Logano, USA (Ford Fusion), +2.400s; **7** Kurt Busch, USA (Ford Fusion), +3.818s; **8** Martin Truex Jr, USA (Toyota Camry), +4.142s; **9** Kevin Harvick, USA (Ford Fusion), +4.900s; **10** Jamie McMurray, USA (Chevrolet SS), +6.397s.
Pole position: Harvick, 29.118s, 190.398mph/306.415km/h.
Championship points
Drivers: 1 Harvick, 90; **2** Busch (Kurt), 86; **3** Keselowski, 84; **4** Elliott, 82; **5** Logano, 80; **6** Larson, 79.

20TH ANNUAL KOBALT 400, Las Vegas Motor Speedway, Nevada, USA, 12 March. Round 3. 267 laps of the 1.500-mile/2.414km circuit, 400.500 miles/644.542km.
1 Martin Truex Jr, USA (Toyota Camry), 2h 56m 39s, 136.032mph/218.922km/h; **2** Kyle Larson, USA (Chevrolet SS), +1.495s; **3** Chase Elliott, USA (Chevrolet SS), +2.346s; **4** Joey Logano, USA (Ford Fusion), +3.501s; **5** Brad Keselowski, USA (Ford Fusion), +3.504s; **6** Denny Hamlin, USA (Toyota Camry), +3.802s; **7** Ryan Blaney, USA (Ford Fusion), +3.926s; **8** Jamie McMurray, USA (Chevrolet SS), +5.014s; **9** Matt Kenseth, USA (Toyota Camry), +5.126s; **10** Clint Bowyer, USA (Ford Fusion), +5.289s.
Pole position: Keselowski, 27.881s, 193.680mph/311.698km/h.
Championship points
Drivers: 1 Keselowski, 132; **2** Larson, 131; **3** Elliott, 129; **4** Truex Jr, 127; **5** Logano, 119; **6** Blaney, 106.

13TH ANNUAL CAMPING WORLD 500, Phoenix-International Raceway, Arizona, USA, 19 March. Round 4. 314 laps of the 1.000-mile/1.609km circuit, 314.000 miles/505.334km.
1 Ryan Newman, USA (Chevrolet SS), 3h 00m 41s, 104.271mph/167.808km/h; **2** Kyle Larson, USA (Chevrolet SS), +0.312s; **3** Kyle Busch, USA (Toyota Camry), +0.768s; **4** Ricky Stenhouse Jr, USA (Ford Fusion), +1.271s; **5** Brad Keselowski, USA (Ford Fusion), +1.286s; **6** Kevin Harvick, USA (Ford Fusion), +1.534s; **7** Daniel Suárez, MEX (Toyota Camry), +1.906s; **8** Erik Jones, USA (Toyota Camry), +2.019s; **9** Jimmie Johnson, USA (Chevrolet SS), +2.100s; **10** Denny Hamlin, USA (Toyota Camry), +2.201s.
Pole position: Joey Logano, USA (Ford Fusion), 26.216s, 137.321mph/220.996km/h.
Championship points
Drivers: 1 Larson, 184; **2** Elliott, 171; **3** Truex Jr, 153; **4** Keselowski, 143; **5** Logano, 135; **6** Blaney, 127.

21ST ANNUAL AUTO CLUB 400, California Speedway, Fontana, California, USA, 26 March. Round 5. 202 laps of the 2.000-mile/3.219km circuit, 404.000 miles/650.175km.
1 Kyle Larson, USA (Chevrolet SS), 2h 57m 46s, 136.359mph/219.448km/h; **2** Brad Keselowski, USA (Ford Fusion), +0.779s; **3** Clint Bowyer, USA (Ford Fusion), +1.030s; **4** Martin Truex Jr, USA (Toyota Camry), +1.513s; **5** Joey Logano, USA (Ford Fusion), +1.935s; **6** Jamie McMurray, USA (Chevrolet SS), +2.101s; **7** Daniel Suárez, MEX (Toyota Camry), +2.281s; **8** Kyle Busch, USA (Toyota Camry), +2.357s; **9** Ryan Blaney, USA (Ford Fusion), +2.402s; **10** Chase Elliott, USA (Chevrolet SS), +2.578s.
Pole position: Larson, 38.493s, 187.047mph/301.023km/h.
Championship points
Drivers: 1 Larson, 243; **2** Elliott, 214; **3** Truex Jr, 205; **4** Keselowski, 179; **5** Logano, 174; **6** McMurray, 162.

68TH ANNUAL STP 500, Martinsville Speedway, Virginia, USA, 2 April. Round 6. 500 laps of the 0.526-mile/0.847km circuit, 263.000 miles/423.257km.
1 Brad Keselowski, USA (Ford Fusion), 3h 44m 59s, 70.139mph/112.877km/h; **2** Kyle Busch, USA (Toyota Camry), +1.806s; **3** Chase Elliott, USA (Chevrolet SS), +2.152s; **4** Joey Logano, USA (Ford Fusion), +4.552s; **5** Austin Dillon, USA (Chevrolet SS), +4.945s; **6** A.J. Allmendinger, USA (Chevrolet SS), +5.882s; **7** Clint Bowyer, USA (Ford Fusion), +9.621s; **8** Ryan Newman, USA (Chevrolet SS), +11.144s; **9** Matt Kenseth, USA (Toyota Camry), +11.287s; **10** Ricky Stenhouse Jr, USA (Ford Fusion), +13.416s.
Pole position: Larson.
Championship points
Drivers: 1 Larson, 268; **2** Elliott, 264; **3** Truex Jr, 236; **4** Keselowski, 234; **5** Logano, 207; **6** Busch (Kyle), 188.

21ST ANNUAL O'REILLY AUTO PARTS 500, Texas Motor Speedway, Fort Worth, Texas, USA, 9 April. Round 7. 334 laps of the 1.500-mile/2.414km circuit, 501.000 miles/806.281km.
1 Jimmie Johnson, USA (Chevrolet SS), 3h 24m 18s, 147.137mph/236.793km/h; **2** Kyle Larson, USA (Chevrolet SS), +0.340s; **3** Joey Logano, USA (Ford Fusion), +1.252s; **4** Kevin Harvick, USA (Ford Fusion), +1.893s; **5** Dale Earnhardt Jr, USA (Chevrolet SS), +2.336s; **6** Brad Keselowski, USA (Ford Fusion), +2.826s; **7** Jamie McMurray, USA (Chevrolet SS), +3.804s; **8** Martin Truex Jr, USA (Toyota Camry), +3.922s; **9** Chase Elliott, USA (Chevrolet SS), +4.565s; **10** Kurt Busch, USA (Ford Fusion), +4.891s.
Pole position: Harvick, 27.217s, 198.405mph/319.303km/h.
Championship points
Drivers: 1 Larson, 315; **2** Elliott, 298; **3** Truex Jr, 275; **4** Keselowski, 274; **5** Logano, 243; **6** Blaney, 224.

57TH ANNUAL FOOD CITY 500, Bristol Motor Speedway, Tennessee, USA, 24 April. Round 8. 500 laps of the 0.533-mile/0.858km circuit, 266.500 miles/428.890km.
1 Jimmie Johnson, USA (Chevrolet SS), 3h 04m 29s, 86.674mph/139.489km/h; **2** Clint Bowyer, USA (Ford Fusion), +1.199s; **3** Kevin Harvick, USA (Ford Fusion), +2.543s; **4** Matt Kenseth, USA (Toyota Camry), +2.726s; **5** Joey Logano, USA (Ford Fusion), +2.837s; **6** Kyle Larson, USA (Chevrolet SS), +3.233s; **7** Chase Elliott, USA (Chevrolet SS), +3.925s; **8** Martin Truex Jr, USA (Toyota Camry), +4.264s; **9** Ricky Stenhouse Jr, USA (Ford Fusion), +4.984s; **10** Denny Hamlin, USA (Toyota Camry), +5.243s.
Pole position: Larson.
Championship points
Drivers: 1 Larson, 360; **2** Elliott, 333; **3** Truex Jr, 323; **4** Logano, 291; **5** Keselowski, 277; **6** Johnson, 244.

63RD ANNUAL TOYOTA OWNERS 400, Richmond International Raceway, Virginia, USA, 30 April. Round 9. 400 laps of the 0.750-mile/1.207km circuit, 300.000 miles/482.803km.
1 Joey Logano, USA (Ford Fusion), 3h 12m 08s, 93.685mph/150.771km/h; **2** Brad Keselowski, USA (Ford Fusion), +0.775s; **3** Denny Hamlin, USA (Toyota Camry), +2.495s; **4** Ricky Stenhouse Jr, USA (Ford Fusion), +6.437s; **5** Kevin Harvick, USA (Ford Fusion), +6.502s; **6** Jamie McMurray, USA (Chevrolet SS), +6.785s; **7** Ryan Newman, USA (Chevrolet SS), +7.954s; **8** Kurt Busch, USA (Ford Fusion), +8.086s; **9** Aric Almirola, USA (Ford Fusion), +8.580s; **10** Martin Truex Jr, USA (Toyota Camry), +10.290s.
Pole position: Matt Kenseth, USA (Toyota Camry), 22.300s, 121.076mph/194.853km/h.
Championship points
Drivers: 1 Larson, 398; **2** Truex Jr, 358; **3** Elliott, 346; **4** Keselowski, 327; **5** Logano, 308; **6** Harvick, 286.

48TH ANNUAL GEICO 500, Talladega Superspeedway, Alabama, USA, 7 May. Round 10. 191 laps of the 2.660-mile/4.281km circuit, 508.060 miles/817.643km.
1 Ricky Stenhouse Jr, USA (Ford Fusion), 3h 29m 16s, 145.669mph/234.431km/h; **2** Jamie McMurray, USA (Chevrolet SS), +0.095s; **3** Kyle Busch, USA (Toyota Camry), +0.099s; **4** Aric Almirola, USA (Ford Fusion), +0.182s; **5** Kasey Kahne, USA (Chevrolet SS), +0.204s; **6** Kurt Busch, USA (Ford Fusion), +0.216s; **7** Brad Keselowski, USA (Ford Fusion), +0.295s; **8** Jimmie Johnson, USA (Chevrolet SS), +0.315s; **9** Paul Menard, USA (Chevrolet SS), +0.330s; **10** David Ragan, USA (Ford Fusion), +0.402s.
Pole position: Stenhouse Jr, 49.993s, 191.547mph/308.265km/h.
Championship points
Drivers: 1 Larson, 428; **2** Truex Jr, 374; **3** Keselowski, 367; **4** Elliott, 353; **5** Logano, 318; **6** McMurray, 318.

7TH ANNUAL GO BOWLING 400, Kansas Speedway, Kansas City, Kansas, USA, 13 May. Round 11. 267 laps of the 1.500-mile/2.414km circuit, 400.500 miles/644.542km.
1 Martin Truex Jr, USA (Toyota Camry), 3h 24m 16s, 117.640mph/189.324km/h; **2** Brad Keselowski, USA (Ford Fusion), +1.100s; **3** Kevin Harvick, USA (Ford Fusion), +1.625s; **4** Ryan Blaney, USA (Ford Fusion), +1.842s; **5** Kyle Busch, USA (Toyota Camry), +2.045s; **6** Kyle Larson, USA (Chevrolet SS), +2.068s; **7** Daniel Suárez, MEX (Toyota Camry), +2.297s; **8** Jamie McMurray, USA (Chevrolet SS), +2.373s; **9** Clint Bowyer, USA (Ford Fusion), +2.800s; **10** Trevor Bayne, USA (Ford Fusion), +3.085s.
Pole position: Blaney, 28.481s, 189.600mph/305.132km/h.
Championship points
Drivers: 1 Larson, 475; **2** Truex Jr, 431; **3** Keselowski, 408; **4** Elliott, 361; **5** McMurray, 354; **6** Harvick, 347.

58TH ANNUAL COCA-COLA 600, Lowe's Motor Speedway, Concord, Charlotte, North Carolina, USA, 28 May. Round 12. 400 laps of the 1.500-mile/2.414km circuit, 600.000 miles/965.606km.
1 Austin Dillon, USA (Chevrolet SS), 4h 19m 22s, 138.800mph/223.376km/h; **2** Kyle Busch, USA (Toyota Camry), +0.835s; **3** Martin Truex Jr, USA (Toyota Camry), +1.152s; **4** Matt Kenseth, USA (Toyota Camry), +5.378s; **5** Denny Hamlin, USA (Toyota Camry), +10.611s; **6** Kurt Busch, USA (Ford Fusion), +11.429s; **7** Erik Jones, USA (Toyota Camry), +14.409s; **8** Kevin Harvick, USA (Ford Fusion), +16.323s; **9** Ryan Newman, USA (Chevrolet SS), +18.703s; **10** Dale Earnhardt Jr, USA (Chevrolet SS), +20.486s.
Pole position: Harvick, 27.918s, 193.424mph/311.285km/h.
Championship points
Drivers: 1 Truex Jr, 491; **2** Larson, 486; **3** Keselowski, 409; **4** Harvick, 388; **5** Busch (Kyle), 386; **6** McMurray, 385.

48TH ANNUAL AAA 400 DRIVE FOR AUTISM, Dover International Speedway, Delaware, USA, 4 June. Round 13. 406 laps of the 1.000-mile/1.609km circuit, 406.000 miles/653.394km.
1 Jimmie Johnson, USA (Chevrolet SS), 3h 52m 06s, 104.955mph/168.908km/h; **2** Kyle Larson, USA (Chevrolet SS), 406 laps; **3** Martin Truex Jr, USA (Toyota Camry), 406; **4** Ryan Newman, USA (Chevrolet SS), 406; **5** Chase Elliott, USA (Chevrolet SS), 406; **6** Daniel Suárez, MEX (Toyota Camry), 406; **7** Jamie McMurray, USA (Chevrolet SS), 406; **8** Denny Hamlin, USA (Toyota Camry), 406; **9** Kevin Harvick, USA (Ford Fusion), 406; **10** Danica Patrick, USA (Ford Fusion), 406.
Pole position: Kyle Busch, USA (Toyota Camry), 22.648s, 158.954mph/255.812km/h.
Championship points
Drivers: 1 Truex Jr, 545; **2** Larson, 536; **3** Harvick, 429; **4** Busch (Kyle), 416; **5** McMurray, 415; **6** Johnson, 414.

36TH ANNUAL POCONO 400, Pocono Raceway, Long Pond, Pennsylvania, USA, 11 June. Round 14. 160 laps of the 2.500-mile/4.023km circuit, 400.000 miles/643.738km.
1 Ryan Blaney, USA (Ford Fusion), 2h 48m 40s, 142.292mph/228.998km/h; **2** Kevin Harvick, USA (Ford Fusion), +0.139s; **3** Erik Jones, USA (Toyota Camry), +1.822s; **4** Kurt Busch, USA (Ford Fusion), +3.112s; **5** Brad Keselowski, USA (Ford Fusion), +3.328s; **6** Martin Truex Jr, USA (Toyota Camry), +4.557s; **7** Kyle Larson, USA (Chevrolet SS), +4.764s; **8** Chase Elliott, USA (Chevrolet SS), +5.889s; **9** Kyle Busch, USA (Toyota Camry), +7.265s; **10** Matt Kenseth, USA (Toyota Camry), +7.625s.
Pole position: Busch, 50.237s, 179.151mph/288.315km/h.
Championship points
Drivers: 1 Truex Jr, 584; **2** Larson, 583; **3** Harvick, 480; **4** Busch (Kyle), 463; **5** Keselowski, 454; **6** Elliott, 438.

49TH ANNUAL FIREKEEPERS CASINO 400, Michigan International Speedway, Brooklyn, Michigan, USA, 18 June. Round 15. 200 laps of the 2.000-mile/3.219km circuit, 400.000 miles/643.738km.
1 Kyle Larson, USA (Chevrolet SS), 2h 47m 24s, 143.369mph/230.730km/h; **2** Chase Elliott, USA (Chevrolet SS), +0.993s; **3** Joey Logano, USA (Ford Fusion), +1.631s; **4** Denny Hamlin, USA (Toyota Camry), +1.917s; **5** Jamie McMurray, USA (Chevrolet SS), +3.199s; **6** Martin Truex Jr, USA (Toyota Camry), +3.333s; **7** Kyle Busch, USA (Toyota Camry), +4.042s; **8** Ricky Stenhouse Jr, USA (Ford Fusion), +4.190s; **9** Dale Earnhardt Jr, USA (Chevrolet SS), +4.617s; **10** Jimmie Johnson, USA (Chevrolet SS), +4.949s.
Pole position: Larson, 35.616s, 202.156mph/325.339km/h.
Championship points
Drivers: 1 Larson, 640; **2** Truex Jr, 635; **3** Busch (Kyle), 510; **4** Harvick, 508; **5** Elliott, 478; **6** Keselowski, 476.

29TH ANNUAL TOYOTA/SAVE MART 350, Infineon Raceway, Sears Point, Sonoma, California, USA, 25 June. Round 16. 110 laps of the 1.990-mile/3.203km circuit, 218.900 miles/352.285km.
1 Kevin Harvick, USA (Ford Fusion), 2h 46m 52s, 78.710mph/126.671km/h; **2** Clint Bowyer, USA (Ford Fusion), 110 laps; **3** Brad Keselowski, USA (Ford Fusion), 110; **4** Denny Hamlin, USA (Toyota Camry), 110; **5** Kyle Busch, USA (Toyota Camry), 110; **6** Dale Earnhardt Jr, USA (Chevrolet SS), 110; **7** Kurt Busch, USA (Ford Fusion), 110; **8** Chase Elliott, USA (Chevrolet SS), 110; **9** Ryan Blaney, USA (Ford Fusion), 110; **10** Jamie McMurray, USA (Chevrolet SS), 110.
Pole position: Kyle Larson, USA (Chevrolet SS), 1m 15.177s, 95.295mph/153.363km/h.
Championship points
Drivers: 1 Larson, 659; **2** Truex Jr, 646; **3** Harvick, 548; **4** Busch (Kyle), 542; **5** Keselowski, 519; **6** Elliott, 509.

59TH ANNUAL COKE ZERO 400 POWERED BY COCA-COLA, Daytona International Speedway, Daytona Beach, Florida, USA, 1 July. Round 17. 163 laps of the 2.500-mile/4.023km circuit, 407.500 miles/655.808km.
1 Ricky Stenhouse Jr, USA (Ford Fusion), 3h 17m 12s, 123.986mph/199.536km/h; **2** Clint Bowyer, USA (Ford Fusion), +0.213s; **3** Paul Menard, USA (Chevrolet SS), +0.269s; **4** Michael McDowell, USA (Chevrolet SS), +0.379s; **5** Ryan Newman, USA (Chevrolet SS), +0.385s; **6** David Ragan, USA (Ford Fusion), +0.466s; **7** Brendan Gaughan, USA (Chevrolet SS), +0.491s; **8** A.J. Allmendinger, USA (Chevrolet SS), +0.540s; **9** Erik Jones, USA (Toyota Camry), +0.562s; **10** Chris Buescher, USA (Chevrolet SS), +0.681s.
Pole position: Dale Earnhardt Jr, USA (Chevrolet SS), 47.127s, 190.973mph/307.342km/h.
Championship points
Drivers: 1 Larson, 667; **2** Truex Jr, 649; **3** Busch (Kyle), 559; **4** Harvick, 557; **5** Keselowski, 535; **6** Elliott, 524.

7TH ANNUAL QUAKER STATE 400 PRESENTED BY ADVANCE AUTO PARTS, Kentucky Speedway, Fort Mitchell, Kentucky, USA, 8 July. Round 18. 274 laps of the 1.500-mile/2.414km circuit, 411.000 miles/661.440km.
1 Martin Truex Jr, USA (Toyota Camry), 2h 57m 55s, 138.604mph/223.062km/h; **2** Kyle Larson, USA (Chevrolet SS), 274 laps; **3** Chase Elliott, USA (Chevrolet SS), 274; **4** Denny Hamlin, USA (Toyota Camry), 274; **5** Kyle Busch, USA (Toyota Camry), 274; **6** Erik Jones, USA (Toyota Camry), 274; **7** Jamie McMurray, USA (Chevrolet SS), 274; **8** Joey Logano, USA (Ford Fusion), 274; **9** Kevin Harvick, USA (Ford Fusion), 274; **10** Ryan Blaney, USA (Ford Fusion), -1.
Pole position: Busch, 28.379s, 190.282mph/306.228km/h.
Championship points
Drivers: 1 Truex Jr, 709; **2** Larson, 675; **3** Busch (Kyle), 609; **4** Harvick, 599; **5** Elliott, 560; **6** McMurray, 545.

25TH ANNUAL OVERTON'S 301, New Hampshire International Speedway, Loudon, New Hampshire, USA, 16 July. Round 19. 301 laps of the 1.058-mile/1.703km circuit, 318.458 miles/512.508km.
1 Denny Hamlin, USA (Toyota Camry), 3h 00m 36s, 105.800mph/170.269km/h; **2** Kyle Larson, USA (Chevrolet SS), +0.509s; **3** Martin Truex Jr, USA (Toyota Camry), +3.297s; **4** Matt Kenseth, USA (Toyota Camry), +4.442s; **5** Kevin Harvick, USA (Ford Fusion), +8.452s; **6** Daniel Suárez, MEX (Toyota Camry), +9.846s; **7** Clint Bowyer, USA (Ford Fusion), +10.618s; **8** Kurt Busch, USA (Ford Fusion), +10.655s; **9** Brad Keselowski, USA (Ford Fusion), +11.451s; **10** Jimmie Johnson, USA (Chevrolet SS), +12.642s.
Pole position: Truex Jr, 28.621s, 133.077mph/214.167km/h.
Championship points
Drivers: 1 Truex Jr, 758; **2** Larson, 720; **3** Busch (Kyle), 650; **4** Harvick, 639; **5** Hamlin, 589; **6** Elliott, 587.

24TH ANNUAL BRICKYARD 400, Indianapolis Motor Speedway, Speedway, Indiana, USA, 23 July. Round 20. 167 laps of the 2.500-mile/4.023km circuit, 417.500 miles/671.901km.
1 Kasey Kahne, USA (Chevrolet SS), 3h 39m 00s, 114.384mph/184.082km/h; **2** Brad Keselowski, USA (Ford Fusion), 167 laps; **3** Ryan Newman, USA (Chevrolet SS), 167; **4** Joey Logano, USA (Ford Fusion), 167; **5** Matt Kenseth, USA (Toyota Camry), 167; **6** Kevin Harvick, USA (Ford Fusion), 167; **7** Daniel Suárez, MEX (Toyota Camry), 167; **8** Matt DiBenedetto, USA (Ford Fusion), 167; **9** Chris Buescher, USA (Chevrolet SS), 167; **10** A.J. Allmendinger, USA (Chevrolet SS), 167.
Pole position: Kyle Busch, USA (Toyota Camry), 48.051s, 187.301mph/301.432km/h.
Championship points
Drivers: 1 Truex Jr, 780; **2** Larson, 732; **3** Harvick, 683; **4** Busch (Kyle), 673; **5** Hamlin, 612; **6** Keselowski, 601.

44TH ANNUAL OVERTON'S 400, Pocono Raceway, Long Pond, Pennsylvania, USA, 30 July. Round 21. 160 laps of the 2.500-mile/4.023km circuit, 400.000 miles/643.738km.
1 Kyle Busch, USA (Toyota Camry), 2h 50m 07s, 141.080mph/227.046km/h; **2** Kevin Harvick, USA (Ford Fusion), +6.178s; **3** Martin Truex Jr, USA (Toyota Camry), +6.821s; **4** Denny Hamlin, USA (Toyota Camry), +8.653s; **5** Brad Keselowski, USA (Ford Fusion), +9.345s; **6** Clint Bowyer, USA (Ford Fusion), +16.363s; **7** Daniel Suárez, MEX (Toyota Camry), +18.969s; **8** Erik Jones, USA (Toyota Camry), +19.327s; **9** Matt Kenseth, USA (Toyota Camry), +21.854s; **10** Chase Elliott, USA (Chevrolet SS), +22.220s.
Pole position: Busch, 50.175s, 179.372mph/288.672km/h.
Championship points
Drivers: 1 Truex Jr, 823; **2** Larson, 738; **3** Harvick, 726; **4** Busch (Kyle), 723; **5** Keselowski, 649; **6** Hamlin, 649.

32ND ANNUAL I LOVE NEW YORK 355 AT THE GLEN, Watkins Glen International, New York, USA, 6 August. Round 22. 90 laps of the 2.450-mile/3.943km circuit, 220.500 miles/354.860km.
1 Martin Truex Jr, USA (Toyota Camry), 2h 07m 03s, 104.132mph/167.585km/h; **2** Matt Kenseth, USA (Toyota Camry), +0.414s; **3** Daniel Suárez, MEX (Toyota Camry), +5.115s; **4** Denny Hamlin, USA (Toyota Camry), +13.989s; **5** Clint Bowyer, USA (Ford Fusion), +14.176s; **6** Kurt

Busch, USA (Ford Fusion), +14.966s; **7** Kyle Busch, USA (Toyota Camry), +17.014s; **8** Ryan Blaney, USA (Ford Fusion), +20.770s; **9** A.J. Allmendinger, USA (Chevrolet SS), +21.505s; **10** Erik Jones, USA (Toyota Camry), +22.694s.
Pole position: Busch, 1m 09.490s, 126.925mph/204.266km/h.
Championship points
Drivers: 1 Truex Jr, 881; **2** Busch (Kyle), 765; **3** Larson, 759; **4** Harvick, 746; **5** Hamlin, 687; **6** Keselowski, 681.

48TH ANNUAL PURE MICHIGAN 400, Michigan International Speedway, Brooklyn, Michigan, USA, 13 August. Round 23. 202 laps of the 2.000-mile/3.219km circuit, 404.000 miles/650.175km.
1 Kyle Larson, USA (Chevrolet SS), 2h 40m 38s, 150.903mph/242.854km/h; **2** Martin Truex Jr, USA (Toyota Camry), +0.310s; **3** Erik Jones, USA (Toyota Camry), +0.970s; **4** Ryan Newman, USA (Chevrolet SS), +1.308s; **5** Trevor Bayne, USA (Ford Fusion), +1.632s; **6** Chris Buescher, USA (Chevrolet SS), +1.777s; **7** Austin Dillon, USA (Chevrolet SS), +2.074s; **8** Chase Elliott, USA (Chevrolet SS), +2.206s; **9** Jamie McMurray, USA (Chevrolet SS), +2.270s; **10** Kyle Busch, USA (Toyota Camry), +2.706s.
Pole position: Brad Keselowski, USA (Ford Fusion), 35.451s, 203.097mph/326.853km/h.
Championship points
Drivers: 1 Truex Jr, 933; **2** Larson, 804; **3** Busch (Kyle), 797; **4** Harvick, 787; **5** Keselowski, 720; **6** Hamlin, 710.

57TH ANNUAL BASS PRO SHOPS NRA NIGHT RACE, Bristol Motor Speedway, Tennessee, USA, 19 August. Round 24. 500 laps of the 0.533-mile/0.858km circuit, 266.500 miles/428.890km.
1 Kyle Busch, USA (Toyota Camry), 2h 46m 37s, 95.969mph/154.447km/h; **2** Erik Jones, USA (Toyota Camry), +1.422s; **3** Denny Hamlin, USA (Toyota Camry), +5.069s; **4** Matt Kenseth, USA (Toyota Camry), +7.391s; **5** Kurt Busch, USA (Ford Fusion), +7.843s; **6** Ryan Newman, USA (Chevrolet SS), +10.140s; **7** Trevor Bayne, USA (Ford Fusion), +10.519s; **8** Kevin Harvick, USA (Ford Fusion), +10.796s; **9** Kyle Larson, USA (Chevrolet SS), +11.109s; **10** Ryan Blaney, USA (Ford Fusion), +12.289s.
Pole position: Jones, 14.981s, 128.082mph/206.128km/h.
Championship points
Drivers: 1 Truex Jr, 951; **2** Busch (Kyle), 850; **3** Larson, 845; **4** Harvick, 824; **5** Hamlin, 753; **6** Keselowski, 728.

68TH ANNUAL BOJANGLES' SOUTHERN 500, Darlington Raceway, South Carolina, USA, 3 September. Round 25. 367 laps of the 1.366-mile/2.198km circuit, 501.322 miles/806.800km.
1 Denny Hamlin, USA (Toyota Camry), 3h 46m 34s, 132.761mph/213.659km/h; **2** Kyle Busch, USA (Toyota Camry), +2.599s; **3** Kurt Busch, USA (Ford Fusion), +11.587s; **4** Austin Dillon, USA (Chevrolet SS), +12.929s; **5** Erik Jones, USA (Toyota Camry), +20.550s; **6** Matt Kenseth, USA (Toyota Camry), 367 laps; **7** Ryan Newman, USA (Chevrolet SS), 367; **8** Martin Truex Jr, USA (Toyota Camry), 367; **9** Kevin Harvick, USA (Ford Fusion), -1; **10** Jamie McMurray, USA (Chevrolet SS), -1.
Pole position: Harvick, 27.669s, 177.730mph/286.028km/h.
Championship points
Drivers: 1 Truex Jr, 1000; **2** Busch (Kyle), 893; **3** Larson, 884; **4** Harvick, 867; **5** Hamlin, 785; **6** Keselowski, 761.

60TH ANNUAL FEDERATED AUTO PARTS 400, Richmond International Raceway, Virginia, USA, 9 September. Round 26. 404 laps of the 0.750-mile/1.207km circuit, 303.000 miles/487.631km.
1 Kyle Larson, USA (Chevrolet SS), 3h 02m 52s, 99.417mph/159.996km/h; **2** Joey Logano, USA (Ford Fusion), 404 laps; **3** Ryan Newman, USA (Chevrolet SS), 404; **4** Kurt Busch, USA (Ford Fusion), 404; **5** Denny Hamlin, USA (Toyota Camry), 404; **6** Erik Jones, USA (Toyota Camry), 404; **7** Daniel Suárez, MEX (Toyota Camry), 404; **8** Jimmie Johnson, USA (Chevrolet SS), 404; **9** Kyle Busch, USA (Toyota Camry), 404; **10** Chase Elliott, USA (Chevrolet SS), 404.
Pole position: Matt Kenseth, USA (Toyota Camry), 22.055s, 122.421mph/197.018km/h.
Championship points
Drivers: 1 Truex Jr, 2053; **2** Larson, 2033; **3** Busch (Kyle), 2029; **4** Keselowski, 2019; **5** Johnson, 2017; **6** Harvick, 2015.

17TH ANNUAL TALES OF THE TURTLES 400, Chicagoland Speedway, Chicago, Illinois, USA, 17 September. Round 27. 267 laps of the 1.500-mile/2.414km circuit, 400.500 miles/644.542km.
1 Martin Truex Jr, USA (Toyota Camry), 2h 45m 16s, 145.401mph/234.001km/h; **2** Chase Elliott, USA (Chevrolet SS), +7.179s; **3** Kevin Harvick, USA (Ford Fusion), +10.200s; **4** Denny Hamlin, USA (Toyota Camry), +11.212s; **5** Kyle Larson, USA (Chevrolet SS), +13.236s; **6** Brad Keselowski, USA (Ford Fusion), +18.232s; **7** Joey Logano, USA (Ford Fusion), +18.363s; **8** Jimmie Johnson, USA (Chevrolet SS), +20.615s; **9** Matt Kenseth, USA (Toyota Camry), +22.217s; **10** Jamie McMurray, USA (Chevrolet SS), 267 laps.
Pole position: Kyle Busch, USA (Toyota Camry), 28.729s, 187.963mph/302.498km/h.
Championship points
Drivers: 1 Truex Jr, 2102; **2** Larson, 2075; **3** Harvick, 2067; **4** Keselowski, 2061; **5** Busch (Kyle), 2061; **6** Hamlin, 2058.

21ST ANNUAL ISM CONNECT 300, New Hampshire International Speedway, Loudon, New Hampshire, USA, 24 September. Round 28. 300 laps of the 1.058-mile/1.703km circuit, 317.400 miles/510.806km.
1 Kyle Busch, USA (Toyota Camry), 2h 54m 47s, 108.958mph/175.351km/h; **2** Kyle Larson, USA (Chevrolet SS), +2.641s; **3** Matt Kenseth, USA (Toyota Camry), +6.936s; **4** Brad Keselowski, USA (Ford Fusion), +7.551s; **5** Martin Truex Jr, USA (Toyota Camry), +8.804s; **6** Erik Jones, USA (Toyota Camry), +9.357s; **7** Clint Bowyer, USA (Ford Fusion), +10.003s; **8** Daniel Suárez, MEX (Toyota Camry), +13.845s; **9** Ryan Blaney, USA (Ford Fusion), +14.374s; **10** Joey Logano, USA (Ford Fusion), +14.725s.
Pole position: Busch, 28.203s, 135.049mph/217.341km/h.
Championship points: Drivers
1 Truex Jr, 2149; **2** Larson, 2125; **3** Busch (Kyle), 2119; **4** Keselowski, 2106; **5** Hamlin, 2088; **6** Kenseth, 2087.

48TH ANNUAL APACHE WARRIOR 400 PRESENTED BY LUCAS OIL, Dover International Speedway, Delaware, USA, 1 October. Round 29. 400 laps of the 1.000-mile/1.609km circuit, 400.000 miles/643.738km.
1 Kyle Busch, USA (Toyota Camry), 3h 05m 48s, 129.171mph/207.881km/h; **2** Chase Elliott, USA (Chevrolet SS), +0.357s; **3** Jimmie Johnson, USA (Chevrolet SS), +4.276s; **4** Martin Truex Jr, USA (Toyota Camry), +9.686s; **5** Kyle Larson, USA (Chevrolet SS), +12.489s; **6** Clint Bowyer, USA (Ford Fusion), +14.840s; **7** Dale Earnhardt Jr, USA (Chevrolet SS), +15.911s; **8** Daniel Suárez, MEX (Toyota Camry), +16.305s; **9** Jamie McMurray, USA (Chevrolet SS), +18.743s; **10** Brad Keselowski, USA (Ford Fusion), +19.469s.
Pole position: Truex Jr, 22.407s, 160.664mph/258.564km/h.
Championship points
Drivers: 1 Truex Jr, 3059; **2** Busch (Kyle), 3041; **3** Larson, 3034; **4** Keselowski, 3020; **5** Johnson, 3017; **6** Harvick, 3015.

58TH ANNUAL BANK OF AMERICA 500, Lowe's Motor Speedway, Concord, Charlotte, North Carolina, USA, 8 October. Round 30. 337 laps of the 1.500-mile/2.414km circuit, 505.500 miles/813.523km.
1 Martin Truex Jr, USA (Toyota Camry), 3h 38m 00s, 139.128mph/223.906km/h; **2** Chase Elliott, USA (Chevrolet SS), +0.911s; **3** Kevin Harvick, USA (Ford Fusion), +1.404s; **4** Denny Hamlin, USA (Toyota Camry), +1.645s; **5** Jamie McMurray, USA (Chevrolet SS), +1.977s; **6** Daniel Suárez, MEX (Toyota Camry), +2.164s; **7** Jimmie Johnson, USA (Chevrolet SS), +2.337s; **8** Ryan Blaney, USA (Ford Fusion), +2.491s; **9** Kasey Kahne, USA (Chevrolet SS), +2.844s; **10** Kyle Larson, USA (Chevrolet SS), +3.234s.
Pole position: Hamlin, 28.184s, 191.598mph/308.347km/h.
Championship points
Drivers: 1 Truex Jr, 3106; **2** Larson, 3072; **3** Harvick, 3069; **4** Elliott, 3059; **5** Hamlin, 3056; **6** Busch (Kyle), 3055.

49TH ANNUAL ALABAMA 500, Talladega Superspeedway, Alabama, USA, 15 October. Round 31. 188 laps of the 2.660-mile/4.281km circuit, 500.080 miles/804.801km.
1 Brad Keselowski, USA (Ford Fusion), 3h 47m 52s, 131.677mph/211.914km/h; **2** Ryan Newman, USA (Chevrolet SS), +0.210s; **3** Trevor Bayne, USA (Ford Fusion), +0.249s; **4** Joey Logano, USA (Ford Fusion), +0.291s; **5** Aric Almirola, USA (Ford Fusion), +0.378s; **6** Denny Hamlin, USA (Toyota Camry), +0.381s; **7** Dale Earnhardt Jr, USA (Chevrolet SS), +0.408s; **8** Kasey Kahne, USA (Chevrolet SS), +0.434s; **9** Gray Gaulding, USA (Toyota Camry), +1.857s; **10** David Ragan, USA (Ford Fusion), +2.052s.
Pole position: Earnhardt Jr, 50.256s, 190.544mph/306.652km/h.
Championship points
Drivers: 1 Truex Jr, 3120; **2** Keselowski, 3101; **3** Larson, 3096; **4** Harvick, 3089; **5** Hamlin, 3088; **6** Elliott, 3087.

17TH ANNUAL HOLLYWOOD CASINO 400, Kansas Speedway, Kansas City, Kansas, USA, 22 October. Round 32. 267 laps of the 1.500-mile/2.414km circuit, 400.500 miles/644.542km.
1 Martin Truex Jr, USA (Toyota Camry), 3h 11m 57s, 125.189mph/201.472km/h; **2** Kurt Busch, USA (Ford Fusion), +2.284s; **3** Ryan Blaney, USA (Ford Fusion), +3.945s; **4** Chase Elliott, USA (Chevrolet SS), +5.362s; **5** Denny Hamlin, USA (Toyota Camry), +8.542s; **6** Chris Buescher, USA (Chevrolet SS), +11.051s; **7** Dale Earnhardt Jr, USA (Chevrolet SS), +11.895s; **8** Kevin Harvick, USA (Ford Fusion), +12.356s; **9** Aric Almirola, USA (Ford Fusion), +14.207s; **10** Kyle Busch, USA (Toyota Camry), +15.046s.
Pole position: Truex Jr, 28.719s, 188.029mph/302.603km/h.
Championship points
Drivers: 1 Truex Jr, 4069; **2** Busch (Kyle), 4042; **3** Keselowski, 4026; **4** Harvick, 4017; **5** Johnson, 4017; **6** Hamlin, 4014.

69TH ANNUAL FIRST DATA 500, Martinsville Speedway, Virginia, USA, 29 October. Round 33. 505 laps of the 0.526-mile/0.847km circuit, 265.630 miles/427.490km.
1 Kyle Busch, USA (Toyota Camry), 3h 32m 47s, 74.902mph/120.542km/h; **2** Martin Truex Jr, USA (Toyota Camry), +0.141s; **3** Clint Bowyer, USA (Ford Fusion), +0.379s; **4** Brad Keselowski, USA (Ford Fusion), +0.991s; **5** Kevin Harvick, USA (Ford Fusion), +1.540s; **6** Trevor Bayne, USA (Ford Fusion), +1.700s; **7** Denny Hamlin, USA (Toyota Camry), +1.905s; **8** Ryan Blaney, USA (Ford Fusion), +1.911s; **9** Matt Kenseth, USA (Toyota Camry), +1.920s; **10** Ricky Stenhouse Jr, USA (Ford Fusion), +1.981s.
Pole position: Joey Logano, USA (Ford Fusion), 19.622s, 96.504mph/155.308km/h.
Championship points
Drivers: 1 Truex Jr, 4117; **2** Busch (Kyle), 4100; **3** Keselowski, 4079; **4** Harvick, 4053; **5** Johnson, 4050; **6** Blaney, 4047.

13TH ANNUAL AAA TEXAS 500, Texas Motor Speedway, Fort Worth, Texas, USA, 5 November. Round 34. 334 laps of the 1.500-mile/2.414km circuit, 501.000 miles/806.281km.
1 Kevin Harvick, USA (Ford Fusion), 3h 29m 52s, 143.234mph/230.512km/h; **2** Martin Truex Jr, USA (Toyota Camry), +1.580s; **3** Denny Hamlin, USA (Toyota Camry), +5.832s; **4** Matt Kenseth, USA (Toyota Camry), +6.024s; **5** Brad Keselowski, USA (Ford Fusion), +8.491s; **6** Ryan Blaney, USA (Ford Fusion), +9.186s; **7** Joey Logano, USA (Ford Fusion), +9.395s; **8** Chase Elliott, USA (Chevrolet SS), +10.585s; **9** Kurt Busch, USA (Ford Fusion), +11.207s; **10** Erik Jones, USA (Toyota Camry), +12.017s.
Pole position: Busch, 26.877s, 200.915mph/323.342km/h.
Championship points
Drivers: 1 Truex Jr, 4168; **2** Busch (Kyle), 4118; **3** Harvick, 4112; **4** Keselowski, 4111; **5** Hamlin, 4092; **6** Blaney, 4089.

30TH ANNUAL CAN-AM 500, Phoenix International Raceway, Arizona, USA, 12 November. Round 35. 312 laps of the 1.000-mile/1.609km circuit, 312.000 miles/502.115km.
1 Matt Kenseth, USA (Toyota Camry), 2h 57m 23s, 105.534mph/169.841km/h; **2** Chase Elliott, USA (Chevrolet SS), +1.207s; **3** Martin Truex Jr, USA (Toyota Camry), +1.358s; **4** Erik Jones, USA (Toyota Camry), +1.435s; **5** Kevin Harvick, USA (Ford Fusion), +1.750s; **6** Jamie McMurray, USA (Chevrolet SS), +3.904s; **7** Kyle Busch, USA (Toyota Camry), +4.428s; **8** Ricky Stenhouse Jr, USA (Ford Fusion), +4.730s; **9** Aric Almirola, USA (Ford Fusion), +5.166s; **10** Dale Earnhardt Jr, USA (Chevrolet SS), +7.267s.
Pole position: Ryan Blaney, USA (Ford Fusion), 26.098s, 137.942mph/221.995km/h.
Championship points
Drivers: 1 Harvick, 5000; **2** Busch (Kyle), 5000; **3** Truex Jr, 5000; **4** Keselowski, 5000; **5** Elliott, 2338; **6** Hamlin, 2321.

19TH ANNUAL FORD ECOBOOST 400, Homestead-Miami Speedway, Florida, USA, 19 November. Round 36. 267 laps of the 1.500-mile/2.414km circuit, 400.500 miles/644.542km.
1 Martin Truex Jr, USA (Toyota Camry), 3h 02m 11s, 131.900mph/212.273km/h; **2** Kyle Busch, USA (Toyota Camry), +0.681s; **3** Kyle Larson, USA (Chevrolet SS), +1.580s; **4** Kevin Harvick, USA (Ford Fusion), +8.150s; **5** Chase Elliott, USA (Chevrolet SS), +10.824s; **6** Joey Logano, USA (Ford Fusion), +13.934s; **7** Brad Keselowski, USA (Ford Fusion), +15.566s; **8** Matt Kenseth, USA (Toyota Camry), +15.765s; **9** Denny Hamlin, USA (Toyota Camry), +16.212s; **10** Ryan Newman, USA (Chevrolet SS), +20.188s.
Pole position: Hamlin, 31.038s, 173.980mph/279.994km/h.

Final championship points
Drivers
1 Martin Truex Jr, USA, 5040; **2** Kyle Busch, USA, 5035; **3** Kevin Harvick, USA, 5033; **4** Brad Keselowski, USA, 5030; **5** Chase Elliott, USA, 2377; **6** Denny Hamlin, USA, 2353; **7** Matt Kenseth, USA, 2344; **8** Kyle Larson, USA, 2320; **9** Ryan Blaney, USA, 2305; **10** Jimmie Johnson, USA, 2260; **11** Austin Dillon, USA, 2224; **12** Jamie McMurray, USA, 2224; **13** Ricky Stenhouse Jr, USA, 2222; **14** Kurt Busch, USA, 2217; **15** Kasey Kahne, USA, 2198; **16** Ryan Newman, USA, 2196; **17** Joey Logano, USA, 930; **18** Clint Bowyer, USA, 871; **19** Erik Jones, USA, 863; **20** Daniel Suárez, MEX, 777; **21** Dale Earnhardt Jr, USA, 668; **22** Trevor Bayne, USA, 660; **23** Paul Menard, USA, 631; **24** Ty Dillon, USA, 593; **25** Chris Buescher, USA, 564; **26** Michael McDowell, USA, 542; **27** A.J. Allmendinger, USA, 531; **28** Danica Patrick, USA, 511; **29** Aric Almirola, USA, 502; **30** David Ragan, USA, 447.

Manufacturers
1 Toyota, 1292; **2** Ford, 1254; **3** Chevrolet, 1247.

Sunoco Rookie of the Year: Erik Jones, USA.

Other NASCAR races

ADVANCE AUTO PARTS CLASH AT DAYTONA, Daytona International Speedway, Daytona Beach, Florida, USA, 19 February. 75 laps of the 2.500-mile/4.023km circuit, 187.500 miles/301.752km.
1 Joey Logano, USA (Ford Fusion) 1h 18m 13s, 143.831mph/231.474km/h; **2** Kyle Busch, USA (Toyota Camry), +1.120s; **3** Alex Bowman, USA (Chevrolet SS), 75 laps; **4** Danica Patrick, USA (Ford Fusion), 75; **5** Kevin Harvick, USA (Ford Fusion), 75; **6** Brad Keselowski, USA (Ford Fusion), 75; **7** Chase Elliott, USA (Chevrolet SS), 75; **8** Daniel Suárez, MEX (Toyota Camry), 75; **9** Chris Buescher, USA (Chevrolet SS), 75; **10** Jamie McMurray, USA (Chevrolet SS), 75.
Pole position: Brad Keselowski (by random draw)
Race scheduled for 18 February, but postponed because of rain.

MONSTER ENERGY NASCAR ALL-STAR RACE, Lowe's Motor Speedway, Concord, Charlotte, North Carolina, USA, 20 May. 70 laps of the 1.500-mile/2.414km circuit, 105.000 miles/168.981km.
1 Kyle Busch, USA (Toyota), 1h 12m 47.0s, 86.558mph/139.302km/h; **2** Kyle Larson, USA (Chevrolet SS), +1,274s; **3** Jimmie Johnson, USA (Chevrolet SS), 70 laps; **4** Kurt Busch, USA (Ford Fusion), 70; **5** Jamie McMurray, USA (Chevrolet SS), 70; **6** Kevin Harvick, USA (Ford Fusion), 70; **7** Chase Elliott, USA (Chevrolet SS), 70; **8** Joey Logano, USA (Ford Fusion), 70; **9** Brad Keselowski, USA (Ford Fusion), 70; **10** Denny Hamlin, USA (Toyota Camry), -4.
Pole position: Larson, 1m 52.626s, 143.839mph/231.486km/h.

Indy Lights Presented by Cooper Tires

All cars are Dallara IL15-Mazda.

MAZDA GRAND PRIX OF ST. PETERSBURG PRESENTED BY COOPER TIRES, St. Petersburg Street Circuit, Florida, USA, 11/12 March. Round 1. 35 and 45 laps of the 1.800-mile/2.897km circuit.
Race 1 (63.000 miles/101.389km).
1 Aaron Telitz, USA, 40m 12.2907s, 94.019mph/151.308km/h; **2** Colton Herta, USA, +11.0330s; **3** Neil Alberico, USA, +13.9925s; **4** Shelby Blackstock, USA, +15.6642s; **5** Patricio O'Ward, MEX, +19.1813s; **6** Kyle Kaiser, USA, +25.4788s; **7** Nicolas Jamin, F, +25.7737s; **8** Zachary Claman, CDN, +25.9800s; **9** Nicolás Dapero, RA, +26.4283s; **10** Ryan Norman, USA, +37.7830s.
Fastest race lap: Herta, 1m 08.1395s, 95.099mph/153.047km/h.
Pole position: Telitz, 1m 07.5844s, 95.880mph/154.304km/h.

Race 2 (81.000 miles/130.357km).
1 Colton Herta, USA, 1h 00m 24.3956s, 80.455mph/129.479km/h; **2** Santiago Urrutia, U, +1.7797s; **3** Patricio O'Ward, MEX, +3.9729s; **4** Kyle Kaiser, USA, +5.6051s; **5** Aaron Telitz, USA, +7.0662s; **6** Shelby Blackstock, USA, +10.4495s; **7** Zachary Claman, CDN, +11.1066s; **8** Nicolás Dapero, RA, +13.4821s; **9** Ryan Norman, USA, +19.7311s; **10** Juan Piedrahita, CO, +21.8159s.
Fastest race lap: Herta, 1m 07.2421s, 96.368mph/155.090km/h.
Pole position: Herta, 1m 06.5465s, 97.376mph/156.711km/h.

MAZDA INDY LIGHTS GP OF ALABAMA, Barber Motorsports Park, Birmingham, Alabama, USA, 22/23 April. Round 2. 30 and 35 laps of the 2.300-mile/3.701km circuit.
Race 1 (69.000 miles/111.045km).
1 Nicolas Jamin, F, 39m 53.9823s, 103.760mph/166.986km/h; **2** Kyle Kaiser, USA, +2.6525s; **3** Neil Alberico, USA, +3.5386s; **4** Matheus Leist, BR, +6.8921s; **5** Zachary Claman, CDN, +7.9310s; **6** Dalton Kellett, CDN, +11.6353s; **7** Shelby Blackstock, USA, +23.4746s; **8** Patricio O'Ward, MEX, +23.6997s; **9** Nicolás Dapero, RA, +24.2379s; **10** Colton Herta, USA, +25.0465s.
Fastest race lap: Jamin, 1m 15.5043s, 109.663mph/176.485km/h.
Pole position: Kaiser, 1m 13.2851s, 112.983mph/181.829km/h.

Race 2 (80.500 miles/129.552km).
1 Colton Herta, USA, 46m 11.4924s, 104.565mph/168.280km/h; **2** Kyle Kaiser, USA, +9.1465s; **3** Nicolas Jamin, F, +11.1006s; **4** Neil Alberico, USA, +11.7478s; **5** Aaron Telitz, USA,

+18.3005s; **6** Nicolás Dapero, RA, +21.1618s; **7** Matheus Leist, BR, +23.7575s; **8** Shelby Blackstock, USA, +33.1064s; **9** Ryan Norman, USA, +35.4034s; **10** Dalton Kellett, CDN, +36.5591s.
Fastest race lap: Santiago Urrutia, U, 1m 14.5774s, 111.026mph/178.678km/h.
Pole position: Kellett.

INDY LIGHTS GP OF INDIANAPOLIS, Indianapolis Motor Speedway, Speedway, Indiana, USA, 12/13 May. Round 3. 30 and 35 laps of the 2.439-mile/3.925km circuit.
Race 1 (73.170 miles/117.756km).
1 Nicolas Jamin, F, 38m 29.3542s, 114.063mph/183.567km/h; **2** Zachary Claman, CDN, +0.8405s; **3** Kyle Kaiser, USA, +2.1150s; **4** Neil Alberico, USA, +3.9264s; **5** Matheus Leist, BR, +8.0926s; **6** Aaron Telitz, USA, +10.8239s; **7** Santiago Urrutia, U, +11.8774s; **8** Ryan Norman, USA, +14.5439s; **9** Shelby Blackstock, USA, +19.0256s; **10** Garth Rickards, USA, +31.1542s.
Fastest race lap: Leist, 1m 16.2644s, 115.131mph/185.285km/h.
Pole position: Jamin, 1m15.2443s, 116.692mph/187.797km/h.

Race 2 (85.365 miles/137.382km).
1 Kyle Kaiser, USA, 45m 11.5257s, 113.336mph/182.397km/h; **2** Santiago Urrutia, U, +6.4768s; **3** Matheus Leist, BR, +13.3677s; **4** Nicolas Jamin, F, +15.9447s; **5** Juan Piedrahita, CO, +18.1266s; **6** Neil Alberico, USA, +19.6149s; **7** Ryan Norman, USA, +19.6779s; **8** Nicolás Dapero, RA, +25.4450s; **9** Dalton Kellett, CDN, +32.1649s; **10** Colton Herta, USA, +33.2296s.
Fastest race lap: Zachary Claman, CDN, 1m 16.8971s, 114.184mph/183.761km/h.
Pole position: Kaiser, 1m14.9629s, 117.130mph/188.502km/h.

FREEDOM 100, Indianapolis Motor Speedway, Speedway, Indiana, USA, 26 May. Round 4. 40 laps of the 2.500-mile/4.023km circuit, 100.000 miles/160.934km.
1 Matheus Leist, BR, 36m 36.6934s, 163.883mph/263.744km/h; **2** Aaron Telitz, USA, +0.7760s; **3** Dalton Kellett, CDN, +0.8401s; **4** Neil Alberico, USA, +2.3748s; **5** Santiago Urrutia, U, +9.9919s; **6** Zachary Claman, CDN, +10.3970s; **7** Garth Rickards, USA, +12.4357s; **8** Juan Piedrahita, CO, +20.4610s; **9** Kyle Kaiser, USA, +25.1065s; **10** Nicolas Jamin, F, +34.9961s.
Fastest race lap: Urrutia, 45.4307s, 198.104mph/318.817km/h.
Pole position: Leist, 1m 30.3625s, 199.198mph/320.578km/h (over 2 laps).

MAZDA INDY LIGHTS GP OF ROAD AMERICA, Road America, Elkhart Lake, Wisconsin, USA, 24/25 June. Round 5. 2 x 20 laps of the 4.014-mile/6.460km circuit.
Race 1 (80.280 miles/129.198km).
1 Matheus Leist, BR, 38m 22.5131s, 125.519mph/202.002km/h; **2** Santiago Urrutia, U, +6.1667s; **3** Kyle Kaiser, USA, +6.2446s; **4** Ryan Norman, USA, +9.2845s; **5** Juan Piedrahita, CO, +11.0644s; **6** Nicolas Jamin, F, +14.5237s; **7** Neil Alberico, USA, +15.9956s; **8** Shelby Blackstock, USA, +17.2422s; **9** Dalton Kellett, CDN, +19.9749s; **10** Zachary Claman, CDN, +20.2927s.
Fastest race lap: Kaiser, 1m 54.4115s, 126.302mph/203.263km/h.
Pole position: Leist, 1m 53.1760s, 127.681mph/205.482km/h.

Race 2 (80.280 miles/129.198km).
1 Zachary Claman, CDN, 38m 03.4595s, 126.566mph/203.688km/h; **2** Kyle Kaiser, USA, +10.5479s; **3** Colton Herta, USA, +12.7612s; **4** Matheus Leist, BR, +15.1694s; **5** Aaron Telitz, USA, +17.5908s; **6** Shelby Blackstock, USA, +24.6336s; **7** Ryan Norman, USA, +26.0311s; **8** Neil Alberico, USA, +28.3206s; **9** Dalton Kellett, CDN, +28.9308s; **10** Juan Piedrahita, CO, +45.2029s.
Fastest race lap: Claman, 1m 53.0138s, 127.864mph/205.777km/h.
Pole position: Herta, 1m 52.0034s, 129.018mph/207.634km/h.

MAZDA IOWA 100, Iowa Speedway, Newton, Iowa, USA, 9 July. Round 6. 100 laps of the 0.894-mile/1.439km circuit, 89.400 miles/143.875km.
1 Matheus Leist, BR, 37m 08.2565s, 144.436mph/232.447km/h; **2** Santiago Urrutia, U, +2.9294s; **3** Dalton Kellett, CDN, +6.7115s; **4** Colton Herta, USA, +13.3736s; **5** Kyle Kaiser, USA, +14.7353s; **6** Zachary Claman, CDN, +15.9305s; **7** Nicolas Jamin, F, +18.7394s; **8** Ryan Norman, USA, +21.9026s; **9** Aaron Telitz, USA, -1 lap; **10** Juan Piedrahita, CO, -1.
Fastest race lap: Kellett, 20.4977s, 157.013mph/252.688km/h.
Pole position: Herta, 39.3279s, 163.670mph/263.401km/h (over 2 laps).

COOPER TIRES INDY LIGHTS GP OF TORONTO, Toronto Street Circuit, Ontario, Canada, 15/16 July. Round 7. 35 and 45 laps of the 1.786-mile/2.874km circuit.
Race 1 (62.510 miles/100.600km).
1 Kyle Kaiser, USA, 41m 28.4746s, 90.431mph/145.535km/h; **2** Zachary Claman, CDN, +3.6118s; **3** Santiago Urrutia, U, +4.7984s; **4** Colton Herta, USA, +5.1149s; **5** Aaron Telitz, USA, +17.1286s; **6** Juan Piedrahita, CO, +35.0434s; **7** Nicolás Dapero, RA, +35.1801s; **8** Neil Alberico, USA, +45.3035s; **9** Garth Rickards, USA, -1 lap; **10** Ryan Norman, USA, -1.
Fastest race lap: Herta, 1m 05.5479s, 98.090mph/157.861km/h.
Pole position: Kaiser, 1m 05.3511s, 98.385mph/158.336km/h.

Race 2 (80.370 miles/129.343km).
1 Kyle Kaiser, USA, 55m 55.5311s, 86.225mph/138.766km/h; **2** Aaron Telitz, USA, +5.8649s; **3** Zachary Claman, CDN, +8.3334s; **4** Juan Piedrahita, CO, +14.9281s; **5** Matheus Leist, BR, +21.9308s; **6** Ryan Norman, USA, +26.2344s; **7** Nicolás Dapero, RA, +52.3313s; **8** Garth Rickards, USA, -1 lap; **9** Dalton Kellett, CDN, -1; **10** Colton Herta, USA, -20 (DNF-mechanical).
Fastest race lap: Kaiser, 1m 05.6533s, 97.933mph/157.607km/h.
Pole position: Herta, 1m 05.0449s, 98.849mph/159.081km/h.

COOPER TIRES INDY LIGHTS GP OF MID-OHIO, Mid-Ohio Sports Car Course, Lexington, Ohio, USA, 29/30 July. Round 8. 30 and 38 laps of the 2.258-mile/3.634km circuit.
Race 1 (67.740 miles/109.017km).
1 Santiago Urrutia, U, 38m 47.4693s, 104.776mph/168.621km/h; **2** Colton Herta, USA, +0.4812s; **3** Nicolas Jamin, F, +2.0408s; **4** Shelby Blackstock, USA, +2.7217s; **5** Zachary Claman, CDN, +3.3116s; **6** Neil Alberico, USA, +9.9257s; **7** Dalton Kellett, CDN, +11.6356s; **8** Aaron Telitz, USA, +13.0471s; **9** Ryan Norman, USA, +31.7669s; **10** Juan Piedrahita, CO, +33.3395s.
Fastest race lap: Blackstock, 1m 12.5798s, 111.998mph/180.243km/h.
Pole position: Urrutia, 1m11.3694s, 113.898mph/183.300km/h.

Race 2 (85.804 miles/138.088km).
1 Nicolas Jamin, F, 46m 35.8335s, 110.484mph/177.806km/h; **2** Santiago Urrutia, U, +0.5026s; **3** Shelby Blackstock, USA, +13.8909s; **4** Zachary Claman, CDN, +14.3358s; **5** Aaron Telitz, USA, +25.1355s; **6** Colton Herta, USA, +26.9240s; **7** Ryan Norman, USA, +34.4449s; **8** Nicolás Dapero, RA, +35.3834s; **9** Neil Alberico, USA, +36.0207s; **10** Matheus Leist, BR, +40.3761s.
Fastest race lap: Urrutia, 1m 12.4486s, 112.201mph/180.570km/h.
Pole position: Herta, 1m 11.1019s, 114.326mph/183.990km/h.

MAZDA ST. LOUIS INDY LIGHTS OVAL CHALLENGE, Gateway Motorsports Park, Madison, Illinois, USA, 26 August. Round 9. 75 laps of the 1.250-mile/2.012km circuit, 93.750 miles/150.876km.
1 Santiago Urrutia, U, 46m 20.0812s, 121.399mph/195.373km/h; **2** Juan Piedrahita, CO, +0.4518s; **3** Colton Herta, USA, +0.9641s; **4** Kyle Kaiser, USA, +2.5437s; **5** Nicolás Dapero, RA, +3.0843s; **6** Zachary Claman, CDN, +3.1337s; **7** Dalton Kellett, CDN, +4.1024s; **8** Ryan Norman, USA, +6.4154s; **9** Shelby Blackstock, USA, -1 lap; **10** Matheus Leist, BR, -2.
Fastest race lap: Claman, 28.0370s, 160.502mph/258.303km/h.
Pole position: Piedrahita, 55.9620s, 160.823mph/258.820km/h (over 2 laps).

MAZDA INDY LIGHTS WATKINS GLEN GP, Watkins Glen International, New York, USA, 3 September. Round 10. 25 laps of the 3.370-mile/5.423km circuit, 84.250 miles/135.587km.
1 Aaron Telitz, USA, 58m 40.9684s, 86.141mph/138.631km/h; **2** Santiago Urrutia, U, +2.1807s; **3** Colton Herta, USA, +9.5449s; **4** Matheus Leist, BR, +10.9795s; **5** Nicolas Jamin, F, +14.2479s; **6** Zachary Claman, CDN, +24.8705s; **7** Kyle Kaiser, USA, +40.9490s; **8** Nicolás Dapero, RA, +43.8622s; **9** Juan Piedrahita, CO, +53.4063s; **10** Ryan Norman, USA, -1 lap 13.4386s.
Fastest race lap: Telitz, 1m 55.3271s, 105.196mph/169.297km/h.
Pole position: Herta, 1m 32.4394s, 131.243mph/211.215km/h.

Final championship points
Drivers
1 Kyle Kaiser, USA, 330; **2** Santiago Urrutia, U, 310; **3** Colton Herta, USA, 300; **4** Matheus Leist, BR, 279; **5** Zachary Claman, CDN, 274; **6** Aaron Telitz, USA, 271; **7** Nicolas Jamin, F, 269; **8** Neil Alberico, USA, 225; **9** Juan Piedrahita, CO, 208; **10** Shelby Blackstock, USA, 207; **11** Ryan Norman, USA, 200; **12** Dalton Kellett, CDN, 198; **13**

Nicolás Dapero, RA, 187; **14** Garth Rickards, USA, 146; **15** Patricio O'Ward, MEX, 58; **16** Chad Boat, USA, 7.

Teams
1 Belardi Auto Racing, 393; **2** Andretti Autosport, 389; **3** Carlin, 365; **4** Juncos Racing, 282; **5** Team Pelfrey, 162.

Atlantic Championship

All cars are Swift 014.a-Toyota.

ATLANTIC CHAMPIONSHIP, Virginia International Raceway, Alton, Virginia, USA, 29/30 April. Round 1. 2 x 22 laps of the 3.270-mile/5.263km circuit.
Race 1 (71.940 miles/115.776km).
1 Keith Grant, USA, 22 laps; **2** David Grant, USA, 22; **3** Peter Portante, USA, 22; **4** Rich Zober, USA, 22; **5** Lee Alexander, USA, 22; **6** Lewis Cooper Jr, USA, 22; **7** Jenna Grillo, USA, 22; **8** Bob Corliss, USA, 22; **9** Bob Corliss, USA, 22; **10** Spencer Brockman, USA, -1.
Fastest race lap: Portante, 1m 42.782s, 114.534mph/184.324km/h.
Pole position: Grant, 1m 42.743s, 114.577mph/184.394km/h.

Race 2 (71.940 miles/115.776km).
1 Peter Portante, USA, 22 laps; **2** David Grant, USA, 22; **3** Keith Grant, USA, 22; **4** Spencer Brockman, USA, 22; **5** Jenna Grillo, USA, 22; **6** Lewis Cooper Jr, USA, 22; **7** Blake Mount, USA, 22; **8** Chris Ash, USA, 22; **9** Mike Jacques, USA, -1; **10** Lee Alexander, USA, -1.
Fastest race lap: Grant, 1m 41.817s, 115.619mph/186.071km/h.
Pole position: Grant, 1m 43.020s, 114.269mph/183.898km/h.

ATLANTIC CHAMPIONSHIP, Mid-Ohio Sports Car Course, Lexington, Ohio, USA, 12/13 May. Round 2. 2 x 29 laps of the 2.258-mile/3.634km circuit.
Race 3 (65.482 miles/105.383km).
1 Peter Portante, USA, 29 laps; **2** Keith Grant, USA, 29; **3** David Grant, USA, 29; **4** Bruce Hamilton, USA, 29; **5** Blake Mount, USA, -1; **6** John Burke, USA, -1; Bill Gillespie, USA, -24 (DNF).
Fastest race lap: Grant, 1m 17.608s, 104.742mph/168.566km/h.
Pole position: Portante, 1m 17.746s, 104.556mph/168.266km/h.

Race 4 (65.482 miles/105.383km).
1 Peter Portante, USA, 29 laps; **2** David Grant, USA, 29; **3** Keith Grant, USA, 29; **4** Blake Mount, USA, -1; **5** Bruce Hamilton, USA, -2; Bruce Hamilton, USA, -21 (DNF); Bill Gillespie, USA, -23 (DNF).
Fastest race lap: Grant, 1m 16.822s, 105.813mph/170.290km/h.
Pole position: Grant, 1m 16.927s, 105.669mph/170.058km/h.

ATLANTIC CHAMPIONSHIP, Indianapolis Motor Speedway, Speedway, Indiana, USA, 10/11 June. Round 3. 9 and 15 laps of the 2.439-mile/3.925km circuit.
Race 5 (21.951 miles/35.327km).
1 Peter Portante, USA, 9 laps; **2** Keith Grant, USA, 9; **3** David Grant, USA, 9; **4** Jimmy Simpson, USA, 9; **5** Dudley Fleck, USA, 9; **6** Mike Jacques, USA, 9; **7** Connor Burke, USA, 9; **8** Bruce Hamilton, USA, 9; **9** Rich Zober, USA, 9; **10** Jenna Grillo, USA, 9.
Fastest race lap: Portante, 1m 22.186s, 106.836mph/171.935km/h.
Pole position: Portante, 1m 21.721s, 107.444mph/172.914km/h.

Race 6 (36.585 miles/58.878km).
1 Peter Portante, USA, 15 laps; **2** Keith Grant, USA, 15; **3** David Grant, USA, 15; **4** Dudley Fleck, USA, 15; **5** Mike Jacques, USA, 15; **6** Jimmy Simpson, USA, 15; **7** Rich Zober, USA, 15; **8** Bruce Hamilton, USA, 15; **9** Kirk Kindsfater, USA, 15; **10** Bob Corliss, USA, 15.
Fastest race lap: Grant, 1m 21.999s, 107.079mph/172.328km/h.
Pole position: Portante, 1m 22.186s, 106.836mph/171.935km/h.

ATLANTIC CHAMPIONSHIP, Mid-Ohio Sports Car Course, Lexington, Ohio, USA, 1/2 July. Round 4. 2 x 29 laps of the 2.258-mile/3.634km circuit.
Race 7 (65.482 miles/105.383km).
1 Peter Portante, USA, 29 laps; **2** Keith Grant, USA, 29; **3** David Grant, USA, 29; **4** Andrew Bujdoso, USA, -1; **5** Bruce Hamilton, USA, -1; **6** Lewis Cooper Jr, USA, -1; **7** Anthony Martin, AUS, -7.
Did not start: Matt Machiko, USA.
Fastest race lap: Portante, 1m 17.452s, 104.953mph/168.905km/h.
Pole position: Martin, 1m 31.134s, 89.196mph/143.547km/h.

Race 8 (65.482 miles/105.383km).
1 David Grant, USA, 29 laps; **2** Keith Grant,

USA, 29; **3** Andrew Bujdoso, USA, 29; **4** Bruce Hamilton, USA, -1; **5** Lewis Cooper Jr, USA, -1; **6** Anthony Martin, AUS, -7; Peter Portante, USA, -27 (DNF).
Fastest race lap: Grant, 1m 17.423s, 104.992mph/168.968km/h.
Pole position: Grant, 1m 16.464s, 106.309mph/171.088km/h.

ATLANTIC CHAMPIONSHIP, Pittsburgh International Race Complex, Pennsylvania, USA, 29/30 July. Round 5. 2 x 24 laps of the 1.600-mile/2.575km circuit.
Race 9 (38.400 miles/61.799km).
1 Keith Grant, USA, 24 laps; **2** Peter Portante, USA, 24; **3** Rich Zober, USA, 24; **4** Chris Ash, USA, 24; **5** Lee Alexander, USA, 24; **6** Bruce Hamilton, USA, -1; **7** Mike Jacques, USA, -1; **8** Bob Corliss, USA, -1; **9** Lewis Cooper Jr, USA, -1; David Grant, USA, -21 (DNF).
Fastest race lap: Portante, 1m 31.880s, 62.690mph/100.891km/h.
Pole position: Grant, 1m 31.031s, 63.275mph/101.831km/h.

Race 10 (38.400 miles/61.799km).
1 David Grant, USA, 24 laps; **2** Peter Portante, USA, 24; **3** Rich Zober, USA, 24; **4** Lee Alexander, USA, 24; **5** Bob Corliss, USA, 24; **6** Chris Ash, USA, 24; **7** Bruce Hamilton, USA, 24; **8** Mike Jacques, USA, 24; Lewis Cooper Jr, USA, -20 (DNF).
Did not start: Keith Grant, USA.
Fastest race lap: Grant, 1m 31.584s, 62.893mph/101.217km/h.
Pole position: Grant, 1m 32.161s, 62.499mph/100.583km/h.

ATLANTIC CHAMPIONSHIP, Summit Point Motorsports Park, Jefferson County, West Virginia, USA, 26/27 August. Round 6. 2 x 35 laps of the 2.000-mile/3.219km circuit.
Race 11 (70.000 miles/112.654km).
1 Peter Portante, USA, 35 laps; **2** David Grant, USA, 35; **3** Matt Miller, USA, 35; **4** John Burke, USA, -1; **5** Christopher Fahan, USA, -2; Keith Grant, USA, -34 (DNF).
Did not start: Connor Burke, USA; Bruce Hamilton, USA.
Fastest race lap: Portante, 1m 05.082s, 110.630mph/178.041km/h.
Pole position: Portante, 1m 03.946s, 112.595mph/181.204km/h.

Race 12 (70.000 miles/112.654km).
1 David Grant, USA, 35 laps; **2** Peter Portante, USA, 35; **3** Keith Grant, USA, 35; **4** Matt Miller, USA, 35; **5** John Burke, USA, -1; **6** Bruce Hamilton, USA, -2; **7** Connor Burke, USA, -3.
Did not start: Christopher Fahan, USA.
Fastest race lap: Grant, 1m 04.893s, 110.952mph/178.560km/h.
Pole position: Portante, 1m 04.021s, 112.463mph/180.992km/h.

ATLANTIC CHAMPIONSHIP, New Jersey Motorsports Park - Thunderbolt, Millville, New Jersey, USA, 7/8 October. Round 7. 24 and 25 laps of the 2.250-mile/3.621km circuit.
Race 13 (54.000 miles/86.905km).
1 Rich Zober, USA, 24 laps; **2** Bruce Hamilton, USA, 24; **3** Theodoras Zorbas, USA, -1; **4** Peter Portante, USA, -2; **5** Michael D'Orlando, USA, -2; **6** John McCusker, USA, -2; **7** Brandon Dixon, USA, -2; **8** Tim Paul, USA, -2; **9** Steve Jenks, USA, -2; **10** David D'Addario, USA, -2.
Fastest race lap: Hamilton, 1m 13.444s, 110.288mph/177.492km/h.
Pole position: Zober, 1m 13.330s, 110.460mph/177.767km/h.

Race 14 (56.250 miles/90.526km).
1 Peter Portante, USA, 25 laps; **2** Rich Zober, USA, -1; **3** Theodoras Zorbas, USA, -2; **4** Brandon Dixon, USA, -3; **5** John McCusker, USA, -3; **6** Steve Jenks, USA, -3; **7** Michael D'Orlando, USA, -3; **8** Peter Gonzalez, USA, -3; **9** Dave Weitzenhof, USA, -3; **10** Bob Reid, USA, -3.
Fastest race lap: Portante, 1m 11.197s, 113.769mph/183.093km/h.
Pole position: Tim Paul, USA, 1m 30.384s, 89.618mph/144.226km/h.

Final championship points
Drivers
1 Peter Portante, USA, 587; **2** David Grant, USA, 491; **3** Keith Grant, USA, 430; **4** Bruce Hamilton, USA, 340; **5** Rich Zober, USA, 254; **6** Lewis Cooper Jr, USA, 166; **7** Lee Alexander, USA, 149; **8** Chris Ash, USA, 143; **9** Mike Jacques, USA, 136; **10** Bob Corliss, USA, 132; **11** John Burke, USA, 125; **12** Blake Mount, USA, 93; **13** Jenna Grillo, USA, 74; **14** Theodoras Zorbas, USA, 74; **15** Andrew Bujdoso, USA, 71; **16** Matt Miller, USA, 68; **17** Dudley Fleck, USA, 65; **18** Connor Burke, USA, 65; **19** Jimmy Simpson, USA, 63; **20** Anthony Martin, AUS, 59; **21** Spencer Brockman, USA, 55; **22** Kirk Kindsfater, USA, 42; **23** Christopher Fahan, USA, 31; **24** Bill Gillespie, USA, 2.